Philips'

WORLD

ATLAS

Philips'

WORLD

ATLAS

GUILD PUBLISHING.LONDON

Edited by
B. M. Willett
Cartographic Editor

The World Today

Contributors
John Chesshire, Science Policy Research Unit, Sussex University; Dr Richard Crockett, Institute of Geological Sciences; Arthur Kilgore, Gordon MacKerron, Science Policy Research Unit, Sussex University; Pauline Marstrand, Science Policy Research Unit, Sussex University; Professor J.H. Paterson, Department of Geography, Leicester University; John Rowley, Editor of *People*, the journal of the International Planned Parenthood Federation; Howard Rush, Science Policy Research Unit, Sussex University; Robert Stewart.

Illustration Acknowledgements
The publishers would like to thank the following individuals and organizations for their kind permission to reproduce the photographs in this section; Ardea, London; Paul Brierley; Camera Press Ltd.; Bruce Coleman Ltd.; *The Daily Telegraph*; Susan Griggs Agency Ltd; Maldwyn Glover; The John Hillelson Agency Ltd.; Alan Hutchison Library; Picturepoint Ltd.; Rex Features Ltd.; John Topham Picture Library; Transworld Feature Syndicate; Zefa Picture Library.

Illustrations on preliminary pages
Contents: harvesting sea salt near Cabo Frio, Brazil *(Bruce Coleman)*; **foreword:** Bora-Bora, an oceanic island fringed with a coral reef in French Polynesia *(Bruce Coleman)*; New York *(Bruce Coleman)*.

First Edition September 1979
Sixth Edition 1987

This edition published 1987 by Book Club Associates by arrangement with George Philip and Son Ltd.

Printed and bound in Hong Kong

Contents

1-32 The World Today

Maps

1 General Reference
World: Physical 1:150M
2-3 World: Political 1:80M
4 Europe: Physical 1:20M
5 Europe: Political 1:20M
6-7 England and Wales 1:2M
8 Scotland 1:2M
9 Ireland 1:2M
10 Great Britain & Ireland: Administrative 1:4M
11 Netherlands, Belgium and Luxembourg 1:2·5M
12 France 1:5M
13 Spain and Portugal 1:5M
14-15 Central Europe 1:5M
Central Europe: Political 1:25M
16-17 Mediterranean Lands 1:10M
18-19 Italy and the Balkan States 1:5M
Malta 1:1M South East Europe: Political 1:25M
20-21 Scandinavia and the Baltic Lands 1:5M
Iceland 1:5M
22-23 U.S.S.R. in Europe 1:10M
24-25 U.S.S.R. 1:20M
26 Asia: Physical 1:50M
27 Asia: Political 1:50M
28 Israel and West Jordan 1:1M
29 Arabia and the Horn of Africa 1:15M
30-31 The Near and Middle East 1:10M
32-33 South Asia 1:10M

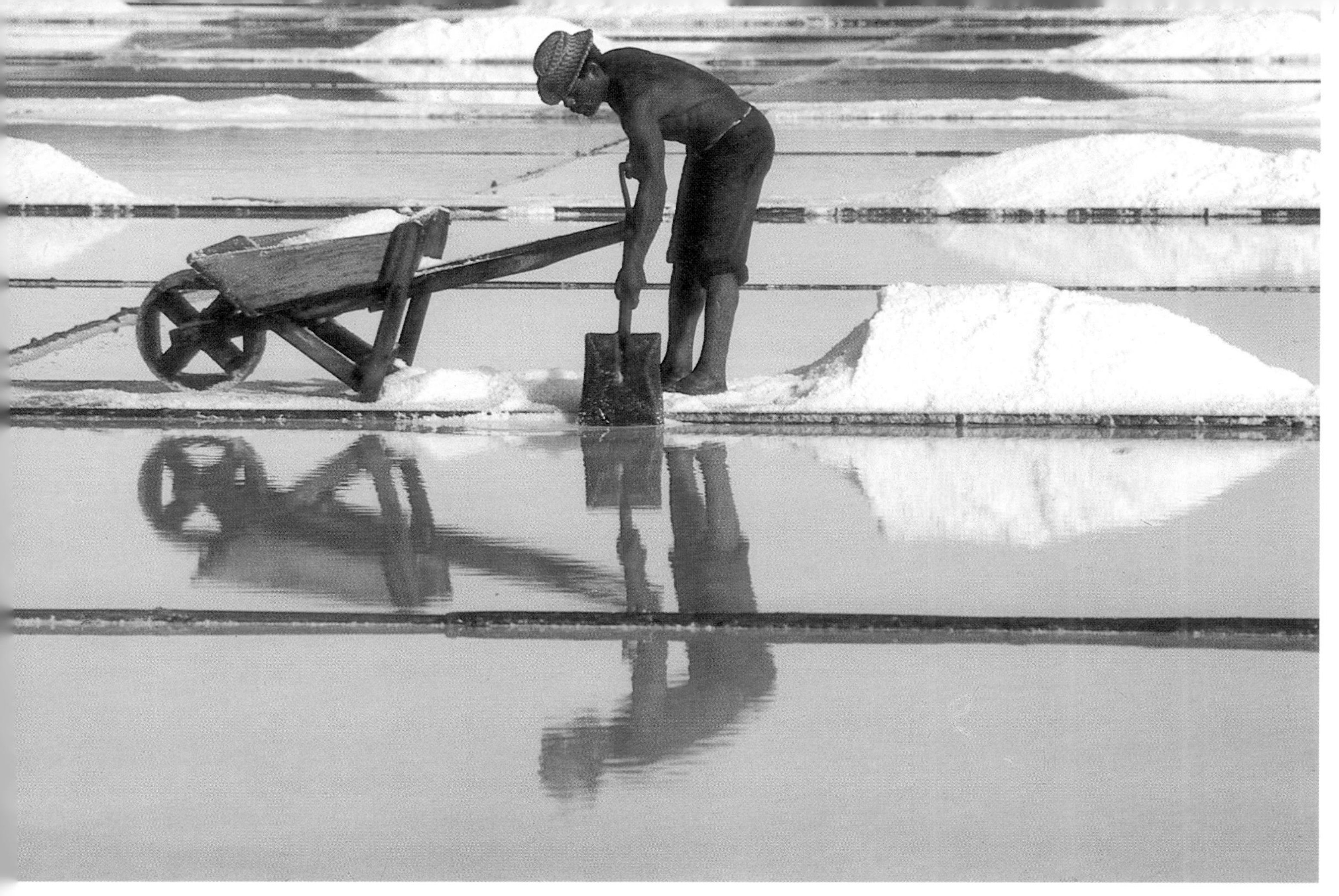

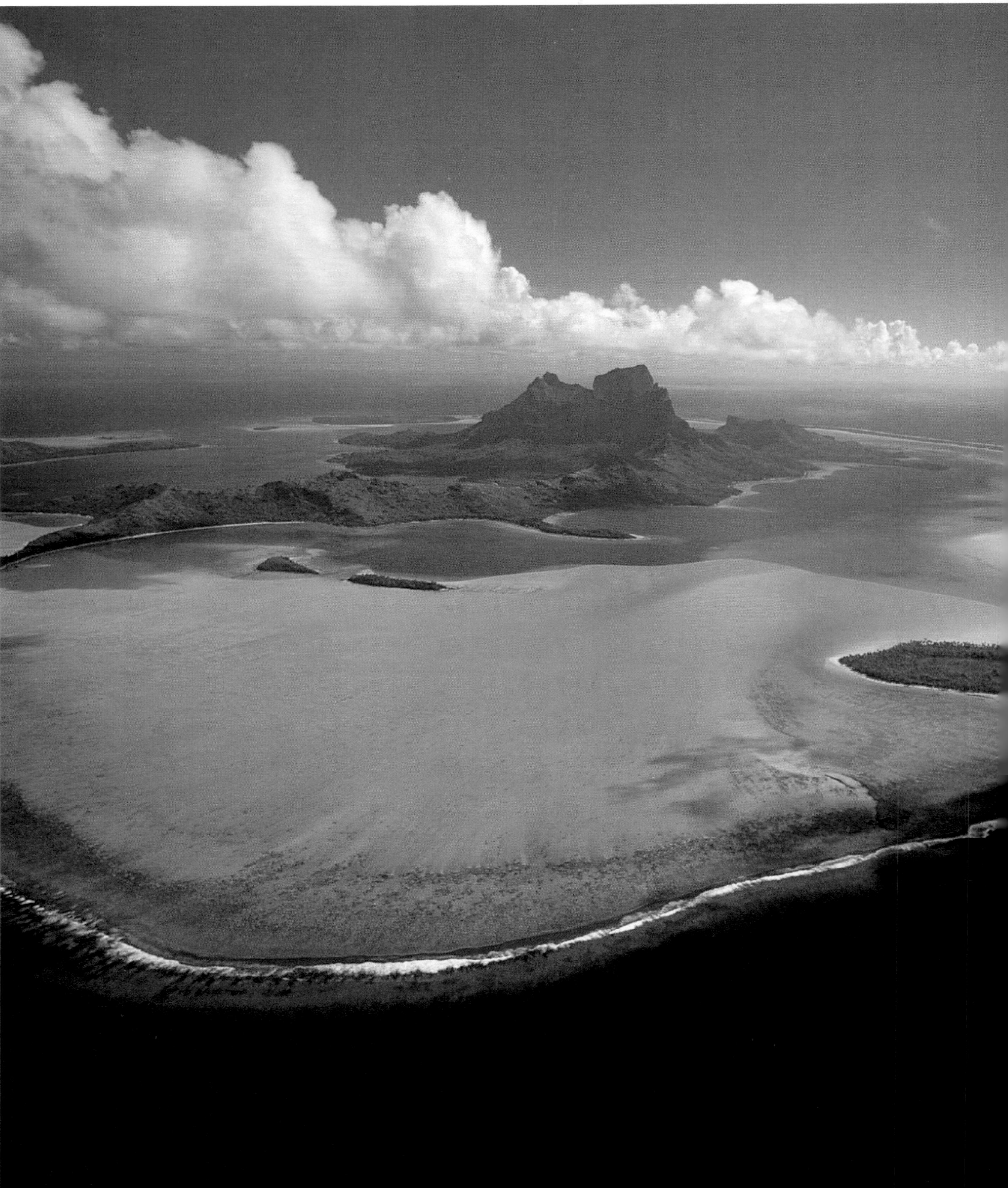

Foreword

Philips' World Atlas presents the reader with two complementary views of the world. The maps and index are a detailed source of reference on the world as it is today while the introductory essays describe many of the important aspects of life on this planet at the end of the twentieth century, and consider what the future may bring in a world where changes take place at an accelerating pace.

The maps are designed to show where places are and to make available a large quantity of information about them.

The Idea of Location There are two related but really quite different kinds of location – absolute and relative. By absolute location is meant the identification of a point on the surface of the earth by reference to a network of lines composed of parallels of latitude and meridians of longitude. The numbering of parallels begins at the Equator and continues as degrees of a quarter circle to the Poles (90°), both North and South. The meridians are numbered from the Prime Meridian, which passes through Greenwich, England, to 180° either East or West.

Relative location means the identification of a place in relation not to the network just described, but to other places or areas. For example, Greenwich is (relatively) located in Great Britain, in England, near the mouth of the River Thames, about 10 miles East of London. If you ask where Greenwich is, any of these answers could be appropriate.

Regional Maps There are 65 pages of regional maps in the atlas, containing a wealth of detail. Information given includes landforms and drainage features and selected aspects of human occupation such as settlements, railways, highways, canals, pipelines, and political boundaries. Surface relief is brought out by combining contours with layer-colouring and relief-shading.

Layer-colouring serves to mark off one range of elevation from the next, and each map contains in its margins an altitude scale which indicates in metres the values of the contours employed. The layer-colouring also extends below sea-level, and shows the continental shelf.

Relief-shading serves to emphasize changes in elevation, and, in addition, contributes a three-dimensional quality to the land surface.

Other natural features such as drainage – rivers, lakes, reservoirs and canals – are shown in conventional blue, and transportation is shown in black for railways, in red for major highways.

The settlements shown on the maps have been classified into nine categories, reflecting size of population and importance.

The regional maps are both physical and political in character. All international boundaries are reinforced with red for clarity and emphasis, and provincial and other sub-national boundaries are shown for a number of major countries.

World and Continental Maps Physical and political maps of the world introduce the atlas and each continental section similarly begins with summary physical and political maps.

Scale The importance of scale, and of distinguishing between maps at different scales, cannot be overestimated. Thus, the map of the continent of Africa (page 48) is shown at a scale of 1:40,000,000 whereas the map of East Africa (page 52) is drawn at a scale of 1:7,500,000. A larger-scale map means that very much more can be shown of terrain, of settlement, of transportation and other features and such scales are used for parts of the world where the users' interests are likely to require them.

The Spelling of Place Names In this atlas, the principle followed is that, for settlements at least, and where the Roman alphabet is employed, the indigenous spellings are used, except for a relatively few places which are so well known that the indigenous spelling would be confusing to the reader. For many of the names in this latter group alternative spellings are also given.

In cases where the Roman alphabet is not employed in the native language, transliteration and romanization are required. In these cases, the recommendations of the U.S. Board on Geographic Names and the U.K. Permanent Committee on Geographical Names are followed wherever possible.

Index The index at the back of the atlas contains over 30,000 place names. Reference is given to the largest-scale map on which the place appears, and this is followed by a description of the absolute location of the place in terms of latitude and longitude.

The World Today

The planet earth

THE earth was formed approximately four-and-a-half billion years ago, although some of the materials that form its surface today may have been laid in place, by the action of rivers for example, only yesterday. By contrast to the age of the planet, the history of man on earth dates back only one million years, and the period of man's occupance of which we have any direct knowledge represents only a minute fraction of this shorter span of time.

During this short period of time, nevertheless, human beings have developed a remarkable variety of races, languages and cultures. Since the earth is a sphere, natural conditions of temperature, landscape and fertility range widely between polar and tropical, and some of the variety of mankind's development is clearly due to this variety in nature. Man has adapted to living in both hot and cold climates, and not only his lifestyle but some of his institutions, such as religion, reflect this adaptation. Yet there is a much greater variety in human life-forms and customs than can be accounted for by environment alone. For one thing, members of the same race, or language group, may be bitterly opposed to one another on political or religious grounds. For another, a sense of belonging draws people together in national or tribal groupings, which develop their own particular means of cultural expression.

Basic resources

Man's primary need is his own life support. Alone among the planets, as far as we know, the earth provides the conditions necessary to sustain life. These conditions we know as resources. Fundamental to the resource structure of the earth is the energy of the sun: it is the power plant that drives all other systems. At a secondary level are the mineral deposits, soils and water on the earth; and thirdly, there are the plants that support animal life, and those animals which exist by preying, species upon species. All these can be classed as the earth's natural resources.

At the highest level, where man exists in total isolation from the natural world, there is a further resource component: what is normally referred to as human resources. These are represented by the ability of man to think, work, invent and find uses for natural materials; to apply skill or power to these materials and transform them. Many animals can build them-

selves a home in ways that display great engineering skill. Most creatures, however, can only build one kind of structure. Man can build a whole range of structures and design new forms to suit his needs as he anticipates them.

Unequal distribution

The distribution of natural resources over the earth's surface is far from even. The whereabouts of mineral deposits depend on random events in a remote geological past; patches of fertile soil depend on events more recent but, to man, equally capricious — the flow of rivers or the movement of ice. When it comes to agriculture, the activity that has been basic to the survival of man and his increase in numbers, we find that, in round figures, 20 per cent of the earth's surface is barred to him by ice or perennially frozen soil; 20 per cent is composed of highlands too cold, rugged or barren for the cultivation of crops; 20 per cent is arid or desert, and between five and 10 per cent of the remainder has no soil, either because it has been scraped by ice or because it is permanently wet or flooded. This leaves only 30-35 per cent of the land surface where food production is possible, together with the oceans and whatever resources may be obtained from that source.

We can think of these natural resources as forming a cover, or coating, of varying thickness over the earth's surface: in some places it is deep and rich; in others it is for all practical purposes non-existent. In the same way, observation shows that human resources vary in quality from place to place. What, in fact, we are observing are different levels of technical ability and equipment among different peoples. Whereas, however, we can accept that natural resource distribution is either random or climatically determined, and therefore unchangeable, the explanation for different development levels of human resources is a much more complex matter.

Why have some nations or groups advanced more rapidly than others in technology? Why have some lost the lead they once had? A number of explanations have been offered in order to answer these questions. One of these is climatic — that some environments are more stimulating to effort and inventiveness than others. Some are racial — and may, in due course, become racist — arguing that one race is more gifted than another. Yet others

▲**The earth in space** was an unfamiliar view we obtained when man first ventured beyond his natural environment: a small, rocky

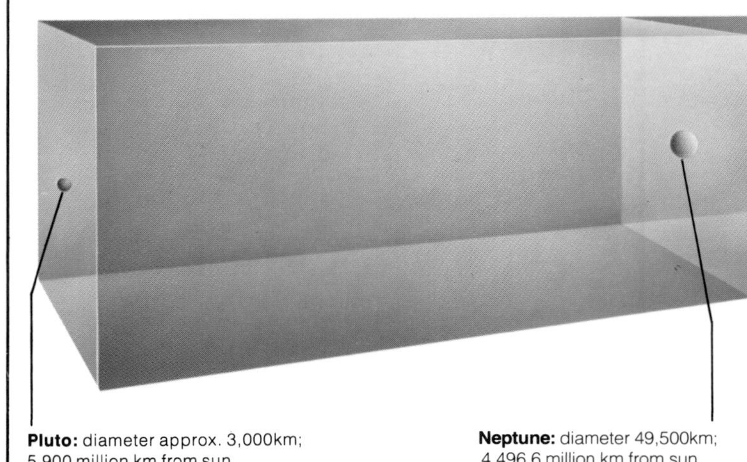

Pluto: diameter approx. 3,000km; 5,900 million km from sun

Neptune: diameter 49,500km; 4,496.6 million km from sun

focus on the structure of society, and the opportunities it affords for the use of individual talents and the freedom to innovate.

The key to exploitation

Each of these theories in isolation can be disproved, simply by pointing out the exceptions to it. Whatever the explanation, however, the fact is clear: that the ability to make use of what nature has provided in the way of resources varies critically from society to society, and that a high level of human resource input can provide a good living for people in areas, such as Scandinavia, where the natural endowment is meagre, while people may live on top of a veritable treasure chest of natural riches, as, it would appear, the Brazilians do, without necessarily obtaining the benefit of

them. It is, after all, only a few years since the oil states of the Middle East were among the world's poorest nations. If we think of the earth as a storehouse of natural wealth, then it is human ingenuity — the human resources represented by technical skills — which provides the key to open it.

Fortunately, no nation today possesses a monopoly of these skills, or is, for that matter, debarred from acquiring them. It is a slow process to do so, but one that can be speeded up if those societies which are relatively advanced will help those that are only at the beginning. Human resources have transformed parts of this planet once judged to be too cold, or too dry, or too poor to support the dense populations, either on the land or in the great cities, that now occupy them.

planet with much surface water and a dense atmosphere.

200 million years ago

135 million years ago

Present day

150 million years' time

Plate Tectonics

The migration of the continents is a feature unique to Planet Earth. The complementary, almost jigsaw-puzzle fit of the coastlines on each side of the Atlantic Ocean inspired Alfred Wegener's theory of continental drift at the beginning of the twentieth century. The theory suggested that an ancient supercontinent, which Wegener named Pangaea, incorporated all of the earth's land masses and gradually split up to form the continents we see today. The modern theory of plate tectonics attributes continental drift to movements in crustal plates underlying the oceans as well as the continents. These movements are caused by the slow but continuous welling-up of material from deep within the earth along a series of mid-ocean ridges. Geological evidence that the continents once formed a single land mass is provided by distinctive rock formations that can be assembled into continuous belts when Africa and South America are lined up next to each other. Distribution of some plants and animals in the past, as well as ancient climatic zones, can only be explained by the theory of plate tectonics.

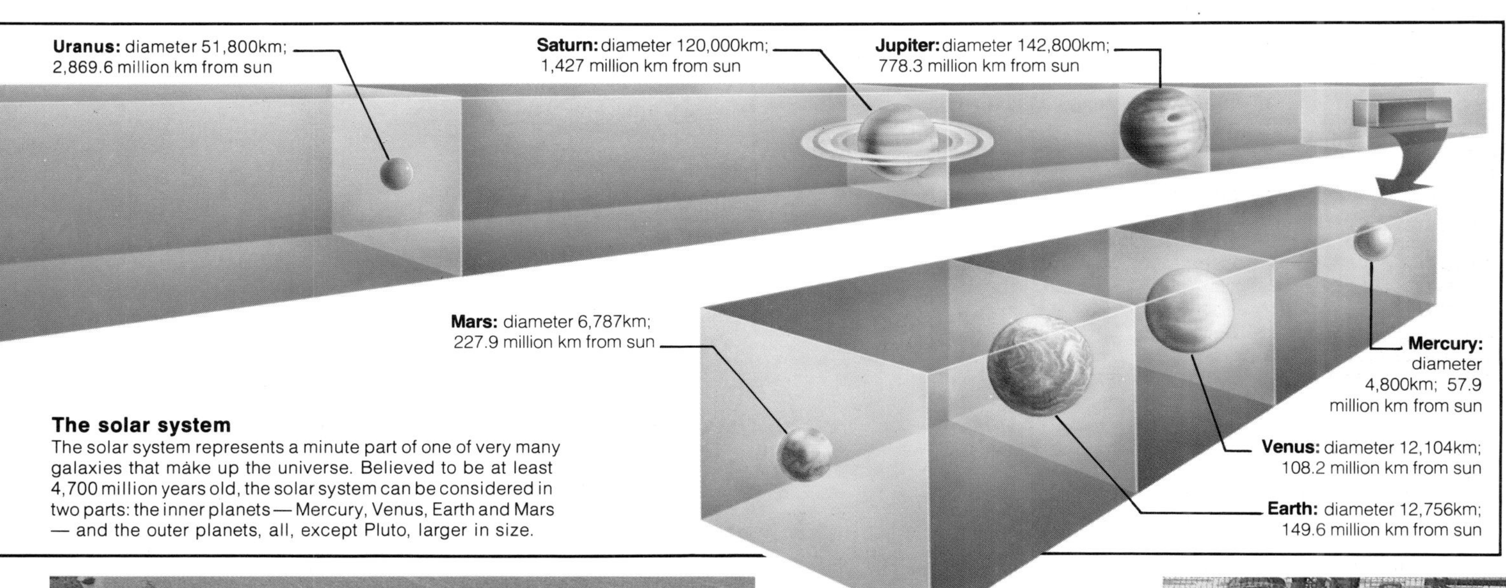

Uranus: diameter 51,800km; 2,869.6 million km from sun

Saturn: diameter 120,000km; 1,427 million km from sun

Jupiter: diameter 142,800km; 778.3 million km from sun

Mars: diameter 6,787km; 227.9 million km from sun

Mercury: diameter 4,800km; 57.9 million km from sun

Venus: diameter 12,104km; 108.2 million km from sun

Earth: diameter 12,756km; 149.6 million km from sun

The solar system

The solar system represents a minute part of one of very many galaxies that make up the universe. Believed to be at least 4,700 million years old, the solar system can be considered in two parts: the inner planets — Mercury, Venus, Earth and Mars — and the outer planets, all, except Pluto, larger in size.

▶ **The evolution of man** *as a unique social and cultural animal has produced a variety of races, languages, religious and social systems. A political rally in China illustrates one aspect of culture.*

◀ **The Amazon basin** *is one of the few remaining wildernesses on earth. Such vast areas of forest play a vital role in global ecology — by helping to maintain the balance of oxygen in the atmosphere.*

▶ **Throughout history** *man has found various ways of expressing his beliefs in supernatural powers. Here, monks follow the teachings of the Dalai Lama in a temple in Tibet — one facet of religion today.*

A crowded planet

FROM man's earliest ancestors on the planet earth, more than one million years ago, until the beginnings of settled agriculture some 10,000 years ago, the number of human beings alive at any one time did not exceed five million. By 1800 the world was home to one billion people. The second billion was reached by 1930, the third by 1960 and the fourth billion by 1970. The likelihood is that the fifth billion will be reached by 1987 and that a sixth billion will be added by the end of the century, when United Nations demographers estimate that the earth will "carry" 6,127,000,000 human beings.

The key to population growth
What happens after that depends on the speed at which the rate of population growth slows down over the coming decade. The annual growth rate is believed to have peaked at about two per cent in 1970, declining to between 1.6 and 1.7 per cent today. This deceptively small statistic is adding some 80 million people to the world's population each year and, because the world's total population includes such a high proportion of young people who have yet to grow up and have children, it is going to take a long time for the population to stabilize at somewhere between eight and 15 billion, some time in the twenty-first century.

The cause of this extraordinary explosion in human numbers over the past 200 years lies essentially in declining death rates rather than in increasing birth rates. Medical advances and improved conditions of life first cut death rates in Europe. The subsequent explosion in the numbers surviving was partly masked by the massive exodus to new countries, with some 60 million migrants travelling to the Americas and elsewhere before World War II. An even greater and faster increase in numbers began in the developing countries of Asia, Africa and Latin America before World War II as a much more rapid drop in death rates followed the spread of scientific technology to prevent and control disease and improvements in the availability of food.

As death rates declined in Europe birth rates also slowly came down, and today population growth in all modern industrialized countries is low or non-existent. In a few cases, such as West Germany and Austria, the population has even begun to decrease. But less than one-third of the world's population

lives in these developed regions, and it is among the two-thirds in the developing countries that population is growing fast. Although the rates of growth have begun to fall in many countries, the proportion of the world's population in the developing countries of Asia, Africa and Latin America will continue to rise until the year 2000.

The distribution of people
At the moment Europe remains the most densely populated area of the globe, with an average of 100 people per square kilometre. The vast territories of southern and eastern Asia are, however, not far behind, and within the next 100 years they are likely to have three times the density of present-day Europe, according to United Nations estimates. In Asia as a whole, population is likely to increase from 2.8 billion to 3.6 billion in the next 20 years. Africa, by contrast, is relatively lightly populated at present, though individual countries such as Egypt, Rwanda and Lesotho have high populations in relation to productive land. The African continent is likely to add another 400 million people to its 1979 population of 455 million by the turn of the century, while Latin America's population will grow from 360 million to some 600 million in the same period.

Of more concern to many governments than overall density of population is the distribution of population within national boundaries. The growth of cities is one of the most striking features of our time. At the beginning of this century there were only 250 million city dwellers in the world. Today 1,500 million people live in urban areas and by the year 2000, it is believed, more than half the world's population, or some 3,000 million people, will be living in towns and cities.

The call of the city
The growth of cities is partly the result of natural increase, but more significantly the result of migration from the countryside, where population growth often coincides with rural stagnation and a shortage of work. Unlike the situation in the nineteenth century, there are few unused fertile areas left in the world. And the only job opportunities are those which appear to beckon from the growing cities. Already one-third of the urban inhabitants in less-developed countries are squatters living on the fringes of cities such as Djakarta, Bombay, Calcutta, Rio de Janeiro, Manila and Mexico City. These are among the fastest grow-

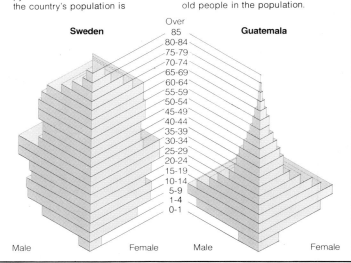

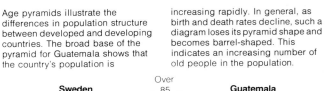

▲ **Most of the world's poor** live in appalling conditions. Having migrated to the cities in the hope of greater opportunities, many people find themselves in even worse surroundings. Shanty towns, such as this one in Sao Paulo, are home to a large proportion of the inhabitants of the world's fastest-growing cities.

Age/sex structure

Age pyramids illustrate the differences in population structure between developed and developing countries. The broad base of the pyramid for Guatemala shows that the country's population is increasing rapidly. In general, as birth and death rates decline, such a diagram loses its pyramid shape and becomes barrel-shaped. This indicates an increasing number of old people in the population.

Sweden **Guatemala**

Over
85
80-84
75-79
70-74
65-69
60-64
55-59
50-54
45-49
40-44
35-39
30-34
25-29
20-24
15-19
10-14
5-9
1-4
0-1

Male Female Male Female

ing settlements in the world today.

Taking both rural and urban areas of the developing world together, more than 40 per cent of the population is either unemployed or underemployed, two billion are continually undernourished and some 1,400 million are illiterate. The causes of such problems are complex, but rapid population growth makes all of them more difficult to solve. As a result, four-fifths of the developing world's population now live in countries which have adopted policies aimed at slowing down the rate of population growth.

Since the world conference on population in Bucharest in 1974, governments have increasingly come to realize that such policies stand the best chance of success if they involve social and development policies which create a wish for smaller families, as well as access to family planning information and services. The motivation for small families involves the reduction of infant and child mortal-

ity, the expansion of basic education, especially for girls, an increase in the income of the rural poor, a more equal distribution of wealth and — of particular importance — the improvement of the status of women in society. Where such measures have been taken along with the provision of family planning services, including access to early abortion and a range of fertility control methods, rapid declines in fertility have taken place. The most spectacular example in recent years has been China.

Millions of people in the developing world, however, have no access to modern birth control methods and, indeed, some governments, on religious grounds or for strategic reasons, actively discourage family planning programmes. With greater pressures being put upon the earth's limited resources, from agricultural land to mineral wealth, and the ever-increasing impact of man's activities on the environment, the prospect of further population growth poses many and varied problems.

▲ **India,** *with the second-largest population in the world, has introduced many birth control methods. At this sterilization clinic many vasectomies are carried out at one session.*

▶ **The status of women** *in a society affects attitudes to population control. In China women are considered to be an essential part of the work force and birth control is encouraged.*

▲ **Birth rates remain high** *in many of the less-developed countries. Large numbers of children are very often encouraged by the societies, for religious, economic and political reasons.*

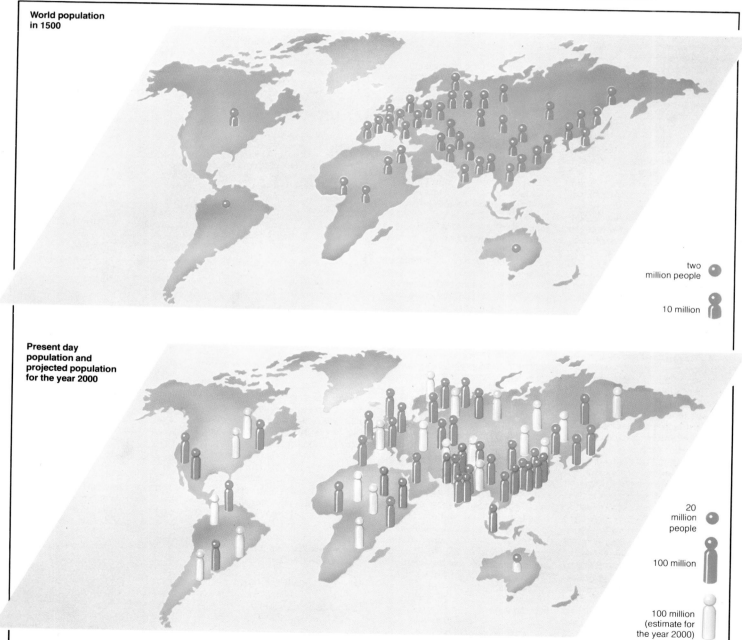

World population in 1500

two million people

10 million

Present day population and projected population for the year 2000

20 million people

100 million

100 million (estimate for the year 2000)

By about 8000 BC there were approximately five million people on earth. From then on, numbers increased by between 0.04 and 0.06 per cent a year until about 1650. The "doubling time" of human numbers had been reduced from 1,500 to 200 years by 1800, by which time world population had reached one billion.

Environment in danger

ALL life on our planet is confined to a thin skin of earth, air and water that is no more than 10 kilometres thick. It depends for its healthy existence on green vegetation which turns sunlight into chemical energy and maintains the balance of oxygen and carbon dioxide in the atmosphere. On this process are based the complex food chains made up of many thousands of plant and animal species, all of which are vulnerable to the activities of man.

The mounting impact of man on the environment is partly the result of his increased numbers. It is also due to the enormous increase in industrial activity and consumption of the earth's resources, particularly in the countries of the northern hemisphere. A two per cent annual increase in population since the middle of this century has been accompanied by a four per cent annual increase in consumption, a rate of growth which, if maintained for a century, will increase consumption 50 times and create an even greater impact on the biological environment.

The impact of man
The oceans, grasslands, croplands and forests have all felt the impact of man's rapidly increasing exploitation of these resources for food, fuel and living space. Forests play a vital role in maintaining the ecological status quo, preserving watersheds, preventing soil erosion and the silting of dams, moderating climate and providing fuel, building materials and paper. But the destruction of trees for farmland and firewood has a long history, and by the middle of this century between one-third and one-half of the earth's original forest cover had gone.

Forest management in western Europe, the Soviet Union and North America now shows an awareness of the need to conserve existing woodland, while China is striving to undo the destruction of past generations. Almost everywhere in the developing world, however, the remaining tree cover is under pressure as the growing population increases the demand for firewood supplies and farmland. Serious deforestation is occurring in the Himalayas, causing erosion and flooding in the plains below, and similar problems are reported from eastern India, Pakistan, Thailand, the Philippines, Malaysia, Tanzania and elsewhere. The tropical forests of southeast Asia, central and west Africa and Amazonia are also severely threatened, and with them the earth's richest store of rare plants and animals.

The loss of farmland
Arable land, which makes up one-tenth of the earth's land surface, is also under great pressure. The area of cropland is being reduced by serious erosion and conversion to non-agricultural use at a faster rate than new land is brought under the plough. Japan, for example, lost six per cent of cropland in the 1960s.

The oceans, too, have recently been exploited more intensively than ever before: the fish catch trebled from 21 to 72 million tonnes between 1950 and 1980. As a result, many areas have been overfished, particularly in the North Atlantic, where there have been sudden declines in catches of cod, haddock, sole and herring. The Peruvian anchovy has been grossly overfished and several species of whale have been hunted almost to the point of extinction.

The oceans are suffering also from another consequence of man's escalating consumption: the generation of excessive and dangerous wastes. The seas, which cover two-thirds of the earth's surface, have become a dustbin for oil, chemicals, radioactive materials, sewage, junk metal, pesticides and detergents, among many other products. Approximately one million tonnes of oil seep into the sea from ships and drilling rigs each year, and many inland seas and estuaries are now so heavily polluted that fish, if they survive at all, are not safe to eat. Pollution is also having its effect on human health through the air we breathe and the food and water we consume. Some 600,000 different chemicals are in daily use and every year several thousand new ones enter into significant use. Among the illnesses they have produced are parasitic infections, emphysema, heart disease and some cancers. With polluted rivers running across national frontiers and acid rain falling over a wide area of Europe, pollution can now be considered an international problem.

A growing concern
The long-term effects of some of man's activities are uncertain. There is considerable concern about the fluorocarbons contained

Environmental pollution
The possibility that the earth's climate may be changing has been a subject much discussed in recent years. Untypical, "freak" weather during the 1970s may well be the result of natural trends of cooling and warming that the earth has experienced throughout its history, but there are suggestions that the activities of man may fundamentally alter the world's climatic patterns. A manifestation of this is what is known as the "greenhouse effect". Carbon dioxide in the atmosphere is transparent to the shortwave infra-red heat radiation from the sun, but opaque to longwave infra-red radiation emitted from warm objects on earth. What this means, in effect, is that heat can get in but it cannot get out as easily. Measurements show that the level of carbon dioxide in the air has increased significantly during this century, possibly by as much as 15 per cent. The combustion of fossil fuels produces carbon dioxide and is the chief culprit, but ploughing land also releases large amounts of soil-held gas into the atmosphere.

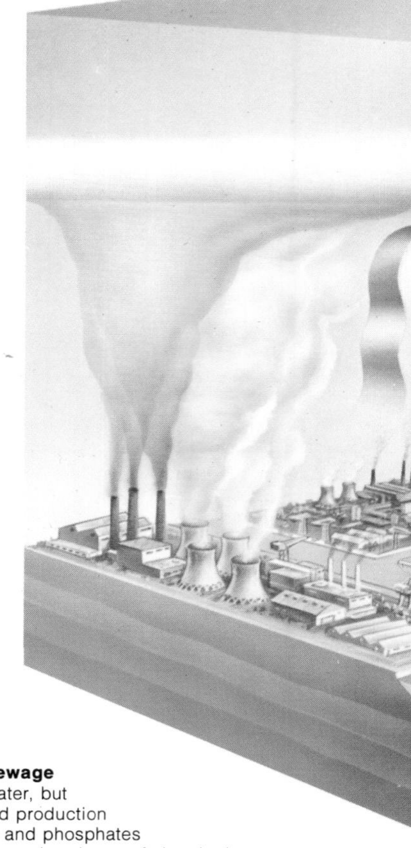

Industrial effluent and untreated sewage
are the most common pollutants of water, but the increasing use of fertilizers in food production means that larger amounts of nitrates and phosphates are leached into river systems. The over-abundance of chemicals such as phosphates in lakes and coastal waters produces an increase in algae on the surface, which blots out the light necessary for plant life. This, in turn, reduces the oxygen content and, ultimately, marine life. More and more water systems are "dying" as a result.

in aerosol cans. Half a million tonnes of these chemicals are released into the atmosphere each year, and it is thought they may be destroying the ozone layer which filters out the harmful ultraviolet radiation from the sun. The result of this could be an increase in the incidence of skin cancer, damage to crops and even a change in climate. The ozone layer may be threatened also by the release of nitrous oxides from nitrogen fertilizers, on which man depends for greater crop yields.

Of more immediate concern is the environmental stress caused by rapid urbanization. By the end of the century more than half the world's six billion people will be city dwellers if present trends continue. The lack of basic services in many cities and the crowding and stress suffered by the majority of urban dwellers in the less-developed countries pose a great environmental problem, albeit local in effect.

There is a rapidly increasing awareness of the environmental impact of man's activities. It is, however, often difficult to put a price on the conservation of nature and the protection of our vulnerable environment.

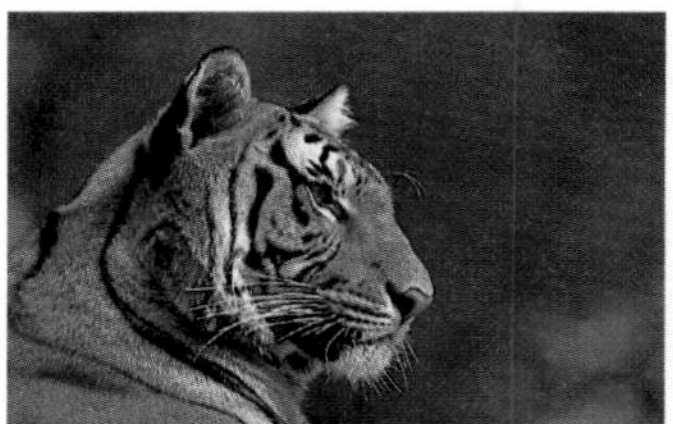

▲ **The world is in danger** of losing some of its rarest fauna as a result of man's activities. Such animals are either hunted into extinction or their habitats are ruined by human encroachment.

▼ **Road vehicles** consume vast amounts of oil and other raw materials, pollute the air and eat up land space for roads and car parks.

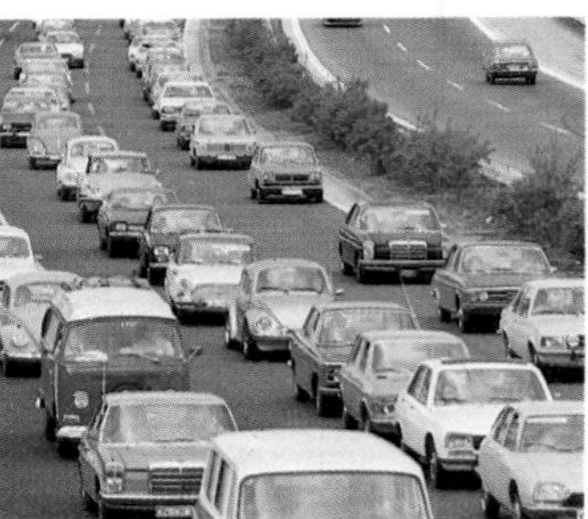

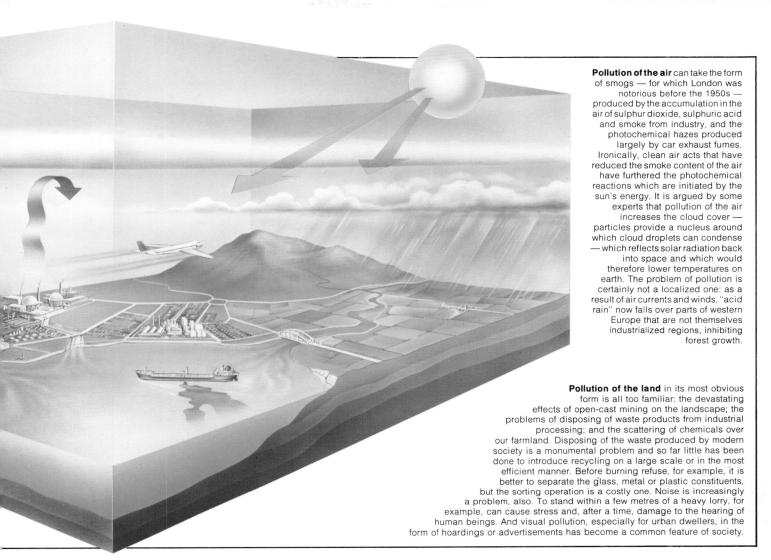

Pollution of the air can take the form of smogs — for which London was notorious before the 1950s — produced by the accumulation in the air of sulphur dioxide, sulphuric acid and smoke from industry, and the photochemical hazes produced largely by car exhaust fumes. Ironically, clean air acts that have reduced the smoke content of the air have furthered the photochemical reactions which are initiated by the sun's energy. It is argued by some experts that pollution of the air increases the cloud cover — particles provide a nucleus around which cloud droplets can condense — which reflects solar radiation back into space and which would therefore lower temperatures on earth. The problem of pollution is certainly not a localized one: as a result of air currents and winds, "acid rain" now falls over parts of western Europe that are not themselves industrialized regions, inhibiting forest growth.

Pollution of the land in its most obvious form is all too familiar: the devastating effects of open-cast mining on the landscape; the problems of disposing of waste products from industrial processing; and the scattering of chemicals over our farmland. Disposing of the waste produced by modern society is a monumental problem and so far little has been done to introduce recycling on a large scale or in the most efficient manner. Before burning refuse, for example, it is better to separate the glass, metal or plastic constituents, but the sorting operation is a costly one. Noise is increasingly a problem, also. To stand within a few metres of a heavy lorry, for example, can cause stress and, after a time, damage to the hearing of human beings. And visual pollution, especially for urban dwellers, in the form of hoardings or advertisements has become a common feature of society.

▶ **Pollution of the air** can be manifested in what is known as a photochemical haze, seen here lingering over a Californian beach. Car exhausts provide many of the raw materials needed for the atmospheric reactions: nitrogen dioxide, hydrocarbons and other organic compounds. Reactions are initiated by the sun's energy.

▼ **The destruction of tree cover,** overgrazing and overcropping contribute to the spread of deserts. The Sahara has crept both north and south – as in the Sahel region shown here – at a rate of almost 100 kilometres in the last 17 years, with the recent loss of 650,000 sq kilometres of productive land.

▲ **The air is still clear** and the land unscarred in regions of the earth that are apparently remote from the industrialized world. Studies of tissues from certain animals in the far northern and southern latitudes, however, shows evidence of pollution in the form of insecticides and other man-made chemicals that are carried to all parts of the globe by the earth's wind and water systems.

Feeding the world

WORLD food supplies have been increasing steadily and, in spite of predictions of impending disaster, have not yet been outstripped by population growth. Although current methods for determining accurately either world population or global food production figures are woefully inadequate, official United Nations statistics estimate that the earth's population has been increasing at less than two per cent annually while food production is growing at 2.9 per cent. While these figures are encouraging they do mask a high level of malnutrition, which is thought to affect between 60 and 400 million people. The cause of this problem is poverty created by an unequal distribution of land, wealth and opportunity rather than actual food shortages.

Nutritional requirements
Over the past two decades, as the young science of nutrition gathered more information, our understanding of nutritional requirements has become more exact. Figures on how many people were inadequately fed were previously based on the assumption that each person needed at least 3,000 kilocalories, including 90 grams of protein, a day. More recent findings have had the effect of revising these figures downwards to 1,990 kilocalories a day for developing countries and 2,320 kilocalories a day for developed countries. These figures are still only an average. Individual nutritional requirements vary, depending on age, sex, level of physical activity and even the climate of the region in which one lives. For example, the range extends from 820 kilocalories for a female child of less than one year to 3,100 kilocalories for a teenage boy.

The new recommended kilocalorie requirements mean that, on average, every individual needs the equivalent of 250 kilograms of grain a year. If the marketed supplies of food could have been equally distributed, then during the early 1970s, when concern about the amount of food available was so high, every person could have had 2,240 kilocalories a day, which is more than enough to engage in a healthy and active life. By the end of the 1970s approximately 1,300 million tonnes of food were reaching the market each year. That would have been enough to feed almost 5,200 million people, more than 1,000 million more than are on earth at the present time.

How much land is available?
During the same period in which nutritional requirements have been revised, our knowledge of how much food can be produced has also improved. Findings based on detailed studies of soil conditions, water availability, climate and crop characteristics indicate that there is the physical capability to produce enough food for even the highest estimate of population in the next 100 years. Studies show that a great deal more land is suitable for agricultural use than was previously believed. In southeast Asia, for example, only about 75 per cent of land which could be put under production is presently farmed.

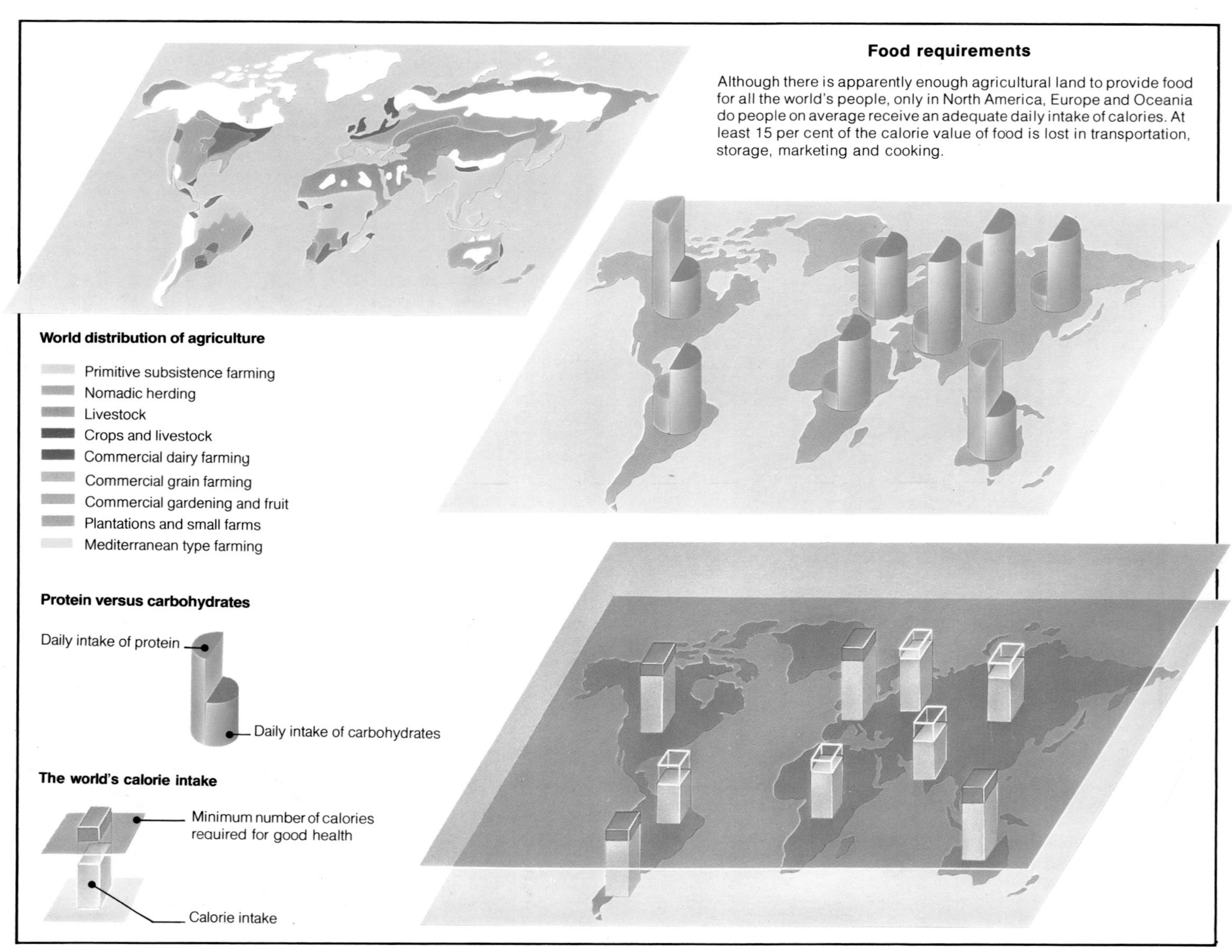

Food requirements

Although there is apparently enough agricultural land to provide food for all the world's people, only in North America, Europe and Oceania do people on average receive an adequate daily intake of calories. At least 15 per cent of the calorie value of food is lost in transportation, storage, marketing and cooking.

World distribution of agriculture

- Primitive subsistence farming
- Nomadic herding
- Livestock
- Crops and livestock
- Commercial dairy farming
- Commercial grain farming
- Commercial gardening and fruit
- Plantations and small farms
- Mediterranean type farming

Protein versus carbohydrates

Daily intake of protein

Daily intake of carbohydrates

The world's calorie intake

Minimum number of calories required for good health

Calorie intake

From the use of United Nations soil maps and studies of crops by the International Biological Programme it is estimated that there are 3,714 million hectares of land suitable for farming. Of these, 1,900 million have the potential for irrigation, a technique which can improve crop yields dramatically. Of course, competing uses for this land and the inability, for social and economic reasons, to gain access to "best-practice" techniques will mean that not all of this area is used to the fullest of its potential. If, however, only 1,208 million hectares were to be irrigated and crop yields were to reach 65 per cent of their potential, then 32,390 million tonnes of grain could be produced each year. That would be enough to feed 30 times the number of people on earth today.

Animal and plant resources

In addition to availability and productivity of land, food production depends on effective utilization of animals and plants. Plant-eating mammals and birds are all potentially edible. There are also numerous other animals, fish, insects and crustaceans which are eaten in some parts of the world but not in others. Many of these are in serious danger of elimination if industrial development takes place without consideration for the environmental requirements of these creatures. We need a world inventory of edible species so that these food sources are not lost by accident and not reduced without replacement.

Many of the hoofed animals thrive better in their home countries than imported sheep and cattle. They can be managed as wild herds by culling a calculated proportion each year for food. A further development would be domestication, as was performed on the original wild cattle of Europe. With modern knowledge of genetics animal breeding programmes could achieve targets in shorter periods than were necessary for the familiar breeds, and such animals as the eland and saiga antelope could be improved to meet the desired characteristics of meat, milk and hides that have been developed successfully in familiar domestic breeds.

More plants to eat

Just as the animal resources of most of the world are hardly yet developed, so too are indigenous plants in many regions where it is urgent that more food is produced locally. The International Biological Programme of 1963-74 identified several hundreds of plants which can fix nitrogen and, therefore, do not need nitrogen fertilizers. Many of these plants produce edible parts and could be improved by selection to become crops. Social anthropological studies show that people eat a much wider variety of plants and parts of plants than is generally supposed. An inventory of these would indicate which have the widest degree of acceptance and these could then be the subject of deliberate programmes of improvement to increase production.

The third factor in food production is technology, and its suitability to the societies that adopt it. So far, wherever a new technology has been introduced into a society where land and other resources are unequally distributed, the effect has been to increase the gap between rich and poor. Even when more food has been produced, poor people seldom get more of it, and there are many documented instances when they have got less.

The future of food production raises many issues, but the overriding aim should be to increase the food supplies available to the millions of people who still go hungry. The problem is to try to ensure that technical advance will for the present keep pace with population growth, and will in the long run overtake it so that those millions can have an adequate diet in the future. The question is what kind of food production is most suitable.

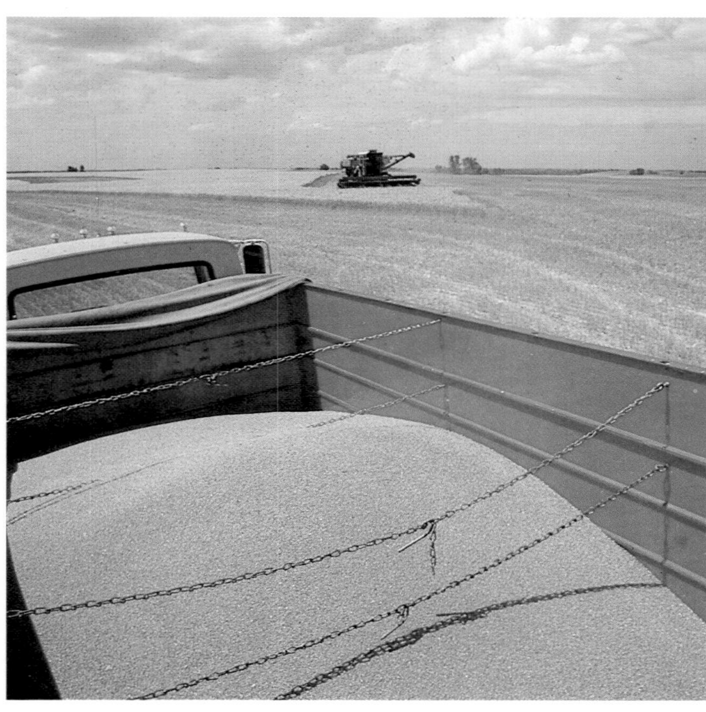

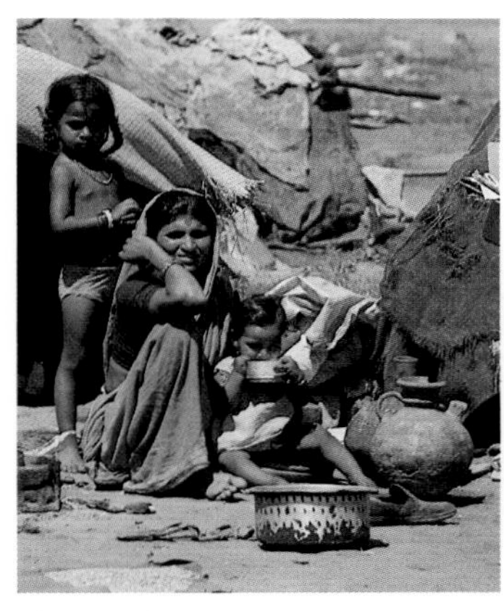

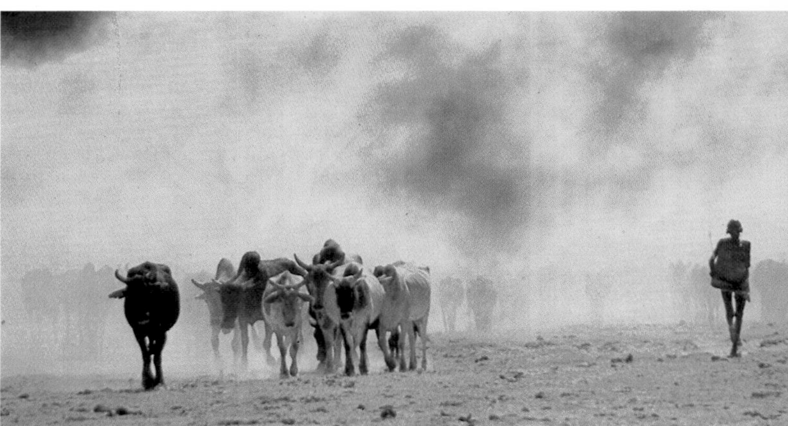

▲ **Nomadic pastoralism** *is practised on marginal lands where extremes of temperature or lack of water make cultivation virtually impossible. Subsistence farming makes no impact on world food markets, but half the world's population lives off the land and produces little or no surplus.*

▲ **The rolling plains** *of the North American continent have made the United States the granary of the world, on which millions of hungry mouths depend. (The USSR is actually the largest grain producer, but also the greatest consumer.) A series of bad harvests in the 1970s reduced world grain reserves to a few days' supply.*

▶ **The dire conditions** *of most of the world's poor — here typified by a mother and her children in the slums of an Indian city — do not offer much opportunity for an adequate diet.*

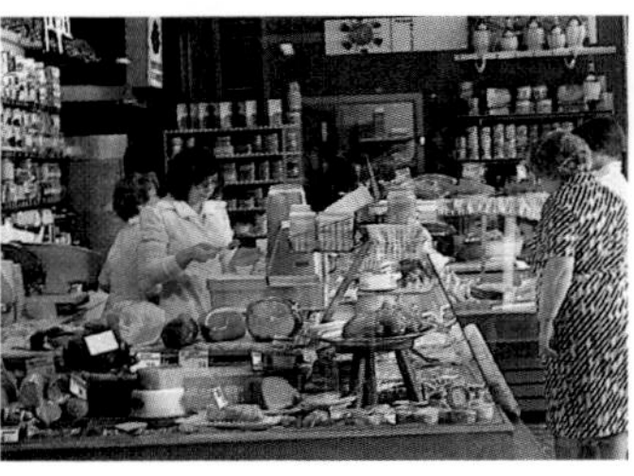

▼ **It is claimed** *that half the food bought in the United States ends up in the waste bin. We are constantly encouraged to buy more even though obesity is an extensive problem in the western world.*

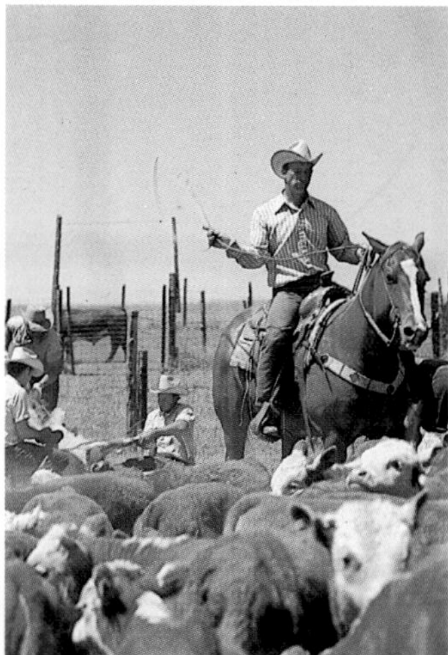

▲ **Commercial livestock ranching** *is big business, especially in North America. It is often argued that we do not need as much meat as we eat and that cattle consume too much grain.*

What kind of food production?

WITH the world's population increasing by 70 or 80 million each year, and with many of the present population living off a totally inadequate diet, there can be little doubt about the urgency of increasing available food supplies. Nor is there any question about the two principal ways of doing so. They are to increase the area at present cultivated or grazed by farmers, and to obtain higher production per unit area from the existing farmlands.

In certain respects, these two objectives overlap. The effective area of cultivation will be doubled, for example, if a single, annual crop can be replaced by double-cropping. To obtain two crops in place of one, however, will probably require either a new breed of plant, which will mature faster, or an addition to the water supply, probably by irrigation, to provide enough water for double-cropping.

Extending the farming frontier
The principal methods by which the cultivated or pastured area can be extended are by clearance of forest, by irrigation, by drainage, by breeding hardier stocks and by removing the barriers presented by disease. The first three date back to antiquity. Irrigation was the basis of the Egyptian, Mesopotamian and some Central American civilizations, while in Europe, where nearly 90 per cent of the potentially arable land is cultivated, forest clearance has historically been the main method of extending the farming frontier, just as it has been for the past three centuries in eastern North America. Forest clearance assumes that the need for, or value of, land under agriculture is greater than the value of land under trees, an assumption that could realistically be made in medieval Europe, but that has ceased to hold good, for example, along the Canadian margins of agriculture. It is probable, in fact, that worldwide at present the forest is advancing on the farmland rather than the reverse. The potential for extra cropland, however, does exist in many areas of the world.

Irrigation and drainage both involve re-directing natural water supplies, and together they have already transformed great areas of Asia (the continent with by far the largest irrigated area, and where the Chinese have been using valley and delta drainage for millennia), the Middle East and North America. The Mississippi Valley and the Central Valley of California are today two of the world's most productive farming regions, yet a century ago one was a tangle of swamps and trees, and the other an area of desert and salt pans. Irrigation and drainage hold out good prospects for further increasing the area of farmland, but the capital costs are enormous, and the more irregular the water supply, the higher those costs become.

The breeding of hardy and quick-maturing plants has already served to push back frontiers by permitting the use of land formerly unsuitable for cultivation because of low temperatures or a short growing season. It is by this means that the great cereal areas of the Canadian prairies and the Soviet steppes have been enlarged still further.

The removal of barriers raised by disease would open up other great areas to the food producer. Africa, one of the most seriously food-deficient regions of the world, would be the principal target in this respect: only 22 per cent of its potentially arable land is cultivated, and much of it is unproductive because of diseases such as sleeping sickness.

A green revolution
The other main method of producing more food is by increasing yields per hectare. If yields worldwide were at the level of those in northwest Europe or the American Midwest, then every hectare of the world's farmland could support between 15 and 20 people on average, instead of the present global figure of between 2.8 and 3.0. The problems are not those of technology, but of supply, economics and education.

On the technical side, the major contribution so far has been made by the plant breeders. The heart of the so-called green revolution of the past four decades has been the scientific creation of high-yielding strains of corn, wheat, rice and other crops, together with improved breeds of livestock. A series of international institutes, most of them located in less-developed countries, now provide a focus for this work. Sometimes the development concerns the period necessary for the plant to mature: a rice that matures in 120 days instead of 160 may permit two crops to be grown each year instead of one. Sometimes it is a case of altering the density of planting: it is possible by scientific breeding to double the number of plants per square metre without overcrowding or loss of growth. Alternatively, the actual structure of the plant may be involved: it must have a shorter stem, for instance, in order to be able to support a heavier head.

Other areas of technical innovation are in the use of chemical fertilizers and pesticides, and in educating the farmer in a wider range of expertise, thus encouraging him to make more innovations. There is, however, the limitation imposed on adopting the new farming techniques by economics. Not only are supplies of seed for the new "wonder crops" limited at present, but the additional fertilizer input and the equipment to harvest and store larger crops have to be paid for. And this cost is not purely financial. Chemical fertilizer production involves far greater energy inputs than the additional food energy yielded by their use. It is necessary, therefore, to possess the raw materials, whose price has been soaring, and to consume other resources, before the farmer can produce more food. It is small wonder that many farmers cling to traditional methods.

Certainly, improvements in food supply can be made: by cutting down losses due to pests and disease; by mariculture, or farming the sea for food; by organizing the marketing of products through co-operatives and re-organizing the tenure of land; and in the future, perhaps, by the development of synthetic food stuffs. Most of these, however, are long-term projects and, like the cross-breeding of plants, cannot be hurried.

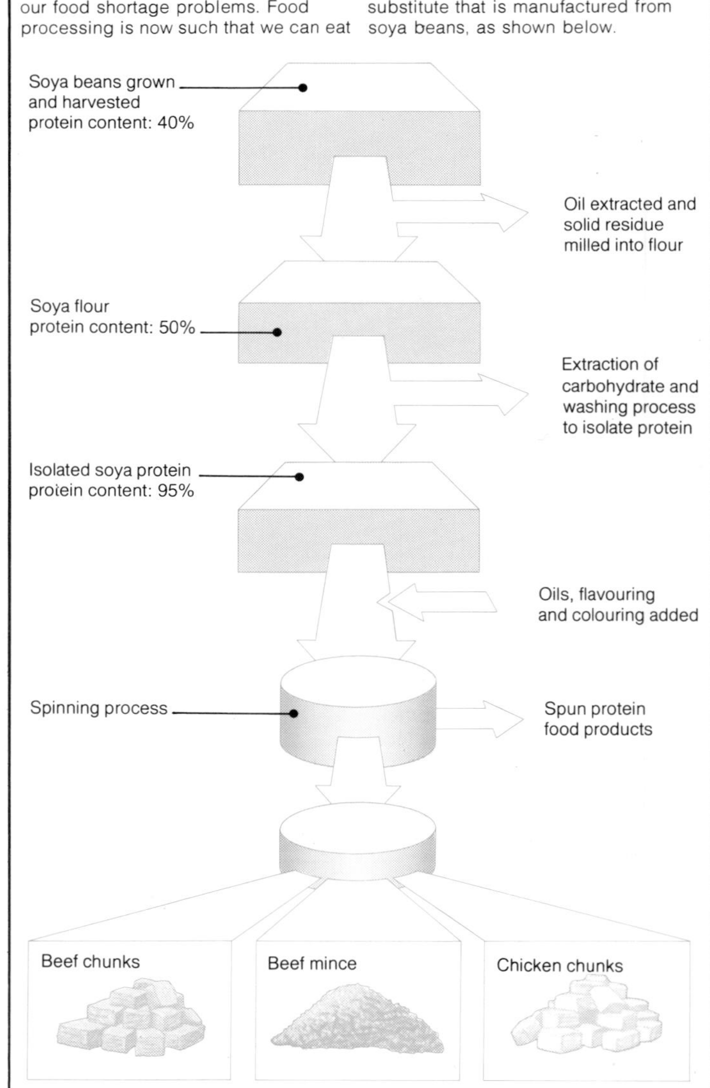

Textured vegetable protein

Textured vegetable protein is thought by many experts to be the answer to our food shortage problems. Food processing is now such that we can eat what appears to be meat but is in fact Kesp, a textured vegetable protein meat substitute that is manufactured from soya beans, as shown below.

Soya beans grown and harvested protein content: 40%

Oil extracted and solid residue milled into flour

Soya flour protein content: 50%

Extraction of carbohydrate and washing process to isolate protein

Isolated soya protein protein content: 95%

Oils, flavouring and colouring added

Spinning process

Spun protein food products

Beef chunks

Beef mince

Chicken chunks

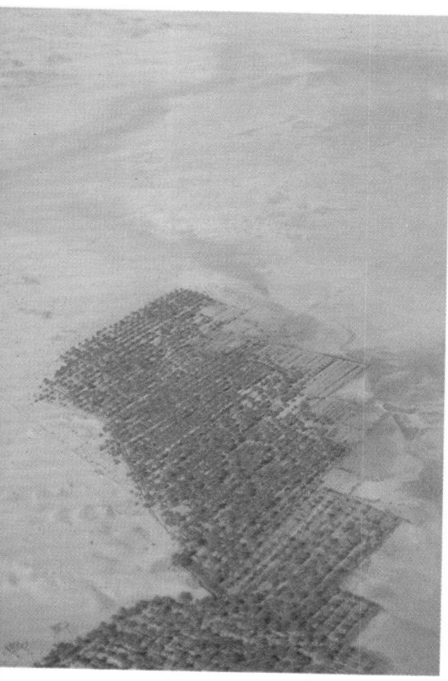

▲ **Deserts** are not necessarily infertile regions and, once water is supplied, they can be transformed into highly productive areas, as in the Algerian Sahara. Water can be pumped from underground reservoirs, or basins can be dug so that the root systems of crops can reach groundwater supplies. Fences protect crops from sand.

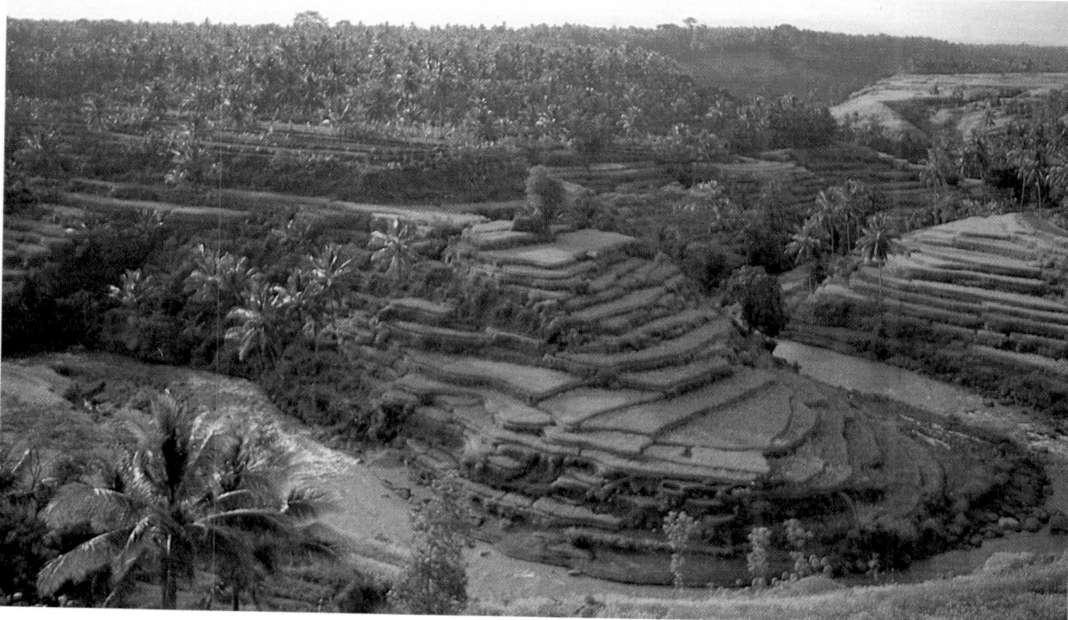

▼ **The world fish catch** reached more than 60 million tonnes a year in the 1970s as a result of greater efficiency and better technology. Some species have been seriously overfished. Attention is now being paid to aquaculture — the artificial culturing of fish — and fish farming, which increases natural stocks in the open sea or seawater tanks.

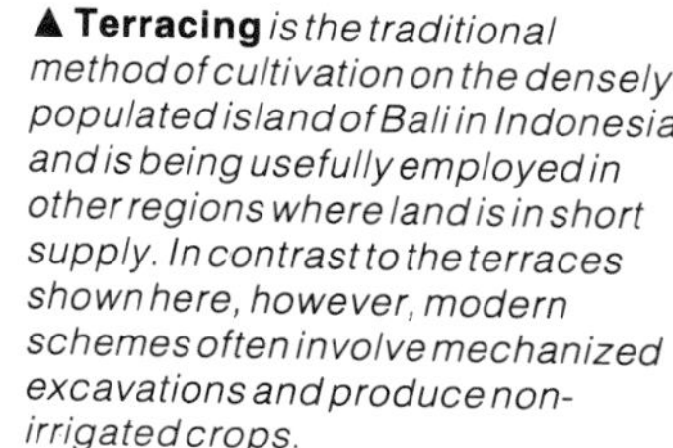

▲ **Terracing** is the traditional method of cultivation on the densely populated island of Bali in Indonesia and is being usefully employed in other regions where land is in short supply. In contrast to the terraces shown here, however, modern schemes often involve mechanized excavations and produce non-irrigated crops.

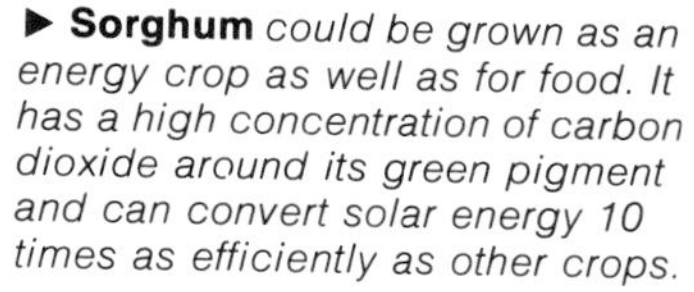

▶ **Sorghum** could be grown as an energy crop as well as for food. It has a high concentration of carbon dioxide around its green pigment and can convert solar energy 10 times as efficiently as other crops.

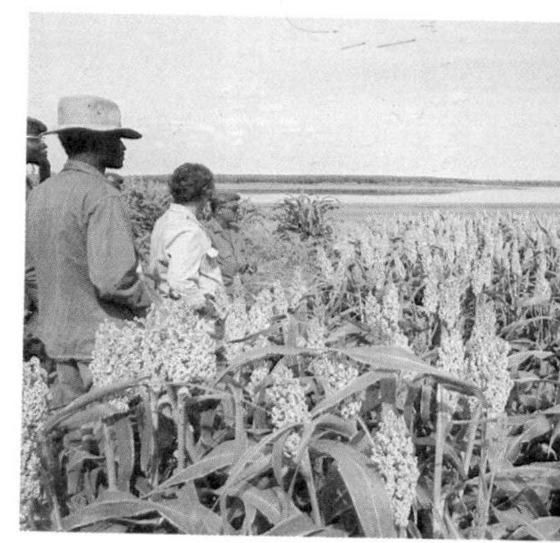

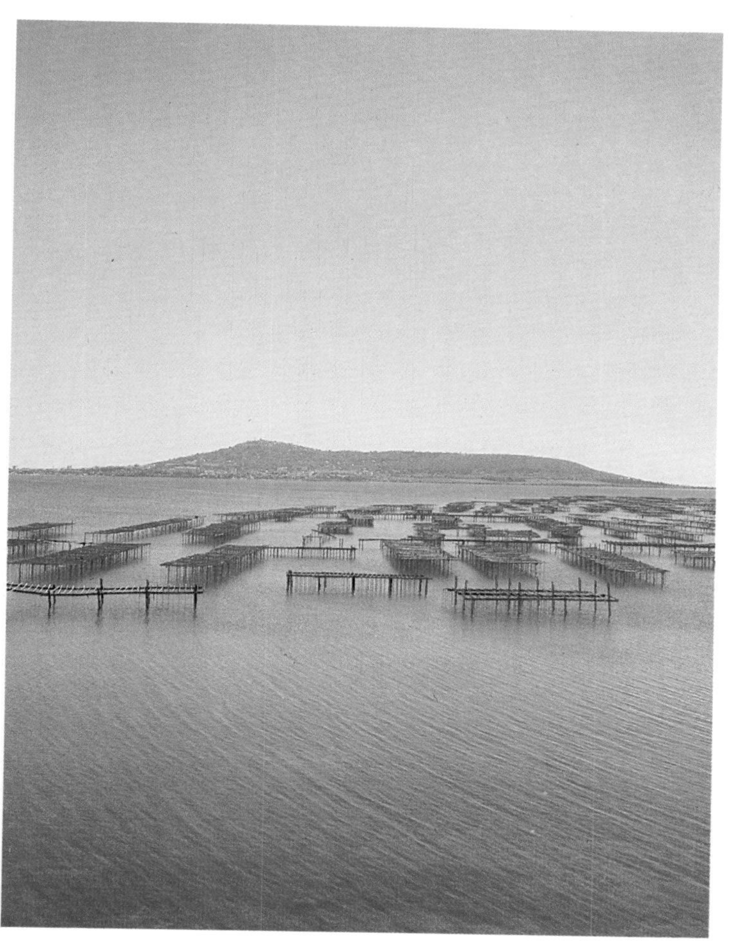

Nutrient film technique

Technology has come to play an increasingly important role in modern agriculture and one new method — the nutrient film technique — means that the farmer can actually grow crops without any soil. This is done with the aid of the device shown here, whereby crops are planted, either outdoors or in greenhouses, in plastic trays. A solution containing all the vital nutrients the plant needs is constantly circulated through the trays. This method — first developed by the Glasshouse Crops Research Institute in England — has proved highly successful and is used in many parts of the world.

Nutrient feed pipe

Flow pipe

Plants supported in plastic gullies

Pump   Nutrient flow   Nutrient solution tank

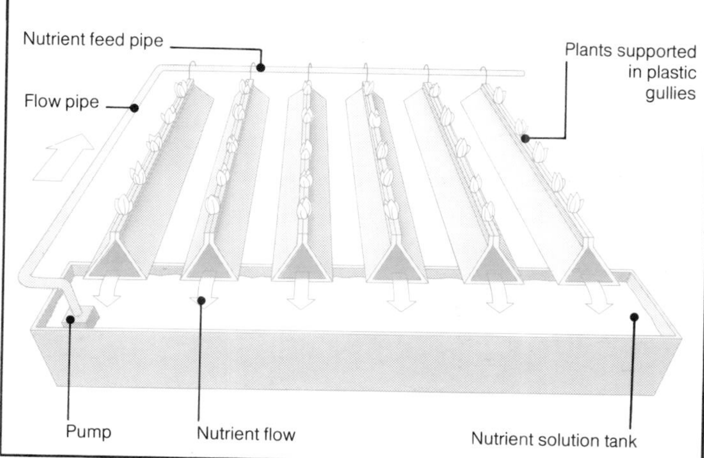

Man's quest for energy

SINCE the Industrial Revolution there has been a close relationship between economic activity and world energy use. For many years a one per cent increase in economic growth has been matched by a similar increase in energy demands. Because of this close, historic relationship, and given fears of impending resource scarcity, energy is very much at the centre of the debate about man's future. Energy underlies everyday life: it heats and lights homes, offices and factories, drives machinery and raises steam for industrial processes, fuels trans-port systems, and is a key require-ment for food production — directly for tractors and food processing and indirectly for the production of fertilizers and pesticides.

Since man learnt to utilize fire, the quest for energy has been a key feature of every civilization. Humans, animals, wood, wind and water were harnessed and the availability of such sources of energy set the limits to economic activity within societies.

First use of fossil fuels

Since the process of industrializa-tion and urbanization began, man has increasingly supplemented the use of renewable sources of energy by exploiting the depletable fossil fuels. At first coal was mined at or near the surface, but as demand grew and technology improved, underground mining complexes were developed. Coal was used in boilers, steam engines and locomo-tives and in open fires to heat homes; converted to coke it fuelled a breakthrough in iron and steel production, and as gas it supplied street lighting and domestic heat-ing; some was used to make chemi-cals, dyes and explosives.

Coal dominated world energy supplies until the 1950s, although oil and natural gas were by then widely used in the United States. In 1900, coal accounted for 94 per cent of the world's use of commer-cial fuels, oil four per cent and natural gas one per cent, and wood and hydroelectric power for the remainder. By 1950, these percen-tages had changed to 62, 25 and nine respectively, and in 1974, the year after the oil crisis, to 32, 45 and 21. Today oil and natural gas account for more than two-thirds of world fossil fuel supplies.

The other dramatic development since the beginning of this century has been a change in the scale of demand for energy. World con-sumption of fossil fuels increased ten-fold between 1900 and 1980 from 760 million tons of coal equi-valent (tce) to 8,500 million tce. The western industrialized economies, mainly North America, Western Europe and Japan, consumed 60 per cent of the total, the USSR and Eastern Europe 23 per cent, and the poorer, less-developed countries (including those with large popula-tions such as India and China) only 17 per cent of the total.

World energy supplies

Coal production reached 4,125 mil-lion tonnes in 1984 and is forecast by the World Energy Conference to double by the year 2000. The main producers are the USSR, USA,

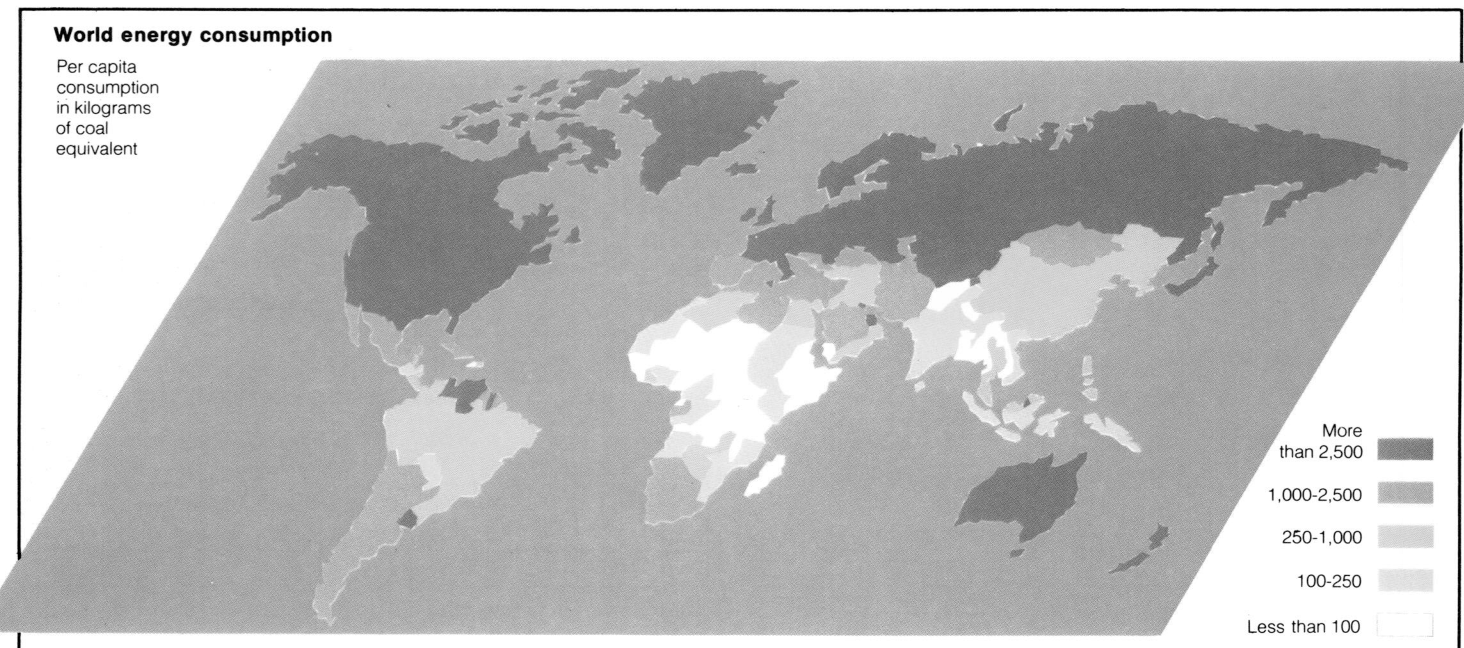

World energy consumption

Per capita consumption in kilograms of coal equivalent

More than 2,500

1,000-2,500

250-1,000

100-250

Less than 100

A continuation of current trends of energy consumption for 75 years would lead to an annual world consumption of about 80,000 million tce in the year 2050: today's poor countries, with 75 per cent of the world's people, would still account for only one-third of total energy consumption.

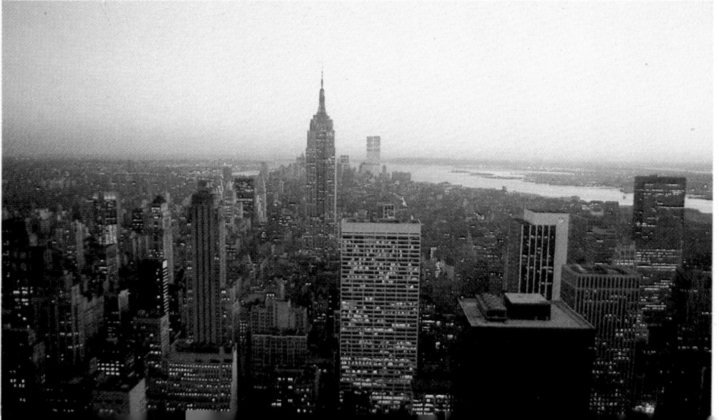

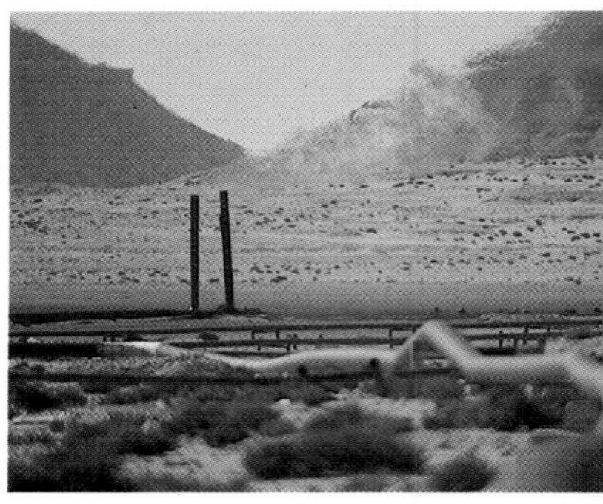

▶ **Large pipelines** — *used here to carry oil across the desert in Qatar — have higher capital costs but lower running costs than other forms of transport. They also raise international political issues.*

◀ **Modern, industrialized society** — *epitomized by the New York skyline — is dependent upon vast supplies of energy. In 1981 the total amount of energy produced commercially was the equivalent of 2.1 tonnes of coal per person.*

China, Poland, the UK and West Germany. Amongst developing countries, India is the major producer. Ultimately recoverable resources are vast — more than one million, million tonnes.

Oil production rose to 4,000 million tce in 1980, the major producers being the USSR, USA, Saudi Arabia, Iran, Venezuela and Iraq. A major recent development has been the exploitation of offshore oil resources. Ultimate crude oil reserves are estimated at between 250 and 300 thousand million tonnes, with a similar quantity in unconventional forms such as oil shales, tar sands and synthetic oils, exploitable at higher costs. Natural gas has become a major world fuel only relatively recently. Proved reserves are estimated at between 70 and 90 thousand million tce, but this is thought to be conservative.

Nuclear power is based on the fission (or splitting) of uranium atoms in a range of reactor types, the dominant categories being water-cooled (mainly in the USA, France, West Germany and Japan) and gas-cooled (mainly in the UK). Future reactor types include fast breeders based on a mixture of uranium and plutonium fuel and the high temperature reactor. Nuclear power at present provides about 11 per cent of world electricity requirements but a substantial increase is planned by 2000. The extent of uranium reserves is subject to considerable uncertainty and this also applies to thorium, which may prove a suitable alternative fuel, although no commerical thorium reactors have been put into operation yet.

Only about 14 per cent of world hydroelectric potential is exploited at present, mainly at sites in industrialized countries. The capital costs of major hydro schemes are often beyond the reach of developing countries unless aided by massive financial assistance.

Industry is the largest consumer of energy in the developed world, accounting for 35-40 per cent of total demand. Those industries concerned with processing of materials — iron and steel, chemicals, aluminium, bricks — account for two-thirds of this total. Technical changes in industrial processes have led to improved energy efficiency and recent fuel price increases will encourage this further. Increased recycling of materials will also reduce the energy demand per unit of output. Public and private services account for 10-15 per cent of energy demands in the developed countries, mainly for heating and lighting.

Energy use in the home

Domestic use accounts for 20-25 per cent of energy demand. Of this about 60 per cent is used for space heating and air conditioning; 20-25 per cent for water heating; 10 per cent for cooking and between five and 10 per cent (almost entirely as electricity) for appliances such as washing machines, televisions and so on. Many appliances, for example hi-fi, use little electricity, but others such as tumble driers and dishwashers may be key future growth areas. Improved insulation of buildings could reduce domestic energy demands.

Transport accounts for 25 per cent of energy demand in the USA and 20 per cent in Western Europe. The largest proportion is used by road transport, especially the private car. A range of new technologies might reduce fuel consumption per mile by 20-40 per cent in the coming decades and there is scope for improving the efficiency of public transport systems.

Over the next 20-30 years, the world will experience a transition from a dependence on oil and gas towards greater use of coal, nuclear power and renewable energy sources. Major technical changes will be necessary and will require a considerable developmental period before widespread application is possible.

How one nuclear reactor works

Certain atoms of uranium break into fragments when a neutron is added to the nucleus. If this occurs, the uranium atom is split into two and energy is released in the form of heat. At the same time neutrons are given off and they continue the process by splitting other nuclei. This is called a chain reaction and it forms the basis of the generation of nuclear power. In a nuclear reactor the chain reaction is kept going at a steady rate and the heat is used to produce steam to drive electricity generators. In order to maintain a steady rate the number of neutrons that continue the reaction has to be controlled. This is done by absorbing excess neutrons in control rods made of boron. If neutrons produced by the reaction are slowed down they can split the nuclei more easily. The slowing down is achieved by surrounding the fuel with a moderator — so-called because it moderates the speed of the neutrons. The reactor is protected by a concrete shield to prevent the escape of dangerous radiation. In a gas-cooled reactor, such as the one shown here, the heat produced by the reaction is removed by circulating carbon dioxide gas. Alternatively, the heat can be removed by circulating water through the system. The heat is used to convert water to steam.

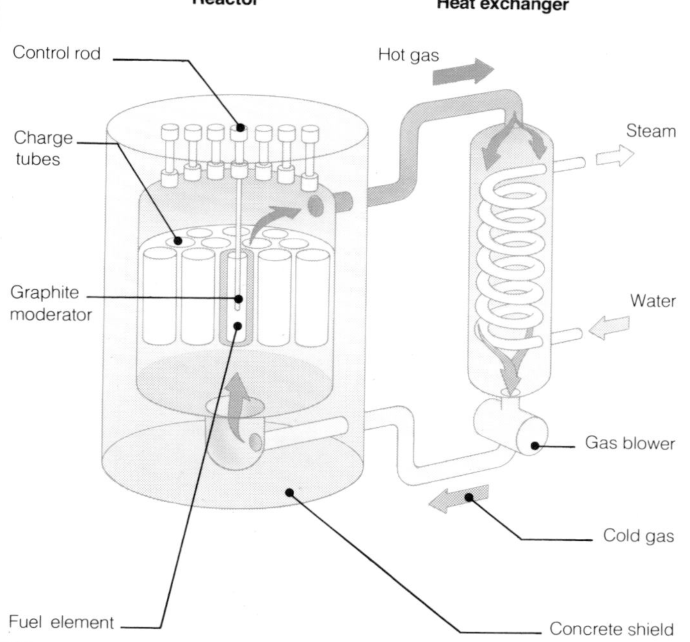

Reactor   **Heat exchanger**

Control rod

Charge tubes

Graphite moderator

Fuel element

Hot gas

Steam

Water

Gas blower

Cold gas

Concrete shield

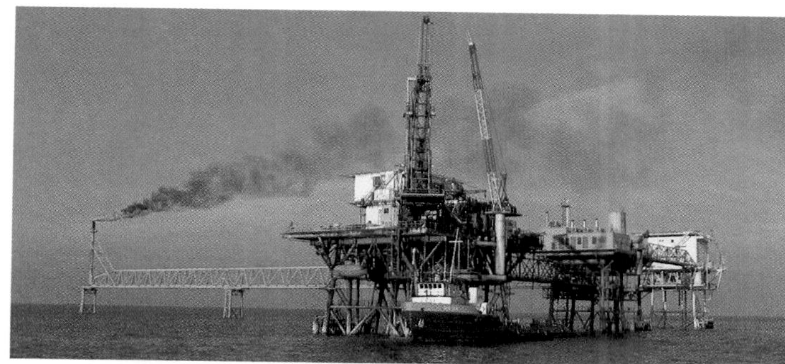

▲ **Natural gas** *was once considered to be a useless by-product of drilling for oil and was burnt off. Today, however, technical developments, such as liquefied natural gas tankers and large pipeline networks, have enabled a rapid growth in its use. Deposits are found in association with oil or on their own, as in this Iranian field.*

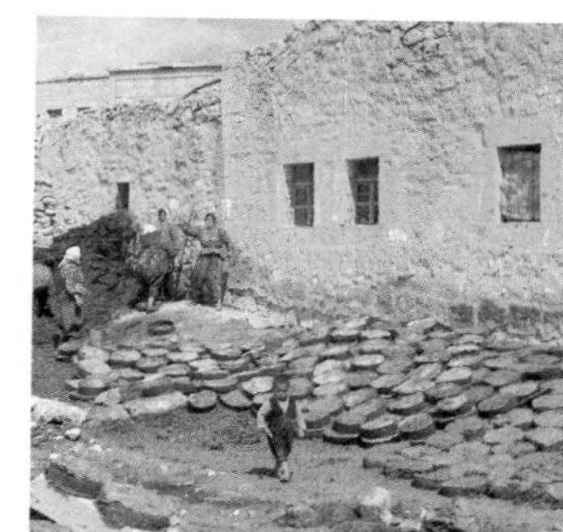

▶ **Millions of people** *in the less-developed countries are dependent for energy on what nature supplies, mainly firewood and dung. Non-commercial consumption of energy is difficult to assess accurately, but is probably in the region of 1,500 tce. Such energy sources are steadily being replaced by fossil fuels, however.*

▶ **Recoverable coal reserves** *are vast enough to last for almost 3,000 years at current rates of consumption. Greater concern for the environment may affect production techniques, however. Open-cast mining — seen here in West Virginia — is one of the most economical mining methods but it usually has a devastating effect on the landscape.*

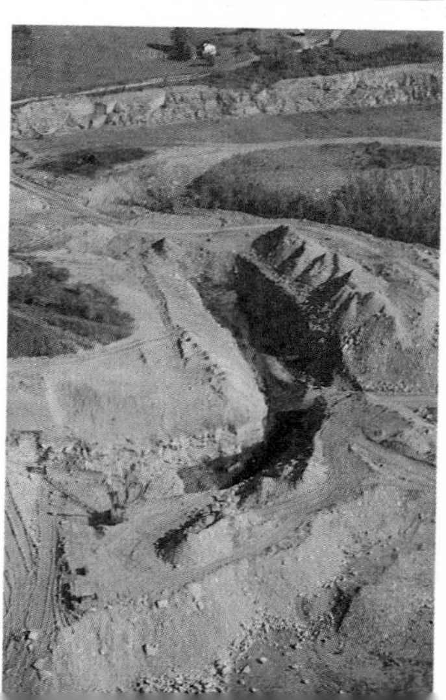

Energy alternatives

AT PRESENT the world depends almost entirely on non-renewable sources for its energy. Nearly 90 per cent of our energy is derived from the major non-renewable fossil fuels: coal, oil and natural gas. A high proportion of the rest, especially in countries of the Third World, comes from wood which, although renewable in principle, is being rapidly depleted. We are never likely to run out of any of these resources completely, but we are already experiencing large increases in the cost of obtaining each unit of fossil fuel. This trend will continue and will impose an ever-increasing strain on the world's systems of production and the societies built on them.

We are at the moment ill-equipped to deal with this eventuality: none of the possible renewable sources of energy are anywhere near ready to start replacing fossil fuels. Moreover, the processes of developing and commercializing major new technologies are extremely difficult and lengthy. Nuclear power, for instance, has been under intensive and massively funded development for more than 30 years, and yet it is still far from being a mature technology and supplies only one per cent of the world's energy demand. Renewable energy, by which we mean direct solar, geothermal, hydroelectric, wind, wave and tidal power, biomass fuels and nuclear breeding and fusion, will require a similar, if not greater, volume and intensity of effort if it is to make a substantial impact on world energy supplies in 50 years' time.

Renewable energy and lifestyles

Renewable energy sources (with the exception of nuclear) are often called "alternative" energy. Alternative energy tends to be linked with the idea of alternative culture — implying a radical change in lifestyle both at an individual level and in the political, economic and social spheres. It is perhaps unfortunate that practitioners of 'alternative culture' in the West are rarely good advertisements for the advantages of their lifestyle but it is certainly true that at their existing (mainly rudimentary) stage of development, most renewable energy sources are most compatible with a low energy-using, rural society with limited industrialization. This is because the majority of renewables provide only diffuse, low-grade energy, which is subject to considerable variability in supply.

Much of the development effort in renewable energy must, therefore, be concentrated on making it as compatible as possible with urban, industrial society. The difficulties of achieving this (through effective storage and the up-grading of low-grade heat, for instance) are what makes the development of renewable energy sources so expensive. In the long term, therefore, widespread reliance on renewable energy will probably not require major and fundamental changes to existing lifestyles. Renewable nuclear sources (breeders and fusion), on the other hand, are specifically designed to fit existing industrial societies and their development in the future may well be compatible only with even more centralized and interdependent societies than exist at present.

Sources of renewable energy

Direct solar energy is the most obviously attractive source because of its abundance. The major problems in its development (common to a number of renewables) concern its low efficiency and its variability, which requires the development of storage technologies. High yields of useful energy from the sun are therefore likely to need heavy capital investment. Domestic space heating technology is reasonably well developed and electricity production from direct solar sources has been demonstrated, but enormous problems remain to be solved.

Hydroelectricity is the only renewable source in significant commercial use, and it provides more than one-fifth of the world's electricity. Its main problems are that it is not a genuinely renewable source in the long term (because of reservoir silting) and that most sites suitable for large-scale development have already been used in

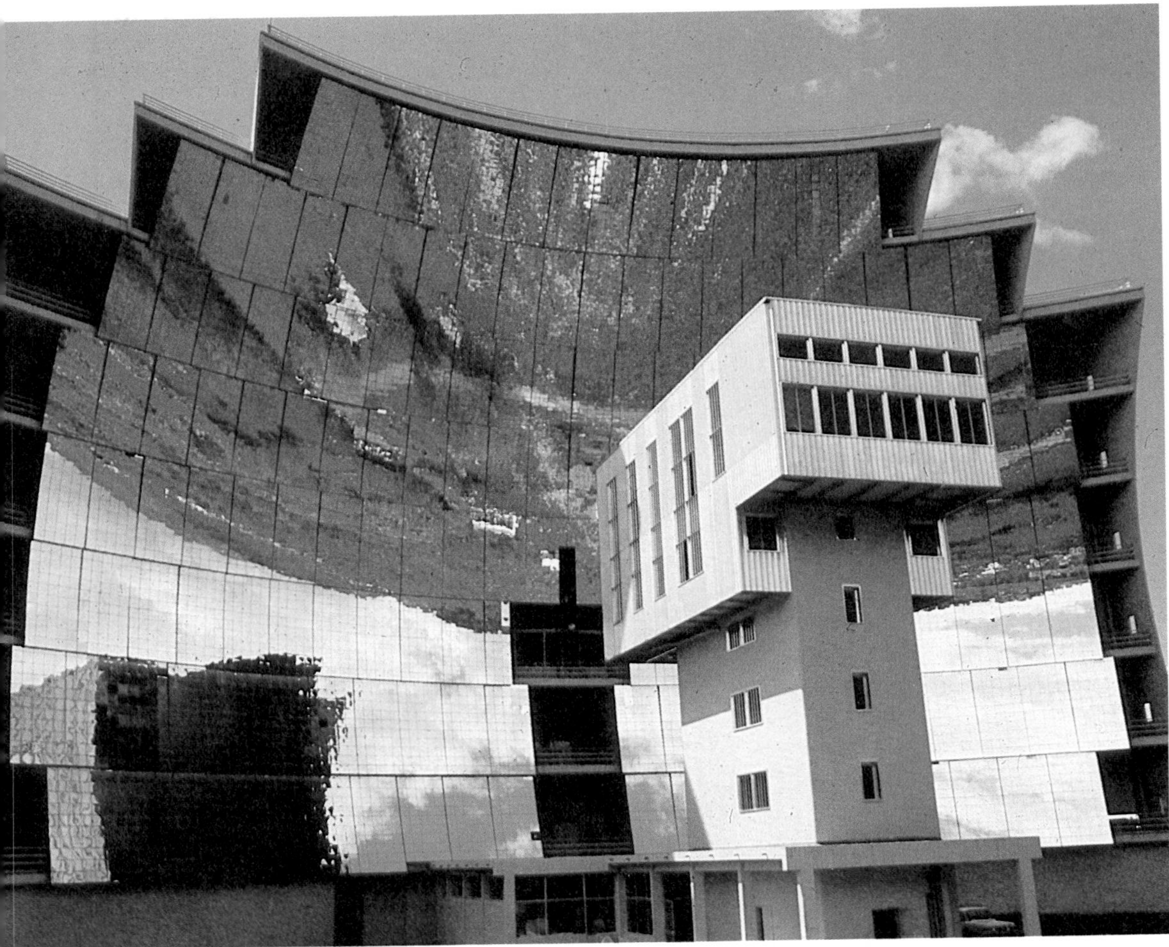

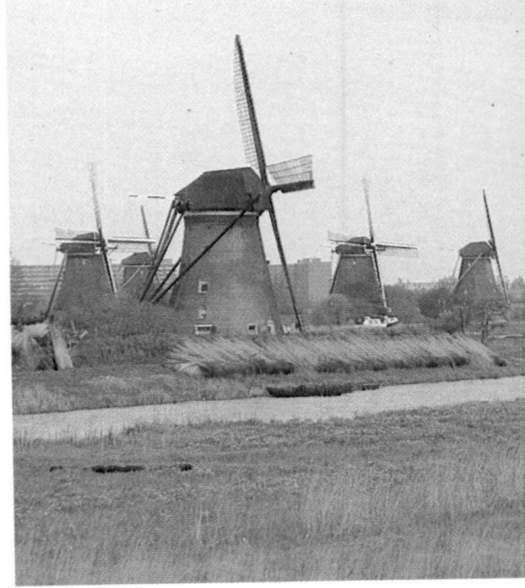

▲ **Wind power** *was used traditionally for pumping water or grinding corn and modern wind power generators have been built in some areas, such as the Orkneys. Wind is an attractive energy source since its use produces no extra heat load on the environment.*

◄ **The world's largest solar furnace,** *at Odeillo in the French Pyrenees, uses a large concave mirror to focus the sun's rays. In regions where there is strong sunshine during the day, solar energy can be used for space heating or to supply hot water to homes or larger buildings that have a low requirement for hot water.*

many industrialized countries. Geothermal sources make use of the earth's internal heat to supply either heat or electricity. Limited commercial development has already taken place. Diffuseness is again a major developmental problem.

Wind power has improved significantly since the heyday of traditional windmills. It may well prove extremely suitable for rural use (pumping and electricity) where climatic conditions are suitable. Wave power could in principle supply large amounts of electricity, but has not yet been substantially demonstrated, and its development faces major technical and economic problems. Tidal power has already been demonstrated on a fairly large scale, but there are few suitable sites in the world.

Biological sources of energy (wood, dung, wastes and crops) are already of vital importance to the Third World, though there are major problems of depletion. The main long-term problem for biomass fuels is competition with food production for the use of land.

The future of nuclear power

Fast breeder nuclear reactors — which "breed" their own fuel in the form of plutonium — and fusion reactors — in which common light elements fuse and release energy — can be considered as renewable sources. Breeders are being built on a commercial scale, but technical, safety and environmental problems remain to be solved. They are, nevertheless, a long-term possibility for electricity production and have massive government backing in both capitalist and communist countries as the main "technical fix" for fossil fuel scarcities. Nuclear fusion is an attempt to reproduce on earth the fusion reaction of the sun, and it would mean an end to the world's energy problems. Fusion occurs, however, at temperatures of about 100 million degrees and the problems of holding the resulting "plasma" stable and then safely extracting energy are currently well beyond our technical capabilities.

The obvious and enormous difficulties that still need to be overcome before renewable energy can by widely used, together with the ever-rising costs of non-renewable sources, lead to two main conclusions: that there is a critical need to promote energy conservation as a way of reducing demand and buying time; and that we will almost certainly need to rely on a combination of a large number of renewable energy sources.

▲ **A considerable number** of sites suitable for hydroelectric power schemes remain unexploited in less-developed countries, but constructing a dam such as the Kariba poses enormous financial, technical and political problems for the developing nations.

Solar power

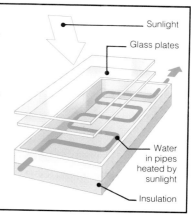

Solar collectors operate in much the same way as a greenhouse. Air inside a metal-backed box with a transparent lid of either glass or plastic is heated by the sun. The glass traps the infra-red radiation and so the box becomes a collector for the heat. Another version has copper pipes in which water is heated instead of air. A solar system can only be effective if the heat can be stored for release when the house needs warming. This is done by means of the heating of a rock store, usually placed beneath the house, or by heating water in a storage tank.

Sunlight
Glass plates
Water in pipes heated by sunlight
Insulation

▲ **Power from geothermal sources** makes use of heat stored in the earth in volcanic regions or deep sedimentary basins. Electricity can be generated from turbines driven by the pressure of underground streams of hot water and steam. Geothermal power is produced commercially in Iceland, the USA, Italy and New Zealand.

Power from the sea

One wave power converter consists of a "duck" that rocks backwards and forwards on a spindle and can extract up to 90 per cent of the energy contained in a wave that it intercepts. No commercial wave power station has yet been built, but to produce power in quantity a long series of ducks in concrete rafts would be needed. They would drive a generator within the axle linking them. It is agreed that, for greatest efficiency, wave power stations should be designed to extract energy not from the biggest waves that occur only a few times a year but from the average-sized waves that flow all the time. The stations will still have to withstand powerful storm waves, however. The average Atlantic wave can produce a power equivalent of about 70 kilowatts per metre. That is enough to heat seven medium-sized houses in a temperate climate for an hour. In a tidal power scheme a basin reservoir is created by constructing a barrage across a tidal estuary. Seawater enters and leaves the basin through ducts containing turbines that power generators. Such schemes are restricted to estuaries whose tidal range between high and low water is extremely large, such as the Rance estuary in northwestern France. The Severn estuary in England is a possible site for the future development of tidal power.

Tidal power

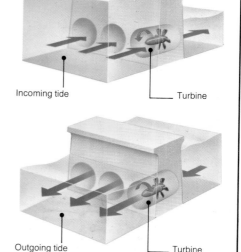

Incoming tide
Turbine
Outgoing tide
Turbine

Wave power

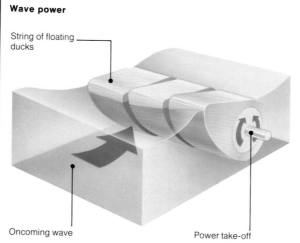

String of floating ducks
Oncoming wave
Power take-off

The earth's mineral wealth

MODERN industrial society is dependent upon an assured supply of a wide variety of mineral commodities besides those that are used as a source of energy. Very few countries are totally devoid of all non-fuel minerals but, conversely, even the few exceptionally mineral-rich nations, such as Australia, Canada and South Africa, usually need to import at least one critically important commodity.

Bulk minerals used for construction purposes, for example crushed stone, sand, gravel, cement and clay, are widely distributed geographically and are therefore unimportant in terms of international trade. Moreover, although they are consumed in large quantities, they have a low intrinsic value and can rarely be transported economically for any great distance even within their countries of origin.

Of other important mineral commodities, some, such as iron ore and bauxite (the raw material of the aluminium industry), are mined and consumed in vast quantities, but because of an unequal global distribution of resources, the considerable cost of transportation has to be borne by the many consumer nations. At the other extreme, minerals such as the various precious metals, diamonds, cobalt, chromium and many others have a high intrinsic value, are not consumed in vast tonnages and, in their case, transportation costs have relatively little significance.

Three categories

When considered in terms of their end-use, the minerals entering international trade fall broadly into three categories. Minerals required as raw materials for the iron and steel industry include, in addition to the iron ore itself, the ores of the alloying metals such as tungsten, nickel, manganese and chromium and sometimes special grades of limestone for smelting purposes.

Non-ferrous metals used in their own right and not mainly as an adjunct to the iron and steel industry form a distinct category of their own. These include the base metals such as copper, lead, tin and zinc and also the precious metals.

A third category includes those substances that are loosely termed industrial minerals, and embraces those which are not utilized as a source of metal. Some, like phos-

phate rock, fluorspar and potash, are essential raw materials in the large-scale manufacture of important chemicals. Others, like ceramic and refractory clays, asbestos, talc and mica, are sought because of certain distinctive physical and chemical properties.

The growth and survival of the world's mineral industry demands considerable expertise at all levels of exploitation, including prospecting, mining, processing and utilization. The widespread search for minerals on and beyond continental limits requires much investment in geological, geophysical and geochemical exploration methods, and reflects the reality that mineral resources are far from being randomly or equally distributed.

A geological revolution

An intellectual revolution in the earth sciences in the last two decades has led to a better understanding of how continental segments or "plates" have evolved and moved relative to each other through more than three billion years of planetary history. In turn, this wider understanding of geological processes has encouraged a broader insight into the mechanism of formation and the reasons for the distribution of many key mineral commodities. For example, the presence of many large copper-bearing ore bodies of the so-called porphyry type along the geologically active western margins of both North and South America can be related to the present-day seismic and volcanic activity in those regions. This kind of correlation provides guidelines for the location of analogous ore bodies in much more ancient terrains.

Other major mineral resources, well exemplified by the major iron ore deposits of Australia, Brazil and South Africa and bauxite in several tropical countries, have a distribution related not so much to deep-seated crustal processes as to climatic or other physical conditions that were prevalent at specific periods in the earth's history. The recognition of the role that such palaeo-environmental factors have had on the formation of these ores serves to focus the search for further mineral deposits.

Exploration for new mineral deposits is also assisted by increasingly refined methods of detection. Discovery of such

deposits is now rarely dependent upon the recognition of visible traces of ore but instead requires detection of the subtle physical and chemical effects which may be the only tangible manifestation of important ore bodies concealed beneath considerable thicknesses of barren rock. Such improvement in prospecting techniques owes much to modern methods of rapid chemical analysis, complex electronic circuitry in geophysical instruments, automatic data processing and remote sensing, using both aircraft and satellite-borne detection devices.

A success story so far

In the fields of mining, handling and milling of ore, economies resulting from the increasingly larger scale of operation have enabled the mining industry to keep pace with ever increasing demand for most commodities. The development of large and highly mechanized open-cast

mining operations at the expense of labour-intensive underground methods has resulted in a significant reduction of the economic ore cut-off grade. Further developments in the processing of low-grade ores, for example by chemical and bacterial leaching, suggest that the process of technical improvement may continue. Mining of sub-sea mineral resources can also be expected to commence in the near future, although there the barriers are of a political nature.

Despite the continuing success of the mining industry, demand for most commodities continues to rise. Investigation of the potential resources that, it is hoped, will provide the necessary margin of reserves ahead of production must therefore be pursued vigorously. Although this search has so far proved successful, some alarm has been expressed that shortages may soon appear in the supply of some key mineral commodities.

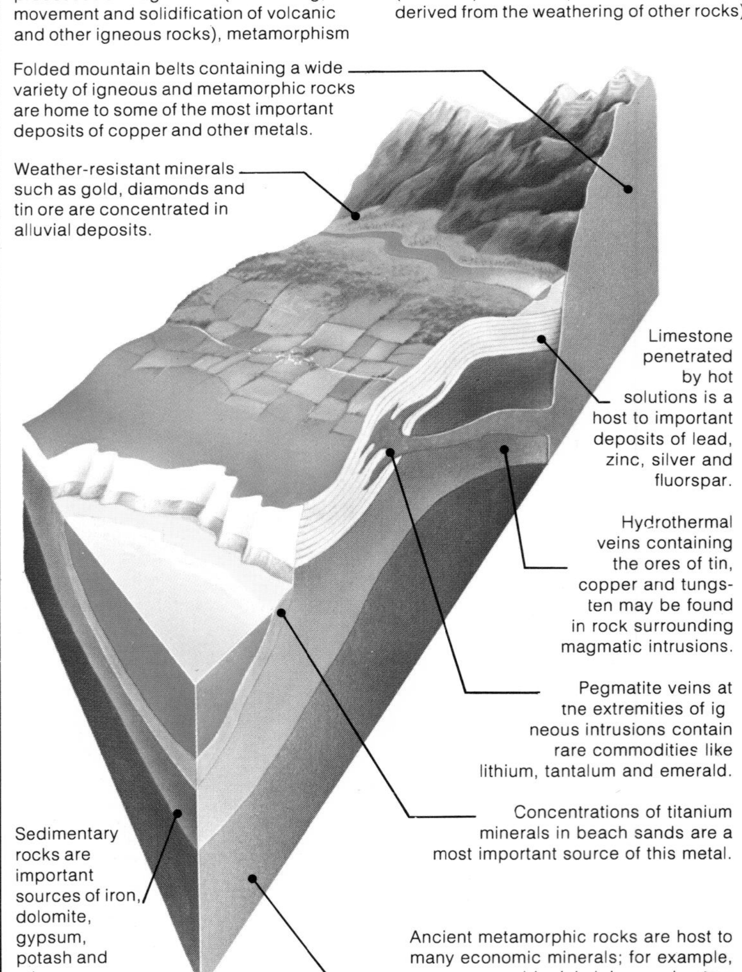

Where economic minerals occur

The distribution and concentration of minerals of economic significance is controlled by the major geological processes of magmatism (the melting, movement and solidification of volcanic and other igneous rocks), metamorphism (chemical and physical changes to rocks brought about by heat and pressure below the zone of weathering) and sedimentation (the transport and deposition of material derived from the weathering of other rocks).

Folded mountain belts containing a wide variety of igneous and metamorphic rocks are home to some of the most important deposits of copper and other metals.

Weather-resistant minerals such as gold, diamonds and tin ore are concentrated in alluvial deposits.

Limestone penetrated by hot solutions is a host to important deposits of lead, zinc, silver and fluorspar.

Hydrothermal veins containing the ores of tin, copper and tungsten may be found in rock surrounding magmatic intrusions.

Pegmatite veins at the extremities of igneous intrusions contain rare commodities like lithium, tantalum and emerald.

Concentrations of titanium minerals in beach sands are a most important source of this metal.

Sedimentary rocks are important sources of iron, dolomite, gypsum, potash and others.

Ancient metamorphic rocks are host to many economic minerals; for example, gold, nickel, iron, asbestos.

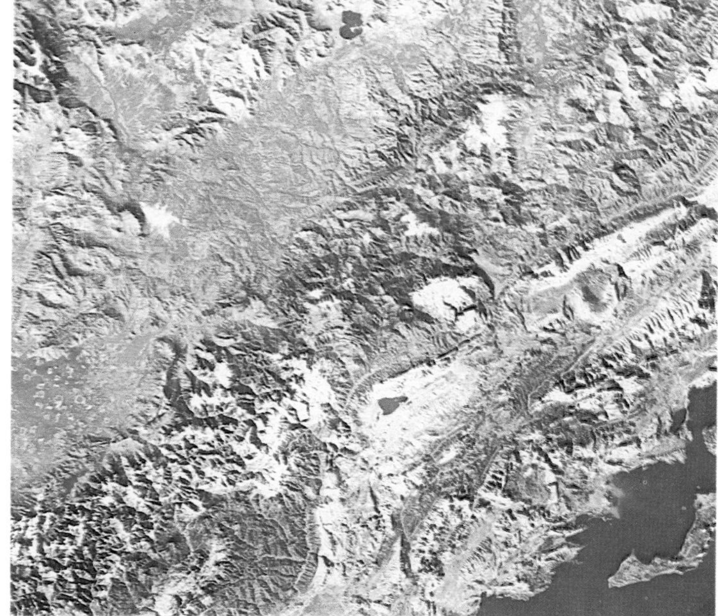

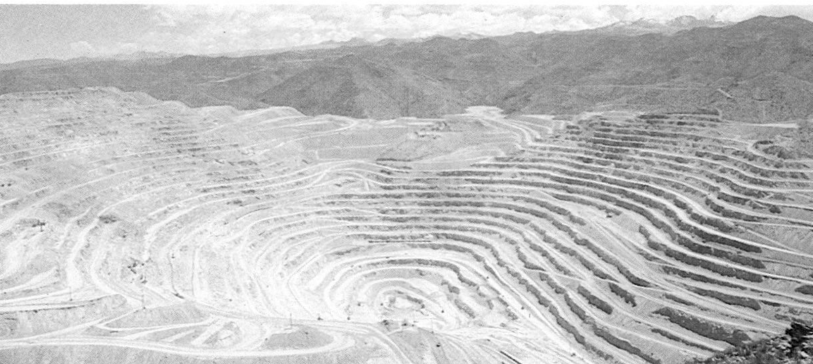

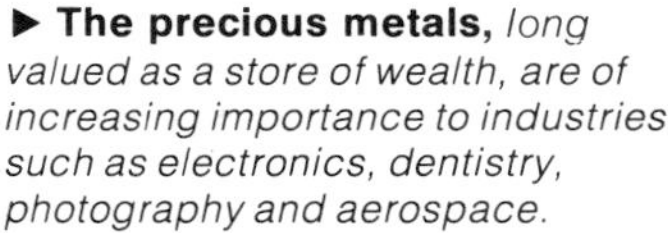

▲ **More than two-thirds** of the world's metallic mineral output is produced by open-cast methods which are cheaper and easier now that technology is available to remove thick overburden.

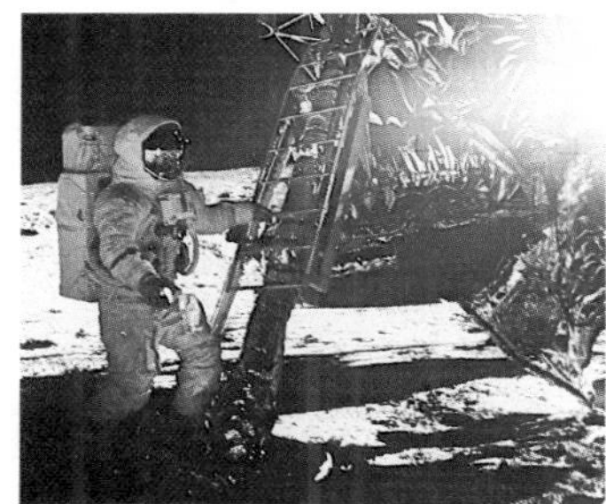

▲ **Satellite surveying** *includes taking photographs that emphasize certain bands of the light spectrum and reveal many large-scale geological features that would be* *unrecognizable from the ground. Satellite-borne detection devices have reduced the time and increased the efficiency of mineral prospecting on the ground.*

▶ **The precious metals,** *long valued as a store of wealth, are of increasing importance to industries such as electronics, dentistry, photography and aerospace.*

Major mineral deposits

Relatively few mineral deposits are of economic value, and of those the metals are the most important. Iron, the fourth most abundant element in the earth's crust, occurs widely and 480 million tonnes are produced annually. Aluminium is the most common metal, but only 17 million tonnes are produced a year. Tin deposits are restricted to a few areas which makes it an expensive metal (production: 210,000 tonnes). Other major metals include copper (8.5 million tonnes), gold (less than 950 tonnes), silver (about 12,000 tonnes), uranium (41,000 tonnes) and lead and zinc, which usually occur together (4.7 & 6.2 million tonnes respectively). The distribution of major deposits of the world's most valuable minerals is shown on the map below.

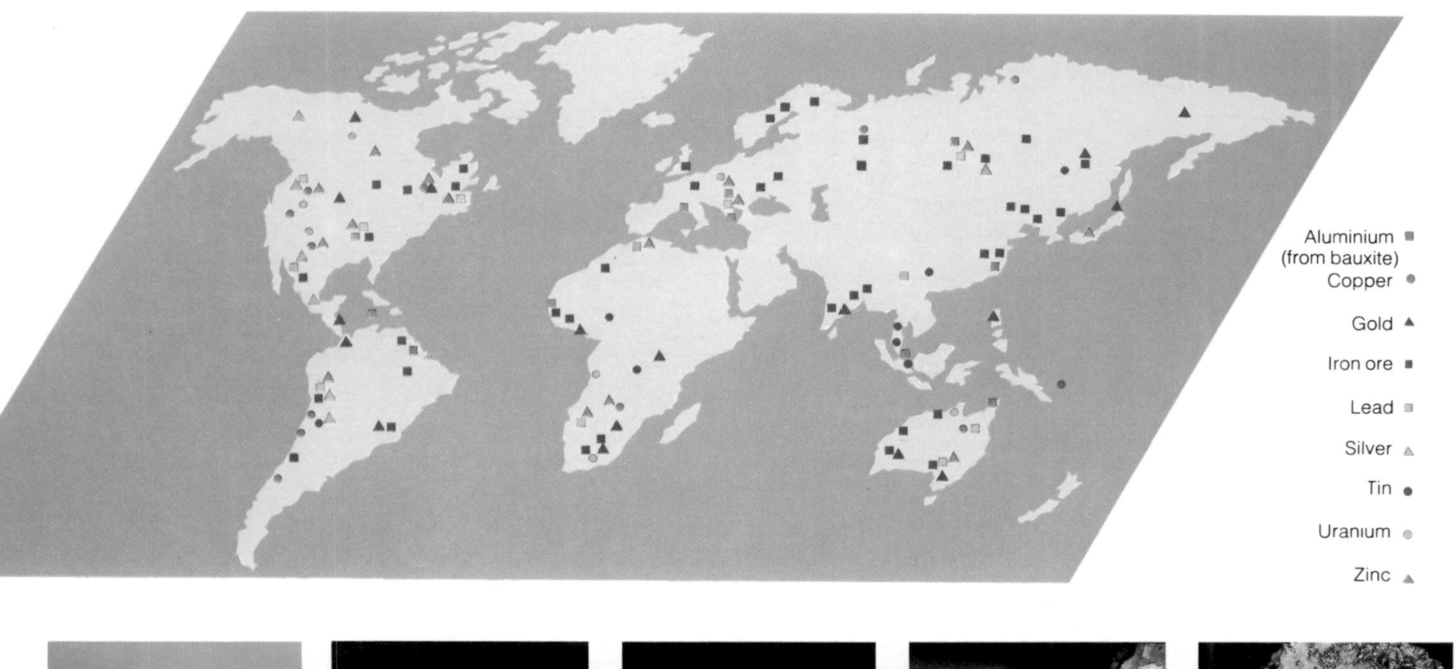

Aluminium ■
(from bauxite)
Copper ●

Gold ▲

Iron ore ■

Lead ▣

Silver △

Tin ●

Uranium ◉

Zinc ▲

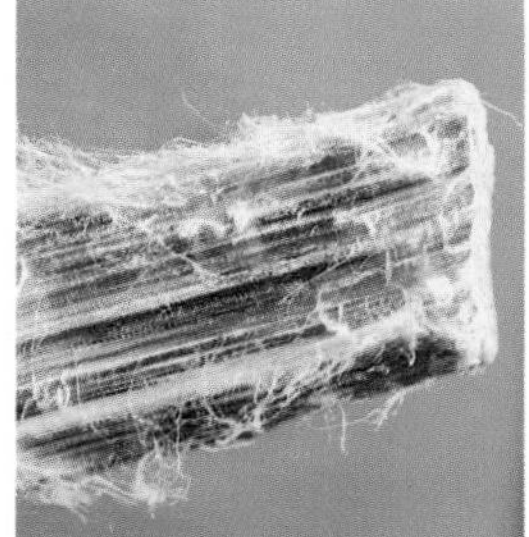

Asbestos (chrysotile)

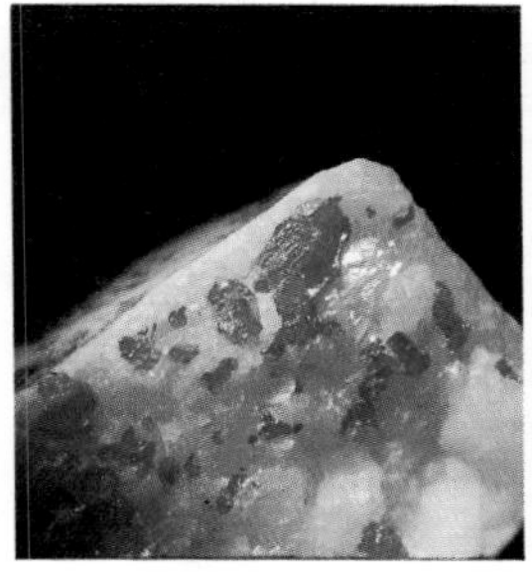

Mercury (cinnabar)

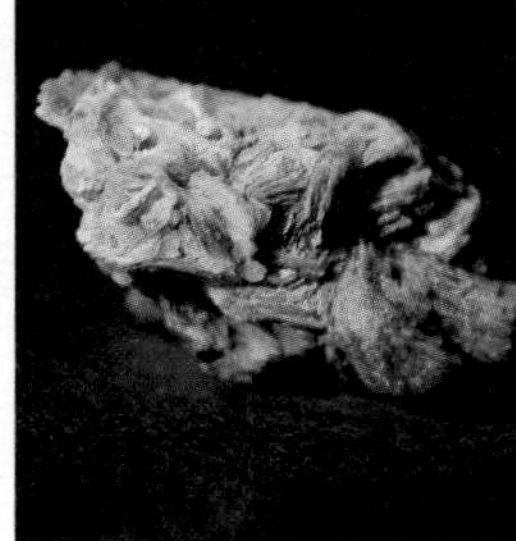

Uranium (autunite)

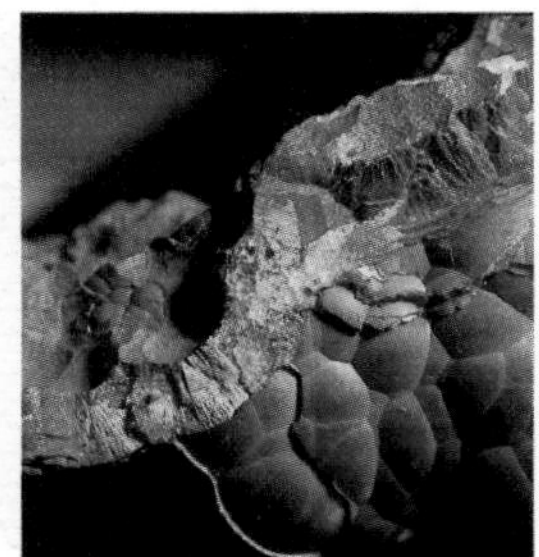

Iron (haematite)

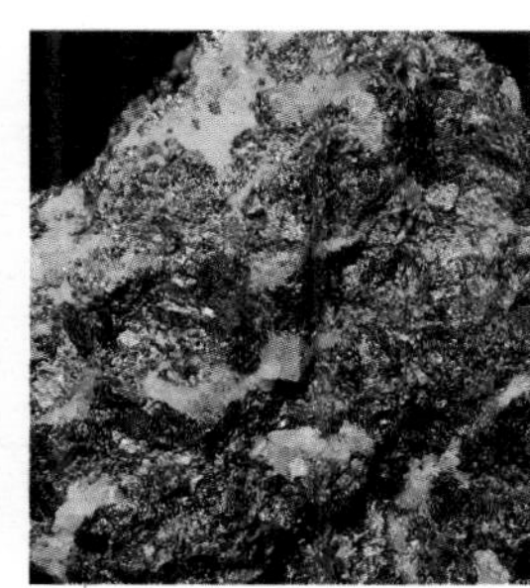

Copper (bornite)

A conserving future

IN THE context of an ever-increasing world population and the consequent rise in demand for living space, food and raw materials, it has been predicted by some economic forecasters that a crisis in the supply of our most important mineral resources is imminent. Although the mining industry has been successful in continuing to discover new resources ahead of demand, it is suggested that the number of new discoveries of ore yet to be made must be finite and that sooner or later mankind will be faced with an absolute shortage of many key commodities which are essential to an industrial society.

The question of conservation
At the simplest level of argument, conservation of minerals is proposed as a desirable object of international co-operation simply to delay for as long as possible the point at which society can no longer rely on supplies. A diametrically opposed view is, however, often supported, not least by the mining industry itself. This argues that the efficient utilization of all resources that are available and can be extracted economically at the present time, far from being discouraged, should be vigorously pursued. Only this will give an innovative society the economic encouragement that it needs to discover technical solutions to the problems of raw material shortages that may occur in the near future.

Expressed in this way, arguments for and against mineral conservation appear to be somewhat academic. However, recent history has shown that for two reasons, political and environmental, conservation or, more accurately, the efficient utilization of mineral resources is a desirable end. In the political sphere, the growth of producer cartels such as OPEC (petroleum), CIPEC (copper) and the IBA (bauxite) may well have the effect of encouraging countries which are net importers of the commodities concerned to examine more closely the efficiency with which those commodities are utilized.

The growing pressure of mining on the environment is partly the result of increased demand requiring bigger mines, but it can also be attributed to the exhaustion of high-grade ore deposits, resulting in a shift of emphasis towards large-scale extractive operations that are able to work vast low-grade deposits at a profit.

Political and environmental pressures, although fundamental in encouraging the efficient use of non-renewable resources, can often act indirectly. For example, the increases imposed for political reasons upon the price of crude petroleum not only encourage less wasteful use of the refinery products themselves but also, at second hand, the efficient use of, say, metals produced in smelters dependent upon oil-based energy.

How to improve efficiency
The efficient use and therefore, ultimately, the conservation of mineral resources involves a critical examination of the way in which they are utilized at all stages from their removal from the ground, through processing, fabrication, usage and recovery as scrap.

At the point at which minerals are mined there is often scope for improvement in recovery ratios. Open-cast mining often permits the recovery of almost 100 per cent of the ore available, but such favourable recoveries are rarely attainable with underground mining. And it must be admitted that in some cases the installation of mechanization to improve the economic performance of underground mining results in a concomitant reduction in the attainable reserves available. Mechanical cutters on longwall faces, for example, can only work on seams that are more than a minimum thickness.

The processing and fabrication stages in the conversion of raw material to finished product offer the opportunity for resource conservation in the way in which energy is used and also in terms of the way in which the final products are designed. Nevertheless, scrutiny of the energy input of manufacturing processes demands a sophisticated degree of analysis. For example, the use of the light metals aluminium and magnesium in automobile components can only be justified if the amount of fuel saved during the lifetime of the vehicle more than offsets the higher energy cost of smelting these substitute metals.

Substitution of many important commodities to meet specific shortages can be envisaged. A good example is aluminium which can substitute for copper as an electrical conductor or for steel in the construction industry. But the physical properties of substitutes are never identical, and in some cases substitution does not appear to be a realistic possibility. Silver, for example, is probably irreplaceable for photographic purposes.

Recycling
It is probable that in the short term recycling of scrap and waste will create more impact than substitution on resource conservation. Once again, however, the trade-offs have to be considered. While little energy input is involved in collecting high-quality process scrap from the floor of a machine shop, the same is not necessarily true if useful materials have to be separated at great expense from general industrial waste. There also tend to be restrictions on the uses to which recovered material can be put. Scrap aluminium usually contains some silicon and can therefore be used for making castings but not for many fabrication purposes. The total efficiency of scrap recovery is closely related to the purpose to which the material is put.

The technical aspects of mineral conservation appear to be fairly well understood. Encouragement for their implementation requires social and political initiative although the operation of the simple law of supply and demand will be effective in time.

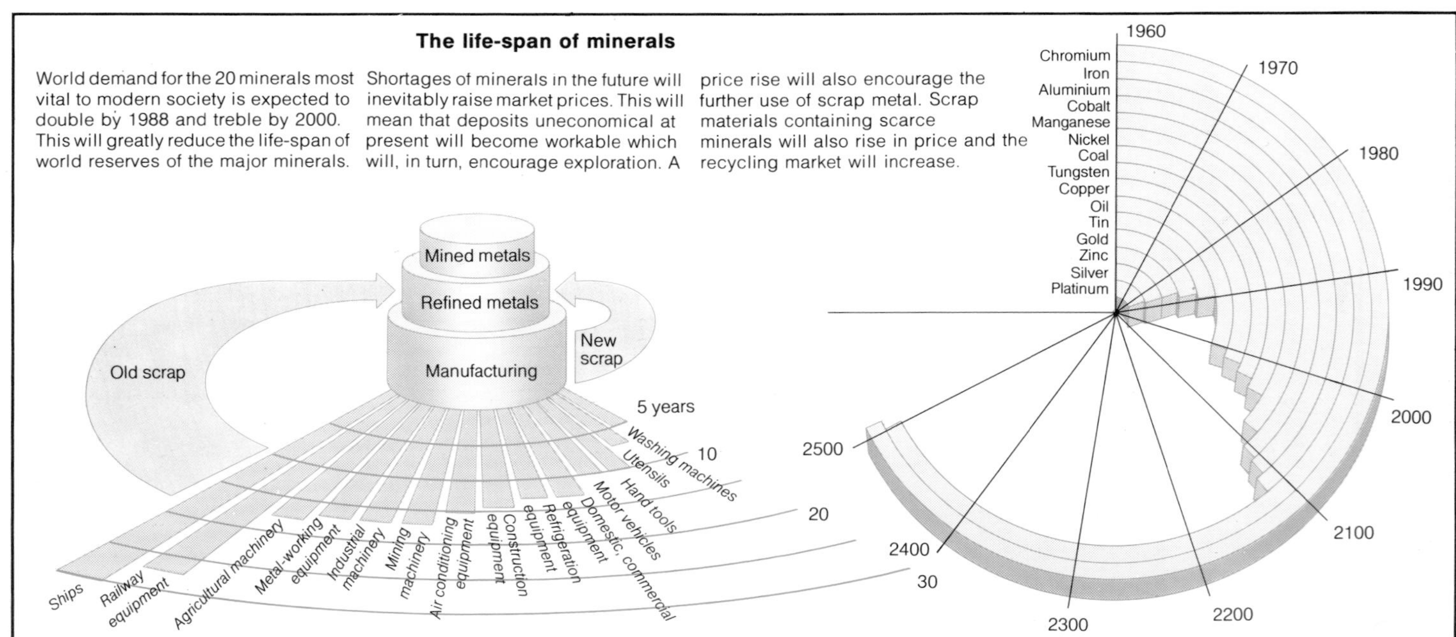

The life-span of minerals

World demand for the 20 minerals most vital to modern society is expected to double by 1988 and treble by 2000. This will greatly reduce the life-span of world reserves of the major minerals. Shortages of minerals in the future will inevitably raise market prices. This will mean that deposits uneconomical at present will become workable which will, in turn, encourage exploration. A price rise will also encourage the further use of scrap metal. Scrap materials containing scarce minerals will also rise in price and the recycling market will increase.

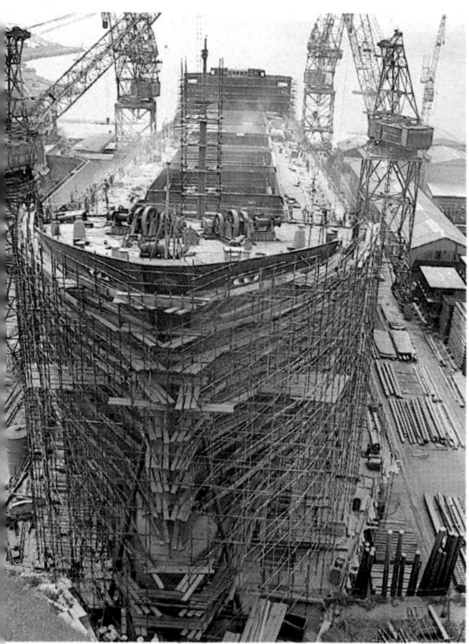

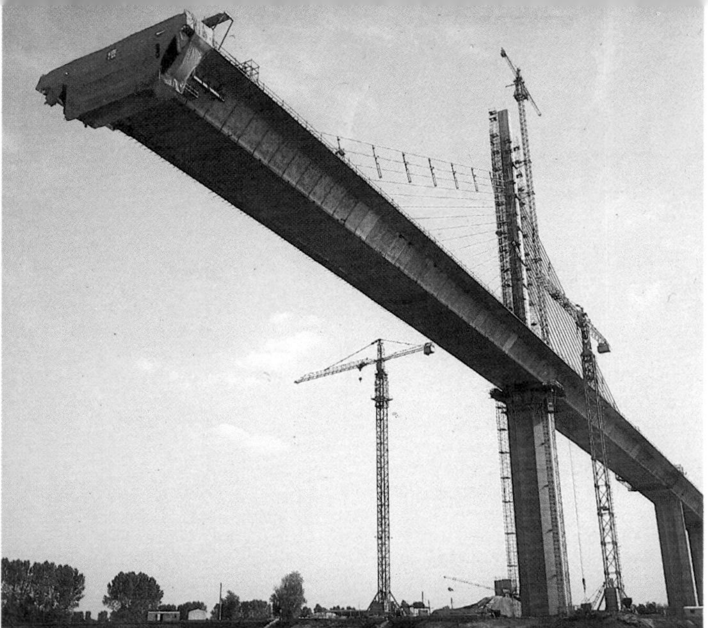

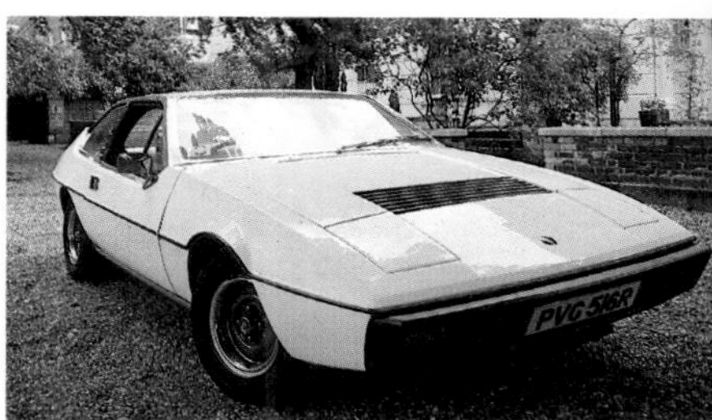

▲ **Iron,** and its principal alloy, steel, are the most important and widely used metals. Iron and steel mills, consuming vast quantities of energy and water as well as raw materials, and the steel-consuming industries such as ship-building represent more than anything else the road to industrialization for the less-developed world.

▶ **More and more** food and drink is sold in non-returnable containers, especially bottles and cans, which create mountains of litter. Aluminium cans, for instance, are no good for composting, they do not degrade and therefore have to be removed. They can be recycled but separation is a costly process.

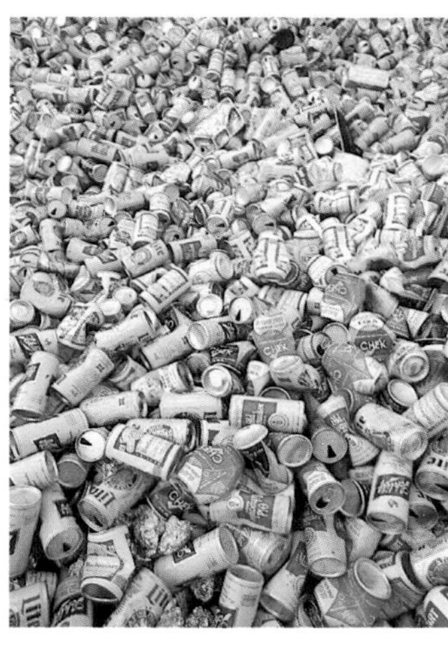

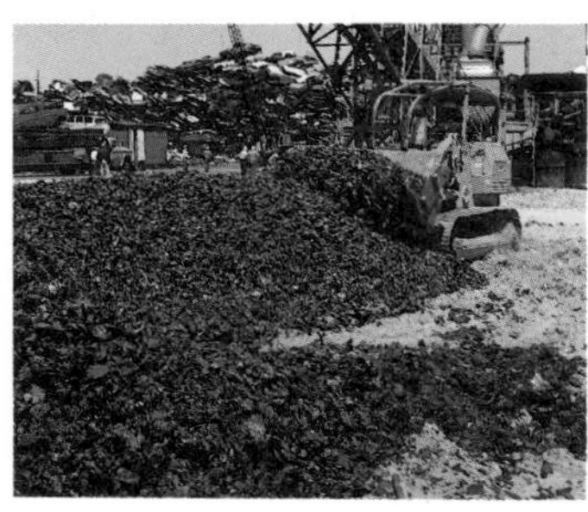

▲ **Millions of cars** are dumped each year when they could be recycled. Since they contain plastic, rubber and other metals as well as steel the end-product from crushing has to be refined before it can be re-used.

▲ **If more motor vehicles** could be produced economically from substitute materials such as glass reinforced plastic, a significant saving of metals would be made.

◀ **Bridges** constructed from reinforced concrete as opposed to metal are another step towards the conservation of minerals.

▼ **Manganese nodules,** found beyond depths of about three kilometres below the surface of the oceans, may be commercially dredged in the future. The origin of these nodules is uncertain, but they may prove an invaluable source of heavy metals as land deposits become increasingly depleted.

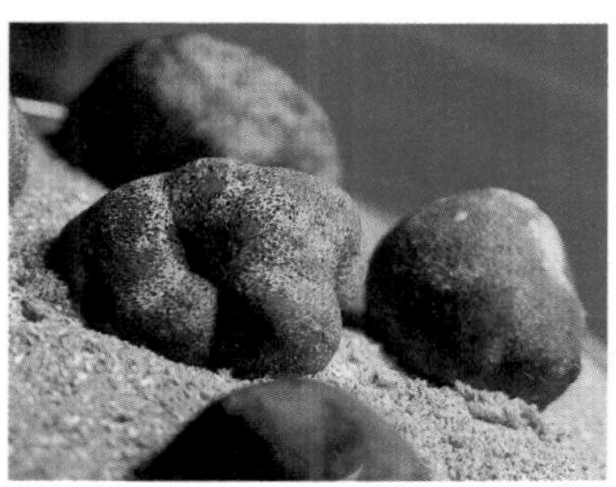

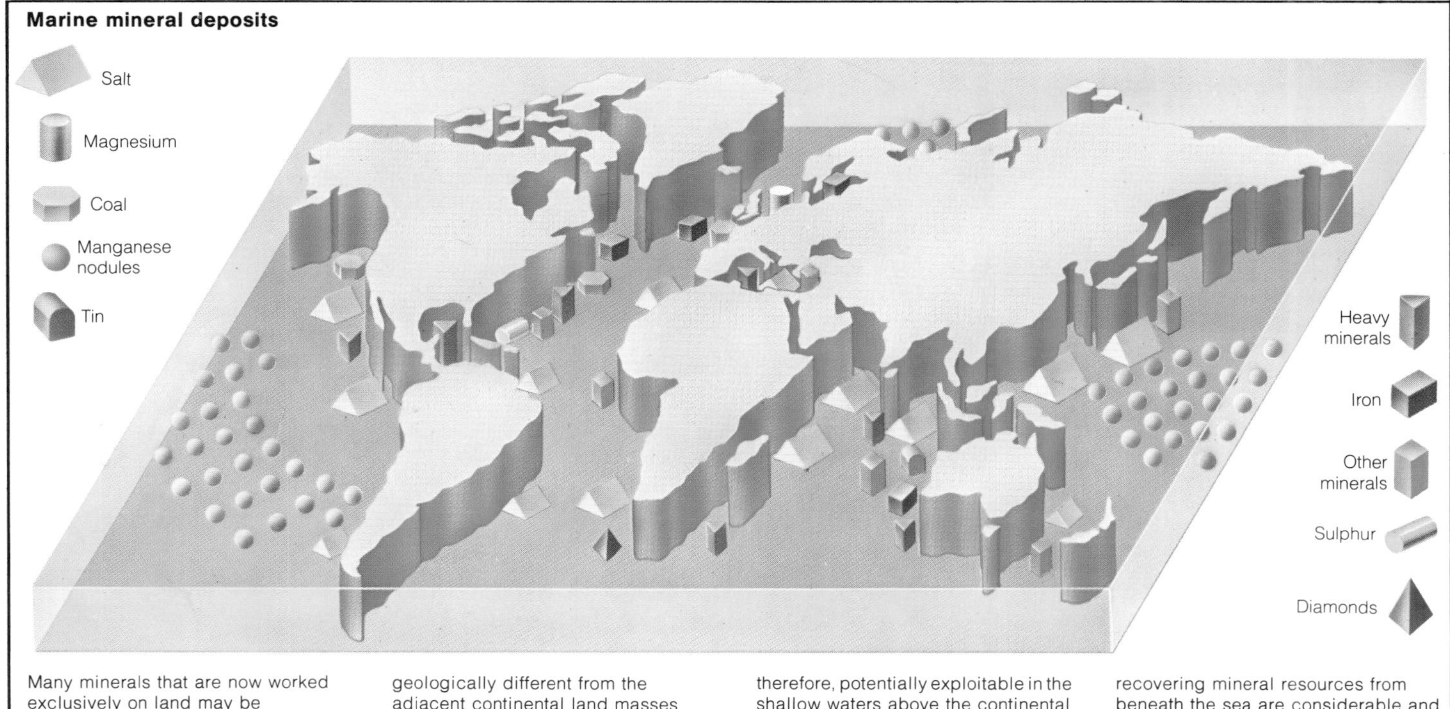

Marine mineral deposits

Salt

Magnesium

Coal

Manganese nodules

Tin

Heavy minerals

Iron

Other minerals

Sulphur

Diamonds

Many minerals that are now worked exclusively on land may be recoverable from the water of the world's oceans. Continental shelves are not geologically different from the adjacent continental land masses above sea level, and all the mineral resources available on land are, therefore, potentially exploitable in the shallow waters above the continental shelves and, in certain cases, beyond. However, the costs involved in recovering mineral resources from beneath the sea are considerable and have limited the commercial development of marine deposits so far.

Economic trends

THE object and function of international trade is to make the world as a whole richer in the supply of material goods, whether they be raw materials (including food) or manufactured products. Two countries will engage in trade only if each of them gains by it, except in circumstances which allow one country to exercise compulsion over the other.

Growth of world trade

In the last 20 years the value of world trade has increased about twenty-fold (although inflation magnifies the real extent of this expansion). In 1948 the value of imports stood at US $62,700 million and exports were valued at $57,000 million. In 1982 the corresponding totals (in millions) were $ 1,955,000 and $1,885,000. Nevertheless, the continuing growth of international trade has done little to bring about a more equal distribution of wealth among the nations of the world. With a few exceptions, such as Australia, New Zealand and Denmark, those countries that have concentrated in the last 100 years or more on developing their manufactures have come to appropriate a disproportionate share of the world's wealth.

In the nineteenth century, the influential German economist Friedrich List argued strongly that only when a country had developed its own national industries could it share in the profits that were the reward of the international division of labour. He went even further and gave his opinion that only a country that exported manufactured products and imported food could rise in the international wealth tables. His influence is still felt today. Most leaders of Third World countries are engaged in an effort to industrialize their economies. Yet it may well be that many of them would profit more from international trade if they ceased to identify prosperity and national pride with steel mills and oil refineries.

A Third World

About 140 countries comprise what has come to be called the Third World. These countries are variously described as ''less-developed'', ''under-developed'' or ''developing'', names that assume Western patterns of development and industrial growth as norms, and desirable norms at that. The people of the Third World, comprising some two-thirds of the world's population, live, for the most part, in dire poverty. National per capita income figures for the seven major regions of the globe show how marked is the divide between the standard of living enjoyed by those living in developed countries and that of the rest of the world. In 1984 annual per capita income was about $14,000 in North America, $9,000 in Europe and Oceania. In stark contrast were the average figures for Africa ($ 300), Asia excluding Japan ($800) and Latin America ($1,000). In the 1970s the national income of some oil-producing countries of the Third World has risen dramatically, but there is no guarantee that their present prosperity will survive the depletion of their oil resources.

It is rare for more than 10 per cent of the gross national product of a Third World country to consist of manufactures. Most developing economies lack the required capital and trained skills for large-scale industry. Their chief pre-occupation is with providing enough food for their people. As a result they contribute only a small part of the total volume of world trade. Again, 1980 import/export figures (in millions of US dollars) reveal large discrepancies between North America (319,359/238,879) or Europe (1,014,128/895,062) and, for instance, Africa (85,513/95,875) or Central and South America (113,824/105,099). The same point is made by comparing the figures for Australia and New Zealand (27,864/27,308) with those for less-developed Oceania (3,539/2,439).

Patterns of trade

A breakdown of world trade figures reveals a number of trends that have become apparent in recent years. Although the developed market economies of the West retain the lion's share of world trade, the volume of their international trade has been growing at a slower rate than that of the Third World and the centrally planned economies (the Soviet bloc members of COMECON and China). Between 1970 and 1976 the volume of world trade rose by 21.2 per cent. The rate of growth in the developed market economies was only 16.7% in the second half of the decade but increased to 22.9% in 1978–9. The comparative figures for the Third World countries were 18.5% and 39.1%.

This dramatic shift in trading patterns reflects, of course, the oil boom enjoyed by those members of OPEC, whose exports rose by 48.2 per cent between 1973 and 1976. That rise is almost entirely explained by exports of oil and was

GNP and world trade

Gross national product and patterns of export trade reveal much about the world economy. The nations with the largest GNPs are those which dominate international trade, and have done so for at least a century. The most apparent feature of patterns of international trade is the fact that approximately 75 per cent of it flows between developed, capitalist countries. Since the distribution of resources is uneven across the globe, the production of goods varies from one region to another and gives some a ''comparative advantage''. Such differences in the cost of production of goods leads, through the development of trade, to specialized areas of production. Some experts argue, however, that this is the result of relationships between developed and under-developed economies. Wealth is extracted from less-developed countries and accumulated in the economic capitals of the developed world. This reflects the free trade philosophy of the nineteenth century when what we now know as the Third World supplied primary products for industrial centres in the Western world. Resource-rich countries. however, have come to command rather more respect in trading agreements today.

Exports _____

Gross national product _____

not shared by the rest of the Third World. It does not, therefore, represent a permanent shift in the patterns of international trade.

More important, in the long run, may be the perceptible rise in the Third World's share of the trade in manufactured goods. World exports of machinery and transport equipment, for example, rose by 19.3 per cent between 1970 and 1979. The developing economies increased their exports of these goods by 35.2 per cent in the same period. Their exports of primary materials and food, on the other hand, moved at exactly the same rate as those of the world as a whole — increasing by about 16 per cent. In time, if this trend continues, the relative wealth of the industrialized West and its partners may decline.

The cry for a new international economic order is an attempt by developing countries to strengthen and realize the potential of their resources and at the same time mitigate the relations of dependency that have characterized their integration into the international economic order. Moves have already been made to stabilize export earnings, increase the flow of aid and technology from the developed to the developing world, and gain favourable trading privileges. But such developments have yet to make a truly significant mark on patterns of international trade and the overwhelming dominance of the Western world in the global economic system.

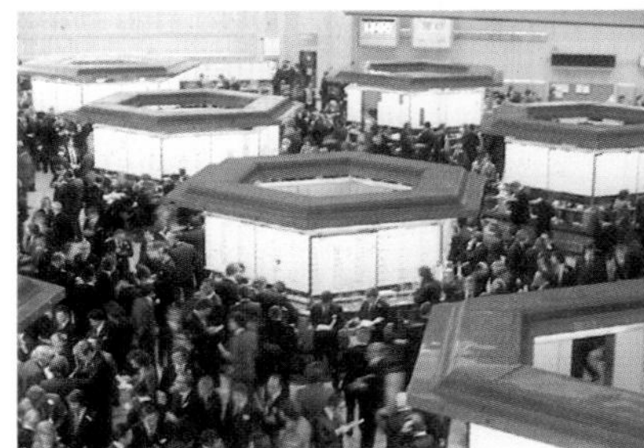

▲ **The London stock exchange** *epitomizes the sophistication and the dominance of developed countries in the world of finance and trade. Bidding and counter-bidding in stock and commodity markets reflect the economic climate of the world.*

▼ **In many parts** *of the developing world, goods are traded in relatively primitive market conditions, such as here in Morocco. For most people economic activity does not extend beyond the local market place.*

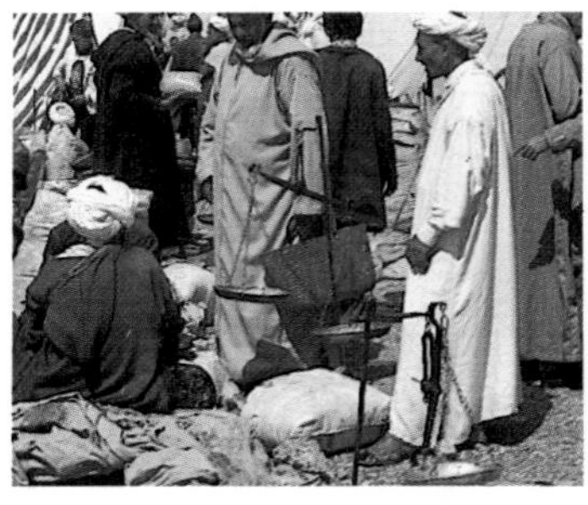

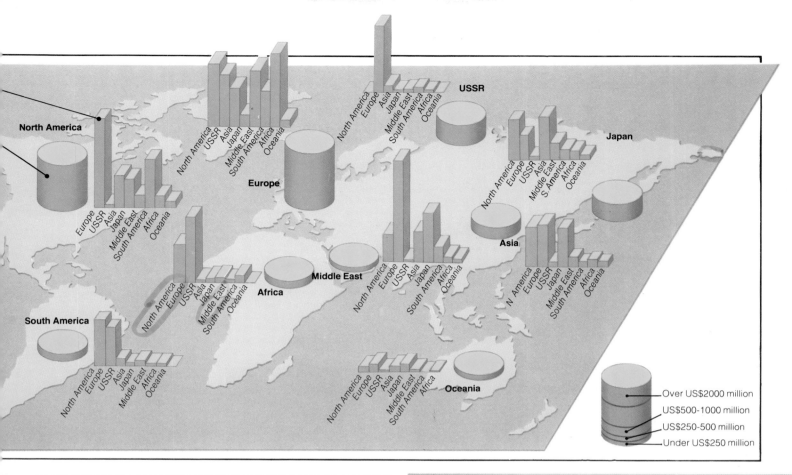

North America

Europe
USSR
Asia
Japan
Middle East
South America
Africa
Oceania

USSR

North America
Europe
Asia
Japan
Middle East
South America
Africa
Oceania

Europe

North America
USSR
Asia
Japan
Middle East
South America
Africa
Oceania

Japan

North America
USSR
Asia
Middle East
Africa
S. America
Oceania

South America

North America
Europe
USSR
Asia
Japan
Middle East
Africa
Oceania

Africa

North America
Europe
USSR
Asia
Japan
Middle East
South America
Oceania

Middle East

North America
Europe
USSR
Asia
Japan
South America
Africa
Oceania

Asia

N America
Europe
USSR
Japan
Middle East
South America
Africa
Oceania

Oceania

North America
Europe
USSR
Asia
Japan
Middle East
South America
Africa

- Over US$2000 million
- US$500-1000 million
- US$250-500 million
- Under US$250 million

The multinationals

The emergence of vast multinational companies is of more than economic and industrial significance. The activities of such organizations affect governmental policy and the relationships between nations. The operations of multinationals span the earth and represent a startling example of international co-operation. Many have annual sales exceeding the gross national product of a small nation.

total sales

profit as proportion of sales (% below)

| Exxon 5.5% | Royal Dutch Shell 6.7% | Mobil Oil 5.5% | General Motors 1.3% loss | Texaco 5.2% |

| British Petroleum 6.9% | Standard Oil (Chevron) 5.9% | Ford 4.2% loss | Gulf Oil 5.3% | IBM 13.6% |

| General Electric 6.1% | Unilever 2.8% | Renault 0.9% | ITT 4.8% | Philips 0.9% |

▲ **The export of luxury goods** *such as motor cars is obviously important for a healthy balance of payments. Another characteristic of developed economies is the export of what is known as "capital" goods — equipment and machinery used in the production of other items, such as farm implements.*

▶ **Regional trading groups** *are formed to stimulate production and trade, but can produce economic anomalies. Certain products can be over-priced because prices are maintained by government subsidies. This leads to wastage. Here French farmers protest against Common Market policies.*

The politics of possession

WHEN the various resource categories — people, land, minerals and energy — are examined in relation to one another, we discover their full political significance. The resources possessed by a nation combine to form the resource structure on which economic and military strength are based. Agriculture, for instance, is essential for a healthy and productive labour force, while substantial energy inputs are required to exploit and develop mineral resources and increase agricultural production.

Resources and power

The power base that is formed by the multifarious links between resources defies the temptation to make a direct correlation between the possession of a single resource and political power. In the case of population, for example, what are regarded as the three most powerful countries in the world — the USA, the USSR and the People's Republic of China — are among the four most populous countries in the world. When one looks to India and Bangladesh, however, with the second- and eighth-largest populations respectively, any direct correlation between power and the size of population breaks down. Quite clearly, the population in these latter countries is out of all proportion to the possession and development of other resources. The access that a population has to other resources, including capital and knowledge, will determine how much it will add to or detract from the political power of the state.

In isolation one can observe the political importance assigned to the categories of resources as links in the power base of a state. In a pariah state such as Israel, self-sufficiency in agriculture is of strategic importance, enabling the country to resist external pressures.

Energy is an increasingly important component of the resource structure, driving countries such as the United Kingdom, France, Brazil and India to develop politically unpopular nuclear power programmes. Industrialized countries such as the United States hold strategic stockpiles of the most important minerals to mitigate any interruption in supply that could arise during political conflicts.

It is bordering on a truism to state that an optimal mix of resources enhances the power of a state while the greater the sum total of that mix, the stronger will be the base from which a state exercises power. The USA and the USSR, as superpowers, derive much of their power from the possession of large amounts of all categories of resources. Saudi Arabia, a country with a sparse population and few agricultural and mineral resources, stands as an

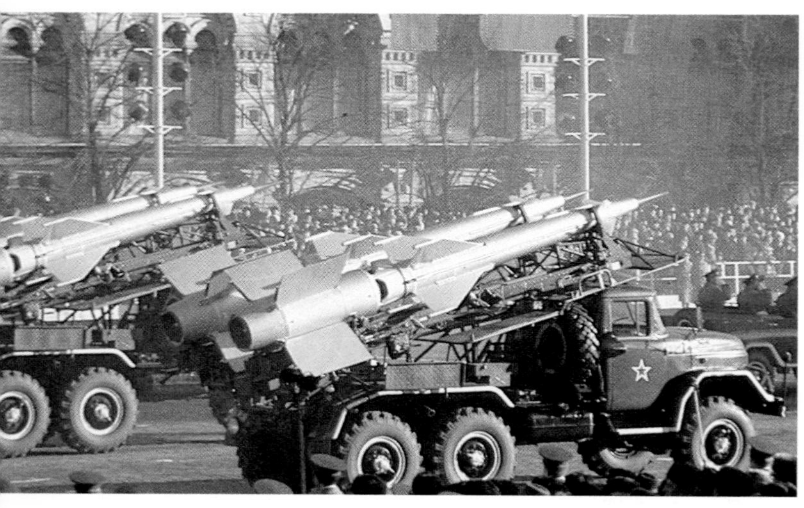

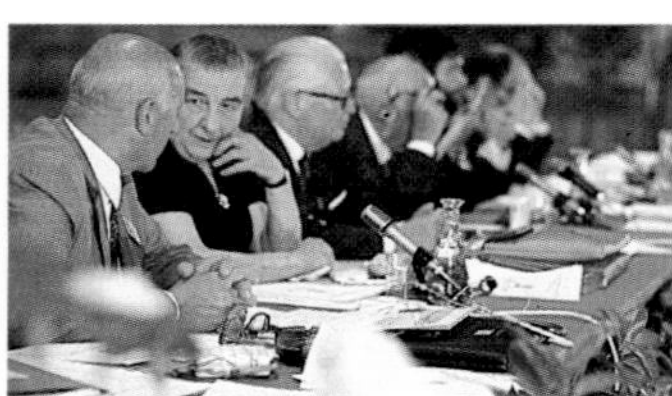

▲ **International conventions,** *whether they be conferences on population or desertification, or political gatherings such as this International Socialist Convention, are a feature of the modern world.*

◄ **Rockets on display** *in Moscow's Red Square during May Day celebrations in fact, through the media, show off the Soviet Union's military might to the world.*

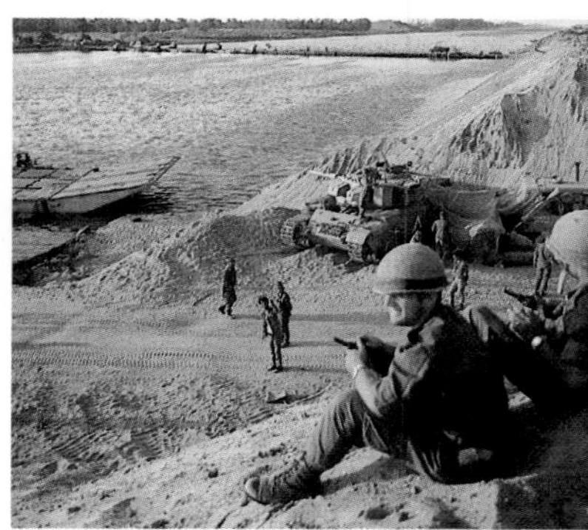

The Arab-Israeli conflict *is a serious threat to world peace. This picture was taken when Israeli-occupied territory extended to the Suez canal.*

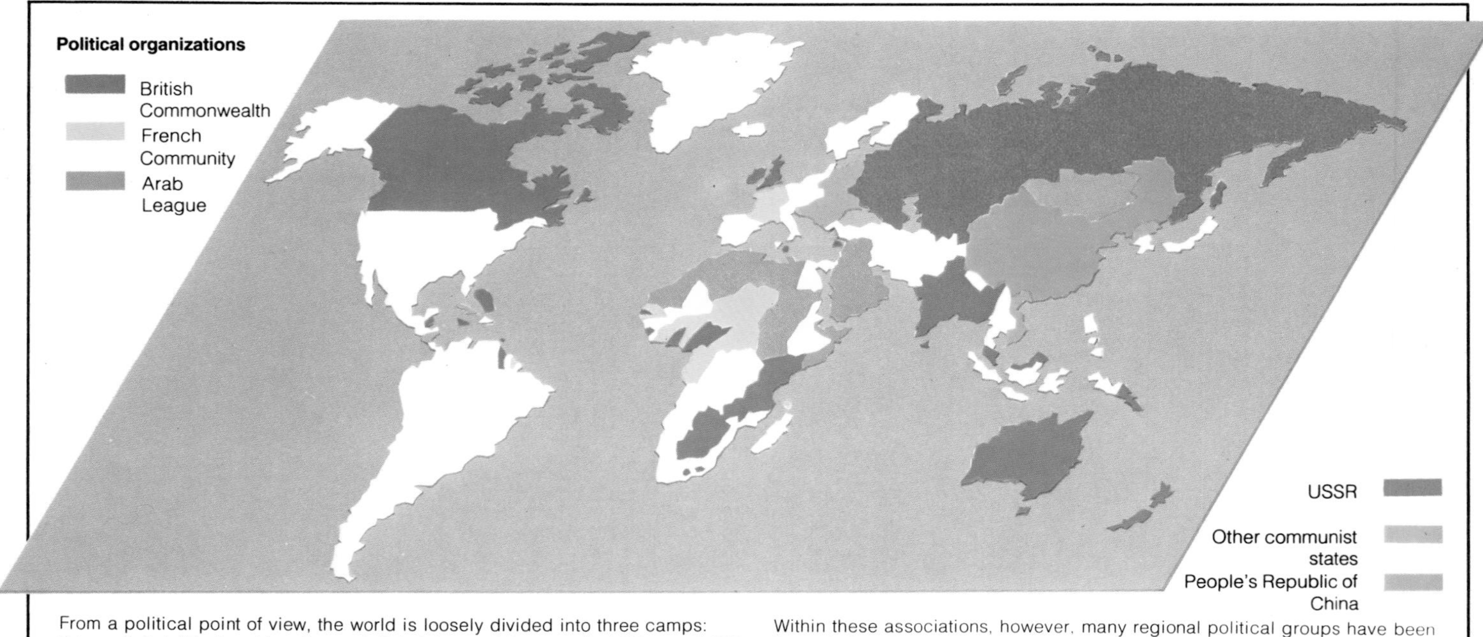

Political organizations

- British Commonwealth
- French Community
- Arab League

- USSR
- Other communist states
- People's Republic of China

From a political point of view, the world is loosely divided into three camps: the capitalist, Western bloc, the socialist states and the so-called "Group of 77". Within these associations, however, many regional political groups have been formed since World War II.

aberration to this pattern. As the world's largest exporter of oil, Saudi Arabia is able to exercise power in world politics far beyond the capability of other single resource states — a power that belies the country's scarcity of resources.

Dependency and power

An abundance or lack of resources is also critical to the dependency structure. A country that is deficient in certain resources often becomes reliant upon external sources. This dependence on external sources for resources is reinforced when a country depends on foreign exchange to finance development and when that foreign exchange is earned primarily by the export of a few commodities. Such nations are forced to look to external sources for aid in financing development and in turn become politically vulnerable as aid is tied to exports

from the donor country or preconditions set by lending institutions.

It is contended by some observers that today's world is one of interdependence, where even the most self-reliant countries such as the USSR and China depend on imports of wheat and high technology from the West, while the West's own power is diminished because of its dependence on developing countries for raw materials.

The lessons of World War II altered the utility of war as a political tool by which a state could seize resources. Total war had become exceptionally costly in terms of the drain on resources and the destruction wrought by modern warfare. What emerged from the War was a bipolar political world characterized by two distinct blocs, with two resource-rich superpowers, the USA and the USSR, serving as respective leaders of each bloc.

The West sought to reduce competition over resources and institutions such as the General Agreement on Tariffs and Trade (GATT) and the International Monetary Fund (IMF) were founded to encourage free trade and stable monetary relations at an international level. The socialist bloc sought a system in which states were to be as self-reliant as possible, with centrally planned economies.

Recent political trends

Two apparent trends have led some to believe that the rift between East and West is diminishing. The first is the disintegration of both political blocs. In 1971 the USA ceased to exchange gold for dollars, marking an end to the post-war monetary system and America's unchallenged leadership of the West. And the socialist bloc has developed rifts within itself. The second trend

is that of convergence between East and West. Western countries such as the UK and Denmark often include a high degree of central planning in their economies, while socialist countries rely on trade with the West to obtain many products.

The rise of a new political bloc of developing countries, otherwise known as the Group of 77, has recently given prominence to a new confrontation over the allocation of resources — the "North-South dialogue". In the mid-1970s the United Nations General Assembly adopted resolutions calling for the transfer of real resources from developed (both capitalist and socialist) to developing countries.

The preoccupation of all countries with political self-interest where ownership and control of resources is concerned shows that resources remain inseparable from the achievement of political ends.

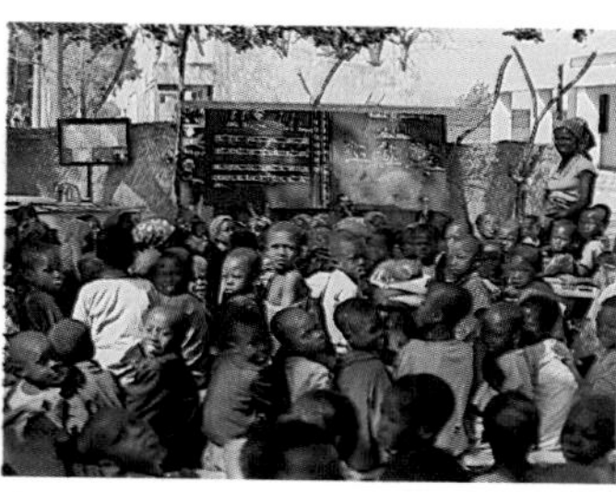

▲ **The education gap** between developed and less-developed countries is of great significance in a world where an educated population is considered to be a vital resource. Practical training rather than theoretical learning is perhaps the most crucial element of education in the Third World.

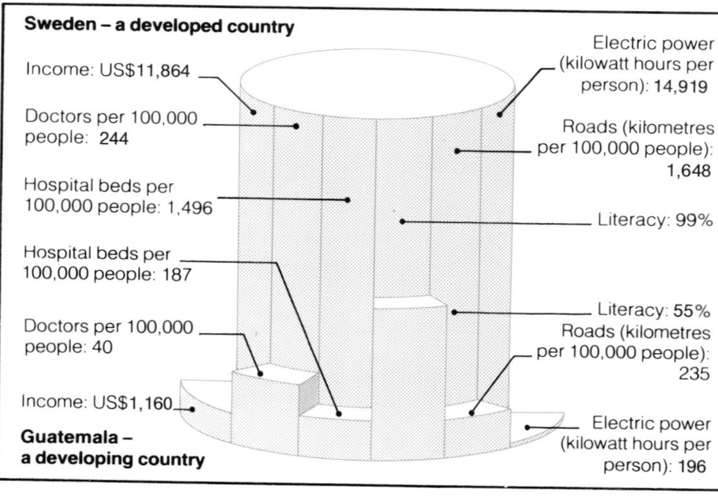

Sweden – a developed country

Income: US$11,864

Doctors per 100,000 people: 244

Hospital beds per 100,000 people: 1,496

Hospital beds per 100,000 people: 187

Doctors per 100,000 people: 40

Income: US$1,160

Guatemala – a developing country

Electric power (kilowatt hours per person): 14,919

Roads (kilometres per 100,000 people): 1,648

Literacy: 99%

Literacy: 55%
Roads (kilometres per 100,000 people): 235

Electric power (kilowatt hours per person): 196

The North/South dialogue

The "haves" versus "have-nots" debate concerning the differences in standards of living or opportunities between the developed and Third worlds has become polarized in what is known as the "North-South dialogue". This is what amounts to a confrontation over the allocation of resources and is an attempt on the part of developing countries to take full advantage of the resources they possess and, at the same time, do away with their dependence on the developed countries which has been a feature of their integration into the international economic system so far. Their goal can only be reached when they have true economic as well as political independence.

Military organizations

▨ NATO

▨ Warsaw Pact

▨ OAS

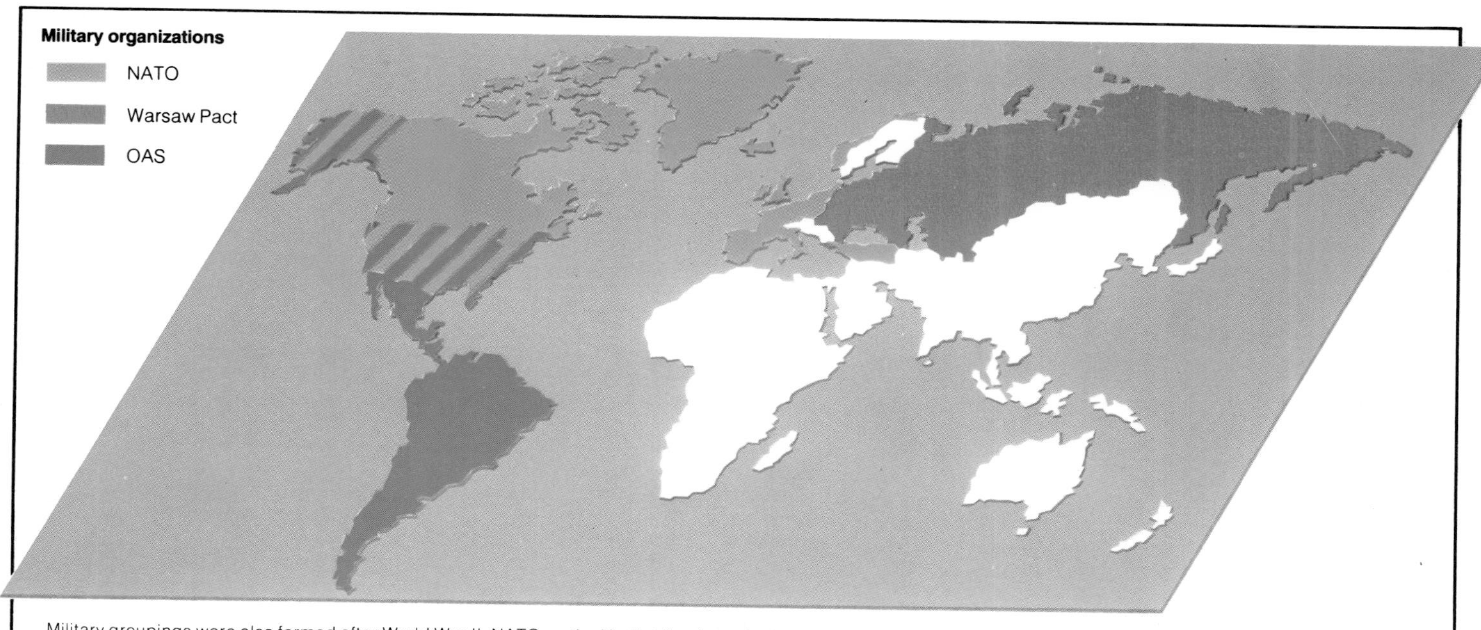

Military groupings were also formed after World War II. NATO, or the North Atlantic Treaty Organization, for example, is a Western defensive alliance that was formed in 1949 to promote military aid and co-operation between Europe and North America during peacetime.

Transport and communication

TWO hundred years ago there began a revolution in the speed, availability and cost of transport. For centuries prior to the end of the eighteenth century, speeds had been limited to those of the horse on land and the sailing vessel at sea, while the carriage of heavy goods was prohibitively expensive and restricted in practice to movement by water. The period since then, however, has seen one transforming event after another — road improvement, canal building, railway construction, the steamship, pipeline, aeroplane and hovercraft. Men who sailed before the mast on the old clipper ship have lived to travel by supersonic jet. Modes of transport have superseded one another rapidly. Since World War II an extensive network of motorways has been built in Britain and much traffic that used to be carried by rail now goes by road, despite the fact that road transport uses energy less efficiently.

The transport revolution
The revolution in transport, in turn, made other changes possible. The Industrial Revolution of the nineteenth century involved, among other things, the assembly of huge quantities of raw materials, such as coal or iron ore. It involved also the transfer of other materials, such as cotton or rubber, from distant parts of the world to the new industrial areas, and the new industry necessitated the concentration of workers near to mines or factories in regions that may previously have had only a sparse population. Basic to all these changes was a transport system that could ensure rapid, predictable flows of traffic to keep industry supplied.

Transport was a key factor also in the "urban revolution" of the same period, as population drained away from the countryside and into the new industrial towns. These new townsmen no longer produced their own food: they had to be supplied from farms elsewhere, and supplied as cheaply as possible. As the nineteenth century drew to a close, the cheapest sources of food were found, on the whole, in countries thousands of miles away from the city markets — in the Americas and Australasia.

Such rapid changes in transport technology have inevitably meant that its development has seen a good deal of waste: waste of capital invested in quickly-outmoded facilities, and waste in the construction of competing routes. Scarcely had the canals in Britain been built when they were superseded by the railways and, in regions such as Britain and North America, not only by one railway but by two or three. Every day, hundreds of empty seats cross the Atlantic in aircraft which fly not so much because there are enough passengers to fill them as for reasons of prestige or competitive pressure. New types of plane, car or train are outdated almost before they can complete the transfer from drawing board to assembly line. A rational transport policy, whereby everybody and everything travelled by the most economical transport mode available, would represent a huge saving in world resources of capital and energy. At present, however, no such policy for transport is in sight.

On land the railway dominated the nineteenth century as road transport has dominated the twentieth. Railways are still being built here and there, but almost exclusively either to tap a particular mineral deposit or for strategic purposes. Some regions have never seen the railway and probably never will. By contrast, every year sees the extension of road networks to accommodate some **430** million motor vehicles that now use them.

This last figure indicates another aspect of the transport revolution. There was a time when travel was the privilege of a few: most people never had the opportunity to travel for pleasure. It is estimated today, however, that there are 300 million tourists worldwide each year: that is, one in 14 of the world's population makes a journey purely for pleasure. Travel has truly been democratized.

Economy of scale
Technical changes in transportation continue, and economies are being made in what has been, in the past, a wasteful industry. The most dramatic of these economies is represented by the rise of the supertanker, the bulk carrier and the jumbo jet — the economies of scale in using a large vehicle. Economies have been made also in loading and unloading techniques as a result of the "container revolution", which has placed small cargoes in easily-handled modules of standard size, and produced the roll-on, roll-off vessel that cuts out trans-

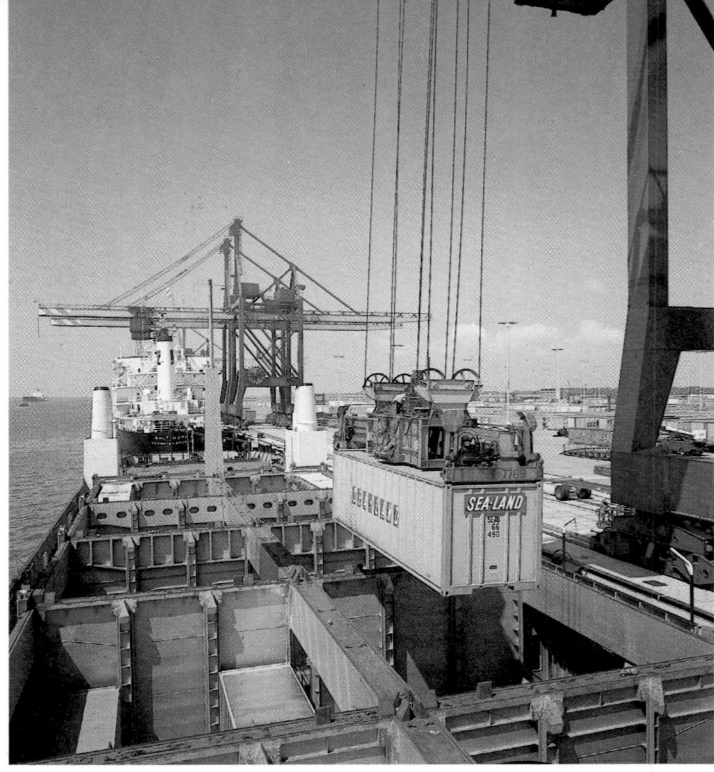

▲ **"Containerization"** has been the major development in the transport of goods in the last two decades. Containers are all of an internationally agreed size and can be quickly loaded into purpose-built vessels.

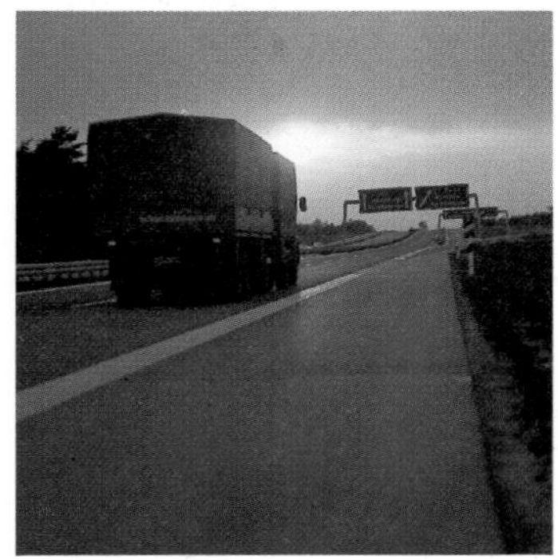

◄ **Road transport** has benefited in the last half-century by the investment by governments in motorway systems. It is, however, not as efficient as rail transport in terms of energy consumption, and threatens the environment.

shipment of cargo altogether. These changes have been necessary if only because of the great increase in international waterborne commerce — from some 900 million tonnes in 1955 to 3.3 billion tonnes in 1984, the bulk of this increase accounted for by the movement of oil.

Communications
If the past two decades have seen revolutionary changes in transport, there have been equally striking developments in communications. These began in 1843 with the transmission of messages by key and code down electric wires: they continued with the telephone, the radio (or wire-less), television and the satellite, and have reached their present degree of sophistication with the involvement of computers, data storage and instant electronic recall of information.

It seems clear that the impact of these changes has still to be fully felt. Already, however, we can see how business structures and, indeed, whole industries, can be transformed by electronics. Branch offices, for example, have immedi-

ate access to central records; executives can "sit in on" conferences at which they are not physically present; and machines are built by other machines rather than by human hand.

The contribution of satellites to the development of communications systems has been particularly dramatic. A number of tasks which previously involved the presence on the ground of a human agent — for example, to map land use or military installations — can now be done much faster and just as effectively from the sky. Satellite pictures help weather forecasters and mineral prospectors, and people across the world can watch an event on television as it happens, instead of the next day or even the following week.

All these developments — whether in transportation or communications systems — are a far cry from the relatively recent days when news was conveyed by runners, goods were moved by barge and empires were administered by issue of orders which could take years to be received and even longer to be implemented.

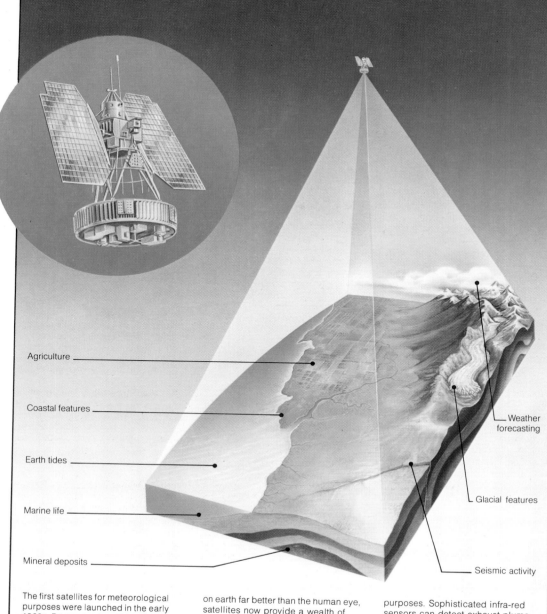

Agriculture

Coastal features

Earth tides

Marine life

Mineral deposits

Weather forecasting

Glacial features

Seismic activity

The first satellites for meteorological purposes were launched in the early 1960s. By means of multi-band cameras and infra-red and microwave sensors that can discriminate conditions on earth far better than the human eye, satellites now provide a wealth of information from their constant surveillance of much of the globe. Satellites can also be used for defence purposes. Sophisticated infra-red sensors can detect exhaust plume emissions from missiles as they are launched and thus give an early warning of possible attack.

▲ **Supertankers** *can be loaded and unloaded quickly with the aid of specialized port facilities and they require few crew members.*

▼ **Transport by air,** *especially of passengers, has increased enormously in the last 30 years, particularly over long distances.*

▲ **Traffic flow** *through the city centre can be monitored from the traffic control room by means of close circuit television cameras mounted in strategic places throughout the city. Details are then relayed to the traffic police in the streets. Highly sophisticated communications systems have revolutionized many industries.*

The shrinking world

As with other aspects of man's activities, from consumption of the earth's resources to the increase in human numbers, the development of transport systems has shown an exponential growth in the speed of the various modes of travel since the take-off point in the nineteenth century. But what of the future of transport? Since social and commercial life depends upon an efficient transport system and as concern for increasingly depleted resources and a threatened environment grows, governments are playing an ever greater role in decision-making within the transport sector. Support for public transport systems, for instance, could see the future development of extensive and rapid mass-transit systems at the expense of private transport which is being made to carry an ever heavier burden of taxation.

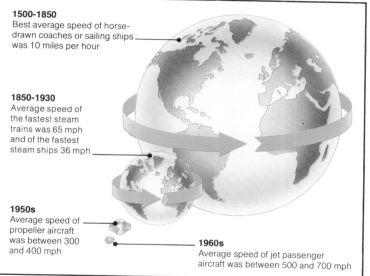

1500-1850
Best average speed of horse-drawn coaches or sailing ships was 10 miles per hour

1850-1930
Average speed of the fastest steam trains was 65 mph and of the fastest steam ships 36 mph

1950s
Average speed of propeller aircraft was between 300 and 400 mph

1960s
Average speed of jet passenger aircraft was between 500 and 700 mph

Industry and technology

WITHIN the last 30 years there have been a number of changes in the overall pattern of world industry or, at least, of industrial science and technology, which are the mainsprings of industrial advance. Before World War II most industrial research was carried out in university laboratories, supported by meagre funds. The technological fruits of that research were, in turn, developed by private companies with their own capital. In both fields — scientific research and technological development — the countries of Western Europe maintained the lead which they had established in the nineteenth century. In the 1950s and 1960s, however, three major changes took place.

Significant developments

In the first place there was an explosive growth in the amount of scientific and technological knowledge and output. Second, there was a massive assumption by government departments and agencies of responsibility for supporting industrial research and development. Third, the United States became the pre-eminent centre of world industry, both in its role as the discoverer of new technologies and in the command which it has come to exercise over worldwide industrial empires. By 1970 the United States was spending 3.5 per cent of its gross national product — about $30 billion, or more than twice the total investment of the rest of the western world — on industrial research and development. This massive capital investment by the government has given the USA its present dominance of industries such as electronics and aerospace.

There have also been changes of direction in other areas. In industries such as chemicals, transport, steel and paper production, there has been a shift away from the simple search for "bigger and better" products. Industry has begun to direct its attention to finding safer chemical products, quieter industrial plants and goods which are both destructible and made from synthetic materials. In such ways industry is beginning to respond to the need for a reduction in the consumption of the earth's natural resources and to the concern of the public that the environment should be protected.

Several trends have manifested themselves in the organization of industry. There has been a move away from adapting organization to technological requirements and towards adapting technology to human and organizational needs. There has been a shift away from plants of maximum size to medium-sized and small units which are more responsive both to market changes and to technological changes in production methods. This change has been especially noticeable in the chemicals and electronics industries and in mechanical engineering works.

In the last 20 years it has been the low-income countries (annual per capita income of less than US $250) and the middle-income countries (more than US $250) that have shown an increase in manufacturing as a percentage of gross domestic product. For all countries, however, the rate of industrial growth has slowed down during the 1970s. A growth rate of 8.9 per cent in low-income countries between 1965 and 1973 fell to 7.4 between 1973 and 1984. In industrial states for the same periods the growth rate fell from 5.1 to 1.8 per cent.

Energy and industrial growth

Undoubtedly, the major cause of this trend has been the increasing cost of energy. Industry will not take strides forward again until alternatives to non-renewable sources of energy (chiefly oil and natural gas) are developed. The high cost of energy in the 1970s is only partly the result of the decision of the oil-exporting countries to raise their prices. It is in the very nature of a non-renewable commodity that the more it is used, the more expensive it becomes. As the most easily exploitable oil fields become exhausted, the cost of developing less accessible and smaller resource deposits automatically rises. This cost is passed on to the major consumer items: housing (fuel and electricity), clothing (synthetic materials based on petroleum) and food (fertilizers and pesticides made from petroleum and natural gas).

This steady and irreversible rise in the price of non-renewable energy sources leads necessarily to industrial stagnation. It produces inflation, a shortage of capital and an unwillingness to invest in high-risk manufacturing enterprises (because the basic cost of energy is so unstable). The future of industry depends upon the current search to find marketable ways of exploiting alternative sources of energy, and the making of plans today for using alternative energy tomorrow.

Technological breakthrough

Two developments, pioneered in the United States, represent a startling technological advance. One is the manufacture of integrated circuits — postage stamp sized chips containing electric currents sufficiently elaborate to operate complex computer systems. Production began in the early 1960s and the results have been successful enough for the product to enter the mass market in the form of digital watches and pocket calculators.

A more recent and equally important development is the photovoltaic cell. This is a thin, chemically-treated slice of silicon, mounted on a metal base. When light hits it, an electric current is generated. This development could eventually provide the answer to a substantial proportion of our electricity demands. The difficulty is to create a market large enough to reduce costs to the point where the cells could be made in large quantities.

Creating a demand

A vicious circle is in operation: because the demand for photovoltaic cells is at present too low to support an efficient scale of production, the cost of the cells remains too high for them to compete on the energy market. The demand has therefore to be created and only governments have the resources to create such a demand. It was huge orders from the American defence department, placed deliberately in order to stimulate production, that made integrated circuits competitive. If any new commodity is to have the same degree of success, a similar stimulation from governments — on a scale that private industry cannot meet — will have to be provided.

This final point helps to explain why, when one looks globally at industrial and technological development, and despite intense efforts in recent decades to transform many Third World countries from subsistence-level, agricultural economies to industrialized, manufacturing economies, the world remains divided into a relatively rich, industrial north and a relatively poor, agricultural south.

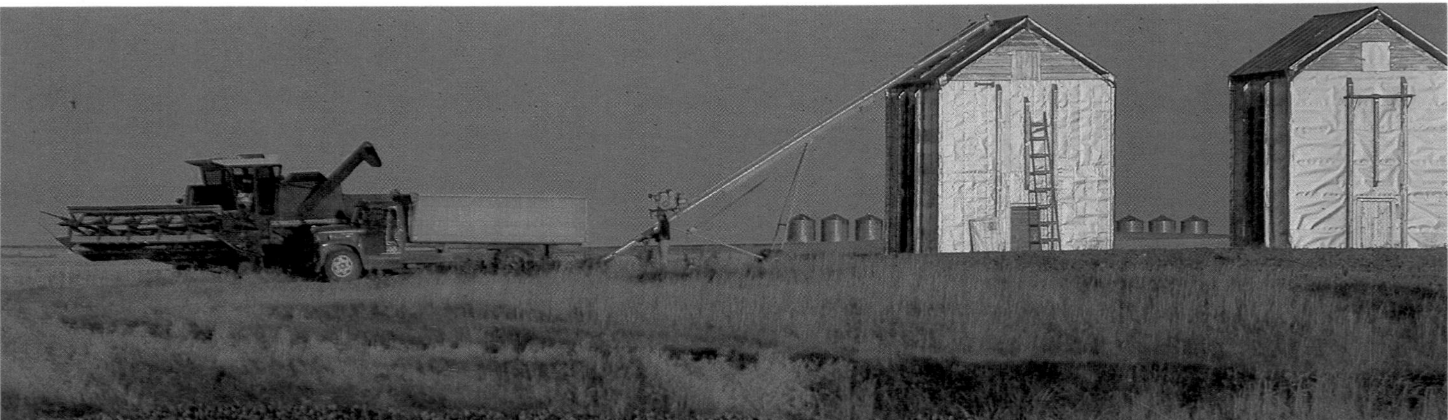

▲ **The North American farmer** has tended to become a small link in a vast agricultural production line that has earned itself the title of agribusiness.

Investment in the farm is massive and trends in food production are dictated by the large food corporations.

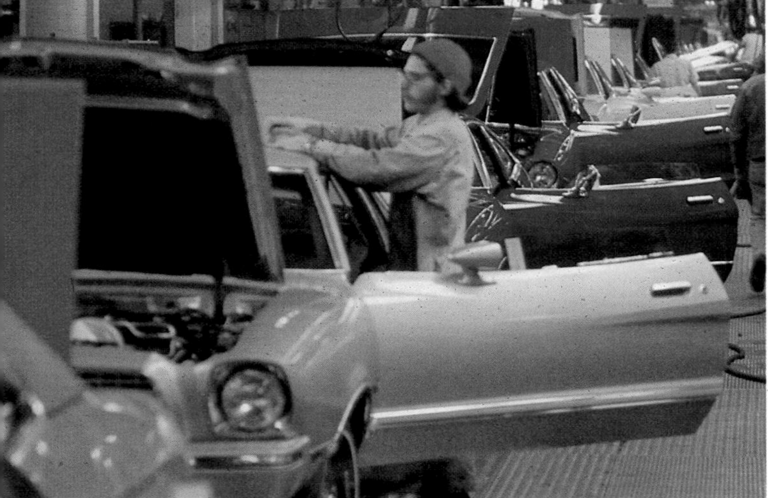

The labour shift

The growth of service industries has been the most significant development within the economic structure of developed countries since World War II. More than 60 per cent of all workers in the United States are employed in the service sector. A service industry is distinguished from other industries in that it supplies the needs of industry or the consumer in the form of such things as banking and insurance, entertainment, education, transport and communications, legal or financial advice, medical and social services, government and the distribution and sale of goods by wholesalers and retailers. The increase in services reflects greater per capita income levels. As people earn more than is required to meet their basic needs they desire and can afford more services. The growth of services does not necessarily reflect a proportional increase in demand. Service industries are labour-intensive and output per worker is not as great as in other sectors. Service industries (personal servants excepted) are of much less significance in developing countries where most growth has been in the retail trade.

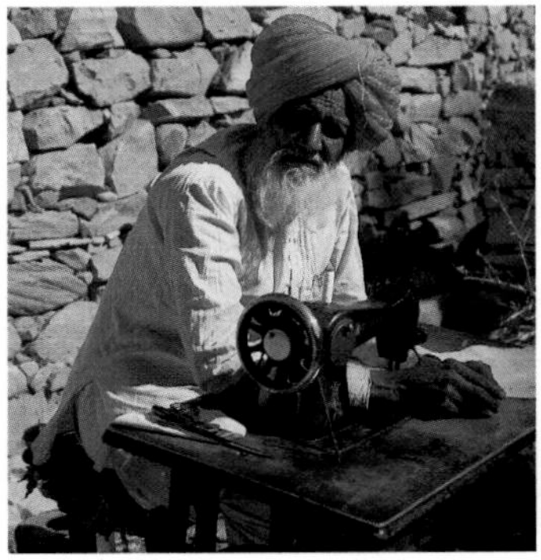

▲ **Assembly line work,** *such as this Ford production line in Detroit, represents for many workers a sophisticated form of drudgery. Wages are high to compensate for the repetitiveness of the work.*

◄ **Textiles** *have played a pioneer role in the economic development of Third World countries. Mechanization exacerbates already high levels of under-employment.*

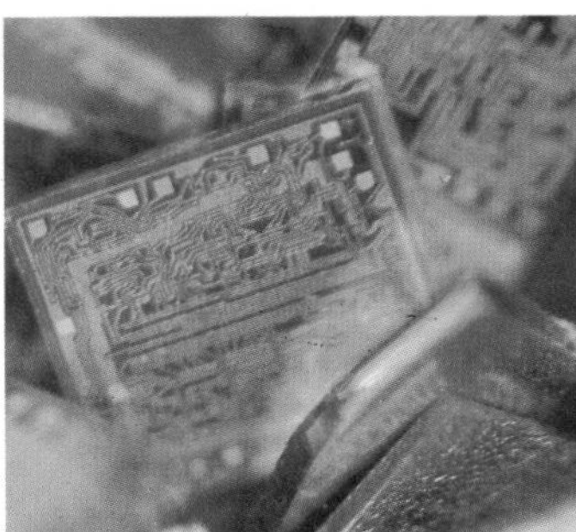

► **Since the advent** *of the transistor radio, electronic devices have become more diverse and increasingly sophisticated. The range of their application today extends from telecommunications to data processing and automatic control. The latter raises serious questions about possibly greater unemployment in the future.*

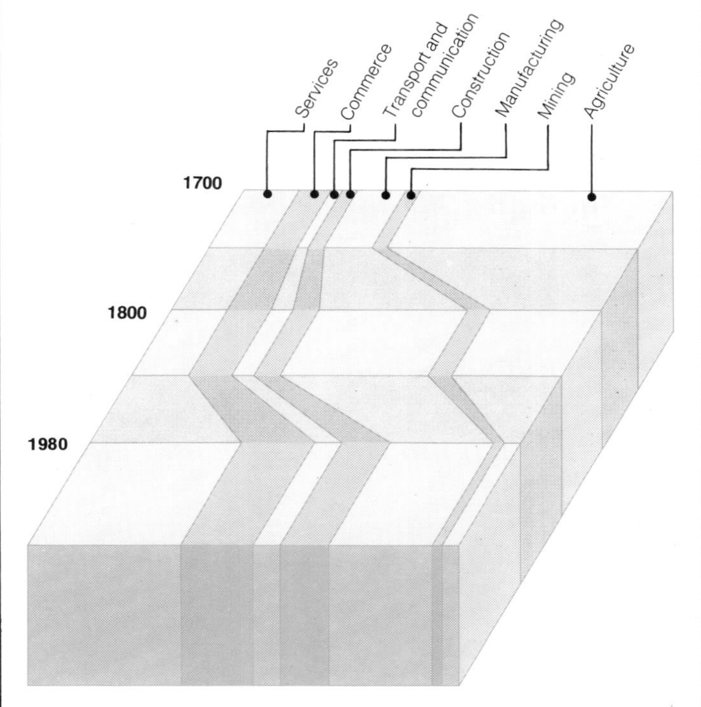

Industrial relations

Good industrial relations have become an increasingly important ingredient for the economic well-being of a nation. The purpose of trade unions is to represent the interests of workers and unions now exist in most countries of the world. The level of organization, however, varies enormously from one country to another. It depends, for instance, on social attitudes, political policies and the economic framework of the country. Disputes and strikes are an inevitable part of a democratic system of industrial relations. Britain does not fare too badly within a league of developed countries, but strikes in Britain differ from many other countries in one important respect: a large proportion of them are unofficial, that is, they are in breach of union rules.

Japan
.13 hrs
55·4 million

France
0·632 hrs
21·2 million

United Kingdom
3·92 hrs
24·4 million

Switzerland
.015 hrs
3·0 million
Working population

Time lost as a result of industrial disputes (working man . . . per year)

Sweden
8·47 hrs
4·2 million

West Germany
0·04 hrs
25·3 million

Australia
4·24 hrs
6·2 million

Canada
6·76 hrs
10·7 million

United States
2·75 hrs
10 20 50 100 million
97·3 million

The quality of life

THAT people should wish for an improvement in the quality of life for themselves and their children seems to most of those people who live in the world's developed countries both reasonable and "normal". For them change is constant and advance is taken for granted. It is important to realize, however, that this state of affairs is relatively recent in the history even of the developed world, and it does not apply, even today, to millions of inhabitants of the developing countries.

The element of choice

What underlies an improvement in the quality of life is the idea of choice: the freedom of human beings, either individually or as communities, to choose among several possibilities the one that best serves their own interests, whether it be type of work, location and kind of dwelling, or use of leisure time. In a society where the dawn to dusk efforts of every single member of the community are required merely to keep starvation at bay, there are no such choices. Everybody must live wherever the work is, in whatever kind of shelter is available, and there is little opportunity for leisure activities.

Sometimes, of course, the absence of choice is imposed not by economic necessity but by political and social restraint. In the feudal society of medieval Europe, for example, most of the population were tied to the soil: they had no right to move from their birthplace, or to withhold their labour when it was required by their overlord. For many centuries, in fact, the only changes that occurred were almost always disastrous — the passage of marauding armies, or the withdrawal of common rights by the landlord. In any totalitarian society, choice is the privilege of those who rule that society.

Industrialization and choice

In the developed world, freedom of choice broadened gradually with the breakdown of feudalism and serfdom, with a growing diversity of work opportunities (especially after the onset of industrialization), with an increasing margin in the economy above the level of mere survival, and with the coming of cheap and rapid movement by public transport. Even so, change was no friend to the first generation or so of the new, freer society. Craftsmen were rendered unemployed by factory-based machines, and small farmers were dispossessed. Thousands of country people found themselves in the new slums of the industrial cities, their only "choice" being to starve on the land or work 12- or 16-hour days in the factories. It has taken time for choice to percolate down through society so that today even the most poorly paid worker has some choice about where he lives or how he spends his leisure hours.

Improvement of the quality of life is a goal also in the centrally planned economies of the Communist world no less than in Western Europe or North America, although the emphasis is on improvement for the community as a whole, rather than for its individual members. Even in these countries, however, it is impossible in practice to eliminate the idea of personal incentive and achievement: in sport, in recreation, in striving for a better job, or in the rewards that come with higher output per worker.

What of the less-developed world, however? There is no reason to suppose that, given the opportunity, millions of inhabitants in developing countries would not welcome the same range of choice that is enjoyed by others. At the moment, most of these people are tied to particular patches of earth which afford their only means of subsistence, and if and when they have the opportunity and the courage to break away, they are as likely as not to find themselves in the shanty towns that have grown up on the outskirts of many large cities in less-developed countries. There they live in appalling conditions and experience great deprivation.

A standard of living

The term normally used to identify differences in the quality of life is standard of living, although the two concepts are subtly different in character. Standard of living is generally expressed by the level of income per person. If we compare nation with nation in this respect, the differences in standards are enormous: $16,330 per person in Switzerland (1984 figures) compared with $260 in India, $360 in Sri Lanka, or $280 per person in Rwanda. Within these countries, needless to say, the range variation about the average figure is great. In many Latin American countries, for example, the idea of an "average" standard of living is meaningless.

Nevertheless, it is the policy of more or less every government, whatever its political complexion, to raise the standard of living of its people. Standards may rise, however, without a corresponding improvement in the quality of life. In general we can say that advance in either will be accompanied by certain signs of change within the society or economy that reflect the improvement of living standards.

Indications of change

As the standard of living rises, it will probably be marked by a decrease in the proportion of the population engaged in primary production — in working on the land, or in forestry, fishing or mining — which implies a broadening variety of other forms of occupation — in manufacturing, transport, education and other service industries. In other words, the society requires fewer people to supply its basic needs. In the United States today only three workers out of ten actually produce anything at all, by farming the land or manufacturing goods.

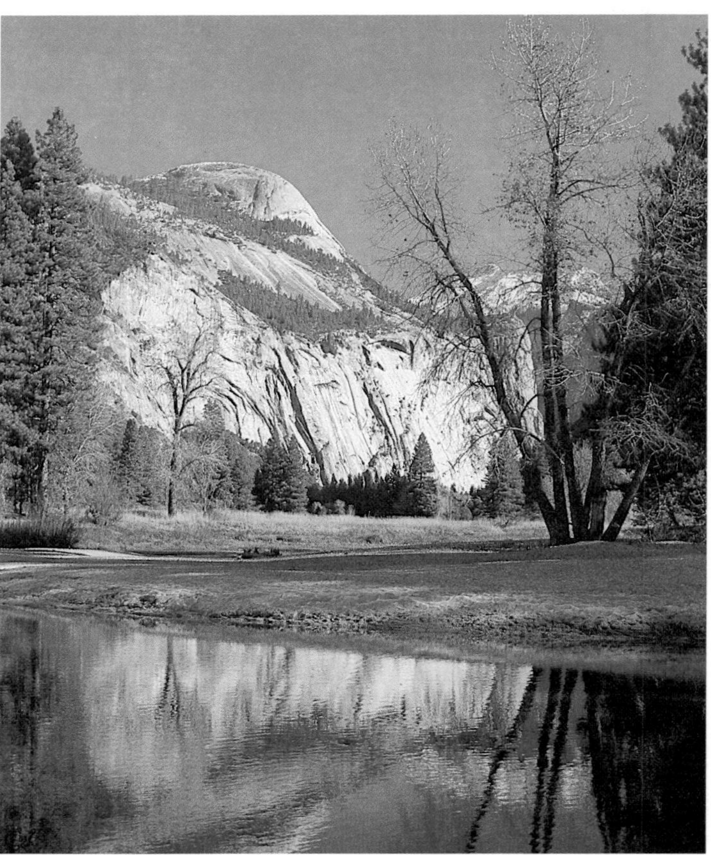

▲ **The clamour** *for extensive, unpolluted open spaces in which to spend our leisure time has meant that millions of hectares in the form of national parks or game reserves have been put aside for just that purpose. Areas of outstanding natural beauty are now protected by law from human encroachment that could damage the environment.*

Another indicator is an increase in the volume of circulation, whether of goods or of people, within society. This implies a greater and wider range of demand for commodities beyond those produced locally, and a greater freedom, financial and personal, to come and go at will. Finally, an improvement in the quality of life will be marked by the increased allocation of resources, especially of land, to leisure pursuits, from golf courses and waterfronts to national parks, in some cases the size of a small country. This involves setting aside some part of land resources from ordinary productive use, and expresses a growing concern for the facilities available to the population when they are not working in offices or factories.

There is an increasing awareness now, however, that the path to industrialization and a higher standard of living in the past will not lead to an improvement in the quality of life in the future. That improvement may well necessitate a fourth indication of change within society — the conservation of the earth's limited resources and the protection of the natural and our man-made environment.

Labour migration

The migration of people has been a recurrent theme throughout history, but a high degree of individual mobility is a characteristic of recent times. Migration has been an essential part of the processes of urbanization and industrialization. To a large extent this has reflected the greater job opportunities and higher income levels in urban centres. For similar reasons, rural-urban migration has been on the increase in less-developed countries. Migration represents one way by which people can improve their standard of living. On the other hand, the post-war prosperity of Europe, for example, has been increased by a vast pool of immigrant labour. The economic recession of recent years, however, has meant that many countries have closed their doors to unlimited foreign labour and only let migrant workers in according to the needs of the country. To some extent, therefore, a migrant workforce may shield the native workforce from the effects of a recessionary period as a contraction in employment will result in fewer migrant workers being admitted or allowed to stay in the host country. In times of growth, on the other hand, immigrant workers will help support economic expansion.

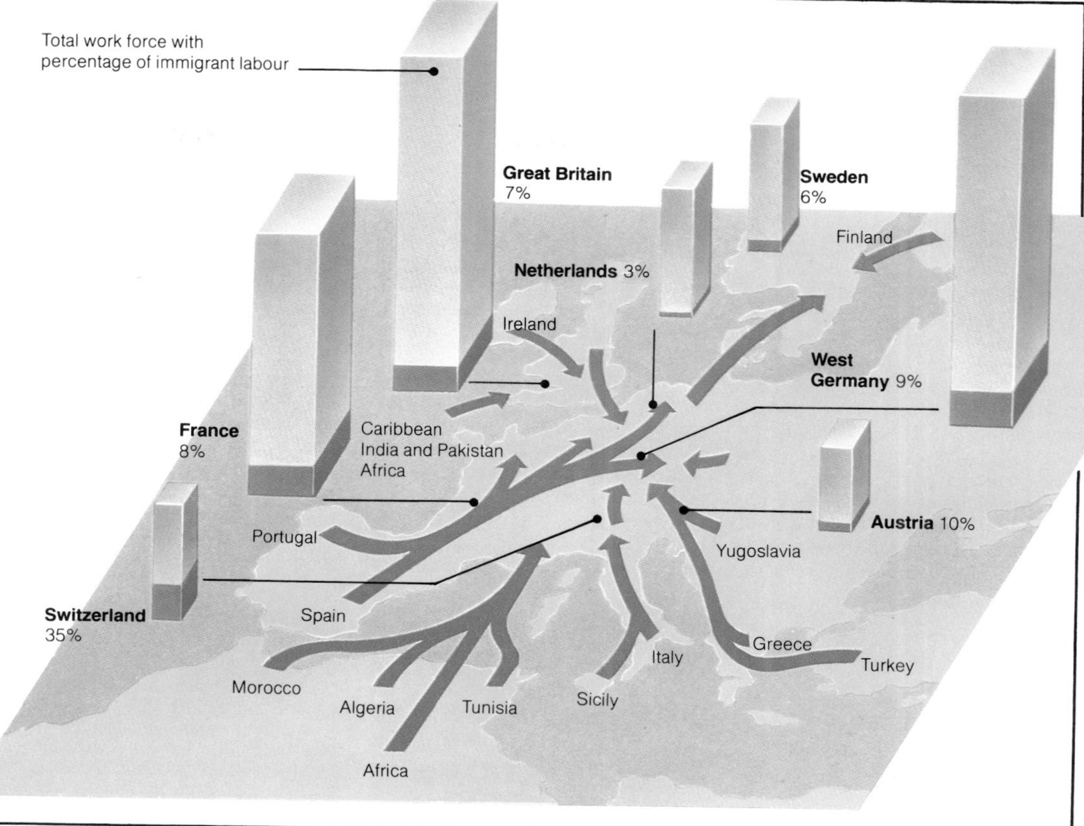

Total work force with percentage of immigrant labour

Great Britain 7%

Sweden 6%

Finland

Netherlands 3%

Ireland

West Germany 9%

France 8%

Caribbean India and Pakistan Africa

Portugal

Yugoslavia

Austria 10%

Switzerland 35%

Spain

Morocco

Algeria

Tunisia

Sicily

Italy

Greece

Turkey

Africa

▶ **The greater opportunities** for migrant workers in post-war Europe has meant an escape from poverty for, for example, millions of Turkish factory workers in West Germany.

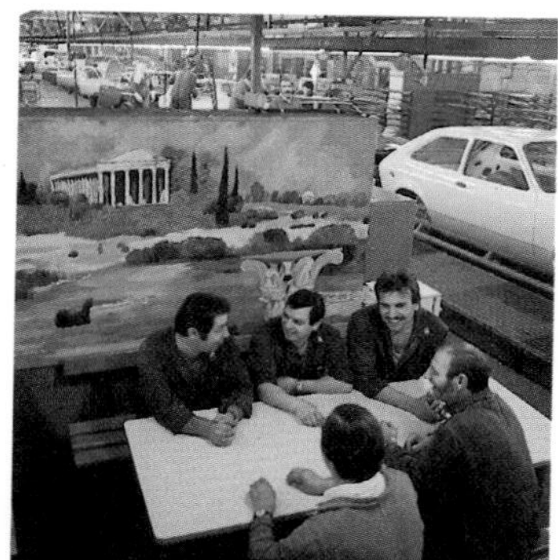

▼ **In the West** we tend to take social improvement for granted, but for the underprivileged in New York's Bowery, life in the developed world offers little opportunity.

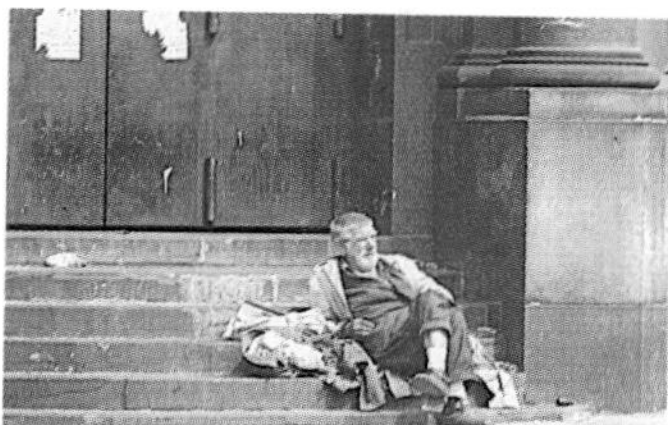

▼ **An ever-shorter** working week and more leisure time leads to increasing demands for leisure facilities. Many sports, such as American baseball, are now big business ventures.

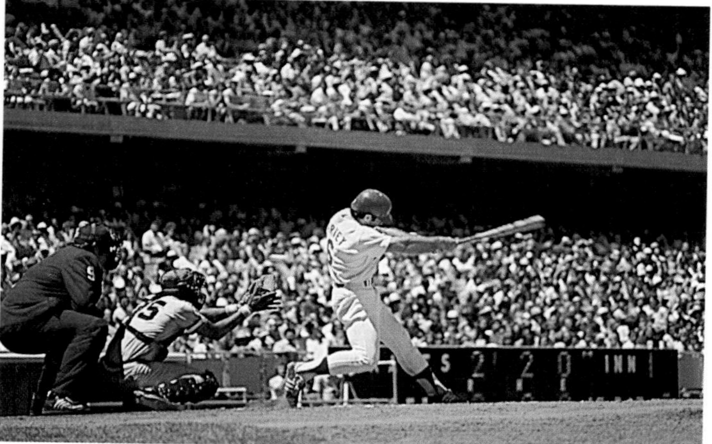

Life expectancy

Not only do we expect better opportunities in life and an ever-higher standard of living, we also expect a healthier and longer life than did our forebears. With the advances of medical science, the length of life the average new-born baby in the developed world can expect has more than doubled in the last two centuries to about 70 years today. Although death rates in many Asian and South American countries have been dramatically reduced, death rates in parts of the African continent have only just begun to decline and remain very high.

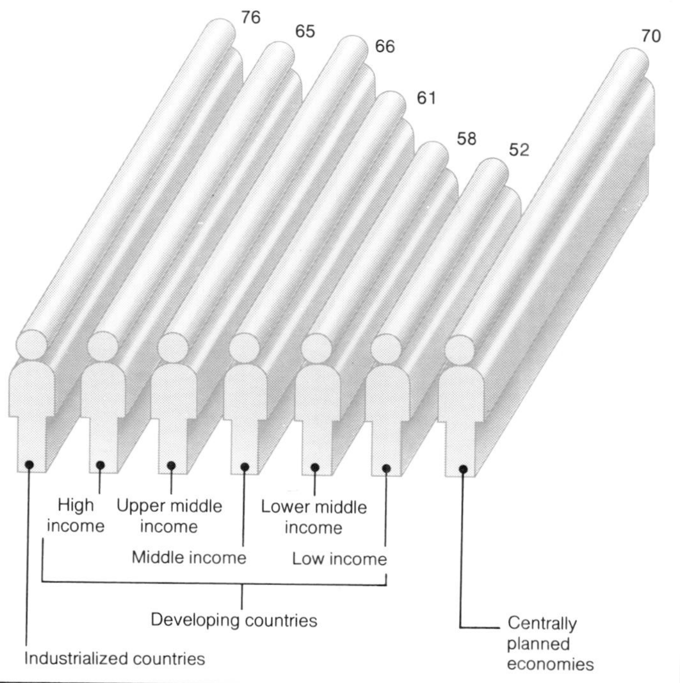

76 65 66 61 58 52 70

High income

Upper middle income

Middle income

Lower middle income

Low income

Developing countries

Industrialized countries

Centrally planned economies

One earth

WITH people everywhere, both in less-developed and developed countries, clamouring for an improved standard of living, it is necessary to appreciate what this implies for an earth whose resources are finite. One way of defining standard of living is as the total amount of resources consumed in a year by the average person in a nation or community. At present, people in countries with a high standard of living are consuming huge and varied quantities of materials derived, in one way or another, from the earth — not only more food per person than their bodies actually require,

but steel and petrol for their cars and a whole range of goods, in fact, that are part of everyday life. Such a community leaves behind it mountains of waste. By contrast, the total resource consumption in a poor community may be represented by small amounts of food and clothing.

Between these levels of consumption there is manifestly no comparison. Yet if we are to visualize that, in the course of time, all living standards will rise and converge upon the highest level we now know, then that implies a colossal drain on the earth's resources. To envisage all of mankind living as North Americans or

Western Europeans currently do, in the present state of our knowledge and technology, is an extremely daunting prospect.

Resources and technology
In past eras, inequalities in living standards were confronted very simply: groups preyed on one another, and the strong grew rich while the poor starved. Not only is this unacceptable by present-day standards, but a new factor has been introduced into the competition for resources — the technical ability to use them. A community with a high level of technology can, in practice, reach out and tap the resources of others: by contrast, a country richly endowed with natural resources may not have the technical expertise to exploit them, and so may have to bring in outsiders and share its wealth with them in return for their assistance. All this means,

however, is that, without resorting to force, the rich grow richer, often at the expense of the poor.

There are several possible remedies for this situation. One is to set up a world organization with sufficient power to introduce some form of international rationing. However, not only would it be exceedingly difficult to decide what constituted "fair shares" for nations with entirely different needs and lifestyles, but such an arrangement could, in practice, only be introduced with the consent and help of the most wealthy nations, and they would naturally be the losers by it.

A question of distribution
The second possibility is that the largest consumers of resources should limit their usage and leave more for the rest of mankind. It has even been agreed that the living standards of the rich would not

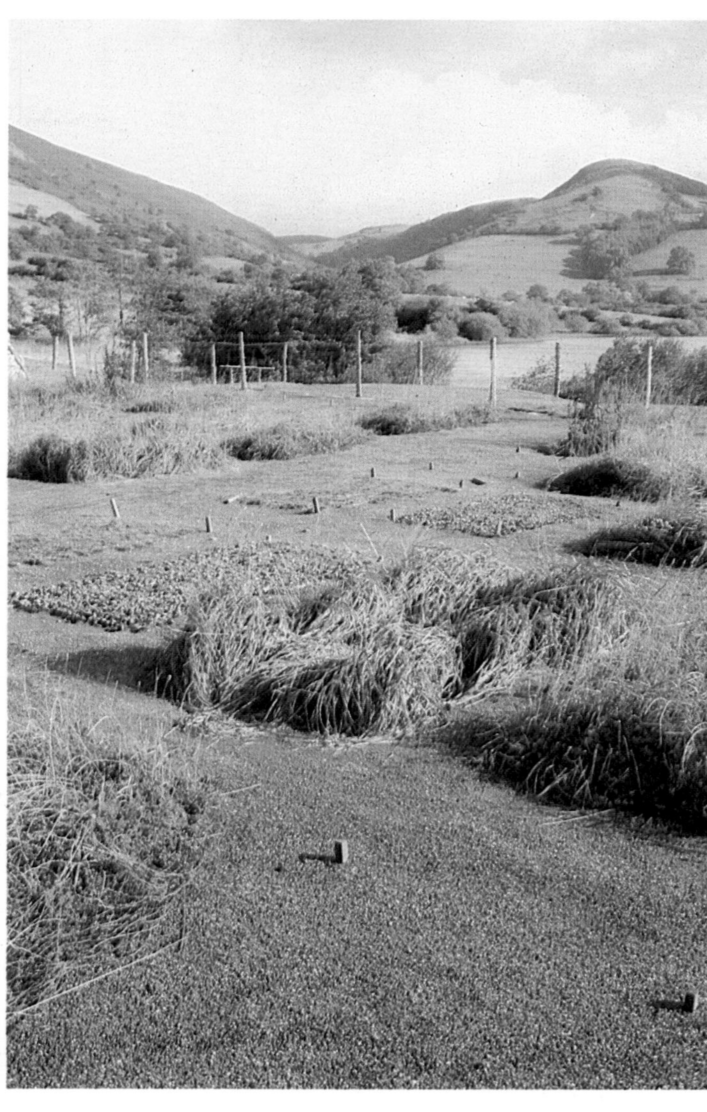

▲ **The rehabilitation** of land spoiled by man's activities has become an exact science. Here in Wales colliery spoil is spread over toxic metal waste and planted with a special strain of grass whose short root system does not reach the toxic soil beneath the top layer.

The United Nations

The United Nations was established in 1948 by 50 nations. It now has three times as many members and stands as a symbol of world unity. The political sector of the UN is the General Assembly and the Security Council. The Economic and Social Council, under the supervision of the General Assembly, co-ordinates the economic and social work of the UN

and 14 specialized agencies. The Trusteeship Council was set up to supervise the affairs of 11 territories all of which except one, the Pacific Islands, are now independent. The International Court of Justice is the principal judicial body and the Secretariat services all other departments and is responsible for implementing their policies.

General Assembly | 1

Security Council | Secretariat | Economic and Social Council | Trusteeship Council | International Court of Justice

2 | 3 | 4 | 5 | 6 | 7 | 8 | 9

IMF International Monetary Fund	IDA International Development Association	ITU International Telecommunications Union
WHO World Health Organization	IBRD International Bank for Reconstruction and Development	WMO World Meteorological Organization
FAO Food and Agriculture Organization	IFC International Finance Corporation	GATT General Agreement on Tariffs and Trade
ILO International Labour Organization	Universal Postal Union	IMCO Inter-Governmental Maritime Consultative Organization
UNESCO Educational, Scientific and Cultural Organization	ICAO International Civil Aviation Organization	

IAEA International Atomic Energy Authority
Peace keeping forces/Military observers
Disarmament Commission

1 UNCTAD Conference on Trade and Development
2 UNIDO Industrial Development Organization
3 UNITAR Institute for Training and Research
4 UNHCR High Commission for Refugees
5 UN Capital Development Fund
6 UNDP Development Programme
7 Trade and Development Board
8 UNICEF Children's Fund
9 UN-FAO World Food Programme

necessarily fall. Their present consumption patterns are so wasteful of resources that any loss in supply could be recouped by the proper use of the resources they still possessed. By eliminating waste, improving efficiency and recycling materials, the developed countries could live on a lot less.

All this is true, and there is no doubt that the average consumer in the developed world today has a far more tender conscience, and a far greater awareness of the needs of others, than was the case a few decades ago, thanks in part to the development of communications and the immediate coverage of famine, catastrophe and living conditions worldwide. Reduced consumption by the well-to-do will not, however, solve the problem of transferring the resources saved by one country in order to supply the needs of another. If the United States were to reduce its consumption of petroleum, this would not necessarily make it cheaper or easier for a poor and oil-less state such as Bangladesh to obtain petroleum. The connection between supply and demand is not that simple. While there is, therefore, an obvious argument that there should be fairness for all, the machinery for achieving this has yet to be created, at least on an international level.

The provision of aid
The only workable alternative to these two ideas, and one which has received a lot of attention in the years since World War II, is that of giving technical aid. Since it is the difference in technical standards and capacities which chiefly distinguish the rich nation from the poor one, a levelling up of those standards ought to lead directly towards an equalization of living standards. Furthermore, it should be possible to do this with a minimum of disturbance to ordinary trade relations, and without the need to move large quantities of food and materials from one place to another. By upgrading the poor nation's ability to make use of its own resources, the poor may gain much and the rich will lose little, at least in the short term. Over a longer period, however, the technically-advanced nation is creating competitors for its own producers. But it is reasonable to expect that, by the time that happens, the advanced economy will have moved on again to different levels of technology.

Experience has shown, however, that aid from the developed countries to the developing has been double-edged. Much of the aid has been in the form of loans, on which interest has to be paid, or there are strings attached, such as the demand that purchases of equipment for the developing economy shall be made only from the aid-granting country. Sometimes technical aid to agriculture benefits only the large farmers and makes life more difficult for the small operator, and industries are established which are not only controlled but also staffed largely by technicians from abroad, so that their presence makes little impact on unemployment in the area.

What this means is not that aid should be stopped, but that it should take carefully chosen forms, and that the basic objective of every aid programme should be to give the maximum assistance to those most in need. In the world today, it is not by the condition of the average man, and certainly not by the wealth of the richest, but by the circumstances of the most needy that future generations will judge us.

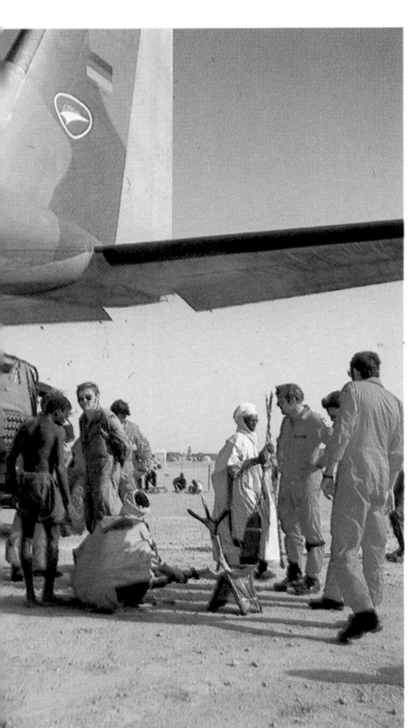

◄ **Massive foreign aid** *is granted to developing countries each year. Aid at times of catastrophe is widely publicized — less well known is the work of the United Nations and other international organizations in assisting economic development in the less developed world.*

► **Proponents of an alternative society** *advocate a return to a pre-industrial way of life in which men live more simply and without generating the problems of modern times. The Amish of Pennsylvania, however, have never succumbed to the pressures of American society and have lived in relative seclusion for the past two centuries.*

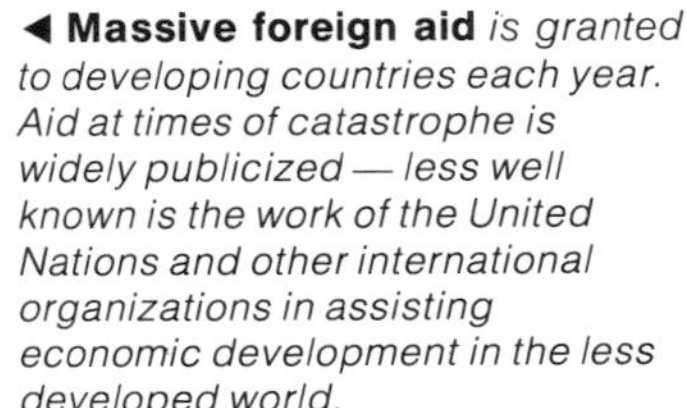

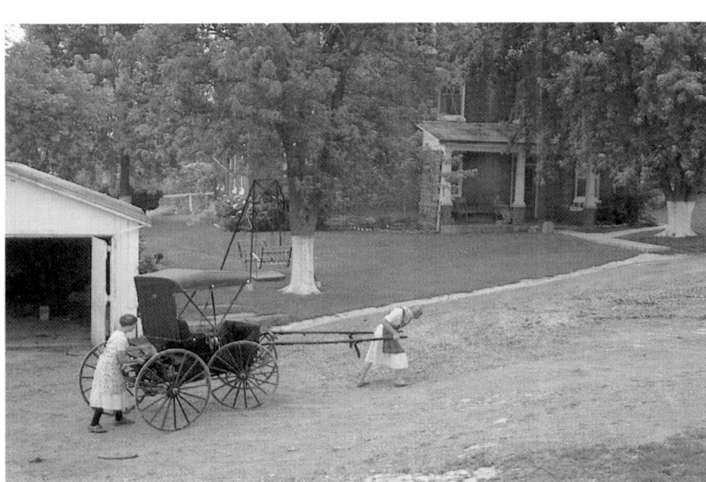

▲ **The most constructive form** *of aid to less-developed countries is education and the introduction of a technology that is best suited to their requirements.*

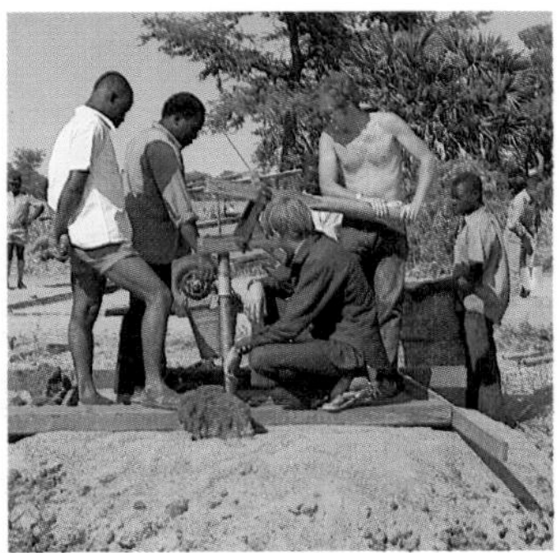
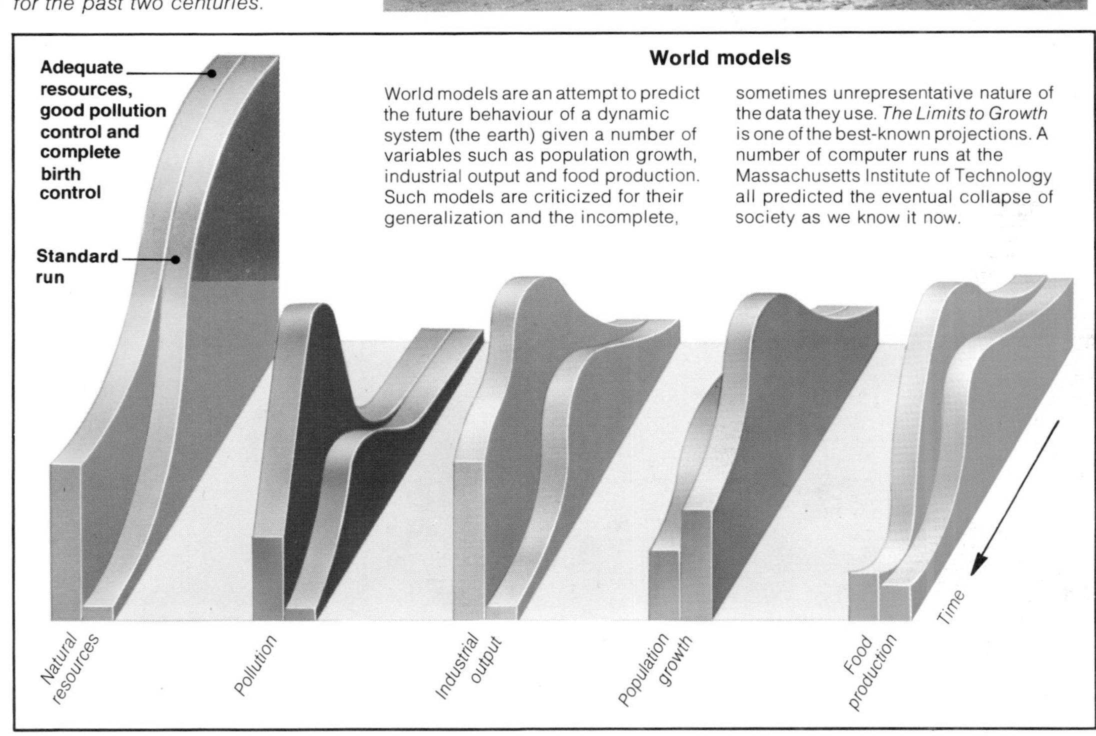

World models
World models are an attempt to predict the future behaviour of a dynamic system (the earth) given a number of variables such as population growth, industrial output and food production. Such models are criticized for their generalization and the incomplete, sometimes unrepresentative nature of the data they use. *The Limits to Growth* is one of the best-known projections. A number of computer runs at the Massachusetts Institute of Technology all predicted the eventual collapse of society as we know it now.

Adequate resources, good pollution control and complete birth control

Standard run

Natural resources

Pollution

Industrial output

Population growth

Food production

Time

Earth data

The earth's dimensions

Superficial area	510,000,000km²
Land surface	149,000,000km²
Land surface as % of total area	29.2%
Water surface	361,000,000km²
Water surface as % of total area	70.8%
Equatorial circumference	40,077km
Meridional circumference	40,009km
Equatorial diameter	12,757km
Polar diameter	12,714km
Volume	$1,083,230 \times 10^6$ km³
Mass	5.9×10^{21} tonnes

The earth's surface

Highest point (Mount Everest, Tibet-Nepal border)	8,848m
Lowest point (Dead Sea, Israel-Jordan)	395m below sea level
Greatest ocean depth (Challenger Deep, Mariana Trench)	11,022m
Average height of land	840m
Average depth of sea	3,808m

The largest oceans and seas

Pacific Ocean	165,721,000km²
Atlantic Ocean	81,660,000km²
Indian Ocean	73,442,000km²
Arctic Ocean	14,351,000km²
Mediterranean Sea	2,966,000km²
Bering Sea	2,274,000km²
Caribbean Sea	1,942,000km²
Mexico, Gulf of	1,813,000km²
Okhotsk, Sea of	1,528,000km²
East China Sea	1,248,000km²

The longest rivers

	LENGTH	LOCATION
Nile	6,669km	Africa
Amazon	6,516km	South America
Mississippi-Missouri	6,050km	North America
Yangtze-Kiang	5,989km	Asia
Ob-Irtysh	5,149km	Asia
Amur	4,666km	Asia
Zaire	4,373km	Africa
Hwang Ho (Yellow River)	4,344km	Asia
Lena	4,256km	Asia
Mackénzie	4,240km	North America

The largest lakes and inland seas

	AREA	LOCATION
Caspian Sea	393,896km²	Asia
Lake Superior	82,413km²	North America
Lake Victoria	69,484km²	Africa
Aral Sea	68,681km²	Asia
Lake Huron	59,596km²	North America
Lake Michigan	58,015km²	North America
Lake Tanganyika	32,893km²	Africa
Great Bear Lake	31,792km²	North America
Lake Baykal	30,510km²	Asia
Lake Nyasa	29,604km²	Africa

The highest mountains

	HEIGHT	LOCATION
Everest	8,848m	Tibet-Nepal
K2 (Godwin Austen)	8,616m	Kashmir
Kanchenjunga	8,591m	Nepal-Sikkim
Makalu	8,481m	Tibet-Nepal
Dhaulagiri	8,177m	Nepal
Nanga Parbat	8,131m	Kashmir
Annapurna	8,078m	Nepal
Gasherbrum	8,073m	Kashmir
Gosainthan	8,019m	Tibet
Nanda Devi	7,822m	India

The largest islands

	AREA	LOCATION
Greenland	2,175,000km²	Atlantic
New Guinea	885,780km²	Pacific
Borneo	743,330km²	Pacific
Madagascar	587,045km²	Indian
Baffin	476,070km²	Arctic
Sumatra	473,600km²	Indian
Honshu	230,540km²	Pacific
Great Britain	218,050km²	Atlantic
Ellesmere	212,690km²	Arctic
Victoria	212,200km²	Arctic

The continents

	AREA
Asia	44,250,000km²
Africa	30,264,000km²
North America	24,398,000km²
South America	17,807,800km²
Antarctica	13,209,000km²
Europe	9,906,000km²
Australia and New Zealand	8,842,400km²

The greatest waterfalls

	HEIGHT	LOCATION
Angel	980m	Venezuela
Tugela	853m	South Africa
Mongefossen	774m	Norway
Yosemite	738m	California
Mardalsfossen	655m	Norway
Cuquenan	610m	Venezuela
Sutherland	579m	New Zealand
Reichenbach	548m	Switzerland
Wollomombi	518m	Australia
Ribbon	491m	California

Notable volcanoes

	HEIGHT	LOCATION
Etna	3,340m	Sicily
Fuji	3,778m	Japan
Mauna Loa	4,160m	Hawaii
Ngaurone	2,290m	New Zealand
Njamiagira	3,059m	Zaire
Nyiragongo	3,472m	Zaire
Pacaya	2,546m	Guatemala
Popocatepetl	5,456m	Mexico
Saint Helens	2,744m	USA
Stromboli	927m	Italy
Tristan da Cunha	2,026m	Atlantic Ocean
Vesuvius	1,278m	Italy

GENERAL REFERENCE

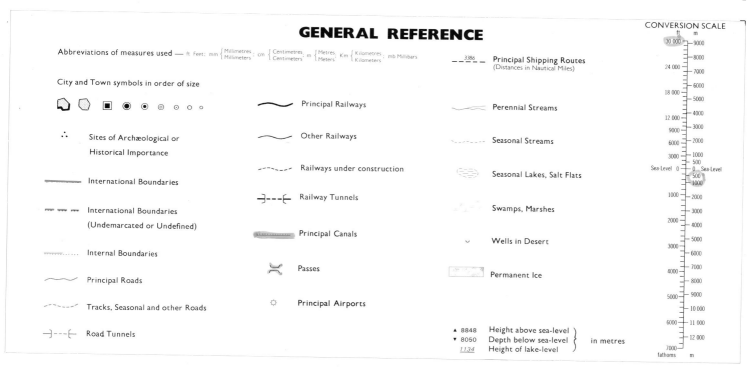

Abbreviations of measures used — ft Feet; mm {Millimetres / Millimeters}; cm {Centimetres / Centimeters}; m {Metres / Meters}; Km {Kilometres / Kilometers}; mb Millibars

City and Town symbols in order of size

Sites of Archæological or Historical Importance

International Boundaries

International Boundaries (Undemarcated or Undefined)

Internal Boundaries

Principal Roads

Tracks, Seasonal and other Roads

Road Tunnels

Principal Railways

Other Railways

Railways under construction

Railway Tunnels

Principal Canals

Passes

Principal Airports

Principal Shipping Routes (Distances in Nautical Miles)

Perennial Streams

Seasonal Streams

Seasonal Lakes, Salt Flats

Swamps, Marshes

Wells in Desert

Permanent Ice

▲ 8848   Height above sea-level
▼ 8050   Depth below sea-level   } in metres
1134   Height of lake-level

CONVERSION SCALE

THE WORLD
Physical
1:150 000 000

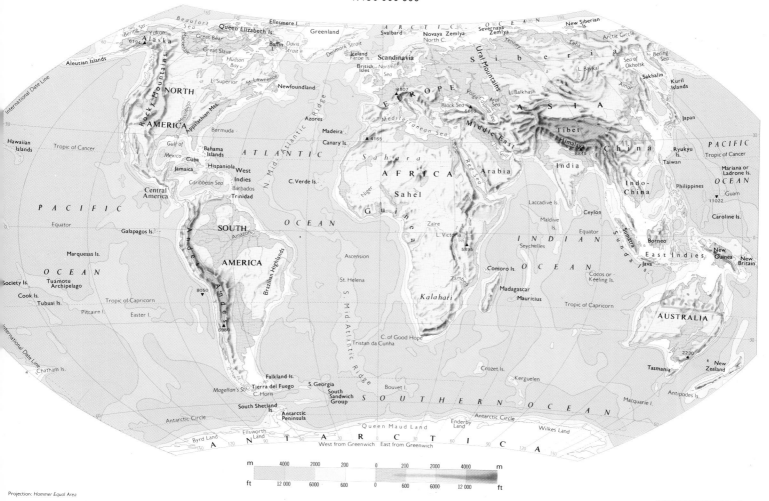

Projection: Hammer Equal Area

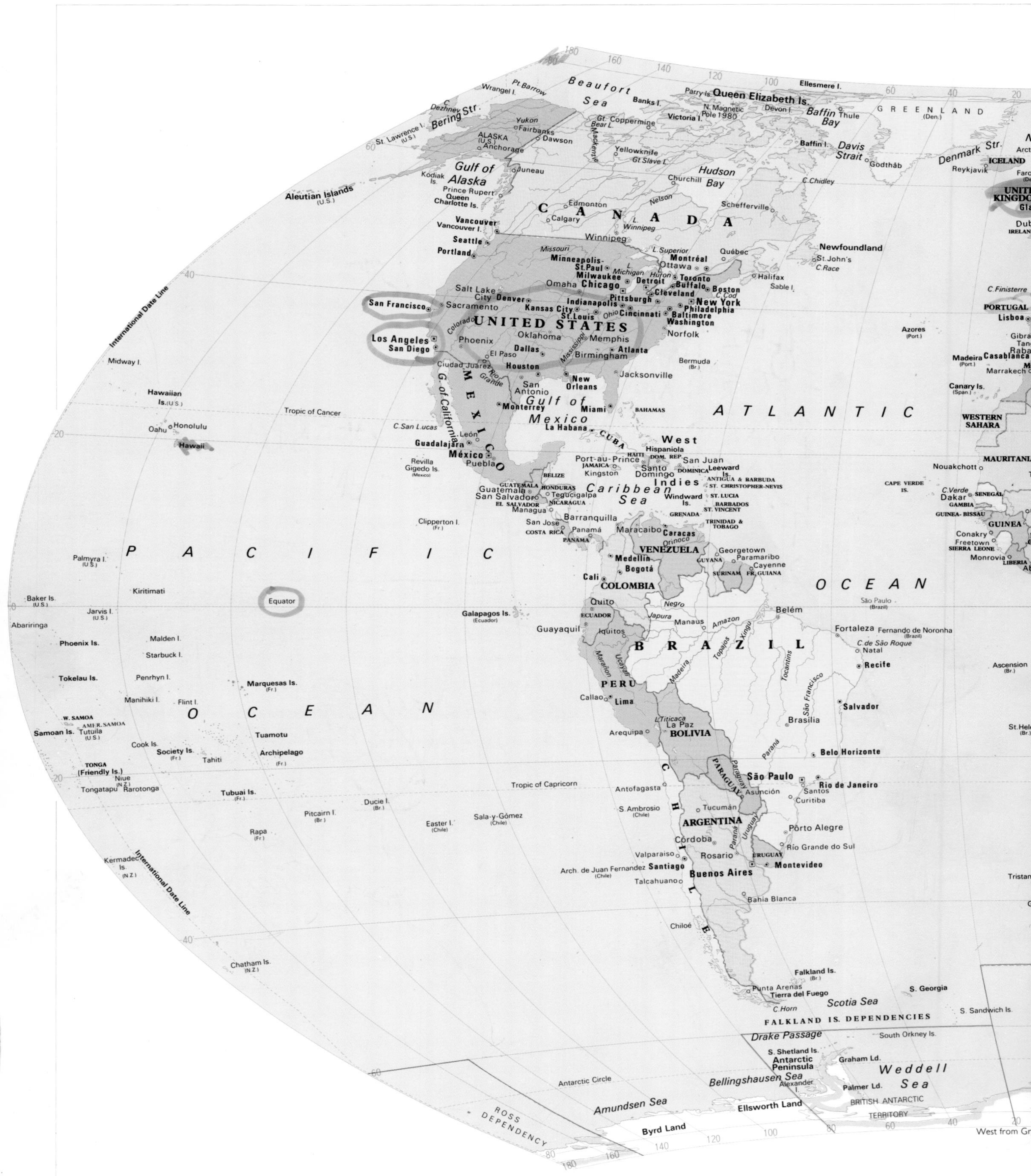

Projection: *Hammer Equal Area*

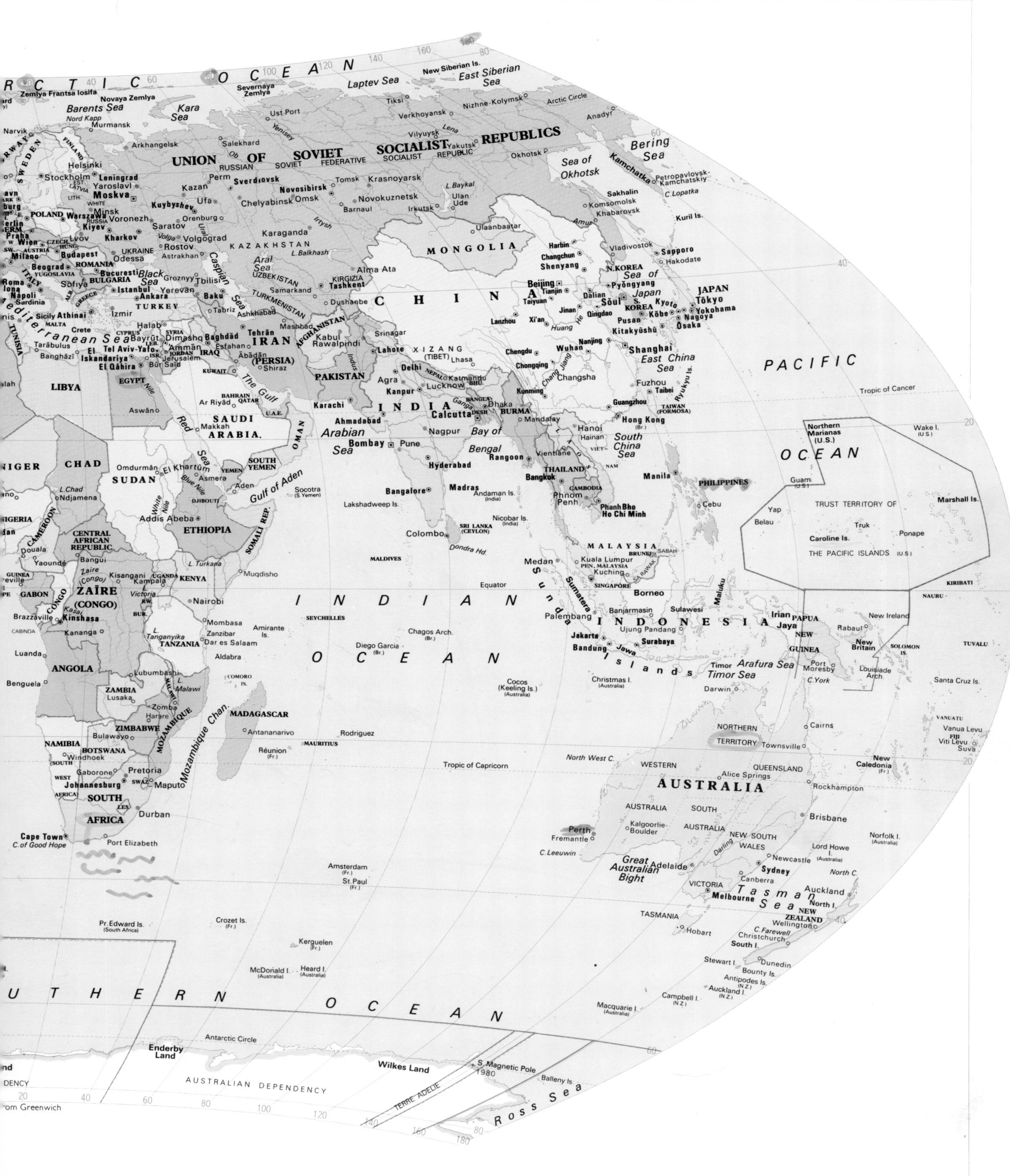

1 : 80 000 000

3

COPYRIGHT GEORGE PHILIP & SON LTD.

ARCTIC OCEAN
Zemlya Frantsa Iosifa
Novaya Zemlya
Severnaya Zemlya
Laptev Sea
New Siberian Is.
East Siberian Sea
Barents Sea
Nord Kapp
Kara Sea
Ust Port
Tiksi
Verkhoyansk
Nizhne-Kolymsk
Arctic Circle
Anadyr
Murmansk
Narvik
Yenisey
Lena
Vilyuysk
Bering Sea
Arkhangelsk
Salekhard
Ob
UNION OF SOVIET SOCIALIST REPUBLICS
RUSSIAN SOVIET FEDERATIVE SOCIALIST REPUBLIC
Yakutsk
Okhotsk
Sea of Okhotsk
Kamchatka
Petropavlovsk-Kamchatskiy
NORWAY
SWEDEN
FINLAND
Helsinki
Stockholm
Leningrad
Yaroslavl
EST.
LATVIA
LITH.
Perm
Sverdlovsk
Novosibirsk
Tomsk
Krasnoyarsk
L. Baykal
Sakhalin
C. Lopatka
Moskva
Kazan
WHITE RUSSIA
Minsk
Kuybyshev
Ufa
Chelyabinsk
Omsk
Novokuznetsk
Barnaul
Irkutsk
Ulan Ude
Komsomolsk
Khabarovsk
Kuril Is.
POLAND
Warszawa
Voronezh
Orenburg
Saratov
Irtysh
Amur
Kiyev
Kharkov
Volga
Volgograd
Ural
Karaganda
Ulaanbaatar
Berlin
Praha
Wien
CZECH.
AUSTRIA
HUNG.
Budapest
UKRAINE
Rostov
Astrakhan
KAZAKHSTAN
L. Balkhash
MONGOLIA
Harbin
Changchun
Shenyang
Vladivostok
Sapporo
Hakodate
Milano
Beograd
YUGOSLAVIA
ROMANIA
Odessa
Bucuresti
BULGARIA
Sofiya
Black Sea
Grozny
Tbilisi
Caspian Sea
Aral Sea
UZBEKISTAN
KIRGIZIA
Alma Ata
Tashkent
N. KOREA
Sea of Japan
Pyongyang
Roma
Napoli
Sardinia
ITALY
ALB.
GREECE
Istanbul
Ankara
TURKEY
Yerevan
Baku
Samarkand
TURKMENISTAN
Dushanbe
CHINA
Beijing
Tianjin
Taiyuan
Dalian
Soul
S. KOREA
Jinan
Qingdao
Pusan
Kyoto
JAPAN
Tokyo
Yokohama
Kobe
Nagoya
Osaka
Kitakyushu
Sicily
Athinai
Izmir
MALTA
Tabriz
Ashkhabad
Mashhad
Lanzhou
Xi'an
Huang He
Halab
SYRIA
Tunis
TUNISIA
Crete
CYPRUS
Bayrut
Dimashq
Baghdad
IRAQ
Tehran
IRAN
(PERSIA)
Esfahan
AFGHANISTAN
Kabul
Rawalpindi
Srinagar
XIZANG
(TIBET)
Lhasa
Chengdu
Nanjing
Wuhan
Shanghai
East China Sea
Mediterranean Sea
Tarabulus
Banghazi
El Iskandariya
Tel Aviv-Yafo
Amman
JORDAN
Jerusalem
ISR.
LEB.
Bur Said
El Qahira
Abadan
Shiraz
Lahore
Indus
Delhi
PAKISTAN
NEPAL
Katmandu
BHU.
Chongqing
Chang Jiang
Changsha
Fuzhou
Taibei
Ryukyu Is.
PACIFIC OCEAN
LIBYA
EGYPT
Nile
KUWAIT
The Gulf
BAHRAIN
QATAR
Ar Riyad
U.A.E.
Karachi
Agra
Kanpur
Lucknow
Ganga
INDIA
BANGLADESH
Dhaka
Calcutta
BURMA
Kunming
Guangzhou
Hong Kong
(Br.)
TAIWAN
(FORMOSA)
Tropic of Cancer
Aswan
Red Sea
Makkah
SAUDI ARABIA
OMAN
Ahmadabad
Arabian Sea
Bombay
Pune
Nagpur
Bay of Bengal
Mandalay
Hanoi
Hainan
VIETNAM
South China Sea
Northern Marianas
(U.S.)
Wake I.
(U.S.)
NIGER
CHAD
SUDAN
Omdurman
El Khartum
Blue Nile
White Nile
Asmera
YEMEN
SOUTH YEMEN
Aden
Gulf of Aden
Socotra
(S. Yemen)
Hyderabad
Rangoon
Vientiane
THAILAND
Bangkok
Manila
PHILIPPINES
Guam
(U.S.)
L. Chad
Ndjamena
DJIBOUTI
Addis Abeba
ETHIOPIA
SOMALI REP.
Bangalore
Madras
Andaman Is.
(India)
Lakshadweep Is.
CAMBODIA
Phnom Penh
Phanh Bho Ho Chi Minh
Cebu
Yap
Belau
TRUST TERRITORY OF THE PACIFIC ISLANDS (U.S.)
Truk
Caroline Is.
Ponape
Marshall Is.
NIGERIA
CAMEROON
CENTRAL AFRICAN REPUBLIC
Douala
Yaounde
Bangui
L. Turkana
Colombo
SRI LANKA
(CEYLON)
Nicobar Is.
(India)
Dondra Hd.
MALDIVES
MALAYSIA
SABAH
BRUNEI
SARAWAK
Medan
Kuala Lumpur
PEN. MALAYSIA
Kuching
SINGAPORE
GUINEA
GABON
CONGO
Zaire
(Congo)
ZAIRE
(CONGO)
Kisangani
UGANDA
Kampala
KENYA
Muqdisho
Equator
Sumatera
Borneo
Maluku
KIRIBATI
NAURU
Kasai
Kinshasa
Brazzaville
CABINDA
Victoria
RW.
BUR.
Nairobi
INDIAN OCEAN
SEYCHELLES
Sunda Islands
Palembang
Banjarmasin
Sulawesi
INDONESIA
Irian Jaya
PAPUA NEW GUINEA
New Ireland
Rabaul
New Britain
SOLOMON IS.
TUVALU
Kananga
L. Tanganyika
TANZANIA
Mombasa
Zanzibar
Dar es Salaam
Amirante Is.
Chagos Arch.
(Br.)
Diego Garcia
(Br.)
Ujung Pandang
Jakarta
Bandung
Jawa
Surabaya
Luanda
ANGOLA
Aldabra
COMORO IS.
Lubumbashi
Cocos
(Keeling Is.)
(Australia)
Christmas I.
(Australia)
Timor
Timor Sea
Arafura Sea
Port Moresby
C. York
Louisiade Arch.
Santa Cruz Is.
Benguela
ZAMBIA
Lusaka
L. Malawi
MALAWI
Mozambique Chan.
MADAGASCAR
Darwin
Zomba
Harare
ZIMBABWE
MOZAMBIQUE
NORTHERN TERRITORY
Cairns
VANUATU
Vanua Levu
FIJI
Viti Levu
Suva
NAMIBIA
Bulawayo
Antananarivo
Rodriguez
MAURITIUS
Townsville
BOTSWANA
Windhoek
SOUTH WEST AFRICA
Reunion
(Fr.)
North West C.
WESTERN AUSTRALIA
QUEENSLAND
New Caledonia
(Fr.)
Gaborone
Pretoria
SWAZ.
Maputo
Tropic of Capricorn
Alice Springs
AUSTRALIA
Johannesburg
SOUTH AFRICA
LES.
Durban
Rockhampton
SOUTH AUSTRALIA
Kalgoorlie-Boulder
Brisbane
Perth
Fremantle
NEW SOUTH WALES
Norfolk I.
(Australia)
Cape Town
C. of Good Hope
Port Elizabeth
C. Leeuwin
Darling
Lord Howe I.
(Australia)
Great Australian Bight
Adelaide
Newcastle
Sydney
North C.
Amsterdam
(Fr.)
St. Paul
(Fr.)
Canberra
VICTORIA
Melbourne
Tasman Sea
Auckland
North I.
NEW ZEALAND
TASMANIA
Hobart
Wellington
C. Farewell
Christchurch
South I.
Pr. Edward Is.
(South Africa)
Crozet Is.
(Fr.)
Kerguelen
(Fr.)
McDonald I.
(Australia)
Heard I.
(Australia)
Stewart I.
Dunedin
Bounty Is.
Antipodes Is.
(N.Z.)
Auckland I.
(N.Z.)
Campbell I.
(N.Z.)
Macquarie I.
(Australia)
SOUTHERN OCEAN
Antarctic Circle
Enderby Land
Wilkes Land
S. Magnetic Pole
1980
AUSTRALIAN DEPENDENCY
TERRE ADELIE
Balleny Is.
Ross Sea
from Greenwich

1:20 000 000

100 0 100 200 300 400 500 miles
100 0 200 400 600 800 km

COPYRIGHT GEORGE PHILIP & SON LTD

Ob

Ural Mountains

Telpos-Iz 1617

Narodnaya 1894

Pechora

Vaygach

Kanin Peninsula

Mezen

N. Dvina

White Sea

Kola Peninsula

Kildin

Lapland

Nordkinn

North Cape

Vesterålen

Lofoten

Tysfjord

Inari

Torne

Ume

Indalsälven

Galdhøpiggen 2469

Jostedal

Skagerrak

Jutland

Kattegat

Lister

Vänern

Vättern

Mälaren

Gotland

Öland

Bornholm

G. of Finland

Neva

Chudskoye

L. Ladoga

L. Onega

Onega

Rybinsk Res.

Volga

Volga Uplands

Kama

Ufa

Central Russian Uplands

Don

Sea of Azov

Kerch

Crimea

BLACK SEA

Dnieper (Dnepr)

Bug

Danube

Ukraine

Pripyat Marshes

Pripyat

Dniestr (Dnester)

Prut

Wallachia

Transylvanian Alps

Carpathians

Sudetes

Plain of Hungary

Danube

Drava

Mures

Tisza

Morava

Danube

Balkans

Rhodope

Balkan Peninsula

Pindus

Morea

C. Matapan 5121

Ionian Is.

Str. of Otranto

Ionian Sea

ADRIATIC SEA

Dinaric Alps

Apennines

Gt. Sasso 2914

Tiber

C. Bon

Sicily

Etna 3263

Malta

Tyrrhenian Sea

Str. of Messina

Calabria

Sardinia

Corsica

Str. of Bonifacio

Ligurian Sea

Po

Alps

Mont Blanc 4807

Jura

Rhône

G. of Lions

Cévennes

Central Massif

Mt. Dore 1886

Gironde

Garonne

Loire

Seine

Rhine

Vosges

Ardennes

Meuse

Eifel

Hunsrück

Black For.

Danube

Taunus

Westerwald

Harz 1142

Erz Geb.

Bohemian For.

Weser

Elbe

Oder (Odra)

Vistula (Wisła)

Niemen

W. Dvina

Baltic Sea

Gulf of Bothnia

Finland

Lapland

Scandinavia

NORWEGIAN SEA

3734

Iceland

Hvannadalshnúkur 2119

Arctic Circle

Faroe Is.

FAEROES

SOUTH EAST ICELAND

Fisher Bank

Rockall

ROCKALL

BAILEY

FASTNET

SHANNON

Valentia I.

C. Clear

FINISTERRE

Bay of Biscay

Biscay

Pico de Aneto 3404

Pyrenees

Old Castile

New Castile

Cantabrian Mts.

Iberian Peninsula

Douro

Sa. de Estrela

Sa. de Guadarrama

Tagus

Sierra Morena

Guadalquivir

Andalusia

Sierra Nevada 3478

C. St. Vincent

C. Trafalgar

Str. of Gibraltar

C. Spartel

Er Rif

Maritime Atlas

Plateau of the Shotts

MEDITERRANEAN SEA

Balearic Is.

ATLANTIC OCEAN

British Isles

Ireland

Great Britain

Ben Nevis 1347

Snowdon 1085

HEBRIDES

Orkney Is.

Shetland Is.

FAIR ISLE

CROMARTY

FORTH

TYNE

HUMBER

DOGGER

Dogger Bank

FORTIES

VIKING

FISHER

GERMAN BIGHT

Helgoland

Netherland

NORTH SEA

THAMES

DOVER

WIGHT

PORTLAND

PLYMOUTH

LUNDY

SOLE

English Channel

Brittany

C. Bizheppe

FAROES

HEBRIDES

BAILEY

Rockall

Lundy

Irish Sea

Piripyat

Türi

Kura

Terek

Caucasus

Elbrus 5633

5165

CASPIAN SEA

-28

Ural

Volga

Manych

Tsimlyansk Res.

Rion

Sulak

Kizil Irmak

Ararat

Anatolia

Taurus 3770

Cyprus 1951

Aegean Sea

Marmara

Bosporus

Dardanelles

Euphrates

m
ft

4000 12000
2000 6000
1000 3000
600   1200
200   600
0   0
200   600
2000 6000
4000 12000

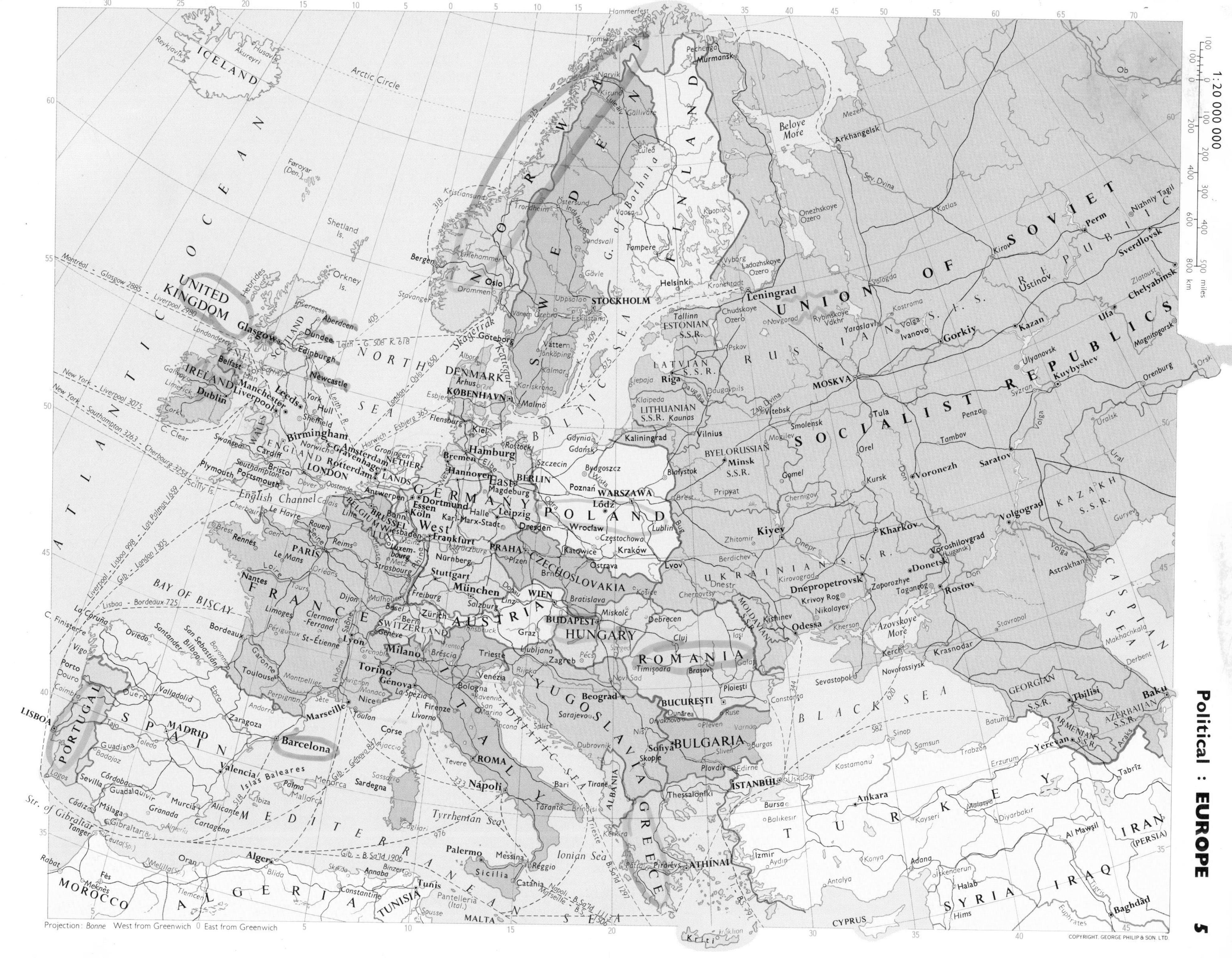
1:20 000 000
100 0 100 200 300 400 500 miles
100 0 200 400 600 800 km
UNION OF SOVIET SOCIALIST REPUBLICS
RUSSIAN S.F.S.R.
UKRAINIAN S.S.R.
BYELORUSSIAN S.S.R.
LITHUANIAN S.S.R.
LATVIAN S.S.R.
ESTONIAN S.S.R.
MOLDAVIAN S.S.R.
GEORGIAN S.S.R.
ARMENIAN S.S.R.
AZERBAIJAN S.S.R.
KAZAKH S.S.R.
ICELAND
FINLAND
SWEDEN
NORWAY
DENMARK
POLAND
GERMANY
East
West
NETHERLANDS
BELGIUM
LUX.
CZECHOSLOVAKIA
HUNGARY
AUSTRIA
SWITZERLAND
ROMANIA
BULGARIA
YUGOSLAVIA
ALBANIA
GREECE
ITALY
FRANCE
SPAIN
PORTUGAL
UNITED KINGDOM
IRELAND
SCOTLAND
WALES
ENGLAND
TURKEY
IRAN (PERSIA)
IRAQ
SYRIA
CYPRUS
MALTA
TUNISIA
ALGERIA
MOROCCO
ATLANTIC OCEAN
NORTH SEA
BALTIC SEA
BLACK SEA
CASPIAN SEA
MEDITERRANEAN SEA
ADRIATIC SEA
Tyrrhenian Sea
Ionian Sea
BAY OF BISCAY
English Channel
G. of Bothnia
Kattegat
Skagerrak
Arctic Circle
Beloye More
Azovskoye More
Str. of Gibraltar
MOSKVA
Leningrad
LONDON
PARIS
BERLIN
WARSZAWA
PRAHA
WIEN
BUDAPEST
BUCUREŞTI
SOFIYA
BEOGRAD
ATHINAI
ROMA
MADRID
LISBOA
STOCKHOLM
OSLO
KØBENHAVN
Helsinki
Dublin
ISTANBUL
Ankara
Projection: Bonne West from Greenwich 0 East from Greenwich
COPYRIGHT. GEORGE PHILIP & SON. LTD.

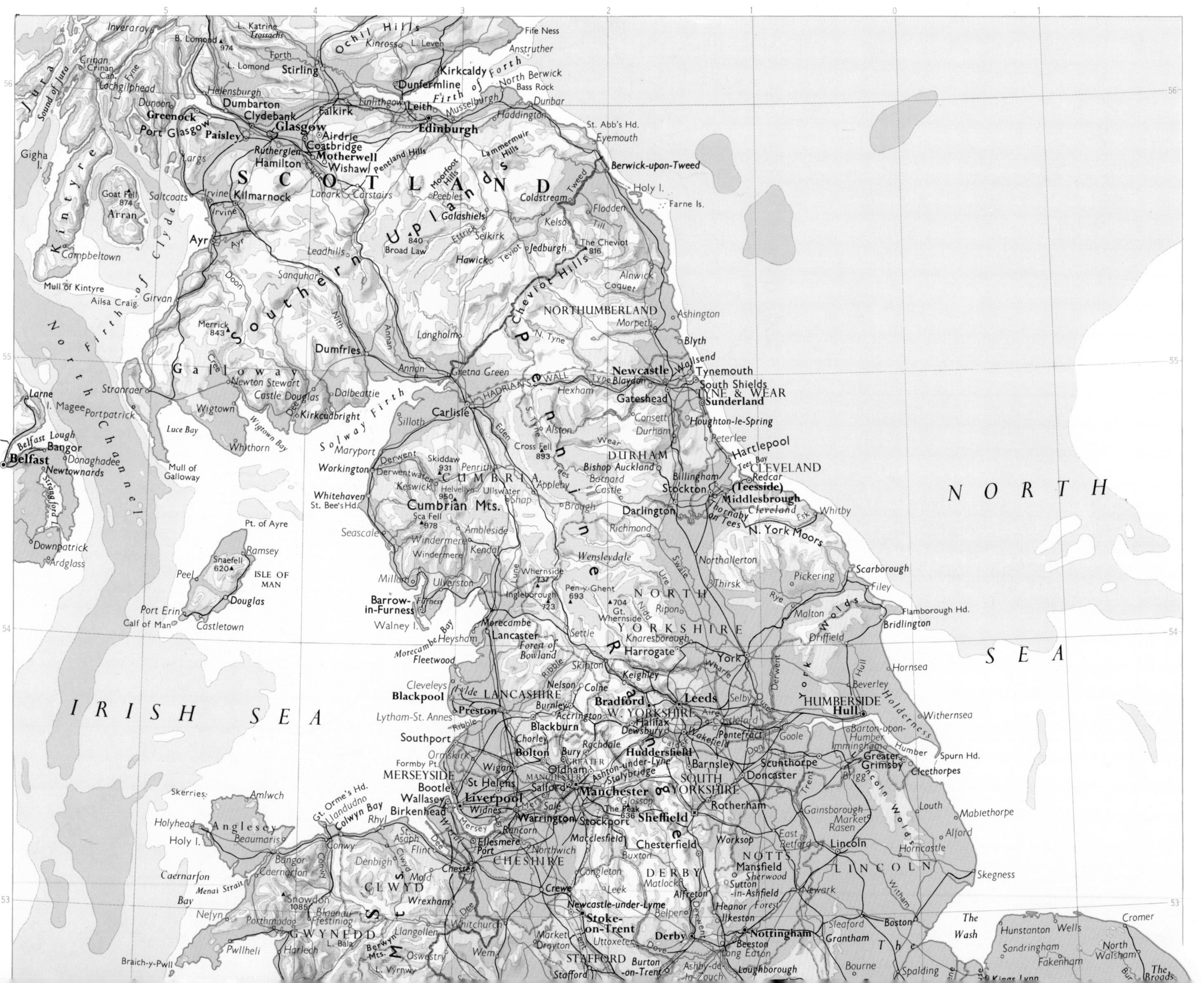
NORTH SEA
IRISH SEA
North Channel
SCOTLAND
Southern Uplands
Galloway
Pennines
Cumbrian Mts.
Cheviot Hills
Hadrian's Wall
N. York Moors
York Wolds
Lincoln Wolds
Holderness
NORTHUMBERLAND
TYNE & WEAR
DURHAM
CLEVELAND
CUMBRIA
NORTH YORKSHIRE
W. YORKSHIRE
SOUTH YORKSHIRE
HUMBERSIDE
LANCASHIRE
GREATER MANCHESTER
MERSEYSIDE
CHESHIRE
DERBY
NOTTS
LINCOLN
STAFFORD
CLWYD
GWYNEDD
ISLE OF MAN
Edinburgh
Glasgow
Leith
Dunfermline
Kirkcaldy
Stirling
Falkirk
Paisley
Greenock
Port Glasgow
Clydebank
Dumbarton
Motherwell
Airdrie
Coatbridge
Hamilton
Kilmarnock
Ayr
Dumfries
Kirkcudbright
Stranraer
Berwick-upon-Tweed
Galashiels
Hawick
Jedburgh
Carlisle
Newcastle
Tynemouth
South Shields
Sunderland
Gateshead
Blyth
Hartlepool
Middlesbrough
(Teesside)
Stockton
Darlington
Bishop Auckland
Scarborough
Bridlington
York
Leeds
Bradford
Harrogate
Halifax
Huddersfield
Wakefield
Barnsley
Sheffield
Rotherham
Doncaster
Scunthorpe
Greater Grimsby
Cleethorpes
Hull
Lincoln
Boston
Grantham
Nottingham
Mansfield
Derby
Chesterfield
Stoke-on-Trent
Newcastle-under-Lyme
Stafford
Manchester
Stockport
Oldham
Bolton
Blackburn
Burnley
Preston
Blackpool
Southport
Liverpool
St Helens
Warrington
Wigan
Birkenhead
Wallasey
Bootle
Chester
Crewe
Lancaster
Morecambe
Barrow-in-Furness
Workington
Whitehaven
Douglas
Ramsey
Castletown
Wrexham
Colwyn Bay
Llandudno
Bangor
Caernarfon
Holyhead
Anglesey
Belfast
Bangor
Larne
The Wash
Skegness
Cromer
Firth of Forth
Firth of Clyde
Solway Firth
Morecambe Bay
Snowdon 1085
Sca Fell 978
Cross Fell 893
The Cheviot 816
Merrick 843
Snaefell 620
Goat Fell 874
Arran
Kintyre
Jura

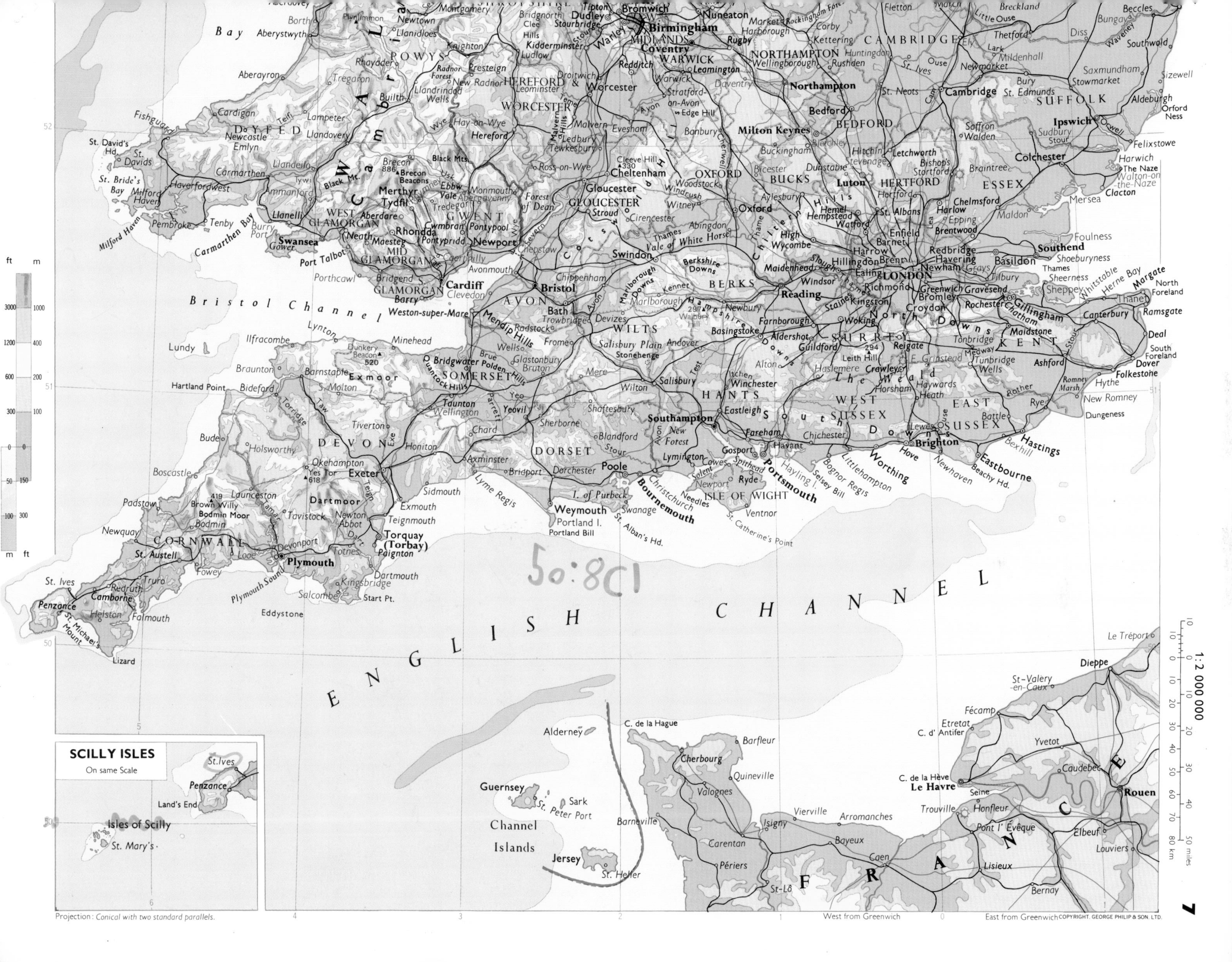
1:2 000 000
10 0 10 20 30 40 50 miles
10 0 10 20 30 40 50 60 70 80 km
ENGLISH CHANNEL
Bristol Channel
Channel Islands
Alderney
Guernsey
Sark
St. Peter Port
Jersey
St. Helier
SCILLY ISLES
On same Scale
Isles of Scilly
St. Mary's
Land's End
Penzance
St. Ives
FRANCE
Dieppe
Rouen
Le Havre
Fécamp
Etretat
C. d' Antifer
C. de la Hève
Honfleur
Trouville
Caen
Bayeux
Arromanches
Lisieux
Bernay
Elbeuf
Louviers
Yvetot
Caudebec
Le Tréport
St-Valery-en-Caux
Cherbourg
C. de la Hague
Barfleur
Quineville
Valognes
Carentan
Isigny
St-Lô
Périers
Barneville
Vierville
LONDON
Brighton
Eastbourne
Hastings
Worthing
Portsmouth
Southampton
Bournemouth
Poole
Weymouth
Exeter
Plymouth
Torquay (Torbay)
Cardiff
Swansea
Newport
Bristol
Bath
Swindon
Oxford
Reading
Gloucester
Cheltenham
Worcester
Hereford
Birmingham
Coventry
Northampton
Bedford
Cambridge
Ipswich
Colchester
Chelmsford
Southend
Canterbury
Dover
Folkestone
Margate
Ramsgate
Deal
Maidstone
Ashford
Gillingham
Luton
Milton Keynes
Salisbury
Winchester
Guildford
ISLE OF WIGHT
CORNWALL
DEVON
DORSET
SOMERSET
WILTS
HANTS
BERKS
SURREY
KENT
EAST SUSSEX
WEST SUSSEX
ESSEX
SUFFOLK
HERTFORD
BUCKS
OXFORD
GLOUCESTER
AVON
GWENT
DYFED
POWYS
WORCESTER
HEREFORD
WARWICK
NORTHAMPTON
BEDFORD
CAMBRIDGE
Dartmoor
Exmoor
Lundy
Lizard
Eddystone
East from Greenwich
West from Greenwich
Projection: Conical with two standard parallels.
COPYRIGHT, GEORGE PHILIP & SON, LTD.
ft m
3000 1000
1200 400
600 200
300 100
0 0
50 150
100 300

1 : 2 000 000

10　　0　　10　　20　　30　　40　　50 miles
10　　0　　10　　20　　30　　40　　50　　60　　70　　80 km

ORKNEY IS.
On same scale

Scapa Flow
Hoy
South Ronaldsay
Orkney Is.
Pentland Firth
Westray
North Ronaldsay
Rousay
Eday
Sanday
Stronsay
Stromness
Mainland
Shapinsay
ORKNEY
Hoy
Kirkwall
Scapa Flow
South Ronaldsay
Pentland Firth
Dunnet Hd.
John o'Groats

C. Wrath
Strathy Pt.
Dunnet Hd.
Thurso
John o'Groats
Orkney Is.
Pentland Firth
Noss Hd.
Wick
Durness
Strathy
Dounreay
Halladale
Tongue
Ben Hope 927
Lybster

Butt of Lewis
Flannan Is.
L. Rodg
Broad Bay
Stornoway
Eye Pen.
Lewis
L. Layford
Eddrachillis Bay
Reay Forest
Ord of Caithness
Helmsdale
L. Assynt
B. More Assynt
Loch Shin
Lairg
Brora
Brora
Golspie
Dornoch
Helmsdale
WESTERN ISLES
Tarbert
L. Seaforth
Harris
Sound of Harris
Lochinver
Enard Bay
Ullapool
Oykell
Dornoch Firth
Tarbat Ness
L. Broom
B. Dearg 1081
Strathpeffer
Dingwall
Conon
Invergordon
Ben Wyvis 1045
Cromarty
Moray Firth
Lossiemouth
Cullen
Portsoy
Banff Macduff
Kinnaird's Head
Fraserburgh
North Uist
Lochmaddy
Rubha Hunish
L. Gairloch
Trotternish
L. Maree
Fannich
Beauly
Nairn
Forres
Elgin
Rothes
Keith
Buckie
Deveron
Turriff
BUCHAN
Rattray Head
Peterhead
Buchan Ness
Benbecula
Skye
Sound of Raasay
Rona
Portree
Raasay
L. Torridon
Farrar
HIGHLAND
Inverness
Culloden Moor
Findhorn
Grantown-on-Spey
Dufftown
Huntly
Elon
Ythan
Monach Is.
Scalpay
Kyle of Lochalsh
Dornie
Glen Affric
Glen Moriston
Fort Augustus
L. Ness
Aviemore
Monadhliath Mts.
Strath Spey
Cairn Gorm
Tomintoul
GRAMPIAN
Inverurie
Don
Alford
Aberdeen
Girdle Ness
South Uist
Lochboisdale
Cuillin Hills
L. Hourn
Glen Garry
L. Oich
Kingussie
Newtonmore
Cairn Toul 1292
Cairngorm Mts.
Ben Macdhui 1311
Ballater
Balmoral
Aboyne
Banchory
Stonehaven
Canna
Rhum
Mallaig
L. Morar
L. Arkaig
Glen Spean
Badenoch
GRAMPIAN HIGHLANDS
Forest of Atholl
Lochnagar 1154
Braemar
N. Esk
Braes of Angus
Laurencekirk
Inverbervie
Eigg
Arisaig
Shiel
L. Eil
Fort William
Ben Nevis 1343
Blair Atholl
Pass of Killiecrankie
Pitlochry
Kirriemuir
S. Esk
Forfar
Brechin
Montrose
Muck
Barra Hd.
Coll
Pt. of Ardnamurchan
Ardgour
Glen Coe
Ballachulish
Rannoch Moor
L. Rannoch
L. Tummel
Aberfeldy
Blairgowrie
Alyth
Strathmore
Arbroath
Tobermory
Morvern
L. Linnhe
Ben Lawers 1214
L. Tay
Tay
Dunkeld
Sidlaw Hills
Broughty Ferry
Tiree
Staffa
Mull
Ben More 966
Iona
Sound of Mull
Ben Cruachan 1124
Breadalbane
Killin
Ben More 983
B. Vorlich
Earn
Crieff
Callander
TAYSIDE
Scone
Perth
Cupar
Dundee
St. Andrews
Firth of Tay
Tayport
Fife Ness
NORTH SEA
ATLANTIC OCEAN
Colonsay
Oban
Inveraray
B. Vorlich 941
L. Awe
Ben Lomond 974
L. Katrine
Trossachs
Dunblane
CENTRAL
Ochil Hills
Kinross
Leven
Glenrothes
Buckhaven
Anstruther
Rubh a' Mhail
Lochgilphead
Crinan
Helensburgh
Dunoon
L. Lomond
Stirling
Bannockburn
Alloa
FIFE
Kirkcaldy
Dunfermline
Bass Rock
North Berwick
Islay
Bowmore
Jura
Sound of Jura
Tarbert
Rothesay
Bute
Port Glasgow
Greenock
Dumbarton
Clydebank
Cumbernauld
Falkirk
Grangemouth
Kirkintilloch
Airdrie
Glasgow
Coatbridge
Bathgate
Linlithgow
Livingston
Rosyth
LOTHIAN
Leith
Edinburgh
Musselburgh
Dalkeith
Haddington
Dunbar
St. Abb's Head
Eyemouth
Port Ellen
Gigha
Paisley
Johnstone
Rutherglen
Motherwell
Wishaw
Hamilton
E. Kilbride
Carstairs
Peebles
Penicuik
Pentland Hills
Moorfoot Hills
Lammermuir Hills
Duns
Berwick-upon-Tweed
Holy I.
Campbeltown
Ardrossan
Saltcoats
Arran
Goat Fell 874
Brodick
Irvine
Kilmarnock
STRATHCLYDE
Lanark
Biggar
Tweed
Coldstream
Galashiels
Melrose
Kelso
Flodden
Till
Rathlin
Fair Hd.
Mull of Kintyre
Troon
Prestwick
Ayr
Cumnock
Leadhills
Broad Law 840
BORDERS
Ettrick
Selkirk
Hawick
Jedburgh
The Cheviot 816
Coquet
Ballycastle
Ailsa Craig
Girvan
Doon
Sanquhar
Nith
Moffat
Teviot
Cheviot Hills
N. Tyne
Hexham
NORTHERN
Trostan 554
Ballymena
Larne
Stranraer
Portpatrick
North Channel
L. Ryan
Newton Stewart
Merrick 843
SOUTHERN UPLANDS
Ken
DUMFRIES AND GALLOWAY
Dumfries
Esk
Langholm
Lockerbie
Gretna Green
Annan
ENGLAND
Esk
Larne
Belfast
Belfast Lough
Bangor
Newtownards
IRELAND
GALLOWAY
Wigtown
Whithorn
Wigtown Bay
Mull of Galloway
Castle Douglas
Dalbeattie
Kirkcudbright
Gatehouse of Fleet
Luce Bay
Solway Firth
Carlisle
HADRIAN'S WALL
S. Tyne
Alston
Cross Fell 893
Wear
Derwent
Skiddaw 931
Ullswater
Penrith
Workington
Tees
Barnard Castle
Cumbrian Mts.
Sumburgh Hd.

SHETLAND IS.
On same scale

Unst
Fetlar
Yell
Yell Sound
Whalsay
SHETLAND
Mainland
Scalloway
Foula
Bressay
Lerwick
Sumburgh Hd.

ft　m
3000　1000
1200　400
600　200
300　100
0　0
50　150
100　300
m　ft

Projection : Conical with two standard parallels.

West from Greenwich

COPYRIGHT. GEORGE PHILIP & SON, LTD.

1:2 000 000

10   10   20   30   40   50 miles
10   0   10   20   30   40   50   60   70   80 km

ATLANTIC OCEAN

NORTHERN IRELAND

IRELAND

Kintyre
Campbeltown
Arran
Mull of Kintyre
Ailsa Craig

Malin Hd.
Giant's Causeway
Rathlin I.
North Channel
Fair Hd.
Tory I. Horn Hd.
Sheep Haven
Carndonagh
Portrush
Ballycastle
Stranraer
Bloody Foreland
Inishowen Pen.
Moville
Ballymoney
Mull of Kintyre
Gweedore Mts.
Errigal 752
Bunerana
Coleraine
Limavady
554 Trostan
Aran I.
Letterkenny
Londonderry
Ballymena
Larne
DONEGAL
Derryveagh Mts.
Sperrin Mts.
Magherafelt
Antrim
I. Magee
Portpatrick
Gweebarra B.
Glenties
Lifford
Strabane
Sawel 683
Carrickfergus
Bluestack
Finn
Mourne
Cookstown
Neagh
Belfast L.
Donaghadee
Rossan Pt.
676
Derg
Bann
16
Bangor
Rathlin O Birne I.
Killybegs
Donegal
Omagh
ULSTER
Dungannon
Newtownards
Ards Pen.
Belfast
Lisburn
Downpatrick Hd.
Killala B.
Ballyshannon
Irvinestown
Blackwater
Portadown
Lurgan (Craigavon)
Broad Haven
Erris Hd.
Killala
Bundoran
Enniskillen
Banbridge
Belmullet
Donegal Bay
L. Erne
Finn
Monaghan
Downpatrick
Dundrum
Mullet Peninsula
Sligo B.
Sligo
Upper Erne
Jones
Newry
Sl. Gullion 577
Slieve Donard 852
Newcastle
Blacksod Bay
Ballina
Collooney
L. Allen
Belturbet
Annalee
Castleblayney
8
Mourne Mts.
Dundrum Bay
Achill Hd.
Moy
Sligo Mts.
Arrow
Leitrim
Cootehill
Warrenpoint
Carling ford L.
Achill I.
Conn
Nephin 806
LEITRIM
Carrick-on-Shannon
CAVAN
Cavan Carrickmacross
Kingscourt
LOUTH
Greenore
Dundalk
Castlebar
MAYO
Boyle
Gowna
L. Sheelin
Louth
Dundalk Bay
Clare I.
Clew Bay
Westport
ROSCOMMON
Castlereagh
Granard
Longford
Oldcastle
Ceanannas Mor (Kells)
Ardee
Croagh Patrick 765
CONNACHT
Claremorris
Robe
Roscommon
An Uaimh (Navan)
Drogheda
Mweelrea 819
L. Mask
Ballinrobe
LONGFORD
L. Ree
Athboy
MEATH
Balbriggan
Inishbofin
Killary Harbour
Twelve Pins
Tuam
Suck
Inny
Trim
Boyne
Lambay I.
Clifden
Connemara
L. Corrib
Clare
WESTMEATH
Mullingar
Swords
Slyne Hd.
GALWAY
IRELAND
Athlone
Maynooth
DUBLIN
Howth Head
Galway
Ballinasloe
Clara
Edenderry
Dublin (Baile Atha Cliath)
Galway Bay
Athenry
Loughrea
Brosna
Tullamore
Daingean
Droichead Nua
Naas
Kippure 754
Dublin Bay
Dun Laoghaire
Inishmore
Gort
OFFALY
Bog
Kildare
Bray
Aran Is.
Slieve Aughty
Portumna
Shannon
Birr
Sl. Bloom
Mountmellick
KILDARE
Poulaphouca Res.
Wicklow
Hags Hd.
L. Derg
Port Laoise
LEINSTER
WICKLOW
Wicklow Hd.
Lisdoonvarna
Ennistymon
Roscrea
LAOIS
Athy
Barrow
Lugnaquillia 923
Rathdrum
Mal Bay
CLARE
Ennis
Nenagh
Templemore
Nore
Carlow
Mizen Hd.
Miltown Malbay
Killaloe
Ballina
Keeper 694
Thurles
Kilkenny
CARLOW
Tullow
Shillelagh
Avoca
Arklow
Kilkee
Rineanna
Ardnacrusha
TIPPERARY
Cashel
KILKENNY
Muine Bheag
Gorey
Loop Hd.
Limerick
Golden Vale
Callan
Mt. Leinster 796
R. Shannon
Foynes
Tipperary
Enniscorthy
WEXFORD
Rathkeale
Galtymore 920
Caher
Slievenamon 722
Cahore Pt.
Kerry Hd.
Listowel
LIMERICK
Galty Mts.
Carrick-on-Suir
Newcastle
Rath Luirc (Charleville)
Mitchelstown
Clonmel
New Ross
Brandon Bay
Tralee Bay
Feale
Knockmealdown Mts.
Comeragh Mts.
Wexford
Tralee
MUNSTER
Newmarket
Blackwater
WATERFORD
Tramore
Rosslare
Brandon Mt. 953
Dingle
Sl. Mish
Maine
Kanturk
Mallow
Fermoy
Lismore
Waterford
Greenore Pt.
Gt. Blasket I.
Laune
KERRY
Killarney
Blackwater
Dungarvan
Tuscar Rock
Dunmore Hd.
Dingle Bay
Macgillycuddy's Reeks
Lakes of Killarney
Boggeragh Mts.
Youghal
Dungarvan Bay
Hook Hd.
Carnsore Pt.
Valentia Harbour
Carrauntuohill 1040
CORK
Youghal Harbour
Saltee Is.
Valentia I.
Cahirciveen
Kenmare
Macroom
Blarney
Lee
Cork
Midleton
St. David's Hd.
Skellig Rocks
Kenmare River
Caha Mts.
Passage West
Cobh
Cork Harbour
Ballinskelligs B.
Glengarriff
Bandon
Crosshaven
Kinsale
Castletown Bearhaven
Bantry
Bandon
Clonakilty
Old Head of Kinsale
Crow Hd.
Bantry Bay
Skull
Skibbereen
Bear I.
Dunmanus Bay
Clonakilty Bay
Galley Hd.
Mizen Hd.
Clear I.
C. Clear
Fastnet Rock
Baltimore

IRISH SEA
St. George's Channel

Towns underlined in Northern Ireland give their
names to the Districts in which they stand
The remaining Districts are:—

1 Fermanagh   5 Castlereagh
2 Moyle   6 Ards
3 Newtownabbey 7 Down
4 North Down   8 Newry & Mourne

ft   m
3000
1200
600
300
0   0
100   300
200   600
m   ft

West from Greenwich

1:4 000 000

20　0　20　40　60 miles
20　0　20　40　60　80 km

ORKNEY
Kirkwall
59
HIGHLAND

SHETLAND
Lerwick
60

The DISTRICTS of Northern Ireland have been numbered and can be identified by reference to this table.

1 Londonderry　14 Craigavon
2 Limavady　15 Armagh
3 Coleraine　16 Newry & Mourne
4 Ballymoney　17 Banbridge
5 Moyle　18 Down
6 Larne　19 Lisburn
7 Ballymena　20 Antrim
8 Magherafelt　21 Newtownabbey
9 Cookstown　22 Carrickfergus
10 Strabane　23 North Down
11 Omagh　24 Ards
12 Fermanagh　25 Castlereagh
13 Dungannon　26 Belfast

Metropolitan Counties :-
On 1st April 1986 the administrative functions of the six metropolitan counties such as planning, education, transportation, libraries and social services were transferred to the city and town boroughs and various non-elected residuary bodies.

WESTERN ISLES
Stornoway

SCOTLAND
HIGHLAND
GRAMPIAN
Inverness
Aberdeen

TAYSIDE
Dundee

FIFE
Glenrothes
CENTRAL
Stirling
STRATHCLYDE
Edinburgh
Glasgow
LOTHIAN

Newtown St. Boswells
BORDERS

ATLANTIC OCEAN

NORTH SEA

NORTHUMBERLAND
DUMFRIES AND GALLOWAY
Dumfries
Newcastle
TYNE AND WEAR
Carlisle
Durham
DURHAM
CUMBRIA
CLEVELAND
Middlesbrough
Northallerton
NORTH YORKSHIRE

North Channel

Lifford
DONEGAL
1 Londonderry
2
3
4
Antrim
10
8
9
7
6
NORTHERN IRELAND
Tyrone
20
21 22
23
26
25 24
Belfast
13
14
19
Down
17 18
Fermanagh
12
Sligo
LEITRIM
Monaghan
Armagh
16
SLIGO
Carrick-on-Shannon
MONAGHAN
Cavan
Dundalk
MAYO
Castlebar
CAVAN
LOUTH
ROSCOMMON
Longford
Roscommon
LONGFORD
An Uaimh (Navan)
Mullingar
WESTMEATH
MEATH

ISLE OF MAN
Douglas

IRISH SEA

LANCASHIRE
Preston
WEST YORKSHIRE
Wakefield
HUMBERSIDE
Hull
GREATER MANCHESTER
Barnsley
SOUTH YORKSHIRE
MERSEYSIDE
Manchester
Liverpool
ENGLAND
Lincoln
DERBYSHIRE
NOTTING-HAMSHIRE
LINCOLNSHIRE
Chester
CHESHIRE
Matlock
Nottingham
Caernarfon
Mold
CLWYD
GWYNEDD
Stafford
STAFFORD-SHIRE
Leicester
LEICESTERSHIRE
NORFOLK
Norwich
Shrewsbury
SHROPSHIRE
WEST MIDLANDS
NORTH-AMPTON-SHIRE
CAMBRIDGE-SHIRE
WALES
Birmingham
Warwick
WARWICK-SHIRE
Northampton
Cambridge
SUFFOLK
Ipswich
POWYS
HEREFORD AND WORCESTER
Worcester
Bedford
BEDFORD-SHIRE
HERTFORD-SHIRE
Hertford
ESSEX
Chelmsford
Llandrindod Wells
Gloucester
GLOUCESTER-SHIRE
Oxford
OXFORDSHIRE
Aylesbury
BUCK-INGHAM-SHIRE
DYFED
Carmarthen
GWENT
Cwmbran
BERKSHIRE
Reading
GREATER LONDON
Kingston
Maidstone
WEST GLAMORGAN
Swansea
MID GLAMORGAN
Cardiff
Bristol
AVON
WILTSHIRE
Trowbridge
SURREY
KENT
SOUTH GLAMORGAN
SOMERSET
Taunton
HAMPSHIRE
Winchester
WEST SUSSEX
Chichester
EAST SUSSEX
Lewes
DEVON
DORSET
Dorchester
Newport
ISLE OF WIGHT
Exeter

GALWAY
Galway
IRELAND
OFFALY
Tullamore
KILDARE
Naas
DUBLIN
Dublin
CLARE
Ennis
LAOIS
Port Laoise
Carlow
CARLOW
WICKLOW
Wicklow
Limerick
LIMERICK
TIPPERARY
Kilkenny
KILKENNY
Tralee
KERRY
Clonmel
WEXFORD
Wexford
WATERFORD
Waterford
CORK
Cork

CELTIC SEA

St. George's Channel

CORNWALL
Truro

ENGLISH CHANNEL

FRANCE

○ Norwich　Administrative headquarters
MERSEYSIDE　Metropolitan counties
Antrim　Former Northern Ireland counties

Projection: Conical with two standard parallels

West from Greenwich　0　East from Greenwich
COPYRIGHT. GEORGE. PHILIP & SON. LTD.

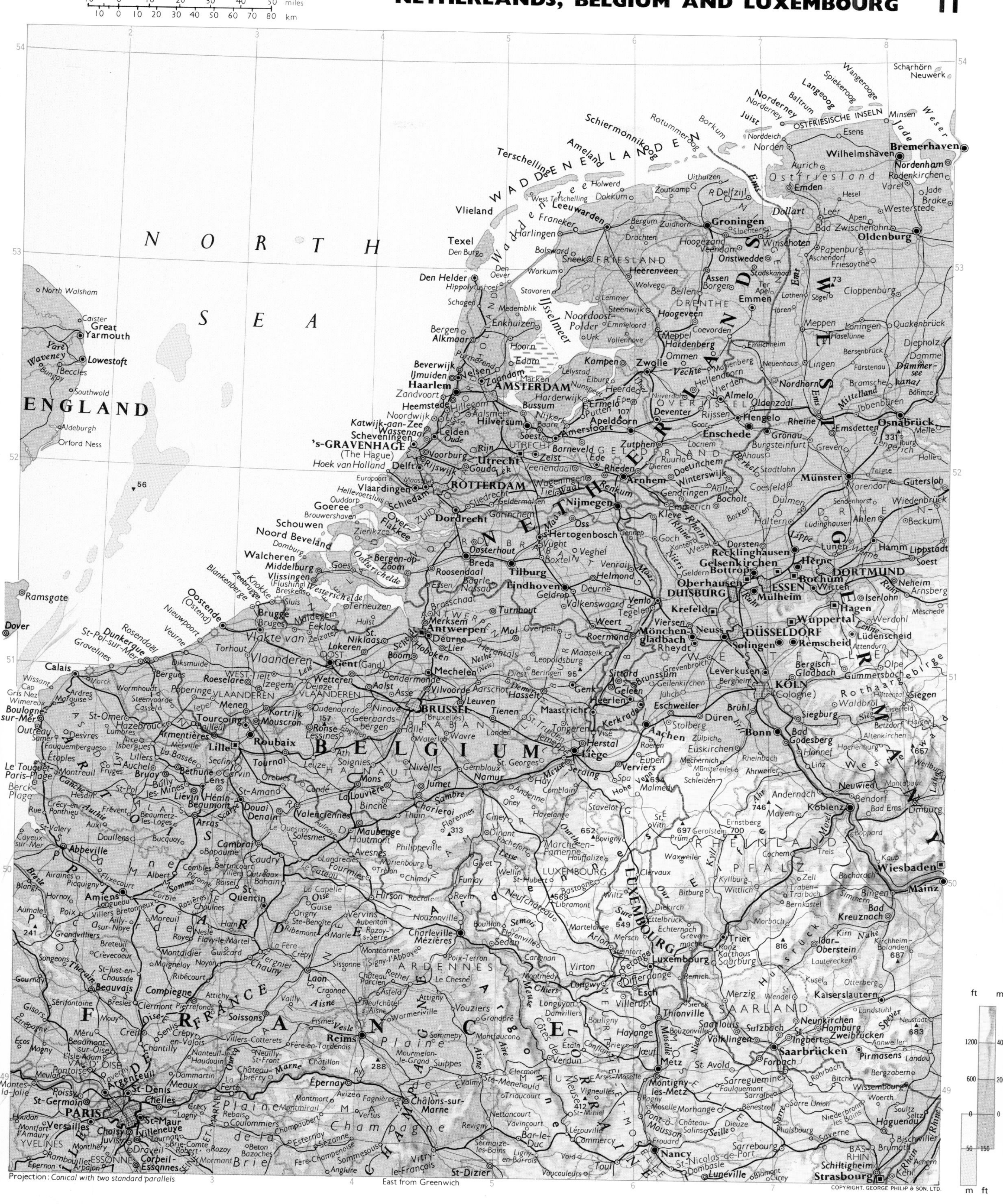

1:2 500 000

Projection: Conical with two standard parallels

East from Greenwich

COPYRIGHT. GEORGE PHILIP & SON. LTD.

1 : 5 000 000

50   0   50   100 miles

50   0   50   100   150 km

FRENCH DEPARTMENTS

Ai.	01	Ain
Ai.	02	Aisne
Al.	03	Allier
A.H.P.	04	Alpes-de-Haute-Provence
H.Alpes	05	Hautes-Alpes
A.M.	06	Alpes-Maritimes
Ard.	07	Ardèche
Ard.	08	Ardennes
Ar.	09	Ariège
Aub.	10	Aube
Aub.	11	Aude
Av.	12	Aveyron
B.Rh.	13	Bouches-du-Rhône
Ca.	14	Calvados
Ca.	15	Cantal
Ch.M.	16	Charente-Maritime
Ch.	17	Charente
Co.	18	Cher
Co.	19	Corrèze
C.O.	20 a)	Corse (a) Haute-Corse b) Corse du Sud
	20b)	
C.O.	21	Côte-d'Or
C.N.	22	Côtes-du-Nord
Cr.	23	Creuse
D.	24	Dordogne
Do.	25	Doubs
Dr.	26	Drôme
E.	27	Eure
E.L.	28	Eure-et-Loir
F.N.	29	Finistère
G.	30	Gard
H.G.	31	Haute-Garonne
Ge.	32	Gers
Gi.	33	Gironde
H.	34	Hérault
I.V.	35	Ille-et-Vilaine
I.	36	Indre
I.L.	37	Indre-et-Loire
Is.	38	Isère
Ju.	39	Jura
La.	40	Landes
L.C.	41	Loir-et-Cher
Loi.	42	Loire
H.Loi.	43	Haute-Loire
L.A.	44	Loire-Atlantique
Loi.	45	Loiret
Lot	46	Lot
L.G.	47	Lot-et-Garonne
Loz.	48	Lozère
M.L.	49	Maine-et-Loire
Ma.	50	Manche
Ma.	51	Marne
H.M.	52	Haute-Marne
May.	53	Mayenne
M.M.	54	Meurthe-et-Moselle
Mos.	55	Meuse
Mos.	56	Morbihan
Mos.	57	Moselle
Ni.	58	Nièvre
No.	59	Nord
Oi.	60	Oise
Or.	61	Orne
P.C.	62	Pas-de-Calais
P.D.	63	Puy-de-Dôme
P.A.	64	Pyrénées-Atlantiques
H.P.	65	Hautes-Pyrénées
P.O.	66	Pyrénées-Orientales
B.Rh.	67	Bas-Rhin
H.Rh.	68	Haut-Rhin
Rh.	69	Rhône
H.S.	70	Haute-Saône
S.L.	71	Saône-et-Loire
Sa.	72	Sarthe
Sa.	73	Savoie
H.Sa.	74	Haute-Savoie
S.Me.	76	Seine-Maritime
S.M²	77	Seine-et-Marne
Y.	78	Yvelines
D.S.	79	Deux-Sèvres
So.	80	Somme
T.	81	Tarn
T.G.	82	Tarn-et-Garonne
Va.	83	Var
Va.	84	Vaucluse
Ve.	85	Vendée
Vi.	86	Vienne
H.V.	87	Haute-Vienne
Vo.	88	Vosges
Y.	89	Yonne
B.	90	Belfort
H.Se.	91	Hauts-de-Seine
S.S.D.	93	Seine-St-Denis
V.M.	94	Val-de-Marne
V.O.	95	Val-d'Oise
Es.	91	Essonne

CORSICA
On same scale

Corse — Haute-Corse — Corse du Sud

COPYRIGHT GEORGE PHILIP & SON LTD.

Projection: Conical with two standard parallels

MEDITERRANEAN SEA

BAY OF BISCAY

ENGLISH CHANNEL

1:5 000 000

50   0   50   100 miles
50   0   50   100   150 km

Projection: Conical with two standard parallels

COPYRIGHT GEORGE PHILIP & SON, LTD.

East from Greenwich

West from Greenwich

FRANCE

Montpellier · Béziers · Narbonne · Perpignan · Toulouse · Bayonne · Biarritz · Pau · San Sebastián · Hendaye

Golfe du Lion · C. Creus · Gerona · Badalona · Barcelona · Sabadell · Tarrasa · Sta. Coloma · Hospitalet

ANDORRA · Pyrénées

BALEARES · Menorca · Mallorca · Palma · Cabrera · Ibiza · Formentera

Bay of Biscay · La Coruña · C. Ortegal · C. Finisterre · El Ferrol · Lugo

GALICIA · Santiago de Compostela · Pontevedra · Vigo · Orense

NAVARRA · Pamplona · Logroño · Zaragoza · Huesca · Lérida · Tarragona · Tortosa

ARAGON · **CATALUÑA**

Bilbao · Baracaldo · Vitoria · Burgos · **PAIS VASCO** · **LA RIOJA** · Sierra de la Demanda

Oviedo · Gijón · Mieres · León · **ASTURIAS** · **CANTABRIA** · Santander · Cordillera Cantábrica

Picos de Europa

CASTILLA Y LEÓN · Palencia · Valladolid · Zamora · Salamanca · Segovia · Ávila

MADRID · Alcalá de Henares · Getafe · Leganés · Guadalajara · Sierra de Guadarrama · Sierra de Gredos

Cuenca · Serranía de Cuenca · Teruel · Mts. de Maestrazgo

VALENCIA · Castellón de la Plana · Golfo de Valencia · Albufera de Valencia · C. Nao · Denia

CASTILLA LA MANCHA · Albacete · Ciudad Real · Montes de Toledo · Toledo

Alicante · Elche · Murcia · Lorca · Cartagena · Cabo de Palos · Mar Menor

MURCIA · Almería · Guadix · Granada · Sa. Nevada · C. de Gata

Jaén · Linares · Córdoba · Sierra Morena · **ANDALUCIA**

Sevilla · Málaga · Vélez Málaga · Marbella · Torremolinos · Antequera

Gibraltar (Br.) · La Línea de la Concepción · Algeciras · Ceuta (Sp.) · Tánger · Tétouan · Strait of Gibraltar

Cádiz · Jerez · Huelva · Golfo de Cádiz · C. Trafalgar · Sanlúcar de Barrameda

EXTREMADURA · Cáceres · Badajoz · Mérida

PORTUGAL · Porto · Coimbra · Lisboa (Lisbon) · Setúbal · Évora · Santarém · Braga

MINHO · **TRAS-OS-MONTES** · **DOURO LITORAL** · **BEIRA ALTA** · **BEIRA BAIXA** · **BEIRA LITORAL** · **ESTREMADURA** · **ALTO ALENTEJO** · **BAIXO ALENTEJO** · **ALGARVE** · **RIBATEJO**

C. de S. Vicente · Sa. de Monchique · Faro · Portimão

MOROCCO · **ALGERIA** · Alger · Blida · Oran · Mostaganem · Ech Cheliff

MEDITERRANEAN SEA · **ATLANTIC OCEAN**

ft   m   9000 6000 4500 3000 1500 1200 600 400 200 0 200 600   ft   m

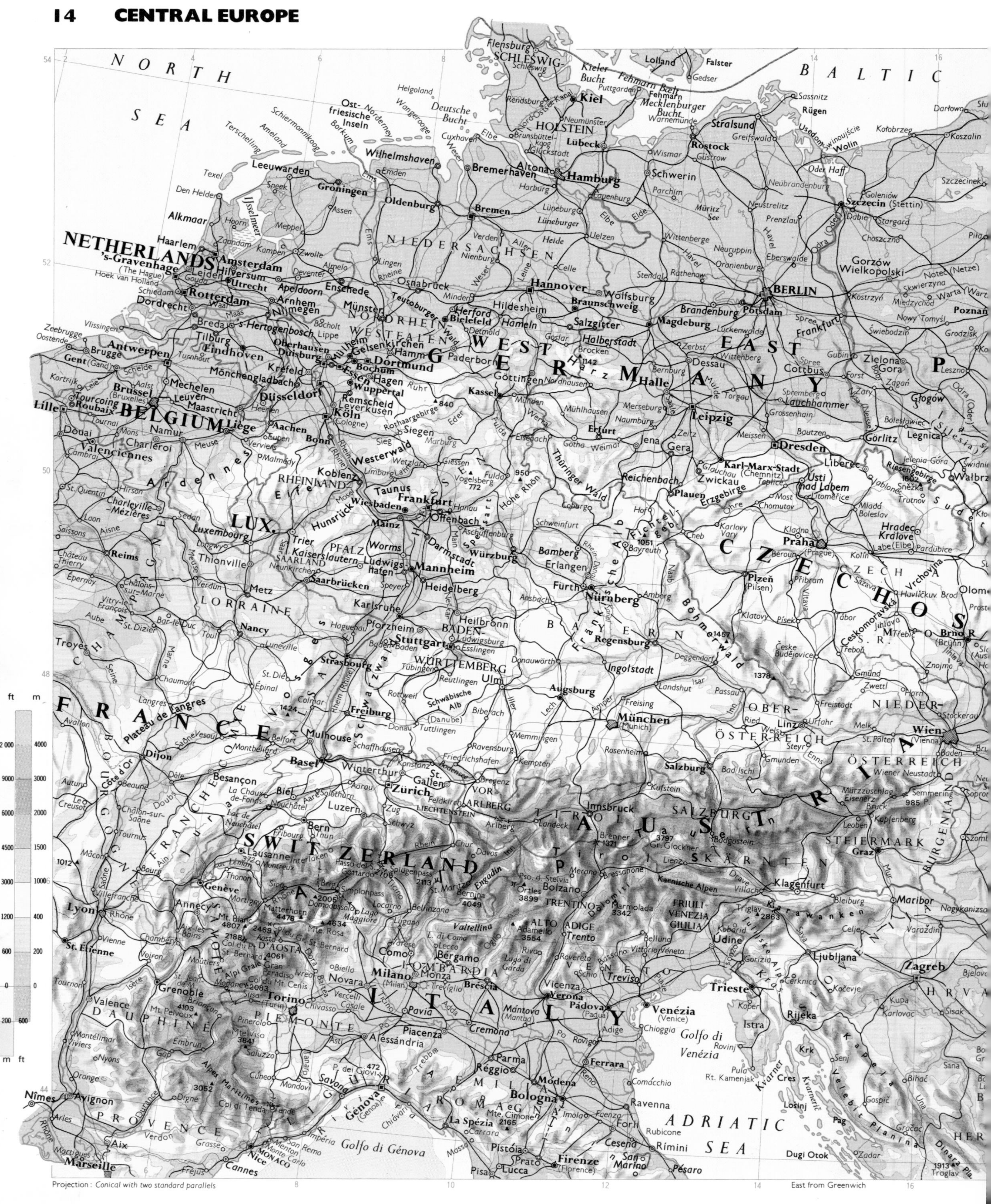
NORTH SEA
BALTIC
NETHERLANDS
BELGIUM
LUX.
WEST GERMANY
EAST GERMANY
CZECHOSLOVAKIA
AUSTRIA
SWITZERLAND
ITALY
FRANCE
ADRIATIC SEA
Golfo di Génova
Golfo di Venézia
Amsterdam
's-Gravenhage (The Hague)
Rotterdam
Utrecht
Antwerpen
Brussel (Bruxelles)
Liège
Luxembourg
Köln (Cologne)
Düsseldorf
Dortmund
Essen
Bonn
Frankfurt
Hamburg
Bremen
Hannover
Kiel
Lübeck
Rostock
BERLIN
Potsdam
Leipzig
Dresden
Halle
Magdeburg
Karl-Marx-Stadt (Chemnitz)
Praha (Prague)
Plzeň (Pilsen)
Brno
Wien (Vienna)
Linz
Salzburg
Innsbruck
Graz
Klagenfurt
München (Munich)
Nürnberg
Stuttgart
Mannheim
Heidelberg
Strasbourg
Metz
Nancy
Reims
Lille
Dijon
Besançon
Lyon
Grenoble
Marseille
Nice
Basel
Zürich
Bern
Lausanne
Genève
Milano (Milan)
Torino (Turin)
Genova (Genoa)
Venézia (Venice)
Verona
Bologna
Firenze (Florence)
Trieste
Ljubljana
Zagreb
Szczecin (Stettin)
Poznań
Ardennes
Harz
Thüringer Wald
Erzgebirge
Schwarzwald
Vosges
Jura
Alpi
Dolomiti
Brocken 1142
Mt. Blanc 4807
Matterhorn 4476
Gr. Glockner 3797
Ortles 3899
Projection: Conical with two standard parallels
East from Greenwich
ft m
12 000 4000
9000 3000
6000 2000
4500 1500
3000 1000
1200 400
600 200
0 0
200 600
m ft

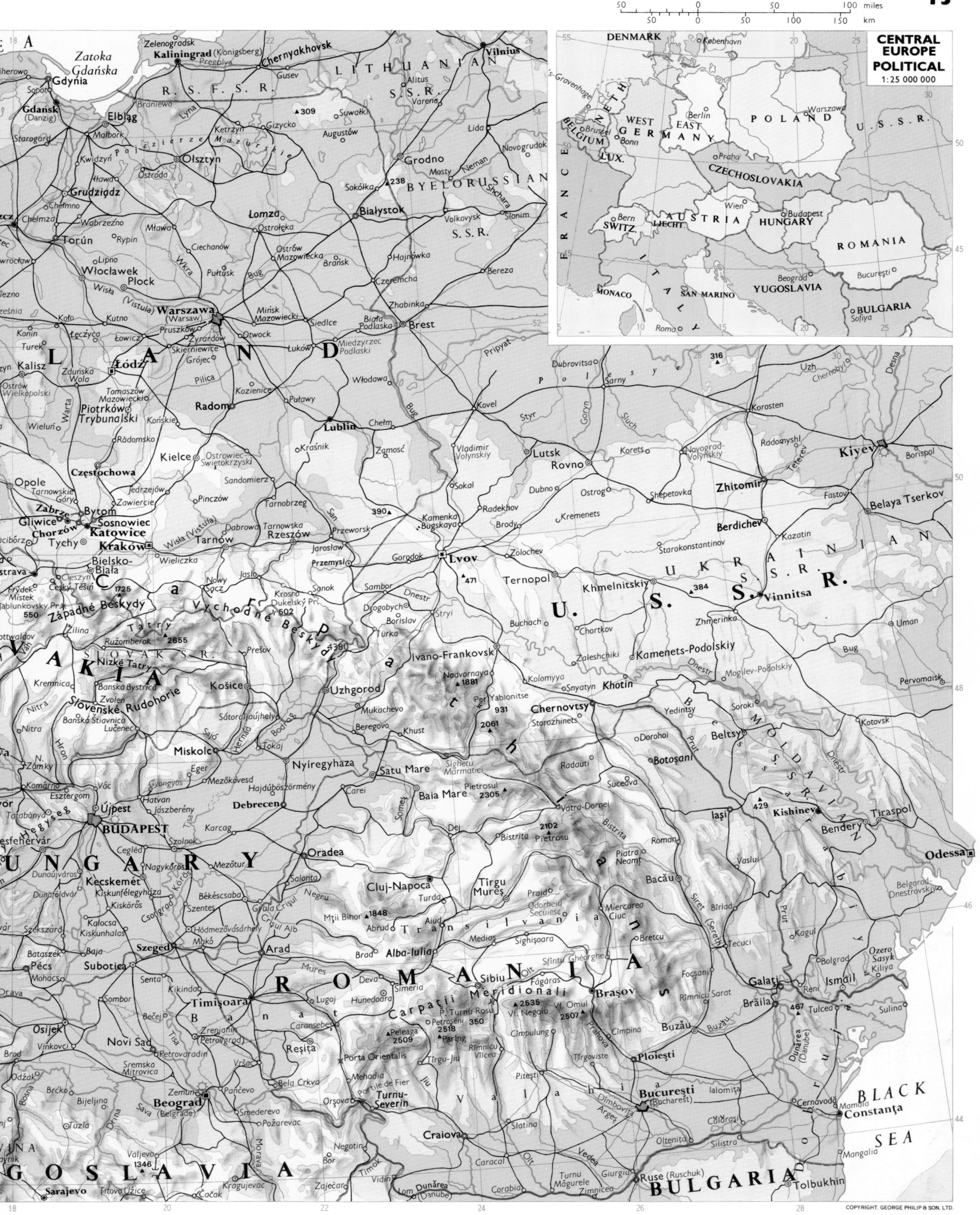

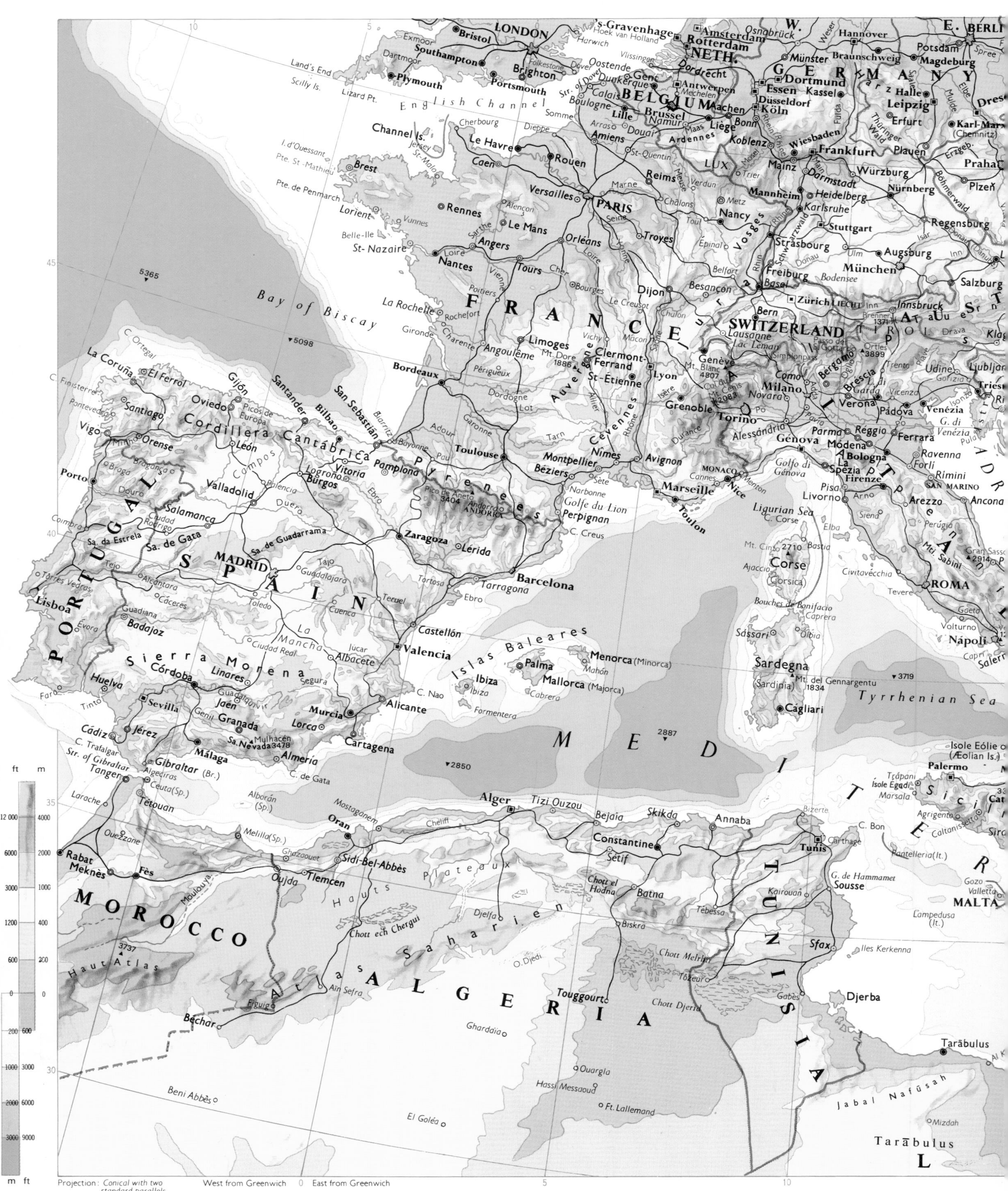

LONDON
Bristol
Exmoor
Southampton
Dartmoor
Plymouth
Portsmouth
Brighton
Folkestone
Dover
Land's End
Scilly Is.
Lizard Pt.
English Channel
's-Gravenhage
Hoek van Holland
Harwich
Amsterdam
Rotterdam
NETH.
Vlissingen
Dordrecht
Oostende
Dunkerque
Gent
Antwerpen
Mechelen
Str. of Dover
Calais
Boulogne
BELGIUM
Lille
Brussel
Namur
Aachen
Liège
Arras
Douai
Amiens
Somme
Ardennes
Maas
Osnabrück
W.
Weser
Hannover
Münster
Braunschweig
GERMANY
Essen
Dortmund
Düsseldorf
Köln
Bonn
Kassel
Halle
Leipzig
Erfurt
Fulda
Thüringer Wald
E.
BERLI
Potsdam
Spree
Magdeburg
Elbe
Mulde
Dres
Karl-Marx
(Chemnitz)
Erzgeb.
Praha
Plzeň
Plauen
Koblenz
Wiesbaden
Frankfurt
Main
Mainz
Rhein
Mosel
Trier
LUX.
Darmstadt
Mannheim
Heidelberg
Würzburg
Nürnberg
Böhmerwald
Regensburg
Karlsruhe
Stuttgart
Isar
Donau
Ulm
Augsburg
Inn
München
Salzburg
Bodensee
Schwarzwald
Freiburg
Basel
Strasbourg
Channel Is.
Jersey
St-Malo
Cherbourg
Dieppe
Le Havre
Rouen
Caen
I. d'Ouessant
Pte. St-Mathieu
Brest
Pte. de Penmarch
Lorient
Vannes
Rennes
Alençon
Le Mans
Sarthe
Angers
Belle-Ile
St-Nazaire
Loire
Nantes
Versailles
PARIS
Seine
Marne
St-Quentin
Reims
Meuse
Verdun
Châlons
Metz
Nancy
Vosges
Toul
Épinal
Troyes
Yonne
Orléans
Tours
Cher
Vienne
Poitiers
Bourges
Belfort
Besançon
Dijon
Le Creusot
Chalon
Mâcon
Saône
Jura
La Rochelle
Rochefort
Charente
Gironde
Angoulême
FRANCE
Limoges
Vichy
Clermont-Ferrand
Mt. Dore 1886
Allier
Auvergne
St-Étienne
Lyon
Rhône
Isère
Bordeaux
Périgueux
Dordogne
Lot
Garonne
Tarn
Adour
Bayonne
Biarritz
Pau
Toulouse
Cévennes
Montpellier
Nîmes
Avignon
Durance
Grenoble
Béziers
Sète
Narbonne
Golfe du Lion
Perpignan
C. Creus
Marseille
Toulon
MONACO
Cannes
Nice
Menton
SWITZERLAND
Bern
Zürich
LIECHT.
Lausanne
Lac Léman
Genève
Mt. Blanc 4807
Simplonpass
Passo del S. Gottardo
Col du Mt. Cenis
2083
Innsbruck
Brenner 1371
AUSTRIA
TIROL
Drava
Ortles 3899
Trento
Udine
Ljubljana
Gorizia
Trieste
Como
Bergamo
Brescia
L. di Garda
Milano
Novara
Vicenza
Verona
Padova
Venézia
G. di Venézia
Isonzo
Torino
Po
Alessándria
Pavia
Parma
Reggio
Ferrara
Genova
Módena
Bologna
Ravenna
Forlì
Rimini
SAN MARINO
La Spezia
Golfo di Génova
Pisa
Firenze
Livorno
Arno
Arezzo
Siena
Perúgia
Ancona
APPENNINO
ITALY
ADRIATIC
Ligurian Sea
C. Corse
Elba
Mt. Cinto 2710
Bastia
Ajaccio
Corse
(Corsica)
Gran Sasso 2914
Mti. Sabini
Civitavécchia
Tevere
ROMA
Gaeta
Volturno
Nápoli
Capri
Salerno
Bouches de Bonifacio
Caprera
Sássari
Olbia
Sardegna
(Sardinia)
Mt. del Gennargentu 1834
Cágliari
3719
Tyrrhenian Sea
Isole Eólie
(Æolian Is.)
Palermo
Trápani
Isole Égadi
Marsala
Sicilia
Agrigento
Caltanissetta
Catania
C. Bon
Pantelleria (It.)
Gozo
Valletta
MALTA
Lampedusa (It.)
5365
Bay of Biscay
5098
C. Ortegal
La Coruña
El Ferrol
C. Finisterre
Pontevedra
Santiago
Gijón
Oviedo
Picos de Europa
Santander
Bilbao
San Sebastián
Cordillera Cantábrica
Vigo
Miño
Orense
León
Bragança
Campos
Braga
Porto
Douro
Valladolid
Palencia
Logroño
Vitoria
Burgos
Pamplona
Ebro
Pyrenees
Pico de Aneto 3404
Andorra
ANDORRA
Duero
Salamanca
Ciudad Rodrigo
Coimbra
Sa. da Estrela
Sa. de Gata
Sa. de Guadarrama
Zaragoza
Lérida
MADRID
Guadalajara
Tajo
Tejo
Alcántara
Tôrres Vedras
Lisboa
PORTUGAL
SPAIN
Cáceres
Toledo
Cuenca
Teruel
Tortosa
Tarragona
Barcelona
Ebro
Guadiana
Badajoz
Évora
La Mancha
Ciudad Real
Júcar
Albacete
Castellón
Valencia
Islas Baleares
Menorca (Minorca)
Mahón
Palma
Mallorca (Majorca)
Ibiza
Cabrera
Formentera
C. Nao
Sierra Morena
Córdoba
Linares
Segura
Huelva
Sevilla
Guadalquivir
Jaén
Genil
Granada
Faro
Tinto
Murcia
Alicante
Lorca
Cartagena
Cádiz
Jérez
Málaga
Mulhacén 3478
Sa. Nevada
Almería
C. de Gata
C. Trafalgar
Str. of Gibraltar
Gibraltar (Br.)
Algeciras
Tangier
Ceuta (Sp.)
Tetouan
Larache
Alborán (Sp.)
2850
2887
MEDITERRANEAN
Alger
Tizi Ouzou
Mostaganem
Oran
Cheliff
Bejaia
Skikda
Annaba
Bizerte
Tunis
Carthage
Constantine
Sétif
Melilla (Sp.)
Ouezzane
Rabat
Meknès
Fès
Ghazaouet
Sidi-Bel-Abbès
Tlemcen
Oujda
Moulouya
Hauts Plateaux
Chott el Hodna
Batna
Tébessa
Kairouan
G. de Hammamet
Sousse
MOROCCO
Djelfa
Chott ech Chergui
Saharien Atlas
Biskra
Chott Melrhir
Sfax
Iles Kerkenna
Tozeur
Gabès
Djerba
3737
Haut Atlas
O. Djedi
Aïn Sefra
Figuig
ALGERIA
Touggourt
Chott Djerid
TUNISIA
Béchar
Ghardaïa
Ouargla
Hassi Messaoud
Ft. Lallemand
Beni Abbès
El Goléa
Tarābulus
Al K
Jabal Nafūsah
Mizdah
Tarābulus
L
10
5
45
40
35
30
0
ft
m
12 000
4000
6000
2000
3000
1000
1200
400
600
200
0
0
200
600
1000
3000
2000
6000
3000
9000
m
ft
Projection: Conical with two standard parallels.
West from Greenwich
East from Greenwich

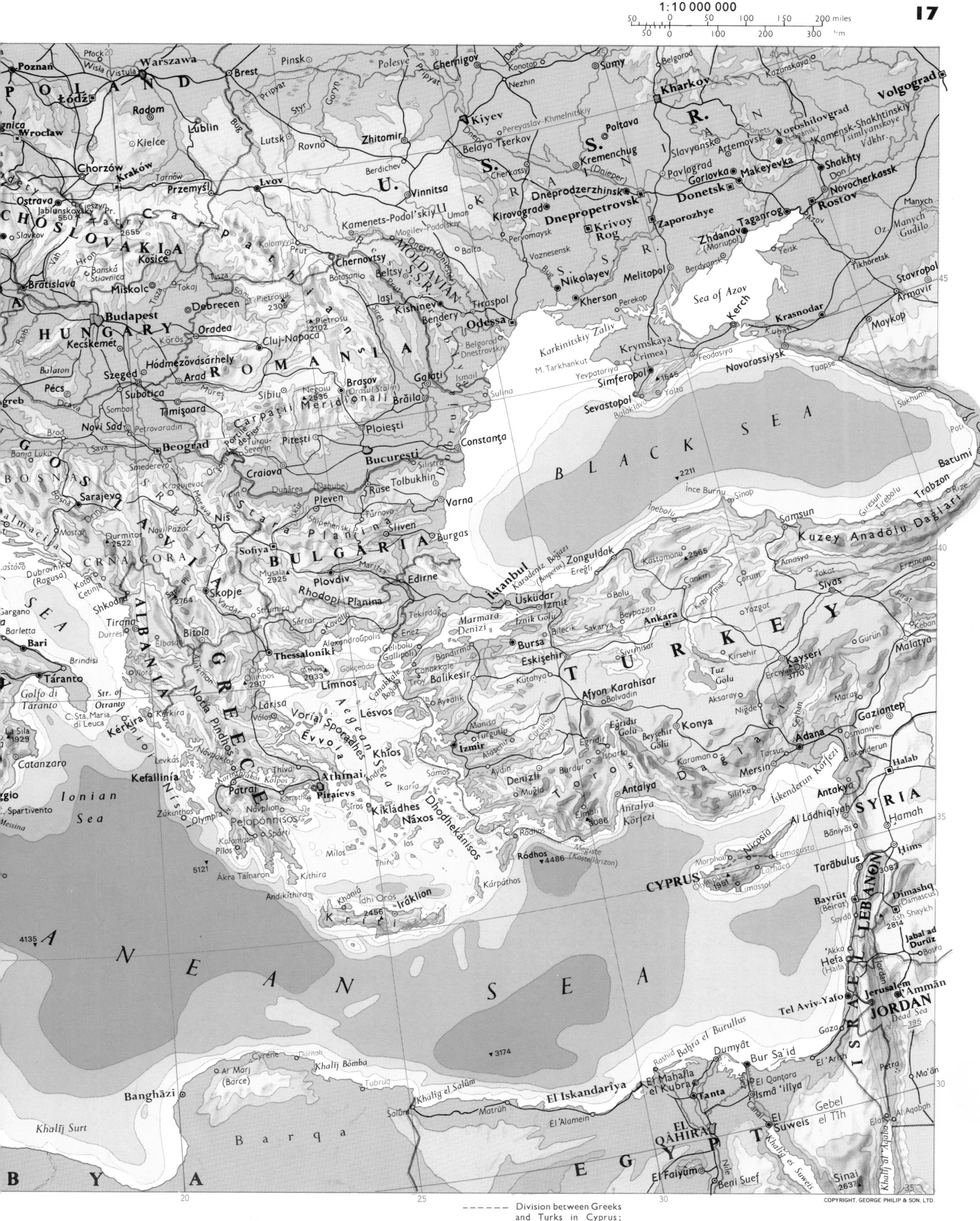

17

1:10 000 000

50   0   50   100   150   200 miles
50   0   100   200   300 km

Division between Greeks
and Turks in Cyprus;
Turks to the north.

COPYRIGHT. GEORGE PHILIP & SON. LTD.

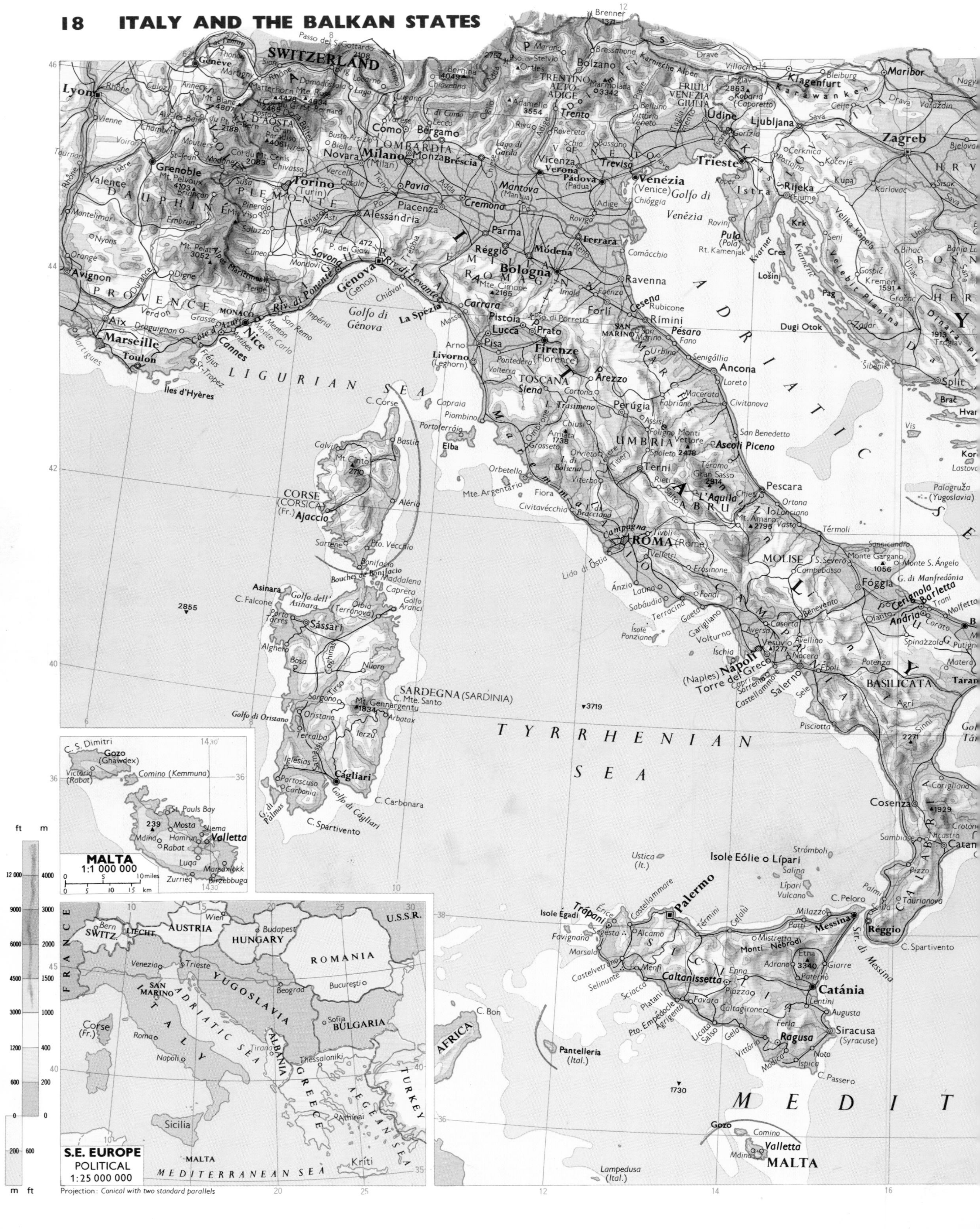

SWITZERLAND

Lyon
Genève
Martigny
Lago
Locarno
Bergamo
Como
Milano (Milan)
Novara
Monza
Bréscia
Varese
OMBARDIA
Torino (Turin)
PIEMONTE
Vercelli
Pavia
Cremona
Piacenza
Alessándria
Asti
Grenoble
DAUPHINÉ
PROVENCE
Cuneo
Savona
Génova (Genoa)
RIVIERA di Ponente
Riv. di Levante
Marseille
Toulon
MONACO
Monte Carlo
Nice
Cannes
Antibes
San Remo
Impéria
Golfo di Génova
La Spézia
LIGURIAN SEA
Carrara
Massa
Pistóia
Lucca
Pisa
Livorno (Leghorn)
Prato
Firenze (Florence)
TOSCANA
Siena
Arezzo
Volterra
Piombino
Elba
Portoferráio
C. Corse
Bastia
Calvi
Mt. Cinto 2710
CORSE (CORSICA) (Fr.)
Ajaccio
Sartène
Pto. Vecchio
Bonifacio
Bouches de Bonifacio
Maddalena
Caprera
Asinara
C. Falcone
Golfo dell' Asinara
Porto Torres
Ólbia (Terranova)
Golfo Aranci
Sássari
Alghero
Bosa
Nuoro
Oristano
Sorgono
Tirso
SARDEGNA (SARDINIA)
Mt. Gennargentu 1834
Arbatax
Iglésias
Carbónia
Golfo di Oristano
Terralba
Iérzu
Golfo di Cágliari
Cágliari
C. Spartivento
C. Carbonara
C. S. Dimitri
Gozo (Ghawdex)
Comino (Kemmuna)
Victoria (Rabat)
239
Mosta
Mdina
Hamrun
Sliema
Valletta
Rabat
St. Pauls Bay
Luqa
Marsaxlokk
Żurrieq
Birżebbuġa

MALTA
1:1 000 000

Brenner
Bressanone
Bolzano
TRENTINO ALTO-ADIGE
Trento
Adamello 3554
Marmolada 3342
Belluno
Vittorio Véneto
VENETO
Vicenza
Verona
Pádova (Padua)
Treviso
Mantova (Mantua)
Rovigo
Venézia (Venice)
Golfo di Venézia
Chióggia
FRIULI VENEZIA GIULIA
Udine
Trieste
Klagenfurt
Maribor
Ljubljana
Zagreb
Cérknica
Rijeka (Fiume)
Pula (Pola)
Cres
Lošinj
Krk
Istra
Senj
Pag
Zadar
Šibenik
Split
Brač
Hvar
Vis
EMILIA
Parma
Réggio
Módena
Bologna
Ferrara
Comácchio
Ravenna
Imola
Fáenza
Forlí
Cesena
Rímini
SAN MARINO
Pésaro
Fano
Senigállia
Ancona
Urbino
Loreto
Macerata
Fabriano
Civitanova
San Benedetto
Ascoli Piceno
Monti Vettore 2478
Áscoli
Téramo
Gran Sasso 2914
Pescara
Ortona
Lanciano
Vasto
Térmoli
ADRIATIC SEA
Dugi Otok
Palagruža (Yugoslavia)
BOSNA
HER
Y
DINARA
UMBRIA
Pisa
Arno
Perúgia
Assisi
Foligno
Terni
Rieti
ABRUZZI
L'Aquila
Chieti
2795
Spoleto
Viterbo
L. di Bolsena
Orvieto
Chiusi
Cortona
L. Trasimeno
Grosseto
Amiata 1738
Mte. Argentário
Fiora
Civitavécchia
L. di Bracciano
ROMA (Rome)
Tivoli
Velletri
Ánzio
Latina
Sabáudia
Terracina
Fondi
Gaeta
Formia
Garigliano
Ísole Ponziane
Ìschia
Capri
Nápoli (Naples)
Torre del Greco
Vesuvio 1277
Nocera
Avellino
Sorrento
Castellammare
Salerno
Éboli
Campobasso
MOLISE
S. Severo
Sannicandro
Monte Gargano
Monte S. Ángelo 1056
G. di Manfredónia
Fóggia
Cerignola
Barletta
Andria
Trani
Molfetta
Corato
Spinazzola
Putignano
BASILICATA
Potenza
Matera
Taran
Agri
Sinni
2271
Pisticci
TYRRHENIAN SEA
3719
CALABRIA
Cosenza
1929
Coriglia
Crotone
Sambiase
Taurianova
Palmi
Scilla
Réggio
Str. di Messina
C. Spartivento
Ústica (It.)
Ísole Eólie o Lípari
Strómboli
Salina
Lípari
Vulcano
Pizzo
Milazzo
Messina
Patti
Mistretta
Monti Nebrodi
Cefalù
Términi
Palermo
Castellammare
Trápani
Érice
Ísole Égadi
Favignana
Alcamo
Segesta
Marsala
Castelvetrano
Selinunte
Menfi
Sciacca
Platani
Pta. Empédocle
Agrigento
Favara
Caltanissetta
Enna
Adrano
Etna 3340
Giarre
Paternò
Catánia
Lentini
Augusta
Siracusa (Syracuse)
Piazza
Caltagirone
Calascibetta
Gela
Licata
Vittória
Comiso
Ragusa
Módica
Noto
Ispica
C. Passero
SICILIA
Pantelleria (It.)
1730
Gozo
Comino
Valletta
MALTA
Mdina
MEDIT

FRANCE
SWITZ.
Bern
LIECHT.
AUSTRIA
Wien
Budapest
HUNGARY
U.S.S.R.
ROMANIA
Bucureşti
Venézia
Trieste
SAN MARINO
ITALY
YUGOSLAVIA
Beograd
Sofija
BULGARIA
Corse (Fr.)
Roma
Nápoli
ADRIATIC SEA
ALBANIA
Tiranë
Thessaloníki
GREECE
Athínai
AEGEAN SEA
TURKEY
C. Bon
AFRICA
Sicília
MALTA
Kríti
MEDITERRANEAN SEA

ft m
12 000 4000
9000 3000
6000 2000
4500 1500
3000 1000
1200 400
600 200
0 0
200 600
m ft

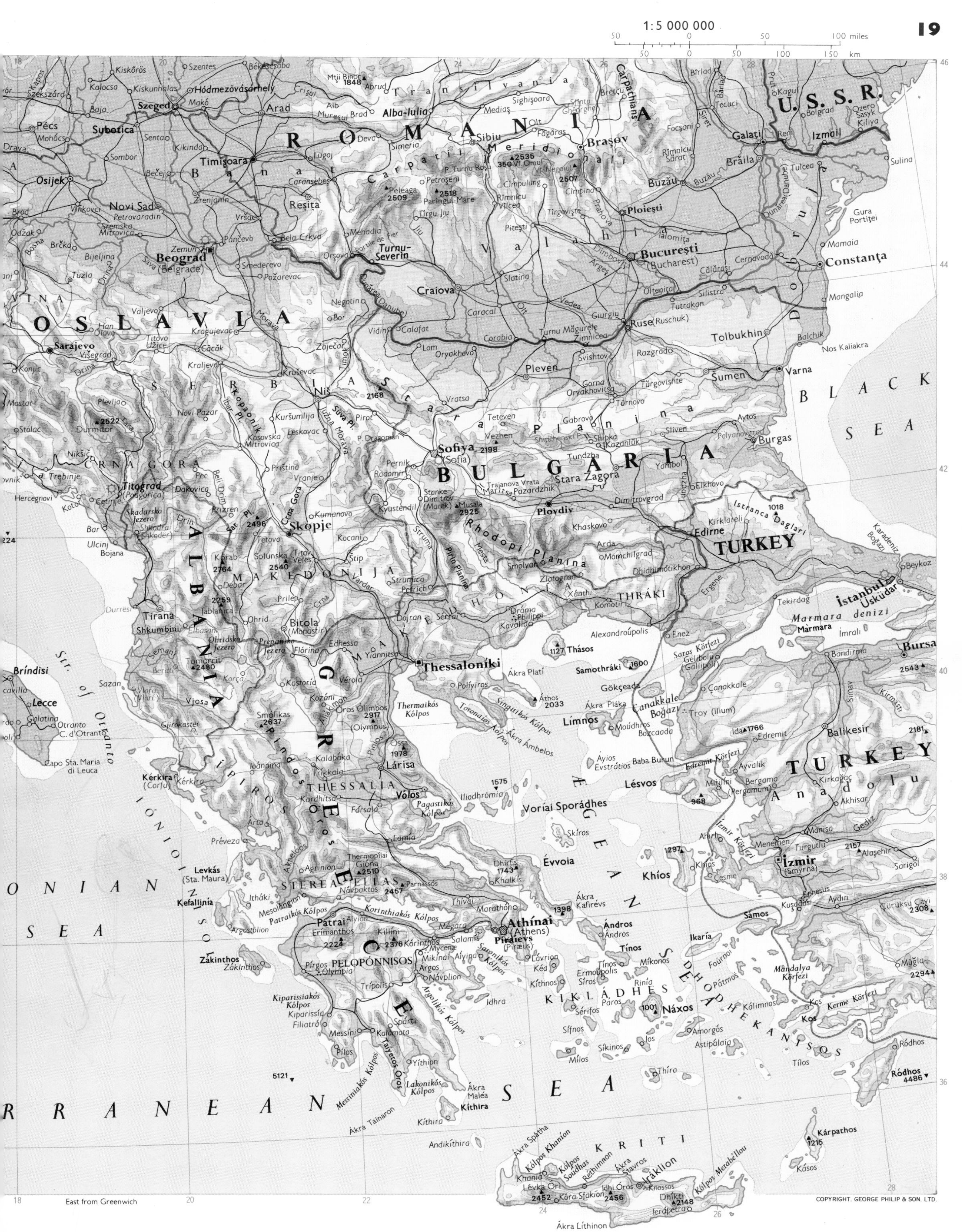
1:5 000 000
50 0 50 100 miles
50 0 50 100 150 km
ROMANIA
U.S.S.R.
BULGARIA
TURKEY
ALBANIA
GREECE
OSLAVIA
BLACK SEA
AEGEAN SEA
IONIAN SEA
RRANEAN SEA
Transilvania
Carpatii Meridionali
Carpathians
Banat
Valahia
Dobrogea
Stara Planina
Rhodopi Planina
Pirin Planina
Pindos Oros
Makedonija
Makedhonia
Thráki
Thessalia
Ípiros
Stereá Ellás
Pelopónnisos
Kikládhes
Dhodhekánisos
Kriti
Anadolu
Srbija
Crna Gora
Voríai Sporádhes
Beograd (Belgrade)
Bucureşti (Bucharest)
Sofiya (Sofia)
Tirana
Athínai (Athens)
Piraiévs (Piraeus)
Thessaloníki
Skopje
Sarajevo
Titograd (Podgorica)
Istanbul
Üsküdar
İzmir (Smyrna)
Bursa
Edirne
Plovdiv
Varna
Burgas
Constanţa
Galaţi
Brăila
Ploieşti
Braşov
Sibiu
Timişoara
Arad
Szeged
Subotica
Novi Sad
Osijek
Pécs
Craiova
Ruse (Ruschuk)
Pleven
Niš
Kragujevac
Lárisa
Vólos
Pátrai
Kórinthos
Iráklion
Khaniá
Marmara denizi
Str. of Otranto
Bríndisi
Lecce
Olimbos 2917 (Olympus)
Musala 2925
Kérkira (Corfu)
Zákinthos
Kefallinía
Levkás (Sta. Maura)
Lésvos
Khíos
Sámos
Ródhos
Kárpathos
Kíthira
Náxos
Thásos
Samothráki
Límnos
Évvoia
Çanakkale Boğazı
Troy (Ilium)
East from Greenwich

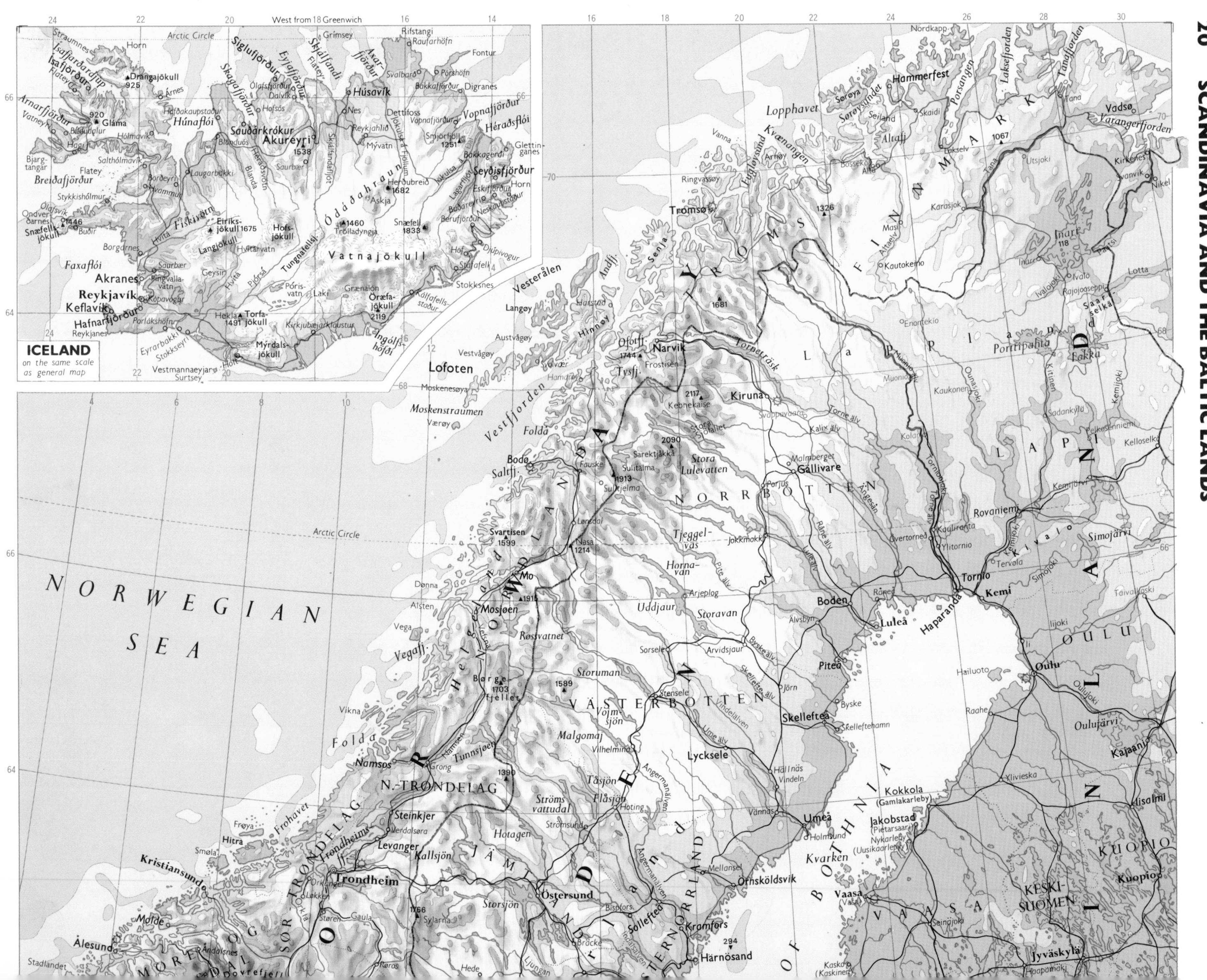
ICELAND
on the same scale as general map
West from 18 Greenwich
Arctic Circle
Vatnajökull
Reykjavík
Keflavík
Hafnarfjörður
Akranes
Faxaflói
Breiðafjörður
Húnaflói
Sauðárkrókur
Akureyri
Húsavík
Seyðisfjörður
Ísafjörður
Siglufjörður
Skagafjörður
Eyjafjörður
Skjálfandi
Vopnafjörður
Héraðsflói
Vestmannaeyjar
Hekla
NORWEGIAN SEA
Lofoten
Vesterålen
Vestfjorden
Moskenstraumen
Tromsø
Narvik
Kiruna
Gällivare
Boden
Luleå
Piteå
Skellefteå
Umeå
Vaasa
Jakobstad
Kokkola
Oulu
Kemi
Tornio
Haparanda
Rovaniemi
Kajaani
Kuopio
Jyväskylä
Hammerfest
Vadsø
Nordkapp
Lopphavet
Lycksele
Östersund
Härnösand
Kramfors
Örnsköldsvik
Trondheim
Namsos
Steinkjer
Levanger
Mosjøen
Bodø
Kristiansund
Ålesund
Molde
Hitra
Frøya
Storsjön
Storuman
Inari
Porttipahta
Lokka
NORRBOTTEN
VÄSTERBOTTEN
N.-TRØNDELAG
SØR-TRØNDELAG
OF BOTHNIA
Kvarken
KESKI-SUOMEN

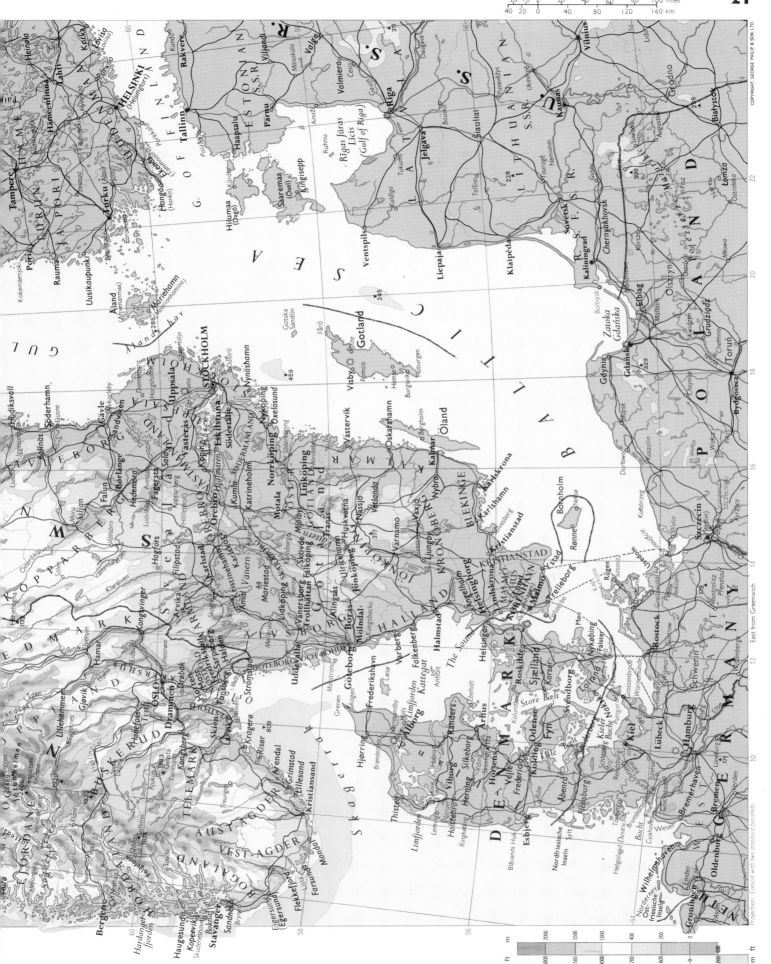

1:5 000 000

20 10 0   40   60   80   100 miles
40 20 0   40   80   120   160 km

COPYRIGHT GEORGE PHILIP & SON LTD.

Projection: Conical with two standard parallels

East from Greenwich

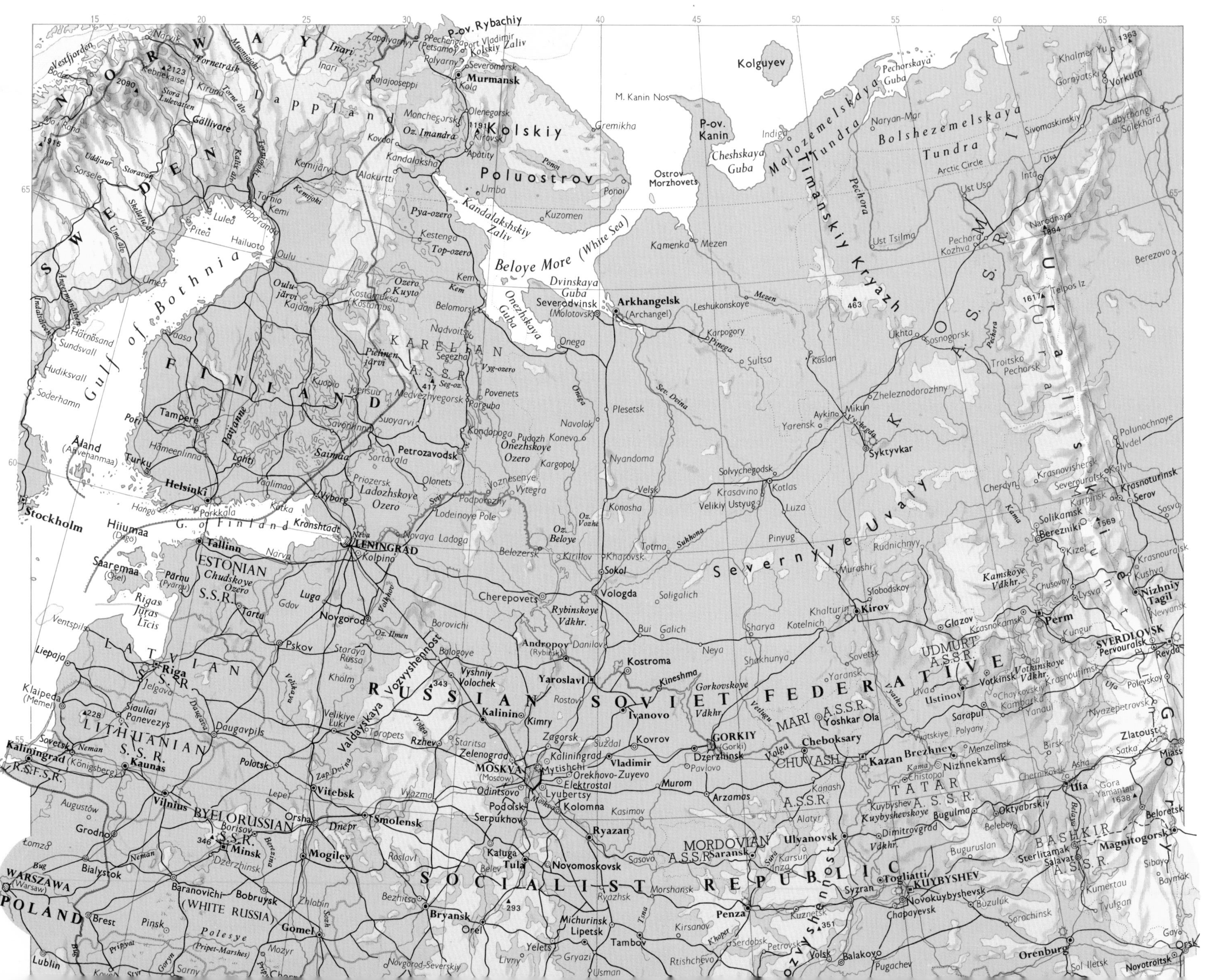

Kolguyev
Timanskiy Kryazh
Bolshezemelskaya Tundra
Malozemelskaya Tundra
Pechora
Pechorskaya Guba
Cheshskaya Guba
P-ov. Kanin
Ostrov Morzhovets
Arctic Circle
Vorkuta
Syktyvkar
Kotlas
Kirov
Perm
SVERDLOVSK
Nizhniy Tagil
Ufa
Orenburg
KUYBYSHEV
Togliatti
Ulyanovsk
Kazan
Ustinov
Penza
Saransk
GORKIY
Dzerzhinsk
Vologda
Yaroslavl
Kostroma
Ivanovo
Vladimir
MOSKVA (Moscow)
Ryazan
Tula
Kaluga
Orel
Bryansk
Smolensk
Kalinin
Novgorod
Pskov
LENINGRAD
Petrozavodsk
Arkhangelsk (Archangel)
Severodvinsk (Molotovsk)
Murmansk
Beloye More (White Sea)
Onezhskaya Guba
Dvinskaya Guba
Kandalakshskiy Zaliv
Kolskiy Poluostrov
Ladozhskoye Ozero
Onezhskoye Ozero
KARELIAN A.S.S.R.
Helsinki
Tampere
Turku
Tallinn
ESTONIAN S.S.R.
Riga
LATVIAN S.S.R.
Vilnius
Kaunas
LITHUANIAN S.S.R.
Minsk
BYELORUSSIAN S.S.R. (WHITE RUSSIA)
Gomel
Mogilev
Vitebsk
Kaliningrad
R.S.F.S.R.
WARSZAWA (Warsaw)
POLAND
Stockholm
Gulf of Bothnia
G. of Finland
FINLAND
SWEDEN
NORWAY
Lappland
Ural
Severnyye Uvaly
Valdayskaya Vozvyshennost
RUSSIAN SOVIET FEDERATIVE SOCIALIST REPUBLIC
TATAR A.S.S.R.
BASHKIR A.S.S.R.
UDMURT A.S.S.R.
CHUVASH A.S.S.R.
MARI A.S.S.R.
MORDOVIAN A.S.S.R.
KOMI A.S.S.R.

1:10 000 000

100 50 0 50 100 150 200 miles
100 0 100 200 300 km

1 Kabardino-Balkar A.S.S.R.
2 North Ossetian A.S.S.R.
3 Nakhichevan A.S.S.R. (Azer.)
4 Checheno-Ingush A.S.S.R.
Karagiye Depression

C A S P I A N   S E A

Zaliv Kara Bogaz Gol

B L A C K   S E A

Azovskoye More (Sea of Azov)

MEDITERRANEAN SEA

Levant

Countries / Regions

K A Z A K H S T A N
Kazakhskaya Nizmennost
STEPPE
KALMYK A.S.S.R.
Ergeni Vozvyshennost
U K R A I N E
MOLDAVIAN S.S.R.
ROMANIA
BULGARIA
T U R K E Y
GEORGIAN S.S.R.
ABKHAZ
ADZHAR
AZERBAIJAN S.S.R.
ARMENIAN S.S.R.
DAGESTAN A.S.S.R.
S Y R I A
I R A Q
P E R S I A (IRAN)
LEBANON
CYPRUS
Anadolu Daglari
Kuzey
Toros Daglari

Cities

Astrakhan, Volgograd (Stalingrad), Rostov, Krasnodar, Stavropol, Groznyy, Ordzhonikidze, Makhachkala, Derbent, Baku, Sumgait, Tbilisi, Yerevan, Kirovakan, Leninakan, Batumi, Sochi, Sukhumi, Novorossiysk, Kerch, Feodosiya, Yalta, Sevastopol, Simferopol, Kherson, Nikolayev, Odessa, Kishinev, KIYEV, KHARKOV, Dnepropetrovsk, Donetsk, Makeyevka, Taganrog, Zaporozhye, Krivoy Rog, BUCURESTI (Bucharest), Brasov, Ploiesti, Varna, Burgas, ISTANBUL, Edirne, Ankara, Konya, Kayseri, Sivas, Samsun, Trabzon, Erzurum, Adana, Mersin, Iskenderun, İzmir (Smyrna), Bursa, Antalya, Tabriz, Qazvin, TEHRAN, Qom, Hamadan, Baghdad, Al Mawsil, Halab, Hama, Hims, DIMASHQ (Damascus), BAYRŪT (Beirut), Tripoli (Tarābulus)

Black Sea
Mediterranean Sea

Division between Greeks and Turks in Cyprus; Turks to the North.

Projection: Conical with two standard parallels

East from Greenwich

ft / m elevation scale:
12 000 / 4000
6000 / 2000
3000 / 1000
1200 / 400
600 / 200
0
200 / -1000
-2000
400 / 12 000

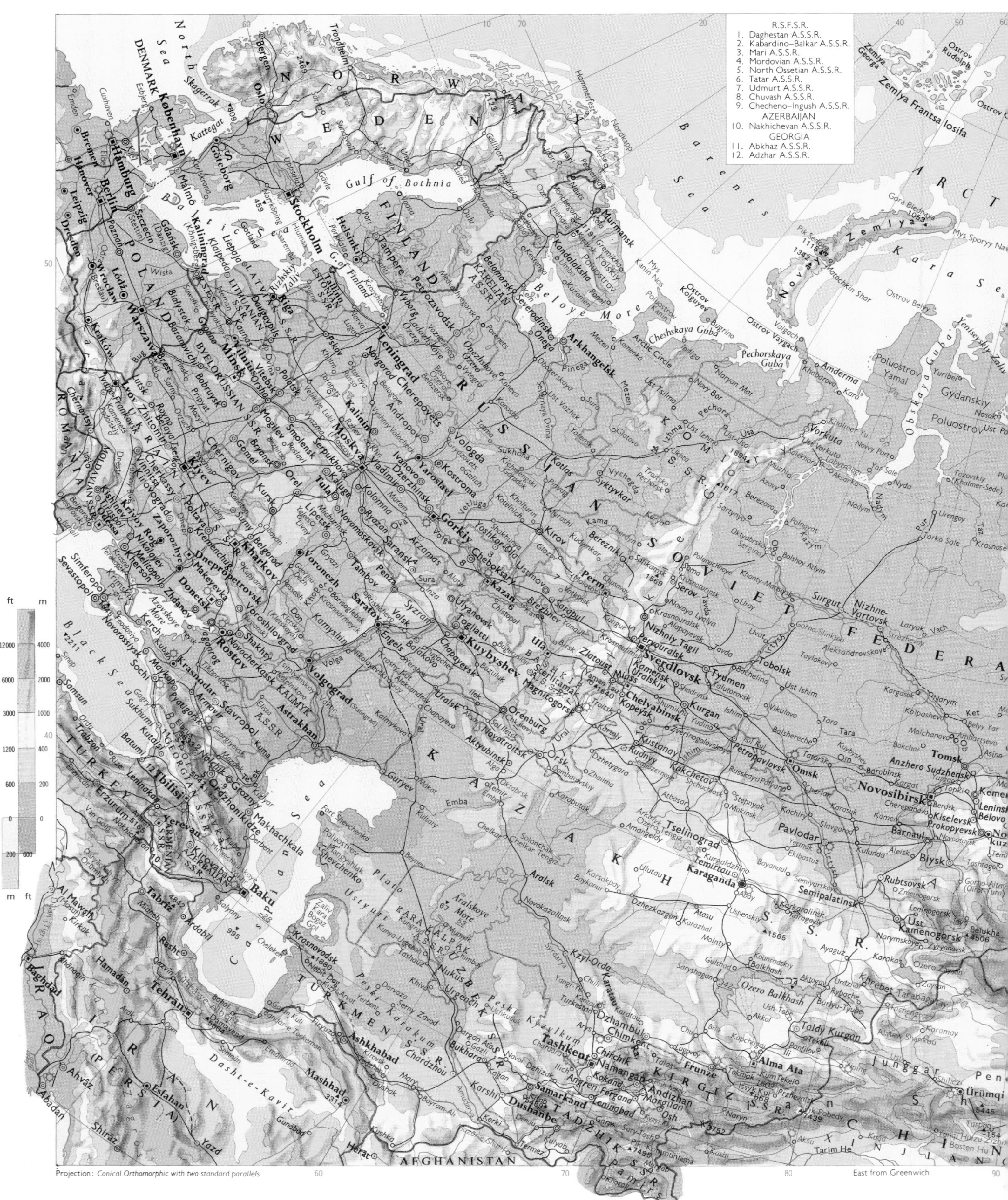

R.S.F.S.R.
1. Daghestan A.S.S.R.
2. Kabardino–Balkar A.S.S.R.
3. Mari A.S.S.R.
4. Mordovian A.S.S.R.
5. North Ossetian A.S.S.R.
6. Tatar A.S.S.R.
7. Udmurt A.S.S.R.
8. Chuvash A.S.S.R.
9. Checheno–Ingush A.S.S.R.
AZERBAIJAN
10. Nakhichevan A.S.S.R.
GEORGIA
11. Abkhaz A.S.S.R.
12. Adzhar A.S.S.R.

Projection: Conical Orthomorphic with two standard parallels

East from Greenwich

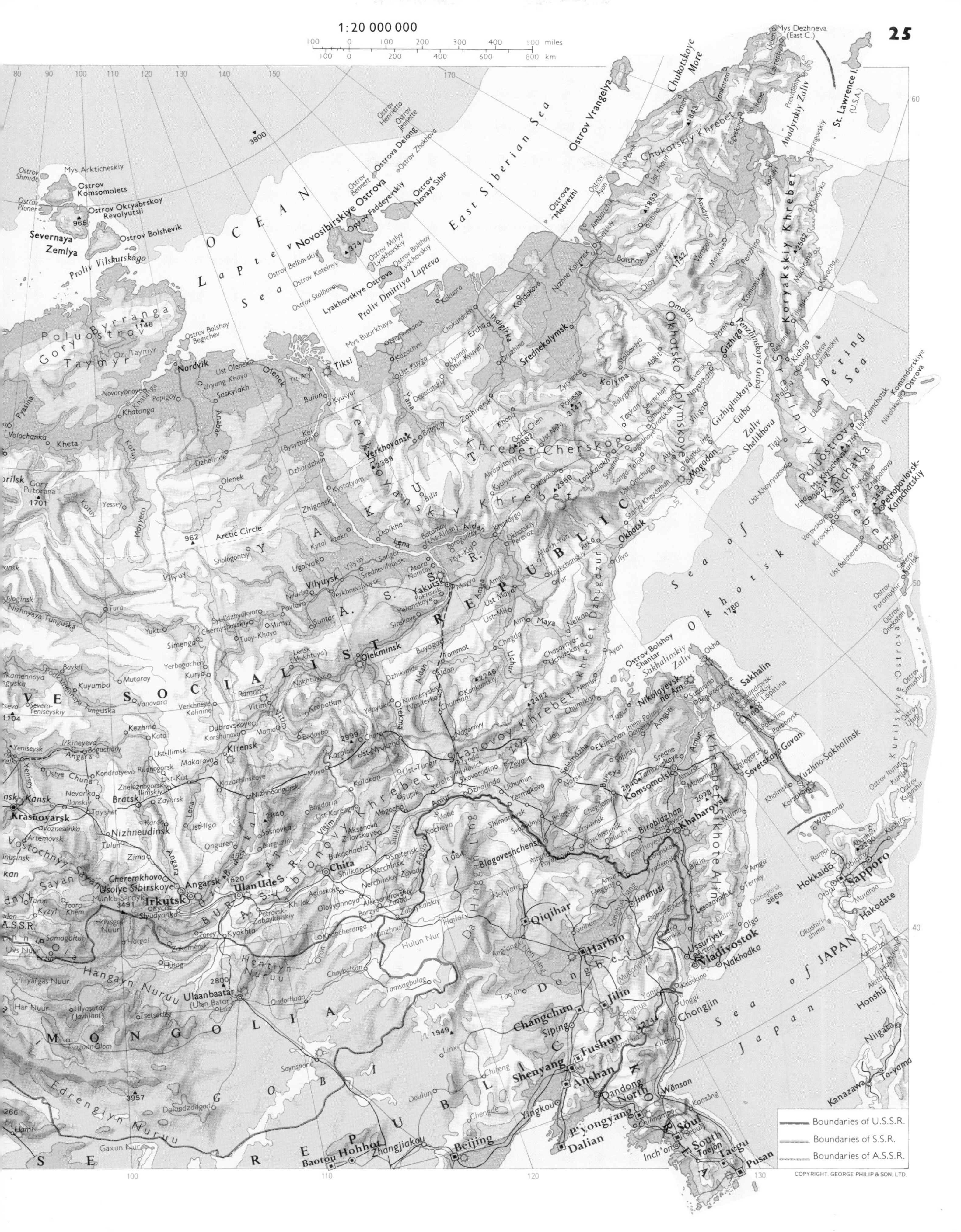
1:20 000 000
100 0 100 200 300 400 500 miles
100 0 200 400 600 800 km
Mys Dezhneva (East C.)
Chukotskoye More
St. Lawrence I. (U.S.A.)
Anadyrskiy Zaliv
Ostrov Vrangelya
East Siberian Sea
Ostrova Medvezhi
Ostrov Henrietta
Ostrov Jeannette
Ostrov Bennett
Ostrova Delong
Ostrov Zhokhova
Novosibirskiye Ostrova
Ostrov Faddeyevskiy
Ostrov Novaya Sibir
Ostrov Malyy Lyakhovskiy
Ostrov Bolshoy Lyakhovskiy
Lyakhovskiye Ostrova
Proliv Dmitriya Lapteva
Ostrov Belkovskiy
Ostrov Kotelnyy
Ostrov Stolbovoy
Laptev Sea
OCEAN
Mys Arkticheskiy
Ostrov Shmidt
Ostrov Komsomolets
Ostrov Pioner
Ostrov Oktyabrskoy Revolyutsii
Ostrov Bolshevik
Severnaya Zemlya
Proliv Vilkitskogo
Gory Byrranga
Poluostrov Taymyr
Oz. Taymyr
Ostrov Bolshoy Begichev
Nordvik
Tiksi
Mys Buorkhaya
Verkhoyansk
Verkhoyanskiy Khrebet
Khrebet Cherskogo
Srednekolymsk
Kolyma
Chukotskiy Khrebet
Koryakskiy Khrebet
Anadyr
Okhotsko Kolymskoye
Gizhiga
Penzhinskaya Guba
Gizhiginskaya Guba
Zaliv Shelikhova
Magadan
Poluostrov Kamchatka
Sredinnyy Khrebet
Petropavlovsk-Kamchatskiy
Komandorskiye Ostrova
Bering Sea
Sea of Okhotsk
Okhotsk
Arctic Circle
YAKUT A.S.S.R.
SOCIALIST REPUBLIC
Yakutsk
Vilyuysk
Olekminsk
Aldan
Lena
Vilyuy
Ostrov Bolshoy Shantar
Sakhalinskiy Zaliv
Sakhalin
Nikolayevsk-na-Amure
Sovetskaya Gavan
Yuzhno-Sakhalinsk
Kurilskiye Ostrova
Stanovoy Khrebet
Khrebet Dzhugdzhur
Kirensk
Bratsk
Kansk
Krasnoyarsk
Nizhneudinsk
Irkutsk
Angarsk
Ulan Ude
Chita
Blagoveshchensk
Komsomolsk
Khabarovsk
Birobidzhan
Khrebet Sikhote Alin
Hokkaido
Sapporo
Hakodate
Vladivostok
Nakhodka
Ussuriysk
Harbin
Qiqihar
Jiamusi
Jilin
Changchun
Fushun
Shenyang
Anshan
Dandong
Dalian
Yingkou
Beijing
Zhangjiakou
Hohhot
Baotou
Chongjin
Wŏnsan
P'yongyang
Sŏul
Inch'on
Taejŏn
Taegu
Pusan
NORTH KOREA
SOUTH KOREA
Sea of Japan
Honshū
Niigata
To-yama
Kanazawa
Da Hinggan Ling
Hulun Nur
Ulaanbaatar (Ulan Bator)
Hentiyn Nuruu
Hangayn Nuruu
MONGOLIA
GOBI
Edrengiyn Nuruu
Gaxun Nur
Hövsgöl Nuur
Vostochnyy Sayan
BURYAT A.S.S.R.
Yablonovyy Khrebet
Noril'sk
Gory Putorana
Nizhnyaya Tunguska
Podkamennaya Tunguska
Yenisey
Angara
Boundaries of U.S.S.R.
Boundaries of S.S.R.
Boundaries of A.S.S.R.

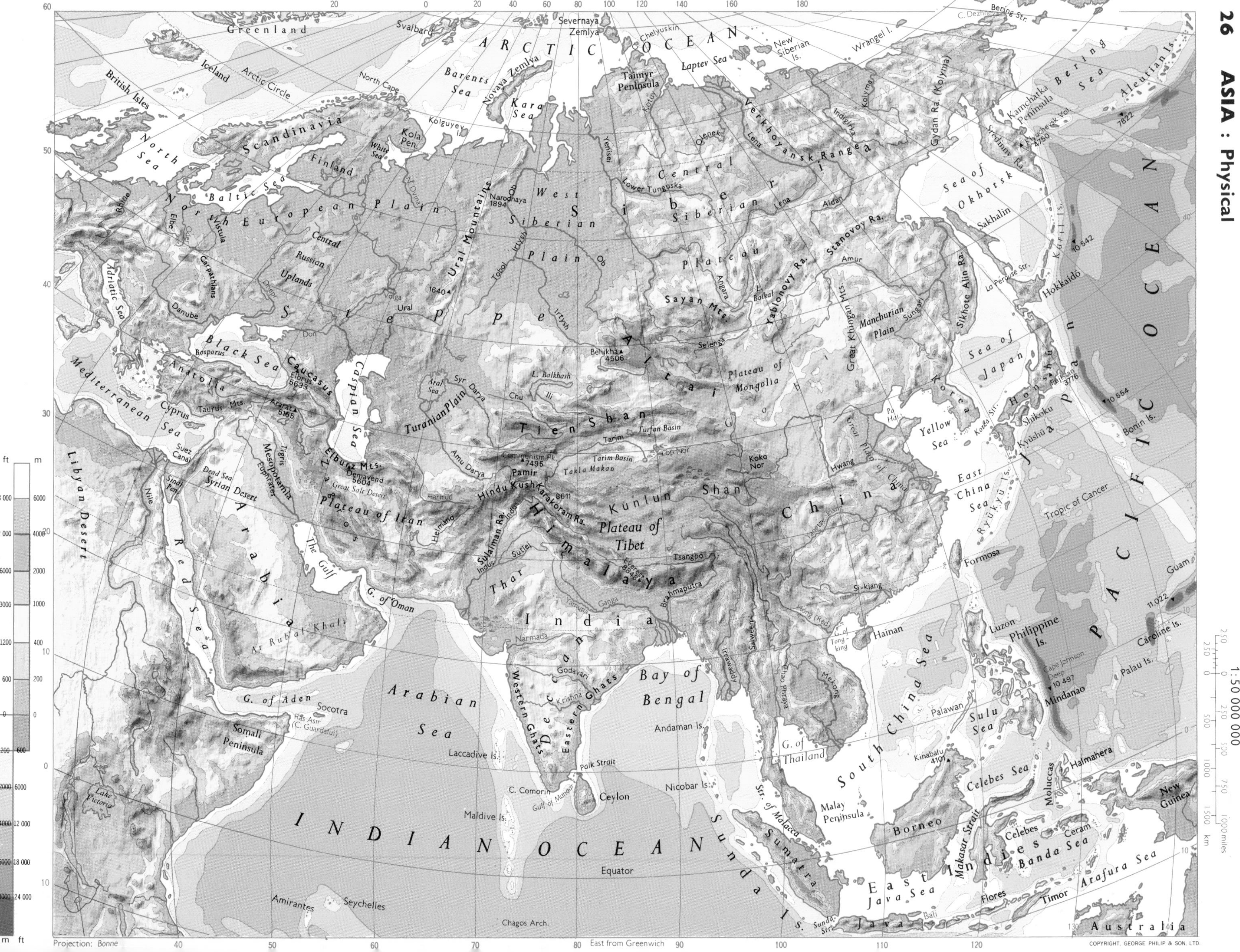

1:50 000 000

ASIA : Physical

miles
km
ARCTIC OCEAN
PACIFIC OCEAN
INDIAN OCEAN
Steppes
Siberia
Arabia
India
China
Japan
Altai
Gobi
Himalaya
Plateau of Tibet
Kunlun Shan
Tien Shan
Plateau of Iran
Plateau of Mongolia
Central Siberian Plateau
West Siberian Plain
North European Plain
Central Russian Uplands
Ural Mountains
Verkhoyansk Range
Stanovoy Ra.
Yablonovy Ra.
Sayan Mts.
Great Khingan Mts.
Manchurian Plain
Sikhote Alin Ra.
Gydan Ra. (Kolyma)
Caucasus
Elburz Mts.
Taurus Mts.
Hindu Kush
Karakoram Ra.
Sulaiman Ra.
Pamir
Deccan
Western Ghats
Eastern Ghats
Thar
Turanian Plain
Takla Makan
Tarim Basin
Turfan Basin
Great Plain of China
Mesopotamia
Syrian Desert
Ar Rub' al Khali
Libyan Desert
Great Salt Desert
Caspian Sea
Black Sea
Mediterranean Sea
Adriatic Sea
Baltic Sea
North Sea
White Sea
Barents Sea
Kara Sea
Laptev Sea
Bering Sea
Sea of Okhotsk
Sea of Japan
Yellow Sea
East China Sea
South China Sea
Sulu Sea
Celebes Sea
Banda Sea
Java Sea
Arafura Sea
Arabian Sea
Bay of Bengal
Red Sea
The Gulf
G. of Oman
G. of Aden
G. of Thailand
G. of Tongking
Gulf of Mannar
Aral Sea
L. Balkhash
Lake Victoria
Dead Sea
Greenland
Iceland
British Isles
Scandinavia
Finland
Svalbard
Novaya Zemlya
Severnaya Zemlya
Taimyr Peninsula
New Siberian Is.
Wrangel I.
Kamchatka Peninsula
Sakhalin
Hokkaido
Honshu
Shikoku
Kyushu
Kuril Is.
Aleutian Is.
Bonin Is.
Ryukyu Is.
Formosa
Hainan
Philippine Is.
Luzon
Mindanao
Palawan
Borneo
Celebes
Moluccas
Halmahera
Ceram
Timor
Flores
Bali
Java
Sumatra
Sunda Is.
East Indies
New Guinea
Australia
Guam
Caroline Is.
Palau Is.
Malay Peninsula
Ceylon
Andaman Is.
Nicobar Is.
Laccadive Is.
Maldive Is.
Chagos Arch.
Seychelles
Amirantes
Socotra
Ras Asir (C. Guardafui)
Somali Peninsula
Sinai Pen.
Suez Canal
Cyprus
Anatolia
Bosporus
Kola Pen.
Kolguyev I.
North Cape
C. Chelyuskin
C. Dezhnev
Bering Str.
La Pérouse Str.
Korea Str.
Str. of Malacca
Palk Strait
Makasar Strait
Sunda Str.
C. Comorin
Korea
Carpathians
Rhine
Elbe
Oder
Vistula
Danube
Dnepr
Don
Volga
Ural
N. Dvina
Ob
Irtysh
Tobol
Yenisei
Lower Tunguska
Angara
Selenga
Olenek
Lena
Aldan
Indigirka
Kolyma
Amur
Sungari
Hwang
Yangtze Kiang
Si-kiang
Hong (Red)
Mekong
Chao Phraya
Salween
Irrawaddy
Brahmaputra
Tsangpo
Ganga
Yamuna
Indus
Sutlej
Narmada
Godavari
Krishna
Helmand
Harirud
Amu Darya
Syr Darya
Chu
Ili
Tarim
Lop Nor
Koko Nor
Baikal
Tigris
Euphrates
Nile
Elbrus 5633
Ararat 5165
Demavend 5604
Communism Pk. 7495
8611
Everest 8848
Belukha 4506
Narodnaya 1894
1640
Klyuchevsk Vol. 4750
Fujisan 3776
Kinabalu 4101
7822
10 542
10 554
11 022
Cape Johnson Deep 10 497
Tropic of Cancer
Arctic Circle
Equator
East from Greenwich
Projection: Bonne
COPYRIGHT, GEORGE PHILIP & SON, LTD.
ft
m
18 000
12 000
6000
3000
1200
600
200
2000
4000
6000
8000
24 000

1:50 000 000

250 0 250 500 750 1000 miles
250 0 500 1000 1500 km

ARCTIC OCEAN

PACIFIC OCEAN

INDIAN OCEAN

U. S. S. R.

CHINA

MONGOLIA

INDIA

IRAN

SAUDI ARABIA

AUSTRALIA

INDONESIA

Beijing
Shanghai
Tokyo
Moskva
Leningrad
London
Paris
Roma
Berlin

Tropic of Cancer

Equator

Arctic Circle

East from Greenwich

Projection: Bonne

1:1 000 000

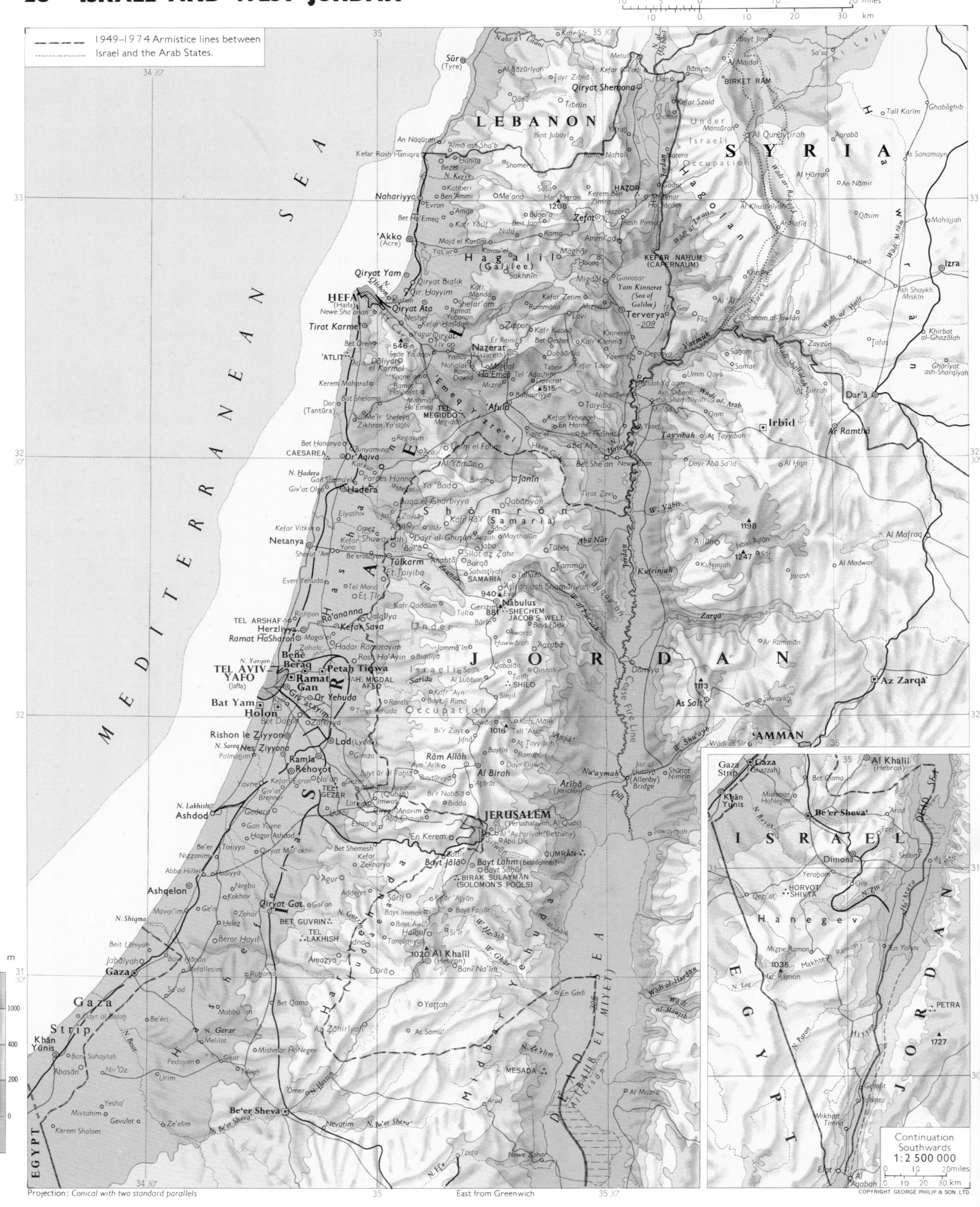

Projection: Conical with two standard parallels

East from Greenwich

COPYRIGHT. GEORGE PHILIP & SON LTD.

Continuation Southwards 1:2 500 000

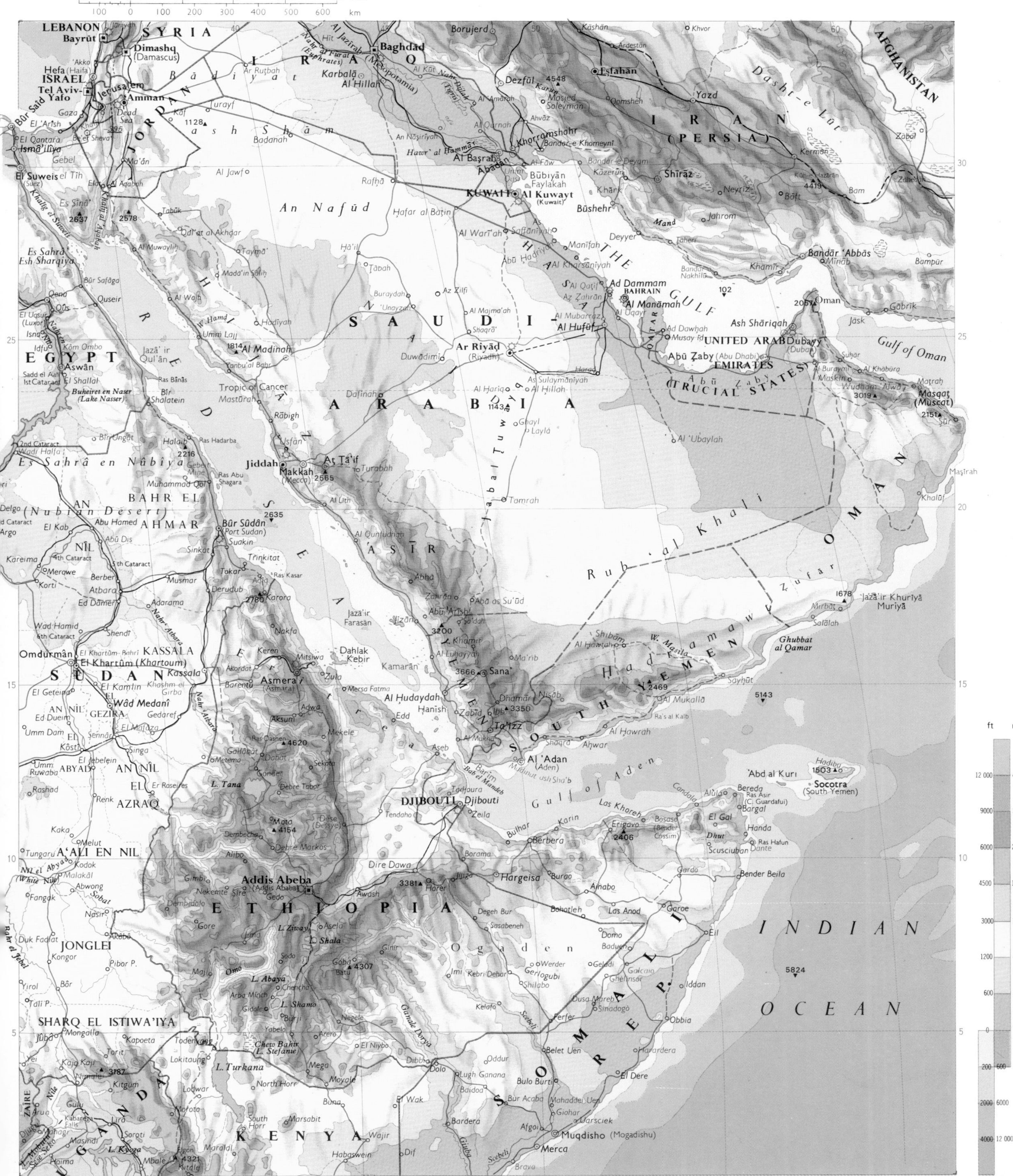

1:15 000 000

Projection: Sanson-Flamsteed's Sinusoidal

COPYRIGHT GEORGE PHILIP & SON LTD

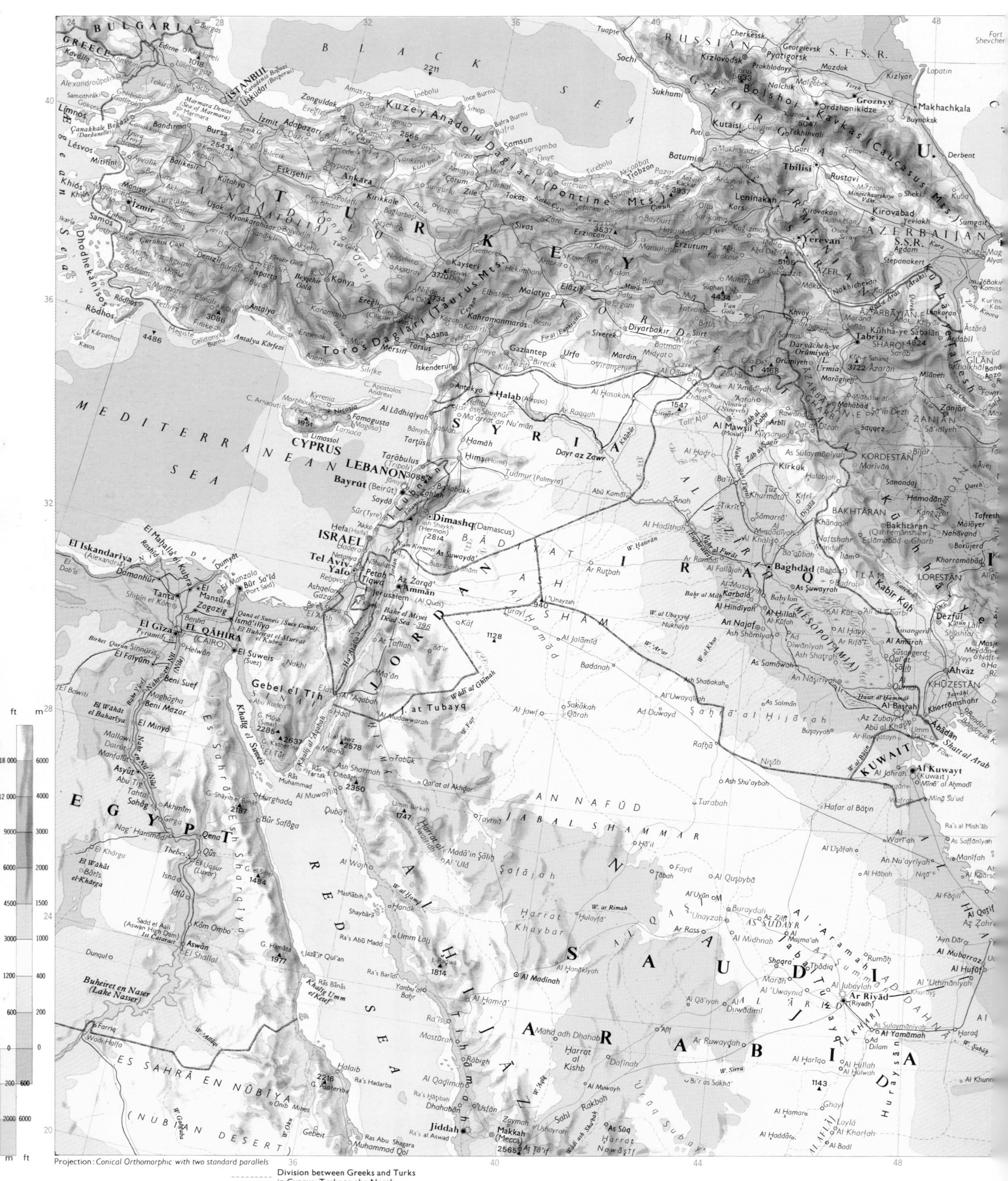

Projection: Conical Orthomorphic with two standard parallels

Division between Greeks and Turks
in Cyprus; Turks to the North.

1:10 000 000

100   0   100   200   300   miles
100   0   100   200   300   400   500   km

KAZAKH S.S.R.

Aralskoye More

Muynak

KARA-KALPAKISCHE A.S.S.R.

PESKI KYZYLKUM

KAZAKH S.S.R.

shevchenko

Ozero Sudoche

Chimbai

Turkestan

Dzhambul

Talas

Naryn

Plato Ustyurt

Nukus

Kungrad

Kazakhski Zaliv

UZBEK S.S.R.

Arys

Chimkent

Lenger 4488

Chakpak

KIRGIZ

Kashi

KoK Yangak

S.S.R.

Tashaus

Turtkul

Urgench

Syrdarya

Tashkent

Chirchik

Angren

Namangan

Andizhan

Osh

Tien Shan

Sartas

Zaliv

Ozero Sarykamysh

Khiva

Kaganu

Yangi Yul

Kokand

Morgelan

Fergana

7579

Kara Bogaz Gol

Darganata

Amu Darya

Gizhduvan

Dzhizak

2169

Ura Tyube

Sulyukta

Isfara

Kanibadam

Leninabad

Kashi Kashgar

7559

Kara Bogaz Gol

Serny Zavod

Bukhara

Kagan

Samarkand

5489

Zarafshan

TADZHIK

Pik Lenina 7134

Uzgen

Murgab

skiyy

Krasnovodski Poluostrov

Karshi

Shakhrisyabz

Dushanbe

Ordzhonikidzeabad

Regar

S.S.R.

Pamir

Krasnovodsk

Krasnovodski Zaliv

TURKMEN S.S.R.

Chardzhou

Guzar

Denau

Kurgan-Kulyab Tyube

Khorog

4409

Poluostrov Cheleken

Nebit Dag

1880

Balkhan

KARA KUM

Kerki

Shirabad

Termez

Qonduz

Nzh Pyandzh

Khanabad

Feyzabad

BADAKHSHAN

7192

Ostrov Ogurchinski

Kizyl Arvat

Kazandzhik

Karakumski Canal

Andkhvoy

Vazirabad

Aqcheh

Baghlan

5203

TAKHAR

Gilgit

Airak

Ashkhabad

Mary (Mery)

Bairam Ali

Iolotan

Sheberghan

Mazar-e-Sharif

Pul-e-Khomri

NORTH

SEA

Kizyl Atrek

Muhammadabad

Tedzhen

Dushak

Serakhs

Tashkepri

BALKH

SAMANGAN

Charikar

Mardan

Islamabad

Rawal-

Bandar-e Torkeman

Gonbad-e Kavus

Bojnurd

Quchan

Kabud Gonbad

3117

Kushka

Maruchak

Meymaneh

FARYAB

Sayghan

BAGHLAN

PARWAN

Kabul

NANGARHAR

Peshawar

pindi

MAZANDARAN

Gorgan

Daregaz

Mashhad (Meshed)

Koh-i-Baba

Jalalabad

Spin Baldak

Kohat

Qa'emshahr

Kuh-e Alborz

Bandar-e Torkeman

Soltanabad

Kuh-e Binalud

3314

Band-e-Torkestan

3494

Koh-i-Baba 5143

Ghazni

WARDAK

LOWGAR

Gardez

PAKTIA

Khost

Bannu

Salt Range

Sargodha

Damavand

Darghan

Neyshabur

Kashaf

Safid Kuh

3216

Panjao

Shotor

Dival Now

PAKTIKA

Miamwali

Chakwal

SEMNAN

Torud

Sabzevar

Kuh-e Sorkh

Fariman

Herat

3588

Safed Koh

Owbeh

Hari Rud

4148

Oruzgan

Mashri

3513

FRONTIER

Kohat

Garmsar

Torbat-e Heydariyeh

Torbat-e Jam

Ghurian

Daryacheh-i-Namakzar

Owbeh

Shindand

FARAH

Doshi

3787

ABOL

Moqor

Zabol

Fort Sandeman

Tank

DASHT-E-KAVIR (Great Salt Desert)

KHORASAN

Naginah

Gonabad

Yazdan

Farah

Kuh

Khash Rud

Ma'ruf

Chaman

Toba Kaka

Hindu Bagh

Musa Khel

Loralai

Dera Ismail

Jhang

Maghiana

Multan

Kashan

Jandaq

Kerman

Boshruyeh

Ferdows

2886

Tabas

Birjand

Sarbisheh

Fash

Lash-e Joveyn

Khanshin

Khughiani

Asp

Gereshk

QANDAHAR

Qandahar

Toba Kaka

Mekhtar

Duki

Barkhan

Rajanpur

Muzaffargarh

IRAN

Zavareh

Anarak

Khur

Mazhan

Deyhuk

3020

Nosratabad

Chakhansur

Zaranj

Dasht-e Margow

Rigestan

Quetta 3593

Nushki

Sibi

Bolan Pass

Dera Ghazi

Jacobabad

Ardestan

Na'in

Nay Band

Yazd

Tabas

Sarbisheh

Nehbandan

Daryacheh-ye Seistan

Zabol

NIMROZ

Char Gay

Kalat

Mastung

1764

Rahimyar-Khan

ESFAHAN

YAZD (YEZD)

4075

Ravar

Zarand

Seistan

Gowd-e Zirreh

2462

Hamun-i-Lora

Dalbandin

Khuzdar

2480

Khanpur

Esfahan

Qomsheh

Nodushan

Shir Kuh

Kerman

3992

Shahdad

Namakzar-e Shahdad

Mirjaveh

Mashki Chah

Nok Kundi

Dasht-i-Tahlab

Baddo

Jacobabad

Sukkur

Shikarpur

Khairpur

GREAT INDIAN DESERT

3723

Abadeh

Kuh-e Dinar 4431

3660

Ardakan

Deh Bid

Lalar Meydan

Shahr-e Babak

4419

Kuh-e Hazaran

Tahrud

4042

Taftan

Tahlab

Hamun-i-Mashkel

Kalat

Dadu

Larkana

Mohenjodaro

INDIA

387

Jaisalmer

Shiraz

Sarvestan

Kuh-e 3962 Barez

Bam

Fahraj

Khash

Kerman

Siareh

Daolg

2146

Siahan Range

Soke Kalat

Panjgur

Bela

Pab Hills

Nawabshah

Hyderabad

Firuzabad

Jahrom

Darab

Dowlatabad

Kahnuj

Halil Rud

Hamun-e Jaz Murian

SISTAN VA

Davar Panah

Khuzdar

Pab Range

Tando Adam

Mirpur Khas

Deyyer

Taheri

Alamarvdasht

3280

Kuh-e Furgun

Shamil

Bampur

Iranshahr

Zaboli

BALUCHESTAN

Panjgur

Rakhshan

Central Makran Ra.

1580

Jhal Jhao

Manjhand

Ghulam

Umarkot

Nay Band

Bastak

Hormoz

2804

Hormoz

Bandar-e

Minab

Remeshk

Qasr-e Qand

Tump R

Turbat

Sonmiani

Las Bela

Karachi

Badin

Nagar Parkar

Bandar-e Nakhilu

Jazireh-ye Lavan

Qeshm

Jask

Bent

Nikshahr

Dasht

Makran Coast Range

Ormara

Hab Nadi Chauki

Rann of Kachchh

KACHCHH

102

Forur

Bandar-e Lengeh

Bostaneh

2163

Qasr-e Qand

Rapch

Polan

Chah Bahar

Gwadar

Astola I.

C. Monze

KARACHI

Mandvi

Gulf of Kachchh

Jamnagar

Sirri

Qeshm

Ra's al Khaymah

Ra's e Meydani

Gavater

Mouths of the Indus

Tatta

Dwarka

Porbandar

Ad Dawhah

Al Wakrah

Musay'id

As Zarqa

Dubayy (Dubai)

Ajman

Al Fujayrah

Shinas

Suhar

Wudham 'Alwa

ARABIAN

SEA

Tropic of Cancer

GULF

Halul

Dalma

Abu Zaby (Abu Dhabi)

EMIRATES

Al Buraymi

Al Khaburah

4122

Sir Bani Yas

Bu Hasa

UNITED

ARAB

Za'by

Al Wahat al Buraymi

1372

Moskin

Masqat (Muscat)

Al Qurayyat

Jiwa

Murban

3019

Ibra

Ra's al Hadd

2151

Tiwi

As Suwayh

OMAN

Al Ashkharah

Porbandar

U.S.S.R.

FĀRYĀB   SAMANGĀN   BADAKHSHĀN
BALKH   TAKHĀR   Mustagh P.   4709
BĀDGHĪSĀT   JOWZJĀN   Hindu Kush   7135
Herāt   BĀMIĀN   Karakoram Range
HERĀT   GHOWR   KĀPISĀ   KONARHA   JAMMU   Saser   7672
    Kabul   NORTH   KASHMIR   Lanak La   5486
    KĀBUL   WEST   Srinagar
A F G H A N I S T A N   WARDAK   FRONTIER   Anantnag
    LOWGAR   Peshawar   Rawalpindi   Islamabad   7026
GHAZNĪ   PAKTIĀ   Khyber Pass   Wah   HIMACHAL   Dankhar
NĪMRŪZ   PAKTĪKĀ   Wana   Jammu   PRADESH   7756
    Gomal Pass   Sialkot   Gujrāt   Kulu   Simla
    Toba Kakar   Gujranwala   Pathankot   Chandigarh
    Quetta   Lahore   Amritsar   Ambala   Dehra Dun
    Bolan Pass   Faisalabad   PUNJAB   Haridwar
B A L U C H I S T A N   Maghiana   Jullundur   Saharanpur   Roorkee
    Kirthar Range   Sahiwal   Ludhiana   Karnal   Najibabad
    Siahan Range   Multan   Patiala   Muzaffarnagar
    Central Makran Range   Bahawalpur   Bikaner   Meerut   Moradabad
    Sukkur   Thar   Sikar   DELHI   Sambhal
    Makran Coast Range   Larkana   Desert   Faridabad   Aligarh
A R A B I A N   S E A   Nawabshah   HARYANA   Mathura   Agra   Firozabad
    Hyderabad   R A J A S T H A N   Jaipur   Gwalior
    KARACHI   Jodhpur   Ajmer   Kota   Jhansi
    Mouths of the Indus   Udaipur   I N D I A   Guna
    Rann of Kachchh   Palanpur   B I H A R   Sagar
GOA   Dharwad   G U J A R A T   Bhopal   MADHYA
    Bellary   Ahmadabad   Ratlam   Ujjain   Indore   PRADESH
K A R N A T A K A   Jamnagar   Rajkot   Vadodara   Nagpur
    Bangalore   Rajkot   (Baroda)   Satpura   Amravati
    Mysore   Junagadh   Bharuch   Khandwa
    Kolar   Surat   Nasik   MAHARASHTRA
T A M I L   N A D U   Diu   Daman   Aurangabad   Nanded
    Salem   Gulf of Khambhat   DADRA & NAGAR HAVELI
    Coimbatore   BOMBAY   Ahmadnagar
    Madurai   Pune   Solapur   Bidar
    Tirunelveli   (Poona)   ANDHRA
    Trivandrum   Kolhapur   Gulbarga   PRADESH
    Cape Comorin   Belgaum   Hyderabad
    GOA   Dharwad   Kurnool
SRI LANKA (CEYLON)
    Colombo   Kandy   Moratuwa
    Galle   Dondra Head

Continuation Southwards on same scale

Projection: Conical with two standard parallels

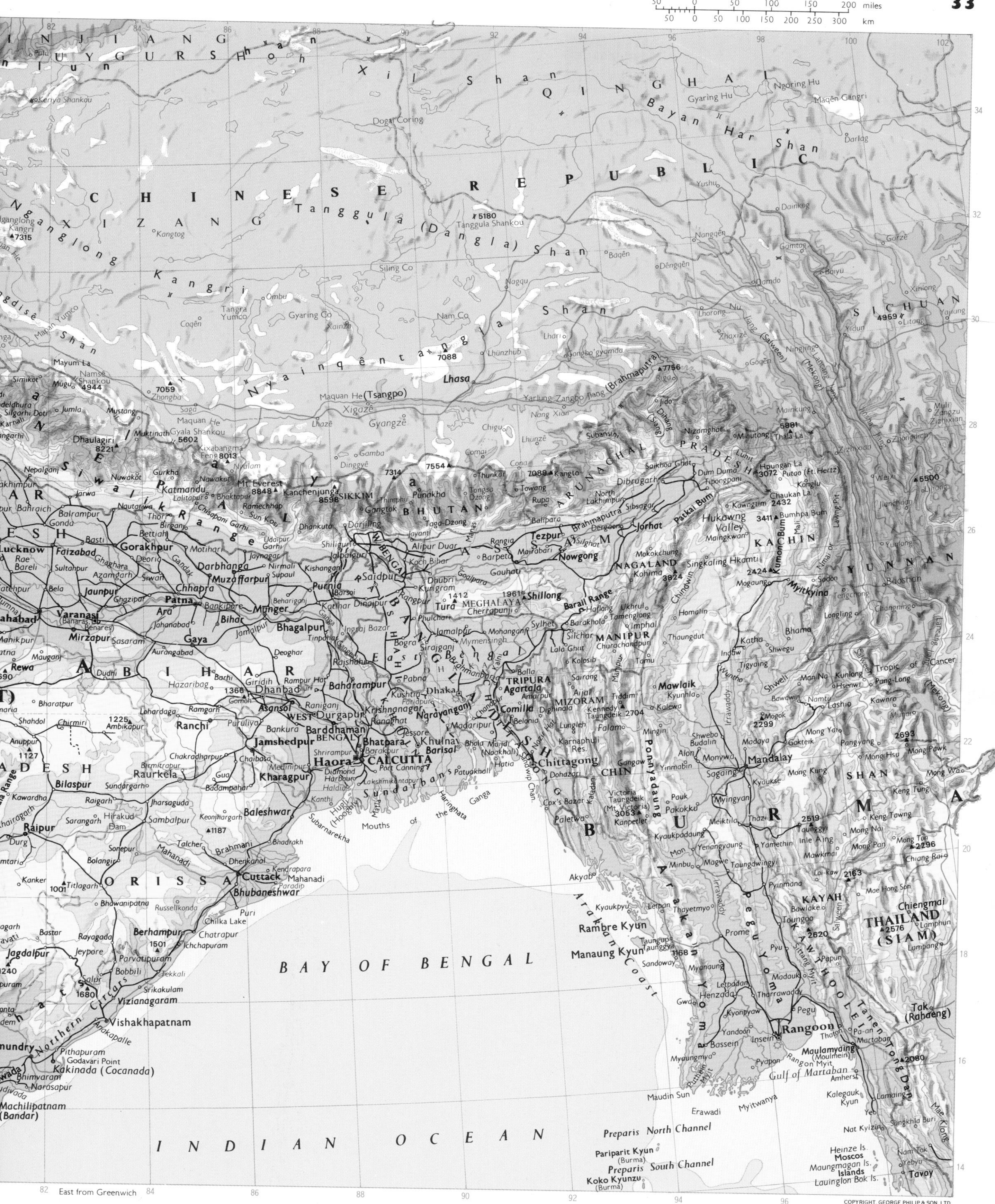

1:10 000 000

50   0   50   100   150   200 miles
50   0   50   100   150   200   250   300 km

CHINESE REPUBLIC

XINJIANG
UYGURS

QINGHAI

XIZANG

SICHUAN

YUNNAN

NEPAL

BHUTAN

ARUNACHAL PRADESH

ASSAM

NAGALAND

MANIPUR

MEGHALAYA

TRIPURA

MIZORAM

WEST BENGAL

BANGLADESH

ORISSA

BIHAR

KACHIN

SHAN

CHIN

KAYAH

THAILAND (SIAM)

BURMA

CALCUTTA

Dhaka

Lhasa

Mandalay

Rangoon

BAY OF BENGAL

INDIAN OCEAN

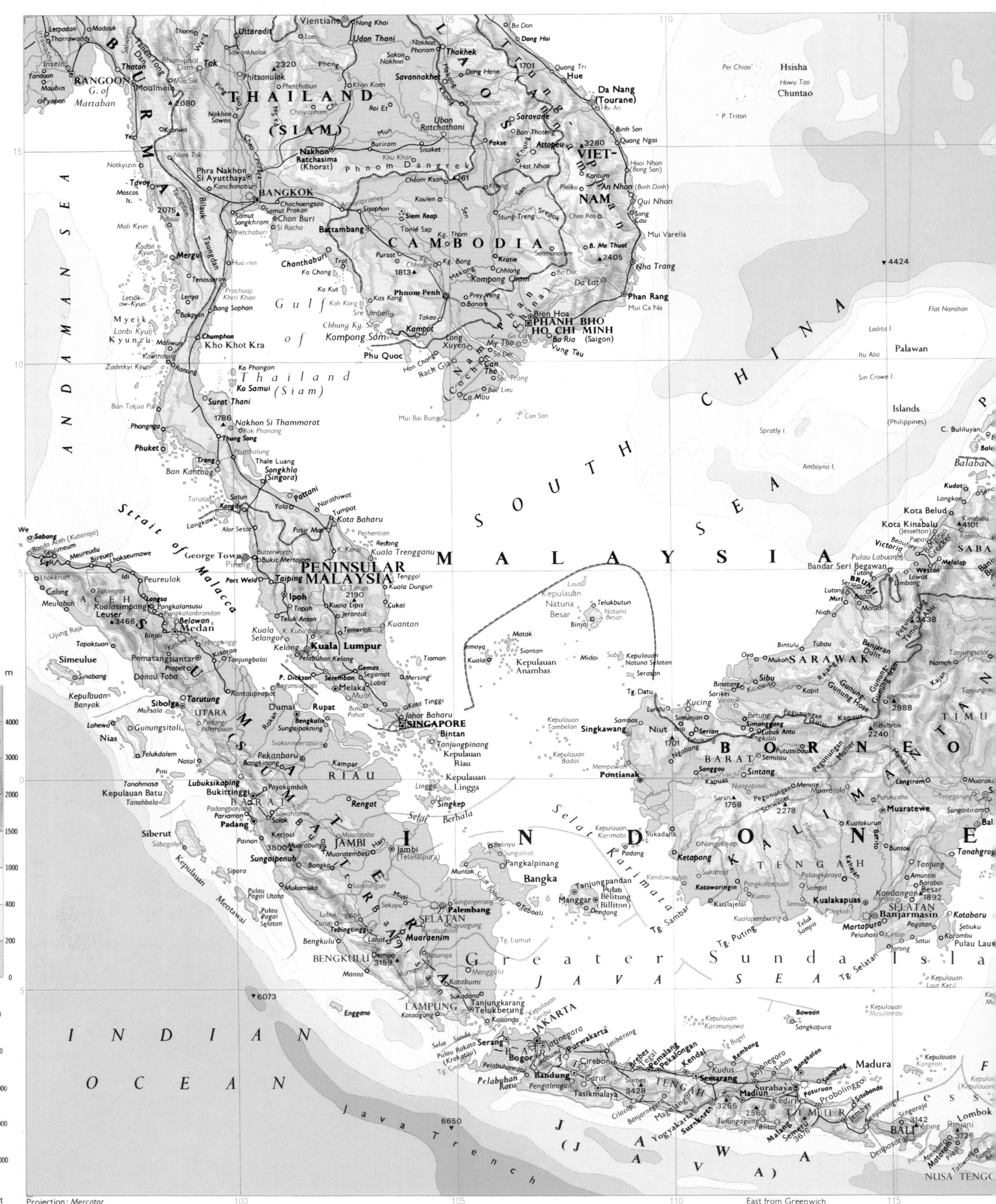
THAILAND
(SIAM)
BURMA
LAOS
CAMBODIA
VIET-NAM
PENINSULAR MALAYSIA
MALAYSIA
SOUTH CHINA SEA
ANDAMAN SEA
INDIAN OCEAN
Gulf of Thailand (Siam)
Strait of Malacca
SUMATERA
BORNEO
KALIMANTAN
JAVA SEA
JAWA (JAVA)
Java Trench
Greater Sunda Islands
BANGKOK
RANGOON
SINGAPORE
JAKARTA
Kuala Lumpur
Phnom Penh
PHANH BHO HO CHI MINH (Saigon)
Vientiane
Medan
Palembang
Bandung
Surabaya
Pontianak
Banjarmasin
Projection: Mercator
East from Greenwich

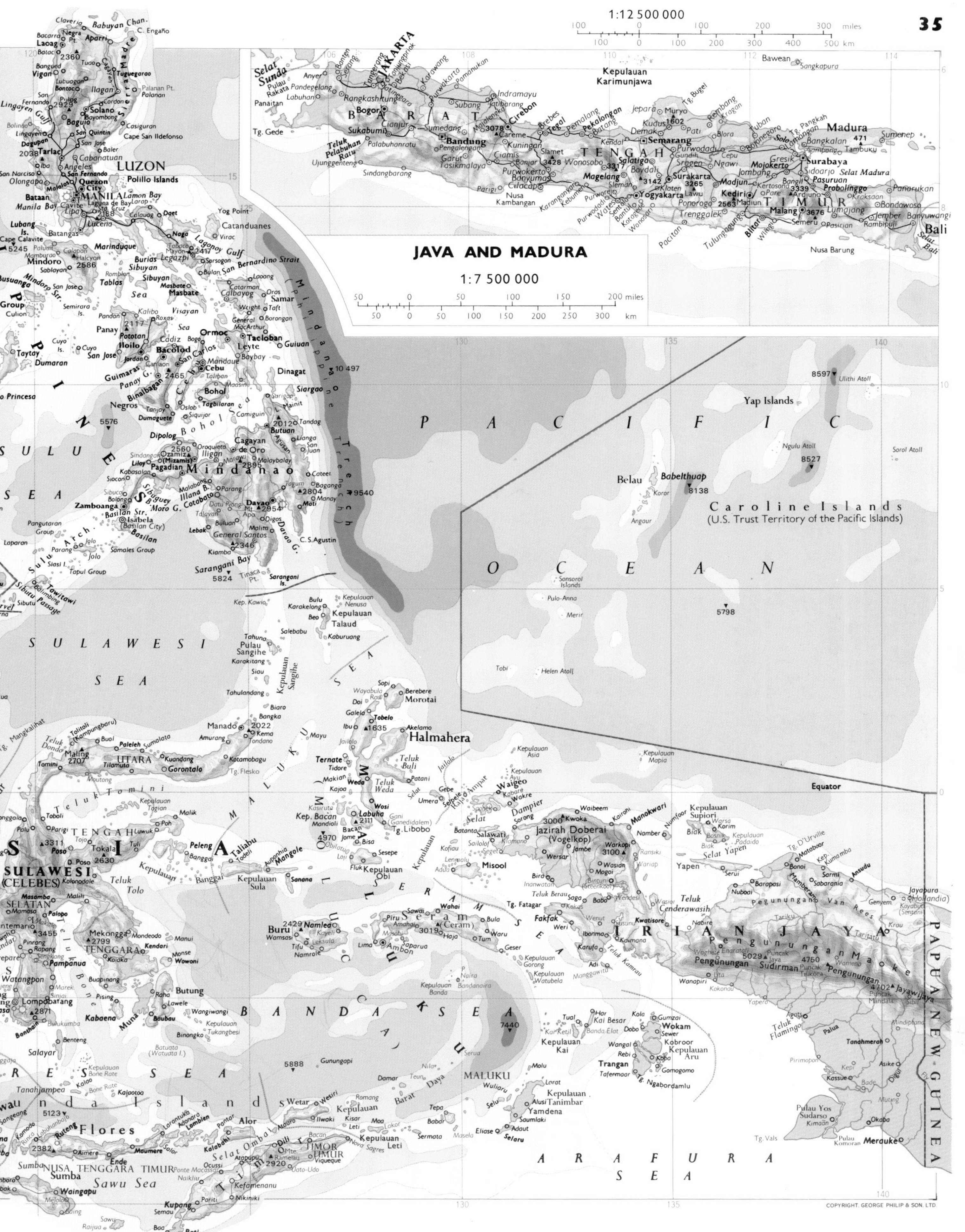
1:12 500 000
miles
km
JAVA AND MADURA
1:7 500 000
miles
km
JAKARTA
Selat Sunda
Bogor
Bandung
Cirebon
Semarang
Surakarta
Yogyakarta
Surabaya
Madura
Malang
Kediri
Kepulauan Karimunjawa
Bawean
Bali
Nusa Barung
BARAT
TENGAH
TIMUR
Babuyan Chan.
Aparri
LUZON
Polillo Islands
MANILA
Quezon City
Manila Bay
Mindoro
Marinduque
Catanduanes
Sibuyan Sea
Masbate
Samar
Visayan Sea
Panay
Negros
Cebu
Leyte
Bohol
Tacloban
Iloilo
Bacolod
Dinagat
Siargao
Mindanao
Zamboanga
Davao
Cagayan de Oro
Basilan
Sulu Arch.
SULU SEA
Mindanao Trench (Philippine Trench)
San Bernardino Strait
PACIFIC OCEAN
Yap Islands
Ulithi Atoll
Sorol Atoll
Ngulu Atoll
Belau
Babelthuap
Koror
Angaur
Caroline Islands
(U.S. Trust Territory of the Pacific Islands)
Sonsorol Islands
Pulo-Anna
Merir
Tobi
Helen Atoll
Kepulauan Talaud
Kepulauan Sangihe
SULAWESI SEA
Manado
Morotai
Halmahera
Ternate
Tidore
Kepulauan Asia
Kepulauan Mapia
Equator
Waigeo
Salawati
Misool
Dampier
Jazirah Doberai (Vogelkop)
Manokwari
Kepulauan Supiori
Biak
Yapen
Teluk Cenderawasih
Gorontalo
UTARA
Teluk Tomini
TENGAH
SULAWESI (CELEBES)
SELATAN
TENGGARA
Kepulauan Banggai
Kepulauan Sula
Obi
Kep. Bacan
MALUKU SEA
Buru
Seram (Ceram)
Ambon
SERAM SEA
Fakfak
IRIAN JAYA
Pegunungan Sudirman
Puncak Jaya 5029
Puncak Trikora 4750
Pegunungan Jayawijaya
Pegunungan Maoke
Pegunungan Van Rees
Jayapura (Hollandia)
Sarmi
BANDA SEA
Kepulauan Banda
Kepulauan Kai
Kepulauan Aru
Kepulauan Tanimbar
Yamdena
MALUKU
Butung
Muna
Kabaena
Salayar
Wetar
Kepulauan Leti
Alor
Flores
Sumba
Sumbawa
Timor
TIMOR TIMUR
Dili
Kupang
Roti
Sawu Sea
NUSA TENGGARA TIMUR
Nusa Tenggara (Lesser Sunda Islands)
ARAFURA SEA
Merauke
Pulau Yos Sudarso
PAPUA NEW GUINEA

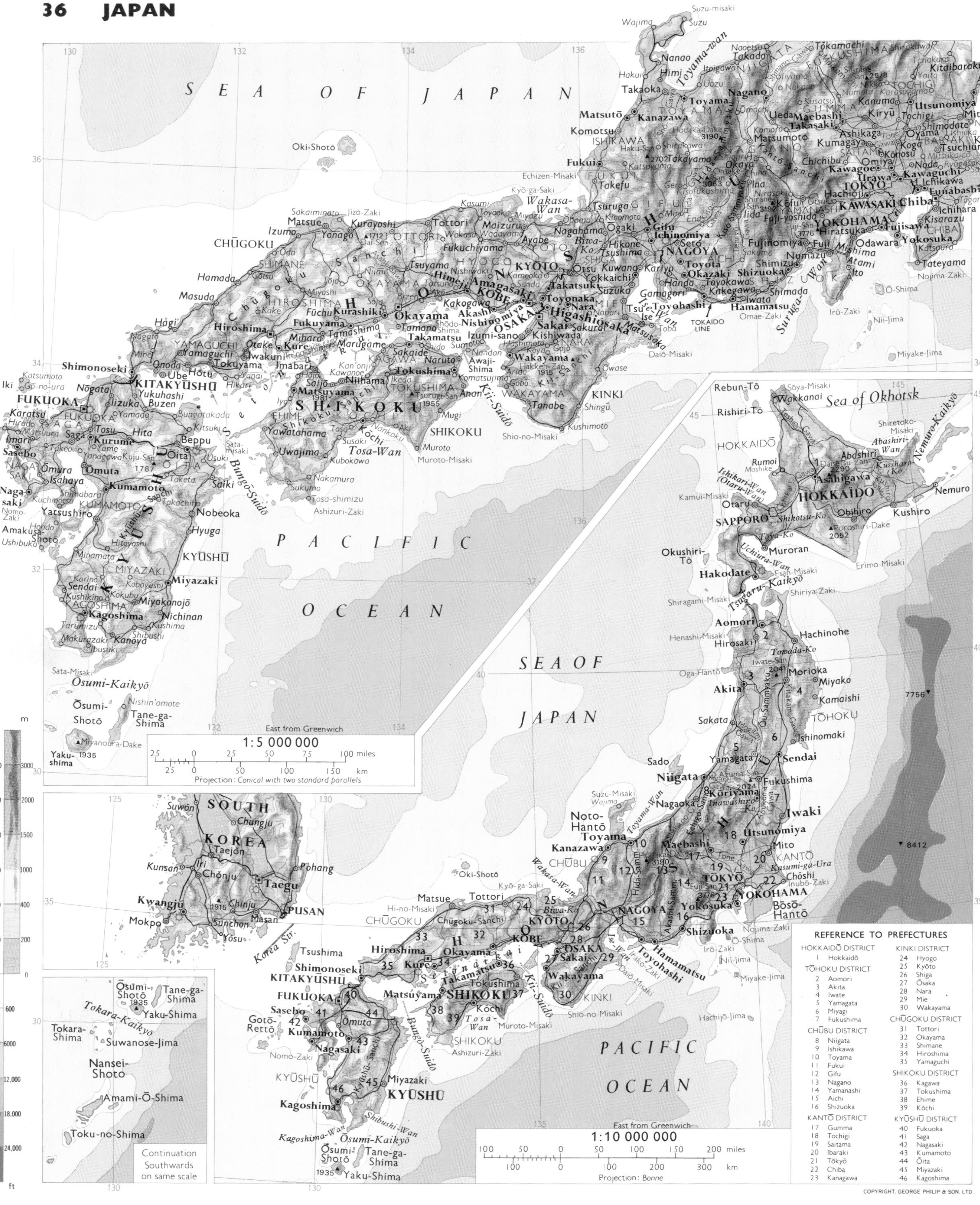
SEA OF JAPAN
PACIFIC OCEAN
East from Greenwich
1:5 000 000
25 0 25 50 75 100 miles
25 0 50 100 150 km
Projection: Conical with two standard parallels
SEA OF JAPAN
Sea of Okhotsk
PACIFIC OCEAN
East from Greenwich
1:10 000 000
100 50 0 50 100 150 200 miles
100 0 100 200 300 km
Projection: Bonne
Continuation Southwards on same scale
SOUTH KOREA
HOKKAIDŌ
SHIKOKU
KYŪSHŪ
Nansei-Shoto
REFERENCE TO PREFECTURES
HOKKAIDŌ DISTRICT
1 Hokkaidō
TŌHOKU DISTRICT
2 Aomori
3 Akita
4 Iwate
5 Yamagata
6 Miyagi
7 Fukushima
CHŪBU DISTRICT
8 Niigata
9 Ishikawa
10 Toyama
11 Fukui
12 Gifu
13 Nagano
14 Yamanashi
15 Aichi
16 Shizuoka
KANTŌ DISTRICT
17 Gumma
18 Tochigi
19 Saitama
20 Ibaraki
21 Tōkyō
22 Chiba
23 Kanagawa
KINKI DISTRICT
24 Hyogo
25 Kyōto
26 Shiga
27 Ōsaka
28 Nara
29 Mie
30 Wakayama
CHŪGOKU DISTRICT
31 Tottori
32 Okayama
33 Shimane
34 Hiroshima
35 Yamaguchi
SHIKOKU DISTRICT
36 Kagawa
37 Tokushima
38 Ehime
39 Kōchi
KYŪSHŪ DISTRICT
40 Fukuoka
41 Saga
42 Nagasaki
43 Kumamoto
44 Ōita
45 Miyazaki
46 Kagoshima

1:20 000 000

Projection: Bonne

East from Greenwich

SEA OF JAPAN

U.S.S.R.

Khabarovsk

Vladivostok

HEILONGJIANG

HARBIN

Qiqihar

Hailar

NEI MONGGOL ZIZHIQU

MONGOLIA

U.S.S.R.

Chita

Ulan-Ude

Irkutsk

Ulaanbaatar (Ulan Bator)

JILIN

Changchun

Jilin

LIAONING

SHENYANG

Fushun

Benxi

Anshan

DALIAN (Lüda)

Lüshun

Jinzhou

Yingkou

NORTH KOREA

Pyŏngyang

SOUTH KOREA

SOUL (Seoul)

Inchŏn

Suwŏn

Taejŏn

Taegu

BEIJING (Peking)

TIANJIN (Tientsin)

Tangshan

Bo Hai (Gulf of Chihli)

YELLOW SEA

Baoding

Shijiazhuang

Zhangjiakou

Datong

Hohhot

Baotou

TAIYUAN

SHANXI

Jinan

Zibo

NINGXIA HUIZU ZIZHIQU

Lanzhou

THE GREAT WALL

Mu Us Shamo (Ordos)

Yinchuan

Huang He

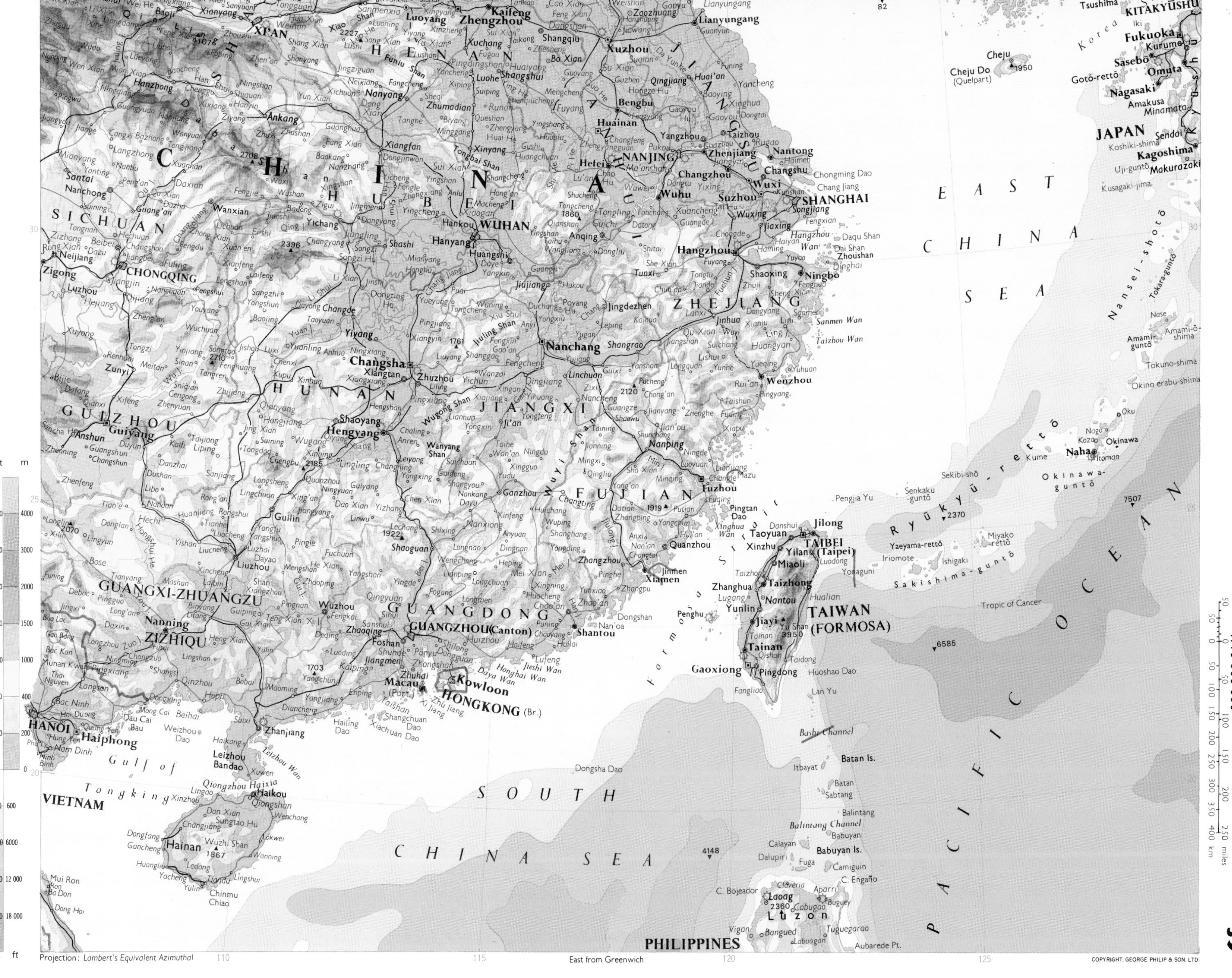

1:10 000 000

50   100   150   200   250 miles
50   0   50   100   150   200   250   300   350   400 km

P A C I F I C   O C E A N

Tropic of Cancer

East China Sea

JAPAN

KITAKYŪSHŪ
Fukuoka
Sasebo
Nagasaki
Kagoshima
Omuta
Kurume
Sendai
Amakusa
Minamata
Makurazaki

Tsushima
Kōshiki-rettō
Gotō-rettō
Iki
Korea Str.

Cheju
Cheju Do
(Quelpart)

Nansei-shotō
Tokara-guntō

Amami-shima
Amami-Ō-shima
Tokuno-shima

Okinawa-guntō
Naha
Okinawa

R y u k y u   I s.

Sakishima-guntō
Yaeyama-rettō
Iriomote
Ishigaki
Miyako-rettō

Senkaku guntō

TAIWAN (FORMOSA)
Jilong
TAIBEI (Taipei)
Taoyuan
Xinzhu
Miaoli
Taizhong
Zhanghua
Nantou
Yunlin
Jiayi
Tainan
Gaoxiong
Pingdong
Ilan

SOUTH CHINA SEA

PHILIPPINES
Batan Is.
Babuyan Is.
Luzon
Laoag
C. Engaño
Aparri
C. Bojeador

SHANGHAI
Nantong
Changshu
Wuxi
Suzhou
Zhenjiang
NANJING
Hangzhou
Shaoxing
Ningbo
Wenzhou

JIANGSU
ANHUI
ZHEJIANG

Lianyungang
Xuzhou
Bengbu
Huainan
Hefei
Wuhu
Anqing

Kaifeng
Zhengzhou
Luoyang
Xian

HENAN
HUBEI
WUHAN
Hankou
Hanyang

Nanchang
JIANGXI

FUJIAN
Nanping
Fuzhou
Quanzhou
Xiamen
Shantou

Changsha
HUNAN
Hengyang
Shaoyang
Yiyang

GUIZHOU
Guiyang
Zunyi

SICHUAN
CHONGQING
Wanxian

GUANGXI-ZHUANGZU ZIZHIQU
Nanning
Liuzhou
Guilin

GUANGDONG
GUANGZHOU (Canton)
Foshan
Kowloon
HONGKONG (Br.)
Macau (Port.)
Zhuhai
Jiangmen
Shaoguan
Zhanjiang

Haikou
Hainan

Gulf of Tongking

VIETNAM
HANOI
Haiphong

East from Greenwich

Projection: Lambert's Equivalent Azimuthal

m
4000
3000
2000
1500
1000
400
200
0

ft
12 000
9000
6000
4500
3000
1200
600
0

ft
18 000
12 000
6000
0

m
6000
4000
2000
0

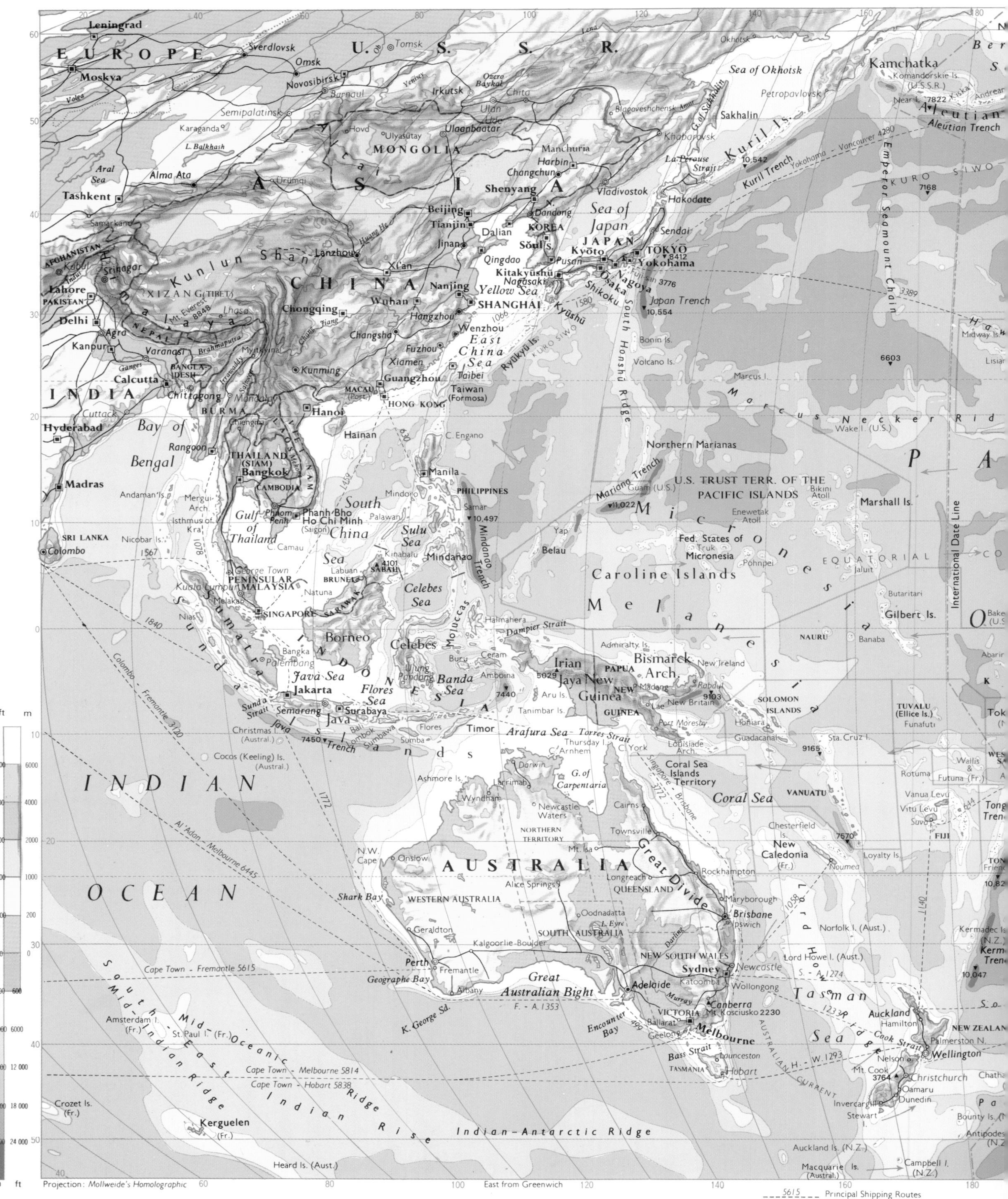
EUROPE
U. S. S. R.
ASIA
MONGOLIA
CHINA
INDIA
INDIAN OCEAN
AUSTRALIA
INDONESIA
Micronesia
Melanesia
Caroline Islands
Leningrad
Moskva
Sverdlovsk
Omsk
Novosibirsk
Tomsk
Irkutsk
Semipalatinsk
Karaganda
L. Balkhash
Aral Sea
Alma Ata
Tashkent
Samarkand
Ulaanbaatar
Hovd
Ulyasutay
Urumqi
Kunlun Shan
XIZANG (TIBET)
Himalaya
Mt. Everest 8848
Lhasa
NEPAL
AFGHANISTAN
PAKISTAN
Lahore
Delhi
Agra
Kanpur
Varanasi
Srinagar
Calcutta
BANGLADESH
Chittagong
Cuttack
Hyderabad
Madras
SRI LANKA
Colombo
Bay of Bengal
Andaman Is.
Nicobar Is.
BURMA
Rangoon
Mandalay
THAILAND (SIAM)
Bangkok
CAMBODIA
LAOS
VIET NAM
Phnom Penh
Ho Chi Minh (Saigon)
Hanoi
Gulf of Thailand
Isthmus of Kra
PENINSULAR MALAYSIA
George Town
Kuala Lumpur
Melaka
SINGAPORE
Sumatra
Nias
Palembang
Bangka
Java Sea
Jakarta
Semarang
Surabaya
Java
Sunda Strait
Java Trench
Bali
Lombok
Sumbawa
Flores
Sumba
Timor
Christmas I. (Austral.)
Cocos (Keeling) Is. (Austral.)
Sunda Islands
Borneo
SARAWAK
SABAH
BRUNEI
Kinabalu 4101
Labuan
Natuna
Celebes
Celebes Sea
Moluccas
Halmahera
Ceram
Buru
Amboina
Banda Sea
Flores Sea
Ujung Pandang
Lanzhou
Xi'an
Chongqing
Wuhan
Nanjing
Hangzhou
Wenzhou
Fuzhou
Xiamen
Guangzhou
Kunming
Changsha
Chang Jiang
Huang He
Beijing
Tianjin
Jinan
Qingdao
Dalian
Shenyang
Changchun
Harbin
Manchuria
SHANGHAI
Yellow Sea
East China Sea
Taibei
Taiwan (Formosa)
MACAU (Port.)
HONG KONG
Hainan
South China Sea
Manila
PHILIPPINES
Mindoro
Palawan
Samar
Mindanao
Mindanao Trench
Sulu Sea
C. Engano
KOREA
Sŏul
Pusan
N. Dandong
Sea of Japan
JAPAN
Kyōto
TOKYO
Yokohama
Nagoya
Osaka
Kitakyūshū
Nagasaki
Kyūshū
Shikoku
Sendai
Hakodate
Fuji-san 3776
Japan Trench
Ryūkyū Is.
Vladivostok
Khabarovsk
Blagoveshchensk
Chita
Ulan Ude
Ozero Baykal
Sakhalin
G. of Sakhalin
Sea of Okhotsk
Okhotsk
Petropavlovsk
Kamchatka
Komandorskie Is. (U.S.S.R.)
Kuril Is.
Kuril Trench
La Perouse Strait
Aleutian Trench
Emperor Seamount Chain
KURO SIWO
Bonin Is.
Volcano Is.
Marcus I.
South Honshu Ridge
Marcus Necker Ridge
Wake I. (U.S.)
Northern Marianas
Mariana Trench
Guam (U.S.)
U.S. TRUST TERR. OF THE PACIFIC ISLANDS
Bikini Atoll
Enewetak Atoll
Marshall Is.
Jaluit
Fed. States of Micronesia
Truk
Pohnpei
Yap
Belau
International Date Line
Gilbert Is.
Butaritari
NAURU
Banaba
Midway Is.
Irian Jaya
Dampier Strait
PAPUA NEW GUINEA
New Guinea
Admiralty Is.
Bismarck Arch.
New Ireland
New Britain
Rabaul
Madang
Lae
Port Moresby
Aru Is.
Tanimbar Is.
Arafura Sea
Torres Strait
Thursday I.
C. York
SOLOMON ISLANDS
Honiara
Guadacanal
Louisiade Arch.
Sta. Cruz I.
TUVALU (Ellice Is.)
Funafuti
VANUATU
Coral Sea Islands Territory
Coral Sea
New Caledonia (Fr.)
Noumea
Chesterfield Is.
Loyalty Is.
FIJI
Vanua Levu
Vitu Levu
Suva
Rotuma
Wallis
Futuna (Fr.)
Darwin
Arnhem
G. of Carpentaria
Ashmore Is.
Wyndham
Newcastle Waters
NORTHERN TERRITORY
Cairns
Townsville
Mt. Isa
Great Divide
Rockhampton
Longreach
QUEENSLAND
Maryborough
Brisbane
Ipswich
Alice Springs
WESTERN AUSTRALIA
Onslow
N.W. Cape
Shark Bay
Geraldton
Kalgoorlie-Boulder
Perth
Fremantle
Geographe Bay
Albany
K. George Sd.
Oodnadatta
L. Eyre
SOUTH AUSTRALIA
Darling
NEW SOUTH WALES
Sydney
Newcastle
Katoomba
Wollongong
Canberra
Mt. Kosciusko 2230
Murray
VICTORIA
Melbourne
Ballarat
Geelong
Adelaide
Encounter Bay
Great Australian Bight
Bass Strait
TASMANIA
Launceston
Hobart
Norfolk I. (Aust.)
Lord Howe I. (Aust.)
Lord Howe Rise
Tasman Sea
EAST AUSTRALIAN CURRENT
Auckland
Hamilton
NEW ZEALAND
Palmerston N.
Wellington
Cook Strait
Nelson
Christchurch
Mt. Cook 3764
Oamaru
Dunedin
Invercargill
Stewart I.
Auckland Is. (N.Z.)
Campbell I. (N.Z.)
Macquarie Is. (Austral.)
Mid-Oceanic Ridge
South-East Indian Ridge
Mid-Indian Ridge
Indian-Antarctic Ridge
Indian Rise
Amsterdam I. (Fr.)
St. Paul I. (Fr.)
Crozet Is. (Fr.)
Kerguelen (Fr.)
Heard Is. (Aust.)
Colombo - Fremantle 3120
Al 'Adan - Melbourne 6445
Cape Town - Fremantle 5615
Cape Town - Melbourne 5814
Cape Town - Hobart 5838
Yokohama - Vancouver 4280
ft m
Projection: Mollweide's Homolographic
East from Greenwich
5615 Principal Shipping Routes (Distances in Nautical Miles)

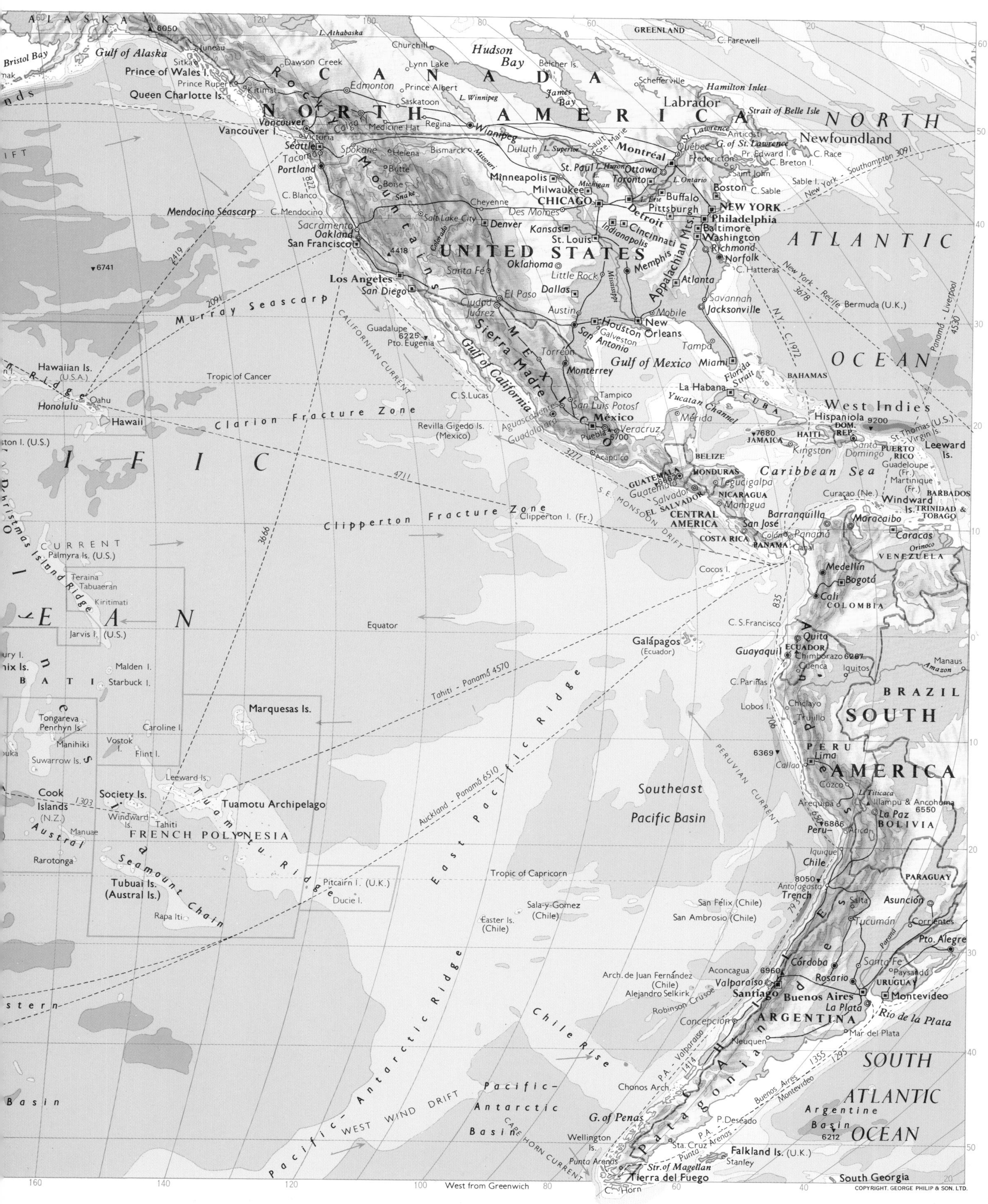

ALASKA
Bristol Bay
Gulf of Alaska
Prince of Wales I.
Prince Rupert
Queen Charlotte Is.
RIFT
Mendocino Seascarp
C. Blanco
C. Mendocino

HAWAIIAN IS. (U.S.A.)
Honolulu   Oahu
Hawaii   Hawaii

Murray Seascarp
Tropic of Cancer

Clarion Fracture Zone

CIFIC

CURRENT
Palmyra Is. (U.S.)
Teraina
Tabuaeran
Kiritimati

Jarvis I. (U.S.)

Equator

Christmas Island Ridge
IS

Phoenix Is.
Malden I.
Starbuck I.
BATI

Marquesas Is.

Tongareva
Penrhyn Is.
Manihiki
Suwarrow Is.
Caroline I.
Vostok
Flint I.

OCEAN

Cook Islands (N.Z.)
Society Is.
Leeward Is.
Windward Is.   Tahiti
Manuae
FRENCH POLYNESIA

Rarotonga
Tubuai (Austral Is.)
Rapa Iti
Austral Seamount Chain

Pitcairn I. (U.K.)
Ducie I.

Tropic of Capricorn

Sala-y-Gomez (Chile)
Easter Is. (Chile)

Tuamotu Archipelago

East Pacific Ridge
Auckland – Panamá 6510
Tahiti – Panamá 4570

Pacific – Antarctic Ridge
WEST WIND DRIFT

Pacific – Antarctic Basin

Basin
stern

CANADA
NORTH AMERICA

Churchill
Lynn Lake
Dawson Creek
Edmonton
Prince Albert
Saskatoon
Medicine Hat
Regina
L. Winnipeg
Winnipeg

L. Athabaska

Hudson Bay
James Bay
Belcher Is.

GREENLAND
C. Farewell

Labrador
Hamilton Inlet
Strait of Belle Isle
Newfoundland

NORTH

Kitimat
Vancouver
Vancouver I.
Victoria
Seattle
Tacoma
Portland
Spokane
Helena
Butte
Boise
Snake

Bismarck
Missouri
Minneapolis
St. Paul
Milwaukee
CHICAGO
L. Michigan
L. Superior
Duluth
Sault Ste. Marie
L. Huron
L. Erie
Detroit
Toronto
Ottawa
Buffalo
Montréal
Québec
Fredericton
Saint John
Pr. Edward I.
C. Breton I.
Sable I.
New York
C. Race
Southampton 3091
Anticosti I.
G. of St. Lawrence
St. Lawrence

UNITED STATES
Cheyenne
Des Moines
Salt Lake City
Colorado
4418
Denver
Kansas
St. Louis
Indianapolis
Cincinnati
Pittsburgh
NEW YORK
Philadelphia
Baltimore
Washington
Richmond
Norfolk
C. Hatteras

Santa Fé
Oklahoma
Memphis
Little Rock
Mississippi
Atlanta
Savannah
Jacksonville

Los Angeles
San Diego

Sierra Madre
CALIFORNIAN CURRENT
Guadalupe 6225
Pto. Eugenia
C.S. Lucas

El Paso
Ciudad Juárez
Dallas
Austin
Houston
San Antonio
Galveston
New Orleans
Mobile
Torreón
Monterrey
Gulf of Mexico
Tampa
Miami
Florida Strait

BAHAMAS

La Habana
Yucatán Channel
CUBA

West Indies
Hispaniola 9200
DOM. REP.
HAITI
JAMAICA 7680
Santo Domingo
St. Thomas (U.S.)
PUERTO RICO
St. Virgin Is.
Leeward Is.
Guadeloupe (Fr.)
Martinique (Fr.)
BARBADOS

Bermuda (U.K.)
New York – Recife 3678
N.Y. 1972
Panamá 4530
Liverpool

ATLANTIC

OCEAN

MEXICO
Aguascalientes
México
Guadalajara
Puebla 5700
Acapulco
3277
Revilla Gigedo Is. (Mexico)
C.S. Francisco
Tampico
San Luis Potosí
Veracruz
Mérida
BELIZE
GUATEMALA
Guatemala
HONDURAS
Tegucigalpa
Salvador
EL SALVADOR
NICARAGUA
Managua
San José
COSTA RICA
Caribbean Sea
Kingston
Curação (Ne.)
Windward Is.
TRINIDAD & TOBAGO

S.E. MONSOON DRIFT
CENTRAL AMERICA
Colón
PANAMÁ
Panamá Canal
Cocos I.

Clipperton Fracture Zone
Clipperton I. (Fr.)
4711
3666

Galápagos (Ecuador)
835

Barranquilla
Caracas
VENEZUELA
Maracaibo
Orinoco
Medellín
Bogotá
Cali
COLOMBIA
Quito
ECUADOR
Guayaquil
Chimborazo 6267
Cuenca
C. Parinas
Iquitos
Manaus
Amazon
BRAZIL
SOUTH

Chiclayo
Lobos Is.
Trujillo
706

PERUVIAN CURRENT
6369
PERU
Lima
Callao
Cozco
Arequipa
L. Titicaca
Illampu & Ancohoma 6550
La Paz
BOLIVIA
Peru
6886
Atico
Iquique
AMERICA

Southeast Pacific Basin

Antofagasta
Trench
8050
San Félix (Chile)
San Ambrosio (Chile)

Salta
Tucumán
Corrientes
Asunción
PARAGUAY
Pto. Alegre

Arch. de Juan Fernández (Chile)
Alejandro Selkirk
Robinson Crusoe
Aconcagua 6960
Valparaíso
Santiago
P.A. – Valparaíso 1474
Córdoba
Rosario
Santa Fe
Buenos Aires
La Plata
Paysandú
URUGUAY
Montevideo
Río de la Plata
ARGENTINA
Neuquén
Concepción
Chile Rise
Buenos Aires – Montevideo
1355
1295
Mar del Plata

SOUTH ATLANTIC
Argentine Basin 6212

Chonos Arch.
P.A.
CAPE HORN CURRENT
G. of Penas
Wellington Is.
Sta. Cruz
Punta Arenas
Stir. of Magellan
Tierra del Fuego
P. Deseado

Falkland Is. (U.K.)
Stanley
South Georgia

OCEAN

C. Horn

1 : 40 000 000

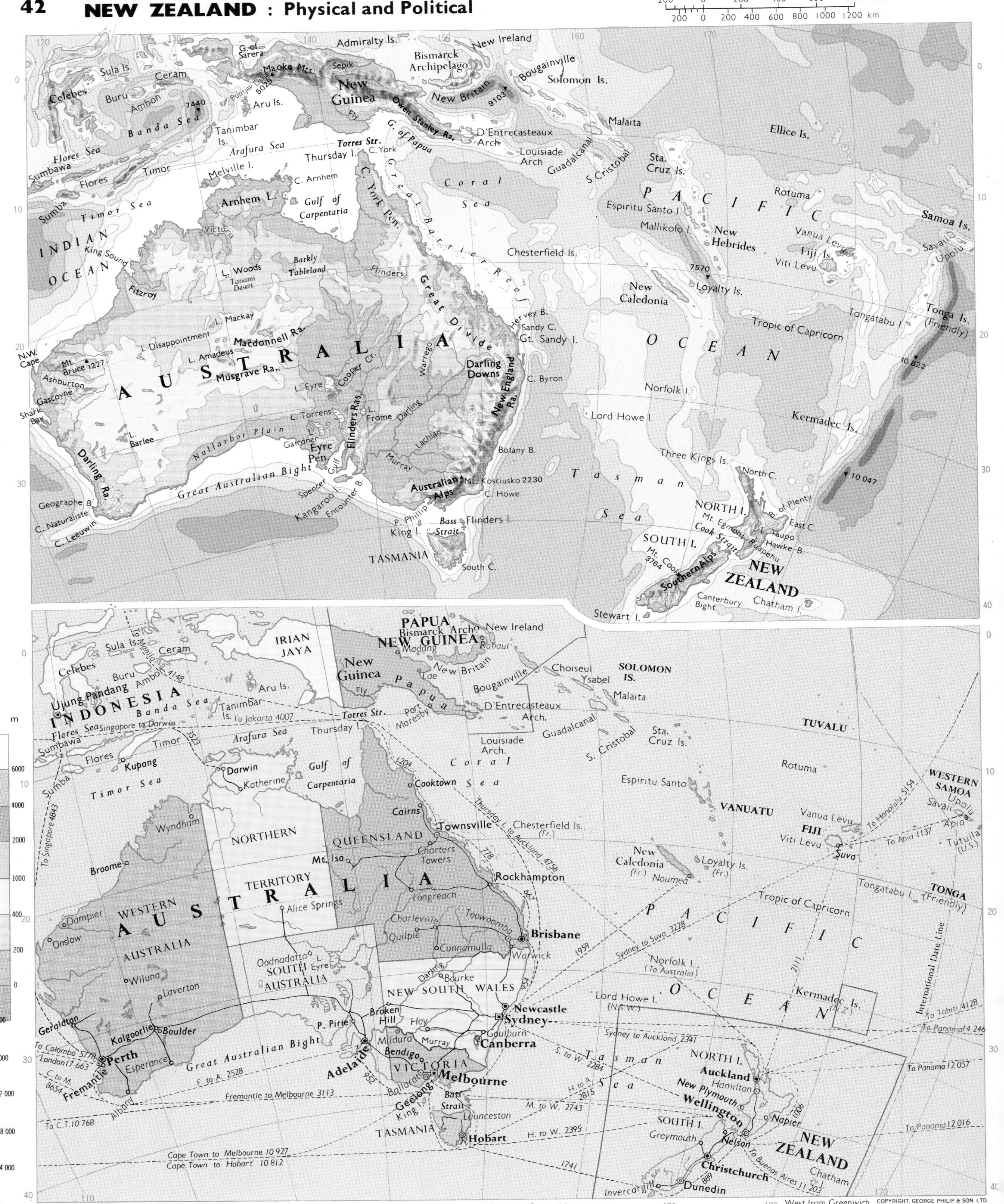

Projection: Bonne

East from Greenwich   West from Greenwich   COPYRIGHT. GEORGE PHILIP & SON. LTD.

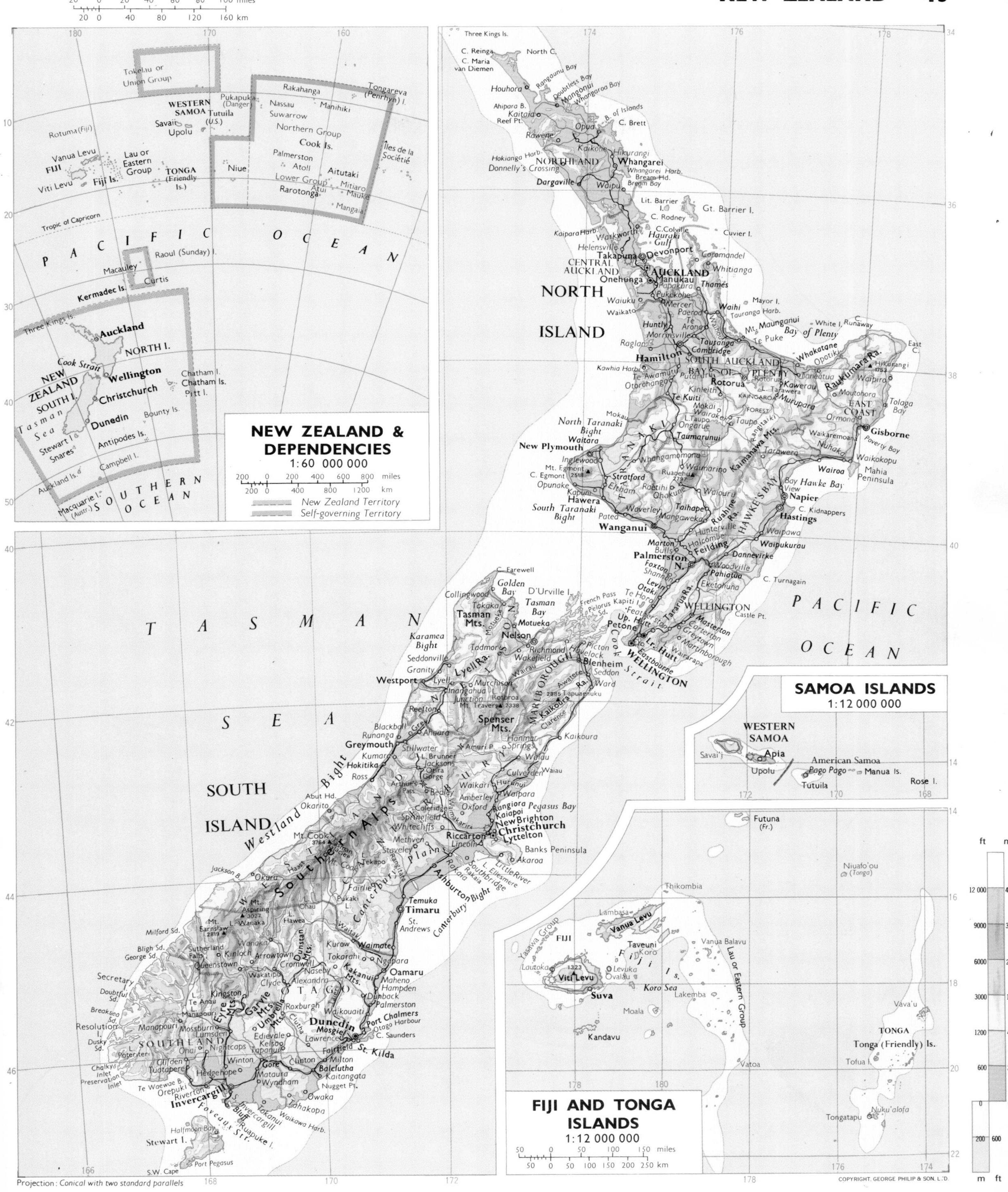

1:6 000 000

20 0 20 40 60 80 100 miles
20 0 40 80 120 160 km

NEW ZEALAND & DEPENDENCIES
1:60 000 000

200 0 200 400 600 800 miles
200 0 200 400 600 800 1000 1200 km

New Zealand Territory
Self-governing Territory

SAMOA ISLANDS
1:12 000 000

WESTERN SAMOA
Savai'i
Upolu
Apia
American Samoa
Pago Pago
Tutuila
Manua Is.
Rose I.

FIJI AND TONGA ISLANDS
1:12 000 000

50 0 50 100 150 miles
50 0 50 100 150 200 250 km

Projection: Conical with two standard parallels

COPYRIGHT. GEORGE PHILIP & SON. L.TD.

ft m
12 000 4000
9000 3000
6000 2000
3000 1000
1200 400
600 200
0 0
200 600
m ft

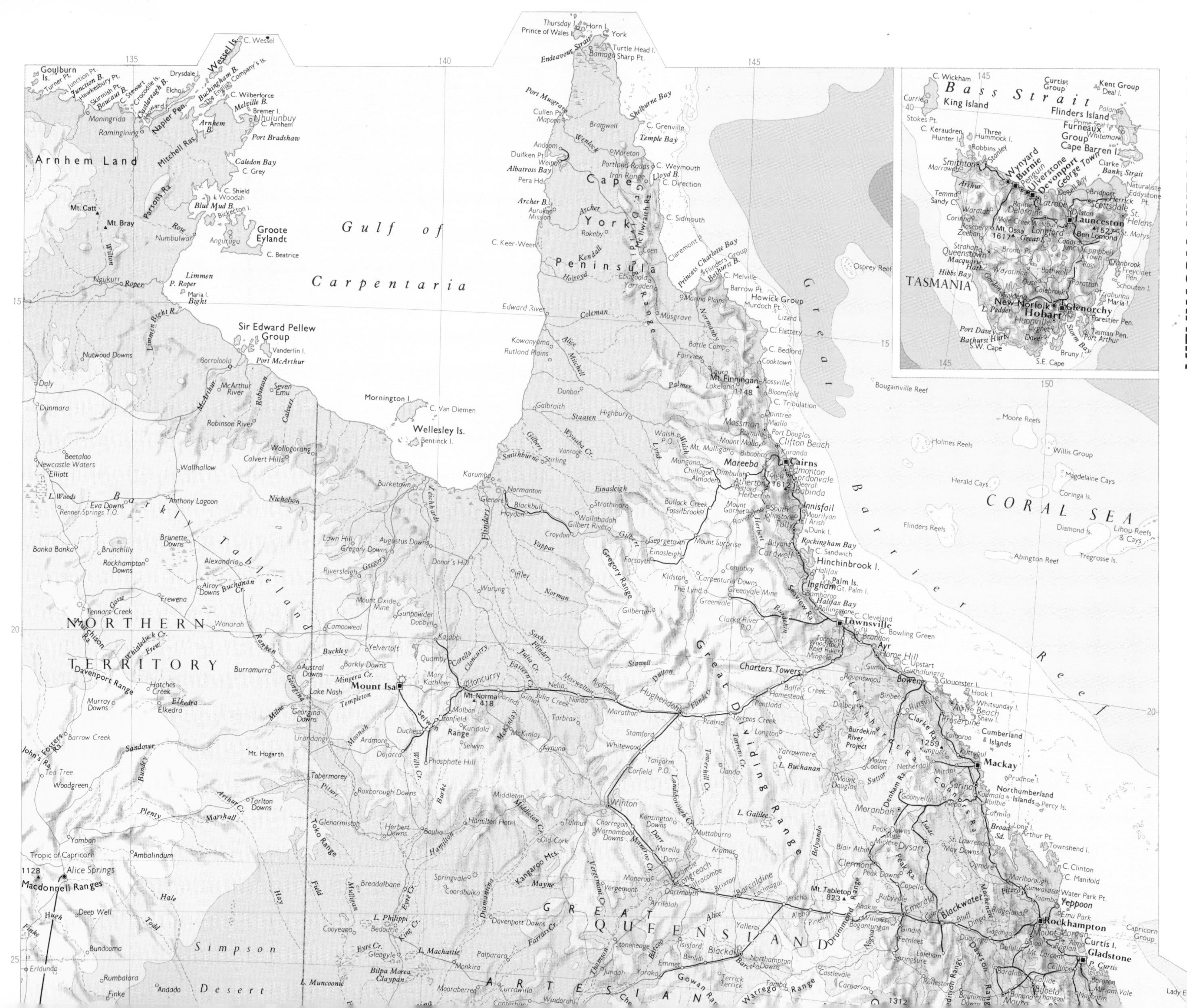

Bass Strait
Flinders Island
King Island
Launceston
Hobart
TASMANIA
CORAL SEA
Great Barrier Reef
Gulf of Carpentaria
Cape York Peninsula
Great Dividing Range
GREAT QUEENSLAND
NORTHERN TERRITORY
Barkly Tableland
Arnhem Land
Groote Eylandt
Wellesley Is.
Sir Edward Pellew Group
Simpson Desert
Cairns
Townsville
Mackay
Rockhampton
Gladstone
Mount Isa
Cloncurry
Charters Towers
Hughenden
Winton
Alice Springs
Macdonnell Ranges

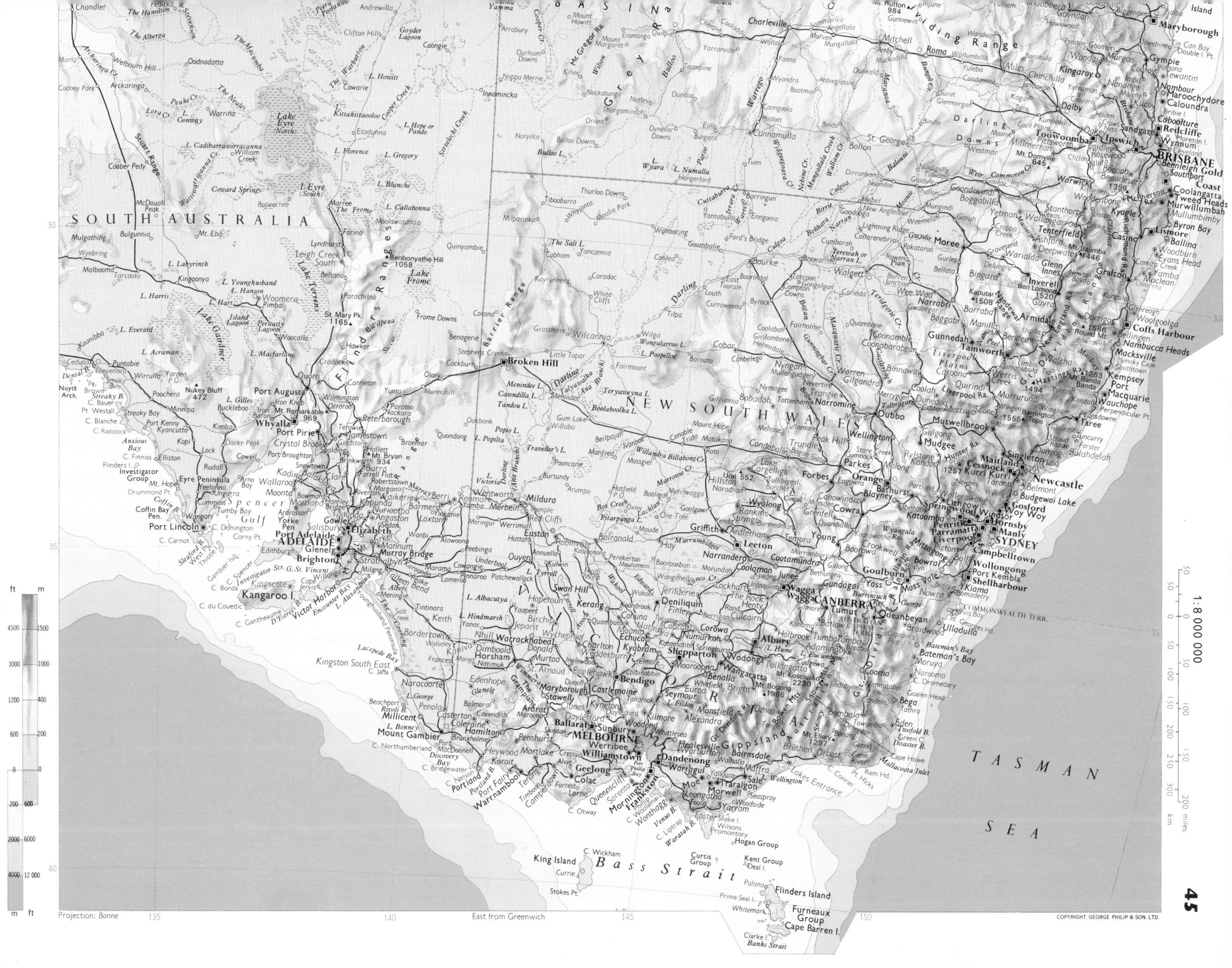

1:8 000 000

TASMAN SEA

NEW SOUTH WALES

BRISBANE

SYDNEY

CANBERRA

SOUTH AUSTRALIA

Great Dividing Range

Darling Downs

Broken Hill

ADELAIDE

MELBOURNE

Bass Strait

King Island

Flinders Island
Furneaux Group
Cape Barren I.

Kangaroo I.

COPYRIGHT GEORGE PHILIP & SON, LTD.

Projection: Bonne

East from Greenwich

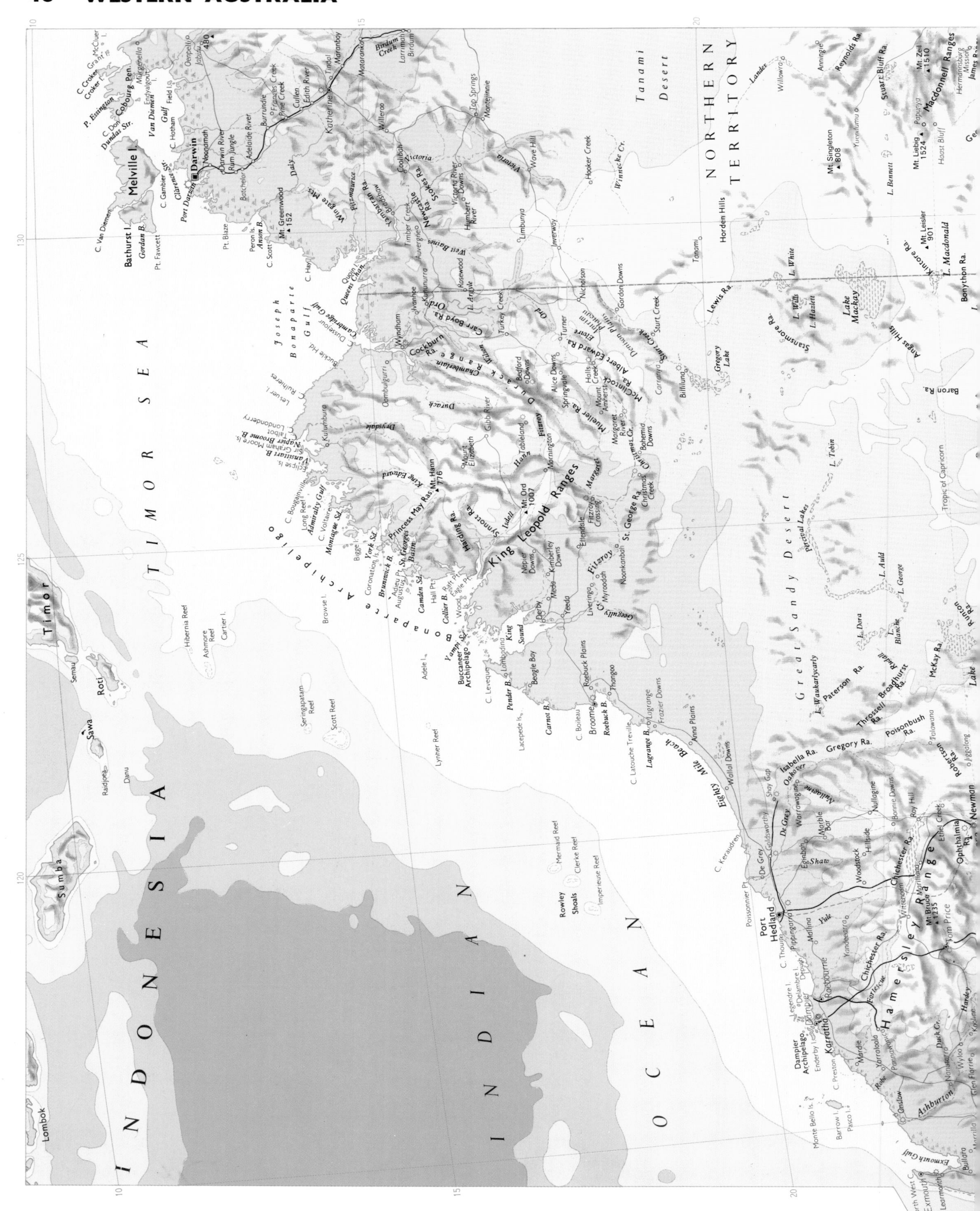
TIMOR SEA
INDONESIA
INDIAN OCEAN
NORTHERN TERRITORY
Tanami Desert
Great Sandy Desert
Joseph Bonaparte Gulf
Bonaparte Archipelago
King Leopold Ranges
Hamersley Range
Melville I.
Bathurst I.
Darwin
Timor
Sumba
Roti
Lombok
Port Hedland
Broome
Derby
Wyndham
Karratha
Newman
Exmouth
Lake Mackay
Eighty Mile Beach
Tropic of Capricorn

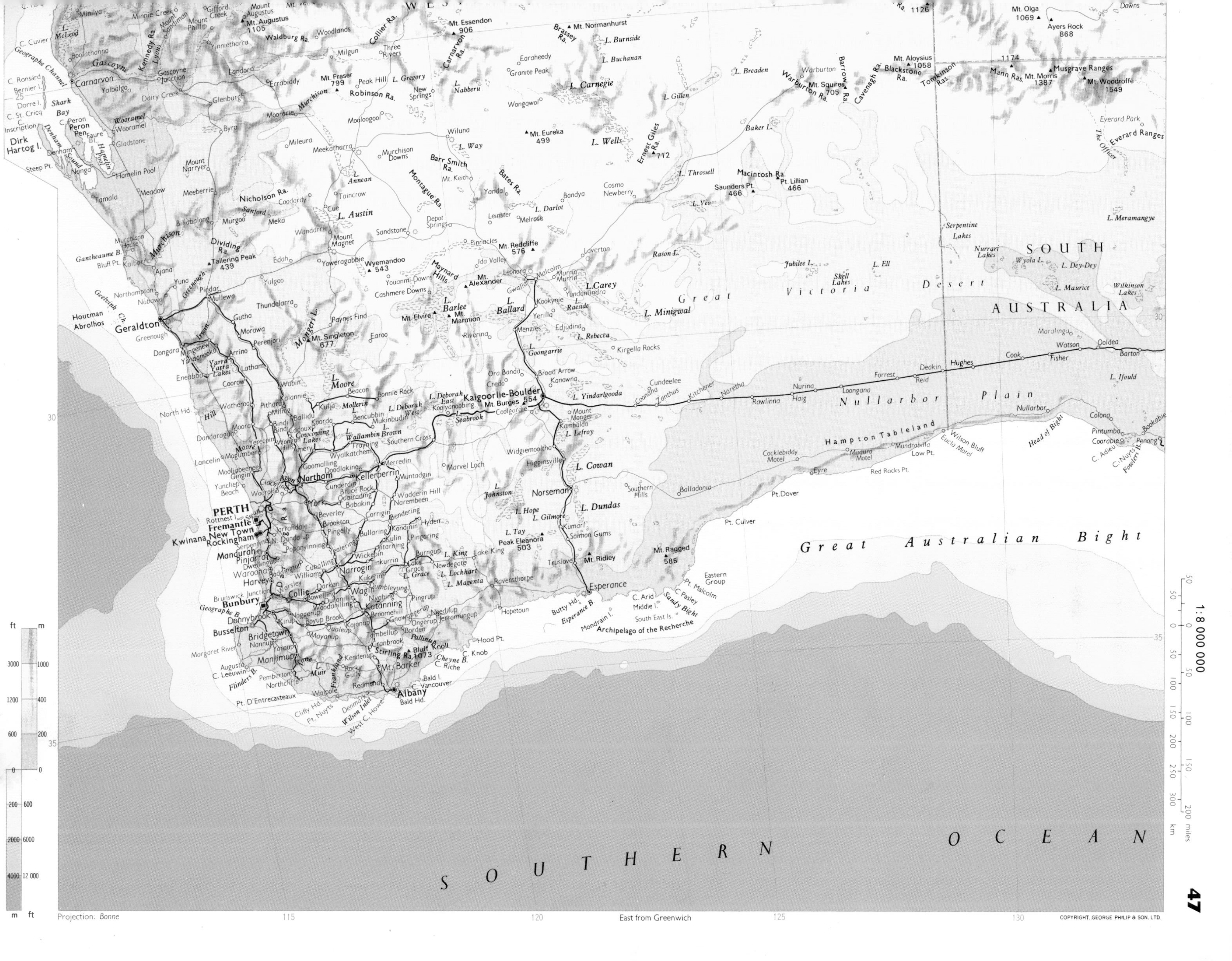

1:8 000 000

50   0   50   100   150   200 miles

50   0   50   100   150   200   250   300 km

S O U T H E R N   O C E A N

G r e a t   A u s t r a l i a n   B i g h t

S O U T H

A U S T R A L I A

W. A.

G r e a t   V i c t o r i a   D e s e r t

N u l l a r b o r   P l a i n

Hampton Tableland

Mt Woodroffe 1549
Ayers Rock 868
Mt Olga 1069
Mann Ras. Mt. Morris 1,387
Everard Ranges
Everard Park
The Officer
1174
Musgrave Ranges
Downs
L. Meramangye
Wilkinson Lakes
Wynola L.
L. Day-Dey
L. Maurice
Serpentine Lakes
Narrari Lakes

Coorabie
C. Nuyts B.
Fowlers B.
Penong
Bookabie
Pintumba
Coobowie
Colona
Wahgunyah
Nullarbor
Eucla Motel
Wilson Bluff
Low Pt.
Mundrabilla Motel
Madura Motel
Red Rocks Pt.
Pt. Culver
Pt. Dover
Eyre
Cocklebiddy Motel
Balladonia
Caiguna
Cook
Fisher
Barton
L. Ifould
Ooldea
Watson
Maralinga
Nurina
Haig
Koonalda
Kitchener
Forrest
Reid
Deakin
Hughes
Mundrabilla
Loongana
Naretha
Rawlinna
Zanthus
Cundeelee

Ra. 1126
Mt Aloysius 1058
Blackstone Ra.
Cavenagh Ra.
Barrow Ra.
Warburton Mt. Squires 705
Warburton Ra.
Baker L.
L. Breaden
L. Gillen
Macintosh Ra.
Saunders Pt. 466
Pt. Lillian 466
L. Throssell
L. Yeo
L. Carnegie
Brassey Ra.
Mt. Normanhurst
L. Burnside
Mt. Eureka 499
L. Wells
Ernest Giles Ra. 712
Jubilee L.
Shell Lakes
L. Ell
Granite Peak
Earaheedy
Cosmo Newberry
Laverton
L. Carey
Bandya
L. Rebecca
L. Minigwal
Kirgella Rocks
Loongara
Balladonia
L. Cowan
L. Dundas
Norseman
L. Lefroy
Kalgoorlie-Boulder 554
East Coolgardie
Mt. Burges
Coolgardie
Kanowna
Broad Arrow
Ora Banda
Menzies
Goongarrie
Gindalbie
Edjudina
Yerilla
Murrin Murrin
Yundamindra
Morapoi
Mt. Remarkable
Malcolm
Leonora
Gwalia

Kingston
Boulder
Widgiemooltha
Higginsville
Norseman
L. Cowan
L. Dundas
Mt. Ridley 249
C. Arid
Sandy Bight
Pt. Pasley
Pt. Malcolm
South East Is.
Middle I.
Eastern Group
Archipelago of the Recherche
Mt. Ragged 585
Peak Eleanora 503
L. Tay
Esperance
Esperance B.
Butty Hd.
Cape Le Grand

Collier Ra.
Mt. Fraser 799
Peak Hill
L. Gregory
Robinson Ra.
New Springs
Three Rivers
Mileura
Barloo
Bar Smith
Montague Ra.
Depot Springs
Youanmi Downs
Cashmere Downs
Sandstone
Mt. Magnet
Mount Keith
L. Mason
Wiluna
Lake Way
L. Nabberu
Mt. Essendon 906
Mt. Carnavon Ra.
Carnarvon Ra.
Waldburg Ra.
Mt. Augustus 1105
Mount Phillip
Kennedy Ra.
Lyons R.
Gascoyne Junction
Minnie Creek
Dairy Creek

Mt. Singleton 677
Mt. Jackson
Bullfinch
Southern Cross
Yellowdine
Marvel Loch
Bonnie Rock
Beacon
Mukinbudin
Bencubbin
Koorda
Bullabulling
Johnston
L. Deborah
Burbanks

L. Barlee
Mt. Elvire
Youanmi
Maynard
Mt. Kenneth
Riverina
L. Ballard
Melrose
Leinster
Lawlers
Bullfinch

Mt. Redcliffe 576
Mt Alexander
Mt. Marmion
Mt. Burlee
Paynes Find
Pindar
Yalgoo
Mount Magnet
Cue
Meekatharra
Mooloogool
Weld Range
Tuckanarra
Nannine
L. Annean
L. Austin

Geraldton
Northampton
Greenough
Dongara
Mingenew
Morawa
Perenjori
Mullewa
Pindar
Yuna
Three Springs
Carnamah
Coorow
Watheroo
Moora
Dalwallinu
Wongan Hills
Goomalling
Wubin

PERTH
Fremantle
Rottnest I.
Rockingham
Kwinana
New Town
Mandurah
Pinjarra
Waroona
Harvey
Collie
Bunbury
Busselton
Donnybrook
Bridgetown
Manjimup
Nannup
Augusta
C. Leeuwin
Pt. D'Entrecasteaux
Pemberton
Northcliffe
Walpole
Nornalup

Northam
York
Beverley
Brookton
Corrigin
Narrogin
Wagin
Katanning
Broomehill
Tambellup
Cranbrook
Mt. Barker
Albany
Bald Hd.
King George Sd.
Stirling Ra. 1073
C. Riche
Cheyne B.
Hopetoun
West Mt. Barren
Ongerup
Gnowangerup
Jerramungup
Ravensthorpe
Hopetoun
Bremer B.
L. King
Lake King
Newdegate
Lake Grace
L. Grace
L. Magenta
Hyden
Corrigin
Kondinin
Kulin
L. Lockhart
Pingrup
Nyabing
Pingelly

Gascoyne
Murchison R.
Avon R.
Swan R.

Mount Augustus 1105
Lyndon
Mt. Vernon
Mt. James
Mt. Labouchere
Lyons R.

Cervantes
Jurien
Lancelin
Gingin
Yanchep
Toodyay
Merredin
Bruce Rock
Narembeen
Kellerberrin
Tammin
Cunderdin
Kellerberrin
Quairading
Wickepin
Williams
Darkan
Boddington
Wandering
Pingelly
Brookton
Beverley

Shark Bay
Denham
Dirk Hartog I.
Dorre I.
Bernier I.
C. Ronsard
C. St. Cricq
C. Cuvier
Steep Pt.
Inscription Pt.
Useless Loop
L. MacLeod
Hamelin Pool
Geographe Channel
Carnarvon
Yalbalgo
Woodleigh
Hamelin
Wooramel
Meedo
Boolathana
Brickhouse

Kalbarri
Murchison R.
Northampton
Ajana
Binnu
North Hd.
Greenough R.
Mingenew
Houtman Abrolhos

W E S T E R N

Projection: Bonne

East from Greenwich

COPYRIGHT GEORGE PHILIP & SON, LTD.

115   120   125   130

30   35

35

ft   m
3000   1000
1200   400
600   200
0
200   600
2000   600
6000   2000
12 000   4000
ft   m

1:40 000 000

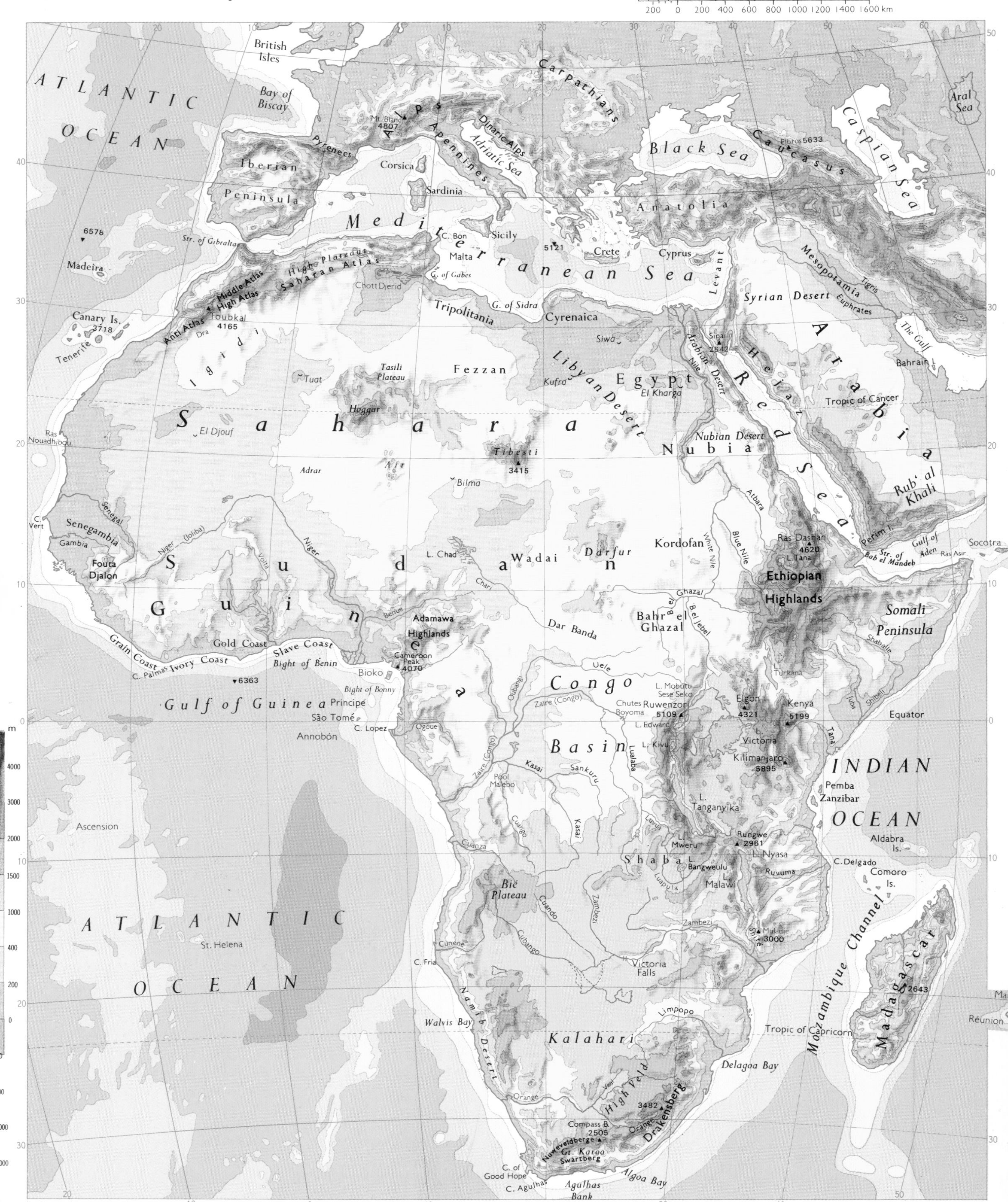
200 0 200 400 600 800 1000 miles
200 0 200 400 600 800 1000 1200 1400 1600 km
ATLANTIC OCEAN
British Isles
Bay of Biscay
Carpathians
Aral Sea
Caspian Sea
Mt. Blanc 4807
Alps
Pyrenees
Dinaric Alps
Apennines
Adriatic Sea
Black Sea
Elbrus 5633
Caucasus
Iberian Peninsula
Corsica
Sardinia
Anatolia
Mediterranean Sea
6576
Str. of Gibraltar
C. Bon
Sicily
5121
Crete
Cyprus
Levant
Malta
Madeira
High Plateaus
Saharan Atlas
G. of Gabes
Middle Atlas
High Atlas
Chott Djerid
Mesopotamia
Tigris
Syrian Desert
Euphrates
Canary Is.
3718
Tenerife
Anti Atlas
Toubkal 4165
Dra
Tripolitania
G. of Sidra
Cyrenaica
Siwa
Sinai 2642
The Gulf
Bahrain I.
Igidi
Tasili Plateau
Fezzan
Libyan Desert
Arabian Desert
Nile
Hejaz
Arabia
Tuat
Hoggar
Kufra
Egypt
El Kharga
Red Sea
Tropic of Cancer
Sahara
Ras Nouadhibou
El Djouf
Tibesti 3415
Nubian Desert
Nubia
Adrar
Air
Bilma
Rub' al Khali
C. Vert
Senegal
Senegambia
Gambia
Niger
(Joliba)
Volta
Atbara
Kordofan
White Nile
Blue Nile
Ras Dashan 4620
L. Tana
Perim I.
Str. of Bab el Mandeb
Gulf of Aden
Socotra
Ras Asir
Fouta Djalon
Sudan
L. Chad
Wadai
Darfur
Chari
Ethiopian Highlands
Somali Peninsula
Guinea
Benue
Adamawa Highlands
Bahr el Ghazal
Bahr el Jebel
Ghazal
Dar Banda
Shabelle
Grain Coast
Gold Coast
Slave Coast
Bight of Benin
Ivory Coast
C. Palmas
Cameroon Peak 4070
6363
Bioko
Bight of Bonny
Uele
Congo
L. Mobutu Sese Seko
Turkana
Gulf of Guinea
Principe
São Tomé
Annobón
C. Lopez
Ogoue
Oubangi
Zaire (Congo)
Chutes Boyoma
Ruwenzori 5109
L. Edward
Elgon 4321
Kenya 5199
Juba
Equator
L. Kivu
L. Victoria
Kilimanjaro 5895
Tana
Basin
Lualaba
Kasai
Sankuru
Zaire (Congo)
Pool Malebo
INDIAN OCEAN
Pemba
Zanzibar
Ascension
Cuango
Kasai
L. Tanganyika
Luvua
L. Mweru
Rungwe 2961
Aldabra Is.
Cuanza
Shaba
L. Bangweulu
L. Nyasa
Ruvuma
C. Delgado
Comoro Is.
Luapula
L. Malawi
Bié Plateau
Cuando
Zambezi
Zambezi
Mulanje 3000
Shire
Mozambique Channel
ATLANTIC OCEAN
St. Helena
Cunene
Cubango
C. Fria
Victoria Falls
Madagascar
2643
Namib Desert
Walvis Bay
Limpopo
Tropic of Capricorn
Réunion
Mau
Kalahari
Delagoa Bay
Vaal
High Veld
Drakensberg
3482
Orange
Orange
Compass B. 2505
Nuweveldberge
Gt. Karoo
Swartberg
C. of Good Hope
C. Agulhas
Agulhas Bank
Algoa Bay
ft m
12 000 4000
9000 3000
6000 2000
4500 1500
3000 1000
1200 400
600 200
0 0
200 600
2000 6000
4000 12 000
6000 18 000
m ft
Projection: Zenithal Equidistant.
West from Greenwich
East from Greenwich
COPYRIGHT GEORGE PHILIP & SON LTD.

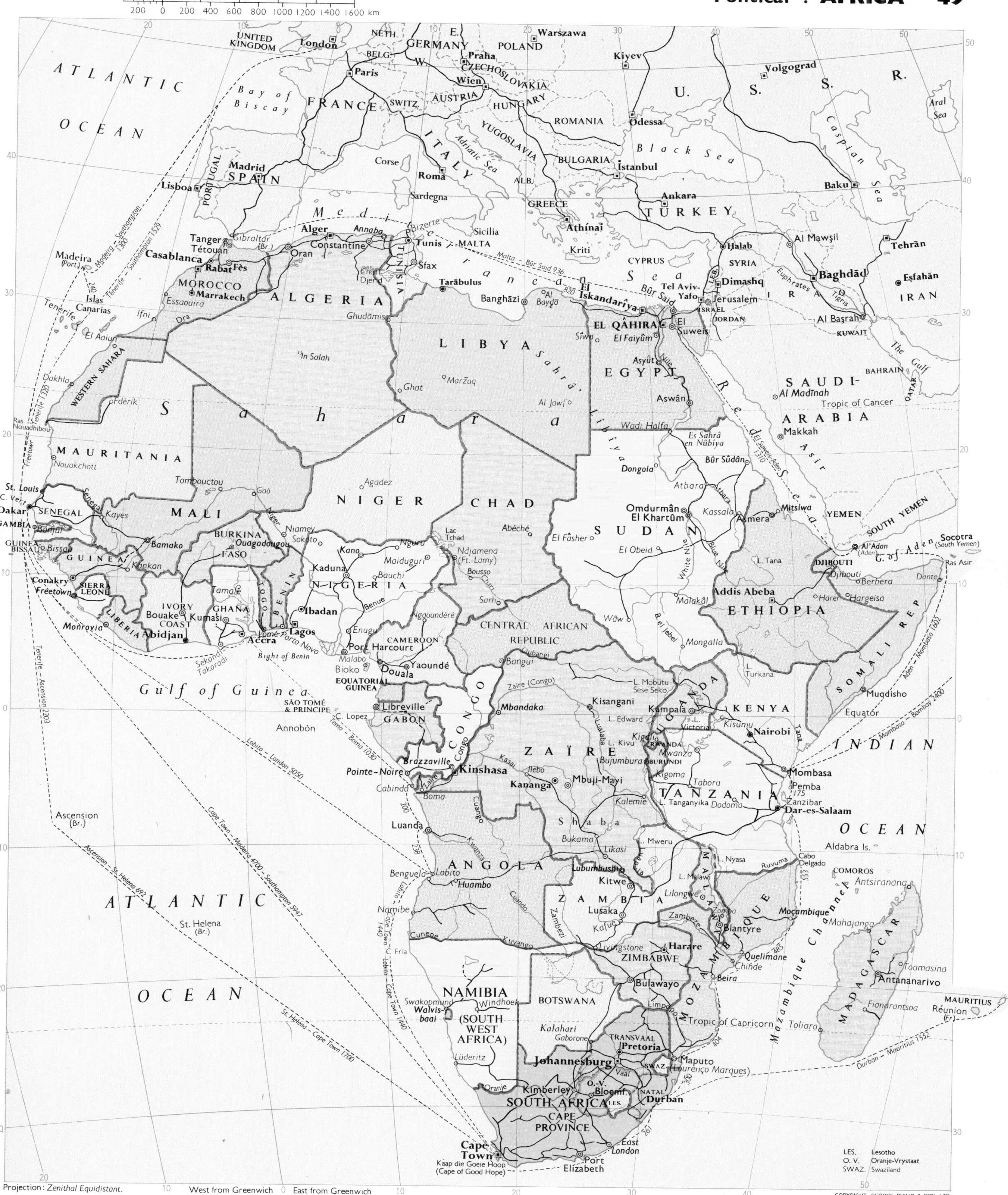

1:40 000 000

200   0   200   400   600   800   1000 miles
200   0   200 400 600 800 1000 1200 1400 1600 km

ATLANTIC
OCEAN

UNITED
KINGDOM   London   NETH.   E.   POLAND
GERMANY   Warszawa
BELG.   W.   Praha   CZECHOSLOVAKIA
Paris   Wien   AUSTRIA   HUNGARY
FRANCE   SWITZ.   Kiyev   Volgograd
Bay of
Biscay   U. S. S. R.

ITALY   YUGOSLAVIA   ROMANIA   Odessa
Madrid   Corse   Roma   ROMANIA   Black Sea   Aral
Lisboa   SPAIN   PORTUGAL   Sardegna   BULGARIA   İstanbul   Caspian   Sea
Madeira   Sicilia   GREECE   Ankara   Baku
(Port.)   Athínai   TURKEY
Islas   Tanger   Alger   Annaba   Bizerte   Kriti   CYPRUS   Halab   Al Mawşil   Tehrân
Canarias   Tétouan   Gibraltar   Constantine   Tunis   MALTA   SYRIA   Baghdâd
Tenérife   Casablanca   Oran   Sfax   Tel Aviv-   Dimashq   Eşfahân
El Aaiun   Rabat   Fès   Tarâbulus   Banghâzî   Yafo   Jerusalem   IRAN   Al Başrah
MOROCCO   Marrakech   ALGERIA   El Iskandarîya   ISRAEL   JORDAN   KUWAIT
Essaouira   Ghudāmis   El QÂHIRA   El Suweis   The   Gulf   BAHRAIN
Ifni   Dra   El Faiyûm   SAUDI-   QATAR
El Aaiun   LIBYA   Sâhrâ Lîbîya   Sîwa   Asyût   ARABIA
WESTERN   In Salah   EGYPT   Aswân   Al Madînah   Tropic of Cancer
SAHARA   Fdérik   Marzûq   Ghat   Al Jawf   Wadi Halfa   Makkah

ATLANTIC   OCEAN

Projection: Zenithal Equidistant.

West from Greenwich   East from Greenwich

LES.   Lesotho
O.V.   Oranje-Vrystaat
SWAZ.   Swaziland

COPYRIGHT. GEORGE PHILIP & SON. LTD.

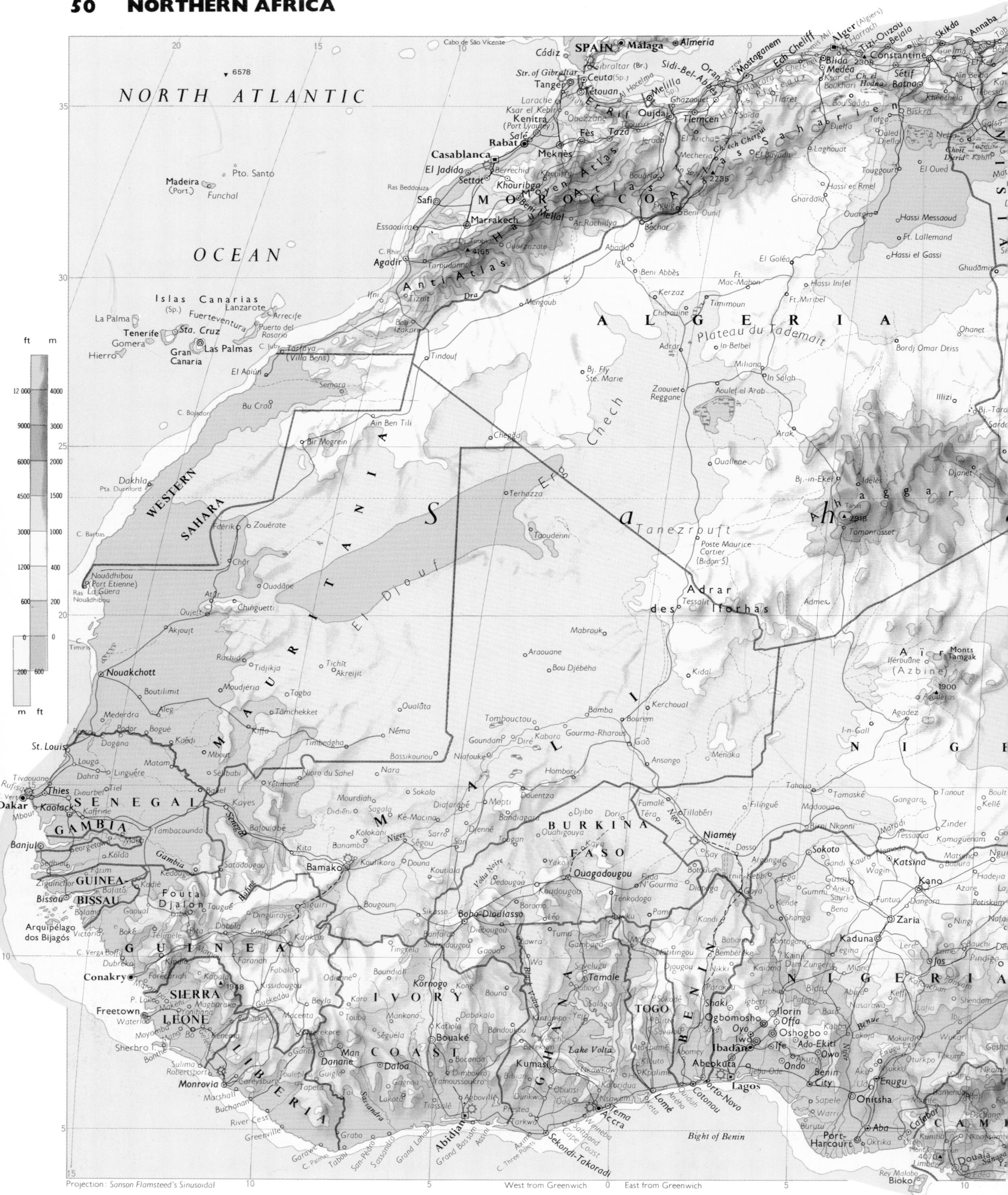
NORTH ATLANTIC
OCEAN
SPAIN
Málaga
Almería
Cádiz
Str. of Gibraltar
Gibraltar (Br.)
Tanger
Ceuta (Sp.)
Tétouan
Melilla (Sp.)
Oran
Mostaganem
Ech Cheliff
Alger (Algiers)
Tizi-Ouzou
Bejaia
Skikda
Annaba
Blida
Medéa
Constantine
Sétif
Batna
Sidi-Bel-Abbès
Tlemcen
Oujda
Kenitra (Port Lyautey)
Salé
Rabat
Fès
Taza
Meknès
Casablanca
El Jadida
Settat
Khouribga
Safi
Essaouira
Marrakech
Agadir
MOROCCO
Haut Atlas
Moyen Atlas
Anti Atlas
Er Rif
Saharien Atlas
Madeira (Port.)
Funchal
Pto. Santo
Islas Canarias (Sp.)
La Palma
Tenerife
Gomera
Hierro
Gran Canaria
Las Palmas
Sta. Cruz
Fuerteventura
Lanzarote
Arrecife
Tarfaya (Villa Bens)
El Aaiún
WESTERN SAHARA
Dakhla
Nouâdhibou (Port Etienne)
ALGERIA
Plateau du Tademait
Tindouf
Béchar
El Goléa
Ghardaïa
Ouargla
Touggourt
Biskra
Hassi Messaoud
Ft. Lallemand
Hassi el Gassi
Timimoun
Adrar
In Salah
Reggane
Erg Chech
Tanezrouft
Ahaggar
Tamanrasset
Djanet
Illizi
Adrar des Iforhas
MAURITANIA
El Djouf
Atar
Nouakchott
Akjoujt
Tidjikja
Néma
St. Louis
SENEGAL
Dakar
Thiès
Kaolack
GAMBIA
Banjul
GUINEA-BISSAU
Bissau
Arquipélago dos Bijagós
GUINEA
Fouta Djalon
Conakry
SIERRA LEONE
Freetown
LIBERIA
Monrovia
MALI
Tombouctou
Gao
Mopti
Ségou
Bamako
Kayes
BURKINA FASO
Ouagadougou
Bobo-Dioulasso
NIGER
Niamey
Aïr (Azbine)
Agadez
Zinder
IVORY COAST
Bouaké
Abidjan
Man
Daloa
GHANA
Kumasi
Tamale
Lake Volta
Accra
Sekondi-Takoradi
TOGO
Lomé
BENIN
Porto-Novo
Cotonou
NIGERIA
Lagos
Ibadan
Abeokuta
Ogbomosho
Oshogbo
Ilorin
Kano
Kaduna
Zaria
Jos
Sokoto
Katsina
Enugu
Onitsha
Benin City
Port Harcourt
Calabar
Bight of Benin
Bioko
Douala
Niger
Gambia
Senegal
Volta Noire
Projection: Sanson Flamsteed's Sinusoidal
West from Greenwich
East from Greenwich
ft
m
12 000
9000
6000
4500
3000
1200
600
0
200
4000
3000
2000
1500
1000
400
200
0
600

1:15 000 000

100   200   300   400 miles
100 0 100 200 300 400 500 600 km

MEDITERRANEAN SEA

TURKEY

Sicily
C. Passero
Ragusa
Pantelleria (It.)
Lampedusa (It.)
MALTA
Kerkenna
Djerba
Gardane
Zuwārah
Tarābulus (Tripoli)
Al Qaddāhīyah
Al Khums
Tājūrā
Mişrātah
Gharyān
Banī Walīd
Mizdah
Jādū
968
Tarābulus
Surt
Khalīj Surt
Zueitina
Ajdābiyah
Marsa Brega
Ra's Al-Unuf
Al' Uqaylah
Banghāzī (Benghazi)
878
Barīnah
Tūkrah
Al Marj
Darnah
Marsā Sūsah (Apollonia)
Shahhāt (Cyrene)
Tulmaythah (Ptolemais)
Khalīj Bunbah
Tubruq (Tobruk)
Bardīa
Sīdī Barrānī
Ra's al Milh
Marsā Matrūh
El 'Alamein
Qāra
Siwa
Al Jaghbūb
Munkhafed el Qattāra (Qattāra Depression)
Al Bawitī
El Faiyum
Beni Suef
LIBYA
Cyrenaica
Sahrâ
Hūn
Marādah
Awjilah
Al 'Irq
Zillah
1200
Sabhah
Fezzan
Brach
Adri
Tasawah
Marzuq
Wāw al Kabīr
Idehan
Marzūq
Al Qatrān
Tropic of Cancer
Rebiana
Al Kufrah
Al Jawf
Al Jazīrah
El Wâhât el-Dakhla
Mût
El Qasr
Bârîs
El Wâhât el-Khârga
El Khârga
Lî bî ye
EGYPT
Es Sahrâ
Qasr Farâfra
El Bawitî
Beni Mazâr
El Minyâ
Mallawi
Dairût
Manfalût
Asyût
Abu Tig
Akhmîm
Sohâg
Girga
El Uqsur (Luxor)
Qena
Qûs
Isna
Idfû
El Qasr
Tahta
1st Cataract
Aswân
(Aswân High Dam)
Sadd el Aali
El Shallal
Dunqul
Buheiret en Naser (Lake Nasser)

Tibesti
Toummo
Abzou
Bardaï
Emi Koussi
3150
Zouar
Gouri
3415
Erdi
Ounianga-Kébir
Ounianga Serir
Faya-Largeau
Anaye
Madama
Bilma
Wour
Borkou
Fada
Ennedi
Djourab
Oum Chalouba
Depression du Mourdi
CHAD
Zigey
Mao
Moussoro
Ati
Rig-Rig
Lac Tchad
Bol
Massakory
Yao
L. Fitri
Bokoro
Ndjamena (Ft. Lamy)
Kousséri
Dikwa
Massaguet
Massénya
Bongor
Melfi
Bitkine
Mongo
Am Dam
Aboudéïa
Oum Hadjer
Abéché
Adré
Goz Beïda
Biltine
Arada
Iriba
Tiné
Kutum
Nyãlã
Nukheila
Bir 'Atrun
Bir Ungat
Laqiya Arba'in
Ma'tan as Sarra
Uweinat
1893
Ayn el 'Uwaynat
El Wâhât el Selîma
2nd Cataract
Wadi Halfa
Es Sahrâ en Nûbîya
Kosha
Abri
Delgo
(Nubian Desert)
3rd Cataract
Argo
Dongola
El Khandaq
Kareima
Merowe
El Debba
Korti
Ed Debba
Abu Hamed
Abū Dis
El Kab
4th Cataract
5th Cataract
Berber
Atbara
Ed Dâmer
Adarama
ESH SHAMALÎYA
AN NÎL
SHAMÂL DÂRFÛR
Malha
Sodiri
Kagmar
El Fasher
Nabkabīyah
El Junaynah
Zalingei
Geneina
Jebel Marra
3088
Dâr Fûr
JANUB DÂRFÛR
Nyãlã
Ghanami
Hajar Banga
Id el Ghanam
Kabkabīyah
Mellit
Umm Keddada
Umm Bel
Wad Banda
En Nahud
Abū Zabad
Er Rahad
El Obeid
Dilling
Rashad
Kadugli
Talodi
Tungaru
Abyei
JANUB KORDOFAN
SHAMÂL KORDOFAN
Hamrato esh Sheykh
Umm Badr
Sodiri
Muglad
Rahad el Bardi
Buram
Abu Matâriq
Kadugli
Heiban
Dilling
El Odaiya
El Laqâwa
Ed Dueim
Umm Dam
Rufa'a
Kosti
Rabak
WAD MEDANÎ
GEZIRA
Sennar
Singa
El Hawata
Gedaref
Gallabât
Er Roseires
Renk
Melut
Kodok
Malakâl
Fangak
AALI EN NIL
AN NÎL EL AZRAQ
SUDAN
KASSALA
El Khartûm Bahrî (Khartoum)
El Khartûm
Omdurmân
6th Cataract
Shendî
Wad Hamid
Geili
Hamato
El Wuz
El Kamlin
NKASSALA
Kassala
Khashm el Girba
Aroma
Hayya Junction
Derudeb
Sinkat
Haiya Junction
Musmar
Tokar
Agig
Trinkitat
Karora
Nakfa
Eritrea
Akordat
Asmera
Adi Ugri
Barentu
Agordat
Kerem
Mersa
Zula
Adwa
Aksum
Mekele
Metema
4620
L. Tana
Debre Tabor
Gonder
Debre Markos
ETHIOPIA
Addis Abeba (Addis Ababa)
Addis Alem
Nekemte
Dembidolo
Gambela
L. Abaya
4200
Chencha
L. Chamo
Yirgalem
Dila
Arba
Asela
 SUDD
BAHR EL GHAZAL
Râga
Wâw
Gogrial
Toni
Tonj
EL BUHEIRAT
Rumbek
Yirol
Bôr
JONGLEI
Kongor
Pibor P.
Akôbo
Nasir
Sobat
Abwong
Fangak
Malakâl
Duk Fuiwil
Bahr el Ghazal
Deim Zubeir
Tambura
Ezo
Yambio
Maridî
GHARB EL ISTIWA'IYA
HARQ EL ISTIWA'IYA
Jûba
Torit
Kapoeta
KENYA
Lokitaung
Todenyang
L. Turkana
Mega
CENTRAL AFRICAN REPUBLIC
Bangui
Bria
Yalinga
Bakala
Ippy
Bambari
Grimari
Fort Sibut
Bossembélé
Damara
Bozoum
Bouca
Kaga Bandoro
Bossangoa
Batangafo
Kabo
Moyenne-Sido
Ndélé
Ouanda Djallé
Birao
Sarh
Kyabé
Moïssala
Goundi
Bédaya
Koumra
Doba
Baïbokoum
Moundou
Bébédja
Gore
Léré
Pala
Bongor
Fianga
ZAÏRE (CONGO)
Bondo
Ango
Bambili
Niangara
Dungu
Faradje
Monga
Libenge
Businga
Bumba
Lisala
Bosobolo
Gbadolite
Yakoma
Bangassou
Obo
Djema
Zémio
Rafaï
Mobaye

JORDAN
ISRAEL
Tel Aviv-Yafo
Jerusalem (Al Quds)
Gaza
Be'er Sheva
'Ammān
Ma'ān
Al 'Aqabah
Be'er Sheva
Bahr el Mayyit (Dead Sea)
Gebel
El 'Arîsh
Bûr Sa'îd
Dumyât
El Mansûra
Damanhûr
Tanta
El Mahalla el Kubra
Buheiret el Manzala
Isma'îlîya
Bûr Taufîq
El Suweis (Suez)
Port Said
El Qantara
Buheirat-Murrat-el-Kubra
El Iskandarîya (Alexandria)
Rosetta
Rashîd
Zagazig
EL QÂHIRA (Cairo)
EL GÎZA
Helwân
Beni Suef
Gebel el Tîh
Sînâ'
Sinnûris
El Faiyum
SYRIA
Halab
Al Mawşil (Mosul)
Nahr Dijla (Tigris)
Mesopotamia
Hamāh
Hims
Tarabulus
LEBANON
Bayrūt
Dimashq (Damascus)
'Akka
Haifa
Nahr al Furat
IRAQ
Ar Rutbah
Bādiyat ash Shām
SAUDI
ARABIA
An Nafūd
Al Jawf
Tabūk
Taymā'
Mada'in Sālih
Al Muwaylih
Al Wajh
Umm Lajj
Yanbu' al Bahr
Al Madînah
Rābigh
Qasr
Makkah (Mecca)
Jiddah
At Tā'if
Al Lith
RED SEA
BAHR EL AHMAR
Bûr Sûdân (Port Sudan)
2635
Suakin
Muḥammad Qol
Ras Abu Shagara
Mine
Halaib
Ras Hadarba
Bîr Shalatein
Ras Banâs
Bûr Safâga
Quseir
Mersa Matrûh
Qasr Farâfra
Bîr Shalatein
El Qusur (Luxor)
Shotûrat (Great)
40
35
30
25
20
15
10
5

COPYRIGHT. GEORGE PHILIP & SON. LTD.

1 : 7 500 000

50   0   50   100   150   miles
50   0   50   100   150   200   250 km

SUDAN   **ETHIOPIA**

KENYA

SOMALI REP.

UGANDA

ZAÏRE

RWANDA

BURUNDI

TANZANIA

ZAMBIA

MALAWI

MOZAMBIQUE

LAKE VICTORIA

LAKE TANGANYIKA

INDIAN OCEAN

Lake Turkana
(Lake Rudolf)
High Lava Plateau

Kampala
Entebbe
Kigali
Bujumbura (Usumbura)
Gitega
Kigoma-Ujiji
Nairobi
Mombasa and Kilindini
Dar-es-Salaam
Zanzibar
Dodoma
Mtwara
Lindi
Kasama
Mbeya
Iringa
Tabora
Mwanza
Bukavu
Kabale

ft   m
12 000   4000
9000   3000
6000   2000
4500   1500
3000   1000
1200   400
600   200
0   0
200   600
m   ft

Projection: *Modified Polyconic*   East from Greenwich   COPYRIGHT. GEORGE PHILIP & SON. LTD.

1:8 000 000

50 0 50 100 150 200 miles
50 0 50 100 150 200 250 300 km

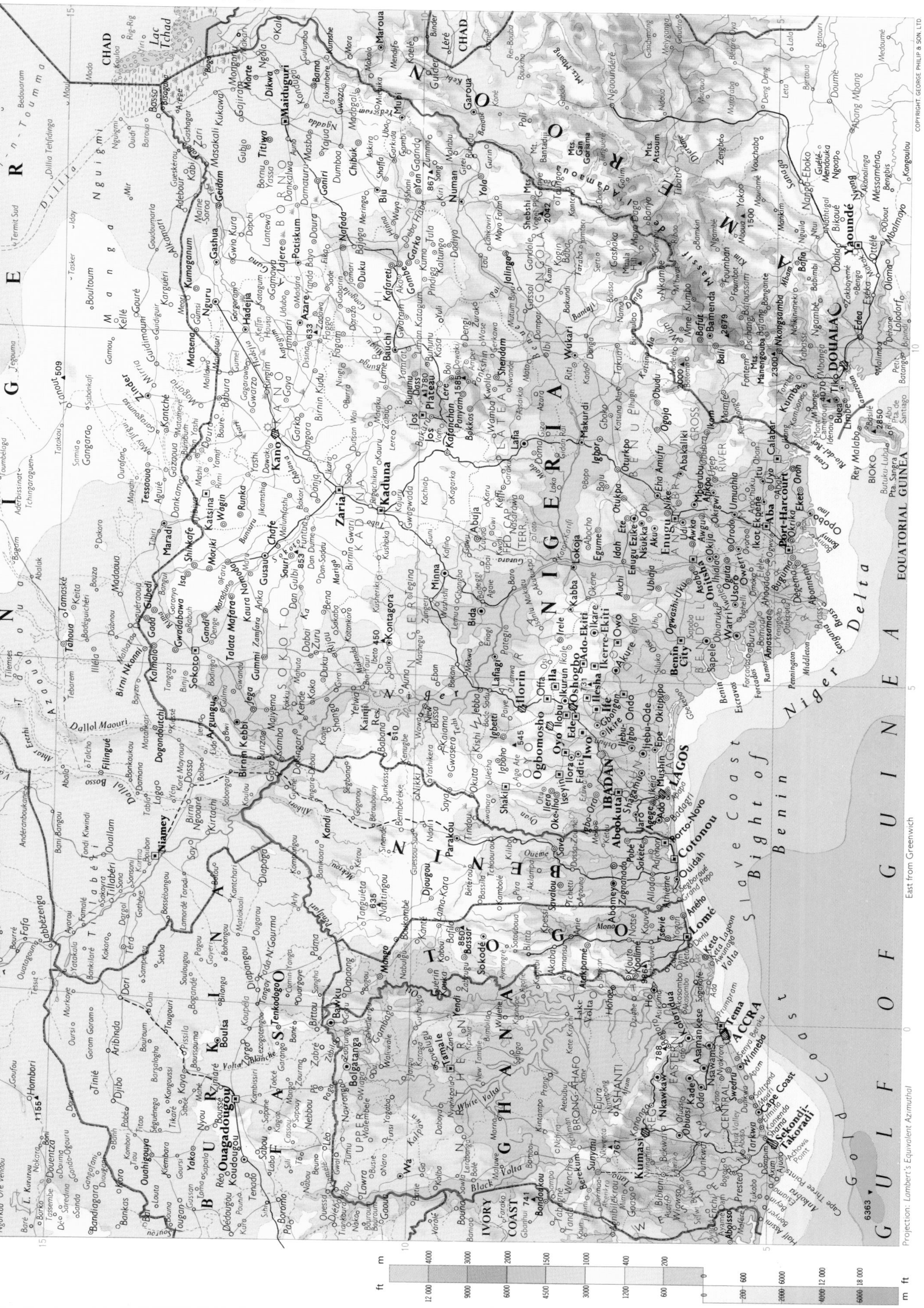

Projection: Lambert's Equivalent Azimuthal

East from Greenwich

CHAD

NIGER

NIGERIA

BENIN

TOGO

GHANA

BURKINA

MALI

CAMEROUN

EQUATORIAL GUINEA

Gulf of Guinea

Bight of Benin

Slave Coast

Niger Delta

LAGOS
IBADAN
ACCRA
Kano
Kaduna
Zaria
Maiduguri
Yaoundé
DOUALA
Port-Harcourt
Ouagadougou
Niamey
Cotonou
Lomé
Tamale
Kumasi
Sekondi-Takoradi

m ft

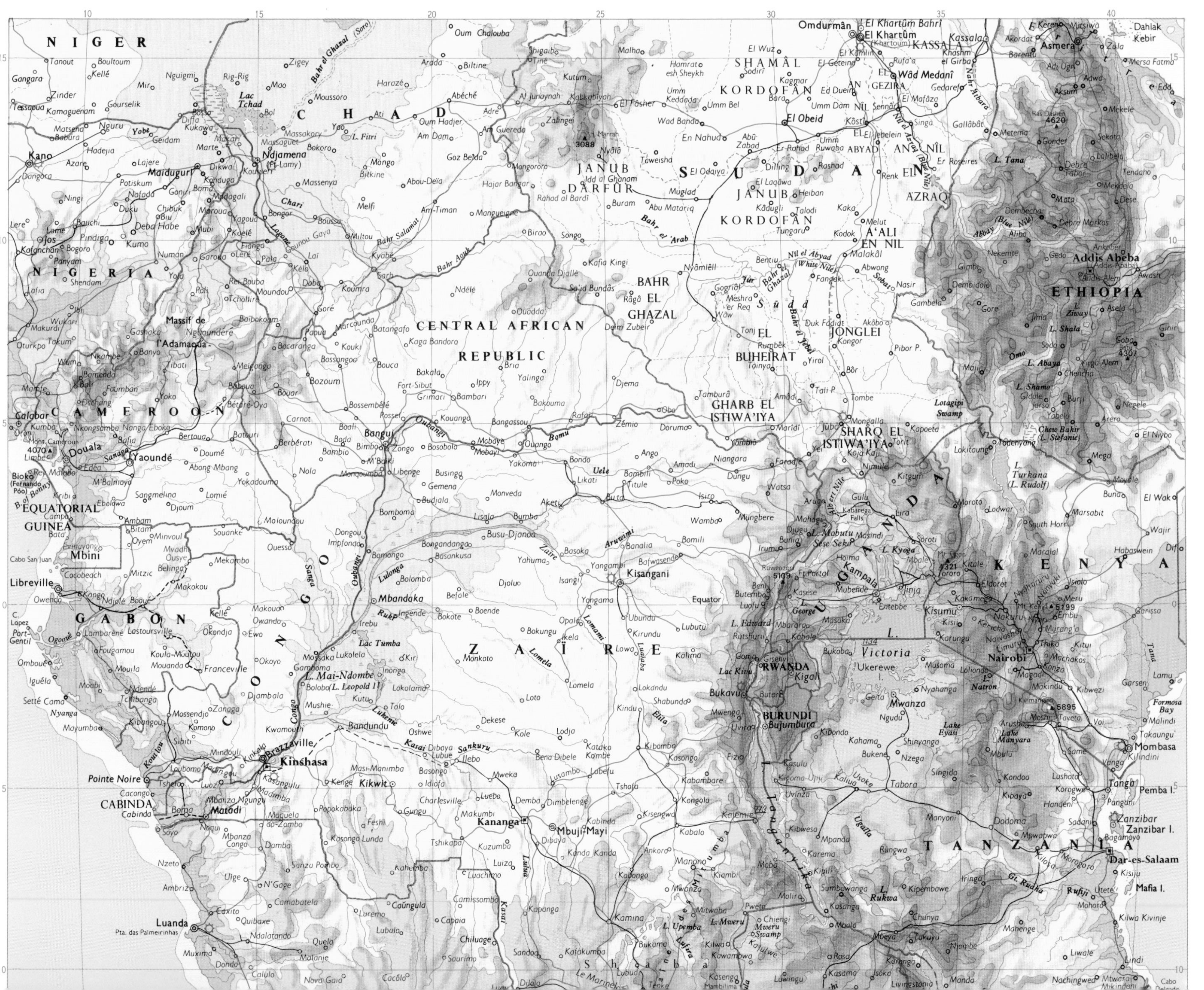

NIGER
CHAD
SUDAN
ETHIOPIA
CENTRAL AFRICAN REPUBLIC
NIGERIA
CAMEROON
EQUATORIAL GUINEA
GABON
CONGO
ZAÏRE
UGANDA
KENYA
RWANDA
BURUNDI
TANZANIA
CABINDA
Addis Abeba
Nairobi
Kinshasa
Brazzaville
Kampala
El Khartûm
Omdurmân
Luanda
Libreville
Yaoundé
Ndjamena
Bangui
Kigali
Bujumbura
Mombasa
Dar-es-Salaam
Asmera
Kisangani
L. Victoria
Lac Tchad

1:15 000 000

100   100   200   300   400 miles
100   0   100   200   300   400   500   600 km

MADAGASCAR
On same scale as General Map

INDIAN OCEAN

INDIAN OCEAN

ATLANTIC OCEAN

Tropic of Capricorn

ZIMBABWE

BOTSWANA
Kalahari

NAMIBIA (SOUTH WEST AFRICA)
Namib Desert
Namaland
Damaraland
Kaokoveld

SOUTH AFRICA

CAPE PROVINCE

ORANGE FREE STATE

TRANSVAAL

NATAL

LESOTHO

SWAZILAND

Caprivi Strip

Okavango Swamps

Harare
Bulawayo
Lusaka
Windhoek
Gaborone
Johannesburg
Pretoria
Bloemfontein
Kimberley
Cape Town
Port Elizabeth
East London
Durban
Pietermaritzburg
Maputo
Beira
Mozambique
Nampula

Mozambique Channel

East from Greenwich

m 6000 4000 3000 2000 1500 1000 400 200 0
ft 18 000 12 000 9000 6000 4500 3000 1200 600 200-500 ft
m

Projection: Sanson Flamsteed's Sinusoidal

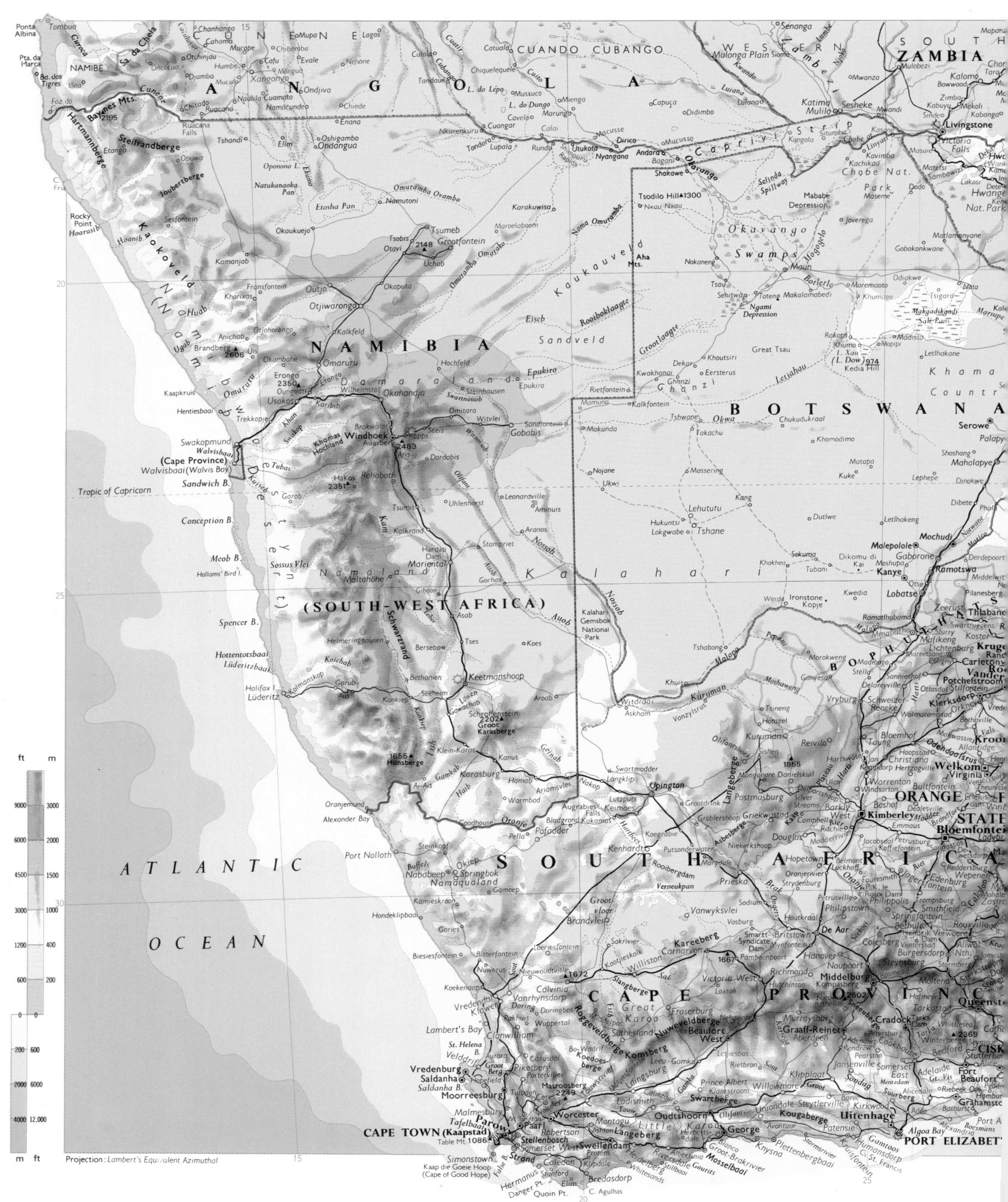

ZAMBIA

ANGOLA

CUANDO CUBANGO

Caprivi Strip

Livingstone

Victoria Falls

Chobe Nat. Park

Okavango Swamps

NAMIBIA

BOTSWANA

Kalahari

(SOUTH-WEST AFRICA)

Tropic of Capricorn

Windhoek

Walvisbaai (Walvis Bay)

ATLANTIC

OCEAN

Lüderitz

SOUTH AFRICA

ORANGE FREE STATE

Kimberley

Bloemfontein

CAPE PROVINCE

Great Karoo

Little Karoo

CAPE TOWN (Kaapstad)
Table Mt 1086

Kaap die Goeie Hoop
(Cape of Good Hope)

C. Agulhas

PORT ELIZABETH

Algoa Bay

CISKEI

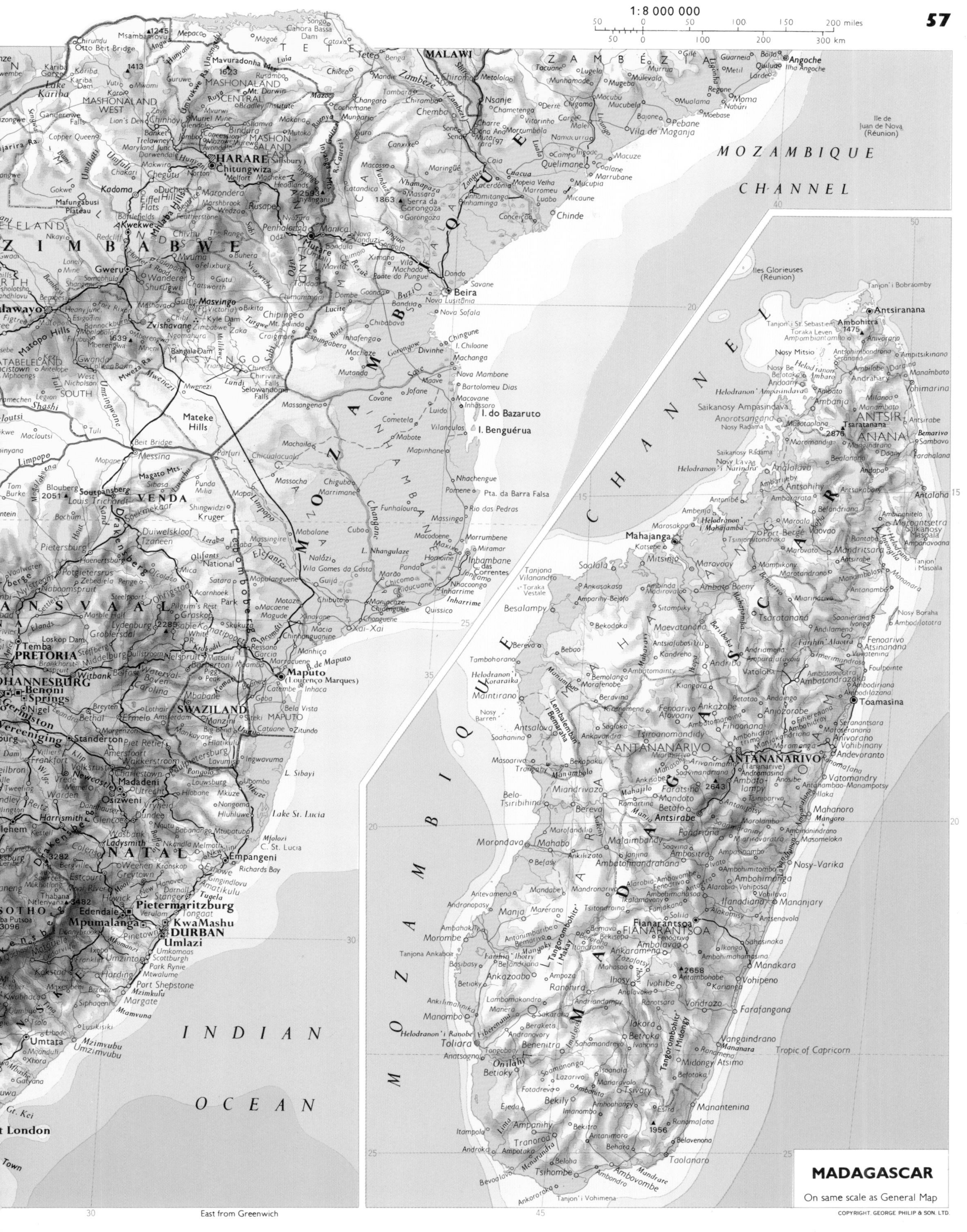

1:8 000 000

50   0   50   100   150   200 miles
50   0   50   100   200   300 km

MOZAMBIQUE

CHANNEL

CHANNEL

INDIAN

OCEAN

MADAGASCAR

On same scale as General Map

COPYRIGHT. GEORGE PHILIP & SON. LTD.

East from Greenwich

1 : 35 000 000

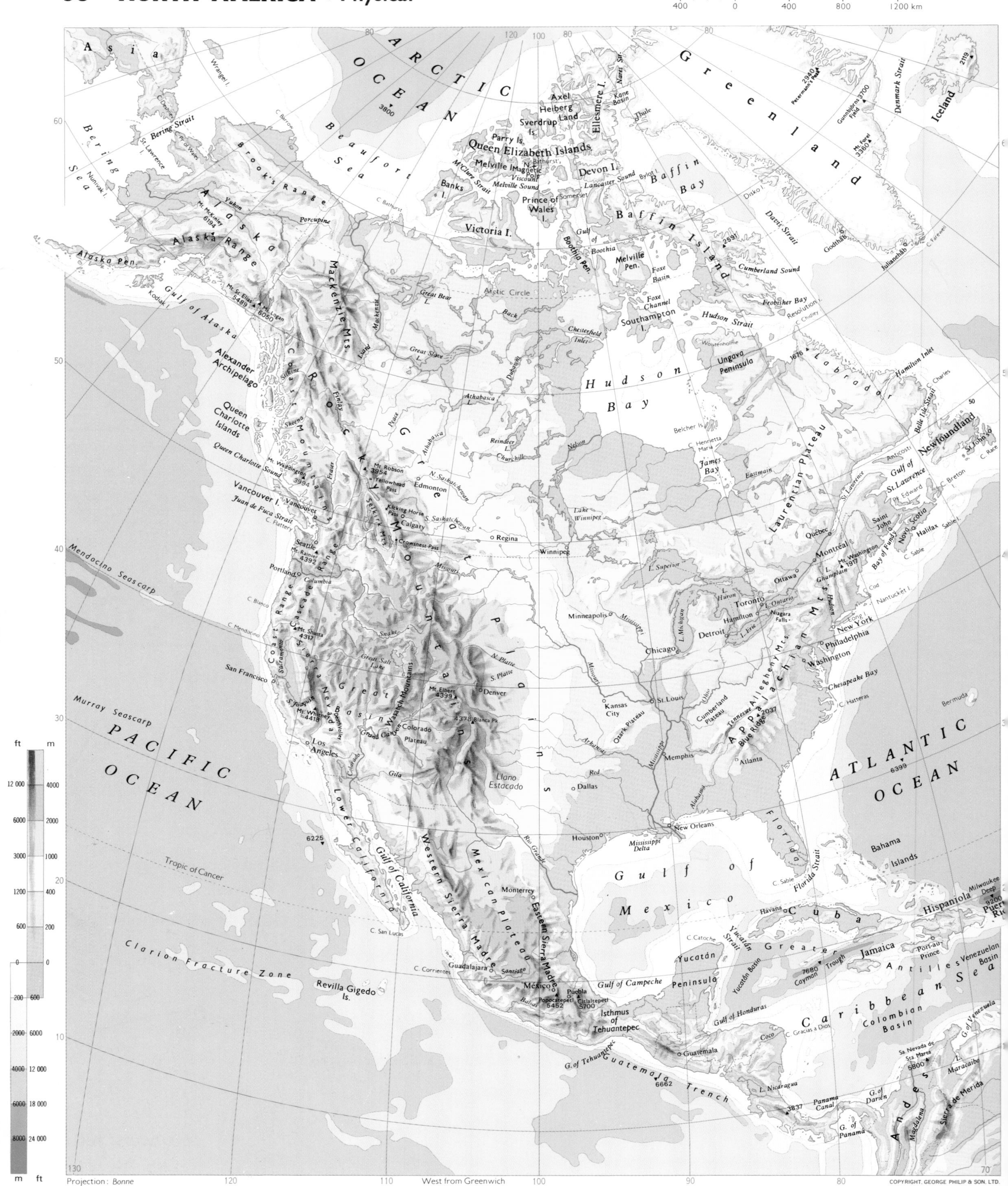

1:35 000 000

200   0   200   400   600   800 miles
400   0   400   800   1200 km

ARCTIC   OCEAN

U.S.S.R.

GREENLAND
(Denmark)

Reykjavik ICELAND
Denmark Strait

Bering Strait
Beaufort Sea

Queen Elizabeth Is.

Ellesmere I.

Bering Sea

Baffin Bay

ALASKA
Yukon
Arctic Circle
Fairbanks
Anchorage

Gulf of Alaska

Porcupine

YUKON TERRITORY
Whitehorse
Juneau

INUVIK

Victoria I.

KITIKMEOT

NORTHWEST TERRITORIES

BAFFIN

Baffin I.

Davis Strait

Godthåb

C. Farell

Mackenzie
Great Bear L.
FORT SMITH
Yellowknife
Great Slave L.
Back
Dubawnt L.

KEEWATIN

Hudson Strait

NEWFOUNDLAND

Hudson Bay

BRITISH COLUMBIA

Skeena
Peace
L. Athabasca
Athabasca

Finlay

ALBERTA
Edmonton
N. Saskatchewan

Fraser

C A N A D A

Churchill
Nelson

MANITOBA

Labrador

Eastmain

QUÉBEC

St. John's

Victoria
Vancouver
Calgary
S. Saskatchewan
Regina

SASKATCHEWAN

L. Winnipeg

ONTARIO

St. Lawrence

PR.
NEW
BRUNS.
EDWARD
WICK
Charlottetown
SPM
NOVA SCOTIA
Halifax

Fredericton
MAINE
Augusta

Quebec
Montréal
Ottawa

WASHINGTON
Seattle
Olympia

Portland
Columbia
Salem
OREGON

IDAHO
Boise
Snake

MONTANA
Helena
Missouri

WYOMING

Winnipeg

NORTH DAKOTA
Bismarck

SOUTH DAKOTA
Pierre

Minneapolis
St. Paul
MINNESOTA

WISCONSIN
Madison
Milwaukee

L. Superior

L. Michigan

MICHIGAN
Lansing

L. Huron

Toronto

L. Ontario
Buffalo
NEW YORK

Montpelier
VER.
Concord
N.H.
Boston
MASS.
Providence
R.I.
Hartford
Albany

Detroit
Cleveland
PENNSYLVANIA
Pittsburgh
Harrisburg

Trenton
N.J.
Philadelphia

Sacramento
San Francisco
San Jose
Carson City
NEVADA

Salt Lake City
UTAH

Cheyenne
N. Platte
NEBRASKA
Lincoln

Des Moines
IOWA

Chicago
ILLINOIS
INDIANA
Indianapolis
Springfield

OHIO
Columbus
Cincinnati
Frankfort

WEST VIRGINIA
Charleston
D.C. Washington
M.D Dover
Annapolis
Baltimore
Richmond
VIRGINIA

CALIFORNIA

Las Vegas

Denver
COLORADO
Arkansas

Topeka
KANSAS
Kansas City

MISSOURI
Jefferson City
St. Louis

KENTUCKY

Nashville
TENNESSEE

Raleigh
NORTH CAROLINA

LOS ANGELES

San Diego

ARIZONA
Phoenix
Tucson
Gila
Colorado

Santa Fe
NEW MEXICO
Albuquerque

OKLAHOMA
Oklahoma City

Little Rock
ARKANSAS
Red River

Memphis

MISSISSIPPI
Jackson

ALABAMA
Birmingham
Montgomery

GEORGIA
Atlanta

Columbia
SOUTH CAROLINA
Charleston

Jacksonville

El Paso
Rio Grande

TEXAS
Austin
Dallas

Houston

LOUISIANA
Baton Rouge
New Orleans

Tallahassee

FLORIDA
Tampa

Miami
C. Sable
Str. of Florida

Bermuda

PACIFIC   OCEAN

ATLANTIC   OCEAN

Tropic of Cancer

M E X I C O

Monterrey

Gulf of Mexico

Havana
CUBA

Nassau
BAHAMAS

Guadalajara

MEXICO

HAITI
Port-au-Prince
DOMINICAN REP.
San Juan
PUERTO RICO
Santo Domingo

JAMAICA
Kingston

Caribbean Sea

Belmopan
BELIZE

GUATEMALA
Guatemala
San Salvador
EL SALVADOR

HONDURAS
Tegucigalpa

NICARAGUA
L. Nicaragua
Managua

COSTA RICA
San José

PANAMA
Panamá

Barranquilla

Maracaibo

VENEZUELA

Medellín
COLOMBIA
Bogotá

SOUTH AMERICA

State capital ⊙

C.	CONNECTICUT	N.H.	NEW HAMPSHIRE
D.	DELAWARE	N.J.	NEW JERSEY
D.C.	DISTRICT OF COLUMBIA	R.I.	RHODE ISLAND
M.	MARYLAND	VER.	VERMONT
MASS.	MASSACHUSETTS	SPM	ST. PIERRE ET MIQUELON

Projection: Bonne

West from Greenwich

COPYRIGHT. GEORGE PHILIP & SON. LTD.

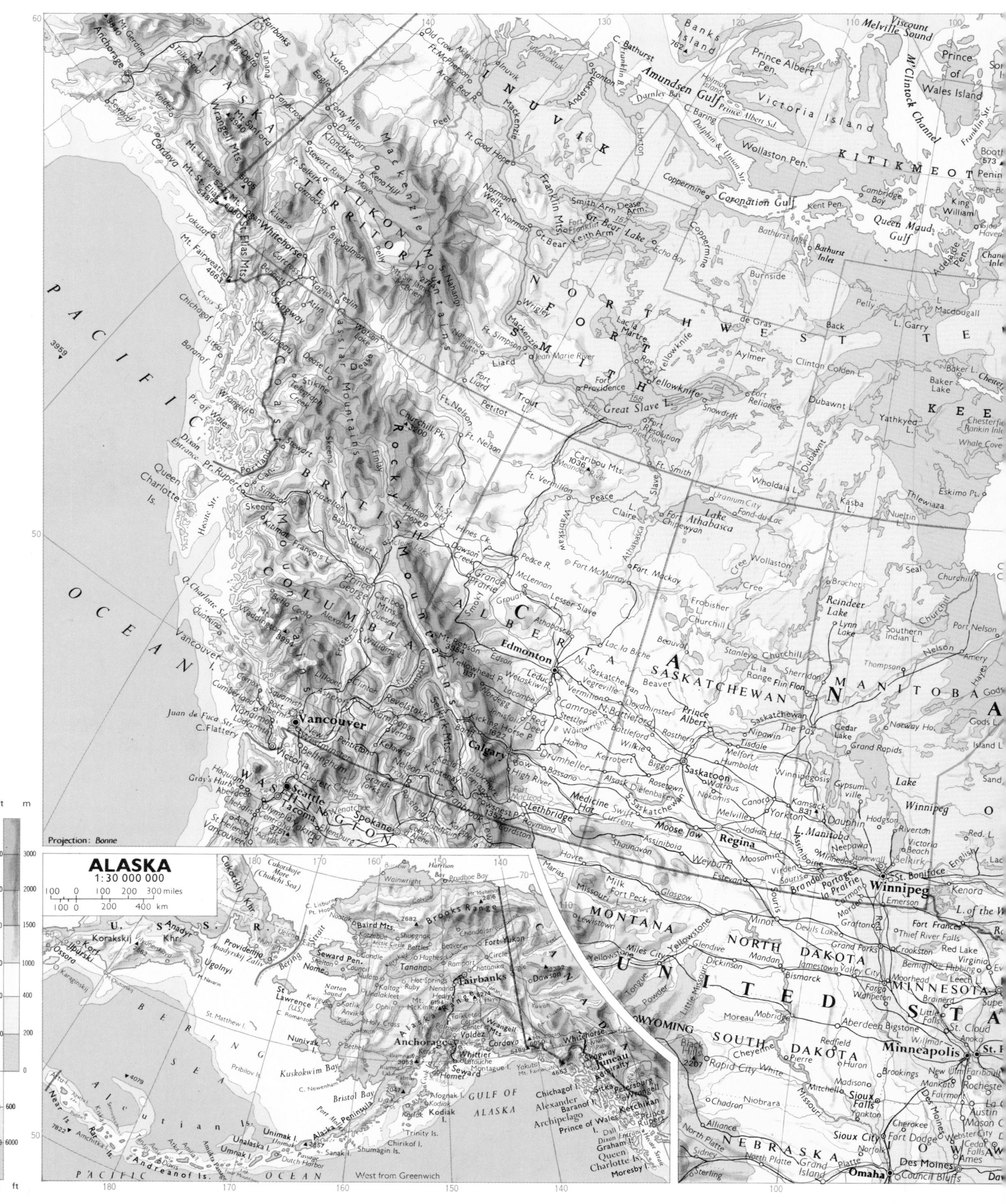

Projection: Bonne

ALASKA
1:30 000 000
100 0 100 200 300 miles
100 0 200 400 km

West from Greenwich

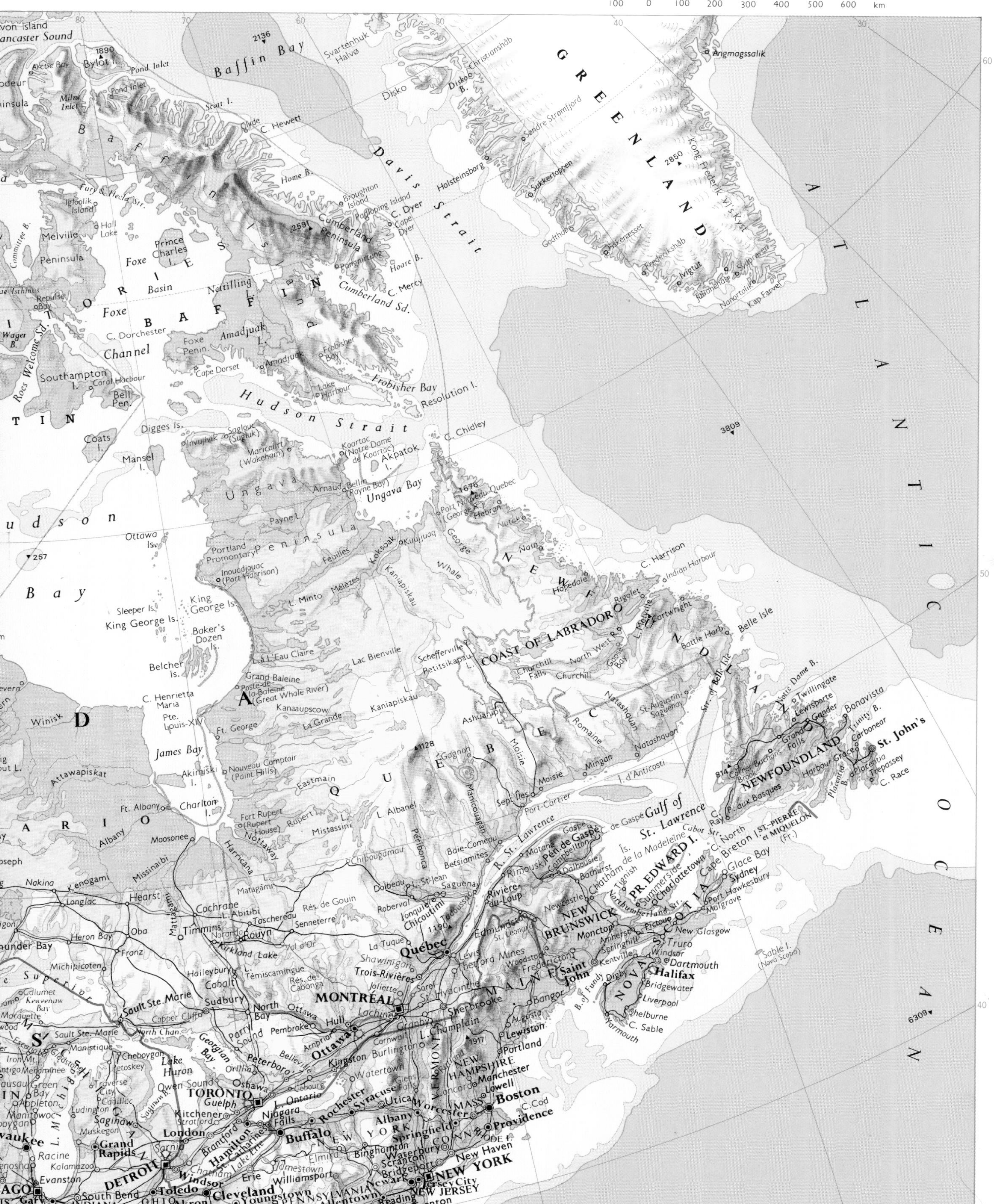

1:15 000 000

100   50   0   100   200   300   400 miles
100   0   100   200   300   400   500   600 km

ATLANTIC

GREENLAND

Angmagssalik

2850

Kong Frederik VI Kyst

Svartenhuk Halvo

Disko

Disko B.

Christianshåb

Sandre Stramfjord

Holsteinsborg

Sukkertoppen

Godthåb

Frederikshåb

Ivigtut

Julianehåb

Nanortalik

Kap Farvel

OCEAN

Baffin Bay

2136

Lancaster Sound

Arctic Bay

Bylot I.

1890

Pond Inlet

Pond Inlet

Scott I.

C. Hewett

Clyde

Home B.

Broughton Island

Pangirtung Island

C. Dyer

Cape Dyer

2591

Cumberland Peninsula

Pangnirtung

C. Mercy

Cumberland Sd.

Hall Lake

Prince Charles I.

Melville Peninsula

Foxe

Basin

Nettilling L.

BAFFIN

Foxe

C. Dorchester

Amadjuak L.

Amadjuak

Cape Dorset

Foxe Penin.

Lake Harbour

Frobisher Bay

Resolution I.

Hudson Strait

C. Chidley

Davis Strait

Repulse Bay

Wager B.

Southampton I.

Roes Welcome Sd.

Coral Harbour

Bell Pen.

Coats I.

Mansel I.

Digges Is.

Inoucdjouac (Saglouc)

Maricourt (Wakeham)

Koartac (Notre Dome de Koartac)

Akpatok I.

3809

Baker's Dozen Is.

King George Is.

Sleeper Is.

Ungava Peninsula

Arnaud (Bellin)

Payne (Bay)

Ungava Bay

Port Nouveau Quebec (George R.)

1676

Hebron

Nutak

Portland Promontory

Inoucdjouac (Port Harrison)

Payne L.

Feuilles

Koksoak

Kuujjuaq

George

Whale

NEW

Nain

Hopedale

C. Harrison

Indian Harbour

Ottawa Isl.

257

Hudson

Bay

King George Is.

Belcher Is.

C. Henrietta Maria

Pte. Louis-XIV

La L'Eau Claire

Lac Bienville

Scheffervile

Petitsikapau L.

L. Minto

Melezes

Kaniapiskau

COAST OF LABRADOR

North West R.

L. Melville

Cartwright

Battle Harb.

Belle Isle

Churchill Falls

Churchill

L

A

B

R

A

D

O

R

Winisk

James Bay

Akimiski I.

Nouveau Comptoir (Paint Hills)

Ft. George

La Grande

Kanaaupscow

Kaniapiskau

Ashuabi

NEWFOUNDLAND

Natashquan

St-Augustin, Saguenay

Romaine

Natashquan

814

Grand Falls

Red Bay

Strs. of Belle Isle

Twillingate

Lewisporte

Gander

Notre Dame B.

Bonavista

Grand Falls

Trinity B.

Carbonear

Harbour Grace

St. John's

Placentia

Trepassey

C. Race

Attawapiskat

Ft. Albany

Charlton I.

Fort Rupert (Rupert House)

Eastmain

Rupert

L. Albanel

Mistassini

L. Albanel

QUEBEC

1128

Gagnon

Moisie

Mingan

J. d'Anticosti

Moosonee

Moose

Nottaway

Harricana

Chibougamau

Peribonca

Baie-Comeau

Betsiamites

R. St. Lawrence

Sept Iles

Port-Cartier

Matane

Gaspé

C. de Gaspé

Gulf of St. Lawrence

Îles de la Madeleine

Cabot Str.

Cape Breton I.

ST-PIERRE et MIQUELON (Fr.)

Missinaibi

Matagami

Rés. de Gouin

Dolbeau

St-Jean

Saguenay

Roberval

Lac St-Jean

Jonquière Chicoutimi

1190

Rimouski

Rivière-du-Loup

Campbellton

Dalhousie

Bathurst

Newcastle

Chatham

NEW BRUNSWICK

Edmundston

St. Leonard

Moncton

Amherst

Springhill

PR. EDWARD I.

Summerside

Charlottetown

C. North

Sydney

Glace Bay

Port Hawkesbury

Mulgrave

New Glasgow

Nakina

Longlac

Hearst

Kenogami

Cochrane

L. Abitibi

Timmins

Rouyn

Kirkland Lake

Val d'Or

Taschereau

Senneterre

La Tuque

Shawinigan

Trois-Rivières

Québec

Lévis

Thetford Mines

Woodstock

Fredericton

Saint John

St-Hyacinthe

Sorel

Granby

Sherbrooke

Bay of Fundy

MAINE

Truro

Windsor

Dartmouth

Halifax

Bridgewater

Liverpool

Shelburne

NOVA SCOTIA

Sable I. (Nova Scotia)

6309

Heron Bay

Oba

Franz

Michipicoten

Sault Ste. Marie

Sault Ste. Marie

Copper Cliff

Sudbury

North Bay

Mattawa

Témiscamingue

Rés. de Cabonga

Haileybury

Cobalt

Thunder Bay

Superior

Keweenaw Bay

Marquette

Iron Mt.

Menominee

Green Bay

Appleton

Oshkosh

Manitowoc

Sheboygan

Racine

Milwaukee

Evanston

CHICAGO

Gary

INDIANA

South Bend

Toledo

Akron

Cleveland

Youngstown

DETROIT

Windsor

Sarnia

London

Chatham

Sault Ste. Marie

Cheboygan

Petoskey

Traverse City

Cadillac

Ludington

Muskegon

Grand Rapids

Kalamazoo

Saginaw

Owen Sound

Georgian Bay

Lake Huron

Parry Sound

Orillia

Barrie

Collingwood

TORONTO

Guelph

Kitchener

Stratford

Brantford

Hamilton

St. Catharines

Niagara Falls

Buffalo

Lake Ontario

Rochester

Syracuse

Utica

NEW YORK

Elmira

Binghamton

Scranton

PENNSYLVANIA

Williamsport

Jamestown

OHIO

Erie

Pembroke

Arnprior

Ottawa

Hull

Lachine

MONTRÉAL

Cornwall

Kingston

Belleville

Cobourg

Oshawa

Peterboro

Lindsay

Watertown

Glens Falls

VERMONT

NEW HAMPSHIRE

Concord

Manchester

Lewiston

Portland

Augusta

Bangor

Burlington

L. Champlain

1917

Albany

Springfield

Worcester

MASS.

Boston

C. Cod

Providence

New Haven

CONN.

Bridgeport

Waterbury

Hartford

Poughkeepsie

Newark

NEW YORK

Jersey City

NEW JERSEY

Trenton

Reading

Allentown

D

RIO

ONTARIO

L. Erie

Joseph

Thunder Bay

West from Greenwich

80   70   60

COPYRIGHT GEORGE PHILIP & SON, LTD

N.W. TERRITORIES

MANITOBA

HUDSON BAY

North Belcher Is.
Baker's Dozen Is.
Kugong I.
Belcher Islands
Flaherty I.
Tukarak I.
Innetalling I.
Merry I.
L. Minto
Nastapoka Is.
Guillaume-Delisle
L. à l'Eau Claire
Petite Baleine
Grand Baleine
Lac Bienville
L. D'Ib...

Polar Bear Provincial Park
Winisk
Wabuk Pt.
C. Lookout
C. Henrietta Maria
Long I.
Pte. Louis-XIV
Kuujjuarapik

JAMES BAY

ONTARIO

Attawapiskat
Akimiski I.
North Twin I.
South Twin I.
Weston I.
Trodely I.
Charlton
Fort George
Nouveau Comptoir
La Grande
Eastmain

Fort Rupert
Rupert House
Broadback
Nemiscau
Némiscau

QUÉBEC

Duluth
Superior
Thunder Bay
Isle Royale
LAKE SUPERIOR
Ashland
Ironwood
Marquette

Timmins
Kirkland Lake
Rouyn
Val-d'Or

WISCONSIN
MICHIGAN

Sault Ste. Marie
Sault Ste. Marie
Elliot Lake
Sudbury
North Bay

LAKE HURON
Georgian Bay
Parry Sound

Green Bay
Traverse City
Manistee
Cadillac

Manitoulin I.
Owen Sound
Barrie
Orillia
Peterborough
Pembroke
Renfrew
OTTAWA
Vanier

Milwaukee
Grand Rapids
Flint
Saginaw
Bay City
Muskegon

TORONTO
HAMILTON
St. Catharines
Niagara Falls
LAKE ONTARIO
Kingston
Brockville
Watertown
ADIRONDACK MOUNTAINS

Madison
Rockford
CHICAGO
Gary
DETROIT
Dearborn
Windsor
London
Sarnia

BUFFALO
Rochester
Syracuse
Utica
Albany

LAKE ERIE
Toledo
CLEVELAND
Lakewood
Sandusky

ILLINOIS   INDIANA   OHIO   PENNSYLVANIA   NEW YORK

Lambert's Equivalent Azimuthal

ft m
4500 1500
3000 1000
1200 400
600 200
0
200 600
2000 6000
4000 12 000
m ft

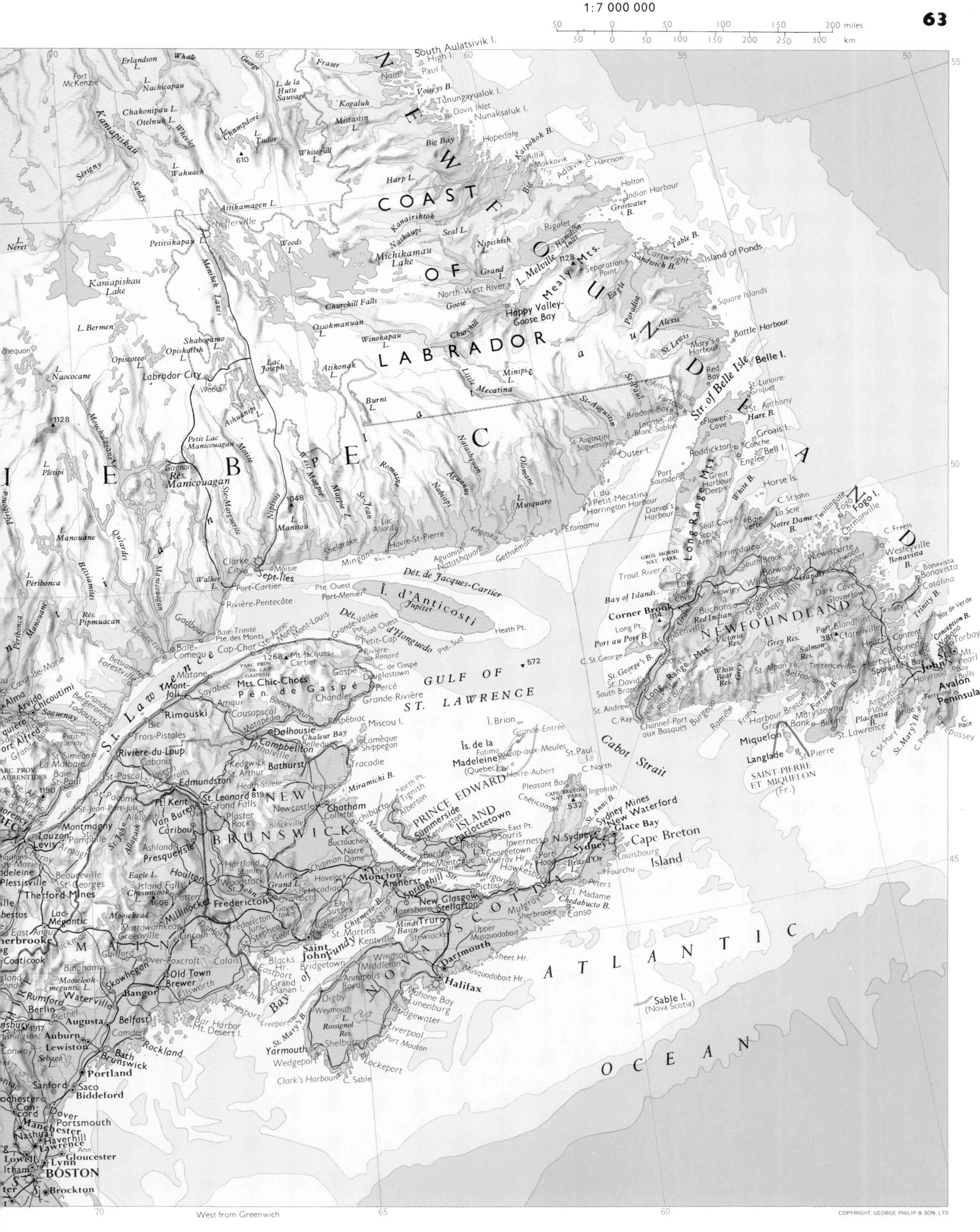

1:7 000 000

50   0   50   100   150   200 miles
50   0   50   100   150   200   250   300   km

N E W   C O A S T   O F   Q U E B E C

L A B R A D O R

Q U E B E C

N E W F O U N D L A N D

South Aulatsivik I.
& High I.
Paul I.
Nain

Fort McKenzie
Erlandson
Whale
George
Fraser
Nachicapau
Kogaluk
Champdoré
I. Tudor
610
Whitegull
Mistastin
Big Bay
Hopedale
Nunaksaluk I.
Davis Inlet
Tunungayualok I.
Voisey's B.
Chakonipau L.
Otelnuk L.
Wheeler

Kaniapiskau

Serigny
Sandy
L. Wakuach
Attikamagen L.
Schefferville
Harp L.
Kanairiktok
Naskaupi
Seal L.
Nipishish
Holton
Indian Harbour
Grosswater B.
Makkovik
Aillik
C. Harrison
Adlavik I.
Bik
Kaipokok B.

L. Neret
Petitsikapau L.
Michikamau Lake
North-West River
Rigolet
Hamilton Inlet
Cartwright
Sandwich B.
Island of Ponds

Kaniapiskau Lake
L. Bermen
Shabogamo L.
Opiscoteo
Opiskottish L.
Churchill Falls
Goose
Happy Valley-Goose Bay
Separation Pt.
Table B.
Square Islands

Chequon
L. Naococane
Labrador City
Wabush
Ossokmanuan
Winokapau
Churchill
Grand
Paradise
Eagle
Alexis
St. Lewis
Mary's Harbour
Battle Harbour

1128
Monoetikona
Gagnon
Rés. Manicouagan
Ashuanipi
Lac Joseph
Atikonak L.
Burnt L.
Little Mecatina
Minipi L.
Mealy Mts. 1128
Red B.
Str. of Belle Isle
Belle I.
St. Lunaire-Griquet
St. Anthony

L. Pletipi
Petit Lac Manicouagan
Moisie
Petit Mécatina
Harrington Harbour
Flower's Cove
Groais I.
Conche
Engle
Bell I.
Roddickton

E   B   E   C
1048
West Maine
Romaine
Nabisipi
Aguanus
St-Augustin
Saguenay
Outer I.
Port Saunders
Long Range Mts.
White B.
Horse Is.
C. St. John
La Scie
Twillingate
Fogo I.

Betsiamites
Manouane
Quitardes
Ste-Marguerite
Clarke City
Moisie
Manitou L.
Sheldrake
Magpie L.
St-Jean L.
Lac Allard
Mingan
Havre-St-Pierre
Aguanish
Natashquan
Kegaska
Gethsémani
Etamamu
Petit-Mécatina
Daniel's Harbour
GROS MORNE NAT. PARK
Baie Verte
Notre Dame Bay
Carmanville
C. Freels

Péribonca
Rés. Pipmuacan
Godbout
Baie-Trinité
Clarke City
Port-Cartier
Rivière-Pentecôte
Pte. Ouest
Port-Menier
Î. d'Anticosti
Jupiter
Dét. de Jacques-Cartier
Heath Pt.
Trout River
Deer Lake
Howley
Springdale
South Brook
Botwood
Lewisporte
Gander
Dark Cove
Glovertown
Bonavista B.
C. Bonavista
Bonavista
Catalina

Péribonca
Betsiamites Forestville
Comeau
Baie-Comeau
Pte. des Monts
Cap-Chat
Mont-Louis
Grande-Vallée
Sud Ouest
Petit-Cap
d'Honguedo
Pte. Sud
572
Bay of Islands
Corner Brook 814
Deer Lake
Pasadena
Buchans
Red Indian L.
Badger
Grand Falls
Bishop's Falls
Gambo
Clarenville
Trinity B.
Bay de Verde
Conception B.

St. Lawrence
Alma
Arvida
Chicoutimi
Baie-St-Marie
1268 Mt. Jacques-Cartier
PARC PROV. DE LA GASPÉSIE
Matane
Mont-Joli
Mts. Chic-Chocs
Gaspé
Douglastown
Percé
GULF OF
ST. LAWRENCE
Long Pt.
Port au Port B.
Stephenville
Victoria L.
Grey Res.
381
Salmon
Terrenceville
C. Pine
Harbour Breton
Placentia
St. John's
Holyrood
Avalon Peninsula

Saguenay
Jonquière
Bergeronnes
Grandes-Bergeronnes
Tadoussac
Sayabec
Amqui
Pén. de Gaspé
Chandler
Grande-Rivière
Bonaventure
Î. Brion
Grande-Entrée
St. George
St. George's B.
St. David's
South Branch
Burgeo
Ramea
Francois
Fortune B.
St. Lawrence
St. Mary's B.
Trepassey
C. Race

Fort Alfred
Petit-Saguenay
La Malbaie
Baie-St-Paul
Trois-Pistoles
Rimouski
Causapscal
Matapédia
Paspébiac
Chaleur Bay
Miscou I.
Lamèque
Shippegan
Tracadie
Îs. de la Madeleine (Quebec)
Cap-aux-Meules
Havre-Aubert
St. Paul
C. North
Cabot Strait
Channel-Port aux Basques
C. Ray
SAINT-PIERRE ET MIQUELON (Fr.)
Miquelon
Langlade
St-Pierre

ARC PROV. LAURENTIDES
St-Siméon
1190
St-Pascal
Dolhousie
Campbellton
Atholville
Kedgwick
St. Arthur
Bathurst
Heath Steele
Negac
Miramichi L.
North Pt.
Alberton
Tignish
PRINCE EDWARD ISLAND
Pleasant Bay
Chéticamp
CAPE BRETON NAT. PARK
532
Ingonish
Inverness
N. Sydney
Sydney Mines
New Waterford
Glace Bay
Cape Breton Island

Rivière-du-Loup
Cabano
Edmundston
St-Léonard 819
Grand Falls
Plaster Rock
N E W
Newcastle
Chatham
Richibucto
Rexton
Buctouche
Summerside
Kensington
Charlottetown
Georgetown
Montague
Souris
East Pt.
Port Hood
Baddeck
Bras d'Or
St. Anns B.
Sydney
Louisbourg

Ft. Kent
Van Buren
Caribou
Presque Isle
Ashland
B R U N S W I C K
Hartland
Woodstock
Minto
Grand L.
Havelock
Petitcodiac
Moncton
Shediac
Cape Tormentine
Borden
Northumberland Str.
Pictou
New Glasgow
Stellarton
Antigonish
Mulgrave
Sherbrooke
Canso
Chedabucto B.
Î. Madame

Houlton
Chesuncook L.
Patten
Millinocket
Fredericton
Oromocto
Gagetown
N O V A
Springhill
Amherst
Parrsboro
Truro
Stewiacke
Upper Musquodoboit
Sheet Hr.
Musquodoboit Hr.

Eagle L.
Island Falls
Moosehead L.
Greenville
Mattawamkeag
Lincoln
M A I N E
St. John
Fredericton Junction
St. Stephen
Calais
St. Martins
S C O T I A
Chignecto B.
Minas Basin
Kentville
Windsor
Dartmouth
Halifax

Dover-Foxcroft
Old Town
Brewer
Bangor
Ellsworth
Machias
Eastport
Grand Manan I.
Blacks Hr.
Saint John
F U N D Y
B A Y   O F
Bridgetown
Annapolis Royal
Middleton
Digby
Weymouth
Mahone Bay
Lunenburg
Bridgewater
A T L A N T I C

Mooselookmeguntic L.
Bingham
Skowhegan
Waterville
Augusta
Belfast
Camden
Rockland
Mt. Desert I.
Bar Harbor
St. Mary's B.
Rossignol L.
Sable I. (Nova Scotia)
Liverpool
Port Mouton

Rumford
Bethel
Auburn
Lewiston
Bath
Brunswick
Portland
Saco
Biddeford
St. Mary's B.
Yarmouth
Wedgeport
Shelburne
Lockeport
Clark's Harbour
C. Sable

Berlin
Conway
Sebago
Sanford
Dover
Portsmouth
Manchester
Nashua
Lawrence
Haverhill
Gloucester
Lynn
Lowell
BOSTON
Brockton

O C E A N

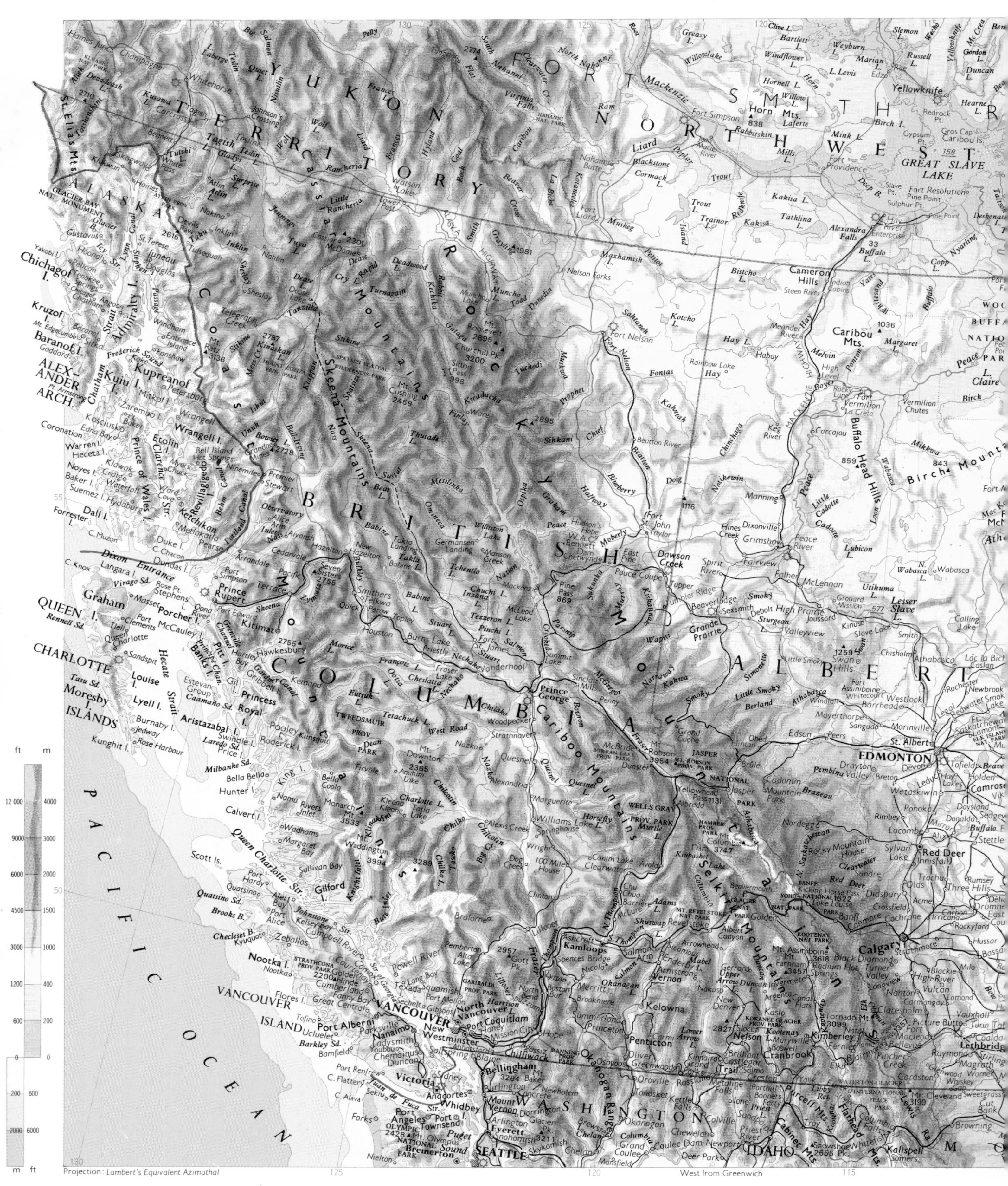
YUKON TERRITORY
NORTHWEST TERRITORIES
BRITISH COLUMBIA
ALBERTA
ALASKA
WASHINGTON
IDAHO
PACIFIC OCEAN
QUEEN CHARLOTTE ISLANDS
VANCOUVER ISLAND
ALEXANDER ARCH.
COAST MOUNTAINS
ROCKY MOUNTAINS
CASSIAR MOUNTAINS
Skeena Mountains
Cariboo Mountains
Selkirk Mountains
Purcell Mts.
Cabinet Mts.
Caribou Mts.
Buffalo Head Hills
Cameron Hills
Horn Mts.
Birch Mountains
GREAT SLAVE LAKE
Yellowknife
Fort Simpson
Fort Providence
Hay River
Fort Resolution
Pine Point
Whitehorse
Carcross
Atlin
Juneau
Skagway
Haines
Sitka
Petersburg
Wrangell
Ketchikan
Prince Rupert
Kitimat
Terrace
Hazelton
Smithers
Prince George
Quesnel
Williams Lake
Fort St. John
Dawson Creek
Fort Nelson
Grande Prairie
Peace River
Edmonton
St. Albert
Red Deer
Calgary
Banff
Jasper
Lethbridge
Kamloops
Vernon
Kelowna
Penticton
Nelson
Trail
Cranbrook
Kimberley
Vancouver
North Vancouver
New Westminster
Port Coquitlam
Victoria
Nanaimo
Port Alberni
Bellingham
Everett
Seattle
Bremerton
Port Angeles
Mt. Robson 3954
Mt. Waddington 3994
Mt. Columbia 3747
Mt. Assiniboine 3618
Mt. Baker 3284
Mt. Roosevelt 2895
Churchill Pk. 3200
Peace
Liard
Fraser
Skeena
Stikine
Athabasca
Mackenzie
Smoky
Dixon Entrance
Hecate Strait
Queen Charlotte Str.
Juan de Fuca Str.
Projection: Lambert's Equivalent Azimuthal
West from Greenwich

1:7 000 000

50   0   50   100   150   200 miles
50 0 50 100 150 200 250 300 km

HUDSON BAY

N TERRITORIES KEEWATIN REGION

SASKATCHEWAN

MANITOBA

ONTARIO

MINNESOTA

NORTH DAKOTA

MONTANA

Lake Athabasca

Reindeer L.
Wollaston L.
Cree L.
Lac la Ronge
Southern Indian L.
Cedar Lake
Lake Winnipegosis
Lake Manitoba
LAKE WINNIPEG
Lake of the Woods

Prince Albert
Saskatoon
Regina
Moose Jaw
Swift Current
Yorkton
Weyburn
Estevan

Flin Flon
The Pas
Dauphin
Brandon
WINNIPEG
Portage la Prairie
Selkirk
Transcona
St. Boniface
Steinbach

Churchill
Thompson
Gillam
Norway House
Island L.
Gods L.
Oxford L.

Kenora
Fort Frances
International Falls
Warroad
Roseau

Minot
Devils Lake
Grand Forks
Williston
Bismarck

Duluth
Bemidji
Grand Rapids
Hibbing

Prince Albert Nat. Park
Riding Mountain National Park
Duck Mtn. Prov. Park
Grass River Prov. Park
Clearwater Prov. Park
Meadow Lake Prov. Park

Fond-du-Lac
Uranium City
Eldorado
Goldfields
Stony Rapids
Key Lake

Hudson Bay
Swan River
Dauphin
Roblin
Russell
Melville
Melfort
Nipawin
Tisdale
Humboldt
Wadena
Wynyard
Watrous
Outlook

Eskimo Point
C. Churchill
Port Nelson
Weir River
York Factory

COPYRIGHT GEORGE PHILIP & SON LTD.

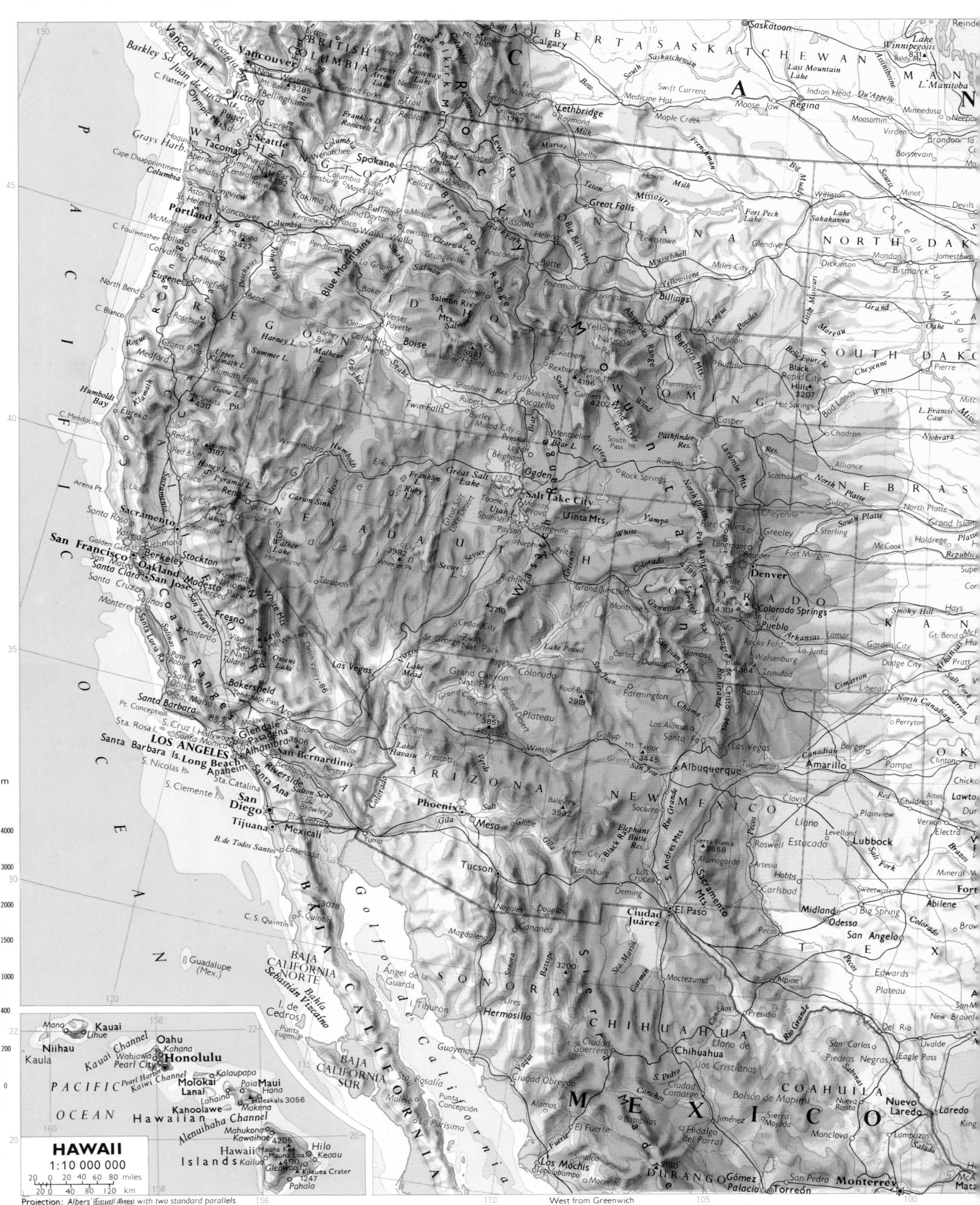

ft   m

12 000   4000

9000   3000

6000   2000

4500   1500

1200   400

600   200

0

200   600

2000   6000

m   ft

HAWAII
1:10 000 000

20 0 20 40 60 80 miles
20 0 40 80 120 km

Projection: Albers' Equal Area with two standard parallels

West from Greenwich

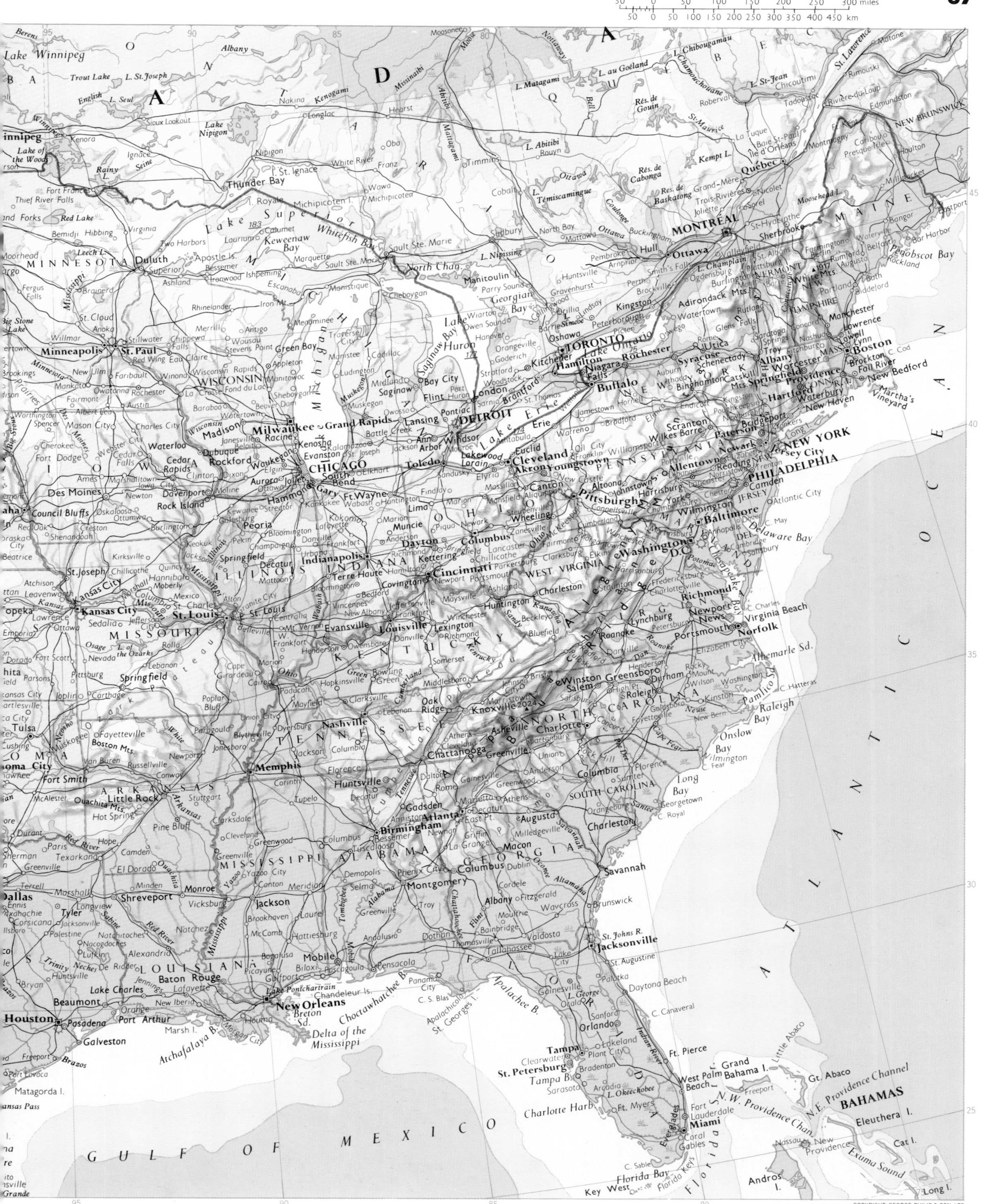

1:12 000 000

50 0 50 100 150 200 250 300 miles
50 0 50 100 150 200 250 300 350 400 450 km

C A N A D A

Lake Winnipeg

MINNESOTA

WISCONSIN

Minneapolis
St. Paul

IOWA

Des Moines

MISSOURI

Kansas City
St. Louis

ARKANSAS
Little Rock

OKLAHOMA

Tulsa

LOUISIANA

Dallas
Shreveport

Houston
Galveston

New Orleans

Baton Rouge

GULF OF MEXICO

MISSISSIPPI

ALABAMA
Birmingham
Montgomery

Memphis

TENNESSEE
Nashville
Chattanooga
Knoxville

Atlanta

GEORGIA

Columbus

Macon

Savannah

FLORIDA

Jacksonville

Orlando

Tampa
St. Petersburg

Miami

BAHAMAS

Lake Superior

Duluth

MICHIGAN

Thunder Bay

Lake Huron

CHICAGO

ILLINOIS

INDIANA

Indianapolis

Milwaukee

Grand Rapids

DETROIT

Lansing

Toledo

OHIO

Columbus

Cincinnati

Louisville

KENTUCKY

Nashville

Springfield

Lake Michigan

Lake Erie

Cleveland

Akron

Pittsburgh

WEST VIRGINIA

Charleston

VIRGINIA

Richmond

NORTH CAROLINA

Charlotte

Raleigh

SOUTH CAROLINA

Columbia

Charleston

Buffalo

TORONTO

Lake Ontario

NEW YORK

PENNSYLVANIA

PHILADELPHIA

Baltimore

Washington

MARYLAND

DELAWARE

Norfolk

Virginia Beach

MONTREAL

Ottawa

MAINE

NEW YORK

Boston

MASS.

NEW BRUNSWICK

Québec

ATLANTIC OCEAN

COPYRIGHT. GEORGE PHILIP & SON. LTD.

QUEBEC

ONTARIO

LAKE SUPERIOR

LAKE HURON

LAKE ONTARIO

LAKE ERIE

Georgian Bay

NEW YORK

VERMONT

NEW HAMPSHIRE

MASS.

CONN.

NEW JERSEY

PENNSYLVANIA

MARYLAND

DELAWARE

WEST VIRGINIA

VIRGINIA

OHIO

INDIANA

KENTUCKY

MICHIGAN

WISCONSIN

ILLINOIS

Chesapeake Bay

MONTREAL

Ottawa

Toronto

Hamilton

Buffalo

Rochester

Syracuse

Albany

BOSTON

NEW YORK

PHILADELPHIA

BALTIMORE

WASHINGTON D.C.

PITTSBURGH

CLEVELAND

DETROIT

TOLEDO

COLUMBUS

Cincinnati

INDIANAPOLIS

CHICAGO

MILWAUKEE

Richmond

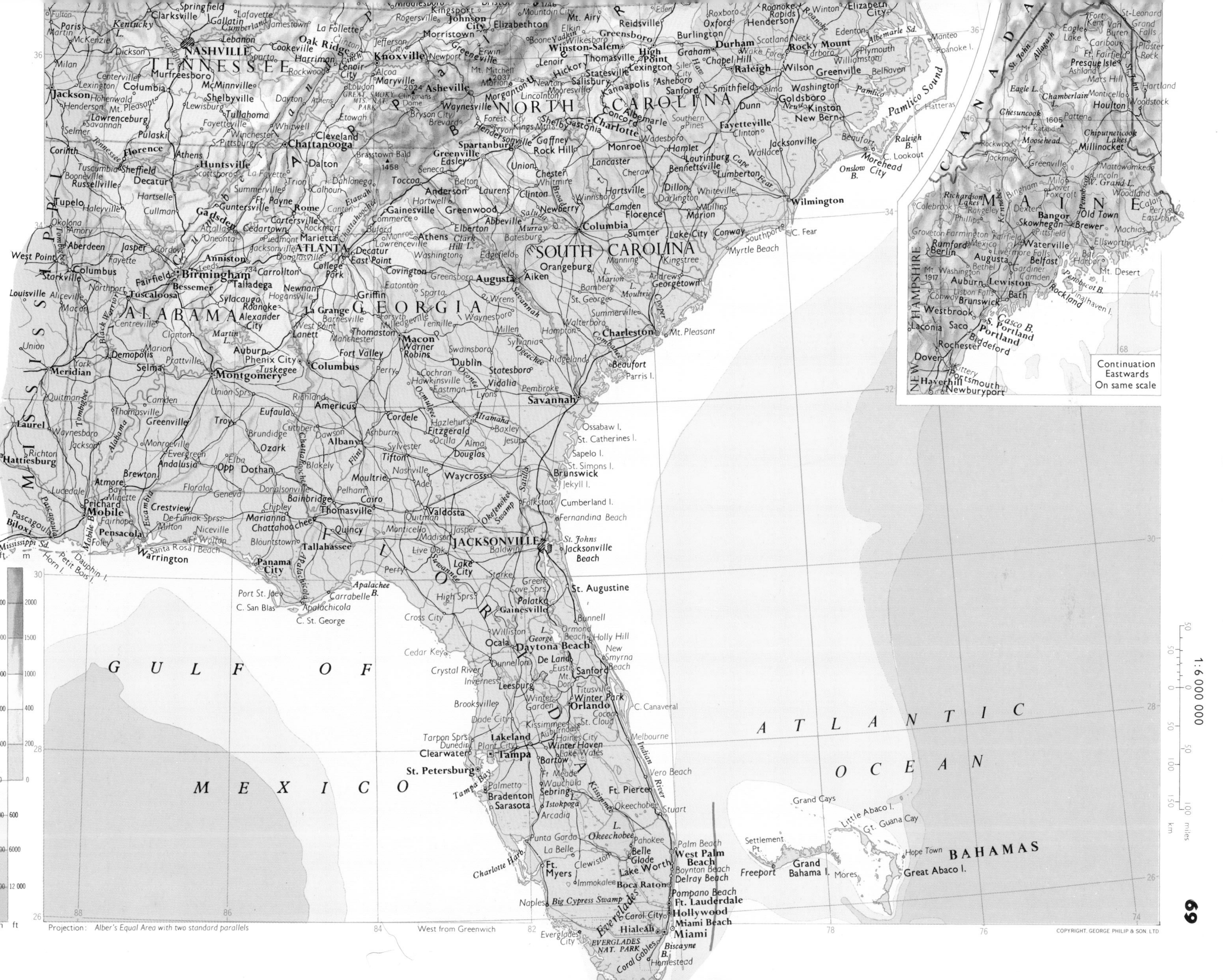

69

1:6 000 000

Continuation Eastwards
On same scale

ATLANTIC OCEAN

BAHAMAS

GULF OF MEXICO

MAINE

NEW HAMPSHIRE

NORTH CAROLINA

SOUTH CAROLINA

GEORGIA

FLORIDA

TENNESSEE

ALABAMA

MISSISSIPPI

KENTUCKY

Projection: Alber's Equal Area with two standard parallels

COPYRIGHT GEORGE PHILIP & SON, LTD

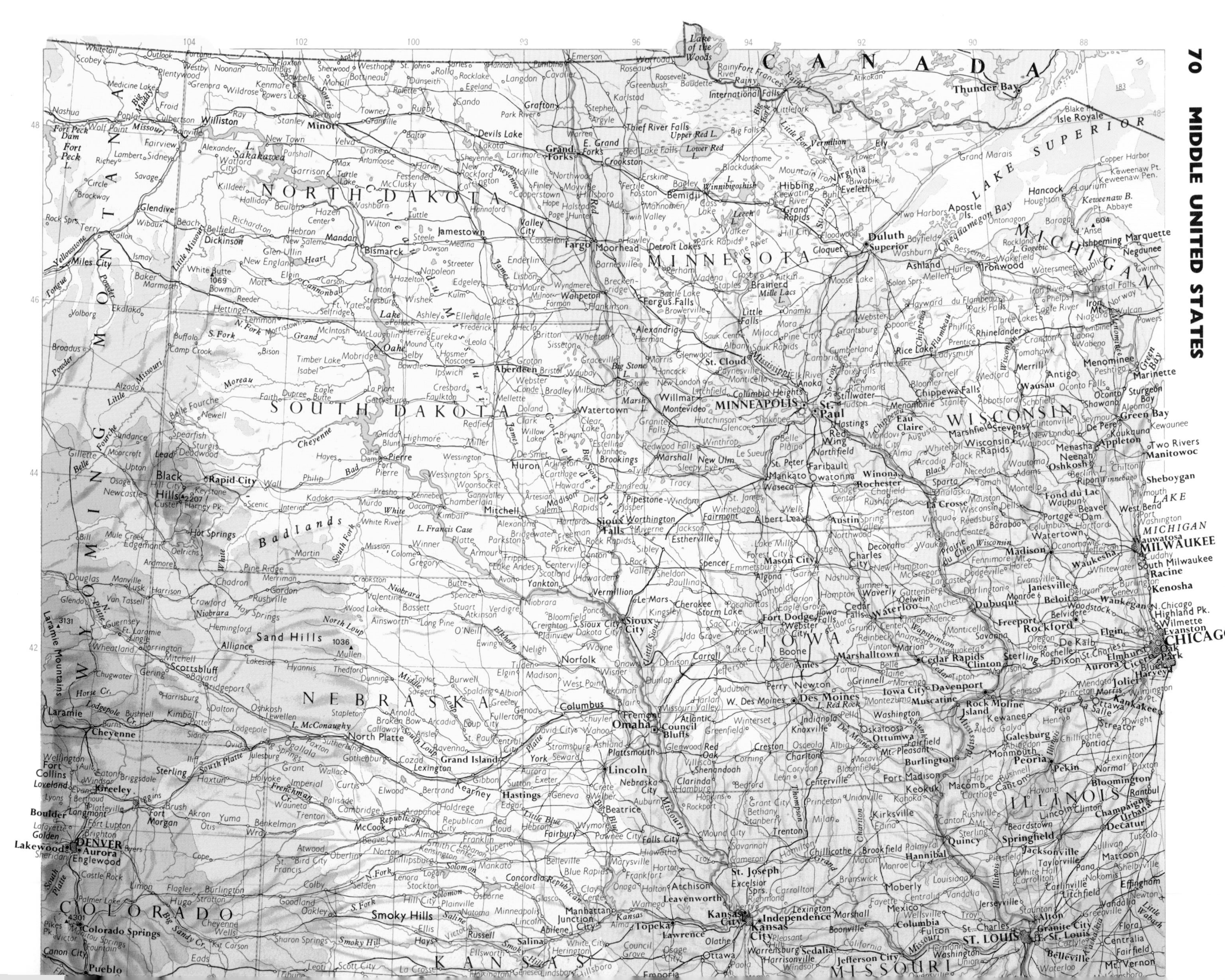
CANADA
LAKE SUPERIOR
LAKE MICHIGAN
MICHIGAN
WISCONSIN
MINNESOTA
NORTH DAKOTA
SOUTH DAKOTA
IOWA
ILLINOIS
MISSOURI
NEBRASKA
KANSAS
COLORADO
WYOMING
MONTANA
CHICAGO
MILWAUKEE
MINNEAPOLIS
St. Paul
Duluth
Superior
Des Moines
Omaha
ST. LOUIS
Kansas City
Lincoln
Topeka
Sioux Falls
Sioux City
Fargo
Bismarck
Pierre
Rapid City
Cheyenne
DENVER
Colorado Springs
Madison
Green Bay
Peoria
Springfield
Rockford
Cedar Rapids
Davenport
Dubuque
Thunder Bay
Lake of the Woods
Black Hills
Badlands
Sand Hills
Laramie Mountains
Smoky Hills
Missouri
Mississippi
Red
Platte

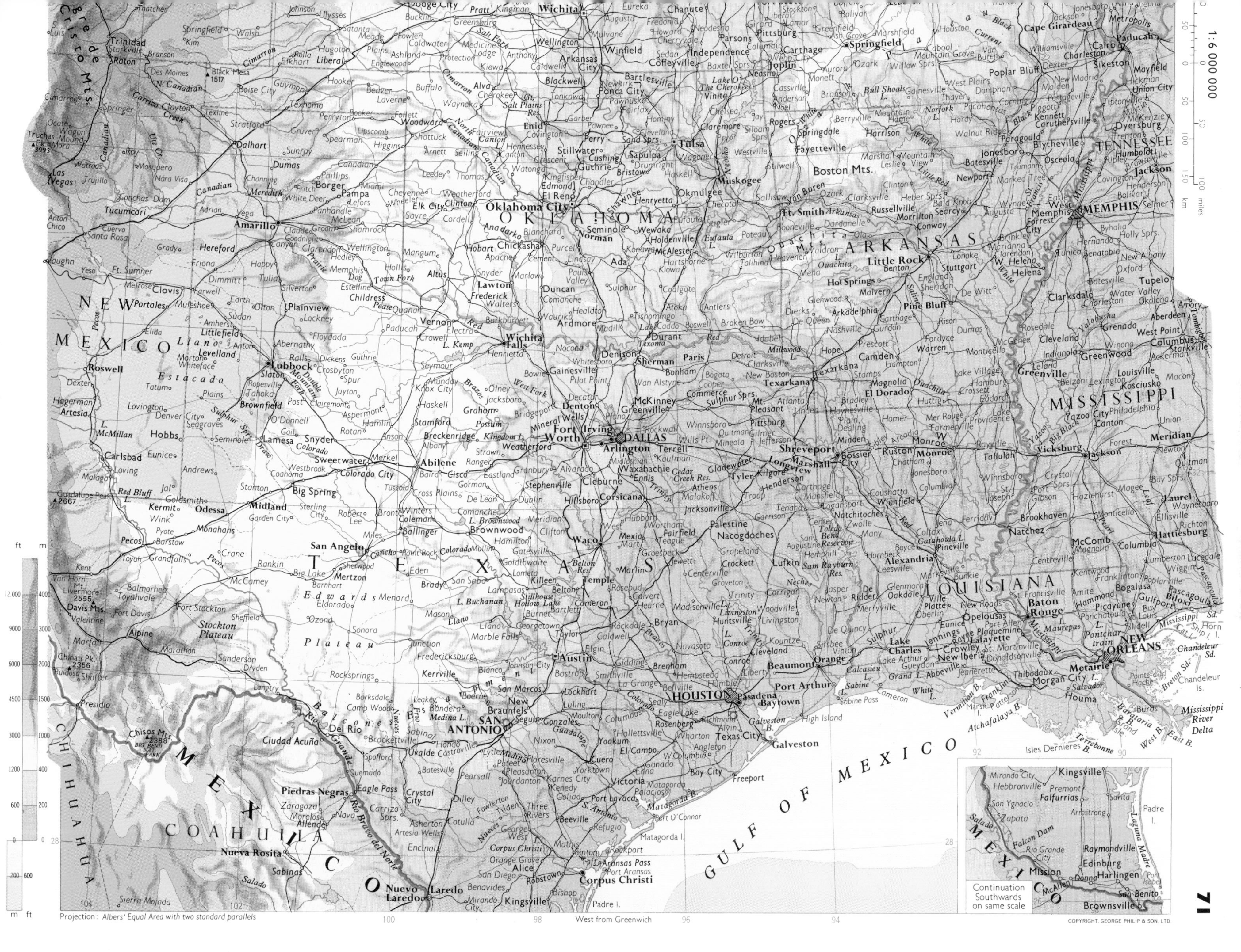
1:6 000 000
0 50 100 miles
0 50 100 150 km
OKLAHOMA
TEXAS
ARKANSAS
LOUISIANA
MISSISSIPPI
TENNESSEE
NEW MEXICO
MEXICO
COAHUILA
CHIHUAHUA
GULF OF MEXICO
Edwards Plateau
Llano Estacado
Ouachita Mts.
Boston Mts.
Stockton Plateau
Sangre de Cristo Mts.
Continuation Southwards on same scale
West from Greenwich
Projection: Albers' Equal Area with two standard parallels
COPYRIGHT GEORGE PHILIP & SON LTD
m 4000 3000 2000 1500 1000 400 200 0
ft 12 000 9000 6000 4500 3000 1200 600 0

1 : 6 000 000

50   50   100 miles
50   0   50   100   150 km

VANCOUVER · **SEATTLE** · **Tacoma** · **Olympia** · **Portland** · **Salem** · **Eugene**

WASHINGTON · **OREGON** · **IDAHO** · **MONTANA** · **WYOMING** · **NEVADA** · **CALIFORNIA** · **UTAH**

BRITISH COLUMBIA · **ALBERTA** · **SASKATCHEWAN**

Bighorn Mountains · Medicine Bow Mts. · Wind River Range · Absaroka Range · Bitterroot Range · Lemhi Range · Salmon River Mountains · Sawtooth Range · Cabinet Mountains · Coeur d'Alene Mountains · Clearwater Mountains · Blue Mountains · Wallowa Mts. · Cascade Range · Coast Range · Olympic Mts. · Shoshone Mountains · Toiyabe Ra. · Independence Mts. · Ruby Mts. · Uinta Mountains

GREAT SALT LAKE · Salt Lake City · Ogden · Provo

Spokane · Billings · Helena · Butte · Bozeman · Missoula · Kalispell · Great Falls · Boise · Pocatello · Idaho Falls · Reno · Carson City · Sacramento · Redding

Yellowstone National Park · Glacier National Park · Crater L. · Columbia · Missouri · Snake · Snake River · Great Sandy Desert · Harney Basin · Alvord Desert · Great Salt Lake Desert

COLORADO

Sangre de Cristo Mts.

San Juan Mts.

NEW MEXICO

TEXAS

CHIHUAHUA

ARIZONA

COLORADO PLATEAU

Grand Canyon

Painted Desert

NEVADA

CALIFORNIA

Death Valley

Mojave Desert

Sonora Desert

LOS ANGELES

Long Beach

SAN DIEGO

PHOENIX

Tucson

MEXICO

SONORA

Golfo de California

BAJA CALIFORNIA

PACIFIC OCEAN

I. de Guadalupe (Mexico)

COPYRIGHT GEORGE PHILIP & SON LTD

Projection : Albers' Equal Area with two standard parallels

West from Greenwich

ft   m   ft

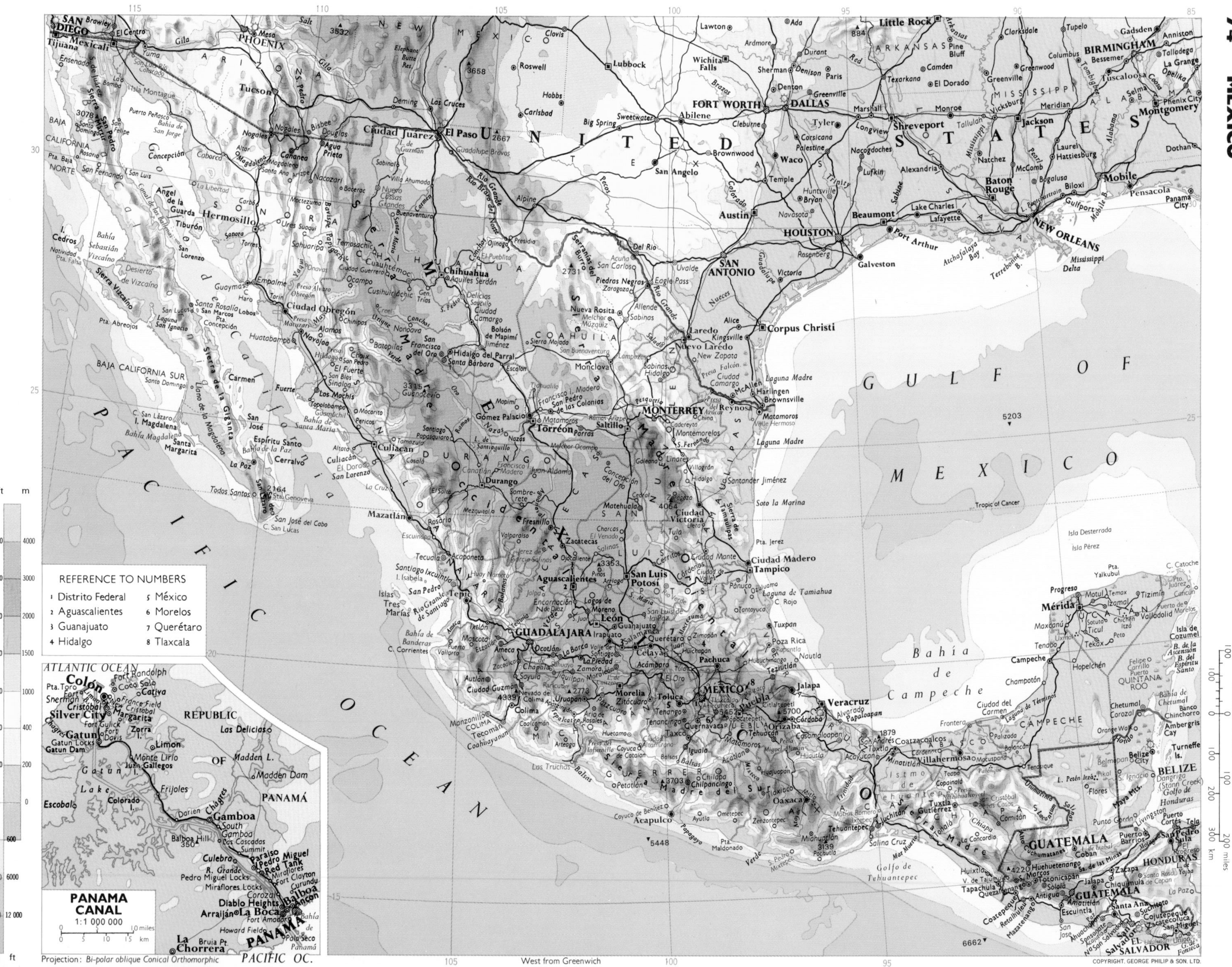

1 : 12 000 000

REFERENCE TO NUMBERS
1 Distrito Federal   5 México
2 Aguascalientes   6 Morelos
3 Guanajuato   7 Querétaro
4 Hidalgo   8 Tlaxcala

PANAMA CANAL
1 : 1 000 000

Projection: Bi-polar oblique Conical Orthomorphic

COPYRIGHT. GEORGE PHILIP & SON. LTD.

1:12 000 000

100   0   100   200 miles
100   0   100   200   300 km

WINDWARD ISLANDS 1:8 000 000

TRINIDAD & TOBAGO 1:8 000 000

JAMAICA 1:8 000 000

LEEWARD ISLANDS 1:8 000 000

BERMUDA 1:1 000 000

ATLANTIC OCEAN

CARIBBEAN SEA

GREATER ANTILLES

LESSER ANTILLES

PACIFIC OCEAN

GULF OF MEXICO

BAHAMAS

CUBA

JAMAICA

HAITI

DOMINICAN REP.

PUERTO RICO

HISPANIOLA

FLORIDA

MEXICO

HONDURAS

NICARAGUA

COSTA RICA

PANAMA

COLOMBIA

VENEZUELA

GUIANA

NETH. ANTILLES

WINDWARD ISLANDS

La Habana
Santiago de Cuba
Kingston
Port-au-Prince
Santo Domingo
San Juan
Caracas
Maracaibo
Barranquilla
Cartagena
Managua
Tegucigalpa
Port of Spain
Bridgetown

Projection: Bi-polar oblique Conical Orthomorphic

West from Greenwich

COPYRIGHT GEORGE PHILIP & SON LTD

1:30 000 000

100 0 100 200 300 400 500 miles
100 0   200   400   600   800 km

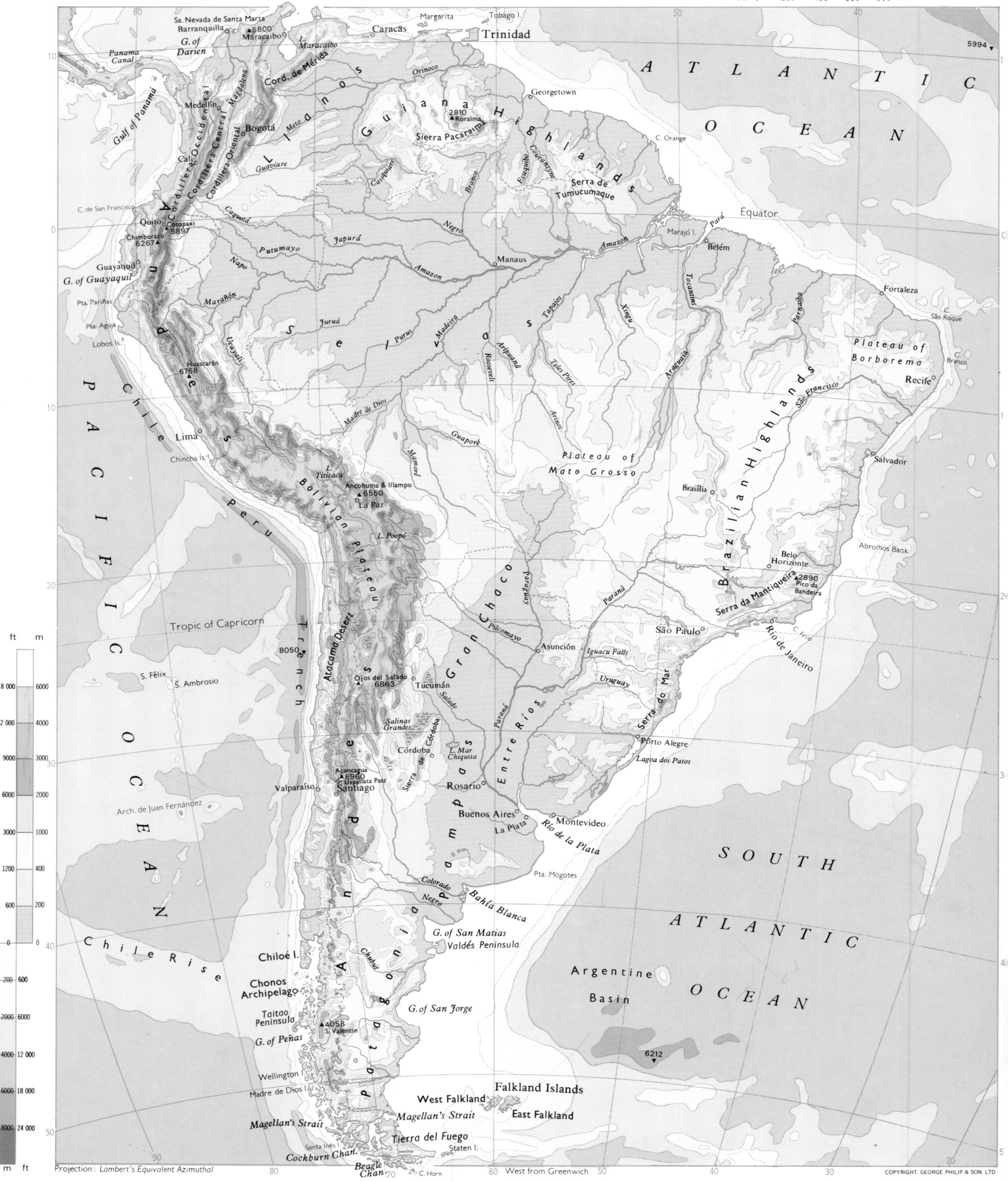

Projection: Lambert's Equivalent Azimuthal

COPYRIGHT. GEORGE PHILIP & SON. LTD.

1 : 30 000 000

100   0   100   200   300   400   500 miles
100   0   200   400   600   800 km

NORTH ATLANTIC OCEAN

PACIFIC OCEAN

SOUTH ATLANTIC OCEAN

COSTA RICA
PANAMA
Golfo de Panamá
San José
David
S.E. 3277
Honolulu 4683

VENEZUELA
COLOMBIA
ECUADOR
PERU
BOLIVIA
PARAGUAY
CHILE
ARGENTINA
URUGUAY
BRAZIL
GUYANA
SURINAM
FRENCH GUIANA
TRINIDAD AND TOBAGO

Barranquilla
Cartagena
Maracaibo
Ciénaga
Cabimas
Barquisimeto
Valencia
Caracas
Cumaná
Maturín
Port of Spain
Trinidad
Isla de Margarita
Punto Fijo
Tobago
Mérida
San Cristóbal
Bucaramanga
Montería
Cúcuta
Golfo de Darién
Medellín
Manizales
Pereira
Ibagué
Bogotá
Cali
Buenaventura
Popayán
Pasto
C. de San Francisco
Quito
Riobamba
Guayaquil
Cuenca
G. de Guayaquil
Ciudad Guayana
Ciudad Bolívar
Orinoco
Meta
Pto. Ayacucho
San Fernando
Georgetown
New Amsterdam
Paramaribo
Cayenne
C. Orange
Macapa
Ilha de Marajó
Belém (Pará)
Equator
São Luís
Manaus
Santarem
Amazon
Tefé
Benjamim Constant
Iquitos
Napo
Putumayo
Japurá
Marañón
Piura
Chiclayo
Trujillo
Chimbote
Cruzeiro do Sul
Ucayali
Juruá
Purus
Madeira
Manicoré
Aripuanã
Tapajós
Xingu
Tocantins
Araguaia
Bacabal
Teresina
Fortaleza (Ceara)
C. de São Roque
Natal
João Pessoa (Paraíba)
Parnaíba
Juazeiro do Norte
Recife (Pernambuco)
Maceió
Aracaju
São Francisco
Salvador (Bahia)
Callao
Lima
Huancayo
Ayacucho
Cuzco
Ica
Islas de Chincha
Pôrto Velho
Rio Branca
Guajará-Mirim
Madre de Dios
Guaporé
Mamoré
Beni
Juliaca
Titicaca
La Paz
Arequipa
Mollendo
Cochabamba
Oruro
Santa Cruz
Corumbá
Culabá
Jataí
Goiânia
Brasília
Montes Claros
Belo Horizonte
Gov. Valadares
Uberaba
Sucre
Tacna
Arica
Iquique
Ulyuni
Tarija
Cuevo
Potosí
Campo Grande
Pedro Juan Caballero
Pres. Prudente
Bauru
Ribeirão Prêto
Juiz de Fora
Campos
Vitória
Niterói
RIO DE JANEIRO
Campinas
Santos
SÃO PAULO
Curitiba
Londrina
Ponta Grossa
Florianópolis
Tropic of Capricorn
Antofagasta
Salta
San Miguel de Tucumán
Resistencia
Posadas
Corrientes
Asunción
Pilcomayo
Paraná
Uruguay
Santa Maria
Pôrto Alegre
Lagoa dos Patos
Pelotas
Uruguaiana
Isla San Félix (Chile)
Isla San Ambrosio (Chile)
Santiago del Estero
Salado
Córdoba
San Juan
Coquimbo
Viña del Mar
Valparaíso
Santiago
Arch. de Juan Fernández (Chile)
Mendoza
San Rafael
Mercedes
Santa Fe
Paraná
Rosario
URUGUAY
Montevideo
La Plata
BUENOS AIRES
Río de la Plata
Talcahuano
Concepción
San Felipe
Talca
Negro
Santa Rosa
Tandil
Mar del Plata
Valdivia
Zapala
Colorado
Bahía Blanca
Puerto Montt
Isla de Chiloé
San Carlos de Bariloche
Viedma
Península Valdés
Trelew
Chubut
Archipiélago de los Chonos
Golfo San Jorge
Comodoro Rivadavia
G. de Penas
I. Wellington
Santa Cruz
Río Gallegos
FALKLAND ISLANDS (ISLAS MALVINAS) (U.K.)
West Falkland
East Falkland
Stanley
Strait of Magellan
Estrecho de Magallanes
Isla Grande de Tierra del Fuego
Cabo de Hornos (Cape Horn)

Projection: Lambert's Equivalent Azimuthal

West from Greenwich

COPYRIGHT. GEORGE PHILIP & SON. LTD.

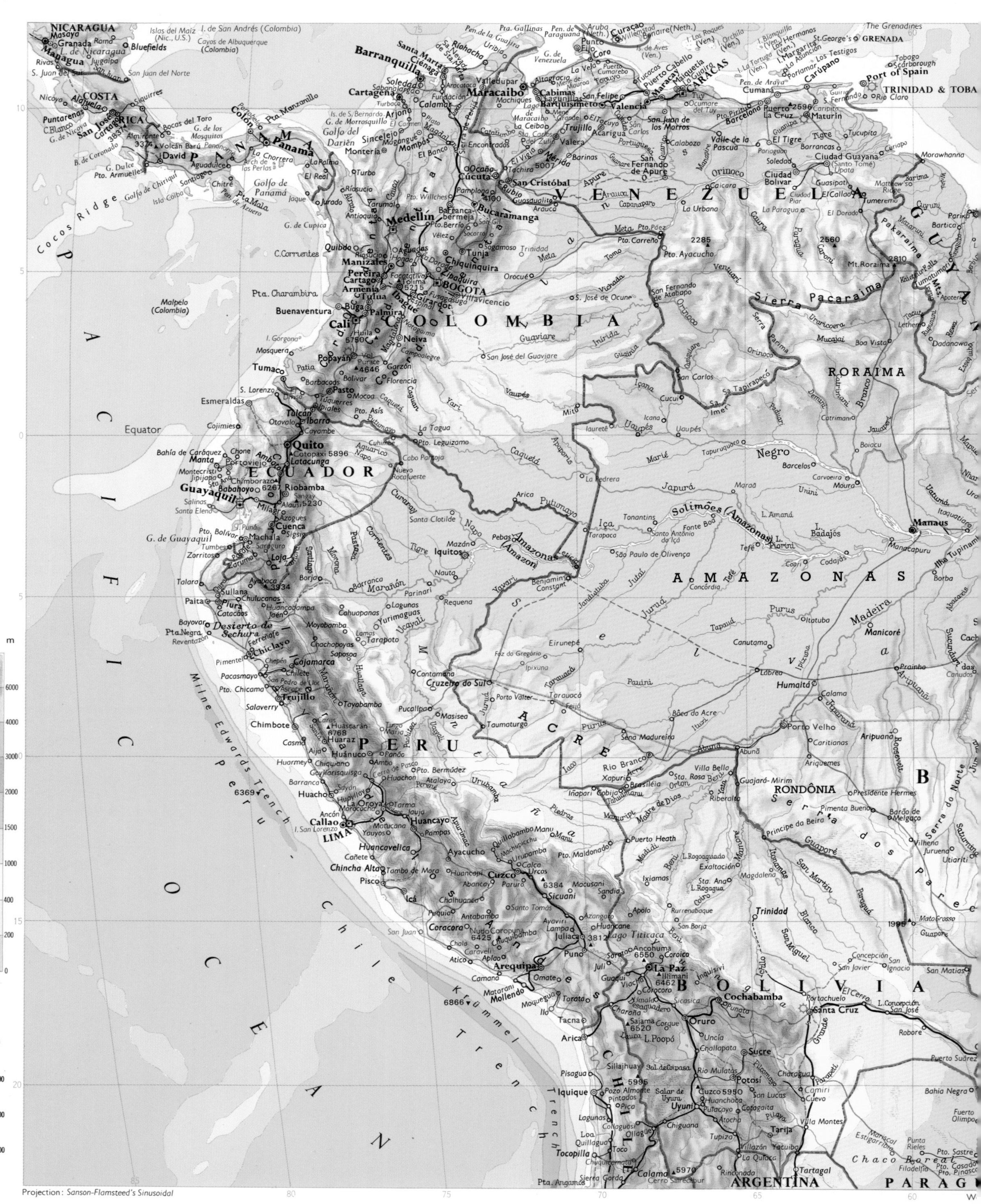

Projection: Sanson-Flamsteed's Sinusoidal

1:16 000 000

100   0   100   200   300   400   500 miles
100   0   100   200   300   400   500   600   700   800 km

A T L A N T I C

O C E A N

Equator

6059

SURINAM
Paramaribo
Nieuw Amsterdam
Moengo   Mana
Albina   St. Laurent   Iracouba   Sinnamary   Kourou
Coronie   Cayenne
Kaw   Approuague
C. Orange

FR. GUIANA
St. Georges   Oiapoque
Camopi
Tumucumaque   Serra
Comani

AMAPÁ
Amapá
Ilha de Maracá
C. do Norte
Araguari
Serra do Navio
Macapá
Estuário do Rio Amazonas
Ilha Caviana
Ilha Mexiana
C. Maguarinho
Curuçá   Salinópolis
Vigia   Igarapé Açu   Bragança
Viseu

Belém (Pará)
Abaetetuba
Turiaçu   Guimarães   São Luís (Maranhão)
Baião   Acará   B. de São Marcos
Cametá   Alcântara   Rosário
Currilinho   Tutóia
Moju   Turiaçu   Breves   Barreirinhas
Igarapé Açu

Santarém
Óbidos   Monte Alegre
Prainha   Almeirim
Gurupá   Afuá   Chaves   Soure
Breves   Muaná

PARÁ
Itaituba   Altamira
Porto de Móz
Jutaí   Baião

Belterra
Aveiro
Brasília Legal

MARANHÃO
Teresina
Bacabal   Codó   Caxias
Coroatá   Timon
Grajaú   Barra do Corda
Imperatriz   Porto Franco   Colinas
Marabá   S. das Carajás
São João dos Patos   Floriano
Carolina   Loreto
Riachão   Amarante
Uruçuí   Nova Iorque
Pedro Afonso   Parnaíba

PIAUÍ
Oeiras
São João do Piauí
Sta. Filomena
Paulistana
Petrolina   Juazeiro
Remanso   Casa Nova
Paulo Afonso

CEARÁ
Fortaleza (Ceará)
Sobral   Cascavel   Aracati
Granja   Itapipoca   Macau
Camocim   Baturité   Russas
Crateús   Quixadá   Mossoró
Iguatu   Orós   Caicó
Crato   Juazeiro do Norte   Cajazeiras

RIO GRANDE DO NORTE
Natal
C. de São Roque
Areia Branca   Ceará Mirim
Currais Novos   Canguaretama
Mamanguape   Cabedelo

PARAÍBA
João Pessoa (Paraíba)
Campina Grande
Caruaru   Limoeiro

PERNAMBUCO
RECIFE
Pernambuco
Olinda
Garanhuns   Pesqueira
Arcoverde   Palmares
Petrolândia   Gouveia
Rio Largo

ALAGOAS
Maceió
Penedo
Arapiraca
Propriá

SERGIPE
Aracaju
São Cristóvão
Estância
Capela

BAHIA
Salvador (Bahia)
Feira de Santana
Santo Amaro
Cachoeira
Alagoinhas
Jacobina   Senhor do Bonfim
Juazeiro   Xique-Xique
Barra   Campo Formoso
Queimadas   Itapicuru
Jequié   Itabuna   Ilhéus
Vitória da Conquista
Canavieiras
Belmonte
Pôrto Seguro
Bom Jesus da Lapa
Barreiras   Paratinga
Caetité   Brumado   Ituaçu
Condeúba   Caravelas
Januária   Salinas

GOIÁS
Brasília
DIST. FED.
Anápolis   Goiânia
Pôrto Nacional
Natividade   Peixe
Manuel Alves
Campos Belos
São Domingos
Posse   Formosa
Niquelândia
Luziânia   Vianópolis
Paracatu

MINAS GERAIS
Belo Horizonte
Uberlândia   Uberaba   Araxá
Divinópolis   Sete Lagoas
Montes Claros
Diamantina
Gov. Valadares
Teófilo Otoni
Nanuque   Prado
Patos de Minas
Patrocínio   Ouro Prêto
Juiz de Fora   Campos
Barbacena   São João del Rei
Poços de Caldas
Caratinga
Ipatinga

ESPÍRITO SANTO
Vitória
Vila Velha
Linhares
São Mateus
Conceição da Barra
Muriaé

RIO DE JANEIRO
Niterói
Petrópolis
Nova Friburgo
Volta Redonda
Cabo Frio

SÃO PAULO
São Paulo
Campinas   Piracicaba
Ribeirão Prêto   Franca
Bauru   Marília
Botucatu   Jaú
Pres. Prudente
Andradina   São Carlos

MATO GROSSO DO SUL
Campo Grande
Três Lagoas
Dourados
Ponta Porã
Água Clara

Planalto do Mato Grosso
GROSSO
Serra do Roncador

B R A Z I L

Rio São Francisco
Chap. do Araripe
Serra do Espinhaço

Fernando de Noronha (Braz.)
Rocas
Atol das Rocas
Abrolhos

Trindade (Braz.)

COPYRIGHT. GEORGE PHILIP & SON, LTD.

1:16 000 000

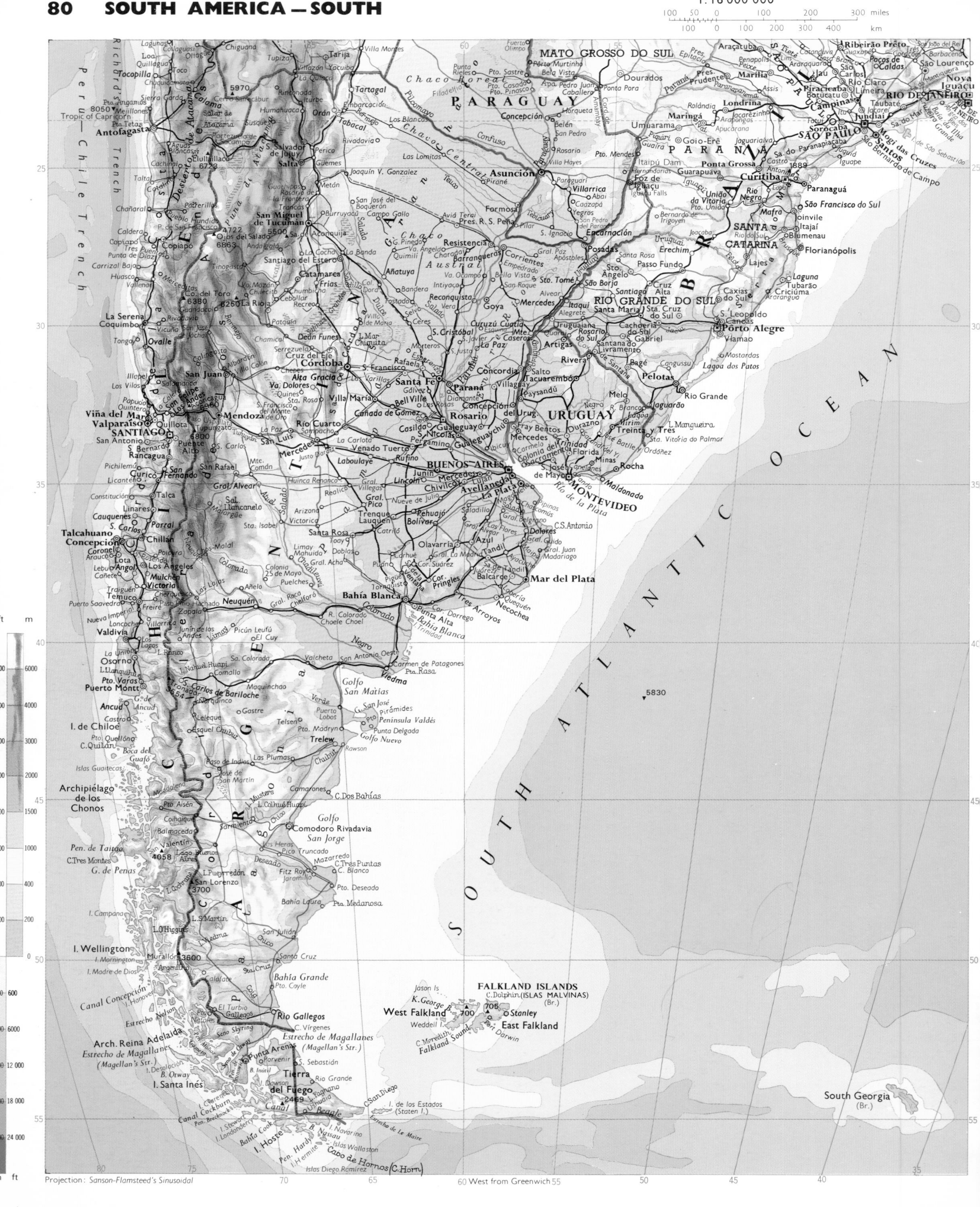

100 50 0   100   200   300 miles
100   0   100   200   300   400 km

Major labels

PARAGUAY

MATO GROSSO DO SUL

BRASIL

PARANÁ

SANTA CATARINA

RIO GRANDE DO SUL

URUGUAY

RIO DE JANEIRO

SÃO PAULO

Tropic of Capricorn

SOUTH ATLANTIC OCEAN

Peru–Chile Trench

FALKLAND ISLANDS (ISLAS MALVINAS) (Br.)
West Falkland
East Falkland
Stanley
Darwin
Jason Is
K. George Bay
Weddell I.
C. Dolphin
C. Meredith
Falkland Sound

South Georgia (Br.)

Cabo de Hornos (C. Horn)
Tierra del Fuego
Estrecho de Magallanes (Magellan's Str.)
Arch. Reina Adelaida
Canal Beagle

Selected cities and towns

Antofagasta, Salta, Asunción, Curitiba, Paranaguá, São Francisco do Sul, Joinvile, Itajaí, Blumenau, Florianópolis, São Paulo, Santos, Campinas, Ribeirão Prêto, Jundiaí, Nova Friburgo, Pôrto Alegre, Pelotas, Rio Grande, Montevideo, Maldonado, Rocha, Buenos Aires, Avellaneda, La Plata, Mar del Plata, Bahía Blanca, Rosario, Santa Fé, Paraná, Córdoba, Mendoza, San Juan, San Luis, Santiago, Valparaíso, Viña del Mar, Concepción, Talcahuano, Temuco, Valdivia, Osorno, Puerto Montt, Ancud, Coihaique, Comodoro Rivadavia, Trelew, Rawson, Viedma, Neuquén, Río Gallegos, Punta Arenas, Río Grande

Elevation scale

ft	m
18 000	6000
12 000	4000
9000	3000
6000	2000
4500	1500
3000	1000
1200	400
600	200
0	0
600	200
6000	2000
12 000	4000
18 000	6000
24 000	8000

Projection: Sanson-Flamsteed's Sinusoidal

West from Greenwich

INDEX

The number in dark type which follows each name in the index refers to the page number where that feature or place will be found.

The geographical co-ordinates which follow the place name are sometimes only approximate but are close enough for the place name to be located.

An open square □ signifies that the name refers to an administrative division of a country while a solid square ■ follows the name of a country.

Rivers have been indexed to their mouth or to where they join another river. All rivers are followed by the symbol →.

The alphabetic order of names composed of two or more words is governed primarily by the first word and then by the second. This is an example of the rule:

> East Tawas
> Eastbourne
> Easter Is.
> Eastern Ghats
> Eastleigh

Names composed of a proper name (*Mexico*) and a description (*Gulf of*) are positioned alphabetically by the proper name. If the same word occurs in the name of a town and a geographical feature, the town name is listed first followed by the name or names of the geographical features.

Names beginning with M', Mc are all indexed as if they were spelled Mac.

Names composed of the definite article (Le, La, Les, L') and a proper name are usually alphabetized by the proper name:

> *Havre, Le*
> *Spezia, La*

If the same place name occurs twice or more in the index and the places are in different countries, they will be followed by the country and be in the latter's alphabetical order:

> *Boston, U.K.*
> *Boston, U.S.A.*

If the same place name occurs two or more times in the index and all are in the same country, each is followed by the name of the administrative subdivision in which it is located. The names are placed in the alphabetical order of the subdivisions. For example:

> *Columbus, Ga., U.S.A.*
> *Columbus, Miss., U.S.A.*
> *Columbus, Ohio, U.S.A.*

If there is a mixture of these situations, the primary order is fixed by the alphabetical sequence of the countries and the secondary order by that of the country subdivisions:

> *Rochester, U.K.*
> *Rochester, Minn., U.S.A.*
> *Rochester, N.Y., U.S.A.*

Below is a list of abbreviations used in the index.

A.S.S.R. – Autonomous Soviet Socialist Republic
Ala. – Alabama
Arch. – Archipelago
Ariz. – Arizona
Ark. – Arkansas
B. – Baie, Bahia, Bay, Boca, Bucht, Bugt
B.C. – British Columbia
Br. – British
C. – Cabo, Cap, Cape
Calif. – California
Chan. – Channel
Col. – Colombia
Colo. – Colorado
Conn. – Connecticut
Cord. – Cordillera
D.C. – District of Columbia
Del. – Delaware
Dep. – Dependency
Des. – Desert
Dist. – District
Dom. Rep. – Dominican Republic
E. – East
Fd. – Fjord

Fed. – Federal, Federation
Fla. – Florida
Fr. – France, French
G. – Golfe, Golfo, Gulf, Guba
Ga. – Georgia
Gt. – Great
Hts. – Heights
I.(s) – Ile, Ilha, Insel, Isla, Island(s)
Ill. – Illinois
Ind. – Indiana
K. – Kap, Kapp
Kans. – Kansas
Ky. – Kentucky
L. – Lac, Lacul, Lago, Lagoa, Lake, Limni, Loch, Lough
La. – Louisiana
Ld. – Land
Mad. P. – Madhya Pradesh
Man. – Manitoba
Mass. – Massachusetts
Md. – Maryland
Mich. – Michigan
Minn. – Minnesota
Miss. – Mississippi
Mo. – Missouri

Mont. – Montana
Mt.(s) – Mont, Monta, Monti, Muntii, Montaña, Mount, Mountain(s)
N. – North, Northern
N.B. – New Brunswick
N.C. – North Carolina
N. Dak. – North Dakota
N.H. – New Hampshire
N.J. – New Jersey
N. Mex. – New Mexico
N.S. – Nova Scotia
N.S.W. – New South Wales
N.Y. – New York
N.Z. – New Zealand
Nat. Park – National Park
Nebr. – Nebraska
Neth. – Netherlands
Nev. – Nevada
Nfld. – Newfoundland
Nic. – Nicaragua
Nig. – Nigeria
Okla. – Oklahoma
Ont. – Ontario
Oreg. – Oregon
P. – Pass, Paso, Pasul

Pa. – Pennsylvania
Pak. – Pakistan
Pass. – Passage
Pen. – Peninsula
Pk. – Peak
Plat. – Plateau
Prov. – Province, Provincial
Pt. – Point
Pta. – Ponta, Punta
Pte. – Pointe
Qué. – Québec
R. – Rio, River
R.S.F.S.R. – Russian Soviet Federative Socialist Republic
Ra.(s) – Range(s)
Rep. – Republic
Res. – Reserve, Reservoir
S. – South
S. Africa – South Africa
S.C. – South Carolina
S. Dak. – South Dakota
S.S.R. – Soviet Socialist Republic
Sa. – Serra, Sierra
Sask. – Saskatchewan

Scot. – Scotland
Sd. – Sound
Sp. – Spain, Spanish
St. – Saint
Str. – Strait, Stretto
Tenn. – Tennessee
Terr. – Territory
Tex. – Texas
U.K. – United Kingdom
U.S.A. – United States of America
U.S.S.R. – Union of Soviet Socialist Republics
Ut. P. – Uttar Pradesh
Va. – Virginia
Vic. – Victoria
Vt. – Vermont
Wash. – Washington
W. – West
W. Va. – West Virginia
Wis. – Wisconsin
Wyo. – Wyoming
Yug. – Yugoslavia

Aachen

A

Aachen 14 50 47N 6 4 E
Aalborg = Ålborg 21 57 2N 9 54 E
A'âli en Nîl □ 51 9 30N 31 30 E
Aalsmeer 11 52 17N 4 43 E
Aalst 11 50 56N 4 2 E
Aalten 11 51 56N 6 35 E
Aarau 14 47 23N 8 4 E
Aare → 14 47 33N 8 14 E
Aarhus = Århus 21 56 8N 10 11 E
Aarschot 11 50 59N 4 49 E
Aba 53 5 10N 7 19 E
Ābādān 30 30 22N 48 20 E
Ābādeh 31 31 8N 52 40 E
Abadla 50 31 2N 2 45W
Abaetetuba 79 1 40S 48 50W
Abagnar Qi 38 43 52N 116 2 E
Abakan 25 53 40N 91 10 E
Abariringa 40 2 50S 171 40W
Abarqū 31 31 10N 53 20 E
'Abasān 28 31 19N 34 21 E
Abashiri 36 44 0N 144 15 E
Abashiri-Wan 36 44 0N 144 30 E
Abay 24 49 38N 72 53 E
Abaya, L. 51 6 30N 37 50 E
Abaza 24 52 39N 90 6 E
Abbay = Nîl el Azraq → 51 15 38N 32 31 E
Abbaye, Pt. 68 46 58N 88 4W
Abbeville, France 12 50 6N 1 49 E
Abbeville, La., U.S.A. 71 30 0N 92 7W
Abbeville, S.C., U.S.A. 69 34 12N 82 21W
Abbieglassie 45 27 15S 147 28 E
Abbotsford, Canada 64 49 5N 122 20W
Abbotsford, U.S.A. 70 44 55N 90 20W
Abbottabad 32 34 10N 73 15 E
Abd al Kūrī 29 12 5N 52 20 E
Abéché 51 13 50N 20 35 E
Åbenrå 21 55 3N 9 25 E
Abeokuta 53 7 3N 3 19 E
Aberaeron 7 52 15N 4 16W
Aberayron = Aberaeron 7 52 15N 4 16W
Abercorn = Mbala 54 8 46S 31 24 E
Abercorn 45 25 12S 151 5 E
Aberdare 7 51 43N 3 27W
Aberdeen, Australia 45 32 9S 150 56 E
Aberdeen, Canada 65 52 20N 106 8W
Aberdeen, S. Africa 56 32 28S 24 2 E
Aberdeen, U.K. 8 57 9N 2 6W
Aberdeen, Ala., U.S.A. 69 33 49N 88 33W
Aberdeen, Idaho, U.S.A. 72 42 57N 112 50W
Aberdeen, S. Dak., U.S.A. 70 45 30N 98 30W
Aberdeen, Wash., U.S.A. 72 47 0N 123 50W
Aberdovey 7 52 33N 4 3W
Aberfeldy 8 56 37N 3 50W
Abergavenny 7 51 49N 3 1W
Abernathy 71 33 49N 101 49W
Abert, L. 72 42 40N 120 8W
Aberystwyth 7 52 25N 4 6W
Abidjan 50 5 26N 3 58W
Abilene, Kans., U.S.A. 70 39 0N 97 16W
Abilene, Tex., U.S.A. 71 32 22N 99 40W
Abingdon, U.K. 7 51 40N 1 17W
Abingdon, Ill., U.S.A. 70 40 53N 90 23W
Abingdon, Va., U.S.A. 69 36 46N 81 56W
Abington Reef 44 18 0S 149 35 E
Abitau → 65 59 53N 109 3W
Abitau L. 65 60 27N 107 15W
Abitibi L. 62 48 40N 79 40W
Abkhaz A.S.S.R. □ 23 43 0N 41 0 E
Abkit 25 64 10N 157 10 E
Abminga 45 26 8S 134 51 E
Abohar 32 30 10N 74 10 E
Abomey 53 7 10N 2 5 E
Abong-Mbang 54 4 0N 13 8 E
Abonnema 53 4 41N 6 49 E
Abou-Deïa 51 11 20N 19 20 E
Aboyne 8 57 4N 2 48W
Abrantes 13 39 24N 8 7W
Abreojos, Pta. 74 26 50N 113 40W
Abri 51 20 50N 30 27 E
Abrolhos, Banka 79 18 0S 38 0W
Abrud 15 46 19N 23 5 E
Abruzzi □ 18 42 15N 14 0 E
Absaroka Ra. 72 44 40N 110 0W
Abū al Khaşīb 30 30 25N 48 0 E
Abū 'Alī 30 27 20N 49 27 E
Abu 'Arīsh 29 16 53N 42 48 E
Abu Dhabi = Abū Ẓāby 31 24 28N 54 22 E
Abū Dīs, Jordan 28 31 47N 35 16 E
Abû Dis, Sudan 51 19 12N 33 38 E
Abū Ghaush 28 31 48N 35 6 E
Abu Hamed 51 19 32N 33 13 E
Abū Kamāl 30 34 30N 41 0 E
Abū Madd, Ra's 30 24 50N 37 7 E
Abu Matariq 51 10 59N 26 9 E
Abu Rudeis 30 28 54N 33 11 E
Abu Tig 51 27 4N 31 15 E
Abû Zabad 51 12 25N 29 10 E
Abū Ẓāby 31 24 28N 54 22 E
Abuja 53 9 16N 7 2 E
Abukuma-Gawa → 36 38 6N 140 52 E
Abunã 78 9 40S 65 20W
Abunã → 78 9 41S 65 20W
Abut Hd. 43 43 7S 170 15 E
Abwong 51 9 2N 32 14 E
Acámbaro 74 20 0N 100 40W
Acaponeta 74 22 30N 105 20W
Acapulco 74 16 51N 99 56W
Acarigua 78 9 33N 69 12W
Acatlán 74 18 10N 98 3W
Acayucan 74 17 59N 94 58W
Accomac 68 37 43N 75 40W
Accra 53 5 35N 0 6W
Accrington 6 53 46N 2 22W
Aceh □ 34 4 15N 97 30 E
Achalpur 32 21 22N 77 32 E
Achill 9 53 56N 9 55W
Achill Hd. 9 53 59N 10 15W
Achill I. 9 53 58N 10 5W
Achill Sound 9 53 53N 9 55W
Achinsk 25 56 20N 90 20 E
Ackerman 71 33 20N 89 8W
Acklins I. 75 22 30N 74 0W
Acme 64 51 33N 113 30W
Aconcagua, Cerro 80 32 39S 70 0W
Aconquija, Mt. 80 27 0S 66 0W
Açores, Is. dos = Azores 2 38 44N 29 0W
Acre = 'Akko 28 32 55N 35 4 E
Acre □ 78 9 1S 71 0W
Acre → 78 8 45S 67 22W
Ad Dahnā 30 24 30N 48 10 E
Ad Dammām 30 26 20N 50 5 E
Ad Dawhah 31 25 15N 51 35 E
Ad Dilam 30 23 55N 47 10 E
Ad Dīwānīyah 30 32 0N 45 0 E
Ada, Minn., U.S.A. 70 47 20N 96 30W
Ada, Okla., U.S.A. 71 34 50N 96 45W
Adaja → 13 41 32N 4 52W
Adam 31 22 15N 57 28 E
Adamaoua, Massif de l' 51 7 20N 12 20 E
Adamawa Highlands = Adamaoua, Massif de l' 51 7 20N 12 20 E
Adamello, Mt. 18 46 10N 10 34 E
Adaminaby 45 36 0S 148 45 E
Adams, N.Y., U.S.A. 68 43 50N 76 3W
Adams, Wis., U.S.A. 70 43 59N 89 50W
Adams, Mt. 72 46 10N 121 28W
Adam's Bridge 32 9 15N 79 40 E
Adams L. 64 51 10N 119 40W
Adam's Peak 32 6 48N 80 30 E
Adana 30 37 0N 35 16 E
Adapazarı 30 40 48N 30 25 E
Adarama 51 17 10N 34 52 E
Adaut 35 8 8S 131 7 E
Adavale 45 25 52S 144 32 E
Adda → 18 45 8N 9 53 E
Addis Ababa = Addis Abeba 51 9 2N 38 42 E
Addis Abeba 51 9 2N 38 42 E
Addis Alem 51 9 0N 38 17 E
Addo 56 33 32S 25 45 E
Adel 69 31 10N 83 28W
Adelaide, Australia 45 34 52S 138 30 E
Adelaide, S. Africa 57 32 42S 26 20 E
Adelaide Pen. 60 68 15N 97 30W
Adelaide River 46 13 15S 131 7 E
Adele, I. 46 15 32S 123 9 E
Aden = Al 'Adan 29 12 45N 45 0 E
Aden, G. of 29 12 30N 47 30 E
Adendorp 56 32 15S 24 30 E
Adi 35 4 15S 133 30 E
Adi Ugri 51 14 58N 38 48 E
Adieu, C. 47 32 0S 132 10 E
Adieu Pt. 46 15 14S 124 35 E
Adige → 18 45 9N 12 20 E
Adilabad 32 19 33N 78 20 E
Adin 72 41 10N 121 0W
Adin Khel 31 32 45N 68 5 E
Adirondack Mts. 68 44 0N 74 15W
Adlavik Is. 63 55 2N 57 45W
Admer 50 20 21N 5 27 E
Admiralty G. 46 14 20S 125 55 E
Admiralty I. 60 57 40N 134 35W
Admiralty Inlet 72 48 0N 122 40W
Admiralty Is. 40 2 0S 147 0 E
Ado 53 6 36N 2 56 E
Ado Ekiti 53 7 38N 5 12 E
Adonara 35 8 15S 123 5 E
Adoni 32 15 33N 77 18W
Adour → 12 43 32N 1 32W
Adra 13 36 43N 3 3W
Adrano 18 37 40N 14 49 E
Adrar 50 27 51N 0 11W
Adré 51 13 40N 22 20 E
Adrī 51 27 32N 13 2 E
Adrian, Mich., U.S.A. 68 41 55N 84 0W
Adrian, Tex., U.S.A. 71 35 19N 102 37W
Adriatic Sea 16 43 0N 16 0 E
Adua 35 1 45S 129 50 E
Adwa 51 14 15N 38 52 E
Adzhar A.S.S.R. □ 23 42 0N 42 0 E
Ægean Sea 17 37 0N 25 0 E
Æolian Is. = Eólie, Is. 18 38 30N 14 50 E
Aerht'ai Shan 37 46 40N 92 45 E
Afars & Issas, Terr. of = Djibouti ■ 29 12 0N 43 0 E
Afghanistan ■ 31 33 0N 65 0 E
Afgoi 29 2 7N 44 59 E
'Afif 30 23 53N 42 56 E
Afognak I. 60 58 10N 152 50W
Africa 48 10 0N 20 0 E
Afuá 79 0 15S 50 20W
Afula 28 32 37N 35 17 E
Afyonkarahisar 30 38 45N 30 33 E
Agadès = Agadez 53 16 58N 7 59 E
Agadez 53 16 58N 7 59 E
Agadir 50 30 28N 9 55W
Agano → 36 37 57N 139 8 E
Agapa 25 71 27N 89 15 E
Agartala 33 23 50N 91 23 E
Agassiz 64 49 14N 121 46W
Agats 35 5 33S 138 0 E
Agattu I. 60 52 25N 172 30 E
Agboville 50 5 55N 4 15W
Agde 12 43 19N 3 28 E
Agen 12 44 12N 0 38 E
Aghil Mts. 32 36 0N 77 0 E
Aginskoye 25 51 6N 114 32 E
Agra 32 27 17N 77 58 E
Agri → 18 40 13N 16 44 E
Ağri Daği 30 39 50N 44 15 E
Ağri Karakose 30 39 44N 43 3 E
Agrigento 18 37 19N 13 33 E
Agrinion 19 38 37N 21 27 E
Água Clara 79 20 25S 52 45W
Agua Prieta 74 31 20N 109 32W
Aguadas 78 5 40N 75 38W
Aguadilla 75 18 27N 67 10W
Aguanish 63 50 14N 62 2W
Aguanus → 63 50 13N 62 5W
Aguarico → 78 0 59S 75 11W
Aguas Blancas 80 24 15S 69 55W
Aguascalientes 74 21 53N 102 12W
Aguascalientes □ 74 22 0N 102 20W
Aguilas 13 37 23N 1 35W
Agulhas, C. 56 34 52S 20 0 E
Agung 34 8 20S 115 28 E
'Agur 28 31 42N 34 55 E
Agusan → 35 9 0N 125 30 E
Aha Mts. 56 19 45S 21 0 E
Ahaggar 50 23 0N 6 30 E
Ahar 30 38 35N 47 0 E
Ahipara B. 43 35 5S 173 5 E
Ahiri 32 19 30N 80 0 E
Ahmadabad 32 23 0N 72 40 E
Ahmadnagar 32 19 7N 74 46 E
Ahmadpur 32 29 12N 71 10 E
Ahmedabad = Ahmadabad 32 23 0N 72 40 E
Ahmednagar = Ahmadnagar 32 19 7N 74 46 E
Ahuachapán 75 13 54N 89 52W
Ahvāz 30 31 20N 48 40 E
Ahvenanmaa = Åland 21 60 15N 20 0 E
Aḥwar 29 13 30N 46 40 E
Aichi □ 36 35 0N 137 15 E
Aigues-Mortes 12 43 35N 4 12 E
Aihui 38 50 10N 127 30 E
Aija 78 9 50S 77 45W
Aiken 69 33 34N 81 50W
Aillik 63 55 11N 59 18W
Ailsa Craig 8 55 15N 5 7W
'Ailūn 28 32 18N 35 47 E
Aim 25 59 0N 133 55 E
Aimere 35 8 45S 121 3 E
Aimorés 79 19 30S 41 4W
Ain □ 12 46 5N 5 20 E
Ain Banaiyan 31 23 0N 51 0 E
Aïn Beïda 50 35 50N 7 29 E
Aïn Ben Tili 50 25 59N 9 27W
Aïn-Sefra 50 32 47N 0 37W
Ainabo 29 9 0N 46 25 E
Ainsworth 70 42 33N 99 52W
Aïr 50 18 30N 8 0 E
Airdrie 8 55 53N 3 57W
Aire → 6 53 42N 0 55W
Airlie Beach 44 20 16S 148 43 E
Aisne □ 12 49 42N 3 40 E
Aisne → 12 49 26N 2 50 E
Aitkin 70 46 32N 93 43W
Aiud 15 46 19N 23 44 E
Aix-en-Provence 12 43 32N 5 27 E
Aix-la-Chapelle = Aachen 14 50 47N 6 4 E
Aiyansh 64 55 17N 129 2W
Aíyina 19 37 45N 23 26 E
Aiyion 19 38 15N 22 5 E
Aizawl 33 23 40N 92 44 E
Aizuwakamatsu 36 37 30N 139 56 E
Ajaccio 12 41 55N 8 40 E
Ajanta Ra. 32 20 28N 75 50 E
Ajdâbiyah 51 30 54N 20 4 E
'Ajmān 31 25 25N 55 30 E
Ajmer 32 26 28N 74 37 E
Ajo 73 32 18N 112 54W
Ak Dağ 30 36 30N 30 0 E
Akaroa 43 43 49S 172 59 E
Akashi 36 34 45N 135 0 E
Akelamo 35 1 35N 129 40 E
Akershus fylke □ 21 60 0N 11 10 E
Aketi 54 2 38N 23 47 E
Akhelóös → 19 38 36N 21 14 E
Akhisar 30 38 56N 27 48 E
Akhmîm 51 26 31N 31 47 E
Akimiski I. 62 52 50N 81 30W
Akita 36 39 45N 140 7 E
Akita □ 36 39 40N 140 30 E
Akjoujt 50 19 45N 14 15W
'Akko 28 32 55N 35 4 E
Akkol 24 45 0N 75 39 E
Aklavik 60 68 12N 135 0W
Akobo → 51 7 48N 33 3 E
Akola 32 20 42N 77 2 E
Akordat 51 15 30N 37 40 E
Akosombo Dam 53 6 20N 0 5 E
Akpatok I. 61 60 25N 68 8W
Akranes 20 64 19N 21 58W
Akreïjit 50 18 19N 9 11W
Akron, Colo., U.S.A. 70 40 13N 103 15W
Akron, Ohio, U.S.A. 68 41 7N 81 31W
Aksai Chih 32 35 15N 79 55 E
Aksaray 30 38 25N 34 2 E
Aksarka 24 66 31N 67 50 E
Aksay 24 51 11N 53 0 E
Akşehir 30 38 18N 31 30 E
Aksenovo Zilovskoye 25 53 20N 117 40 E
Aksu 37 41 5N 80 10 E
Aksum 51 14 5N 38 40 E
Aktogay 24 46 57N 79 40 E
Aktyubinsk 23 50 17N 57 10 E
Aku 53 6 40N 7 18 E
Akure 53 7 15N 5 5 E
Akureyri 20 65 40N 18 6W
Akyab = Sittwe 33 20 18N 92 45 E
Al 'Adan 29 12 45N 45 0 E
Al Aḥsā 30 25 50N 49 0 E
Al Amādīyah 30 37 5N 43 30 E
Al Amārah 30 31 55N 47 15 E
Al 'Aqabah 28 29 31N 35 0 E
Al 'Aramah 30 25 30N 46 0 E
Al Ashkhara 31 21 50N 59 30 E
Al 'Ayzarīyah 28 31 47N 35 15 E
Al Badī' 30 22 0N 46 35 E
Al Başrah 30 30 30N 47 50 E
Al Bāzūrīyah 28 33 15N 35 16 E
Al Bīrah 28 31 55N 35 12 E
Al Bu'ayrāt 51 31 24N 15 44 E
Al Buqay'ah 28 32 15N 35 30 E
Al Fallūjah 30 33 20N 43 55 E
Al Fāw 30 30 0N 48 30 E
Al Fujayrah 31 25 7N 56 18 E
Al Hābah 30 27 10N 47 0 E
Al Haddār 30 21 58N 45 57 E
Al Ḥadīthah 30 34 0N 41 13 E
Al Hāmad 30 31 30N 39 30 E
Al Ḥamar 30 22 23N 46 6 E
Al Ḥamrā' 30 24 2N 38 55 E
Al Ḥarīq 30 23 29N 46 27 E
Al Ḥarīr, W. → 28 32 44N 35 59 E
Al Ḥasakah 30 36 35N 40 45 E
Al Ḥawrah 29 13 50N 47 35 E
Al Ḥayy 30 32 5N 46 5 E
Al Ḥijāz 29 26 0N 37 30 E
Al Ḥillah, Iraq 30 32 30N 44 25 E
Al Ḥillah, Si. Arabia 30 23 35N 46 50 E
Al Hindīyah 30 32 30N 44 10 E
Al Ḥişn 28 32 29N 35 52 E
Al Hoceïma 50 35 8N 3 58W
Al Ḥudaydah 29 14 50N 43 0 E
Al Hufūf 30 25 25N 49 45 E
Al Ḥulwah 30 23 24N 46 48 E
Al Irq 51 29 5N 21 35 E
Al Ittihad = Madīnat ash Sha'b 29 12 50N 45 0 E
Al Jāfūrah 30 25 0N 50 15 E
Al Jaghbūb 51 29 42N 24 38 E
Al Jahrah 30 29 25N 47 40 E
Al Jalāmīd 30 31 20N 39 45 E
Al Jawf, Libya 51 24 10N 23 24 E
Al Jawf, Si. Arabia 30 29 55N 39 40 E
Al Jazirah, Asia 30 33 30N 44 0 E
Al Jazirah, Libya 51 26 10N 21 20 E
Al Jubayl 30 27 0N 49 50 E
Al Jubaylah 30 24 55N 46 25 E
Al Junaynah 51 13 27N 22 45 E
Al Khābūra 31 23 57N 57 5 E
Al Khalīl 28 31 32N 35 6 E
Al Khalūf 29 20 30N 58 13 E
Al Kharfah 30 22 0N 46 35 E
Al Kharj 30 24 0N 47 0 E
Al Kufrah 51 24 17N 23 15 E
Al Kūt 30 32 30N 46 0 E
Al Kuwayt 30 29 30N 48 0 E
Al Lādhiqīyah 30 35 30N 35 45 E
Al Lubban 28 32 9N 35 14 E
Al Luḥayyah 29 15 45N 42 40 E
Al Madīnah 29 24 35N 39 52 E
Al-Mafraq 28 32 17N 36 14 E
Al Majma'ah 30 25 57N 45 22 E
Al Manāmah 31 26 10N 50 30 E
Al Marj 51 32 25N 20 30 E
Al Mawşil 30 36 15N 43 5 E
Al Mazra 28 31 16N 35 31 E
Al Midhnab 30 25 50N 44 18 E
Al Miqdādīyah 30 34 0N 45 0 E
Al Mish'āb 30 28 12N 48 36 E
Al Mubarraz 30 25 30N 49 40 E
Al Muḥarraq 31 26 15N 50 40 E
Al Mukallā 29 14 33N 49 2 E
Al Mukhā 29 13 18N 43 15 E
Al Musayyib 30 32 40N 44 25 E
Al Muwayliḥ 30 27 40N 35 30 E
Al Owuho = Otukpa 53 7 9N 7 41 E
Al Qaḍīmah 30 22 20N 39 13 E
Al Qā'iyah 30 24 33N 43 15 E
Al Qāmishli 30 37 10N 41 10 E
Al Qaşabát 51 32 39N 14 1 E
Al Qaşīm 30 26 0N 43 0 E
Al Qaţīf 30 26 35N 50 0 E
Al Qaţrūn 51 24 56N 15 3 E
Al Quaisūmah 30 28 10N 46 20 E
Al Quds = Jerusalem 28 31 47N 35 10 E
Al Qurayyāt 31 23 17N 58 53 E
Al Qurnah 30 31 1N 47 25 E
Al 'Ulā 30 26 35N 38 0 E
Al Uqaylah ash Sharqīgah 51 30 12N 19 10 E
Al Uqayr 30 25 40N 50 15 E
Al 'Uthmānīyah 30 25 5N 49 22 E
Al 'Uwaynid 30 24 50N 46 0 E
Al' 'Uwayqīlah 30 30 30N 42 10 E
Al 'Uyūn 30 26 30N 43 50 E
Al Wakrah 31 25 10N 51 40 E
Al Wari'āh 30 27 51N 47 25 E
Al Yamāmah 30 24 5N 47 30 E
Al Yāmūn 28 32 29N 35 14 E
Alabama □ 69 33 0N 87 0W
Alabama → 69 31 8N 87 57W
Alagoa Grande 79 7 3S 35 35W
Alagoas □ 79 9 0S 36 0W
Alagoinhas 79 12 7S 38 20W
Alajuela 75 10 2N 84 8W
Alakamisy 57 21 19S 47 14 E
Alakurtti 22 67 0N 30 30 E
Alameda 73 35 10N 106 43W
Alamo 73 36 21N 115 10W
Alamogordo 73 32 59N 106 0W
Alamos 74 27 0N 109 0W
Alamosa 73 37 30N 106 0W
Åland 21 60 15N 20 0 E
Ålands hav 21 60 0N 19 30 E
Alandur 32 13 0N 80 15 E
Alanya 30 36 38N 32 0 E
Alaotra, Farihin' 57 17 30S 48 30 E
Alapayevsk 24 57 52N 61 42 E
Alaşehir 23 38 23N 28 30 E
Alaska □ 60 65 0N 150 0W
Alaska, G. of 60 58 0N 145 0W
Alaska Highway 64 60 0N 130 0W
Alaska Pen. 60 56 0N 160 0W
Alaska Range 60 62 50N 151 0W
Alataw Shankou 37 45 5N 81 57 E
Alatyr 22 54 45N 46 35 E
Alausi 78 2 0S 78 50W
Alava, C. 72 48 10N 124 40W
Alawoona 45 34 45S 140 30 E
Alba 18 44 41N 8 1 E
Alba Iulia 15 46 8N 23 39 E
Albacete 13 39 0N 1 50W
Albacutya, L. 45 35 45S 141 58 E
Albania ■ 19 41 0N 20 0 E
Albany, Australia 47 35 1S 117 58 E
Albany, Ga., U.S.A. 69 31 40N 84 10W
Albany, Minn., U.S.A. 70 45 37N 94 38W
Albany, N.Y., U.S.A. 68 42 35N 73 47W
Albany, Oreg., U.S.A. 72 44 41N 123 0W
Albany, Tex., U.S.A. 71 32 45N 99 20W
Albany → 62 52 17N 81 31W
Albardón 80 31 20S 68 30W
Albarracín, Sierra de 13 40 30N 1 30W
Albatross B. 44 12 45S 141 30 E
Albemarle 69 35 27N 80 15W
Albemarle Sd. 69 36 0N 76 30W
Alberche → 13 39 58N 4 46W

Angellala

Albert, L. = Mobutu Sese Seko, L. ... 54 1 30N 31 0 E
Albert, L. .... 45 35 30S 139 10 E
Albert Canyon 64 51 8N 117 41W
Albert Edward Ra. . 46 18 17S 127 57 E
Albert Lea 70 43 32N 93 20W
Albert Nile → .... 54 3 36N 32 2 E
Alberta □ 64 54 40N 115 0W
Albertinia .... 56 34 11S 21 34 E
Alberton 63 46 50N 64 0W
Albertville = Kalemie 54 5 55S 29 9 E
Albi .... 12 43 56N 2 9 E
Albia 70 41 0N 92 50W
Albina 79 5 37N 54 15W
Albina, Ponta ..... 56 15 52S 11 44 E
Albion, Idaho, U.S.A. 72 42 21N 113 37W
Albion, Mich., U.S.A. 68 42 15N 84 45W
Albion, Nebr., U.S.A. 70 41 47N 98 0W
Ålborg .... 21 57 2N 9 54 E
Alborz, Reshteh-ye Kūhhā-ye ...... 31 36 0N 52 0 E
Albreda 64 52 35N 119 10W
Albuquerque 73 35 5N 106 47W
Albuquerque, Cayos de 75 12 10N 81 50W
Alburquerque 13 39 15N 6 59W
Albury .... 45 36 3S 146 56 E
Alcalá de Henares . 13 40 28N 3 22W
Alcalá la Real 13 37 27N 3 57W
Alcamo .... 18 37 59N 12 55 E
Alcañiz 13 41 2N 0 8W
Alcântara, Brazil .. 79 2 20S 44 30W
Alcántara, Spain .. 13 39 41N 6 57W
Alcantara L. 65 60 57N 108 9W
Alcaraz, Sierra de . 13 38 40N 2 20W
Alcaudete 13 37 35N 4 5W
Alcázar de San Juan 13 39 24N 3 12W
Alcira 13 39 9N 0 30W
Alcoa 69 35 50N 84 0W
Alcobaça 13 39 32N 9 0W
Alcova 72 42 37N 106 52W
Alcoy 13 38 43N 0 30W
Aldabra Is. .... 3 9 22S 46 28 E
Aldan .... 25 58 40N 125 30 E
Aldan → .... 25 63 28N 129 35 E
Aldeburgh .... 7 52 9N 1 35 E
Alder 72 45 27N 112 3W
Alderney 7 49 42N 2 12W
Aldershot 7 51 15N 0 43W
Aledo 70 41 10N 90 50W
Aleg 50 17 3N 13 55W
Alegrete 80 29 40S 56 0W
Aleisk .... 24 52 40N 83 0 E
Alejandro Selkirk, I. 41 33 50S 80 15W
Aleksandrovsk-Sakhalinskiy .... 25 50 50N 142 20 E
Aleksandrovskiy Zavod .... 25 50 40N 117 50 E
Aleksandrovskoye . 24 60 35N 77 50 E
Alemania 80 25 40S 65 30W
Alençon .... 12 48 27N 0 4 E
Alenuihaha Chan. . 66 20 25N 156 0W
Aleppo = Ḥalab ... 30 36 10N 37 15 E
Aléria .... 18 42 5N 9 26 E
Alert Bay 64 50 30N 126 55W
Alès .... 12 44 9N 4 5 E
Alessándria ...... 18 44 54N 8 37 E
Ålesund .... 20 62 28N 6 12 E
Aleutian Is. 60 52 0N 175 0W
Aleutian Trench ... 40 48 0N 180 0 E
Alexander 70 47 51N 103 40W
Alexander, Mt. .... 47 28 58S 120 16 E
Alexander Arch. 60 57 0N 135 0W
Alexander B. ...... 56 28 36S 16 33 E
Alexander Bay .... 56 28 40S 16 30 E
Alexander City 69 32 58N 85 57W
Alexandra, Australia 45 37 8S 145 40 E
Alexandra, N.Z. ... 43 45 14S 169 25 E
Alexandra Falls ... 64 60 29N 116 18W
Alexandretta = İskenderun ..... 30 36 32N 36 10 E
Alexandria = El Iskandarîya ..... 51 31 0N 30 0 E
Alexandria, Australia 44 19 5S 136 40 E
Alexandria, B.C., Canada 64 52 35N 122 27W
Alexandria, Ont., Canada 62 45 19N 74 38W
Alexandria, S. Africa 56 33 38S 26 28 E
Alexandria, Ind., U.S.A. 68 40 18N 85 40W
Alexandria, La., U.S.A. 71 31 20N 92 30W
Alexandria, Minn., U.S.A. 70 45 50N 95 20W
Alexandria, S. Dak., U.S.A. 70 43 40N 97 45W
Alexandria, Va., U.S.A. 68 38 47N 77 1W
Alexandria Bay 68 44 20N 75 52W
Alexandrina, L. .... 45 35 25S 139 10 E
Alexandroúpolis ... 19 40 50N 25 54 E
Alexis → 63 52 33N 56 8W
Alexis Creek 64 52 10N 123 20W
Alford 8 57 13N 2 42W
Alfreton 6 53 6N 1 22W
Alga .... 23 49 53N 57 20 E
Algarve 13 36 58N 8 20W
Algeciras 13 36 9N 5 28W
Algemesí 13 39 11N 0 27W
Alger .... 50 36 42N 3 8 E
Algeria ■ .... 50 28 30N 2 0 E
Alghero .... 18 40 34N 8 20 E
Algiers = Alger ... 50 36 42N 3 8 E
Algoa B. .... 56 33 50S 25 45 E
Algoma 68 44 35N 87 27W
Algona 70 43 4N 94 14W
Alhama de Murcia . 13 37 51N 1 25W
Alhambra 73 34 2N 118 10W
Alhucemas = Al Hoceïma 50 35 8N 3 58W
'Alī al Gharbī ..... 30 32 30N 46 45 E
'Alī Khēl .... 32 33 57N 69 43 E
Aliákmon → ..... 19 40 30N 22 36 E
Alibo .... 51 9 52N 37 5 E
Alicante 13 38 23N 0 30W
Alice, S. Africa .... 56 32 48S 26 55 E
Alice, U.S.A. 71 27 47N 98 1W
Alice →, Queens., Australia .... 44 24 2S 144 50 E
Alice →, Queens., Australia .... 44 15 35S 142 20 E
Alice Arm 64 55 29N 129 31W
Alice Downs ...... 46 17 45S 127 56 E
Alice Springs ..... 44 23 40S 133 50 E
Alicedale .... 56 33 15S 26 4 E
Aliceville 69 33 9N 88 10W
Alick Cr. → ..... 44 20 55S 142 20 E
Alida 65 49 25N 101 55W
Aligarh, Ut. P., India 32 27 55N 78 10 E
Aligarh, India ..... 32 27 55N 78 10 E
Alīgūdarz .... 30 33 25N 49 45 E
Alingsås .... 21 57 56N 12 31 E
Alipur .... 32 29 25N 70 55 E
Alipur Duar .... 33 26 30N 89 35 E
Aliquippa 68 40 38N 80 18W
Aliwal North ...... 56 30 45S 26 45 E
Alix 64 52 24N 113 11W
Aljustrel 13 37 55N 8 10W
Alkmaar .... 11 52 37N 4 45 E
All American Canal 73 32 45N 115 0W
Allahabad .... 33 25 25N 81 58 E
Allakh-Yun .... 25 60 50N 137 5 E
Allan 65 51 53N 106 4W
Allanmyo .... 33 19 30N 95 17 E
Allanridge .... 56 27 45S 26 40 E
Allanwater 62 50 14N 90 10W
Allegan 68 42 32N 85 52W
Allegheny → 68 40 27N 80 0W
Allegheny Mts. 68 38 0N 80 0W
Allen, Bog of 9 53 15N 7 0W
Allen, L. 9 54 12N 8 5W
Allenby Br. = Jisr al Ḥusayn .... 28 31 53N 35 33 E
Allende 74 28 20N 100 50W
Allentown 68 40 36N 75 30W
Alleppey .... 32 9 30N 76 28 E
Alliance, Nebr., U.S.A. 70 42 10N 102 50W
Alliance, Ohio, U.S.A. 68 40 53N 81 7W
Allier □ .... 12 46 25N 3 0 E
Allier → .... 12 46 57N 3 4 E
Alliston 62 44 9N 79 52W
Alloa 8 56 7N 3 49W
Allora .... 45 28 2S 152 0 E
Alma, Canada 63 48 35N 71 40W
Alma, Ga., U.S.A. .. 69 31 33N 82 28W
Alma, Kans., U.S.A. 70 39 1N 96 22W
Alma, Mich., U.S.A. 68 43 25N 84 40W
Alma, Nebr., U.S.A. 70 40 10N 99 25W
Alma, Wis., U.S.A. . 70 44 19N 91 54W
'Almā ash Sha'b .. 28 33 7N 35 9 E
Alma Ata .... 24 43 15N 76 57 E
Almada 13 38 40N 9 9W
Almaden, Australia 44 17 22S 144 40 E
Almadén, Spain ... 13 38 49N 4 52W
Almanor, L. 72 40 15N 121 11W
Almansa 13 38 51N 1 5W
Almanzor, Pico de . 13 40 15N 5 18W
Almanzora → ... 13 37 14N 1 46W
Almazán 13 41 30N 2 30W
Almeirim 79 1 30S 52 34W
Almelo .... 11 52 22N 6 42 E
Almendralejo 13 38 41N 6 26W
Almería 13 36 52N 2 27W
Almirante 75 9 10N 82 30W
Almora .... 32 29 38N 79 40 E
Alnwick 6 55 25N 1 42W
Alon .... 33 22 12N 95 5 E
Alor .... 35 8 15S 124 30 E
Alor Setar .... 34 6 7N 100 22 E
Aloysius Mt. ...... 47 26 0S 128 38 E
Alpena 68 45 6N 83 24W
Alpes-de-Haute-Provence □ .... 12 44 8N 6 10 E
Alpes-Maritimes □ 12 43 55N 7 10 E
Alpha .... 44 23 39S 146 37 E
Alphonse .... 3 7 0S 52 45 E
Alpine, Ariz., U.S.A. 73 33 57N 109 4W
Alpine, Tex., U.S.A. 71 30 25N 103 35W
Alps .... 14 47 0N 8 0 E
Alroy Downs ..... 44 19 20S 136 5 E
Alsace .... 12 48 15N 7 25 E
Alsask 65 51 21N 109 59W
Alsásua 13 42 54N 2 10W
Alsten .... 20 65 58N 12 40 E
Alta .... 20 69 57N 23 10 E
Alta Gracia 80 31 40S 64 30W
Alta Lake 64 50 10N 123 0W
Altaelva → ...... 20 69 46N 23 45 E
Altafjorden .... 20 70 5N 23 5 E
Altagracia 78 10 45N 71 30W
Altai = Aerht'ai Shan .... 37 46 40N 92 45 E
Altai Mts. .... 26 46 40N 92 45 E
Altamaha → 69 31 19N 81 17W
Altamira 79 3 12S 52 10W
Altanbulag .... 37 50 16N 106 30 E
Altar 74 30 40N 111 50W
Altata 74 24 30N 108 0W
Altavista 68 37 9N 79 22W
Altay .... 37 47 48N 88 10 E
Alto Adige = Trentino-Alto Adige □ .... 18 46 30N 11 0 E
Alto-Alentejo 13 39 0N 7 40W
Alto Araguaia 79 17 15S 53 20W
Alto Cuchumatanes = Cuchumatanes, Sierra de los 75 15 35N 91 25W
Alto Molocue ..... 55 15 50S 37 35 E
Alton 70 38 55N 90 5W
Alton Downs ..... 45 26 7S 138 57 E
Altona .... 14 53 32N 9 56 E
Altoona 68 40 32N 78 24W
Altun Shan .... 37 38 30N 88 0 E
Alturas 72 41 36N 120 37W
Altus 71 34 30N 99 25W
Alùla .... 29 11 50N 50 45 E
Alusi .... 35 7 35S 131 40 E
Alva 71 36 50N 98 50W
Alvarado, Mexico .. 74 18 40N 95 50W
Alvarado, U.S.A. .. 71 32 25N 97 15W
Alvaro Obregón, Presa 74 27 55N 109 52W
Alvear 80 29 5S 56 30W
Alvesta .... 21 56 54N 14 35 E
Alvie .... 45 38 14S 143 30 E
Alvin 71 29 23N 95 12W
Älvkarleby .... 21 60 34N 17 26 E
Älvsborgs län □ ... 21 58 30N 12 30 E
Älvsbyn .... 20 65 40N 21 0 E
Alwar .... 32 27 38N 76 34 E
Alxa Zuoqi .... 38 38 50N 105 40 E
Alyaskitovyy ...... 25 64 45N 141 30 E
Alyata .... 23 39 58N 49 25 E
Alyth 8 56 38N 3 15W
Alzada 70 45 3N 104 22W
Am Dam .... 51 12 40N 20 35 E
Am-Timan .... 51 11 0N 20 10 E
Amadeus, L. ...... 47 24 54S 131 0 E
Amâdi, Sudan ..... 51 5 29N 30 25 E
Amadi, Zaïre ...... 54 3 40N 26 40 E
Amadjuak 61 64 0N 72 39W
Amadjuak L. 61 65 0N 71 8W
Amagasaki .... 36 34 42N 135 20 E
Amakusa-Shotō ... 36 32 15N 130 10 E
Amalner .... 32 21 5N 75 5 E
Amambay, Cordillera de 80 23 0S 55 45W
Amangeldy .... 24 50 10N 65 10 E
Amapá 79 2 5N 50 50W
Amapá □ 79 1 40N 52 0W
Amarante 79 6 14S 42 50W
Amaranth 65 50 36N 98 43W
Amargosa 79 13 2S 39 36W
Amarillo 71 35 14N 101 46W
Amaro, Mt. .... 18 42 5N 14 6 E
Amasra .... 30 41 45N 32 30 E
Amassama .... 53 5 1N 6 2 E
Amasya .... 30 40 40N 35 50 E
Amatikulu .... 57 29 3S 31 33 E
Amatitlán 75 14 29N 90 38W
Amazon = Amazonas → .. 79 0 5S 50 0W
Amazonas □ 78 4 0S 62 0W
Amazonas → 79 0 5S 50 0W
Ambahakily ...... 57 21 36S 43 41 E
Ambala .... 32 30 23N 76 56 E
Ambalavao ...... 57 21 50S 46 56 E
Ambalindum ..... 44 23 23S 135 0 E
Ambam .... 54 2 20N 11 15 E
Ambanja .... 57 13 40S 48 27 E
Ambarchik .... 25 69 40N 162 20 E
Ambarijeby ...... 57 14 56S 47 41 E
Ambaro, Helodranon' .... 57 13 23S 48 38 E
Ambartsevo ...... 24 57 30N 83 52 E
Ambato 78 1 5S 78 42W
Ambato Boeny .... 57 16 28S 46 43 E
Ambatofinandrahana 57 20 33S 46 48 E
Ambatolampy ..... 57 19 20S 47 35 E
Ambatondrazaka .. 57 17 55S 48 28 E
Ambatosoratra .... 57 17 37S 48 31 E
Ambenja .... 57 15 17S 46 58 E
Amberg .... 14 49 25N 11 52 E
Ambergris Cay 74 18 0N 88 0W
Amberley .... 43 43 9S 172 44 E
Ambikapur .... 33 23 15N 83 15 E
Ambilobé .... 57 13 10S 49 3 E
Ambinanindrano .. 57 20 5S 48 23 E
Ambleside 6 54 26N 2 58W
Ambo 78 10 5S 76 10W
Ambodifototra .... 57 16 59S 49 52 E
Ambodilazana .... 57 18 6S 49 10 E
Ambohimahasoa .. 57 21 7S 47 13 E
Ambohimanga .... 57 20 52S 47 36 E
Ambohitra .... 57 12 30S 49 10 E
Ambon .... 35 3 35S 128 20 E
Ambositra .... 57 20 31S 47 25 E
Ambovombé ..... 57 25 11S 46 5 E
Amboy 73 34 33N 115 51W
Amboyna I. .... 34 7 50N 112 50 E
Ambriz .... 54 7 48S 13 8 E
Amby .... 45 26 30S 148 11 E
Amchitka I. 60 51 30N 179 0W
Amderma .... 24 69 45N 61 30 E
Ameca 74 20 30N 104 0W
Ameca → 74 20 40N 105 15W
Amecameca 74 19 7N 98 46W
Ameland .... 11 53 27N 5 45 E
Amen .... 25 68 45N 180 0 E
American Falls 72 42 46N 112 56W
American Falls Res. 72 43 0N 112 50W
American Samoa ■ 43 14 20S 170 40W
Americus 69 32 0N 84 10W
Amersfoort, Neth. . 11 52 9N 5 23 E
Amersfoort, S. Africa 57 26 59S 29 53 E
Amery, Australia .. 47 31 9S 117 5 E
Amery, Canada ... 65 56 34N 94 3W
Ames 70 42 0N 93 40W
Amga .... 25 60 50N 132 0 E
Amga → .... 25 62 38N 134 32 E
Amgu .... 25 45 45N 137 15 E
Amgun → ...... 25 52 56N 139 38 E
Amherst, Burma ... 33 16 2N 97 20 E
Amherst, Canada .. 63 45 48N 64 8W
Amherst, U.S.A. ... 71 34 0N 102 24W
Amherstburg 62 42 6N 83 6W
Amiata, Mte. ...... 18 42 54N 11 40 E
Amiens .... 12 49 54N 2 16 E
Amirante Is. ...... 3 6 0S 53 0 E
Amisk L. 65 54 35N 102 15W
Amite 71 30 47N 90 31W
Amlwch 6 53 24N 4 21W
'Ammān .... 28 31 57N 35 52 E
Ammanford 7 51 48N 4 0W
Ammi'ad .... 28 32 55N 35 32 E
Amorgós .... 19 36 50N 25 57 E
Amory 69 33 59N 88 29W
Amos 62 48 35N 78 5W
Amoy = Xiamen .. 38 24 25N 118 4 E
Ampanihy .... 57 24 40S 44 45 E
Ampasindava, Helodranon' .... 57 13 40S 48 15 E
Ampasindava, Saikanosy ...... 57 13 42S 47 55 E
Ampenan .... 34 8 35S 116 13 E
Ampotaka .... 57 25 3S 44 41 E
Ampoza .... 57 22 20S 44 44 E
Amqa .... 28 32 59N 35 10 E
Amqui 63 48 28N 67 27W
Amravati .... 32 20 55N 77 45 E
Amreli .... 32 21 35N 71 17 E
Amritsar .... 32 31 35N 74 57 E
Amroha .... 32 28 53N 78 30 E
Amsterdam, Neth. . 11 52 23N 4 54 E
Amsterdam, U.S.A. 68 42 58N 74 10W
Amsterdam, I. .... 3 38 30S 77 30 E
Amudarya → .... 24 43 40N 59 0 E
Amundsen Gulf ... 60 71 0N 124 0W
Amuntai .... 34 2 28S 115 25 E
Amur → .... 25 52 56N 141 10 E
Amurang .... 35 1 5N 124 40 E
Amuri Pass ...... 43 42 31S 172 11 E
Amursk .... 25 50 14N 136 54 E
Amurzet .... 25 47 50N 131 5 E
An Nafūd .... 30 28 15N 41 0 E
An Najaf .... 30 32 3N 44 15 E
An Nāqūrah ...... 28 33 7N 35 8 E
An Nāṣirīyah ..... 30 31 0N 46 15 E
An Nhon .... 34 13 55N 109 7 E
An Nîl □ .... 51 19 30N 33 0 E
An Nîl el Abyad □ . 51 14 0N 32 15 E
An Nîl el Azraq □ .. 51 12 30N 34 30 E
An Nu'ayrīyah .... 30 27 30N 48 30 E
An Uaimh 9 53 39N 6 40W
Anabar → ...... 25 73 8N 113 36 E
'Anabtā .... 28 32 19N 35 7 E
Anaconda 72 46 7N 113 0W
Anacortes 72 48 30N 122 40W
Anadarko 71 35 4N 98 15W
Anadolu .... 30 38 0N 30 0 E
Anadyr .... 25 64 35N 177 20 E
Anadyr → ...... 25 64 55N 176 5 E
Anadyrskiy Zaliv .. 25 64 0N 180 0 E
'Ānah .... 30 34 25N 42 0 E
Anaheim 73 33 50N 118 0W
Anahim Lake 64 52 28N 125 18W
Anáhuac 74 27 14N 100 9W
Anakapalle .... 33 17 42N 83 6 E
Anakie .... 44 23 32S 147 45 E
Analalava .... 57 14 35S 48 0 E
Anambas, Kepulauan ..... 34 3 20N 106 30 E
Anamoose 70 47 55N 100 20W
Anamosa 70 42 7N 91 30W
Anamur .... 30 36 8N 32 58 E
Anan .... 36 33 54N 134 40 E
Anantnag .... 32 33 45N 75 10 E
Anápolis 79 16 15S 48 50W
Anār .... 31 30 55N 55 13 E
Anārak .... 31 33 25N 53 40 E
Anatolia = Anadolu 30 38 0N 30 0 E
Anatone 72 46 9N 117 4W
Anatsogno .... 57 23 33S 43 46 E
Añatuya 80 28 20S 62 50W
Anaunethad L. 65 60 55N 104 25W
Anaye .... 51 19 15N 12 50 E
Anchorage 60 61 10N 149 50W
Ancohuma, Nevada 78 16 0S 68 50W
Ancón 78 11 50S 77 10W
Ancona .... 18 43 37N 13 30 E
Ancud 80 42 0S 73 50W
Ancud, G. de 80 42 0S 73 0W
Anda .... 38 46 24N 125 19 E
Andado .... 44 25 25S 135 15 E
Andalgalá 80 27 40S 66 30W
Åndalsnes .... 20 62 35N 7 43 E
Andalucía □ 13 37 35N 5 0W
Andalusia 69 31 19N 86 30W
Andalusia □ = Andalucía □ 13 37 35N 5 0W
Andaman Is. ...... 3 12 30N 92 30 E
Andaman Sea .... 34 13 0N 96 0 E
Andara .... 56 18 2S 21 9 E
Andenne .... 11 50 30N 5 5 E
Anderson, Calif., U.S.A. 72 40 30N 122 19W
Anderson, Ind., U.S.A. 68 40 5N 85 40W
Anderson, Mo., U.S.A. 71 36 43N 94 29W
Anderson, S.C., U.S.A. 69 34 32N 82 40W
Anderson → 60 69 42N 129 0W
Anderson, Mt. .... 57 25 5S 30 42 E
Andes 78 5 40N 75 53W
Andes, Cord. de los 78 20 0S 68 0W
Andfjorden .... 20 69 10N 16 20 E
Andhra Pradesh □ 32 16 0N 79 0 E
Andikíthira .... 19 35 52N 23 15 E
Andizhan .... 24 41 10N 72 0 E
Andkhvoy .... 31 36 52N 65 8 E
Andoany .... 57 13 25S 48 16 E
Andong .... 38 36 40N 128 43 E
Andorra ■ .... 13 42 30N 1 30 E
Andorra La Vella .. 13 42 31N 1 32 E
Andover 7 51 13N 1 29W
Andrahary, Mt. .... 57 13 37S 49 17 E
Andramasina ..... 57 19 11S 47 35 E
Andranopasy ..... 57 21 17S 43 44 E
Andreanof Is. 60 52 0N 178 0W
Andrewilla .... 45 26 31S 139 17 E
Andrews, S.C., U.S.A. 69 33 29N 79 30W
Andrews, Tex., U.S.A. 71 32 18N 102 33W
Ándria .... 18 41 13N 16 17 E
Andriba .... 57 17 30S 46 58 E
Androka .... 57 24 58S 44 2 E
Andropov .... 22 58 5N 38 50 E
Ándros .... 19 37 50N 24 57 E
Andros I. 75 24 30N 78 0W
Andros Town 75 24 43N 77 47W
Andújar 13 38 3N 4 5W
Andulo .... 54 11 25S 16 45 E
Anegada I. 75 18 45N 64 20W
Anegada Passage . 75 18 15N 63 45W
Anécho .... 53 6 12N 1 34 E
Aneto, Pico de .... 13 42 37N 0 40 E
Angamos, Punta .. 80 23 1S 70 32W
Ang'angxi .... 38 47 10N 123 48 E
Angara → .... 25 58 30N 97 0 E
Angarsk .... 25 52 30N 104 0 E
Angas Downs .... 47 25 2S 132 14 E
Angas Hills ...... 46 23 0S 127 50 E
Angaston .... 45 34 30S 139 8 E
Ånge .... 20 62 31N 15 35 E
Ángel de la Guarda, I. 74 29 30N 113 30W
Angeles .... 35 15 9N 120 33 E
Ängelholm .... 21 56 15N 12 58 E
Angellala .... 45 26 24S 146 54 E

Angels Camp

Angels Camp **73** 38 8N 120 30W
Ångermanälven → **20** 62 40N 18 0 E
Angers **12** 47 30N 0 35W
Ängesån → **20** 66 50N 22 15 E
Angikuni L. **65** 62 0N 100 0W
Anglesey **6** 53 17N 4 20W
Angleton **71** 29 12N 95 23W
Ango **54** 4 10N 26 5 E
Angola **68** 41 40N 85 0W
Angola ■ **55** 12 0S 18 0 E
Angoon **64** 57 40N 134 40W
Angoulême **12** 45 39N 0 10 E
Angoumois **12** 45 50N 0 25 E
Angra dos Reis **80** 23 0S 44 10W
Angren **24** 41 1N 70 12 E
Anguilla **75** 18 14N 63 5W
Angurugu **44** 14 0S 136 25 E
Angus, Braes of **8** 56 51N 3 10W
Anholt **21** 56 42N 11 33 E
Anhua **39** 28 23N 111 12 E
Anhui □ **39** 32 0N 117 0 E
Anhwei □ = Anhui □ **39** 32 0N 117 0 E
Anichab **56** 21 0S 14 46 E
Animas **73** 31 58N 108 58W
Anivorano **57** 18 44S 48 58 E
Anjidiv I. **32** 14 40N 74 10 E
Anjou **12** 47 20N 0 15W
Anjozorobe **57** 18 22S 47 52 E
Anju **38** 39 36N 125 40 E
Anka **53** 12 13N 5 58 E
Ankaboa, Tanjona **57** 21 58S 43 20 E
Ankang **39** 32 40N 109 1 E
Ankara **30** 40 0N 32 54 E
Ankaramena **57** 21 57S 46 39 E
Ankazoabo **57** 22 18S 44 31 E
Ankazobe **57** 18 20S 47 10 E
Ankisabe **57** 19 17S 46 29 E
Ankoro **54** 6 45S 26 55 E
Anlu **39** 31 15N 113 45 E
Ann, C. **68** 42 39N 70 37W
Ann Arbor **68** 42 17N 83 45W
Anna **71** 37 28N 89 10W
Anna Plains **46** 19 17S 121 37 E
Annaba **50** 36 50N 7 46 E
Annalee → **9** 54 3N 7 15W
Annam = Trung-Phan **34** 16 0N 108 0 E
Annan **8** 55 0N 3 17W
Annan → **8** 54 58N 3 18W
Annapolis **68** 39 0N 76 30W
Annapolis Royal **63** 44 44N 65 32W
Annean, L. **47** 26 54S 118 14 E
Annecy **12** 45 55N 6 8 E
Anning **37** 24 55N 102 26 E
Anningie **46** 21 50S 133 7 E
Anniston **69** 33 45N 85 50W
Annobón **48** 1 25S 5 36 E
Annonciation, L' **62** 46 25N 74 55W
Annotto Bay **75** 18 17N 77 3W
Annuello **45** 34 53S 142 55 E
Anoka **70** 45 10N 93 26W
Anorotsangana **57** 13 56S 47 55 E
Anqing **39** 30 30N 117 3 E
Anren **39** 26 43N 113 18 E
Ansāb **30** 29 11N 44 43 E
Ansai **38** 36 50N 109 20 E
Ansbach **14** 49 17N 10 34 E
Anse, L' **62** 46 47N 88 28W
Anse au Loup, L' **63** 51 32N 56 50W
Anshan **38** 41 5N 122 58 E
Anshun **39** 26 18N 105 57 E
Ansirabe **57** 19 55S 47 2 E
Ansley **70** 41 19N 99 24W
Anson **71** 32 46N 99 54W
Anson B. **46** 13 20S 130 6 E
Ansongo **53** 15 25N 0 35 E
Anstruther **8** 56 14N 2 40W
Ansudu **35** 2 11S 139 22 E
Antabamba **78** 14 40S 73 0W
Antakya **30** 36 14N 36 10 E
Antalaha **57** 14 57S 50 20 E
Antalya **30** 36 52N 30 45 E
Antalya Körfezi **30** 36 15N 31 30 E
Antananarivo **57** 18 55S 47 31 E
Antananarivo □ **57** 19 0S 47 0 E
Antanimbaribe **57** 21 30S 44 48 E
Antequera **13** 37 5N 4 33W
Antero Mt. **73** 38 45N 106 15W
Anthony, Kans., U.S.A. **71** 37 8N 98 2W
Anthony, N. Mex., U.S.A. **73** 32 1N 106 37W
Anthony Lagoon **44** 18 0S 135 30 E
Anti Atlas **50** 30 0N 8 30W
Anticosti, I. d' **63** 49 30N 63 0W
Antigo **70** 45 8N 89 5W
Antigonish **63** 45 38N 61 58W
Antigua, Guat. **75** 14 34N 90 41W
Antigua, W. Indies **75** 17 0N 61 50W
Antigua & Barbuda ■ **75** 17 20N 61 48W
Antilla **75** 20 40N 75 50W
Antimony **73** 38 7N 112 0W
Antioch **72** 38 0N 121 45W
Antioquia **78** 6 40N 75 55W
Antipodes Is. **40** 49 45S 178 40 E
Antler **70** 48 58N 101 18W
Antler → **65** 49 8N 101 0W
Antlers **71** 34 15N 95 35W
Antofagasta **80** 23 50S 70 30W
Antofagasta de la Sierra **80** 26 5S 67 20W
Anton **71** 33 49N 102 5W
Anton Chico **73** 35 12N 105 5W
Antongila, Helodrano **57** 15 30S 49 50 E
Antonibé **57** 15 7S 47 24 E
Antonibé, Presqu'île d' **57** 14 55S 47 20 E
Antonina **80** 25 26S 48 42W
Antonito **73** 37 4N 106 1W
Antrim **9** 54 43N 6 13W
Antrim □ **9** 54 55N 6 20W
Antrim, Mts. of **9** 54 57N 6 8W
Antrim Plateau **46** 18 8S 128 20 E
Antsalova **57** 18 40S 44 37 E
Antsiranana **57** 12 25S 49 20 E
Antsohihy **57** 14 50S 47 59 E
Antsohimbondrona Seranana **57** 13 7S 48 48 E
Antwerp = Antwerpen **11** 51 13N 4 25 E
Antwerpen **11** 51 13N 4 25 E
Antwerpen □ **11** 51 15N 4 40 E
Anupgarh **32** 29 10N 73 10 E
Anuradhapura **32** 8 22N 80 28 E
Anvers = Antwerpen **11** 51 13N 4 25 E
Anvik **60** 62 37N 160 20W
Anxi, Fujian, China **39** 25 2N 118 12 E
Anxi, Gansu, China **37** 40 30N 95 43 E
Anxious B. **45** 33 24S 134 45 E
Anyang **38** 36 5N 114 21 E
Anyi, Jiangxi, China **39** 28 49N 115 25 E
Anyi, Shanxi, China **39** 35 2N 111 2 E
Anyuan **39** 25 9N 115 21 E
'Anzah **28** 32 22N 35 12 E
Anzhero-Sudzhensk **24** 56 10N 86 0 E
Ánzio **18** 41 28N 12 37 E
Aomori **36** 40 45N 140 45 E
Aomori □ **36** 40 45N 140 40 E
Aosta **18** 45 43N 7 20 E
Aoudéras **50** 17 45N 8 20 E
Aoulef el Arab **50** 26 55N 1 2 E
Apache **71** 34 53N 98 22W
Apalachee B. **69** 30 0N 84 0W
Apalachicola **69** 29 40N 85 0W
Apalachicola → **69** 29 40N 85 0W
Apaporis → **78** 1 23S 69 25W
Aparri **35** 18 22N 121 38 E
Apàtity **22** 67 34N 33 22 E
Apatzingán **74** 19 0N 102 20W
Apeldoorn **11** 52 13N 5 57 E
Apia **43** 13 50S 171 50W
Apiacás, Serra dos **78** 9 50S 57 0W
Apizaco **74** 19 26N 98 9W
Aplao **78** 16 0S 72 40W
Apo, Mt. **35** 6 53N 125 14 E
Apollonia = Marsá Susah **51** 32 52N 21 59 E
Apolo **78** 14 30S 68 30W
Apostle Is. **70** 47 0N 90 30W
Apoteri **78** 4 2N 58 32W
Appalachian Mts. **68** 38 0N 80 0W
Appenines = Appennini **18** 41 0N 15 0 E
Appennini **18** 41 0N 15 0 E
Appleby **6** 54 35N 2 29W
Appleton **68** 44 17N 88 25W
Approuague **79** 4 20N 52 0W
Apucarana **80** 23 55S 51 33W
Apulia = Púglia □ **18** 41 0N 16 30 E
Apure → **78** 7 37N 66 25W
Apurimac → **78** 12 17S 73 56W
Aqabah = Al 'Aqabah **28** 29 31N 35 0 E
'Aqabah, Khalīj al **30** 28 15N 33 20 E
Āqcheh **31** 37 0N 66 5 E
Aqīq **51** 18 14N 38 12 E
Aqrabā **28** 32 9N 35 20 E
Aqrah **30** 36 46N 43 45 E
Aquidauana **79** 20 30S 55 50W
Áquila, L' **18** 42 21N 13 24 E
Aquiles Serdán **74** 28 37N 105 54W
Ar Rachidiya **50** 31 58N 4 20W
Ar Rafid **28** 32 57N 35 52 E
Ar Ramādī **30** 33 25N 43 20 E
Ar Ramthā **28** 32 34N 36 0 E
Ar Raqqah **30** 36 0N 38 55 E
Ar Rass **30** 25 50N 43 40 E
Ar Rifa'i **30** 31 50N 46 10 E
Ar Riyāḍ **29** 24 41N 46 42 E
Ar Rummān **28** 32 9N 35 48 E
Ar Ruṭbah **30** 33 0N 40 15 E
Ar Ruwayḍah **30** 23 40N 44 40 E
Ara **33** 25 35N 84 32 E
'Arab, Bahr el → **51** 9 0N 29 30 E
Arab, Shatt al **30** 30 0N 48 31 E
Arabia **29** 25 0N 45 0 E
Arabian Desert = Es Sahrâ' Esh Sharqîya **51** 27 30N 32 30 E
Arabian Gulf = Gulf, The **31** 27 0N 50 0 E
Arabian Sea **26** 16 0N 65 0 E
Arac **30** 41 15N 33 21 E
Aracaju **79** 10 55S 37 4W
Aracataca **78** 10 38N 74 9W
Aracati **79** 4 30S 37 44W
Araçatuba **79** 21 10S 50 30W
Aracena **13** 37 53N 6 38W
Araçuaí **79** 16 52S 42 4W
'Arad, Israel **28** 31 15N 35 12 E
Arad, Romania **15** 46 10N 21 20 E
Arada **51** 15 0N 20 20 E
Arafura Sea **35** 9 0S 135 0 E
Aragón □ **13** 41 25N 1 0W
Aragón → **13** 42 13N 1 44W
Araguacema **79** 8 50S 49 20W
Araguaia → **79** 5 21S 48 41W
Araguari **79** 18 38S 48 11W
Araguari → **79** 1 15N 49 55W
Arak, Algeria **50** 25 20N 3 45 E
Arāk, Iran **30** 34 0N 49 40 E
Arakan Coast **33** 19 0N 94 0 E
Arakan Yoma **33** 20 0N 94 40 E
Araks = Aras, Rūd-e → **30** 39 10N 47 10 E
Aral Sea = Aralskoye More **24** 44 30N 60 0 E
Aralsk **24** 46 50N 61 20 E
Aralskoye More **24** 44 30N 60 0 E
Aramac **44** 22 58S 145 14 E
Aran I. **9** 55 0N 8 30W
Aran Is. **9** 53 5N 9 42W
Aranjuez **13** 40 1N 3 40W
Aranos **56** 24 9S 19 7 E
Aransas Pass **71** 27 55N 97 9W
Araouane **50** 18 55N 3 30W
Arapahoe **70** 40 22N 99 53W
Arapiraca **79** 9 45S 36 39W
Arapkir **30** 39 5N 38 30 E
Arapongas **80** 23 29S 51 28W
Araranguá **80** 29 0S 49 30W
Araraquara **79** 21 50S 48 0W
Ararat **45** 37 16S 143 0 E
Ararat, Mt. = Ağri Daği **30** 39 50N 44 15 E
Araripe, Chapada do **79** 7 20S 40 0W
Aras, Rūd-e → **30** 39 10N 47 10 E
Arauca **78** 7 0N 70 40W
Arauca → **78** 7 24N 66 35W
Arauco **80** 37 16S 73 25W
Araxá **79** 19 35S 46 55W
Araya, Pen. de **78** 10 40N 64 0W
Arbatax **18** 39 57N 9 42 E
Arbaza **25** 52 40N 92 30 E
Arbīl **30** 36 15N 44 5 E
Arborfield **65** 53 6N 103 39W
Arborg **65** 50 54N 97 13W
Arbroath **8** 56 34N 2 35W
Arbuckle **72** 39 3N 122 2W
Arcachon **12** 44 40N 1 10W
Arcadia, Fla., U.S.A. **69** 27 20N 81 50W
Arcadia, La., U.S.A. **71** 32 34N 92 53W
Arcadia, Nebr., U.S.A. **70** 41 29N 99 4W
Arcadia, Wis., U.S.A. **70** 44 13N 91 29W
Arcata **72** 40 55N 124 4W
Archangel = Arkhangelsk **22** 64 40N 41 0 E
Archer → **44** 13 28S 141 41 E
Archer B. **44** 13 20S 141 30 E
Arcila = Asilah **50** 35 29N 6 0W
Arckaringa **45** 27 56S 134 45 E
Arckaringa Cr. → **45** 28 10S 135 22 E
Arco **72** 43 45N 113 16W
Arcola **65** 49 40N 102 30W
Arcos **13** 41 12N 2 16W
Arcot **32** 12 53N 79 20 E
Arcoverde **79** 8 25S 37 4W
Arctic Bay **61** 73 1N 85 7W
Arctic Red River **60** 67 15N 134 0W
Arda → **19** 41 40N 26 29 E
Ardabīl **30** 38 15N 48 18 E
Ardahan **30** 41 7N 42 41 E
Ardakān = Sepīdān **31** 30 20N 52 5 E
Ardèche □ **12** 44 42N 4 16 E
Ardee **9** 53 51N 6 32W
Ardenne **11** 50 0N 5 10 E
Ardennes □ **12** 49 35N 4 40 E
Ardestān **31** 33 20N 52 25 E
Ardgour **8** 56 45N 5 25W
Ardlethan **45** 34 22S 146 53 E
Ardmore, Australia **44** 21 39S 139 11 E
Ardmore, Okla., U.S.A. **71** 34 10N 97 5W
Ardmore, S. Dak., U.S.A. **70** 43 0N 103 40W
Ardnacrusha **9** 52 43N 8 38W
Ardnamurchan, Pt. of **8** 56 44N 6 14W
Ardrossan, Australia **45** 34 26S 137 53 E
Ardrossan, U.K. **8** 55 39N 4 50W
Ards □ **9** 54 35N 5 30W
Ards Pen. **9** 54 30N 5 25W
Arecibo **75** 18 29N 66 42W
Areia Branca **79** 5 0S 37 0W
Arendal **21** 58 28N 8 46 E
Arequipa **78** 16 20S 71 30W
Arero **51** 4 41N 38 50 E
Arévalo **13** 41 3N 4 43W
Arezzo **18** 43 28N 11 50 E
Argamakmur **34** 3 35S 102 0 E
Argentário, Mte. **18** 42 23N 11 11 E
Argentia **63** 47 18N 53 58W
Argentina ■ **80** 35 0S 66 0W
Argentino, L. **80** 50 10S 73 0W
Argeş → **15** 44 12N 26 14 E
Arghandab → **32** 31 30N 64 15 E
Argo **51** 19 28N 30 30 E
Argolikós Kólpos **19** 37 20N 22 52 E
Argonne **12** 49 10N 5 0 E
Árgos **19** 37 40N 22 43 E
Argostólion **19** 38 12N 20 33 E
Arguello, Pt. **73** 34 34N 120 40W
Argun → **25** 53 20N 121 28 E
Argungu **53** 12 40N 4 31 E
Argyle **70** 48 23N 96 49W
Argyle, L. **46** 16 20S 128 40 E
Århus **21** 56 8N 10 11 E
Ariamsvlei **56** 28 9S 19 51 E
Arica, Chile **78** 18 32S 70 20W
Arica, Colombia **78** 2 0S 71 50W
Arid, C. **47** 34 1S 123 10 E
Aridh **30** 25 0N 46 0 E
Ariège □ **12** 42 56N 1 30 E
Arima **75** 10 38N 61 17W
Arinos → **78** 10 25S 58 20W
Ario de Rosales **74** 19 12N 102 0W
Aripuanā **78** 9 25S 60 30W
Aripuanā → **78** 5 7S 60 25W
Ariquemes **78** 9 55S 63 6W
Arisaig **8** 56 55N 5 50W
Aristazabal I. **64** 52 40N 129 10W
Arivaca **73** 31 37N 111 25W
Arivonimamo **57** 19 1S 47 11 E
Ariza **36** 41 19N 2 3W
Arizona **80** 35 45S 65 25W
Arizona □ **73** 34 20N 111 30W
Arizpe **74** 30 20N 110 11W
Arjeplog **20** 66 3N 18 2 E
Arjona **78** 10 14N 75 22W
Arjuno **35** 7 49S 112 34 E
Arka **25** 60 15N 142 0 E
Arkadelphia **71** 34 5N 93 0W
Arkaig, L. **8** 56 58N 5 10W
Arkalyk **24** 50 13N 66 50 E
Arkansas □ **71** 35 0N 92 30W
Arkansas → **71** 33 48N 91 4W
Arkansas City **71** 37 4N 97 3W
Arkhangelsk **22** 64 40N 41 0 E
Arklow **9** 52 48N 6 10W
Arkticheskiy, Mys **25** 81 10N 95 0 E
Arlanzón → **13** 42 3N 4 17W
Arlberg Pass **14** 47 9N 10 12 E
Arlee **72** 47 10N 114 4W
Arles **12** 43 41N 4 40 E
Arlington, S. Africa **57** 28 1S 27 53 E
Arlington, Oreg., U.S.A. **72** 45 48N 120 6W
Arlington, S. Dak., U.S.A. **70** 44 25N 97 4W
Arlington, Va., U.S.A. **68** 38 52N 77 5W
Arlington, Wash., U.S.A. **72** 48 11N 122 4W
Arlon **11** 49 42N 5 49 E
Armagh **9** 54 22N 6 40W
Armagh □ **9** 54 18N 6 37W
Armagnac **12** 43 50N 0 10 E
Armavir **23** 45 2N 41 7 E
Armenia **78** 4 35N 75 45W
Armenian S.S.R. □ **23** 40 0N 44 0 E
Armidale **45** 30 30S 151 40 E
Armour **70** 43 20N 98 25W
Armstrong, B.C., Canada **64** 50 25N 119 10W
Armstrong, Ont., Canada **62** 50 18N 89 4W
Armstrong, U.S.A. **71** 26 59N 97 48W
Armstrong Cr. → **46** 16 35S 131 40 E
Arnaouti, C. **30** 35 6N 32 17 E
Arnarfjörður **20** 65 48N 23 40W
Arnaud → **61** 60 0N 70 0W
Árnes **20** 66 1N 21 31W
Arnett **71** 36 0N 99 44W
Arnhem **11** 51 58N 5 55 E
Arnhem, C. **44** 12 20S 137 30 E
Arnhem B. **44** 12 20S 136 10 E
Arnhem Land **44** 13 10S 134 30 E
Arno → **18** 43 41N 10 17 E
Arno Bay **45** 33 54S 136 34 E
Arnold **70** 41 29N 100 10W
Arnot **65** 55 56N 96 41W
Arnøy **20** 70 9N 20 40 E
Arnprior **62** 45 26N 76 21W
Aroab **56** 26 41S 19 39 E
Arrabury **45** 26 45S 141 0 E
Arraiján **74** 8 56N 79 36W
Arran **8** 55 34N 5 12W
Arrandale **64** 54 57N 130 0W
Arras **12** 50 17N 2 46 E
Arrecife **50** 28 57N 13 37W
Arrée, Mts. d' **12** 48 26N 3 55W
Arriaga **74** 21 55N 101 23W
Arrilalah P.O. **44** 23 43S 143 54 E
Arrino **47** 29 30S 115 40 E
Arrow, L. **9** 54 3N 8 20W
Arrow Rock Res. **72** 43 45N 115 50W
Arrowhead **64** 50 40N 117 55W
Arrowtown **43** 44 57S 168 50 E
Arroyo Grande **73** 35 9N 120 32W
Arsenault L. **65** 55 6N 108 32W
Árta **19** 39 8N 21 2 E
Arteaga **74** 18 50N 102 20W
Artemovsk **25** 54 45N 93 35 E
Artesia = Mosomane **56** 24 2S 26 19 E
Artesia **71** 32 55N 104 25W
Artesia Wells **71** 28 17N 99 18W
Artesian **70** 44 2N 97 54W
Arthur → **44** 41 2S 144 40 E
Arthur Cr. → **44** 22 30S 136 25 E
Arthur Pt. **44** 22 7S 150 3 E
Arthur's Pass **43** 42 54S 171 35 E
Artigas **80** 30 20S 56 30W
Artillery L. **65** 63 9N 107 52W
Artois **12** 50 20N 2 30 E
Artvin **30** 41 14N 41 44 E
Aru, Kepulauan **35** 6 0S 134 30 E
Arua **54** 3 1N 30 58 E
Aruanā **79** 14 54S 51 10W
Aruba **75** 12 30N 70 0W
Arumpo **45** 33 48S 142 55 E
Arunachal Pradesh □ **33** 28 0N 95 0 E
Arusha **54** 3 20S 36 40 E
Aruwimi → **54** 1 13N 23 36 E
Arvada **72** 44 43N 106 6W
Arvayheer **37** 46 15N 102 48 E
Arvida **63** 48 25N 71 14W
Arvidsjaur **20** 65 35N 19 10 E
Arvika **21** 59 40N 12 36 E
Arxan **38** 47 11N 119 57 E
Arys **24** 42 26N 68 48 E
Arzamas **22** 55 27N 43 55 E
Arzew **50** 35 50N 0 23W
'As Saffānīyah **30** 28 5N 48 50 E
Aş Şāfī **28** 31 2N 35 28 E
As Salt **28** 32 2N 35 43 E
As Samāwah **30** 31 15N 45 15 E
As Samū' **28** 31 24N 35 4 E
As Sanamayn **28** 33 3N 36 10 E
As Sulaymānīyah, Iraq **30** 35 35N 45 29 E
As Sulaymānīyah, Si. Arabia **30** 24 9N 47 18 E
As Summān **30** 25 0N 47 0 E
As Sūq **30** 21 58N 42 3 E
As Suwaydā' **30** 32 40N 36 30 E
As Suwayh **31** 22 10N 59 33 E
As Şuwayrah **30** 32 55N 45 0 E
Asab **56** 25 30S 18 0 E
Asahigawa **36** 43 46N 142 22 E
Asamankese **53** 5 50N 0 40W
Asansol **33** 23 40N 87 1 E
Asbesberge **56** 29 0S 23 0 E
Asbestos **63** 45 47N 71 58W
Asbury Park **68** 40 15N 74 1W
Ascensión, B. de la **74** 19 50N 87 20W
Ascension I. **2** 8 0S 14 15W
Aschaffenburg **14** 49 58N 9 8 E
Áscoli Piceno **18** 42 51N 13 34 E
Ascope **78** 7 46S 79 8W
Aseb **29** 13 0N 42 40 E
Asela **51** 8 0N 39 0 E
Ash Fork **73** 35 14N 112 32W
Ash Grove **71** 37 21N 93 36W
Ash Shām, Bādiyat **30** 32 0N 40 0 E
Ash Shāmīyah **30** 31 55N 44 35 E
Ash Shāriqah **31** 25 23N 55 26 E
Ash Shaṭrah **30** 31 30N 46 10 E
Ash Shaykh, J. **30** 33 25N 35 50 E
Ash Shu'aybah **30** 27 53N 44 43 E
Ash Shu'bah **30** 28 54N 44 44 E
Ash Shūnah ash Shamālīyah **28** 32 37N 35 34 E
Asha **22** 55 0N 57 16 E
Ashburn **69** 31 42N 83 40W
Ashburton **43** 43 53S 171 48 E
Ashburton → **46** 21 40S 114 56 E
Ashburton Downs **46** 23 25S 117 4 E
Ashby-de-la-Zouch **6** 52 45N 1 29W
Ashcroft **64** 50 40N 121 20W
Ashdod **28** 31 49N 34 35 E

Balashov

Ashdot Yaaqov **28** 32 39N 35 35 E
Asheboro **69** 35 43N 79 46W
Asherton **71** 28 25N 99 43W
Asheville **69** 35 39N 82 30W
Asheweig → **62** 54 17N 87 12W
Ashford, Australia **45** 29 15S 151 3 E
Ashford, U.K. **7** 51 8N 0 53 E
Ashford, U.S.A. **72** 46 45N 122 2W
Ashikaga **36** 36 28N 139 29 E
Ashizuri-Zaki **36** 32 44N 133 0 E
Ashkhabad **24** 38 0N 57 50 E
Ashland, Kans., U.S.A. **71** 37 13N 99 43W
Ashland, Ky., U.S.A. **68** 38 25N 82 40W
Ashland, Maine, U.S.A. **63** 46 34N 68 26W
Ashland, Mont., U.S.A. **72** 45 41N 106 12W
Ashland, Nebr., U.S.A. **70** 41 5N 96 27W
Ashland, Ohio, U.S.A. **68** 40 52N 82 20W
Ashland, Oreg., U.S.A. **72** 42 10N 122 38W
Ashland, Va., U.S.A. **68** 37 46N 77 30W
Ashland, Wis., U.S.A. **70** 46 40N 90 52W
Ashley **70** 46 3N 99 23W
Ashmont **64** 54 7N 111 35W
Ashmore Reef **46** 12 14S 123 5 E
Ashq'elon **28** 31 42N 34 35 E
Ashtabula **68** 41 52N 80 50W
Ashton, S. Africa **56** 33 50S 20 5 E
Ashton, U.S.A. **72** 44 6N 111 30W
Ashton-under-Lyne **6** 53 30N 2 8W
Ashuanipi, L. **63** 52 45N 66 15W
Asia **26** 45 0N 75 0 E
Asia, Kepulauan **35** 1 0N 131 13 E
Asifabad **32** 19 20N 79 24 E
Asike **35** 6 39S 140 24 E
Asilah **50** 35 29N 6 0W
Asinara **18** 41 5N 8 15 E
Asinara, G. dell' **18** 41 0N 8 30 E
Asino **24** 57 0N 86 0 E
'Asīr □ **29** 18 40N 42 30 E
Asir, Ras **29** 11 55N 51 10 E
Askersund **21** 58 53N 14 55 E
Askham **56** 26 59S 20 47 E
Askja **20** 65 3N 16 48W
Āsmār **31** 35 10N 71 27 E
Asmara = Asmera **51** 15 19N 38 55 E
Asmera **51** 15 19N 38 55 E
Aso **36** 33 0N 131 5 E
Asotin **72** 46 20N 117 3W
Aspen **73** 39 12N 106 56W
Aspermont **71** 33 11N 100 15W
Aspiring, Mt. **43** 44 23S 168 46 E
Asquith **65** 52 8N 107 13W
Assam □ **33** 26 0N 93 0 E
Asse **11** 50 24N 4 10 E
Assen **11** 53 0N 6 35 E
Assini **50** 5 9N 3 17W
Assiniboia **65** 49 40N 105 59W
Assiniboine → **65** 49 53N 97 8W
Assis **80** 22 40S 50 20W
Assisi **18** 43 4N 12 36 E
Assynt, L. **8** 58 25N 5 15W
Astara **23** 38 30N 48 50 E
Asti **18** 44 54N 8 11 E
Astipálaia **19** 36 32N 26 22 E
Astorga **13** 42 29N 6 8W
Astoria **72** 46 16N 123 50W
Astrakhan **23** 46 25N 48 5 E
Astrakhan-Bazàr **23** 39 14N 48 30 E
Asturias **13** 43 15N 6 0W
Asunción **80** 25 10S 57 30W
Asunción, La **78** 11 2N 63 53W
Aswân **51** 24 4N 32 57 E
Aswân High Dam = Sadd el Aali **51** 23 54N 32 54 E
Asyût **51** 27 11N 31 4 E
At Ţafilah **30** 30 45N 35 30 E
At Tā'if **29** 21 5N 40 27 E
Aţ Ţur **28** 31 47N 35 14 E
Aţ Ţurrah **28** 32 39N 35 59 E
Atacama, Desierto de **80** 24 0S 69 20W
Atacama, Salar de **80** 23 30S 68 20W
Atakpamé **53** 7 31N 1 13 E
Atalaya **78** 10 45S 73 50W
Atami **36** 35 5N 139 4 E
Atapupu **35** 9 0S 124 51 E
Atâr **50** 20 30N 13 5W
Atara **25** 63 10N 129 10 E
Atascadero **73** 35 32N 120 44W
Atasu **24** 48 30N 71 0 E
Atauro **35** 8 10S 125 30 E
Atbara **51** 17 42N 33 59 E
'Atbara → **51** 17 40N 33 56 E
Atbasar **24** 51 48N 68 20 E
Atchafalaya B. **71** 29 30N 91 20W
Atchison **70** 39 40N 95 10W
Ath **11** 50 38N 3 47 E
Athabasca **64** 54 45N 113 20W
Athabasca → **65** 58 40N 110 50W
Athabasca, L. **65** 59 15N 109 15W
Athboy **9** 53 37N 6 55W
Athenry **9** 53 18N 8 45W
Athens = Athínai **19** 37 58N 23 46 E
Athens, Ala., U.S.A. **69** 34 49N 86 58W
Athens, Ga., U.S.A. **69** 33 56N 83 24W
Athens, Ohio, U.S.A. **68** 39 25N 82 6W
Athens, Tenn., U.S.A. **69** 35 45N 84 38W
Athens, Tex., U.S.A. **71** 32 11N 95 48W
Atherton **44** 17 17S 145 30 E
Athínai **19** 37 58N 23 46 E
Athlone **9** 53 26N 7 57W
Atholl, Forest of **8** 56 51N 3 50W
Atholville **63** 47 59N 66 43W
Áthos **19** 40 9N 24 22 E
Athy **9** 53 0N 7 0W
Ati **51** 13 13N 18 20 E
Atico **78** 16 14S 73 40W
Atikokan **62** 48 45N 91 37W
Atikonak L. **63** 52 40N 64 32W
Atka **25** 60 50N 151 48 E
Atkinson **70** 42 35N 98 59W
Atlanta, Ga., U.S.A. **69** 33 50N 84 24W
Atlanta, Tex., U.S.A. **71** 33 7N 94 8W
Atlantic **70** 41 25N 95 0W
Atlantic City **68** 39 25N 74 25W
Atlantic Ocean **2** 0 0 20 0W
Atlas Mts. = Haut Atlas **50** 32 30N 5 0W
Atlin **60** 59 31N 133 41W
Atlin, L. **64** 59 26N 133 45W
'Atlit **28** 32 42N 34 56 E
Atmore **69** 31 2N 87 30W
Atoka **71** 34 22N 96 10W
Atoyac → **74** 16 30N 97 31W
Atrak → **31** 37 50N 57 0 E
Atsuta **36** 43 24N 141 26 E
Attalla **69** 34 2N 86 5W
Attawapiskat **62** 52 56N 82 24W
Attawapiskat → **62** 52 57N 82 18W
Attawapiskat, L. **62** 52 18N 87 54W
Attica **68** 40 20N 87 15W
Attikamagen L. **63** 55 0N 66 30W
'Attīl **28** 32 23N 35 4 E
Attleboro **68** 41 56N 71 18W
Attock **32** 33 52N 72 20 E
Attopeu **34** 14 48N 106 50 E
Attur **32** 11 35N 78 30 E
Atuel → **80** 36 17S 66 50W
Åtvidaberg **21** 58 12N 16 0 E
Atwater **73** 37 21N 120 37W
Atwood **70** 39 52N 101 3W
Au Sable → **68** 44 25N 83 20W
Au Sable Pt. **62** 46 40N 86 10W
Aube □ **12** 48 15N 4 10 E
Aube → **12** 48 34N 3 43 E
Auburn, Ala., U.S.A. **69** 32 37N 85 30W
Auburn, Calif., U.S.A. **72** 38 53N 121 4W
Auburn, Ind., U.S.A. **68** 41 20N 85 0W
Auburn, N.Y., U.S.A. **68** 42 57N 76 39W
Auburn, Nebr., U.S.A. **70** 40 25N 95 50W
Auburn Range **45** 25 15S 150 30 E
Auburndale **69** 28 5N 81 45W
Aubusson **12** 45 57N 2 11 E
Auch **12** 43 39N 0 36 E
Auckland **43** 36 52S 174 46 E
Auckland Is. **40** 50 40S 166 5 E
Aude □ **12** 43 8N 2 28 E
Aude → **12** 43 13N 3 14 E
Auden **62** 50 14N 87 53W
Audubon **70** 41 43N 94 56W
Augathella **45** 25 48S 146 35 E
Augrabies Falls **56** 28 35S 20 20 E
Augsburg **14** 48 22N 10 54 E
Augusta, Italy **18** 37 14N 15 12 E
Augusta, Ark., U.S.A. **71** 35 17N 91 25W
Augusta, Ga., U.S.A. **69** 33 29N 81 59W
Augusta, Kans., U.S.A. **71** 37 40N 97 0W
Augusta, Maine, U.S.A. **63** 44 20N 69 46W
Augusta, Mont., U.S.A. **72** 47 30N 112 29W
Augusta, Wis., U.S.A. **70** 44 41N 91 8W
Augustów **15** 53 51N 23 0 E
Augustus, Mt. **47** 24 20S 116 50 E
Augustus Downs **44** 18 35S 139 55 E
Augustus I. **46** 15 20S 124 30 E
Ault **70** 40 40N 104 42W
Aunis **12** 46 5N 0 50W
Auponhia **35** 1 58S 125 27 E
Aurangabad, Bihar, India **33** 24 45N 84 18 E
Aurangabad, Maharashtra, India **32** 19 50N 75 23 E
Aurillac **12** 44 55N 2 26 E
Aurora, S. Africa **56** 32 40S 18 29 E
Aurora, Colo., U.S.A. **70** 39 44N 104 55W
Aurora, Ill., U.S.A. **68** 41 42N 88 12W
Aurora, Mo., U.S.A. **71** 36 58N 93 42W
Aurora, Nebr., U.S.A. **70** 40 55N 98 0W
Aurukun Mission **44** 13 20S 141 45 E
Aus **56** 26 35S 16 12 E
Aust-Agder fylke □ **21** 58 55N 7 40 E
Austerlitz = Slavkov **14** 49 10N 16 52 E
Austin, Minn., U.S.A. **70** 43 37N 92 59W
Austin, Nev., U.S.A. **72** 39 30N 117 1W
Austin, Tex., U.S.A. **71** 30 20N 97 45W
Austin, L. **47** 27 40S 118 0 E
Austral Downs **44** 20 30S 137 45 E
Austral Is. = Tubuai Is. **41** 25 0S 150 0W
Austral Seamount Chain **41** 24 0S 150 0W
Australia ■ **3** 23 0S 135 0 E
Australian Alps **45** 36 30S 148 30 E
Australian Cap. Terr. □ **45** 35 30S 149 0 E
Austria ■ **14** 47 0N 14 0 E
Austvågøy **20** 68 20N 14 40 E
Autlán **74** 19 40N 104 30W
Autun **12** 46 58N 4 17 E
Auvergne, Australia **46** 15 39S 130 1 E
Auvergne, France **12** 45 20N 3 15 E
Auxerre **12** 47 48N 3 32 E
Avallon **12** 47 30N 3 53 E
Avalon Pen. **63** 47 30N 53 20W
Aveiro, Brazil **79** 3 10S 55 5W
Aveiro, Portugal **13** 40 37N 8 38W
Āvej **30** 35 40N 49 15 E
Avellaneda **80** 34 50S 58 10W
Avellino **18** 40 54N 14 46 E
Aversa **18** 40 58N 14 11 E
Avery **72** 47 22N 115 56W
Aves, I. de **75** 15 45N 63 55W
Aves, Is. de **75** 12 0N 67 30W
Avesta **21** 60 9N 16 10 E
Aveyron □ **12** 44 22N 2 45 E
Aviá Terai **80** 26 45S 60 50W
Avignon **12** 43 57N 4 50 E
Ávila **13** 40 39N 4 43W
Avilés **13** 43 35N 5 57W
Avoca, Australia **45** 37 5S 143 26 E
Avoca, Ireland **9** 52 52N 6 13W
Avoca → **45** 35 40S 143 43 E
Avola **64** 51 45N 119 19W
Avon **70** 43 0N 98 3W
Avon □ **7** 51 30N 2 40W
Avon →, Australia **47** 31 40S 116 7 E
Avon →, Avon, U.K. **7** 51 30N 2 43W
Avon →, Hants., U.K. **7** 50 44N 1 45W
Avon →, Warwick, U.K. **7** 52 0N 2 9W
Avonlea **65** 50 0N 105 0W
Avonmouth **7** 51 30N 2 42W
Avranches **12** 48 40N 1 20W
'Awālī **31** 26 0N 50 30 E
'Awartā **28** 32 10N 35 17 E
Awash **29** 9 1N 40 10 E
Awatere → **43** 41 37S 174 10 E
Awbārī **51** 26 46N 12 57 E
Awe, L. **8** 56 15N 5 15W
Awgu **53** 6 4N 7 24 E
Awjilah **51** 29 8N 21 7 E
Axarfjörður **20** 66 15N 16 45W
Axel Heiberg I. **58** 80 0N 90 0W
Axim **50** 4 51N 2 15W
Axminster **7** 50 47N 3 1W
Ayabaca **78** 4 40S 79 53W
Ayabe **36** 35 20N 135 20 E
Ayacucho, Argentina **80** 37 5S 58 20W
Ayacucho, Peru **78** 13 0S 74 0W
Ayaguz **24** 48 10N 80 0 E
Ayamonte **13** 37 12N 7 24W
Ayan **25** 56 30N 138 16 E
Ayaviri **78** 14 50S 70 35W
Āybak **31** 36 15N 68 5 E
Ayers Rock **47** 25 23S 131 5 E
Ayios Evstrátios **19** 39 34N 24 58 E
Aykin **22** 62 15N 49 56 E
Aylesbury **7** 51 48N 0 49W
Aylmer L. **60** 64 0N 110 8W
'Ayn 'Arīk **28** 31 54N 35 8 E
Ayn Dār **30** 25 55N 49 10 E
Ayn Zālah **30** 36 45N 42 35 E
Ayon, Ostrov **25** 69 50N 169 0 E
Ayr, Australia **44** 19 35S 147 25 E
Ayr, U.K. **8** 55 28N 4 37W
Ayr → **8** 55 29N 4 40W
Ayre, Pt. of **6** 54 27N 4 21W
Aytos **19** 42 42N 27 16 E
Ayu, Kepulauan **35** 0 35N 131 5 E
Ayutla **74** 16 58N 99 17W
Ayvalık **30** 39 20N 26 46 E
Az Zahrān **30** 26 10N 50 7 E
Az Zarqā **28** 32 5N 36 4 E
Az-Zilfī **30** 26 12N 44 52 E
Az Zubayr **30** 30 20N 47 50 E
Azamgarh **33** 26 5N 83 13 E
Āzarbāyjān-e Gharbī □ **30** 37 0N 44 30 E
Āzarbāyjān-e Sharqī □ **30** 37 20N 47 0 E
Azare **53** 11 55N 10 10 E
Azbine = Aïr **50** 18 30N 8 0 E
Azerbaijan S.S.R. □ **23** 40 20N 48 0 E
Azogues **78** 2 35S 78 0W
Azor **28** 32 2N 34 48 E
Azores **2** 38 44N 29 0W
Azov **23** 47 3N 39 25 E
Azov Sea = Azovskoye More **24** 46 0N 36 30 E
Azovskoye More **24** 46 0N 36 30 E
Azovy **24** 64 55N 64 35 E
Aztec **73** 36 54N 108 0W
Azúa de Compostela **75** 18 25N 70 44W
Azuaga **13** 38 16N 5 39W
Azuero, Pen. de **75** 7 30N 80 30W
Azul **80** 36 42S 59 43W

B

Ba Don **34** 17 45N 106 26 E
Ba Ria **34** 10 30N 107 10 E
Ba Xian **38** 39 8N 116 22 E
Baa **35** 10 50S 123 0 E
Baarle Nassau **11** 51 27N 4 56 E
Baarn **11** 52 12N 5 17 E
Bab el Mandeb **29** 12 35N 43 25 E
Babahoyo **78** 1 40S 79 30W
Babakin **47** 32 7S 118 1 E
Babana **53** 10 31N 3 46 E
Babar **35** 8 0S 129 30 E
Babb **72** 48 56N 113 27W
Babinda **44** 17 20S 145 56 E
Babine **64** 55 22N 126 37W
Babine → **64** 55 45N 127 44W
Babine L. **64** 54 48N 126 0W
Babo **35** 2 30S 133 30 E
Bābol **31** 36 40N 52 50 E
Bābol Sar **31** 36 45N 52 45 E
Baboua **54** 5 49N 14 58 E
Babura **53** 12 51N 8 59 E
Babuyan Chan. **35** 18 40N 121 30 E
Babylon **30** 32 40N 44 30 E
Bacabal **79** 4 15S 44 45W
Bacan **35** 8 27S 126 27 E
Bacan, Kepulauan **35** 0 35S 127 30 E
Bacan, Pulau **35** 0 50S 127 30 E
Bacarra **35** 18 15N 120 37 E
Bacău **15** 46 35N 26 55 E
Bacerac **74** 30 18N 108 50W
Bachelina **24** 57 45N 67 20 E
Back → **60** 65 10N 104 0W
Backstairs Passage **45** 35 40S 138 5 E
Bacolod **35** 10 40N 122 57 E
Bad → **70** 44 22N 100 22W
Bad Axe **68** 43 48N 82 59W
Bad Ischl **14** 47 44N 13 38 E
Bad Lands **70** 43 40N 102 10W
Badagara **32** 11 35N 75 40 E
Badajoz **13** 38 50N 6 59W
Badakhshān □ **31** 36 30N 71 0 E
Badalona **13** 41 26N 2 15 E
Badalzai **32** 29 50N 65 35 E
Badampahar **33** 22 10N 86 10 E
Badanah **30** 30 58N 41 30 E
Badarinath **32** 30 45N 79 30 E
Badas **34** 4 33N 114 25 E
Badas, Kepulauan **34** 0 45N 107 5 E
Baddo → **31** 28 0N 64 20 E
Bade **35** 7 10S 139 35 E
Baden **14** 48 1N 16 13 E
Baden-Baden **14** 48 45N 8 15 E
Baden-Württemberg □ **14** 48 40N 9 0 E
Badgastein **14** 47 7N 13 9 E
Badger **63** 49 0N 56 4W
Bādghīsāt □ **31** 35 0N 63 0 E
Badin **32** 24 38N 68 54 E
Badong **39** 31 1N 110 23 E
Baduen **29** 7 15N 47 40 E
Badulla **32** 7 1N 81 7 E
Baeza **13** 37 57N 3 25W
Bafatá **50** 12 8N 14 40W
Baffin B. **58** 72 0N 64 0W
Baffin I. **61** 68 0N 75 0W
Bafia **54** 4 40N 11 10 E
Bafing → **50** 13 49N 10 50W
Bafoulabé **50** 13 50N 10 55W
Bāfq **31** 31 40N 55 25 E
Bafra **30** 41 34N 35 54 E
Bāft **31** 29 15N 56 38 E
Bafut **53** 6 6N 10 2 E
Bafwasende **54** 1 3N 27 5 E
Bagamoyo **54** 6 28S 38 55 E
Baganga **35** 7 34N 126 33 E
Bagani **56** 18 7S 21 41 E
Bagansiapiapi **34** 2 12N 100 50 E
Bagdarin **25** 54 26N 113 36 E
Bagé **80** 31 20S 54 15W
Bagenalstown = Muine Bheag **9** 52 42N 6 57W
Baggs **72** 41 8N 107 46W
Baghdād **30** 33 20N 44 30 E
Baghlān **31** 36 12N 69 0 E
Baghlān □ **31** 36 0N 68 30 E
Bagley **70** 47 30N 95 22W
Bagotville **63** 48 22N 70 54W
Baguio **35** 16 26N 120 34 E
Bahama, Canal Viejo de **75** 22 10N 77 30W
Bahamas ■ **75** 24 0N 75 0W
Baharampur **33** 24 2N 88 27 E
Bahawalpur **32** 29 24N 71 40 E
Bahía = Salvador **79** 13 0S 38 30W
Bahía □ **79** 12 0S 42 0W
Bahía, Is. de la **75** 16 45N 86 15W
Bahía Blanca **80** 38 35S 62 13W
Bahía de Caráquez **78** 0 40S 80 27W
Bahía Laura **80** 48 10S 66 30W
Bahía Negra **78** 20 5S 58 5W
Bahr Aouk → **54** 8 40N 19 0 E
Bahr el Ahmar □ **51** 20 0N 35 0 E
Bahr el Ghazâl □ **51** 7 0N 28 0 E
Bahr Salamat → **51** 9 20N 18 0 E
Bahraich **33** 27 38N 81 37 E
Bahrain ■ **31** 26 0N 50 35 E
Baia Mare **15** 47 40N 23 35 E
Baïbokoum **51** 7 46N 15 43 E
Baicheng **38** 45 38N 122 42 E
Baidoa **29** 3 8N 43 30 E
Baie Comeau **63** 49 12N 68 10W
Baie-St-Paul **63** 47 28N 70 32W
Baie Trinité **63** 49 25N 67 20W
Baie Verte **63** 49 55N 56 12W
Ba'ījī **30** 35 0N 43 30 E
Baikal, L. = Baykal, Oz. **25** 53 0N 108 0 E
Baile Atha Cliath = Dublin **9** 53 20N 6 18W
Bailundo **55** 12 10S 15 50 E
Bainbridge **69** 30 53N 84 34W
Baing **35** 10 14S 120 34 E
Bainville **70** 48 8N 104 10W
Bā'ir **30** 30 45N 36 55 E
Baird **71** 32 25N 99 25W
Baird Mts. **60** 67 10N 160 15W
Bairin Youqi **38** 43 30N 118 35 E
Bairin Zuoqi **38** 43 58N 119 15 E
Bairnsdale **45** 37 48S 147 36 E
Baitadi **33** 29 35N 80 25 E
Baixo-Alentejo **13** 38 0N 8 30W
Baiyin **38** 36 45N 104 14 E
Baiyu Shan **38** 37 15N 107 30 E
Baja **15** 46 12N 18 59 E
Baja, Pta. **74** 29 50N 116 0W
Baja California **74** 31 10N 115 12W
Bajimba, Mt. **45** 29 17S 152 6 E
Bajo Nuevo **75** 15 40N 78 50W
Bajool **44** 23 40S 150 35 E
Bakala **51** 6 15N 20 20 E
Bakchar **24** 57 1N 82 5 E
Bakel **50** 14 56N 12 20W
Baker, Calif., U.S.A. **73** 35 16N 116 8W
Baker, Mont., U.S.A. **70** 46 22N 104 12W
Baker, Oreg., U.S.A. **72** 44 50N 117 55W
Baker, L., Australia **47** 26 54S 126 5 E
Baker, L., Canada **60** 64 0N 96 0W
Baker I. **40** 0 10N 176 35W
Baker Lake **60** 64 20N 96 3W
Baker Mt. **72** 48 50N 121 49W
Bakers Creek **44** 21 13S 149 7 E
Baker's Dozen Is. **62** 56 45N 78 45W
Bakersfield **73** 35 25N 119 0W
Bākhtarān **30** 34 23N 47 0 E
Bākhtarān □ **30** 34 0N 46 30 E
Bakinskikh Komissarov, im. 26 **30** 39 20N 49 15 E
Bakkafjörður **20** 66 2N 14 48W
Bakkagerði **20** 65 31N 13 49W
Bakony Forest = Bakony Hegyseg **15** 47 10N 17 30 E
Bakony Hegyseg **15** 47 10N 17 30 E
Bakouma **51** 5 40N 22 56 E
Baku **23** 40 25N 49 45 E
Bal'ā **28** 32 20N 35 6 E
Bala, L. = Tegid, L. **6** 52 53N 3 38W
Balabac, Str. **34** 7 53N 117 5 E
Balabac I. **34** 8 0N 117 0 E
Balabakk **30** 34 0N 36 10 E
Balabalangan, Kepulauan **34** 2 20S 117 30 E
Balaghat **32** 21 49N 80 12 E
Balaghat Ra. **32** 18 50N 76 30 E
Balaguer **13** 41 50N 0 50 E
Balaklava, Australia **45** 34 7S 138 22 E
Balaklava, U.S.S.R. **23** 44 30N 33 30 E
Balakovo **22** 52 4N 47 55 E
Balashov **22** 51 30N 43 10 E

Balasore

Balasore = Baleshwar 33 21 35N 87 3 E
Balaton 15 46 50N 17 40 E
Balboa 75 9 0N 79 30W
Balboa Hill 74 9 6N 79 44W
Balbriggan 9 53 35N 6 10W
Balcarce 80 38 0S 58 10W
Balcarres 65 50 50N 103 35W
Balchik 19 43 28N 28 11 E
Balclutha 43 46 15S 169 45 E
Bald Hd. 47 35 6S 118 1 E
Bald I. 47 34 57S 118 27 E
Bald Knob 71 35 20N 91 35W
Baldock L. 65 56 33N 97 57W
Baldwin, Fla., U.S.A. 69 30 15N 82 10W
Baldwin, Mich., U.S.A. 68 43 54N 85 53W
Baldwinsville 68 43 10N 76 19W
Baleares, Is. 13 39 30N 3 0 E
Balearic Is. = Baleares, Is. 13 39 30N 3 0 E
Baler 35 15 46N 121 34 E
Baleshwar 33 21 35N 87 3 E
Balfe's Creek 44 20 12S 145 55 E
Balfour 57 26 38S 28 35 E
Balfouriyya 28 32 38N 35 18 E
Bali, Cameroon 53 5 54N 10 0 E
Bali, Indonesia 34 8 20S 115 0 E
Bali □ 34 8 20S 115 0 E
Bali, Selat 35 8 18S 114 25 E
Balikesir 30 39 35N 27 58 E
Balikpapan 34 1 10S 116 55 E
Balimbing 35 5 5N 119 58 E
Balipara 33 26 50N 92 45 E
Baliza 79 16 0S 52 20W
Balkan Mts. = Stara Planina 19 43 15N 23 0 E
Balkan Pen. 4 42 0N 22 0 E
Balkh 31 36 44N 66 47 E
Balkh □ 31 36 30N 67 0 E
Balkhash 24 46 50N 74 50 E
Balkhash, Ozero 24 46 0N 74 50 E
Balla 33 24 10N 91 35 E
Ballachulish 8 56 40N 5 10W
Balladonia 47 32 27S 123 51 E
Ballarat 45 37 33S 143 50 E
Ballard, L. 47 29 20S 120 10 E
Ballater 8 57 2N 3 2W
Ballenas, Canal de 74 29 10N 113 45W
Ballenas, Canal de 74 29 10N 113 45W
Ballidu 47 30 35S 116 45 E
Ballina, Australia 45 28 50S 153 31 E
Ballina, Mayo, Ireland 9 54 7N 9 10W
Ballina, Tipp., Ireland 9 52 49N 8 27W
Ballinasloe 9 53 20N 8 12W
Ballinger 71 31 45N 99 58W
Ballinrobe 9 53 36N 9 13W
Ballinskelligs B. 9 51 46N 10 11W
Ballycastle 9 55 12N 6 15W
Ballymena 9 54 53N 6 18W
Ballymena □ 9 54 53N 6 18W
Ballymoney 9 55 5N 6 30W
Ballymoney □ 9 55 5N 6 23W
Ballyshannon 9 54 30N 8 10W
Balmaceda 80 46 0S 71 50W
Balmoral, Australia 45 37 15S 141 48 E
Balmoral, U.K. 8 57 3N 3 13W
Balmorhea 71 31 2N 103 41W
Balonne → 45 28 47S 147 56 E
Balrampur 33 27 30N 82 20 E
Balranald 45 34 38S 143 33 E
Balsas → 74 17 55N 102 10W
Balta, U.S.A. 70 48 12N 100 7W
Balta, U.S.S.R. 23 48 2N 29 45 E
Baltic Sea 21 56 0N 20 0 E
Baltimore, Ireland 9 51 29N 9 22W
Baltimore, U.S.A. 68 39 18N 76 37W
Baluchistan □ 31 27 30N 65 0 E
Balygychan 25 63 56N 154 12 E
Bam 31 29 7N 58 14 E
Bama 53 11 33N 13 41 E
Bamako 50 12 34N 7 55W
Bamba 50 17 5N 1 24W
Bambari 51 5 40N 20 35 E
Bambaroo 44 18 50S 146 10 E
Bamberg, Germany 14 49 54N 10 53 E
Bamberg, U.S.A. 69 33 19N 81 1W
Bambili 54 3 40N 26 0 E
Bamenda 53 5 57N 10 11 E
Bamfield 64 48 45N 125 10W
Bāmīān □ 31 35 0N 67 0 E
Bamiancheng 38 43 15N 124 2 E
Bampūr 31 27 15N 60 21 E
Ban Don = Surat Thani 34 9 6N 99 20 E
Banaba 40 0 45S 169 50 E
Banalia 54 1 32N 25 5 E
Banam 34 11 20N 105 17 E
Banamba 50 13 29N 7 22W
Banana 44 24 28S 150 8 E
Bananal, I. do 79 11 30S 50 30W
Banaras = Varanasi 33 25 22N 83 0 E
Banbridge 9 54 21N 6 17W
Banbridge □ 9 54 21N 6 16W
Banbury 7 52 4N 1 21W
Banchory 8 57 3N 2 30W
Bancroft 62 45 3N 77 51W
Band-e Torkestān 31 35 30N 64 0 E
Banda 32 25 30N 80 26 E
Banda, Kepulauan 35 4 37S 129 50 E
Banda, La 80 27 45S 64 10W
Banda Aceh 34 5 35N 95 20 E
Banda Banda, Mt. 45 31 10S 152 28 E
Banda Elat 35 5 40S 133 5 E
Banda Sea 35 6 0S 130 0 E
Bandai-San 36 37 36N 140 4 E
Bandanaira 35 4 32S 129 54 E
Bandar = Machilipatnam 33 16 12N 81 8 E
Bandār 'Abbās 31 27 15N 56 15 E
Bandar-e Anzalī 30 37 30N 49 30 E
Bandar-e Chārak 31 26 45N 54 20 E
Bandar-e Deylam 30 30 5N 50 10 E
Bandar-e Khomeyni 30 30 30N 49 5 E
Bandar-e Lengeh 31 26 35N 54 58 E
Bandar-e Ma'shur 30 30 35N 49 10 E
Bandar-e Nakhīlū 31 26 58N 53 30 E
Bandar-e Rīg 31 29 29N 50 38 E
Bandar-e Torkeman 31 37 0N 54 10 E
Bandar Maharani = Muar 34 2 3N 102 34 E
Bandar Penggaram = Batu Pahat 34 1 50N 102 56 E
Bandar Seri Begawan 34 4 52N 115 0 E
Bandawe 55 11 58S 34 5 E
Bandeira, Pico da 79 20 26S 41 47W
Bandera, Argentina 80 28 55S 62 20W
Bandera, U.S.A. 71 29 45N 99 3W
Banderas, B. de 74 20 40N 105 30W
Bandiagara 50 14 12N 3 29W
Bandırma 30 40 20N 28 0 E
Bandon 9 51 44N 8 45W
Bandon → 9 51 40N 8 41W
Bandundu 54 3 15S 17 22 E
Bandung 35 6 54S 107 36 E
Bandya 47 27 40S 122 5 E
Banes 75 21 0N 75 42W
Banff, Canada 64 51 10N 115 34W
Banff, U.K. 8 57 40N 2 32W
Banff Nat. Park 64 51 30N 116 15W
Banfora 50 10 40N 4 40W
Bang Saphan 34 11 14N 99 28 E
Bangalore 32 12 59N 77 40 E
Bangassou 54 4 55N 23 7 E
Banggai 35 1 40S 123 30 E
Banggi, P. 34 7 17N 117 12 E
Banghāzī 51 32 11N 20 3 E
Bangil 35 7 36S 112 50 E
Bangka, Pulau, Sulawesi, Indonesia 35 1 50N 125 5 E
Bangka, Pulau, Sumatera, Indonesia 34 2 0S 105 50 E
Bangka, Selat 34 2 30S 105 30 E
Bangkalan 35 7 2S 112 46 E
Bangkinang 34 0 18N 101 5 E
Bangko 34 2 5S 102 9 E
Bangkok 34 13 45N 100 35 E
Bangladesh ■ 33 24 0N 90 0 E
Bangong Tso 32 34 0N 78 20 E
Bangor, N. Ireland, U.K. 9 54 40N 5 40W
Bangor, Wales, U.K. 6 53 13N 4 9W
Bangor, U.S.A. 63 44 48N 68 42W
Bangued 35 17 40N 120 37 E
Bangui 54 4 23N 18 35 E
Bangweulu, L. 54 11 0S 30 0 E
Bani 75 18 16N 70 22W
Banī Na'īm 28 31 31N 35 10 E
Banī Suhaylah 28 31 21N 34 19 E
Banī Walīd 51 31 36N 13 53 E
Banīnah 51 32 0N 20 12 E
Bāniyās 30 35 10N 36 0 E
Banja Luka 18 44 49N 17 11 E
Banjar 35 7 24S 108 30 E
Banjarmasin 34 3 20S 114 35 E
Banjarnegara 35 7 24S 109 42 E
Banjul 50 13 28N 16 40W
Banka Banka 44 18 50S 134 0 E
Bankipore 33 25 35N 85 10 E
Banks I., B.C., Canada 64 53 20N 130 0W
Banks I., N.W.T., Canada 60 73 15N 121 30W
Banks Pen. 43 43 45S 173 15 E
Banks Str. 44 40 40S 148 10 E
Bankura 33 23 11N 87 18 E
Bann →, Down, U.K. 9 54 30N 6 31W
Bann →, Londonderry, U.K. 9 55 10N 6 34W
Banning 73 33 58N 116 52W
Banningville = Bandundu 54 3 15S 17 22 E
Bannockburn 8 56 5N 3 55W
Bannu 32 33 0N 70 18 E
Banská Bystrica 15 48 46N 19 14 E
Banská Štiavnica 15 48 25N 18 55 E
Banswara 32 23 32N 74 24 E
Banten 35 6 5S 106 8 E
Bantry 9 51 40N 9 28W
Bantry, B. 9 51 35N 9 50W
Bantul 35 7 55S 110 19 E
Banu 32 35 35N 69 5 E
Banyak, Kepulauan 34 2 10N 97 10 E
Banyo 53 6 52N 11 45 E
Banyumas 35 7 32S 109 18 E
Banyuwangi 35 8 13S 114 21 E
Banzyville = Mobayi 54 4 15N 21 8 E
Baocheng 39 33 12N 106 56 E
Baode 38 39 1N 111 5 E
Baoding 38 38 50N 115 28 E
Baoji 39 34 20N 107 5 E
Baojing 39 28 45N 109 41 E
Baokang 39 31 54N 111 12 E
Baoshan 37 25 10N 99 5 E
Baotou 38 40 32N 110 2 E
Baoying 39 33 17N 119 20 E
Bapatla 33 15 55N 80 30 E
Bâqa el Gharbîyya 28 32 25N 35 2 E
Ba'qūbah 30 33 45N 44 50 E
Bar 19 42 8N 19 8 E
Bar Harbor 63 44 15N 68 20W
Bar-le-Duc 12 48 47N 5 10 E
Barabai 34 2 32S 115 34 E
Barabinsk 24 55 20N 78 20 E
Baraboo 70 43 28N 89 46W
Baracaldo 13 43 18N 2 59W
Baracoa 75 20 20N 74 30W
Baraga 70 46 49N 88 29W
Barahona 75 18 13N 71 7W
Barail Range 33 25 15N 93 20 E
Barakhola 33 25 0N 92 45 E
Barakpur 33 22 44N 88 30 E
Barakula 45 26 30S 150 33 E
Baralaba 44 24 13S 149 50 E
Baralzon L. 65 60 0N 98 3W
Baramula 32 34 15N 74 20 E
Baran 32 25 9N 76 40 E
Baranof I. 60 57 0N 135 10W
Baranovichi 22 53 10N 26 0 E
Barão de Melgaço 78 11 50S 60 45W
Barapasi 35 2 15S 137 5 E
Barat Daya, Kepulauan 35 7 30S 128 0 E
Barataria B. 71 29 15N 89 45W
Barbacena 79 21 15S 43 56W
Barbacoas 78 1 45N 78 0W
Barbados ■ 75 13 0N 59 30W
Barberton, S. Africa 57 25 42S 31 2 E
Barberton, U.S.A. 68 41 0N 81 40W
Barbourville 69 36 57N 83 52W
Barbuda I. 75 17 30N 61 40W
Barca, La 74 20 20N 102 40W
Barcaldine 44 23 43S 145 6 E
Barcelona, Spain 13 41 21N 2 10 E
Barcelona, Venezuela 78 10 10N 64 40W
Barcelos 78 1 0S 63 0W
Barcoo → 44 25 30S 142 50 E
Barddhaman 33 23 14N 87 39 E
Bardera 29 2 20N 42 27 E
Bardi, Ra's 30 24 17N 37 31 E
Bardia 51 31 45N 25 0 E
Bardsey I. 6 52 46N 4 47W
Bardstown 68 37 50N 85 29W
Bareilly 32 28 22N 79 27 E
Barentu 51 15 2N 37 35 E
Barga 37 30 40N 81 20 E
Bargal 29 11 25N 51 0 E
Bargara 44 24 50S 152 25 E
Barge, La 72 42 12N 110 4W
Barguzin 25 53 37N 109 37 E
Barhi 33 24 15N 85 25 E
Bari 18 41 6N 16 52 E
Bari Doab 32 30 20N 73 0 E
Barīm 29 12 39N 43 25 E
Barinas 78 8 36N 70 15W
Baring, C. 60 70 0N 117 30W
Bârîs 51 24 42N 30 31 E
Barisal 33 22 45N 90 20 E
Barisan, Bukit 34 3 30S 102 15 E
Barito → 34 4 0S 114 50 E
Barkā' 31 23 40N 58 0 E
Barkley Sound 64 48 50N 125 10W
Barkly Downs 44 20 30S 138 30 E
Barkly East 56 30 58S 27 33 E
Barkly Tableland 44 17 50S 136 40 E
Barkly West 56 28 5S 24 31 E
Barksdale 71 29 47N 100 2W
Barlee, L. 47 29 15S 119 30 E
Barletta 18 41 20N 16 17 E
Barlow L. 65 62 0N 103 0W
Barmedman 45 34 9S 147 21 E
Barmer 32 25 45N 71 20 E
Barmera 45 34 15S 140 28 E
Barmouth 6 52 44N 4 3W
Barnard Castle 6 54 33N 1 55W
Barnato 45 31 38S 145 0 E
Barnaul 24 53 20N 83 40 E
Barnesville 69 33 6N 84 9W
Barnet 7 51 37N 0 15W
Barneveld 11 52 7N 5 36 E
Barngo 44 25 3S 147 20 E
Barnhart 71 31 10N 101 8W
Barnsley 6 53 33N 1 29W
Barnstaple 7 51 5N 4 3W
Barnsville 70 46 43N 96 28W
Baro 53 8 35N 6 18 E
Baroda = Vadodara 32 22 20N 73 10 E
Baroe 56 33 13S 24 33 E
Baron Ra. 46 23 30S 127 45 E
Barpeta 33 26 20N 91 10 E
Barques, Pte. aux 68 44 5N 82 55W
Barquísimeto 78 10 4N 69 19W
Barra, Brazil 79 11 5S 43 10W
Barra, U.K. 8 57 0N 7 30W
Barra, Sd. of 8 57 4N 7 25W
Barra do Corda 79 5 30S 45 10W
Barra do Piraí 79 22 30S 43 50W
Barra Falsa, Pta. da 57 22 58S 35 37 E
Barra Hd. 8 56 47N 7 40W
Barraba 45 30 21S 150 35 E
Barrackpur = Barakpur 33 22 44N 88 30 E
Barranca, Lima, Peru 78 10 45S 77 50W
Barranca, Loreto, Peru 78 4 50S 76 50W
Barrancabermeja 78 7 0N 73 50W
Barrancas 78 8 55N 62 5W
Barrancos 13 38 10N 6 58W
Barranqueras 80 27 30S 59 0W
Barranquilla 78 11 0N 74 50W
Barras 79 4 15S 42 18W
Barraute 62 48 26N 77 38W
Barre 68 44 15N 72 30W
Barreiras 79 12 8S 45 0W
Barreirinhas 79 2 30S 42 50W
Barreiro 13 38 40N 9 6W
Barreiros 79 8 49S 35 12W
Barren, Nosy 57 18 25S 43 40 E
Barretos 79 20 30S 48 35W
Barrhead 64 54 10N 114 24W
Barrie 62 44 24N 79 40W
Barrier Ra. 45 31 0S 141 30 E
Barrière 64 51 12N 120 7W
Barrington L. 65 56 55N 100 15W
Barrington Tops 45 32 6S 151 28 E
Barringun 45 29 1S 145 41 E
Barrow 60 71 16N 156 50W
Barrow → 9 52 10N 6 57W
Barrow Creek 44 21 30S 133 55 E
Barrow I. 46 20 45S 115 20 E
Barrow-in-Furness 6 54 8N 3 15W
Barrow Pt. 44 14 20S 144 40 E
Barrow Ra. 47 26 0S 127 40 E
Barry 7 51 23N 3 19W
Barry's Bay 62 45 29N 77 41W
Barsi 32 18 10N 75 50 E
Barsoi 33 25 48N 87 57 E
Barstow, Calif., U.S.A. 73 34 58N 117 2W
Barstow, Tex., U.S.A. 71 31 28N 103 24W
Bartica 78 6 25N 58 40W
Bartin 30 41 38N 32 21 E
Bartlesville 71 36 50N 95 58W
Bartlett 71 30 46N 97 30W
Bartlett, L. 64 63 5N 118 20W
Barton 47 30 31S 132 39 E
Barton-upon-Humber 6 53 41N 0 27W
Bartow 69 27 53N 81 49W
Barú, Volcan 75 8 55N 82 35W
Bas-Rhin □ 12 48 40N 7 30 E
Bāsa'idū 31 26 35N 55 20 E
Basankusa 54 1 5N 19 50 E
Basel 14 47 35N 7 35 E
Bashkir A.S.S.R. □ 22 54 0N 57 0 E
Basilan 35 6 35N 122 0 E
Basilan Str. 35 6 50N 122 0 E
Basildon 7 51 34N 0 29 E
Basilicata □ 18 40 30N 16 0 E
Basim = Washim 32 20 3N 77 0 E
Basin 72 44 22N 108 2W
Basingstoke 7 51 15N 1 5W
Baskatong, Rés. 62 46 46N 75 50W
Basle = Basel 14 47 35N 7 35 E
Basoka 54 1 16N 23 40 E
Basongo 54 4 15S 20 20 E
Basque Provinces = Vascongadas □ 13 42 50N 2 45W
Basra = Al Başrah 30 30 30N 47 50 E
Bass Rock 8 56 5N 2 40W
Bass Str. 44 39 15S 146 30 E
Bassano 64 50 48N 112 20W
Bassano del Grappa 18 45 45N 11 45 E
Bassar 53 9 19N 0 57 E
Bassas da India 55 22 0S 39 0 E
Basse-Terre 75 16 0N 61 40W
Bassein 33 16 45N 94 30 E
Basseterre 75 17 17N 62 43W
Bassett, Nebr., U.S.A. 70 42 37N 99 30W
Bassett, Va., U.S.A. 69 36 48N 79 59W
Bassigny 12 48 0N 5 30 E
Bassikounou 50 15 55N 6 1W
Bastak 31 27 15N 54 25 E
Bastar 33 19 15N 81 40 E
Basti 33 26 52N 82 55 E
Bastia 12 42 40N 9 30 E
Bastogne 11 50 1N 5 43 E
Bastrop 71 30 5N 97 22W
Bat Yam 28 32 2N 34 44 E
Bata 54 1 57N 9 50 E
Bataan 35 14 40N 120 25 E
Batabanó 75 22 40N 82 20W
Batabanó, G. de 75 22 30N 82 30W
Batac 35 18 3N 120 34 E
Batagoy 25 67 38N 134 38 E
Batalha 13 39 40N 8 50W
Batamay 25 63 30N 129 15 E
Batang, China 37 30 1N 99 0 E
Batang, Indonesia 35 6 55S 109 45 E
Batangafo 51 7 25N 18 20 E
Batangas 35 13 35N 121 10 E
Batanta 35 0 55S 130 40 E
Batavia 68 43 0N 78 10W
Batchelor 46 13 4S 131 1 E
Bateman's B. 45 35 40S 150 12 E
Batemans Bay 45 35 44S 150 11 E
Batesburg 69 33 54N 81 32W
Batesville, Ark., U.S.A. 71 35 48N 91 40W
Batesville, Miss., U.S.A. 71 34 17N 89 58W
Batesville, Tex., U.S.A. 71 28 59N 99 38W
Bath, U.K. 7 51 22N 2 22W
Bath, Maine, U.S.A. 63 43 50N 69 49W
Bath, N.Y., U.S.A. 68 42 20N 77 17W
Bathgate 8 55 54N 3 38W
Bathurst = Banjul 50 13 28N 16 40W
Bathurst, Australia 45 33 25S 149 31 E
Bathurst, Canada 63 47 37N 65 43W
Bathurst, S. Africa 56 33 30S 26 50 E
Bathurst, C. 60 70 34N 128 0W
Bathurst B. 44 14 16S 144 25 E
Bathurst Harb. 44 43 15S 146 10 E
Bathurst I. 46 11 30S 130 10 E
Bathurst Inlet 60 66 50N 108 1W
Batinah 31 24 0N 56 0 E
Batlow 45 35 31S 148 9 E
Batman 30 37 55N 41 5 E
Batna 50 35 34N 6 15 E
Baton Rouge 71 30 30N 91 5W
Batopilas 74 27 0N 107 45W
Batouri 54 4 30N 14 25 E
Battambang 34 13 7N 103 12 E
Batticaloa 32 7 43N 81 45 E
Battīr 28 31 44N 35 8 E
Battle 7 50 55N 0 30 E
Battle → 65 52 43N 108 15W
Battle Camp 44 15 20S 144 40 E
Battle Creek 68 42 20N 85 6W
Battle Harbour 63 52 16N 55 35W
Battle Lake 70 46 20N 95 43W
Battle Mountain 72 40 45N 117 0W
Battleford 65 52 45N 108 15W
Batu 29 6 55N 39 45 E
Batu, Kepulauan 34 0 30S 98 25 E
Batu Pahat 34 1 50N 102 56 E
Batuata 35 6 12S 122 42 E
Batumi 23 41 30N 41 30 E
Baturaja 34 4 11S 104 15 E
Baturité 79 4 28S 38 45W
Bau 34 1 25N 110 9 E
Baubau 35 5 25S 122 38 E
Bauchi 53 10 22N 9 48 E
Bauchi □ 53 10 30N 10 0 E
Baudette 70 48 46N 94 35W
Bauer, C. 45 32 44S 134 4 E
Bauhinia Downs 44 24 35S 149 18 E
Bauru 79 22 10S 49 0W
Baús 79 18 22S 52 47W
Bautzen 14 51 11N 14 25 E
Bavaria = Bayern □ 14 49 7N 11 30 E
Bavispe → 74 29 30N 109 11W
Bawdwin 33 23 5N 97 20 E
Bawean 34 5 46S 112 35 E
Bawku 53 11 3N 0 19W
Bawlake 33 19 11N 97 21 E
Baxley 69 31 43N 82 23W
Baxter Springs 71 37 3N 94 45W
Bay, L. de 35 14 20N 121 11 E
Bay Bulls 63 47 19N 52 50W
Bay City, Mich., U.S.A. 68 43 35N 83 51W

Bettiah

Bay City, Oreg., U.S.A. **72** 45 45N 123 58W
Bay City, Tex., U.S.A. **71** 28 59N 95 55W
Bay de Verde **63** 48 5N 52 54W
Bay Minette **69** 30 54N 87 43W
Bay St. Louis **71** 30 18N 89 22W
Bay Springs **71** 31 58N 89 18W
Bay View **43** 39 25S 176 50 E
Bayamo **75** 20 20N 76 40W
Bayamón **75** 18 24N 66 10W
Bayan **38** 46 5N 127 24 E
Bayan Har Shan **37** 34 0N 98 0 E
Bayan Hot = Alxa Zuoqi **38** 38 50N 105 40 E
Bayan Obo **38** 41 52N 109 59 E
Bayanaul **24** 50 45N 75 45 E
Bayanhongor **37** 46 8N 102 43 E
Bayard **70** 41 48N 103 17W
Bayázeh **31** 33 30N 54 40 E
Baybay **35** 10 40N 124 55 E
Bayburt **30** 40 15N 40 20 E
Bayern □ **14** 49 7N 11 30 E
Bayeux **12** 49 17N 0 42W
Bayfield **70** 46 50N 90 48W
Baykal, Oz. **25** 53 0N 108 0 E
Baykit **25** 61 50N 95 50 E
Baykonur **24** 47 48N 65 50 E
Baymak **22** 52 36N 58 19 E
Baynes Mts. **56** 17 15S 13 0 E
Bayombong **35** 16 30N 121 10 E
Bayonne **12** 43 30N 1 28W
Bayovar **78** 5 50S 81 0W
Bayram-Ali **24** 37 37N 62 10 E
Bayreuth **14** 49 56N 11 35 E
Bayrūt **30** 33 53N 35 31 E
Bayt Awlá **28** 31 37N 35 2 E
Bayt Fajjār **28** 31 38N 35 9 E
Bayt Fūrīk **28** 32 11N 35 20 E
Bayt Ḥānūn **28** 31 32N 34 32 E
Bayt Jālā **28** 31 43N 35 11 E
Bayt Lahm **28** 31 43N 35 12 E
Bayt Rīma **28** 32 2N 35 6 E
Bayt Sāḥūr **28** 31 42N 35 13 E
Bayt Ummar **28** 31 38N 35 7 E
Bayt 'ūr al Taḥtā **28** 31 54N 35 5 E
Baytīn **28** 31 56N 35 14 E
Baytown **71** 29 42N 94 57W
Baytūniyā **28** 31 54N 35 10 E
Baza **13** 37 30N 2 47W
Bazaruto, I. do **57** 21 40S 35 28 E
Bazhong **39** 31 52N 106 46 E
Beach **70** 46 57N 103 58W
Beachport **45** 37 29S 140 0 E
Beachy Head **7** 50 44N 0 16 E
Beacon, Australia **47** 30 26S 117 52 E
Beacon, U.S.A. **68** 41 32N 73 58W
Beaconia **65** 50 25N 96 31W
Beagle, Canal **80** 55 0S 68 30W
Beagle Bay **46** 16 58S 122 40 E
Bealanana **57** 14 33N 48 44 E
Bear I. **9** 51 38N 9 50W
Bear L., B.C., Canada **64** 56 10N 126 52W
Bear L., Man., Canada **65** 55 8N 96 0W
Bear L., U.S.A. **72** 42 0N 111 20W
Bearcreek **72** 45 11N 109 6W
Beardmore **62** 49 36N 87 57W
Beardstown **70** 40 0N 90 25W
Béarn **12** 43 20N 0 30W
Bearpaw Mts. **72** 48 15N 109 30W
Bearskin Lake **62** 53 58N 91 2W
Beata, C. **75** 17 40N 71 30W
Beatrice **70** 40 20N 96 40W
Beatrice, C. **44** 14 20S 136 55 E
Beatton → **64** 56 15N 120 45W
Beatton River **64** 57 26N 121 20W
Beatty **73** 36 58N 116 46W
Beauce, Plaine de la **12** 48 10N 1 45 E
Beauceville **63** 46 13N 70 46W
Beaudesert **45** 27 59S 153 0 E
Beaufort, Malaysia **34** 5 30N 115 40 E
Beaufort, N.C., U.S.A. **69** 34 45N 76 40W
Beaufort, S.C., U.S.A. **69** 32 25N 80 40W
Beaufort Sea **58** 72 0N 140 0W
Beaufort West **56** 32 18S 22 36 E
Beauharnois **62** 45 20N 73 52W
Beaulieu → **64** 62 3N 113 11W
Beauly **8** 57 29N 4 27W
Beauly → **8** 57 26N 4 28W
Beaumaris **6** 53 16N 4 7W
Beaumont **71** 30 5N 94 8W
Beaune **12** 47 2N 4 50 E
Beauséjour **65** 50 5N 96 35W
Beauvais **12** 49 25N 2 8 E
Beauval **65** 55 9N 107 37W
Beaver, Alaska, U.S.A. **60** 66 20N 147 30W
Beaver, Okla., U.S.A. **71** 36 52N 100 31W
Beaver, Utah, U.S.A. **73** 38 20N 112 45W
Beaver →, B.C., Canada **64** 59 52N 124 20W
Beaver →, Ont., Canada **62** 55 55N 87 48W
Beaver →, Sask., Canada **65** 55 26N 107 45W
Beaver City **70** 40 13N 99 50W
Beaver Dam **70** 43 28N 88 50W
Beaver Falls **68** 40 44N 80 20W
Beaver Hill L. **65** 54 5N 94 50W
Beaver I. **68** 45 40N 85 31W
Beaverhill L., Alta., Canada **64** 53 27N 112 32W
Beaverhill L., N.W.T., Canada **65** 63 2N 104 22W
Beaverlodge **64** 55 11N 119 29W
Beavermouth **64** 51 32N 117 23W
Beaverstone → **62** 54 59N 89 25W
Beawar **32** 26 3N 74 18 E
Beboa **57** 17 22S 44 33 E
Beccles **7** 52 27N 1 33 E
Bečej **19** 45 36N 20 3 E
Béchar **50** 31 38N 2 18W
Beckley **68** 37 50N 81 8W
Bedford, Canada **62** 45 7N 72 59W
Bedford, S. Africa **56** 32 40S 26 10 E
Bedford, U.K. **7** 52 8N 0 29W
Bedford, Ind., U.S.A. **68** 38 50N 86 30W
Bedford, Iowa, U.S.A. **70** 40 40N 94 41W
Bedford, Ohio, U.S.A. **68** 41 23N 81 32W
Bedford, Va., U.S.A. **68** 37 25N 79 30W
Bedford □ **7** 52 4N 0 28W
Bedford, C. **44** 15 14S 145 21 E
Bedford Downs **46** 17 19S 127 20 E
Bedourie **44** 24 30S 139 30 E
Beech Grove **68** 39 40N 86 2W
Beechworth **45** 36 22S 146 43 E
Beechy **65** 50 53N 107 24W
Beenleigh **45** 27 43S 153 10 E
Be'er Sheva' **28** 31 15N 34 48 E
Be'er Sheva' → **28** 31 12N 34 40 E
Be'er Toviyya **28** 31 44N 34 42 E
Be'eri **28** 31 25N 34 30 E
Be'erotayim **28** 32 19N 34 59 E
Beersheba = Be'er Sheva' **28** 31 15N 34 48 E
Beeston **6** 52 55N 1 11W
Beetaloo **44** 17 15S 133 50 E
Beeville **71** 28 27N 97 44W
Befale **54** 0 25N 20 45 E
Befandriana **57** 21 55S 44 0 E
Befotaka **57** 23 49S 47 0 E
Bega **45** 36 41S 149 51 E
Behara **57** 24 55S 46 20 E
Behbehān **30** 30 30N 50 15 E
Behshahr **31** 36 45N 53 35 E
Bei Jiang → **39** 23 2N 112 58 E
Bei'an **38** 48 10N 126 20 E
Beibei **39** 29 47N 106 22 E
Beihai **39** 21 28N 109 6 E
Beijing **38** 39 55N 116 20 E
Beijing □ **38** 39 55N 116 20 E
Beilen **11** 52 52N 6 27 E
Beilpajah **45** 32 54S 143 52 E
Beira **55** 19 50S 34 52 E
Beira-Alta **13** 40 35N 7 35W
Beira-Baixa **13** 40 2N 7 30W
Beira-Litoral **13** 40 5N 8 30W
Beirut = Bayrūt **30** 33 53N 35 31 E
Beit Lāhiyah **28** 31 32N 34 30 E
Beitaolaizhao **38** 44 58N 125 58 E
Beitbridge **55** 22 12S 30 0 E
Beizhen **38** 37 20N 118 2 E
Beja, Portugal **13** 38 2N 7 53W
Béja, Tunisia **50** 36 43N 9 12 E
Bejaia **50** 36 42N 5 2 E
Bejestān **31** 34 30N 58 5 E
Bekasi **35** 6 14S 106 59 E
Békéscsaba **15** 46 40N 21 5 E
Bekily **57** 24 13S 45 19 E
Bela, India **33** 25 50N 82 0 E
Bela, Pakistan **32** 26 12N 66 20 E
Bela Crkva **19** 44 55N 21 27 E
Bela Vista, Brazil **80** 22 12S 56 20W
Bela Vista, Mozam. **57** 26 10S 32 44 E
Belau Is. **40** 7 30N 134 30 E
Belavenona **57** 24 50S 47 4 E
Belawan **34** 3 33N 98 32 E
Belaya → **22** 56 0N 54 32 E
Belaya Tserkov **23** 49 45N 30 10 E
Belcher Is. **62** 56 15N 78 45W
Belebey **22** 54 7N 54 7 E
Belém **79** 1 20S 48 30W
Belén, Paraguay **80** 23 30S 57 6W
Belen, U.S.A. **73** 34 40N 106 50W
Belet Uen **29** 4 30N 45 5 E
Belev **22** 53 50N 36 5 E
Belfast, S. Africa **57** 25 42S 30 2 E
Belfast, U.K. **9** 54 35N 5 56W
Belfast, U.S.A. **63** 44 30N 69 0W
Belfast □ **9** 54 35N 5 56W
Belfast, L. **9** 54 40N 5 50W
Belfield **70** 46 54N 103 11W
Belfort **12** 47 38N 6 50 E
Belfry **72** 45 10N 109 2W
Belgaum **32** 15 55N 74 35 E
Belgium ■ **11** 50 30N 5 0 E
Belgorod **23** 50 35N 36 35 E
Belgorod-Dnestrovskiy **23** 46 11N 30 23 E
Belgrade = Beograd **19** 44 50N 20 37 E
Belgrade **72** 45 50N 111 10W
Belhaven **69** 35 34N 76 35W
Beli Drim → **19** 42 6N 20 25 E
Belinga **54** 1 10N 13 2 E
Belinyu **34** 1 35S 105 50 E
Belitung **34** 3 10S 107 50 E
Belize ■ **74** 17 0N 88 30W
Belize City **74** 17 25N 88 0W
Belkovskiy, Ostrov **25** 75 32N 135 44 E
Bell → **62** 49 48N 77 38W
Bell Bay **44** 41 6S 146 53 E
Bell I. **63** 50 46N 55 35W
Bell-Irving → **64** 56 12N 129 5W
Bell Peninsula **61** 63 50N 82 0W
Bell Ville **80** 32 40S 62 40W
Bella Bella **64** 52 10N 128 10W
Bella Coola **64** 52 25N 126 40W
Bella Unión **80** 30 15S 57 40W
Bella Vista **80** 28 33S 59 0W
Bellaire **68** 40 1N 80 46W
Bellary **32** 15 10N 76 56 E
Bellata **45** 29 53S 149 46 E
Belle, La **69** 26 45N 81 22W
Belle Fourche **70** 44 43N 103 52W
Belle Fourche → **70** 44 25N 102 19W
Belle Glade **69** 26 43N 80 38W
Belle-Ile **12** 47 20N 3 10W
Belle Isle **63** 51 57N 55 25W
Belle Isle, Str. of **63** 51 30N 56 30W
Belle Plaine, Iowa, U.S.A. **70** 41 51N 92 18W
Belle Plaine, Minn., U.S.A. **70** 44 35N 93 48W
Belledune **63** 47 55N 65 50W
Bellefontaine **68** 40 20N 83 45W
Bellefonte **68** 40 56N 77 45W
Belleoram **63** 47 31N 55 25W
Belleville, Canada **62** 44 10N 77 23W
Belleville, Ill., U.S.A. **70** 38 30N 90 0W
Belleville, Kans., U.S.A. **70** 39 51N 97 38W
Bellevue, Canada **64** 49 35N 114 22W
Bellevue, U.S.A. **72** 43 25N 114 23W
Bellin **61** 60 0N 70 0W
Bellingen **45** 30 25S 152 50 E
Bellingham **72** 48 45N 122 27W
Bellinzona **14** 46 11N 9 1 E
Bello **78** 6 20N 75 33W
Bellows Falls **68** 43 10N 72 30W
Belluno **18** 46 8N 12 13 E
Bellville **71** 29 58N 96 18W
Bélmez **13** 38 17N 5 17W
Belmont, Australia **45** 33 4S 151 42 E
Belmont, S. Africa **56** 29 28S 24 22 E
Belmonte **79** 16 0S 39 0W
Belmopan **74** 17 18N 88 30W
Belmullet **9** 54 13N 9 58W
Belo Horizonte **79** 19 55S 43 56W
Belo-sur-Mer **57** 20 42S 44 0 E
Belo-Tsiribihina **57** 19 40S 44 30 E
Belogorsk **25** 51 0N 128 20 E
Beloha **57** 25 10S 45 3 E
Beloit, Kans., U.S.A. **70** 39 32N 98 9W
Beloit, Wis., U.S.A. **70** 42 35N 89 0W
Belomorsk **22** 64 35N 34 30 E
Belonia **33** 23 15N 91 30 E
Beloretsk **22** 53 58N 58 24 E
Belovo **24** 54 30N 86 0 E
Beloye, Oz. **22** 60 10N 37 35 E
Beloye More **22** 66 30N 38 0 E
Belozersk **22** 60 0N 37 30 E
Beltana **45** 30 48S 138 25 E
Belterra **79** 2 45S 55 0W
Belton, S.C., U.S.A. **69** 34 31N 82 39W
Belton, Tex., U.S.A. **71** 31 4N 97 30W
Belton Res. **71** 31 8N 97 32W
Beltsy **23** 47 48N 28 0 E
Belturbet **9** 54 6N 7 28W
Belukha **24** 49 50N 86 50 E
Beluran **34** 5 48N 117 35 E
Belvidere **70** 42 15N 88 55W
Belyando → **44** 21 38S 146 50 E
Belyy, Ostrov **24** 73 30N 71 0 E
Belyy Yar **24** 58 26N 84 39 E
Belzoni **71** 33 12N 90 30W
Bemaraha, Lembalemban' i **57** 18 40S 44 45 E
Bemarivo **57** 21 45S 44 45 E
Bemarivo → **57** 15 27S 47 40 E
Bemavo **57** 21 33S 45 25 E
Bembéréke **53** 10 11N 2 43 E
Bemidji **70** 47 30N 94 50W
Ben 'Ammi **28** 33 0N 35 7 E
Ben Cruachan **8** 56 26N 5 8W
Ben Dearg **8** 57 47N 4 58W
Ben Gardane **51** 33 11N 11 11 E
Ben Hope **8** 58 24N 4 36W
Ben Lawers **8** 56 33N 4 13W
Ben Lomond, N.S.W., Australia **45** 30 1S 151 43 E
Ben Lomond, Tas., Australia **44** 41 38S 147 42 E
Ben Lomond, U.K. **8** 56 12N 4 39W
Ben Macdhui **8** 57 4N 3 40W
Ben Mhor **8** 57 16N 7 21W
Ben More, Central, U.K. **8** 56 23N 4 31W
Ben More, Strathclyde, U.K. **8** 56 26N 6 2W
Ben More Assynt **8** 58 7N 4 51W
Ben Nevis **8** 56 48N 5 0W
Ben Vorlich **8** 56 22N 4 15W
Ben Wyvis **8** 57 40N 4 35W
Bena **53** 11 20N 5 50 E
Bena Dibele **54** 4 4S 22 50 E
Benagerie **45** 31 25S 140 22 E
Benalla **45** 36 30S 146 0 E
Benares = Varanasi **33** 25 22N 83 0 E
Benavides **71** 27 35N 98 28W
Benbecula **8** 57 26N 7 21W
Benbonyathe, Mt. **45** 30 25S 139 11 E
Bencubbin **47** 30 48S 117 52 E
Bend **72** 44 2N 121 15W
Bendel □ **53** 6 0N 6 0 E
Bender Beila **29** 9 30N 50 48 E
Bendering **47** 32 23S 118 18 E
Bendery **23** 46 50N 29 30 E
Bendigo **45** 36 40S 144 15 E
Benē Beraq **28** 32 6N 34 51 E
Benenitra **57** 23 27S 45 5 E
Benevento **18** 41 7N 14 45 E
Bengal, Bay of **33** 15 0N 90 0 E
Bengbu **39** 32 58N 117 20 E
Benghazi = Banghāzī **51** 32 11N 20 3 E
Bengkalis **34** 1 30N 102 10 E
Bengkulu **34** 3 50S 102 12 E
Bengkulu □ **34** 3 48S 102 16 E
Bengough **65** 49 25N 105 10W
Benguela **55** 12 37S 13 25 E
Benguérua, I. **57** 21 58S 35 28 E
Beni **54** 0 30N 29 27 E
Beni → **78** 10 23S 65 24W
Beni Abbès **50** 30 5N 2 5W
Beni Mazâr **51** 28 32N 30 44 E
Beni Mellal **50** 32 21N 6 21W
Beni Ounif **50** 32 0N 1 10W
Beni Suef **51** 29 5N 31 6 E
Beniah L. **64** 63 23N 112 17W
Benidorm **13** 38 33N 0 9W
Benin ■ **53** 10 0N 2 0 E
Benin, Bight of **53** 5 0N 3 0 E
Benin City **53** 6 20N 5 31 E
Benjamin Constant **78** 4 40S 70 15W
Benkelman **70** 40 7N 101 32W
Benlidi **44** 24 35S 144 50 E
Bennett **64** 59 56N 134 53W
Bennett, Ostrov **25** 76 21N 148 56 E
Bennettsville **69** 34 38N 79 39W
Bennington **68** 42 52N 73 12W
Benoni **57** 26 11S 28 18 E
Benson **73** 31 59N 110 19W
Bent **31** 26 20N 59 31 E
Benteng **35** 6 10S 120 30 E
Bentinck I. **44** 17 3S 139 35 E
Benton, Ark., U.S.A. **71** 34 30N 92 35W
Benton, Ill., U.S.A. **70** 38 0N 88 55W
Benton Harbor **68** 42 10N 86 28W
Benue □ **53** 7 30N 7 30 E
Benue → **53** 7 48N 6 46 E
Benxi **38** 41 20N 123 48 E
Beo **35** 4 25N 126 50 E
Beograd **19** 44 50N 20 37 E
Beowawe **72** 40 35N 116 30W
Beppu **36** 33 15N 131 30 E
Berau, Teluk **35** 2 30S 132 30 E
Berber **51** 18 0N 34 0 E
Berbera **29** 10 30N 45 2 E
Berbérati **54** 4 15N 15 40 E
Berbice → **78** 6 20N 57 32W
Berdichev **23** 49 57N 28 30 E
Berdsk **24** 54 47N 83 2 E
Berdyansk **23** 46 45N 36 50 E
Berea **68** 37 35N 84 18W
Berebere **35** 2 25N 128 45 E
Bereda **29** 11 45N 51 0 E
Berekum **50** 7 29N 2 34W
Berens → **65** 52 25N 97 2W
Berens I. **65** 52 18N 97 18W
Berens River **65** 52 25N 97 0W
Berevo, Mahajanga, Madag. **57** 17 14S 44 17 E
Berevo, Toliara, Madag. **57** 19 44S 44 58 E
Berezina → **22** 52 33N 30 14 E
Berezniki **24** 59 24N 56 46 E
Berezovo **22** 64 0N 65 0 E
Bergama **30** 39 8N 27 15 E
Bérgamo **18** 45 42N 9 40 E
Bergen, Neth. **11** 52 40N 4 43 E
Bergen, Norway **21** 60 23N 5 20 E
Bergen-op-Zoom **11** 51 30N 4 18 E
Bergerac **12** 44 51N 0 30 E
Bergum **11** 53 13N 5 59 E
Bergville **57** 28 52S 29 18 E
Berhala, Selat **34** 1 0S 104 15 E
Berhampore = Baharampur **33** 24 2N 88 27 E
Berhampur **33** 19 15N 84 54 E
Bering Sea **60** 58 0N 167 0 E
Bering Str. **60** 66 0N 170 0W
Beringen **11** 51 3N 5 14 E
Beringovskiy **25** 63 3N 179 19 E
Berja **13** 36 50N 2 56W
Berkeley, U.K. **7** 51 41N 2 28W
Berkeley, U.S.A. **72** 37 52N 122 20W
Berkeley Springs **68** 39 38N 78 12W
Berkshire □ **7** 51 30N 1 20W
Berland → **64** 54 0N 116 50W
Berlin, Germany **14** 52 32N 13 24 E
Berlin, Md., U.S.A. **68** 38 19N 75 12W
Berlin, N.H., U.S.A. **68** 44 29N 71 10W
Berlin, Wis., U.S.A. **68** 43 58N 88 55W
Bermejo →, Formosa, Argentina **80** 26 51S 58 23W
Bermejo →, San Juan, Argentina **80** 32 30S 67 30W
Bermuda ■ **2** 32 45N 65 0W
Bern **14** 46 57N 7 28 E
Bernado **73** 34 30N 106 53W
Bernalillo **73** 35 17N 106 37W
Bernardo de Irigoyen **80** 26 15S 53 40W
Bernburg **14** 51 40N 11 42 E
Berne = Bern **14** 46 57N 7 28 E
Bernier I. **47** 24 50S 113 12 E
Beror Hayil **28** 31 34N 34 38 E
Beroroha **57** 21 40S 45 10 E
Beroun **14** 49 57N 14 5 E
Berrechid **50** 33 18N 7 36W
Berri **45** 34 14S 140 35 E
Berry, Australia **45** 34 46S 150 43 E
Berry, France **12** 46 50N 2 0 E
Berry Is. **75** 25 40N 77 50W
Berryville **71** 36 23N 93 35W
Berthold **70** 48 19N 101 45W
Berthoud **70** 40 21N 105 5W
Bertoua **54** 4 30N 13 45 E
Bertrand **70** 40 35N 99 38W
Berufjörður **20** 64 48N 14 29W
Berwick **68** 41 4N 76 17W
Berwick-upon-Tweed **6** 55 47N 2 0W
Berwyn Mts. **6** 52 54N 3 26W
Besalampy **57** 16 43S 44 29 E
Besançon **12** 47 15N 6 0 E
Besar **34** 2 40S 116 0 E
Besnard L. **65** 55 25N 106 0W
Besni **30** 37 41N 37 52 E
Besor, N. → **28** 31 28N 34 22 E
Bessemer, Ala., U.S.A. **69** 33 25N 86 57W
Bessemer, Mich., U.S.A. **70** 46 27N 90 0W
Bet Alfa **28** 32 31N 35 25 E
Bet Dagan **28** 32 1N 34 49 E
Bet Guvrin **28** 31 37N 34 54 E
Bet Ha'Emeq **28** 32 58N 35 8 E
Bet Hashitta **28** 32 31N 35 27 E
Bet Qeshet **28** 32 41N 35 21 E
Bet She'an **28** 32 30N 35 30 E
Bet Shemesh **28** 31 44N 35 0 E
Bet Yosef **28** 32 34N 35 33 E
Betafo **57** 19 50S 46 51 E
Bétaré Oya **54** 5 40N 14 5 E
Bethal **57** 26 27S 29 28 E
Bethanien **56** 26 31S 17 8 E
Bethany = Al 'Ayzarīyah **28** 31 47N 35 15 E
Bethany, S. Africa **56** 29 34S 25 59 E
Bethany, U.S.A. **70** 40 18N 94 0W
Bethel **60** 60 50N 161 50W
Bethlehem = Bayt Lahm **28** 31 43N 35 12 E
Bethlehem, S. Africa **57** 28 14S 28 18 E
Bethlehem, U.S.A. **68** 40 39N 75 24W
Bethulie **56** 30 30S 25 59 E
Béthune **12** 50 30N 2 38 E
Bethungra **45** 34 45S 147 51 E
Betioky **57** 23 48S 44 20 E
Betoota **44** 25 45S 140 42 E
Betroka **57** 23 16S 46 0 E
Betsiamites **63** 48 56N 68 40W
Betsiamites → **63** 48 56N 68 38W
Betsiboka → **57** 16 3S 46 36 E
Betsjoeanaland **56** 26 30S 22 30 E
Bettiah **33** 26 48N 84 33 E

Betul

Betul 32 21 58N 77 59 E
Betung 34 1 24N 111 31 E
Beulah 70 47 18N 101 47W
Beverley, Australia 47 32 9S 116 56 E
Beverley, U.K. 6 53 52N 0 26W
Beverly 72 46 55N 119 59W
Beverly Hills 73 34 4N 118 29W
Beverwijk 11 52 28N 4 38 E
Beyla 50 8 30N 8 38W
Beyneu 23 45 10N 55 3 E
Beypazarı 30 40 10N 31 56 E
Beyşehir Gölü 30 37 40N 31 45 E
Bezet 28 33 4N 35 8 E
Bezhitsa 22 53 19N 34 17 E
Béziers 12 43 20N 3 12 E
Bezwada = Vijayawada 33 16 31N 80 39 E
Bhachau 32 23 20N 70 16 E
Bhadrakh 32 21 10N 86 30 E
Bhadravati 32 13 49N 75 40 E
Bhagalpur 33 25 10N 87 0 E
Bhakra Dam 32 31 30N 76 45 E
Bhamo 33 24 15N 97 15 E
Bhandara 32 21 5N 79 42 E
Bhanrer Ra. 32 23 40N 79 45 E
Bharat = India ■ 32 20 0N 78 0 E
Bharatpur 32 27 15N 77 30 E
Bhatpara 33 22 50N 88 25 E
Bhaunagar = Bhavnagar 32 21 45N 72 10 E
Bhavnagar 32 21 45N 72 10 E
Bhawanipatna 33 19 55N 80 10 E
Bhilsa = Vidisha 32 23 28N 77 53 E
Bhilwara 32 25 25N 74 38 E
Bhima → 32 16 25N 77 17 E
Bhimavaram 33 16 30N 81 30 E
Bhind 32 26 30N 78 46 E
Bhiwandi 32 19 20N 73 0 E
Bhiwani 32 28 50N 76 9 E
Bhola 33 22 45N 90 35 E
Bhopal 32 23 20N 77 30 E
Bhubaneshwar 33 20 15N 85 50 E
Bhuj 32 23 15N 69 49 E
Bhumibol Dam 34 17 15N 98 58 E
Bhusaval 32 21 3N 75 46 E
Bhutan ■ 33 27 25N 90 30 E
Biafra, B. of = Bonny, Bight of 54 3 30N 9 20 E
Biak 35 1 10S 136 6 E
Biała Podlaska 15 52 4N 23 6 E
Białystok 15 53 10N 23 10 E
Biaro 35 2 5N 125 26 E
Biarritz 12 43 29N 1 33W
Bibai 36 43 19N 141 52 E
Bibala 55 14 44S 13 24 E
Bibby I. 65 61 55N 93 0W
Biberach 14 48 5N 9 49 E
Bibiani 50 6 30N 2 8W
Biboohra 44 16 56S 145 25 E
Bic 63 48 20N 68 41W
Biche, La → 64 59 57N 123 50W
Bickerton I. 44 13 45S 136 10 E
Bicknell, Ind., U.S.A. 68 38 50N 87 20W
Bicknell, Utah, U.S.A. 73 38 16N 111 35W
Bida 53 9 3N 5 58 E
Bidar 32 17 55N 77 35 E
Biddeford 63 43 30N 70 28W
Biddiyā 28 32 7N 35 4 E
Biddū 28 31 50N 35 8 E
Bideford 7 51 1N 4 13W
Bidon 5 = Poste Maurice Cortier 50 22 14N 1 2 E
Bié, Planalto de 55 12 0S 16 0 E
Bieber 72 41 4N 121 6W
Biel 14 47 8N 7 14 E
Bielé Karpaty 15 49 5N 18 0 E
Bielefeld 14 52 2N 8 31 E
Biella 18 45 33N 8 3 E
Bielsko-Biała 15 49 50N 19 2 E
Bien Hoa 34 10 57N 106 49 E
Bienfait 65 49 10N 102 50W
Bienne = Biel 14 47 8N 7 14 E
Bienville, L. 62 55 5N 72 40W
Biesiesfontein 56 30 57S 17 58 E
Big → 63 54 50N 58 55W
Big B. 63 55 43N 60 35W
Big Beaver 65 49 10N 105 10W
Big Belt Mts. 72 46 50N 111 30W
Big Bend 57 26 50S 31 58 E
Big Bend Nat. Park 71 29 15N 103 15W
Big Black → 71 32 0N 91 5W
Big Blue → 70 39 11N 96 40W
Big Cr. → 64 51 42N 122 41W
Big Cypress Swamp 69 26 12N 81 10W
Big Falls 70 48 11N 93 48W
Big Fork → 70 48 31N 93 43W
Big Horn Mts. = Bighorn Mts. 72 44 30N 107 30W
Big Lake 71 31 12N 101 25W
Big Muddy → 70 48 8N 104 36W
Big Pine 73 37 12N 118 17W
Big Piney 72 42 32N 110 3W
Big Quill L. 65 51 55N 104 50W
Big Rapids 68 43 42N 85 27W
Big River 65 53 50N 107 0W
Big Sable Pt. 68 44 5N 86 30W
Big Sand L. 65 57 45N 99 45W
Big Sandy 72 48 12N 110 9W
Big Sandy Cr. → 70 38 6N 102 29W
Big Sioux → 70 42 30N 96 25W
Big Spring 71 32 10N 101 25W
Big Springs 70 41 4N 102 3W
Big Stone City 70 45 20N 96 30W
Big Stone Gap 69 36 52N 82 45W
Big Stone L. 70 45 30N 96 35W
Big Timber 72 45 53N 110 0W
Big Trout L. 62 53 40N 90 0W
Bigfork 72 48 3N 114 2W
Biggar, Canada 65 52 4N 108 0W
Biggar, U.K. 8 55 38N 3 31W
Bigge I. 46 14 35S 125 10 E
Biggenden 45 25 31S 152 4 E
Bighorn 72 46 11N 107 25W
Bighorn → 72 46 9N 107 28W
Bighorn Mts. 72 44 30N 107 30W
Bigorre 12 43 10N 0 5 E
Bigstone L. 65 53 42N 95 44W
Bihać 18 44 49N 15 57 E
Bihar 33 25 5N 85 40 E
Bihar □ 33 25 0N 86 0 E
Bijagós, Arquipélago dos 50 11 15N 16 10W
Bijapur, Karnataka, India 32 16 50N 75 55 E
Bijapur, Mad. P., India 33 18 50N 80 50 E
Bījār 30 35 52N 47 35 E
Bijeljina 19 44 46N 19 17 E
Bijie 39 27 20N 105 16 E
Bijnor 32 29 27N 78 11 E
Bikaner 32 28 2N 73 18 E
Bikin 25 46 50N 134 20 E
Bikini Atoll 40 12 0N 167 30 E
Bilara 32 26 14N 73 53 E
Bilaspur 33 22 2N 82 15 E
Bilauk Taungdan 34 13 0N 99 0 E
Bilbao 13 43 16N 2 56W
Bíldudalur 20 65 41N 23 36W
Bilecik 30 40 5N 30 5 E
Bilibino 25 68 3N 166 20 E
Bilir 25 65 40N 131 20 E
Bill 70 43 18N 105 18W
Billabalong 47 27 25S 115 49 E
Billiluna 46 19 37S 127 41 E
Billingham 6 54 36N 1 18W
Billings 72 45 43N 108 29W
Billiton Is. = Belitung 34 3 10S 107 50 E
Bilma 51 18 50N 13 30 E
Biloela 44 24 24S 150 31 E
Biloxi 71 30 24N 88 53W
Bilpa Morea Claypan 44 25 0S 140 0 E
Biltine 51 14 40N 20 50 E
Bilyana 44 18 5S 145 50 E
Bima 35 8 22S 118 49 E
Bimbo 54 4 15N 18 33 E
Bimini Is. 75 25 42N 79 25W
Bin Xian 39 35 2N 108 4 E
Bina-Etawah 32 24 13N 78 14 E
Binalbagan 35 10 12N 122 50 E
Bīnālūd, Kūh-e 31 36 30N 58 30 E
Binatang 34 2 10N 111 40 E
Binbee 44 20 19S 147 56 E
Binche 11 50 26N 4 10 E
Binda 45 27 52S 147 21 E
Bindi Bindi 47 30 37S 116 22 E
Bindle 45 27 40S 148 45 E
Bindura 55 17 18S 31 18 E
Bingara, N.S.W., Australia 45 29 52S 150 36 E
Bingara, Queens., Australia 45 28 10S 144 37 E
Bingham 63 45 5N 69 50W
Bingham Canyon 72 40 31N 112 10W
Binghamton 68 42 9N 75 54W
Bingöl 30 38 53N 40 29 E
Binh Dinh = An Nhon 34 13 55N 109 7 E
Binh Son 34 15 20N 108 40 E
Binjai 34 3 20N 98 30 E
Binnaway 45 31 28S 149 24 E
Binongko 35 5 55S 123 55 E
Binscarth 65 50 37N 101 17W
Bint Jubayl 28 33 8N 35 25 E
Bintan 34 1 0N 104 0 E
Bintulu 34 3 10N 113 0 E
Bintuni 35 2 7S 133 32 E
Binyamina 28 32 32N 34 56 E
Binyang 39 23 12N 108 47 E
Binzert = Bizerte 50 37 15N 9 50 E
Bioko 53 3 30N 8 40 E
Biq'at Bet Netofa 28 32 49N 35 22 E
Bir 32 19 0N 75 54 E
Bir Autrun 51 18 15N 26 40 E
Bir Mogrein 50 25 10N 11 25W
Bi'r Nabālā 28 31 52N 35 12 E
Bîr Ungât 51 22 8N 33 48 E
Bi'r Zayt 28 31 59N 35 11 E
Bira 35 2 3S 132 2 E
Birak Sulaymān 28 31 42N 35 7 E
Birao 51 10 20N 22 47 E
Birch Hills 65 52 59N 105 25W
Birch I. 65 52 26N 99 54W
Birch L., N.W.T., Canada 64 62 4N 116 33W
Birch L., Ont., Canada 62 51 23N 92 18W
Birch L., U.S.A. 62 47 48N 91 43W
Birch Mts. 64 57 30N 113 10W
Birch River 65 52 24N 101 6W
Birchip 45 35 56S 142 55 E
Bird 65 56 30N 94 13W
Bird City 70 39 48N 101 33W
Bird I. = Aves, I. de 75 15 45N 63 55W
Bird I. 56 32 3S 18 17 E
Birdlip 7 51 50N 2 7W
Birdsville 44 25 51S 139 20 E
Birdum 46 15 39S 133 13 E
Birecik 30 37 0N 38 0 E
Bireuen 34 5 14N 96 39 E
Birkenhead 6 53 24N 3 1W
Bîrlad 15 46 15N 27 38 E
Birmingham, U.K. 7 52 30N 1 55W
Birmingham, U.S.A. 69 33 31N 86 50W
Birmitrapur 33 22 24N 84 46 E
Birni Nkonni 50 13 55N 5 15 E
Birnin Kebbi 53 12 32N 4 12 E
Birnin Kudu 53 11 30N 9 29 E
Birobidzhan 25 48 50N 132 50 E
Birqīn 28 32 27N 35 15 E
Birr 9 53 7N 7 55W
Birrie → 45 29 43S 146 37 E
Birsk 22 55 25N 55 30 E
Birtle 65 50 30N 101 5W
Birur 32 13 30N 75 55 E
Bisa 35 1 15S 127 28 E
Bisbee 73 31 30N 110 0W
Biscay, B. of 16 45 0N 2 0W
Biscayne B. 69 25 40N 80 12W
Biscostasing 62 47 18N 82 9W
Bisho 57 32 50S 27 23 E
Bishop, Calif., U.S.A. 73 37 20N 118 26W
Bishop, Tex., U.S.A. 71 27 35N 97 49W
Bishop Auckland 6 54 40N 1 40W
Bishop's Falls 63 49 2N 55 30W
Bishop's Stortford 7 51 52N 0 11 E
Biskra 50 34 50N 5 44 E
Bislig 35 8 15N 126 27 E
Bismarck 70 46 49N 100 49W
Bismarck Arch. 40 2 30S 150 0 E
Bison 70 45 34N 102 28W
Bispfors 20 63 1N 16 37 E
Bissagos = Bijagós, Arquipélago dos 50 11 15N 16 10W
Bissau 50 11 45N 15 45W
Bissett 65 51 2N 95 41W
Bistcho L. 64 59 45N 118 50W
Bistriţa 15 47 9N 24 35 E
Bistriţa → 15 46 30N 26 57 E
Bitam 54 2 5N 11 25 E
Bitkine 51 11 59N 18 13 E
Bitlis 30 38 20N 42 3 E
Bitola 19 41 5N 21 10 E
Bitolj = Bitola 19 41 5N 21 10 E
Bitter Creek 72 41 39N 108 36W
Bitter L. = Buheirat-Murrat-el-Kubra 51 30 15N 32 40 E
Bitterfontein 56 31 1S 18 32 E
Bitterroot → 72 46 52N 114 6W
Bitterroot Range 72 46 0N 114 20W
Biu 51 10 40N 12 3 E
Biwa-Ko 36 35 15N 136 10 E
Biwabik 70 47 33N 92 19W
Biyang 39 32 38N 113 21 E
Biysk 24 52 40N 85 0 E
Bizana 57 30 50S 29 52 E
Bizerte 50 37 15N 9 50 E
Bjargtangar 20 65 30N 24 30W
Bjelovar 18 45 56N 16 49 E
Black →, Ark., U.S.A. 71 35 38N 91 19W
Black →, Wis., U.S.A. 70 43 52N 91 22W
Black Diamond 64 50 45N 114 14W
Black Forest = Schwarzwald 14 48 0N 8 0 E
Black Hills 70 44 0N 103 50W
Black I. 65 51 12N 96 30W
Black L., Canada 65 59 12N 105 15W
Black L., U.S.A. 68 45 28N 84 15W
Black Mesa, Mt. 71 36 57N 102 55W
Black Mt. = Mynydd Du 7 51 45N 3 45W
Black Mts. 7 51 52N 3 5W
Black Range 73 33 30N 107 55W
Black River 75 18 0N 77 50W
Black River Falls 70 44 23N 90 52W
Black Sea 17 43 30N 35 0 E
Black Volta → 50 8 41N 1 33W
Black Warrior → 69 32 32N 87 51W
Blackall 44 24 25S 145 45 E
Blackball 43 42 22S 171 26 E
Blackbull 44 17 55S 141 45 E
Blackburn 6 53 44N 2 30W
Blackduck 70 47 43N 94 32W
Blackfoot 72 43 13N 112 12W
Blackfoot → 72 46 52N 113 53W
Blackfoot Res. 72 43 0N 111 35W
Blackie 64 50 36N 113 37W
Blackpool 6 53 48N 3 3W
Blacks Harbour 63 45 3N 66 49W
Blacksburg 68 37 17N 80 23W
Blacksod B. 9 54 6N 10 0W
Blackstone 68 37 6N 78 0W
Blackstone → 64 61 5N 122 55W
Blackstone Ra. 47 26 0S 128 30 E
Blackville 63 46 44N 65 50W
Blackwater 44 23 35S 148 53 E
Blackwater →, Ireland 9 51 55N 7 50W
Blackwater →, U.K. 9 54 31N 6 35W
Blackwater Cr. → 45 25 56S 144 30 E
Blackwell 71 36 55N 97 20W
Blaenau Ffestiniog 6 53 0N 3 57W
Blagodarnoye 23 45 7N 43 37 E
Blagoveshchensk 25 50 20N 127 30 E
Blaine 72 48 59N 122 43W
Blaine Lake 65 52 51N 106 52W
Blair 70 41 38N 96 10W
Blair Athol 44 22 42S 147 31 E
Blair Atholl 8 56 46N 3 50W
Blairgowrie 8 56 36N 3 20W
Blairmore 64 49 40N 114 25W
Blake Pt. 70 48 12N 88 27W
Blakely 69 31 22N 85 0W
Blanc, Mont 12 45 48N 6 50 E
Blanca, B. 80 39 10S 61 30W
Blanca Peak 73 37 35N 105 29W
Blanchard 71 35 8N 97 40W
Blanche, C. 45 33 1S 134 9 E
Blanche L., S. Austral., Australia 45 29 15S 139 40 E
Blanche L., W. Austral., Australia 46 22 25S 123 17 E
Blanco, S. Africa 56 33 55S 22 23 E
Blanco, U.S.A. 71 30 7N 98 30W
Blanco, C., C. Rica 75 9 34N 85 8W
Blanco, C., U.S.A. 72 42 50N 124 40W
Blanda → 20 65 20N 19 40W
Blandford Forum 7 50 52N 2 10W
Blanding 73 37 35N 109 30W
Blankenberge 11 51 20N 3 9 E
Blantyre 55 15 45S 35 0 E
Blarney 9 51 57N 8 35W
Blåvands Huk 21 55 33N 8 4 E
Blaydon 6 54 56N 1 47W
Blayney 45 33 32S 149 14 E
Blaze, Pt. 46 12 56S 130 11 E
Blednaya, Gora 24 76 20N 65 0 E
Bleiburg 14 46 35N 14 49 E
Blekinge län □ 21 56 20N 15 20 E
Blenheim 43 41 38S 173 57 E
Bletchley 7 51 59N 0 44W
Blida 50 36 30N 2 49 E
Bligh Sound 43 44 47S 167 32 E
Blind River 62 46 10N 82 58W
Blitar 35 8 5S 112 11 E
Blitta 53 8 23N 1 6 E
Block I. 68 41 11N 71 35W
Bloemfontein 56 29 6S 26 7 E
Bloemhof 56 27 38S 25 32 E
Blois 12 47 35N 1 20 E
Blönduós 20 65 40N 20 12W
Bloodvein → 65 51 47N 96 43W
Bloody Foreland 9 55 10N 8 18W
Bloomer 70 45 8N 91 30W
Bloomfield, Australia 44 15 56S 145 22 E
Bloomfield, Iowa, U.S.A. 70 40 44N 92 26W
Bloomfield, N. Mex., U.S.A. 73 36 46N 107 59W
Bloomfield, Nebr., U.S.A. 70 42 38N 97 40W
Bloomington, Ill., U.S.A. 70 40 27N 89 0W
Bloomington, Ind., U.S.A. 68 39 10N 86 30W
Bloomsburg 68 41 0N 76 30W
Blora 35 6 57S 111 25 E
Blouberg 57 23 8S 28 59 E
Blountstown 69 30 28N 85 5W
Blue Island 68 41 40N 87 40W
Blue Lake 72 40 53N 124 0W
Blue Mesa Res. 73 38 30N 107 15W
Blue Mts., Oreg., U.S.A. 72 45 15N 119 0W
Blue Mts., Pa., U.S.A. 68 40 30N 76 30W
Blue Mud B. 44 13 30S 136 0 E
Blue Nile = An Nîl el Azraq □ 51 12 30N 34 30 E
Blue Nile = Nîl el Azraq → 51 15 38N 32 31 E
Blue Rapids 70 39 41N 96 39W
Blue Ridge Mts. 69 36 30N 80 15W
Blue Stack Mts. 9 54 46N 8 5W
Blueberry → 64 56 45N 120 49W
Bluefield 68 37 18N 81 14W
Bluefields 75 12 20N 83 50W
Bluff, Australia 44 23 35S 149 4 E
Bluff, N.Z. 43 46 37S 168 20 E
Bluff, U.S.A. 73 37 17N 109 33W
Bluff Knoll 47 34 24S 118 15 E
Bluff Pt. 47 27 50S 114 5 E
Bluffton 68 40 43N 85 9W
Blumenau 80 27 0S 49 0W
Blunt 70 44 32N 100 0W
Bly 72 42 23N 121 0W
Blyth 6 55 8N 1 32W
Blythe 73 33 40N 114 33W
Bo 50 7 55N 11 50W
Bo Duc 34 11 58N 106 50 E
Bo Hai 38 39 0N 120 0 E
Bo Xian 39 33 50N 115 45 E
Boa Vista 78 2 48N 60 30W
Boaco 75 12 29N 85 35W
Boatman 45 27 16S 146 55 E
Bobadah 45 32 19S 146 41 E
Bobai 39 22 17N 109 59 E
Bobbili 33 18 35N 83 30 E
Bobcaygeon 62 44 33N 78 33W
Bobo-Dioulasso 50 11 8N 4 13W
Bóbr → 14 52 4N 15 4 E
Bobraomby, Tanjon' i 57 12 40S 49 10 E
Bobruysk 22 53 10N 29 15 E
Boca, La 74 8 56N 79 30W
Bôca do Acre 78 8 50S 67 27W
Boca Raton 69 26 21N 80 5W
Bocaiúva 79 17 7S 43 49W
Bocanda 50 7 5N 4 31W
Bocaranga 51 7 0N 15 35 E
Bocas del Toro 75 9 15N 82 20W
Bocholt 14 51 50N 6 35 E
Bochum 14 51 28N 7 12 E
Boda 54 4 19N 17 26 E
Bodaybo 25 57 50N 114 0 E
Boddington 47 32 50S 116 30 E
Boden 20 65 50N 21 42 E
Bodensee 14 47 35N 9 25 E
Bodhan 32 18 40N 77 44 E
Bodmin 7 50 28N 4 44W
Bodmin Moor 7 50 33N 4 36W
Bodrog → 15 48 15N 21 35 E
Bodrum 30 37 5N 27 30 E
Boegoebergdam 56 29 7S 22 9 E
Boende 54 0 24S 21 12 E
Boerne 71 29 48N 98 41W
Boffa 50 10 16N 14 3W
Bogalusa 71 30 50N 89 55W
Bogan → 45 29 59S 146 17 E
Bogan Gate 45 33 7S 147 49 E
Bogantungan 44 23 41S 147 17 E
Bogata 71 33 26N 95 10W
Boggabilla 45 28 36S 150 24 E
Boggabri 45 30 45S 150 0 E
Boggeragh Mts. 9 52 2N 8 55W
Bognor Regis 7 50 47N 0 40W
Bogo 35 11 3N 124 0 E
Bogong, Mt. 45 36 47S 147 17 E
Bogor 35 6 36S 106 48 E
Bogorodskoye 25 52 22N 140 30 E
Bogotá 78 4 34N 74 0W
Bogotol 24 56 15N 89 50 E
Bogra 33 24 51N 89 22 E
Boguchany 25 58 40N 97 30 E
Bogué 50 16 45N 14 10W
Bohemia Downs 46 18 53S 126 14 E
Bohemian Forest = Böhmerwald 14 49 30N 12 40 E
Bohena Cr. → 45 30 17S 149 42 E
Böhmerwald 14 49 30N 12 40 E
Bohol 35 9 50N 124 10 E
Bohol Sea 35 9 0N 124 0 E
Bohotleh 29 8 20N 46 25 E
Boileau, C. 46 17 40S 122 7 E
Boise 72 43 43N 116 9W
Boise City 71 36 45N 102 30W
Boissevain 65 49 15N 100 5W
Bojador C. 50 26 0N 14 30W
Bojana → 19 41 52N 19 22 E
Bojnūrd 31 37 30N 57 20 E
Bojonegoro 35 7 11S 111 54 E
Boju 53 7 22N 7 55 E
Boké 50 10 50N 14 17W
Bokhara → 45 29 55S 146 42 E
Bokkos 53 9 17N 9 1 E
Boknafjorden 21 59 14N 5 40 E
Bokoro 51 12 25N 17 14 E
Bokote 54 0 12S 21 8 E
Bokungu 54 0 35S 22 50 E

Bronte Park

Bol 51 13 30N 15 0 E
Bolama 50 11 30N 15 30W
Bolan Pass 31 29 50N 67 20 E
Bolaños → 74 21 14N 104 8W
Bolbec 12 49 30N 0 30 E
Bole 37 45 11N 81 37 E
Bolesławiec 14 51 17N 15 37 E
Bolgatanga 53 10 44N 0 53W
Boli 38 45 46N 130 31 E
Bolinao C. 35 16 23N 119 55 E
Bolívar, Argentina 80 36 15S 60 53W
Bolívar, Colombia 78 2 0N 77 0W
Bolivar, Mo., U.S.A. 71 37 38N 93 22W
Bolivar, Tenn., U.S.A. 71 35 14N 89 0W
Bolivia ■ 78 17 6S 64 0W
Bolivian Plateau 76 20 0S 67 30W
Bollnäs 21 61 21N 16 24 E
Bollon 45 28 2S 147 29 E
Bolobo 54 2 6S 16 20 E
Bologna 18 44 30N 11 20 E
Bologoye 22 57 55N 34 0 E
Bolomba 54 0 35N 19 0 E
Bolong 35 7 6N 122 14 E
Bolsena, L. di 18 42 35N 11 55 E
Bolshereche 24 56 4N 74 45 E
Bolshevik, Ostrov 25 78 30N 102 0 E
Bolshezemelskaya Tundra 22 67 0N 56 0 E
Bolshoi Kavkas 23 42 50N 44 0 E
Bolshoy Anyuy → 25 68 30N 160 49 E
Bolshoy Atlym 24 62 25N 66 50 E
Bolshoy Begichev, Ostrov 25 74 20N 112 30 E
Bolshoy Lyakhovskiy, Ostrov 25 73 35N 142 0 E
Bolsward 11 53 3N 5 32 E
Bolton 6 53 35N 2 26W
Bolu 30 40 45N 31 35 E
Bolvadin 30 38 45N 31 4 E
Bolzano 18 46 30N 11 20 E
Bom Despacho 79 19 43S 45 15W
Bom Jesus da Lapa 79 13 15S 43 25W
Boma 54 5 50S 13 4 E
Bomaderry 45 34 52S 150 37 E
Bombala 45 36 56S 149 15 E
Bombay 32 18 55N 72 50 E
Bomboma 54 2 25N 18 55 E
Bomili 54 1 45N 27 5 E
Bomongo 54 1 27N 18 21 E
Bomu → 54 4 40N 22 30 E
Bon, C. 51 37 1N 11 2 E
Bonaire 75 12 10N 68 15W
Bonang 45 37 11S 148 41 E
Bonanza 75 13 54N 84 35W
Bonaparte Archipelago 46 14 0S 124 30 E
Bonaventure 63 48 5N 65 32W
Bonavista 63 48 40N 53 5W
Bonavista, C. 63 48 42N 53 5W
Bondo 54 3 55N 23 53 E
Bondoukou 50 8 2N 2 47W
Bondowoso 35 7 55S 113 49 E
Bone, Teluk 35 4 10S 120 50 E
Bone Rate 35 7 25S 121 5 E
Bone Rate, Kepulauan 35 6 30S 121 10 E
Bo'ness 8 56 0N 3 38W
Bong Son = Hoai Nhon 34 14 28N 109 1 E
Bongandanga 54 1 24N 21 3 E
Bongor 51 10 35N 15 20 E
Bonham 71 33 30N 96 10W
Bonifacio 12 41 24N 9 10 E
Bonifacio, Bouches de 18 41 12N 9 15 E
Bonin Is. 40 27 0N 142 0 E
Bonn 14 50 43N 7 6 E
Bonne Terre 71 37 57N 90 33W
Bonners Ferry 72 48 38N 116 21W
Bonney, L. 45 37 50S 140 20 E
Bonnie Downs 44 22 7S 143 50 E
Bonnie Rock 47 30 29S 118 22 E
Bonny, Bight of 54 3 30N 9 20 E
Bonnyville 65 54 20N 110 45W
Bonoi 35 1 45S 137 41 E
Bontang 34 0 10N 117 30 E
Bonthain 35 5 34S 119 56 E
Bonthe 50 7 30N 12 33W
Bontoc 35 17 7N 120 58 E
Bonython Ra. 46 23 40S 128 45 E
Boogardie 47 28 2S 117 45 E
Bookabie 47 31 50S 132 41 E
Booker 71 36 29N 100 30W
Boolaboolka, L. 45 32 38S 143 10 E
Booligal 45 33 58S 144 53 E
Boom 11 51 6N 4 20 E
Boonah 45 27 58S 152 41 E
Boone, Iowa, U.S.A. 70 42 5N 93 53W
Boone, N.C., U.S.A. 69 36 14N 81 43W
Booneville, Ark., U.S.A. 71 35 10N 93 54W
Booneville, Miss., U.S.A. 69 34 39N 88 34W
Boonville, Ind., U.S.A. 68 38 3N 87 13W
Boonville, Mo., U.S.A. 70 38 57N 92 45W
Boonville, N.Y., U.S.A. 68 43 31N 75 20W
Boorindal 45 30 22S 146 11 E
Boorowa 45 34 28S 148 44 E
Boothia, Gulf of 61 71 0N 90 0W
Boothia Pen. 60 71 0N 94 0W
Bootle, Cumbria, U.K. 6 54 17N 3 24W
Bootle, Merseyside, U.K. 6 53 28N 3 1W
Booué 54 0 5S 11 55 E
Bophuthatswana □ 56 25 49S 25 30 E
Boquilla, Presa de la 74 27 40N 105 30W
Bôr, Sudan 51 6 10N 31 40 E
Bor, Yugoslavia 19 44 8N 22 7 E
Borah, Pk. 72 44 19N 113 46W
Borama 29 9 55N 43 7 E
Borås 21 57 43N 12 56 E
Borāzjān 31 29 22N 51 10 E
Borba 78 4 12S 59 34W
Borda, C. 45 35 45S 136 34 E
Bordeaux 12 44 50N 0 36W
Borden, Australia 47 34 3S 118 12 E
Borden, Canada 63 46 18N 63 47W
Borders □ 8 55 35N 2 50W
Bordertown 45 36 19S 140 45 E
Borðeyri 20 65 12N 21 6W
Bordj Fly Ste. Marie 50 27 19N 2 32W
Bordj-in-Eker 50 24 9N 5 3 E
Bordj Omar Driss 50 28 10N 6 40 E
Bordj-Tarat 50 25 55N 9 3 E
Borgarnes 20 64 32N 21 55W
Børgefjellet 20 65 20N 13 45 E
Borger, Neth. 11 52 54N 6 44 E
Borger, U.S.A. 71 35 40N 101 20W
Borgholm 21 56 52N 16 39 E
Borisoglebsk 23 51 27N 42 5 E
Borisov 22 54 17N 28 28 E
Borja 78 4 20S 77 40W
Borkou 51 18 15N 18 50 E
Borkum 14 53 36N 6 42 E
Borlänge 21 60 29N 15 26 E
Borneo 34 1 0N 115 0 E
Bornholm 21 55 10N 15 0 E
Borno □ 53 12 30N 12 30 E
Borobudur 35 7 36S 110 13 E
Borogontsy 25 62 42N 131 8 E
Boromo 50 11 45N 2 58W
Borongan 35 11 37N 125 26 E
Bororen 44 24 13S 151 33 E
Borovichi 22 58 25N 33 55 E
Borroloola 44 16 4S 136 17 E
Borth 7 52 29N 4 3W
Borujerd 30 33 55N 48 50 E
Borzya 25 50 24N 116 31 E
Bosa 18 40 17N 8 32 E
Bosanska Gradiška 18 45 10N 17 15 E
Bosaso 29 11 12N 49 18 E
Boscastle 7 50 42N 4 42W
Bose 39 23 53N 106 35 E
Boshan 38 36 28N 117 49 E
Boshoek 56 25 30S 27 9 E
Boshof 56 28 31S 25 13 E
Boshrūyeh 31 33 50N 57 30 E
Bosna → 19 45 4N 18 29 E
Bosna i Hercegovina □ 18 44 0N 18 0 E
Bosnia = Bosna i Hercegovina □ 18 44 0N 18 0 E
Bosnik 35 1 5S 136 10 E
Bōsō-Hantō 36 35 20N 140 20 E
Bosobolo 54 4 15N 19 50 E
Bosporus = Karadeniz Boğazı 30 41 10N 29 10 E
Bossangoa 51 6 35N 17 30 E
Bossekop 20 69 57N 23 15 E
Bossembélé 51 5 25N 17 40 E
Bossier City 71 32 28N 93 48W
Bosso 51 13 43N 13 19 E
Bosten Hu 37 41 55N 87 40 E
Boston, U.K. 6 52 59N 0 2W
Boston, U.S.A. 68 42 20N 71 0W
Boston Bar 64 49 52N 121 30W
Boswell, Canada 64 49 28N 116 45W
Boswell, U.S.A. 71 34 1N 95 50W
Botany Bay 45 34 0S 151 14 E
Bothaville 56 27 23S 26 34 E
Bothnia, G. of 20 63 0N 20 0 E
Bothwell 44 42 20S 147 1 E
Botletle → 56 20 10S 23 15 E
Botoşani 15 47 42N 26 41 E
Botswana ■ 56 22 0S 24 0 E
Bottineau 70 48 49N 100 25W
Bottrop 11 51 34N 6 59 E
Botucatu 80 22 55S 48 30W
Botwood 63 49 6N 55 23W
Bou Djébéha 50 18 25N 2 45W
Bou Izakarn 50 29 12N 9 46W
Bouaké 50 7 40N 5 2W
Bouar 54 6 0N 15 40 E
Bouârfa 50 32 32N 1 58 E
Bouca 51 6 45N 18 25 E
Boucaut B. 44 12 0S 134 25 E
Bouches-du-Rhône □ 12 43 37N 5 2 E
Bougainville C. 46 13 57S 126 4 E
Bougainville Reef 44 15 30S 147 5 E
Bougie = Bejaia 50 36 42N 5 2 E
Bougouni 50 11 30N 7 20W
Bouillon 11 49 44N 5 3 E
Boulder, Colo., U.S.A. 70 40 3N 105 10W
Boulder, Mont., U.S.A. 72 46 14N 112 4W
Boulder City 73 35 58N 114 50W
Boulder Dam = Hoover Dam 73 36 0N 114 45W
Boulia 44 22 52S 139 51 E
Boulogne-sur-Mer 12 50 42N 1 36 E
Boultoum 53 14 45N 10 25 E
Bouna 50 9 10N 3 0W
Boundiali 50 9 30N 6 20W
Bountiful 72 40 57N 111 58W
Bounty I. 40 48 0S 178 30 E
Bourbonnais 12 46 28N 3 0 E
Bourem 53 17 0N 0 24W
Bourg-en-Bresse 12 46 13N 5 12 E
Bourges 12 47 9N 2 25 E
Bourgogne 12 47 0N 4 50 E
Bourke 45 30 8S 145 55 E
Bournemouth 7 50 43N 1 53W
Bousso 51 10 34N 16 52 E
Boutilimit 50 17 45N 14 40W
Bouvet I. = Bouvetøya 3 54 26S 3 24 E
Bouvetøya 3 54 26S 3 24 E
Bovigny 11 50 12N 5 55 E
Bovill 72 46 58N 116 27W
Bow Island 64 49 50N 111 23W
Bowbells 70 48 47N 102 19W
Bowdle 70 45 30N 99 40W
Bowelling 47 33 25S 116 30 E
Bowen 44 20 0S 148 16 E
Bowen Mts. 45 37 0S 148 0 E
Bowie, Ariz., U.S.A. 73 32 15N 109 30W
Bowie, Tex., U.S.A. 71 33 33N 97 50W
Bowland, Forest of 6 54 0N 2 30W
Bowling Green, Ky., U.S.A. 68 37 0N 86 25W
Bowling Green, Ohio, U.S.A. 68 41 22N 83 40W
Bowling Green, C. 44 19 19S 147 25 E
Bowman 70 46 12N 103 21W
Bowmans 45 34 10S 138 17 E
Bowmanville 62 43 55N 78 41W
Bowmore 8 55 45N 6 18W
Bowral 45 34 26S 150 27 E
Bowraville 45 30 37S 152 52 E
Bowron → 64 54 3N 121 50W
Bowser L. 64 56 30N 129 30W
Bowsman 65 52 14N 101 12W
Boxtel 11 51 36N 5 20 E
Boyce 71 31 25N 92 39W
Boyer → 64 58 27N 115 57W
Boyle 9 53 58N 8 19W
Boyne → 9 53 43N 6 15W
Boyne City 68 45 13N 85 1W
Boyni Qara 31 36 20N 67 0 E
Boynton Beach 69 26 31N 80 3W
Boyoma, Chutes 48 0 35N 25 23 E
Boyup Brook 47 33 50S 116 23 E
Bozeman 72 45 40N 111 0W
Bozen = Bolzano 18 46 30N 11 20 E
Bozoum 51 6 25N 16 35 E
Brabant □ 11 50 46N 4 30 E
Brabant L. 65 55 58N 103 43W
Brač 18 43 20N 16 40 E
Bracadale, L. 8 57 20N 6 30W
Bracciano, L. di 18 42 8N 12 11 E
Bracebridge 62 45 2N 79 19W
Brach 51 27 31N 14 20 E
Bräcke 20 62 45N 15 26 E
Brackettville 71 29 21N 100 20W
Brad 15 46 10N 22 50 E
Bradenton 69 27 25N 82 35W
Bradford, U.K. 6 53 47N 1 45W
Bradford, U.S.A. 68 41 58N 78 41W
Bradley, Ark., U.S.A. 71 33 7N 93 39W
Bradley, S. Dak., U.S.A. 70 45 10N 97 40W
Bradore Bay 63 51 27N 57 18W
Bradshaw 46 15 21S 130 16 E
Brady 71 31 8N 99 25W
Braemar 45 33 12S 139 35 E
Braga 13 41 35N 8 25W
Bragança, Brazil 79 1 0S 47 2W
Bragança, Portugal 13 41 48N 6 50W
Brahmanbaria 33 23 58N 91 15 E
Brahmani → 33 20 39N 86 46 E
Brahmaputra → 33 24 2N 90 59 E
Braich-y-pwll 6 52 47N 4 46W
Braidwood 45 35 27S 149 49 E
Brăila 15 45 19N 27 59 E
Brainerd 70 46 20N 94 10W
Braintree 7 51 53N 0 34 E
Brak → 56 29 35S 22 55 E
Brakwater 56 22 28S 17 3 E
Bralorne 64 50 50N 122 50W
Brampton 62 43 45N 79 45W
Bramwell 44 12 8S 142 37 E
Branco → 78 1 20S 61 50W
Brandenburg 14 52 24N 12 33 E
Brandfort 56 28 40S 26 30 E
Brandon 65 49 50N 99 57W
Brandon, Mt. 9 52 15N 10 15W
Brandon B. 9 52 17N 10 8W
Brandvlei 56 30 25S 20 30 E
Braniewo 15 54 25N 19 50 E
Brańsk 15 52 45N 22 50 E
Branson, Colo., U.S.A. 71 37 4N 103 53W
Branson, Mo., U.S.A. 71 36 40N 93 18W
Brantford 62 43 10N 80 15W
Branxholme 45 37 52S 141 49 E
Bras d'Or, L. 63 45 50N 60 50W
Brasil, Planalto 76 18 0S 46 30W
Brasiléia 78 11 0S 68 45W
Brasília 79 15 47S 47 55W
Braşov 15 45 38N 25 35 E
Brasschaat 11 51 19N 4 27 E
Brassey, Banjaran 34 5 0N 117 15 E
Brassey Ra. 47 25 8S 122 15 E
Brasstown Bald, Mt. 69 34 54N 83 45W
Bratislava 14 48 10N 17 7 E
Bratsk 25 56 10N 101 30 E
Brattleboro 68 42 53N 72 37W
Braunschweig 14 52 17N 10 28 E
Braunton 7 51 6N 4 9W
Brava 29 1 20N 44 8 E
Bravo del Norte → 74 25 57N 97 9W
Brawley 73 32 58N 115 30W
Bray 9 53 12N 6 6W
Bray, Mt. 44 14 0S 134 30 E
Bray-sur-Seine 12 48 25N 3 14 E
Brazeau → 64 52 55N 115 14W
Brazil 68 39 32N 87 8W
Brazil ■ 79 12 0S 50 0W
Brazilian Highlands = Brasil, Planalto 76 18 0S 46 30W
Brazos → 71 28 53N 95 23W
Brazzaville 54 4 9S 15 12 E
Brčko 19 44 54N 18 46 E
Breadalbane, Australia 44 23 50S 139 35 E
Breadalbane, U.K. 8 56 30N 4 15W
Breaden, L. 47 25 51S 125 28 E
Breaksea Sd. 43 45 35S 166 35 E
Bream Bay 43 35 56S 174 28 E
Bream Head 43 35 51S 174 36 E
Brebes 35 6 52S 109 3 E
Brechin 8 56 44N 2 40W
Breckenridge, Colo., U.S.A. 72 39 30N 106 2W
Breckenridge, Minn., U.S.A. 70 46 20N 96 36W
Breckenridge, Tex., U.S.A. 71 32 48N 98 55W
Brecon 7 51 57N 3 23W
Brecon Beacons 7 51 53N 3 27W
Breda 11 51 35N 4 45 E
Bredasdorp 56 34 33S 20 2 E
Bredbo 45 35 58S 149 10 E
Bregenz 14 47 30N 9 45 E
Breiðafjörður 20 65 15N 23 15W
Brejo 79 3 41S 42 47W
Bremen 14 53 4N 8 47 E
Bremer I. 44 12 5S 136 45 E
Bremerhaven 14 53 34N 8 35 E
Bremerton 72 47 30N 122 38W
Brenham 71 30 5N 96 27W
Brenner Pass 14 47 0N 11 30 E
Brent, Canada 62 46 2N 78 29W
Brent, U.K. 7 51 33N 0 18W
Brentwood 7 51 37N 0 19 E
Bréscia 18 45 33N 10 13 E
Breskens 11 51 23N 3 33 E
Breslau = Wrocław 14 51 5N 17 5 E
Bressanone 18 46 43N 11 40 E
Bressay I. 8 60 10N 1 5W
Bresse 12 46 50N 5 10 E
Brest, France 12 48 24N 4 31W
Brest, U.S.S.R. 22 52 10N 23 40 E
Bretagne 12 48 0N 3 0W
Bretçu 15 46 7N 26 18 E
Breton 64 53 7N 114 28W
Breton Sd. 71 29 40N 89 12W
Brett, C. 43 35 10S 174 20 E
Brevard 69 35 19N 82 42W
Brewarrina 45 30 0S 146 51 E
Brewer 63 44 43N 68 50W
Brewster 72 48 10N 119 51W
Brewton 69 31 9N 87 2W
Breyten 57 26 16S 30 0 E
Brezhnev 24 55 42N 52 19 E
Bria 51 6 30N 21 58 E
Briançon 12 44 54N 6 39 E
Bribie I. 45 27 0S 152 58 E
Bridgend 7 51 30N 3 35W
Bridgeport, Calif., U.S.A. 73 38 14N 119 15W
Bridgeport, Conn., U.S.A. 68 41 12N 73 12W
Bridgeport, Nebr., U.S.A. 70 41 42N 103 10W
Bridgeport, Tex., U.S.A. 71 33 15N 97 45W
Bridger 72 45 20N 108 58W
Bridgeton 68 39 29N 75 10W
Bridgetown, Australia 47 33 58S 116 7 E
Bridgetown, Barbados 75 13 0N 59 30W
Bridgetown, Canada 63 44 55N 65 18W
Bridgewater, Canada 63 44 25N 64 31W
Bridgewater, U.S.A. 70 43 34N 97 29W
Bridgewater, C. 45 38 23S 141 23 E
Bridgnorth 7 52 33N 2 25W
Bridgwater 7 51 7N 3 0W
Bridlington 6 54 6N 0 11W
Bridport, Australia 44 40 59S 147 23 E
Bridport, U.K. 7 50 43N 2 45W
Brie, Plaine de la 12 48 35N 3 10 E
Brig 14 46 18N 7 59 E
Brigg 6 53 33N 0 30W
Briggsdale 70 40 40N 104 20W
Brigham City 72 41 30N 112 1W
Bright 45 36 42S 146 56 E
Brighton, Australia 45 35 5S 138 30 E
Brighton, Canada 62 44 2N 77 44W
Brighton, U.K. 7 50 50N 0 9W
Brighton, U.S.A. 70 39 59N 104 50W
Brilliant 64 49 19N 117 38W
Bríndisi 19 40 39N 17 55 E
Brinkley 71 34 55N 91 15W
Brinkworth 45 33 42S 138 26 E
Brion, I. 63 47 46N 61 26W
Brisbane 45 27 25S 153 2 E
Brisbane → 45 27 24S 153 9 E
Bristol, U.K. 7 51 26N 2 35W
Bristol, Conn., U.S.A. 68 41 44N 72 57W
Bristol, S. Dak., U.S.A. 70 45 25N 97 43W
Bristol, Tenn., U.S.A. 69 36 36N 82 11W
Bristol B. 60 58 0N 160 0W
Bristol Channel 7 51 18N 4 30W
Bristol L. 73 34 23N 116 50W
Bristow 71 35 55N 96 28W
British Columbia □ 64 55 0N 125 15W
British Guiana = Guyana ■ 78 5 0N 59 0W
British Honduras = Belize ■ 74 17 0N 88 30W
British Isles 4 55 0N 4 0W
Brits 57 25 37S 27 48 E
Britstown 56 30 37S 23 30 E
Britt 62 45 46N 80 34W
Brittany = Bretagne 12 48 0N 3 0W
Britton 70 45 50N 97 47W
Brixton 44 23 32S 144 57 E
Brlik 24 43 40N 73 49 E
Brno 14 49 10N 16 35 E
Broad → 69 33 59N 82 39W
Broad Arrow 47 30 23S 121 15 E
Broad B. 8 58 14N 6 16W
Broad Haven 9 54 20N 9 55W
Broad Law 8 55 30N 3 22W
Broad Sd. 44 22 0S 149 45 E
Broadhurst Ra. 46 22 30S 122 30 E
Broads, The 6 52 45N 1 30 E
Broadus 70 45 28N 105 27W
Broadview 65 50 22N 102 35W
Brochet 65 57 53N 101 40W
Brochet, L. 65 58 36N 101 35W
Brock 65 51 26N 108 43W
Brocken 14 51 48N 10 40 E
Brockport 68 43 12N 77 56W
Brockville 62 44 35N 75 41W
Brockway 70 47 18N 105 46W
Brodeur Pen. 61 72 30N 88 10W
Brodick 8 55 34N 5 9W
Brogan 72 44 14N 117 32W
Broken Bow, Nebr., U.S.A. 70 41 25N 99 35W
Broken Bow, Okla., U.S.A. 71 34 2N 94 43W
Broken Hill = Kabwe 55 14 30S 28 29 E
Broken Hill 45 31 58S 141 29 E
Bromfield 7 52 25N 2 45W
Bromley 7 51 20N 0 5 E
Brønderslev 21 57 16N 9 57 E
Bronkhorstspruit 57 25 46S 28 45 E
Bronte 71 31 54N 100 18W
Bronte Park 44 42 8S 146 30 E

Brookfield

Brookfield 70 39 50N 93 4W
Brookhaven 71 31 40N 90 25W
Brookings, Oreg., U.S.A. 72 42 4N 124 10W
Brookings, S. Dak., U.S.A. 70 44 20N 96 45W
Brookmere 64 49 52N 120 53W
Brooks 64 50 35N 111 55W
Brooks B. 64 50 15N 127 55W
Brooks L. 65 61 55N 106 35W
Brooks Ra. 60 68 40N 147 0W
Brooksville 69 28 32N 82 21W
Brookville 68 39 25N 85 0W
Brooloo 45 26 30S 152 43 E
Broom, L. 8 57 55N 5 15W
Broome 46 18 0S 122 15 E
Broomehill 47 33 51S 117 39 E
Brora 8 58 0N 3 50W
Brora → 8 58 4N 3 52W
Brosna → 9 53 8N 8 0W
Brothers 72 43 56N 120 39W
Broughton Island 61 67 33N 63 0W
Broughty Ferry 8 56 29N 2 50W
Brouwershaven 11 51 45N 3 55 E
Browerville 70 46 3N 94 50W
Brown, Pt. 45 32 32S 133 50 E
Brown Willy 7 50 35N 4 34W
Brownfield 71 33 10N 102 15W
Browning 72 48 35N 113 0W
Brownlee 65 50 43N 106 1W
Brownsville, Oreg., U.S.A. 72 44 29N 123 0W
Brownsville, Tenn., U.S.A. 71 35 35N 89 15W
Brownsville, Tex., U.S.A. 71 25 56N 97 25W
Brownwood 71 31 45N 99 0W
Brownwood, L. 71 31 51N 98 35W
Browse I. 46 14 7S 123 33 E
Bruay-en-Artois 12 50 29N 2 33 E
Bruce, Mt. 46 22 37S 118 8 E
Bruce Rock 47 31 52S 118 8 E
Bruck an der Leitha 14 48 1N 16 47 E
Brue → 7 51 10N 2 59W
Bruges = Brugge 11 51 13N 3 13 E
Brugge 11 51 13N 3 13 E
Brûlé 64 53 15N 117 58W
Brumado 79 14 14S 41 40W
Brunchilly 44 18 50S 134 30 E
Brundidge 69 31 43N 85 45W
Bruneau 72 42 57N 115 55W
Bruneau → 72 42 57N 115 58W
Brunei = Bandar Seri Begawan 34 4 52N 115 0 E
Brunei ■ 34 4 50N 115 0 E
Brunette Downs 44 18 40S 135 55 E
Brunner, L. 43 42 37S 171 27 E
Bruno 65 52 20N 105 30W
Brunsbüttelkoog 14 53 52N 9 13 E
Brunswick = Braunschweig 14 52 17N 10 28 E
Brunswick, Ga., U.S.A. 69 31 10N 81 30W
Brunswick, Maine, U.S.A. 63 43 53N 69 50W
Brunswick, Md., U.S.A. 68 39 20N 77 38W
Brunswick, Mo., U.S.A. 70 39 26N 93 10W
Brunswick, Pen. de 80 53 30S 71 30W
Brunswick B. 46 15 15S 124 50 E
Brunswick Junction 47 33 15S 115 50 E
Bruny I. 44 43 20S 147 15 E
Brush 70 40 17N 103 33W
Brusque 80 27 5S 49 0W
Brussel 11 50 51N 4 21 E
Brussels = Brussel 11 50 51N 4 21 E
Bruthen 45 37 42S 147 50 E
Bruxelles = Brussel 11 50 51N 4 21 E
Bryan, Ohio, U.S.A. 68 41 30N 84 30W
Bryan, Tex., U.S.A. 71 30 40N 96 27W
Bryan, Mt. 45 33 30S 139 0 E
Bryansk 22 53 13N 34 25 E
Bryant 70 44 35N 97 28W
Bryne 21 58 44N 5 38 E
Bryson City 69 35 28N 83 25W
Bu Craa 50 26 45N 12 50W
Buapinang 35 4 40S 121 30 E
Buayan 35 6 3N 125 6 E
Bucak 30 37 28N 30 36 E
Bucaramanga 78 7 0N 73 0W
Buccaneer Arch. 46 16 7S 123 20 E
Buchan 8 57 32N 2 8W
Buchan Ness 8 57 29N 1 48W
Buchanan, Canada 65 51 40N 102 45W
Buchanan, Liberia 50 5 57N 10 2W
Buchanan, L., Queens., Australia 44 21 35S 145 52 E
Buchanan, L., W. Austral., Australia 47 25 33S 123 2 E
Buchanan, L., U.S.A. 71 30 50N 98 25W
Buchans 63 48 50N 56 52W
Bucharest = Bucureşti 15 44 27N 26 10 E
Buckeye 73 33 28N 112 40W
Buckhannon 68 39 2N 80 10W
Buckhaven 8 56 10N 3 2W
Buckie 8 57 40N 2 58W
Buckingham, Canada 62 45 37N 75 24W
Buckingham, U.K. 7 52 0N 0 59W
Buckingham □ 7 51 50N 0 55W
Buckingham B. 44 12 10S 135 40 E
Buckland Newton 7 50 45N 2 25W
Buckle Hd. 46 14 26S 127 52 E
Buckleboo 45 32 54S 136 12 E
Buckley 72 47 10N 122 2W
Bucklin 71 37 37N 99 40W
Buctouche 63 46 30N 64 45W
Bucureşti 15 44 27N 26 10 E
Bucyrus 68 40 48N 83 0W
Budalin 33 22 20N 95 10 E
Budapest 15 47 29N 19 5 E
Bude 7 50 49N 4 33W
Budennovsk 23 44 50N 44 10 E
Budgewoi Lake 45 33 13S 151 34 E
Búðareyri 20 65 2N 14 13W
Búðir 20 64 49N 23 23W
Budjala 54 2 50N 19 40 E
Buea 53 4 10N 9 9 E
Buena Vista, Colo., U.S.A. 73 38 56N 106 6W
Buena Vista, Va., U.S.A. 68 37 47N 79 23W
Buena Vista L. 73 35 15N 119 21W
Buenaventura, Colombia 78 3 53N 77 4W
Buenaventura, Mexico 74 29 50N 107 30W
Buenos Aires 80 34 30S 58 20W
Buenos Aires, L. 80 46 35S 72 30W
Buffalo, Mo., U.S.A. 71 37 40N 93 5W
Buffalo, N.Y., U.S.A. 68 42 55N 78 50W
Buffalo, Okla., U.S.A. 71 36 55N 99 42W
Buffalo, S. Dak., U.S.A. 70 45 39N 103 31W
Buffalo, Wyo., U.S.A. 72 44 25N 106 50W
Buffalo → 64 60 5N 115 5W
Buffalo Head Hills 64 57 25N 115 55W
Buffalo L. 64 52 27N 112 54W
Buffalo Narrows 65 55 51N 108 29W
Buffels → 56 29 36S 17 3 E
Buford 69 34 5N 84 0W
Bug →, Poland 15 52 31N 21 5 E
Bug →, U.S.S.R. 23 46 59N 31 58 E
Buga 78 4 0N 76 15W
Bugel, Tanjung 34 6 26S 111 3 E
Bugsuk 34 8 15N 117 15 E
Bugt 38 48 47N 121 56 E
Bugulma 22 54 33N 52 48 E
Buguma 53 4 42N 6 55 E
Buguruslan 22 53 39N 52 26 E
Buheirat-Murrat-el-Kubra 51 30 15N 32 40 E
Buhl, Idaho, U.S.A. 72 42 35N 114 54W
Buhl, Minn., U.S.A. 70 47 30N 92 46W
Buick 71 37 38N 91 2W
Builth Wells 7 52 10N 3 26W
Buir Nur 37 47 50N 117 42 E
Bujumbura 54 3 16S 29 18 E
Bukachacha 25 52 55N 116 50 E
Bukama 54 9 10S 25 50 E
Bukavu 54 2 20S 28 52 E
Bukene 54 4 15S 32 48 E
Bukhara 24 39 48N 64 25 E
Bukittinggi 34 0 20S 100 20 E
Bukoba 54 1 20S 31 49 E
Bukombe 52 3 31S 32 4 E
Bula 35 3 6S 130 30 E
Bulahdelah 45 32 23S 152 13 E
Bulan 35 12 40N 123 52 E
Bulandshahr 32 28 28N 77 51 E
Bulawayo 55 20 7S 28 32 E
Bulgan 37 48 45N 103 34 E
Bulgaria ■ 19 42 35N 25 30 E
Bulgroo 45 25 47S 143 58 E
Bulgunnia 45 30 10S 134 53 E
Bulhar 29 10 25N 44 30 E
Buli, Teluk 35 1 5N 128 25 E
Buliluyan, C. 34 8 20N 117 15 E
Bulkley → 64 55 15N 127 40W
Bull Shoals L. 71 36 40N 93 5W
Bullara 46 22 40S 114 3 E
Bullaring 47 32 30S 117 45 E
Buller → 43 41 44S 171 36 E
Bulli 45 34 15S 150 57 E
Bullock Creek 44 17 43S 144 31 E
Bulloo → 45 28 43S 142 30 E
Bulloo Downs, Queens., Australia 45 28 31S 142 57 E
Bulloo Downs, W. Austral., Australia 47 24 0S 119 32 E
Bulloo L. 45 28 43S 142 25 E
Bulls 43 40 10S 175 24 E
Bulo Burti 29 3 50N 45 33 E
Bulsar = Valsad 32 20 40N 72 58 E
Bultfontein 56 28 18S 26 10 E
Bulu Karakelong 35 4 35N 126 50 E
Bulukumba 35 5 33S 120 11 E
Bulun 25 70 37N 127 30 E
Bumba 54 2 13N 22 30 E
Bumhpa Bum 33 26 51N 97 14 E
Buna 54 2 58N 39 30 E
Bunbah, Khalīj 51 32 20N 23 15 E
Bunbury 47 33 20S 115 35 E
Buncrana 9 55 8N 7 28W
Bundaberg 45 24 54S 152 22 E
Bundey → 44 21 46S 135 37 E
Bundi 32 25 30N 75 35 E
Bundooma 44 24 54S 134 16 E
Bundoran 9 54 24N 8 17W
Bungil Cr. → 44 27 5S 149 5 E
Bungo-Suidō 36 33 0N 132 15 E
Bungun Shara 37 49 0N 104 0 E
Bunia 54 1 35N 30 20 E
Bunji 32 35 45N 74 40 E
Bunkie 71 31 1N 92 12W
Bunnell 69 29 28N 81 12W
Buntok 34 1 40S 114 58 E
Bununu Dass 53 10 0N 9 31 E
Bunyu 34 3 35N 117 50 E
Buol 35 1 15N 121 32 E
Buon Me Thuot 34 12 40N 108 3 E
Buorkhaya, Mys 25 71 50N 132 40 E
Buqayq 30 26 0N 49 45 E
Buqei'a 28 32 58N 35 20 E
Bur Acaba 29 3 12N 44 20 E
Bûr Safâga 51 26 43N 33 57 E
Bûr Sa'îd 51 31 16N 32 18 E
Bûr Sûdân 51 19 32N 37 9 E
Bura 52 1 4S 39 58 E
Burao 29 9 32N 45 32 E
Buras 71 29 20N 89 33W
Buraydah 30 26 20N 44 8 E
Buraymī, Al Wāhāt al 31 24 10N 55 43 E
Burbank 73 34 9N 118 23W
Burcher 45 33 30S 147 16 E
Burdekin → 44 19 38S 147 25 E
Burdett 64 49 50N 111 32W
Burdur 30 37 45N 30 22 E
Burdwan = Barddhaman 33 23 14N 87 39 E
Bure → 6 52 38N 1 45 E
Bureya → 25 49 27N 129 30 E
Burgas 19 42 33N 27 29 E
Burgenland □ 14 47 20N 16 20 E
Burgeo 63 47 37N 57 38W
Burgersdorp 56 31 0S 26 20 E
Burges, Mt. 47 30 50S 121 5 E
Burgos 13 42 21N 3 41W
Burgsvik 21 57 3N 18 19 E
Burgundy = Bourgogne 12 47 0N 4 50 E
Burias 35 12 55N 123 5 E
Burica, Pta. 75 8 3N 82 51W
Burin, Canada 63 47 1N 55 14W
Būrīn, Jordan 28 32 11N 35 15 E
Buriram 34 15 0N 103 0 E
Burji 51 5 29N 37 51 E
Burkburnett 71 34 7N 98 35W
Burke 72 47 31N 115 56W
Burke → 44 23 12S 139 33 E
Burketown 44 17 45S 139 33 E
Burkina Faso ■ 50 12 0N 1 0W
Burk's Falls 62 45 37N 79 24W
Burley 72 42 37N 113 55W
Burlington, Colo., U.S.A. 70 39 21N 102 18W
Burlington, Iowa, U.S.A. 70 40 50N 91 5W
Burlington, Kans., U.S.A. 70 38 15N 95 47W
Burlington, N.C., U.S.A. 69 36 7N 79 27W
Burlington, N.J., U.S.A. 68 40 5N 74 50W
Burlington, Vt., U.S.A. 68 44 27N 73 14W
Burlington, Wash., U.S.A. 72 48 29N 122 19W
Burlington, Wis., U.S.A. 68 42 41N 88 18W
Burlyu-Tyube 24 46 30N 79 10 E
Burma ■ 33 21 0N 96 30 E
Burnaby I. 64 52 25N 131 19W
Burnet 71 30 45N 98 11W
Burney 72 40 56N 121 41W
Burngup 47 33 2S 118 42 E
Burnie 44 41 4S 145 56 E
Burnley 6 53 47N 2 15W
Burns, Oreg., U.S.A. 72 43 40N 119 4W
Burns, Wyo., U.S.A. 70 41 13N 104 18W
Burns Lake 64 54 20N 125 45W
Burnside → 60 66 51N 108 4W
Burnside, L. 47 25 22S 123 0 E
Burntwood → 65 56 8N 96 34W
Burntwood L. 65 55 22N 100 26W
Burqâ 28 32 18N 35 11 E
Burqān 30 29 0N 47 57 E
Burqin 37 47 43N 87 0 E
Burra 45 33 40S 138 55 E
Burramurra 44 20 25S 137 15 E
Burren Junction 45 30 7S 148 59 E
Burrendong Dam 45 32 39S 149 6 E
Burrinjuck Res. 45 35 0S 148 36 E
Burro, Serranías del 74 29 0N 102 0W
Burrundie 46 13 32S 131 42 E
Burruyacú 80 26 30S 64 40W
Burry Port 7 51 41N 4 17W
Bursa 30 40 15N 29 5 E
Burstall 65 50 39N 109 54W
Burton L. 62 54 45N 78 20W
Burton-upon-Trent 6 52 48N 1 39W
Burtundy 45 33 45S 142 15 E
Buru 35 3 30S 126 30 E
Burundi ■ 54 3 15S 30 0 E
Burutu 53 5 20N 5 29 E
Burwell 70 41 49N 99 8W
Bury 6 53 36N 2 19W
Bury St. Edmunds 7 52 15N 0 42 E
Buryat A.S.S.R. □ 25 53 0N 110 0 E
Buşayyah 30 30 0N 46 10 E
Būshehr 31 28 55N 50 55 E
Būshehr □ 31 28 20N 51 45 E
Bushell 65 59 31N 108 45W
Bushire = Būshehr 31 28 55N 50 55 E
Bushnell, Ill., U.S.A. 70 40 32N 90 30W
Bushnell, Nebr., U.S.A. 70 41 18N 103 50W
Businga 54 3 16N 20 59 E
Buskerud fylke □ 21 60 13N 9 0 E
Busra ash Shām 30 32 30N 36 25 E
Busselton 47 33 42S 115 15 E
Bussum 11 52 16N 5 10 E
Busto Arsizio 18 45 40N 8 50 E
Busu-Djanoa 54 1 43N 21 23 E
Busuanga 35 12 10N 120 0 E
Buta 54 2 50N 24 53 E
Butare 54 2 31S 29 52 E
Butaritari 40 3 30N 174 0 E
Bute 8 55 48N 5 2W
Bute Inlet 64 50 40N 124 53W
Butembo 54 0 9N 29 18 E
Butha Qi 38 48 0N 122 32 E
Butler, Mo., U.S.A. 70 38 17N 94 18W
Butler, Pa., U.S.A. 68 40 52N 79 52W
Butte, Mont., U.S.A. 72 46 0N 112 31W
Butte, Nebr., U.S.A. 70 42 56N 98 54W
Butterworth = Gcuwa 57 32 20S 28 11 E
Butterworth 34 5 24N 100 23 E
Buttfield, Mt. 47 24 45S 128 9 E
Button B. 65 58 45N 94 23W
Butty Hd. 47 33 54S 121 39 E
Butuan 35 8 57N 125 33 E
Butung 35 5 0S 122 45 E
Buturlinovka 23 50 50N 40 35 E
Buxton, S. Africa 56 27 38S 24 42 E
Buxton, U.K. 6 53 16N 1 54W
Buy 22 58 28N 41 28 E
Buyaga 25 59 50N 127 0 E
Buzău 15 45 10N 26 50 E
Buzău → 15 45 26N 27 44 E
Buzen 36 33 35N 131 5 E
Buzi → 55 19 50S 34 43 E
Buzuluk 22 52 48N 52 12 E
Buzzards Bay 68 41 45N 70 38W
Bydgoszcz 15 53 10N 18 0 E
Byelorussian S.S.R. □ 22 53 30N 27 0 E
Byers 70 39 46N 104 13W
Byhalia 71 34 53N 89 41W
Bylas 73 33 11N 110 9W
Bylot I. 61 73 13N 78 34W
Byro 47 26 5S 116 11 E
Byrock 45 30 40S 146 27 E
Byron Bay 45 28 43S 153 37 E
Byrranga, Gory 25 75 0N 100 0 E
Byske 20 64 57N 21 11 E
Byske älv → 20 64 57N 21 13 E
Bytom 15 50 25N 18 54 E

C

Ca Mau = Quan Long 34 9 7N 105 8 E
Caála 55 12 46S 15 30 E
Caamano Sd. 64 52 55N 129 25W
Cabanatuan 35 15 30N 120 58 E
Cabano 63 47 40N 68 56W
Cabedelo 79 7 0S 34 50W
Cabimas 78 10 23N 71 25W
Cabinda 54 5 33S 12 11 E
Cabinda □ 54 5 0S 12 30 E
Cabinet Mts. 72 48 0N 115 30W
Cabo Blanco 80 47 15S 65 47W
Cabo Frio 79 22 51S 42 3W
Cabo Pantoja 78 1 0S 75 10W
Cabonga, Réservoir 62 47 20N 76 40W
Cabool 71 37 10N 92 8W
Caboolture 45 27 5S 152 58 E
Cabora Bassa Dam 55 15 20S 32 50 E
Caborca 74 30 40N 112 10W
Cabot Strait 63 47 15N 59 40W
Cabrera, I. 13 39 8N 2 57 E
Cabri 65 50 35N 108 25W
Cabriel → 13 39 14N 1 3W
Čačak 19 43 54N 20 20 E
Cáceres, Brazil 78 16 5S 57 40W
Cáceres, Spain 13 39 26N 6 23W
Cache Bay 62 46 22N 80 0W
Cachimbo, Serra do 79 9 30S 55 0W
Cachoeira 79 12 30S 39 0W
Cachoeira de Itapemirim 79 20 51S 41 7W
Cachoeira do Sul 80 30 3S 52 53W
Cacólo 54 10 9S 19 21 E
Caconda 55 13 48S 15 8 E
Cacongo 54 5 11S 12 5 E
Caddo 71 34 8N 96 18W
Cadell Cr. → 44 22 35S 141 51 E
Cader Idris 6 52 43N 3 56W
Cadibarrawirracanna, L. 45 28 52S 135 27 E
Cadillac, Canada 62 48 14N 78 23W
Cadillac, U.S.A. 68 44 16N 85 25W
Cadiz, Phil. 35 10 57N 123 15 E
Cádiz, Spain 13 36 30N 6 20W
Cádiz, G. de 13 36 40N 7 0W
Cadney Park 45 27 55S 134 3 E
Cadomin 64 53 2N 117 20W
Cadotte → 64 56 43N 117 10W
Cadoux 47 30 46S 117 7 E
Caen 12 49 10N 0 22W
Caernarfon 6 53 8N 4 17W
Caernarfon B. 6 53 4N 4 40W
Caernarvon = Caernarfon 6 53 8N 4 17W
Caerphilly 7 51 34N 3 13W
Caesarea 28 32 30N 34 53 E
Caeté 79 19 55S 43 40W
Caetité 79 13 50S 42 32W
Cafu 56 16 30S 15 8 E
Cagayan → 35 18 25N 121 42 E
Cagayan de Oro 35 8 30N 124 40 E
Cágliari 18 39 15N 9 6 E
Cágliari, G. di 18 39 8N 9 10 E
Caguas 75 18 14N 66 4W
Caha Mts. 9 51 45N 9 40W
Cahama 56 16 17S 14 19 E
Caher 9 52 23N 7 56W
Cahersiveen 9 51 57N 10 13W
Cahore Pt. 9 52 34N 6 11W
Cahors 12 44 27N 1 27 E
Cahuapanas 78 5 15S 77 0W
Caia 55 17 51S 35 24 E
Caibarién 75 22 30N 79 30W
Caicara 78 7 38N 66 10W
Caicó 79 6 20S 37 0W
Caicos Is. 75 21 40N 71 40W
Caicos Passage 75 22 45N 72 45W
Cairn Gorm 8 57 7N 3 40W
Cairn Toul 8 57 3N 3 44W
Cairngorm Mts. 8 57 6N 3 42W
Cairns 44 16 57S 145 45 E
Cairo = El Qâhira 51 30 1N 31 14 E
Cairo, Ga., U.S.A. 69 30 52N 84 12W
Cairo, Ill., U.S.A. 71 37 0N 89 10W
Caithness, Ord of 8 58 9N 3 37W
Caiundo 55 15 50S 17 28 E
Caiza 78 20 2S 65 40W
Cajamarca 78 7 5S 78 28W
Cajàzeiras 79 6 52S 38 30W
Calabar 53 4 57N 8 20 E
Calábria □ 18 39 24N 16 30 E
Calafate 80 50 19S 72 15W
Calahorra 13 42 18N 1 59W
Calais, France 12 50 57N 1 56 E
Calais, U.S.A. 63 45 11N 67 20W
Calama, Brazil 78 8 0S 62 50W
Calama, Chile 80 22 30S 68 55W
Calamar, Bolívar, Colombia 78 10 15N 74 55W
Calamar, Vaupés, Colombia 78 1 58N 72 32W
Calamian Group 35 11 50N 119 55 E
Calamocha 13 40 50N 1 17W
Calang 34 4 37N 95 37 E
Calapan 35 13 25N 121 7 E
Calatayud 13 41 20N 1 40W
Calauag 35 13 55N 122 15 E
Calavite, Cape 35 13 26N 120 20 E
Calbayog 35 12 4N 124 38 E
Calca 78 13 22S 72 0W
Calcasieu L. 71 30 0N 93 17W
Calcutta 33 22 36N 88 24 E
Calder → 6 53 44N 1 21W
Caldera 80 27 5S 70 55W
Caldwell, Idaho, U.S.A. 72 43 45N 116 42W

Caspian Sea

Caspian Sea 23 43 0N 50 0 E
Cass City 68 43 34N 83 24W
Cass Lake 70 47 23N 94 38W
Casselton 70 47 0N 97 15W
Cassiar 64 59 16N 129 40W
Cassiar Mts. 64 59 30N 130 30W
Cassinga 55 15 5S 16 4 E
Cassville 71 36 45N 93 52W
Castellammare del Golfo 18 38 2N 12 53 E
Castellammare di Stábia 18 40 47N 14 29 E
Castellón de la Plana 13 39 58N 0 3W
Castelo Branco 13 39 50N 7 31W
Castelvetrano 18 37 40N 12 46 E
Casterton 45 37 30S 141 30 E
Castilla La Mancha □ 13 39 30N 3 30W
Castilla La Nueva 13 39 45N 3 20W
Castilla La Vieja 13 41 55N 4 0W
Castilla y Leon □ 13 42 0N 5 0W
Castle Dale 72 39 11N 111 1W
Castle Douglas 8 54 57N 3 57W
Castle Point 43 40 54S 176 15 E
Castle Rock, Colo., U.S.A. 70 39 26N 104 50W
Castle Rock, Wash., U.S.A. 72 46 20N 122 58W
Castlebar 9 53 52N 9 17W
Castleblaney 9 54 7N 6 44W
Castlegar 64 49 20N 117 40W
Castlemaine 45 37 2S 144 12 E
Castlereagh 9 53 47N 8 30W
Castlereagh □ 9 54 33N 5 53W
Castlereagh → 45 30 12S 147 32 E
Castlereagh B. 44 12 10S 135 10 E
Castletown 6 54 4N 4 40W
Castletown Bearhaven 9 51 40N 9 54W
Castlevale 44 24 30S 146 48 E
Castor 64 52 15N 111 50W
Castres 12 43 37N 2 13 E
Castries 75 14 0N 60 50W
Castro 80 42 30S 73 50W
Castro Alves 79 12 46S 39 33W
Castro del Río 13 37 41N 4 29W
Castroville 71 29 20N 98 53W
Casummit Lake 62 51 29N 92 22W
Cat I., Bahamas 75 24 30N 75 30W
Cat I., U.S.A. 71 30 15N 89 7W
Cat L. 62 51 40N 91 50W
Catacáos 78 5 20S 80 45W
Catahoula L. 71 31 30N 92 5W
Catalão 79 18 10S 47 57W
Catalina 63 48 31N 53 4W
Catalonia = Cataluña □ 13 41 40N 1 15 E
Cataluña □ 13 41 40N 1 15 E
Catamarca 80 28 30S 65 50W
Catanduanes 35 13 50N 124 20 E
Catanduva 79 21 5S 48 58W
Catánia 18 37 31N 15 4 E
Catanzaro 18 38 54N 16 38 E
Catarman 35 12 28N 124 35 E
Cateel 35 7 47N 126 24 E
Cathcart 56 32 18S 27 10 E
Cathlamet 72 46 12N 123 23W
Cativa 74 9 21N 79 49W
Catlettsburg 68 38 23N 82 38W
Catoche, C. 74 21 40N 87 8W
Catrimani 78 0 27N 61 41W
Catskill 68 42 14N 73 52W
Catskill Mts. 68 42 15N 74 15W
Catt, Mt. 44 13 49S 134 23 E
Catuala 56 16 25S 19 2 E
Cauca → 78 8 54N 74 28W
Caucaia 79 3 40S 38 35W
Caucasus 4 43 0N 44 0 E
Caucasus Mts. = Bolshoi Kavkas 23 42 50N 44 0 E
Caúngula 54 8 26S 18 38 E
Cauquenes 80 36 0S 72 22W
Caura → 78 7 38N 64 53W
Causapscal 63 48 19N 67 12W
Cauvery → 32 11 9N 78 52 E
Caux, Pays de 12 49 38N 0 35 E
Cavalier 70 48 50N 97 39W
Cavan 9 54 0N 7 22W
Cavan □ 9 53 58N 7 10W
Cave City 68 37 13N 85 57W
Cavenagh Range 47 26 12S 127 55 E
Cavendish 45 37 31S 142 2 E
Caviana, I. 79 0 10N 50 10W
Cavite 35 14 29N 120 55 E
Cawndilla, L. 45 32 30S 142 15 E
Cawnpore = Kanpur 32 26 28N 80 20 E
Caxias 79 4 55S 43 20W
Caxias do Sul 80 29 10S 51 10W
Caxito 54 8 30S 13 30 E
Cay Sal Bank 75 23 45N 80 0W
Cayambe 78 0 3N 78 8W
Cayenne 79 5 0N 52 18W
Cayes, Les 75 18 15N 73 46W
Cayman Is. 75 19 40N 80 30W
Cayo Romano 75 22 0N 78 0W
Cayuga L. 68 42 45N 76 45W
Cazombo 55 11 54S 22 56 E
Ceanannus Mor 9 53 42N 6 53W
Ceará = Fortaleza 79 3 45S 38 35W
Ceará □ 79 5 0S 40 0W
Ceará Mirim 79 5 38S 35 25W
Cebollar 80 29 10S 66 35W
Cebu 35 10 18N 123 54 E
Cecil Plains 45 27 30S 151 11 E
Cedar → 70 41 17N 91 21W
Cedar City 73 37 41N 113 3W
Cedar Creek Res. 71 32 4N 96 5W
Cedar Falls 70 42 39N 92 29W
Cedar Key 69 29 9N 83 5W
Cedar L. 65 53 10N 100 0W
Cedar Rapids 70 42 0N 91 38W
Cedartown 69 34 1N 85 15W
Cedarvale 64 55 1N 128 22W
Cedarville, S. Africa 57 30 23S 29 3 E
Cedarville, U.S.A. 72 41 37N 120 13W
Cedral 74 23 50N 100 42W
Cedro 79 6 34S 39 3W
Cedros, I. de 74 28 10N 115 20W
Ceduna 45 32 7S 133 46 E
Cefalù 18 38 3N 14 1 E
Cegléd 15 47 11N 19 47 E
Cehegín 13 38 6N 1 48W
Ceiba, La 75 15 40N 86 50W
Celaya 74 20 31N 100 37W
Celbridge 9 53 20N 6 33W
Celebes = Sulawesi □ 35 2 0S 120 0 E
Celebes Sea 35 3 0N 123 0 E
Celina 68 40 32N 84 31W
Celje 18 46 16N 15 18 E
Celle 14 52 37N 10 4 E
Cement 71 34 56N 98 8W
Cengong 39 27 13N 108 44 E
Center, N. Dak., U.S.A. 70 47 9N 101 17W
Center, Tex., U.S.A. 71 31 50N 94 10W
Centerfield 73 39 9N 111 56W
Centerville, Iowa, U.S.A. 70 40 45N 92 57W
Centerville, S. Dak., U.S.A. 70 43 10N 96 58W
Centerville, Tenn., U.S.A. 69 35 46N 87 29W
Centerville, Tex., U.S.A. 71 31 15N 95 56W
Central 73 32 46N 108 9W
Central □ 8 56 10N 4 30W
Central, Cordillera, Colombia 78 5 0N 75 0W
Central, Cordillera, C. Rica 75 10 10N 84 5W
Central African Republic ■ 54 7 0N 20 0 E
Central City, Ky., U.S.A. 68 37 20N 87 7W
Central City, Nebr., U.S.A. 70 41 8N 98 0W
Central Makran Range 31 26 30N 64 15 E
Central Patricia 62 51 30N 90 9W
Central Russian Uplands 4 54 0N 36 0 E
Central Siberian Plateau 26 65 0N 105 0 E
Centralia, Ill., U.S.A. 70 38 32N 89 5W
Centralia, Mo., U.S.A. 70 39 12N 92 6W
Centralia, Wash., U.S.A. 72 46 46N 122 59W
Centreville, Ala., U.S.A. 69 32 55N 87 7W
Centreville, Miss., U.S.A. 71 31 10N 91 3W
Cephalonia = Kefallinía 19 38 20N 20 30 E
Cepu 35 7 9S 111 35 E
Ceram = Seram 35 3 10S 129 0 E
Ceram Sea = Seram Sea 35 2 30S 128 30 E
Ceres, Argentina 80 29 55S 61 55W
Ceres, S. Africa 56 33 21S 19 18 E
Cerignola 18 41 17N 15 53 E
Cerigo = Kíthira 19 36 9N 23 0 E
Çerkeş 30 40 49N 32 52 E
Cerknica 18 45 48N 14 21 E
Cernavodă 15 44 22N 28 3 E
Cerralvo 74 24 20N 109 45 E
Cerritos 74 22 27N 100 20W
Cervera 13 41 40N 1 16 E
Cervera del Río Alhama 13 42 2N 1 58W
Cesena 18 44 9N 12 14 E
České Budějovice 14 48 55N 14 25 E
Ceskomoravská Vrchovina 14 49 30N 15 40 E
Český Těšin 15 49 45N 18 39 E
Cessnock 45 32 50S 151 21 E
Cetinje 19 42 23N 18 59 E
Ceuta 50 35 52N 5 18W
Cévennes 12 44 10N 3 50 E
Ceyhan 30 37 4N 35 47 E
Ceyhan → 23 36 38N 35 40 E
Ceylon = Sri Lanka ■ 32 7 30N 80 50 E
Chablais 12 46 20N 6 36 E
Chachapoyas 78 6 15S 77 50W
Chachran 32 28 55N 70 30 E
Chad ■ 51 15 0N 17 15 E
Chad, L. = Tchad, L. 51 13 30N 14 30 E
Chadan 25 51 17N 91 35 E
Chadileuvú → 80 37 46S 66 0W
Chadron 70 42 50N 103 0W
Chagai Hills 32 29 30N 63 0 E
Chagda 25 58 45N 130 38 E
Chagos Arch. 3 6 0S 72 0 E
Chágres → 74 9 10N 79 40W
Chāh Bahār 31 25 20N 60 40 E
Chāh Gay Hills 31 29 30N 64 0 E
Chahar Burjak 32 30 15N 62 0 E
Chahār Mahāll va Bakhtīarī □ 30 32 0N 49 0 E
Chaibasa 33 22 42N 85 49 E
Chake Chake 52 5 15S 39 45 E
Chakhānsūr 31 31 10N 62 0 E
Chakonipau, L. 63 56 18N 68 30W
Chakradharpur 33 22 45N 85 40 E
Chakwal 32 32 56N 72 53 E
Chala 78 15 48S 74 20W
Chalcis = Khalkís 19 38 27N 23 42 E
Chaleur B. 63 47 55N 65 30W
Chalhuanca 78 14 15S 73 15W
Chaling 39 26 58N 113 30 E
Chalisgaon 32 20 30N 75 10 E
Chalky Inlet 43 46 3S 166 31 E
Challapata 78 18 53S 66 50W
Challis 72 44 32N 114 25W
Châlons-sur-Marne 12 48 58N 4 20 E
Chama 73 36 54N 106 35W
Chaman 31 30 58N 66 25 E
Chamba, India 32 32 35N 76 10 E
Chamba, Tanzania 55 11 37S 37 0 E
Chambal → 32 26 29N 79 15 E
Chamberlain 70 43 50N 99 21W
Chamberlain → 46 15 30S 127 54 E
Chambers 73 35 13N 109 30W
Chambersburg 68 39 53N 77 41W
Chambéry 12 45 34N 5 55 E
Chambord 63 48 25N 72 6W
Chamical 80 30 22S 66 27W
Chamonix-Mont-Blanc 12 45 55N 6 51 E
Champagne 64 60 49N 136 30W
Champagne, Plaine de 12 49 0N 4 30 E
Champaign 68 40 8N 88 14W
Champlain, Canada 68 46 27N 72 24W
Champlain, U.S.A. 68 44 59N 73 27W
Champlain, L. 68 44 30N 73 20W
Champotón 74 19 20N 90 50W
Chañaral 80 26 23S 70 40W
Chandalar 60 67 30N 148 35W
Chandeleur Is. 71 29 48N 88 51W
Chandeleur Sd. 71 29 58N 88 40W
Chandigarh 32 30 43N 76 47 E
Chandler, Australia 45 27 0S 133 19 E
Chandler, Canada 63 48 18N 64 46W
Chandler, Ariz., U.S.A. 73 33 20N 111 56W
Chandler, Okla., U.S.A. 71 35 43N 96 53W
Chandmani 37 45 22N 98 2 E
Chandpur 33 23 8N 90 45 E
Chandrapur 32 19 57N 79 25 E
Chang Jiang → 39 31 48N 121 10 E
Changanacheri 32 9 25N 76 31 E
Changane → 57 24 30S 33 30 E
Changbai 38 41 25N 128 5 E
Changbai Shan 38 42 20N 129 0 E
Changchiak'ou = Zhangjiakou 38 40 48N 114 55 E
Ch'angchou = Changzhou 39 31 47N 119 58 E
Changchun 38 43 57N 125 17 E
Changde 39 29 4N 111 35 E
Changfeng 39 32 28N 117 10 E
Changhai = Shanghai 38 31 15N 121 26 E
Changjiang 39 19 20N 108 55 E
Changjin-chŏsuji 38 40 30N 127 15 E
Changle 39 25 59N 119 27 E
Changli 38 39 40N 119 13 E
Changning 39 26 28N 112 22 E
Changping 38 40 14N 116 12 E
Changsha 39 28 12N 113 0 E
Changshou 39 29 51N 107 8 E
Changshu 39 31 38N 120 43 E
Changshun 39 26 3N 106 25 E
Changtai 39 24 35N 117 42 E
Changting 39 25 50N 116 22 E
Changyang 39 30 30N 111 10 E
Changzhi 38 36 10N 113 6 E
Changzhou 39 31 47N 119 58 E
Chanhanga 56 16 0S 14 8 E
Channapatna 32 12 40N 77 15 E
Channel Is., U.K. 7 49 30N 2 40W
Channel Is., U.S.A. 73 33 55N 119 26W
Channel-Port aux Basques 63 47 30N 59 9W
Channing, Mich., U.S.A. 68 46 9N 88 1W
Channing, Tex., U.S.A. 71 35 45N 102 20W
Chantada 13 42 36N 7 46W
Chanthaburi 34 12 38N 102 12 E
Chantrey Inlet 60 67 48N 96 20W
Chanute 71 37 45N 95 25W
Chao Hu 39 31 30N 117 30 E
Chao Phraya → 34 13 32N 100 36 E
Chao'an 39 23 42N 116 32 E
Chaoyang, Guangdong, China 39 23 17N 116 30 E
Chaoyang, Liaoning, China 38 41 35N 120 22 E
Chapala, L. de 74 20 10N 103 20W
Chapayevo 23 50 25N 51 10 E
Chapayevsk 22 53 0N 49 40 E
Chapel Hill 69 35 53N 79 3W
Chapleau 62 47 50N 83 24W
Chaplin 65 50 28N 106 40W
Châr 50 21 32N 12 45 E
Chara 25 56 54N 118 20 E
Charadai 80 27 35S 60 0W
Charagua 78 19 45S 63 10W
Charaña 78 17 30S 69 25W
Charcas 74 23 10N 101 20W
Charcoal L. 65 58 49N 102 22W
Chard 7 50 52N 2 59W
Chardara 24 41 16N 67 59 E
Chardzhou 24 39 6N 63 34 E
Charente □ 12 45 50N 0 16 E
Charente-Maritime □ 12 45 45N 0 45W
Chari → 51 12 58N 14 31 E
Chārīkār 31 35 0N 69 10 E
Chariton → 70 39 19N 92 58W
Charleroi 11 50 24N 4 27 E
Charles, C. 68 37 10N 75 59W
Charles City 70 43 2N 92 41W
Charles L. 65 59 50N 110 33W
Charles Town 68 39 20N 77 50W
Charleston, Ill., U.S.A. 68 39 30N 88 10W
Charleston, Miss., U.S.A. 71 34 2N 90 3W
Charleston, Mo., U.S.A. 71 36 52N 89 20W
Charleston, S.C., U.S.A. 69 32 47N 79 56W
Charleston, W. Va., U.S.A. 68 38 24N 81 36W
Charlestown, S. Africa 57 27 26S 29 53 E
Charlestown, U.S.A. 68 38 29N 85 40W
Charlesville 54 5 27S 20 59 E
Charleville = Rath Luirc 9 52 21N 8 40W
Charleville 45 26 24S 146 15 E
Charleville-Mézières 12 49 44N 4 40 E
Charlevoix 68 45 19N 85 14W
Charlotte, Mich., U.S.A. 68 42 36N 84 48W
Charlotte, N.C., U.S.A. 69 35 16N 80 46W
Charlotte Amalie 75 18 22N 64 56W
Charlotte Harbor 69 26 58N 82 4W
Charlottesville 68 38 1N 78 30W
Charlottetown 63 46 14N 63 8W
Charlton, Australia 45 36 16S 143 24 E
Charlton, U.S.A. 70 40 59N 93 20W
Charlton I. 62 52 0N 79 20W
Charny 63 46 43N 71 15W
Charolles 12 46 27N 4 16 E
Charouine 50 29 0N 0 15W
Charters Towers 44 20 5S 146 13 E
Chartres 12 48 29N 1 30 E
Chascomús 80 35 30S 58 0W
Chasovnya-Uchurskaya 25 57 15N 132 50 E
Château-Salins 12 48 50N 6 30 E
Châteaubriant 12 47 43N 1 23W
Châteauroux 12 46 50N 1 40 E
Châtellerault 12 46 50N 0 30 E
Chatfield 70 43 15N 91 58W
Chatham, N.B., Canada 63 47 2N 65 28W
Chatham, Ont., Canada 62 42 24N 82 11W
Chatham, U.K. 7 51 22N 0 32 E
Chatham, U.S.A. 71 32 22N 92 26W
Chatham Is. 40 44 0S 176 40W
Chatham Str. 64 57 0N 134 40W
Chatrapur 33 19 22N 85 2 E
Chattahoochee → 69 30 43N 84 51W
Chattanooga 69 35 2N 85 17W
Chauk 33 20 53N 94 49 E
Chaukan La 33 27 0N 97 15 E
Chaumont 12 48 7N 5 8 E
Chauvin 65 52 45N 110 10W
Chaux-de-Fonds, La 14 47 7N 6 50 E
Chaves, Brazil 79 0 15S 49 55W
Chaves, Portugal 13 41 45N 7 32W
Chavuma 55 13 4S 22 40 E
Chaykovskiy 22 56 47N 54 9 E
Cheb 14 50 9N 12 28 E
Cheboksary 22 56 8N 47 12 E
Cheboygan 68 45 38N 84 29W
Chech, Erg 50 25 0N 2 15W
Checheno-Ingush A.S.S.R. □ 23 43 30N 45 29 E
Checleset B. 64 50 5N 127 35W
Checotah 71 35 31N 95 30W
Chedabucto B. 63 45 25N 61 8W
Cheduba I. 33 18 45N 93 40 E
Cheepie 45 26 33S 145 1 E
Chegdomyn 25 51 7N 133 1 E
Chegga 50 25 27N 5 40W
Chegutu 55 18 10S 30 14 E
Chehalis 72 46 44N 122 59W
Cheju Do 39 33 29N 126 34 E
Chekiang = Zhejiang □ 39 29 0N 120 0 E
Chela, Sa. da 56 16 20S 13 20 E
Chelan 72 47 49N 120 0W
Chelan, L. 72 48 5N 120 30W
Cheleken 23 39 26N 53 7 E
Chelforó 80 39 0S 66 33W
Chelkar 24 47 48N 59 39 E
Chelkar Tengiz, Solonchak 24 48 0N 62 30 E
Chełm 15 51 8N 23 30 E
Chełmno 15 53 20N 18 30 E
Chelmsford 7 51 44N 0 29 E
Chelmsford Dam 57 27 55S 29 59 E
Chełmża 15 53 10N 18 39 E
Chelsea 71 36 35N 95 35W
Cheltenham 7 51 55N 2 5W
Chelyabinsk 24 55 10N 61 24 E
Chelyuskin, C. 26 77 30N 103 0 E
Chemainus 64 48 55N 123 42W
Chemnitz = Karl-Marx-Stadt 14 50 50N 12 55 E
Chemult 72 43 14N 121 47W
Chen, Gora 25 65 16N 141 50 E
Chen Xian 39 25 47N 113 1 E
Chenab → 32 30 23N 71 2 E
Chencha 51 6 15N 37 32 E
Chenchiang = Zhenjiang 39 32 11N 119 26 E
Cheney 72 47 29N 117 34W
Chengbu 39 26 18N 110 16 E
Chengcheng 39 35 8N 109 56 E
Chengchou = Zhengzhou 39 34 45N 113 34 E
Chengde 38 40 59N 117 58 E
Chengdu 37 30 38N 104 2 E
Chenggu 39 33 10N 107 21 E
Chengjiang 37 24 39N 103 0 E
Ch'engtu = Chengdu 37 30 38N 104 2 E
Chengyang 38 36 18N 120 21 E
Chenxi 39 28 2N 110 12 E
Cheo Reo 34 13 25N 108 28 E
Cheom Ksan 34 14 13N 104 56 E
Chepén 78 7 15S 79 23W
Chepes 80 31 20S 66 35W
Chepo 75 9 10N 79 6W
Chequamegon B. 70 46 40N 90 30W
Cher □ 12 47 10N 2 30 E
Cher → 12 47 21N 0 29 E
Cheraw 69 34 42N 79 54W
Cherbourg 12 49 39N 1 40W
Cherchell 50 36 35N 2 12 E
Cherdyn 22 60 24N 56 29 E
Cheremkhovo 25 53 8N 103 1 E
Cherepanovo 24 54 15N 83 30 E
Cherepovets 22 59 5N 37 55 E
Chergui, Chott ech 50 34 21N 0 25 E
Cherkassy 23 49 27N 32 4 E
Cherlak 24 54 15N 74 55 E
Chernigov 22 51 28N 31 20 E
Chernikovsk 22 54 48N 56 8 E
Chernogorsk 25 53 49N 91 18 E
Chernovtsy 23 48 15N 25 52 E
Chernoye 25 70 30N 89 10 E
Chernyshovskiy 25 63 0N 112 30 E
Cherokee, Iowa, U.S.A. 70 42 40N 95 30W
Cherokee, Okla., U.S.A. 71 36 45N 98 25W
Cherokees, L. O'The 71 36 50N 95 12W
Cherquenco 80 38 35S 72 0W
Cherrapunji 33 25 17N 91 47 E
Cherry Creek 72 39 50N 114 58W

Clipperton, I.

Cherryvale 71 37 20N 95 33W
Cherskiy 25 68 45N 161 18 E
Cherskogo Khrebet 25 65 0N 143 0 E
Cherwell —► 7 51 46N 1 18W
Chesapeake 68 36 43N 76 15W
Chesapeake Bay 68 38 0N 76 12W
Cheshire □ 6 53 14N 2 30W
Cheshskaya Guba 22 67 20N 47 0 E
Cheslatta L. 64 53 49N 125 20W
Chester, U.K. 6 53 12N 2 53W
Chester, Calif., U.S.A. 72 40 22N 121 14W
Chester, Ill., U.S.A. 71 37 58N 89 50W
Chester, Mont., U.S.A. 72 48 31N 111 0W
Chester, Pa., U.S.A. 68 39 54N 75 20W
Chester, S.C., U.S.A. 69 34 44N 81 13W
Chesterfield 6 53 14N 1 26W
Chesterfield, Îles 40 19 52S 158 15 E
Chesterfield Inlet 60 63 30N 90 45W
Chesterton Range 45 25 30S 147 27 E
Chesuncook L. 63 46 0N 69 10W
Chéticamp 63 46 37N 60 59W
Chetumal 74 18 30N 88 20W
Chetumal, B. de 74 18 40N 88 10W
Chetwynd 64 55 45N 121 36W
Cheviot, The 6 55 29N 2 8W
Cheviot Hills 6 55 20N 2 30W
Cheviot Ra. 44 25 20S 143 45 E
Chew Bahir 51 4 40N 36 50 E
Chewelah 72 48 17N 117 43W
Cheyenne, Okla., U.S.A. 71 35 35N 99 40W
Cheyenne, Wyo., U.S.A. 70 41 9N 104 49W
Cheyenne —► 70 44 40N 101 15W
Cheyenne Wells 70 38 51N 102 10W
Cheyne B. 47 34 35S 118 50 E
Chhapra 33 25 48N 84 44 E
Chhatarpur 32 24 55N 79 35 E
Chhindwara 32 22 2N 78 59 E
Chhlong 34 12 15N 105 58 E
Chi —► 34 15 11N 104 43 E
Chiamis 35 7 20S 108 21 E
Chiamussu = Jiamusi 38 46 40N 130 26 E
Chiange 55 15 35S 13 40 E
Chiapa —► 74 16 42N 93 0W
Chiapas □ 74 17 0N 92 45W
Chiba 36 35 30N 140 7 E
Chiba □ 36 35 30N 140 20 E
Chibabava 57 20 17S 33 35 E
Chibatu 35 7 6S 107 59 E
Chibemba, Cunene, Angola 55 15 48S 14 8 E
Chibemba, Huila, Angola 56 16 20S 15 20 E
Chibia 55 15 10S 13 42 E
Chibougamau 62 49 56N 74 24W
Chibougamau L. 62 49 50N 74 20W
Chibuk 53 10 52N 12 50 E
Chic-Chocs, Mts. 63 48 55N 66 0W
Chicacole = Srikakulam 33 18 14N 83 58 E
Chicago 68 41 53N 87 40W
Chicago Heights 68 41 29N 87 37W
Chichagof I. 64 58 0N 136 0W
Chichester 7 50 50N 0 47W
Chichibu 36 36 5N 139 10 E
Ch'ich'ihaerh = Qiqihar 38 47 26N 124 0 E
Chickasha 71 35 0N 98 0W
Chiclana de la Frontera 13 36 26N 6 9W
Chiclayo 78 6 42S 79 50W
Chico 72 39 45N 121 54W
Chico —►, Chubut, Argentina 80 44 0S 67 0W
Chico —►, Santa Cruz, Argentina 80 50 0S 68 30W
Chicomo 57 24 31S 34 6 E
Chicopee 68 42 6N 72 37W
Chicoutimi 63 48 28N 71 5W
Chicualacuala 57 22 6S 31 42 E
Chidambaram 32 11 20N 79 45 E
Chidenguele 57 24 55S 34 11 E
Chidley, C. 61 60 23N 64 26W
Chiede 56 17 15S 16 22 E
Chiengi 54 8 45S 29 10 E
Chiese —► 18 45 8N 10 25 E
Chieti 18 42 22N 14 10 E
Chifeng 38 42 18N 118 58 E
Chignecto B. 63 45 30N 64 40W
Chiguana 78 21 0S 67 58W
Chihli, G. of = Bo Hai 38 39 0N 120 0 E
Chihuahua 74 28 40N 106 3W
Chihuahua □ 74 28 40N 106 3W
Chiili 24 44 20N 66 15 E
Chik Bollapur 32 13 25N 77 45 E
Chikmagalur 32 13 15N 75 45 E
Chilako —► 64 53 53N 122 57W
Chilapa 74 17 40N 99 11W
Chilas 32 35 25N 74 5 E
Chilaw 32 7 30N 79 50 E
Chilcotin —► 64 51 44N 122 23W
Childers 45 25 15S 152 17 E
Childress 71 34 30N 100 15W
Chile ■ 80 35 0S 72 0W
Chile Rise 41 38 0S 92 0W
Chilete 78 7 10S 78 50W
Chililabombwe 55 12 18S 27 43 E
Chilin = Jilin 38 43 44N 126 30 E
Chilka L. 33 19 40N 85 25 E
Chilko —► 64 52 0N 123 40W
Chilko, L. 64 51 20N 124 10W
Chillagoe 44 17 7S 144 33 E
Chillán 80 36 40S 72 10W
Chillicothe, Ill., U.S.A. 70 40 55N 89 32W
Chillicothe, Mo., U.S.A. 70 39 45N 93 30W
Chillicothe, Ohio, U.S.A. 68 39 20N 82 58W
Chilliwack 64 49 10N 121 54W
Chiloane, I. 57 20 40S 34 55 E
Chiloé, I. de 80 42 30S 73 50W
Chilpancingo 74 17 30N 99 30W
Chiltern Hills 7 51 44N 0 42W
Chilton 68 44 1N 88 12W
Chiluage 54 9 30S 21 50 E
Chilumba 52 10 28S 34 12 E
Chilwa, L. 55 15 15S 35 40 E
Chimay 11 50 3N 4 20 E
Chimbay 24 42 57N 59 47 E
Chimborazo 78 1 29S 78 55W
Chimbote 78 9 0S 78 35W
Chimkent 24 42 18N 69 36 E
Chimoio 55 19 4S 33 30 E
Chin □ 33 22 0N 93 0 E
Chin Ling Shan = Qinling Shandi 39 33 50N 108 10 E
China 74 25 40N 99 20W
China ■ 37 30 0N 110 0 E
Chinan = Jinan 38 36 38N 117 1 E
Chinandega 75 12 35N 87 12W
Chinati Pk. 71 30 0N 104 25W
Chincha Alta 78 13 25S 76 7W
Chinchilla 45 26 45S 150 38 E
Chinchón 13 40 9N 3 26W
Chinchorro, Banco 74 18 35N 87 20W
Chinchou = Jinzhou 38 41 5N 121 3 E
Chincoteague 68 37 58N 75 21W
Chinde 55 18 35S 36 30 E
Chindwin —► 33 21 26N 95 15 E
Chingola 55 12 31S 27 53 E
Ch'ingtao = Qingdao 38 36 5N 120 20 E
Chinguetti 50 20 25N 12 24W
Chingune 57 20 33S 35 0 E
Chinhae 38 35 9N 128 47 E
Chinhanguanine 57 25 21S 32 30 E
Chinhoyi 55 17 20S 30 8 E
Chiniot 32 31 45N 73 0 E
Chinju 38 35 12N 128 2 E
Chinle 73 36 14N 109 38W
Chinnampo 38 38 52N 125 10 E
Chino Valley 73 34 54N 112 28W
Chinon 12 47 10N 0 15 E
Chinook, Canada 65 51 28N 110 59W
Chinook, U.S.A. 72 48 35N 109 19W
Chinsali 54 10 30S 32 2 E
Chinteche 52 11 50S 34 5 E
Chióggia 18 45 13N 12 15 E
Chíos = Khíos 19 38 27N 26 9 E
Chipata 55 13 38S 32 28 E
Chipatujah 35 7 45S 108 0 E
Chipewyan L. 65 58 0N 98 27W
Chipley 69 30 45N 85 32W
Chipman 63 46 6N 65 53W
Chippenham 7 51 27N 2 7W
Chippewa —► 70 44 25N 92 10W
Chippewa Falls 70 44 55N 91 22W
Chiquián 78 10 10S 77 0W
Chiquimula 75 14 51N 89 37W
Chiquinquira 78 5 37N 73 50W
Chirala 32 15 50N 80 26 E
Chirchik 24 41 29N 69 35 E
Chiricahua Pk. 73 31 53N 109 14W
Chirikof I. 60 55 50N 155 40W
Chiriquí, G. de 75 8 0N 82 10W
Chiriquí, L. de 75 9 10N 82 0W
Chirmiri 33 23 15N 82 20 E
Chiromo 55 16 30S 35 7 E
Chirripó Grande, Cerro 75 9 29N 83 29W
Chisamba 55 14 55S 28 20 E
Chisapani Garhi 33 27 30N 84 2 E
Chisholm 64 54 55N 114 10W
Chisos Mts. 71 29 20N 103 15W
Chistopol 22 55 25N 50 38 E
Chita 25 52 0N 113 35 E
Chitado 55 17 10S 14 8 E
Chitembo 55 13 30S 16 50 E
Chitral 31 35 50N 71 56 E
Chitré 75 7 59N 80 27W
Chittagong 33 22 19N 91 48 E
Chittagong □ 33 24 5N 91 0 E
Chittaurgarh 32 24 52N 74 38 E
Chittoor 32 13 15N 79 5 E
Chiusi 18 43 1N 11 58 E
Chivasso 18 45 10N 7 52 E
Chivilcoy 80 34 55S 60 0W
Chkalov = Orenburg 22 51 45N 55 6 E
Chobe National Park 56 18 0S 25 0 E
Choele Choel 80 39 11S 65 40W
Choix 74 26 40N 108 23W
Chojnice 15 53 42N 17 32 E
Chokurdakh 25 70 38N 147 55 E
Cholet 12 47 4N 0 52W
Choluteca 75 13 20N 87 14W
Choma 55 16 48S 26 59 E
Chomutov 14 50 28N 13 23 E
Chon Buri 34 13 21N 101 1 E
Chonan 38 36 48N 127 9 E
Chone 78 0 40S 80 0W
Chong'an 39 27 45N 118 0 E
Chongde 39 30 32N 120 26 E
Chongjin 38 41 47N 129 50 E
Chŏngju, N. Korea 38 39 40N 125 5 E
Chŏngju, S. Korea 38 36 39N 127 27 E
Chongli 38 40 58N 115 15 E
Chongming Dao 39 31 40N 121 30 E
Chongqing 39 29 35N 106 25 E
Chongzuo 39 22 23N 107 20 E
Chŏnju 38 35 50N 127 4 E
Chonos, Arch. de los 80 45 0S 75 0W
Chorley 6 53 39N 2 39W
Chorregon 44 22 40S 143 32 E
Chorrera, La 74 8 50N 79 50W
Chŏrwŏn 38 38 15N 127 10 E
Chorzów 15 50 18N 18 57 E
Chos-Malal 80 37 20S 70 15W
Chosan 38 40 50N 125 47 E
Chōshi 36 35 45N 140 51 E
Choszczno 14 53 7N 15 25 E
Choteau 72 47 50N 112 10W
Chotila 32 22 23N 71 15 E
Chowchilla 73 37 11N 120 12W
Choybalsan 37 48 4N 114 30 E
Christchurch, N.Z. 43 43 33S 172 47 E
Christchurch, U.K. 7 50 44N 1 33W
Christiana 56 27 52S 25 8 E
Christie B. 65 62 32N 111 10W
Christina —► 65 56 40N 111 3W
Christmas Cr. —► 46 18 29S 125 23 E
Christmas Creek 46 18 29S 125 23 E
Christmas I. = Kiritimati 2 1 58N 157 27W
Christmas I. 3 10 30S 105 40 E
Christopher L. 47 24 49S 127 42 E
Chu 24 43 36N 73 42 E
Chu Chua 64 51 22N 120 10W
Ch'uanchou = Quanzhou 39 24 55N 118 34 E
Chūbu □ 36 36 45N 137 30 E
Chubut —► 80 43 20S 65 5W
Chuchi L. 64 55 12N 124 30W
Chudskoye, Oz. 22 58 13N 27 30 E
Chūgoku □ 36 35 0N 133 0 E
Chūgoku-Sanchi 36 35 0N 133 0 E
Chugwater 70 41 48N 104 47W
Chuka 52 0 23S 37 38 E
Chukotskiy Khrebet 25 68 0N 175 0 E
Chukotskoye More 25 68 0N 175 0W
Chula Vista 73 32 39N 117 8W
Chulman 25 56 52N 124 52 E
Chulucanas 78 5 8S 80 10W
Chulym —► 24 57 43N 83 51 E
Chumbicha 80 29 0S 66 10W
Chumikan 25 54 40N 135 10 E
Chumphon 34 10 35N 99 14 E
Chuna —► 25 57 47N 94 37 E
Chun'an 39 29 35N 119 3 E
Chunchŏn 38 37 58N 127 44 E
Chungking = Chongqing 39 29 35N 106 25 E
Chunya 54 8 30S 33 27 E
Chuquibamba 78 15 47S 72 44W
Chuquicamata 80 22 15S 69 0W
Chuquisaca □ 78 23 30S 63 30W
Chur 14 46 52N 9 32 E
Churachandpur 33 24 20N 93 40 E
Churchill 65 58 47N 94 11W
Churchill —►, Man., Canada 65 58 47N 94 12W
Churchill —►, Nfld., Canada 63 53 19N 60 10W
Churchill, C. 65 58 46N 93 12W
Churchill Falls 63 53 36N 64 19W
Churchill L. 65 55 55N 108 20W
Churchill Pk. 64 58 10N 125 10W
Churu 32 28 20N 74 50 E
Chushal 32 33 40N 78 40 E
Chusovoy 22 58 15N 57 40 E
Chuvash A.S.S.R.□ 22 55 30N 47 0 E
Ci Xian 38 36 20N 114 25 E
Cianjur 35 6 49S 107 8 E
Cibadok 35 6 53S 106 47 E
Cibatu 35 7 8S 107 59 E
Cicero 68 41 48N 87 48W
Ciechanów 15 52 52N 20 38 E
Ciego de Avila 75 21 50N 78 50W
Ciénaga 78 11 1N 74 15W
Cienfuegos 75 22 10N 80 30W
Cieszyn 15 49 45N 18 35 E
Cieza 13 38 17N 1 23W
Cijulang 35 7 42S 108 27 E
Cikajang 35 7 25S 107 48 E
Cikampek 35 6 23S 107 28 E
Cilacap 35 7 43S 109 0 E
Cilician Gates P. 30 37 20N 34 52 E
Cimahi 35 6 53S 107 33 E
Cimarron, Kans., U.S.A. 71 37 50N 100 20W
Cimarron, N. Mex., U.S.A. 71 36 30N 104 52W
Cimarron —► 71 36 10N 96 17W
Cimone, Mte. 18 44 10N 10 40 E
Cîmpina 15 45 10N 25 45 E
Cîmpulung 15 45 17N 25 3 E
Cinca —► 13 41 26N 0 21 E
Cincinnati 68 39 10N 84 26W
Ciney 11 50 18N 5 5 E
Cinto, Mte. 12 42 24N 8 54 E
Circle, Alaska, U.S.A. 60 65 50N 144 10W
Circle, Mont., U.S.A. 70 47 26N 105 35W
Circleville, Ohio, U.S.A. 68 39 35N 82 57W
Circleville, Utah, U.S.A. 73 38 12N 112 24W
Cirebon 35 6 45S 108 32 E
Cirencester 7 51 43N 1 59W
Cisco 71 32 25N 99 0W
Ciskei □ 57 33 0S 27 0 E
Citlaltépetl 74 19 0N 97 20W
Citrusdal 56 32 35S 19 0 E
Ciudad Altamirano 74 18 20N 100 40W
Ciudad Bolívar 78 8 5N 63 36W
Ciudad Camargo 74 27 41N 105 10W
Ciudad de Valles 74 22 0N 99 0W
Ciudad del Carmen 74 18 38N 91 50W
Ciudad Delicias = Delicias 74 28 10N 105 30W
Ciudad Guayana 78 8 0N 62 30W
Ciudad Guerrero 74 28 33N 107 28W
Ciudad Guzmán 74 19 40N 103 30W
Ciudad Juárez 74 31 40N 106 28W
Ciudad Madero 74 22 19N 97 50W
Ciudad Mante 74 22 50N 99 0W
Ciudad Obregón 74 27 28N 109 59W
Ciudad Real 13 38 59N 3 55W
Ciudad Rodrigo 13 40 35N 6 32W
Ciudad Trujillo = Santo Domingo 75 18 30N 69 59W
Ciudad Victoria 74 23 41N 99 9W
Civitanova Marche 18 43 18N 13 41 E
Civitavécchia 18 42 6N 11 46 E
Çivril 30 38 20N 29 43 E
Cizre 30 37 19N 42 10 E
Clackline 47 31 40S 116 32 E
Clacton-on-Sea 7 51 47N 1 10 E
Claire, L. 64 58 35N 112 5W
Clairemont 71 33 9N 100 44W
Clanton 69 32 48N 86 36W
Clanwilliam 56 32 11S 18 52 E
Clara 9 53 20N 7 38W
Clara —► 44 19 8S 142 30 E
Clare, Australia 45 33 50S 138 37 E
Clare, U.S.A. 68 43 47N 84 45W
Clare □ 9 52 20N 9 0W
Clare —► 9 53 22N 9 5W
Clare I. 9 53 48N 10 0W
Claremont 68 43 23N 72 20W
Claremont Pt. 44 14 1S 143 41 E
Claremore 71 36 40N 95 37W
Claremorris 9 53 45N 9 0W
Clarence —►, Australia 45 29 25S 153 22 E
Clarence —►, N.Z. 43 42 10S 173 56 E
Clarence, I. 80 54 0S 72 0W
Clarence Str., Australia 46 12 0S 131 0 E
Clarence Str., U.S.A. 64 55 40N 132 10W
Clarendon, Ark., U.S.A. 71 34 41N 91 20W
Clarendon, Tex., U.S.A. 71 34 58N 100 54W
Clarenville 63 48 10N 54 1W
Claresholm 64 50 0N 113 33W
Clarinda 70 40 45N 95 0W
Clarion 70 42 41N 93 46W
Clarion Fracture Zone 41 20 0N 120 0W
Clark 70 44 55N 97 45W
Clark Fork 72 48 9N 116 9W
Clark Fork —► 72 48 9N 116 15W
Clark Hill Res. 69 33 45N 82 20W
Clarkdale 73 34 53N 112 3W
Clarke City 63 50 12N 66 38W
Clarke I. 44 40 32S 148 10 E
Clarke L. 65 54 24N 106 54W
Clarke Ra. 44 20 45S 148 20 E
Clark's Fork —► 72 45 39N 108 43W
Clark's Harbour 63 43 25N 65 38W
Clarksburg 68 39 18N 80 21W
Clarksdale 71 34 12N 90 33W
Clarkston 72 46 28N 117 2W
Clarksville, Ark., U.S.A. 71 35 29N 93 27W
Clarksville, Tenn., U.S.A. 69 36 32N 87 20W
Clarksville, Tex., U.S.A. 71 33 37N 94 59W
Clatskanie 72 46 9N 123 12W
Claude 71 35 8N 101 22W
Claveria 35 18 37N 121 4 E
Clay Center 70 39 27N 97 9W
Claypool 73 33 27N 110 55W
Clayton, Idaho, U.S.A. 72 44 12N 114 31W
Clayton, N. Mex., U.S.A. 71 36 30N 103 10W
Cle Elum 72 47 15N 120 57W
Clear, C. 9 51 26N 9 30W
Clear I. 9 51 26N 9 30W
Clear L. 72 39 5N 122 47W
Clear Lake, S. Dak., U.S.A. 70 44 48N 96 41W
Clear Lake, Wash., U.S.A. 72 48 27N 122 15W
Clear Lake Res. 72 41 55N 121 10W
Clearfield, Pa., U.S.A. 68 41 0N 78 27W
Clearfield, Utah, U.S.A. 72 41 10N 112 0W
Clearmont 72 44 43N 106 29W
Clearwater, Canada 64 51 38N 120 2W
Clearwater, U.S.A. 69 27 58N 82 45W
Clearwater —►, Alta., Canada 64 52 22N 114 57W
Clearwater —►, Alta., Canada 65 56 44N 111 23W
Clearwater Cr. —► 64 61 36N 125 30W
Clearwater Mts. 72 46 20N 115 30W
Clearwater Prov. Park 65 54 0N 101 0W
Cleburne 71 32 18N 97 25W
Cleethorpes 6 53 33N 0 2W
Cleeve Cloud 7 51 56N 2 0W
Clerke Reef 46 17 22S 119 20 E
Clermont 44 22 49S 147 39 E
Clermont-Ferrand 12 45 46N 3 4 E
Clervaux 11 50 4N 6 2 E
Cleveland, Australia 45 27 30S 153 15 E
Cleveland, Miss., U.S.A. 71 33 43N 90 43W
Cleveland, Ohio, U.S.A. 68 41 28N 81 43W
Cleveland, Okla., U.S.A. 71 36 21N 96 33W
Cleveland, Tenn., U.S.A. 69 35 9N 84 52W
Cleveland, Tex., U.S.A. 71 30 18N 95 0W
Cleveland □ 6 54 35N 1 8 E
Cleveland, C. 44 19 11S 147 1 E
Clew B. 9 53 54N 9 50W
Clewiston 69 26 44N 80 50W
Clifden, Ireland 9 53 30N 10 2W
Clifden, N.Z. 43 46 1S 167 42 E
Clifton, Australia 45 27 59S 151 53 E
Clifton, Ariz., U.S.A. 73 33 8N 109 23W
Clifton, Tex., U.S.A. 71 31 46N 97 35W
Clifton Beach 44 16 46S 145 39 E
Clifton Forge 68 37 49N 79 51W
Clifton Hills 45 27 1S 138 54 E
Climax 65 49 10N 108 20W
Clinch —► 69 36 0N 84 29W
Clingmans Dome 69 35 35N 83 30W
Clint 73 31 37N 106 11W
Clinton, B.C., Canada 64 51 6N 121 35W
Clinton, Ont., Canada 62 43 37N 81 32W
Clinton, N.Z. 43 46 12S 169 23 E
Clinton, Ark., U.S.A. 71 35 37N 92 30W
Clinton, Ill., U.S.A. 70 40 8N 89 0W
Clinton, Ind., U.S.A. 68 39 40N 87 22W
Clinton, Iowa, U.S.A. 70 41 50N 90 12W
Clinton, Mass., U.S.A. 68 42 26N 71 40W
Clinton, Mo., U.S.A. 70 38 20N 93 46W
Clinton, N.C., U.S.A. 69 35 5N 78 15W
Clinton, Okla., U.S.A. 71 35 30N 99 0W
Clinton, S.C., U.S.A. 69 34 30N 81 54W
Clinton, Tenn., U.S.A. 69 36 6N 84 10W
Clinton C. 44 22 30S 150 45 E
Clinton Colden L. 60 63 58N 107 27W
Clintonville 70 44 35N 88 46W
Clipperton, I. 41 10 18N 109 13W

Dankhar Gompa

Corque ... **78** 18 20S 67 41W
Correntes, C. das . **57** 24 6S 35 34 E
Corrèze □ ... **12** 45 20N 1 45 E
Corrib, L. ... **9** 53 5N 9 10W
Corrientes ... **80** 27 30S 58 45W
Corrientes → ... **78** 3 43S 74 35W
Corrientes, C., Colombia ... **78** 5 30N 77 34W
Corrientes, C., Cuba **75** 21 43N 84 30W
Corrientes, C., Mexico ... **74** 20 25N 105 42W
Corrigan ... **71** 31 0N 94 48W
Corrigin ... **47** 32 20S 117 53 E
Corry ... **68** 41 55N 79 39W
Corse ... **12** 42 0N 9 0 E
Corse, C. ... **18** 43 1N 9 25 E
Corse-du-Sud □ .. **12** 41 45N 9 0 E
Corsica = Corse .. **12** 42 0N 9 0 E
Corsicana ... **71** 32 5N 96 30W
Cortez ... **73** 37 24N 108 35W
Cortland ... **68** 42 35N 76 11W
Cortona ... **18** 43 16N 12 0 E
Çorum ... **30** 40 30N 34 57 E
Corumbá ... **78** 19 0S 57 30W
Corumbá de Goiás **79** 16 0S 48 50W
Coruña, La ... **13** 43 20N 8 25W
Corunna = Coruña, La ... **13** 43 20N 8 25W
Corvallis ... **72** 44 36N 123 15W
Corvette, L. de la .. **62** 53 25N 74 3W
Corydon ... **70** 40 42N 93 22W
Cosalá ... **74** 24 28N 106 40W
Cosamaloapan ... **74** 18 23N 95 50W
Cosenza ... **18** 39 17N 16 14 E
Coshocton ... **68** 40 17N 81 51W
Cosmo Newberry .. **47** 28 0S 122 54 E
Costa Blanca ... **13** 38 25N 0 10W
Costa Brava ... **13** 41 30N 3 0 E
Costa del Sol ... **13** 36 30N 4 30W
Costa Dorada ... **13** 40 45N 1 15 E
Costa Rica ■ ... **75** 10 0N 84 0W
Costilla ... **73** 37 0N 105 30W
Cotabato ... **35** 7 14N 124 15 E
Cotagaita ... **78** 20 45S 65 40W
Côte-d'Or □ ... **12** 47 30N 4 50 E
Coteau des Prairies **70** 44 30N 97 0W
Coteau du Missouri **70** 47 0N 101 0W
Cotentin ... **12** 49 15N 1 30W
Côtes-du-Nord □ . **12** 48 25N 2 40W
Cotonou ... **53** 6 20N 2 25 E
Cotopaxi, Vol. ... **76** 0 40S 78 30W
Cotswold Hills ... **7** 51 42N 2 10W
Cottage Grove ... **72** 43 48N 123 2W
Cottbus ... **14** 51 44N 14 20 E
Cottonwood ... **73** 34 48N 112 1W
Cotulla ... **71** 28 26N 99 14W
Coudersport ... **68** 41 45N 78 1W
Couedic, C. du ... **45** 36 5S 136 40 E
Coulee City ... **72** 47 36N 119 18W
Coulonge → ... **62** 45 52N 76 46W
Council, Alaska, U.S.A. ... **60** 64 55N 163 45W
Council, Idaho, U.S.A. ... **72** 44 44N 116 26W
Council Bluffs ... **70** 41 20N 95 50W
Council Grove ... **70** 38 41N 96 30W
Courantyne → ... **78** 5 55N 57 5W
Courtenay ... **64** 49 45N 125 0W
Courtrai = Kortrijk . **11** 50 50N 3 17 E
Coushatta ... **71** 32 0N 93 21W
Coutts ... **64** 49 0N 111 57W
Coventry ... **7** 52 25N 1 31W
Coventry L. ... **65** 61 15N 106 15W
Covilhã ... **13** 40 17N 7 31W
Covington, Ga., U.S.A. ... **69** 33 36N 83 50W
Covington, Ky., U.S.A. ... **68** 39 5N 84 30W
Covington, Okla., U.S.A. ... **71** 36 21N 97 36W
Covington, Tenn., U.S.A. ... **71** 35 34N 89 39W
Cowal, L. ... **45** 33 40S 147 25 E
Cowan ... **65** 52 5N 100 45W
Cowan, L. ... **47** 31 45S 121 45 E
Cowan L. ... **65** 54 0N 107 15W
Cowangie ... **45** 35 12S 141 26 E
Cowarie ... **45** 27 45S 138 15 E
Cowcowing Lakes . **47** 30 55S 117 20 E
Cowdenbeath ... **8** 56 7N 3 20W
Cowell ... **45** 33 39S 136 56 E
Cowes ... **7** 50 45N 1 18W
Cowra ... **45** 33 49S 148 42 E
Coxim ... **79** 18 30S 54 55W
Cox's Bazar ... **33** 21 26N 91 59 E
Cox's Cove ... **63** 49 7N 58 5W
Coyuca de Benítez **74** 17 1N 100 8W
Coyuca de Catalan **74** 18 18N 100 41W
Cozad ... **70** 40 55N 99 57W
Cozumel, I. de ... **74** 20 30N 86 40W
Craboon ... **45** 32 3S 149 30 E
Cracow = Kraków . **15** 50 4N 19 57 E
Cracow ... **45** 25 17S 150 17 E
Cradock ... **56** 32 8S 25 36 E
Craig, Alaska, U.S.A. **64** 55 30N 133 5W
Craig, Colo., U.S.A. **72** 40 32N 107 33W
Craiova ... **15** 44 21N 23 48 E
Cramsie ... **44** 23 20S 144 15 E
Cranberry Portage . **65** 54 35N 101 23W
Cranbrook, Tas., Australia ... **44** 42 0S 148 5 E
Cranbrook, W. Austral., Australia ... **47** 34 18S 117 33 E
Cranbrook, Canada **64** 49 30N 115 46W
Crandon ... **70** 45 32N 88 52W
Crane, Oreg., U.S.A. **72** 43 21N 118 39W
Crane, Tex., U.S.A. **71** 31 26N 102 27W
Crater, L. ... **72** 42 55N 122 3W
Crateús ... **79** 5 10S 40 39W
Crato ... **79** 7 10S 39 25W
Crawford ... **70** 42 40N 103 25W
Crawfordsville ... **68** 40 2N 86 51W
Crawley ... **7** 51 7N 0 10W
Crazy Mts. ... **72** 46 14N 110 30W
Crean L. ... **65** 54 5N 106 9W
Crécy-en-Ponthieu **12** 50 15N 1 53 E
Credo ... **47** 30 28S 120 45 E
Cree →, Canada . **65** 58 57N 105 47W
Cree →, U.K. ... **8** 54 51N 4 24W
Cree L. ... **65** 57 30N 106 30W
Creede ... **73** 37 56N 106 59W
Creel ... **74** 27 45N 107 38W
Creighton ... **70** 42 30N 97 52W
Cremona ... **18** 45 8N 10 2 E
Cres ... **18** 44 58N 14 25 E
Cresbard ... **70** 45 13N 98 57W
Crescent, Okla., U.S.A. ... **71** 35 58N 97 36W
Crescent, Oreg., U.S.A. ... **72** 43 30N 121 37W
Crescent City ... **72** 41 45N 124 12W
Cressy ... **45** 38 2S 143 40 E
Crested Butte ... **73** 38 57N 107 0W
Creston, Canada .. **64** 49 10N 116 31W
Creston, Iowa, U.S.A. ... **70** 41 0N 94 20W
Creston, Wash., U.S.A. ... **72** 47 47N 118 36W
Crestview ... **69** 30 45N 86 35W
Crete = Kríti ... **19** 35 15N 25 0 E
Crete ... **70** 40 38N 96 58W
Crete, La ... **64** 58 11N 116 24W
Creus, C. ... **13** 42 20N 3 19 E
Creuse □ ... **12** 46 10N 2 0 E
Creuse → ... **12** 47 0N 0 34 E
Creusot, Le ... **12** 46 48N 4 24 E
Crewe ... **6** 53 6N 2 28W
Crib Point ... **45** 38 22S 145 13 E
Criciúma ... **80** 28 40S 49 23W
Crieff ... **8** 56 22N 3 50W
Crimea = Krymskiy Poluostrov ... **23** 45 0N 34 0 E
Crinan ... **8** 56 6N 5 34W
Cristóbal ... **74** 9 19N 79 54W
Crişu Alb → ... **15** 46 42N 21 17 E
Crişu Negru → .. **15** 46 42N 21 16 E
Crna Gora ... **19** 42 10N 21 30 E
Crna Gora □ ... **19** 42 40N 19 20 E
Crna Reka → ... **19** 41 33N 21 59 E
Croaghpatrick ... **9** 53 46N 9 40W
Crocker, Banjaran . **34** 5 40N 116 30 E
Crocker I. ... **47** 11 12S 132 32 E
Crockett ... **71** 31 20N 95 30W
Crocodile = Krokodil → ... **57** 25 14S 32 18 E
Crocodile Is. ... **44** 12 3S 134 58 E
Croix, La, L. ... **62** 48 20N 92 15W
Croker, C. ... **46** 10 58S 132 35 E
Cromarty, Canada . **65** 58 3N 94 9W
Cromarty, U.K. ... **8** 57 40N 4 2W
Cromer ... **6** 52 56N 1 18 E
Cromwell ... **43** 45 3S 169 14 E
Cronulla ... **45** 34 3S 151 8 E
Crooked →, Canada ... **64** 54 50N 122 54W
Crooked →, U.S.A. **72** 44 30N 121 16W
Crooked I. ... **75** 22 50N 74 10W
Crookston, Minn., U.S.A. ... **70** 47 50N 96 40W
Crookston, Nebr., U.S.A. ... **70** 42 56N 100 45W
Crooksville ... **68** 39 45N 82 8W
Crookwell ... **45** 34 28S 149 24 E
Crosby, Minn., U.S.A. ... **70** 46 28N 93 57W
Crosby, N. Dak., U.S.A. ... **65** 48 55N 103 18W
Crosbyton ... **71** 33 37N 101 12W
Cross City ... **69** 29 35N 83 5W
Cross Fell ... **6** 54 44N 2 29W
Cross L. ... **65** 54 45N 97 30W
Cross Plains ... **71** 32 8N 99 7W
Cross River □ ... **53** 6 0N 8 0 E
Cross Sound ... **60** 58 20N 136 30W
Crosse, La, Kans., U.S.A. ... **70** 38 33N 99 20W
Crosse, La, Wis., U.S.A. ... **70** 43 48N 91 13W
Crossett ... **71** 33 10N 91 57W
Crossfield ... **64** 51 25N 114 0W
Crosshaven ... **9** 51 48N 8 19W
Crotone ... **18** 39 5N 17 6 E
Crow → ... **64** 59 41N 124 20W
Crow Agency ... **72** 45 40N 107 30W
Crow Hd. ... **9** 51 34N 10 9W
Crowell ... **71** 33 59N 99 45W
Crowley ... **71** 30 15N 92 20W
Crown Point ... **68** 41 24N 87 23W
Crows Nest ... **45** 27 16S 152 4 E
Crowsnest Pass ... **64** 49 40N 114 40W
Croydon, Australia . **44** 18 13S 142 14 E
Croydon, U.K. ... **7** 51 18N 0 5W
Crozet Is. ... **3** 46 27S 52 0 E
Cruz, C. ... **75** 19 50N 77 50W
Cruz, La ... **74** 23 55N 106 54W
Cruz Alta ... **80** 28 45S 53 40W
Cruz del Eje ... **80** 30 45S 64 50W
Cruzeiro ... **79** 22 33S 45 0W
Cruzeiro do Sul ... **78** 7 35S 72 35W
Cry L. ... **64** 58 45N 129 0W
Crystal Brook ... **45** 33 21S 138 12 E
Crystal City, Mo., U.S.A. ... **70** 38 15N 90 23W
Crystal City, Tex., U.S.A. ... **71** 28 40N 99 50W
Crystal Falls ... **68** 46 9N 88 11W
Crystal River ... **69** 28 54N 82 35W
Crystal Springs ... **71** 31 59N 90 25W
Csongrád ... **15** 46 43N 20 12 E
Cuamato ... **56** 17 2S 15 7 E
Cuamba ... **55** 14 45S 36 22 E
Cuando → ... **55** 17 30S 23 15 E
Cuando Cubango □ **56** 16 25S 20 0 E
Cuangar ... **56** 17 36S 18 39 E
Cuanza → ... **48** 9 2S 13 30 E
Cuarto → ... **80** 33 25S 63 2W
Cuauhtémoc ... **74** 28 25N 106 52W
Cuba ... **73** 36 0N 107 0W
Cuba ■ ... **75** 22 0N 79 0W
Cuballing ... **47** 32 50S 117 10 E
Cubango → ... **56** 18 50S 22 25 E
Cuchi ... **55** 14 37S 16 58 E
Cuchumatanes, Sierra de los ... **75** 15 35N 91 25W
Cúcuta ... **78** 7 54N 72 31W
Cudahy ... **68** 42 54N 87 50W
Cuddalore ... **32** 11 46N 79 45 E
Cuddapah ... **32** 14 30N 78 47 E
Cuddapan, L. ... **44** 25 45S 141 26 E
Cudgewa ... **45** 36 10S 147 42 E
Cue ... **47** 27 25S 117 54 E
Cuenca, Ecuador .. **78** 2 50S 79 9W
Cuenca, Spain ... **13** 40 5N 2 10W
Cuenca, Serranía de **13** 39 55N 1 50W
Cuernavaca ... **74** 18 50N 99 20W
Cuero ... **71** 29 5N 97 17W
Cuervo ... **71** 35 5N 104 25W
Cuevas del Almanzora ... **13** 37 18N 1 58W
Cuevo ... **78** 20 15S 63 30W
Cuiabá ... **79** 15 30S 56 0W
Cuiabá → ... **79** 17 5S 56 36W
Cuillin Hills ... **8** 57 14N 6 15W
Cuillin Sd. ... **8** 57 4N 6 20W
Cuiluan ... **38** 47 51N 128 32 E
Cuima ... **55** 13 25S 15 45 E
Cuito → ... **56** 18 1S 20 48 E
Cuitzeo, L. de ... **74** 19 55N 101 5W
Cukai ... **34** 4 13N 103 25 E
Culbertson ... **70** 48 9N 104 30W
Culcairn ... **45** 35 41S 147 3 E
Culebra, Sierra de la **13** 41 55N 6 20W
Culgoa → ... **45** 29 56S 146 20 E
Culiacán ... **74** 24 50N 107 23W
Culion ... **35** 11 54N 120 1 E
Cullarin Range ... **45** 34 30S 149 30 E
Cullen, Australia .. **46** 13 58S 131 54 E
Cullen, U.K. ... **8** 57 45N 2 50W
Cullen Pt. ... **44** 11 57S 141 54 E
Cullera ... **13** 39 9N 0 17W
Cullman ... **69** 34 13N 86 50W
Culloden Moor ... **8** 57 29N 4 7W
Culpeper ... **68** 38 29N 77 59W
Culuene → ... **79** 12 56S 52 51W
Culver, Pt. ... **47** 32 54S 124 43 E
Culverden ... **43** 42 47S 172 49 E
Cumaná ... **78** 10 30N 64 5W
Cumberland, Canada ... **64** 49 40N 125 0W
Cumberland, Md., U.S.A. ... **68** 39 40N 78 43W
Cumberland, Wis., U.S.A. ... **70** 45 32N 92 3W
Cumberland → .. **69** 36 15N 87 0W
Cumberland I. ... **69** 30 52N 81 30W
Cumberland Is. ... **44** 20 35S 149 10 E
Cumberland L. ... **65** 54 3N 102 18W
Cumberland Pen. .. **61** 67 0N 64 0W
Cumberland Plateau **69** 36 0N 84 30W
Cumberland Sd. ... **61** 65 30N 66 0W
Cumborah ... **45** 29 40S 147 45 E
Cumbria □ ... **6** 54 35N 2 55W
Cumbrian Mts. ... **6** 54 30N 3 0W
Cumbum ... **32** 15 40N 79 10 E
Cummins ... **45** 34 16S 135 43 E
Cumnock, Australia **45** 32 59S 148 46 E
Cumnock, U.K. ... **8** 55 27N 4 18W
Cundeelee ... **47** 30 43S 123 26 E
Cunderdin ... **47** 31 37S 117 12 E
Cunene → ... **56** 17 20S 11 50 E
Cúneo ... **18** 44 23N 7 31 E
Cunnamulla ... **45** 28 2S 145 38 E
Cupar, Canada ... **65** 50 57N 104 10W
Cupar, U.K. ... **8** 56 20N 3 0W
Cupica, G. de ... **78** 6 25N 77 30W
Curaçao ... **75** 12 10N 69 0W
Curaray → ... **78** 2 20S 74 5W
Curiapo ... **78** 8 33N 61 5W
Curicó ... **80** 34 55S 71 20W
Curitiba ... **80** 25 20S 49 10W
Currabubula ... **45** 31 16S 150 44 E
Currais Novos ... **79** 6 13S 36 30W
Curralinho ... **79** 1 45S 49 46W
Currant ... **72** 38 51N 115 32W
Curraweena ... **45** 30 47S 145 54 E
Currawilla ... **44** 25 10S 141 20 E
Current → ... **71** 37 15N 91 10W
Currie, Australia ... **44** 39 56S 143 53 E
Currie, U.S.A. ... **72** 40 16N 114 45W
Currie, Mt. ... **57** 30 29S 29 21 E
Currituck Sd. ... **69** 36 20N 75 50W
Curtis ... **70** 40 41N 100 32W
Curtis Group ... **44** 39 30S 146 37 E
Curtis I. ... **44** 23 35S 151 10 E
Curuápanema → . **79** 2 25S 55 2W
Curuçá ... **79** 0 43S 47 50W
Çürüksu Çayi → . **23** 37 27N 27 11 E
Curundu ... **74** 8 59N 79 38W
Curup ... **34** 4 26S 102 13 E
Cururupu ... **79** 1 50S 44 50W
Curuzú Cuatiá ... **80** 29 50S 58 5W
Cushing ... **71** 35 59N 96 46W
Cushing, Mt. ... **64** 57 35N 126 57W
Cusihuiriáchic ... **74** 28 10N 106 50W
Custer ... **70** 43 45N 103 38W
Cut Bank ... **72** 48 40N 112 15W
Cuthbert ... **69** 31 47N 84 47W
Cuttaburra → .. **45** 29 43S 144 22 E
Cuttack ... **33** 20 25N 85 57 E
Cuvier, C. ... **47** 23 14S 113 22 E
Cuvier I. ... **43** 36 27S 175 50 E
Cuxhaven ... **14** 53 51N 8 41 E
Cuyahoga Falls ... **68** 41 8N 81 30W
Cuyo ... **35** 10 50N 121 5 E
Cuzco, Bolivia ... **78** 20 0S 66 50W
Cuzco, Peru ... **78** 13 32S 72 0W
Cwmbran ... **7** 51 39N 3 0W
Cyclades = Kikládhes ... **19** 37 20N 24 30 E
Cygnet ... **44** 43 8S 147 1 E
Cynthiana ... **68** 38 23N 84 10W
Cypress Hills ... **65** 49 40N 109 30W
Cyprus ■ ... **30** 35 0N 33 0 E
Cyrenaica ... **51** 27 0N 23 0 E
Cyrene = Shaḥḥāt . **51** 32 48N 21 54 E
Czar ... **65** 52 27N 110 50W
Czechoslovakia ■ . **14** 49 0N 17 0 E
Czeremcha ... **15** 52 31N 23 21 E
Częstochowa ... **15** 50 49N 19 7 E

D

Da Hinggan Ling .. **38** 48 0N 121 0 E
Da Lat ... **34** 11 56N 108 25 E
Da Nang ... **34** 16 4N 108 13 E
Da Qaidam ... **37** 37 50N 95 15 E
Da Yunhe → ... **39** 34 25N 120 5 E
Da'an ... **38** 45 30N 124 7 E
Daba Shan ... **39** 32 0N 109 0 E
Dabakala ... **50** 8 15N 4 20W
Dabbūrīya ... **28** 32 42N 35 22 E
Dąbie ... **14** 53 27N 14 45 E
Dabo ... **34** 0 30S 104 33 E
Dabola ... **50** 10 50N 11 5W
Daboya ... **53** 9 30N 1 20W
Dabrowa Tarnówska **15** 50 10N 20 59 E
Dacca = Dhaka ... **33** 23 43N 90 26 E
Dacca □ = Dhaka □ **33** 24 25N 90 25 E
Dadanawa ... **78** 2 50N 59 30W
Dade City ... **69** 28 20N 82 12W
Dadiya ... **53** 9 35N 11 24 E
Dadra and Nagar Haveli □ ... **32** 20 5N 73 0 E
Dadu ... **32** 26 45N 67 45 E
Daet ... **35** 14 2N 122 55 E
Dafang ... **39** 27 9N 105 39 E
Dagana ... **50** 16 30N 15 35W
Daghestan A.S.S.R. □ ... **23** 42 30N 47 0 E
Dagö = Hiiumaa .. **22** 58 50N 22 45 E
Dagupan ... **35** 16 3N 120 20 E
Dahlak Kebir ... **29** 15 50N 40 10 E
Dahlonega ... **69** 34 35N 83 59W
Dahod ... **32** 22 50N 74 15 E
Dahomey = Benin ■ **53** 10 0N 2 0 E
Dahra ... **50** 15 22N 15 30W
Dai Shan ... **39** 30 25N 122 10 E
Dai Xian ... **38** 39 4N 112 58 E
Daingean ... **9** 53 18N 7 15W
Daintree ... **44** 16 20S 145 20 E
Daiō-Misaki ... **36** 34 15N 136 45 E
Dairût ... **51** 27 34N 30 43 E
Daisetsu-Zan ... **36** 43 30N 142 57 E
Dajarra ... **44** 21 42S 139 30 E
Dakar ... **50** 14 34N 17 29W
Dakhla ... **50** 23 50N 15 53W
Dakhla, El Wâhât el- **51** 25 30N 28 50 E
Dakhovskaya ... **23** 44 13N 40 13 E
Dakingari ... **53** 11 37N 4 1 E
Dakota City ... **70** 42 27N 96 28W
Đakovica ... **19** 42 22N 20 26 E
Dalachi ... **38** 36 48N 105 0 E
Dalai Nur ... **38** 43 20N 116 45 E
Dalälven ... **21** 60 12N 16 43 E
Dalandzadgad ... **37** 43 27N 104 30 E
Dalarö ... **21** 59 8N 18 24 E
Dālbandīn ... **31** 29 0N 64 23 E
Dalbeattie ... **8** 54 55N 3 50W
Dalby ... **45** 27 10S 151 17 E
Dalgaranger, Mt. .. **47** 27 50S 117 5 E
Dalhart ... **71** 36 10N 102 30W
Dalhousie ... **63** 48 5N 66 26W
Dali, Shaanxi, China **39** 34 48N 109 58 E
Dali, Yunnan, China **37** 25 40N 100 10 E
Dalian ... **38** 38 50N 121 40 E
Daliang Shan ... **37** 28 0N 102 45 E
Dāliyat el Karmel .. **28** 32 43N 35 2 E
Dalkeith ... **8** 55 54N 3 5W
Dall I. ... **64** 54 59N 133 25W
Dallarnil ... **45** 25 19S 152 2 E
Dallas, Oreg., U.S.A. **72** 45 0N 123 15W
Dallas, Tex., U.S.A. **71** 32 50N 96 50W
Dalmacija □ ... **18** 43 20N 17 0 E
Dalmatia = Dalmacija □ ... **18** 43 20N 17 0 E
Dalmellington ... **8** 55 20N 4 25W
Dalnegorsk ... **25** 44 32N 135 33 E
Dalneretchensk ... **25** 45 50N 133 40 E
Daloa ... **50** 7 0N 6 30W
Dalton, Canada ... **62** 48 11N 84 1W
Dalton, Ga., U.S.A. **69** 34 47N 84 58W
Dalton, Nebr., U.S.A. **70** 41 27N 103 0W
Dalvík ... **20** 65 58N 18 32W
Daly → ... **46** 13 35S 130 19 E
Daly L. ... **65** 56 32N 105 39W
Daly Waters ... **44** 16 15S 133 24 E
Daman ... **32** 20 25N 72 57 E
Damanhûr ... **51** 31 0N 30 30 E
Damar ... **35** 7 7S 128 40 E
Damaraland ... **56** 21 0S 17 0 E
Damascus = Dimashq ... **30** 33 30N 36 18 E
Damaturu ... **53** 11 45N 11 55 E
Damāvand ... **31** 35 47N 52 0 E
Damāvand, Qolleh-ye ... **31** 35 56N 52 10 E
Damba ... **54** 6 44S 15 20 E
Dāmghān ... **31** 36 10N 54 17 E
Damietta = Dumyât **51** 31 24N 31 48 E
Daming ... **38** 36 15N 115 6 E
Dāmīya ... **28** 32 6N 35 34 E
Damoh ... **32** 23 50N 79 28 E
Dampier ... **46** 20 41S 116 42 E
Dampier, Selat ... **35** 0 40S 131 0 E
Dampier Arch. ... **46** 20 38S 116 32 E
Dan Xian ... **39** 19 31N 109 33 E
Dana ... **35** 11 0S 122 52 E
Dana, L. ... **62** 50 53N 77 20W
Danbury ... **68** 41 23N 73 29W
Danby L. ... **73** 34 17N 115 0W
Dandaragan ... **47** 30 40S 115 40 E
Dandeldhura ... **33** 29 20N 80 35 E
Dandeli ... **32** 15 5N 74 30 E
Dandenong ... **45** 38 0S 145 15 E
Dandong ... **38** 40 10N 124 20 E
Danforth ... **63** 45 39N 67 57W
Danger Is. = Pukapuka ... **41** 10 53S 165 49W
Danger Pt. ... **56** 34 40S 19 17 E
Dangora ... **53** 11 30N 8 7 E
Dangriga ... **74** 17 0N 88 13W
Dangshan ... **39** 34 27N 116 22 E
Dangtu ... **39** 31 32N 118 25 E
Dangyang ... **39** 30 52N 111 44 E
Daniel ... **72** 42 56N 110 2W
Daniel's Harbour .. **63** 50 13N 57 35W
Danielskuil ... **56** 28 11S 23 33 E
Danilov ... **22** 58 16N 40 13 E
Dankalwa ... **53** 11 52N 12 12 E
Dankhar Gompa .. **32** 32 10N 78 10 E

Danlí

Danlí 75 14 4N 86 35W
Dannemora, Sweden 21 60 12N 17 51 E
Dannemora, U.S.A. 68 44 41N 73 44W
Dannevirke 43 40 12S 176 8 E
Dannhauser 57 28 0S 30 3 E
Danshui 39 25 12N 121 25 E
Dansville 68 42 32N 77 41W
Dante 29 10 25N 51 16 E
Danube → 15 45 20N 29 40 E
Danville, Ill., U.S.A. 68 40 10N 87 40W
Danville, Ky., U.S.A. 68 37 40N 84 45W
Danville, Va., U.S.A. 69 36 40N 79 20W
Danzhai 39 26 11N 107 48 E
Danzig = Gdańsk 15 54 22N 18 40 E
Dao 35 10 30N 121 57 E
Dao Xian 39 25 36N 111 31 E
Daoud = Aïn Beïda 50 35 50N 7 29 E
Daqing Shan 38 40 40N 111 0 E
Daqu Shan 39 30 25N 122 20 E
Dar-es-Salaam, Tanzania 52 6 50S 39 12 E
Dar es Salaam, Tanzania 54 6 50S 39 12 E
Dar'ā 28 32 36N 36 7 E
Dārāb 31 28 50N 54 30 E
Daraj 50 30 10N 10 28 E
Darband 32 34 20N 72 50 E
Darbhanga 33 26 15N 85 55 E
Darby 72 46 2N 114 7W
Dardanelle 71 35 12N 93 9W
Dardanelles = Çanakkale Boğazı 30 40 3N 26 12 E
Dârfûr 51 13 40N 24 0 E
Dargai 32 34 25N 71 55 E
Dargan Ata 24 40 29N 62 10 E
Dargaville 43 35 57S 173 52 E
Darhan Muminggan Lianheqi 38 41 40N 110 28 E
Darien 74 9 7N 79 46W
Darién, G. del 78 9 0N 77 0W
Darjeeling = Darjiling 33 27 3N 88 18 E
Darjiling 33 27 3N 88 18 E
Dark Cove 63 48 47N 54 13W
Darkan 47 33 20S 116 43 E
Darling → 45 34 4S 141 54 E
Darling Downs 45 27 30S 150 30 E
Darling Ra. 47 32 30S 116 0 E
Darlington, U.K. 6 54 33N 1 33W
Darlington, S.C., U.S.A. 69 34 18N 79 50W
Darlington, Wis., U.S.A. 70 42 43N 90 7W
Darlot, L. 47 27 48S 121 35 E
Darłowo 14 54 25N 16 25 E
Darmstadt 14 49 51N 8 40 E
Darnah 51 32 40N 22 35 E
Darnall 57 29 23S 31 18 E
Darnley B. 60 69 30N 123 30W
Darr 44 23 13S 144 7 E
Darr → 44 23 39S 143 50 E
Darrington 72 48 14N 121 37W
Darror → 29 10 30N 50 0 E
Dart → 7 50 24N 3 36W
Dartmoor 7 50 36N 4 0W
Dartmouth, Australia 44 23 31S 144 44 E
Dartmouth, Canada 63 44 40N 63 30W
Dartmouth, U.K. 7 50 21N 3 35W
Dartmouth, L. 45 26 4S 145 18 E
Darvaza 24 40 11N 58 24 E
Darvel, Teluk 35 4 50N 118 20 E
Darwha 32 20 15N 77 45 E
Darwin 46 12 25S 130 51 E
Darwin River 46 12 50S 130 58 E
Dās 31 25 20N 53 30 E
Dasht → 31 25 10N 61 40 E
Dasht-e Kavīr 31 34 30N 55 0 E
Dasht-e Lūt 31 31 30N 58 0 E
Dasht-e Mārgow 31 30 40N 62 30 E
Dasseneiland 56 33 25S 18 3 E
Datia 32 25 39N 78 27 E
Datian 39 25 40N 117 50 E
Datong, Anhui, China 39 30 48N 117 44 E
Datong, Shanxi, China 38 40 6N 113 18 E
Datu, Tanjung 34 2 5N 109 39 E
Datu Piang 35 7 2N 124 30 E
Daugava → 22 57 4N 24 3 E
Daugavpils 22 55 53N 26 32 E
Daulpur 32 26 45N 77 59 E
Dauphin 65 51 9N 100 5W
Dauphin I. 69 30 16N 88 10W
Dauphin L. 65 51 20N 99 45W
Dauphiné 12 45 15N 5 25 E
Daura 53 11 31N 11 24 E
Davangere 32 14 25N 75 55 E
Davao 35 7 0N 125 40 E
Davao, G. of 35 6 30N 125 48 E
Dāvar Panāh 31 27 25N 62 15 E
Davenport, Iowa, U.S.A. 70 41 30N 90 40W
Davenport, Wash., U.S.A. 72 47 40N 118 5W
Davenport Downs 44 24 8S 141 7 E
Davenport Ra. 44 20 28S 134 0 E
David 75 8 30N 82 30W
David City 70 41 18N 97 10W
Davidson 65 51 16N 105 59W
Davis 72 38 33N 121 44W
Davis Dam 73 35 11N 114 35W
Davis Inlet 63 55 50N 60 59W
Davis Mts. 71 30 42N 104 15W
Davis Str. 61 65 0N 58 0W
Davos 14 46 48N 9 49 E
Davy L. 65 58 53N 108 18W
Dawes Ra. 44 24 40S 150 40 E
Dawson, Canada 60 64 10N 139 30W
Dawson, Ga., U.S.A. 69 31 45N 84 28W
Dawson, N. Dak., U.S.A. 70 46 56N 99 45W
Dawson, I. 80 53 50S 70 50W
Dawson Creek 64 55 45N 120 15W
Dawson Inlet 65 61 50N 93 25W
Dawson Range 44 24 30S 149 48 E
Daxian 39 31 15N 107 23 E
Daxin 39 22 50N 107 11 E
Daxue Shan 37 30 30N 101 30 E
Daye 39 30 6N 114 58 E
Dayong 39 29 11N 110 30 E
Dayr Abū Sa'īd 28 32 30N 35 42 E
Dayr al-Ghuṣūn 28 32 21N 35 4 E
Dayr az Zawr 30 35 20N 40 5 E
Dayr Dirwān 28 31 55N 35 15 E
Daysland 64 52 50N 112 20W
Dayton, Ohio, U.S.A. 68 39 45N 84 10W
Dayton, Tenn., U.S.A. 69 35 30N 85 1W
Dayton, Wash., U.S.A. 72 46 20N 118 10W
Daytona Beach 69 29 14N 81 0W
Dayu 39 25 24N 114 22 E
Dayville 72 44 33N 119 37W
Dazhu 39 30 41N 107 15 E
Dazu 39 29 40N 105 42 E
De Aar 56 30 39S 24 0 E
De Funiak Springs 69 30 42N 86 10W
De Grey 46 20 12S 119 12 E
De Grey → 46 20 12S 119 13 E
De Kalb 70 41 55N 88 45W
De Land 69 29 1N 81 19W
De Leon 71 32 9N 98 35W
De Pere 68 44 28N 88 1W
De Queen 71 34 3N 94 24W
De Quincy 71 30 30N 93 27W
De Ridder 71 30 48N 93 15W
De Smet 70 44 25N 97 35W
De Soto 70 38 7N 90 33W
De Tour 68 45 59N 83 56W
De Witt 71 34 19N 91 20W
Dead Sea 28 31 30N 35 30 E
Deadwood 70 44 23N 103 44W
Deadwood L. 64 59 10N 128 30W
Deakin 47 30 46S 128 58 E
Deal 7 51 13N 1 25 E
Deal I. 44 39 30S 147 20 E
Dealesville 56 28 41S 25 44 E
Dean, Forest of 7 51 50N 2 35W
Deán Funes 80 30 20S 64 20W
Dearborn 62 42 18N 83 15W
Dease → 64 59 56N 128 32W
Dease L. 64 58 40N 130 5W
Dease Lake 64 58 25N 130 6W
Death Valley 73 36 19N 116 52W
Death Valley Junc. 73 36 21N 116 30W
Death Valley Nat. Monument 73 36 30N 117 0W
Deba Habe 53 10 14N 11 20 E
Debao 39 23 21N 106 46 E
Debar 19 41 31N 20 30 E
Debden 65 53 30N 106 50W
Debolt 64 55 12N 118 1W
Deborah East, L. 47 30 45S 119 0 E
Deborah West, L. 47 30 45S 118 50 E
Debre Markos 51 10 20N 37 40 E
Debre Tabor 51 11 50N 38 26 E
Debrecen 15 47 33N 21 42 E
Decatur, Ala., U.S.A. 69 34 35N 87 0W
Decatur, Ga., U.S.A. 69 33 47N 84 17W
Decatur, Ill., U.S.A. 70 39 50N 89 0W
Decatur, Ind., U.S.A. 68 40 50N 84 56W
Decatur, Tex., U.S.A. 71 33 15N 97 35W
Deccan 32 18 0N 79 0 E
Deception L. 65 56 33N 104 13W
Decorah 70 43 20N 91 50W
Dedéagach = Alexandroúpolis 19 40 50N 25 54 E
Dédougou 50 12 30N 3 25W
Dee →, Scotland, U.K. 8 57 4N 2 7W
Dee →, Wales, U.K. 6 53 15N 3 7W
Deep B. 64 61 15N 116 35W
Deep Well 44 24 20S 134 0 E
Deepwater 45 29 25S 151 51 E
Deer → 65 58 23N 94 13W
Deer Lake, Nfld., Canada 63 49 11N 57 27W
Deer Lake, Ont., Canada 65 52 36N 94 20W
Deer Lodge 72 46 25N 112 40W
Deer Park 72 47 55N 117 21W
Deer River 70 47 21N 93 44W
Deeral 44 17 14S 145 55 E
Deerdepoort 56 24 37S 26 27 E
Defiance 68 41 20N 84 20W
Deganya 28 32 43N 35 34 E
Degeh Bur 29 8 11N 43 31 E
Degema 53 4 50N 6 48 E
Deggendorf 14 48 49N 12 59 E
Deh Bīd 31 30 39N 53 11 E
Dehi Titan 32 33 45N 63 50 E
Dehibat 50 32 0N 10 47 E
Dehkareqan 30 37 43N 45 55 E
Dehra Dun 32 30 20N 78 4 E
Dehui 38 44 30N 125 40 E
Deinze 11 50 59N 3 32 E
Dej 15 47 10N 23 52 E
Dekese 54 3 24S 21 24 E
Del Norte 73 37 40N 106 27W
Del Rio 71 29 23N 100 50W
Delano 73 35 48N 119 13W
Delareyville 56 26 41S 25 26 E
Delavan 70 42 40N 88 39W
Delaware 68 40 20N 83 0W
Delaware □ 68 39 0N 75 40W
Delaware → 68 39 20N 75 25W
Delegate 45 37 4S 148 56 E
Delft 11 52 1N 4 22 E
Delfzijl 11 53 20N 6 55 E
Delgado, C. 54 10 45S 40 40 E
Delgo 51 20 6N 30 40 E
Delhi 32 28 38N 77 17 E
Delia 64 51 38N 112 23W
Delice → 30 39 45N 34 15 E
Delicias 74 28 10N 105 30W
Dell City 73 31 58N 105 19W
Dell Rapids 70 43 53N 96 44W
Delmiro Gouveia 79 9 24S 38 6W
Delong, Ostrova 25 76 40N 149 20 E
Deloraine, Australia 44 41 30S 146 40 E
Deloraine, Canada 65 49 15N 100 29W
Delphi 68 40 37N 86 40W
Delphos 68 40 51N 84 17W
Delportshoop 56 28 22S 24 20 E
Delray Beach 69 26 27N 80 4W
Delta, Colo., U.S.A. 73 38 44N 108 5W
Delta, Utah, U.S.A. 72 39 21N 112 29W
Delungra 45 29 39S 150 51 E
Demanda, Sierra de la 13 42 15N 3 0W
Demba 54 5 28S 22 15 E
Dembecha 51 10 32N 37 30 E
Dembidolo 51 8 34N 34 50 E
Demer → 11 50 57N 4 42 E
Deming 73 32 10N 107 50W
Demini → 78 0 46S 62 56W
Demopolis 69 32 30N 87 48W
Dempo, Mt. 34 4 2S 103 15 E
Den Burg 11 53 3N 4 47 E
Den Haag = 's-Gravenhage 11 52 7N 4 17 E
Den Helder 11 52 57N 4 45 E
Den Oever 11 52 56N 5 2 E
Denain 11 50 20N 3 22 E
Denau 24 38 16N 67 54 E
Denbigh 6 53 12N 3 26W
Dendang 34 3 7S 107 56 E
Dendermonde 11 51 2N 4 5 E
Deng Xian 39 32 34N 112 4 E
Dengi 53 9 25N 9 55 E
Denham 47 25 56S 113 31 E
Denham Ra. 44 21 55S 147 46 E
Denham Sd. 47 25 45S 113 15 E
Denia 13 38 49N 0 8 E
Denial B. 45 32 14S 133 32 E
Deniliquin 45 35 30S 144 58 E
Denison, Iowa, U.S.A. 70 42 0N 95 18W
Denison, Tex., U.S.A. 71 33 50N 96 40W
Denison Plains 46 18 35S 128 0 E
Denizli 30 37 42N 29 2 E
Denmark 47 34 59S 117 25 E
Denmark ■ 21 55 30N 9 0 E
Denmark Str. 2 66 0N 30 0W
Denpasar 34 8 45S 115 14 E
Denton, Mont., U.S.A. 72 47 25N 109 56W
Denton, Tex., U.S.A. 71 33 12N 97 10W
D'Entrecasteaux Pt. 47 34 50S 115 57 E
Denver 70 39 45N 105 0W
Denver City 71 32 58N 102 48W
Deoghar 33 24 30N 86 42 E
Deolali 32 19 58N 73 50 E
Deoria 33 26 31N 83 48 E
Deosai Mts. 32 35 40N 75 0 E
Deping 38 37 25N 116 58 E
Depot Springs 47 27 55S 120 3 E
Deputatskiy 25 69 18N 139 54 E
Dêqên 37 28 34N 98 51 E
Deqing 39 23 8N 111 42 E
Dera Ghazi Khan 32 30 5N 70 43 E
Dera Ismail Khan 32 31 50N 70 50 E
Derbent 23 42 5N 48 15 E
Derby, Australia 46 17 18S 123 38 E
Derby, U.K. 6 52 55N 1 28W
Derby □ 6 52 55N 1 28W
Derg → 9 54 42N 7 26W
Derg, L. 9 53 0N 8 20W
Dergaon 33 26 45N 94 0 E
Dernieres Isles 71 29 0N 90 45W
Derry = Londonderry 9 55 0N 7 20W
Derryveagh Mts. 9 55 0N 8 40W
Derudub 51 17 31N 36 7 E
Derwent 65 53 41N 110 58W
Derwent →, Derby, U.K. 6 52 53N 1 17W
Derwent →, N. Yorks., U.K. 6 53 45N 0 57W
Derwent Water, L. 6 54 35N 3 9W
Des Moines, Iowa, U.S.A. 70 41 35N 93 37W
Des Moines, N. Mex., U.S.A. 71 36 50N 103 51W
Des Moines → 70 40 23N 91 25W
Desaguadero → 78 18 24S 67 5W
Deschaillons 63 46 32N 72 7W
Descharme → 65 56 51N 109 13W
Deschutes → 72 45 30N 121 0W
Dese 29 11 5N 39 40 E
Desert Center 73 33 45N 115 27W
Deskenatlata L. 64 60 55N 112 3W
Desna → 22 50 33N 30 32 E
Desolación, I. 80 53 0S 74 0W
Despeñaperros, Paso 13 38 24N 3 30W
Dessau 14 51 49N 12 15 E
Dessye = Dese 29 11 5N 39 40 E
D'Estrees B. 45 35 55S 137 45 E
Detmold 14 51 55N 8 50 E
Detour Pt. 68 45 37N 86 35W
Detroit, Mich., U.S.A. 62 42 23N 83 5W
Detroit, Tex., U.S.A. 71 33 40N 95 10W
Detroit Lakes 70 46 50N 95 50W
Deurne, Belgium 11 51 12N 4 24 E
Deurne, Neth. 11 51 27N 5 49 E
Deutsche Bucht 14 54 0N 8 0 E
Deux-Sèvres □ 12 46 35N 0 20W
Deva 15 45 53N 22 55 E
Devakottai 32 9 55N 78 45 E
Deventer 11 52 15N 6 10 E
Deveron → 8 57 40N 2 31W
Devils Lake 70 48 5N 98 50W
Devils Paw 64 58 47N 134 0W
Devizes 7 51 21N 2 0W
Devon 64 53 24N 113 44W
Devon I. 58 75 10N 85 0W
Devonport, Australia 44 41 10S 146 22 E
Devonport, N.Z. 43 36 49S 174 49 E
Devonport, U.K. 7 50 23N 4 11W
Devonshire □ 7 50 50N 3 40W
Dewas 32 22 59N 76 3 E
Dewetsdorp 56 29 33S 26 39 E
Dewsbury 6 53 42N 1 38W
Dexter, Mo., U.S.A. 71 36 50N 90 0W
Dexter, N. Mex., U.S.A. 71 33 15N 104 25W
Dey-Dey, L. 47 29 12S 131 4 E
Deyhūk 31 33 15N 57 30 E
Deyyer 31 27 55N 51 55 E
Dezadeash L. 64 60 28N 136 58W
Dezfūl 30 32 20N 48 30 E
Dezhneva, Mys 25 66 5N 169 40W
Dezhou 38 37 26N 116 18 E
Dhafra 31 23 20N 54 0 E
Dhahira 31 23 40N 57 0 E
Dhahran = Aẓ Ẓahrān 30 26 10N 50 7 E
Dhaka 33 23 43N 90 26 E
Dhaka □ 33 24 25N 90 25 E
Dhamar 29 14 30N 44 20 E
Dhamtari 33 20 42N 81 35 E
Dhanbad 33 23 50N 86 30 E
Dhangarhi 33 28 55N 80 40 E
Dhankuta 33 26 55N 87 40 E
Dhar 32 22 35N 75 26 E
Dharmapuri 32 12 10N 78 10 E
Dharwad 32 15 22N 75 15 E
Dharwar 32 15 43N 75 1 E
Dhaulagiri 33 28 39N 83 28 E
Dhenkanal 33 20 45N 85 35 E
Dhidhimótikhon 19 41 22N 26 29 E
Dhíkti 19 35 8N 25 22 E
Dhírfis 19 38 40N 23 54 E
Dhodhekánisos 19 36 35N 27 0 E
Dhrol 32 22 33N 70 25 E
Dhubaibah 31 23 25N 54 35 E
Dhuburi 33 26 2N 89 59 E
Dhule 32 20 58N 74 50 E
Diablo Heights 74 8 58N 79 34W
Diafarabé 50 14 9N 4 57W
Diamantina 79 18 17S 43 40W
Diamantina → 45 26 45S 139 10 E
Diamantino 79 14 30S 56 30W
Diamond Harbour 33 22 11N 88 14 E
Diamond Is. 44 17 25S 151 5 E
Diamond Mts. 72 40 0N 115 58W
Diamondville 72 41 51N 110 30W
Diancheng 39 21 30N 111 4 E
Diapaga 53 12 5N 1 46 E
Dībā 31 25 45N 56 16 E
Dibaya 54 6 30S 22 57 E
Dibaya-Lubue 54 4 12S 19 54 E
Dibbi 29 4 10N 41 52 E
Dibete 56 23 45S 26 32 E
Dibrugarh 33 27 29N 94 55 E
Dickinson 70 46 50N 102 48W
Dickson, U.S.A. 69 36 5N 87 22W
Dickson, U.S.S.R. 24 73 40N 80 5 E
Didiéni 50 13 53N 8 6W
Didsbury 64 51 35N 114 10W
Diébougou 50 11 0N 3 15W
Diefenbaker L. 65 51 0N 106 55W
Diego Garcia 3 7 50S 72 50 E
Diekirch 11 49 52N 6 10 E
Dieppe 12 49 54N 1 4 E
Dieren 11 52 3N 6 6 E
Dierks 71 34 9N 94 0W
Diest 11 50 58N 5 4 E
Differdange 11 49 31N 5 54 E
Digby 63 44 38N 65 50W
Digges 65 58 40N 94 0W
Digges Is. 61 62 40N 77 50W
Dighinala 33 23 15N 92 5 E
Dighton 70 38 30N 100 26W
Digne 12 44 5N 6 12 E
Digos 35 6 45N 125 20 E
Digranes 20 66 4N 14 44 E
Digul → 35 7 7S 138 42 E
Dihang → 33 27 48N 95 30 E
Dijlah, Nahr → 30 31 0N 47 25 E
Dijon 12 47 20N 5 0 E
Dikomu di Kai 56 24 58S 24 36 E
Diksmuide 11 51 2N 2 52 E
Dikson = Dickson 24 73 40N 80 5 E
Dikwa 53 12 4N 13 30 E
Dili 35 8 39S 125 34 E
Dilley 71 28 40N 99 12W
Dilling 51 12 3N 29 35 E
Dillon, Canada 65 55 56N 108 35W
Dillon, Mont., U.S.A. 72 45 9N 112 36W
Dillon, S.C., U.S.A. 69 34 26N 79 20W
Dillon → 65 55 56N 108 56W
Dilolo 54 10 28S 22 18 E
Dilston 44 41 22S 147 10 E
Dimashq 30 33 30N 36 18 E
Dimbaza 57 32 50S 27 14 E
Dimbokro 50 6 45N 4 46W
Dimboola 45 36 28S 142 7 E
Dîmboviţa → 15 44 5N 26 35 E
Dimbulah 44 17 8S 145 4 E
Dimitrovgrad, Bulgaria 19 42 5N 25 35 E
Dimitrovgrad, U.S.S.R. 22 54 14N 49 39 E
Dimmitt 71 34 36N 102 16W
Dimona 28 31 2N 35 1 E
Dinagat 35 10 10N 125 40 E
Dinajpur 33 25 33N 88 43 E
Dinan 12 48 28N 2 2W
Dinant 11 50 16N 4 55 E
Dinar 30 38 5N 30 15 E
Dinara Planina 18 44 0N 16 30 E
Dinard 12 48 38N 2 6W
Dinaric Alps = Dinara Planina 18 44 0N 16 30 E
Dindigul 32 10 25N 78 0 E
Ding Xian 38 38 30N 114 59 E
Dingbian 38 37 35N 107 32 E
Dinghai 39 30 1N 122 6 E
Dingle 9 52 9N 10 17W
Dingle B. 9 52 3N 10 20W
Dingnan 39 24 45N 115 0 E
Dingo 44 23 38S 149 19 E
Dingtao 39 35 5N 115 35 E
Dinguiraye 50 11 18N 10 49W
Dingwall 8 57 36N 4 26W
Dingxi 38 35 30N 104 33 E
Dingxiang 38 38 30N 112 58 E
Dinokwe 56 23 29S 26 37 E
Dinosaur National Monument 72 40 30N 108 58W
Dinuba 73 36 31N 119 22W
Diourbel 50 14 39N 16 12W
Dipolog 35 8 36N 123 20 E
Dir 31 35 8N 71 59 E
Diré 50 16 20N 3 25W
Dire Dawa 29 9 35N 41 45 E
Diriamba 75 11 51N 86 19W
Dirico 55 17 50S 20 42 E
Dirk Hartog I. 47 25 50S 113 5 E
Dirranbandi 45 28 33S 148 17 E

Eagle Pt.

Disa . . . . **32** 24 18N 72 10 E
Disappointment, C. **72** 46 20N 124 0W
Disappointment L. . **46** 23 20S 122 40 E
Disaster B. . . . . **45** 37 15S 150 0 E
Discovery B. . . . . . **45** 38 10S 140 40 E
Disko **58** 69 45N 53 30W
Disteghil Sar . . . . . **32** 36 20N 75 12 E
Distrito Federal □ . **79** 15 45S 47 45W
Diu . . . . **32** 20 45N 70 58 E
Divide **72** 45 48N 112 47W
Dividing Ra. . . . . . . **47** 27 45S 116 0 E
Divinópolis **79** 20 10S 44 54W
Divnoye . . . . **23** 45 55N 43 21 E
Dīwāl Kol . . . . **32** 34 23N 67 52 E
Dixon, Ill., U.S.A. . . **70** 41 50N 89 30W
Dixon, Mont., U.S.A. **72** 47 19N 114 25W
Dixon, N. Mex., U.S.A. **73** 36 15N 105 57W
Dixon Entrance . . . **64** 54 30N 132 0W
Dixonville **64** 56 32N 117 40W
Diyarbakir . . . . **30** 37 55N 40 18 E
Diz Chah . . . . **31** 35 30N 55 30 E
Djado . . . . **51** 21 4N 12 14 E
Djakarta = Jakarta **35** 6 9S 106 49 E
Djamba . . . . **56** 16 45S 13 58 E
Djambala . . . . **54** 2 32S 14 30 E
Djanet . . . . **50** 24 35N 9 32 E
Djawa = Jawa . . . . **35** 7 0S 110 0 E
Djelfa . . . . **50** 34 40N 3 15 E
Djema . . . . **54** 6 3N 25 15 E
Djenné **50** 14 0N 4 30W
Djerid, Chott . . . . . **50** 33 42N 8 30 E
Djibo **53** 14 9N 1 35W
Djibouti . . . . **29** 11 30N 43 5 E
Djibouti ■ . . . . **29** 12 0N 43 0 E
Djolu . . . . **54** 0 35N 22 5 E
Djougou . . . . **53** 9 40N 1 45 E
Djoum . . . . **54** 2 41N 12 35 E
Djourab . . . . **51** 16 40N 18 50 E
Djugu . . . . **54** 1 55N 30 35 E
Djúpivogur **20** 64 39N 14 17W
Dmitriya Lapteva, Proliv . . . . **25** 73 0N 140 0 E
Dnepr → . . . . **23** 46 30N 32 18 E
Dneprodzerzhinsk . **23** 48 32N 34 37 E
Dnepropetrovsk . . . **23** 48 30N 35 0 E
Dnestr → . . . . **23** 46 18N 30 17 E
Dnestrovski = Belgorod . . . . **23** 50 35N 36 35 E
Dnieper = Dnepr → . . . . . **23** 46 30N 32 18 E
Dniester = Dnestr → . . . . . **23** 46 18N 30 17 E
Doba . . . . **51** 8 40N 16 50 E
Dobbyn . . . . **44** 19 44S 140 2 E
Doberai, Jazirah . . **35** 1 25S 133 0 E
Doblas **80** 37 5S 64 0W
Dobo . . . . **35** 5 45S 134 15 E
Dobruja . . . . **15** 44 30N 28 15 E
Dodecanese = Dhodhekánisos . **19** 36 35N 27 0 E
Dodge Center **70** 44 1N 92 50W
Dodge City **71** 37 42N 100 0W
Dodge L. **65** 59 50N 105 36W
Dodgeville **70** 42 55N 90 8W
Dodoma . . . . **54** 6 8S 35 45 E
Dodsland **65** 51 50N 108 45W
Dodson **72** 48 23N 108 16W
Doetinchem . . . . . . **11** 51 59N 6 18 E
Dog Creek **64** 51 35N 122 14W
Dog L., Man., Canada **65** 51 2N 98 31W
Dog L., Ont., Canada **62** 48 48N 89 30W
Dogger Bank . . . . . **4** 54 50N 2 0 E
Dogi . . . . **32** 32 20N 62 50 E
Dogondoutchi . . . . . **53** 13 38N 4 2 E
Dohazari . . . . **33** 22 10N 92 5 E
Doi . . . . **35** 2 14N 127 49 E
Doig → **64** 56 25N 120 40W
Dois Irmãos, Sa. . . **79** 9 0S 42 30W
Dokka . . . . **21** 60 49N 10 7 E
Dokkum . . . . **11** 53 20N 5 59 E
Doland **70** 44 55N 98 5W
Dolbeau **63** 48 53N 72 18W
Dole . . . . **12** 47 7N 5 31 E
Dolgellau **6** 52 44N 3 53W
Dolgelley = Dolgellau **6** 52 44N 3 53W
Dollart . . . . **11** 53 20N 7 10 E
Dolomites = Dolomiti . . . . **18** 46 30N 11 40 E
Dolomiti . . . . **18** 46 30N 11 40 E
Dolores, Argentina . **80** 36 20S 57 40W
Dolores, U.S.A. . . . **73** 37 30N 108 30W
Dolores → **73** 38 49N 108 17W
Dolphin, C. **80** 51 10S 59 0W
Dolphin and Union Str. **60** 69 5N 114 45W
Dombarovskiy . . . . **24** 50 46N 59 32 E
Dombås . . . . **21** 62 4N 9 8 E
Dombes . . . . **12** 46 0N 5 0 E
Domburg . . . . **11** 51 34N 3 30 E
Dominica ■ **75** 15 20N 61 20W
Dominican Rep. ■ . **75** 19 0N 70 30W
Domo . . . . **29** 7 50N 47 10 E
Domodóssola . . . . . **18** 46 6N 8 19 E
Domville, Mt. . . . . . **45** 28 1S 151 15 E
Don →, England, U.K. **6** 53 41N 0 51W
Don →, Scotland, U.K. **8** 57 14N 2 5W
Don →, U.S.S.R. . **23** 47 4N 39 18 E
Don, C. . . . . **46** 11 18S 131 46 E
Don Benito **13** 38 53N 5 51W
Don Martín, Presa de **74** 27 30N 100 50W
Donaghadee **9** 54 38N 5 32W
Donald . . . . **45** 36 23S 143 0 E
Donalda **64** 52 35N 112 34W
Donaldsonville **71** 30 2N 91 0W
Donalsonville **69** 31 3N 84 52W
Donau → . . . . **14** 48 10N 17 0 E
Donauwörth . . . . . . **14** 48 42N 10 47 E
Doncaster **6** 53 31N 1 9W
Dondo, Angola . . . . **54** 9 45S 14 25 E
Dondo, Mozam. . . . **55** 19 33S 34 46 E
Dondo, Teluk . . . . . **35** 0 29N 120 30 E
Dondra Head . . . . . **32** 5 55N 80 40 E
Donegal **9** 54 39N 8 8W
Donegal □ **9** 54 53N 8 0W
Donegal B. **9** 54 30N 8 35W
Donets → . . . . **23** 47 33N 40 55 E
Donetsk . . . . **23** 48 0N 37 45 E
Dongara . . . . **47** 29 14S 114 57 E
Dongfang . . . . **39** 18 50N 108 33 E
Donggala . . . . **35** 0 30S 119 40 E
Donggou . . . . **38** 39 52N 124 10 E
Dongguan . . . . **39** 22 58N 113 44 E
Dongguang . . . . **38** 37 50N 116 30 E
Dongjingcheng . . . . **38** 44 0N 129 10 E
Donglan . . . . **39** 24 30N 107 21 E
Dongliu . . . . **39** 30 13N 116 55 E
Dongola . . . . **51** 19 9N 30 22 E
Dongou . . . . **54** 2 0N 18 5 E
Dongping . . . . **38** 35 55N 116 20 E
Dongshan . . . . **39** 23 43N 117 30 E
Dongsheng . . . . **38** 39 50N 110 0 E
Dongtai . . . . **39** 32 51N 120 21 E
Dongting Hu . . . . . . **37** 29 18N 112 45 E
Dongxing . . . . **39** 21 34N 108 0 E
Dongyang . . . . **39** 29 13N 120 15 E
Donington, C. . . . . . **45** 34 45S 136 0 E
Doniphan **71** 36 40N 90 50W
Dønna, Norway . . . **20** 66 6N 12 30 E
Donna, U.S.A. **71** 26 12N 98 2W
Donnaconna **63** 46 41N 71 41W
Donnelly's Crossing **43** 35 42S 173 38 E
Donnybrook, Australia . . . . **47** 33 34S 115 48 E
Donnybrook, S. Africa . . . . **57** 29 59S 29 48 E
Donor's Hill . . . . . . **44** 18 42S 140 33 E
Doon → **8** 55 26N 4 41W
Dor . . . . **28** 32 37N 34 55 E
Dora, L. . . . . **46** 22 0S 123 0 E
Dora Báltea → . . . **18** 45 11N 8 5 E
Dorada, La **78** 5 30N 74 40W
Doran L. **65** 61 13N 108 6W
Dorchester **7** 50 42N 2 28W
Dorchester, C. **61** 65 27N 77 27W
Dordogne □ . . . . . . **12** 45 5N 0 40 E
Dordogne → **12** 45 2N 0 36W
Dordrecht, Neth. . . **11** 51 48N 4 39 E
Dordrecht, S. Africa **56** 31 20S 27 3 E
Dore, Mts. . . . . **12** 45 32N 2 50 E
Doré L. **65** 54 46N 107 17W
Doré Lake **65** 54 38N 107 36W
Dori **53** 14 3N 0 2W
Doring → . . . . **56** 31 54S 18 39 E
Doringbos . . . . **56** 31 59S 19 16 E
Dorion **62** 45 23N 74 3W
Dornoch **8** 57 52N 4 0W
Dornoch Firth **8** 57 52N 4 0W
Dorohoi . . . . **15** 47 56N 26 30 E
Döröö Nuur . . . . . . **37** 48 0N 93 0 E
Dorre I. . . . . **47** 25 13S 113 12 E
Dorrigo . . . . **45** 30 20S 152 44 E
Dorris **72** 41 59N 121 58W
Dorset □ **7** 50 48N 2 25W
Dortmund . . . . **14** 51 32N 7 28 E
Doruma . . . . **54** 4 42N 27 33 E
Dos Bahías, C. **80** 44 58S 65 32W
Dosso . . . . **53** 13 0N 3 13 E
Dothan **69** 31 10N 85 25W
Douai . . . . **12** 50 21N 3 4 E
Douala . . . . **54** 4 0N 9 45 E
Douarnenez **12** 48 6N 4 21W
Double Island Pt. . . **45** 25 56S 153 11 E
Doubs □ . . . . **12** 47 10N 6 20 E
Doubs → . . . . **12** 46 53N 5 1 E
Doubtful Sd. . . . . . . **43** 45 20S 166 49 E
Doubtless B. . . . . . . **43** 34 55S 173 26 E
Douentza **50** 14 58N 2 48W
Douglas, S. Africa . **56** 29 4S 23 46 E
Douglas, U.K. **6** 54 9N 4 29W
Douglas, Alaska, U.S.A. **64** 58 23N 134 24W
Douglas, Ariz., U.S.A. **73** 31 21N 109 30W
Douglas, Ga., U.S.A. **69** 31 32N 82 52W
Douglas, Wyo., U.S.A. **70** 42 45N 105 20W
Douglastown **63** 48 46N 64 24W
Douglasville **69** 33 46N 84 43W
Doumé . . . . **54** 4 15N 13 25 E
Dounreay **8** 58 34N 3 44W
Dourados **80** 22 9S 54 50W
Douro → **13** 41 8N 8 40W
Douro Litoral □ . . . **13** 41 10N 8 20W
Dove → **6** 52 51N 1 36W
Dove Creek **73** 37 46N 108 59W
Dover, Australia . . . **44** 43 18S 147 2 E
Dover, U.K. . . . . . . **7** 51 7N 1 19 E
Dover, Del., U.S.A. . **68** 39 10N 75 31W
Dover, N.H., U.S.A. . **68** 43 12N 70 51W
Dover, Ohio, U.S.A. **68** 40 32N 81 30W
Dover, Pt. . . . . **47** 32 32S 125 32 E
Dover, Str. of . . . . . **12** 51 0N 1 30 E
Dover-Foxcroft . . . **63** 45 14N 69 14W
Dovey → **7** 52 32N 4 0W
Dovrefjell . . . . **20** 62 15N 9 33 E
Dowagiac **68** 41 58N 86 8W
Dowlat Yār . . . . **31** 34 30N 65 45 E
Dowlatābād **31** 28 20N 56 40W
Down □ **9** 54 20N 6 0W
Downey **72** 42 29N 112 3W
Downham Market . **7** 52 36N 0 22 E
Downieville **72** 39 34N 120 50W
Downpatrick **9** 54 20N 5 43W
Downpatrick Hd. . . **9** 54 20N 9 21W
Dowshī . . . . **31** 35 35N 68 43 E
Draa, Oued → . . . **50** 28 40N 11 10W
Drachten . . . . **11** 53 7N 6 5 E
Dragoman, Prokhod **19** 43 0N 22 53 E
Draguignan . . . . . . **12** 43 32N 6 27 E
Drain **72** 43 45N 123 17W
Drake, Australia . . . **45** 28 55S 152 25 E
Drake, U.S.A. **70** 47 56N 100 21W
Drakensberg . . . . . **57** 31 0S 28 0 E
Dráma . . . . **19** 41 9N 24 10 E
Drammen . . . . **21** 59 42N 10 12 E
Drangajökull **20** 66 9N 22 15W
Drau = Drava → . **19** 45 33N 18 55 E
Drava → . . . . **19** 45 33N 18 55 E
Drayton Valley **64** 53 12N 114 58W
Drenthe □ . . . . **11** 52 52N 6 40 E
Dresden . . . . **14** 51 2N 13 45 E
Dreux . . . . **12** 48 44N 1 23 E
Driffield **6** 54 0N 0 25W
Driggs **72** 43 50N 111 8W
Drina → . . . . **19** 44 53N 19 21 E
Drøbak . . . . **21** 59 39N 10 39 E
Drogheda **9** 53 45N 6 20W
Drogobych . . . . **23** 49 20N 23 30 E
Droichead Nua **9** 53 11N 6 50W
Droitwich **7** 52 16N 2 10W
Drôme □ . . . . **12** 44 38N 5 15 E
Dromedary, C. . . . . **45** 36 17S 150 10 E
Dronfield . . . . **44** 21 12S 140 3 E
Drumheller **64** 51 25N 112 40W
Drummond **72** 46 40N 113 4W
Drummond I. **62** 46 0N 83 40W
Drummond Pt. . . . . **45** 34 9S 135 16 E
Drummond Ra. . . . . **44** 23 45S 147 10 E
Drummondville **62** 45 55N 72 25W
Drumright **71** 35 59N 96 38W
Druzhina . . . . **25** 68 14N 145 18 E
Dry Tortugas **75** 24 38N 82 55W
Dryden, Canada . . . **65** 49 47N 92 50W
Dryden, U.S.A. **71** 30 3N 102 3W
Drysdale → . . . . . . **46** 13 59S 126 51 E
Drysdale I. . . . . **44** 11 41S 136 0 E
Dschang . . . . **53** 5 32N 10 3 E
Du Bois **68** 41 8N 78 46W
Du Quoin **70** 38 0N 89 10W
Duaringa . . . . **44** 23 42S 149 42 E
Ḑubā . . . . **30** 27 10N 35 40 E
Dubai = Dubayy . . . **31** 25 18N 55 20 E
Dubawnt → **65** 64 33N 100 6W
Dubawnt, L. **65** 63 4N 101 42W
Dubayy . . . . **31** 25 18N 55 20 E
Dubbo . . . . **45** 32 11S 148 35 E
Dublin, Ireland **9** 53 20N 6 18W
Dublin, Ga., U.S.A. . **69** 32 30N 82 34W
Dublin, Tex., U.S.A. **71** 32 0N 98 20W
Dublin □ **9** 53 24N 6 20W
Dublin B. **9** 53 18N 6 5W
Dubois **72** 44 7N 112 9W
Dubovka . . . . **23** 49 5N 44 50 E
Dubréka **50** 9 46N 13 31W
Dubrovnik . . . . **19** 42 39N 18 6 E
Dubrovskoye . . . . . **25** 58 55N 111 10 E
Dubuque **70** 42 30N 90 41W
Duchang . . . . **39** 29 18N 116 12 E
Duchesne **72** 40 14N 110 22W
Duchess . . . . **44** 21 20S 139 50 E
Ducie I. **41** 24 40S 124 48W
Duck Cr. → . . . . . . **46** 22 37S 116 53 E
Duck Lake **65** 52 50N 106 16W
Duck Mt. Prov. Parks **65** 51 45N 101 0W
Dudhi . . . . **33** 24 15N 83 10 E
Dudinka . . . . **25** 69 30N 86 13 E
Dudley **7** 52 30N 2 5W
Duero → **13** 41 8N 8 40W
Dufftown **8** 57 26N 3 9W
Dugi Otok . . . . **18** 44 0N 15 0 E
Duifken Pt. . . . . **44** 12 33S 141 38 E
Duisburg . . . . **14** 51 27N 6 42 E
Duiwelskloof . . . . . **57** 23 42S 30 10 E
Duke I. **64** 54 50N 131 20W
Dukhān . . . . **31** 25 25N 50 50 E
Duki . . . . **32** 30 14N 68 25 E
Duku . . . . **53** 10 43N 10 43 E
Dulce → **80** 30 32S 62 33W
Dulce, G. **75** 8 40N 83 20W
Dulit, Banjaran . . . . **34** 3 15N 114 30 E
Dululu . . . . **44** 23 48S 150 15 E
Duluth **70** 46 48N 92 10W
Dum Duma . . . . **33** 27 40N 95 40 E
Dum Hadjer . . . . . . **51** 13 18N 19 41 E
Dumaguete . . . . **35** 9 17N 123 15 E
Dumai . . . . **34** 1 35N 101 28 E
Dumaran . . . . **35** 10 33N 119 50 E
Dumas, Ark., U.S.A. **71** 33 52N 91 30W
Dumas, Tex., U.S.A. **71** 35 50N 101 58W
Dumbarton **8** 55 58N 4 35W
Dumbleyung . . . . . . **47** 33 17S 117 42 E
Dumfries **8** 55 4N 3 37W
Dumfries & Galloway □ **8** 55 0N 4 0W
Dumoine → **62** 46 13N 77 51W
Dumoine L. **62** 46 55N 77 55W
Dumyât . . . . **51** 31 24N 31 48 E
Dun Laoghaire **9** 53 17N 6 9W
Dunaföldvár . . . . . . **15** 46 50N 18 57 E
Dunărea → . . . . . . **15** 45 20N 29 40 E
Dunback . . . . **43** 45 23S 170 36 E
Dunbar, Australia . . **44** 16 0S 142 22 E
Dunbar, U.K. **8** 56 0N 2 32W
Dunblane **8** 56 10N 3 58W
Duncan, Canada . . **64** 48 45N 123 40W
Duncan, Ariz., U.S.A. **73** 32 46N 109 6W
Duncan, Okla., U.S.A. **71** 34 25N 98 0W
Duncan, L. **62** 53 29N 77 58W
Duncan L. **64** 62 51N 113 58W
Duncan Town **75** 22 15N 75 45W
Dundalk **9** 54 1N 6 25W
Dundalk Bay **9** 53 55N 6 15W
Dundas **62** 43 17N 79 59W
Dundas, L. . . . . **47** 32 35S 121 50 E
Dundas I. **64** 54 30N 130 50W
Dundas Str. . . . . . . **46** 11 15S 131 35 E
Dundee, S. Africa . **57** 28 11S 30 15 E
Dundee, U.K. **8** 56 29N 3 0W
Dundoo . . . . **45** 27 40S 144 37 E
Dundrum **9** 54 17N 5 50W
Dundrum B. **9** 54 12N 5 40W
Dunedin, N.Z. . . . . . **43** 45 50S 170 33 E
Dunedin, U.S.A. . . . **69** 28 1N 82 45W
Dunedin → **64** 59 30N 124 5W
Dunfermline **8** 56 5N 3 28W
Dungannon **9** 54 30N 6 47W
Dungannon □ **9** 54 30N 6 55W
Dungarvan **9** 52 6N 7 40W
Dungarvan Bay . . . **9** 52 5N 7 35W
Dungeness . . . . **7** 50 54N 0 59 E
Dungo, L. do . . . . . **56** 17 15S 19 0 E
Dungog . . . . **45** 32 22S 151 46 E
Dungu . . . . **54** 3 40N 28 32 E
Dunhua . . . . **38** 43 20N 128 14 E
Dunhuang . . . . **37** 40 8N 94 36 E
Dunk I. . . . . **44** 17 59S 146 29 E
Dunkeld **8** 56 34N 3 36W
Dunkerque . . . . **12** 51 2N 2 20 E
Dunkery Beacon . . **7** 51 15N 3 37W
Dunkirk = Dunkerque . . . . . **12** 51 2N 2 20 E
Dunkirk **68** 42 30N 79 18W
Dunkwa **50** 6 0N 1 47W
Dunlap **70** 41 50N 95 36W
Dúnleary = Dun Laoghaire **9** 53 17N 6 9W
Dunmanus B. **9** 51 31N 9 50W
Dunmara . . . . **44** 16 42S 133 25 E
Dunmore **68** 41 27N 75 38W
Dunmore Hd. **9** 52 10N 10 35W
Dunn **69** 35 18N 78 36W
Dunnellon **69** 29 4N 82 28W
Dunnet Hd. **8** 58 38N 3 22W
Dunning **70** 41 52N 100 4W
Dunolly . . . . **45** 36 51S 143 44 E
Dunoon **8** 55 57N 4 56W
Dunqul . . . . **51** 23 26N 31 37 E
Duns **8** 55 47N 2 20W
Dunseith **70** 48 49N 100 2W
Dunsmuir **72** 41 10N 122 18W
Dunstable **7** 51 53N 0 31W
Dunstan Mts. . . . . . **43** 44 53S 169 35 E
Dunster **64** 53 8N 119 50W
Dunvegan L. **65** 60 8N 107 10W
Duolun . . . . **38** 42 12N 116 28 E
Dupree **70** 45 4N 101 35W
Dupuyer **72** 48 11N 112 31W
Dūrā . . . . **28** 31 31N 35 1 E
Durack → . . . . **46** 15 33S 127 52 E
Durack Range . . . . **46** 16 50S 127 40 E
Durance → . . . . . . **12** 43 55N 4 45 E
Durand **68** 42 54N 83 58W
Durango, Spain . . . **13** 43 13N 2 40W
Durango, U.S.A. . . . **73** 37 16N 107 50W
Durango □ **74** 25 0N 105 0W
Duranillin . . . . **47** 33 30S 116 45 E
Durant **71** 34 0N 96 25W
Durazno **80** 33 25S 56 31W
Durazzo = Durrësi . **19** 41 19N 19 28 E
Durban . . . . **57** 29 49S 31 1 E
Durg . . . . **33** 21 15N 81 22 E
Durgapur . . . . **33** 23 30N 87 20 E
Durham, Canada . . **62** 44 10N 80 49W
Durham, U.K. **6** 54 47N 1 34W
Durham, U.S.A. . . . **69** 36 0N 78 55W
Durham □ **6** 54 42N 1 45W
Durham Downs . . . **45** 26 6S 141 47 E
Durmitor . . . . **16** 43 10N 19 0 E
Durness **8** 58 34N 4 45W
Durrësi . . . . **19** 41 19N 19 28 E
Durrie . . . . **44** 25 40S 140 15 E
D'Urville, Tanjung . **35** 1 28S 137 54 E
D'Urville I. . . . . **43** 40 50S 173 55 E
Dusa Mareb . . . . . . **29** 5 30N 46 15 E
Dushak . . . . **24** 37 13N 60 1 E
Dushan . . . . **39** 25 48N 107 30 E
Dushanbe . . . . **24** 38 33N 68 48 E
Dusky Sd. . . . . **43** 45 47S 166 30 E
Dussejour, C. . . . . . **46** 14 45S 128 13 E
Düsseldorf . . . . **14** 51 15N 6 46 E
Dutch Harbor **60** 53 54N 166 35W
Dutlwe . . . . **56** 23 58S 23 46 E
Dutton → . . . . **44** 20 44S 143 10 E
Duwādimi . . . . **30** 24 35N 44 15 E
Duyun . . . . **39** 26 18N 107 29 E
Duzce . . . . **30** 40 50N 31 10 E
Duzdab = Zāhedān **31** 29 30N 60 50 E
Dvina, Sev. → . . . **22** 64 32N 40 30 E
Dvinsk = Daugavpils **22** 55 53N 26 32 E
Dvinskaya Guba . . **22** 65 0N 39 0 E
Dwarka . . . . **32** 22 18N 69 8 E
Dwellingup . . . . **47** 32 43S 116 4 E
Dwight **68** 41 5N 88 25W
Dyer, C. **61** 66 40N 61 0W
Dyersburg **71** 36 2N 89 20W
Dyfed □ **7** 52 0N 4 30W
Dynevor Downs . . . **45** 28 10S 144 20 E
Dysart **65** 50 57N 104 2W
Dzamin Üüd . . . . . **37** 43 50N 111 58 E
Dzerzhinsk, Byelorussian S.S.R., U.S.S.R. . . . . . . **22** 53 40N 27 1 E
Dzerzhinsk, R.S.F.S.R., U.S.S.R. . . . . . . **22** 56 14N 43 30 E
Dzhalinda . . . . **25** 53 26N 124 0 E
Dzhambul . . . . **24** 42 54N 71 22 E
Dzhankoi . . . . **23** 45 40N 34 20 E
Dzhardzhan . . . . . . **25** 68 10N 124 10 E
Dzhelinde . . . . **25** 70 0N 114 20 E
Dzhetygara . . . . . . **24** 52 11N 61 12 E
Dzhezkazgan . . . . . **24** 47 44N 67 40 E
Dzhikimde . . . . **25** 59 1N 121 47 E
Dzhizak . . . . **24** 40 6N 67 50 E
Dzhugdzur, Khrebet **25** 57 30N 138 0 E
Dzhungarskiye Vorota . . . . **24** 45 0N 82 0 E
Dzungaria = Junggar Pendi . . **37** 44 30N 86 0 E
Dzungarian Gate = Alataw Shankou . **37** 45 5N 81 57 E
Dzungarian Gates = Dzhungarskiye Vorota . . . . **24** 45 0N 82 0 E
Dzuumod . . . . **37** 47 45N 106 58 E

E

Eabamet, L. **62** 51 30N 87 46W
Eads **70** 38 30N 102 46W
Eagle, Alaska, U.S.A. **60** 64 44N 141 7W
Eagle, Colo., U.S.A. **72** 39 39N 106 55W
Eagle → **63** 53 36N 57 26W
Eagle Butt **70** 45 1N 101 12W
Eagle Grove **70** 42 37N 93 53W
Eagle L., Calif., U.S.A. **72** 40 35N 120 50W
Eagle L., Maine, U.S.A. **63** 46 23N 69 22W
Eagle Lake **71** 29 35N 96 21W
Eagle Nest **73** 36 33N 105 13W
Eagle Pass **71** 28 45N 100 35W
Eagle Pt. . . . . **46** 16 11S 124 23 E

Eagle River

Eagle River 70 45 55N 89 17W
Ealing 7 51 30N 0 19W
Earaheedy 47 25 34S 121 29 E
Earl Grey 65 50 57N 104 43W
Earle 71 35 18N 90 26W
Earlimart 73 35 53N 119 16W
Earn → 8 56 20N 3 19W
Earn, L. 8 56 23N 4 14W
Earnslaw, Mt. 43 44 32S 168 27 E
Earoo 47 29 34S 118 22 E
Earth 71 34 18N 102 30W
Easley 69 34 52N 82 35W
East Angus 63 45 30N 71 40W
East B. 71 29 2N 89 16W
East Bengal 33 24 0N 90 0 E
East Beskids = Vychodné Beskydy 15 49 30N 22 0 E
East C. 43 37 42S 178 35 E
East Chicago 68 41 40N 87 30W
East China Sea 37 30 5N 126 0 E
East Coulee 64 51 23N 112 27W
East Falkland 80 51 30S 58 30W
East Germany ■ 14 52 0N 12 0 E
East Grand Forks 70 47 55N 97 5W
East Helena 72 46 37N 111 58W
East Indies 34 0 0 120 0 E
East Jordan 68 45 10N 85 7W
East Kilbride 8 55 46N 4 10W
East Lansing 68 42 44N 84 29W
East Liverpool 68 40 39N 80 35W
East London 57 33 0S 27 55 E
East Main = Eastmain 62 52 10N 78 30W
East Orange 68 40 46N 74 13W
East Pacific Ridge 41 15 0S 110 0W
East Pakistan = Bangladesh ■ 33 24 0N 90 0 E
East Pine 64 55 48N 120 12W
East Pt. 63 46 27N 61 58W
East Point 69 33 40N 84 28W
East Retford 6 53 19N 0 55W
East St. Louis 70 38 37N 90 4W
East Schelde → = Oosterschelde 11 51 33N 4 0 E
East Siberian Sea 25 73 0N 160 0 E
East Sussex □ 7 51 0N 0 20 E
East Tawas 68 44 17N 83 31W
East Toorale 45 30 27S 145 28 E
Eastbourne, N.Z. 43 41 19S 174 55 E
Eastbourne, U.K. 7 50 46N 0 18 E
Eastend 65 49 32N 108 50W
Easter Islands 41 27 0S 109 0W
Eastern Cr. → 44 20 40S 141 35 E
Eastern Ghats 32 14 0N 78 50 E
Eastern Group = Lau 43 17 0S 178 30W
Eastern Group 47 33 30S 124 30 E
Easterville 65 53 8N 99 49W
Eastland 71 32 26N 98 45W
Eastleigh 7 50 58N 1 21W
Eastmain 62 52 10N 78 30W
Eastmain → 62 52 27N 78 26W
Eastman 69 32 13N 83 20W
Easton, Md., U.S.A. 68 38 47N 76 7W
Easton, Pa., U.S.A. 68 40 41N 75 15W
Easton, Wash., U.S.A. 72 47 14N 121 8W
Eastport 63 44 57N 67 0W
Eaton 70 40 35N 104 42W
Eatonia 65 51 13N 109 25W
Eatonton 69 33 22N 83 24W
Eau Claire 70 44 46N 91 30W
Ebagoola 44 14 15S 143 12 E
Ebbw Vale 7 51 47N 3 12W
Ebeltoft 21 56 12N 10 41 E
Eberswalde 14 52 49N 13 50 E
Eboli 18 40 39N 15 2 E
Ebolowa 54 2 55N 11 10 E
Ebro → 13 40 43N 0 54 E
Ech Cheliff 50 36 10N 1 20 E
Echo Bay, N.W.T., Canada 60 66 5N 117 55W
Echo Bay, Ont., Canada 62 46 29N 84 4W
Echoing → 65 55 51N 92 5W
Echternach 11 49 49N 6 25 E
Echuca 45 36 10S 144 20 E
Ecija 13 37 30N 5 10W
Eclipse Is. 46 13 54S 126 19 E
Ecuador ■ 78 2 0S 78 0W
Ed Dâmer 51 17 27N 34 0 E
Ed Debba 51 18 0N 30 51 E
Ed Dueim 51 14 0N 32 10 E
Edah 47 28 16S 117 10 E
Edam, Canada 65 53 11N 108 46W
Edam, Neth. 11 52 31N 5 3 E
Eday 8 59 11N 2 47W
Edd 29 14 0N 41 38 E
Eddrachillis B. 8 58 16N 5 10W
Eddystone 7 50 11N 4 16W
Eddystone Pt. 44 40 59S 148 20 E
Ede, Neth. 11 52 4N 5 40 E
Ede, Nigeria 53 7 45N 4 29 E
Édea 54 3 51N 10 9 E
Edehon L. 65 60 25N 97 15W
Eden, Australia 45 37 3S 149 55 E
Eden, N.C., U.S.A. 69 36 29N 79 53W
Eden, Tex., U.S.A. 71 31 16N 99 50W
Eden, Wyo., U.S.A. 72 42 2N 109 27W
Eden → 6 54 57N 3 2W
Eden L. 65 56 38N 100 15W
Edenburg 56 29 43S 25 58 E
Edendale 57 29 39S 30 18 E
Edenderry 9 53 21N 7 3W
Edenton 69 36 5N 76 36W
Edenville 57 27 37S 27 34 E
Edgar 70 40 25N 98 0W
Edge Hill 7 52 7N 1 28W
Edgefield 69 33 50N 81 59W
Edgeley 70 46 27N 98 41W
Edgemont 70 43 15N 103 53W
Edhessa 19 40 48N 22 5 E
Edievale 43 45 49S 169 22 E
Edina 70 40 6N 92 10W
Edinburg 71 26 22N 98 10W
Edinburgh 8 55 57N 3 12W
Edirne 30 41 40N 26 34 E
Edithburgh 45 35 5S 137 43 E
Edjudina 47 29 48S 122 23 E
Edmond 71 35 37N 97 30W
Edmonds 72 47 47N 122 22W
Edmonton, Australia 44 17 2S 145 46 E
Edmonton, Canada 64 53 30N 113 30W
Edmund L. 65 54 45N 93 17W
Edmundston 63 47 23N 68 20W
Edna 71 29 0N 96 40W
Edna Bay 64 55 55N 133 40W
Edremit 30 39 34N 27 0 E
Edson 64 53 35N 116 28W
Edward → 45 35 0S 143 30 E
Edward, L. 54 0 25S 29 40 E
Edward I. 62 48 22N 88 37W
Edwards Plateau 71 30 30N 101 5W
Edzo 64 62 49N 116 4W
Eekloo 11 51 11N 3 33 E
Ef'e, Nahal 28 31 9N 35 13 E
Effingham 68 39 8N 88 30W
Égadi, Ísole 18 37 55N 12 16 E
Eganville 62 45 32N 77 5W
Egeland 70 48 42N 99 6W
Egenolf L. 65 59 3N 100 0W
Eger = Cheb 14 50 9N 12 28 E
Eger 15 47 53N 20 27 E
Egersund 21 58 26N 6 1 E
Egg L. 65 55 5N 105 30W
Eginbah 46 20 53S 119 47 E
Egmont, C. 43 39 16S 173 45 E
Egmont, Mt. 43 39 17S 174 5 E
Eğridir 30 37 52N 30 51 E
Eğridir Gölü 30 37 53N 30 50 E
Egume 53 7 30N 7 14 E
Egvekinot 25 66 19N 179 50W
Egypt ■ 51 28 0N 31 0 E
Eha Amufu 53 6 30N 7 46 E
Ehime □ 36 33 30N 132 40 E
Eidsvold 45 25 25S 151 12 E
Eidsvoll 21 60 19N 11 14 E
Eifel 14 50 10N 6 45 E
Eigg 8 56 54N 6 10W
Eighty Mile Beach 46 19 30S 120 40 E
Eil 29 8 0N 49 50 E
Eil, L. 8 56 50N 5 15W
Eildon, L. 45 37 10S 146 0 E
Eileen L. 65 62 16N 107 37W
Einasleigh 44 18 32S 144 5 E
Einasleigh → 44 17 30S 142 17 E
Eindhoven 11 51 26N 5 30 E
Eire ■ 9 53 0N 8 0W
Eiríksjökull 20 64 46N 20 24W
Eirunepé 78 6 35S 69 53W
Eisenach 14 50 58N 10 18 E
Eisenerz 14 47 32N 14 54 E
Ekalaka 70 45 55N 104 30W
Eket 53 4 38N 7 56 E
Eketahuna 43 40 38S 175 43 E
Ekibastuz 24 51 50N 75 10 E
Ekimchan 25 53 0N 133 0W
Ekwan → 62 53 12N 82 15W
Ekwan Pt. 62 53 16N 82 7W
El Aaiún 50 27 9N 13 12W
El Aat 28 32 50N 35 45 E
El Alamein 51 30 48N 28 58 E
El Aricha 50 34 13N 1 10W
El Arīhā 28 31 52N 35 27 E
El Arish, Australia 44 17 35S 146 1 E
El 'Arîsh, Egypt 51 31 8N 33 50 E
El Asnam = Ech Cheliff 50 36 10N 1 20 E
El Bawiti 51 28 25N 28 45 E
El Bayadh 50 33 40N 1 1 E
El Bluff 75 11 59N 83 40W
El Buheirat □ 51 7 0N 30 0 E
El Cajon 73 32 49N 117 0W
El Callao 78 7 18N 61 50W
El Campo 71 29 10N 96 20W
El Centro 73 32 50N 115 40W
El Cerro 78 17 30S 61 40W
El Cuy 80 39 55S 68 25W
El Cuyo 74 21 30N 87 40W
El Dere 29 3 50N 47 8 E
El Diviso 78 1 22N 78 14W
El Djouf 50 20 0N 9 0W
El Dorado, Ark., U.S.A. 71 33 10N 92 40W
El Dorado, Kans., U.S.A. 71 37 55N 96 56W
El Dorado, Venezuela 78 6 55N 61 37W
El Escorial 13 40 35N 4 7W
El Faiyûm 51 29 19N 30 50 E
El Fâsher 51 13 33N 25 26 E
El Ferrol 13 43 29N 8 15W
El Fuerte 74 26 30N 108 40W
El Gal 29 10 58N 50 20 E
El Geteina 51 14 50N 32 27 E
El Gezira □ 51 15 0N 33 0 E
El Gîza 51 30 0N 31 10 E
El Goléa 50 30 30N 2 50 E
El Harrach 50 36 45N 3 5 E
El Iskandarîya 51 31 0N 30 0 E
El Jadida 50 33 11N 8 17W
El Jebelein 51 12 40N 32 55 E
El Kab 51 19 27N 32 46 E
El Kala 50 36 50N 8 30 E
El Kamlin 51 15 3N 33 11 E
El Kef 50 36 12N 8 47 E
El Khandaq 51 18 30N 30 30 E
El Khârga 51 25 30N 30 33 E
El Khartûm 51 15 31N 32 35 E
El Khartûm Bahrî 51 15 40N 32 31 E
El Laqâwa 51 11 25N 29 1 E
El Mafâza 51 13 38N 34 30 E
El Mahalla el Kubra 51 31 0N 31 0 E
El Mansûra 30 31 0N 31 19 E
El Minyâ 51 28 7N 30 33 E
El Obeid 51 13 8N 30 10 E
El Odaiya 51 12 8N 28 12 E
El Oro 74 19 48N 100 8W
El Oued 50 33 20N 6 58 E
El Palmito, Presa 74 25 40N 105 30W
El Paso 73 31 50N 106 30W
El Portal 73 37 44N 119 49W
El Progreso 75 15 26N 87 51W
El Pueblito 74 29 3N 105 4W
El Qâhira 51 30 1N 31 14 E
El Qantara 51 30 51N 32 20 E
El Qasr 51 25 44N 28 42 E
El Reno 71 35 30N 98 0W
El Salvador ■ 75 13 50N 89 0W
El Sauce 75 13 0N 86 40W
El Shallal 51 24 0N 32 53 E
El Suweis 51 29 58N 32 31 E
El Tigre 78 8 44N 64 15W
El Tocuyo 78 9 47N 69 48W
El Turbio 80 51 45S 72 5W
El Uqsur 51 25 41N 32 38 E
El Venado 74 22 56N 101 10W
El Vigía 78 8 38N 71 39W
El Wak 54 2 49N 40 56 E
El Wuz 51 15 0N 30 7 E
Elandsvlei 56 32 19S 19 31 E
Elat 28 29 30N 34 56 E
Elâzığ 30 38 37N 39 14 E
Elba, Italy 18 42 48N 10 15 E
Elba, U.S.A. 69 31 27N 86 4W
Elbasani 19 41 9N 20 9 E
Elbe → 14 53 50N 9 0 E
Elbert, Mt. 73 39 5N 106 27W
Elberta 68 44 35N 86 14W
Elberton 69 34 7N 82 51W
Elbeuf 12 49 17N 1 2 E
Elbidtan 30 38 13N 37 12 E
Elbing = Elbląg 15 54 10N 19 25 E
Elbląg 15 54 10N 19 25 E
Elbow 65 51 7N 106 35W
Elbrus 23 43 21N 42 30 E
Elburg 11 52 26N 5 50 E
Elburz Mts. = Alborz, Reshteh-ye Kūhhā-ye 31 36 0N 52 0 E
Elche 13 38 15N 0 42W
Elcho I. 44 11 55S 135 45 E
Eldon 70 38 20N 92 38W
Eldora 70 42 20N 93 5W
Eldorado, Canada 65 59 35N 108 30W
Eldorado, Mexico 74 24 20N 107 22W
Eldorado, Ill., U.S.A. 68 37 50N 88 25W
Eldorado, Tex., U.S.A. 71 30 52N 100 35W
Eldorado Springs 71 37 54N 93 59W
Eldoret 54 0 30N 35 17 E
Electra 71 34 0N 99 0W
Elefantes → 57 24 10S 32 40 E
Elektrostal 22 55 41N 38 32 E
Elephant Butte Res. 73 33 45N 107 30W
Eleuthera 75 25 0N 76 20W
Elgin, Canada 63 45 48N 65 10W
Elgin, U.K. 8 57 39N 3 20W
Elgin, Ill., U.S.A. 68 42 0N 88 20W
Elgin, N. Dak., U.S.A. 70 46 24N 101 46W
Elgin, Nebr., U.S.A. 70 41 58N 98 3W
Elgin, Nev., U.S.A. 73 37 21N 114 20W
Elgin, Oreg., U.S.A. 72 45 37N 118 0W
Elgin, Tex., U.S.A. 71 30 21N 97 22W
Elgon, Mt. 54 1 10N 34 30 E
Eliase 35 8 21S 130 48 E
Elida 71 33 56N 103 41W
Elim 56 34 35S 19 45 E
Elisabethville = Lubumbashi 55 11 40S 27 28 E
Elista 23 46 16N 44 14 E
Elizabeth, Australia 45 34 42S 138 41 E
Elizabeth, U.S.A. 68 40 37N 74 12W
Elizabeth City 69 36 18N 76 16W
Elizabethton 69 36 20N 82 13W
Elizabethtown 68 37 40N 85 54W
Elk City 71 35 25N 99 25W
Elk Island Nat. Park 64 53 35N 112 59W
Elk Lake 62 47 40N 80 25W
Elk Point 65 53 54N 110 55W
Elk River, Idaho, U.S.A. 72 46 50N 116 8W
Elk River, Minn., U.S.A. 70 45 17N 93 34W
Elkedra 44 21 9S 135 33 E
Elkedra → 44 21 8S 136 22 E
Elkhart, Ind., U.S.A. 68 41 42N 85 55W
Elkhart, Kans., U.S.A. 71 37 3N 101 54W
Elkhorn 65 49 59N 101 14W
Elkhorn → 70 41 7N 98 15W
Elkhovo 19 42 10N 26 40 E
Elkin 69 36 17N 80 50W
Elkins 68 38 53N 79 53W
Elko, Canada 64 49 20N 115 10W
Elko, U.S.A. 72 40 50N 115 50W
Ell, L. 47 29 13S 127 46 E
Ellendale, Australia 46 17 56S 124 48 E
Ellendale, U.S.A. 70 46 3N 98 30W
Ellensburg 72 47 0N 120 30W
Ellenville 68 41 42N 74 23W
Ellery, Mt. 45 37 28S 148 47 E
Ellesmere I. 58 79 30N 80 0W
Ellice Is. = Tuvalu ■ 3 8 0S 178 0 E
Ellinwood 70 38 27N 98 37W
Elliot, Australia 44 17 33S 133 32 E
Elliot, S. Africa 57 31 22S 27 48 E
Elliot Lake 62 46 25N 82 35W
Elliotdale = Xhora 57 31 55S 28 38 E
Ellis 70 39 0N 99 39W
Ellisville 71 31 38N 89 12W
Ellon 8 57 21N 2 5W
Ellore = Eluru 33 16 48N 81 8 E
Ells → 64 57 18N 111 40W
Ellsworth 70 38 47N 98 15W
Ellwood City 68 40 52N 80 19W
Elma, Canada 65 49 52N 95 55W
Elma, U.S.A. 72 47 0N 123 30W
Elmalı 30 36 44N 29 56 E
Elmenteita 52 0 32S 36 14 E
Elmhurst 68 41 52N 87 58W
Elmira 68 42 8N 76 49W
Elmore 45 36 30S 144 37 E
Eloy 73 32 46N 111 33W
Elrose 65 51 12N 108 0W
Elsas 62 48 32N 82 55W
Elsinore = Helsingør 21 56 2N 12 35 E
Elsinore 73 38 40N 112 2W
Eltham 43 39 26S 174 19 E
Eluru 33 16 48N 81 8 E
Elvas 13 38 50N 7 10W
Elverum 21 60 53N 11 34 E
Elvire → 46 17 51S 128 11 E
Elwood, Ind., U.S.A. 68 40 20N 85 50W
Elwood, Nebr., U.S.A. 70 40 38N 99 51W
Ely, U.K. 7 52 24N 0 16 E
Ely, Minn., U.S.A. 70 47 54N 91 52W
Ely, Nev., U.S.A. 72 39 10N 114 50W
Elyashiv 28 32 23N 34 55 E
Elyria 68 41 22N 82 8W
Emāmrūd 31 36 30N 55 0 E
Emba 24 48 50N 58 8 E
Emba → 23 46 38N 53 14 E
Embarcación 80 23 10S 64 0W
Embarras Portage 65 58 27N 111 28W
Embetsu 36 44 44N 141 47 E
Embrun 12 44 34N 6 30 E
Embu 54 0 32S 37 38 E
Emden 14 53 22N 7 12 E
'Emeq Yizre'el 28 32 35N 35 12 E
Emerald 44 23 32S 148 10 E
Emerson 65 49 0N 97 10W
Emery 73 38 59N 111 17W
Emilia-Romagna □ 18 44 33N 10 40 E
Emmeloord 11 52 44N 5 46 E
Emmen 11 52 48N 6 57 E
Emmet 44 24 45S 144 30 E
Emmetsburg 70 43 3N 94 40W
Emmett 72 43 51N 116 33W
Empalme 74 28 1N 110 49W
Empangeni 57 28 50S 31 52 E
Empedrado 80 28 0S 58 46W
Emperor Seamount Chain 40 40 0N 170 0 E
Emporia, Kans., U.S.A. 70 38 25N 96 10W
Emporia, Va., U.S.A. 69 36 41N 77 32W
Emporium 68 41 30N 78 17W
Empress 65 50 57N 110 0W
Ems → 14 53 22N 7 15 E
Emu 38 43 40N 128 6 E
Emu Park 44 23 13S 150 50 E
En Gedi 28 31 28N 35 25 E
En Gev 28 32 47N 35 38 E
En Harod 28 32 33N 35 22 E
'En Kerem 28 31 47N 35 6 E
En Nahud 51 12 45N 28 25 E
Enana 56 17 30S 16 23 E
Enaratoli 35 3 55S 136 21 E
Enard B. 8 58 5N 5 20W
Encanto, C. 35 15 45N 121 38 E
Encarnación 80 27 15S 55 50W
Encarnación de Diaz 74 21 30N 102 13W
Encinal 71 28 3N 99 25W
Encino 73 34 38N 105 40W
Encounter B. 45 35 45S 138 45 E
Ende 35 8 45S 121 40 E
Endeavour 65 52 10N 102 39W
Endeavour Str. 44 10 45S 142 0 E
Enderbury I. 40 3 8S 171 5W
Enderby 64 50 35N 119 10W
Enderby I. 46 20 35S 116 30 E
Enderlin 70 46 37N 97 41W
Endicott, N.Y., U.S.A. 68 42 6N 76 2W
Endicott, Wash., U.S.A. 72 47 0N 117 45W
Endyalgout I. 46 11 40S 132 35 E
Enez 23 40 45N 26 5 E
Enfield 7 51 39N 0 4W
Engadin 14 46 45N 10 10 E
Engaño, C., Dom. Rep. 75 18 30N 68 20W
Engaño, C., Phil. 35 18 35N 122 23 E
Engcobo 57 31 37S 28 0 E
Engels 22 51 28N 46 6 E
Engemann L. 65 58 0N 106 55W
Enggano 34 5 20S 102 40 E
Enghien 11 50 37N 4 2 E
Engkilili 34 1 3N 111 42 E
England 71 34 30N 91 58W
England □ 5 53 0N 2 0W
Englee 63 50 45N 56 5W
Englehart 62 47 49N 79 52W
Engler L. 65 59 8N 106 52W
Englewood, Colo., U.S.A. 70 39 40N 105 0W
Englewood, Kans., U.S.A. 71 37 7N 99 59W
English → 65 50 35N 93 30W
English Bazar = Ingraj Bazar 33 24 58N 88 10 E
English Channel 7 50 0N 2 0W
English River 62 49 14N 91 0W
Enid 71 36 26N 97 52W
Enkhuizen 11 52 42N 5 17 E
Enna 18 37 34N 14 15 E
Ennadai 65 61 8N 100 53W
Ennadai L. 65 61 0N 101 0W
Ennedi 51 17 15N 22 0 E
Enngonia 45 29 21S 145 50 E
Ennis, Ireland 9 52 51N 8 59W
Ennis, Mont., U.S.A. 72 45 20N 111 42W
Ennis, Tex., U.S.A. 71 32 15N 96 40W
Enniscorthy 9 52 30N 6 35W
Enniskillen 9 54 20N 7 40W
Ennistimon 9 52 56N 9 18W
Enns → 14 48 14N 14 32 E
Enontekiö 20 68 23N 23 37 E
Enping 39 22 16N 112 21 E
Enriquillo, L. 75 18 20N 72 5W
Enschede 11 52 13N 6 53 E
Ensenada 74 31 50N 116 50W
Enshi 39 30 18N 109 29 E
Entebbe 54 0 4N 32 28 E
Enterprise, Canada 64 60 47N 115 45W
Enterprise, Oreg., U.S.A. 72 45 30N 117 18W
Enterprise, Utah, U.S.A. 73 37 37N 113 36W
Entrecasteaux, Pt. d' 47 34 50S 115 56 E
Enugu 53 6 20N 7 30 E
Enugu Ezike 53 7 0N 7 29 E
Enumclaw 72 47 12N 122 0W
Éolie, Is. 18 38 30N 14 50 E
Epe, Neth. 11 52 21N 5 59 E
Epe, Nigeria 53 6 36N 3 59 E
Épernay 12 49 3N 3 56 E
Ephesus 30 37 50N 27 33 E
Ephraim 72 39 21N 111 37W
Ephrata 72 47 20N 119 32W
Épinal 12 48 10N 6 27 E

Feuilles

Epping 7 51 42N 0 8 E
Epukiro 56 21 40S 19 9 E
Equatorial Guinea ■ 54 2 0N 8 0 E
Er Rahad 51 12 45N 30 32 E
Er Rif 50 35 1N 4 1W
Er Roseires 51 11 55N 34 30 E
Erâwadī Myit → = Irrawaddy → 33 15 50N 95 6 E
Ercha 25 69 45N 147 20 E
Erciyaş Daği 30 38 30N 35 30 E
Erdao Jiang → 38 43 0N 127 0 E
Erechim 80 27 35S 52 15W
Ereğli, Konya, Turkey 30 37 31N 34 4 E
Ereğli, Zonguldak, Turkey 30 41 15N 31 30 E
Erenhot 38 43 48N 111 59 E
Eresma → 13 41 26N 40 45W
Erewadi Myitwanya 33 15 30N 95 0 E
Erfenisdam 56 28 30S 26 50 E
Erfurt 14 50 58N 11 2 E
Ergani 30 38 17N 39 49 E
Ergene → 19 41 1N 26 22 E
Ergeni Vozvyshennost 23 47 0N 44 0 E
Ergun Zuoqi 38 50 47N 121 31 E
Eriboll, L. 8 58 28N 4 41W
Érice 18 38 4N 12 34 E
Erie 68 42 10N 80 7W
Erie, L. 68 42 15N 81 0W
Erigavo 29 10 35N 47 20 E
Eriksdale 65 50 52N 98 7W
Erímanthos 19 37 57N 21 50 E
Erimo-misaki 36 41 50N 143 15 E
Eritrea □ 51 14 0N 38 30 E
Erlangen 14 49 35N 11 0 E
Erldunda 44 25 14S 133 12 E
Ermelo, Neth. 11 52 18N 5 35 E
Ermelo, S. Africa 57 26 31S 29 59 E
Ermenak 30 36 38N 33 0 E
Ermoúpolis = Síros 19 37 28N 24 57 E
Ernakulam = Cochin 32 9 59N 76 22 E
Erne → 9 54 30N 8 16W
Erne, Lough 9 54 26N 7 46W
Ernest Giles Ra. 47 27 0S 123 45 E
Erode 32 11 24N 77 45 E
Eromanga 45 26 40S 143 11 E
Erongo 56 21 39S 15 58 E
Errabiddy 47 25 25S 117 5 E
Erramala Hills 32 15 30N 78 15 E
Errigal, Mt. 9 55 2N 8 8W
Erris Hd. 9 54 19N 10 0W
Erskine 70 47 37N 96 0W
Erwin 69 36 10N 82 28W
Erzgebirge 14 50 25N 13 0 E
Erzin 25 50 15N 95 10 E
Erzincan 30 39 46N 39 30 E
Erzurum 30 39 57N 41 15 E
Es Sahrâ' Esh Sharqîya 51 27 30N 32 30 E
Es Sînâ' 51 29 0N 34 0 E
Esan-Misaki 36 41 40N 141 10 E
Esbjerg 21 55 29N 8 29 E
Escalante 73 37 47N 111 37W
Escalante → 73 37 17N 110 53W
Escalón 74 26 46N 104 20W
Escambia → 69 30 32N 87 15W
Escanaba 68 45 44N 87 5W
Esch-sur-Alzette 11 49 32N 6 0 E
Escobal 74 9 6N 80 1W
Escondido 73 33 9N 117 4W
Escuinapa 74 22 50N 105 50W
Escuintla 75 14 20N 90 48W
Eşfahān 31 33 0N 51 30 E
Esh Sham = Dimashq 30 33 30N 36 18 E
Esh Shamâlîya □ 51 19 0N 29 0 E
Eshowe 57 28 50S 31 30 E
Eshta'ol 28 31 47N 35 0 E
Esk →, Dumf. & Gall., U.K. 8 54 58N 3 4W
Esk →, N. Yorks., U.K. 6 54 27N 0 36W
Eskifjörður 20 65 3N 13 55W
Eskilstuna 21 59 22N 16 32 E
Eskimo Pt. 65 61 10N 94 15W
Eskişehir 30 39 50N 30 35 E
Esla → 13 41 29N 6 3W
Eslāmābād-e Gharb 30 34 10N 46 30 E
Esmeraldas 78 1 0N 79 40W
Espanola 62 46 15N 81 46W
Esperance 47 33 45S 121 55 E
Esperance B. 47 33 48S 121 55 E
Esperanza 80 31 29S 61 3W
Espichel, C. 13 38 22N 9 16W
Espinal 78 4 9N 74 53W
Espinazo, Sierra del = Espinhaço, Serra do 79 17 30S 43 30W
Espinhaço, Serra do 79 17 30S 43 30W
Espírito Santo □ 79 20 0S 40 45W
Espíritu Santo, B. del 74 19 15N 87 0W
Espíritu Santo, I. 74 24 30N 110 23W
Espungabera 57 20 29S 32 45 E
Esquel 80 42 55S 71 20W
Esquina 80 30 0S 59 30W
Essaouira 50 31 32N 9 42W
Essen, Belgium 11 51 28N 4 28 E
Essen, W. Germany 14 51 28N 6 59 E
Essequibo → 78 6 50N 58 30W
Essex □ 7 51 48N 0 30 E
Esslingen 14 48 43N 9 19 E
Essonne □ 12 48 30N 2 20 E
Estados, I. de Los 80 54 40S 64 30W
Estância, Brazil 79 11 16S 37 26W
Estancia, U.S.A. 73 34 50N 106 1W
Estcourt 57 29 0S 29 53 E
Estelí 75 13 9N 86 22W
Estelline, S. Dak., U.S.A. 70 44 39N 96 52W
Estelline, Tex., U.S.A. 71 34 35N 100 27W
Esterhazy 65 50 37N 102 5W
Estevan 65 49 10N 102 59W
Estevan Group 64 53 3N 129 38W
Estherville 70 43 25N 94 50W
Eston 65 51 8N 108 40W
Estonian S.S.R. □ 22 58 30N 25 30 E
Estoril 13 38 42N 9 23W
Estrada, La 13 42 43N 8 27W
Estrêla, Serra da 13 40 10N 7 45W
Estremadura 13 39 0N 9 0W
Estrondo, Serra do 79 7 20S 48 0W
Esztergom 15 47 47N 18 44 E
Eţ Ţîra 28 32 14N 34 56 E
Etadunna 45 28 43S 138 38 E
Etamamu 63 50 18N 59 59W
Etanga 56 17 55S 13 0 E
Etawah 32 26 48N 79 6 E
Etawah → 69 34 20N 84 15W
Etawney L. 65 57 50N 96 50W
Ete 53 7 2N 7 28 E
Ethel Creek 46 23 5S 120 11 E
Ethelbert 65 51 32N 100 25W
Ethiopia ■ 29 8 0N 40 0 E
Ethiopian Highlands 48 10 0N 37 0 E
Etive, L. 8 56 30N 5 12W
Etna 18 37 45N 15 0 E
Etolin I. 64 56 5N 132 20W
Etosha Pan 56 18 40S 16 30 E
Etowah 69 35 20N 84 30W
Étroits, Les 63 47 24N 68 54W
Ettrick Water 8 55 31N 2 55W
Etzatlán 74 20 48N 104 5W
Euboea = Évvoia 19 38 30N 24 0 E
Euclid 68 41 32N 81 31W
Eucumbene, L. 45 36 2S 148 40 E
Eudora 71 33 5N 91 17W
Eufaula, Ala., U.S.A. 69 31 55N 85 11W
Eufaula, Okla., U.S.A. 71 35 20N 95 33W
Eufaula, L. 71 35 15N 95 28W
Eugene 72 44 0N 123 8W
Eugowra 45 33 22S 148 24 E
Eulo 45 28 10S 145 3 E
Eunice, La., U.S.A. 71 30 35N 92 28W
Eunice, N. Mex., U.S.A. 71 32 30N 103 10W
Eupen 11 50 37N 6 3 E
Euphrates = Furāt, Nahr al → 30 31 0N 47 25 E
Eure □ 12 49 10N 1 0 E
Eure-et-Loir □ 12 48 22N 1 30 E
Eureka, Calif., U.S.A. 72 40 50N 124 0W
Eureka, Kans., U.S.A. 71 37 50N 96 20W
Eureka, Mont., U.S.A. 72 48 53N 115 6W
Eureka, Nev., U.S.A. 72 39 32N 116 2W
Eureka, S. Dak., U.S.A. 70 45 49N 99 38W
Eureka, Utah, U.S.A. 72 40 0N 112 9W
Eureka, Mt. 47 26 35S 121 35 E
Euroa 45 36 44S 145 35 E
Europa, I. 55 22 20S 40 22 E
Europa, Picos de 13 43 10N 4 49W
Europa, Pta. de 13 36 3N 5 21W
Europa Pt. = Europa, Pta. de 13 36 3N 5 21W
Europe 4 50 0N 20 0 E
Europoort 11 51 57N 4 10 E
Eustis 69 28 54N 81 36W
Eutsuk L. 64 53 20N 126 45W
Eva Downs 44 18 1S 134 52 E
Eval 28 32 15N 35 15 E
Evale 56 16 33S 15 44 E
Evans 70 40 25N 104 43W
Evans Head 45 29 7S 153 27 E
Evans L. 62 50 50N 77 0W
Evanston, Ill., U.S.A. 68 42 0N 87 40W
Evanston, Wyo., U.S.A. 72 41 10N 111 0W
Evansville, Ind., U.S.A. 68 38 0N 87 35W
Evansville, Wis., U.S.A. 70 42 47N 89 18W
Eveleth 70 47 29N 92 46W
Even Yahuda 28 32 16N 34 53 E
Evensk 25 62 12N 159 30 E
Everard, L. 45 31 30S 135 0 E
Everard Ras. 47 27 5S 132 28 E
Everest, Mt. 33 28 5N 86 58 E
Everett 72 48 0N 122 10W
Everglades 69 26 0N 80 30W
Everglades City 69 25 52N 81 23W
Everglades Nat. Park. 69 25 27N 80 53W
Evergreen 69 31 28N 86 55W
Everson 72 48 57N 122 22W
Evesham 7 52 6N 1 57W
Evinayong 54 1 26N 10 35 E
Évora 13 38 33N 7 57W
Évreux 12 49 0N 1 8 E
Évvoia 19 38 30N 24 0 E
Ewe, L. 8 57 49N 5 38W
Ewing 70 42 18N 98 22W
Ewo 54 0 48S 14 45 E
Exaltación 78 13 10S 65 20W
Excelsior Springs 70 39 20N 94 10W
Exe → 7 50 38N 3 27W
Exeter, U.K. 7 50 43N 3 31W
Exeter, Calif., U.S.A. 73 36 17N 119 9W
Exeter, Nebr., U.S.A. 70 40 43N 97 30W
Exmoor 7 51 10N 3 59W
Exmouth, Australia 46 21 54S 114 10 E
Exmouth, U.K. 7 50 37N 3 26W
Exmouth G. 46 22 15S 114 15 E
Expedition Range 44 24 30S 149 12 E
Extremadura □ 13 39 30N 6 5W
Exuma Sound 75 24 30N 76 20W
Eyasi, L. 54 3 30S 35 0 E
Eyeberry L. 65 63 8N 104 43W
Eyemouth 8 55 53N 2 5W
Eyjafjörður 20 66 15N 18 30W
Eyrarbakki 20 63 52N 21 9W
Eyre 47 32 15S 126 18 E
Eyre (North), L. 45 28 30S 137 20 E
Eyre (South), L. 45 29 18S 137 25 E
Eyre Cr. → 45 26 40S 139 0 E
Eyre Mts. 43 45 25S 168 25 E
Eyre Pen. 45 33 30S 137 17 E

F

Fabens 73 31 30N 106 8W
Fabriano 18 43 20N 12 52 E
Facatativá 78 4 49N 74 22W
Fachi 50 18 6N 11 34 E
Fada 51 17 13N 21 34 E
Fada-n-Gourma 53 12 10N 0 30 E
Faddeyevskiy, Ostrov 25 76 0N 150 0 E
Fāḍilī 30 26 55N 49 10 E
Faenza 18 44 17N 11 53 E
Fagam 53 11 1N 10 1 E
Făgăras 15 45 48N 24 58 E
Fagernes 21 60 59N 9 14 E
Fagersta 21 60 1N 15 46 E
Fagnano, L. 80 54 30S 68 0W
Fahraj 31 29 0N 59 0 E
Fahūd 31 22 18N 56 28 E
Fair Hd. 9 55 14N 6 10W
Fairbank 73 31 44N 110 12W
Fairbanks 60 64 50N 147 50W
Fairbury 70 40 5N 97 5W
Fairfax 71 36 37N 96 45W
Fairfield, Ala., U.S.A. 69 33 30N 87 0W
Fairfield, Calif., U.S.A. 72 38 14N 122 1W
Fairfield, Idaho, U.S.A. 72 43 21N 114 46W
Fairfield, Ill., U.S.A. 68 38 20N 88 20W
Fairfield, Iowa, U.S.A. 70 41 0N 91 58W
Fairfield, Mont., U.S.A. 72 47 40N 112 0W
Fairfield, Tex., U.S.A. 71 31 40N 96 0W
Fairford 65 51 37N 98 38W
Fairhope 69 30 35N 87 50W
Fairlie 43 44 5S 170 49 E
Fairmont, Minn., U.S.A. 70 43 37N 94 30W
Fairmont, W. Va., U.S.A. 68 39 29N 80 10W
Fairplay 73 39 9N 105 40W
Fairport 68 43 8N 77 29W
Fairview, Australia 44 15 31S 144 17 E
Fairview, Canada 64 56 5N 118 25W
Fairview, N. Dak., U.S.A. 70 47 49N 104 7W
Fairview, Okla., U.S.A. 71 36 19N 98 30W
Fairview, Utah, U.S.A. 72 39 50N 111 0W
Fairweather, Mt. 60 58 55N 137 45W
Faisalabad 32 31 30N 73 5 E
Faith 70 45 2N 102 4W
Faizabad 33 26 45N 82 10 E
Fajardo 75 18 20N 65 39W
Fakfak 35 3 0S 132 15 E
Faku 38 42 32N 123 21 E
Falaise 12 48 54N 0 12W
Falam 33 23 0N 93 45 E
Falcon Dam 71 26 50N 99 20W
Falfurrias 71 27 14N 98 8W
Falher 64 55 44N 117 15W
Falkenberg 21 56 54N 12 30 E
Falkirk 8 56 0N 3 47W
Falkland Is. 80 51 30S 59 0W
Falkland Sd. 80 52 0S 60 0W
Falköping 21 58 12N 13 33 E
Fall River 68 41 45N 71 5W
Fall River Mills 72 41 1N 121 30W
Fallbrook 73 33 25N 117 12W
Fallon, Mont., U.S.A. 70 46 52N 105 8W
Fallon, Nev., U.S.A. 72 39 31N 118 51W
Falls City, Nebr., U.S.A. 70 40 0N 95 40W
Falls City, Oreg., U.S.A. 72 44 54N 123 29W
Falmouth, Jamaica 75 18 30N 77 40W
Falmouth, U.K. 7 50 9N 5 5W
Falmouth, U.S.A. 68 38 40N 84 20W
False B. 56 34 15S 18 40 E
Falso, C. 75 15 12N 83 21W
Falster 21 54 45N 11 55 E
Falsterbo 21 55 23N 12 50 E
Falun 21 60 37N 15 37 E
Famagusta 30 35 8N 33 55 E
Family L. 65 51 54N 95 27W
Fan Xian 38 35 55N 115 38 E
Fandriana 57 20 14S 47 21 E
Fang Xian 39 32 3N 110 40 E
Fangchang 39 31 5N 118 4 E
Fangcheng 39 33 18N 112 59 E
Fangliao 39 22 22N 120 38 E
Fangzheng 38 49 50N 128 48 E
Fanjiatun 38 43 40N 125 0 E
Fannich, L. 8 57 40N 5 0W
Fanny Bay 64 49 37N 124 48W
Fano 18 43 50N 13 0 E
Fanshaw 64 57 11N 133 30W
Fao = Al Fāw 30 30 0N 48 30 E
Faradje 54 3 50N 29 45 E
Farafangana 57 22 49S 47 50 E
Farāh 31 32 20N 62 7 E
Farāh □ 31 32 25N 62 10 E
Farahalana 57 14 26S 50 10 E
Faranah 50 10 3N 10 45W
Farasān, Jazā'ir 29 16 45N 41 55 E
Faratsiho 57 19 24S 46 57 E
Fareham 7 50 52N 1 11W
Farewell, C. 43 40 29S 172 43 E
Farewell C. = Farvel, Kap 58 59 48N 43 55W
Fargo 70 46 52N 96 40W
Fari'a → 28 32 12N 35 27 E
Faribault 70 44 15N 93 19W
Farim 50 12 27N 15 9W
Farīmān 31 35 40N 59 49 E
Farina 45 30 3S 138 15 E
Farmerville 71 32 48N 92 23W
Farmington, N. Mex., U.S.A. 73 36 45N 108 28W
Farmington, Utah, U.S.A. 72 41 0N 111 12W
Farmville 68 37 19N 78 22W
Farnborough 7 51 17N 0 46W
Farne Is. 6 55 38N 1 37W
Faro, Brazil 79 2 10S 56 39W
Faro, Portugal 13 37 2N 7 55W
Fårö, Sweden 21 57 55N 19 5 E
Faroe Is. = Føroyar 5 62 0N 7 0W
Farquhar, C. 47 23 50S 113 36 E
Farquhar Is. 3 11 0S 52 0 E
Farrar → 8 57 30N 4 30W
Farrars Cr. → 44 25 35S 140 43 E
Farrāshband 31 28 57N 52 5 E
Farrell 68 41 13N 80 29W
Farrell Flat 45 33 48S 138 48 E
Farrukhabad-cum-Fatehgarh 32 27 30N 79 32 E
Fārs □ 31 29 30N 55 0 E
Fársala 19 39 17N 22 23 E
Farsund 21 58 5N 6 55 E
Fartak, Râs 30 28 5N 34 34 E
Farvel, Kap 58 59 48N 43 55W
Farwell 71 34 25N 103 0W
Faryab 32 28 7N 57 14 E
Fāryāb □ 31 36 0N 65 0 E
Fasā 31 29 0N 53 39 E
Fastnet Rock 9 51 22N 9 37W
Fatagar, Tanjung 35 2 46S 131 57 E
Fatehgarh 32 27 25N 79 35 E
Fatehpur, Raj., India 32 28 0N 74 40 E
Fatehpur, Ut. P., India 33 25 56N 81 13 E
Fatima 63 47 24N 61 53W
Faulkton 70 45 4N 99 8W
Faure I. 47 25 52S 113 50 E
Fauresmith 56 29 44S 25 17 E
Fauske 20 67 17N 15 25 E
Favara 18 37 19N 13 39 E
Favignana 18 37 56N 12 18 E
Favourable Lake 62 52 50N 93 39W
Fawn → 62 55 20N 87 35W
Faxaflói 20 64 29N 23 0W
Faya-Largeau 51 17 58N 19 6 E
Fayd 30 27 1N 42 52 E
Fayette, Ala., U.S.A. 69 33 40N 87 50W
Fayette, Mo., U.S.A. 70 39 10N 92 40W
Fayetteville, Ark., U.S.A. 71 36 0N 94 5W
Fayetteville, N.C., U.S.A. 69 35 0N 78 58W
Fayetteville, Tenn., U.S.A. 69 35 8N 86 30W
Fazilka 32 30 27N 74 2 E
Fdérik 50 22 40N 12 45W
Feale → 9 52 26N 9 40W
Fear, C. 69 33 51N 78 0W
Feather → 72 38 47N 121 36W
Featherston 43 41 6S 175 20 E
Fécamp 12 49 45N 0 22 E
Fehmarn 14 54 26N 11 10 E
Fehmarn Bælt 14 54 35N 11 20 E
Fei Xian 39 35 18N 117 59 E
Feilding 43 40 13S 175 35 E
Feira de Santana 79 12 15S 38 57W
Feldkirch 14 47 15N 9 37 E
Felipe Carrillo Puerto 74 19 38N 88 3W
Felixstowe 7 51 58N 1 22 E
Femunden 20 62 10N 11 53 E
Fen He → 38 35 36N 110 42 E
Feng Xian, Jiangsu, China 39 34 43N 116 35 E
Feng Xian, Shaanxi, China 39 33 54N 106 40 E
Fengcheng, Jiangxi, China 39 28 12N 115 48 E
Fengcheng, Liaoning, China 38 40 28N 124 5 E
Fengdu 39 29 55N 107 41 E
Fengfeng 38 36 28N 114 8 E
Fenghua 39 29 40N 121 25 E
Fenghuang 39 27 57N 109 29 E
Fengjie 39 31 5N 109 36 E
Fengkai 39 23 24N 111 30 E
Fengle 39 31 29N 112 29 E
Fengning 38 41 10N 116 33 E
Fengtai 38 39 50N 116 18 E
Fengxian 39 30 55N 121 26 E
Fengxiang 39 34 29N 107 25 E
Fengxin 39 28 41N 115 18 E
Fengyang 39 32 51N 117 29 E
Fengzhen 38 40 25N 113 2 E
Fenit 9 52 17N 9 51W
Fennimore 70 42 58N 90 41W
Fenoarivo Afovoany 57 18 26S 46 34 E
Fenoarivo Atsinanana 57 17 22S 49 25 E
Fens, The 6 52 45N 0 2 E
Fenton 68 42 47N 83 44W
Fenyang 38 37 18N 111 48 E
Feodosiya 23 45 2N 35 28 E
Ferdows 31 33 58N 58 2 E
Ferfer 29 5 4N 45 9 E
Fergana 24 40 23N 71 19 E
Fergus 62 43 43N 80 24W
Fergus Falls 70 46 18N 96 7W
Ferland 62 50 19N 88 27W
Fermanagh □ 9 54 21N 7 40W
Fermoy 9 52 4N 8 18W
Fernandina Beach 69 30 40N 81 30W
Fernando de Noronha 79 4 0S 33 10W
Fernando Póo = Bioko 53 3 30N 8 40 E
Ferndale, Calif., U.S.A. 72 40 37N 124 12W
Ferndale, Wash., U.S.A. 72 48 51N 122 41W
Fernie 64 49 30N 115 5W
Fernlees 44 23 51S 148 7 E
Fernley 72 39 36N 119 14W
Ferozepore = Firozpur 32 30 55N 74 40 E
Ferrara 18 44 50N 11 36 E
Ferreñafe 78 6 42S 79 50W
Ferriday 71 31 35N 91 33W
Ferron 73 39 3N 111 3W
Ferryland 63 47 2N 52 53W
Fertile 70 47 31N 96 18W
Fès 50 34 0N 5 0W
Feshi 54 6 8S 18 10 E
Fessenden 70 47 42N 99 38W
Fethiye 30 36 36N 29 10 E
Fetlar 8 60 36N 0 52W
Feuilles → 61 58 47N 70 4W

Feyzābād

Feyzābād **31** 37 7N 70 33 E
Fezzan **51** 27 0N 15 0 E
Ffestiniog **6** 52 58N 3 56W
Fianarantsoa **57** 21 26S 47 5 E
Fianarantsoa □ **57** 19 30S 47 0 E
Fianga **51** 9 55N 15 9 E
Fichtelgebirge **14** 50 10N 12 0 E
Ficksburg **57** 28 51S 27 53 E
Fiditi **53** 7 45N 3 53 E
Field **62** 46 31N 80 1W
Field → **44** 23 48S 138 0 E
Field I. **46** 12 5S 132 23 E
Fife □ **8** 56 13N 3 2W
Fife Ness **8** 56 17N 2 35W
Figeac **12** 44 37N 2 2 E
Figueira da Foz **13** 40 7N 8 54W
Figueras **13** 42 18N 2 58 E
Figuig **50** 32 5N 1 11W
Fihaonana **57** 18 36S 47 12 E
Fiherenana **57** 18 29S 48 24 E
Fiherenana → **57** 23 19S 43 37 E
Fiji ■ **43** 17 20S 179 0 E
Filer **72** 42 30N 114 35W
Filey **6** 54 13N 0 18W
Filiatrá **19** 37 9N 21 35 E
Filipstad **21** 59 43N 14 9 E
Fillmore, Canada **65** 49 50N 103 25W
Fillmore, Calif., U.S.A. **73** 34 23N 118 58W
Fillmore, Utah, U.S.A. **73** 38 58N 112 20W
Filyos → **30** 41 35N 32 10 E
Findhorn → **8** 57 38N 3 38W
Findlay **68** 41 0N 83 41W
Finger L. **65** 53 33N 93 30W
Fíngõe **55** 14 55S 31 50 E
Finike **30** 36 21N 30 10 E
Finistère □ **12** 48 20N 4 0W
Finisterre, C. **13** 42 50N 9 19W
Finke **44** 25 34S 134 35 E
Finke → **45** 27 0S 136 10 E
Finland ■ **22** 63 0N 27 0 E
Finland, G. of **22** 60 0N 26 0 E
Finlay → **64** 57 0N 125 10W
Finley, Australia **45** 35 38S 145 35 E
Finley, U.S.A. **70** 47 35N 97 50W
Finn → **9** 54 50N 7 55W
Finnigan, Mt. **44** 15 49S 145 17 E
Finniss, C. **45** 33 8S 134 51 E
Finnmark fylke □ **20** 69 30N 25 0 E
Fiora → **18** 42 20N 11 35 E
Fiq **28** 32 46N 35 41 E
Fire River **62** 48 47N 83 21W
Firebag → **65** 57 45N 111 21W
Firedrake L. **65** 61 25N 104 30W
Firenze **18** 43 47N 11 15 E
Firozabad **32** 27 10N 78 25 E
Firozpur **32** 30 55N 74 40 E
Fīrūzābād **31** 28 52N 52 35 E
Fīrūzkūh **31** 35 50N 52 50 E
Firvale **64** 52 27N 126 13W
Fish →, Namibia **56** 28 7S 17 10 E
Fish →, S. Africa **56** 31 30S 20 16 E
Fisher **47** 30 30S 131 0 E
Fisher B. **65** 51 35N 97 13W
Fishguard **7** 51 59N 4 59W
Fishing L. **65** 52 10N 95 24W
Fitchburg **68** 42 35N 71 47W
Fitri, L. **51** 12 50N 17 28 E
Fitz Roy **80** 47 0S 67 0W
Fitzgerald, Canada **64** 59 51N 111 36W
Fitzgerald, U.S.A. **69** 31 45N 83 16W
Fitzmaurice → **46** 14 45S 130 5 E
Fitzroy →, Queens., Australia **44** 23 32S 150 52 E
Fitzroy →, W. Austral., Australia **46** 17 31S 123 35 E
Fitzroy Crossing **46** 18 9S 125 38 E
Fiume = Rijeka **18** 45 20N 14 21 E
Fizi **54** 4 17S 28 55 E
Flagler **70** 39 20N 103 4W
Flagstaff **73** 35 10N 111 40W
Flaherty I. **62** 56 15N 79 15W
Flåm **21** 60 50N 7 7 E
Flambeau → **70** 45 18N 91 15W
Flamborough Hd. **6** 54 8N 0 4W
Flaming Gorge Dam **72** 40 50N 109 46W
Flaming Gorge Res. **72** 41 15N 109 30W
Flamingo, Teluk **35** 5 30S 138 0 E
Flanders = West-Vlaanderen □ **11** 51 0N 3 0 E
Flandre Occidentale □ = West-Vlaanderen □ **11** 51 0N 3 0 E
Flandre Orientale □ = Oost-Vlaanderen □ **11** 51 5N 3 50 E
Flandreau **70** 44 5N 96 38W
Flåsjön **20** 64 5N 15 40 E
Flat → **64** 61 33N 125 18W
Flat River **71** 37 50N 90 30W
Flatey, Barðastrandarsýsla, Iceland **20** 66 10N 17 52W
Flatey, Suður-þingeyjarsýsla, Iceland **20** 65 22N 22 56W
Flathead L. **72** 47 50N 114 0W
Flattery, C., Australia **44** 14 58S 145 21 E
Flattery, C., U.S.A. **72** 48 21N 124 43W
Flaxton **70** 48 52N 102 24W
Fleetwood **6** 53 55N 3 1W
Flekkefjord **21** 58 18N 6 39 E
Flensburg **14** 54 46N 9 28 E
Flesko, Tanjung **35** 0 29N 124 30 E
Fletton **7** 52 34N 0 13W
Flin Flon **65** 54 46N 101 53W
Flinders → **44** 17 36S 140 36 E
Flinders B. **47** 34 19S 115 19 E
Flinders Group **44** 14 11S 144 15 E
Flinders I. **44** 40 0S 148 0 E
Flinders Ranges **45** 31 30S 138 30 E
Flinders Reefs **44** 17 37S 148 31 E
Flint, U.K. **6** 53 15N 3 7W
Flint, U.S.A. **68** 43 5N 83 40W
Flint → **69** 30 52N 84 38W
Flint, I. **41** 11 26S 151 48W
Flinton **45** 27 55S 149 32 E
Flodden **6** 55 37N 2 8W
Floodwood **70** 46 55N 92 55W
Flora **68** 38 40N 88 30W
Florala **69** 31 0N 86 20W
Florence = Firenze **18** 43 47N 11 15 E
Florence, Ala., U.S.A. **69** 34 50N 87 40W
Florence, Ariz., U.S.A. **73** 33 0N 111 25W
Florence, Colo., U.S.A. **70** 38 26N 105 0W
Florence, Oreg., U.S.A. **72** 44 0N 124 3W
Florence, S.C., U.S.A. **69** 34 12N 79 44W
Florence, L. **45** 28 53S 138 9 E
Florennes **11** 50 15N 4 35 E
Florenville **11** 49 40N 5 19 E
Flores, Guat. **75** 16 59N 89 50W
Flores, Indonesia **35** 8 35S 121 0 E
Flores I. **64** 49 20N 126 10W
Flores Sea **34** 6 30S 124 0 E
Floresville **71** 29 10N 98 10W
Floriano **79** 6 50S 43 0W
Florianópolis **80** 27 30S 48 30W
Florida, Cuba **75** 21 32N 78 14W
Florida, Uruguay **80** 34 7S 56 10W
Florida □ **69** 28 30N 82 0W
Florida, Straits of **75** 25 0N 80 0W
Florida B. **75** 25 0N 81 20W
Florida Keys **75** 25 0N 80 40W
Florø **21** 61 35N 5 1 E
Flower's Cove **63** 51 14N 56 46W
Floydada **71** 33 58N 101 18W
Fluk **35** 1 42S 127 44 E
Flushing = Vlissingen **11** 51 26N 3 34 E
Fly → **40** 8 25S 143 0 E
Foam Lake **65** 51 40N 103 32W
Fogang **39** 23 52N 113 30 E
Fóggia **18** 41 28N 15 31 E
Foggo **53** 11 21N 9 57 E
Fogo **63** 49 43N 54 17W
Fogo I. **63** 49 40N 54 5W
Foix **12** 42 58N 1 38 E
Folda, Nord-Trøndelag, Norway **20** 64 41N 10 50 E
Folda, Nordland, Norway **20** 67 38N 14 50 E
Foleyet **62** 48 15N 82 25W
Folgefonn **21** 60 3N 6 23 E
Folkestone **7** 51 5N 1 11 E
Folkston **69** 30 55N 82 0W
Follett **71** 36 30N 100 12W
Follette, La **69** 36 23N 84 9W
Fond-du-Lac, Canada **65** 59 19N 107 12W
Fond du Lac, U.S.A. **70** 43 46N 88 26W
Fond-du-Lac → **65** 59 17N 106 0W
Fonseca, G. de **75** 13 10N 87 40W
Fontainebleau **12** 48 24N 2 40 E
Fontas → **64** 58 14N 121 48W
Fonte Boa **78** 2 33S 66 0W
Fontenay-le-Comte **12** 46 28N 0 48W
Fontur **20** 66 23N 14 32W
Foochow = Fuzhou **39** 26 5N 119 16 E
Foping **39** 33 41N 108 0 E
Forbes **45** 33 22S 148 0 E
Ford's Bridge **45** 29 41S 145 29 E
Fordyce **71** 33 50N 92 20W
Forécariah **50** 9 28N 13 10W
Foremost **64** 49 26N 111 34W
Forest **71** 32 21N 89 27W
Forest City, Iowa, U.S.A. **70** 43 12N 93 39W
Forest City, N.C., U.S.A. **69** 35 23N 81 50W
Forest Grove **72** 45 31N 123 4W
Forestburg **64** 52 35N 112 1W
Forestier Pen. **44** 43 0S 148 0 E
Forestville, Canada **63** 48 48N 69 2W
Forestville, U.S.A. **68** 44 41N 87 29W
Forez, Mts. du **12** 45 40N 3 50 E
Forfar **8** 56 40N 2 53W
Forks **72** 47 56N 124 23W
Forlì **18** 44 14N 12 2 E
Forman **70** 46 9N 97 43W
Formby Pt. **6** 53 33N 3 7W
Formentera **13** 38 43N 1 27 E
Formosa = Taiwan ■ **39** 23 30N 121 0 E
Formosa **80** 26 15S 58 10W
Formosa, Serra **79** 12 0S 55 0W
Formosa Bay **54** 2 40S 40 20 E
Føroyar **5** 62 0N 7 0W
Forres **8** 57 37N 3 38W
Forrest, Vic., Australia **45** 38 33S 143 47 E
Forrest, W. Austral., Australia **47** 30 51S 128 6 E
Forrest, Mt. **47** 24 48S 127 45 E
Forrest City **71** 35 0N 90 50W
Forsayth **44** 18 33S 143 34 E
Forster **45** 32 12S 152 31 E
Forsyth, Ga., U.S.A. **69** 33 4N 83 55W
Forsyth, Mont., U.S.A. **72** 46 14N 106 37W
Fort Albany **62** 52 15N 81 35W
Fort Amador **74** 8 56N 79 32W
Fort Apache **73** 33 50N 110 0W
Fort Assiniboine **64** 54 20N 114 45W
Fort Augustus **8** 57 9N 4 40W
Fort Beaufort **56** 32 46S 26 40 E
Fort Benton **72** 47 50N 110 40W
Fort Bragg **72** 39 28N 123 50W
Fort Bridger **72** 41 22N 110 20W
Fort Chipewyan **65** 58 42N 111 8W
Fort Clayton **74** 9 0N 79 35W
Fort Collins **70** 40 30N 105 4W
Fort-Coulonge **62** 45 50N 76 45W
Fort Davis, Panama **74** 9 17N 79 56W
Fort Davis, U.S.A. **71** 30 38N 103 53W
Fort-de-France **75** 14 36N 61 2W
Fort de Possel = Possel **54** 5 5N 19 10 E
Fort Defiance **73** 35 47N 109 4W
Fort Dodge **70** 42 29N 94 10W
Fort Frances **65** 48 36N 93 24W
Fort Franklin **60** 65 10N 123 30W
Fort Garland **73** 37 28N 105 30W
Fort George **62** 53 50N 79 0W
Fort Good-Hope **60** 66 14N 128 40W
Fort Hancock **73** 31 19N 105 56W
Fort Hertz = Putao **33** 27 28N 97 30 E
Fort Hope **62** 51 30N 88 0W
Fort Jameson = Chipata **55** 13 38S 32 28 E
Fort Kent **63** 47 12N 68 30W
Fort Klamath **72** 42 45N 122 0W
Fort Lallemand **50** 31 13N 6 17 E
Fort-Lamy = Ndjamena **51** 12 10N 14 59 E
Fort Laramie **70** 42 15N 104 30W
Fort Lauderdale **69** 26 10N 80 5W
Fort Liard **64** 60 14N 123 30W
Fort Liberté **75** 19 42N 71 51W
Fort Lupton **70** 40 8N 104 48W
Fort Mackay **64** 57 12N 111 41W
Fort McKenzie **63** 57 20N 69 0W
Fort Macleod **64** 49 45N 113 30W
Fort MacMahon **50** 29 43N 1 45 E
Fort McMurray **64** 56 44N 111 7W
Fort McPherson **60** 67 30N 134 55W
Fort Madison **70** 40 39N 91 20W
Fort Meade **69** 27 45N 81 45W
Fort Miribel **50** 29 25N 2 55 E
Fort Morgan **70** 40 10N 103 50W
Fort Myers **69** 26 39N 81 51W
Fort Nelson **64** 58 50N 122 44W
Fort Nelson → **64** 59 32N 124 0W
Fort Norman **60** 64 57N 125 30W
Fort Payne **69** 34 25N 85 44W
Fort Peck **72** 48 1N 106 30W
Fort Peck Dam **72** 48 0N 106 38W
Fort Peck L. **72** 47 40N 107 0W
Fort Pierce **69** 27 29N 80 19W
Fort Pierre **70** 44 25N 100 25W
Fort Portal **54** 0 40N 30 20 E
Fort Providence **64** 61 3N 117 40W
Fort Qu'Appelle **65** 50 45N 103 50W
Fort Randolph **74** 9 23N 79 53W
Fort Resolution **64** 61 10N 113 40W
Fort Roseberry = Mansa **54** 11 13S 28 55 E
Fort Rupert **62** 51 30N 78 40W
Fort St. James **64** 54 30N 124 10W
Fort St. John **64** 56 15N 120 50W
Fort Sandeman **32** 31 20N 69 31 E
Fort Saskatchewan **64** 53 40N 113 15W
Fort Scott **71** 37 50N 94 40W
Fort Severn **62** 56 0N 87 40W
Fort Sherman **74** 9 22N 79 56W
Fort Shevchenko **23** 43 40N 51 20 E
Fort-Sibut **51** 5 46N 19 10 E
Fort Simpson **64** 61 45N 121 15W
Fort Smith, Canada **64** 60 0N 111 51W
Fort Smith, U.S.A. **71** 35 25N 94 25W
Fort Stanton **73** 33 33N 105 36W
Fort Stockton **71** 30 54N 102 54W
Fort Sumner **71** 34 24N 104 16W
Fort Trinquet = Bir Mogrein **50** 25 10N 11 25W
Fort Valley **69** 32 33N 83 52W
Fort Vermilion **64** 58 24N 116 0W
Fort Walton Beach **69** 30 25N 86 40W
Fort Wayne **68** 41 5N 85 10W
Fort William **8** 56 48N 5 8W
Fort Worth **71** 32 45N 97 25W
Fort Yates **70** 46 8N 100 38W
Fort Yukon **60** 66 35N 145 20W
Fortaleza **79** 3 45S 38 35W
Forteau **63** 51 28N 56 58W
Forth, Firth of **8** 56 5N 2 55W
Fortrose **8** 57 35N 4 10W
Fortuna, Calif., U.S.A. **72** 40 38N 124 8W
Fortuna, N. Dak., U.S.A. **70** 48 55N 103 48W
Fortune B. **63** 47 30N 55 22W
Forūr **31** 26 20N 54 30 E
Foshan **39** 23 4N 113 5 E
Fossil **72** 45 0N 120 9W
Fossilbrook **44** 17 47S 144 29 E
Fosston **70** 47 33N 95 39W
Foster → **65** 55 47N 105 49W
Fosters Ra. **44** 21 35S 133 48 E
Fostoria **68** 41 8N 83 25W
Fougamou **54** 1 16S 10 30 E
Fougères **12** 48 21N 1 14W
Foul Pt. **32** 8 35N 81 18 E
Foulness I. **7** 51 36N 0 55 E
Foulpointe **57** 17 41S 49 31 E
Foumban **53** 5 45N 10 50 E
Fountain, Colo., U.S.A. **70** 38 42N 104 40W
Fountain, Utah, U.S.A. **72** 39 41N 111 37W
Fourchu **63** 45 43N 60 17W
Fouriesburg **56** 28 38S 28 14 E
Fouta Djalon **50** 11 20N 12 10W
Foux, Cap-à- **75** 19 43N 73 27W
Foveaux Str. **43** 46 42S 168 10 E
Fowey **7** 50 20N 4 39W
Fowler, Calif., U.S.A. **73** 36 41N 119 41W
Fowler, Colo., U.S.A. **70** 38 10N 104 0W
Fowler, Kans., U.S.A. **71** 37 28N 100 7W
Fowlers B. **47** 31 59S 132 34 E
Fowlerton **71** 28 26N 98 50W
Fownhope **7** 52 0N 2 37W
Fox → **65** 56 3N 93 18W
Fox Valley **65** 50 30N 109 25W
Foxe Basin **61** 66 0N 77 0W
Foxe Chan. **61** 65 0N 80 0W
Foxe Pen. **61** 65 0N 76 0W
Foxpark **72** 41 4N 106 6W
Foxton **43** 40 29S 175 18 E
Foyle, Lough **9** 55 6N 7 8W
Foynes **9** 52 37N 9 5W
Fóz do Cunene **56** 17 15S 11 48 E
Foz do Gregório **78** 6 47S 70 44W
Foz do Iguaçu **80** 25 30S 54 30W
Franca **79** 20 33S 47 30W
Francavilla Fontana **19** 40 32N 17 35 E
France ■ **12** 47 0N 3 0 E
Frances **45** 36 41S 140 55 E
Frances → **64** 60 16N 129 10W
Frances L. **64** 61 23N 129 30W
Franceville **54** 1 40S 13 32 E
Franche-Comté **12** 46 50N 5 55 E
Francisco I. Madero, Coahuila, Mexico **74** 25 48N 103 18W
Francisco I. Madero, Durango, Mexico **74** 24 32N 104 22W
Francistown **57** 21 7S 27 33 E
François, Canada **63** 47 35N 56 45W
François, Mart. **75** 14 38N 60 57W
François L. **64** 54 0N 125 30W
Franeker **11** 53 12N 5 33 E
Frankfort, S. Africa **57** 27 17S 28 30 E
Frankfort, Ind., U.S.A. **68** 40 20N 86 33W
Frankfort, Kans., U.S.A. **70** 39 42N 96 26W
Frankfort, Ky., U.S.A. **68** 38 12N 84 52W
Frankfort, Mich., U.S.A. **68** 44 38N 86 14W
Frankfurt am Main **14** 50 7N 8 40 E
Frankfurt an der Oder **14** 52 50N 14 31 E
Fränkische Alb **14** 49 20N 11 30 E
Frankland → **47** 35 0S 116 48 E
Franklin, Ky., U.S.A. **69** 36 40N 86 30W
Franklin, La., U.S.A. **71** 29 45N 91 30W
Franklin, N.H., U.S.A. **68** 43 28N 71 39W
Franklin, Nebr., U.S.A. **70** 40 9N 98 55W
Franklin, Pa., U.S.A. **68** 41 22N 79 45W
Franklin, Tenn., U.S.A. **69** 35 54N 86 53W
Franklin, Va., U.S.A. **69** 36 40N 76 58W
Franklin, W. Va., U.S.A. **68** 38 38N 79 21W
Franklin, L. **72** 40 20N 115 26W
Franklin B. **60** 69 45N 126 0W
Franklin D. Roosevelt L. **72** 48 30N 118 16W
Franklin Mts. **60** 65 0N 125 0W
Franklin Str. **60** 72 0N 96 0W
Franklinton **71** 30 53N 90 10W
Franks Peak **72** 43 50N 109 5W
Frankston **45** 38 8S 145 8 E
Frantsa Iosifa, Zemlya **24** 82 0N 55 0 E
Franz **62** 48 25N 84 30W
Franz Josef Land = Frantsa Iosifa, Zemlya **24** 82 0N 55 0 E
Fraser →, B.C., Canada **64** 49 7N 123 11W
Fraser →, Nfld., Canada **63** 56 39N 62 10W
Fraser, Mt. **47** 25 35S 118 20 E
Fraser I. **45** 25 15S 153 10 E
Fraser Lake **64** 54 0N 124 50W
Fraserburg **56** 31 55S 21 30 E
Fraserburgh **8** 57 41N 2 0W
Fraserdale **62** 49 55N 81 37W
Fray Bentos **80** 33 10S 58 15W
Frazier Downs **46** 18 48S 121 42 E
Fredericia **21** 55 34N 9 45 E
Frederick, Md., U.S.A. **68** 39 25N 77 23W
Frederick, Okla., U.S.A. **71** 34 22N 99 0W
Frederick, S. Dak., U.S.A. **70** 45 55N 98 29W
Frederick Sd. **64** 57 10N 134 0W
Fredericksburg, Tex., U.S.A. **71** 30 17N 98 55W
Fredericksburg, Va., U.S.A. **68** 38 16N 77 29W
Frederickstown **71** 37 35N 90 15W
Fredericton **63** 45 57N 66 40W
Fredericton Junc. **63** 45 41N 66 40W
Frederikshavn **21** 57 28N 10 31 E
Fredonia, Ariz., U.S.A. **73** 36 59N 112 36W
Fredonia, Kans., U.S.A. **71** 37 34N 95 50W
Fredonia, N.Y., U.S.A. **68** 42 26N 79 20W
Fredrikstad **21** 59 13N 10 57 E
Freels, C. **63** 49 15N 53 30W
Freeman **70** 43 25N 97 20W
Freeport, Bahamas **75** 26 30N 78 47W
Freeport, Canada **63** 44 15N 66 20W
Freeport, Ill., U.S.A. **70** 42 18N 89 40W
Freeport, N.Y., U.S.A. **68** 40 39N 73 35W
Freeport, Tex., U.S.A. **71** 28 55N 95 22W
Freetown **50** 8 30N 13 17W
Frégate, L. **62** 53 15N 74 45W
Freiburg **14** 48 0N 7 52 E
Freire **80** 38 54S 72 38W
Freising **14** 48 24N 11 47 E
Freistadt **14** 48 30N 14 30 E
Fréjus **12** 43 25N 6 44 E
Fremantle **47** 32 7S 115 47 E
Fremont, Calif., U.S.A. **73** 37 32N 122 1W
Fremont, Mich., U.S.A. **68** 43 29N 85 59W
Fremont, Nebr., U.S.A. **70** 41 30N 96 30W
Fremont, Ohio, U.S.A. **68** 41 20N 83 5W
Fremont → **73** 38 15N 110 20W
Fremont, L. **72** 43 0N 109 50W
French Cr. → **68** 41 22N 79 50W
French Guiana ■ **79** 4 0N 53 0W
French Polynesia □ **41** 20 0S 145 0 E
French Terr. of Afars & Issas = Djibouti ■ **29** 12 0N 43 0 E
Frenchglen **72** 42 48N 119 0W
Frenchman → **72** 48 24N 107 5W
Frenchman Butte **65** 53 35N 109 38W
Frenchman Creek → **70** 40 13N 100 50W
Fresco → **79** 7 15S 51 30W
Fresnillo **74** 23 10N 103 0W

Gerede

Fresno **73** 36 47N 119 50W
Fresno Res. **72** 48 40N 110 0W
Frew → **44** 20 0S 135 38 E
Frewena **44** 19 25S 135 25 E
Freycinet Pen. **44** 42 10S 148 25 E
Fria, C. **56** 18 0S 12 0 E
Frías **80** 28 40S 65 5W
Friedrichshafen **14** 47 39N 9 29 E
Friendly, Is. = Tonga ■ **43** 19 50S 174 30W
Friesland □ **11** 53 5N 5 50 E
Frijoles **74** 9 11N 79 48W
Frio → **71** 28 30N 98 10W
Friona **71** 34 40N 102 42W
Frisian Is. **4** 53 30N 6 0 E
Fritch **71** 35 40N 101 35W
Friuli-Venezia Giulia □ **18** 46 0N 13 0 E
Frobisher B. **61** 62 30N 66 0W
Frobisher Bay **61** 63 44N 68 31W
Frobisher L. **65** 56 20N 108 15W
Frohavet **20** 63 50N 9 35 E
Froid **70** 48 20N 104 29W
Fromberg **72** 42 25N 108 58W
Frome **7** 51 16N 2 17W
Frome, L. **45** 30 45S 139 45 E
Frome Downs **45** 31 13S 139 45 E
Front Range **72** 40 0N 105 40W
Front Royal **68** 38 55N 78 10W
Frontera **74** 18 30N 92 40W
Frosinone **18** 41 38N 13 20 E
Frostburg **68** 39 43N 78 57W
Frostisen **20** 68 14N 17 10 E
Frøya **20** 63 43N 8 40 E
Frunze **24** 42 54N 74 46 E
Frutal **79** 20 0S 49 0W
Frýdek-Místek **15** 49 40N 18 20 E
Fu Xian, Liaoning, China **38** 39 38N 121 58 E
Fu Xian, Shaanxi, China **38** 36 0N 109 20 E
Fucheng **38** 37 50N 116 10 E
Fuchou = Fuzhou **39** 26 5N 119 16 E
Fuchū **36** 34 34N 133 14 E
Fuchuan **39** 24 50N 111 5 E
Fuchun Jiang → **39** 30 5N 120 5 E
Fuding **39** 27 20N 120 12 E
Fuente Ovejuna **13** 38 15N 5 25W
Fuentes de Oñoro **13** 40 33N 6 52W
Fuerte → **74** 25 50N 109 25W
Fuerte Olimpo **78** 21 0S 57 51W
Fuerteventura **50** 28 30N 14 0W
Fugløysund **20** 70 15N 20 20 E
Fugou **39** 34 3N 114 25 E
Fuhai **37** 47 2N 87 25 E
Fuji **36** 35 9N 138 39 E
Fuji-no-miya **36** 35 10N 138 40 E
Fuji-San **36** 35 22N 138 44 E
Fujian □ **39** 26 0N 118 0 E
Fujin **38** 47 16N 132 1 E
Fujisawa **36** 35 22N 139 29 E
Fukien = Fujian □ **39** 26 0N 118 0 E
Fukuchiyama **36** 35 19N 135 9 E
Fukue-Shima **36** 32 40N 128 45 E
Fukui **36** 36 0N 136 10 E
Fukui □ **36** 36 0N 136 12 E
Fukuoka **36** 33 39N 130 21 E
Fukuoka □ **36** 33 30N 131 0 E
Fukushima **36** 37 44N 140 28 E
Fukushima □ **36** 37 30N 140 15 E
Fukuyama **36** 34 35N 133 20 E
Fulda **14** 50 32N 9 41 E
Fulda → **14** 51 27N 9 40 E
Fuling **39** 29 40N 107 20 E
Fullerton, Calif., U.S.A. **73** 33 52N 117 58W
Fullerton, Nebr., U.S.A. **70** 41 25N 98 0W
Fulton, Mo., U.S.A. **70** 38 50N 91 55W
Fulton, N.Y., U.S.A. **68** 43 20N 76 22W
Fulton, Tenn., U.S.A. **69** 36 31N 88 53W
Funabashi **36** 35 45N 140 0 E
Funafuti **40** 8 30S 179 0 E
Funchal **50** 32 38N 16 54W
Fundación **78** 10 31N 74 11W
Fundão **13** 40 8N 7 30W
Fundy, B. of **63** 45 0N 66 0W
Funing, Jiangsu, China **39** 33 45N 119 50 E
Funing, Yunnan, China **39** 23 35N 105 45 E
Funiu Shan **39** 33 30N 112 20 E
Funtua **53** 11 30N 7 18 E
Fuping **38** 38 48N 114 12 E
Fuqing **39** 25 41N 119 21 E
Furāt, Nahr al → **30** 31 0N 47 25 E
Furneaux Group **44** 40 10S 147 50 E
Furness **6** 54 12N 3 10W
Fürth **14** 49 29N 11 0 E
Fury and Hecla Str. **61** 69 56N 84 0W
Fusagasuga **78** 4 21N 74 22W
Fushan **38** 37 30N 121 15 E
Fushun **38** 41 50N 123 56 E
Fusong **38** 42 20N 127 15 E
Fusui **39** 22 40N 107 56 E
Futuna **43** 14 25S 178 20 E
Fuxin **38** 42 5N 121 48 E
Fuyang, Anhui, China **39** 33 0N 115 48 E
Fuyang, Zhejiang, China **39** 30 5N 119 57 E
Fuyu **38** 45 12N 124 43 E
Fuyuan **38** 48 20N 134 5 E
Fuzhou **39** 26 5N 119 16 E
Fylde **6** 53 50N 2 58W
Fyn **21** 55 20N 10 30 E
Fyne, L. **8** 56 0N 5 20W

G

Gaanda **53** 10 10N 12 27 E
Gabela **54** 11 0S 14 24 E
Gabès **50** 33 53N 10 2 E
Gabès, G. de **51** 34 0N 10 30 E
Gabon ■ **54** 0 10S 10 0 E
Gaborone **56** 24 45S 25 57 E
Gabrovo **19** 42 52N 25 19 E
Gachsārān **31** 30 15N 50 45 E
Gadag **32** 15 30N 75 45 E
Gadarwara **32** 22 50N 78 50 E
Gadhada **32** 22 0N 71 35 E
Gadsden, Ala., U.S.A. **69** 34 1N 86 0W
Gadsden, Ariz., U.S.A. **73** 32 35N 114 47W
Gadwal **32** 16 10N 77 50 E
Gaffney **69** 35 3N 81 40W
Gafsa **50** 34 24N 8 43 E
Gagetown **63** 45 46N 66 10W
Gagnoa **50** 6 56N 5 16W
Gagnon **63** 51 50N 68 5W
Gagnon, L. **65** 62 3N 110 27W
Gai Xian **38** 40 22N 122 20 E
Gail **71** 32 48N 101 25W
Gainesville, Fla., U.S.A. **69** 29 38N 82 20W
Gainesville, Ga., U.S.A. **69** 34 17N 83 47W
Gainesville, Mo., U.S.A. **71** 36 35N 92 26W
Gainesville, Tex., U.S.A. **71** 33 40N 97 10W
Gainsborough **6** 53 23N 0 46W
Gairdner L. **45** 31 30S 136 0 E
Gairloch, L. **8** 57 43N 5 45W
Galangue **55** 13 42S 16 9 E
Galápagos **41** 0 0 89 0W
Galashiels **8** 55 37N 2 50W
Galaţi **15** 45 27N 28 2 E
Galatina **19** 40 10N 18 10 E
Galax **69** 36 42N 80 57W
Galbraith **44** 16 25S 141 30 E
Galcaio **29** 6 30N 47 30 E
Galdhøpiggen **21** 61 38N 8 18 E
Galela **35** 1 50N 127 49 E
Galesburg **70** 40 57N 90 23W
Galich **22** 58 23N 42 12 E
Galicia □ **13** 42 43N 7 45W
Galilee = Hagalil **28** 32 53N 35 18 E
Galilee, L. **44** 22 20S 145 50 E
Galilee, Sea of = Yam Kinneret **28** 32 45N 35 35 E
Galiuro Mts. **73** 32 40N 110 30W
Gallabat **51** 12 58N 36 11 E
Gallatin **69** 36 24N 86 27W
Galle **32** 6 5N 80 10 E
Gállego → **13** 41 39N 0 51W
Gallegos → **80** 51 35S 69 0W
Galley Hd. **9** 51 32N 8 56W
Gallinas, Pta. **78** 12 28N 71 40W
Gallipoli = Gelibolu **30** 40 28N 26 43 E
Gallípoli **19** 40 8N 18 0 E
Gallipolis **68** 38 50N 82 10W
Gällivare **20** 67 9N 20 40 E
Galloway **8** 55 0N 4 25W
Galloway, Mull of **8** 54 38N 4 50W
Gallup **73** 35 30N 108 45W
Gal'on **28** 31 38N 34 51 E
Galong **45** 34 37S 148 34 E
Galoya **32** 8 10N 80 55 E
Galty Mts. **9** 52 22N 8 10W
Galtymore **9** 52 22N 8 12W
Galula **52** 8 40S 33 0 E
Galva **70** 41 10N 90 0W
Galveston **71** 29 15N 94 48W
Galveston B. **71** 29 30N 94 50W
Gálvez **80** 32 0S 61 14W
Galway **9** 53 16N 9 4W
Galway □ **9** 53 16N 9 3W
Galway B. **9** 53 10N 9 20W
Gambaga **53** 10 30N 0 28W
Gambela **51** 8 14N 34 38 E
Gambia ■ **50** 13 25N 16 0W
Gambia → **50** 13 28N 16 34W
Gambier, C. **46** 11 56S 130 57 E
Gambier Is. **45** 35 3S 136 30 E
Gamboa **74** 9 8N 79 42W
Gamboma **54** 1 55S 15 52 E
Gamerco **73** 35 33N 108 56W
Gamlakarleby = Kokkola **20** 63 50N 23 8 E
Gammon → **65** 51 24N 95 44W
Gan Jiang → **37** 29 15N 116 0 E
Gan Shemu'el **28** 32 28N 34 56 E
Gan Yavne **28** 31 48N 34 42 E
Ganado, Ariz., U.S.A. **73** 35 46N 109 41W
Ganado, Tex., U.S.A. **71** 29 4N 96 31W
Gananoque **62** 44 20N 76 10W
Ganaveh **31** 29 35N 50 35 E
Gancheng **39** 18 51N 108 37 E
Gand = Gent **11** 51 2N 3 42 E
Ganda **55** 13 3S 14 35 E
Gandak → **33** 25 39N 85 13 E
Gandava **32** 28 32N 67 32 E
Gander **63** 48 58N 54 35W
Gander L. **63** 48 58N 54 35W
Gandhi Sagar **32** 24 40N 75 40 E
Gandi **53** 12 55N 5 49 E
Ganedidalem = Gani **35** 0 48S 128 14 E
Ganga → **33** 23 20N 90 30 E
Ganganagar **32** 29 56N 73 56 E
Gangara **53** 14 35N 8 29 E
Gangaw **33** 22 5N 94 5 E
Gangdisê Shan **33** 31 20N 81 0 E
Ganges = Ganga → **33** 23 20N 90 30 E
Gangtok **33** 27 20N 88 37 E
Gani **35** 0 48S 128 14 E
Gannett Pk. **72** 43 15N 109 38W
Gannvalley **70** 44 3N 98 57W
Ganquan **38** 36 20N 109 20 E
Gansu □ **38** 36 0N 104 0 E
Ganta **50** 7 15N 8 59W
Gantheaume, C. **45** 36 4S 137 32 E
Gantheaume B. **47** 27 40S 114 10 E
Ganyem **35** 2 46S 140 12 E
Ganyu **39** 34 50N 119 8 E
Ganzhou **39** 25 51N 114 56 E
Gao'an **39** 28 26N 115 17 E
Gaomi **38** 36 20N 119 42 E
Gaoping **38** 35 45N 112 55 E
Gaoua **50** 10 20N 3 8W
Gaoual **50** 11 45N 13 25W
Gaoxiong **39** 22 38N 120 18 E
Gaoyou **39** 32 47N 119 26 E
Gaoyou Hu **39** 32 45N 119 20 E
Gaoyuan **38** 37 8N 117 58 E
Gap **12** 44 33N 6 5 E
Gar **37** 32 10N 79 58 E
Garachiné **75** 8 0N 78 12W
Garanhuns **79** 8 50S 36 30W
Garawe **50** 4 35N 8 0W
Garber **71** 36 30N 97 36W
Garberville **72** 40 11N 123 50W
Gard **29** 9 30N 49 6 E
Gard □ **12** 44 2N 4 10 E
Garda, L. di **18** 45 40N 10 40 E
Garde L. **65** 62 50N 106 13W
Garden City, Kans., U.S.A. **71** 38 0N 100 45W
Garden City, Tex., U.S.A. **71** 31 52N 101 28W
Garden Grove **73** 33 47N 117 55W
Gardēz **31** 33 37N 69 9 E
Gardiner **72** 45 3N 110 42W
Gardner **68** 42 35N 72 0W
Gardner Canal **64** 53 27N 128 8W
Gardnerville **72** 38 59N 119 47W
Garfield **72** 47 3N 117 8W
Gargano, Mte. **18** 41 43N 15 43 E
Garibaldi Prov. Park **64** 49 50N 122 40W
Garies **56** 30 32S 17 59 E
Garigliano → **18** 41 13N 13 44 E
Garissa **52** 0 25S 39 40 E
Garland **72** 41 47N 112 10W
Garm **24** 39 0N 70 20 E
Garmsār **31** 35 20N 52 25 E
Garner **70** 43 4N 93 37W
Garnett **70** 38 18N 95 12W
Garoe **29** 8 25N 48 33 E
Garonne → **12** 45 2N 0 36W
Garoua **53** 9 19N 13 21 E
Garrison, Mont., U.S.A. **72** 46 30N 112 56W
Garrison, N. Dak., U.S.A. **70** 47 39N 101 27W
Garrison, Tex., U.S.A. **71** 31 50N 94 28W
Garrison Res. = Sakakawea, L. **70** 47 30N 102 0W
Garry → **8** 56 47N 3 47W
Garry L. **60** 65 58N 100 18W
Garsen **54** 2 20S 40 5 E
Garson L. **65** 56 19N 110 2W
Garub **56** 26 37S 16 0 E
Garut **35** 7 14S 107 53 E
Garvie Mts. **43** 45 30S 168 50 E
Garwa = Garoua **53** 9 19N 13 21 E
Gary **68** 41 35N 87 20W
Garzê **37** 31 39N 99 58 E
Garzón **78** 2 10N 75 40W
Gasan Kuli **24** 37 40N 54 20 E
Gascogne **12** 43 45N 0 20 E
Gascogne, G. de **12** 44 0N 2 0W
Gascony = Gascogne **12** 43 45N 0 20 E
Gascoyne → **47** 24 52S 113 37 E
Gascoyne Junc. T.O. **47** 25 2S 115 17 E
Gashaka **53** 7 20N 11 29 E
Gashua **53** 12 54N 11 0 E
Gaspé **63** 48 52N 64 30W
Gaspé, C. de **63** 48 48N 64 7W
Gaspé, Pén. de **63** 48 45N 65 40W
Gaspésie, Parc Prov. de la **63** 48 55N 65 50W
Gassaway **68** 38 42N 80 43W
Gastonia **69** 35 17N 81 10W
Gastre **80** 42 20S 69 15W
Gata, C. de **13** 36 41N 2 13W
Gata, Sierra de **13** 40 20N 6 45W
Gataga → **64** 58 35N 126 59W
Gateshead **6** 54 57N 1 37W
Gatesville **71** 31 29N 97 45W
Gâtinais **12** 48 5N 2 40 E
Gatineau → **62** 45 27N 75 42W
Gatineau, Parc de la **62** 45 40N 76 0W
Gatun **74** 9 16N 79 55W
Gatun, L. **75** 9 7N 79 56W
Gatun Dam **74** 9 16N 79 55W
Gatun Locks **74** 9 16N 79 55W
Gatyana **57** 32 16S 28 31 E
Gau **43** 18 2S 179 18 E
Gauer L. **65** 57 0N 97 50W
Gauhati **33** 26 10N 91 45 E
Gaula → **20** 63 21N 10 14 E
Gausta, Mt. **21** 59 48N 8 40 E
Gavāter **31** 25 10N 61 31 E
Gävleborgs län □ **21** 61 30N 16 15 E
Gawachab **56** 27 4S 17 55 E
Gawilgarh Hills **32** 21 15N 76 45 E
Gawler **45** 34 30S 138 42 E
Gaxun Nur **37** 42 22N 100 30 E
Gay **22** 51 27N 58 27 E
Gaya, India **33** 24 47N 85 4 E
Gaya, Niger **53** 11 52N 3 28 E
Gaylord **68** 45 1N 84 41W
Gayndah **45** 25 35S 151 32 E
Gaza **28** 31 30N 34 28 E
Gaza □ **57** 23 10S 32 45 E
Gaza Strip **28** 31 29N 34 25 E
Gazaoua **53** 13 32N 7 55 E
Gaziantep **30** 37 6N 37 23 E
Gazli **24** 40 14N 63 24 E
Gboko **53** 7 17N 9 4 E
Gbongan **53** 7 28N 4 20 E
Gcuwa **57** 32 20S 28 11 E
Gdańsk **15** 54 22N 18 40 E
Gdańska, Zatoka **15** 54 30N 19 20 E
Gdov **22** 58 48N 27 55 E
Gdynia **15** 54 35N 18 33 E
Ge'a **28** 31 38N 34 37 E
Gebe **35** 0 5N 129 25 E
Gebeit Mine **51** 21 3N 36 29 E
Gebel Mûsa **30** 28 32N 33 59 E
Gedaref **51** 14 2N 35 28 E
Gede, Tanjung **34** 6 46S 105 12 E
Gedera **28** 31 49N 34 46 E
Gedser **21** 54 35N 11 55 E
Geelong **45** 38 10S 144 22 E
Geelvink Chan. **47** 28 30S 114 0 E
Geidam **51** 12 57N 11 57 E
Geikie → **65** 57 45N 103 52W
Geili **51** 16 1N 32 37 E
Geita **54** 2 48S 32 12 E
Gejiu **37** 23 20N 103 10 E
Gela **18** 37 6N 14 18 E
Geladi **29** 6 59N 46 30 E
Gelderland □ **11** 52 5N 6 10 E
Geldermalsen **11** 51 53N 5 17 E
Geldrop **11** 51 25N 5 32 E
Geleen **11** 50 57N 5 49 E
Gelehun **50** 8 20N 11 40W
Gelibolu **30** 40 28N 26 43 E
Gelsenkirchen **14** 51 30N 7 5 E
Gemas **34** 2 37N 102 36 E
Gembloux **11** 50 34N 4 43 E
Gemena **54** 3 13N 19 48 E
Gemerek **30** 39 15N 36 10 E
Gen He → **38** 50 16N 119 32 E
Gendringen **11** 51 52N 6 21 E
General Acha **80** 37 20S 64 38W
General Alvear, Buenos Aires, Argentina **80** 36 0S 60 0W
General Alvear, Mendoza, Argentina **80** 35 0S 67 40W
General Artigas **80** 26 52S 56 16W
General Belgrano **80** 36 35S 58 47W
General Guido **80** 36 40S 57 50W
General Juan Madariaga **80** 37 0S 57 0W
General La Madrid **80** 37 17S 61 20W
General MacArthur **35** 11 18N 125 28 E
General Martin Miguel de Güemes **80** 24 50S 65 0W
General Paz **80** 27 45S 57 36W
General Pico **80** 35 45S 63 50W
General Pinedo **80** 27 15S 61 20W
General Santos **35** 6 5N 125 14 E
General Trías **74** 28 21N 106 22W
General Villegas **80** 35 0S 63 0W
Genesee **72** 46 31N 116 59W
Genesee → **68** 43 16N 77 36W
Geneseo, Ill., U.S.A. **70** 41 25N 90 10W
Geneseo, Kans., U.S.A. **70** 38 32N 98 8W
Geneva = Genève **14** 46 12N 6 9 E
Geneva, Ala., U.S.A. **69** 31 2N 85 52W
Geneva, N.Y., U.S.A. **68** 42 53N 77 0W
Geneva, Nebr., U.S.A. **70** 40 35N 97 35W
Geneva, Ohio, U.S.A. **68** 41 49N 80 58W
Geneva, L. = Léman, Lac **14** 46 26N 6 30 E
Geneva, L. **68** 42 38N 88 30W
Genève **14** 46 12N 6 9 E
Genil → **13** 37 42N 5 19W
Genk **11** 50 58N 5 32 E
Gennargentu, Mti. del **18** 40 0N 9 10 E
Gennep **11** 51 41N 5 59 E
Genoa = Génova **18** 44 24N 8 56 E
Genoa, Australia **45** 37 29S 149 35 E
Genoa, U.S.A. **70** 41 31N 97 44W
Génova **18** 44 24N 8 56 E
Génova, G. di **18** 44 0N 9 0 E
Gent **11** 51 2N 3 42 E
Geographe B. **47** 33 30S 115 15 E
Geographe Chan. **47** 24 30S 113 0 E
Georga, Zemlya **24** 80 30N 49 0 E
George **56** 33 58S 22 29 E
George → **63** 58 49N 66 10W
George, L., N.S.W., Australia **45** 35 10S 149 25 E
George, L., S. Austral., Australia **45** 37 25S 140 0 E
George, L., W. Austral., Australia **46** 22 45S 123 40 E
George, L., Uganda **54** 0 5N 30 10 E
George, L., U.S.A. **69** 29 15N 81 35W
George River = Port Nouveau-Québec **61** 58 30N 65 59W
George Sound **43** 44 52S 167 25 E
George Town, Australia **44** 41 5S 146 49 E
George Town, Bahamas **75** 23 33N 75 47W
George Town, Malaysia **34** 5 25N 100 15 E
George West **71** 28 18N 98 5W
Georgetown, Australia **44** 18 17S 143 33 E
Georgetown, Ont., Canada **62** 43 40N 79 56W
Georgetown, P.E.I., Canada **63** 46 13N 62 24W
Georgetown, Gambia **50** 13 30N 14 47W
Georgetown, Guyana **78** 6 50N 58 12W
Georgetown, Colo., U.S.A. **72** 39 46N 105 49W
Georgetown, Ky., U.S.A. **68** 38 13N 84 33W
Georgetown, Ohio, U.S.A. **68** 38 50N 83 50W
Georgetown, S.C., U.S.A. **69** 33 22N 79 15W
Georgetown, Tex., U.S.A. **71** 30 40N 97 45W
Georgia □ **69** 32 0N 82 0W
Georgia, Str. of **64** 49 25N 124 0W
Georgian B. **62** 45 15N 81 0W
Georgian S.S.R. □ **23** 42 0N 43 0 E
Georgievsk **23** 44 12N 43 28 E
Georgina → **44** 23 30S 139 47 E
Georgina Downs **44** 21 10S 137 40 E
Georgiu-Dezh **23** 51 3N 39 30 E
Gera **14** 50 53N 12 11 E
Geraardsbergen **11** 50 45N 3 53 E
Geral, Serra **80** 26 25S 50 0W
Geral de Goiás, Serra **79** 12 0S 46 0W
Geraldine **72** 47 36N 110 18W
Geraldton, Australia **47** 28 48S 114 32 E
Geraldton, Canada **62** 49 44N 86 59W
Gerede **30** 40 45N 32 10 E

Gypsumville

Grande, B. 80 50 30S 68 20W
Grande, La 72 45 15N 118 0W
Grande Baie 63 48 19N 70 52W
Grande Baleine, R. de la → 62 55 16N 77 47W
Grande Cache 64 53 53N 119 8W
Grande de Santiago → ... 74 21 20N 105 50W
Grande-Entrée 63 47 30N 61 40W
Grande Prairie 64 55 10N 118 50W
Grande-Rivière 63 48 26N 64 30W
Grande-Vallée 63 49 14N 65 8W
Grandes-Bergeronnes 63 48 16N 69 35W
Grandfalls 71 31 21N 102 51W
Grandoe Mines ... 64 56 29N 129 54W
Grandview 72 46 13N 119 58W
Grange, La, Ga., U.S.A. 69 33 4N 85 0W
Grange, La, Ky., U.S.A. 68 38 20N 85 20W
Grange, La, Tex., U.S.A. 71 29 54N 96 52W
Grangemouth 8 56 1N 3 43W
Granger, Wash., U.S.A. 72 46 25N 120 5W
Granger, Wyo., U.S.A. 72 41 35N 109 58W
Grangeville 72 45 57N 116 4W
Granite City 70 38 45N 90 3W
Granite Falls 70 44 45N 95 35W
Granite Peak ..... 47 25 40S 121 20 E
Granite Pk. 72 45 8N 109 52W
Granity .... 43 41 39S 171 51 E
Granja 79 3 7S 40 50W
Granja de Torrehermosa ... 13 38 19N 5 35W
Granollers .... 13 41 39N 2 18 E
Grant 70 40 53N 101 42W
Grant, I. .... 46 11 10S 132 52 E
Grant, Mt. 72 38 34N 118 48W
Grant City 70 40 30N 94 25W
Grant Range Mts. . 73 38 30N 115 30W
Grantham 6 52 55N 0 39W
Grantown-on-Spey 8 57 19N 3 36W
Grants 73 35 14N 107 51W
Grants Pass 72 42 30N 123 22W
Grantsburg 70 45 46N 92 44W
Grantsville 72 40 35N 112 32W
Granville, France .. 12 48 50N 1 35W
Granville, N. Dak., U.S.A. 70 48 18N 100 48W
Granville, N.Y., U.S.A. 68 43 24N 73 16W
Granville L. 65 56 18N 100 30W
Grapeland 71 31 30N 95 31W
Gras, L. de 60 64 30N 110 30W
Graskop .... 57 24 56S 30 49 E
Grass → 65 56 3N 96 33W
Grass Range 72 47 0N 109 0W
Grass River Prov. Park 65 54 40N 100 50W
Grass Valley, Calif., U.S.A. 72 39 18N 121 0W
Grass Valley, Oreg., U.S.A. 72 45 22N 120 48W
Grasse .... 12 43 38N 6 56 E
Grassmere .... 45 31 24S 142 38 E
Gravelbourg 65 49 50N 106 35W
's-Gravenhage .... 11 52 7N 4 17 E
Gravesend, Australia 45 29 35S 150 20 E
Gravesend, U.K. .. 7 51 25N 0 22 E
Gravois, Pointe-à- . 75 16 15N 73 56W
Grayling 68 44 40N 84 42W
Grayling → 64 59 21N 125 0W
Grays Harbor 72 46 55N 124 8W
Grays L. 72 43 8N 111 30W
Grayson 65 50 45N 102 40W
Graz .... 14 47 4N 15 27 E
Greasy L. 64 62 55N 122 12W
Great Abaco I. 75 26 25N 77 10W
Great Australia Basin .... 44 26 0S 140 0 E
Great Australian Bight .... 47 33 30S 130 0 E
Great Bahama Bank 75 23 15N 78 0W
Great Barrier I. .... 43 36 11S 175 25 E
Great Barrier Reef . 44 18 0S 146 50 E
Great Basin 72 40 0N 116 30W
Great Bear → ... 60 65 0N 124 0W
Great Bear L. 60 65 30N 120 0W
Great Bend 70 38 25N 98 55W
Great Blasket I. ... 9 52 5N 10 30W
Great Britain 4 54 0N 2 15W
Great Central 64 49 20N 125 10W
Great Dividing Ra. . 44 23 0S 146 0 E
Great Exuma I. 75 23 30N 75 50W
Great Falls, Canada 65 50 27N 96 1W
Great Falls, U.S.A. . 72 47 27N 111 12W
Great Fish → = Groot Vis → ... 56 33 28S 27 5 E
Great Guana Cay .. 75 24 0N 76 20W
Great Harbour Deep 63 50 25N 56 32W
Great Inagua I. 75 21 0N 73 20W
Great Indian Desert = Thar Desert .. 32 28 0N 72 0 E
Great I. 65 58 53N 96 35W
Great Karoo ...... 56 31 55S 21 0 E
Great Lake .... 44 41 50S 146 40 E
Great Orme's Head 6 53 20N 3 52W
Great Ouse → ... 6 52 47N 0 22 E
Great Palm I. ..... 44 18 45S 146 40 E
Great Plains 58 47 0N 105 0W
Great Ruaha → .. 54 7 56S 37 52 E
Great Saint Bernard P. = Grand St-Bernard, Col du . 14 45 50N 7 10 E
Great Salt Lake ... 72 41 0N 112 30W
Great Salt Lake Desert 72 40 20N 113 50W
Great Salt Plains Res. 71 36 40N 98 15W
Great Sandy Desert 46 21 0S 124 0 E
Great Slave L. 64 61 23N 115 38W
Great Smoky Mts. Nat. Park 69 35 39N 83 30W
Great Stour = Stour → ...... 7 51 15N 1 20 E
Great Victoria Desert 47 29 30S 126 30 E
Great Wall .... 38 38 30N 109 30 E
Great Whernside .. 6 54 9N 1 59W
Great Yarmouth ... 6 52 40N 1 45 E
Greater Antilles ... 75 17 40N 74 0W
Greater London □ . 7 51 30N 0 5W
Greater Manchester □ .. 6 53 30N 2 15W
Greater Sunda Is. . 34 7 0S 112 0 E
Gredos, Sierra de . 13 40 20N 5 0W
Greece ■ .... 19 40 0N 23 0 E
Greeley, Colo., U.S.A. 70 40 30N 104 40W
Greeley, Nebr., U.S.A. 70 41 36N 98 32W
Green →, Ky., U.S.A. 68 37 54N 87 30W
Green →, Utah, U.S.A. 73 38 11N 109 53W
Green B. 68 45 0N 87 30W
Green Bay 68 44 30N 88 0W
Green C. .... 45 37 13S 150 1 E
Green Cove Springs 69 29 59N 81 40W
Green Hd. .... 47 30 5S 114 56 E
Green Island ...... 43 45 55S 170 26 E
Green River 73 38 59N 110 10W
Greenbush 70 48 46N 96 10W
Greencastle 68 39 40N 86 48W
Greenfield, Ind., U.S.A. 68 39 47N 85 51W
Greenfield, Iowa, U.S.A. 70 41 18N 94 28W
Greenfield, Mass., U.S.A. 68 42 38N 72 38W
Greenfield, Miss., U.S.A. 71 37 28N 93 50W
Greenland ■ 2 66 0N 45 0W
Greenock 8 55 57N 4 46W
Greenore 9 54 2N 6 8W
Greenore Pt. 9 52 15N 6 20W
Greenough → ... 47 28 51S 114 38 E
Greensboro, Ga., U.S.A. 69 33 34N 83 12W
Greensboro, N.C., U.S.A. 69 36 7N 79 46W
Greensburg, Ind., U.S.A. 68 39 20N 85 30W
Greensburg, Kans., U.S.A. 71 37 38N 99 20W
Greensburg, Pa., U.S.A. 68 40 18N 79 31W
Greenville, Liberia . 50 5 1N 9 6W
Greenville, Ala., U.S.A. 69 31 50N 86 37W
Greenville, Calif., U.S.A. 72 40 8N 120 57W
Greenville, Ill., U.S.A. 70 38 53N 89 22W
Greenville, Maine, U.S.A. 63 45 30N 69 32W
Greenville, Mich., U.S.A. 68 43 12N 85 14W
Greenville, Miss., U.S.A. 71 33 25N 91 0W
Greenville, N.C., U.S.A. 69 35 37N 77 26W
Greenville, Ohio, U.S.A. 68 40 5N 84 38W
Greenville, Pa., U.S.A. 68 41 23N 80 22W
Greenville, S.C., U.S.A. 69 34 54N 82 24W
Greenville, Tenn., U.S.A. 69 36 13N 82 51W
Greenville, Tex., U.S.A. 71 33 5N 96 5W
Greenwater Lake Prov. Park 65 52 32N 103 30W
Greenwich .... 7 51 28N 0 0 E
Greenwood, Canada 64 49 10N 118 40W
Greenwood, Miss., U.S.A. 71 33 30N 90 4W
Greenwood, S.C., U.S.A. 69 34 13N 82 13W
Greenwood, Mt. ... 46 13 48S 130 4 E
Gregory 70 43 14N 99 20W
Gregory → ...... 44 17 53S 139 17 E
Gregory, L., S. Austral., Australia ...... 45 28 55S 139 0 E
Gregory, L., W. Austral., Australia ...... 47 25 38S 119 58 E
Gregory Downs ... 44 18 35S 138 45 E
Gregory Ra., Queens., Australia 44 19 30S 143 40 E
Gregory Ra., W. Austral., Australia ...... 46 21 20S 121 12 E
Greifswald .... 14 54 6N 13 23 E
Gremikha .... 22 67 50N 39 40 E
Grenada 71 33 45N 89 50W
Grenada ■ 75 12 10N 61 40W
Grenadines 75 12 40N 61 20W
Grenen .... 21 57 44N 10 40 E
Grenfell, Australia . 45 33 52S 148 8 E
Grenfell, Canada .. 65 50 30N 102 56W
Grenoble .... 12 45 12N 5 42 E
Grenora 70 48 38N 103 54W
Grenville, C. ...... 44 12 0S 143 13 E
Grenville Chan. ... 64 53 40N 129 46W
Gresham 72 45 30N 122 25W
Gresik .... 35 7 13S 112 38 E
Gretna Green 8 55 0N 3 3W
Grevenmacher ..... 11 49 41N 6 26 E
Grey → .... 43 42 27S 171 12 E
Grey, C. .... 44 13 0S 136 35 E
Grey Range ...... 45 27 0S 143 30 E
Grey Res. 63 48 20N 56 30W
Greybull 72 44 30N 108 3W
Greymouth .... 43 42 29S 171 13 E
Greytown, N.Z. .... 43 41 5S 175 29 E
Greytown, S. Africa 57 29 1S 30 36 E
Gribbell I. 64 53 23N 129 0W
Gridley 72 39 27N 121 47W
Griekwastad ...... 56 28 49S 23 15 E
Griffin 69 33 17N 84 14W
Griffith .... 45 34 18S 146 2 E
Grimari .... 51 5 43N 20 6 E
Grimsby 6 53 35N 0 5W
Grímsey 20 66 33N 18 0W
Grimshaw 64 56 10N 117 40W
Grimstad .... 21 58 22N 8 35 E
Grinnell 70 41 45N 92 43W
Gris-Nez, C. ...... 12 50 52N 1 35 E
Groais I. 63 50 55N 55 35W
Groblersdal ...... 57 25 15S 29 25 E
Grodno .... 22 53 42N 23 52 E
Grodzisk Wielkopolski .... 14 52 15N 16 22 E
Groesbeck 71 31 32N 96 34W
Grójec .... 15 51 50N 20 58 E
Grong .... 20 64 25N 12 8 E
Groningen .... 11 53 15N 6 35 E
Groningen □ ..... 11 53 16N 6 40 E
Groom 71 35 12N 100 59W
Groot → .... 56 33 45S 24 36 E
Groot Berg → ... 56 32 47S 18 8 E
Groot-Brakrivier ... 56 34 2S 22 18 E
Groot-Kei → .... 57 32 41S 28 22 E
Groot Vis → ..... 56 33 28S 27 5 E
Groote Eylandt .... 44 14 0S 136 40 E
Grootfontein ...... 56 19 31S 18 6 E
Grootlaagte → .. 56 20 55S 21 27 E
Grootvloer .... 56 30 0S 20 40 E
Gros C. 64 61 59N 113 32W
Gross Glockner ... 14 47 5N 12 40 E
Grossenhain ...... 14 51 17N 13 32 E
Grosseto .... 18 42 45N 11 7 E
Groswater B. 63 54 20N 57 40W
Groton 70 45 27N 98 6W
Grouard Mission .. 64 55 33N 116 9W
Groundhog → .. 62 48 45N 82 58W
Grouse Creek 72 41 44N 113 57W
Groveton, N.H., U.S.A. 68 44 34N 71 30W
Groveton, Tex., U.S.A. 71 31 5N 95 4W
Groznyy .... 23 43 20N 45 45 E
Grudziądz .... 15 53 30N 18 47 E
Grundy Center 70 42 22N 92 45W
Gruver 71 36 19N 101 20W
Gryazi .... 22 52 30N 39 58 E
Gua .... 33 22 18N 85 20 E
Guacanayabo, G. de 75 20 40N 77 20W
Guadalajara, Mexico 74 20 40N 103 20W
Guadalajara, Spain 13 40 37N 3 12W
Guadalcanal ...... 40 9 32S 160 12 E
Guadalete → 13 36 35N 6 13W
Guadalhorce → .. 13 36 41N 4 27W
Guadalquivir → .. 13 36 47N 6 22W
Guadalupe = Guadeloupe ■ .. 75 16 20N 61 40W
Guadalupe 73 34 59N 120 33W
Guadalupe → ... 71 28 30N 96 53W
Guadalupe, Sierra de 13 39 28N 5 30W
Guadalupe Bravos . 74 31 20N 106 10W
Guadalupe I. 41 29 0N 118 50W
Guadalupe Pk. 73 31 50N 105 30W
Guadarrama, Sierra de 13 41 0N 4 0W
Guadeloupe ■ 75 16 20N 61 40W
Guadeloupe Passage 75 16 50N 62 15W
Guadiana → 13 37 14N 7 22W
Guadix 13 37 18N 3 11W
Guafo, Boca del .. 80 43 35S 74 0W
Guaíra 80 24 5S 54 10W
Guaira, La 78 10 36N 66 56W
Guaitecas, Is. 80 44 0S 74 30W
Guajará-Mirim 78 10 50S 65 20W
Guajira, Pen. de la . 78 12 0N 72 0W
Gualeguay 80 33 10S 59 14W
Gualeguaychú 80 33 3S 59 31W
Guam .... 3 13 27N 144 45 E
Guamúchil 74 25 25N 108 3W
Guan Xian .... 37 31 2N 103 38 E
Guanabacoa 75 23 8N 82 18W
Guanacaste, Cordillera del ... 75 10 40N 85 4W
Guanaceví 74 25 40N 106 0W
Guanahani = San Salvador 75 24 0N 74 40W
Guanajay 75 22 56N 82 42W
Guanajuato 74 21 0N 101 20W
Guanajuato □ 74 20 40N 101 20W
Guandacol 80 29 30S 68 40W
Guane 75 22 10N 84 7W
Guang'an .... 39 30 28N 106 35 E
Guangde .... 39 30 54N 119 25 E
Guangdong □ .... 39 23 0N 113 0 E
Guanghua .... 39 32 22N 111 38 E
Guangshun .... 39 26 8N 106 21 E
Guangxi Zhuangzu Zizhiqu □ ...... 39 24 0N 109 0 E
Guangyuan .... 39 32 26N 105 51 E
Guangze .... 39 27 30N 117 12 E
Guangzhou .... 39 23 5N 113 10 E
Guanipa → 78 9 56N 62 26W
Guantánamo 75 20 10N 75 14W
Guantao .... 38 36 42N 115 25 E
Guanyun .... 39 34 20N 119 18 E
Guápiles 75 10 10N 83 46W
Guaporé → 78 11 55S 65 4W
Guaqui 78 16 41S 68 54W
Guarapuava 80 25 20S 51 30W
Guarda 13 40 32N 7 20W
Guardafui, C. = Asir, Ras .... 29 11 55N 51 10 E
Guasdualito 78 7 15N 70 44W
Guasipati 78 7 28N 61 54W
Guatemala 75 14 40N 90 22W
Guatemala ■ 75 15 40N 90 30W
Guatire 78 10 28N 66 32W
Guaviare → 78 4 3N 67 44W
Guaxupé 79 21 10S 47 5W
Guayama 75 17 59N 66 7W
Guayaquil 78 2 15S 79 52W
Guayaquil, G. de .. 78 3 10S 81 0W
Guaymas 74 27 59N 110 54W
Guazhou .... 39 32 17N 119 21 E
Gudbrandsdalen .. 21 61 33N 10 0 E
Guddu Barrage ... 32 28 30N 69 50 E
Gudivada .... 33 16 30N 81 3 E
Gudur .... 32 14 12N 79 55 E
Guecho 13 43 21N 2 59W
Guékédou 50 8 40N 10 5W
Guelma .... 50 36 25N 7 29 E
Guelph 62 43 35N 80 20W
Güera, La 50 20 51N 17 0W
Guéréda .... 51 14 31N 22 5 E
Guéret .... 12 46 11N 1 51 E
Guernica 13 43 19N 2 40W
Guernsey, U.K. 7 49 30N 2 35W
Guernsey, U.S.A. .. 70 42 19N 104 45W
Guerrero □ 74 17 30N 100 0W
Gueydan 71 30 3N 92 30W
Gui Jiang → .... 39 23 30N 111 15 E
Gui Xian .... 39 23 8N 109 35 E
Guichi .... 39 30 39N 117 27 E
Guidong .... 39 26 7N 113 57 E
Guiglo 50 6 45N 7 30W
Guijá .... 57 24 27S 33 0 E
Guildford 7 51 14N 0 34W
Guilford 63 45 12N 69 25W
Guilin .... 39 25 18N 110 15 E
Guilvinec 12 47 48N 4 17W
Guimarães 79 2 9S 44 42W
Guimaras .... 35 10 35N 122 37 E
Guinea ■ 50 10 20N 11 30W
Guinea, Gulf of ... 3 3 0N 2 30 E
Guinea-Bissau ■ .. 50 12 0N 15 0W
Güines 75 22 50N 82 0W
Guingamp 12 48 34N 3 10W
Guiping .... 39 23 21N 110 2 E
Güiria 78 10 32N 62 18W
Guiuan .... 35 11 5N 125 55 E
Guixi .... 39 28 16N 117 15 E
Guiyang, Guizhou, China .... 39 26 32N 106 40 E
Guiyang, Hunan, China .... 39 25 46N 112 42 E
Guizhou □ .... 39 27 0N 107 0 E
Gujarat □ .... 32 23 20N 71 0 E
Gujranwala .... 32 32 10N 74 12 E
Gujrat .... 32 32 40N 74 2 E
Gulbarga .... 32 17 20N 76 50 E
Gulf, The .... 31 27 0N 50 0 E
Gulfport 71 30 21N 89 3W
Gulgong .... 45 32 20S 149 49 E
Gull Lake 65 50 10N 108 29W
Gulshad .... 24 46 45N 74 25 E
Gulu .... 54 2 48N 32 17 E
Gum Lake .... 45 32 42S 143 9 E
Gumlu .... 44 19 53S 147 41 E
Gumma □ .... 36 36 30N 138 20 E
Gummi .... 53 12 4N 5 9 E
Gümüşane .... 30 40 30N 39 30 E
Gumzai .... 35 5 28S 134 42 E
Guna .... 32 24 40N 77 19 E
Gundagai .... 45 35 3S 148 6 E
Gundih .... 35 7 10S 110 56 E
Gungu .... 54 5 43S 19 20 E
Gunisao → 65 53 56N 97 53W
Gunisao L. 65 53 33N 96 15W
Gunnbjørn Fjeld ... 58 68 45N 31 0W
Gunnedah .... 45 30 59S 150 15 E
Gunningbar Cr. → 45 31 14S 147 6 E
Gunnison, Colo., U.S.A. 73 38 32N 106 56W
Gunnison, Utah, U.S.A. 72 39 11N 111 48W
Gunnison → 73 39 3N 108 30W
Guntakal .... 32 15 11N 77 27 E
Guntersville 69 34 18N 86 16W
Guntur .... 33 16 23N 80 30 E
Gunungapi .... 35 6 45S 126 30 E
Gunungsitoli ...... 34 1 15N 97 30 E
Gunza .... 54 10 50S 13 50 E
Guo He → ...... 39 32 59N 117 10 E
Guoyang .... 39 33 32N 116 12 E
Gupis .... 32 36 15N 73 20 E
Gûrchañ .... 30 34 55N 49 25 E
Gurdaspur .... 32 32 5N 75 31 E
Gurdon 71 33 55N 93 10W
Gurgaon .... 32 28 27N 77 1 E
Gurkha .... 33 28 5N 84 40 E
Gurley .... 45 29 45S 149 48 E
Gurupá 79 1 25S 51 35W
Gurupá, I. Grande de 79 1 25S 51 45W
Gurupi → 79 1 13S 46 6W
Guryev .... 23 47 5N 52 0 E
Gusau .... 53 12 12N 6 40 E
Gushan .... 38 39 50N 123 35 E
Gushi .... 39 32 11N 115 41 E
Gustine 73 37 14N 121 0W
Güstrow .... 14 53 47N 12 12 E
Gutha .... 47 28 58S 115 55 E
Guthalongra ...... 44 19 52S 147 50 E
Guthrie 71 35 55N 97 30W
Guttenberg 70 42 46N 91 10W
Guyana ■ 78 5 0N 59 0W
Guyang .... 38 41 0N 110 5 E
Guyenne .... 12 44 30N 0 40 E
Guymon 71 36 45N 101 30W
Guyra .... 45 30 15S 151 40 E
Guyuan .... 38 36 0N 106 20 E
Guzhen .... 39 33 22N 117 18 E
Guzinozersk ...... 25 51 20N 106 35 E
Guzmán, L. de 74 31 25N 107 25W
Gwa .... 33 17 36N 94 34 E
Gwaai .... 55 19 15S 27 45 E
Gwabegar .... 45 30 31S 149 0 E
Gwadabawa ...... 53 13 28N 5 15 E
Gwādar .... 31 25 10N 62 18 E
Gwalia .... 47 28 54S 121 20 E
Gwalior .... 32 26 12N 78 10 E
Gwanda .... 55 20 55S 29 0 E
Gwaram .... 53 10 15N 10 25 E
Gwarzo .... 53 12 20N 8 55 E
Gweebarra B. 9 54 52N 8 21W
Gweedore 9 55 4N 8 15W
Gwent □ 7 51 45N 2 55W
Gweru .... 55 19 28S 29 45 E
Gwinn 68 46 15N 87 29W
Gwoza .... 53 11 5N 13 40 E
Gwydir → .... 45 29 27S 149 48 E
Gwynedd □ 6 53 0N 4 0W
Gyaring Hu ...... 37 34 50N 97 40 E
Gydanskiy P-ov. .. 24 70 0N 78 0 E
Gympie .... 45 26 11S 152 38 E
Gyoda .... 36 36 10N 139 30 E
Gyöngyös .... 15 47 48N 19 56 E
Györ .... 15 47 41N 17 40 E
Gypsum Pt. 64 61 53N 114 35W
Gypsumville 65 51 45N 98 40W

Ha 'Arava

H

Ha 'Arava → 28 30 50N 35 20 E
Haapamäki 20 62 18N 24 28 E
Haarlem 11 52 23N 4 39 E
Haast → 43 43 50S 169 2 E
Hab Nadi Chauki 32 25 0N 66 50 E
Habana, La 75 23 8N 82 22W
Habaswein 54 1 2N 39 30 E
Habay 64 58 50N 118 44W
Hachijō-Jima 36 33 5N 139 45 E
Hachinohe 36 40 30N 141 29 E
Hachiōji 36 35 40N 139 20 E
Hadarba, Ras 51 22 4N 36 51 E
Hadd, Ras al 31 22 35N 59 50 E
Haddington 8 55 57N 2 48W
Hadejia 53 12 30N 10 5 E
Haden 45 27 13S 151 54 E
Hadera 28 32 27N 34 55 E
Hadera, N. → 28 32 28N 34 52 E
Hadhramaut = Hadramawt 29 15 30N 49 30 E
Hadramawt 29 15 30N 49 30 E
Hadrians Wall 6 55 0N 2 30W
Haeju 38 38 3N 125 45 E
Haerhpin = Harbin 38 45 48N 126 40 E
Hafar al Bāṭin 30 28 25N 46 0 E
Hafizabad 32 32 5N 73 40 E
Haflong 33 25 10N 93 5 E
Hafnarfjörður 20 64 4N 21 57W
Haft-Gel 30 31 30N 49 32 E
Hafun, Ras 29 10 29N 51 30 E
Hagalil 28 32 53N 35 18 E
Hagen 14 51 21N 7 29 E
Hagerman 71 33 5N 104 22W
Hagerstown 68 39 39N 77 46W
Hagfors 21 60 3N 13 45 E
Hagi, Iceland 20 65 28N 23 25W
Hagi, Japan 36 34 30N 131 22 E
Hagolan 28 33 0N 35 45 E
Hagondange-Briey 12 49 16N 6 11 E
Hags Hd. 9 52 57N 9 30W
Hague, C. de la 12 49 44N 1 56W
Hague, The = 's-Gravenhage 11 52 7N 4 17 E
Haguenau 12 48 49N 7 47 E
Haicheng 38 40 50N 122 45 E
Haifa = Hefa 28 32 46N 35 0 E
Haifeng 39 22 58N 115 10 E
Haig 47 30 55S 126 10 E
Haikang 39 20 52N 110 8 E
Haikou 39 20 1N 110 16 E
Ḥā'il 30 27 28N 41 45 E
Hailar 38 49 10N 119 38 E
Hailar He → 38 49 30N 117 50 E
Hailey 72 43 30N 114 15W
Haileybury 62 47 30N 79 38W
Hailin 38 44 37N 129 30 E
Hailing Dao 39 21 35N 111 47 E
Hailong 38 42 32N 125 40 E
Hailun 38 47 28N 126 50 E
Hailuoto 20 65 3N 24 45 E
Haimen 39 31 52N 121 10 E
Hainan Dao 39 19 0N 109 30 E
Hainaut □ 11 50 30N 4 0 E
Haines 72 44 51N 117 59W
Haines City 69 28 6N 81 35W
Haines Junction 64 60 45N 137 30W
Haining 39 30 28N 120 40 E
Haiphong 39 20 47N 106 41 E
Haiti ■ 75 19 0N 72 30W
Haiya Junction 51 18 20N 36 21 E
Haiyan 39 30 28N 120 58 E
Haiyang 38 36 47N 121 9 E
Haiyuan 38 36 35N 105 52 E
Haja 35 3 19S 129 37 E
Hajar Bangar 51 10 40N 22 45 E
Hajdúböszörmény 15 47 40N 21 30 E
Hajówka 15 52 47N 23 35 E
Hajr 31 24 0N 56 34 E
Hakken-Zan 36 34 10N 135 54 E
Hakodate 36 41 45N 140 44 E
Hala 32 25 43N 68 20 E
Ḥalab 30 36 10N 37 15 E
Ḥalabjah 30 35 10N 45 58 E
Halaib 51 22 12N 36 30 E
Halberstadt 14 51 53N 11 2 E
Halcombe 43 40 8S 175 30 E
Halcon, Mt. 35 13 0N 121 30 E
Halden 21 59 9N 11 23 E
Haldia 33 22 5N 88 3 E
Haldwani 32 29 31N 79 30 E
Hale → 44 24 56S 135 53 E
Haleakala Crater 66 20 43N 156 12W
Haleyville 69 34 15N 87 40W
Halfway → 64 56 12N 121 32W
Ḥalḥul 28 31 35N 35 7 E
Haliburton 62 45 3N 78 30W
Halifax, Australia 44 18 32S 146 22 E
Halifax, Canada 63 44 38N 63 35W
Halifax, U.K. 6 53 43N 1 51W
Halifax B. 44 18 50S 147 0 E
Halifax I. 56 26 38S 15 4 E
Halīl → 31 27 40N 58 30 E
Hall Beach 61 68 46N 81 12W
Hall Pt. 46 15 40S 124 23 E
Hallands län □ 21 56 50N 12 50 E
Halle, Belgium 11 50 44N 4 13 E
Halle, Germany 14 51 29N 12 0 E
Hällefors 21 59 47N 14 31 E
Hallett 45 33 25S 138 55 E
Hallettsville 71 29 28N 96 57W
Halliday 70 47 20N 102 25W
Halliday L. 65 61 21N 108 56W
Hallingdal → 21 60 34N 9 12 E
Hällnäs 20 64 19N 19 36 E
Hallock 65 48 47N 97 0W
Halls Creek 46 18 16S 127 38 E
Halmahera 35 0 40N 128 0 E
Halmstad 21 56 41N 12 52 E
Halq el Oued 51 36 53N 10 18 E
Hals 21 56 59N 10 18 E
Hälsingborg = Helsingborg 21 56 3N 12 42 E
Halstad 70 47 21N 96 50W
Halul 31 25 40N 52 40 E
Hamab 56 28 7S 19 16 E
Hamada 36 34 56N 132 4 E
Hamadān 30 34 52N 48 32 E
Hamadān □ 30 35 0N 49 0 E
Hamāh 30 35 5N 36 40 E
Hamamatsu 36 34 45N 137 45 E
Hamar 21 60 48N 11 7 E
Hamarøy 20 68 5N 15 38 E
Hambantota 32 6 10N 81 10 E
Hamber Prov. Park 64 52 20N 118 0W
Hamburg, Germany 14 53 32N 9 59 E
Hamburg, Ark., U.S.A. 71 33 15N 91 47W
Hamburg, Iowa, U.S.A. 70 40 37N 95 38W
Hame 21 61 30N 24 0 E
Hämeenlinna 20 61 0N 24 28 E
Hamelin Pool 47 26 22S 114 20 E
Hamelin Pool Bay 47 26 10S 114 5 E
Hameln 14 52 7N 9 24 E
Hamersley Ra. 46 22 0S 117 45 E
Hamhung 38 39 54N 127 30 E
Hami 37 42 55N 93 25 E
Hamilton, Australia 45 37 45S 142 2 E
Hamilton, Canada 62 43 15N 79 50W
Hamilton, N.Z. 43 37 47S 175 19 E
Hamilton, U.K. 8 55 47N 4 2W
Hamilton, Mo., U.S.A. 70 39 45N 93 59W
Hamilton, Mont., U.S.A. 72 46 20N 114 6W
Hamilton, N.Y., U.S.A. 68 42 49N 75 31W
Hamilton, Ohio, U.S.A. 68 39 20N 84 35W
Hamilton, Tex., U.S.A. 71 31 40N 98 5W
Hamilton → 44 23 30S 139 47 E
Hamilton Hotel 44 22 45S 140 40 E
Hamilton Inlet 63 54 0N 57 30W
Hamiota 65 50 11N 100 38W
Hamlet 69 34 56N 79 40W
Hamley Bridge 45 34 17S 138 35 E
Hamlin 71 32 58N 100 8W
Hamm 14 51 40N 7 49 E
Hammerfest 20 70 39N 23 41 E
Hammond, Ind., U.S.A. 68 41 40N 87 30W
Hammond, La., U.S.A. 71 30 32N 90 30W
Hammonton 68 39 40N 74 47W
Hampden 43 45 18S 170 50 E
Hampshire □ 7 51 3N 1 20W
Hampshire Downs 7 51 10N 1 10W
Hampton, Ark., U.S.A. 71 33 35N 92 29W
Hampton, Iowa, U.S.A. 70 42 42N 93 12W
Hampton, S.C., U.S.A. 69 32 52N 81 2W
Hampton, Va., U.S.A. 68 37 4N 76 18W
Hampton Tableland 47 32 0S 127 0 E
Hamrat esh Sheykh 51 14 38N 27 55 E
Han Jiang → 39 23 25N 116 40 E
Han Shui → 39 30 35N 114 18 E
Ḥana 66 20 45N 155 59W
Hanamaki 36 39 23N 141 7 E
Hanau 14 50 8N 8 56 E
Hancheng 38 35 31N 110 25 E
Hancock, Mich., U.S.A. 70 47 10N 88 40W
Hancock, Minn., U.S.A. 70 45 26N 95 46W
Handa, Japan 36 34 53N 137 0 E
Handa, Somalia 29 10 37N 51 2 E
Handan 38 36 35N 114 28 E
Handeni 54 5 25S 38 2 E
Hanegev 28 30 50N 35 0 E
Haney 64 49 12N 122 40W
Hanford 73 36 23N 119 39W
Hangang → 38 37 50N 126 30 E
Hangayn Nuruu 37 47 30N 100 0 E
Hangchou = Hangzhou 39 30 18N 120 11 E
Hanggin Houqi 38 40 58N 107 4 E
Hangklip, K. 56 34 26S 18 48 E
Hangö 21 59 50N 22 57 E
Hangu 38 39 18N 117 53 E
Hangzhou 39 30 18N 120 11 E
Hangzhou Wan 39 30 15N 120 45 E
Ḥanīsh 29 13 45N 42 46 E
Hanita 28 33 5N 35 10 E
Hankinson 70 46 9N 96 58W
Hanko 21 59 59N 22 57 E
Hankou 39 30 35N 114 30 E
Hanksville 73 38 19N 110 45W
Hanle 32 32 42N 79 4 E
Hanmer Springs 43 42 32S 172 50 E
Hann → 46 17 26S 126 17 E
Hann, Mt. 46 15 45S 126 0 E
Hanna 64 51 40N 111 54W
Hannaford 70 47 23N 98 11W
Hannah 70 48 58N 98 42W
Hannah B. 62 51 40N 80 0W
Hannibal 70 39 42N 91 22W
Hannover 14 52 23N 9 43 E
Hanoi 39 21 5N 105 55 E
Hanover = Hannover 14 52 23N 9 43 E
Hanover, S. Africa 56 31 4S 24 29 E
Hanover, N.H., U.S.A. 68 43 43N 72 17W
Hanover, Pa., U.S.A. 68 39 46N 76 59W
Hanover, I. 80 51 0S 74 50W
Hansi 32 29 10N 75 57 E
Hanson, L. 45 31 0S 136 15 E
Hanyang 39 30 35N 114 2 E
Hanyin 39 32 54N 108 28 E
Hanzhong 39 33 10N 107 1 E
Hanzhuang 39 34 33N 117 23 E
Haora 33 22 37N 88 20 E
Haparanda 20 65 52N 24 8 E
Happy 71 34 47N 101 50W
Happy Camp 72 41 52N 123 22W
Happy Valley-Goose Bay 63 53 15N 60 20W
Hapur 32 28 45N 77 45 E
Ḥaql 30 29 10N 35 0 E
Har 35 5 16S 133 14 E
Har Hu 37 38 20N 97 38 E
Har Us Nuur 37 48 0N 92 0 E
Har Yehuda 28 31 35N 34 57 E
Ḥaraḍ 30 24 22N 49 0 E
Haraisan Plateau 30 23 0N 47 40 E
Harardera 29 4 33N 47 38 E
Harare 55 17 43S 31 2 E
Harazé 51 14 20N 19 12 E
Harbin 38 45 48N 126 40 E
Harbor Beach 68 43 50N 82 38W
Harbor Springs 68 45 28N 85 0W
Harbour Breton 63 47 29N 55 50W
Harbour Grace 63 47 40N 53 22W
Harburg 14 53 27N 9 58 E
Hardangerfjorden 21 60 15N 6 0 E
Hardap Dam 56 24 32S 17 50 E
Hardenberg 11 52 34N 6 37 E
Harderwijk 11 52 21N 5 38 E
Hardey → 46 22 45S 116 8 E
Hardin 72 45 44N 107 35W
Harding 57 30 35S 29 55 E
Harding Ra. 46 16 17S 124 55 E
Hardisty 64 52 40N 111 18W
Hardman 72 45 12N 119 40W
Hardoi 32 27 26N 80 6 E
Hardwar = Haridwar 32 29 58N 78 9 E
Hardy 71 36 20N 91 30W
Hardy, Pen. 80 55 30S 68 20W
Hare B. 63 51 15N 55 45W
Hare Gilboa 28 32 31N 35 25 E
Hare Meron 28 32 59N 35 24 E
Harer 29 9 20N 42 8 E
Hargeisa 29 9 30N 44 2 E
Hargshamn 21 60 12N 18 30 E
Hari → 34 1 16S 104 5 E
Haridwar 32 29 58N 78 9 E
Haringhata → 33 22 0N 89 58 E
Harīrūd 31 35 0N 61 0 E
Harīrūd → 31 34 20N 62 30 E
Harlan, Iowa, U.S.A. 70 41 37N 95 20W
Harlan, Tenn., U.S.A. 69 36 50N 83 20W
Harlech 6 52 52N 4 7W
Harlem 72 48 29N 108 47W
Harlingen, Neth. 11 53 11N 5 25 E
Harlingen, U.S.A. 71 26 20N 97 50W
Harlowton 72 46 30N 109 54W
Harney Basin 72 43 30N 119 0W
Harney L. 72 43 0N 119 0W
Harney Pk. 70 43 52N 103 33W
Härnösand 20 62 38N 18 0 E
Harp L. 63 55 5N 61 50W
Harpe, La 70 40 30N 91 0W
Ḥarrat al Kishb 30 22 30N 40 15 E
Harrat al 'Uwairidh 30 26 50N 38 0 E
Harriman 69 36 0N 84 35W
Harrington Harbour 63 50 31N 59 30W
Harris 8 57 50N 6 55W
Harris, Sd. of 8 57 44N 7 6W
Harris L. 45 31 10S 135 10 E
Harrisburg, Ill., U.S.A. 71 37 42N 88 30W
Harrisburg, Nebr., U.S.A. 70 41 36N 103 46W
Harrisburg, Oreg., U.S.A. 72 44 16N 123 10W
Harrisburg, Pa., U.S.A. 68 40 18N 76 52W
Harrismith 57 28 15S 29 8 E
Harrison, Ark., U.S.A. 71 36 10N 93 4W
Harrison, Idaho, U.S.A. 72 47 30N 116 51W
Harrison, Nebr., U.S.A. 70 42 42N 103 52W
Harrison, C. 63 54 55N 57 55W
Harrison B. 60 70 25N 151 30W
Harrison L. 64 49 33N 121 50W
Harrisonburg 68 38 28N 78 52W
Harrisonville 70 38 39N 94 21W
Harriston 62 43 57N 80 53W
Harrisville 68 44 40N 83 19W
Harrogate 6 53 59N 1 32W
Harrow 7 51 35N 0 15W
Harstad 20 68 48N 16 30 E
Hart 68 43 42N 86 21W
Hart, L. 45 31 10S 136 25 E
Hartbees → 56 28 45S 20 32 E
Hartford, Conn., U.S.A. 68 41 47N 72 41W
Hartford, Ky., U.S.A. 68 37 26N 86 50W
Hartford, S. Dak., U.S.A. 70 43 40N 96 58W
Hartford, Wis., U.S.A. 70 43 18N 88 25W
Hartford City 68 40 22N 85 20W
Hartland 63 46 20N 67 32W
Hartland Pt. 7 51 2N 4 32W
Hartlepool 6 54 42N 1 11W
Hartley Bay 64 53 25N 129 15W
Hartmannberge 56 17 0S 13 0 E
Hartney 65 49 30N 100 35W
Harts → 56 28 24S 24 17 E
Hartselle 69 34 25N 86 55W
Hartshorne 71 34 51N 95 30W
Hartsville 69 34 23N 80 2W
Hartwell 69 34 21N 82 52W
Harvey, Australia 47 33 5S 115 54 E
Harvey, Ill., U.S.A. 68 41 40N 87 40W
Harvey, N. Dak., U.S.A. 70 47 50N 99 58W
Harwich 7 51 56N 1 18 E
Haryana □ 32 29 0N 76 10 E
Harz 14 51 40N 10 40 E
Hasa 30 26 0N 49 0 E
Hasharon 28 32 12N 34 49 E
Hashefela 28 31 30N 34 43 E
Haskell, Okla., U.S.A. 71 35 51N 95 40W
Haskell, Tex., U.S.A. 71 33 10N 99 45W
Hasselt 11 50 56N 5 21 E
Hassi Inifel 50 29 50N 3 41 E
Hassi Messaoud 50 31 43N 6 8 E
Hastings, N.Z. 43 39 39S 176 52 E
Hastings, U.K. 7 50 51N 0 36 E
Hastings, Mich., U.S.A. 68 42 40N 85 20W
Hastings, Minn., U.S.A. 70 44 41N 92 51W
Hastings, Nebr., U.S.A. 70 40 34N 98 22W
Hastings Ra. 45 31 15S 152 14 E
Hatch 73 32 45N 107 8W
Hatches Creek 44 20 56S 135 12 E
Hatchet L. 65 58 36N 103 40W
Hatfield P.O. 45 33 54S 143 49 E
Hatgal 37 50 26N 100 9 E
Hathras 32 27 36N 78 6 E
Hatia 33 22 30N 91 5 E
Hattah 45 34 48S 142 17 E
Hatteras, C. 69 35 10N 75 30W
Hattiesburg 71 31 20N 89 20W
Hatvan 15 47 40N 19 45 E
Hau Bon = Cheo Reo 34 13 25N 108 28 E
Haugesund 21 59 23N 5 13 E
Haultain → 65 55 51N 106 46W
Hauraki Gulf 43 36 35S 175 5 E
Hauran 28 32 50N 36 15 E
Haut Atlas 50 32 30N 5 0W
Haut-Rhin □ 12 48 0N 7 15 E
Hautah, Wahāt al 30 23 40N 47 0 E
Haute-Corse □ 12 42 30N 9 30 E
Haute-Garonne □ 12 43 30N 1 30 E
Haute-Loire □ 12 45 5N 3 50 E
Haute-Marne □ 12 48 10N 5 20 E
Haute-Saône □ 12 47 45N 6 10 E
Haute-Savoie □ 12 46 0N 6 20 E
Haute-Vienne □ 12 45 50N 1 10 E
Hauterive 63 49 10N 68 16W
Hautes-Alpes □ 12 44 42N 6 20 E
Hautes-Pyrénées □ 12 43 0N 0 10 E
Hauts-de-Seine □ 12 48 52N 2 15 E
Hauts Plateaux 50 35 0N 1 0 E
Havana = Habana, La 75 23 8N 82 22W
Havana 70 40 19N 90 3W
Havant 7 50 51N 0 59W
Havasu, L. 73 34 18N 114 28W
Havel → 14 52 40N 12 1 E
Havelange 11 50 23N 5 15 E
Havelock, N.B., Canada 63 46 2N 65 24W
Havelock, Ont., Canada 62 44 26N 77 53W
Havelock, N.Z. 43 41 17S 173 48 E
Haverfordwest 7 51 48N 4 59W
Haverhill 68 42 50N 71 2W
Havering 7 51 33N 0 20 E
Havlíčkův Brod 14 49 36N 15 33 E
Havre 72 48 34N 109 40W
Havre, Le 12 49 30N 0 5 E
Havre-Aubert 63 47 12N 61 56W
Havre-St.-Pierre 63 50 18N 63 33W
Havza 30 41 0N 35 35 E
Haw → 69 35 36N 79 3W
Hawaii □ 66 20 30N 157 0W
Hawaii I. 66 20 0N 155 0W
Hawaiian Is. 66 20 30N 156 0W
Hawaiian Ridge 41 24 0N 165 0W
Hawarden, Canada 65 51 25N 106 36W
Hawarden, U.S.A. 70 43 2N 96 28W
Hawea Lake 43 44 28S 169 19 E
Hawera 43 39 35S 174 19 E
Hawick 8 55 25N 2 48W
Hawk Junction 62 48 5N 84 38W
Hawke B. 43 39 25S 177 20 E
Hawke's Bay □ 43 39 45S 176 35 E
Hawkesbury 62 45 37N 74 37W
Hawkesbury I. 64 53 37N 129 3W
Hawkesbury Pt. 44 11 55S 134 5 E
Hawkinsville 69 32 17N 83 30W
Hawkwood 45 25 45S 150 50 E
Hawley 70 46 58N 96 20W
Hawrān 28 32 45N 36 15 E
Hawthorne 72 38 31N 118 37W
Haxtun 70 40 40N 102 39W
Hay 45 34 30S 144 51 E
Hay →, Australia 44 24 50S 138 0 E
Hay →, Canada 64 60 50N 116 26W
Hay, C. 46 14 5S 129 29 E
Hay L. 64 58 50N 118 50W
Hay Lakes 64 53 12N 113 2W
Hay-on-Wye 7 52 4N 3 9W
Hay River 64 60 51N 115 44W
Hay Springs 70 42 40N 102 38W
Hayden, Ariz., U.S.A. 73 33 2N 110 48W
Hayden, Colo., U.S.A. 72 40 30N 107 22W
Haydon 44 18 0S 141 30 E
Hayes 70 44 22N 101 1W
Hayes → 65 57 3N 92 12W
Haynesville 71 33 0N 93 7W
Hays, Canada 64 50 6N 111 48W
Hays, U.S.A. 70 38 55N 99 25W
Hayward 70 46 2N 91 30W
Hayward's Heath 7 51 0N 0 5W
Hazard 68 37 18N 83 10W
Hazaribag 33 23 58N 85 26 E
Hazelton, Canada 64 55 20N 127 42W
Hazelton, U.S.A. 70 46 30N 100 15W
Hazen, N. Dak., U.S.A. 70 47 18N 101 38W
Hazen, Nev., U.S.A. 72 39 37N 119 2W
Hazlehurst, Ga., U.S.A. 69 31 50N 82 35W
Hazlehurst, Miss., U.S.A. 71 31 52N 90 24W
Hazleton 68 40 58N 76 0W
Hazlett, L. 46 21 30S 128 48 E
Hazor 28 33 2N 35 32 E
He Xian 39 24 27N 111 30 E
Head of Bight 47 31 30S 131 25 E
Healdsburg 72 38 33N 122 51W
Healdton 71 34 16N 97 31W
Healesville 45 37 35S 145 30 E
Heanor 6 53 1N 1 20W
Heard I. 3 53 0S 74 0 E
Hearne 71 30 54N 96 35W
Hearne B. 65 60 10N 99 10W
Hearne L. 64 62 20N 113 10W
Hearst 62 49 40N 83 41W
Heart → 70 46 40N 100 51W
Heart's Content 63 47 54N 53 27W
Heath Pt. 63 49 8N 61 40W
Heath Steele 63 47 17N 66 5W
Heavener 71 34 54N 94 36W
Hebbronville 71 27 20N 98 40W
Hebei □ 38 39 0N 116 0 E
Hebel 45 28 58S 147 47 E

Hospet

Heber Springs **71** 35 29N 91 59W
Hebert **65** 50 30N 107 10W
Hebgen, L. **72** 44 50N 111 15W
Hebi **38** 35 57N 114 7 E
Hebrides **8** 57 30N 7 0W
Hebrides, Inner Is. **8** 57 20N 6 40W
Hebrides, Outer Is. **8** 57 30N 7 40W
Hebron = Al Khalīl **28** 31 32N 35 6 E
Hebron, Canada **61** 58 5N 62 30W
Hebron, N. Dak., U.S.A. **70** 46 56N 102 2W
Hebron, Nebr., U.S.A. **70** 40 15N 97 33W
Hecate Str. **64** 53 10N 130 30W
Hechi **39** 24 40N 108 2 E
Hechuan **39** 30 2N 106 12 E
Hecla **70** 45 56N 98 8W
Hecla I. **65** 51 10N 96 43W
Hede **20** 62 23N 13 30 E
Hedemora **21** 60 18N 15 58 E
Hedley **71** 34 53N 100 39W
Heemstede **11** 52 22N 4 37 E
Heerde **11** 52 24N 6 2 E
Heerenveen **11** 52 57N 5 55 E
Heerlen **11** 50 55N 6 0 E
Hefa **28** 32 46N 35 0 E
Hefei **39** 31 52N 117 18 E
Hegang **38** 47 20N 130 19 E
Heidelberg, Germany **14** 49 23N 8 41 E
Heidelberg, C. Prov., S. Africa **56** 34 6S 20 59 E
Heidelberg, Trans., S. Africa **57** 26 30S 28 23 E
Heilbron **57** 27 16S 27 59 E
Heilbronn **14** 49 8N 9 13 E
Heilongjiang □ **38** 48 0N 126 0 E
Heilunkiang = Heilongjiang □ **38** 48 0N 126 0 E
Heinola **21** 61 13N 26 2 E
Heinze Is. **33** 14 25N 97 45 E
Hejaz = Al Ḥijāz **29** 26 0N 37 30 E
Hejian **38** 38 25N 116 5 E
Hejiang **39** 28 43N 105 46 E
Hekimhan **30** 38 50N 38 0 E
Hekla **20** 63 56N 19 35W
Hekou **37** 22 30N 103 59 E
Helan Shan **38** 39 0N 105 55 E
Helena, Ark., U.S.A. **71** 34 30N 90 35W
Helena, Mont., U.S.A. **72** 46 40N 112 0W
Helensburgh **8** 56 0N 4 44W
Helensville **43** 36 41S 174 29 E
Helez **28** 31 36N 34 39 E
Helgoland **14** 54 10N 7 51 E
Heligoland = Helgoland **14** 54 10N 7 51 E
Hellendoorn **11** 52 24N 6 27 E
Hellevoetsluis **11** 51 50N 4 8 E
Hellín **13** 38 31N 1 40W
Helmand □ **31** 31 20N 64 0 E
Helmand → **31** 31 12N 61 34 E
Helmand, Hamun **31** 31 15N 61 15 E
Helmond **11** 51 29N 5 41 E
Helmsdale **8** 58 7N 3 40W
Helper **72** 39 44N 110 56W
Helsingborg **21** 56 3N 12 42 E
Helsingfors **21** 60 15N 25 3 E
Helsingør **21** 56 2N 12 35 E
Helsinki **21** 60 15N 25 3 E
Helston **7** 50 7N 5 17W
Helvellyn **6** 54 31N 3 1W
Helwân **51** 29 50N 31 20 E
Hemet **73** 33 45N 116 59W
Hemingford **70** 42 21N 103 4W
Hemphill **71** 31 21N 93 49W
Hempstead **71** 30 5N 96 5W
Hemse **21** 57 15N 18 22 E
Henan □ **39** 34 0N 114 0 E
Henares → **13** 40 24N 3 30W
Henderson, Ky., U.S.A. **68** 37 50N 87 38W
Henderson, N.C., U.S.A. **69** 36 20N 78 25W
Henderson, Nev., U.S.A. **73** 36 2N 115 0W
Henderson, Pa., U.S.A. **69** 35 25N 88 40W
Henderson, Tex., U.S.A. **71** 32 5N 94 49W
Hendersonville **69** 35 21N 82 28W
Hendon **45** 28 5S 151 50 E
Heng Xian **39** 22 40N 109 17 E
Hengdaohezi **38** 44 52N 129 0 E
Hengelo **11** 52 3N 6 19 E
Hengshan, Hunan, China **39** 27 16N 112 45 E
Hengshan, Shaanxi, China **38** 37 58N 109 5 E
Hengshui **38** 37 41N 115 40 E
Hengyang **39** 26 52N 112 33 E
Henlopen, C. **68** 38 48N 75 5W
Hennenman **56** 27 59S 27 1 E
Hennessey **71** 36 8N 97 53W
Henrietta **71** 33 50N 98 15W
Henrietta, Ostrov **25** 77 6N 156 30 E
Henrietta Maria C. **62** 55 9N 82 20W
Henry **70** 41 5N 89 20W
Henryetta **71** 35 30N 96 0W
Hentiyn Nuruu **37** 48 30N 108 30 E
Henty **45** 35 30S 147 0 E
Henzada **33** 17 38N 95 26 E
Heping **39** 24 29N 115 0 E
Heppner **72** 45 21N 119 34W
Hepu **39** 21 40N 109 12 E
Héraðsflói **20** 65 42N 14 12W
Héraðsvötn → **20** 65 45N 19 25W
Herald Cays **44** 16 58S 149 9 E
Herāt **31** 34 20N 62 7 E
Herāt □ **31** 35 0N 62 0 E
Hérault □ **12** 43 34N 3 15 E
Herbert → **44** 18 31S 146 17 E
Herbert Downs **44** 23 7S 139 9 E
Herberton **44** 17 20S 145 25 E
Hercegnovi **19** 42 30N 18 33 E
Hercegovina = Bosna i Hercegovina □ **18** 44 0N 18 0 E
Herðubreið **20** 65 11N 16 21W
Hereford, U.K. **7** 52 4N 2 42W
Hereford, U.S.A. **71** 34 50N 102 28W
Hereford and Worcester □ **7** 52 10N 2 30W
Herentals **11** 51 12N 4 51 E
Herford **14** 52 7N 8 40 E
Herington **70** 38 43N 97 0W
Herjehogna **21** 61 43N 12 7 E
Herkimer **68** 43 0N 74 59W
Herman **70** 45 51N 96 8W
Hermann **70** 38 40N 91 25W
Hermannsburg Mission **46** 23 57S 132 45 E
Hermanus **56** 34 27S 19 12 E
Hermidale **45** 31 30S 146 42 E
Hermiston **72** 45 50N 119 16W
Hermitage **43** 43 44S 170 5 E
Hermite, I. **80** 55 50S 68 0W
Hermon, Mt. = Ash Shaykh, J. **30** 33 25N 35 50 E
Hermosillo **74** 29 10N 111 0W
Hernád → **15** 47 56N 21 8 E
Hernandarias **80** 25 20S 54 40W
Hernando **71** 34 50N 89 59W
Herne **11** 51 33N 7 12 E
Herne Bay **7** 51 22N 1 8 E
Herning **21** 56 8N 8 58 E
Heroica = Caborca **74** 30 40N 112 10W
Heroica Nogales = Nogales **74** 31 20N 110 56W
Heron Bay **62** 48 40N 86 25W
Herreid **70** 45 53N 100 5W
Herrera **13** 37 26N 4 55W
Herrick **44** 41 5S 147 55 E
Herrin **71** 37 50N 89 0W
Herstal **11** 50 40N 5 38 E
Hertford **7** 51 47N 0 4W
Hertford □ **7** 51 51N 0 5W
's-Hertogenbosch **11** 51 42N 5 17 E
Hertzogville **56** 28 9S 25 30 E
Hervey Bay **44** 25 3S 153 5 E
Herzliyya **28** 32 10N 34 50 E
Hesse = Hessen □ **14** 50 40N 9 20 E
Hessen □ **14** 50 40N 9 20 E
Hettinger **70** 46 0N 102 38W
Hevron → **28** 31 12N 34 42 E
Hewett, C. **61** 70 16N 67 45W
Hexham **6** 54 58N 2 7W
Hexigten Qi **38** 43 18N 117 30 E
Hexrivier **56** 33 30S 19 35 E
Heysham **6** 54 5N 2 53W
Heywood **45** 38 8S 141 37 E
Hi-no-Misaki **36** 35 26N 132 38 E
Hialeah **69** 25 49N 80 17W
Hiawatha, Kans., U.S.A. **70** 39 55N 95 33W
Hiawatha, Utah, U.S.A. **72** 39 29N 111 1W
Hibbing **70** 47 30N 93 0W
Hibbs B. **44** 42 35S 145 15 E
Hibernia Reef **46** 12 0S 123 23 E
Hickory **69** 35 46N 81 17W
Hicks Pt. **45** 37 49S 149 17 E
Hida-Sammyaku **36** 36 30N 137 40 E
Hidalgo **74** 24 15N 99 26W
Hidalgo, Presa M. **74** 26 30N 108 35W
Hidalgo del Parral **74** 26 58N 105 40W
Hierro **50** 27 44N 18 0 E
Higashiōsaka **36** 34 40N 135 37 E
Higgins **71** 36 9N 100 1W
Higginsville **47** 31 42S 121 38 E
High Atlas = Haut Atlas **50** 32 30N 5 0W
High I. **63** 56 40N 61 10W
High Island **71** 29 32N 94 22W
High Level **64** 58 31N 117 8W
High Point **69** 35 57N 79 58W
High Prairie **64** 55 30N 116 30W
High River **64** 50 30N 113 50W
High Springs **69** 29 50N 82 40W
High Wycombe **7** 51 37N 0 45W
Highbury **44** 16 25S 143 9 E
Highland □ **8** 57 30N 5 0W
Highland Park **68** 42 10N 87 50W
Highmore **70** 44 35N 99 26W
Highrock L. **65** 57 5N 105 32W
Hiiumaa **22** 58 50N 22 45 E
Ḥijārah, Şaḩrā' al **30** 30 25N 44 30 E
Ḥijāz □ **29** 24 0N 40 0 E
Hijo = Tagum **35** 7 33N 125 53 E
Hiko **73** 37 30N 115 13W
Hikone **36** 35 15N 136 10 E
Hildesheim **14** 52 9N 9 55 E
Hill → **47** 30 23S 115 3 E
Hill City, Idaho, U.S.A. **72** 43 20N 115 2W
Hill City, Kans., U.S.A. **70** 39 25N 99 51W
Hill City, Minn., U.S.A. **70** 46 57N 93 35W
Hill City, S. Dak., U.S.A. **70** 43 58N 103 35W
Hill Island L. **65** 60 30N 109 50W
Hillegom **11** 52 18N 4 35 E
Hillingdon **7** 51 33N 0 29W
Hillman **68** 45 5N 83 52W
Hillmond **65** 53 26N 109 41W
Hillsboro, Kans., U.S.A. **70** 38 22N 97 10W
Hillsboro, N. Dak., U.S.A. **70** 47 23N 97 9W
Hillsboro, N.H., U.S.A. **68** 43 8N 71 56W
Hillsboro, N. Mex., U.S.A. **73** 33 0N 107 35W
Hillsboro, Oreg., U.S.A. **72** 45 31N 123 0W
Hillsboro, Tex., U.S.A. **71** 32 0N 97 10W
Hillsdale **68** 41 55N 84 40W
Hillside **46** 21 45S 119 23 E
Hillsport **62** 49 27N 85 34W
Hillston **45** 33 30S 145 31 E
Hilo **66** 19 44N 155 5W
Hilversum **11** 52 14N 5 10 E
Himachal Pradesh □ **32** 31 30N 77 0 E
Himalaya, Mts. **33** 29 0N 84 0 E
Himatnagar **32** 23 37N 72 57 E
Himeji **36** 34 50N 134 40 E
Himi **36** 36 50N 137 0 E
Ḥimş **30** 34 40N 36 45 E
Hinchinbrook I. **44** 18 20S 146 15 E
Hinckley, U.K. **7** 52 33N 1 21W
Hinckley, U.S.A. **72** 39 18N 112 41W
Hindmarsh L. **45** 36 5S 141 55 E
Hindu Kush **31** 36 0N 71 0 E
Hindubagh **32** 30 56N 67 57 E
Hindupur **32** 13 49N 77 32 E
Hines Creek **64** 56 20N 118 40W
Hinganghat **32** 20 30N 78 52 E
Hingham **72** 48 34N 110 29W
Hingoli **32** 19 41N 77 15 E
Hinna = Imi **29** 6 28N 42 10 E
Hinsdale **72** 48 26N 107 2W
Hinton, Canada **64** 53 26N 117 34W
Hinton, U.S.A. **68** 37 40N 80 51W
Hippolytushoef **11** 52 54N 4 58 E
Hirakud Dam **33** 21 32N 83 45 E
Hiratsuka **36** 35 19N 139 21 E
Hirosaki **36** 40 34N 140 28 E
Hiroshima **36** 34 24N 132 30 E
Hiroshima □ **36** 34 50N 133 0 E
Hisar **32** 29 12N 75 45 E
Hispaniola **75** 19 0N 71 0W
Hita **36** 33 20N 130 58 E
Hitachi **36** 36 36N 140 39 E
Hitchin **7** 51 57N 0 16W
Hitoyoshi **36** 32 13N 130 45 E
Hitra **20** 63 30N 8 45 E
Ḥiyyon, N. → **28** 30 25N 35 10 E
Hjalmar L. **65** 61 33N 109 25W
Hjälmaren **21** 59 18N 15 40 E
Hjørring **21** 57 29N 9 59 E
Hluhluwe **57** 28 1S 32 15 E
Ho **53** 6 37N 0 27 E
Ho Chi Minh City = Phanh Bho Ho Chi Minh **34** 10 58N 106 40 E
Hoai Nhon **34** 14 28N 109 1 E
Hoare B. **61** 65 17N 62 30W
Hobart, Australia **44** 42 50S 147 21 E
Hobart, U.S.A. **71** 35 0N 99 5W
Hobbs **71** 32 40N 103 3W
Hoboken **11** 51 11N 4 21 E
Hobro **21** 56 39N 9 46 E
Hoburgen **21** 56 55N 18 7 E
Hodgson **65** 51 13N 97 36W
Hódmezövásárhely **15** 46 28N 20 22 E
Hodna, Chott el **50** 35 30N 5 0 E
Hodonín **14** 48 50N 17 10 E
Hoek van Holland **11** 52 0N 4 7 E
Hoëveld **57** 26 30S 30 0 E
Hof, Germany **14** 50 18N 11 55 E
Hof, Iceland **20** 64 33N 14 40W
Höfðakaupstaður **20** 65 50N 20 19W
Hofmeyr **56** 31 39S 25 50 E
Hofsjökull **20** 64 49N 18 48W
Hofsós **20** 65 53N 19 26W
Hōfu **36** 34 3N 131 34 E
Hogan Group **44** 39 13S 147 1 E
Hogansville **69** 33 14N 84 50W
Hogeland **72** 48 51N 108 40W
Hoh Xil Shan **37** 35 0N 89 0 E
Hohe Rhön **14** 50 24N 9 58 E
Hohe Venn **11** 50 30N 6 5 E
Hohenwald **69** 35 35N 87 30W
Hohhot **38** 40 52N 111 40 E
Hoi An **34** 15 30N 108 19 E
Hoisington **70** 38 33N 98 50W
Hokianga Harbour **43** 35 31S 173 22 E
Hokitika **43** 42 42S 171 0 E
Hokkaidō □ **36** 43 30N 143 0 E
Holbrook, Australia **45** 35 42S 147 18 E
Holbrook, U.S.A. **73** 35 54N 110 10W
Holden, Canada **64** 53 13N 112 11W
Holden, U.S.A. **72** 39 0N 112 26W
Holdenville **71** 35 5N 96 25W
Holderness **6** 53 45N 0 5W
Holdfast **65** 50 58N 105 25W
Holdrege **70** 40 26N 99 22W
Holguín **75** 20 50N 76 20W
Hollams Bird I. **56** 24 40S 14 30 E
Holland **68** 42 47N 86 7W
Hollandia = Jayapura **35** 2 28S 140 38 E
Holleton **47** 31 55S 119 0 E
Hollidaysburg **68** 40 26N 78 25W
Hollis **71** 34 45N 99 55W
Hollister, Calif., U.S.A. **73** 36 51N 121 24W
Hollister, Idaho, U.S.A. **72** 42 21N 114 40W
Holly **70** 38 7N 102 7W
Holly Hill **69** 29 15N 81 3W
Holly Springs **71** 34 45N 89 25W
Hollywood, Calif., U.S.A. **66** 34 7N 118 25W
Hollywood, Fla., U.S.A. **69** 26 0N 80 9W
Holman Island **60** 70 42N 117 41W
Hólmavík **20** 65 42N 21 40W
Holmes Reefs **44** 16 27S 148 0 E
Holmsund **20** 63 41N 20 20 E
Holon **28** 32 2N 34 47 E
Holroyd → **44** 14 10S 141 36 E
Holstebro **21** 56 22N 8 37 E
Holsworthy **7** 50 48N 4 21W
Holt **20** 63 33N 19 48W
Holton, Canada **63** 54 31N 57 12W
Holton, U.S.A. **70** 39 28N 95 44W
Holtville **73** 32 50N 115 27W
Holwerd **11** 53 22N 5 54 E
Holy Cross **60** 62 10N 159 52W
Holy I., England, U.K. **6** 55 42N 1 48W
Holy I., Wales, U.K. **6** 53 17N 4 37W
Holyhead **6** 53 18N 4 38W
Holyoke, Colo., U.S.A. **70** 40 39N 102 18W
Holyoke, Mass., U.S.A. **68** 42 14N 72 37W
Holyrood **63** 47 27N 53 8W
Homalin **33** 24 55N 95 0 E
Hombori **53** 15 20N 1 38W
Home B. **61** 68 40N 67 10W
Home Hill **44** 19 43S 147 25 E
Homedale **72** 43 42N 116 59W
Homer, Alaska, U.S.A. **60** 59 40N 151 35W
Homer, La., U.S.A. **71** 32 50N 93 4W
Homestead, Australia **44** 20 20S 145 40 E
Homestead, Fla., U.S.A. **69** 25 29N 80 27W
Homestead, Oreg., U.S.A. **72** 45 5N 116 57W
Hominy **71** 36 26N 96 24W
Homoine **57** 23 55S 35 8 E
Homs = Ḥimş **30** 34 40N 36 45 E
Hon Chong **34** 10 25N 104 30 E
Honan = Henan □ **39** 34 0N 114 0 E
Honbetsu **36** 43 7N 143 37 E
Honda **78** 5 12N 74 45W
Hondeklipbaai **56** 30 19S 17 17 E
Hondo **71** 29 22N 99 6W
Hondo → **74** 18 25N 88 21W
Honduras ■ **75** 14 40N 86 30W
Honduras, G. de **75** 16 50N 87 0W
Hønefoss **21** 60 10N 10 18 E
Honey L. **72** 40 13N 120 14W
Honfleur **12** 49 25N 0 13 E
Hong → **26** 20 17N 106 34 E
Hong Kong ■ **39** 22 11N 114 14 E
Hong'an **39** 31 20N 114 40 E
Honghai Wan **39** 22 40N 115 0 E
Honghu **39** 29 50N 113 30 E
Hongjiang **39** 27 7N 109 59 E
Hongshui He → **39** 23 48N 109 30 E
Hongtong **38** 36 16N 111 40 E
Honguedo, Détroit d' **63** 49 15N 64 0W
Hongze Hu **39** 33 15N 118 35 E
Honiara **40** 9 27S 159 57 E
Honiton **7** 50 48N 3 11W
Honjō **36** 39 23N 140 3 E
Honolulu **66** 21 19N 157 52W
Honshū **36** 36 0N 138 0 E
Hood, Pt. **47** 34 23S 119 34 E
Hood Mt. **72** 45 24N 121 41W
Hood River **72** 45 45N 121 31W
Hoodsport **72** 47 24N 123 7W
Hoogeveen **11** 52 44N 6 30 E
Hoogezand **11** 53 11N 6 45 E
Hooghly → = Hughli → **33** 21 56N 88 4 E
Hook Hd. **9** 52 8N 6 57W
Hook I. **44** 20 4S 149 0 E
Hook of Holland = Hoek van Holland **11** 52 0N 4 7 E
Hooker **71** 36 55N 101 10W
Hooker Creek **46** 18 23S 130 38 E
Hoopeston **68** 40 30N 87 40W
Hoopstad **56** 27 50S 25 55 E
Hoorn **11** 52 38N 5 4 E
Hoover Dam **73** 36 0N 114 45W
Hope, Canada **64** 49 25N 121 25 E
Hope, Ark., U.S.A. **71** 33 40N 93 36W
Hope, N. Dak., U.S.A. **70** 47 21N 97 42W
Hope, L. **45** 28 24S 139 18 E
Hope Pt. **60** 68 20N 166 50W
Hope Town **75** 26 35N 76 57W
Hopedale **63** 55 28N 60 13W
Hopefield **56** 33 3S 18 22 E
Hopei = Hebei □ **38** 39 0N 116 0 E
Hopelchén **74** 19 46N 89 50W
Hopetoun, Vic., Australia **45** 35 42S 142 22 E
Hopetoun, W. Austral., Australia **47** 33 57S 120 7 E
Hopetown **56** 29 34S 24 3 E
Hopkins **70** 40 31N 94 45W
Hopkins, L. **46** 24 15S 128 35 E
Hopkinsville **69** 36 52N 87 26W
Hopland **72** 39 0N 123 7W
Hoquiam **72** 46 50N 123 55W
Hordaland fylke □ **21** 60 25N 6 15 E
Horden Hills **46** 20 15S 130 0 E
Hormoz **31** 27 35N 55 0 E
Hormoz, Jaz. ye **31** 27 8N 56 28 E
Hormozgān □ **31** 27 30N 56 0 E
Hormuz Str. **31** 26 30N 56 30 E
Horn, Austria **14** 48 39N 15 40 E
Horn, Ísafjarðarsýsla, Iceland **20** 66 28N 22 28W
Horn, Suður-Múlasýsla, Iceland **20** 65 10N 13 31W
Horn → **64** 61 30N 118 1W
Horn, Cape = Hornos, C. de **80** 55 50S 67 30W
Horn Head **9** 55 13N 8 0W
Horn I., Australia **44** 10 37S 142 17 E
Horn I., U.S.A. **69** 30 17N 88 40W
Horn Mts. **64** 62 15N 119 15W
Hornavan **20** 66 15N 17 30 E
Hornbeck **71** 31 22N 93 20W
Hornbrook **72** 41 58N 122 37W
Horncastle **6** 53 13N 0 8W
Hornell **68** 42 23N 77 41W
Hornell L. **64** 62 20N 119 25W
Hornepayne **62** 49 14N 84 48W
Hornos, C. de **80** 55 50S 67 30W
Hornsby **45** 33 42S 151 2 E
Hornsea **6** 53 55N 0 10W
Horqin Youyi Qianqi **38** 46 5N 122 3 E
Horqueta **80** 23 15S 56 55W
Horse Cr. → **70** 41 57N 103 58W
Horse Is. **63** 50 15N 55 50W
Horsefly L. **64** 52 25N 121 0W
Horsens **21** 55 52N 9 51 E
Horsham, Australia **45** 36 44S 142 13 E
Horsham, U.K. **7** 51 4N 0 20W
Horten **21** 59 25N 10 32 E
Horton **70** 39 42N 95 30W
Horton → **60** 69 56N 126 52W
Horwood, L. **62** 48 5N 82 20W
Hose, Gunung-Gunung **34** 2 5N 114 6 E
Hoshangabad **32** 22 45N 77 45 E
Hoshiarpur **32** 31 30N 75 58 E
Hosmer **70** 45 36N 99 29W
Hospet **32** 15 15N 76 20 E

Hospitalet de Llobregat

Hospitalet de Llobregat 13 41 21N 2 6 E
Hoste, I. 80 55 0S 69 0W
Hot Creek Ra. 72 39 0N 116 0W
Hot Springs, Ark., U.S.A. 71 34 30N 93 0W
Hot Springs, S. Dak., U.S.A. 70 43 25N 103 30W
Hotagen 20 63 50N 14 30 E
Hotan 37 37 25N 79 55 E
Hotazel 56 27 17S 22 58 E
Hotchkiss 73 38 47N 107 47W
Hotham, C. 46 12 2S 131 18 E
Hoting 20 64 8N 16 15 E
Hottentotsbaai 56 26 8S 14 59 E
Houck 73 35 15N 109 15W
Houffalize 11 50 8N 5 48 E
Houghton 70 47 9N 88 39W
Houghton L. 68 44 20N 84 40W
Houghton-le-Spring 6 54 51N 1 28W
Houhora 43 34 49S 173 9 E
Houlton 63 46 5N 67 50W
Houma 71 29 35N 90 44W
Houston, Canada 64 54 25N 126 39W
Houston, Mo., U.S.A. 71 37 20N 92 0W
Houston, Tex., U.S.A. 71 29 50N 95 20W
Houtman Abrolhos 47 28 43S 113 48 E
Hovd 37 48 2N 91 37 E
Hove 7 50 50N 0 10W
Hövsgöl Nuur 37 51 0N 100 30 E
Howard, Australia 45 25 16S 152 32 E
Howard, Kans., U.S.A. 71 37 30N 96 16W
Howard, S. Dak., U.S.A. 70 44 2N 97 30W
Howard I. 44 12 10S 135 24 E
Howard L. 65 62 15N 105 57W
Howatharra 47 28 29S 114 33 E
Howe 72 43 48N 113 0W
Howe, C. 45 37 30S 150 0 E
Howell 68 42 38N 83 56W
Howick 57 29 28S 30 14 E
Howick Group 44 14 20S 145 30 E
Howitt, L. 45 27 40S 138 40 E
Howley 63 49 12N 57 2W
Howrah = Haora 33 22 37N 88 20 E
Howth Hd. 9 53 21N 6 0W
Hoy I. 8 58 50N 3 15W
Høyanger 21 61 13N 6 4 E
Hpungan Pass 33 27 30N 96 55 E
Hradec Králové 14 50 15N 15 50 E
Hron → 15 47 49N 18 45 E
Hrvatska 18 45 20N 16 0 E
Hsenwi 33 23 22N 97 55 E
Hsiamen = Xiamen 38 24 25N 118 4 E
Hsian = Xi'an 39 34 15N 109 0 E
Hsinhailien = Lianyungang 39 34 40N 119 11 E
Hsüchou = Xuzhou 39 34 18N 117 10 E
Hua Hin 34 12 34N 99 58 E
Hua Xian, Henan, China 39 35 30N 114 30 E
Hua Xian, Shaanxi, China 39 34 30N 109 48 E
Huacheng 39 24 4N 115 37 E
Hiacho 78 11 10S 77 35W
Huachón 78 10 35S 76 0W
Huachuan 38 46 50N 130 21 E
Huade 38 41 55N 113 59 E
Huadian 38 43 0N 126 40 E
Huai He → 39 33 0N 118 30 E
Huai'an 39 33 30N 119 10 E
Huaide 38 43 30N 124 40 E
Huainan 39 32 38N 116 58 E
Huaiyang 39 33 40N 114 52 E
Huaiyuan 39 24 31N 108 22 E
Huajianzi 38 41 23N 125 20 E
Huajuapan de Leon 74 17 50N 97 48W
Hualapai Pk. 73 35 8N 113 58W
Hualian 39 23 59N 121 37 E
Huallaga → 78 5 0S 75 30W
Huambo 55 12 42S 15 54 E
Huan Jiang → 38 34 28N 109 0 E
Huan Xian 38 36 33N 107 7 E
Huancabamba 78 5 10S 79 15W
Huancane 78 15 10S 69 44W
Huancapi 78 13 40S 74 0W
Huancavelica 78 12 50S 75 5W
Huancayo 78 12 5S 75 12W
Huang Hai = Yellow Sea 38 35 0N 123 0 E
Huang He → 38 37 55N 118 50 E
Huangchuan 39 32 15N 115 10 E
Huangliu 39 18 20N 108 50 E
Huanglong 38 35 30N 109 59 E
Huangshi 39 30 10N 115 3 E
Huangyan 39 28 38N 121 19 E
Huánuco 78 9 55S 76 15W
Huaraz 78 9 30S 77 32W
Huarmey 78 10 5S 78 5W
Huascarán 78 9 8S 77 36W
Huascarán, Nevado 76 9 7S 77 37W
Huasco 80 28 30S 71 15W
Huatabampo 74 26 50N 109 50W
Huay Namota 74 21 56N 104 30W
Huayllay 78 11 3S 76 21W
Hubbard 71 31 50N 96 50W
Hubbart Pt. 65 59 21N 94 41W
Hubei □ 39 31 0N 112 0 E
Hubli-Dharwad = Dharwad 32 15 22N 75 15 E
Huddersfield 6 53 38N 1 49W
Hudiksvall 21 61 43N 17 10 E
Hudson, Canada 65 50 6N 92 9W
Hudson, Mich., U.S.A. 68 41 50N 84 20W
Hudson, N.Y., U.S.A. 68 42 15N 73 46W
Hudson, Wis., U.S.A. 70 44 57N 92 45W
Hudson, Wyo., U.S.A. 72 42 54N 108 37W
Hudson → 68 40 42N 74 2W
Hudson Bay 61 52 51N 102 23W
Hudson Falls 68 43 18N 73 34W
Hudson Str. 61 62 0N 70 0W
Hudson's Hope 64 56 0N 121 54W
Hue 34 16 30N 107 35 E
Huelva 13 37 18N 6 57W
Huesca 13 42 8N 0 25W
Huetamo 74 18 36N 100 54W
Hugh → 44 25 1S 134 1 E
Hughenden 44 20 52S 144 10 E
Hughes, Australia 47 30 42S 129 31 E
Hughes, U.S.A. 60 66 0N 154 20W
Hughli → 33 21 56N 88 4 E
Hugo 70 39 12N 103 27W
Hugoton 71 37 11N 101 22W
Hui Xian 38 35 27N 113 12 E
Hui'an 39 25 1N 118 43 E
Huichang 39 25 32N 115 45 E
Huichapán 74 20 24N 99 40W
Huihe 38 48 12N 119 17 E
Huila, Nevado del 78 3 0N 76 0W
Huilai 39 23 0N 116 18 E
Huimin 38 37 27N 117 28 E
Huinan 38 42 40N 126 2 E
Huinca Renancó 80 34 51S 64 22W
Huining 38 35 38N 105 0 E
Huinong 38 39 5N 106 35 E
Huize 37 26 24N 103 15 E
Huizhou 39 23 0N 114 23 E
Hukawng Valley 33 26 30N 96 30 E
Hukou 39 29 45N 116 21 E
Hukuntsi 56 23 58S 21 45 E
Hulan 38 46 1N 126 37 E
Ḥulayfā' 30 25 58N 40 45 E
Huld 37 45 5N 105 30 E
Hulda 28 31 50N 34 51 E
Hulin 38 45 48N 132 59 E
Hull, Canada 62 45 25N 75 44W
Hull, U.K. 6 53 45N 0 20W
Hull → 6 53 43N 0 25W
Hulst 11 51 17N 4 2 E
Hulun Nur 38 49 0N 117 30 E
Huma 38 51 43N 126 38 E
Huma He → 38 51 42N 126 42 E
Humahuaca 80 23 10S 65 25W
Humaitá, Brazil 78 7 35S 63 1W
Humaitá, Paraguay 80 27 2S 58 31W
Humansdorp 56 34 2S 24 46 E
Humbe 56 16 40S 14 55 E
Humber → 6 53 40N 0 10W
Humberside □ 6 53 50N 0 30W
Humbert River 46 16 30S 130 45 E
Humble 71 29 59N 93 18W
Humboldt, Canada 65 52 15N 105 9W
Humboldt, Iowa, U.S.A. 70 42 42N 94 15W
Humboldt, Tenn., U.S.A. 71 35 50N 88 55W
Humboldt → 72 40 2N 118 31W
Hume, L. 45 36 0S 147 0 E
Humphreys Pk. 73 35 24N 111 38W
Hūn 51 29 2N 16 0 E
Húnaflói 20 65 50N 20 50W
Hunan □ 39 27 30N 112 0 E
Hunchun 38 42 52N 130 28 E
Hundred Mile House 64 51 38N 121 18W
Hunedoara 15 45 40N 22 50 E
Hungary ■ 15 47 20N 19 20 E
Hungary, Plain of 4 47 0N 20 0 E
Hungerford 45 28 58S 144 24 E
Hŭngnam 38 39 49N 127 45 E
Hunsberge 56 27 45S 17 12 E
Hunsrück 14 49 30N 7 0 E
Hunstanton 6 52 57N 0 30 E
Hunter 70 47 12N 97 17W
Hunter I., Australia 44 40 30S 144 45 E
Hunter I., Canada 64 51 55N 128 0W
Hunter Ra. 45 32 45S 150 15 E
Hunterville 43 39 56S 175 35 E
Huntingburg 68 38 20N 86 58W
Huntingdon, Canada 62 45 6N 74 10W
Huntingdon, U.K. 7 52 20N 0 11W
Huntingdon, U.S.A. 68 40 28N 78 1W
Huntington, Ind., U.S.A. 68 40 52N 85 30W
Huntington, Oreg., U.S.A. 72 44 22N 117 21W
Huntington, Utah, U.S.A. 72 39 24N 111 1W
Huntington, W. Va., U.S.A. 68 38 20N 82 30W
Huntington Beach 73 33 40N 118 0W
Huntington Park 73 33 58N 118 15W
Huntly, N.Z. 43 37 34S 175 11 E
Huntly, U.K. 8 57 27N 2 48W
Huntsville, Canada 62 45 20N 79 14W
Huntsville, Ala., U.S.A. 69 34 45N 86 35W
Huntsville, Tex., U.S.A. 71 30 45N 95 35W
Huo Xian 38 36 36N 111 42 E
Huonville 44 43 0S 147 5 E
Huoqiu 39 32 20N 116 12 E
Huoshao Dao 39 22 40N 121 30 E
Hupeh □ = Hubei □ 39 31 0N 112 0 E
Hure Qi 38 42 45N 121 45 E
Hurley, N. Mex., U.S.A. 73 32 45N 108 7W
Hurley, Wis., U.S.A. 70 46 26N 90 10W
Huron 70 44 22N 98 12W
Huron, L. 68 45 0N 83 0W
Hurricane 73 37 10N 113 12W
Hurunui → 43 42 54S 173 18 E
Húsavík 20 66 3N 17 21W
Huskvarna 21 57 47N 14 15 E
Hussar 64 51 3N 112 41W
Hutchinson, Kans., U.S.A. 71 38 3N 97 59W
Hutchinson, Minn., U.S.A. 70 44 50N 94 22W
Hutou 38 45 58N 133 38 E
Huttig 71 33 5N 92 10W
Hutton, Mt. 45 25 51S 148 20 E
Ḥuwwārah 28 32 9N 35 15 E
Huy 11 50 31N 5 15 E
Hvammur 20 65 13N 21 49W
Hvar 18 43 11N 16 28 E
Hvítá 20 64 40N 21 5W
Hvítá → 20 64 0N 20 58W
Hvítárvatn 20 64 37N 19 50W
Hwang Ho = Huang He → 38 37 55N 118 50 E
Hwange 55 18 18S 26 30 E
Hwange Nat. Park 56 19 0S 26 30 E
Hyannis 70 42 0N 101 45W
Hyargas Nuur 37 49 0N 93 0 E
Hyden 47 32 24S 118 53 E
Hyderabad, India 32 17 22N 78 29 E
Hyderabad, Pakistan 32 25 23N 68 24 E
Hyères 12 43 8N 6 9 E
Hyesan 38 41 20N 128 10 E
Hyland → 64 59 52N 128 12W
Hyndman Pk. 72 43 50N 114 10W
Hyōgo □ 36 35 15N 135 0 E
Hyrum 72 41 35N 111 56W
Hysham 72 46 21N 107 11W
Hythe 7 51 4N 1 5 E
Hyvinge = Hyvinkää 21 60 38N 24 50 E
Hyvinkää 21 60 38N 24 50 E

I

I-n-Gall 53 16 51N 7 1 E
Iaco → 78 9 3S 68 34W
Iakora 57 23 6S 46 40 E
Ialomiţa → 15 44 42N 27 51 E
Iaşi 17 47 10N 27 40 E
Iba 35 15 22N 120 0 E
Ibadan 53 7 22N 3 58 E
Ibagué 78 4 20N 75 20W
Ibar → 19 43 43N 20 45 E
Ibaraki □ 36 36 10N 140 10 E
Ibarra 78 0 21N 78 7W
Iberian Peninsula 4 40 0N 5 0W
Iberville 62 45 19N 73 17W
Iberville, Lac D' 62 55 55N 73 15W
Ibi 53 8 15N 9 44 E
Ibiá 79 19 30S 46 30W
Ibicuy 80 33 55S 59 10W
Ibioapaba, Sa. da 79 4 0S 41 30W
Ibiza 13 38 54N 1 26 E
Ibonma 35 3 29S 133 31 E
Ibotirama 79 12 13S 43 12W
Ibu 35 1 35N 127 33 E
Icá 78 14 0S 75 48W
Içá → 78 2 55S 67 58W
Içana 78 0 21N 67 19W
Iceland ■ 20 65 0N 19 0W
Icha 25 55 30N 156 0 E
Ich'ang = Yichang 39 30 40N 111 20 E
Ichchapuram 33 19 10N 84 40 E
Ichihara 36 35 28N 140 5 E
Ichikawa 36 35 44N 139 55 E
Ichilo → 78 15 57S 64 50W
Ichinomiya 36 35 18N 136 48 E
Ichinoseki 36 38 55N 141 8 E
Icy Str. 64 58 20N 135 30W
Ida Grove 70 42 20N 95 25W
Ida Valley 47 28 42S 120 29 E
Idabel 71 33 53N 94 50W
Idaho □ 72 44 10N 114 0W
Idaho City 72 43 50N 115 52W
Idaho Falls 72 43 30N 112 1W
Idaho Springs 72 39 49N 105 30W
Idd el Ghanam 51 11 30N 24 19 E
Iddan 29 6 10N 48 55 E
Idehan 51 27 10N 11 30 E
Idehan Marzūq 51 24 50N 13 51 E
Idelès 50 23 50N 5 53 E
Idfû 51 25 0N 32 49 E
Ídhi Óros 19 35 15N 24 45 E
Ídhra 19 37 20N 23 28 E
Idi 34 5 2N 97 37 E
Idiofa 54 4 55S 19 42 E
Idlip 30 35 55N 36 38 E
Idna 28 31 34N 34 58 E
Idutywa 57 32 8S 28 18 E
Ieper 11 50 51N 2 53 E
Ierápetra 19 35 0N 25 44 E
Ierzu 18 39 48N 9 32 E
Ifanadiana 57 21 19S 47 39 E
Ife 53 7 30N 4 31 E
Iffley 44 18 53S 141 12 E
Ifni 50 29 29N 10 12W
Iforas, Adrar des 50 19 40N 1 40 E
Igarapava 79 20 3S 47 47W
Igarapé Açu 79 1 4S 47 33W
Igarka 25 67 30N 86 33 E
Igbetti 53 8 44N 4 8 E
Igbo-Ora 53 7 29N 3 15 E
Iggesund 21 61 39N 17 10 E
Iglésias 18 39 19N 8 27 E
Igli 50 30 25N 2 19W
Igloolik 61 69 20N 81 49W
Ignace 62 49 30N 91 40W
Iguaçu → 80 25 36S 54 36W
Iguaçu, Cat. del 80 25 41S 54 26W
Iguaçu Falls = Iguaçu, Cat. del 80 25 41S 54 26W
Iguala 74 18 20N 99 40W
Igualada 13 41 37N 1 37 E
Iguassu = Iguaçu → 80 25 36S 54 36W
Iguatu 79 6 20S 39 18W
Iguéla 54 2 0S 9 16 E
Ihiala 53 5 51N 6 55 E
Ihosy 57 22 24S 46 8 E
Ihotry, L. 57 21 56S 43 41 E
Ii 20 65 19N 25 22 E
Iida 36 35 35N 137 50 E
Iijoki → 20 65 20N 25 20 E
Iisalmi 20 63 32N 27 10 E
Iizuka 36 33 38N 130 42 E
Ijebu-Igbo 53 6 56N 4 1 E
Ijebu-Ode 53 6 47N 3 58 E
IJmuiden 11 52 28N 4 35 E
IJssel → 11 52 35N 5 50 E
IJsselmeer 11 52 45N 5 20 E
Ikare 53 7 32N 5 40 E
Ikaría 19 37 35N 26 10 E
Ikeja 53 6 36N 3 23 E
Ikela 54 1 6S 23 6 E
Ikerre-Ekiti 53 7 25N 5 19 E
Iki 36 33 45N 129 42 E
Ikire 53 7 23N 4 15 E
Ikopa → 57 16 45S 46 40 E
Ikot Ekpene 53 5 12N 7 40 E
Ikurun 53 7 54N 4 40 E
Ila 53 8 0N 4 39 E
Ilagan 35 17 7N 121 53 E
Īlām 30 33 0N 46 0 E
Ilanskiy 25 56 14N 96 3 E
Ilbilbie 44 21 45S 149 20 E
Île-à-la Crosse 65 55 27N 107 53W
Île-à-la-Crosse, Lac 65 55 40N 107 45W
Île-de-France 12 49 0N 2 20 E
Ilebo 54 4 17S 20 55 E
Ilek 24 51 32N 53 21 E
Ilek → 22 51 30N 53 22 E
Ilero 53 8 0N 3 20 E
Ilesha 53 7 37N 4 40 E
Ilford 65 56 4N 95 35W
Ilfracombe, Australia 44 23 30S 144 30 E
Ilfracombe, U.K. 7 51 13N 4 8W
Ilhéus 79 14 49S 39 2W
Ili → 24 45 53N 77 10 E
Ilich 24 40 50N 68 27 E
Iliff 70 40 50N 103 3W
Iligan 35 8 12N 124 13 E
Iliodhrómia 19 39 12N 23 50 E
Ilion 68 43 0N 75 3W
Ilkeston 6 52 59N 1 19W
Illampu = Ancohuma, Nevada 78 16 0S 68 50W
Illana B. 35 7 35N 123 45 E
Illapel 80 32 0S 71 10W
'Illār 28 32 23N 35 7 E
Ille-et-Vilaine □ 12 48 10N 1 30W
Iller → 14 48 23N 9 58 E
Illimani 78 16 30S 67 50W
Illinois □ 67 40 15N 89 30W
Illinois → 67 38 55N 90 28W
Illium = Troy 30 39 57N 26 12 E
Ilmen, Oz. 22 58 15N 31 10 E
Ilo 78 17 40S 71 20W
Ilobu 53 7 45N 4 25 E
Iloilo 35 10 45N 122 33 E
Ilora 53 7 45N 3 50 E
Ilorin 53 8 30N 4 35 E
Ilwaki 35 7 55S 126 30 E
Imabari 36 34 4N 133 0 E
Imaloto → 57 23 27S 45 13 E
Imandra, Oz. 22 67 30N 33 0 E
Imari 36 33 15N 129 52 E
Imbler 72 45 31N 118 0W
imeni 26 Bakinskikh Komissarov, Azerbaijan, U.S.S.R. 23 39 19N 49 12 E
imeni 26 Bakinskikh Komissarov, Turkmen S.S.R., U.S.S.R. 23 39 22N 54 10 E
Imeni Poliny Osipenko 25 52 30N 136 29 E
Imeri, Serra 78 0 50N 65 25W
Imerimandroso 57 17 26S 48 35 E
Imi 29 6 28N 42 10 E
Imlay 72 40 45N 118 9W
Immingham 6 53 37N 0 12W
Immokalee 69 26 25N 81 26W
Imo □ 53 5 15N 7 20 E
Imola 18 44 20N 11 42 E
Imperatriz 79 5 30S 47 29W
Impéria 18 43 52N 8 0 E
Imperial, Canada 65 51 21N 105 28W
Imperial, Calif., U.S.A. 73 32 52N 115 34W
Imperial, Nebr., U.S.A. 70 40 38N 101 39W
Imperial Dam 73 32 50N 114 30W
Imperieuse Reef 46 17 36S 118 50 E
Impfondo 54 1 40N 18 0 E
Imphal 33 24 48N 93 56 E
Imuruan B. 35 10 40N 119 10 E
In Belbel 50 27 55N 1 12 E
In Salah 50 27 10N 2 32 E
Ina 36 35 50N 138 0 E
Ina-Bonchi 36 35 45N 137 58 E
Inangahua Junc. 43 41 52S 171 59 E
Inanwatan 35 2 10S 132 14 E
Iñapari 78 11 0S 69 40W
Inari 20 68 54N 27 5 E
Inarijärvi 20 69 0N 28 0 E
Inawashiro-Ko 36 37 29N 140 6 E
Inca 13 39 43N 2 54 E
İnce-Burnu 30 42 7N 34 56 E
Inchon 38 37 27N 126 40 E
Incomáti → 57 25 46S 32 43 E
Indalsälven → 20 62 36N 17 30 E
Indaw 33 24 15N 96 5 E
Independence, Calif., U.S.A. 73 36 51N 118 14W
Independence, Iowa, U.S.A. 70 42 27N 91 52W
Independence, Kans., U.S.A. 71 37 10N 95 43W
Independence, Mo., U.S.A. 70 39 3N 94 25W
Independence, Oreg., U.S.A. 72 44 53N 123 12W
Independence Mts. 72 41 30N 116 2W
India ■ 32 20 0N 78 0 E
Indian → 69 27 59N 80 34W
Indian-Antarctic Ridge 40 49 0S 120 0 E
Indian Cabins 64 59 52N 117 40W
Indian Harbour 63 54 27N 57 13W
Indian Head 65 50 30N 103 41W
Indian Ocean 3 5 0S 75 0 E
Indiana 68 40 38N 79 9W
Indiana □ 68 40 0N 86 0W
Indianapolis 68 39 42N 86 10W
Indianola, Iowa, U.S.A. 70 41 20N 93 32W
Indianola, Miss., U.S.A. 71 33 27N 90 40W
Indiga 22 67 50N 48 50 E
Indigirka → 25 70 48N 148 54 E
Indio 73 33 46N 116 15W
Indonesia ■ 34 5 0S 115 0 E
Indore 32 22 42N 75 53 E
Indramayu 35 6 20S 108 19 E
Indravati → 33 19 20N 80 20 E
Indre □ 12 46 50N 1 39 E
Indre-et-Loire □ 12 47 20N 0 40 E
Indus → 32 24 20N 67 47 E
İnebolu 30 41 55N 33 40 E

Jenkins

İnegöl 30 40 5N 29 31 E
Infante, Kaap 56 34 27S 20 51 E
Infiernillo, Presa del 74 18 9N 102 0W
Ingende 54 0 12S 18 57 E
Ingham 44 18 43S 146 10 E
Ingleborough 6 54 11N 2 23W
Inglewood, Queens., Australia 45 28 25S 151 2 E
Inglewood, Vic., Australia 45 36 29S 143 53 E
Inglewood, N.Z. 43 39 9S 174 14 E
Inglewood, U.S.A. 73 33 58N 118 21W
Ingólfshöfði 20 63 48N 16 39W
Ingolstadt 14 48 45N 11 26 E
Ingomar 72 46 35N 107 21W
Ingonish 63 46 42N 60 18W
Ingraj Bazar 33 24 58N 88 10 E
Ingulec 23 47 42N 33 14 E
Ingwavuma 57 27 9S 31 59 E
Inhaca, I. 57 26 1S 32 57 E
Inhafenga 57 20 36S 33 53 E
Inhambane 57 23 54S 35 30 E
Inhambane □ 57 22 30S 34 20 E
Inhaminga 55 18 26S 35 0 E
Inharrime 57 24 30S 35 0 E
Inharrime → 57 24 30S 35 0 E
Ining = Yining 37 43 58N 81 10 E
Inírida → 78 3 55N 67 52W
Inishbofin 9 53 35N 10 12W
Inishmore 9 53 8N 9 45W
Inishowen 9 55 14N 7 15W
Injune 45 25 53S 148 32 E
Inklin 64 58 56N 133 5W
Inklin → 64 58 50N 133 10W
Inkom 72 42 51N 112 15W
Inle L. 33 20 30N 96 58 E
Inn → 14 48 35N 13 28 E
Innamincka 45 27 44S 140 46 E
Inner Hebrides 8 57 0N 6 30W
Inner Mongolia = Nei Monggol Zizhiqu □ 38 42 0N 112 0 E
Inner Sound 8 57 30N 5 55W
Innetalling I. 62 56 0N 79 0W
Innisfail, Australia 44 17 33S 146 5 E
Innisfail, Canada 64 52 0N 113 57W
Innsbruck 14 47 16N 11 23 E
Inny → 9 53 30N 7 50W
Inongo 54 1 55S 18 30 E
Inoucdjouac 61 58 25N 78 15W
Inowrocław 15 52 50N 18 12 E
Inquisivi 78 16 50S 67 10W
Inscription, C. 47 25 29S 112 59 E
Insein 33 16 50N 96 5 E
Inta 22 66 5N 60 8 E
Interior 70 43 46N 101 59W
International Falls 70 48 36N 93 25W
Intiyaco 80 28 43S 60 5W
Inútil, B. 80 53 30S 70 15W
Inuvik 60 68 16N 133 40W
Inveraray 8 56 13N 5 5W
Inverbervie 8 56 50N 2 17W
Invercargill 43 46 24S 168 24 E
Inverell 45 29 45S 151 8 E
Invergordon 8 57 41N 4 10W
Invermere 64 50 30N 116 2W
Inverness, Canada 63 46 15N 61 19W
Inverness, U.K. 8 57 29N 4 12W
Inverness, U.S.A. 69 28 50N 82 20W
Inverurie 8 57 15N 2 21W
Inverway 46 17 50S 129 38 E
Investigator Group 45 34 45S 134 20 E
Investigator Str. 45 35 30S 137 0 E
Inya 24 50 28N 86 37 E
Inyo Mts. 73 37 0N 118 0W
Inyokern 73 35 38N 117 48W
Inza 22 53 55N 46 25 E
Iola 71 38 0N 95 20W
Iona 8 56 20N 6 25W
Ione, Calif., U.S.A. 72 38 20N 120 56W
Ione, Wash., U.S.A. 72 48 44N 117 29W
Ionia 68 42 59N 85 7W
Ionian Is. = Iónioi Nísoi 19 38 40N 20 0 E
Ionian Sea 17 37 30N 17 30 E
Iónioi Nísoi 19 38 40N 20 0 E
Íos 19 36 41N 25 20 E
Iowa □ 70 42 18N 93 30W
Iowa City 70 41 40N 91 35W
Iowa Falls 70 42 30N 93 15W
Ipameri 79 17 44S 48 9W
Ipatinga 79 19 32S 42 30W
Ipiales 78 0 50N 77 37W
Ipin = Yibin 37 28 45N 104 32 E
Ípiros □ 19 39 30N 20 30 E
Ipixuna 78 7 0S 71 40W
Ipoh 34 4 35N 101 5 E
Ippy 51 6 5N 21 7 E
Ipswich, Australia 45 27 35S 152 40 E
Ipswich, U.K. 7 52 4N 1 9 E
Ipswich, U.S.A. 70 45 28N 99 1W
Ipu 79 4 23S 40 44W
Iquique 78 20 19S 70 5W
Iquitos 78 3 45S 73 10W
Iracoubo 79 5 30N 53 10W
Iráklion 19 35 20N 25 12 E
Iran ■ 31 33 0N 53 0 E
Iran, Gunung-Gunung 34 2 20N 114 50 E
Īrānshahr 31 27 15N 60 40 E
Irapuato 74 20 40N 101 30W
Iraq ■ 30 33 0N 44 0 E
Irbid 28 32 35N 35 48 E
Irebu 54 0 40S 17 46 E
Ireland ■ 9 53 0N 8 0W
Ireland's Eye 9 53 25N 6 4W
Irele 53 7 40N 5 40 E
Iret 25 60 3N 154 20 E
Iri 38 35 59N 127 0 E
Irian Jaya □ 35 4 0S 137 0 E
Iringa 54 7 48S 35 43 E
Iriri → 79 3 52S 52 37W
Irish Republic ■ 9 53 0N 8 0W
Irish Sea 6 54 0N 5 0W
Irkineyeva 25 58 30N 96 49 E
Irkutsk 25 52 18N 104 20 E
Irma 65 52 55N 111 14W
Iron Baron 45 32 58S 137 11 E
Iron Gate = Portile de Fier 15 44 42N 22 30 E
Iron Knob 45 32 46S 137 8 E
Iron Mountain 68 45 49N 88 4W
Iron River 70 46 6N 88 40W
Ironbridge 7 52 38N 2 29W
Ironstone Kopje 56 25 17S 24 5 E
Ironton, Mo., U.S.A. 71 37 40N 90 40W
Ironton, Ohio, U.S.A. 68 38 35N 82 40W
Ironwood 70 46 30N 90 10W
Iroquois Falls 62 48 46N 80 41W
Irrara Cr. → 45 29 35S 145 31 E
Irrawaddy □ 33 17 0N 95 0 E
Irrawaddy → 33 15 50N 95 6 E
Irtysh → 24 61 4N 68 52 E
Irumu 54 1 32N 29 53 E
Irún 13 43 20N 1 52W
Irvine, Canada 65 49 57N 110 16W
Irvine, U.K. 8 55 37N 4 40W
Irvine, U.S.A. 68 37 42N 83 58W
Irvinestown 9 54 28N 7 38W
Irwin → 47 29 15S 114 54 E
Irwin, Pt. 47 35 5S 116 55 E
Irymple 45 34 14S 142 8 E
Isa 53 13 14N 6 24 E
Isaac → 44 22 55S 149 20 E
Isabel 70 45 27N 101 22W
Isabela, I. 74 21 51N 105 55W
Isabella 35 6 40N 122 10 E
Isabella, Cord. 75 13 30N 85 25W
Isabella Ra. 46 21 0S 121 4 E
Ísafjarðardjúp 20 66 10N 23 0W
Ísafjörður 20 66 5N 23 9W
Isangi 54 0 52N 24 10 E
Isar → 14 48 49N 12 58 E
Íschia 18 40 45N 13 51 E
Isdell → 46 16 27S 124 51 E
Ise 36 34 25N 136 45 E
Ise-Wan 36 34 43N 136 43 E
Isère □ 12 45 15N 5 40 E
Isère → 12 44 59N 4 51 E
Iseyin 53 8 0N 3 36 E
Ishikari-Wan 36 43 25N 141 1 E
Ishikawa □ 36 36 30N 136 30 E
Ishim 24 56 10N 69 30 E
Ishim → 24 57 45N 71 10 E
Ishinomaki 36 38 32N 141 20 E
Ishkuman 32 36 30N 73 50 E
Ishpeming 68 46 30N 87 40W
Isil Kul 24 54 55N 71 16 E
Isiolo 54 0 24N 37 33 E
Isipingo Beach 57 30 0S 30 57 E
Isiro 54 2 53N 27 40 E
Isisford 44 24 15S 144 21 E
İskenderun 30 36 32N 36 10 E
İskenderun Körfezi 23 36 40N 35 50 E
Iskut → 64 56 45N 131 49W
Isla → 8 56 32N 3 20W
Islamabad 32 33 40N 73 10 E
Island → 64 60 25N 121 12W
Island Falls, Canada 62 49 35N 81 20W
Island Falls, U.S.A. 63 46 0N 68 16W
Island L. 65 53 47N 94 25W
Island Lagoon 45 31 30S 136 40 E
Island Pt. 47 30 20S 115 1 E
Island Pond 68 44 50N 71 50W
Islands, B. of 63 49 11N 58 15W
Islay 8 55 46N 6 10W
Isle aux Morts 63 47 35N 59 0W
Isle of Wight □ 7 50 40N 1 20W
Isle Royale 70 48 0N 88 50W
Isleta 73 34 58N 106 46W
Ismail 23 45 22N 28 46 E
Ismâ'ilîya 30 30 37N 32 18 E
Ismay 70 46 33N 104 44W
Isna 51 25 17N 32 30 E
Isoka 52 10 4S 32 42 E
Isparta 30 37 47N 30 30 E
Íspica 18 36 47N 14 53 E
Israel ■ 28 32 0N 34 50 E
Isseka 47 28 30S 114 35 E
Issyk-Kul, Ozero 24 42 25N 77 15 E
İstanbul 30 41 0N 29 0 E
Istokpoga, L. 69 27 22N 81 14W
Istra 18 45 10N 14 0 E
Istria = Istra 18 45 10N 14 0 E
Itabaiana 79 7 18S 35 19W
Itaberaba 79 12 32S 40 18W
Itabira 79 19 37S 43 13W
Itabuna 79 14 48S 39 16W
Itaipu Dam 80 25 30S 54 30W
Itaituba 79 4 10S 55 50W
Itajaí 80 27 50S 48 39W
Italy ■ 18 42 0N 13 0 E
Itampolo 57 24 41S 43 57 E
Itapecuru-Mirim 79 3 24S 44 20W
Itaperuna 79 21 10S 41 54W
Itapicuru →, Bahia, Brazil 79 11 47S 37 32W
Itapicuru →, Maranhão, Brazil 79 2 52S 44 12W
Itapipoca 79 3 30S 39 35W
Itaquatiara 78 2 58S 58 30W
Itaquí 80 29 8S 56 30W
Itatuba 78 5 46S 63 20W
Itchen → 7 50 57N 1 20W
Ithaca = Itháki 19 38 25N 20 40 E
Ithaca 68 42 25N 76 30W
Itháki 19 38 25N 20 40 E
Ito 36 34 58N 139 5 E
Itonamas → 78 12 28S 64 24W
Itu 53 5 10N 7 58 E
Ituaçu 79 13 50S 41 18W
Ituiutaba 79 19 0S 49 25W
Itumbiara 79 18 20S 49 10W
Ituna 65 51 10N 103 24W
Iturbe 80 23 0S 65 25W
Iturup, Ostrov 25 45 0N 148 0 E
Ivalo 20 68 38N 27 35 E
Ivalojoki → 20 68 40N 27 40 E
Ivanhoe, N.S.W., Australia 45 32 56S 144 20 E
Ivanhoe, N. Terr., Australia 46 15 41S 128 41 E
Ivanhoe L. 65 60 25N 106 30W
Ivano-Frankovsk 23 48 40N 24 40 E
Ivanovo 22 57 5N 41 0 E
Ivato 57 20 37S 47 10 E
Ivdel 22 60 42N 60 24 E
Iviza = Ibiza 13 38 54N 1 26 E
Ivohibe 57 22 31S 46 57 E
Ivory Coast ■ 50 7 30N 5 0W
Ivrea 18 45 30N 7 52 E
Ivugivik 61 62 24N 77 55W
Iwahig 34 8 36N 117 32 E
Iwaki 36 37 3N 140 55 E
Iwakuni 36 34 15N 132 8 E
Iwamizawa 36 43 12N 141 46 E
Iwanai 36 42 58N 140 30 E
Iwanuma 36 38 7N 140 51 E
Iwata 36 34 42N 137 51 E
Iwate □ 36 39 30N 141 30 E
Iwate-San 36 39 51N 141 0 E
Iwo 53 7 39N 4 9 E
Ixiamas 78 13 50S 68 5W
Ixopo 57 30 11S 30 5 E
Ixtepec 74 16 32N 95 10W
Ixtlán del Río 74 21 5N 104 21W
Izabel, L. de 75 15 30N 89 10W
Izamal 74 20 56N 89 1W
Izegem 11 50 55N 3 12 E
Izhevsk = Ustinov 22 56 51N 53 14 E
İzmir 23 38 25N 27 8 E
İzmit 30 40 45N 29 50 E
Izra 28 32 51N 36 15 E
Izumi-sano 36 34 23N 135 18 E
Izumo 36 35 20N 132 46 E

J

Jaba' 28 32 20N 35 13 E
Jabalpur 32 23 9N 79 58 E
Jabālyah 28 31 32N 34 27 E
Jablah 30 35 20N 36 0 E
Jablonec 14 50 43N 15 10 E
Jaboatão 79 8 7S 35 1W
Jaburu 78 5 30S 64 0W
Jaca 13 42 35N 0 33W
Jacareí 80 23 20S 46 0W
Jacarèzinho 80 23 5S 50 0W
Jackman 63 45 35N 70 17W
Jacksboro 71 33 14N 98 15W
Jackson, Australia 45 26 39S 149 39 E
Jackson, Ala., U.S.A. 69 31 32N 87 53W
Jackson, Calif., U.S.A. 72 38 19N 120 47W
Jackson, Ky., U.S.A. 68 37 35N 83 22W
Jackson, Mich., U.S.A. 68 42 18N 84 25W
Jackson, Minn., U.S.A. 70 43 35N 95 0W
Jackson, Miss., U.S.A. 71 32 20N 90 10W
Jackson, Mo., U.S.A. 71 37 25N 89 42W
Jackson, Ohio, U.S.A. 68 39 0N 82 40W
Jackson, Tenn., U.S.A. 69 35 40N 88 50W
Jackson, Wyo., U.S.A. 72 43 30N 110 49W
Jackson, L. 72 43 55N 110 40W
Jackson Bay 43 43 58S 168 42 E
Jacksons 43 42 46S 171 32 E
Jacksonville, Ala., U.S.A. 69 33 49N 85 45W
Jacksonville, Fla., U.S.A. 69 30 15N 81 38W
Jacksonville, Ill., U.S.A. 70 39 42N 90 15W
Jacksonville, N.C., U.S.A. 69 34 50N 77 29W
Jacksonville, Oreg., U.S.A. 72 42 19N 122 56W
Jacksonville, Tex., U.S.A. 71 31 58N 95 19W
Jacksonville Beach 69 30 19N 81 26W
Jacmel 75 18 14N 72 32W
Jacob Lake 73 36 45N 112 12W
Jacobabad 32 28 20N 68 29 E
Jacobina 79 11 11S 40 30W
Jacob's Well 28 32 13N 35 13 E
Jacques-Cartier, Mt. 63 48 57N 66 0W
Jacundá → 79 1 57S 50 26W
Jadotville = Likasi 54 10 55S 26 48 E
Jādū 51 32 0N 12 0 E
Jaén, Peru 78 5 25S 78 40W
Jaén, Spain 13 37 44N 3 43W
Jaffa = Tel Aviv-Yafo 28 32 4N 34 48 E
Jaffa, C. 45 36 58S 139 40 E
Jaffna 32 9 45N 80 2 E
Jagadhri 32 30 10N 77 20 E
Jagdalpur 33 19 3N 82 0 E
Jagersfontein 56 29 44S 25 27 E
Jagraon 32 30 50N 75 25 E
Jagtial 32 18 50N 79 0 E
Jaguariaíva 80 24 10S 49 50W
Jaguaribe → 79 4 25S 37 45W
Jagüey Grande 75 22 35N 81 7W
Jahrom 31 28 30N 53 31 E
Jailolo 35 1 5N 127 30 E
Jailolo, Selat 35 0 5N 129 5 E
Jaipur 32 27 0N 75 50 E
Jakarta 35 6 9S 106 49 E
Jakobstad 20 63 40N 22 43 E
Jal 71 32 8N 103 8W
Jalai Nur 38 49 27N 117 42 E
Jalalabad 31 34 30N 70 29 E
Jalapa 75 14 39N 89 59W
Jalapa Enríquez 74 19 32N 96 55W
Jalas, Jabal al 30 27 30N 36 30 E
Jalgaon, Maharashtra, India 32 21 2N 76 31 E
Jalgaon, Maharashtra, India 32 21 0N 75 42 E
Jalingo 53 8 55N 11 25 E
Jalisco □ 74 20 0N 104 0W
Jalna 32 19 48N 75 38 E
Jalón → 13 41 47N 1 4W
Jalpa 74 21 38N 102 58W
Jalpaiguri 33 26 32N 88 46 E
Jalq 31 27 35N 62 46 E
Jaluit I. 40 6 0N 169 30 E
Jamaari 53 11 44N 9 53 E
Jamaica ■ 75 18 10N 77 30W
Jamalpur, Bangla. 33 24 52N 89 56 E
Jamalpur, India 33 25 18N 86 28 E
Jamanxim → 79 4 43S 56 18W
Jambe 35 1 15S 132 10 E
Jambi 34 1 38S 103 30 E
Jambi □ 34 1 30S 102 30 E
James → 70 42 52N 97 18W
James B. 62 51 30N 80 0W
James Ranges 46 24 10S 132 30 E
Jamestown, Australia 45 33 10S 138 32 E
Jamestown, S. Africa 56 31 6S 26 45 E
Jamestown, Ky., U.S.A. 68 37 0N 85 5W
Jamestown, N. Dak., U.S.A. 70 46 54N 98 42W
Jamestown, N.Y., U.S.A. 68 42 5N 79 18W
Jamestown, Tenn., U.S.A. 69 36 25N 85 0W
Jamkhandi 32 16 30N 75 15 E
Jammā'īn 28 32 8N 35 12 E
Jammu 32 32 43N 74 54 E
Jammu & Kashmir □ 32 34 25N 77 0 E
Jamnagar 32 22 30N 70 6 E
Jamrud 32 33 59N 71 24 E
Jamshedpur 33 22 44N 86 12 E
Jämtlands län □ 20 62 40N 13 50 E
Jan Kempdorp 56 27 55S 24 51 E
Jan L. 65 54 56N 102 55W
Jand 32 33 30N 72 6 E
Jandaq 31 34 3N 54 22 E
Jandowae 45 26 45S 151 7 E
Janesville 70 42 39N 89 1W
Janīn 28 32 28N 35 18 E
Januária 79 15 25S 44 25W
Janub Dârfûr □ 51 11 0N 25 0 E
Janub Kordofân □ 51 12 0N 30 0 E
Jaora 32 23 40N 75 10 E
Japan ■ 36 36 0N 136 0 E
Japan, Sea of 36 40 0N 135 0 E
Japan Trench 40 32 0N 142 0 E
Japen = Yapen 35 1 50S 136 0 E
Japurá → 78 3 8S 64 46W
Jaque 78 7 27N 78 8W
Jara, La 73 37 16N 106 0W
Jarama → 13 40 2N 3 39W
Jarash 28 32 17N 35 54 E
Jardines de la Reina, Is. 75 20 50N 78 50W
Jargalant = Hovd 37 48 2N 91 37 E
Jargalant 37 48 2N 91 37 E
Jarosław 15 50 2N 22 42 E
Jarrahdale 47 32 24S 116 5 E
Jarso 51 5 15N 37 30 E
Jarvis I. 41 0 15S 159 55W
Jarwa 33 27 38N 82 30 E
Jāsk 31 25 38N 57 45 E
Jasło 15 49 45N 21 30 E
Jasper, Canada 64 52 55N 118 5W
Jasper, Ala., U.S.A. 69 33 48N 87 16W
Jasper, Fla., U.S.A. 69 30 31N 82 58W
Jasper, Minn., U.S.A. 70 43 52N 96 22W
Jasper, Tex., U.S.A. 71 30 59N 93 58W
Jasper Nat. Park 64 52 50N 118 8W
Jassy = Iaşi 17 47 10N 27 40 E
Jászberény 15 47 30N 19 55 E
Jataí 79 17 58S 51 48W
Jatibarang 35 6 28S 108 18 E
Jatinegara 35 6 13S 106 52 E
Játiva 13 39 0N 0 32W
Jatt 28 32 24N 35 2 E
Jaú 79 22 10S 48 30W
Jauja 78 11 45S 75 15W
Jaunpur 33 25 46N 82 44 E
Java = Jawa 35 7 0S 110 0 E
Java Sea 34 4 35S 107 15 E
Java Trench 40 10 0S 110 0W
Javhlant = Ulyasutay 37 47 56N 97 28 E
Jawa 35 7 0S 110 0 E
Jay 71 36 25N 94 46W
Jaya, Puncak 35 3 57S 137 17 E
Jayanti 33 26 45N 89 40 E
Jayapura 35 2 28S 140 38 E
Jayawijaya, Pegunungan 35 5 0S 139 0 E
Jaynagar 33 26 43N 86 9 E
Jayton 71 33 17N 100 35W
Jean 73 35 47N 115 20W
Jean Marie River 60 61 32N 120 38W
Jean Rabel 75 19 50N 73 5W
Jeanerette 71 29 52N 91 38W
Jeanette, Ostrov 25 76 43N 158 0 E
Jebba 53 9 9N 4 48 E
Jebel, Bahr el → 51 9 30N 30 25 E
Jedburgh 8 55 28N 2 33W
Jedda = Jiddah 29 21 29N 39 10 E
Jędrzejów 15 50 35N 20 15 E
Jedway 64 52 17N 131 14W
Jefferson, Iowa, U.S.A. 70 42 3N 94 25W
Jefferson, Tex., U.S.A. 71 32 45N 94 23W
Jefferson, Wis., U.S.A. 70 43 0N 88 49W
Jefferson, Mt., Nev., U.S.A. 72 38 51N 117 0W
Jefferson, Mt., Oreg., U.S.A. 72 44 45N 121 50W
Jefferson City, Mo., U.S.A. 70 38 34N 92 10W
Jefferson City, Tenn., U.S.A. 69 36 8N 83 30W
Jeffersonville 68 38 20N 85 42W
Jega 53 12 15N 4 23 E
Jelenia Góra 14 50 50N 15 45 E
Jelgava 22 56 41N 23 49 E
Jellicoe 62 49 40N 87 30W
Jemaja 34 3 5N 105 45 E
Jember 35 8 11S 113 41 E
Jembongan 34 6 45N 117 20 E
Jemeppe 11 50 37N 5 30 E
Jena, Germany 14 50 56N 11 33 E
Jena, U.S.A. 71 31 41N 92 7W
Jenkins 68 37 13N 82 41W

Jennings

Jennings 71 30 10N 92 45W
Jennings → 64 59 38N 132 5W
Jeparit 45 36 8S 142 1 E
Jequié 79 13 51S 40 5W
Jequitinhonha 79 16 30S 41 0W
Jequitinhonha → 79 15 51S 38 53W
Jerada 50 34 17N 2 10W
Jerantut 34 3 56N 102 22 E
Jérémie 75 18 40N 74 10W
Jerez, Punta 74 22 58N 97 40W
Jerez de García Salinas 74 22 39N 103 0W
Jerez de la Frontera 13 36 41N 6 7W
Jerez de los Caballeros 13 38 20N 6 45W
Jericho = El Arīḩā 28 31 52N 35 27 E
Jericho 44 23 38S 146 6 E
Jerilderie 45 35 20S 145 41 E
Jerome 73 34 50N 112 0W
Jersey, I. 7 49 13N 2 7W
Jersey City 68 40 41N 74 8W
Jersey Shore 68 41 17N 77 18W
Jerseyville 70 39 5N 90 20W
Jerusalem 28 31 47N 35 10 E
Jervis B. 45 35 8S 150 46 E
Jesselton = Kota Kinabalu 34 6 0N 116 4 E
Jessore 33 23 10N 89 10 E
Jesup 69 31 36N 81 54W
Jetmore 71 38 10N 99 57W
Jewett 71 31 20N 96 8W
Jeypore 33 18 50N 82 38 E
Jhal Jhao 31 26 20N 65 35 E
Jhalawar 32 24 40N 76 10 E
Jhang Maghiana 32 31 15N 72 22 E
Jhansi 32 25 30N 78 36 E
Jharsaguda 33 21 50N 84 5 E
Jhelum 32 33 0N 73 45 E
Jhelum → 32 31 20N 72 10 E
Jhunjhunu 32 28 10N 75 30 E
Ji Xian 38 36 7N 110 40 E
Jia Xian 38 38 12N 110 28 E
Jiamusi 38 46 40N 130 26 E
Ji'an 39 27 6N 114 59 E
Jianchuan 37 26 38N 99 55 E
Jiande 39 29 23N 119 15 E
Jiangbei 39 29 40N 106 34 E
Jiange 39 32 4N 105 32 E
Jiangjin 39 29 14N 106 14 E
Jiangling 39 30 25N 112 12 E
Jiangmen 39 22 32N 113 0 E
Jiangshan 39 28 40N 118 37 E
Jiangsu □ 39 33 0N 120 0 E
Jiangxi □ 39 27 30N 116 0 E
Jiangyin 39 31 54N 120 17 E
Jiangyong 39 25 20N 111 22 E
Jiangyou 39 31 44N 104 43 E
Jianning 39 26 50N 116 50 E
Jian'ou 39 27 3N 118 17 E
Jianshi 39 30 37N 109 38 E
Jianshui 37 23 36N 102 43 E
Jianyang 39 27 20N 118 5 E
Jiao Xian 38 36 18N 120 1 E
Jiaohe 38 38 2N 116 20 E
Jiaozhou Wan 38 36 5N 120 10 E
Jiaozuo 39 35 16N 113 12 E
Jiawang 39 34 28N 117 26 E
Jiaxing 39 30 49N 120 45 E
Jiayi 39 23 30N 120 24 E
Jibuti = Djibouti ■ 29 12 0N 43 0 E
Jiddah 29 21 29N 39 10 E
Jido 33 29 2N 94 58 E
Jifnā 28 31 58N 35 13 E
Jihlava 14 49 28N 15 35 E
Jihlava → 14 48 55N 16 36 E
Jijel 50 36 52N 5 50 E
Jijiga 29 9 20N 42 50 E
Jilin 38 43 44N 126 30 E
Jilin □ 38 44 0N 124 0 E
Jiloca → 13 41 21N 1 39W
Jilong 39 25 8N 121 42 E
Jima 51 7 40N 36 47 E
Jiménez 74 27 10N 104 54W
Jimo 38 36 23N 120 30 E
Jin Xian 38 38 55N 121 42 E
Jinan 38 36 38N 117 1 E
Jincheng 38 35 29N 112 50 E
Jindabyne 45 36 25S 148 35 E
Jing He → 39 34 27N 109 4 E
Jing Xian 39 26 33N 109 40 E
Jingchuan 38 35 20N 107 20 E
Jingdezhen 39 29 20N 117 11 E
Jinggu 37 23 35N 100 41 E
Jinghai 38 38 55N 116 55 E
Jingle 38 38 20N 111 55 E
Jingmen 39 31 0N 112 10 E
Jingning 38 35 30N 105 43 E
Jingshan 39 31 1N 113 7 E
Jingtai 38 37 10N 104 6 E
Jingxi 39 23 8N 106 27 E
Jingyu 38 42 25N 126 45 E
Jingyuan 38 36 30N 104 40 E
Jingziguan 39 33 15N 111 0 E
Jinhe 38 51 18N 121 32 E
Jinhua 39 29 8N 119 38 E
Jining, Nei Mongol Zizhiqu, China 38 41 5N 113 0 E
Jining, Shandong, China 39 35 22N 116 34 E
Jinja 54 0 25N 33 12 E
Jinmen Dao 39 24 25N 118 25 E
Jinnah Barrage 31 32 58N 71 33 E
Jinotega 75 13 6N 85 59W
Jinotepe 75 11 50N 86 10W
Jinshi 39 29 40N 111 50 E
Jinxiang 39 35 5N 116 22 E
Jinzhou 38 41 5N 121 3 E
Jiparaná → 78 8 3S 62 52W
Jipijapa 78 1 0S 80 40W
Jiquilpan 74 19 57N 102 42W
Jishou 39 28 21N 109 43 E
Jisr al Ḩusayn 28 31 53N 35 33 E
Jisr ash Shughūr 30 35 49N 36 18 E
Jitarning 47 32 48S 117 57 E
Jiu → 15 43 47N 23 48 E
Jiudengkou 38 39 56N 106 40 E
Jiujiang 39 29 42N 115 58 E
Jiuling Shan 39 28 40N 114 40 E
Jiuquan 37 39 50N 98 20 E
Jixi 38 45 20N 130 50 E
Jīzān 29 17 0N 42 20 E
Joaçaba 80 27 5S 51 31W
João Pessoa 79 7 10S 34 52W
Joaquín V. González 80 25 10S 64 0W
Jodhpur 32 26 23N 73 8 E
Joensuu 22 62 37N 29 49 E
Jofane 57 21 15S 34 18 E
Joggins 63 45 42N 64 27W
Jogjakarta = Yogyakarta 35 7 49S 110 22 E
Johannesburg 57 26 10S 28 2 E
John Day 72 44 25N 118 57W
John Day → 72 45 44N 120 39W
John H. Kerr Res. 69 36 20N 78 30W
John o' Groats 8 58 39N 3 3W
Johnson 71 37 35N 101 48W
Johnson City, N.Y., U.S.A. 68 42 7N 75 57W
Johnson City, Tenn., U.S.A. 69 36 18N 82 21W
Johnson City, Tex., U.S.A. 71 30 15N 98 24W
Johnson's Crossing 64 60 29N 133 18W
Johnston, L. 47 32 25S 120 30 E
Johnston Falls = Mambilima Falls 54 10 31S 28 45 E
Johnston I. 41 17 10N 169 8W
Johnstone Str. 64 50 28N 126 0W
Johnstown, N.Y., U.S.A. 68 43 1N 74 20W
Johnstown, Pa., U.S.A. 68 40 19N 78 53W
Johor Baharu 34 1 28N 103 46 E
Joinvile 80 26 15S 48 55W
Jokkmokk 20 66 35N 19 50 E
Jökulsá á Dal → 20 65 40N 14 16W
Jökulsá Fjöllum → 20 66 10N 16 30W
Joliet 68 41 30N 88 0W
Joliette 62 46 3N 73 24W
Jolo 35 6 0N 121 0 E
Jombang 35 7 33S 112 14 E
Jome 35 1 16S 127 30 E
Jonesboro, Ark., U.S.A. 71 35 50N 90 45W
Jonesboro, Ill., U.S.A. 71 37 26N 89 18W
Jonesboro, La., U.S.A. 71 32 15N 92 41W
Jonesport 63 44 32N 67 38W
Jonglei □ 51 7 30N 32 30 E
Jönköping 21 57 45N 14 10 E
Jönköpings län □ 21 57 30N 14 30 E
Jonquière 63 48 27N 71 14W
Joplin 71 37 0N 94 31W
Jordan 72 47 25N 106 58W
Jordan ■ 30 31 0N 36 0 E
Jordan → 28 31 48N 35 32 E
Jordan Valley 72 43 0N 117 2W
Jorhat 33 26 45N 94 12 E
Jorm 31 36 50N 70 52 E
Jörn 20 65 4N 20 1 E
Jorong 34 3 58S 114 56 E
Jos 53 9 53N 8 51 E
Joseph 72 45 27N 117 13W
Joseph, L. 63 52 45N 65 18W
Joseph Bonaparte G. 46 14 35S 128 50 E
Joseph City 73 35 0N 110 16W
Jostedal 21 61 35N 7 15 E
Jotunheimen 21 61 35N 8 25 E
Jourdanton 71 28 54N 98 32W
Joussard 64 55 22N 115 50W
Jovellanos 75 22 40N 81 10W
Jowzjān □ 31 36 10N 66 0 E
Ju Xian 39 36 35N 118 20 E
Juan Aldama 74 24 20N 103 23W
Juan de Fuca Str. 72 48 15N 124 0W
Juan de Nova 57 17 3S 43 45 E
Juan Fernández, Arch. de 76 33 50S 80 0W
Juárez 80 37 40S 59 43W
Juárez, Sierra de 74 32 0N 116 0W
Juàzeiro 79 9 30S 40 30W
Juàzeiro do Norte 79 7 10S 39 18W
Jubbulpore = Jabalpur 32 23 9N 79 58 E
Jubilee L. 47 29 0S 126 50 E
Juby, C. 50 28 0N 12 59W
Júcar → 13 39 5N 0 10W
Juchitán 74 16 27N 95 5W
Judaea = Har Yehuda 28 31 35N 34 57 E
Judith → 72 47 44N 109 38W
Judith Gap 72 46 40N 109 46W
Jugoslavia = Yugoslavia ■ 19 44 0N 20 0 E
Juigalpa 75 12 6N 85 26W
Juiz de Fora 79 21 43S 43 19W
Julesburg 70 41 0N 102 20W
Juli 78 16 10S 69 25W
Julia Cr. → 44 20 0S 141 11 E
Julia Creek 44 20 39S 141 44 E
Juliaca 78 15 25S 70 10W
Julian 73 33 4N 116 38W
Julianehåb 2 60 43N 46 0W
Jullundur 32 31 20N 75 40 E
Julu 38 37 15N 115 2 E
Jumentos Cays 75 23 0N 75 40 E
Jumet 11 50 27N 4 25 E
Jumilla 13 38 28N 1 19W
Jumla 33 29 15N 82 13 E
Jumna = Yamuna → 33 25 30N 81 53 E
Junagadh 32 21 30N 70 30 E
Junction, Tex., U.S.A. 71 30 29N 99 48W
Junction, Utah, U.S.A. 73 38 10N 112 15W
Junction B. 44 11 52S 133 55 E
Junction City, Kans., U.S.A. 70 39 4N 96 55W
Junction City, Oreg., U.S.A. 72 44 14N 123 12W
Junction Pt. 44 11 45S 133 50 E
Jundah 44 24 46S 143 2 E
Jundiaí 80 24 30S 47 0W
Juneau 60 58 20N 134 20W
Junee 45 34 53S 147 35 E
Junggar Pendi 37 44 30N 86 0 E
Junín 80 34 33S 60 57W
Junín de los Andes 80 39 45S 71 0W
Jūniyah 30 33 59N 35 38 E
Junta, La 71 38 0N 103 30W
Juntura 72 43 44N 118 4W
Jupiter → 63 49 29N 63 37W
Jur, Nahr el → 51 8 45N 29 15 E
Jura 8 56 0N 5 50W
Jura □ 12 46 47N 5 45 E
Jura, Mts. 12 46 40N 6 5 E
Jura, Sd. of 8 55 57N 5 45W
Jurado 78 7 7N 77 46W
Juruá → 78 2 37S 65 44W
Juruena → 78 7 20S 58 3W
Juruti 79 2 9S 56 4W
Justo Daract 80 33 52S 65 12W
Juticalpa 75 14 40N 86 12W
Jutland = Jylland 21 56 25N 9 30 E
Juventud, I. de la 75 21 40N 82 40W
Juwain 31 31 45N 61 30 E
Jylland 21 56 25N 9 30 E
Jyväskylä 20 62 14N 25 50 E

K

K2, Mt. 32 35 58N 76 32 E
Kaap die Goeie Hoop 56 34 24S 18 30 E
Kaap Plateau 56 28 30S 24 0 E
Kaapkruis 56 21 55S 13 57 E
Kaapstad = Cape Town 56 33 55S 18 22 E
Kabaena 35 5 15S 122 0 E
Kabala 50 9 38N 11 37W
Kabale 54 1 15S 30 0 E
Kabalo 54 6 0S 27 0 E
Kabambare 54 4 41S 27 39 E
Kabanjahe 34 3 6N 98 30 E
Kabara 50 16 40N 2 50W
Kabardino-Balkar-A.S.S.R. □ 23 43 30N 43 30 E
Kabare 35 0 4S 130 58 E
Kabarega Falls 54 2 15N 31 30 E
Kabarnet 52 0 31N 35 44 E
Kabasalan 35 7 47N 122 44 E
Kabba 53 7 50N 6 3 E
Kabinakagami L. 62 48 54N 84 25W
Kabīr, Zab al → 30 36 0N 43 0 E
Kabīr Kūh 30 33 0N 47 30 E
Kabkabīyah 51 13 50N 24 0 E
Kabompo → 55 14 10S 23 11 E
Kabongo 54 7 22S 25 33 E
Kabra 44 23 25S 150 25 E
Kabūd Gonbad 31 37 5N 59 45 E
Kābul 31 34 28N 69 11 E
Kābul □ 31 34 30N 69 0 E
Kabul → 32 33 55N 72 14 E
Kaburuang 35 3 50N 126 30 E
Kabwe 55 14 30S 28 29 E
Kachchh, Gulf of 32 22 50N 69 15 E
Kachchh, Rann of 32 24 0N 70 0 E
Kachin □ 33 26 0N 97 30 E
Kachiry 24 53 10N 75 50 E
Kackar 30 40 45N 41 10 E
Kadan Kyun 34 12 30N 98 20 E
Kade 53 6 7N 0 56W
Kadina 45 34 0S 137 43 E
Kadirli 30 37 23N 36 5 E
Kadiyevka = Stakhanov 23 48 35N 38 40 E
Kadoka 70 43 50N 101 31W
Kadoma 55 18 20S 29 52 E
Kâdugli 51 11 0N 29 45 E
Kaduna 53 10 30N 7 21 E
Kaduna □ 53 11 0N 7 30 E
Kaédi 50 16 9N 13 28W
Kaelé 53 10 7N 14 27 E
Kaesŏng 38 37 58N 126 35 E
Kāf 30 31 25N 37 29 E
Kafakumba 54 9 38S 23 46 E
Kafan 23 39 18N 46 15 E
Kafanchan 53 9 40N 8 20 E
Kafareti 53 10 25N 11 12 E
Kaffrine 50 14 8N 15 36W
Kafia Kingi 51 9 20N 24 25 E
Kafirévs, Ákra 19 38 9N 24 38 E
Kafr 'Ayn 28 32 3N 35 7 E
Kafr Kammā 28 32 44N 35 26 E
Kafr Kannā 28 32 45N 35 20 E
Kafr Mālik 28 32 0N 35 18 E
Kafr Mandā 28 32 49N 35 15 E
Kafr Quaddūm 28 32 14N 35 7 E
Kafr Rā'ī 28 32 23N 35 9 E
Kafr Şīr 28 33 19N 35 23 E
Kafr Yāsīf 28 32 58N 35 10 E
Kafue → 55 15 30S 29 0 E
Kafulwe 54 9 0S 29 1 E
Kaga Bandoro 51 7 0N 19 10 E
Kagade 52 0 58N 30 48 E
Kagan 24 39 43N 64 33 E
Kagawa □ 36 34 15N 134 0 E
Kağizman 30 40 5N 43 10 E
Kagoshima 36 31 35N 130 33 E
Kagoshima □ 36 31 30N 130 30 E
Kagoshima-Wan 36 31 25N 130 40 E
Kahama 54 4 8S 32 30 E
Kahayan → 34 3 40S 114 0 E
Kahe 52 3 30S 37 25 E
Kahemba 54 7 18S 18 55 E
Kahniah → 64 58 15N 120 55W
Kahnūj 31 27 55N 57 40 E
Kahoka 70 40 25N 91 42W
Kahoolawe 66 20 33N 156 35W
Kahramanmaras 30 37 37N 36 53 E
Kai, Kepulauan 35 5 55S 132 45W
Kai Besar 35 5 35S 133 0 E
Kai-Ketil 35 5 45S 132 40 E
Kaiama 53 9 36N 4 1 E
Kaiapoi 43 42 24S 172 40 E
Kaieteur Falls 78 5 1N 59 10W
Kaifeng 39 34 48N 114 21 E
Kaihua 39 29 12N 118 20 E
Kaiingveld 56 30 0S 22 0 E
Kaikohe 43 35 25S 173 49 E
Kaikoura 43 42 25S 173 43 E
Kaikoura Pen. 43 42 25S 173 43 E
Kaikoura Ra. 43 41 59S 173 41 E
Kaili 39 26 33N 107 59 E
Kailu 38 43 38N 121 18 E
Kailua 66 19 39N 156 0W
Kaimana 35 3 39S 133 45 E
Kaimanawa Mts. 43 39 15S 175 56 E
Kaingaroa Forest 43 38 24S 176 30 E
Kainji Res. 53 10 1N 4 40 E
Kaipara Harbour 43 36 25S 174 14 E
Kaiping 39 22 23N 112 42 E
Kaipokok B. 63 54 54N 59 47W
Kaironi 35 0 47S 133 40 E
Kairouan 50 35 45N 10 5 E
Kaiserslautern 14 49 30N 7 43 E
Kaitaia 43 35 8S 173 17 E
Kaitangata 43 46 17S 169 51 E
Kaiwi Channel 66 21 13N 157 30W
Kaiyuan 38 42 28N 124 1 E
Kajaani 20 64 17N 27 46 E
Kajabbi 44 20 0S 140 1 E
Kajana = Kajaani 20 64 17N 27 46 E
Kajo Kaji 51 3 58N 31 40 E
Kaka 51 10 38N 32 10 E
Kakabeka Falls 62 48 24N 89 37W
Kakamas 56 28 45S 20 33 E
Kakamega 54 0 20N 34 46 E
Kakanui Mts. 43 45 10S 170 30 E
Kakegawa 36 34 45N 138 1 E
Kakhovka 23 46 40N 33 15 E
Kakhovskoye Vdkhr. 23 47 5N 34 16 E
Kakinada 33 16 57N 82 11 E
Kakisa → 64 61 3N 118 10W
Kakisa L. 64 60 56N 117 43W
Kakogawa 36 34 46N 134 51 E
Kakwa → 64 54 37N 118 28W
Kala 53 12 2N 14 40 E
Kalabagh 32 33 0N 71 28 E
Kalabahi 35 8 13S 124 31 E
Kalabáka 19 39 42N 21 39 E
Kalabo 55 14 58S 22 40 E
Kalach 23 50 22N 41 0 E
Kaladan → 33 20 20N 93 5 E
Kalahari 56 24 0S 21 30 E
Kalahari Gemsbok Nat. Park 56 25 30S 20 30 E
Kalakamati 57 20 40S 27 25 E
Kalakan 25 55 15N 116 45 E
Kalama 72 46 0N 122 55W
Kalamata 19 37 3N 22 10 E
Kalamazoo 68 42 20N 85 35W
Kalamazoo → 68 42 40N 86 12W
Kalan 30 39 7N 39 32 E
Kalannie 47 30 22S 117 5 E
Kalao 35 7 21S 121 0 E
Kalaotoa 35 7 20S 121 50 E
Kalat 31 29 8N 66 31 E
Kalbarri 47 27 40S 114 10 E
Kalegauk Kyun 33 15 33N 97 35 E
Kalemie 54 5 55S 29 9 E
Kalewa 33 23 10N 94 15 E
Kálfafellsstaður 20 64 11N 15 53W
Kalgan = Zhangjiakou 38 40 48N 114 55 E
Kalgoorlie-Boulder 47 30 40S 121 22 E
Kaliakra, Nos 19 43 21N 28 30 E
Kalianda 34 5 50S 105 45 E
Kalibo 35 11 43N 122 22 E
Kalima 54 2 33S 26 32 E
Kalimantan 34 0 0 114 0 E
Kalimantan Barat □ 34 0 0 110 30 E
Kalimantan Selatan □ 34 2 30S 115 30 E
Kalimantan Tengah □ 34 2 0S 113 30 E
Kalimantan Timur □ 34 1 30N 116 30 E
Kálimnos 19 37 0N 27 0 E
Kalinin 22 56 55N 35 55 E
Kaliningrad, R.S.F.S.R., U.S.S.R. 22 55 58N 37 54 E
Kaliningrad, R.S.F.S.R., U.S.S.R. 22 54 42N 20 32 E
Kalispell 72 48 10N 114 22W
Kalisz 15 51 45N 18 8 E
Kaliua 54 5 5S 31 48 E
Kalix → 20 65 50N 23 11 E
Kalkaska 68 44 44N 85 11W
Kalkfeld 56 20 57S 16 14 E
Kalkfontein 56 22 4S 20 57 E
Kalkrand 56 24 1S 17 35 E
Kallia 28 31 46N 35 30 E
Kallsjön 20 63 38N 13 0 E
Kalmalo 53 13 40N 5 20 E
Kalmar 21 56 40N 16 20 E
Kalmyk A.S.S.R. □ 23 46 5N 46 1 E
Kalmykovo 23 49 0N 51 47 E
Kalocsa 15 46 32N 19 0 E
Kalomo 55 17 0S 26 30 E
Kaluga 22 54 35N 36 10 E
Kalundborg 21 55 41N 11 5 E
Kalutara 32 6 35N 80 0 E
Kalya 22 60 15N 59 59 E
Kama → 22 55 45N 52 0 E
Kamaishi 36 39 20N 142 0 E
Kamandorskiye Ostrava 25 55 0N 167 0 E
Kamaran 29 15 21N 42 35 E
Kambalda 47 31 10S 121 37 E
Kambarka 22 56 15N 54 11 E
Kamchatka, P-ov. 25 57 0N 160 0 E
Kamen 24 53 50N 81 30 E
Kamenets-Podolskiy 23 48 45N 26 10 E
Kamenjak, Rt. 18 44 47N 13 55 E
Kamenka 22 65 58N 44 0 E
Kamensk Uralskiy 24 56 25N 62 2 E
Kamenskoye 25 62 45N 165 30 E
Kamiah 72 46 12N 116 2W
Kamieskroon 56 30 9S 17 56 E
Kamilukuak, L. 65 62 22N 101 40W
Kamina 54 8 45S 25 0 E
Kaminak L. 65 62 10N 95 0W
Kamloops 64 50 40N 120 20W
Kampala 54 0 20N 32 30 E
Kampar → 34 0 30N 103 8 E
Kampen 11 52 33N 5 53 E

Khalmer Yu

Kampot **34** 10 36N 104 10 E
Kampuchea = Cambodia ■ **34** 12 15N 105 0 E
Kampung → **35** 5 44S 138 24 E
Kampungbaru = Tolitoli **35** 1 5N 120 50 E
Kamrau, Teluk **35** 3 30S 133 36 E
Kamsack **65** 51 34N 101 54W
Kamskoye Vdkhr. **22** 58 0N 56 0 E
Kamuchawie L. **65** 56 18N 101 59W
Kamui-Misaki **36** 43 20N 140 21 E
Kamyshin **23** 50 10N 45 24 E
Kanaaupscow **62** 54 2N 76 30W
Kanab **73** 37 3N 112 29W
Kanab Creek **73** 37 0N 112 40W
Kanagawa □ **36** 35 20N 139 20 E
Kanairiktok → **63** 55 2N 60 18W
Kananga **54** 5 55S 22 18 E
Kanarraville **73** 37 34N 113 12W
Kanash **22** 55 30N 47 32 E
Kanawha → **68** 38 50N 82 8W
Kanazawa **36** 36 30N 136 38 E
Kanchanaburi **34** 14 2N 99 31 E
Kanchenjunga **33** 27 50N 88 10 E
Kanchipuram **32** 12 52N 79 45 E
Kanda Kanda **54** 6 52S 23 48 E
Kandahar = Qandahār **31** 31 32N 65 30 E
Kandalaksha **22** 67 9N 32 30 E
Kandalakshkiy Zaliv **22** 66 0N 35 0 E
Kandalu **32** 29 55N 63 20 E
Kandangan **34** 2 50S 115 20 E
Kandi **53** 11 7N 2 55 E
Kandla **32** 23 0N 70 10 E
Kandos **45** 32 45S 149 58 E
Kandy **32** 7 18N 80 43 E
Kane **68** 41 39N 78 53W
Kane Basin **58** 79 1N 73 0W
Kangaroo I. **45** 35 45S 137 0 E
Kangaroo Mts. **44** 23 25S 142 0 E
Kangavar **30** 34 40N 48 0 E
Kangean, Kepulauan **34** 6 55S 115 23 E
Kanggye **38** 41 0N 126 35 E
Kangnŭng **38** 37 45N 128 54 E
Kango **54** 0 11N 10 5 E
Kangto **33** 27 50N 92 35 E
Kaniapiskau → **63** 56 40N 69 30W
Kaniapiskau L. **63** 54 10N 69 55W
Kanin, P-ov. **22** 68 0N 45 0 E
Kanin Nos, Mys **22** 68 45N 43 20 E
Kaniva **45** 36 22S 141 18 E
Kankakee **68** 41 6N 87 50W
Kankakee → **68** 41 23N 88 16W
Kankan **50** 10 23N 9 15W
Kanker **33** 20 10N 81 40 E
Kankunskiy **25** 57 37N 126 8 E
Kannapolis **69** 35 32N 80 37W
Kannauj **32** 27 3N 79 56 E
Kannod **32** 22 45N 76 40 E
Kano **53** 12 2N 8 30 E
Kano □ **53** 11 45N 9 0 E
Kanowit **34** 2 14N 112 20 E
Kanowna **47** 30 32S 121 31 E
Kanoya **36** 31 25N 130 50 E
Kanpetlet **33** 21 10N 93 59 E
Kanpur **32** 26 28N 80 20 E
Kansas □ **70** 38 40N 98 0W
Kansas → **70** 39 7N 94 36W
Kansas City, Kans., U.S.A. **70** 39 0N 94 40W
Kansas City, Mo., U.S.A. **70** 39 3N 94 30W
Kansk **25** 56 20N 95 37 E
Kansu = Gansu □ **38** 36 0N 104 0 E
Kantang **34** 7 25N 99 31 E
Kantché **53** 13 31N 8 30 E
Kanturk **9** 52 10N 8 55W
Kanuma **36** 36 34N 139 42 E
Kanus **56** 27 50S 18 39 E
Kanye **56** 25 0S 25 28 E
Kaohsiung = Gaoxiong **39** 22 38N 120 18 E
Kaokoveld **56** 19 15S 14 30 E
Kaolack **50** 14 5N 16 8W
Kapanga **54** 8 30S 22 40 E
Kapchagai **24** 43 51N 77 14 E
Kapela **18** 44 40N 15 40 E
Kapfenberg **14** 47 26N 15 18 E
Kapiri Mposhi **55** 13 59S 28 43 E
Kāpīsā □ **31** 35 0N 69 20 E
Kapiskau → **62** 52 47N 81 55W
Kapit **34** 2 0N 112 55 E
Kapiti I. **43** 40 50S 174 56 E
Kapoeta **51** 4 50N 33 35 E
Kaposvár **15** 46 25N 17 47 E
Kapps **56** 22 32S 17 18 E
Kapuas → **34** 0 25S 109 20 E
Kapuas Hulu, Pegunungan **34** 1 30N 113 30 E
Kapunda **45** 34 20S 138 56 E
Kapuskasing **62** 49 25N 82 30W
Kapuskasing → **62** 49 49N 82 0W
Kaputar, Mt. **45** 30 15S 150 10 E
Kara **24** 69 10N 65 0 E
Kara Bogaz Gol, Zaliv **23** 41 0N 53 30 E
Kara Kalpak A.S.S.R. □ **24** 43 0N 60 0 E
Kara Kum = Karakum, Peski **24** 39 30N 60 0 E
Kara Sea **24** 75 0N 70 0 E
Karabük **30** 41 12N 32 37 E
Karabutak **24** 49 59N 60 14 E
Karachi **32** 24 53N 67 0 E
Karad **32** 17 15N 74 10 E
Karadeniz Boğazı **30** 41 10N 29 10 E
Karaganda **24** 49 50N 73 10 E
Karagayly **24** 49 26N 76 0 E
Karaginskiy, Ostrov **25** 58 45N 164 0 E
Karagiye Depression **23** 43 27N 51 45 E
Karaikal **32** 10 59N 79 50 E
Karaikkudi **32** 10 0N 78 45 E
Karaj **31** 35 48N 51 0 E
Karakas **24** 48 20N 83 30 E
Karakitang **35** 3 14N 125 28 E
Karakoram Pass **32** 35 33N 77 50 E
Karakoram Ra. **32** 35 30N 77 0 E
Karakum, Peski **24** 39 30N 60 0 E
Karalon **25** 57 5N 115 50 E
Karaman **30** 37 14N 33 13 E
Karamay **37** 45 30N 84 58 E
Karambu **34** 3 53S 116 6 E
Karamea Bight **43** 41 22S 171 40 E
Karanganyar **35** 7 38S 109 37 E
Karasburg **56** 28 0S 18 44 E
Karasino **24** 66 50N 86 50 E
Karasjok **20** 69 27N 25 30 E
Karasuk **24** 53 44N 78 2 E
Karatau **24** 43 10N 70 28 E
Karatau, Khrebet **24** 43 30N 69 30 E
Karawanken **18** 46 30N 14 40 E
Karazhal **24** 48 2N 70 49 E
Karbalā **30** 32 36N 44 3 E
Karcag **15** 47 19N 20 57 E
Karda **25** 55 0N 103 16 E
Kardhítsa **19** 39 23N 21 54 E
Kareeberge **56** 30 59S 21 50 E
Karelian A.S.S.R. □ **22** 65 30N 32 30 E
Kargānrūd **30** 37 55N 49 0 E
Kargasok **24** 59 3N 80 53 E
Kargat **24** 55 10N 80 15 E
Kargil **32** 34 32N 76 12 E
Kargopol **22** 61 30N 38 58 E
Kariba Dam **55** 16 30S 28 35 E
Kariba Gorge **55** 16 30S 28 50 E
Kariba L. **55** 16 40S 28 25 E
Karibib **56** 22 0S 15 56 E
Karimata, Kepulauan **34** 1 25S 109 0 E
Karimata, Selat **34** 2 0S 108 40 E
Karimnagar **32** 18 26N 79 10 E
Karimunjawa, Kepulauan **34** 5 50S 110 30 E
Karin **29** 10 50N 45 52 E
Kariya **36** 34 58N 137 1 E
Karkaralinsk **24** 49 26N 75 30 E
Karkinitskiy Zaliv **23** 45 56N 33 0 E
Karkur **28** 32 29N 34 57 E
Karl-Marx-Stadt **14** 50 50N 12 55 E
Karlovac **18** 45 31N 15 36 E
Karlovy Vary **14** 50 13N 12 51 E
Karlsborg **21** 58 33N 14 33 E
Karlshamn **21** 56 10N 14 51 E
Karlskoga **21** 59 22N 14 33 E
Karlskrona **21** 56 10N 15 35 E
Karlsruhe **14** 49 3N 8 23 E
Karlstad, Sweden **21** 59 23N 13 30 E
Karlstad, U.S.A. **70** 48 38N 96 30W
Karnal **32** 29 42N 77 2 E
Karnali → **33** 29 0N 83 20 E
Karnaphuli Res. **33** 22 40N 92 20 E
Karnataka □ **32** 13 15N 77 0 E
Karnes City **71** 28 53N 97 53W
Karnische Alpen **14** 46 36N 13 0 E
Kärnten □ **14** 46 52N 13 30 E
Karonga **54** 9 57S 33 55 E
Karoonda **45** 35 1S 139 59 E
Karora **51** 17 44N 38 15 E
Kárpathos **19** 35 37N 27 10 E
Karpinsk **22** 59 45N 60 1 E
Karpogory **22** 63 59N 44 27 E
Kars **30** 40 40N 43 5 E
Karsakpay **24** 47 55N 66 40 E
Karshi **24** 38 53N 65 48 E
Karsun **22** 54 14N 46 57 E
Kartaly **24** 53 3N 60 40 E
Karufa **35** 3 50S 133 20 E
Karumba **44** 17 31S 140 50 E
Karungu **54** 0 50S 34 10 E
Karwar **32** 14 55N 74 13 E
Kasai → **54** 3 30S 16 10 E
Kasama **54** 10 16S 31 9 E
Kasane **56** 17 34S 24 50 E
Kasanga **54** 8 30S 31 10 E
Kasangulu **54** 4 33S 15 15 E
Kasaragod **32** 12 30N 74 58 E
Kasba L. **65** 60 20N 102 10W
Kasempa **55** 13 30S 25 44 E
Kasenga **54** 10 20S 28 45 E
Kashabowie **62** 48 40N 90 26W
Kāshān **31** 34 5N 51 30 E
Kashi **37** 39 30N 76 2 E
Kashiwazaki **36** 37 22N 138 33 E
Kashk-e Kohneh **31** 34 55N 62 30 E
Kāshmar **31** 35 16N 58 26 E
Kashmir **32** 34 0N 76 0 E
Kashun Noerh = Gaxun Nur **37** 42 22N 100 30 E
Kasimov **22** 54 55N 41 20 E
Kasiruta **35** 0 25S 127 12 E
Kaskaskia → **70** 37 58N 89 57W
Kaskattama → **65** 57 3N 90 4W
Kaskinen **20** 62 22N 21 15 E
Kaskö **20** 62 22N 21 15 E
Kaslo **64** 49 55N 116 55W
Kasmere L. **65** 59 34N 101 10W
Kasongo **54** 4 30S 26 33 E
Kasongo Lunda **54** 6 35S 16 49 E
Kásos **19** 35 20N 26 55 E
Kassala **51** 15 30N 36 0 E
Kassalâ □ **51** 15 20N 36 26 E
Kassel **14** 51 19N 9 32 E
Kassue **35** 6 58S 139 21 E
Kastamonu **30** 41 25N 33 43 E
Kastellorizon = Megiste **17** 36 8N 29 34 E
Kastoría **19** 40 30N 21 19 E
Kasulu **54** 4 37S 30 5 E
Kasur **32** 31 5N 74 25 E
Kata **25** 58 46N 102 40 E
Katako Kombe **54** 3 25S 24 20 E
Katamatite **45** 36 6S 145 41 E
Katangi **32** 21 56N 79 50 E
Katangli **25** 51 42N 143 14 E
Katha **33** 24 10N 96 30 E
Katherine **46** 14 27S 132 20 E
Kathiawar **32** 22 20N 71 0 E
Katihar **33** 25 34N 87 36 E
Katima Mulilo **56** 17 28S 24 13 E
Katingan = Mendawai → **34** 3 30S 113 0 E
Katiola **50** 8 10N 5 10W
Katkopberg **56** 30 0S 20 0 E
Katmandu **33** 27 45N 85 20 E
Katoomba **45** 33 41S 150 19 E
Katowice **15** 50 17N 19 5 E
Katrine, L. **8** 56 15N 4 30W
Katrineholm **21** 59 9N 16 12 E
Katsepe **57** 15 45S 46 15 E
Katsina **53** 13 0N 7 32 E
Katsuura **36** 35 10N 140 20 E
Kattegatt **21** 57 0N 11 20 E
Katwe **52** 0 8S 29 52 E
Katwijk-aan-Zee **11** 52 12N 4 24 E
Kauai **66** 22 0N 159 30W
Kauai Chan. **66** 21 45N 158 50W
Kaufman **71** 32 35N 96 20W
Kaukauna **68** 44 20N 88 13W
Kaukauveld **56** 20 0S 20 15 E
Kaukonen **20** 67 31N 24 53 E
Kauliranta **20** 66 27N 23 41 E
Kaunas **22** 54 54N 23 54 E
Kaura Namoda **53** 12 37N 6 33 E
Kautokeino **20** 69 0N 23 4 E
Kavacha **25** 60 16N 169 51 E
Kavali **32** 14 55N 80 1 E
Kavála **19** 40 57N 24 28 E
Kavkaz, Bolshoi **23** 42 50N 44 0 E
Kaw **79** 4 30N 52 15W
Kawagoe **36** 35 55N 139 29 E
Kawaguchi **36** 35 52N 139 45 E
Kawaihae **66** 20 3N 155 50W
Kawambwa **54** 9 48S 29 3 E
Kawardha **33** 22 0N 81 17 E
Kawasaki **36** 35 35N 139 42 E
Kawene **62** 48 45N 91 15W
Kawerau **43** 38 7S 176 42 E
Kawhia Harbour **43** 38 5S 174 51 E
Kawio, Kepulauan **35** 4 30N 125 30 E
Kawnro **33** 22 48N 99 8 E
Kawthoolei □ = Kawthule □ **33** 18 0N 97 30 E
Kawthule □ **33** 18 0N 97 30 E
Kaya **53** 13 4N 1 10W
Kayah □ **33** 19 15N 97 15 E
Kayan → **34** 2 55N 117 35 E
Kaycee **72** 43 45N 106 46W
Kayeli **35** 3 20S 127 10 E
Kayenta **73** 36 46N 110 15W
Kayes **50** 14 25N 11 30W
Kayoa **35** 0 1N 127 28 E
Kayrunnera **45** 30 40S 142 30 E
Kayseri **30** 38 45N 35 30 E
Kaysville **72** 41 2N 111 58W
Kayuagung **34** 3 24S 104 50 E
Kazachinskoye **25** 56 16N 107 36 E
Kazachye **25** 70 52N 135 58 E
Kazakh S.S.R. □ **23** 50 0N 70 0 E
Kazan **22** 55 48N 49 3 E
Kazanlúk **19** 42 38N 25 20 E
Kāzerūn **31** 29 38N 51 40 E
Kazumba **54** 6 25S 22 5 E
Kazym → **24** 63 54N 65 50 E
Ké-Macina **50** 13 58N 5 22W
Kéa **19** 37 35N 24 22 E
Keams Canyon **73** 35 53N 110 9W
Kearney **70** 40 45N 99 3W
Keban **23** 38 50N 38 50 E
Kebnekaise **20** 67 53N 18 33 E
Kebri Dehar **29** 6 45N 44 17 E
Kebumen **35** 7 42S 109 40 E
Kechika → **64** 59 41N 127 12W
Kecskemét **15** 46 57N 19 42 E
Kedgwick **63** 47 40N 67 20W
Kedia Hill **56** 21 28S 24 37 E
Kediri **35** 7 51S 112 1 E
Kédougou **50** 12 35N 12 10W
Keeley L. **65** 54 54N 108 8W
Keeling Is. = Cocos Is. **3** 12 10S 96 55 E
Keene **68** 42 57N 72 17W
Keeper Hill **9** 52 46N 8 17W
Keer-Weer, C. **44** 14 0S 141 32 E
Keetmanshoop **56** 26 35S 18 8 E
Keewatin **70** 47 23N 93 0W
Keewatin □ **65** 63 20N 95 0W
Keewatin → **65** 56 29N 100 46W
Kefallinía **19** 38 20N 20 30 E
Kefamenanu **35** 9 28S 124 29 E
Kefar 'Eqron **28** 31 52N 34 49 E
Kefar Hasīdim **28** 32 47N 35 5 E
Kefar Nahum **28** 32 54N 35 34 E
Kefar Sava **28** 32 11N 34 54 E
Kefar Szold **28** 33 11N 35 39 E
Kefar Vitkin **28** 32 22N 34 53 E
Kefar Yehezqel **28** 32 34N 35 22 E
Kefar Yona **28** 32 20N 34 54 E
Kefar Zekharya **28** 31 43N 34 57 E
Kefar Zetim **28** 32 48N 35 27 E
Keffi **53** 8 55N 7 43 E
Keflavík **20** 64 2N 22 35W
Keg River **64** 57 54N 117 55W
Kegaska **63** 50 9N 61 18W
Keighley **6** 53 52N 1 54W
Keimoes **56** 28 41S 20 59 E
Keith, Australia **45** 36 6S 140 20 E
Keith, U.K. **8** 57 33N 2 58W
Keith Arm **60** 64 20N 122 15W
Kekri **32** 26 0N 75 10 E
Kël **25** 69 30N 124 10 E
Kelan **38** 38 43N 111 31 E
Kelang **34** 3 2N 101 26 E
Kelibia **51** 36 50N 11 3 E
Kellé **54** 0 8S 14 38 E
Keller **72** 48 2N 118 44W
Kellerberrin **47** 31 36S 117 38 E
Kellogg **72** 47 30N 116 5W
Kelloselkä **20** 66 56N 28 53 E
Kells = Ceanannus Mor **9** 53 42N 6 53W
Kélo **51** 9 10N 15 45 E
Kelowna **64** 49 50N 119 25W
Kelsey Bay **64** 50 25N 126 0W
Kelso, N.Z. **43** 45 54S 169 15 E
Kelso, U.K. **8** 55 36N 2 27W
Kelso, U.S.A. **72** 46 10N 122 57W
Keluang **34** 2 3N 103 18 E
Kelvington **65** 52 10N 103 30W
Kem **22** 65 0N 34 38 E
Kem → **22** 64 57N 34 41 E
Kema **35** 1 22N 125 8 E
Kemah **30** 39 32N 39 5 E
Kemano **64** 53 35N 128 0W
Kemerovo **24** 55 20N 86 5 E
Kemi **20** 65 44N 24 34 E
Kemi älv = Kemijoki → **20** 65 47N 24 32 E
Kemijärvi **20** 66 43N 27 22 E
Kemijoki → **20** 65 47N 24 32 E
Kemmerer **72** 41 52N 110 30W
Kemmuna = Comino **18** 36 0N 14 20 E
Kemp L. **71** 33 45N 99 15W
Kempsey **45** 31 1S 152 50 E
Kempt, L. **62** 47 25N 74 22W
Kempten **14** 47 42N 10 18 E
Kemptville **62** 45 0N 75 38W
Kendal, Indonesia **34** 6 56S 110 14 E
Kendal, U.K. **6** 54 19N 2 44W
Kendall **45** 31 35S 152 44 E
Kendall → **44** 14 4S 141 35 E
Kendallville **68** 41 25N 85 15W
Kendari **35** 3 50S 122 30 E
Kendawangan **34** 2 32S 110 17 E
Kende **53** 11 30N 4 12 E
Kendenup **47** 34 30S 117 38 E
Kendrapara **33** 20 35N 86 30 E
Kendrew **56** 32 32S 24 30 E
Kendrick **72** 46 43N 116 41W
Kenedy **71** 28 49N 97 51W
Kenema **50** 7 50N 11 14W
Keng Tawng **33** 20 45N 98 18 E
Keng Tung **33** 21 0N 99 30 E
Kenge **54** 4 50S 17 4 E
Kenhardt **56** 29 19S 21 12 E
Kenitra **50** 34 15N 6 40W
Kenmare, Ireland **9** 51 52N 9 35W
Kenmare, U.S.A. **70** 48 40N 102 4W
Kenmare → **9** 51 40N 10 0W
Kennebec **70** 43 56N 99 54W
Kennedy Ra. **47** 24 45S 115 10 E
Kennedy Taungdeik **33** 23 15N 93 45 E
Kennet → **7** 51 24N 0 58W
Kenneth Ra. **47** 23 50S 117 8 E
Kennett **71** 36 7N 90 0W
Kennewick **72** 46 11N 119 2W
Kénogami **63** 48 25N 71 15W
Kenogami → **62** 51 6N 84 28W
Kenora **65** 49 47N 94 29W
Kenosha **68** 42 33N 87 48W
Kensington, Canada **63** 46 28N 63 34W
Kensington, U.S.A. **70** 39 48N 99 2W
Kensington Downs **44** 22 31S 144 19 E
Kent, Ohio, U.S.A. **68** 41 8N 81 20W
Kent, Oreg., U.S.A. **72** 45 11N 120 45W
Kent, Tex., U.S.A. **71** 31 5N 104 12W
Kent □ **7** 51 12N 0 40 E
Kent Group **44** 39 30S 147 20 E
Kent Pen. **60** 68 30N 107 0W
Kentau **24** 43 32N 68 36 E
Kentland **68** 40 45N 87 25W
Kenton **68** 40 40N 83 35W
Kentucky □ **68** 37 20N 85 0W
Kentucky → **68** 38 41N 85 11W
Kentucky L. **69** 36 25N 88 0W
Kentville **63** 45 6N 64 29W
Kentwood **71** 31 0N 90 30W
Kenya ■ **54** 1 0N 38 0 E
Kenya, Mt. **54** 0 10S 37 18 E
Keokuk **70** 40 25N 91 24W
Kepi **35** 6 32S 139 19 E
Kepsut **30** 39 40N 28 9 E
Kerala □ **32** 11 0N 76 15 E
Kerang **45** 35 40S 143 55 E
Keraudren, C. **46** 19 58S 119 45 E
Kerch **23** 45 20N 36 20 E
Kerchoual **50** 17 12N 0 20 E
Kerem Maharal **28** 32 39N 34 59 E
Keren **51** 15 45N 38 28 E
Kerguelen **3** 49 15S 69 10 E
Kericho **54** 0 22S 35 15 E
Kerinci **34** 1 40S 101 15 E
Kerki **24** 37 50N 65 12 E
Kérkira **19** 39 38N 19 50 E
Kerkrade **11** 50 53N 6 4 E
Kermadec Is. **40** 30 0S 178 15W
Kermadec Trench **40** 30 30S 176 0W
Kermān **31** 30 15N 57 1 E
Kermān □ **31** 30 0N 57 0 E
Kermānshāh = Bākhtarān **30** 34 23N 47 0 E
Kermit **71** 31 56N 103 3W
Kern → **73** 35 16N 119 18W
Kerrobert **65** 51 56N 109 8W
Kerrville **71** 30 1N 99 8W
Kerry □ **9** 52 7N 9 35W
Kerry Hd. **9** 52 26N 9 56W
Kertosono **35** 7 38S 112 9 E
Kerulen → **37** 48 48N 117 0 E
Kerzaz **50** 29 29N 1 37W
Kesagami → **62** 51 40N 79 45W
Kesagami L. **62** 50 23N 80 15W
Keski-Suomen lääni □ **20** 62 0N 25 30 E
Kestell **57** 28 17S 28 42 E
Kestenga **22** 66 0N 31 50 E
Keswick **6** 54 35N 3 9W
Ket → **24** 58 55N 81 32 E
Keta **53** 5 49N 1 0 E
Ketapang **34** 1 55S 110 0 E
Ketchikan **60** 55 25N 131 40W
Ketchum **72** 43 41N 114 27W
Kettering **7** 52 24N 0 44W
Kettle → **65** 56 40N 89 34W
Kettle Falls **72** 48 41N 118 2W
Kevin **72** 48 45N 111 58W
Kewanee **70** 41 18N 89 55W
Kewaunee **68** 44 27N 87 30W
Keweenaw B. **68** 46 56N 88 23W
Keweenaw Pen. **68** 47 30N 88 0W
Keweenaw Pt. **68** 47 26N 87 40W
Key Harbour **62** 45 50N 80 45W
Key West **75** 24 33N 82 0W
Keyser **68** 39 26N 79 0W
Keystone **70** 43 54N 103 27W
Kezhma **25** 58 59N 101 9 E
Khabarovo **24** 69 30N 60 30 E
Khabarovsk **25** 48 30N 135 5 E
Khābūr → **30** 35 0N 40 30 E
Khairpur **32** 27 32N 68 49 E
Khakhea **56** 24 48S 23 22 E
Khalkhāl **30** 37 37N 48 32 E
Khalkís **19** 38 27N 23 42 E
Khalmer-Sede = Tazovskiy **24** 67 30N 78 44 E
Khalmer Yu **22** 67 58N 65 1 E

Lafia

Kong **50** 8 54N 4 36W
Kong, Koh **34** 11 20N 103 0 E
Kongju **38** 36 30N 127 0 E
Konglu **33** 27 13N 97 57 E
Kongolo **54** 5 22S 27 0 E
Kongor **51** 7 1N 31 27 E
Kongsberg **21** 59 39N 9 39 E
Kongsvinger **21** 60 12N 12 2 E
Königsberg = Kaliningrad **22** 54 42N 20 32 E
Konin **15** 52 12N 18 15 E
Konjic **19** 43 42N 17 58 E
Konkiep **56** 26 49S 17 15 E
Konosha **22** 61 0N 40 5 E
Konotop **23** 51 12N 33 7 E
Konqi He → **37** 40 45N 90 10 E
Końskie **15** 51 15N 20 23 E
Konstanz **14** 47 39N 9 10 E
Kontagora **53** 10 23N 5 27 E
Kontum **34** 14 24N 108 0 E
Konya **30** 37 52N 32 35 E
Konya Ovasi **30** 38 30N 33 0 E
Konza **54** 1 45S 37 7 E
Kookynie **47** 29 17S 121 22 E
Kooline **46** 22 57S 116 20 E
Kooloonong **45** 34 48S 143 10 E
Koolyanobbing **47** 30 48S 119 36 E
Koondrook **45** 35 33S 144 8 E
Koorawatha **45** 34 2S 148 33 E
Koorda **47** 30 48S 117 35 E
Kooskia **72** 46 9N 115 59W
Kootenai → **72** 49 15N 117 39W
Kootenay L. **64** 49 45N 116 50W
Kootenay Nat. Park **64** 51 0N 116 0W
Kootjieskolk **56** 31 15S 20 21 E
Kopaonik Planina **19** 43 10N 21 50 E
Kópavogur **20** 64 6N 21 55W
Koper **18** 45 31N 13 44 E
Kopervik **21** 59 17N 5 17 E
Kopeysk **24** 55 7N 61 37 E
Kopi **45** 33 24S 135 40 E
Köping **21** 59 31N 16 3 E
Kopparberg **21** 59 52N 15 0 E
Kopparbergs län □ **21** 61 20N 14 15 E
Koppeh Dāgh **31** 38 0N 58 0 E
Koppies **57** 27 20S 27 30 E
Korab **19** 41 44N 20 40 E
Korça **19** 40 37N 20 50 E
Korce = Korça **19** 40 37N 20 50 E
Korčula **18** 42 57N 17 8 E
Kordestan **30** 35 30N 42 0 E
Kordestān □ **30** 36 0N 47 0 E
Korea, North ■ **38** 40 0N 127 0 E
Korea, South ■ **38** 36 0N 128 0 E
Korea Bay **38** 39 0N 124 0 E
Korea Strait **39** 34 0N 129 30 E
Koreh Wells **52** 0 3N 38 45 E
Korhogo **50** 9 29N 5 28W
Korim **35** 0 58S 136 10 E
Korinthiakós Kólpos **19** 38 16N 22 30 E
Kórinthos **19** 37 56N 22 55 E
Kōriyama **36** 37 24N 140 23 E
Koro, Fiji **43** 17 19S 179 23 E
Koro, Ivory C. **50** 8 32N 7 30W
Koro, Mali **50** 14 1N 2 58W
Koro Sea **43** 17 30S 179 45W
Korogwe **54** 5 5S 38 25 E
Koroit **45** 38 18S 142 24 E
Körös → **15** 46 43N 20 12 E
Korraraika, Helodranon' i **57** 17 45S 43 57 E
Korsakov **25** 46 36N 142 42 E
Korshunovo **25** 58 37N 110 10 E
Korsör **21** 55 20N 11 9 E
Korti **51** 18 6N 31 33 E
Kortrijk **11** 50 50N 3 17 E
Koryakskiy Khrebet **25** 61 0N 171 0 E
Kos **19** 36 50N 27 15 E
Koschagyl **23** 46 40N 54 0 E
Kościan **14** 52 5N 16 40 E
Kosciusko **71** 33 3N 89 34W
Kosciusko, Mt. **45** 36 27S 148 16 E
Kosciusko I. **64** 56 0N 133 40W
Kosha **51** 20 50N 30 30 E
K'oshih = Kashi **37** 39 30N 76 2 E
Kosi-meer **57** 27 0S 32 50 E
Košice **15** 48 42N 21 15 E
Koslan **22** 63 28N 48 52 E
Kosŏng **38** 38 40N 128 22 E
Kosovska-Mitrovica **19** 42 54N 20 52 E
Kostamuksa **22** 62 34N 32 44 E
Koster **56** 25 52S 26 54 E
Kôstî **51** 13 8N 32 43 E
Kostroma **22** 57 50N 40 58 E
Koszalin **14** 54 11N 16 8 E
Kota **32** 25 14N 75 49 E
Kota Baharu **34** 6 7N 102 14 E
Kota Belud **34** 6 21N 116 26 E
Kota Kinabalu **34** 6 0N 116 4 E
Kota Tinggi **34** 1 44N 103 53 E
Kotaagung **34** 5 38S 104 29 E
Kotabaru **34** 3 20S 116 20 E
Kotabumi **34** 4 49S 104 54 E
Kotagede **35** 7 54S 110 26 E
Kotamobagu **35** 0 57N 124 31 E
Kotaneelee → **64** 60 11N 123 42W
Kotawaringin **34** 2 28S 111 27 E
Kotcho L. **64** 59 7N 121 12W
Kotelnich **22** 58 20N 48 10 E
Kotelnyy, Ostrov **25** 75 10N 139 0 E
Kotka **21** 60 28N 26 58 E
Kotlas **22** 61 15N 47 0 E
Kotli **32** 33 30N 73 55 E
Kotor **19** 42 25N 18 47 E
Kotri **32** 25 22N 68 22 E
Kottayam **32** 9 35N 76 33 E
Kotturu **32** 14 45N 76 10 E
Kotuy → **25** 71 54N 102 6 E
Kotzebue **60** 66 50N 162 40W
Kouango **54** 5 0N 20 10 E
Koudougou **50** 12 10N 2 20W
Kougaberge **56** 33 48S 23 50 E
Kouilou → **54** 4 10S 12 5 E
Kouki **54** 7 22N 17 3 E
Koula Moutou **54** 1 15S 12 25 E
Koulen **34** 13 50N 104 40 E
Koulikoro **50** 12 40N 7 50W
Koumala **44** 21 38S 149 15 E
Koumra **51** 8 50N 17 35 E
Kounradskiy **24** 46 59N 75 0 E
Kountze **71** 30 20N 94 22W
Kouroussa **50** 10 45N 9 45W
Kousseri **51** 12 0N 14 55 E
Koutiala **50** 12 25N 5 23W
Kovdor **22** 67 34N 30 24 E
Kovel **22** 51 10N 24 20 E
Kovrov **22** 56 25N 41 25 E
Kowkash **62** 50 20N 87 12W
Kowloon **39** 22 20N 114 15 E
Koyabuti **35** 2 36S 140 37 E
Koyuk **60** 64 55N 161 20W
Koyukuk → **60** 64 56N 157 30W
Kozan **30** 37 35N 35 50 E
Kozáni **19** 40 19N 21 47 E
Kozhikode = Calicut **32** 11 15N 75 43 E
Kozhva **22** 65 10N 57 0 E
Kpalimé **53** 6 57N 0 44 E
Kra, Isthmus of = Kra, Kho Khot **34** 10 15N 99 30 E
Kra, Kho Khot **34** 10 15N 99 30 E
Kragan **35** 6 43S 111 38 E
Kragerø **21** 58 52N 9 25 E
Kragujevac **19** 44 2N 20 56 E
Krakatau = Rakata, Pulau **34** 6 10S 105 20 E
Kraków **15** 50 4N 19 57 E
Kraksaan **35** 7 43S 113 23 E
Kraljevo **19** 43 44N 20 41 E
Kramatorsk **23** 48 50N 37 30 E
Kramfors **20** 62 55N 17 48 E
Krankskop **57** 28 0S 30 47 E
Krasavino **22** 60 58N 46 29 E
Kraskino **25** 42 44N 130 48 E
Kraśnik **15** 50 55N 22 5 E
Krasnodar **23** 45 5N 39 0 E
Krasnokamsk **22** 58 4N 55 48 E
Krasnoselkupsk **24** 65 20N 82 10 E
Krasnoturinsk **22** 59 46N 60 12 E
Krasnoufimsk **22** 56 57N 57 46 E
Krasnouralsk **22** 58 21N 60 3 E
Krasnovishersk **22** 60 23N 57 3 E
Krasnovodsk **23** 40 0N 52 52 E
Krasnoyarsk **25** 56 8N 93 0 E
Krasnyy Luch **23** 48 13N 39 0 E
Krasnyy Yar **23** 46 43N 48 23 E
Kratie **34** 12 32N 106 10 E
Krau **35** 3 19S 140 5 E
Krawang **35** 6 19N 107 18 E
Krefeld **14** 51 20N 6 32 E
Kremenchug **23** 49 5N 33 25 E
Kremenchugskoye Vdkhr. **23** 49 20N 32 30 E
Kremmling **72** 40 10N 106 30W
Kremnica **15** 48 45N 18 50 E
Kribi **54** 2 57N 9 56 E
Krishna → **33** 15 57N 80 59 E
Krishnanagar **33** 23 24N 88 33 E
Kristiansand **21** 58 9N 8 1 E
Kristianstad **21** 56 2N 14 9 E
Kristianstads län □ **21** 56 15N 14 0 E
Kristiansund **20** 63 7N 7 45 E
Kristiinankaupunki **20** 62 16N 21 21 E
Kristinehamn **21** 59 18N 14 13 E
Kristinestad **20** 62 16N 21 21 E
Kríti **19** 35 15N 25 0 E
Krivoy Rog **23** 47 51N 33 20 E
Krk **18** 45 8N 14 40 E
Krokodil → **57** 25 14S 32 18 E
Kronobergs län □ **21** 56 45N 14 30 E
Kronshtadt **22** 60 5N 29 45 E
Kroonstad **56** 27 43S 27 19 E
Kropotkin, R.S.F.S.R., U.S.S.R. **23** 45 28N 40 28 E
Kropotkin, R.S.F.S.R., U.S.S.R. **25** 59 0N 115 30 E
Krosno **15** 49 42N 21 46 E
Krotoszyn **15** 51 42N 17 23 E
Kruger Nat. Park **57** 23 30S 31 40 E
Krugersdorp **57** 26 5S 27 46 E
Kruisfontein **56** 33 59S 24 43 E
Krung Thep = Bangkok **34** 13 45N 100 35 E
Kruševac **19** 43 35N 21 28 E
Kruzof I. **64** 57 10N 135 40W
Krymskiy Poluostrov **23** 45 0N 34 0 E
Ksar el Boukhari **50** 35 51N 2 52 E
Ksar el Kebir **50** 35 0N 6 0W
Ksar es Souk = Ar Rachidiya **50** 31 58N 4 20W
Kuala **34** 2 55N 105 47 E
Kuala Kubu Baharu **34** 3 34N 101 39 E
Kuala Lipis **34** 4 10N 102 3 E
Kuala Lumpur **34** 3 9N 101 41 E
Kuala Trengganu **34** 5 20N 103 8 E
Kualajelai **34** 2 58S 110 46 E
Kualakapuas **34** 2 55S 114 20 E
Kualakurun **34** 1 10S 113 50 E
Kualapembuang **34** 3 14S 112 38 E
Kualasimpang **34** 4 17N 98 3 E
Kuandang **35** 0 56N 123 1 E
Kuandian **38** 40 45N 124 45 E
Kuangchou = Guangzhou **39** 23 5N 113 10 E
Kuantan **34** 3 49N 103 20 E
Kuba **23** 41 21N 48 32 E
Kubak **31** 27 10N 63 10 E
Kuban → **23** 45 20N 37 30 E
Kucing **34** 1 33N 110 25 E
Kuda **32** 23 10N 71 15 E
Kudat **34** 6 55N 116 55 E
Kudus **35** 6 48S 110 51 E
Kudymkar **24** 59 1N 54 39 E
Kueiyang = Guiyang **39** 26 32N 106 40 E
Kufrinjah **28** 32 20N 35 41 E
Kufstein **14** 47 35N 12 11 E
Kugong I. **62** 56 18N 79 50W
Kūh-e 'Alijūq **31** 31 30N 51 41 E
Kūh-e Dīnār **31** 30 40N 51 0 E
Kūh-e-Hazārām **31** 29 35N 57 20 E
Kūh-e-Jebāl Bārez **31** 29 0N 58 0 E
Kūh-e Sorkh **31** 35 30N 58 45 E
Kūh-e Taftān **31** 28 40N 61 0 E
Kūhak **31** 27 12N 63 10 E
Kūhhā-ye-Bashākerd **31** 26 45N 59 0 E
Kūhhā-ye Sabalān **30** 38 15N 47 45 E
Kūhpāyeh **31** 32 44N 52 20 E
Kuile He → **38** 49 32N 124 42 E
Kuito **55** 12 22S 16 55 E
Kuji **36** 40 11N 141 46 E
Kukawa **51** 12 58N 13 27 E
Kukerin **47** 33 13S 118 0 E
Kulasekarappattinam **32** 8 20N 78 0 E
Kuldja = Yining **37** 43 58N 81 10 E
Kulin **47** 32 40S 118 2 E
Kulja **47** 30 28S 117 18 E
Kulm **70** 46 22N 98 58W
Kulsary **23** 46 59N 54 1 E
Kulumbura **46** 13 55S 126 35 E
Kulunda **24** 52 35N 78 57 E
Kulwin **45** 35 0S 142 42 E
Kulyab **24** 37 55N 69 50 E
Kum Tekei **24** 43 10N 79 30 E
Kuma → **23** 44 55N 47 0 E
Kumaganum **53** 13 8N 10 38 E
Kumagaya **36** 36 9N 139 22 E
Kumai **34** 2 44S 111 43 E
Kumamba, Kepulauan **35** 1 36S 138 45 E
Kumamoto **36** 32 45N 130 45 E
Kumamoto □ **36** 32 55N 130 55 E
Kumanovo **19** 42 9N 21 42 E
Kumara **43** 42 37S 171 12 E
Kumarl **47** 32 47S 121 33 E
Kumasi **50** 6 41N 1 38W
Kumba **54** 4 36N 9 24 E
Kumbarilla **45** 27 15S 150 55 E
Kumertau **22** 52 46N 55 47 E
Kumla **21** 59 8N 15 10 E
Kumo **53** 10 1N 11 12 E
Kumon Bum **33** 26 30N 97 15 E
Kunama **45** 35 35S 148 4 E
Kunashir, Ostrov **25** 44 0N 146 0 E
Kundip **47** 33 42S 120 10 E
Kungala **45** 29 58S 153 7 E
Kunghit I. **64** 52 6N 131 3W
Kungrad **24** 43 6N 58 54 E
Kungsbacka **21** 57 30N 12 5 E
Kungur **22** 57 25N 56 57 E
Kungurri **44** 21 3S 148 46 E
Kuningan **35** 6 59S 108 29 E
Kunlong **33** 23 20N 98 50 E
Kunlun Shan **33** 36 0N 86 30 E
Kunming **37** 25 1N 102 41 E
Kunsan **38** 35 59N 126 45 E
Kunshan **39** 31 22N 120 58 E
Kununurra **46** 15 40S 128 50 E
Kunwarara **44** 22 55S 150 9 E
Kunya-Urgench **24** 42 19N 59 10 E
Kuopio **20** 62 53N 27 35 E
Kuopion lääni □ **20** 63 25N 27 10 E
Kupa → **18** 45 28N 16 24 E
Kupang **35** 10 19S 123 39 E
Kuqa **37** 41 35N 82 30 E
Kura → **23** 39 50N 49 20 E
Kuranda **44** 16 48S 145 35 E
Kurashiki **36** 34 40N 133 50 E
Kurayoshi **36** 35 26N 133 50 E
Kure **36** 34 14N 132 32 E
Kurgaldzhino **24** 50 35N 70 20 E
Kurgan **24** 55 26N 65 18 E
Kuria Maria Is. = Khūrīyā Mūrīyā, Jazā 'ir **29** 17 30N 55 58 E
Kuridala **44** 21 16S 140 29 E
Kurigram **33** 25 49N 89 39 E
Kuril Is. = Kurilskiye Ostrova **25** 45 0N 150 0 E
Kuril Trench **40** 44 0N 153 0 E
Kurilsk **25** 45 14N 147 53 E
Kurilskiye Ostrova **25** 45 0N 150 0 E
Kurmuk **51** 10 33N 34 21 E
Kurnool **32** 15 45N 78 0 E
Kurow **43** 44 44S 170 29 E
Kurrajong **45** 33 33S 150 42 E
Kurri Kurri **45** 32 50S 151 28 E
Kursk **22** 51 42N 36 11 E
Kuršumlija **19** 43 9N 21 19 E
Kuruktag **37** 41 0N 89 0 E
Kuruman **56** 27 28S 23 28 E
Kuruman → **56** 26 56S 20 39 E
Kurume **36** 33 15N 130 30 E
Kurunegala **32** 7 30N 80 23 E
Kurya **25** 61 15N 108 10 E
Kusawa L. **64** 60 20N 136 13W
Kushiro **36** 43 0N 144 25 E
Kushiro → **36** 42 59N 144 23 E
Kushka **24** 35 20N 62 18 E
Kushtia **33** 23 55N 89 5 E
Kushva **22** 58 18N 59 45 E
Kuskokwim → **60** 60 17N 162 27W
Kuskokwim Bay **60** 59 50N 162 56W
Kussharo-Ko **36** 43 38N 144 21 E
Kustanay **24** 53 10N 63 35 E
Kütahya **30** 39 30N 30 2 E
Kutaisi **23** 42 19N 42 40 E
Kutaraja = Banda Aceh **34** 5 35N 95 20 E
Kutch, Gulf of = Kachchh, Gulf of **32** 22 50N 69 15 E
Kutch, Rann of = Kachchh, Rann of **32** 24 0N 70 0 E
Kutno **15** 52 15N 19 23 E
Kuttabul **44** 21 5S 148 48 E
Kutu **54** 2 40S 18 11 E
Kutum **51** 14 10N 24 40 E
Kuujjuaq **61** 58 6N 68 15W
Kuwait = Al Kuwayt **30** 29 30N 48 0 E
Kuwait ■ **30** 29 30N 47 30 E
Kuwana **36** 35 0N 136 43 E
Kuybyshev, R.S.F.S.R., U.S.S.R. **22** 53 8N 50 6 E
Kuybyshev, R.S.F.S.R., U.S.S.R. **24** 55 27N 78 19 E
Kuybyshevskoye Vdkhr. **22** 55 2N 49 30 E
Kūysanjaq **30** 36 5N 44 38 E
Kuyto, Oz. **22** 64 40N 31 0 E
Kuyumba **25** 60 58N 96 59 E
Kuzey Anadolu Dağlari **30** 41 30N 35 0 E
Kuznetsk **22** 53 12N 46 40 E
Kuzomen **22** 66 22N 36 50 E
Kvænangen **20** 70 5N 21 15 E
Kvarner **18** 44 50N 14 10 E
Kvarnerič **18** 44 43N 14 37 E
Kwabhaca **57** 30 51S 29 0 E
Kwadacha → **64** 57 28N 125 38W
Kwakhanai **56** 21 39S 21 16 E
Kwakoegron **79** 5 12N 55 25W
KwaMashu **57** 29 45S 30 58 E
Kwamouth **54** 3 9S 16 12 E
Kwando → **56** 18 27S 23 32 E
Kwangju **38** 35 9N 126 54 E
Kwangsi-Chuang = Guangxi Zhuangzu Zizhiqu □ **39** 24 0N 109 0 E
Kwangtung = Guangdong □ **39** 23 0N 113 0 E
Kwara □ **53** 8 0N 5 0 E
Kwataboahegan → **62** 51 9N 80 50W
Kwatisore **35** 3 18S 134 50 E
Kweichow = Guizhou □ **39** 27 0N 107 0 E
Kwekwe **55** 18 58S 29 48 E
Kwiguk **60** 63 45N 164 35W
Kwinana New Town **47** 32 15S 115 47 E
Kwoka **35** 0 31S 132 27 E
Kyabé **51** 9 30N 19 0 E
Kyabra Cr. → **45** 25 36S 142 55 E
Kyabram **45** 36 19S 145 4 E
Kyakhta **25** 50 30N 106 25 E
Kyangin **33** 18 20N 95 20 E
Kyaukpadaung **33** 20 52N 95 8 E
Kyaukpyu **33** 19 28N 93 30 E
Kyaukse **33** 21 36N 96 10 E
Kyle Dam **55** 20 15S 31 0 E
Kyle of Lochalsh **8** 57 17N 5 43W
Kyneton **45** 37 10S 144 29 E
Kynuna **44** 21 37S 141 55 E
Kyō-ga-Saki **36** 35 45N 135 15 E
Kyoga, L. **54** 1 35N 33 0 E
Kyogle **45** 28 40S 153 0 E
Kyongju **38** 35 51N 129 14 E
Kyongpyaw **33** 17 12N 95 10 E
Kyōto **36** 35 0N 135 45 E
Kyōto □ **36** 35 15N 135 45 E
Kyren **25** 51 45N 101 45 E
Kyrenia **30** 35 20N 33 20 E
Kystatyam **25** 67 20N 123 10 E
Kytal Ktakh **25** 65 30N 123 40 E
Kyulyunken **25** 64 10N 137 5 E
Kyunhla **33** 23 25N 95 15 E
Kyuquot **64** 50 3N 127 25W
Kyūshū **36** 33 0N 131 0 E
Kyūshū-Sanchi **36** 32 35N 131 17 E
Kyustendil **19** 42 16N 22 41 E
Kyusyur **25** 70 39N 127 15 E
Kywong **45** 34 58S 146 44 E
Kyzyl **25** 51 50N 94 30 E
Kyzyl-Kiya **24** 40 16N 72 8 E
Kyzylkum, Peski **24** 42 30N 65 0 E
Kzyl-Orda **24** 44 48N 65 28 E

L

Labak **35** 6 32N 124 5 E
Labe = Elbe → **14** 53 50N 9 0 E
Labé **50** 11 24N 12 16W
Laberge, L. **64** 61 11N 135 12W
Labis **34** 2 22N 103 2 E
Laboulaye **80** 34 10S 63 30W
Labrador, Coast of □ **63** 53 20N 61 0W
Labrador City **63** 52 57N 66 55W
Lábrea **78** 7 15S 64 51W
Labuan, Pulau **34** 5 21N 115 13 E
Labuha **35** 0 30S 127 30 E
Labuhan **35** 6 22S 105 50 E
Labuhanbajo **35** 8 28S 120 1 E
Labuk, Telok **34** 6 10N 117 50 E
Labytnangi **22** 66 39N 66 21 E
Lac Allard **63** 50 33N 63 24W
Lac Bouchette **63** 48 16N 72 11W
Lac du Flambeau **70** 46 1N 89 51W
Lac Édouard **62** 47 40N 72 16W
Lac La Biche **64** 54 45N 111 58W
Lac la Martre **60** 63 8N 117 16W
Lac-Mégantic **63** 45 35N 70 53W
Lac Seul, Res. **62** 50 25N 92 30W
Lacantúm → **74** 16 36N 90 40W
Laccadive Is. = Lakshadweep Is. **3** 10 0N 72 30 E
Lacepede B. **45** 36 40S 139 40 E
Lacepede Is. **46** 16 55S 122 0 E
Lachine **62** 45 30N 73 40W
Lachlan → **45** 34 22S 143 55 E
Lachute **62** 45 39N 74 21W
Lackawanna **68** 42 49N 78 50W
Lacombe **64** 52 30N 113 44W
Laconia **68** 43 32N 71 30W
Lacrosse **72** 46 51N 117 58W
Ladakh Ra. **32** 34 0N 78 0 E
Ladismith **56** 33 28S 21 15 E
Lādīz **31** 28 55N 61 15 E
Ladoga, L. = Ladozhskoye Ozero **22** 61 15N 30 30 E
Ladozhskoye Ozero **22** 61 15N 30 30 E
Lady Grey **56** 30 43S 27 13 E
Ladybrand **56** 29 9S 27 29 E
Ladysmith, Canada **64** 49 0N 123 49W
Ladysmith, S. Africa **57** 28 32S 29 46 E
Ladysmith, U.S.A. **70** 45 27N 91 4W
Lae **40** 6 40S 147 2 E
Læsø **21** 57 15N 10 53 E
Lafayette, Colo., U.S.A. **70** 40 0N 105 2W
Lafayette, Ga., U.S.A. **69** 34 44N 85 15W
Lafayette, Ind., U.S.A. **68** 40 22N 86 52W
Lafayette, La., U.S.A. **71** 30 18N 92 0W
Lafayette, Tenn., U.S.A. **69** 36 35N 86 0W
Laferte → **64** 61 53N 117 44W
Lafia **53** 8 30N 8 34 E

Longxi

Lévis **63** 46 48N 71 9W
Levis, L. **64** 62 37N 117 58W
Levkás **19** 38 40N 20 43 E
Levkôsia = Nicosia **30** 35 10N 33 25 E
Lewellen **70** 41 22N 102 5W
Lewes, U.K. **7** 50 53N 0 2 E
Lewes, U.S.A. **68** 38 45N 75 8W
Lewis **8** 58 10N 6 40W
Lewis, Butt of **8** 58 30N 6 12W
Lewis Ra., Australia **46** 20 3S 128 50 E
Lewis Ra., U.S.A. **72** 48 0N 113 15W
Lewisburg **69** 35 29N 86 46W
Lewisporte **63** 49 15N 55 3W
Lewiston **72** 46 25N 117 0W
Lewistown, Mont., U.S.A. **72** 47 0N 109 25W
Lewistown, Pa., U.S.A. **68** 40 37N 77 33W
Lexington, Ill., U.S.A. **70** 40 37N 88 47W
Lexington, Ky., U.S.A. **68** 38 6N 84 30W
Lexington, Miss., U.S.A. **71** 33 8N 90 2W
Lexington, Mo., U.S.A. **70** 39 7N 93 55W
Lexington, N.C., U.S.A. **69** 35 50N 80 13W
Lexington, Nebr., U.S.A. **70** 40 48N 99 45W
Lexington, Oreg., U.S.A. **72** 45 29N 119 46W
Lexington, Tenn., U.S.A. **69** 35 38N 88 25W
Lexington Park **68** 38 16N 76 27W
Leyte **35** 11 0N 125 0 E
Lhasa **37** 29 25N 90 58 E
Lhazê **37** 29 5N 87 38 E
Lhokkruet **34** 4 55N 95 24 E
Lhokseumawe **34** 5 10N 97 10 E
Lhuntsi Dzong **33** 27 39N 91 10 E
Li Shui → **39** 29 24N 112 1 E
Li Xian, Gansu, China **39** 34 10N 105 5 E
Li Xian, Hunan, China **39** 29 36N 111 42 E
Lianga **35** 8 38N 126 6 E
Liangdang **39** 33 56N 106 18 E
Lianhua **39** 27 3N 113 54 E
Lianjiang **39** 26 12N 119 27 E
Lianping **39** 24 26N 114 30 E
Lianshanguan **38** 40 53N 123 43 E
Lianyungang **39** 34 40N 119 11 E
Liao He → **38** 41 0N 121 50 E
Liaocheng **38** 36 28N 115 58 E
Liaodong Bandao **38** 40 0N 122 30 E
Liaodong Wan **38** 40 20N 121 10 E
Liaoning □ **38** 42 0N 122 0 E
Liaoyang **38** 41 15N 122 58 E
Liaoyuan **38** 42 58N 125 2 E
Liaozhong **38** 41 23N 122 50 E
Liard → **64** 61 51N 121 18W
Libau = Liepaja **22** 56 30N 21 0 E
Libby **72** 48 20N 115 33W
Libenge **54** 3 40N 18 55 E
Liberal, Kans., U.S.A. **71** 37 4N 101 0W
Liberal, Mo., U.S.A. **71** 37 35N 94 30W
Liberec **14** 50 47N 15 7 E
Liberia **75** 10 40N 85 30W
Liberia ■ **50** 6 30N 9 30W
Libertad, La **74** 29 55N 112 41W
Liberty, Mo., U.S.A. **70** 39 15N 94 24W
Liberty, Tex., U.S.A. **71** 30 5N 94 50W
Libo **39** 25 22N 107 53 E
Libobo, Tanjung **35** 0 54S 128 28 E
Libode **57** 31 33S 29 2 E
Libonda **55** 14 28S 23 12 E
Libourne **12** 44 55N 0 14W
Libramont **11** 49 55N 5 23 E
Libreville **54** 0 25N 9 26 E
Libya ■ **51** 27 0N 17 0 E
Libyan Desert **48** 25 0N 25 0 E
Licantén **80** 35 55S 72 0W
Licata **18** 37 6N 13 55 E
Lichfield **6** 52 40N 1 50W
Lichtenburg **56** 26 8S 26 8 E
Lichuan **39** 30 18N 108 57 E
Lida **73** 37 30N 117 30W
Lidköping **21** 58 31N 13 14 E
Liechtenstein ■ **14** 47 8N 9 35 E
Liège **11** 50 38N 5 35 E
Liège □ **11** 50 32N 5 35 E
Liegnitz = Legnica **14** 51 12N 16 10 E
Lienyünchiangshih = Lianyungang **39** 34 40N 119 11 E
Lienz **14** 46 50N 12 46 E
Liepaja **22** 56 30N 21 0 E
Lier **11** 51 7N 4 34 E
Lièvre → **62** 45 31N 75 26W
Liffey → **9** 53 21N 6 20W
Lifford **9** 54 50N 7 30W
Lightning Ridge **45** 29 22S 148 0 E
Liguria □ **18** 44 30N 9 0 E
Ligurian Sea **18** 43 20N 9 0 E
Lihou Reefs and Cays **44** 17 25S 151 40 E
Lihue **66** 21 59N 159 24W
Lijiang **37** 26 55N 100 20 E
Likasi **54** 10 55S 26 48 E
Likati **54** 3 20N 24 0 E
Liling **39** 27 42N 113 29 E
Lille **12** 50 38N 3 3 E
Lille Bælt **21** 55 20N 9 45 E
Lillehammer **21** 61 8N 10 30 E
Lillesand **21** 58 15N 8 23 E
Lilleshall **7** 52 45N 2 22W
Lillestrøm **21** 59 58N 11 5 E
Lillian Point, Mt. **47** 27 40S 126 6 E
Lillooet → **64** 49 15N 121 57W
Lilongwe **55** 14 0S 33 48 E
Liloy **35** 8 4N 122 39 E
Lima, Indonesia **35** 3 37S 128 4 E
Lima, Peru **78** 12 0S 77 0W
Lima, Mont., U.S.A. **72** 44 41N 112 38W
Lima, Ohio, U.S.A. **68** 40 42N 84 5W
Limassol **30** 34 42N 33 1 E
Limavady **9** 55 3N 6 58W
Limavady □ **9** 55 0N 6 55W
Limay → **80** 39 0S 68 0W
Limay Mahuida **80** 37 10S 66 45W
Limbang **34** 4 42N 115 6 E
Limbe **54** 4 1N 9 10 E
Limbri **45** 31 3S 151 5 E
Limbunya **46** 17 14S 129 50 E
Limburg □, Belgium **11** 51 2N 5 25 E
Limburg □, Neth. **11** 51 20N 5 55 E
Limeira **80** 22 35S 47 28W
Limerick **9** 52 40N 8 38W
Limerick □ **9** 52 30N 8 50W
Limestone → **65** 56 31N 94 7W
Limfjorden **21** 56 55N 9 0 E
Limia → **13** 41 41N 8 50W
Limmen Bight **44** 14 40S 135 35 E
Limmen Bight → **44** 15 7S 135 44 E
Límnos **19** 39 50N 25 5 E
Limoeiro do Norte **79** 5 5S 38 0W
Limoges **12** 45 50N 1 15 E
Limón, C. Rica **75** 10 0N 83 2W
Limon, Panama **74** 9 17N 79 45W
Limon, U.S.A. **70** 39 18N 103 38W
Limon B. **74** 9 22N 79 56W
Limousin **12** 45 30N 1 30 E
Limpopo → **57** 25 5S 33 30 E
Limuru **54** 1 2S 36 35 E
Linares, Chile **80** 35 50S 71 40W
Linares, Mexico **74** 24 50N 99 40W
Linares, Spain **13** 38 10N 3 40W
Lincheng **38** 37 25N 114 30 E
Linchuan **39** 27 57N 116 15 E
Lincoln, Argentina **80** 34 55S 61 30W
Lincoln, N.Z. **43** 43 38S 172 30 E
Lincoln, U.K. **6** 53 14N 0 32W
Lincoln, Ill., U.S.A. **70** 40 10N 89 20W
Lincoln, Kans., U.S.A. **70** 39 6N 98 9W
Lincoln, Maine, U.S.A. **63** 45 27N 68 29W
Lincoln, N. Mex., U.S.A. **73** 33 30N 105 26W
Lincoln, Nebr., U.S.A. **70** 40 50N 96 42W
Lincoln □ **6** 53 14N 0 32W
Lincoln Wolds **6** 53 20N 0 5W
Lincolnton **69** 35 30N 81 15W
Lind **72** 47 0N 118 33W
Linden, Guyana **78** 6 0N 58 10W
Linden, U.S.A. **71** 33 0N 94 20W
Lindi **54** 9 58S 39 38 E
Lindian **38** 47 11N 124 52 E
Lindsay, Canada **62** 44 22N 78 43W
Lindsay, Calif., U.S.A. **73** 36 14N 119 6W
Lindsay, Okla., U.S.A. **71** 34 51N 97 37W
Lindsborg **70** 38 35N 97 40W
Línea de la Concepción, La **13** 36 15N 5 23W
Linfen **38** 36 3N 111 30 E
Ling Xian **38** 37 22N 116 30 E
Lingao **39** 19 56N 109 42 E
Lingayen **35** 16 1N 120 14 E
Lingayen G. **35** 16 10N 120 15 E
Lingchuan **39** 25 26N 110 21 E
Lingen **14** 52 32N 7 21 E
Lingga **34** 0 12S 104 37 E
Lingga, Kepulauan **34** 0 10S 104 30 E
Lingle **70** 42 10N 104 18W
Lingling **39** 26 17N 111 37 E
Lingshan **39** 22 25N 109 18 E
Lingshi **38** 36 48N 111 48 E
Lingshui **39** 18 27N 110 0 E
Lingtai **39** 35 0N 107 40 E
Linguéré **50** 15 25N 15 5W
Lingyuan **38** 41 10N 119 15 E
Lingyun **39** 25 2N 106 35 E
Linhai **39** 28 50N 121 8 E
Linhares **79** 19 25S 40 4W
Linhe **38** 40 48N 107 20 E
Linjiang **38** 41 50N 127 0 E
Linköping **21** 58 28N 15 36 E
Linkou **38** 45 15N 130 18 E
Linlithgow **8** 55 58N 3 38W
Linnhe, L. **8** 56 36N 5 25W
Linqing **38** 36 50N 115 42 E
Lins **80** 21 40S 49 44W
Lintao **38** 35 18N 103 52 E
Lintlaw **65** 52 4N 103 14W
Linton, Canada **63** 47 15N 72 16W
Linton, Ind., U.S.A. **68** 39 0N 87 10W
Linton, N. Dak., U.S.A. **70** 46 21N 100 12W
Linville **45** 26 50S 152 11 E
Linwu **39** 25 19N 112 31 E
Linxi **38** 43 36N 118 2 E
Linxia **37** 35 36N 103 10 E
Linyanti → **56** 17 50S 25 5 E
Linyi **39** 35 5N 118 21 E
Linz **14** 48 18N 14 18 E
Lion, G. du **12** 43 0N 4 0 E
Lion's Head **62** 44 58N 81 15W
Lipa **35** 13 57N 121 10 E
Lípari, Is. **18** 38 30N 14 50 E
Lipetsk **22** 52 37N 39 35 E
Liping **39** 26 15N 109 7 E
Lippe → **14** 51 39N 6 38 E
Lipscomb **71** 36 16N 100 16W
Liptrap C. **45** 38 50S 145 55 E
Lira **54** 2 17N 32 57 E
Liria **13** 39 37N 0 35W
Lisala **54** 2 12N 21 38 E
Lisboa **13** 38 42N 9 10W
Lisbon = Lisboa **13** 38 42N 9 10W
Lisbon **70** 46 30N 97 46W
Lisburn **9** 54 30N 6 9W
Lisburne, C. **60** 68 50N 166 0W
Liscannor, B. **9** 52 57N 9 24W
Lishi **38** 37 31N 111 8 E
Lishui **39** 28 28N 119 54 E
Lisianski I. **40** 26 2N 174 0W
Lisichansk **23** 48 55N 38 30 E
Lisieux **12** 49 10N 0 12 E
Lismore, Australia **45** 28 44S 153 21 E
Lismore, Ireland **9** 52 8N 7 58W
Lisse **11** 52 16N 4 33 E
Lista, Norway **21** 58 7N 6 39 E
Lista, Sweden **21** 59 19N 16 16 E
Liston **45** 28 39S 152 6 E
Listowel, Canada **62** 43 44N 80 58W
Listowel, Ireland **9** 52 27N 9 30W
Litang, China **39** 23 12N 109 8 E
Litang, Malaysia **35** 5 27N 118 31 E
Litani →, Lebanon **28** 33 20N 35 14 E
Litani →, Surinam **30** 3 40N 54 0W
Litchfield, Ill., U.S.A. **70** 39 10N 89 40W
Litchfield, Minn., U.S.A. **70** 45 5N 94 31W
Lithgow **45** 33 25S 150 8 E
Líthinon, Ákra **19** 34 55N 24 44 E
Lithuanian S.S.R. □ **22** 55 30N 24 0 E
Litoměřice **14** 50 33N 14 10 E
Little Abaco I. **75** 26 50N 77 30W
Little Barrier I. **43** 36 12S 175 8 E
Little Belt Mts. **72** 46 50N 111 0W
Little Blue → **70** 39 41N 96 40W
Little Bushman Land **56** 29 10S 18 10 E
Little Cadotte → **64** 56 41N 117 6W
Little Churchill → **65** 57 30N 95 22W
Little Colorado → **73** 36 11N 111 48W
Little Current **62** 45 55N 82 0W
Little Current → **62** 50 57N 84 36W
Little Falls, Minn., U.S.A. **70** 45 58N 94 19W
Little Falls, N.Y., U.S.A. **68** 43 3N 74 50W
Little Fork → **70** 48 31N 93 35W
Little Grand Rapids **65** 52 0N 95 29W
Little Humboldt → **72** 41 0N 117 43W
Little Inagua I. **75** 21 40N 73 50W
Little Karoo **56** 33 45S 21 0 E
Little Lake **73** 35 58N 117 58W
Little Minch **8** 57 35N 6 45W
Little Missouri → **70** 47 30N 102 25W
Little Namaqualand **56** 29 0S 17 9 E
Little Ouse → **7** 52 25N 0 50 E
Little Red → **71** 35 11N 91 27W
Little River **43** 43 45S 172 49 E
Little Rock **71** 34 41N 92 10W
Little Sable Pt. **68** 43 40N 86 32W
Little Sioux → **70** 41 49N 96 4W
Little Smoky → **64** 54 44N 117 11W
Little Snake → **72** 40 27N 108 26W
Little Wabash → **68** 37 54N 88 5W
Littlefield **71** 33 57N 102 17W
Littlefork **70** 48 24N 93 35W
Littlehampton **7** 50 48N 0 32W
Littleton **68** 44 19N 71 47W
Liuba **39** 33 38N 106 55 E
Liucheng **39** 24 38N 109 14 E
Liukang Tenggaja **35** 6 45S 118 50 E
Liuwa Plain **55** 14 20S 22 30 E
Liuyang **39** 28 10N 113 37 E
Liuzhou **39** 24 22N 109 22 E
Live Oak **69** 30 17N 83 0W
Liveringa **46** 18 3S 124 10 E
Livermore, Mt. **71** 30 45N 104 8W
Liverpool, Australia **45** 33 54S 150 58 E
Liverpool, Canada **63** 44 5N 64 41W
Liverpool, U.K. **6** 53 25N 3 0W
Liverpool Plains **45** 31 15S 150 15 E
Liverpool Ra. **45** 31 50S 150 30 E
Livingston, Guat. **75** 15 50N 88 50W
Livingston, Mont., U.S.A. **72** 45 40N 110 40W
Livingston, Tex., U.S.A. **71** 30 44N 94 54W
Livingstone **55** 17 46S 25 52 E
Livingstone Mts. **52** 9 40S 34 20 E
Livingstonia **54** 10 38S 34 5 E
Livny **22** 52 30N 37 30 E
Livonia **68** 42 25N 83 23W
Livorno **18** 43 32N 10 18 E
Livramento **80** 30 55S 55 30W
Liwale **54** 9 48S 37 58 E
Lizard I. **44** 14 42S 145 30 E
Lizard Pt. **7** 49 57N 5 11W
Ljubljana **18** 46 4N 14 33 E
Ljungan → **20** 62 18N 17 23 E
Ljungby **21** 56 49N 13 55 E
Ljusdal **21** 61 46N 16 3 E
Ljusnan → **21** 61 12N 17 8 E
Ljusne **21** 61 13N 17 7 E
Llancanelo, Salina **80** 35 40S 69 8W
Llandeilo **7** 51 53N 4 0W
Llandovery **7** 51 59N 3 49W
Llandrindod Wells **7** 52 15N 3 23W
Llandudno **6** 53 19N 3 51W
Llanelli **7** 51 41N 4 11W
Llanes **13** 43 25N 4 50W
Llangollen **6** 52 58N 3 10W
Llanidloes **7** 52 28N 3 31W
Llano **71** 30 45N 98 41W
Llano → **71** 30 50N 98 25W
Llano Estacado **71** 34 0N 103 0W
Llanos **78** 5 0N 71 35W
Llera **74** 23 19N 99 1W
Llobregat → **13** 41 19N 2 9 E
Lloret de Mar **13** 41 41N 2 53 E
Lloyd B. **44** 12 45S 143 27 E
Lloyd L. **65** 57 22N 108 57W
Lloydminster **65** 53 17N 110 0W
Llullaillaco, Volcán **80** 24 43S 68 30W
Loa **73** 38 18N 111 40W
Loa → **80** 21 26S 70 41W
Lobatse **56** 25 12S 25 40 E
Lobería **80** 38 10S 58 40W
Lobito **55** 12 18S 13 35 E
Lobos, I. **74** 27 15N 110 30W
Lobos, Is. **76** 6 57S 80 45W
Locarno **14** 46 10N 8 47 E
Lochaber **8** 56 55N 5 0W
Lochcarron **8** 57 25N 5 30W
Loche, La **65** 56 29N 109 26W
Lochem **11** 52 9N 6 26 E
Loches **12** 47 7N 1 0 E
Lochgelly **8** 56 7N 3 18W
Lochgilphead **8** 56 2N 5 37W
Lochinver **8** 58 9N 5 15W
Lochnagar, Australia **44** 23 33S 145 38 E
Lochnagar, U.K. **8** 56 57N 3 14W
Lochy → **8** 56 52N 5 3W
Lock **45** 33 34S 135 46 E
Lock Haven **68** 41 7N 77 31W
Lockeport **63** 43 47N 65 4W
Lockerbie **8** 55 7N 3 21W
Lockhart **71** 29 55N 97 40W
Lockhart, L. **47** 33 15S 119 3 E
Lockney **71** 34 7N 101 27W
Lockport **68** 43 12N 78 42W
Lod **28** 31 57N 34 54 E
Lodeinoye Pole **22** 60 44N 33 33 E
Lodge Grass **72** 45 21N 107 20W
Lodgepole **70** 41 12N 102 40W
Lodgepole Cr. → **70** 41 20N 104 30W
Lodhran **32** 29 32N 71 30 E
Lodi **72** 38 12N 121 16W
Lodja **54** 3 30S 23 23 E
Lodwar **54** 3 10N 35 40 E
Łódź **15** 51 45N 19 27 E
Loeriesfontein **56** 31 0S 19 26 E
Lofoten **20** 68 30N 15 0 E
Logan, Kans., U.S.A. **70** 39 40N 99 35W
Logan, Ohio, U.S.A. **68** 39 25N 82 22W
Logan, Utah, U.S.A. **72** 41 45N 111 50W
Logan, W. Va., U.S.A. **68** 37 51N 81 59W
Logan, Mt. **60** 60 31N 140 22W
Logan Pass **64** 48 41N 113 44W
Logansport, Ind., U.S.A. **68** 40 45N 86 21W
Logansport, La., U.S.A. **71** 31 58N 93 58W
Logroño **13** 42 28N 2 27W
Lohardaga **33** 23 27N 84 45 E
Loi-kaw **33** 19 40N 97 17 E
Loimaa **21** 60 50N 23 5 E
Loir → **12** 47 33N 0 32W
Loir-et-Cher □ **12** 47 40N 1 20 E
Loire □ **12** 45 40N 4 5 E
Loire → **12** 47 16N 2 10W
Loire-Atlantique □ **12** 47 25N 1 40W
Loiret □ **12** 47 55N 2 30 E
Loja, Ecuador **78** 3 59S 79 16W
Loja, Spain **13** 37 10N 4 10W
Loji **35** 1 38S 127 28 E
Lokandu **54** 2 30S 25 45 E
Lokeren **11** 51 6N 3 59 E
Lokichokio **52** 4 19N 34 13 E
Lokitaung **54** 4 12N 35 48 E
Lokka **20** 67 55N 27 35 E
Løkken Verk **20** 63 7N 9 43 E
Lokoja **53** 7 47N 6 45 E
Lokolama **54** 2 35S 19 50 E
Lokwei **39** 19 5N 110 31 E
Loliondo **54** 2 2S 35 39 E
Lolland **21** 54 45N 11 30 E
Lolo **72** 46 50N 114 8W
Lom **19** 43 48N 23 12 E
Loma **72** 47 59N 110 29W
Lomami → **54** 0 46N 24 16 E
Lombadina **46** 16 31S 122 54 E
Lombardia □ **18** 45 35N 9 45 E
Lombardy = Lombardia □ **18** 45 35N 9 45 E
Lomblen **35** 8 30S 123 32 E
Lombok **34** 8 45S 116 30 E
Lomé **53** 6 9N 1 20 E
Lomela **54** 2 19S 23 15 E
Lomela → **54** 0 15S 20 40 E
Lometa **71** 31 15N 98 25W
Lomié **54** 3 13N 13 38 E
Lomond **64** 50 24N 112 36W
Lomond, L. **8** 56 8N 4 38W
Lompobatang **35** 5 24S 119 56 E
Lompoc **73** 34 41N 120 32W
Łomza **15** 53 10N 22 2 E
Loncoche **80** 39 20S 72 50W
Londa **32** 15 30N 74 30 E
Londiani **52** 0 10S 35 33 E
London, Canada **62** 42 59N 81 15W
London, U.K. **7** 51 30N 0 5W
London, Ky., U.S.A. **68** 37 11N 84 5W
London, Ohio, U.S.A. **68** 39 54N 83 28W
London, Greater □ **7** 51 30N 0 5W
Londonderry **9** 55 0N 7 20W
Londonderry □ **9** 55 0N 7 20W
Londonderry, C. **46** 13 45S 126 55 E
Londonderry, I. **80** 55 0S 71 0W
Londrina **80** 23 18S 51 10W
Lone Pine **73** 36 35N 118 2W
Long Beach, Calif., U.S.A. **73** 33 46N 118 12W
Long Beach, Wash., U.S.A. **72** 46 20N 124 1W
Long Branch **68** 40 19N 74 0W
Long Creek **72** 44 43N 119 6W
Long Eaton **6** 52 54N 1 16W
Long I., Australia **44** 22 8S 149 53 E
Long I., Bahamas **75** 23 20N 75 10W
Long I., U.S.A. **68** 40 50N 73 20W
Long L. **62** 49 30N 86 50W
Long Pine **70** 42 33N 99 41W
Long Pt. **63** 48 47N 58 46W
Long Range Mts. **63** 49 30N 57 30W
Long Xian **39** 34 55N 106 55 E
Long Xuyen **34** 10 19N 105 28 E
Long'an **39** 23 10N 107 40 E
Longchuan **39** 24 5N 115 17 E
Longde **38** 35 30N 106 20 E
Longford, Australia **44** 41 32S 147 3 E
Longford, Ireland **9** 53 43N 7 50W
Longford □ **9** 53 42N 7 45W
Longhua **38** 41 18N 117 45 E
Longiram **34** 0 5S 115 45 E
Longjiang **38** 47 20N 123 12 E
Longkou **38** 37 40N 120 18 E
Longlac **62** 49 45N 86 25W
Longlin **39** 24 47N 105 20 E
Longmen **39** 23 40N 114 18 E
Longmont **70** 40 10N 105 4W
Longnan **39** 24 55N 114 47 E
Longnawan **34** 1 51N 114 55 E
Longone → **51** 10 0N 15 40 E
Longquan **39** 28 7N 119 10 E
Longreach **44** 23 28S 144 14 E
Longshan **39** 29 29N 109 25 E
Longsheng **39** 25 48N 110 0 E
Longton **44** 20 58S 145 55 E
Longtown **7** 51 58N 2 59W
Longview, Canada **64** 50 32N 114 10W
Longview, Tex., U.S.A. **71** 32 30N 94 45W
Longview, Wash., U.S.A. **72** 46 9N 122 58W
Longxi **38** 34 53N 104 40 E

Maracay

Madre, Sierra, Phil. 35 17 0N 122 0 E
Madre de Dios → 78 10 59S 66 8W
Madre de Dios, I. 80 50 20S 75 10W
Madre del Sur, Sierra 74 17 30N 100 0W
Madre Occidental, Sierra 74 27 0N 107 0W
Madre Oriental, Sierra 74 25 0N 100 0W
Madrid 13 40 25N 3 45W
Madura, Selat 35 7 30S 113 20 E
Madura Motel 47 31 55S 127 0 E
Madurai 32 9 55N 78 10 E
Madurantakam 32 12 30N 79 50 E
Mae Sot 34 16 43N 98 34 E
Maebashi 36 36 24N 139 4 E
Maesteg 7 51 36N 3 40W
Maestra, Sierra 75 20 15N 77 0W
Maestrazgo, Mts. del 13 40 30N 0 25W
Maevatanana 57 16 56S 46 49 E
Mafeking 65 52 40N 101 10W
Mafeteng 56 29 51S 27 15 E
Maffra 45 37 53S 146 58 E
Mafia I. 54 7 45S 39 50 E
Mafikeng 56 25 50S 25 38 E
Mafra, Brazil 80 26 10S 50 0W
Mafra, Portugal 13 38 55N 9 20W
Magadan 25 59 38N 150 50 E
Magadi 54 1 54S 36 19 E
Magaliesburg 57 26 0S 27 32 E
Magallanes, Estrecho de 80 52 30S 75 0W
Magangué 78 9 14N 74 45W
Magburaka 50 8 47N 12 0W
Magdalena, Argentina 80 35 5S 57 30W
Magdalena, Bolivia 78 13 13S 63 57W
Magdalena, Malaysia 34 4 25N 117 55 E
Magdalena, Mexico 74 30 50N 112 0W
Magdalena, U.S.A. 73 34 10N 107 20W
Magdalena →, Colombia 78 11 6N 74 51W
Magdalena →, Mexico 74 30 40N 112 25W
Magdalena, B. 74 24 30N 112 10W
Magdalena, Llano de la 74 25 0N 111 30W
Magdeburg 14 52 8N 11 36 E
Magdelaine Cays 44 16 33S 150 18 E
Magdi'el 28 32 10N 34 54 E
Magee 71 31 53N 89 45W
Magee, I. 9 54 48N 5 44W
Magelang 35 7 29S 110 13 E
Magellan's Str. = Magallanes, Estrecho de 80 52 30S 75 0W
Magenta, L. 47 33 30S 119 2 E
Maggiore, L. 18 46 0N 8 35 E
Maghâr 28 32 54N 35 24 E
Magherafelt 9 54 44N 6 37W
Magnitogorsk 22 53 27N 59 4 E
Magnolia, Ark., U.S.A. 71 33 18N 93 12W
Magnolia, Miss., U.S.A. 71 31 8N 90 28W
Magog 63 45 18N 72 9W
Magosa = Famagusta 30 35 8N 33 55 E
Magpie L. 63 51 0N 64 41W
Magrath 64 49 25N 112 50W
Maguarinho, C. 79 0 15S 48 30W
Maguse L. 65 61 40N 95 10W
Maguse Pt. 65 61 20N 93 50W
Magwe 33 20 10N 95 0 E
Mahābād 30 36 50N 45 45 E
Mahabo 57 20 23S 44 40 E
Mahagi 54 2 20N 31 0 E
Mahajamba → 57 15 33S 47 8 E
Mahajamba, Helodranon' i 57 15 24S 47 5 E
Mahajanga 57 15 40S 46 25 E
Mahajanga □ 57 17 0S 47 0 E
Mahajilo → 57 19 42S 45 22 E
Mahakam → 34 0 35S 117 17 E
Mahalapye 56 23 1S 26 51 E
Maḥallāt 31 33 55N 50 30 E
Mahanadi → 33 20 20N 86 25 E
Mahanoro 57 19 54S 48 48 E
Maharashtra □ 32 20 30N 75 30 E
Mahari Mts. 52 6 20S 30 0 E
Mahasolo 57 19 7S 46 22 E
Mahbubnagar 32 16 45N 77 59 E
Mahdia 51 35 28N 11 0 E
Mahé 3 5 0S 55 30 E
Mahenge 54 8 45S 36 41 E
Maheno 43 45 10S 170 50 E
Mahesana 32 23 39N 72 26 E
Mahia Pen. 43 39 9S 177 55 E
Mahnomen 70 47 22N 95 57W
Mahón 13 39 53N 4 16 E
Mahone Bay 63 44 30N 64 20W
Mai-Ndombe, L. 54 2 0S 18 20 E
Maicurú → 79 2 14S 54 17W
Maidenhead 7 51 31N 0 42W
Maidstone, Canada 65 53 5N 109 20W
Maidstone, U.K. 7 51 16N 0 31 E
Maiduguri 53 12 0N 13 20 E
Maijdi 33 22 48N 91 10 E
Maikala Ra. 33 22 0N 81 0 E
Main →, Germany 14 50 0N 8 18 E
Main →, U.K. 9 54 49N 6 20W
Main Centre 65 50 35N 107 21W
Maine 12 48 0N 0 0 E
Maine □ 63 45 20N 69 0W
Maine → 9 52 10N 9 40W
Maine-et-Loire □ 12 47 31N 0 30W
Maingkwan 33 26 15N 96 37 E
Mainit, L. 35 9 31N 125 30 E
Mainland, Orkney, U.K. 8 59 0N 3 10W
Mainland, Shetland, U.K. 8 60 15N 1 22W
Maintirano 57 18 3S 44 1 E
Mainz 14 50 0N 8 17 E
Maipú 80 36 52S 57 50W
Maiquetía 78 10 36N 66 57W
Mairabari 33 26 30N 92 22 E
Maisi, Pta. de 75 20 10N 74 10W
Maitland, N.S.W., Australia 45 32 33S 151 36 E
Maitland, S. Austral., Australia 45 34 23S 137 40 E
Maiz, Is. del 75 12 15N 83 4W
Maizuru 36 35 25N 135 22 E
Majalengka 35 6 50S 108 13 E
Majd el Kurūm 28 32 56N 35 15 E
Majene 35 3 38S 118 57 E
Maji 51 6 12N 35 30 E
Major 65 51 52N 109 37W
Majorca, I. = Mallorca 13 39 30N 3 0 E
Maka 50 13 40N 14 10W
Makale 35 3 6S 119 51 E
Makari 54 12 35N 14 28 E
Makarikari = Makgadikgadi Salt Pans 56 20 40S 25 45 E
Makarovo 25 57 40N 107 45 E
Makasar = Ujung Pandang 35 5 10S 119 20 E
Makasar, Selat 35 1 0S 118 20 E
Makat 23 47 39N 53 19 E
Makedhonía □ 19 40 39N 22 0 E
Makedonija □ 19 41 53N 21 40 E
Makena 66 20 39N 156 27W
Makeni 50 8 55N 12 5W
Makeyevka 23 48 0N 38 0 E
Makgadikgadi Salt Pans 56 20 40S 25 45 E
Makhachkala 23 43 0N 47 30 E
Makian 35 0 20N 127 20 E
Makindu 54 2 18S 37 50 E
Makinsk 24 52 37N 70 26 E
Makkah 29 21 30N 39 54 E
Makkovik 63 55 10N 59 10W
Maklakovo 25 58 16N 92 29 E
Makó 15 46 14N 20 33 E
Makokou 54 0 40N 12 50 E
Makoua 54 0 5S 15 50 E
Makrai 32 22 2N 77 0 E
Makran 31 26 13N 61 30 E
Makran Coast Range 31 25 40N 64 0 E
Maksimkin Yar 24 58 42N 86 50 E
Mākū 30 39 15N 44 31 E
Makumbi 54 5 50S 20 43 E
Makunda 56 22 30S 20 7 E
Makurazaki 36 31 15N 130 20 E
Makurdi 53 7 43N 8 35 E
Makwassie 56 27 17S 26 0 E
Mal B. 9 52 50N 9 30W
Mala, Pta. 75 7 28N 80 2W
Malabang 35 7 36N 124 3 E
Malabar Coast 32 11 0N 75 0 E
Malacca, Str. of 34 3 0N 101 0 E
Malad City 72 42 10N 112 20 E
Málaga, Spain 13 36 43N 4 23W
Malaga, U.S.A. 71 32 12N 104 2W
Málaga □ 13 36 38N 4 58W
Malaimbandy 57 20 20S 45 36 E
Malakâl 51 9 33N 31 40 E
Malakand 32 34 40N 71 55 E
Malakoff 71 32 10N 95 55W
Malamyzh 25 50 0N 136 50 E
Malang 35 7 59S 112 45 E
Malange 54 9 36S 16 17 E
Mälaren 21 59 30N 17 10 E
Malargüe 80 35 32S 69 30W
Malartic 62 48 9N 78 9W
Malatya 30 38 25N 38 20 E
Malawi ■ 55 11 55S 34 0 E
Malawi, L. 55 12 30S 34 30 E
Malay Pen. 34 7 25N 100 0 E
Malaybalay 35 8 5N 125 7 E
Malāyer 30 34 19N 48 51 E
Malaysia ■ 34 5 0N 110 0 E
Malazgirt 30 39 10N 42 33 E
Malbaie, La 63 47 40N 70 10W
Malbon 44 21 5S 140 17 E
Malbooma 45 30 41S 134 11 E
Malbork 15 54 3N 19 1 E
Malcolm 47 28 51S 121 25 E
Malcolm, Pt. 47 33 48S 123 45 E
Maldegem 11 51 14N 3 26 E
Malden 71 36 35N 90 0W
Malden I. 41 4 3S 155 1W
Maldives ■ 3 5 0N 73 0 E
Maldonado 80 35 0S 55 0W
Maldonado, Punta 74 16 19N 98 35W
Malé Karpaty 14 48 30N 17 20 E
Maléa, Ákra 19 36 28N 23 7 E
Malegaon 32 20 30N 74 38 E
Malema 55 14 57S 37 20 E
Malgomaj 20 64 40N 16 30 E
Malha 51 15 8N 25 10 E
Malhão, Sa. do 13 37 25N 8 0W
Malheur → 72 44 3N 116 59W
Malheur L. 72 43 19N 118 42W
Mali ■ 50 17 0N 3 0W
Mali → 33 25 40N 97 40 E
Malih → 28 32 20N 35 34 E
Malik 35 0 39S 123 16 E
Malili 35 2 42S 121 6 E
Malindi 54 3 12S 40 5 E
Malines = Mechelen 11 51 2N 4 29 E
Maling 35 1 0N 121 0 E
Malita 35 6 19N 125 39 E
Mallacoota Inlet 45 37 34S 149 40 E
Mallaig 8 57 0N 5 50W
Mallawi 51 27 44N 30 44 E
Mallorca 13 39 30N 3 0 E
Mallow 9 52 8N 8 40W
Malmberget 20 67 11N 20 40 E
Malmédy 11 50 25N 6 2 E
Malmesbury 56 33 28S 18 41 E
Malmö 21 55 36N 12 59 E
Malmöhus län □ 21 55 45N 13 30 E
Malolos 35 14 50N 120 49 E
Malone 68 44 50N 74 19W
Malozemelskaya Tundra 22 67 0N 50 0 E
Malpelo 78 4 3N 81 35W
Malta, Idaho, U.S.A. 72 42 15N 113 30W
Malta, Mont., U.S.A. 72 48 20N 107 55W
Malta ■ 18 35 50N 14 30 E
Maltahöhe 56 24 55S 17 0 E
Malton 6 54 9N 0 48W
Maluku 35 1 0S 127 0 E
Maluku □ 35 3 0S 128 0 E
Malvan 32 16 2N 73 30 E
Malvern, U.K. 7 52 7N 2 19W
Malvern, U.S.A. 71 34 22N 92 50W
Malvern Hills 7 52 0N 2 19W
Malvinas, Is. = Falkland Is. 80 51 30S 59 0W
Malyy Lyakhovskiy, Ostrov 25 74 7N 140 36 E
Mama 25 58 18N 112 54 E
Mamahatun 30 39 50N 40 23 E
Mamaia 15 44 18N 28 37 E
Mamanguape 79 6 50S 35 4W
Mamasa 35 2 55S 119 20 E
Mambasa 52 1 22N 29 3 E
Mamberamo → 35 2 0S 137 50 E
Mambilima Falls 54 10 31S 28 45 E
Mamburao 35 13 13N 120 39 E
Mameigwess L. 62 52 35N 87 50W
Mamfe 53 5 50N 9 15 E
Mammoth 73 32 46N 110 43W
Mamoré → 78 10 23S 65 53W
Mamou 50 10 15N 12 0W
Mamuju 35 2 41S 118 50 E
Man 50 7 30N 7 40W
Man, I. of 6 54 15N 4 30W
Man Na 33 23 27N 97 19 E
Mana 79 5 45N 53 55W
Manaar, Gulf of = Mannar, G. of 32 8 30N 79 0 E
Manacapuru 78 3 16S 60 37W
Manacor 13 39 34N 3 13 E
Manado 35 1 29N 124 51 E
Managua 75 12 6N 86 20W
Managua, L. 75 12 20N 86 30W
Manakara 57 22 8S 48 1 E
Manambao → 57 17 35S 44 0 E
Manambato 57 13 43S 49 7 E
Manambolo → 57 19 18S 44 22 E
Manambolosy 57 16 2S 49 40 E
Mananara 57 16 10S 49 46 E
Mananara → 57 23 21S 47 42 E
Mananjary 57 21 13S 48 20 E
Manantenina 57 24 17S 47 19 E
Manaos = Manaus 78 3 0S 60 0W
Manapouri 43 45 34S 167 39 E
Manapouri, L. 43 45 32S 167 32 E
Manas 37 44 17N 85 56 E
Manas → 33 26 12N 90 40 E
Manasir 31 24 30N 51 10 E
Manassa 73 37 12N 105 58W
Manaung 33 18 45N 93 40 E
Manaus 78 3 0S 60 0W
Manawan L. 65 55 24N 103 14W
Manay 35 7 17N 126 33 E
Mancelona 68 44 54N 85 5W
Mancha, La 13 39 10N 2 54W
Manche □ 12 49 10N 1 20W
Manchegorsk 22 67 40N 32 40 E
Manchester, U.K. 6 53 30N 2 15W
Manchester, Conn., U.S.A. 68 41 47N 72 30W
Manchester, Ga., U.S.A. 69 32 53N 84 32W
Manchester, Iowa, U.S.A. 70 42 28N 91 27W
Manchester, Ky., U.S.A. 68 37 9N 83 45W
Manchester, N.H., U.S.A. 68 42 58N 71 29W
Manchester L. 65 61 28N 107 29W
Mand → 31 28 20N 52 30 E
Manda 54 10 30S 34 40 E
Mandabé 57 21 0S 44 55 E
Mandal 21 58 2N 7 25 E
Mandalay 33 22 0N 96 4 E
Mandale = Mandalay 33 22 0N 96 4 E
Mandalī 30 33 43N 45 28 E
Mandan 70 46 50N 101 0W
Mandar, Teluk 35 3 35S 119 15 E
Mandasor = Mandsaur 32 24 3N 75 8 E
Mandaue 35 10 20N 123 56 E
Mandi 32 31 39N 76 58 E
Mandimba 55 14 20S 35 40 E
Mandioli 35 0 40S 127 20 E
Mandla 33 22 39N 80 30 E
Mandoto 57 19 34S 46 17 E
Mandrare → 57 25 10S 46 30 E
Mandritsara 57 15 50S 48 49 E
Mandsaur 32 24 3N 75 8 E
Mandurah 47 32 36S 115 48 E
Mandvi 32 22 51N 69 22 E
Mandya 32 12 30N 77 0 E
Maneroo 44 23 22S 143 53 E
Maneroo Cr. → 44 23 21S 143 53 E
Manfalût 51 27 20N 30 52 E
Manfred 45 33 19S 143 45 E
Mangaia 43 21 55S 157 55W
Mangalia 15 43 50N 28 35 E
Mangalore 32 12 55N 74 47 E
Manggar 34 2 50S 108 10 E
Manggawitu 35 4 8S 133 32 E
Mangkalihat, Tanjung 35 1 2N 118 59 E
Mangla Dam 32 33 9N 73 44 E
Mangnai 37 37 52N 91 43 E
Mango 53 10 20N 0 30 E
Mangoche 55 14 25S 35 16 E
Mangoky → 57 21 29S 43 41 E
Mangole 35 1 50S 125 55 E
Mangonui 43 35 1S 173 32 E
Mangueigne 51 10 30N 21 15 E
Mangueira, L. da 80 33 0S 52 50W
Mangum 71 34 50N 99 30W
Manhattan 70 39 10N 96 40W
Manhiça 57 25 23S 32 49 E
Manhuaçu 79 20 15S 42 2W
Mania → 57 19 42S 45 22 E
Manica 57 18 58S 32 59 E
Manica e Sofala □ 57 19 10S 33 45 E
Manicoré 78 5 48S 61 16W
Manicouagan → 63 49 30N 68 30W
Manīfah 30 27 44N 49 0 E
Manifold 44 22 41S 150 40 E
Manifold, C. 44 22 41S 150 50 E
Manigotagan 65 51 6N 96 18W
Manihiki 41 10 24S 161 1W
Manila, Phil. 35 14 40N 121 3 E
Manila, U.S.A. 72 41 0N 109 44W
Manila Bay 35 14 0N 120 0 E
Manilla 45 30 45S 150 43 E
Manipur □ 33 25 0N 94 0 E
Manipur → 33 23 45N 94 20 E
Manisa 30 38 38N 27 30 E
Manistee 68 44 15N 86 20W
Manistee → 68 44 15N 86 21W
Manistique 68 45 59N 86 18W
Manito L. 65 52 43N 109 43W
Manitoba □ 65 55 30N 97 0W
Manitoba, L. 65 51 0N 98 45W
Manitou 65 49 15N 98 32W
Manitou I. 62 47 22N 87 30W
Manitou Is. 68 45 8N 86 0W
Manitou L. 63 50 55N 65 17W
Manitou Springs 70 38 52N 104 55W
Manitoulin I. 62 45 40N 82 30W
Manitowaning 62 45 46N 81 49W
Manitowoc 68 44 8N 87 40W
Manizales 78 5 5N 75 32W
Manja 57 21 26S 44 20 E
Manjacaze 57 24 45S 34 0 E
Manjakandriana 57 18 55S 47 47 E
Manjhand 32 25 50N 68 10 E
Manjil 30 36 46N 49 30 E
Manjimup 47 34 15S 116 6 E
Manjra → 32 18 49N 77 52 E
Mankato, Kans., U.S.A. 70 39 49N 98 11W
Mankato, Minn., U.S.A. 70 44 8N 93 59W
Mankayane 57 26 40S 31 4 E
Mankono 50 8 1N 6 10W
Mankota 65 49 25N 107 5W
Manly 45 33 48S 151 17 E
Manmad 32 20 18N 74 28 E
Mann Ranges, Mts. 47 26 6S 130 5 E
Manna 34 4 25S 102 55 E
Mannahill 45 32 25S 140 0 E
Mannar 32 9 1N 79 54 E
Mannar, G. of 32 8 30N 79 0 E
Mannar I. 32 9 5N 79 45 E
Mannheim 14 49 28N 8 29 E
Manning, Canada 64 56 53N 117 39W
Manning, U.S.A. 69 33 40N 80 9W
Manning Prov. Park 64 49 5N 120 45W
Mannington 68 39 35N 80 25W
Mannum 45 34 50S 139 20 E
Mano 50 8 3N 12 2W
Manokwari 35 0 54S 134 0 E
Manombo 57 22 57S 43 28 E
Manono 54 7 15S 27 25 E
Manouane, L. 63 50 45N 70 45W
Manresa 13 41 48N 1 50 E
Mans, Le 12 48 0N 0 10 E
Mansa 54 11 13S 28 55 E
Mansel I. 61 62 0N 80 0W
Mansfield, Australia 45 37 4S 146 6 E
Mansfield, U.K. 6 53 8N 1 12W
Mansfield, La., U.S.A. 71 32 2N 93 40W
Mansfield, Ohio, U.S.A. 68 40 45N 82 30W
Mansfield, Wash., U.S.A. 72 47 51N 119 44W
Manson Creek 64 55 37N 124 32W
Manta 78 1 0S 80 40W
Mantalingajan, Mt. 34 8 55N 117 45 E
Manteca 73 37 50N 121 12W
Manteo 69 35 55N 75 41W
Mantes-la-Jolie 12 49 0N 1 41 E
Manthani 32 18 40N 79 35 E
Manti 72 39 23N 111 32W
Mantiqueira, Serra da 79 22 0S 44 0W
Manton 68 44 23N 85 25W
Mántova 18 45 20N 10 42 E
Mänttä 20 62 0N 24 40 E
Mantua = Mántova 18 45 20N 10 42 E
Manu 78 12 10S 70 51W
Manua Is. 43 14 13S 169 35W
Manuae 41 19 30S 159 0W
Manuel Alves → 79 11 19S 48 28W
Manui 35 3 35S 123 5 E
Manville 70 42 48N 104 36W
Many 71 31 36N 93 28W
Manyara, L. 54 3 40S 35 50 E
Manych-Gudilo, Oz. 23 46 24N 42 38 E
Manyoni 54 5 45S 34 55 E
Manzai 32 32 12N 70 15 E
Manzanares 13 39 0N 3 22W
Manzanillo, Cuba 75 20 20N 77 31W
Manzanillo, Mexico 74 19 0N 104 20W
Manzanillo, Pta. 75 9 30N 79 40W
Manzano Mts. 73 34 30N 106 45W
Manzhouli 38 49 35N 117 25 E
Manzini 57 26 30S 31 25 E
Mao 51 14 4N 15 19 E
Maoke, Pegunungan 35 3 40S 137 30 E
Maoming 39 21 50N 110 54 E
Mapam Yumco 33 30 45N 81 28 E
Mapia, Kepulauan 35 0 50N 134 20 E
Mapimí 74 25 50N 103 50W
Mapimí, Bolsón de 74 27 30N 104 15W
Mapinhane 57 22 20S 35 0 E
Maple Creek 65 49 55N 109 29W
Mapleton 72 44 4N 123 58W
Mapuera → 78 1 5S 57 2W
Maputo 57 25 58S 32 32 E
Maputo, B. de 57 25 50S 32 45 E
Maqnā 30 28 25N 34 50 E
Maquela do Zombo 54 6 0S 15 15 E
Maquinchao 80 41 15S 68 50W
Maquoketa 70 42 4N 90 40W
Mar, Serra do 80 25 30S 49 0W
Mar Chiquita, L. 80 30 40S 62 50W
Mar del Plata 80 38 0S 57 30W
Mara 52 1 30S 34 32 E
Maraã 78 1 52S 65 25W
Marabá 79 5 20S 49 5W
Maracá, I. de 79 2 10N 50 30W
Maracaibo 78 10 40N 71 37W
Maracaibo, L. de 78 9 40N 71 30W
Maracay 78 10 15N 67 28W

Marādah

Marādah **51** 29 15N 19 15 E
Maradi **53** 13 29N 7 20 E
Marāgheh **30** 37 30N 46 12 E
Marāh **30** 25 0N 45 35 E
Marajó, I. de **79** 1 0S 49 30W
Maralal **54** 1 0N 36 38 E
Maralinga **47** 30 13S 131 32 E
Marama **45** 35 10S 140 10 E
Marampa **50** 8 45N 12 28W
Marana **73** 32 30N 111 9W
Maranboy **46** 14 40S 132 39 E
Marand **30** 38 30N 45 45 E
Maranguape **79** 3 55S 38 50W
Maranhão = São Luís **79** 2 39S 44 15W
Maranhão □ **79** 5 0S 46 0W
Maranoa → **45** 27 50S 148 37 E
Marañón → **78** 4 30S 73 35W
Marão **57** 24 18S 34 2 E
Marathon, Australia **44** 20 51S 143 32 E
Marathon, Canada **62** 48 44N 86 23W
Marathón, Greece **19** 38 11N 23 58 E
Marathon, U.S.A. **71** 30 15N 103 15W
Maratua **35** 2 10N 118 35 E
Marbella **13** 36 30N 4 57W
Marble Bar **46** 21 9S 119 44 E
Marble Falls **71** 30 30N 98 15W
Marburg **14** 50 49N 8 36 E
March **7** 52 33N 0 5 E
Marche **12** 46 5N 1 20 E
Marche □ **18** 43 22N 13 10 E
Marche-en-Famenne **11** 50 14N 5 19 E
Marches = Marche □ **18** 43 22N 13 10 E
Marcus **40** 24 0N 153 45 E
Marcus Necker Ridge **40** 20 0N 175 0 E
Mardan **32** 34 20N 72 0 E
Mardie **46** 21 12S 115 59 E
Mardin **30** 37 20N 40 43 E
Maree L. **8** 57 40N 5 30W
Mareeba **44** 16 59S 145 28 E
Marek = Stanke Dimitrov **19** 42 17N 23 9 E
Marek **35** 4 41S 120 24 E
Maremma **18** 42 45N 11 15 E
Marengo **70** 41 42N 92 5W
Marerano **57** 21 23S 44 52 E
Marfa **71** 30 15N 104 0W
Margaret Bay **64** 51 20N 127 35W
Margaret L. **64** 58 56N 115 25W
Margarita **74** 9 20N 79 55W
Margarita, I. de **78** 11 0N 64 0W
Margate, S. Africa **57** 30 50S 30 20 E
Margate, U.K. **7** 51 23N 1 24 E
Margelan **24** 40 27N 71 42 E
Marguerite **64** 52 30N 122 25W
Mari A.S.S.R. □ **22** 56 30N 48 0 E
Maria I., N. Terr., Australia **44** 14 52S 135 45 E
Maria I., Tas., Australia **44** 42 35S 148 0 E
Maria van Diemen, C. **43** 34 29S 172 40 E
Marian L. **64** 63 0N 116 15W
Mariana Trench **40** 13 0N 145 0 E
Marianao **75** 23 8N 82 24W
Marianna, Ark., U.S.A. **71** 34 48N 90 48W
Marianna, Fla., U.S.A. **69** 30 45N 85 15W
Marias → **72** 47 56N 110 30W
Mariato, Punta **75** 7 12N 80 52W
Ma'rib **29** 15 25N 45 21 E
Maribor **18** 46 36N 15 40 E
Marico → **56** 23 35S 26 57 E
Maricopa, Ariz., U.S.A. **73** 33 5N 112 2W
Maricopa, Calif., U.S.A. **73** 35 7N 119 27W
Marîdî **51** 4 55N 29 25 E
Marie-Galante **75** 15 56N 61 16W
Mariecourt **61** 61 30N 72 0W
Mariehamn **21** 60 5N 19 55 E
Marienberg **11** 52 30N 6 35 E
Marienbourg **11** 50 6N 4 31 E
Mariental **56** 24 36S 18 0 E
Mariestad **21** 58 43N 13 50 E
Marietta, Ga., U.S.A. **69** 34 0N 84 30W
Marietta, Ohio, U.S.A. **68** 39 27N 81 27W
Mariinsk **24** 56 10N 87 20 E
Marília **79** 22 13S 50 0W
Marillana **46** 22 37S 119 16 E
Marín **13** 42 23N 8 42W
Marina Plains **44** 14 37S 143 57 E
Marinduque **35** 13 25N 122 0 E
Marine City **68** 42 45N 82 29W
Marinel, Le **54** 10 25S 25 17 E
Marinette **68** 45 4N 87 40W
Maringá **80** 23 26S 52 2W
Marion, Ala., U.S.A. **69** 32 33N 87 20W
Marion, Ill., U.S.A. **71** 37 45N 88 55W
Marion, Ind., U.S.A. **68** 40 35N 85 40W
Marion, Iowa, U.S.A. **70** 42 2N 91 36W
Marion, Kans., U.S.A. **70** 38 25N 97 2W
Marion, Mich., U.S.A. **68** 44 7N 85 8W
Marion, N.C., U.S.A. **69** 35 42N 82 0W
Marion, Ohio, U.S.A. **68** 40 38N 83 8W
Marion, S.C., U.S.A. **69** 34 11N 79 22W
Marion, Va., U.S.A. **69** 36 51N 81 29W
Marion, L. **69** 33 30N 80 15W
Marion I. **3** 47 0S 38 0 E
Mariposa **73** 37 31N 119 59W
Mariscal Estigarribia **78** 22 3S 60 40W
Maritsa → **19** 41 40N 26 34 E
Marīvān **30** 35 30N 46 25 E
Markazī □ **31** 35 0N 49 30 E
Marked Tree **71** 35 35N 90 24W
Marken **11** 52 26N 5 12 E
Market Drayton **6** 52 55N 2 30W
Market Harborough **7** 52 29N 0 55W
Markham L. **65** 62 30N 102 35W
Markovo **25** 64 40N 169 40 E
Marks **22** 51 45N 46 50 E
Marksville **71** 31 10N 92 2W
Marla **45** 27 19S 133 33 E
Marlborough **44** 22 46S 149 52 E
Marlborough □ **43** 41 45S 173 33 E
Marlborough Downs **7** 51 25N 1 55W
Marlin **71** 31 25N 96 50W
Marlow **71** 34 40N 97 58W
Marmagao **32** 15 25N 73 56 E
Marmara **30** 40 35N 27 38 E
Marmara, Sea of = Marmara Denizi **30** 40 45N 28 15 E
Marmara Denizi **30** 40 45N 28 15 E
Marmaris **30** 36 50N 28 14 E
Marmarth **70** 46 21N 103 52W
Marmion L. **62** 48 55N 91 20W
Marmion Mt. **47** 29 16S 119 50 E
Marmolada, Mte. **18** 46 25N 11 55 E
Marmora **62** 44 28N 77 41W
Marne □ **12** 48 50N 4 10 E
Marne → **12** 48 48N 2 24 E
Maroala **57** 15 23S 47 59 E
Maroantsetra **57** 15 26S 49 44 E
Maromandia **57** 14 13S 48 5 E
Marondera **55** 18 5S 31 42 E
Maroni → **79** 5 30N 54 0W
Maroochydore **45** 26 29S 153 5 E
Maroona **45** 37 27S 142 54 E
Marosakoa **57** 15 26S 46 38 E
Maroua **53** 10 40N 14 20 E
Marovoay **57** 16 6S 46 39 E
Marquard **56** 28 40S 27 28 E
Marquesas Is. **41** 9 30S 140 0W
Marquette **68** 46 30N 87 21W
Marracuene **57** 25 45S 32 35 E
Marrakech **50** 31 9N 8 0W
Marrawah **44** 40 55S 144 42 E
Marree **45** 29 39S 138 1 E
Marrilla **46** 22 31S 114 25 E
Marrimane **57** 22 58S 33 34 E
Marromeu **57** 18 15S 36 25 E
Marrowie Creek **45** 33 23S 145 40 E
Marrupa **55** 13 8S 37 30 E
Mars, Le **70** 43 0N 96 0W
Marsá Matrûh **51** 31 19N 27 9 E
Marsá Susah **51** 32 52N 21 59 E
Marsabit **54** 2 18N 38 0 E
Marsala **18** 37 48N 12 25 E
Marsaxlokk **18** 35 47N 14 32 E
Marsden **45** 33 47S 147 32 E
Marseille **12** 43 18N 5 23 E
Marseilles = Marseille **12** 43 18N 5 23 E
Marsh I. **71** 29 35N 91 50W
Marsh L. **70** 45 5N 96 0W
Marshall, Liberia **50** 6 8N 10 22W
Marshall, Ark., U.S.A. **71** 35 58N 92 40W
Marshall, Mich., U.S.A. **68** 42 17N 84 59W
Marshall, Minn., U.S.A. **70** 44 25N 95 45W
Marshall, Mo., U.S.A. **70** 39 8N 93 15W
Marshall, Tex., U.S.A. **71** 32 29N 94 20W
Marshall → **44** 22 59S 136 59 E
Marshall Is. **40** 9 0N 171 0 E
Marshalltown **70** 42 5N 92 56W
Marshfield, Mo., U.S.A. **71** 37 20N 92 58W
Marshfield, Wis., U.S.A. **70** 44 42N 90 10W
Marstrand **21** 57 53N 11 35 E
Mart **71** 31 34N 96 51W
Martaban **33** 16 30N 97 35 E
Martaban, G. of **33** 16 5N 96 30 E
Martapura, Kalimantan, Indonesia **34** 3 22S 114 47 E
Martapura, Sumatera, Indonesia **34** 4 19S 104 22 E
Marte **53** 12 23N 13 46 E
Martelange **11** 49 49N 5 43 E
Martha's Vineyard **68** 41 25N 70 35W
Martin, S. Dak., U.S.A. **70** 43 11N 101 45W
Martin, Tenn., U.S.A. **71** 36 23N 88 51W
Martin, L. **69** 32 45N 85 50W
Martinborough **43** 41 14S 175 29 E
Martinique **75** 14 40N 61 0W
Martinique Passage **75** 15 15N 61 0W
Martinsburg **68** 39 30N 77 57W
Martinsville, Ind., U.S.A. **68** 39 29N 86 23W
Martinsville, Va., U.S.A. **69** 36 41N 79 52W
Marton **43** 40 4S 175 23 E
Martos **13** 37 44N 3 58W
Marudi **34** 4 11N 114 19 E
Ma'ruf **31** 31 30N 67 6 E
Marugame **36** 34 15N 133 40 E
Marulan **45** 34 43S 150 3 E
Marunga **56** 17 28S 20 2 E
Marwar **32** 25 43N 73 45 E
Mary **24** 37 40N 61 50 E
Mary Frances L. **65** 63 19N 106 13W
Mary Kathleen **44** 20 44S 139 48 E
Maryborough = Port Laoise **9** 53 2N 7 20W
Maryborough, Queens., Australia **45** 25 31S 152 37 E
Maryborough, Vic., Australia **45** 37 0S 143 44 E
Maryfield **65** 49 50N 101 35W
Maryland □ **68** 39 10N 76 40W
Maryport **6** 54 43N 3 30W
Mary's Harbour **63** 52 18N 55 51W
Marystown **63** 47 10N 55 10W
Marysvale **73** 38 25N 112 17W
Marysville, Canada **64** 49 35N 116 0W
Marysville, Calif., U.S.A. **72** 39 14N 121 40W
Marysville, Kans., U.S.A. **70** 39 50N 96 49W
Marysville, Ohio, U.S.A. **68** 40 15N 83 20W
Maryvale **45** 28 4S 152 12 E
Maryville **69** 35 50N 84 0W
Marzūq **51** 25 53N 13 57 E
Masada = Mesada **28** 31 20N 35 19 E
Masai Steppe **52** 4 30S 36 30 E
Masaka **54** 0 21S 31 45 E
Masalembo, Kepulauan **34** 5 35S 114 30 E
Masalima, Kepulauan **34** 5 4S 117 5 E
Masamba **35** 2 30S 120 15 E
Masan **38** 35 11N 128 32 E
Masandam, Ras **31** 26 30N 56 30 E
Masasi **54** 10 45S 38 52 E
Masaya **75** 12 0N 86 7W
Masbate **35** 12 21N 123 36 E
Mascara **50** 35 26N 0 6 E
Mascarene Is. **3** 22 0S 55 0 E
Mascota **74** 20 30N 104 50W
Masela **35** 8 9S 129 51 E
Maseru **56** 29 18S 27 30 E
Mashābih **30** 25 35N 36 30 E
Mashan **39** 23 40N 108 11 E
Mashhad **31** 36 20N 59 35 E
Mashike **36** 43 31N 141 30 E
Mashkel, Hamun-i- **31** 28 30N 63 0 E
Mashki Chāh **31** 29 5N 62 30 E
Mashonaland Central □ **57** 17 30S 31 0 E
Mashonaland East □ **57** 18 0S 32 0 E
Mashonaland West □ **57** 17 30S 29 30 E
Masi **20** 69 26N 23 40 E
Masi Manimba **54** 4 40S 17 54 E
Masindi **54** 1 40N 31 43 E
Masisea **78** 8 35S 74 22W
Masisi **52** 1 23S 28 49 E
Masjed Soleyman **30** 31 55N 49 18 E
Mask, L. **9** 53 36N 9 24W
Masoala, Tanjon' i **57** 15 59S 50 13 E
Masoarivo **57** 19 3S 44 19 E
Masohi **35** 3 20S 128 55 E
Masomeloka **57** 20 17S 48 37 E
Mason **71** 30 45N 99 15W
Mason City **70** 43 9N 93 12W
Masqat **31** 23 37N 58 36 E
Massa **18** 44 2N 10 7 E
Massachusetts □ **68** 42 25N 72 0W
Massada **28** 33 41N 35 36 E
Massaguet **51** 12 28N 15 26 E
Massakory **51** 13 0N 15 49 E
Massangena **57** 21 34S 33 0 E
Massawa = Mitsiwa **51** 15 35N 39 25 E
Massena **68** 44 52N 74 55W
Massénya **51** 11 21N 16 9 E
Masset **64** 54 2N 132 10W
Massif Central **12** 45 30N 3 0 E
Massillon **68** 40 47N 81 30W
Massinga **57** 23 15S 35 22 E
Masterton **43** 40 56S 175 39 E
Mastuj **32** 36 20N 72 36 E
Mastung **31** 29 50N 66 56 E
Masuda **36** 34 40N 131 51 E
Masvingo **55** 20 8S 30 49 E
Mataboor **35** 1 41S 138 3 E
Matachewan **62** 47 56N 80 39W
Matad **37** 47 11N 115 27 E
Matadi **54** 5 52S 13 31 E
Matagalpa **75** 13 0N 85 58W
Matagami **62** 49 45N 77 34W
Matagami, L. **62** 49 50N 77 40W
Matagorda **71** 28 43N 96 0W
Matagorda B. **71** 28 30N 96 15W
Matagorda I. **71** 28 10N 96 40W
Matak, P. **34** 3 18N 106 16 E
Matakana **45** 32 59S 145 54 E
Matam **50** 15 34N 13 17W
Matamoros, Coahuila, Mexico **74** 25 33N 103 15W
Matamoros, Puebla, Mexico **74** 18 2N 98 17W
Matamoros, Tamaulipas, Mexico **74** 25 50N 97 30W
Ma'ṭan as Sarra **51** 21 45N 22 0 E
Matane **63** 48 50N 67 33W
Matanuska **60** 61 39N 149 19W
Matanzas **75** 23 0N 81 40W
Matapan, C. = Taínaron, Ákra **19** 36 22N 22 27 E
Matapédia **63** 48 0N 66 59W
Matara **32** 5 58N 80 30 E
Mataram **34** 8 41S 116 10 E
Matarani **78** 77 0S 72 10W
Mataranka **46** 14 55S 133 4 E
Matatiele **57** 30 20S 28 49 E
Mataura **43** 46 11S 168 51 E
Matehuala **74** 23 40N 100 40W
Matera **18** 40 40N 16 37 E
Matheson Island **65** 51 45N 96 56W
Mathis **71** 28 4N 97 48W
Mathura **32** 27 30N 77 40 E
Mati **35** 6 55N 126 15 E
Matías Romero **74** 16 53N 95 2W
Matima **56** 20 15S 24 26 E
Matlock **6** 53 8N 1 32W
Matmata **50** 33 37N 9 59 E
Mato Grosso □ **79** 14 0S 55 0W
Mato Grosso, Planalto do **79** 15 0S 55 0W
Matochkin Shar **24** 73 10N 56 40 E
Matosinhos **13** 41 11N 8 42W
Matrah **31** 23 37N 58 30 E
Matsena **53** 13 5N 10 5 E
Matsue **36** 35 25N 133 10 E
Matsumae **36** 41 26N 140 7 E
Matsumoto **36** 36 15N 138 0 E
Matsusaka **36** 34 34N 136 32 E
Matsutō **36** 36 31N 136 34 E
Matsuyama **36** 33 45N 132 45 E
Mattagami → **62** 50 43N 81 29W
Mattancheri **32** 9 50N 76 15 E
Mattawa **62** 46 20N 78 45W
Mattawamkeag **63** 45 30N 68 21W
Matterhorn **14** 45 58N 7 39 E
Matthew Town **75** 20 57N 73 40W
Matthew's Ridge **78** 7 37N 60 10W
Mattice **62** 49 40N 83 20W
Matuba **57** 24 28S 32 49 E
Matucana **78** 11 55S 76 25W
Matun **32** 33 22N 69 58 E
Maturín **78** 9 45N 63 11W
Mau Ranipur **32** 25 16N 79 8 E
Maud, Pt. **46** 23 6S 113 45 E
Maude **45** 34 29S 144 18 E
Maudin Sun **33** 16 0N 94 30 E
Maués **78** 3 20S 57 45W
Mauganj **33** 24 50N 81 55 E
Maui **66** 20 45N 156 20 E
Mauke **43** 20 9S 157 20W
Maulamyaing **33** 16 30N 97 40 E
Maumee **68** 41 35N 83 40W
Maumee → **68** 41 42N 83 28W
Maumere **35** 8 38S 122 13 E
Maun **56** 20 0S 23 26 E
Mauna Kea **66** 19 50N 155 28W
Mauna Loa **66** 21 8N 157 10W
Maungmagan Kyunzu **33** 14 0N 97 48 E
Maupin **72** 45 12N 121 9W
Maurepas L. **71** 30 18N 90 35W
Maures **12** 43 15N 6 15 E
Maurice L. **47** 29 30S 131 0 E
Mauritania ■ **50** 20 50N 10 0W
Mauritius ■ **3** 20 0S 57 0 E
Mauston **70** 43 48N 90 5W
Mavinga **55** 15 50S 20 21 E
Mavqi'im **28** 31 38N 34 32 E
Mawk Mai **33** 20 14N 97 37 E
Mawlaik **33** 23 40N 94 26 E
Max **70** 47 50N 101 20W
Maxcanú **74** 20 40N 92 0W
Maxesibeni **57** 30 49S 29 23 E
Maxhamish L. **64** 59 50N 123 17W
Maxixe **57** 23 54S 35 17 E
Maxwelton **44** 20 43S 142 41 E
May Downs **44** 22 38S 148 55 E
May Pen **75** 17 58N 77 15W
Maya → **25** 54 31N 134 41 E
Maya Mts. **74** 16 30N 89 0W
Mayaguana **75** 22 30N 72 44W
Mayagüez **75** 18 12N 67 9W
Mayarí **75** 20 40N 75 41W
Maybell **72** 40 30N 108 4W
Maydena **44** 42 45S 146 30 E
Mayenne **12** 48 20N 0 38W
Mayenne □ **12** 48 10N 0 40W
Mayer **73** 34 28N 112 17W
Mayerthorpe **64** 53 57N 115 8W
Mayfield **69** 36 45N 88 40W
Mayhill **73** 32 58N 105 30W
Maykop **23** 44 35N 40 25 E
Maynard Hills **47** 28 28S 119 49 E
Mayne → **44** 23 40S 141 55 E
Maynooth **9** 53 22N 6 38W
Mayo **60** 63 38N 135 57W
Mayo □ **9** 53 47N 9 7W
Mayo L. **60** 63 45N 135 0W
Mayon Volcano **35** 13 15N 123 41 E
Mayor I. **43** 37 16S 176 17 E
Mayson L. **65** 57 55N 107 10W
Maysville **68** 38 39N 83 46W
Maythalūn **28** 32 21N 35 16 E
Mayu **35** 1 30N 126 30 E
Mayville **70** 47 30N 97 23W
Mayya **25** 61 44N 130 18 E
Mazabuka **55** 15 52S 27 44 E
Mazagán = El Jadida **50** 33 11N 8 17W
Mazagão **79** 0 7S 51 16W
Mazán **78** 3 30S 73 0W
Māzandarān □ **31** 36 30N 52 0 E
Mazar-e Sharīf **31** 36 41N 67 0 E
Mazarredo **80** 47 10S 66 50W
Mazarrón **13** 37 38N 1 19W
Mazaruni → **78** 6 25N 58 35W
Mazatenango **75** 14 35N 91 30W
Mazatlán **74** 23 10N 106 30W
Māzhān **31** 32 30N 59 0 E
Mazīnān **31** 36 19N 56 56 E
Mazoe → **55** 16 20S 33 30 E
Mazu Dao **39** 26 10N 119 55 E
Mazurian Lakes = Mazurski, Pojezierze **15** 53 50N 21 0 E
Mazurski, Pojezierze **15** 53 50N 21 0 E
Mbabane **57** 26 18S 31 6 E
Mbaïki **54** 3 53N 18 1 E
Mbala **54** 8 46S 31 24 E
Mbale **54** 1 8N 34 12 E
Mbalmayo **54** 3 33N 11 33 E
Mbamba Bay **54** 11 13S 34 49 E
Mbandaka **54** 0 1N 18 18 E
Mbanza Congo **54** 6 18S 14 16 E
Mbanza Ngungu **54** 5 12S 14 53 E
Mbarara **54** 0 35S 30 40 E
Mbashe → **57** 32 15S 28 54 E
Mbeya **54** 8 54S 33 29 E
Mbini □ **54** 1 30N 10 0 E
Mbour **50** 14 22N 16 54W
Mbout **50** 16 1N 12 38W
Mbuji-Mayi **54** 6 9S 23 40 E
Mbulu **54** 3 45S 35 30 E
Mchinji **55** 13 47S 32 58 E
Mdina **18** 35 51N 14 25 E
Mead, L. **73** 36 1N 114 44W
Meade **71** 37 18N 100 25W
Meadow **47** 26 35S 114 40 E
Meadow Lake **65** 54 10N 108 26W
Meadow Lake Prov. Park **65** 54 27N 109 0W
Meadow Valley Wash → **73** 36 39N 114 35W
Meadville **68** 41 39N 80 9W
Meaford **62** 44 36N 80 35W
Mealy Mts. **63** 53 10N 58 0W
Meander River **64** 59 2N 117 42W
Meares, C. **72** 45 37N 124 0W
Mearim → **79** 3 4S 44 35W
Meath □ **9** 53 32N 6 40W
Meath Park **65** 53 27N 105 22W
Meaux **12** 48 58N 2 50 E
Mecca = Makkah **29** 21 30N 39 54 E
Mecca **73** 33 37N 116 3W
Mechelen **11** 51 2N 4 29 E
Mecheria **50** 33 35N 0 18W
Mecklenburger Bucht **14** 54 20N 11 40 E
Meconta **55** 14 59S 39 50 E
Meda **46** 17 22S 123 59 E

Miranda

Medan 34 3 40N 98 38 E
Medanosa, Pta. 80 48 8S 66 0W
Medéa 50 36 12N 2 50 E
Medellín 78 6 15N 75 35W
Medemblik 11 52 46N 5 8 E
Mederdra 50 17 0N 15 38W
Medford, Oreg., U.S.A. 72 42 20N 122 52W
Medford, Wis., U.S.A. 70 45 9N 90 21W
Mediaş 15 46 9N 24 22 E
Medical Lake 72 47 35N 117 42W
Medicine Bow 72 41 56N 106 11W
Medicine Bow Pk. 72 41 21N 106 19W
Medicine Bow Ra. 72 41 10N 106 25W
Medicine Hat 65 50 0N 110 45W
Medicine Lake 70 48 30N 104 30W
Medicine Lodge 71 37 20N 98 37W
Medina = Al Madīnah 29 24 35N 39 52 E
Medina, N. Dak., U.S.A. 70 46 57N 99 20W
Medina, N.Y., U.S.A. 68 43 15N 78 27W
Medina, Ohio, U.S.A. 68 41 9N 81 50W
Medina → 71 29 10N 98 20W
Medina del Campo 13 41 18N 4 55W
Medina L. 71 29 35N 98 58W
Medina-Sidonia 13 36 28N 5 57W
Medinipur 33 22 25N 87 21 E
Mediterranean Sea 16 35 0N 15 0 E
Medley 65 54 25N 110 16W
Médoc 12 45 10N 0 50W
Medport = Marsaxlokk 18 35 47N 14 32 E
Medstead 65 53 19N 108 5W
Medveditsa → 23 49 35N 42 41 E
Medvezhi, Ostrava 25 71 0N 161 0 E
Medvezhyegorsk 22 63 0N 34 25 E
Medway → 7 51 28N 0 45 E
Meeberrie 47 26 57S 115 51 E
Meekatharra 47 26 32S 118 29 E
Meeker 72 40 1N 107 58W
Meerut 32 29 1N 77 42 E
Meeteetse 72 44 10N 108 56W
Mega 51 3 57N 38 19 E
Mégara 19 37 58N 23 22 E
Meghalaya □ 33 25 50N 91 0 E
Megiddo 28 32 36N 35 11 E
Mégiscane, L. 62 48 35N 75 55W
Megiste 17 36 8N 29 34 E
Mehadia 15 44 56N 22 23 E
Mei Jiang → 39 24 25N 116 35 E
Mei Xian 39 24 16N 116 6 E
Meiganga 54 6 30N 14 25 E
Meiktila 33 20 53N 95 54 E
Me'ir Shefeya 28 32 35N 34 58 E
Meissen 14 51 10N 13 29 E
Meitan 39 27 45N 107 29 E
Mejillones 80 23 10S 70 30W
Meka 47 27 25S 116 48 E
Mékambo 54 1 2N 13 50 E
Mekdela 51 11 24N 39 10 E
Mekhtar 32 30 30N 69 15 E
Meknès 50 33 57N 5 33W
Mekong → 34 9 30N 106 15 E
Mekongga 35 3 39S 121 15 E
Melagiri Hills 32 12 20N 77 30 E
Melaka 34 2 15N 102 15 E
Melalap 34 5 10N 116 5 E
Melanesia 40 4 0S 155 0 E
Melbourne, Australia 45 37 50S 145 0 E
Melbourne, U.S.A. 69 28 4N 80 35W
Melchor Múzquiz 74 27 50N 101 30W
Melchor Ocampo 74 24 52N 101 40W
Mélèzes → 61 57 30N 71 0W
Melfi 51 11 0N 17 59 E
Melfort 65 52 50N 104 37W
Melilla 50 35 21N 2 57W
Melilot 28 31 22N 34 37 E
Melita 65 49 15N 101 0W
Melitopol 23 46 50N 35 22 E
Melk 14 48 13N 15 20 E
Mellansel 20 63 25N 18 17 E
Mellen 70 46 19N 90 36W
Mellerud 21 58 41N 12 28 E
Mellette 70 45 11N 98 29W
Melo 80 32 20S 54 10W
Melolo 35 9 53S 120 40 E
Melrose, N.S.W., Australia 45 32 42S 146 57 E
Melrose, W. Austral., Australia 47 27 50S 121 15 E
Melrose, U.K. 8 53 35N 2 44W
Melrose, U.S.A. 71 34 27N 103 33W
Melstone 72 46 36N 107 50W
Melton Mowbray 6 52 46N 0 52W
Melun 12 48 32N 2 39 E
Melut 51 10 30N 32 13 E
Melville 65 50 55N 102 50W
Melville, C. 44 14 11S 144 30 E
Melville, L. 63 53 30N 60 0W
Melville B. 44 12 0S 136 45 E
Melville I., Australia 46 11 30S 131 0 E
Melville I., Canada 58 75 30N 112 0W
Melville Pen. 61 68 0N 84 0W
Melvin → 64 59 11N 117 31W
Memba 55 14 11S 40 30 E
Memboro 35 9 30S 119 30 E
Memel = Klaipeda 22 55 43N 21 10 E
Memel 57 27 38S 29 36 E
Memmingen 14 47 59N 10 12 E
Mempawah 34 0 30N 109 5 E
Memphis, Tenn., U.S.A. 71 35 7N 90 0W
Memphis, Tex., U.S.A. 71 34 45N 100 30W
Mena 71 34 40N 94 15W
Menai Strait 6 53 14N 4 10W
Ménaka 53 15 59N 2 18 E
Menan = Chao Phraya → 34 13 32N 100 36 E
Menarandra → 57 25 17S 44 30 E
Menard 71 30 57N 99 48W
Menasha 68 44 13N 88 27W
Menate 34 0 12S 113 3 E
Mendawai → 34 3 30S 113 0 E
Mende 12 44 31N 3 30 E
Menderes → 30 37 25N 28 45 E
Mendip Hills 7 51 17N 2 40W
Mendocino 72 39 26N 123 50W
Mendocino, C. 72 40 26N 124 25W
Mendocino Seascarp 41 41 0N 140 0W
Mendota, Calif., U.S.A. 73 36 46N 120 24W
Mendota, Ill., U.S.A. 70 41 35N 89 5W
Mendoza 80 32 50S 68 52W
Mene Grande 78 9 49N 70 56W
Menemen 30 38 34N 27 3 E
Menen 11 50 47N 3 7 E
Menfi 18 37 36N 12 57 E
Mengcheng 39 33 18N 116 31 E
Menggala 34 4 30S 105 15 E
Mengshan 39 24 14N 110 55 E
Mengzi 37 23 20N 103 22 E
Menihek L. 63 54 0N 67 0W
Menin = Menen 11 50 47N 3 7 E
Menindee 45 32 20S 142 25 E
Menindee, L. 45 32 20S 142 25 E
Meningie 45 35 35S 139 0 E
Menominee 68 45 9N 87 39W
Menominee → 68 45 5N 87 36W
Menomonie 70 44 50N 91 54W
Menongue 55 14 48S 17 52 E
Menorca 13 40 0N 4 0 E
Mentawai, Kepulauan 34 2 0S 99 0 E
Menton 12 43 50N 7 29 E
Mentz Dam 56 33 10S 25 9 E
Menzelinsk 22 55 53N 53 1 E
Menzies 47 29 40S 120 58 E
Me'ona 28 33 1N 35 15 E
Meppel 68 52 42N 6 12 E
Mer Rouge 71 32 47N 91 48W
Merabéllou, Kólpos 19 35 10N 25 50 E
Meramangye, L. 47 28 25S 132 13 E
Meran = Merano 18 46 40N 11 10 E
Merano 18 46 40N 11 10 E
Merauke 35 8 29S 140 24 E
Merbabu 35 7 30S 110 40 E
Merbein 45 34 10S 142 2 E
Merca 29 1 48N 44 50 E
Merced 73 37 18N 120 30W
Mercedes, Buenos Aires, Argentina 80 34 40S 59 30W
Mercedes, Corrientes, Argentina 80 29 10S 58 5W
Mercedes, San Luis, Argentina 80 33 40S 65 21W
Mercedes, Uruguay 80 33 12S 58 0W
Merceditas 80 28 20S 70 35W
Mercer 43 37 16S 175 5 E
Mercy C. 61 65 0N 63 30W
Meredith, C. 80 52 15S 60 40W
Meredith, L. 71 35 30N 101 35W
Merga = Nukheila 51 19 1N 26 21 E
Mergui Arch. = Myeik Kyunzu 34 11 30N 97 30 E
Mérida, Mexico 74 20 9N 89 40W
Mérida, Spain 13 38 55N 6 25W
Mérida, Venezuela 78 8 24N 71 8W
Mérida, Cord. de 76 9 0N 71 0W
Meriden 68 41 33N 72 47W
Meridian, Idaho, U.S.A. 72 43 41N 116 25W
Meridian, Miss., U.S.A. 69 32 20N 88 42W
Meridian, Tex., U.S.A. 71 31 55N 97 37W
Meriruma 79 1 15N 54 50W
Merkel 71 32 30N 100 0W
Merksem 11 51 16N 4 25 E
Mermaid Reef 46 17 6S 119 36 E
Merowe 51 18 29N 31 46 E
Merredin 47 31 28S 118 18 E
Merrick 8 55 8N 4 30W
Merrill, Oreg., U.S.A. 72 42 2N 121 37W
Merrill, Wis., U.S.A. 70 45 11N 89 41W
Merriman 70 42 55N 101 42W
Merritt 64 50 10N 120 45W
Merriwa 45 32 6S 150 22 E
Merriwagga 45 33 47S 145 43 E
Merry I. 62 55 29N 77 31W
Merrygoen 45 31 51S 149 12 E
Merryville 71 30 47N 93 31W
Mersa Fatma 29 14 57N 40 17 E
Mersch 11 49 44N 6 7 E
Merseburg 14 51 20N 12 0 E
Mersey → 6 53 20N 2 56W
Merseyside □ 6 53 25N 2 55W
Mersin 30 36 51N 34 36 E
Mersing 34 2 25N 103 50 E
Merthyr Tydfil 7 51 45N 3 23W
Mértola 13 37 40N 7 40 E
Mertzon 71 31 17N 100 48W
Meru 54 0 3N 37 40 E
Mesa 73 33 20N 111 56W
Mesa, La, Calif., U.S.A. 73 32 48N 117 5W
Mesa, La, N. Mex., U.S.A. 73 32 6N 106 48W
Mesada 28 31 20N 35 19 E
Mesgouez, L. 62 51 20N 75 0W
Meshed = Mashhad 31 36 20N 59 35 E
Meshra er Req 51 8 25N 29 18 E
Mesick 68 44 24N 85 42W
Mesilinka → 64 56 6N 124 30W
Mesilla 73 32 20N 106 50W
Mesolóngion 19 38 21N 21 28 E
Mesopotamia = Al Jazirah 30 33 30N 44 0 E
Mesquite 73 36 47N 114 6W
Mess Cr. → 64 57 55N 131 14W
Messina, Italy 18 38 10N 15 32 E
Messina, S. Africa 57 22 20S 30 0 E
Messina, Str. di 18 38 5N 15 35 E
Messíni 19 37 4N 22 1 E
Messiniakós, Kólpos 19 36 45N 22 5 E
Mesta → 19 41 30N 24 0 E
Meta → 78 6 12N 67 28W
Metairie 71 29 59N 90 9W
Metaline Falls 72 48 52N 117 22W
Metán 80 25 30S 65 0W
Metangula 55 12 40S 34 50 E
Metema 51 12 56N 36 13 E
Methven 43 43 38S 171 40 E
Methy L. 65 56 28N 109 30W
Metil 55 16 24S 39 0 E
Metlakatla 64 55 10N 131 33W
Metropolis 71 37 10N 88 47W
Mettur Dam 32 11 45N 77 45 E
Metulla 28 33 17N 35 34 E
Metz 12 49 8N 6 10 E
Meulaboh 34 4 11N 96 3 E
Meureudu 34 5 19N 96 10 E
Meurthe-et-Moselle □ 12 48 52N 6 0 E
Meuse □ 12 49 8N 5 25 E
Meuse → 11 50 45N 5 41 E
Mexborough 6 53 29N 1 18W
Mexia 71 31 38N 96 32W
Mexiana, I. 79 0 0 49 30W
Mexicali 74 32 40N 115 30W
México, Mexico 74 19 20N 99 10W
Mexico, U.S.A. 70 39 10N 91 55W
México □ 74 19 20N 99 10W
Mexico ■ 74 25 0N 105 0W
Mexico, G. of 74 25 0N 90 0W
Meymaneh 31 35 53N 64 38 E
Mezen 22 65 50N 44 20 E
Mezen → 22 66 11N 43 59 E
Mezőkövesd 15 47 49N 20 35 E
Mezőtúr 15 47 0N 20 41 E
Mezquital 74 23 29N 104 23W
Mhow 32 22 33N 75 50 E
Miahuatlán 74 16 21N 96 36W
Miallo 44 16 28S 145 22 E
Miami, Ariz., U.S.A. 73 33 25N 110 54W
Miami, Fla., U.S.A. 69 25 45N 80 15W
Miami, Tex., U.S.A. 71 35 44N 100 38W
Miami → 68 39 20N 84 40W
Miami Beach 69 25 49N 80 6W
Miamisburg 68 39 40N 84 11W
Mian Xian 39 33 10N 106 32 E
Mianchi 39 34 48N 111 48 E
Miāndowāb 30 37 0N 46 5 E
Miandrivazo 57 19 31S 45 29 E
Mīāneh 30 37 30N 47 40 E
Mianwali 32 32 38N 71 28 E
Mianyang, Hubei, China 39 30 25N 113 25 E
Mianyang, Sichuan, China 39 31 22N 104 47 E
Miaoli 39 24 37N 120 49 E
Miarinarivo 57 18 57S 46 55 E
Miass 22 54 59N 60 6 E
Michigan □ 67 44 40N 85 40W
Michigan, L. 68 44 0N 87 0W
Michigan City 68 41 42N 86 56W
Michikamau L. 63 54 20N 63 10W
Michipicoten 62 47 55N 84 55W
Michipicoten I. 62 47 40N 85 40W
Michoacan □ 74 19 0N 102 0W
Michurinsk 22 52 58N 40 27 E
Miclere 44 22 34S 147 32 E
Mico, Pta. 75 12 0N 83 30W
Micronesia 40 11 0N 160 0 E
Mid Glamorgan □ 7 51 40N 3 25W
Mid-Indian Ridge 40 40 0S 75 0 E
Mid-Oceanic Ridge 40 42 0S 90 0 E
Midai, P. 34 3 0N 107 47 E
Midale 65 49 25N 103 20W
Middelburg, Neth. 11 51 30N 3 36 E
Middelburg, C. Prov., S. Africa 56 31 30S 25 0 E
Middelburg, Trans., S. Africa 57 25 49S 29 28 E
Middelwit 56 24 51S 27 3 E
Middle Alkali L. 72 41 30N 120 3W
Middle Loup → 70 41 17N 98 23W
Middleport 68 39 0N 82 5W
Middlesboro 69 36 36N 83 43W
Middlesbrough 6 54 35N 1 14W
Middleton, Australia 44 22 22S 141 32 E
Middleton, Canada 63 44 57N 65 4W
Middletown, Conn., U.S.A. 68 41 37N 72 40W
Middletown, N.Y., U.S.A. 68 41 28N 74 28W
Middletown, Ohio, U.S.A. 68 39 29N 84 25W
Midi, Canal du → 12 43 45N 1 21 E
Midland, Australia 45 31 54S 115 59 E
Midland, Canada 62 44 45N 79 50W
Midland, Mich., U.S.A. 68 43 37N 84 17W
Midland, Tex., U.S.A. 71 32 0N 102 3W
Midleton 9 51 52N 8 12W
Midlothian 71 32 30N 97 0W
Midongy, Tangorombohitr' i 57 23 30S 47 0 E
Midongy Atsimo 57 23 35S 47 1 E
Midway Is. 2 28 13N 177 22W
Midwest 72 43 27N 106 19W
Midyat 30 37 25N 41 23 E
Mie □ 36 34 30N 136 10 E
Międzychód 14 52 35N 15 53 E
Międzyrzec Podlaski 15 51 58N 22 45 E
Mienga 56 17 12S 19 48 E
Miercurea Ciuc 15 46 21N 25 48 E
Mieres 13 43 18N 5 48W
Migdāl 28 32 51N 35 30 E
Migdal Afeq 28 32 5N 34 58 E
Miguel Alemán, Presa 74 18 15N 96 40W
Miguel Alves 79 4 11S 42 55W
Mihara 36 34 24N 133 5 E
Mikínai 19 37 43N 22 46 E
Mikkeli 21 61 43N 27 15 E
Mikkeli □ 20 62 0N 28 0 E
Mikkwa → 64 58 25N 114 46W
Míkonos 19 37 30N 25 25 E
Mikun 22 62 20N 50 0 E
Mikura-Jima 36 33 52N 139 36 E
Milaca 70 45 45N 93 40W
Milagro 78 2 11S 79 36W
Milan = Milano 18 45 28N 9 10 E
Milan, Mo., U.S.A. 70 40 10N 93 5W
Milan, Tenn., U.S.A. 69 35 55N 88 45W
Milang 45 32 2S 139 10 E
Milano 18 45 28N 9 10 E
Milâs 30 37 20N 27 50 E
Milazzo 18 38 13N 15 13 E
Milbank 70 45 17N 96 38W
Milden 65 51 29N 107 32W
Mildura 45 34 13S 142 9 E
Miles, Australia 45 26 40S 150 9 E
Miles, U.S.A. 71 31 39N 100 11W
Miles City 70 46 24N 105 50W
Milestone 65 49 59N 104 31W
Mileura 47 26 22S 117 20 E
Milford, Del., U.S.A. 68 38 52N 75 27W
Milford, Utah, U.S.A. 73 38 20N 113 0W
Milford Haven 7 51 43N 5 2W
Milford Sd. 43 44 41S 167 47 E
Milgun 47 25 6S 118 18 E
Milḥ, Baḥr al 30 32 40N 43 35 E
Milḥ, Ras al 51 31 54N 25 6 E
Miliana 50 27 20N 2 32 E
Miling 47 30 30S 116 17 E
Milk → 72 48 5N 106 15W
Milk River 64 49 10N 112 5W
Mill City 72 44 45N 122 28W
Mille 69 33 7N 83 15W
Mille Lacs, L. 70 46 10N 93 30W
Mille Lacs, L. des 62 48 45N 90 35W
Millen 69 32 50N 81 57W
Miller 70 44 35N 98 59W
Millicent 45 37 34S 140 21 E
Millinocket 63 45 45N 68 45W
Millmerran 45 27 53S 151 16 E
Mills L. 64 61 30N 118 20W
Milltown Malbay 9 52 51N 9 25W
Millville 68 39 22N 75 0W
Millwood Res. 71 33 45N 94 0W
Milne → 44 21 10S 137 33 E
Milne Inlet 61 72 30N 80 0W
Milnor 70 46 19N 97 29W
Milo 64 50 34N 112 53W
Mílos 19 36 44N 24 25 E
Milparinka 45 29 46S 141 57 E
Milton, N.Z. 43 46 7S 169 59 E
Milton, U.K. 8 57 18N 4 32W
Milton, Fla., U.S.A. 69 30 38N 87 0W
Milton, Pa., U.S.A. 68 41 0N 76 53W
Milton-Freewater 72 45 57N 118 24W
Milton Keynes 7 52 3N 0 42W
Miltou 51 10 14N 17 26 E
Milwaukee 68 43 9N 87 58W
Milwaukie 72 45 27N 122 39W
Min Jiang →, Fujian, China 39 26 0N 119 35 E
Min Jiang →, Sichuan, China 37 28 45N 104 40 E
Min Xian 39 34 25N 104 0 E
Mina 73 38 21N 118 9W
Mina Pirquitas 80 22 40S 66 30W
Mīnā Su'ud 30 28 45N 48 28 E
Mīnā'al Aḥmadī 30 29 5N 48 10 E
Mīnāb 31 27 10N 57 1 E
Minago → 65 54 33N 98 59W
Minaki 65 49 59N 94 40W
Minamata 36 32 10N 130 30 E
Minas 80 34 20S 55 10W
Minas, Sierra de las 75 15 9N 89 31W
Minas Basin 63 45 20N 64 12W
Minas de Rio Tinto 13 37 42N 6 35W
Minas Gerais □ 79 18 50S 46 0W
Minatitlán 74 17 58N 94 35W
Minbu 33 20 10N 94 52 E
Mindanao 35 8 0N 125 0 E
Mindanao Sea = Bohol Sea 35 9 0N 124 0 E
Mindanao Trench 35 8 0N 128 0 E
Minden, Germany 14 52 18N 8 45 E
Minden, U.S.A. 71 32 40N 93 20W
Mindiptana 35 5 55S 140 22 E
Mindoro 35 13 0N 121 0 E
Mindoro Strait 35 12 30N 120 30 E
Mindouli 54 4 12S 14 28 E
Minehead 7 51 12N 3 29W
Mineola 71 32 40N 95 30W
Mineral Wells 71 32 50N 98 5W
Minersville 73 38 14N 112 58W
Mingan 63 50 20N 64 0W
Mingechaurskoye Vdkhr. 23 40 56N 47 20 E
Mingela 44 19 52S 146 38 E
Mingenew 47 29 12S 115 21 E
Mingera Cr. → 44 20 38S 137 45 E
Minggang 39 32 24N 114 3 E
Mingin 33 22 50N 94 30 E
Mingxi 39 26 18N 117 12 E
Minho □ 13 41 25N 8 20W
Minho → 13 41 58N 8 40W
Minidoka 72 42 47N 113 34W
Minigwal L. 47 29 31S 123 14 E
Minilya 47 23 55S 114 0 E
Minilya → 47 23 45S 114 0 E
Minipi, L. 63 52 25N 60 45W
Mink L. 64 61 54N 117 40W
Minna 53 9 37N 6 30 E
Minneapolis, Kans., U.S.A. 70 39 11N 97 40W
Minneapolis, Minn., U.S.A. 70 44 58N 93 20W
Minnedosa 65 50 14N 99 50W
Minnesota □ 70 46 40N 94 0W
Minnie Creek 47 24 3S 115 42 E
Minnitaki L. 62 49 57N 92 10W
Miño → 13 41 52N 8 40W
Minorca = Menorca 13 40 0N 4 0 E
Minore 45 32 14S 148 27 E
Minot 70 48 10N 101 15W
Minqing 39 26 15N 118 50 E
Minsk 22 53 52N 27 30 E
Mińsk Mazowiecki 15 52 10N 21 33 E
Mintaka Pass 32 37 0N 74 58 E
Minto 60 64 55N 149 20W
Minton 65 49 10N 104 35W
Minturn 72 39 35N 106 25W
Minusinsk 25 53 50N 91 20 E
Minutang 33 28 15N 96 30 E
Minvoul 54 2 9N 12 8 E
Mir 51 14 5N 11 59 E
Miraflores Locks 74 8 59N 79 36W
Miraj 32 16 50N 74 45 E
Miram 44 21 15S 148 55 E
Miram Shah 32 33 0N 70 2 E
Miramar 57 23 50S 35 35 E
Miramichi B. 63 47 15N 65 0W
Miranda 79 20 10S 56 15W

Miranda de Ebro

Miranda de Ebro **13** 42 41N 2 57W
Mirando City **71** 27 28N 98 59W
Mirbāṭ **29** 17 0N 54 45 E
Miri **34** 4 23N 113 59 E
Miriam Vale **44** 24 20S 151 33 E
Mirim, L. **80** 32 45S 52 50W
Mirnyy **25** 62 33N 113 53 E
Mirond L. **65** 55 6N 102 47W
Mirpur Khas **32** 25 30N 69 0 E
Mirror **64** 52 30N 113 7W
Miryang **38** 35 31N 128 44 E
Mirzapur **33** 25 10N 82 34 E
Mirzapur-cum-Vindhyachal = Mirzapur **33** 25 10N 82 34 E
Miscou I. **63** 47 57N 64 31W
Mish'āb, Ra'as al **30** 28 15N 48 43 E
Mishan **38** 45 37N 131 48 E
Mishawaka **68** 41 40N 86 8W
Mishima **36** 35 10N 138 52 E
Mishmar Ayyalon **28** 31 52N 34 57 E
Mishmar Ha' Emeq **28** 32 37N 35 7 E
Mishmar Ha Negev **28** 31 22N 34 48 E
Mishmar Ha Yarden **28** 33 0N 35 36 E
Miskīn **31** 23 44N 56 52 E
Miskitos, Cayos **75** 14 26N 82 50W
Miskolc **15** 48 7N 20 50 E
Misool **35** 1 52S 130 10 E
Misrātah **51** 32 24N 15 3 E
Misriç **30** 37 55N 41 40 E
Missanabie **62** 48 20N 84 6W
Missinaibi → **62** 50 43N 81 29W
Missinaibi L. **62** 48 23N 83 40W
Mission, S. Dak., U.S.A. **70** 43 21N 100 36W
Mission, Tex., U.S.A. **71** 26 15N 98 20W
Mission City **64** 49 10N 122 15W
Missisa L. **62** 52 20N 85 7W
Mississagi → **62** 46 15N 83 9W
Mississippi → **71** 29 0N 89 15W
Mississippi, Delta of the **71** 29 15N 90 30W
Mississippi Sd. **71** 30 25N 89 0W
Missoula **72** 46 52N 114 0W
Missouri □ **70** 38 25N 92 30W
Missouri → **70** 38 50N 90 8W
Missouri Valley **70** 41 33N 95 53W
Mistake B. **65** 62 8N 93 0W
Mistassini → **63** 48 42N 72 20W
Mistassini L. **62** 51 0N 73 30W
Mistastin L. **63** 55 57N 63 20W
Mistatim **65** 52 52N 103 22W
Mistretta **18** 37 56N 14 20 E
Misty L. **65** 58 53N 101 40W
Mitchell, Australia **45** 26 29S 147 58 E
Mitchell, Ind., U.S.A. **68** 38 42N 86 25W
Mitchell, Nebr., U.S.A. **70** 41 58N 103 45W
Mitchell, Oreg., U.S.A. **72** 44 31N 120 8W
Mitchell, S. Dak., U.S.A. **70** 43 40N 98 0W
Mitchell → **44** 15 12S 141 35 E
Mitchell, Mt. **69** 35 40N 82 20W
Mitchelstown **9** 52 16N 8 18W
Mitiaro, I. **43** 19 49S 157 43W
Mito **36** 36 20N 140 30 E
Mitsinjo **57** 16 1S 45 52 E
Mitsiwa **51** 15 35N 39 25 E
Mittagong **45** 34 28S 150 29 E
Mitú **78** 1 8N 70 3W
Mitumba, Chaîne des **54** 7 0S 27 30 E
Mitwaba **54** 8 2S 27 17 E
Mitzic **54** 0 45N 11 40 E
Mixteco → **74** 18 11N 98 30W
Miyagi □ **36** 38 15N 140 45 E
Miyake-Jima **36** 34 0N 139 30 E
Miyako **36** 39 40N 141 59 E
Miyakonojō **36** 31 40N 131 5 E
Miyazaki **36** 31 56N 131 30 E
Miyazaki □ **36** 32 30N 131 30 E
Miyazu **36** 35 35N 135 10 E
Miyet, Bahr el = Dead Sea **28** 31 30N 35 30 E
Miyun **38** 40 28N 116 50 E
Mizal **30** 23 59N 45 11 E
Mizamis = Ozamis **35** 8 15N 123 50 E
Mizdah **51** 31 30N 13 0 E
Mizen Hd., Cork, Ireland **9** 51 27N 9 50W
Mizen Hd., Wicklow, Ireland **9** 52 52N 6 4W
Mizhi **38** 37 47N 110 12 E
Mizoram □ **33** 23 30N 92 40 E
Mizpe Ramon **28** 30 34N 34 49 E
Mjanji **52** 0 16N 34 0 E
Mjölby **21** 58 20N 15 10 E
Mjøsa **21** 60 48N 11 0 E
Mkomazi → **57** 30 12S 30 50 E
Mkuze **57** 27 10S 32 0 E
Mkuze → **57** 27 45S 32 30 E
Mladá Boleslav **14** 50 27N 14 53 E
Mława **15** 53 9N 20 25 E
Mmabatho **56** 25 49S 25 30 E
Mme **53** 6 18N 10 14 E
Mo i Rana **20** 66 15N 14 7 E
Moa **35** 8 0S 128 0 E
Moab **73** 38 40N 109 35W
Moabi **54** 2 24S 10 59 E
Moala **43** 18 36S 179 53 E
Moalie Park **45** 29 42S 143 3 E
Moba **54** 7 0S 29 48 E
Mobaye **54** 4 25N 21 5 E
Mobayi **54** 4 15N 21 8 E
Moberly **70** 39 25N 92 25W
Moberly → **64** 56 12N 120 55W
Mobile **69** 30 41N 88 3W
Mobile B. **69** 30 30N 88 0W
Mobridge **70** 45 31N 100 28W
Mobutu Sese Seko, L. **54** 1 30N 31 0 E
Moçambique **55** 15 3S 40 42 E
Moçâmedes = Namibe **55** 15 7S 12 11 E
Mochudi **56** 24 27S 26 7 E
Mocimboa da Praia **54** 11 25S 40 20 E
Moclips **72** 47 14N 124 10W
Mocoa **78** 1 7N 76 35W
Mocorito **74** 25 30N 107 53W
Moctezuma **74** 29 50N 109 0W
Moctezuma → **74** 21 59N 98 34W
Mocuba **55** 16 54S 36 57 E
Mocúzari, Presa **74** 27 10N 109 10W
Modane **12** 45 12N 6 40 E
Modder → **56** 29 2S 24 37 E
Modderrivier **56** 29 2S 24 38 E
Módena, Italy **18** 44 39N 10 55 E
Modena, U.S.A. **73** 37 55N 113 56W
Modesto **73** 37 43N 121 0W
Módica **18** 36 52N 14 45 E
Moe **45** 38 12S 146 19 E
Moengo **79** 5 45N 54 20W
Moffat **8** 55 20N 3 27W
Mogadishu = Muqdisho **29** 2 2N 45 25 E
Mogador = Essaouira **50** 31 32N 9 42W
Mogalakwena → **57** 22 38S 28 40 E
Mogami → **36** 38 45N 140 0 E
Mogaung **33** 25 20N 97 0 E
Mogi das Cruzes **80** 23 31S 46 11W
Mogi-Mirim **80** 22 29S 47 0W
Mogilev **22** 53 55N 30 18 E
Mogilev-Podolskiy **23** 48 20N 27 40 E
Mogocha **25** 53 40N 119 50 E
Mogoi **35** 1 55S 133 10 E
Mogok **33** 23 0N 96 40 E
Mogumber **47** 31 2S 116 3 E
Mohács **15** 45 58N 18 41 E
Mohales Hoek **56** 30 7S 27 26 E
Mohall **70** 48 46N 101 30W
Moḥammadābād **31** 37 52N 59 5 E
Mohe **38** 53 28N 122 17 E
Mohoro **54** 8 6S 39 8 E
Moidart, L. **8** 56 47N 5 40W
Mointy **24** 47 10N 73 18 E
Moisie **63** 50 12N 66 1W
Moisie → **63** 50 14N 66 5W
Moïssala **51** 8 21N 17 46 E
Mojave **73** 35 8N 118 8W
Mojave Desert **73** 35 0N 116 30W
Mojokerto **35** 7 28S 112 26 E
Mokai **43** 38 32S 175 56 E
Mokhotlong **57** 29 22S 29 2 E
Mokokchung **33** 26 15N 94 30 E
Mol **11** 51 11N 5 5 E
Molchanovo **24** 57 40N 83 50 E
Mold **6** 53 10N 3 10W
Moldavian S.S.R. □ **23** 47 0N 28 0 E
Molde **20** 62 45N 7 9 E
Molepolole **56** 24 28S 25 28 E
Molfetta **18** 41 12N 16 35 E
Moline **70** 41 30N 90 30W
Moliro **54** 8 12S 30 30 E
Molise □ **18** 41 45N 14 30 E
Mollendo **78** 17 0S 72 0W
Mollerin, L. **47** 30 30S 117 35 E
Mölndal **21** 57 40N 12 3 E
Molokai **66** 21 8N 157 0W
Molong **45** 33 5S 148 54 E
Molopo → **56** 27 30S 20 13 E
Molotov = Perm **22** 58 0N 57 10 E
Moloundou **54** 2 8N 15 15 E
Molson L. **65** 54 22N 96 40W
Molteno **56** 31 22S 26 22 E
Molu **35** 6 45S 131 40 E
Molucca Sea **35** 4 0S 124 0 E
Moluccas = Maluku **35** 1 0S 127 0 E
Moma **55** 16 47S 39 4 E
Mombasa **54** 4 2S 39 43 E
Mombetsu **36** 42 27N 142 4 E
Mompós **78** 9 14N 74 26W
Møn **21** 54 57N 12 15 E
Mon → **33** 20 25N 94 30 E
Mona, Canal de la **75** 18 30N 67 45W
Mona, I. **75** 18 5N 67 54W
Mona, Pta. **75** 9 37N 82 36W
Monach Is. **8** 57 32N 7 40W
Monaco ■ **12** 43 46N 7 23 E
Monadhliath Mts. **8** 57 10N 4 4W
Monaghan **9** 54 15N 6 58W
Monaghan □ **9** 54 10N 7 0W
Monahans **71** 31 35N 102 50W
Monarch Mt. **64** 51 55N 125 57W
Monastir = Bitola **19** 41 5N 21 10 E
Monastir **51** 35 50N 10 49 E
Monbetsu **36** 44 21N 143 22 E
Moncayo, Sierra del **13** 41 48N 1 50W
Mönchengladbach **14** 51 12N 6 23 E
Monchique **13** 37 19N 8 38W
Monchique, Sa. de **13** 37 18N 8 39W
Monclova **74** 26 50N 101 30W
Moncton **63** 46 7N 64 51W
Mondego → **13** 40 9N 8 52W
Mondeodo **35** 3 34S 122 9 E
Mondoví, Italy **18** 44 23N 7 49 E
Mondovi, U.S.A. **70** 44 37N 91 40W
Mondrain I. **47** 34 9S 122 14 E
Monessen **68** 40 9N 79 50W
Monett **71** 36 55N 93 56W
Monforte **13** 39 6N 7 25W
Mong Hsu **33** 21 54N 98 30 E
Mong Kung **33** 21 35N 97 35 E
Mong Nai **33** 20 32N 97 46 E
Mong Pawk **33** 22 4N 99 16 E
Mong Ton **33** 20 17N 98 45 E
Mong Wa **33** 21 26N 100 27 E
Mong Yai **33** 22 21N 98 3 E
Mongalla **51** 5 8N 31 42 E
Mongers, L. **47** 29 25S 117 5 E
Monghyr = Munger **33** 25 23N 86 30 E
Mongo **51** 12 14N 18 43 E
Mongolia ■ **37** 47 0N 103 0 E
Mongororo **51** 12 3N 22 26 E
Mongu **55** 15 16S 23 12 E
Môngua **56** 16 43S 15 20 E
Monkira **44** 24 46S 140 30 E
Monkoto **54** 1 38S 20 35 E
Monmouth, U.K. **7** 51 48N 2 43W
Monmouth, U.S.A. **70** 40 50N 90 40W
Mono, L. **73** 38 0N 119 9W
Monópoli **18** 40 57N 17 18 E
Monqoumba **54** 3 33N 18 40 E
Monroe, Ga., U.S.A. **69** 33 47N 83 43W
Monroe, La., U.S.A. **71** 32 32N 92 4W
Monroe, Mich., U.S.A. **68** 41 55N 83 26W
Monroe, N.C., U.S.A. **69** 35 2N 80 37W
Monroe, Utah, U.S.A. **73** 38 45N 112 5W
Monroe, Wis., U.S.A. **70** 42 38N 89 40W
Monroe City **70** 39 40N 91 40W
Monroeville **69** 31 33N 87 15W
Monrovia, Liberia **50** 6 18N 10 47W
Monrovia, U.S.A. **73** 34 7N 118 1W
Mons **11** 50 27N 3 58 E
Monse **35** 4 0S 123 10 E
Mont-de-Marsan **12** 43 54N 0 31W
Mont-Joli **63** 48 37N 68 10W
Mont-Laurier **62** 46 35N 75 30W
Mont-St.-Michel, Le **12** 48 40N 1 30W
Mont Tremblant Prov. Park **62** 46 30N 74 30W
Montagu **56** 33 45S 20 8 E
Montague, Canada **63** 46 10N 62 39W
Montague, U.S.A. **72** 41 47N 122 30W
Montague, I. **74** 31 40N 114 56W
Montague I. **60** 60 0N 147 0W
Montague Ra. **47** 27 15S 119 30 E
Montague Sd. **46** 14 28S 125 20 E
Montalbán **13** 40 50N 0 45W
Montaña **78** 6 0S 73 0W
Montana □ **66** 47 0N 110 0W
Montargis **12** 47 59N 2 43 E
Montauban **12** 44 0N 1 21 E
Montauk **68** 41 3N 71 57W
Montbéliard **12** 47 31N 6 48 E
Monte Alegre **79** 2 0S 54 0W
Monte Azul **79** 15 9S 42 53W
Monte Bello Is. **46** 20 30S 115 45 E
Monte-Carlo **12** 43 46N 7 23 E
Monte Caseros **80** 30 10S 57 50W
Monte Comán **80** 34 40S 67 53W
Monte Sant' Ángelo **18** 41 42N 15 59 E
Monte Santu, C. di **18** 40 5N 9 42 E
Monte Vista **73** 37 40N 106 8W
Montebello **62** 45 40N 74 55W
Montecristi **78** 1 0S 80 40W
Montego Bay **75** 18 30N 78 0W
Montejinnie **46** 16 40S 131 38 E
Montélimar **12** 44 33N 4 45 E
Montello **70** 43 49N 89 21W
Montemorelos **74** 25 11N 99 42W
Montenegro = Crna Gora □ **19** 42 40N 19 20 E
Montepuez **55** 13 8S 38 59 E
Monterey **73** 36 35N 121 57W
Montería **78** 8 46N 75 53W
Monterrey **74** 25 40N 100 30W
Montes Claros **79** 16 30S 43 50W
Montesano **72** 46 58N 123 39W
Montevideo, Uruguay **80** 34 50S 56 11W
Montevideo, U.S.A. **70** 44 55N 95 40W
Montezuma **70** 41 32N 92 35W
Montgomery = Sahiwal **32** 30 45N 73 8 E
Montgomery, U.K. **7** 52 34N 3 9W
Montgomery, Ala., U.S.A. **69** 32 20N 86 20W
Montgomery, W. Va., U.S.A. **68** 38 9N 81 21W
Monticello, Ark., U.S.A. **71** 33 40N 91 48W
Monticello, Fla., U.S.A. **69** 30 35N 83 50W
Monticello, Ind., U.S.A. **68** 40 40N 86 45W
Monticello, Iowa, U.S.A. **70** 42 18N 91 12W
Monticello, Ky., U.S.A. **69** 36 52N 84 50W
Monticello, Minn., U.S.A. **70** 45 17N 93 52W
Monticello, Miss., U.S.A. **71** 31 35N 90 8W
Monticello, Utah, U.S.A. **73** 37 55N 109 27W
Montijo **13** 38 52N 6 39W
Montilla **13** 37 36N 4 40W
Montluçon **12** 46 22N 2 36 E
Montmagny **63** 46 58N 70 34W
Montmartre **65** 50 14N 103 27W
Montmorency **63** 46 53N 71 11W
Monto **44** 24 52S 151 6 E
Montoro **13** 38 1N 4 27W
Montpelier, Idaho, U.S.A. **72** 42 15N 111 20W
Montpelier, Ohio, U.S.A. **68** 41 34N 84 40W
Montpelier, Vt., U.S.A. **68** 44 15N 72 38W
Montpellier **12** 43 37N 3 52 E
Montréal **62** 45 31N 73 34W
Montreal L. **65** 54 20N 105 45W
Montreal Lake **65** 54 3N 105 46W
Montreuil **12** 50 27N 1 45 E
Montreux **14** 46 26N 6 55 E
Montrose, U.K. **8** 56 43N 2 28W
Montrose, U.S.A. **73** 38 30N 107 52W
Monts, Pte. des **63** 49 20N 67 12W
Montserrat **75** 16 40N 62 10W
Monveda **54** 2 52N 21 30 E
Monywa **33** 22 7N 95 11 E
Monza **18** 45 35N 9 15 E
Monze **55** 16 17S 27 29 E
Monze, C. **32** 24 47N 66 37 E
Monzón **13** 41 52N 0 10 E
Mooi River **57** 29 13S 29 50 E
Moolawatana **45** 29 55S 139 45 E
Mooliabeenee **47** 31 20S 116 2 E
Mooloogool **47** 26 2S 119 5 E
Moomin, Cr. → **45** 29 44S 149 20 E
Moonah → **44** 22 3S 138 33 E
Moonbeam **62** 49 20N 82 10W
Moonie **45** 27 46S 150 20 E
Moonie → **45** 29 19S 148 43 E
Moonta **45** 34 6S 137 32 E
Moora **47** 30 37S 115 58 E
Mooraberree **44** 25 13S 140 54 E
Moorarie **47** 25 56S 117 35 E
Moorcroft **70** 44 17N 104 58W
Moore → **47** 31 22S 115 30 E
Moore, L. **47** 29 50S 117 35 E
Moore Reefs **44** 16 0S 149 5 E
Moorefield **68** 39 5N 78 59W
Mooresville **69** 35 36N 80 45W
Moorfoot Hills **8** 55 44N 3 8W
Moorhead **70** 46 51N 96 44W
Mooroopna **45** 36 25S 145 22 E
Moorreesburg **56** 33 6S 18 38 E
Moose → **62** 51 20N 80 25W
Moose Factory **62** 51 16N 80 32W
Moose I. **65** 51 42N 97 10W
Moose Jaw **65** 50 24N 105 30W
Moose Jaw → **65** 50 34N 105 18W
Moose Lake, Canada **65** 53 43N 100 20W
Moose Lake, U.S.A. **70** 46 27N 92 48W
Moose Mountain Cr. → **65** 49 13N 102 12W
Moose Mountain Prov. Park **65** 49 48N 102 25W
Moose River **62** 50 48N 81 17W
Moosehead L. **63** 45 34N 69 40W
Moosomin **65** 50 9N 101 40W
Moosonee **62** 51 17N 80 39W
Mopeia Velha **55** 17 30S 35 40 E
Mopipi **56** 21 6S 24 55 E
Mopti **50** 14 30N 4 0W
Moquegua **78** 17 15S 70 46W
Mora, Sweden **21** 61 2N 14 38 E
Mora, Minn., U.S.A. **70** 45 52N 93 19W
Mora, N. Mex., U.S.A. **73** 35 58N 105 21W
Moradabad **32** 28 50N 78 50 E
Morafenobe **57** 17 50S 44 53 E
Moramanga **57** 18 56S 48 12 E
Moran, Kans., U.S.A. **71** 37 53N 94 35W
Moran, Wyo., U.S.A. **72** 43 53N 110 37W
Moranbah **44** 22 1S 148 6 E
Morant Cays **75** 17 22N 76 0W
Morant Pt. **75** 17 55N 76 12W
Morar L. **8** 56 57N 5 40W
Moratuwa **32** 6 45N 79 55 E
Morava → **14** 48 10N 16 59 E
Moravia **70** 40 50N 92 50W
Moravian Hts. = Ceskomoravská Vrchovina **14** 49 30N 15 40 E
Morawa **47** 29 13S 116 0 E
Morawhanna **78** 8 30N 59 40W
Moray Firth **8** 57 50N 3 30W
Morbihan □ **12** 47 55N 2 50W
Morden **65** 49 15N 98 10W
Mordovian A.S.S.R. □ **22** 54 20N 44 30 E
Møre og Romsdal fylke □ **20** 62 30N 8 0 E
Morea, Australia **45** 36 45S 141 18 E
Morea, Greece **4** 37 45N 22 10 E
Moreau → **70** 45 15N 100 43W
Morecambe **6** 54 5N 2 52W
Morecambe B. **6** 54 7N 3 0W
Moree **45** 29 28S 149 54 E
Morehead **68** 38 12N 83 22W
Morehead City **69** 34 46N 76 44W
Morelia **74** 19 40N 101 11W
Morella, Australia **44** 23 0S 143 52 E
Morella, Spain **13** 40 35N 0 5W
Morelos □ **74** 18 40N 99 10W
Morena, Sierra **13** 38 20N 4 0W
Morenci **73** 33 7N 109 20W
Moresby I. **64** 52 30N 131 40W
Moreton **44** 12 22S 142 30 E
Moreton I. **45** 27 10S 153 25 E
Morgan, Australia **45** 34 0S 139 35 E
Morgan, U.S.A. **72** 41 3N 111 44W
Morgan City **71** 29 40N 91 15W
Morganfield **68** 37 40N 87 55W
Morganton **69** 35 46N 81 48W
Morgantown **68** 39 39N 79 58W
Morgenzon **57** 26 45S 29 36 E
Morice L. **64** 53 50N 127 40W
Moriki **53** 12 52N 6 30 E
Morinville **64** 53 49N 113 41W
Morioka **36** 39 45N 141 8 E
Morlaix **12** 48 36N 3 52W
Mornington, Vic., Australia **45** 38 15S 145 5 E
Mornington, W. Austral., Australia **46** 17 31S 126 6 E
Mornington, I. **80** 49 50S 75 30W
Mornington I. **44** 16 30S 139 30 E
Moro G. **35** 6 30N 123 0 E
Morocco ■ **50** 32 0N 5 50W
Morococha **78** 11 40S 76 5W
Morogoro **54** 6 50S 37 40 E
Moroleón **74** 20 8N 101 32W
Morombe **57** 21 45S 43 22 E
Morón **75** 22 8N 78 39W
Mörön → **37** 47 14N 110 37 E
Morón de la Frontera **13** 37 6N 5 28W
Morondava **57** 20 17S 44 17 E
Morotai **35** 2 10N 128 30 E
Moroto **54** 2 28N 34 42 E
Morpeth **6** 55 11N 1 41W
Morphou **30** 35 12N 32 59 E
Morrilton **71** 35 10N 92 45W
Morrinhos **79** 17 45S 49 10W
Morrinsville **43** 37 40S 175 32 E
Morris, Canada **65** 49 25N 97 22W
Morris, Ill., U.S.A. **68** 41 20N 88 20W
Morris, Minn., U.S.A. **70** 45 33N 95 56W
Morris, Mt. **47** 26 9S 131 4 E
Morrisburg **62** 44 55N 75 7W
Morrison **70** 41 47N 90 0W
Morristown, Ariz., U.S.A. **73** 33 54N 112 35W
Morristown, S. Dak., U.S.A. **70** 45 57N 101 44W
Morristown, Tenn., U.S.A. **69** 36 18N 83 20W
Morro Bay **73** 35 27N 120 54W
Morrosquillo, G. de **75** 9 35N 75 40W
Morrumbene **57** 23 31S 35 16 E
Morshansk **22** 53 28N 41 50 E
Morteros **80** 30 50S 62 0W
Mortes, R. das → **79** 11 45S 50 44W
Mortlake **45** 38 5S 142 50 E
Morton, Tex., U.S.A. **71** 33 39N 102 49W

Nairn

Morton, Wash., U.S.A. 72 46 33N 122 17W
Morundah 45 34 57S 146 19 E
Moruya 45 35 58S 150 3 E
Morvan 12 47 5N 4 0 E
Morven 45 26 22S 147 5 E
Morvern 8 56 38N 5 44W
Morwell 45 38 10S 146 22 E
Morzhovets, Ostrov 22 66 44N 42 35 E
Moscos Is. 34 14 0N 97 30 E
Moscow = Moskva 22 55 45N 37 35 E
Moscow 72 46 45N 116 59W
Mosel → 11 50 22N 7 36 E
Moselle = Mosel → 11 50 22N 7 36 E
Moselle □ 12 48 59N 6 33 E
Moses Lake 72 47 9N 119 17W
Mosgiel 43 45 53S 170 21 E
Moshi 54 3 22S 37 18 E
Moshupa 56 24 46S 25 29 E
Mosjøen 20 65 51N 13 12 E
Moskenesøya 20 67 58N 13 0 E
Moskenstraumen 20 67 47N 12 45 E
Moskva 22 55 45N 37 35 E
Moskva → 22 55 5N 38 51 E
Mosomane 56 24 2S 26 19 E
Mosquera 78 2 35N 78 24W
Mosquero 71 35 48N 103 57W
Mosquitos, G. de los 75 9 15N 81 10W
Moss 21 59 27N 10 40 E
Moss Vale 45 34 32S 150 25 E
Mossaka 54 1 15S 16 45 E
Mossbank 65 49 56N 105 56W
Mossburn 43 45 41S 168 15 E
Mosselbaai 56 34 11S 22 8 E
Mossendjo 54 2 55S 12 42 E
Mossgiel 45 33 15S 144 5 E
Mossman 44 16 21S 145 15 E
Mossoró 79 5 10S 37 15W
Mossuril 55 14 58S 40 42 E
Mossy → 65 54 5N 102 58W
Most 14 50 31N 13 38 E
Mosta 18 35 54N 14 24 E
Mostaganem 50 35 54N 0 5 E
Mostar 19 43 22N 17 50 E
Mostardas 80 31 2S 50 51W
Mosul = Al Mawşil 30 36 15N 43 5 E
Motagua → 75 15 44N 88 14W
Motala 21 58 32N 15 1 E
Motherwell 8 55 48N 4 0W
Motihari 33 26 30N 84 55 E
Motozintla de Mendoza 74 15 21N 92 14W
Mott 70 46 25N 102 29W
Motueka 43 41 7S 173 1 E
Motul 74 21 0N 89 20W
Mouanda 54 1 28S 13 7 E
Mouchalagane → 63 50 56N 68 41W
Moúdhros 19 39 50N 25 18 E
Moudjeria 50 17 50N 12 28W
Mouila 54 1 50S 11 0 E
Moulamein 45 35 3S 144 1 E
Moule 75 16 20N 61 22W
Moulins 12 46 35N 3 19 E
Moulmein 33 16 30N 97 40 E
Moulton 71 29 35N 97 8W
Moultrie 69 31 11N 83 47W
Moultrie, L. 69 33 25N 80 10W
Mound City, Mo., U.S.A. 70 40 2N 95 25W
Mound City, S. Dak., U.S.A. 70 45 46N 100 3W
Moundou 51 8 40N 16 10 E
Moundsville 68 39 53N 80 43W
Mount Airy 69 36 31N 80 37W
Mount Amherst 46 18 24S 126 58 E
Mount Angel 72 45 4N 122 46W
Mount Augustus 47 24 20S 116 56 E
Mount Barker, S. Austral., Australia 45 35 5S 138 52 E
Mount Barker, W. Austral., Australia 47 34 38S 117 40 E
Mount Carmel 68 38 20N 87 48W
Mount Clemens 62 42 35N 82 50W
Mount Coolon 44 21 25S 147 25 E
Mount Darwin 55 16 47S 31 38 E
Mount Desert I. 63 44 15N 68 25W
Mount Dora 69 28 49N 81 32W
Mount Douglas 44 21 35S 146 50 E
Mount Edgecumbe 64 57 8N 135 22W
Mount Elizabeth 46 16 0S 125 50 E
Mount Fletcher 57 30 40S 28 30 E
Mount Forest 62 43 59N 80 43W
Mount Gambier 45 37 50S 140 46 E
Mount Garnet 44 17 37S 145 6 E
Mount Hope, N.S.W., Australia 45 32 51S 145 51 E
Mount Hope, S. Austral., Australia 45 34 7S 135 23 E
Mount Hope, U.S.A. 68 37 52N 81 9W
Mount Horeb 70 43 0N 89 42W
Mount Howitt 45 26 31S 142 16 E
Mount Isa 44 20 42S 139 26 E
Mount Keith 47 27 15S 120 30 E
Mount Larcom 44 23 48S 150 59 E
Mount Lofty Ra. 45 34 35S 139 5 E
Mount McKinley Nat. Park 60 64 0N 150 0W
Mount Magnet 47 28 2S 117 47 E
Mount Margaret 45 26 54S 143 21 E
Mount Maunganui 43 37 40S 176 14 E
Mount Molloy 44 16 42S 145 20 E
Mount Monger 47 31 0S 122 0 E
Mount Morgan 44 23 40S 150 25 E
Mount Morris 68 42 43N 77 50W
Mount Mulligan 44 16 45S 144 47 E
Mount Narryer 47 26 30S 115 55 E
Mount Oxide Mine 44 19 30S 139 29 E
Mount Pearl 63 47 31N 52 47W
Mount Perry 45 25 13S 151 42 E
Mount Phillips 47 24 25S 116 15 E
Mount Pleasant, Iowa, U.S.A. 70 40 58N 91 35W
Mount Pleasant, Mich., U.S.A. 68 43 35N 84 47W
Mount Pleasant, S.C., U.S.A. 69 32 45N 79 48W
Mount Pleasant, Tenn., U.S.A. 69 35 31N 87 11W
Mount Pleasant, Tex., U.S.A. 71 33 5N 95 0W
Mount Pleasant, Utah, U.S.A. 72 39 40N 111 29W
Mount Rainier Nat. Park. 72 46 50N 121 43W
Mount Revelstoke Nat. Park 64 51 5N 118 30W
Mount Robson Prov. Park 64 53 0N 119 0W
Mount Sandiman 47 24 25S 115 30 E
Mount Shasta 72 41 20N 122 18W
Mount Sterling, Ill., U.S.A. 70 39 59N 90 40W
Mount Sterling, Ky., U.S.A. 68 38 3N 83 57W
Mount Surprise 44 18 10S 144 17 E
Mount Vernon, Australia 47 24 9S 118 2 E
Mount Vernon, Ind., U.S.A. 70 38 17N 88 57W
Mount Vernon, N.Y., U.S.A. 68 40 57N 73 49W
Mount Vernon, Ohio, U.S.A. 68 40 20N 82 30W
Mount Vernon, Wash., U.S.A. 72 48 25N 122 20W
Mountain City, Nev., U.S.A. 72 41 54N 116 0W
Mountain City, Tenn., U.S.A. 69 36 30N 81 50W
Mountain Grove 71 37 5N 92 20W
Mountain Home, Ark., U.S.A. 71 36 20N 92 25W
Mountain Home, Idaho, U.S.A. 72 43 11N 115 45W
Mountain Iron 70 47 30N 92 37W
Mountain Park 64 52 50N 117 15W
Mountain View, Ark., U.S.A. 71 35 52N 92 10W
Mountain View, Calif., U.S.A. 73 37 26N 122 5W
Mountainair 73 34 35N 106 15W
Mountmellick 9 53 7N 7 20W
Moura, Australia 44 24 35S 149 58 E
Moura, Brazil 78 1 32S 61 38W
Mourdi, Dépression du 51 18 10N 23 0 E
Mourdiah 50 14 35N 7 25W
Moure, La 70 46 27N 98 17W
Mourilyan 44 17 35S 146 3 E
Mourne → 9 54 45N 7 39W
Mourne Mts. 9 54 10N 6 0W
Mouscron 11 50 45N 3 12 E
Moussoro 51 13 41N 16 35 E
Moutong 35 0 28N 121 13 E
Moville 9 55 11N 7 3W
Moy → 9 54 5N 8 50W
Moyale, Ethiopia 29 3 34N 39 4 E
Moyale, Kenya 54 3 30N 39 0 E
Moyamba 50 8 4N 12 30W
Moyen Atlas 50 33 0N 5 0W
Moyle □ 9 55 10N 6 15W
Moyo 34 8 10S 117 40 E
Moyobamba 78 6 0S 77 0W
Moyyero → 25 68 44N 103 42 E
Mozambique = Moçambique 55 15 3S 40 42 E
Mozambique ■ 55 19 0S 35 0 E
Mozambique Chan. 57 17 30S 42 30 E
Mozdok 23 43 45N 44 48 E
Mozyr 22 52 0N 29 15 E
Mpanda 54 6 23S 31 1 E
Mpika 55 11 51S 31 25 E
Mporokoso 52 9 25S 30 5 E
Mpumalanga 57 29 50S 30 33 E
Mpwapwa 54 6 23S 36 30 E
Msaken 51 35 49N 10 33 E
Msoro 55 13 35S 31 50 E
Mtubatuba 57 28 30S 32 8 E
Mtwara-Mikindani 52 10 20S 40 20 E
Mu Us Shamo 38 39 0N 109 0 E
Muaná 79 1 25S 49 15W
Muar 34 2 3N 102 34 E
Muarabungo 34 1 28S 102 52 E
Muaraenim 34 3 40S 103 50 E
Muarajuloi 34 0 12S 114 3 E
Muarakaman 34 0 2S 116 45 E
Muaratebo 34 1 30S 102 26 E
Muaratembesi 34 1 42S 103 8 E
Muaratewe 34 0 58S 114 52 E
Mubende 54 0 33N 31 22 E
Mubi 53 10 18N 13 16 E
Muck 8 56 50N 6 15W
Muckadilla 45 26 35S 148 23 E
Muconda 54 10 31S 21 15 E
Mucuri 79 18 0S 39 36W
Mucusso 56 18 1S 21 25 E
Mudanjiang 38 44 38N 129 30 E
Muddy → 73 38 0N 110 22W
Mudgee 45 32 32S 149 31 E
Mudjatik → 65 56 1N 107 36W
Muêda 52 11 36S 39 28 E
Mueller Ra. 46 18 18S 126 46 E
Muerto, Mar 74 16 10N 94 10W
Mufulira 55 12 32S 28 15 E
Muğla 30 37 15N 28 22 E
Mugu 33 29 45N 82 30 E
Muhammad Qol 51 20 53N 37 9 E
Muharraqa = Sa'ad 28 31 28N 34 33 E
Muikamachi 36 37 15N 138 50 E
Muine Bheag 9 52 42N 6 57W
Muir, L. 47 34 30S 116 40 E
Mukah 34 2 55N 112 5 E
Mukden = Shenyang 38 41 48N 123 27 E
Mukhtuya = Lensk 25 60 48N 114 55 E
Mukinbudin 47 30 55S 118 5 E
Mukomuko 34 2 30S 101 10 E
Muktsar 32 30 30N 74 30 E
Mukur 32 32 50N 67 42 E
Mukutawa → 65 53 10N 97 24W
Mulchén 80 37 45S 72 20W
Mulde → 14 51 50N 12 15 E
Mule Creek 70 43 19N 104 8W
Muleba 52 1 50S 31 37 E
Muleshoe 71 34 17N 102 42W
Mulgathing 45 30 15S 134 8 E
Mulgrave 63 45 38N 61 31W
Mulhacén 13 37 4N 3 20W
Mülheim 14 51 26N 6 53 E
Mulhouse 14 47 40N 7 20 E
Muling He → 38 45 53N 133 30 E
Mull 8 56 27N 6 0W
Mullaittvu 32 9 15N 80 49 E
Mullen 70 42 5N 101 0W
Mullengudgery 45 31 43S 147 23 E
Mullens 68 37 34N 81 22W
Muller, Pegunungan 34 0 30N 113 30 E
Mullet Pen. 9 54 10N 10 2W
Mullewa 47 28 29S 115 30 E
Mulligan → 45 26 40S 139 0 E
Mullin 71 31 33N 98 38W
Mullingar 9 53 31N 7 20W
Mullins 69 34 12N 79 15W
Mullumbimby 45 28 30S 153 30 E
Multan 32 30 15N 71 36 E
Mulvane 71 37 30N 97 15W
Mumbwa 55 15 0S 27 0 E
Muna 35 5 0S 122 30 E
München 14 48 8N 11 33 E
Munchen-Gladbach = Mönchengladbach 14 51 12N 6 23 E
Muncho Lake 64 59 0N 125 50W
Muncie 68 40 10N 85 20W
Mundala 35 4 30S 141 0 E
Mundare 64 53 35N 112 20W
Munday 71 33 26N 99 39W
Münden 14 51 25N 9 42 E
Mundiwindi 46 23 47S 120 9 E
Mundo Novo 79 11 50S 40 29W
Mundrabilla 47 31 52S 127 51 E
Mungallala 45 26 28S 147 34 E
Mungallala Cr. → 45 28 53S 147 5 E
Mungana 44 17 8S 144 27 E
Mungbere 54 2 36N 28 28 E
Munger 33 25 23N 86 30 E
Mungindi 45 28 58S 149 1 E
Munhango 55 12 10S 18 38 E
Munich = München 14 48 8N 11 33 E
Munising 68 46 25N 86 39W
Munku-Sardyk 25 51 45N 100 20 E
Muñoz Gamero, Pen. 80 52 30S 73 5 E
Munroe L. 65 59 13N 98 35W
Münster 14 51 58N 7 37 E
Munster □ 9 52 20N 8 40W
Muntadgin 47 31 45S 118 33 E
Muntok 34 2 5S 105 10 E
Munyak 24 43 30N 59 15 E
Muonio 20 67 57N 23 40 E
Mupa 55 16 5S 15 50 E
Muping 38 37 22N 121 36 E
Muqdisho 29 2 2N 45 25 E
Mur → 14 46 35N 16 3 E
Murallón, Cuerro 80 49 48S 73 30W
Murang'a 54 0 45S 37 9 E
Murashi 22 59 30N 49 0 E
Murchison → 47 27 45S 114 0 E
Murchison Falls = Kabarega Falls 54 2 15N 31 30 E
Murchison House 47 27 39S 114 14 E
Murchison Ra. 44 20 0S 134 10 E
Murcia 13 38 20N 1 10W
Murcia □ 13 37 50N 1 30W
Murdo 70 43 56N 100 43W
Murdoch Pt. 44 14 37S 144 55 E
Mureş → 15 46 15N 20 13 E
Mureşul = Mureş → 15 46 15N 20 13 E
Murfreesboro 69 35 50N 86 21W
Murgab 24 38 10N 74 2 E
Murgon 45 26 15S 151 54 E
Murgoo 47 27 24S 116 28 E
Muria 35 6 36S 110 53 E
Müritz See 14 53 25N 12 40 E
Murmansk 22 68 57N 33 10 E
Murom 22 55 35N 42 3 E
Muroran 36 42 25N 141 0 E
Muroto-Misaki 36 33 15N 134 10 E
Murphy 72 43 11N 116 33W
Murphysboro 71 37 50N 89 20W
Murray, Ky., U.S.A. 69 36 40N 88 20W
Murray, Utah, U.S.A. 72 40 41N 111 58W
Murray →, Australia 45 35 20S 139 22 E
Murray →, Canada 64 56 11N 120 45W
Murray, L. 69 34 8N 81 30W
Murray Bridge 45 35 6S 139 14 E
Murray Downs 44 21 4S 134 40 E
Murray Harbour 63 46 0N 62 28W
Murray Seascarp 41 30 0N 135 0W
Murraysburg 56 31 58S 23 47 E
Murree 32 33 56N 73 28 E
Murrin Murrin 47 28 58S 121 33 E
Murrumbidgee → 45 34 43S 143 12 E
Murrumburrah 45 34 32S 148 22 E
Murrurundi 45 31 42S 150 51 E
Mursala 34 1 41N 98 28 E
Murtle L. 64 52 8N 119 38W
Murtoa 45 36 35S 142 28 E
Murwara 33 23 46N 80 28 E
Murwillumbah 45 28 18S 153 27 E
Mürzzuschlag 14 47 36N 15 41 E
Muş 30 38 45N 41 30 E
Mûsa, G. 30 28 33N 33 59 E
Musa Khel 32 30 59N 69 52 E
Mūsá Qal'eh 31 32 20N 64 50 E
Musaffargarh 32 30 10N 71 10 E
Musala 19 42 13N 23 37 E
Musan 38 42 12N 129 12 E
Musay'īd 31 25 0N 51 33 E
Muscat = Masqat 31 23 37N 58 36 E
Muscat & Oman = Oman ■ 29 23 0N 58 0 E
Muscatine 70 41 25N 91 5W
Musgrave Ras. 47 26 0S 132 0 E
Mushie 54 2 56S 16 55 E
Mushin 53 6 32N 3 21 E
Musi → 34 2 20S 104 56 E
Muskeg → 64 60 20N 123 20W
Muskegon 68 43 15N 86 17W
Muskegon → 68 43 25N 86 0W
Muskegon Hts. 68 43 12N 86 17W
Muskogee 71 35 50N 95 25W
Muskwa → 64 58 47N 122 48W
Musmar 51 18 13N 35 40 E
Musoma 54 1 30S 33 48 E
Musquaro, L. 63 50 38N 61 5W
Musquodoboit Harbour 63 44 50N 63 9W
Musselburgh 8 55 57N 3 3W
Musselshell → 72 47 21N 107 58W
Mussoorie 32 30 27N 78 6 E
Mussuco 56 17 2S 19 3 E
Mustang 33 29 10N 83 55 E
Musters, L. 80 45 20S 69 25W
Muswellbrook 45 32 16S 150 56 E
Mût, Egypt 51 25 28N 28 58 E
Mut, Turkey 30 36 40N 33 28 E
Mutanda 57 21 0S 33 34 E
Mutaray 25 60 56N 101 0 E
Mutare 55 18 58S 32 38 E
Muting 35 7 23S 140 20 E
Mutsu-Wan 36 41 5N 140 55 E
Muttaburra 44 22 38S 144 29 E
Muxima 54 9 33S 13 58 E
Muya 25 56 27N 115 50 E
Muzaffarabad 32 34 25N 73 30 E
Muzaffarnagar 32 29 26N 77 40 E
Muzaffarpur 33 26 7N 85 23 E
Muzhi 24 65 25N 64 40 E
Muzon C. 64 54 40N 132 40W
Muztag 37 36 20N 87 28 E
Mvuma 55 19 16S 30 30 E
Mwanza, Tanzania 54 2 30S 32 58 E
Mwanza, Zaïre 54 7 55S 26 43 E
Mweelrea 9 53 37N 9 48W
Mweka 54 4 50S 21 34 E
Mwenezi 55 21 15S 30 48 E
Mwenga 54 3 1S 28 28 E
Mweru, L. 54 9 0S 28 40 E
Mwinilunga 55 11 43S 24 25 E
Mwirasandu 52 0 56S 30 22 E
My Tho 34 10 29N 106 23 E
Myanaung 33 18 18N 95 22 E
Myaungmya 33 16 30N 94 40 E
Mycenae = Mikínai 19 37 43N 22 46 E
Myeik Kyunzu 34 11 30N 97 30 E
Myingyan 33 21 30N 95 20 E
Myitkyina 33 25 24N 97 26 E
Mymensingh 33 24 45N 90 24 E
Mynydd Du 7 51 45N 3 45W
Mýrdalsjökull 20 63 40N 19 6W
Myrtle Beach 69 33 43N 78 50W
Myrtle Creek 72 43 0N 123 9W
Myrtle Point 72 43 0N 124 4W
Mysore 32 12 17N 76 41 E
Mysore □ = Karnataka □ 32 13 15N 77 0 E
Myton 72 40 10N 110 2W
Mývatn 20 65 36N 17 0W
Mzimkulu → 57 30 44S 30 28 E
Mzimvubu → 57 31 38S 29 33 E

N

Naab → 14 49 1N 12 2 E
Na'an 28 31 53N 34 52 E
Naantali 21 60 29N 22 2 E
Naas 9 53 12N 6 40W
Nababiep 56 29 36S 17 46 E
Nabawa 47 28 30S 114 48 E
Nabberu, L. 47 25 50S 120 30 E
Nabeul 51 36 30N 10 44 E
Nabire 35 3 15S 135 26 E
Nabisipi → 63 50 14N 62 13W
Nablus = Nābulus 28 32 14N 35 15 E
Naboomspruit 57 24 32S 28 40 E
Nābulus 28 32 14N 35 15 E
Naches 72 46 48N 120 42W
Nachingwea 54 10 23S 38 49 E
Nackara 45 32 48S 139 12 E
Naco 73 31 24N 109 58W
Nacogdoches 71 31 33N 94 39W
Nacozari 74 30 24N 109 39W
Nadiad 32 22 41N 72 56 E
Nadūshan 31 32 2N 53 35 E
Nadvoitsy 22 63 52N 34 14 E
Nadym 24 65 35N 72 42 E
Nadym → 24 66 12N 72 0 E
Nafada 53 11 8N 11 20 E
Naftshahr 30 34 0N 45 30 E
Nafūd ad Dahy 30 22 0N 45 0 E
Naga 35 13 38N 123 15 E
Naga Hills 33 26 0N 94 30 E
Nagagami → 62 49 40N 84 40W
Nagaland □ 33 26 0N 94 30 E
Nagano 36 36 40N 138 10 E
Nagano □ 36 36 15N 138 0 E
Nagaoka 36 37 27N 138 51 E
Nagappattinam 32 10 46N 79 51 E
Nagar Parkar 32 24 30N 70 35 E
Nagasaki 36 32 47N 129 50 E
Nagasaki □ 36 32 50N 129 40 E
Nagaur 32 27 15N 73 45 E
Nagercoil 32 8 12N 77 26 E
Nagīneh 31 34 20N 57 15 E
Nagoorin 44 24 17S 151 15 E
Nagornyy 25 55 58N 124 57 E
Nagoya 36 35 10N 136 50 E
Nagpur 32 21 8N 79 10 E
Nagykanizsa 14 46 28N 17 0 E
Nagykōrös 15 47 5N 19 48 E
Naha 39 26 13N 127 42 E
Nahalal 28 32 41N 35 12 E
Nahanni Butte 64 61 2N 123 31W
Nahanni Nat. Park 64 61 15N 125 0W
Nahariyya 28 33 1N 35 5 E
Nahāvand 30 34 10N 48 22 E
Nahf 28 32 56N 35 18 E
Nahlin 64 58 55N 131 38W
Naicam 65 52 30N 104 30W
Nā'ifah 29 19 59N 50 46 E
Nain, Canada 63 56 34N 61 40W
Nā'īn, Iran 31 32 54N 53 0 E
Nainpur 32 22 30N 80 10 E
Naira 35 4 28S 130 0 E
Nairn 8 57 35N 3 54W

Nairobi

Nairobi 54 1 17S 36 48 E
Naivasha 54 0 40S 36 30 E
Najafābād 31 32 40N 51 15 E
Najd 30 26 30N 42 0 E
Najibabad 32 29 40N 78 20 E
Najin 38 42 12N 130 15 E
Nakadōri-Shima 36 32 57N 129 4 E
Nakamura 36 33 0N 133 0 E
Nakfa 51 16 40N 38 32 E
Nakhichevan A.S.S.R. □ 23 39 14N 45 30 E
Nakhodka 25 42 53N 132 54 E
Nakhon Phanom 34 17 23N 104 43 E
Nakhon Ratchasima 34 14 59N 102 12 E
Nakhon Sawan 34 15 35N 100 10 E
Nakhon Si Thammarat 34 8 29N 100 0 E
Nakina, B.C., Canada 64 59 12N 132 52W
Nakina, Ont., Canada 62 50 10N 86 40W
Nakskov 21 54 50N 11 8 E
Naktong → 38 35 7N 128 57 E
Nakuru 54 0 15S 36 4 E
Nakusp 64 50 20N 117 45W
Nal → 32 25 20N 65 30 E
Nalchik 23 43 30N 43 33 E
Nalgonda 32 17 6N 79 15 E
Nallamalai Hills 32 15 30N 78 50 E
Nalón → 13 43 32N 6 4W
Nālūt 51 31 54N 11 0 E
Nam Co 37 30 30N 90 45 E
Nam-Phan 34 10 30N 106 0 E
Namacunde 56 17 18S 15 50 E
Namacurra 57 17 30S 36 50 E
Namak, Daryācheh-ye 31 34 30N 52 0 E
Namak, Kavir-e 31 34 30N 57 30 E
Namaland 56 24 30S 17 0 E
Namangan 24 41 0N 71 40 E
Namapa 55 13 43S 39 50 E
Namaqualand 56 30 0S 17 25 E
Namasagali 52 1 2N 33 0 E
Namber 35 1 2S 134 49 E
Nambour 45 26 32S 152 58 E
Nambucca Heads 45 30 37S 153 0 E
Nameh 34 2 34N 116 21 E
Namew L. 65 54 14N 101 56W
Namib Desert = Namibwoestyn 56 22 30S 15 0 E
Namibe 55 15 7S 12 11 E
Namibe □ 56 16 35S 12 30 E
Namibia ■ 56 22 0S 18 9 E
Namibwoestyn 56 22 30S 15 0 E
Namlea 35 3 18S 127 5 E
Namoi → 45 30 12S 149 30 E
Nampa 72 43 34N 116 34W
Nampula 55 15 6S 39 15 E
Namrole 35 3 46S 126 46 E
Namse Shankou 33 30 0N 82 25 E
Namsen → 20 64 27N 11 42 E
Namsos 20 64 29N 11 30 E
Namtay 25 62 43N 129 37 E
Namtu 33 23 5N 97 28 E
Namu 64 51 52N 127 50W
Namur 11 50 27N 4 52 E
Namur □ 11 50 17N 5 0 E
Namutoni 56 18 49S 16 55 E
Namwala 55 15 44S 26 30 E
Nanaimo 64 49 10N 124 0W
Nanam 38 41 44N 129 40 E
Nanan 39 24 59N 118 21 E
Nanango 45 26 40S 152 0 E
Nan'ao, China 39 23 28N 117 5 E
Nanao, Japan 36 37 0N 137 0 E
Nanbu 39 31 18N 106 3 E
Nanchang 39 28 42N 115 55 E
Nancheng 39 27 33N 116 35 E
Nanching = Nanjing 39 32 2N 118 47 E
Nanchong 39 30 43N 106 2 E
Nanchuan 39 29 9N 107 6 E
Nancy 12 48 42N 6 12 E
Nanda Devi 32 30 23N 79 59 E
Nandan 39 24 58N 107 29 E
Nanded 32 19 10N 77 20 E
Nandewar Ra. 45 30 15S 150 35 E
Nandi 43 17 42S 177 20 E
Nandurbar 32 21 20N 74 15 E
Nandyal 32 15 30N 78 30 E
Nanga 47 26 7S 113 45 E
Nanga-Eboko 54 4 41N 12 22 E
Nanga Parbat 32 35 10N 74 35 E
Nangapinoh 34 0 20S 111 44 E
Nangarhár □ 31 34 20N 70 0 E
Nangatayap 34 1 32S 110 34 E
Nanjiang 39 32 28N 106 51 E
Nanjing 39 32 2N 118 47 E
Nankang 39 25 40N 114 45 E
Nanking = Nanjing 39 32 2N 118 47 E
Nanning 39 22 48N 108 20 E
Nannup 47 33 59S 115 48 E
Nanpi 38 38 2N 116 45 E
Nanping 39 26 38N 118 10 E
Nansei-Shotō 37 26 0N 128 0 E
Nantes 12 47 12N 1 33W
Nanticoke 68 41 12N 76 1W
Nanton 64 50 21N 113 46W
Nantong 39 32 1N 120 52 E
Nantucket I. 58 41 16N 70 3W
Nanuque 79 17 50S 40 21W
Nanutarra 46 22 32S 115 30 E
Nanxiong 39 25 6N 114 15 E
Nanyang 39 33 11N 112 30 E
Nanyuan 38 39 44N 116 22 E
Nanyuki 54 0 2N 37 4 E
Nanzhang 39 31 45N 111 50 E
Náo, C. de la 13 38 44N 0 14 E
Naococane L. 63 52 50N 70 45W
Naoetsu 36 37 12N 138 10 E
Naoli He → 38 47 18N 134 9 E
Napa 72 38 18N 122 17W
Napanee 62 44 15N 77 0W
Napier 43 39 30S 176 56 E
Napier Broome B. 46 14 2S 126 37 E
Napier Downs 46 17 11S 124 36 E
Napier Pen. 44 12 4S 135 43 E
Naples = Nápoli 18 40 50N 14 17 E
Naples 69 26 10N 81 45W
Napo → 78 3 20S 72 40W
Napoleon, N. Dak., U.S.A. 70 46 32N 99 49W
Napoleon, Ohio, U.S.A. 68 41 24N 84 7W
Nápoli 18 40 50N 14 17 E
Nappa Merrie 45 27 36S 141 7 E
Nara, Japan 36 34 40N 135 49 E
Nara, Mali 50 15 10N 7 20W
Nara □ 36 34 30N 136 0 E
Nara Visa 71 35 39N 103 10W
Naracoorte 45 36 58S 140 45 E
Naradhan 45 33 34S 146 17 E
Narasapur 33 16 26N 81 40 E
Narathiwat 34 6 30N 101 48 E
Narayanganj 33 23 40N 90 33 E
Narayanpet 32 16 45N 77 30 E
Narbonne 12 43 11N 3 0 E
Nardò 19 40 10N 18 0 E
Narembeen 47 32 7S 118 24 E
Nares Strӕde 58 80 0N 70 0W
Naretha 47 31 0S 124 45 E
Narin 32 36 5N 69 0 E
Narindra, Helodranon' i 57 14 55S 47 30 E
Narmada → 32 21 38N 72 36 E
Narodnaya 22 65 5N 60 0 E
Narok 52 1 55S 35 52 E
Narooma 45 36 14S 150 4 E
Narrabri 45 30 19S 149 46 E
Narran → 45 28 37S 148 12 E
Narrandera 45 34 42S 146 31 E
Narraway → 64 55 44N 119 55W
Narrogin 47 32 58S 117 14 E
Narromine 45 32 12S 148 12 E
Narsimhapur 32 22 54N 79 14 E
Narva 22 59 23N 28 12 E
Narvik 20 68 28N 17 26 E
Naryan-Mar 22 68 0N 53 0 E
Naryilco 45 28 37S 141 53 E
Narym 24 59 0N 81 30 E
Narymskoye 24 49 10N 84 15 E
Naryn 24 41 26N 75 58 E
Nasa 20 66 29N 15 23 E
Nasarawa 53 8 32N 7 41 E
Naseby 43 45 1S 170 10 E
Naser, Buheirat en 51 23 0N 32 30 E
Nashua, Iowa, U.S.A. 70 42 55N 92 34W
Nashua, Mont., U.S.A. 72 48 10N 106 25W
Nashua, N.H., U.S.A. 68 42 50N 71 25W
Nashville, Ark., U.S.A. 71 33 56N 93 50W
Nashville, Ga., U.S.A. 69 31 3N 83 15W
Nashville, Tenn., U.S.A. 69 36 12N 86 46W
Nasik 32 19 58N 73 50 E
Nasirabad 32 26 15N 74 45 E
Naskaupi → 63 53 47N 60 51W
Nass → 64 55 0N 129 40W
Nassau 75 25 0N 77 20W
Nassau, B. 80 55 20S 68 0W
Nasser, L. = Naser, Buheirat en 51 23 0N 32 30 E
Nässjö 21 57 39N 14 42 E
Nat Kyizin 33 14 57N 97 59 E
Nata 56 20 12S 26 12 E
Natagaima 78 3 37N 75 6W
Natal, Brazil 79 5 47S 35 13W
Natal, Canada 64 49 43N 114 51W
Natal, Indonesia 34 0 35N 99 7 E
Natal □ 57 28 30S 30 30 E
Naṭanz 31 33 30N 51 55 E
Natashquan 63 50 14N 61 46W
Natashquan → 63 50 7N 61 50W
Natchez 71 31 35N 91 25W
Natchitoches 71 31 47N 93 4W
Nathalia 45 36 1S 145 13 E
Nathdwara 32 24 55N 73 50 E
Natimuk 45 36 42S 142 0 E
Nation → 64 55 30N 123 32W
National City 73 32 39N 117 7W
Natitingou 53 10 20N 1 26 E
Natividad, I. 74 27 50N 115 10W
Natoma 70 39 14N 99 0W
Natron, L. 54 2 20S 36 0 E
Natuna Besar, Kepulauan 34 4 0N 108 15 E
Natuna Selatan, Kepulauan 34 2 45N 109 0 E
Naturaliste C. 44 40 50S 148 15 E
Naubinway 62 46 7N 85 27W
Naumburg 14 51 10N 11 48 E
Nauru ■ 3 1 0S 166 0 E
Naushahra = Nowshera 32 34 0N 72 0 E
Nauta 78 4 31S 73 35W
Nautanwa 33 27 20N 83 25 E
Nautla 74 20 20N 96 50W
Navajo Res. 73 36 55N 107 30W
Navalcarnero 13 40 17N 4 5W
Navan = An Uaimh 9 53 39N 6 40W
Navarino, I. 80 55 0S 67 40W
Navarra □ 13 42 40N 1 40W
Navasota 71 30 20N 96 5W
Navassa 75 18 30N 75 0W
Naver → 8 58 34N 4 15W
Navoi 24 40 9N 65 22 E
Navojoa 74 27 0N 109 30W
Navolok 22 62 33N 39 57 E
Návpaktos 19 38 23N 21 50 E
Návplion 19 37 33N 22 50 E
Navsari 32 20 57N 72 59 E
Nawabshah 32 26 15N 68 25 E
Nawakot 33 27 55N 85 10 E
Nawalgarh 32 27 50N 75 15 E
Nawāsīf, Harrat 30 21 20N 42 10 E
Náxos 19 37 8N 25 25 E
Nāy Band 31 27 20N 52 40 E
Nayakhan 25 61 56N 159 0 E
Nayarit □ 74 22 0N 105 0W
Nazareth = Naẕerat 28 32 42N 35 17 E
Nazas 74 25 10N 104 6W
Nazas → 74 25 35N 103 25W
Naze, The 7 51 53N 1 19 E
Naẕerat 28 32 42N 35 17 E
Nazir Hat 33 22 35N 91 49 E
Nazko 64 53 1N 123 37W
Nazko → 64 53 7N 123 34W
Ncheu 55 14 50S 34 47 E
Ndala 52 4 45S 33 15 E
Ndalatando 54 9 12S 14 48 E
Ndélé 51 8 25N 20 36 E
Ndendé 54 2 22S 11 23 E
Ndjamena 51 12 10N 14 59 E
Ndjolé 54 0 10S 10 45 E
Ndola 55 13 0S 28 34 E
Neagh, Lough 9 54 35N 6 25W
Neah Bay 72 48 25N 124 40W
Neale L. 46 24 15S 130 0 E
Near Is. 60 53 0N 172 0 E
Neath 7 51 39N 3 49W
Nebine Cr. → 45 29 27S 146 56 E
Nebit Dag 23 39 30N 54 22 E
Nebo 44 59 12N 32 25 E
Nebraska □ 70 41 30N 100 0W
Nebraska City 70 40 40N 95 52W
Nébrodi, Monti 18 37 55N 14 50 E
Necedah 70 44 2N 90 7W
Nechako → 64 53 30N 122 44W
Neches → 71 29 55N 93 52W
Neckar → 14 49 31N 8 26 E
Necochea 80 38 30S 58 50W
Needles 73 34 50N 114 35W
Needles, The 7 50 39N 1 35W
Neemuch = Nimach 32 24 30N 74 56 E
Neenah 68 44 10N 88 30W
Neepawa 65 50 15N 99 30W
Neft-chala = imeni 26 Bakinskikh Komissarov 23 39 19N 49 12 E
Nefta 50 33 53N 7 50 E
Neftyannyye Kamni 23 40 20N 50 55 E
Negapatam = Nagappattinam 32 10 46N 79 51 E
Negaunee 68 46 30N 87 36W
Negba 28 31 40N 34 41 E
Negele 29 5 20N 39 36 E
Negev Desert = Hanegev 28 30 50N 35 0 E
Negoiul, Vf. 15 45 38N 24 35 E
Negombo 32 7 12N 79 50 E
Negotin 19 44 16N 22 37 E
Negra Pt. 35 18 40N 120 50 E
Negro →, Argentina 80 41 2S 62 47W
Negro →, Brazil 78 3 0S 60 0W
Negro →, Uruguay 80 33 24S 58 22W
Negros 35 9 30N 122 40 E
Nehbandān 31 31 35N 60 5 E
Nei Monggol Zizhiqu □ 38 42 0N 112 0 E
Neidpath 65 50 12N 107 20W
Neihart 72 47 0N 110 44W
Neijiang 39 29 35N 104 55 E
Neilton 72 17 24N 123 52W
Neisse → 14 52 4N 14 46 E
Neiva 78 2 56N 75 18W
Neixiang 39 33 10N 111 52 E
Nejanilini L. 65 59 33N 97 48W
Nekemte 51 9 4N 36 30 E
Neksø 21 55 4N 15 8 E
Nelia 44 20 39S 142 12 E
Neligh 70 42 11N 98 2W
Nelkan 25 57 40N 136 4 E
Nellore 32 14 27N 79 59 E
Nelma 25 47 39N 139 0 E
Nelson, Canada 64 49 30N 117 20W
Nelson, N.Z. 43 41 18S 173 16 E
Nelson, U.K. 6 53 50N 2 14W
Nelson, U.S.A. 73 35 35N 113 16W
Nelson □ 43 42 11S 172 15 E
Nelson → 65 54 33N 98 2W
Nelson, C. 45 38 26S 141 32 E
Nelson, Estrecho 80 51 30S 75 0W
Nelson Forks 64 59 30N 124 0W
Nelson House 65 55 47N 98 51W
Nelson L. 65 55 48N 100 7W
Nelspoort 56 32 7S 23 0 E
Nelspruit 57 25 29S 30 59 E
Néma 50 16 40N 7 15W
Neman → 22 55 25N 21 10 E
Nemeiben L. 65 55 20N 105 20W
Nemunas = Neman → 22 55 25N 21 10 E
Nemuro 36 43 20N 145 35 E
Nemuro-Kaikyō 36 43 30N 145 30 E
Nemuy 25 55 40N 136 9 E
Nen Jiang → 38 45 28N 124 30 E
Nenagh 9 52 52N 8 11W
Nenana 60 64 30N 149 20W
Nene → 6 52 38N 0 13 E
Nenjiang 38 49 10N 125 10 E
Nenusa, Kepulauan 35 4 45N 127 1 E
Neodesha 71 37 30N 95 37W
Neosho 71 36 56N 94 28W
Neosho → 71 35 59N 95 10W
Nepal ■ 33 28 0N 84 30 E
Nepalganj 33 28 5N 81 40 E
Nephi 72 39 43N 111 52W
Nephin 9 54 1N 9 21W
Nerchinsk 25 52 0N 116 39 E
Nerchinskiy Zavod 25 51 20N 119 40 E
Néret L. 63 54 45N 70 44W
Neretva → 19 43 1N 17 27 E
Nerva 13 37 42N 6 30W
Nes 20 65 53N 17 24W
Nes Ziyyona 28 31 56N 34 48W
Neskaupstaður 20 65 9N 13 42W
Ness, Loch 8 57 15N 4 30W
Nesttun 21 60 19N 5 21 E
Netanya 28 32 20N 34 51 E
Nète → 11 51 7N 4 14 E
Nether Stowey 7 51 0N 3 10W
Netherbury 7 50 46N 2 45W
Netherdale 44 21 10S 148 33 E
Netherlands ■ 11 52 0N 5 30 E
Netherlands Antilles ■ 78 12 15N 69 0W
Netherlands Guiana = Surinam ■ 79 4 0N 56 0W
Nettilling L. 61 66 30N 71 0W
Netzahualcoyotl, Presa 74 17 10N 93 30W
Neubrandenburg 14 53 33N 13 17 E
Neuchâtel 14 47 0N 6 55 E
Neuchâtel, Lac de 14 46 53N 6 50 E
Neufchâteau 11 49 50N 5 25 E
Neumünster 14 54 4N 9 58 E
Neunkirchen 14 49 23N 7 12 E
Neuquén 80 38 55S 68 0W
Neuruppin 14 52 56N 12 48 E
Neuse → 69 35 5N 76 30W
Neusiedler See 14 47 50N 16 47 E
Neuss 11 51 12N 6 39 E
Neustrelitz 14 53 22N 13 4 E
Neva → 22 59 50N 30 30 E
Nevada 71 37 51N 94 22W
Nevada □ 72 39 20N 117 0W
Nevada, Sierra, Spain 13 37 3N 3 15W
Nevada, Sierra, U.S.A. 72 39 0N 120 30W
Nevada City 72 39 20N 121 0W
Nevada de Sta. Marta, Sa. 78 10 55N 73 50W
Nevanka 25 56 31N 98 55 E
Nevers 12 47 0N 3 9 E
Nevertire 45 31 50S 147 44 E
Neville 65 49 58N 107 39W
Nevinnomyssk 23 44 40N 42 0 E
Nevis 75 17 0N 62 30W
Nevşehir 30 38 33N 34 40 E
Nevyansk 22 57 30N 60 13 E
New Albany, Ind., U.S.A. 68 38 20N 85 50W
New Albany, Miss., U.S.A. 71 34 30N 89 0W
New Amsterdam 78 6 15N 57 36W
New Angledool 45 29 5S 147 55 E
New Bedford 68 41 40N 70 52W
New Bern 69 35 8N 77 3W
New Boston 71 33 27N 94 21W
New Braunfels 71 29 43N 98 9W
New Brighton 43 43 29S 172 43 E
New Britain, Papua N. G. 40 5 50S 150 20 E
New Britain, U.S.A. 68 41 41N 72 47W
New Brunswick 68 40 30N 74 28W
New Brunswick □ 63 46 50N 66 30W
New Bussa 53 9 53N 4 31 E
New Caledonia 40 21 0S 165 0 E
New Castile = Castilla La Nueva 13 39 45N 3 20W
New Castle, Ind., U.S.A. 68 39 55N 85 23W
New Castle, Pa., U.S.A. 68 41 0N 80 20W
New Cristóbal 74 9 22N 79 40W
New Delhi 32 28 37N 77 13 E
New Denver 64 50 0N 117 25W
New England 70 46 36N 102 47W
New England Ra. 45 30 20S 151 45 E
New Forest 7 50 53N 1 40W
New Glasgow 63 45 35N 62 36W
New Guinea 40 4 0S 136 0 E
New Hampshire □ 68 43 40N 71 40W
New Hampton 70 43 2N 92 20W
New Hanover 57 29 22S 30 31 E
New Haven 68 41 20N 72 54W
New Hazelton 64 55 20N 127 30W
New Hebrides = Vanuatu ■ 3 15 0S 168 0 E
New Iberia 71 30 2N 91 54W
New Ireland 40 3 20S 151 50 E
New Jersey □ 68 40 30N 74 10W
New Kensington 68 40 36N 79 43W
New Lexington 68 39 40N 82 15W
New Liskeard 62 47 31N 79 41W
New London, Conn., U.S.A. 68 41 23N 72 8W
New London, Minn., U.S.A. 70 45 17N 94 55W
New London, Wis., U.S.A. 70 44 23N 88 43W
New Madrid 71 36 40N 89 30W
New Meadows 72 45 0N 116 32W
New Mexico □ 66 34 30N 106 0W
New Norcia 47 30 57S 116 13 E
New Norfolk 44 42 46S 147 2 E
New Orleans 71 30 0N 90 5W
New Philadelphia 68 40 29N 81 25W
New Plymouth, N.Z. 43 39 4S 174 5 E
New Plymouth, U.S.A. 72 43 58N 116 49W
New Providence 75 25 25N 78 35W
New Radnor 7 52 15N 3 10W
New Richmond 70 45 6N 92 34W
New Roads 71 30 43N 91 30W
New Rockford 70 47 44N 99 7W
New Ross 9 52 24N 6 58W
New Salem 70 46 51N 101 25W
New Siberian Is. = Novosibirskiye Ostrava 25 75 0N 142 0 E
New Smyrna Beach 69 29 0N 80 50W
New South Wales □ 45 33 0S 146 0 E
New Springs 47 25 49S 120 1 E
New Town 70 48 0N 102 30W
New Ulm 70 44 15N 94 30W
New Waterford 63 46 13N 60 4W
New Westminster 64 49 13N 122 55W
New York □ 68 42 40N 76 0W
New York City 68 40 45N 74 0W
New Zealand ■ 43 40 0S 176 0 E
Newala 54 10 58S 39 18 E
Newark, Del., U.S.A. 68 39 42N 75 45W
Newark, N.J., U.S.A. 68 40 41N 74 12W
Newark, N.Y., U.S.A. 68 43 2N 77 10W
Newark, Ohio, U.S.A. 68 40 5N 82 24W
Newark-on-Trent 6 53 6N 0 48W
Newaygo 68 43 25N 85 48W
Newberg 72 45 22N 123 0W
Newberry, Mich., U.S.A. 68 46 20N 85 32W
Newberry, S.C., U.S.A. 69 34 17N 81 37W
Newbrook 64 54 24N 112 57W
Newburgh 68 41 30N 74 1W
Newbury 7 51 24N 1 19W
Newburyport 68 42 48N 70 50W
Newcastle, Australia 45 33 0S 151 46 E
Newcastle, Canada 63 47 1N 65 38W
Newcastle, S. Africa 57 27 45S 29 58 E
Newcastle, U.K. 9 54 13N 5 54W

Novaya Ladoga

Newcastle, U.S.A. **70** 43 50N 104 12W
Newcastle Emlyn **7** 52 2N 4 29W
Newcastle Ra. **46** 15 45S 130 15 E
Newcastle-under-Lyme **6** 53 2N 2 15W
Newcastle-upon-Tyne **6** 54 59N 1 37W
Newcastle Waters **44** 17 30S 133 28 E
Newdegate **47** 33 6S 119 0 E
Newe Etan **28** 32 30N 35 32 E
Newe Sha'anan **28** 32 47N 34 59 E
Newe Zohar **28** 31 9N 35 21 E
Newell **70** 44 48N 103 25W
Newenham, C. **60** 58 40N 162 15W
Newfoundland □ **61** 53 0N 58 0W
Newhalem **64** 48 41N 121 16W
Newham **7** 51 31N 0 2 E
Newhaven **7** 50 47N 0 4 E
Newkirk **71** 36 52N 97 3W
Newman **46** 23 18S 119 45 E
Newmarket, Ireland **9** 52 13N 9 0W
Newmarket, U.K. **7** 52 15N 0 23 E
Newnan **69** 33 22N 84 48W
Newport, Gwent, U.K. **7** 51 35N 3 0W
Newport, I. of W., U.K. **7** 50 42N 1 18W
Newport, Salop, U.K. **7** 52 47N 2 22W
Newport, Ark., U.S.A. **71** 35 38N 91 15W
Newport, Ky., U.S.A. **68** 39 5N 84 23W
Newport, N.H., U.S.A. **68** 43 23N 72 8W
Newport, Oreg., U.S.A. **72** 44 41N 124 2W
Newport, R.I., U.S.A. **68** 41 13N 71 19W
Newport, Tenn., U.S.A. **69** 35 59N 83 12W
Newport, Vt., U.S.A. **68** 44 57N 72 17W
Newport, Wash., U.S.A. **72** 48 11N 117 2W
Newport Beach **73** 33 40N 117 58W
Newport News **68** 37 2N 76 30W
Newquay **7** 50 24N 5 6W
Newry **9** 54 10N 6 20W
Newry & Mourne □ **9** 54 10N 6 15W
Newton, Iowa, U.S.A. **70** 41 40N 93 3W
Newton, Mass., U.S.A. **68** 42 21N 71 10W
Newton, Miss., U.S.A. **71** 32 19N 89 10W
Newton, N.C., U.S.A. **69** 35 42N 81 10W
Newton, N.J., U.S.A. **68** 41 3N 74 46W
Newton, Tex., U.S.A. **71** 30 54N 93 42W
Newton Abbot **7** 50 32N 3 37W
Newton Boyd **45** 29 45S 152 16 E
Newton Stewart **8** 54 57N 4 30W
Newtonmore **8** 57 4N 4 7W
Newtown **7** 52 31N 3 19W
Newtownabbey **9** 54 40N 5 55W
Newtownabbey □ **9** 54 45N 6 0W
Newtownards **9** 54 37N 5 40W
Neya **22** 58 21N 43 49 E
Neyrīz **31** 29 15N 54 19 E
Neyshābūr **31** 36 10N 58 50 E
Nezhin **23** 51 5N 31 55 E
Nezperce **72** 46 13N 116 15W
Ngabang **34** 0 23N 109 55 E
Ngabordamlu, Tanjung **35** 6 56S 134 11 E
Ngami Depression **56** 20 30S 22 46 E
Nganglong Kangri **33** 33 0N 81 0 E
Nganjuk **35** 7 32S 111 55 E
Ngaoundéré **54** 7 15N 13 35 E
Ngapara **43** 44 57S 170 46 E
Ngawi **35** 7 24S 111 26 E
Ngoring Hu **37** 34 55N 97 5 E
Ngorongoro **52** 3 11S 35 32 E
Ngozi **52** 2 54S 29 50 E
Ngudu **54** 2 58S 33 25 E
Nguigmi **51** 14 20N 13 20 E
Ngukurr **44** 14 44S 134 44 E
Nguru **53** 12 56N 10 29 E
Nha Trang **34** 12 16N 109 10 E
Nhacoongo **57** 24 18S 35 14 E
Nhangutazi, L. **57** 24 0S 34 30 E
Nhill **45** 36 18S 141 40 E
Nhulunbuy **44** 12 10S 137 20 E
Niafounké **50** 16 0N 4 5W
Niagara **68** 45 45N 88 0W
Niagara Falls, Canada **62** 43 7N 79 5W
Niagara Falls, U.S.A. **68** 43 5N 79 0W
Niah **34** 3 58N 113 46 E
Niamey **53** 13 27N 2 6 E
Niangara **54** 3 42N 27 50 E
Nianzishan **38** 47 31N 122 53 E
Nias **34** 1 0N 97 30 E
Nicaragua ■ **75** 11 40N 85 30W
Nicaragua, L. de **75** 12 0N 85 30W
Nicastro **18** 39 0N 16 18 E
Nice **12** 43 42N 7 14 E
Niceville **69** 30 30N 86 30W
Nichinan **36** 31 38N 131 23 E
Nicholás, Canal **75** 23 30N 80 5W
Nicholasville **68** 37 54N 84 31W
Nicholson **46** 18 2S 128 54 E
Nicholson → **44** 17 31S 139 36 E
Nicholson Ra. **47** 27 15S 116 45 E
Nicobar Is. **3** 9 0N 93 0 E
Nicola **64** 50 12N 120 40W
Nicolet **62** 46 17N 72 35W
Nicolls Town **75** 25 8N 78 0W
Nicosia **30** 35 10N 33 25 E
Nicoya, G. de **75** 10 0N 85 0W
Nicoya, Pen. de **75** 9 45N 85 40W
Nidd → **6** 54 1N 1 32W
Niekerkshoop **56** 29 19S 22 51 E
Nienburg **14** 52 38N 9 15 E
Nieu Bethesda **56** 31 51S 24 34 E
Nieuw Amsterdam **79** 5 53N 55 5W
Nieuw Nickerie **79** 6 0N 56 59W
Nieuwoudtville **56** 31 23S 19 7 E
Nieuwpoort **11** 51 8N 2 45 E
Nièvre □ **12** 47 10N 3 40 E
Niğde **30** 38 0N 34 40 E
Nigel **57** 26 27S 28 25 E
Niger □ **53** 10 0N 5 0 E
Niger ■ **50** 17 30N 10 0 E
Niger → **53** 5 33N 6 33 E
Nigeria ■ **53** 8 30N 8 0 E
Nightcaps **43** 45 57S 168 2 E
Nii-Jima **36** 34 20N 139 15 E
Niigata **36** 37 58N 139 0 E
Niigata □ **36** 37 15N 138 45 E
Niihama **36** 33 55N 133 16 E
Niihau **66** 21 55N 160 10W
Nijkerk **11** 52 13N 5 30 E
Nijmegen **11** 51 50N 5 52 E
Nijverdal **11** 52 22N 6 28 E
Nike **53** 6 26N 7 29 E
Nikel **20** 69 24N 30 12 E
Nikiniki **35** 9 49S 124 30 E
Nikki **53** 9 58N 3 12 E
Nikkō **36** 36 45N 139 35 E
Nikolayev **23** 46 58N 32 0 E
Nikolayevsk **23** 50 0N 45 35 E
Nikolayevsk-na-Amur **25** 53 8N 140 44 E
Nikolskoye **25** 55 12N 166 0 E
Nikopol **23** 47 35N 34 25 E
Nīkshahr **31** 26 15N 60 10 E
Nîl, Nahr en → **51** 30 10N 31 6 E
Nîl el Abyad → **51** 15 38N 32 31 E
Nîl el Azraq → **51** 15 38N 32 31 E
Niland **73** 33 16N 115 30W
Nile = Nîl, Nahr en → **51** 30 10N 31 6 E
Niles **68** 41 8N 80 40W
Nimach **32** 24 30N 74 56 E
Nîmes **12** 43 50N 4 23 E
Nimmitabel **45** 36 29S 149 15 E
Nimneryskiy **25** 57 50N 125 10 E
Nimrūz □ **31** 30 0N 62 0 E
Nimule **54** 3 32N 32 3 E
Nīnawá **30** 36 25N 43 10 E
Nindigully **45** 28 21S 148 50 E
Ninemile **64** 56 0N 130 7W
Nineveh = Nīnawá **30** 36 25N 43 10 E
Ningaloo **46** 22 41S 113 41 E
Ning'an **38** 44 22N 129 20 E
Ningbo **39** 29 51N 121 28 E
Ningde **39** 26 38N 119 23 E
Ningdu **39** 26 25N 115 59 E
Ningjin **38** 37 35N 114 57 E
Ningming **39** 22 8N 107 4 E
Ningpo = Ningbo **39** 29 51N 121 28 E
Ningqiang **39** 32 47N 106 15 E
Ningshan **39** 33 21N 108 21 E
Ningsia Hui A.R. = Ningxia Huizu Zizhiqu □ **38** 38 0N 106 0 E
Ningwu **38** 39 0N 112 18 E
Ningxia Huizu Zizhiqu □ **38** 38 0N 106 0 E
Ningxiang **39** 28 15N 112 30 E
Ningyuan **39** 25 37N 111 57 E
Ninove **11** 50 51N 4 2 E
Niobrara **70** 42 48N 97 59W
Niobrara → **70** 42 45N 98 0W
Nioro du Sahel **50** 15 15N 9 30W
Niort **12** 46 19N 0 29W
Nipawin **65** 53 20N 104 0W
Nipawin Prov. Park **65** 54 0N 104 37W
Nipigon **62** 49 0N 88 17W
Nipigon, L. **62** 49 50N 88 30W
Nipin → **65** 55 46N 108 35W
Nipishish L. **63** 54 12N 60 45W
Nipissing L. **62** 46 20N 80 0W
Nipomo **73** 35 4N 120 29W
Niquelândia **79** 14 33S 48 23W
Nirmal **32** 19 3N 78 20 E
Nirmali **33** 26 20N 86 35 E
Niš **19** 43 19N 21 58 E
Nişāb **29** 14 25N 46 29 E
Nishinomiya **36** 34 45N 135 20 E
Niskibi → **62** 56 29N 88 9W
Nisutlin → **64** 60 14N 132 34W
Nitā' **30** 27 15N 48 35 E
Nitchequon **63** 53 10N 70 58W
Niterói **79** 22 52S 43 0W
Nith → **8** 55 20N 3 5W
Nitra **15** 48 19N 18 4 E
Nitra → **15** 47 46N 18 10 E
Niuafo'ou **43** 15 30S 175 58W
Niue I. **2** 19 2S 169 54W
Niut **34** 0 55N 110 6 E
Nivelles **11** 50 35N 4 20 E
Nivernais **12** 47 0N 3 20 E
Nixon **71** 29 17N 97 45W
Nizamabad **32** 18 45N 78 7 E
Nizamghat **33** 28 20N 95 45 E
Nizhne Kolymsk **25** 68 34N 160 55 E
Nizhneangarsk **25** 55 47N 109 30 E
Nizhnekamsk **22** 55 38N 51 49 E
Nizhneudinsk **25** 54 54N 99 3 E
Nizhnevartovsk **24** 60 56N 76 38 E
Nizhneyansk **25** 71 26N 136 4 E
Nizhniy Novgorod = Gorkiy **22** 56 20N 44 0 E
Nizhniy Tagil **22** 57 55N 59 57 E
Nizhnyaya Tunguska → **25** 64 20N 93 0 E
Nizip **30** 37 5N 37 50 E
Nizké Tatry **15** 48 55N 20 0 E
Njombe **54** 9 20S 34 50 E
Nkambe **53** 6 35N 10 40 E
Nkawkaw **53** 6 36N 0 49W
Nkhata Bay **54** 11 33S 34 16 E
Nkhota Kota **55** 12 56S 34 15 E
Nkongsamba **54** 4 55N 9 55 E
Nkurenkuru **56** 17 42S 18 32 E
Nmai → **33** 25 30N 97 25 E
Noakhali = Maijdi **33** 22 48N 91 10 E
Noatak **60** 67 32N 162 59W
Nobeoka **36** 32 36N 131 41 E
Noblesville **68** 40 1N 85 59W
Nocera Inferiore **18** 40 45N 14 37 E
Nockatunga **45** 27 42S 142 42 E
Nocona **71** 33 48N 97 45W
Noel **71** 36 36N 94 29W
Nogales, Mexico **74** 31 20N 110 56W
Nogales, U.S.A. **73** 31 33N 110 56W
Nōgata **36** 33 48N 130 44 E
Noggerup **47** 33 32S 116 5 E
Noginsk **25** 64 30N 90 50 E
Nogoa → **44** 23 40S 147 55 E
Noirmoutier, I. de **12** 46 58N 2 10W
Nojane **56** 23 15S 20 14 E
Nok Kundi **31** 28 50N 62 45 E
Nokaneng **56** 19 40S 22 17 E
Nokhtuysk **25** 60 0N 117 45 E
Nokomis **65** 51 35N 105 0W
Nokomis L. **65** 57 0N 103 0W
Nola **54** 3 35N 16 4 E
Noma Omuramba → **56** 18 52S 20 53 E
Noman L. **65** 62 15N 108 55W
Nome **60** 64 30N 165 24W
Nonacho L. **65** 61 42N 109 40W
Nonda **44** 20 40S 142 28 E
Nong Khai **34** 17 50N 102 46 E
Nong'an **38** 44 25N 125 5 E
Nongoma **57** 27 58S 31 35 E
Nonoava **74** 27 28N 106 44W
Noonamah **46** 12 40S 131 4 E
Noonan **70** 48 51N 102 59W
Noondoo **45** 28 35S 148 30 E
Noonkanbah **46** 18 30S 124 50 E
Noord Brabant □ **11** 51 40N 5 0 E
Noord Holland □ **11** 52 30N 4 45 E
Noordbeveland **11** 51 35N 3 50 E
Noordoostpolder **11** 52 45N 5 45 E
Noordwijk aan Zee **11** 52 14N 4 26 E
Nootka **64** 49 38N 126 38W
Nootka I. **64** 49 32N 126 42W
Nóqui **54** 5 55S 13 30 E
Noranda **62** 48 20N 79 0W
Nord □ **12** 50 15N 3 30 E
Nord-Ostsee Kanal **14** 54 15N 9 40 E
Nord-Trøndelag fylke □ **20** 64 20N 12 0 E
Nordegg **64** 52 29N 116 5W
Nordhausen **14** 51 29N 10 47 E
Nordkapp **20** 71 10N 25 44 E
Nordkinn **4** 71 8N 27 40 E
Nordland fylke □ **20** 65 40N 13 0 E
Nordrhein-Westfalen □ **14** 51 45N 7 30 E
Nordvik **25** 74 2N 111 32 E
Nore → **9** 52 40N 7 20W
Norembega **62** 48 59N 80 43W
Norfolk, Nebr., U.S.A. **70** 42 3N 97 25W
Norfolk, Va., U.S.A. **68** 36 40N 76 15W
Norfolk □ **6** 52 39N 1 0 E
Norfolk Broads **6** 52 30N 1 15 E
Norfolk I. **3** 28 58S 168 3 E
Norfork Res. **71** 36 13N 92 15W
Norilsk **25** 69 20N 88 6 E
Norley **45** 27 45S 143 48 E
Norma, Mt. **44** 20 55S 140 42 E
Normal **70** 40 30N 89 0W
Norman **71** 35 12N 97 30W
Norman → **44** 17 28S 140 49 E
Norman Wells **60** 65 17N 126 51W
Normanby → **44** 14 23S 144 10 E
Normandie **12** 48 45N 0 10 E
Normandin **62** 48 49N 72 31W
Normandy = Normandie **12** 48 45N 0 10 E
Normanhurst, Mt. **47** 25 4S 122 30 E
Normanton **44** 17 40S 141 10 E
Norquay **65** 51 53N 102 5W
Norquinco **80** 41 51S 70 55W
Norrbotten □ **20** 66 30N 22 30 E
Norrby **20** 64 55N 18 15 E
Nørresundby **21** 57 5N 9 52 E
Norris **72** 45 40N 111 40W
Norristown **68** 40 9N 75 21W
Norrköping **21** 58 37N 16 11 E
Norrland □ **20** 66 50N 18 0 E
Norrtälje **21** 59 46N 18 42 E
Norseman **47** 32 8S 121 43 E
Norsk **25** 52 30N 130 0 E
North Adams **68** 42 42N 73 6W
North America **58** 40 0N 100 0W
North Battleford **65** 52 50N 108 17W
North Bay **62** 46 20N 79 30W
North Belcher Is. **62** 56 50N 79 50W
North Bend, Canada **64** 49 50N 121 27W
North Bend, U.S.A. **72** 43 28N 124 14W
North Berwick **8** 56 4N 2 44W
North Canadian → **71** 35 17N 95 31W
North C., Canada **63** 47 2N 60 20W
North C., N.Z. **43** 34 23S 173 4 E
North Caribou L. **62** 52 50N 90 40W
North Carolina □ **69** 35 30N 80 0W
North Channel, Br. Is. **8** 55 0N 5 30W
North Channel, Canada **62** 46 0N 83 0W
North Chicago **68** 42 19N 87 50W
North Dakota □ **70** 47 30N 100 0W
North Dandalup **47** 32 30S 115 57 E
North Down □ **9** 54 40N 5 45W
North Downs **7** 51 17N 0 30 E
North East Frontier Agency = Arunachal Pradesh □ **33** 28 0N 95 0 E
North East Providence Chan. **75** 26 0N 76 0W
North Esk → **8** 56 44N 2 25W
North European Plain **4** 55 0N 20 0 E
North Foreland **7** 51 22N 1 28 E
North Henik L. **65** 61 45N 97 40W
North I. **43** 38 0S 175 0 E
North Knife → **65** 58 53N 94 45W
North Korea ■ **38** 40 0N 127 0 E
North Lakhimpur **33** 27 14N 94 7 E
North Las Vegas **73** 36 15N 115 6W
North Loup → **70** 41 17N 98 23W
North Minch **8** 58 5N 5 55W
North Nahanni → **64** 62 15N 123 20W
North Ossetian A.S.S.R. □ **23** 43 30N 44 30 E
North Palisade **73** 37 6N 118 32W
North Platte **70** 41 10N 100 50W
North Platte → **70** 41 15N 100 45W
North Pt. **63** 47 5N 64 0W
North Portal **65** 49 0N 102 33W
North Powder **72** 45 2N 117 59W
North Ronaldsay **8** 59 20N 2 30W
North Saskatchewan → **65** 53 15N 105 5W
North Sea **4** 56 0N 4 0 E
North Sporades = Voríai Sporádhes **19** 39 15N 23 30 E
North Sydney **63** 46 12N 60 15W
North Thompson → **64** 50 40N 120 20W
North Tonawanda **68** 43 5N 78 50W
North Truchas Pk. **73** 36 0N 105 30W
North Twin I. **62** 53 20N 80 0W
North Tyne → **6** 54 59N 2 7W
North Uist **8** 57 40N 7 15W
North Vancouver **64** 49 25N 123 3W
North Vernon **68** 39 0N 85 35W
North Wabasca L. **64** 56 0N 113 55W
North Walsham **6** 52 49N 1 22 E
North West C. **46** 21 45S 114 9 E
North West Christmas I. Ridge **41** 6 30N 165 0W
North West Frontier □ **32** 34 0N 71 0 E
North West Highlands **8** 57 35N 5 2W
North West Providence Channel **75** 26 0N 78 0W
North West River **63** 53 30N 60 10W
North West Territories □ **60** 67 0N 110 0W
North York Moors **6** 54 25N 0 50W
North Yorkshire □ **6** 54 15N 1 25W
Northallerton **6** 54 20N 1 26W
Northam **56** 24 56S 27 18 E
Northampton, Australia **47** 28 27S 114 33 E
Northampton, U.K. **7** 52 14N 0 54W
Northampton, U.S.A. **68** 42 22N 72 31W
Northampton □ **7** 52 16N 0 55W
Northampton Downs **44** 24 35S 145 48 E
Northcliffe **47** 34 39S 116 7 E
Northern Circars **33** 17 30N 82 30 E
Northern Group **43** 10 0S 160 0W
Northern Indian L. **65** 57 20N 97 20W
Northern Ireland □ **9** 54 45N 7 0W
Northern Light, L. **62** 48 15N 90 39W
Northern Marianas **40** 17 0N 145 0 E
Northern Territory □ **46** 16 0S 133 0 E
Northfield **70** 44 30N 93 10W
Northland □ **43** 35 30S 173 30 E
Northome **70** 47 53N 94 15W
Northport, Ala., U.S.A. **69** 33 15N 87 35W
Northport, Mich., U.S.A. **68** 45 8N 85 39W
Northport, Wash., U.S.A. **72** 48 55N 117 48W
Northumberland □ **6** 55 12N 2 0W
Northumberland, C. **45** 38 5S 140 40 E
Northumberland Is. **44** 21 30S 149 50 E
Northumberland Str. **63** 46 20N 64 0W
Northwich **6** 53 16N 2 30W
Northwood, Iowa, U.S.A. **70** 43 27N 93 0W
Northwood, N. Dak., U.S.A. **70** 47 44N 97 30W
Norton **70** 39 50N 99 53W
Norton Sd. **60** 64 0N 164 0W
Norwalk, Conn., U.S.A. **68** 41 9N 73 25W
Norwalk, Ohio, U.S.A. **68** 41 13N 82 38W
Norway **68** 45 46N 87 57W
Norway ■ **21** 63 0N 11 0 E
Norway House **65** 53 59N 97 50W
Norwegian Sea **21** 66 0N 1 0 E
Norwich, U.K. **6** 52 38N 1 17 E
Norwich, U.S.A. **68** 42 32N 75 30W
Noshiro **36** 40 12N 140 0 E
Nosok **24** 70 10N 82 20 E
Noşratābād **31** 29 55N 60 0 E
Noss Hd. **8** 58 29N 3 4W
Nossob → **56** 26 55S 20 45 E
Nosy Bé **55** 13 25S 48 15 E
Nosy Boraha **57** 16 50S 49 55 E
Nosy Mitsio **55** 12 54S 48 36 E
Nosy Varika **57** 20 35S 48 32 E
Notigi Dam **65** 56 40N 99 10W
Notikewin → **64** 57 2N 117 38W
Noto **18** 36 52N 15 4 E
Noto-Hanto **36** 37 0N 137 0 E
Notre-Dame **63** 46 18N 64 46W
Notre Dame B. **63** 49 45N 55 30W
Notre Dame de Koartac = Koartac **61** 60 55N 69 40W
Notre Dame d'Ivugivic = Ivugivik **61** 62 24N 77 55W
Nottaway → **62** 51 22N 78 55W
Nottingham **6** 52 57N 1 10W
Nottingham □ **6** 53 10N 1 0W
Nottoway → **68** 36 33N 76 55W
Notwane → **56** 23 35S 26 58 E
Nouâdhibou **50** 20 54N 17 0W
Nouâdhibou, Ras **50** 20 50N 17 0W
Nouakchott **50** 18 9N 15 58W
Nouméa **40** 22 17S 166 30 E
Noupoort **56** 31 10S 24 57 E
Nouveau Comptoir **62** 53 0N 78 49W
Nouvelle Calédonie = New Caledonia **40** 21 0S 165 0 E
Nova Casa Nova **79** 9 25S 41 5W
Nova Cruz **79** 6 28S 35 25W
Nova Friburgo **79** 22 16S 42 30W
Nova Gaia **54** 10 10S 17 35 E
Nova Iguaçu **79** 22 45S 43 28W
Nova Iorque **79** 7 0S 44 5W
Nova Lima **79** 19 59S 43 51W
Nova Lisboa = Huambo **55** 12 42S 15 54 E
Nova Mambone **57** 21 0S 35 3 E
Nova Scotia □ **63** 45 10N 63 0W
Nova Sofala **57** 20 7S 34 42 E
Nova Venécia **79** 18 45S 40 24W
Noval Iorque **79** 6 48S 44 0W
Novara **18** 45 27N 8 36 E
Novaya Ladoga **22** 60 7N 32 16 E

Novaya Lyalya

Novaya Lyalya .... 24 59 10N 60 35 E
Novaya Sibir, Ostrov 25 75 10N 150 0 E
Novaya Zemlya ... 24 75 0N 56 0 E
Nové Zámky ...... 15 48 2N 18 8 E
Novgorod .... 22 58 30N 31 25 E
Novgorod-Severskiy 22 52 2N 33 10 E
Novi Sad .... 19 45 18N 19 52 E
Novo Remanso ... 79 9 41S 42 4W
Novoaltaysk ...... 24 53 30N 84 0 E
Novocherkassk ... 23 47 27N 40 5 E
Novokazalinsk .... 24 45 48N 62 6 E
Novokuybyshevsk . 22 53 7N 49 58 E
Novokuznetsk .... 24 53 45N 87 10 E
Novomoskovsk ... 22 54 5N 38 15 E
Novorossiysk .... 23 44 43N 37 46 E
Novorybnoye ..... 25 72 50N 105 50 E
Novoshakhtinsk ... 23 47 46N 39 58 E
Novosibirsk ...... 24 55 0N 83 5 E
Novosibirskiye
Ostrava .... 25 75 0N 142 0 E
Novotroitsk ...... 22 51 10N 58 15 E
Novouzensk ...... 23 50 32N 48 17 E
Novska .... 18 45 19N 17 0 E
Novvy Port .... 24 67 40N 72 30 E
Now Shahr .... 31 36 40N 51 30 E
Nowgong .... 33 26 20N 92 50 E
Nowra .... 45 34 53S 150 35 E
Nowshera .... 32 34 0N 72 0 E
Nowy Sącz .... 15 49 40N 20 41 E
Nowy Tomyśl ..... 14 52 19N 16 10 E
Noxon 72 48 0N 115 43W
Noyes I. 64 55 30N 133 40W
Nsanje .... 55 16 55S 35 12 E
Nsawam 53 5 50N 0 24W
Nsukka .... 53 6 51N 7 29 E
Nûbîya, Es Sahrâ En 51 21 30N 33 30 E
Nuboai .... 35 2 10S 136 30 E
Nueces → 71 27 50N 97 30W
Nueima → ...... 28 31 54N 35 25 E
Nueltin L. 65 60 30N 99 30W
Nueva Gerona 75 21 53N 82 49W
Nueva Imperial ... 80 38 45S 72 58W
Nueva Rosita 74 28 0N 101 11W
Nueva San Salvador 75 13 40N 89 18W
Nuéve de Julio 80 35 30S 61 0W
Nuevitas 75 21 30N 77 20W
Nuevo, G. 80 43 0S 64 30W
Nuevo Laredo 74 27 30N 99 30W
Nuevo León □ 74 25 0N 100 0W
Nugget Pt. .... 43 46 27S 169 50 E
Nuhaka .... 43 39 3S 177 45 E
Nukey Bluff, Mt. ... 45 32 26S 135 29 E
Nukheila .... 51 19 1N 26 21 E
Nuku'alofa 43 21 10S 174 0W
Nukus .... 24 42 20N 59 7 E
Nulato 60 64 40N 158 10W
Nullagine → ..... 46 21 20S 120 20 E
Nullarbor .... 47 31 28S 130 55 E
Nullarbor Plain .. 47 31 10S 129 0 E
Numalla, L. .... 45 28 43S 144 20 E
Numan .... 53 9 29N 12 3 E
Numata .... 36 36 45N 139 4 E
Numazu .... 36 35 7N 138 51 E
Numbulwar .... 44 14 15S 135 45 E
Numfoor .... 35 1 0S 134 50 E
Numurkah .... 45 36 5S 145 26 E
Nunaksaluk I. 63 55 49N 60 20W
Nuneaton 7 52 32N 1 29W
Nunivak 60 60 0N 166 0W
Nunkun .... 32 33 57N 76 2 E
Nunspeet .... 11 52 21N 5 45 E
Nuomin He → ... 38 46 45N 126 55 E
Nuremburg =
Nürnberg ...... 14 49 26N 11 5 E
Nurina .... 47 30 56S 126 33 E
Nuriootpa .... 45 34 27S 139 0 E
Nürnberg .... 14 49 26N 11 5 E
Nurran, L. =
Terewah, L. ..... 45 29 52S 147 35 E
Nurrari Lakes .... 47 29 1S 130 5 E
Nusa Barung ..... 35 8 10S 113 30 E
Nusa Kambangan . 35 7 40S 108 10 E
Nusa Tenggara
Barat □ .... 34 8 50S 117 30 E
Nusa Tenggara
Timur □ .... 35 9 30S 122 0 E
Nusaybin .... 23 37 3N 41 10 E
Nushki .... 32 29 35N 66 0 E
Nutak 61 57 28N 61 59W
Nutwood Downs .. 44 15 49S 134 10 E
Nuwakot .... 33 28 10N 83 55 E
Nuweveldberge ... 56 32 10S 21 45 E
Nuyts, C. .... 47 32 2S 132 21 E
Nuyts Arch. ...... 45 32 35S 133 20 E
Nxau-Nxau ...... 56 18 57S 21 4 E
Nyah West ...... 45 35 16S 143 21 E
Nyahanga .... 54 2 20S 33 37 E
Nyahururu .... 54 0 2N 36 27 E
Nyainqentanglha
Shan .... 37 30 0N 90 0 E
Nyakanazi .... 52 3 2S 31 10 E
Nyakanyasi .... 52 1 10S 31 13 E
Nyâlâ .... 51 12 2N 24 58 E
Nyandoma .... 22 61 40N 40 12 E
Nyangana .... 56 18 0S 20 40 E
Nyanza .... 52 4 21S 29 36 E
Nyarling → 64 60 41N 113 23W
Nyasa, L. = Malawi,
L. .... 55 12 30S 34 30 E
Nyazepetrovsk .... 22 56 3N 59 36 E
Nybro .... 21 56 44N 15 55 E
Nyda .... 24 66 40N 72 58 E
Nyeri .... 54 0 23S 36 56 E
Nyíregyháza ...... 15 47 58N 21 47 E
Nykarleby .... 20 63 22N 22 31 E
Nykøbing .... 21 54 56N 11 52 E
Nyköping .... 21 58 45N 17 0 E
Nylstroom .... 57 24 42S 28 22 E
Nymagee .... 45 32 7S 146 20 E
Nynäshamn ...... 21 58 54N 17 57 E
Nyngan .... 45 31 30S 147 8 E
Nysa .... 15 50 30N 17 22 E
Nysa → .... 14 52 4N 14 46 E
Nyssa 72 43 56N 117 2W
Nyurba .... 25 63 17N 118 28 E
Nzega .... 54 4 10S 33 12 E
N'Zérékoré 50 7 49N 8 48W
Nzeto .... 54 7 10S 12 52 E
Nzubuka .... 52 4 45S 32 50 E

O

Ō-Shima .... 36 34 44N 139 24 E
Oacoma 70 43 50N 99 26W
Oahe Dam 70 44 28N 100 25W
Oahe L. 70 45 30N 100 25W
Oahu 66 21 30N 158 0W
Oak Creek 72 40 15N 106 59W
Oak Harb. 72 48 20N 122 38W
Oak Hill 68 38 0N 81 7W
Oak Park 68 41 55N 87 45W
Oak Ridge 69 36 1N 84 12W
Oakbank .... 45 33 4S 140 33 E
Oakdale, Calif.,
U.S.A. 73 37 45N 120 55W
Oakdale, La., U.S.A. 71 30 50N 92 38W
Oakengates 6 52 42N 2 29W
Oakes 70 46 14N 98 4W
Oakesdale 72 47 11N 117 15W
Oakey .... 45 27 25S 151 43 E
Oakham 6 52 40N 0 43W
Oakland, Calif.,
U.S.A. 73 37 50N 122 18W
Oakland, Oreg.,
U.S.A. 72 43 23N 123 18W
Oakland City 68 38 20N 87 20W
Oakley, Idaho,
U.S.A. 72 42 14N 113 55W
Oakley, Kans.,
U.S.A. 70 39 8N 100 51W
Oakover → ..... 46 21 0S 120 40 E
Oakridge 72 43 47N 122 31W
Oamaru .... 43 45 5S 170 59 E
Oatman 73 35 1N 114 19W
Oaxaca 74 17 2N 96 40W
Oaxaca □ 74 17 0N 97 0W
Ob → .... 24 66 45N 69 30 E
Oba 62 49 4N 84 7W
Oban 8 56 25N 5 30W
Obbia .... 29 5 25N 48 30 E
Obed 64 53 30N 117 10W
Oberhausen ...... 14 51 28N 6 50 E
Oberlin, Kans.,
U.S.A. 70 39 52N 100 31W
Oberlin, La., U.S.A. 71 30 42N 92 42W
Oberon .... 45 33 45S 149 52 E
Obi, Kepulauan ... 35 1 23S 127 45 E
Óbidos 79 1 50S 55 30W
Obihiro .... 36 42 56N 143 12 E
Obilatu .... 35 1 25S 127 20 E
Obluchye .... 25 49 1N 131 4 E
Obo .... 54 5 20N 26 32 E
Observatory Inlet .. 64 55 10N 129 54W
Obshchi Syrt ..... 4 52 0N 53 0 E
Obskaya Guba ... 24 69 0N 73 0 E
Obuasi 53 6 17N 1 40W
Ocala 69 29 11N 82 5W
Ocampo 74 28 9N 108 24W
Ocaña 13 39 55N 3 30W
Oconomowoc 70 43 7N 88 30W
Ocate 71 36 12N 104 59W
Occidental,
Cordillera 78 5 0N 76 0W
Ocean, I. = Banaba 40 0 45S 169 50 E
Ocean City 68 39 18N 74 34W
Ocean Park 72 46 30N 124 2W
Oceanside 73 33 13N 117 26W
Ochil Hills 8 56 14N 3 40W
Ochre River 65 51 4N 99 47W
Ocilla 69 31 35N 83 15W
Ocmulgee → 69 31 58N 82 32W
Oconee → 69 31 58N 82 32W
Oconto 68 44 52N 87 53W
Oconto Falls 68 44 52N 88 10W
Ocotal 75 13 41N 86 31W
Ocotlán 74 20 21N 102 42W
Octave 73 34 10N 112 43W
Ocumare del Tuy .. 78 10 7N 66 46W
Oda 53 5 50N 0 51W
Ódáðahraun 20 65 5N 17 0W
Odate .... 36 40 16N 140 34 E
Odawara .... 36 35 20N 139 6 E
Odda .... 21 60 3N 6 35 E
Oddur .... 29 4 11N 43 52 E
Odei → 65 56 6N 96 54W
Ödemiş .... 30 38 15N 28 0 E
Odendaalsrus ..... 56 27 48S 26 45 E
Odense .... 21 55 22N 10 23 E
Oder → .... 14 53 33N 14 38 E
Odessa, Tex., U.S.A. 71 31 51N 102 23W
Odessa, Wash.,
U.S.A. 72 47 19N 118 35W
Odessa, U.S.S.R. .. 23 46 30N 30 45 E
Odiakwe .... 56 20 12S 25 17 E
Odienné 50 9 30N 7 34W
Odintsovo .... 22 55 39N 37 15 E
O'Donnell 71 33 0N 101 48W
Odorheiu Secuiesc 15 46 21N 25 21 E
Odra → .... 14 53 33N 14 38 E
Odžak .... 19 45 3N 18 18 E
Odzi .... 57 19 0S 32 20 E
Oeiras 79 7 0S 42 8W
Oelrichs 70 43 11N 103 14W
Oelwein 70 42 41N 91 55W
Oenpelli .... 46 12 20S 133 4 E
Ofanto → .... 18 41 22N 16 13 E
Offa .... 53 8 13N 4 42 E
Offaly □ 9 53 15N 7 30W
Offenbach .... 14 50 6N 8 46 E
Ofotfjorden ...... 20 68 27N 16 40 E
Oga-Hantō ...... 36 39 58N 139 47 E
Ogahalla 62 50 6N 85 51W
Ōgaki .... 36 35 21N 136 37 E
Ogallala 70 41 12N 101 40W
Ogbomosho ..... 53 8 1N 4 11 E
Ogden, Iowa, U.S.A. 70 42 3N 94 0W
Ogden, Utah, U.S.A. 72 41 13N 112 1W
Ogdensburg 68 44 40N 75 27W
Ogeechee → 69 31 51N 81 6W
Oglio → .... 18 45 2N 10 39 E
Ogmore .... 44 22 37S 149 35 E
Ogoja .... 53 6 38N 8 39 E
Ogoki → 62 51 38N 85 57W
Ogoki L. 62 50 50N 87 10W
Ogoki Res. 62 50 45N 88 15W
Ogooué → ...... 54 1 0S 9 0 E
Ogowe =
Ogooué → .... 54 1 0S 9 0 E
Oguta .... 53 5 44N 6 44 E
Ogwashi-Uku ..... 53 6 15N 6 30 E
Ohai .... 43 44 55S 168 0 E
Ohakune .... 43 39 24S 175 24 E
Ohanet .... 50 28 44N 8 46 E
Ohau, L. .... 43 44 15S 169 53 E
Ohey .... 11 50 26N 5 8 E
Ohio □ 68 40 20N 84 10W
Ohio → 68 38 0N 86 0W
Ohre → .... 14 50 30N 14 10 E
Ohridsko, Jezero .. 19 41 8N 20 52 E
Ohrigstad .... 57 24 39S 30 36 E
Oil City 68 41 26N 79 40W
Oise □ .... 12 49 28N 2 30 E
Ōita .... 36 33 14N 131 36 E
Ōita □ .... 36 33 15N 131 30 E
Oiticica 79 5 3S 41 5W
Ojai 73 34 28N 119 16W
Ojinaga 74 29 34N 104 25W
Ojos del Salado,
Cerro 80 27 0S 68 40W
Okaba .... 35 8 6S 139 42 E
Okahandja .... 56 22 0S 16 59 E
Okahukura .... 40 38 48S 175 14 E
Okanagan L. 64 50 0N 119 30W
Okandja .... 54 0 35S 13 45 E
Okanogan 72 48 6N 119 43W
Okanogan → 72 48 6N 119 43W
Okaputa .... 56 20 5S 17 0 E
Okara .... 32 30 50N 73 31 E
Okarito .... 43 43 15S 170 9 E
Okaukuejo .... 56 19 10S 16 0 E
Okavango Swamps 56 18 45S 22 45 E
Okaya .... 36 36 0N 138 10 E
Okayama .... 36 34 40N 133 54 E
Okayama □ ...... 36 35 0N 133 50 E
Okazaki .... 36 34 57N 137 10 E
Oke-Iho .... 53 8 1N 3 18 E
Okeechobee 69 27 16N 80 46W
Okeechobee, L. ... 69 27 0N 80 50W
Okefenokee Swamp 69 30 50N 82 15W
Okehampton 7 50 44N 4 1W
Okene .... 53 7 32N 6 11 E
Okha .... 25 53 40N 143 0 E
Okhotsk .... 25 59 20N 143 10 E
Okhotsk, Sea of ... 25 55 0N 145 0 E
Okhotskiy Perevoz 25 61 52N 135 35 E
Okhotsko
Kolymskoye .... 25 63 0N 157 0 E
Oki-Shotō .... 36 36 5N 133 15 E
Okiep .... 56 29 39S 17 53 E
Okigwi .... 53 5 52N 7 20 E
Okija .... 53 5 54N 6 55 E
Okitipupa .... 53 6 31N 4 50 E
Oklahoma □ 71 35 20N 97 30W
Oklahoma City 71 35 25N 97 30W
Okmulgee 71 35 38N 96 0W
Okolona 71 34 0N 88 45W
Okrika .... 53 4 40N 7 10 E
Oktabrsk .... 23 49 28N 57 25 E
Oktyabrskiy ...... 22 54 28N 53 28 E
Oktyabrskoy
Revolyutsii, Os. . 25 79 30N 97 0 E
Oktyabrskoye ..... 24 62 28N 66 3 E
Okuru .... 43 43 55S 168 55 E
Okushiri-Tō ...... 36 42 15N 139 30 E
Okuta .... 53 9 14N 3 12 E
Okwa → .... 56 22 30S 23 0 E
Ola 71 35 2N 93 10W
Ólafsfjörður 20 66 4N 18 39W
Ólafsvík 20 64 53N 23 43W
Olancha 73 36 15N 118 1W
Olanchito 75 15 30N 86 30W
Öland .... 21 56 45N 16 38 E
Olary .... 45 32 18S 140 19 E
Olathe 70 38 50N 94 50W
Olavarría 80 36 55S 60 20W
Ólbia .... 18 40 55N 9 30 E
Old Bahama Chan.
= Bahama, Canal
Viejo de 75 22 10N 77 30W
Old Castile =
Castilla La Vieja . 13 41 55N 4 0W
Old Castle 9 53 46N 7 10W
Old Cork .... 44 22 57S 141 52 E
Old Crow .... 60 67 30N 140 5 E
Old Fort → 65 58 36N 110 24W
Old Town 63 45 0N 68 41W
Old Wives L. 65 50 5N 106 0W
Oldbury 7 51 38N 2 30W
Oldenburg .... 14 53 10N 8 10 E
Oldenzaal .... 11 52 19N 6 53 E
Oldham 6 53 33N 2 8W
Oldman → 64 49 57N 111 42W
Olds 64 51 50N 114 10W
Olean 68 42 8N 78 25W
Olekma → ...... 25 60 22N 120 42 E
Olekminsk .... 25 60 25N 120 30 E
Olenegorsk ...... 22 68 9N 33 18 E
Olenek .... 25 68 28N 112 18 E
Olenek → .... 25 73 0N 120 10 E
Oléron, I. d' 12 45 55N 1 15W
Oleśnica .... 15 51 13N 17 22 E
Olga .... 25 43 50N 135 14 E
Olga, L. 62 49 47N 77 15W
Olga, Mt. .... 47 25 20S 130 50 E
Olifants → ...... 57 23 57S 31 58 E
Olifantshoek ...... 56 27 57S 22 42 E
Ólimbos, Óros .... 19 40 6N 22 23 E
Olinda 79 8 1S 34 51W
Oliveira 79 20 39S 44 50W
Olivenza 13 38 41N 7 9W
Oliver 64 49 13N 119 37W
Oliver L. 65 56 56N 103 22W
Ollagüe 78 21 15S 68 10W
Olney, Ill., U.S.A. .. 68 38 40N 88 0W
Olney, Tex., U.S.A. 71 33 25N 98 45W
Olomane → 63 50 14N 60 37W
Olomouc .... 14 49 38N 17 12 E
Olonets .... 22 61 10N 33 0 E
Olongapo .... 35 14 50N 120 18 E
Olovo .... 19 44 0N 19 0 E
Olovyannaya ..... 25 50 58N 115 35 E
Oloy → .... 25 66 29N 159 29 E
Olsztyn .... 15 53 48N 20 29 E
Olt → .... 15 43 43N 24 51 E
Olteniţa .... 15 44 7N 26 42 E
Olton 71 34 16N 102 7W
Oltu .... 30 40 35N 41 58 E
Olympia, Greece .. 19 37 39N 21 39 E
Olympia, U.S.A. ... 72 47 0N 122 58W
Olympic Mts. 72 47 50N 123 45W
Olympic Nat. Park . 72 47 48N 123 30W
Olympus, Mt. =
Ólimbos, Óros .. 19 40 6N 22 23 E
Olympus, Mt. 72 47 52N 123 40W
Om → .... 24 54 59N 73 22 E
Ōmachi .... 36 36 30N 137 50 E
Omagh 9 54 36N 7 20W
Omagh □ 9 54 35N 7 15W
Omaha 70 41 15N 96 0W
Omak 72 48 24N 119 31W
Oman ■ .... 29 23 0N 58 0 E
Oman, G. of ...... 31 24 30N 58 30 E
Omaruru .... 56 21 26S 16 0 E
Omaruru → ..... 56 22 7S 14 15 E
Omate 78 16 45S 71 0W
Ombai, Selat ..... 35 8 30S 124 50 E
Omboué .... 54 1 35S 9 15 E
Ombrone → ..... 18 42 39N 11 0 E
Omdurmân .... 51 15 40N 32 28 E
Ometepe, I. de 75 11 32N 85 35W
Ometepec 74 16 39N 98 23W
Omez .... 28 32 22N 35 0 E
Omineca → 64 56 3N 124 16W
Omitara .... 56 22 16S 18 2 E
Ōmiya .... 36 35 54N 139 38 E
Ommen .... 11 52 31N 6 26 E
Omo → .... 51 6 25N 36 10 E
Omolon → ...... 25 68 42N 158 36 E
Omono-Gawa → . 36 39 46N 140 3 E
Omsk .... 24 55 0N 73 12 E
Omsukchan ...... 25 62 32N 155 48 E
Omul, Vf. .... 15 45 27N 25 29 E
Ōmura .... 36 32 56N 130 0 E
Omuramba
Omatako → ... 55 17 45S 20 25 E
Ōmuta .... 36 33 0N 130 26 E
Onaga 70 39 32N 96 12W
Onalaska 70 43 53N 91 14W
Onamia 70 46 4N 93 38W
Onancock 68 37 42N 75 49W
Onang .... 35 3 2S 118 49 E
Onaping L. 62 47 3N 81 30W
Onarhā .... 31 35 30N 71 0 E
Onavas 74 28 28N 109 30W
Onawa 70 42 2N 96 2W
Onaway 68 45 21N 84 11W
Oncócua .... 56 16 30S 13 25 E
Onda 13 39 55N 0 17W
Ondangua .... 56 17 57S 16 4 E
Ondjiva .... 56 16 48S 15 50 E
Ondo .... 53 7 4N 4 47 E
Ondo □ .... 53 7 0N 5 0 E
Öndörhaan .... 37 47 19N 110 39 E
Öndverðarnes 20 64 52N 24 0W
Onega .... 22 64 0N 38 10 E
Onega → .... 22 63 58N 37 55 E
Onega, G. of =
Onezhskaya Guba 22 64 30N 37 0 E
Onega, L. =
Onezhskoye
Ozero .... 22 62 0N 35 30 E
Onehunga .... 43 36 55S 174 48 E
Oneida 68 43 5N 75 40W
Oneida L. 68 43 12N 76 0W
O'Neill 70 42 30N 98 38W
Onekotan, Ostrov . 25 49 25N 154 45 E
Oneonta, Ala.,
U.S.A. 69 33 58N 86 29W
Oneonta, N.Y.,
U.S.A. 68 42 26N 75 5W
Onezhskaya Guba . 22 64 30N 37 0 E
Onezhskoye Ozero 22 62 0N 35 30 E
Ongarue .... 43 38 42S 175 19 E
Ongerup .... 47 33 58S 118 28 E
Ongniud Qi ...... 38 43 0N 118 38 E
Ongole .... 32 15 33N 80 2 E
Onguren .... 25 53 38N 107 36 E
Onida 70 44 42N 100 5W
Onilahy → ...... 57 23 34S 43 45 E
Onitsha .... 53 6 6N 6 42 E
Onoda .... 36 34 2N 131 25 E
Onslow .... 46 21 40S 115 12 E
Onslow B. 69 34 20N 77 20W
Onstwedde .... 11 53 2N 7 4 E
Ontake-San ...... 36 35 53N 137 29 E
Ontario, Calif.,
U.S.A. 73 34 2N 117 40W
Ontario, Oreg.,
U.S.A. 72 44 1N 117 1W
Ontario □ 62 52 0N 88 10W
Ontario, L. 62 43 40N 78 0W
Ontonagon 70 46 52N 89 19W
Oodnadatta ...... 45 27 33S 135 30 E
Ooldea .... 47 30 27S 131 50 E
Oombulgurri ..... 46 15 15S 127 45 E
Oona River 64 53 57N 130 16W
Oorindi .... 44 20 40S 141 1 E
Oost-Vlaanderen □ 11 51 5N 3 50 E
Oostende .... 11 51 15N 2 54 E
Oosterhout .... 11 51 39N 4 47 E
Oosterschelde .... 11 51 33N 4 0 E
Ootacamund ...... 32 11 30N 76 44 E
Ootsa L. 64 53 50N 126 2W
Opala, U.S.S.R. ... 25 51 58N 156 30 E
Opala, Zaïre ..... 54 0 40S 24 20 E
Opanake .... 32 6 35N 80 40 E
Opasatika 62 49 30N 82 50W
Opasquia 65 53 16N 93 34W
Opava .... 15 49 57N 17 58 E
Opelousas 71 30 35N 92 7W
Opémisca, L. 62 49 56N 74 52W
Opheim 72 48 52N 106 30W
Ophir 60 63 10N 156 40W
Ophthalmia Ra. ... 46 23 15S 119 30 E
Opi .... 53 6 36N 7 28 E
Opinaca → 62 52 15N 78 2W
Opinaca L. 62 52 39N 76 20W
Opiskotish, L. 63 53 10N 67 50W
Opobo .... 53 4 35N 7 34 E
Opole .... 15 50 42N 17 58 E
Oporto = Porto ... 13 41 8N 8 40W

Panama Canal

Opotiki **43** 38 1S 177 19 E
Opp **69** 31 19N 86 13W
Oppland fylke □ **21** 61 15N 9 40 E
Opua **43** 35 19S 174 9 E
Opunake **43** 39 26S 173 52 E
Or Yehuda **28** 32 2N 34 50 E
Ora **28** 30 55N 35 1 E
Ora Banda **47** 30 20S 121 0 E
Oracle **73** 32 36N 110 46W
Oradea **17** 47 2N 21 58 E
Öræfajökull **20** 64 2N 16 39W
Orai **32** 25 58N 79 30 E
Oran, Algeria **50** 35 45N 0 39W
Oran, Argentina **80** 23 10S 64 20W
Orange, Australia **45** 33 15S 149 7 E
Orange, France **12** 44 8N 4 47 E
Orange, Tex., U.S.A. **71** 30 10N 93 50W
Orange, Va., U.S.A. **68** 38 17N 78 5W
Orange → =
Oranje → **56** 28 41S 16 28 E
Orange, C. **79** 4 20N 51 30W
Orange Free State □ **56** 28 30S 27 0 E
Orange Grove **71** 27 57N 97 57W
Orange Walk **74** 18 6N 88 33W
Orangeburg **69** 33 35N 80 53W
Orangeville **62** 43 55N 80 5W
Oranienburg **14** 52 45N 13 15 E
Oranje → **56** 28 41S 16 28 E
Oranje Vrystaat □ =
Orange Free
State □ **56** 28 30S 27 0 E
Oranjemund **56** 28 38S 16 29 E
Oranjerivier **56** 29 40S 24 12 E
Or'Aquiva **28** 32 30N 34 54 E
Oras **35** 12 9N 125 28 E
Oraşul Stalin =
Braşov **15** 45 38N 25 35 E
Orbetello **18** 42 26N 11 11 E
Orbost **45** 37 40S 148 29 E
Orchila, I. **78** 11 48N 66 10W
Ord → **46** 15 33S 138 15 E
Ord, Mt. **46** 17 20S 125 34 E
Orderville **73** 37 18N 112 43W
Ordos = Mu Us
Shamo **38** 39 0N 109 0 E
Ordu **30** 40 55N 37 53 E
Ordway **70** 38 15N 103 42W
Ordzhonikidze **23** 43 0N 44 35 E
Ore Mts. =
Erzgebirge **14** 50 25N 13 0 E
Örebro **21** 59 20N 15 18 E
Örebro län □ **21** 59 27N 15 0 E
Oregon **70** 42 1N 89 20W
Oregon □ **72** 44 0N 121 0W
Oregon City **72** 45 21N 122 35W
Orekhovo-Zuyevo **22** 55 50N 38 55 E
Orel **22** 52 57N 36 3 E
Orem **72** 40 20N 111 45W
Orenburg **22** 51 45N 55 6 E
Orense **13** 42 19N 7 55W
Orepuki **43** 46 19S 167 46 E
Orford Ness **7** 52 6N 1 31 E
Orgūn **31** 32 55N 69 12 E
Orhon Gol → **37** 49 30N 106 0 E
Orient **45** 28 7S 142 50 E
Oriental, Cordillera **78** 6 0N 73 0W
Orihuela **13** 38 7N 0 55W
Orinoco → **78** 9 15N 61 30W
Orissa □ **33** 20 0N 84 0 E
Oristano **18** 39 54N 8 35 E
Oristano, G. di **18** 39 50N 8 22 E
Orizaba **74** 18 50N 97 10W
Orkanger **20** 63 18N 9 52 E
Orkla → **20** 63 18N 9 51 E
Orkney **56** 26 58S 26 40 E
Orkney □ **8** 59 0N 3 0W
Orkney Is. **8** 59 0N 3 0W
Orland **72** 39 46N 122 12W
Orlando **69** 28 30N 81 25W
Orléanais **12** 48 0N 2 0 E
Orléans **12** 47 54N 1 52 E
Orléans, I. d' **63** 46 54N 70 58W
Orlik **25** 52 30N 99 55 E
Ormara **31** 25 16N 64 33 E
Ormoc **35** 11 0N 124 37 E
Ormond **43** 38 33S 177 56 E
Ormond Beach **69** 29 13N 81 5W
Orne □ **12** 48 40N 0 5 E
Örnsköldsvik **20** 63 17N 18 40 E
Oro → **74** 25 35N 105 2W
Orocué **78** 4 48N 71 20W
Orodo **53** 5 34N 7 4 E
Orogrande **73** 32 20N 106 4W
Oromocto **63** 45 54N 66 29W
Oron **53** 4 48N 8 14 E
Oroqen Zizhiqi **38** 50 34N 123 43 E
Oroquieta **35** 8 32N 123 44 E
Orós **79** 6 15S 38 55W
Orotukan **25** 62 16N 151 42 E
Oroville, Calif.,
U.S.A. **72** 39 31N 121 30W
Oroville, Wash.,
U.S.A. **72** 48 58N 119 30W
Orroroo **45** 32 43S 138 38 E
Orsha **22** 54 30N 30 25 E
Orsk **22** 51 12N 58 34 E
Orşova **15** 44 41N 22 25 E
Ortegal, C. **13** 43 43N 7 52W
Orthez **12** 43 29N 0 48W
Ortigueira **13** 43 40N 7 50W
Ortles **18** 46 31N 10 33 E
Ortón → **78** 10 50S 67 0W
Ortona **18** 42 21N 14 24 E
Orūmīyeh **30** 37 40N 45 0 E
Orūmīyeh,
Daryācheh-ye **30** 37 50N 45 30 E
Oruro **78** 18 0S 67 9W
Oruzgān □ **31** 33 30N 66 0 E
Orvieto **18** 42 43N 12 8 E
Orwell → **7** 52 2N 1 12 E
Oryakhovo **19** 43 40N 23 57 E
Osa **22** 57 17N 55 26 E
Osa, Pen. de **75** 8 0N 84 0W
Osage, Iowa, U.S.A. **70** 43 15N 92 50W
Osage, Wyo., U.S.A. **70** 43 59N 104 25W
Osage → **70** 38 35N 91 57W
Osage City **70** 38 43N 95 51W
Ōsaka **36** 34 40N 135 30 E
Ōsaka □ **36** 34 30N 135 30 E
Osawatomie **70** 38 30N 94 55W
Osborne **70** 39 30N 98 45W
Osceola, Ark., U.S.A. **71** 35 40N 90 0W
Osceola, Iowa,
U.S.A. **70** 41 0N 93 20W
Oscoda **68** 44 26N 83 20W
Ösel = Saaremaa **22** 58 30N 22 30 E
Osh **24** 40 37N 72 49 E
Oshawa **62** 43 50N 78 50W
Oshkosh, Nebr.,
U.S.A. **70** 41 27N 102 20W
Oshkosh, Wis.,
U.S.A. **70** 44 3N 88 35W
Oshogbo **53** 7 48N 4 37 E
Oshwe **54** 3 25S 19 28 E
Osijek **19** 45 34N 18 41 E
Osipenko =
Berdyansk **23** 46 45N 36 50 E
Osizweni **57** 27 49S 30 7 E
Oskaloosa **70** 41 18N 92 40W
Oskarshamn **21** 57 15N 16 27 E
Oskélanéo **62** 48 5N 75 15W
Oslo **21** 59 55N 10 45 E
Oslob **35** 9 31N 123 26 E
Oslofjorden **21** 59 20N 10 35 E
Osmanabad **32** 18 5N 76 10 E
Osmaniye **30** 37 5N 36 10 E
Osnabrück **14** 52 16N 8 2 E
Osorio **80** 29 53S 50 17W
Osorno **80** 40 25S 73 0W
Osoyoos **64** 49 0N 119 30W
Ospika → **64** 56 20N 124 0W
Osprey Reef **44** 13 52S 146 36 E
Oss **11** 51 46N 5 32 E
Ossa, Mt. **44** 41 52S 146 3 E
Óssa, Oros **19** 39 47N 22 42 E
Ossabaw I. **69** 31 45N 81 8W
Ossining **68** 41 9N 73 50W
Ossokmanuan L. **63** 53 25N 65 0W
Ossora **25** 59 20N 163 13 E
Ostend = Oostende **11** 51 15N 2 54 E
Österdalälven → **21** 61 30N 13 45 E
Östergötlands län □ **21** 58 35N 15 45 E
Östersund **20** 63 10N 14 38 E
Østfold fylke □ **21** 59 25N 11 25 E
Ostfriesische Inseln **14** 53 45N 7 15 E
Ostrava **15** 49 51N 18 18 E
Ostróda **15** 53 42N 19 58 E
Ostrołęka **15** 53 4N 21 32 E
Ostrów Mazowiecka **15** 52 50N 21 51 E
Ostrów Wielkopolski **15** 51 36N 17 44 E
Ostrowiec-
Świętokrzyski **15** 50 55N 21 22 E
Ōsumi-Kaikyō **36** 30 55N 131 0 E
Osuna **13** 37 14N 5 8W
Oswego **68** 43 29N 76 30W
Oswestry **6** 52 52N 3 3W
Otago □ **43** 44 44S 169 10 E
Otago Harb. **43** 45 47S 170 42 E
Ōtake **36** 34 12N 132 13 E
Otaki **43** 40 45S 175 10 E
Otaru **36** 43 10N 141 0 E
Otaru-Wan =
Ishikari-Wan **36** 43 25N 141 1 E
Otavalo **78** 0 13N 78 20W
Otavi **56** 19 40S 17 24 E
Otchinjau **56** 16 30S 13 56 E
Othello **72** 46 53N 119 8W
Otira Gorge **43** 42 53S 171 33 E
Otis **70** 40 12N 102 58W
Otjiwarongo **56** 20 30S 16 33 E
Otoineppu **36** 44 44N 142 16 E
Otorohanga **43** 38 12S 175 14 E
Otoskwin → **62** 52 13N 88 6W
Otosquen **65** 53 17N 102 1W
Otranto **19** 40 9N 18 28 E
Otranto, C. d' **19** 40 7N 18 30 E
Otranto, Str. of **19** 40 15N 18 40 E
Otse **56** 25 2S 25 45 E
Ōtsu **36** 35 0N 135 50 E
Ottawa, Canada **62** 45 27N 75 42W
Ottawa, Ill., U.S.A. **70** 41 20N 88 55W
Ottawa, Kans.,
U.S.A. **70** 38 40N 95 6W
Ottawa → =
Outaouais → **62** 45 27N 74 8W
Ottawa Is. **61** 59 35N 80 10W
Otter L. **65** 55 35N 104 39W
Otter Rapids, Ont.,
Canada **62** 50 11N 81 39W
Otter Rapids, Sask.,
Canada **65** 55 38N 104 44W
Ottosdal **56** 26 46S 25 59 E
Ottoshoop **56** 25 45S 25 58 E
Ottumwa **70** 41 0N 92 25W
Otukpa **53** 7 9N 7 41 E
Oturkpo **53** 7 16N 8 8 E
Otway, B. **80** 53 30S 74 0W
Otway, C. **45** 38 52S 143 30 E
Otwock **15** 52 5N 21 20 E
Ou-Sammyaku **36** 39 20N 140 35 E
Ouachita → **71** 31 38N 91 49W
Ouachita, L. **71** 34 40N 93 25W
Ouachita Mts. **71** 34 50N 94 30W
Ouadâne **50** 20 50N 11 40W
Ouadda **51** 8 15N 22 20 E
Ouagadougou **53** 12 25N 1 30W
Ouahran = Oran **50** 35 45N 0 39W
Ouallene **50** 24 41N 1 11 E
Ouanda Djallé **51** 8 55N 22 53 E
Ouango **54** 4 19N 22 30 E
Ouargla **50** 31 59N 5 16 E
Ouarzazate **50** 30 55N 6 50W
Oubangi → **54** 0 30S 17 50 E
Ouddorp **11** 51 50N 3 57 E
Oude Rijn → **11** 52 12N 4 24 E
Oudenaarde **11** 50 50N 3 37 E
Oudtshoorn **56** 33 35S 22 14 E
Ouessant, I. d' **12** 48 28N 5 6W
Ouesso **54** 1 37N 16 5 E
Ouest, Pte. **63** 49 52N 64 40W
Ouezzane **50** 34 51N 5 35W
Ouidah **53** 6 25N 2 0 E
Oujda **50** 34 41N 1 55W
Oujeft **50** 20 2N 13 0W
Ouled Djellal **50** 34 28N 5 2 E
Oulu **20** 65 1N 25 29 E
Oulu □ **20** 65 10N 27 20 E
Oulujärvi **20** 64 25N 27 15 E
Oulujoki → **20** 65 1N 25 30 E
Oum Chalouba **51** 15 48N 20 46 E
Ounguati **56** 22 0S 15 46 E
Ounianga-Kébir **51** 19 4N 20 29 E
Ounianga Sérir **51** 18 54N 20 51 E
Our → **11** 49 55N 6 5 E
Ouray **73** 38 3N 107 40W
Ouricuri **79** 7 53S 40 5W
Ouro Prêto **79** 20 20S 43 30W
Ourthe → **11** 50 29N 5 35 E
Ouse **44** 42 38S 146 42 E
Ouse →,
E. Sussex, U.K. **7** 50 43N 0 3 E
Ouse →, N. Yorks.,
U.K. **6** 54 3N 0 7 E
Outaouais → **62** 45 27N 74 8W
Outardes → **63** 49 24N 69 30W
Outer Hebrides **8** 57 30N 7 40W
Outer I. **63** 51 10N 58 35W
Outjo **56** 20 5S 16 7 E
Outlook, Canada **65** 51 30N 107 0W
Outlook, U.S.A. **70** 48 53N 104 46W
Ouyen **45** 35 1S 142 22 E
Ovalau **43** 17 40S 178 48 E
Ovalle **80** 30 33S 71 18W
Ovar **13** 40 51N 8 40W
Overflakkee **11** 51 44N 4 10 E
Overijssel □ **11** 52 25N 6 35 E
Overpelt **11** 51 12N 5 20 E
Overton **73** 36 32N 114 31W
Övertorneå **20** 66 23N 23 38 E
Ovid **70** 41 0N 102 17W
Oviedo **13** 43 25N 5 50W
Owaka **43** 46 27S 169 40 E
Owase **36** 34 7N 136 12 E
Owatonna **70** 44 3N 93 10W
Owbeh **31** 34 28N 63 10 E
Owego **68** 42 6N 76 17W
Owen Falls **52** 0 30N 33 5 E
Owen Sound **62** 44 35N 80 55W
Owendo **54** 0 17N 9 30 E
Owens L. **73** 36 20N 118 0W
Owensboro **68** 37 40N 87 5W
Owensville **70** 38 20N 91 30W
Owerri **53** 5 29N 7 0 E
Owl → **65** 57 51N 92 44W
Owo **53** 7 10N 5 39 E
Owosso **68** 43 0N 84 10W
Owyhee **72** 42 0N 116 3W
Owyhee → **72** 43 46N 117 2W
Owyhee, L. **72** 43 40N 117 16W
Ox Mts. **9** 54 6N 9 0W
Oxelösund **21** 58 43N 17 15 E
Oxford, N.Z. **43** 43 18S 172 11 E
Oxford, U.K. **7** 51 45N 1 15W
Oxford, Miss., U.S.A. **71** 34 22N 89 30W
Oxford, N.C., U.S.A. **69** 36 19N 78 36W
Oxford, Ohio, U.S.A. **68** 39 30N 84 40W
Oxford □ **7** 51 45N 1 15W
Oxford L. **65** 54 51N 95 37W
Oxley **45** 34 11S 144 6 E
Oxnard **73** 34 10N 119 14W
Oya **34** 2 55N 111 55 E
Oyama **36** 36 18N 139 48 E
Oyem **54** 1 34N 11 31 E
Oyen **65** 51 22N 110 28W
Oykel → **8** 57 55N 4 26W
Oymyakon **25** 63 25N 142 44 E
Oyo **53** 7 46N 3 56 E
Oyo □ **53** 8 0N 3 30 E
Ozamis **35** 8 15N 123 50 E
Ozark, Ala., U.S.A. **69** 31 29N 85 39W
Ozark, Ark., U.S.A. **71** 35 30N 93 50W
Ozark, Mo., U.S.A. **71** 37 0N 93 15W
Ozark Plateau **71** 37 20N 91 40W
Ozarks, L. of the **70** 38 10N 92 40W
Ozona **71** 30 43N 101 11W
Ozuluama **74** 21 40N 97 50W

P

P.K. le Roux Dam **56** 30 4S 24 40 E
Pa-an **33** 16 51N 97 40 E
Paarl **56** 33 45S 18 56 E
Paatsi → **20** 68 55N 29 0 E
Paauilo **66** 20 3N 155 22W
Pab Hills **32** 26 30N 66 45 E
Pabna **33** 24 1N 89 18 E
Pacaja → **79** 1 56S 50 50W
Pacaraima, Sierra **78** 4 0N 62 30W
Pacasmayo **78** 7 20S 79 35W
Pachpadra **32** 25 58N 72 10 E
Pachuca **74** 20 10N 98 40W
Pacific **64** 54 48N 128 28W
Pacific-Antarctic
Basin **41** 46 0S 95 0W
Pacific-Antarctic
Ridge **41** 43 0S 115 0W
Pacific Grove **73** 36 38N 121 58W
Pacific Ocean **2** 10 0N 140 0W
Pacitan **35** 8 12S 111 7 E
Padaido, Kepulauan **35** 1 5S 138 0 E
Padang **34** 1 0S 100 20 E
Padangpanjang **34** 0 40S 100 20 E
Padangsidempuan **34** 1 30N 99 15 E
Paddockwood **65** 53 30N 105 30W
Paderborn **14** 51 42N 8 44 E
Padloping Island **61** 67 0N 62 50W
Pádova **18** 45 24N 11 52 E
Padre I. **71** 27 0N 97 20W
Padstow **6** 50 33N 4 57W
Padua = Pádova **18** 45 24N 11 52 E
Paducah, Ky., U.S.A. **68** 37 0N 88 40W
Paducah, Tex.,
U.S.A. **71** 34 3N 100 16W
Paeroa **43** 37 23S 175 41 E
Pag **18** 44 30N 14 50 E
Pagadian **35** 7 55N 123 30 E
Pagai Selatan **34** 3 0S 100 15W
Pagai Utara **34** 2 35S 100 0 E
Pagalu = Annobón **48** 1 25S 5 36 E
Pagastikós Kólpos **19** 39 15N 23 0 E
Pagatan **34** 3 33S 115 59 E
Page, Ariz., U.S.A. **73** 36 57N 111 27W
Page, N. Dak.,
U.S.A. **70** 47 11N 97 37W
Pago Pago **43** 14 16S 170 43W
Pagosa Springs **73** 37 16N 107 4W
Pagwa River **62** 50 2N 85 14W
Pahala **66** 19 12N 155 25W
Pahiatua **43** 40 27S 175 50 E
Pahokee **69** 26 50N 80 40W
Pahrump **73** 36 15N 116 0W
Paia **66** 20 54N 156 22W
Paignton **7** 50 26N 3 33W
Päijänne, L. **21** 61 30N 25 30 E
Painan **34** 1 21S 100 34 E
Painesville **68** 41 42N 81 18W
Paint Hills =
Nouveau Comptoir **62** 53 0N 78 49W
Paint L. **65** 55 28N 97 57W
Paint Rock **71** 31 30N 99 56W
Painted Desert **73** 36 0N 111 30W
Paintsville **68** 37 50N 82 50W
Pais Vasco □ **13** 43 0N 2 30W
Paisley, U.K. **8** 55 51N 4 27W
Paisley, U.S.A. **72** 42 43N 120 40W
Paita **78** 5 11S 81 9W
Pakaraima Mts. **78** 6 0N 60 0W
Pakistan ■ **31** 30 0N 70 0 E
Pakistan, East =
Bangladesh ■ **33** 24 0N 90 0 E
Pakokku **33** 21 20N 95 0 E
Pakse **34** 15 5N 105 52 E
Paktīā □ **31** 33 0N 69 15 E
Pala **51** 9 25N 15 5 E
Palacios **71** 28 44N 96 12W
Palagruža **18** 42 24N 16 15 E
Palam **32** 19 0N 77 0 E
Palamós **13** 41 50N 3 10 E
Palampur **32** 32 10N 76 30 E
Palana, Australia **44** 39 45S 147 55 E
Palana, U.S.S.R. **25** 59 10N 159 59 E
Palanan **35** 17 8N 122 29 E
Palanan Pt. **35** 17 17N 122 30 E
Palangkaraya **34** 2 16S 113 56 E
Palani Hills **32** 10 14N 77 33 E
Palanpur **32** 24 10N 72 25 E
Palapye **56** 22 30S 27 7 E
Palatka, U.S.A. **69** 29 40N 81 40W
Palatka, U.S.S.R. **25** 60 6N 150 54 E
Palawan **34** 9 30N 118 30 E
Palayankottai **32** 8 45N 77 45 E
Paleleh **35** 1 10N 121 50 E
Palembang **34** 3 0S 104 50 E
Palencia **13** 42 1N 4 34W
Palermo, Italy **18** 38 8N 13 20 E
Palermo, U.S.A. **72** 39 30N 121 37W
Palestine, Asia **28** 32 0N 35 0 E
Palestine, U.S.A. **71** 31 42N 95 35W
Paletwa **33** 21 10N 92 50 E
Palghat **32** 10 46N 76 42 E
Palgrave, Mt. **46** 23 22S 115 58 E
Pali **32** 25 50N 73 20 E
Palisade **70** 40 21N 101 10W
Palitana **32** 21 32N 71 49 E
Palizada **74** 18 18N 92 8W
Palk Bay **32** 9 30N 79 15 E
Palk Strait **32** 10 0N 79 45 E
Palla Road =
Dinokwe **56** 23 29S 26 37 E
Pallinup **47** 34 0S 117 55 E
Palm Beach **69** 26 46N 80 0W
Palm Is. **44** 18 40S 146 35 E
Palm Springs **73** 33 51N 116 35W
Palma **54** 10 46S 40 29 E
Palma → **79** 12 33S 47 52W
Palma, B. de **13** 39 30N 2 39 E
Palma, La,
Canary Is. **50** 28 40N 17 50W
Palma, La, Panama **75** 8 15N 78 0W
Palma, La, Spain **13** 37 21N 6 38W
Palma de Mallorca **13** 39 35N 2 39 E
Palma Soriano **75** 20 15N 76 0W
Palmaḥim **28** 31 56N 34 44 E
Palmares **79** 8 41S 35 28W
Palmas, C. **50** 4 27N 7 46W
Pálmas, G. di **18** 39 0N 8 30 E
Palmdale **73** 34 36N 118 7W
Palmeira dos Índios **79** 9 25S 36 37W
Palmeirinhas, Pta.
das **54** 9 2S 12 57 E
Palmer **60** 61 35N 149 10W
Palmer → **44** 15 34S 142 26 E
Palmer Lake **70** 39 10N 104 52W
Palmerston North **43** 40 21S 175 39 E
Palmetto **69** 27 33N 82 33W
Palmi **18** 38 21N 15 51 E
Palmira **78** 3 32N 76 16W
Palmyra = Tudmur **30** 34 36N 38 15 E
Palmyra **70** 39 45N 91 30W
Palmyra Is. **41** 5 52N 162 5W
Palo Alto **73** 37 25N 122 8W
Palopo **35** 3 0S 120 16 E
Palos, C. de **13** 37 38N 0 40W
Palouse **72** 46 59N 117 5W
Palparara **44** 24 47S 141 28 E
Palu, Indonesia **35** 1 0S 119 52 E
Palu, Turkey **30** 38 45N 40 0 E
Paluan **35** 13 26N 120 29 E
Pama **53** 11 19N 0 44 E
Pamanukan **35** 6 16S 107 49 E
Pamekasan **35** 7 10S 113 28 E
Pamirs **24** 37 40N 73 0 E
Pamlico → **69** 35 25N 76 30W
Pamlico Sd. **69** 35 20N 76 0W
Pampa **71** 35 35N 100 58W
Pampa de las
Salinas **80** 32 1S 66 58W
Pampanua **35** 4 16S 120 8 E
Pampas, Argentina **80** 35 0S 63 0W
Pampas, Peru **78** 12 20S 74 50W
Pamplona, Colombia **78** 7 23N 72 39W
Pamplona, Spain **13** 42 48N 1 38W
Pampoenpoort **56** 31 3S 22 40 E
Pana **70** 39 25N 89 10W
Panaca **73** 37 51N 114 23W
Panaitan **35** 6 36S 105 12 E
Panaji **32** 15 25N 73 50 E
Panamá **75** 9 0N 79 25W
Panama ■ **75** 8 48N 79 55W
Panamá, G. de **75** 8 4N 79 20W
Panama Canal **75** 9 10N 79 37W

Panama City

Panama City 69 30 10N 85 41W
Panamint Ra. 73 36 30N 117 20W
Panão 78 9 55S 75 55W
Panarukan 35 7 42S 113 56 E
Panay 35 11 10N 122 30 E
Panay, G. 35 11 0N 122 30 E
Pancake Ra. 73 38 30N 116 0W
Pančevo 19 44 52N 20 41 E
Pancorbo, Paso 13 42 32N 3 5W
Pandan 35 11 45N 122 10 E
Pandegelang 35 6 25S 106 0 E
Pandharpur 32 17 41N 75 20 E
Pando 80 34 44S 56 0W
Pando, L. = Hope, L. 45 28 24S 139 18 E
Panevezys 22 55 42N 24 25 E
Panfilov 24 44 10N 80 0 E
Pang-Long 33 23 11N 98 45 E
Pang-Yang 33 22 7N 98 48 E
Pangalanes, Canal des 57 22 48S 47 50 E
Pangani 54 5 25S 38 58 E
Pangfou = Bengbu 39 32 58N 117 20 E
Pangkah, Tanjung 35 6 51S 112 33 E
Pangkajene 35 4 46S 119 34 E
Pangkalanbrandan 34 4 1N 98 20 E
Pangkalanbuun 34 2 41S 111 37 E
Pangkalansusu 34 4 2N 98 13 E
Pangkalpinang 34 2 0S 106 0 E
Pangkoh 34 3 5S 114 8 E
Pangnirtung 61 66 8N 65 54W
Pangrango 35 6 46S 107 1 E
Panguitch 73 37 52N 112 30W
Pangutaran Group 35 6 18N 120 34 E
Panhandle 71 35 23N 101 23W
Panjgur 31 27 0N 64 5 E
Panjim = Panaji 32 15 25N 73 50 E
Panjinad Barrage 31 29 22N 71 15 E
Panna 32 24 40N 80 15 E
Panorama 80 21 21S 51 51W
Panshan 38 41 3N 122 2 E
Panshi 38 42 58N 126 5 E
Pantar 35 8 28S 124 10 E
Pantelleria 18 36 52N 12 0 E
Pánuco 74 22 0N 98 15W
Panyam 53 9 27N 9 8 E
Panyu 39 22 51N 113 20 E
Paola 70 38 36N 94 50W
Paonia 73 38 56N 107 37W
Paoting = Baoding 38 38 50N 115 28 E
Paot'ou = Baotou 38 40 32N 110 2 E
Paoua 51 7 9N 16 20 E
Pápa 15 47 22N 17 30 E
Papagayo → 74 16 36N 99 43W
Papagayo, G. de 75 10 30N 85 50W
Papakura 43 37 4S 174 59 E
Papantla 74 20 30N 97 30W
Papar 34 5 45N 116 0 E
Paparoa 43 36 6S 174 16 E
Papigochic → 74 29 9N 109 40W
Paposo 80 25 0S 70 30W
Papua New Guinea ■ 40 8 0S 145 0 E
Papudo 80 32 29S 71 27W
Papun 33 18 0N 97 30 E
Pará = Belém 79 1 20S 48 30W
Pará □ 79 3 20S 52 0W
Paraburdoo 46 23 14S 117 32 E
Paracatu 79 17 10S 46 50W
Parachilna 45 31 10S 138 21 E
Parachinar 32 33 55N 70 5 E
Paradip 33 20 15N 86 35 E
Paradise 72 47 27N 114 17W
Paradise → 63 53 27N 57 19W
Paradise Valley 72 41 30N 117 28W
Parado 35 8 42S 118 30 E
Paragould 71 36 5N 90 30W
Paragua → 78 6 55N 62 55W
Paragua, La 78 6 50N 63 20W
Paraguaçu → 79 12 45S 38 54W
Paraguaná, Pen. de 78 12 0N 70 0W
Paraguarí 80 25 36S 57 0W
Paraguay ■ 80 23 0S 57 0W
Paraguay → 80 27 18S 58 38W
Paraíba = João Pessoa 79 7 10S 34 52W
Paraíba □ 79 7 0S 36 0W
Paraíba do Sul → 79 21 37S 41 3W
Parainen 21 60 18N 22 18 E
Parakou 53 9 25N 2 40 E
Paramaribo 79 5 50N 55 10W
Paramushir, Ostrov 25 50 24N 156 0 E
Paran → 28 30 20N 35 10 E
Paraná, Argentina 80 31 45S 60 30W
Paranã, Brazil 79 12 30S 47 48W
Paraná □ 80 24 30S 51 0W
Paraná → 80 33 43S 59 15W
Paranaguá 80 25 30S 48 30W
Paranaíba → 79 20 6S 51 4W
Paranapanema → 80 22 40S 53 9W
Paranapiacaba, Serra do 80 24 31S 48 35W
Parang, Jolo, Phil. 35 5 55N 120 54 E
Parang, Mindanao, Phil. 35 7 23N 124 16 E
Paratinga 79 12 40S 43 10W
Paratoo 45 32 42S 139 40 E
Parattah 44 42 22S 147 23 E
Parbhani 32 19 8N 76 52 E
Parchim 14 53 25N 11 50 E
Pardes Hanna 28 32 28N 34 57 E
Pardo →, Bahia, Brazil 79 15 40S 39 0W
Pardo →, Mato Grosso, Brazil 79 21 46S 52 9W
Pardo →, São Paulo, Brazil 79 20 10S 48 38W
Pardubice 14 50 3N 15 45 E
Pare 35 7 43S 112 12 E
Parecis, Serra dos 78 13 0S 60 0W
Paren 25 62 30N 163 15 E
Parent 62 47 55N 74 35W
Parent, Lac 62 48 31N 77 1W
Parepare 35 4 0S 119 40 E
Parfuri 57 22 28S 31 17 E
Parguba 22 62 20N 34 27 E
Pariaguán 78 8 51N 64 34W
Pariaman 34 0 47S 100 11 E
Paricutín, Cerro 74 19 28N 102 15W
Parigi, Java, Indonesia 35 7 42S 108 29 E
Parigi, Sulawesi, Indonesia 35 0 50S 120 5 E
Parika 78 6 50N 58 20W
Parima, Serra 78 2 30N 64 0W
Parinari 78 4 35S 74 25W
Parîng 15 45 20N 23 37 E
Parintins 79 2 40S 56 50W
Pariparit Kyun 33 14 55S 93 45 E
Paris, Canada 62 43 12N 80 25W
Paris, France 12 48 50N 2 20 E
Paris, Idaho, U.S.A. 72 42 13N 111 30W
Paris, Ky., U.S.A. 68 38 12N 84 12W
Paris, Tenn., U.S.A. 69 36 20N 88 20W
Paris, Tex., U.S.A. 71 33 40N 95 30W
Paris, Ville de □ 12 48 50N 2 20 E
Pariti 35 10 15S 123 45 E
Park City 72 40 42N 111 35W
Park Falls 70 45 58N 90 27W
Park Range 72 40 0N 106 30W
Park Rapids 70 46 56N 95 0W
Park River 70 48 25N 97 43W
Park Rynie 57 30 25S 30 45 E
Parker, Ariz., U.S.A. 73 34 8N 114 16W
Parker, S. Dak., U.S.A. 70 43 25N 97 7W
Parker Dam 73 34 13N 114 5W
Parkersburg 68 39 18N 81 31W
Parkerview 65 51 21N 103 18W
Parkes 45 33 9S 148 11 E
Parkside 65 53 10N 106 33W
Parkston 70 43 25N 98 0W
Parksville 64 49 20N 124 21W
Parma, Italy 18 44 50N 10 20 E
Parma, U.S.A. 72 43 49N 116 59W
Parnaguá 79 10 10S 44 38W
Parnaíba, Piauí, Brazil 79 2 54S 41 47W
Parnaíba, São Paulo, Brazil 79 19 34S 51 14W
Parnaíba → 79 3 0S 41 50W
Parnassós 19 38 35N 22 30 E
Pärnu 22 58 28N 24 33 E
Paroo → 45 31 28S 143 32 E
Páros 19 37 5N 25 12 E
Parowan 73 37 54N 112 56W
Parral 80 36 10S 71 52W
Parramatta 45 33 48S 151 1 E
Parras 74 25 30N 102 20W
Parrett → 7 51 7N 2 58W
Parris I. 69 32 20N 80 30W
Parrsboro 63 45 30N 64 25W
Parry Is. 58 77 0N 110 0W
Parry Sound 62 45 20N 80 0W
Parshall 70 47 56N 102 11W
Parsnip → 64 55 10N 123 2W
Parsons 71 37 20N 95 17W
Parsons Ra. 44 13 30S 135 15 E
Paru → 79 1 33S 52 38W
Paruro 78 13 45S 71 50W
Parvān □ 31 35 0N 69 0 E
Parvatipuram 33 18 50N 83 25 E
Parys 56 26 52S 27 29 E
Pas-de-Calais □ 12 50 30N 2 10 E
Pasadena, Calif., U.S.A. 73 34 5N 118 9W
Pasadena, Tex., U.S.A. 71 29 45N 95 14W
Pasaje 78 3 23S 79 50W
Pascagoula 71 30 21N 88 30W
Pascagoula → 71 30 21N 88 35W
Pasco 72 46 10N 119 0W
Pasco, Cerro de 78 10 45S 76 10W
Pasfield L. 65 58 24N 105 20W
Pashmakli = Smolyan 19 41 36N 24 38 E
Pasirian 35 8 13S 113 8 E
Pasley, C. 47 33 52S 123 35 E
Pasni 31 25 15N 63 27 E
Paso de Indios 80 43 55S 69 0W
Paso Robles 73 35 40N 120 45W
Paspébiac 63 48 3N 65 17W
Passage West 9 51 52N 8 20W
Passau 14 48 34N 13 27 E
Passero, C. 18 36 42N 15 8 E
Passo Fundo 80 28 10S 52 20W
Passos 79 20 45S 46 37W
Pastaza → 78 4 50S 76 52W
Pasto 78 1 13N 77 17W
Pasuruan 35 7 40S 112 44 E
Patagonia, Argentina 80 45 0S 69 0W
Patagonia, U.S.A. 73 31 35N 110 45W
Patan, India 32 23 54N 72 14 E
Patan, Nepal 33 27 40N 85 20 E
Patani 35 0 20N 128 50 E
Patchewollock 45 35 22S 142 12 E
Patchogue 68 40 46N 73 1W
Patea 43 39 45S 174 30 E
Pategi 53 8 50N 5 45 E
Patensie 56 33 46S 24 49 E
Paternò 18 37 34N 14 53 E
Pateros 72 48 4N 119 58W
Paterson 68 40 55N 74 10W
Paterson Ra. 46 21 45S 122 10 E
Pathankot 32 32 18N 75 45 E
Pathfinder Res. 72 42 30N 107 0W
Pati 35 6 45S 111 1 E
Patiala 32 30 23N 76 26 E
Patkai Bum 33 27 0N 95 30 E
Pátmos 19 37 21N 26 36 E
Patna 33 25 35N 85 12 E
Patos, L. dos 80 31 20S 51 0W
Patos de Minas 79 18 35S 46 32W
Patquía 80 25 30N 102 11W
Pátrai 19 38 14N 21 47 E
Pátraikós, Kólpos 19 38 17N 21 30 E
Patrocínio 79 18 57S 47 0W
Pattani 34 6 48N 101 15 E
Patten 63 45 59N 68 28W
Patterson, Calif., U.S.A. 73 37 30N 121 9W
Patterson, La., U.S.A. 71 29 44N 91 20W
Patti 18 38 8N 14 57 E
Patuakhali 33 22 20N 90 25 E
Patuca → 75 15 50N 84 18W
Patuca, Punta 75 15 49N 84 14W
Pátzcuaro 74 19 30N 101 40W
Pau 12 43 19N 0 25W
Pauillac 12 45 11N 0 46W
Pauini → 78 1 42S 62 50W
Pauk 33 21 27N 94 30 E
Paul I. 63 56 30N 61 20W
Paulis = Isiro 54 2 53N 27 40 E
Paulistana 79 8 9S 41 9W
Paullina 70 42 55N 95 40W
Paulo Afonso 79 9 21S 38 15W
Paulpietersburg 57 27 23S 30 50 E
Pauls Valley 71 34 40N 97 17W
Pavia 18 45 10N 9 10 E
Pavlodar 24 52 33N 77 0 E
Pavlograd 23 48 30N 35 52 E
Pavlovo, Gorkiy, U.S.S.R. 22 55 58N 43 5 E
Pavlovo, Yakut A.S.S.R., U.S.S.R. 25 63 5N 115 25 E
Pavlovsk 23 50 26N 40 5 E
Pawhuska 71 36 40N 96 25W
Pawnee 71 36 24N 96 50W
Pawnee City 70 40 8N 96 10W
Pawtucket 68 41 51N 71 22W
Paxton, Ill., U.S.A. 68 40 25N 88 7W
Paxton, Nebr., U.S.A. 70 41 12N 101 27W
Payakumbuh 34 0 20S 100 35 E
Payette 72 44 0N 117 0W
Payne Bay = Bellin 61 60 0N 70 0W
Payne L. 61 59 30N 74 30W
Paynes Find 47 29 15S 117 42 E
Paynesville 70 45 21N 94 44W
Paysandú 80 32 19S 58 8W
Payson, Ariz., U.S.A. 73 34 17N 111 15W
Payson, Utah, U.S.A. 72 40 8N 111 41W
Paz → 75 13 44N 90 10W
Paz, B. de la 74 24 15N 110 25W
Paz, La, Entre Ríos, Argentina 80 30 50S 59 45W
Paz, La, San Luis, Argentina 80 33 30S 67 20W
Paz, La, Bolivia 78 16 20S 68 10W
Paz, La, Hond. 75 14 20N 87 47W
Paz, La, Mexico 74 24 10N 110 20W
Pazar 30 41 10N 40 50 E
Pazardzhik 19 42 12N 24 20 E
Pe Ell 72 46 30N 123 18W
Peace → 64 59 0N 111 25W
Peace Point 64 59 7N 112 27W
Peace River 64 56 15N 117 18W
Peach Springs 73 35 36N 113 30W
Peak, The 6 53 24N 1 53W
Peak Downs 44 22 14S 148 0 E
Peak Downs Mine 44 22 17S 148 11 E
Peak Hill, N.S.W., Australia 45 32 47S 148 11 E
Peak Hill, W. Austral., Australia 47 25 35S 118 43 E
Peak Range 44 22 50S 148 20 E
Peake 45 35 25S 140 0 E
Peake Cr. → 45 28 2S 136 7 E
Peale Mt. 73 38 25N 109 12W
Pearl → 71 30 23N 89 45W
Pearl City 66 21 24N 158 0W
Pearsall 71 28 55N 99 8W
Pearse I. 64 54 52N 130 14W
Pease → 71 34 12N 99 7W
Pebane 55 17 10S 38 8 E
Pebas 78 3 10S 71 46W
Peč 19 42 40N 20 17 E
Pechenga 22 69 30N 31 25 E
Pechora → 22 68 13N 54 15 E
Pechorskaya Guba 22 68 40N 54 0 E
Pecos 71 31 25N 103 35W
Pecos → 71 29 42N 102 30W
Pécs 15 46 5N 18 15 E
Pedder, L. 44 42 55S 146 10 E
Peddie 57 33 14S 27 7 E
Pedirka 45 26 40S 135 14 E
Pedra Azul 79 16 2S 41 17W
Pedreiras 79 4 32S 44 40W
Pedrera, La 78 1 18S 69 43W
Pedro Afonso 79 9 0S 48 10W
Pedro Cays 75 17 5N 77 48W
Pedro Juan Caballero 80 22 30S 55 40W
Pedro Miguel Locks 74 9 1N 79 36W
Peduyim 28 31 20N 34 37 E
Peebinga 45 34 52S 140 57 E
Peebles 8 55 40N 3 12W
Peekskill 68 41 18N 73 57W
Peel 6 54 14N 4 40W
Peel →, Australia 45 30 50S 150 29 E
Peel →, Canada 60 67 0N 135 0W
Peera Peera Poolanna L. 45 26 30S 138 0 E
Peers 64 53 40N 116 0W
Pegasus Bay 43 43 20S 173 10 E
Pegu 33 17 20N 96 29 E
Pegu Yoma 33 19 0N 96 0 E
Pehuajó 80 35 45S 62 0W
Peip'ing = Beijing 38 39 55N 116 20 E
Peixe 79 12 0S 48 40W
Pekalongan 35 6 53S 109 40 E
Pekanbaru 34 0 30N 101 15 E
Pekin 70 40 35N 89 40W
Peking = Beijing 38 39 55N 116 20 E
Pelabuhan Kelang 34 3 0N 101 23 E
Pelabuhan Ratu, Teluk 35 7 5S 106 30 E
Pelabuhanratu 35 7 0S 106 32 E
Pelaihari 34 3 55S 114 45 E
Peleaga 15 45 22N 22 55 E
Pelée, Mt. 75 14 48N 61 0W
Pelee, Pt. 62 41 54N 82 31W
Pelee I. 62 41 47N 82 40W
Peleng 35 1 20S 123 30 E
Pelham 69 31 5N 84 6W
Pelican L. 65 52 28N 100 20W
Pelican Narrows 65 55 10N 102 56W
Pelican Rapids 65 52 45N 100 42W
Pelkosenniemi 20 67 6N 27 28 E
Pella, S. Africa 56 29 1S 19 6 E
Pella, U.S.A. 70 41 30N 93 0W
Pelly → 60 62 47N 137 19W
Pelly Bay 61 68 38N 89 50W
Pelly L. 60 66 0N 102 0W
Peloponnese = Pelopónnisos □ 19 37 10N 22 0 E
Pelopónnisos □ 19 37 10N 22 0 E
Peloro, C. 18 38 15N 15 40 E
Pelorus Sound 43 40 59S 173 59 E
Pelotas 80 31 42S 52 23W
Pelvoux, Massif de 12 44 52N 6 20 E
Pemalang 35 6 53S 109 23 E
Pematangsiantar 34 2 57N 99 5 E
Pemba I. 54 5 0S 39 45 E
Pemberton, Australia 47 34 30S 116 0 E
Pemberton, Canada 64 50 25N 122 50W
Pembina 65 48 58N 97 15W
Pembina → 65 49 0N 98 12W
Pembine 68 45 38N 87 59W
Pembino 70 48 58N 97 15W
Pembroke, Canada 62 45 50N 77 7W
Pembroke, U.K. 7 51 41N 4 57W
Pembroke, U.S.A. 69 32 5N 81 32W
Pen-y-Ghent 6 54 10N 2 15W
Peña de Francia, Sierra de 13 40 32N 6 10W
Peñalara, Pico 13 40 51N 3 57W
Penang = Pinang 34 5 25N 100 15 E
Penápolis 80 21 30S 50 0W
Peñarroya-Pueblonuevo 13 38 19N 5 16W
Peñas, C. de 13 43 42N 5 52W
Penas, G. de 80 47 0S 75 0W
Pench'i = Benxi 38 41 20N 123 48 E
Pend Oreille → 72 49 4N 117 37W
Pend Oreille, L. 72 48 0N 116 30W
Pendembu 50 9 7N 12 14W
Pender B. 46 16 45S 122 42 E
Pendleton 72 45 35N 118 50W
Penedo 79 10 15S 36 36W
Penetanguishene 62 44 50N 79 55W
Pengalengan 35 7 9S 107 30 E
Penglai 38 37 48N 120 42 E
Pengshui 39 29 17N 108 12 E
Penguin 44 41 8S 146 6 E
Peniche 13 39 19N 9 22W
Penicuik 8 55 50N 3 14W
Penida 34 8 45S 115 30 E
Peninsular Malaysia □ 34 4 0N 102 0 E
Penmarch, Pte. de 12 47 48N 4 22W
Penn Yan 68 42 39N 77 7W
Pennant 65 50 32N 108 14W
Penner → 32 14 35N 80 10 E
Pennines 6 54 50N 2 20W
Pennsylvania □ 68 40 50N 78 0W
Penny 64 53 51N 121 20W
Penola 45 37 25S 140 21 E
Penonomé 75 8 31N 80 21W
Penrhyn Is. 41 9 0S 158 30W
Penrith, Australia 45 33 43S 150 38 E
Penrith, U.K. 6 54 40N 2 45W
Pensacola 69 30 30N 87 10W
Pense 65 50 25N 104 59W
Penshurst 45 37 49S 142 20 E
Penticton 64 49 30N 119 38W
Pentland 44 20 32S 145 25 E
Pentland Firth 8 58 43N 3 10W
Pentland Hills 8 55 48N 3 25W
Penylan L. 65 61 50N 106 20W
Penza 22 53 15N 45 5 E
Penzance 7 50 7N 5 32W
Penzhino 25 63 30N 167 55 E
Penzhinskaya Guba 25 61 30N 163 0 E
Peoria, Ariz., U.S.A. 73 33 40N 112 15W
Peoria, Ill., U.S.A. 70 40 40N 89 40W
Pera Hd. 44 12 55S 141 37 E
Perabumilih 34 3 27S 104 15 E
Percé 63 48 31N 64 13W
Perche 12 48 31N 1 1 E
Percival Lakes 46 21 25S 125 0 E
Percy Is. 44 21 39S 150 16 E
Perdido, Mte. 13 42 40N 0 5 E
Perdu, Mt. = Perdido, Mte. 13 42 40N 0 5 E
Pereira 78 4 49N 75 43W
Perekerten 45 34 55S 143 40 E
Perekop 23 46 10N 33 42 E
Perenjori 47 29 26S 116 16 E
Pereyaslav Khmelnitskiy 23 50 3N 31 28 E
Pérez, I. 74 22 24N 89 42W
Pergamino 80 33 52S 60 30W
Perham 70 46 36N 95 36W
Péribonca → 63 48 45N 72 5W
Péribonca, L. 63 50 1N 71 10W
Perico 80 24 20S 65 5W
Pericos 74 25 3N 107 42W
Périgord 12 45 0N 0 40 E
Périgueux 12 45 10N 0 42 E
Perijá, Sierra de 78 9 30N 73 3W
Perlas, Arch. de las 75 8 41N 79 7W
Perlas, Punta de 75 12 30N 83 30W
Perm 22 58 0N 57 10 E
Pernambuco = Recife 79 8 0S 35 0W
Pernambuco □ 79 8 0S 37 0W
Pernatty Lagoon 45 31 30S 137 12 E
Peron, C. 47 25 30S 113 30 E
Peron Is. 46 13 9S 130 4 E
Peron Pen. 47 26 0S 113 10 E
Perouse Str., La 40 45 40N 142 0 E
Perow 64 54 35N 126 10W
Perpendicular Pt. 45 31 37S 152 52 E
Perpignan 12 42 42N 2 53 E
Perry, Fla., U.S.A. 69 30 9N 83 40W
Perry, Ga., U.S.A. 69 32 25N 83 41W
Perry, Iowa, U.S.A. 70 41 48N 94 5W
Perry, Maine, U.S.A. 69 44 59N 67 20W
Perry, Okla., U.S.A. 71 36 20N 97 20W
Perryton 71 36 28N 100 48W
Perryville 71 37 42N 89 50W
Persepolis 31 29 55N 52 50 E
Persia = Iran ■ 31 33 0N 53 0 E
Persian Gulf = Gulf, The 31 27 0N 50 0 E
Perth, Australia 47 31 57S 115 52 E
Perth, Canada 62 44 55N 76 15W
Perth, U.K. 8 56 24N 3 27W
Perth Amboy 68 40 31N 74 16W

Port Alice

Peru, Ill., U.S.A. 70 41 18N 89 12W
Peru, Ind., U.S.A. 68 40 42N 86 0W
Peru ■ 78 8 0S 75 0W
Peru-Chile Trench 41 20 0S 72 0W
Perúgia 18 43 6N 12 24 E
Pervomaysk 23 48 10N 30 46 E
Pervouralsk 22 56 55N 60 0 E
Pésaro 18 43 55N 12 53 E
Pescara 18 42 28N 14 13 E
Peshawar 32 34 2N 71 37 E
Peshtigo 68 45 4N 87 46W
Pesqueira 79 8 20S 36 42W
Petah Tiqwa 28 32 6N 34 53 E
Petaluma 72 38 13N 122 39W
Petange 11 49 33N 5 55 E
Petatlán 74 17 31N 101 16W
Petauke 55 14 14S 31 20 E
Petawawa 62 45 54N 77 17W
Petén Itzá, L. 75 16 58N 89 50W
Peter Pond L. 65 55 55N 108 44W
Peterbell 62 48 36N 83 21W
Peterborough, Australia 45 32 58S 138 51 E
Peterborough, U.K. 7 52 35N 0 14W
Peterhead 8 57 30N 1 49W
Petersburg, Alaska, U.S.A. 60 56 50N 133 0W
Petersburg, Ind., U.S.A. 68 38 30N 87 15W
Petersburg, Va., U.S.A. 68 37 17N 77 26W
Petersburg, W. Va., U.S.A. 68 38 59N 79 10W
Petford 44 17 20S 144 58 E
Petit Bois I. 69 30 16N 88 25W
Petit-Cap 63 49 3N 64 30W
Petit Goâve 75 18 27N 72 51W
Petit Lac Manicouagan 63 51 25N 67 40W
Petitcodiac 63 45 57N 65 11W
Petite Baleine → 62 56 0N 76 45W
Petite Saguenay 63 48 15N 70 4W
Petitsikapau, L. 63 54 37N 66 25W
Petlad 32 22 30N 72 45 E
Peto 74 20 10N 88 53W
Petone 43 41 13S 174 53 E
Petoskey 68 45 22N 84 57W
Petra 28 30 20N 35 22 E
Petrich 19 41 24N 23 13 E
Petrolândia 79 9 5S 38 20W
Petrolia 62 42 54N 82 9W
Petrolina 79 9 24S 40 30W
Petropavlovsk 24 54 53N 69 13 E
Petropavlovsk-Kamchatskiy 25 53 3N 158 43 E
Petrópolis 79 22 33S 43 9W
Petroşeni 15 45 28N 23 20 E
Petroskey 68 45 22N 84 57W
Petrovaradin 19 45 16N 19 55 E
Petrovsk 22 52 22N 45 19 E
Petrovsk-Zabaykalskiy 25 51 20N 108 55 E
Petrozavodsk 22 61 41N 34 20 E
Petrus Steyn 57 27 38S 28 8 E
Petrusburg 56 29 4S 25 26 E
Peureulak 34 4 48N 97 45 E
Pevek 25 69 41N 171 19 E
Pforzheim 14 48 53N 8 43 E
Phagwara 32 31 10N 75 40 E
Phala 56 23 45S 26 50 E
Phalodi 32 27 12N 72 24 E
Phan Rang 34 11 34N 109 0 E
Phangan, Ko 34 9 45N 100 0 E
Phangnga 34 8 28N 98 30 E
Phanh Bho Ho Chi Minh 34 10 58N 106 40 E
Phatthalung 34 7 39N 100 6 E
Phelps 70 46 2N 89 2W
Phelps L. 65 59 15N 103 15W
Phenix City 69 32 30N 85 0W
Phetchabun 34 16 25N 101 8 E
Philadelphia, Miss., U.S.A. 71 32 47N 89 5W
Philadelphia, Pa., U.S.A. 68 40 0N 75 10W
Philip 70 44 4N 101 42W
Philippeville 11 50 12N 4 33 E
Philippi L. 44 24 20S 138 55 E
Philippines ■ 35 12 0N 123 0 E
Philippolis 56 30 15S 25 16 E
Philippopolis = Plovdiv 19 42 8N 24 44 E
Philipsburg 72 46 20N 113 21W
Philipstown 56 30 28S 24 30 E
Phillip, I. 45 38 30S 145 12 E
Phillips, Tex., U.S.A. 71 35 48N 101 17W
Phillips, Wis., U.S.A. 70 45 41N 90 22W
Phillipsburg 70 39 48N 99 20W
Phillott 45 27 53S 145 50 E
Philomath 72 44 28N 123 21W
Phitsanulok 34 16 50N 100 12 E
Phnom Dangrek 34 14 20N 104 0 E
Phnom Penh 34 11 33N 104 55 E
Phoenix 73 33 30N 112 10W
Phoenix Is. 40 3 30S 172 0W
Phra Nakhon Si Ayutthaya 34 14 25N 100 30 E
Phuket 34 7 52N 98 22 E
Piacenza 18 45 2N 9 42 E
Pialba 45 25 20S 152 45 E
Pian Cr. → 45 30 2S 148 12 E
Piapot 65 49 59N 109 8W
Piatra Neamţ 15 46 56N 26 21 E
Piauí □ 79 7 0S 43 0W
Piave → 18 45 32N 12 44 E
Piazza Ármerina 18 37 21N 14 20 E
Pibor Post 51 6 47N 33 3 E
Pica 78 20 35S 69 25W
Picardie 12 49 50N 3 0 E
Picardy = Picardie 12 49 50N 3 0 E
Picayune 71 30 31N 89 40W
Pichilemu 80 34 22S 72 0W
Pickerel L. 62 48 40N 91 25W
Pickle Lake 62 51 30N 90 12W
Pico Truncado 80 46 40S 68 0W
Picton, Australia 45 34 12S 150 34 E
Picton, Canada 62 44 1N 77 9W
Picton, N.Z. 43 41 18S 174 3 E
Pictou 63 45 41N 62 42W
Picture Butte 64 49 55N 112 45W
Picún Leufú 80 39 30S 69 5W
Pidurutalagala 32 7 10N 80 50 E
Piedad, La 74 20 20N 102 1W
Piedmont = Piemonte □ 18 45 0N 7 30 E
Piedmont 69 33 55N 85 39W
Piedmont Plateau 69 34 0N 81 30W
Piedras, R. de las → 78 12 30S 69 15W
Piedras Negras 74 28 35N 100 35W
Piemonte □ 18 45 0N 7 30 E
Pierce 72 46 29N 115 53W
Pierre 70 44 23N 100 20W
Piet Retief 57 27 1S 30 50 E
Pietarsaari = Jakobstad 20 63 40N 22 43 E
Pietermaritzburg 57 29 35S 30 25 E
Pietersburg 57 23 54S 29 25 E
Pietrosul 15 47 35N 24 43 E
Pigeon 68 43 50N 83 17W
Piggott 71 36 20N 90 10W
Pigüe 80 37 36S 62 25W
Pikes Peak 70 38 50N 105 10W
Piketberg 56 32 55S 18 40 E
Pikeville 68 37 30N 82 30W
Pikwitonei 65 55 35N 97 9W
Pilar, Brazil 79 9 36S 35 56W
Pilar, Paraguay 80 26 50S 58 20W
Pilas Group 35 6 45N 121 35 E
Pilbara 46 21 15S 118 16 E
Pilcomayo → 80 25 21S 57 42W
Pilibhit 32 28 40N 79 50 E
Pilica → 15 51 52N 21 17 E
Pílos 19 36 55N 21 42 E
Pilot Mound 65 49 15N 98 54W
Pilot Point 71 33 26N 97 0W
Pilot Rock 72 45 30N 118 50W
Pilsen = Plzeň 14 49 45N 13 22 E
Pima 73 32 54N 109 50W
Pimba 45 31 18S 136 46 E
Pimenta Bueno 78 11 35S 61 10W
Pimentel 78 6 45S 79 55W
Pinang 34 5 25N 100 15 E
Pinar del Río 75 22 26N 83 40W
Pincher Creek 64 49 30N 113 57W
Pinchi L. 64 54 38N 124 30W
Pinckneyville 70 38 5N 89 20W
Pińczów 15 50 32N 20 32 E
Pindar 47 28 30S 115 47 E
Pindiga 53 9 58N 10 53 E
Pindos Óros 19 40 0N 21 0 E
Pindus Mts. = Pindos Óros 19 40 0N 21 0 E
Pine 73 34 27N 111 30W
Pine → 65 58 50N 105 38W
Pine, C. 63 46 37N 53 32W
Pine, La 72 43 40N 121 30W
Pine Bluff 71 34 10N 92 0W
Pine City 70 45 46N 93 0W
Pine Falls 65 50 34N 96 11W
Pine Pass 64 55 25N 122 42W
Pine Point 64 60 50N 114 28W
Pine Ridge 70 43 0N 102 35W
Pine River, Canada 65 51 45N 100 30W
Pine River, U.S.A. 70 46 43N 94 24W
Pinega → 22 64 8N 46 54 E
Pinehill 44 23 38S 146 57 E
Pinerolo 18 44 47N 7 21 E
Pinetop 73 34 10N 109 57W
Pinetown 57 29 48S 30 54 E
Pinetree 72 43 42N 105 52W
Pineville, Ky., U.S.A. 69 36 42N 83 42W
Pineville, La., U.S.A. 71 31 22N 92 30W
Ping → 34 15 42N 100 9 E
Pingaring 47 32 40S 118 32 E
Pingding 38 37 47N 113 38 E
Pingdingshan 39 33 43N 113 27 E
Pingdong 39 22 39N 120 30 E
Pingdu 38 36 42N 119 59 E
Pingelly 47 32 32S 117 5 E
Pingguo 39 23 19N 107 36 E
Pinghe 39 24 17N 117 21 E
Pingjiang 39 28 45N 113 36 E
Pingle 39 24 40N 110 40 E
Pingliang 38 35 35N 106 31 E
Pingluo 38 38 52N 106 30 E
Pingnan 39 23 33N 110 22 E
Pingrup 47 33 32S 118 29 E
Pingtan Dao 39 25 29N 119 47 E
Pingwu 39 32 25N 104 30 E
Pingxiang, Guangxi Zhuangzu, China 39 22 6N 106 46 E
Pingxiang, Jiangxi, China 39 27 43N 113 48 E
Pingyao 38 37 12N 112 10 E
Pinhel 13 40 50N 7 1W
Pini 34 0 10N 98 40 E
Piniós → 19 39 55N 22 10 E
Pinjarra 47 32 37S 115 52 E
Pink → 65 56 50N 103 50W
Pinnacles 47 28 12S 120 26 E
Pinnaroo 45 35 17S 140 53 E
Pinos 74 22 20N 101 40W
Pinos Pt. 73 36 38N 121 57W
Pinrang 35 3 46S 119 41 E
Pinsk 22 52 10N 26 1 E
Pintados 78 20 35S 69 40W
Pintumba 47 31 30S 132 12 E
Pinyang 39 27 42N 120 31 E
Pinyug 22 60 5N 48 0 E
Pioche 73 38 0N 114 35W
Piombino 18 42 54N 10 30 E
Pioner, Os. 25 79 50N 92 0 E
Piorini, L. 78 3 15S 62 35W
Piotrków Trybunalski 15 51 23N 19 43 E
Pip 31 26 45N 60 10 E
Pipestone 70 44 0N 96 20W
Pipestone → 62 52 53N 89 23W
Pipestone Cr. → 65 49 38N 100 15W
Pipmuacan, Rés. 63 49 45N 70 30W
Pippingarra 46 20 27S 118 42 E
Piqua 68 40 10N 84 10W
Piquiri → 80 24 3S 54 14W
Piracicaba 80 22 45S 47 40W
Piracuruca 79 3 50S 41 50W
Piræus = Piraiévs 19 37 57N 23 42 E
Piraiévs 19 37 57N 23 42 E
Pirané 80 25 42S 59 6W
Pirapora 79 17 20S 44 56W
Pírgos 19 37 40N 21 27 E
Pirin Planina 19 41 40N 23 30 E
Pirineos 13 42 40N 1 0 E
Piripiri 79 4 15S 41 46W
Pirot 19 43 9N 22 39 E
Piru 35 3 4S 128 12 E
Pisa 18 43 43N 10 23 E
Pisagua 78 19 40S 70 15W
Pisco 78 13 50S 76 12W
Písek 14 49 19N 14 10 E
Pishan 37 37 30N 78 33 E
Pising 35 5 8S 121 53 E
Pistóia 18 43 57N 10 53 E
Pistol B. 65 62 25N 92 37W
Pisuerga → 13 41 33N 4 52W
Pitarpunga, L. 45 34 24S 143 30 E
Pitcairn I. 2 25 5S 130 5W
Pite älv → 20 65 20N 21 25 E
Piteå 20 65 20N 21 25 E
Piteşti 15 44 52N 24 54 E
Pithapuram 33 17 10N 82 15 E
Pithara 47 30 20S 116 35 E
Pitlochry 8 56 43N 3 43W
Pitt I. 64 53 30N 129 50W
Pittsburg, Kans., U.S.A. 71 37 21N 94 43W
Pittsburg, Tex., U.S.A. 71 32 59N 94 58W
Pittsburgh 68 40 25N 79 55W
Pittsfield, Ill., U.S.A. 70 39 35N 90 46W
Pittsfield, Mass., U.S.A. 68 42 28N 73 17W
Pittston 68 41 19N 75 50W
Pittsworth 45 27 41S 151 37 E
Pituri → 44 22 35S 138 30 E
Piura 78 5 15S 80 38W
Pizzo 18 38 44N 16 10 E
Placentia 63 47 20N 54 0W
Placentia B. 63 47 0N 54 40W
Placerville 72 38 47N 120 51W
Placetas 75 22 15N 79 44W
Plain Dealing 71 32 56N 93 41W
Plainfield 68 40 37N 74 28W
Plains, Kans., U.S.A. 71 37 20N 100 35W
Plains, Mont., U.S.A. 72 47 27N 114 57W
Plains, Tex., U.S.A. 71 33 11N 102 50W
Plainview, Nebr., U.S.A. 70 42 25N 97 48W
Plainview, Tex., U.S.A. 71 34 10N 101 40W
Plainville 70 39 18N 99 19W
Plainwell 68 42 28N 85 40W
Plakhino 24 67 45N 86 5 E
Plankinton 70 43 45N 98 27W
Plano 71 33 0N 96 45W
Plant, La 70 45 11N 100 40W
Plant City 69 28 0N 82 8W
Plaquemine 71 30 20N 91 15W
Plasencia 13 40 3N 6 8W
Plaster Rock 63 46 53N 67 22W
Plata, La 80 35 0S 57 55W
Plata, Río de la 80 34 45S 57 30W
Platani → 18 37 23N 13 16 E
Plateau □ 53 8 0N 8 30 E
Plateau du Coteau du Missouri 70 47 9N 101 5W
Platí, Ákra 19 40 27N 24 0 E
Plato 78 9 47N 74 47W
Platte 70 43 28N 98 50W
Platte → 70 39 16N 94 50W
Platteville 70 40 18N 104 47W
Plattsburg 68 44 41N 73 30W
Plattsmouth 70 41 0N 95 50W
Plauen 14 50 29N 12 9 E
Playgreen L. 65 54 0N 98 15W
Pleasant Bay 63 46 51N 60 48W
Pleasant Hill 70 38 48N 94 14W
Pleasanton 71 29 0N 98 30W
Pleasantville 68 39 25N 74 30W
Pleiku 34 13 57N 108 0 E
Plenty → 44 23 25S 136 31 E
Plenty, Bay of 43 37 45S 177 0 E
Plentywood 70 48 45N 104 35W
Plesetsk 22 62 40N 40 10 E
Plessisville 63 46 14N 71 47W
Pletipi L. 63 51 44N 70 6W
Pleven 19 43 26N 24 37 E
Plevlja 19 43 21N 19 21 E
Płock 15 52 32N 19 40 E
Ploieşti 15 44 57N 26 5 E
Plonge, Lac la 65 55 8N 107 20W
Plovdiv 19 42 8N 24 44 E
Plummer 72 47 21N 116 59W
Plumtree 55 20 27S 27 55 E
Plymouth, U.K. 7 50 23N 4 9W
Plymouth, Ind., U.S.A. 68 41 20N 86 19W
Plymouth, N.C., U.S.A. 69 35 54N 76 46W
Plymouth, Wis., U.S.A. 68 43 42N 87 58W
Plymouth Sd. 7 50 20N 4 10W
Plynlimon = Pumlumon Fawr 7 52 29N 3 47W
Plzeň 14 49 45N 13 22 E
Po → 18 44 57N 12 4 E
Po Hai = Bo Hai 38 39 0N 120 0 E
Pobé 53 7 0N 2 56 E
Pobeda 25 65 12N 146 12 E
Pobedino 25 49 51N 142 49 E
Pobedy Pik 24 40 45N 79 58 E
Pocahontas, Ark., U.S.A. 71 36 18N 91 0W
Pocahontas, Iowa, U.S.A. 70 42 41N 94 42W
Pocatello 72 42 50N 112 25W
Pochutla 74 15 50N 96 31W
Pocomoke City 68 38 4N 75 32W
Poços de Caldas 79 21 50S 46 33W
Podgorica = Titograd 19 42 30N 19 19 E
Podkamennaya Tunguska → 25 61 50N 90 13 E
Podolsk 22 55 25N 37 30 E
Podor 50 16 40N 15 2W
Podporozhy 22 60 55N 34 2 E
Pofadder 56 29 10S 19 22 E
Pogamasing 62 46 55N 81 50W
Poh 35 0 46S 122 51 E
Pohang 38 36 1N 129 23 E
Point Edward 62 43 0N 82 30W
Point Pedro 32 9 50N 80 15 E
Point Pleasant 68 38 50N 82 7W
Pointe-à-la Hache 71 29 35N 89 55W
Pointe-à-Pitre 75 16 10N 61 30W
Pointe Noire 54 4 48S 11 53 E
Poisonbush Ra. 46 22 30S 121 30 E
Poitiers 12 46 35N 0 20 E
Pojoaque Valley 73 35 55N 106 0W
Pokaran 32 27 0N 71 50 E
Pokataroo 45 29 30S 148 36 E
Pokrovsk 25 61 29N 126 12 E
Polacca 73 35 52N 110 25W
Polan 31 25 30N 61 10 E
Poland ■ 15 52 0N 20 0 E
Polcura 80 37 17S 71 43W
Polden Hills 7 51 7N 2 50W
Polesye 22 52 0N 28 10 E
Polevskoy 22 56 26N 60 11 E
Polewali 35 3 21S 119 23 E
Poli 54 8 34N 13 15 E
Polillo Is. 35 14 56N 122 0 E
Políyiros 19 40 23N 23 25 E
Pollachi 32 10 35N 77 0 E
Pollock 70 45 58N 100 18W
Polnovat 24 63 50N 65 54 E
Polo 70 41 59N 89 38W
Polotsk 22 55 30N 28 50 E
Polson 72 47 45N 114 12W
Poltava 23 49 35N 34 35 E
Polunochnoye 22 60 52N 60 25 E
Polyarny 22 69 8N 33 20 E
Polynesia 41 10 0S 162 0W
Pombal, Brazil 79 6 45S 37 50W
Pombal, Portugal 13 39 55N 8 40W
Pomeroy, Ohio, U.S.A. 68 39 0N 82 0W
Pomeroy, Wash., U.S.A. 72 46 30N 117 33W
Pomona 73 34 2N 117 49W
Pompano Beach 69 26 12N 80 6W
Pompeys Pillar 72 46 0N 108 0W
Ponape 40 6 55N 158 10 E
Ponask, L. 62 54 0N 92 41W
Ponass L. 65 52 16N 103 58W
Ponca 70 42 38N 96 41W
Ponca City 71 36 40N 97 5W
Ponce 75 18 1N 66 37W
Ponchatoula 71 30 27N 90 25W
Poncheville, L. 62 50 10N 76 55W
Pond Inlet 61 72 40N 77 0W
Pondicherry 32 11 59N 79 50 E
Ponds, I. of 63 53 27N 55 52W
Ponferrada 13 42 32N 6 35W
Ponnani 32 10 45N 75 59 E
Ponnyadaung 33 22 0N 94 10 E
Ponoi 22 67 0N 41 0 E
Ponoi → 22 66 59N 41 17 E
Ponoka 64 52 42N 113 40W
Ponorogo 35 7 52S 111 27 E
Ponta Grossa 80 25 7S 50 10W
Ponta Pora 80 22 20S 55 35W
Pontarlier 12 46 54N 6 20 E
Pontchartrain, L. 71 30 12N 90 0W
Ponte Macassar 35 9 30S 123 58 E
Ponte Nova 79 20 25S 42 54W
Pontedera 18 43 40N 10 37 E
Pontefract 6 53 42N 1 19W
Ponteix 65 49 46N 107 29W
Pontevedra 13 42 26N 8 40W
Pontiac, Ill., U.S.A. 70 40 50N 88 40W
Pontiac, Mich., U.S.A. 68 42 40N 83 20W
Pontianak 34 0 3S 109 15 E
Pontine Is. = Ponziane, Isole 18 40 55N 13 0 E
Pontine Mts. = Kuzey Anadolu Dağlari 30 41 30N 35 0 E
Ponton → 64 58 27N 116 11W
Pontypool 7 51 42N 3 1W
Pontypridd 7 51 36N 3 21W
Ponziane, Isole 18 40 55N 13 0 E
Poochera 45 32 43S 134 51 E
Poole 7 50 42N 1 58W
Pooley I. 64 52 45N 128 15W
Poona = Pune 32 18 29N 73 57 E
Pooncarie 45 33 22S 142 31 E
Poopelloe, L. 45 31 40S 144 0 E
Poopó, L. de 78 18 30S 67 35W
Popanyinning 47 32 40S 117 2 E
Popayán 78 2 27N 76 36W
Poperinge 11 50 51N 2 42 E
Popigay 25 72 1N 110 39 E
Popilta, L. 45 33 10S 141 42 E
Popio, L. 45 33 10S 141 52 E
Poplar 70 48 3N 105 9W
Poplar →, Man., Canada 65 53 0N 97 19W
Poplar →, N.W.T., Canada 64 61 22N 121 52W
Poplar Bluff 71 36 45N 90 22W
Poplarville 71 30 55N 89 30W
Popocatepetl 74 19 10N 98 40W
Popokabaka 54 5 41S 16 40 E
Porbandar 32 21 44N 69 43 E
Porcher I. 64 53 50N 130 30W
Porcupine →, Canada 65 59 11N 104 46W
Porcupine →, U.S.A. 60 66 35N 145 15W
Pori 21 61 29N 21 48 E
Porjus 20 66 57N 19 50 E
Porkkala 21 59 59N 24 26 E
Porlamar 78 10 57N 63 51W
Poronaysk 25 49 13N 143 0 E
Poroshiri-Dake 36 42 41N 142 52 E
Porretta, Passo di 18 44 2N 10 56 E
Porsangen 20 70 40N 25 40 E
Port Adelaide 45 34 46S 138 30 E
Port Alberni 64 49 14N 124 50W
Port Alfred, Canada 63 48 18N 70 53W
Port Alfred, S. Africa 56 33 36S 26 55 E
Port Alice 64 50 20N 127 25W

Port Allegany

Port Allegany 68 41 49N 78 17W
Port Allen 71 30 30N 91 15W
Port Alma 44 23 38S 150 53 E
Port Angeles 72 48 7N 123 30W
Port Antonio 75 18 10N 76 30W
Port Aransas 71 27 49N 97 4W
Port Arthur = Lüshun 38 38 45N 121 15 E
Port Arthur, Australia 44 43 7S 147 50 E
Port Arthur, U.S.A. 71 30 0N 94 0W
Port au Port B. 63 48 40N 58 50W
Port-au-Prince 75 18 40N 72 20W
Port Augusta 45 32 30S 137 50 E
Port Augusta West 45 32 29S 137 29 E
Port Austin 68 44 3N 82 59W
Port Bergé Vaovao 57 15 33S 47 40 E
Port Blandford 63 48 20N 54 10W
Port Bradshaw 44 12 30S 137 20 E
Port Broughton 45 33 37S 137 56 E
Port Burwell 62 42 40N 80 48W
Port-Cartier 63 50 2N 66 50W
Port Chalmers 43 45 49S 170 30 E
Port Chester 68 41 0N 73 41W
Port Clements 64 53 40N 132 10W
Port Clinton 68 41 30N 82 58W
Port Colborne 62 42 50N 79 10W
Port Coquitlam 64 49 15N 122 45W
Port Curtis 44 23 57S 151 20 E
Port Darwin, Australia 46 12 24S 130 45 E
Port Darwin, Falk. Is. 80 51 50S 59 0W
Port Davey 44 43 16S 145 55 E
Port-de-Paix 75 19 50N 72 50W
Port Dickson 34 2 30N 101 49 E
Port Douglas 44 16 30S 145 30 E
Port Edward 64 54 12N 130 10W
Port Elgin 62 44 25N 81 25W
Port Elizabeth 56 33 58S 25 40 E
Port Ellen 8 55 38N 6 10W
Port-en-Bessin 12 49 21N 0 45W
Port Erin 6 54 5N 4 45W
Port Essington 46 11 15S 132 10 E
Port Etienne = Nouâdhibou 50 20 54N 17 0W
Port Fairy 45 38 22S 142 12 E
Port-Gentil 54 0 40S 8 50 E
Port Gibson 71 31 57N 91 0W
Port Glasgow 8 55 57N 4 40W
Port Harcourt 53 4 40N 7 10 E
Port Hardy 64 50 41N 127 30W
Port Harrison = Inoucdjouac 61 58 25N 78 15W
Port Hawkesbury 63 45 36N 61 22W
Port Hedland 46 20 25S 118 35 E
Port Henry 68 44 0N 73 30W
Port Hood 63 46 0N 61 32W
Port Hope 62 43 56N 78 20W
Port Huron 68 43 0N 82 28W
Port Isabel 71 26 4N 97 9W
Port Jefferson 68 40 58N 73 5W
Port Kembla 45 34 52S 150 49 E
Port-la-Nouvelle 12 43 1N 3 3 E
Port Laoise 9 53 2N 7 20W
Port Lavaca 71 28 38N 96 38W
Port Lincoln 45 34 42S 135 52 E
Port Loko 50 8 48N 12 46W
Port Louis 3 20 10S 57 30 E
Port Lyautey = Kenitra 50 34 15N 6 40W
Port Macdonnell 45 38 0S 140 48 E
Port Macquarie 45 31 25S 152 25 E
Port Maria 75 18 25N 77 5W
Port Mellon 64 49 32N 123 31W
Port-Menier 63 49 51N 64 15W
Port Moresby 40 9 24S 147 8 E
Port Mouton 63 43 58N 64 50W
Port Musgrave 44 11 55S 141 50 E
Port Nelson 65 57 3N 92 36W
Port Nolloth 56 29 17S 16 52 E
Port Nouveau-Québec 61 58 30N 65 59W
Port O'Connor 71 28 26N 96 24W
Port of Spain 75 10 40N 61 31W
Port Orchard 72 47 31N 122 38W
Port Orford 72 42 45N 124 28W
Port Pegasus 43 47 12S 167 41 E
Port Perry 62 44 6N 78 56W
Port Phillip B. 45 38 10S 144 50 E
Port Pirie 45 33 10S 138 1 E
Port Radium = Echo Bay 60 66 5N 117 55W
Port Renfrew 64 48 30N 124 20W
Port Roper 44 14 45S 135 25 E
Port Rowan 62 42 40N 80 30W
Port Safaga = Bûr Safâga 51 26 43N 33 57 E
Port Said = Bûr Sa'îd 51 31 16N 32 18 E
Port St. Joe 69 29 49N 85 20W
Port St. Johns 57 31 38S 29 33 E
Port-St.-Louis-du-Rhône 12 43 23N 4 49 E
Port Sanilac 62 43 26N 82 33W
Port Saunders 63 50 40N 57 18W
Port Shepstone 57 30 44S 30 28 E
Port Simpson 64 54 30N 130 20W
Port Stanley 62 42 40N 81 10W
Port Sudan = Bûr Sûdân 51 19 32N 37 9 E
Port Talbot 7 51 35N 3 48W
Port Townsend 72 48 7N 122 50W
Port-Vendres 12 42 32N 3 8 E
Port Vladimir 22 69 25N 33 6 E
Port Wakefield 45 34 12S 138 10 E
Port Washington 68 43 25N 87 52W
Port Weld 34 4 50N 100 38 E
Portachuelo 78 17 10S 63 20W
Portadown 9 54 27N 6 26W
Portage 70 43 31N 89 25W
Portage La Prairie 65 49 58N 98 18W
Portageville 71 36 25N 89 40W
Portalegre 13 39 19N 7 25W
Portalegre □ 13 39 20N 7 40W
Portales 71 34 12N 103 25W
Portarlington 9 53 10N 7 10W
Porte, La 68 41 36N 86 43W
Porter L., N.W.T., Canada 65 61 41N 108 5W
Porter L., Sask., Canada 65 56 20N 107 20W
Porterville, S. Africa 56 33 0S 19 0 E
Porterville, U.S.A. 73 36 5N 119 0W
Porthcawl 7 51 28N 3 42W
Porthill 72 49 0N 116 30W
Portile de Fier 15 44 42N 22 30 E
Portimão 13 37 8N 8 32W
Portland, N.S.W., Australia 45 33 20S 150 0 E
Portland, Vic., Australia 45 38 20S 141 35 E
Portland, Maine, U.S.A. 63 43 40N 70 15W
Portland, Mich., U.S.A. 68 42 52N 84 58W
Portland, Oreg., U.S.A. 72 45 35N 122 40W
Portland, Bill of 7 50 31N 2 27W
Portland, I. of 7 50 32N 2 25W
Portland B. 45 38 15S 141 45 E
Portland Prom. 61 58 40N 78 33W
Portneuf 63 46 43N 71 55W
Porto 13 41 8N 8 40W
Pôrto Alegre 80 30 5S 51 10W
Porto Amboim = Gunza 54 10 50S 13 50 E
Pôrto de Móz 79 1 41S 52 13W
Porto Empédocle 18 37 18N 13 30 E
Porto Esperança 78 19 37S 57 29W
Pôrto Franco 79 6 20S 47 24W
Porto Mendes 80 24 30S 54 15W
Pôrto Murtinho 78 21 45S 57 55W
Pôrto Nacional 79 10 40S 48 30W
Porto Novo 53 6 23N 2 42 E
Porto Santo 50 33 45N 16 25W
Pôrto Seguro 79 16 26S 39 5W
Porto Tórres 18 40 50N 8 23 E
Pôrto União 80 26 10S 51 10W
Pôrto Válter 78 8 15S 72 40W
Porto-Vecchio 12 41 35N 9 16 E
Pôrto Velho 78 8 46S 63 54W
Portoferráio 18 42 50N 10 20 E
Portola 72 39 49N 120 28W
Portoscuso 18 39 12N 8 22 E
Portoviejo 78 1 7S 80 28W
Portpatrick 8 54 50N 5 7W
Portree 8 57 25N 6 11W
Portrush 9 55 13N 6 40W
Portsmouth, Domin. 75 15 34N 61 27W
Portsmouth, U.K. 7 50 48N 1 6W
Portsmouth, N.H., U.S.A. 68 43 5N 70 45W
Portsmouth, Ohio, U.S.A. 68 38 45N 83 0W
Portsmouth, Va., U.S.A. 68 36 50N 76 20W
Portsoy 8 57 41N 2 41W
Porttipahta 20 68 5N 26 40 E
Portugal ■ 13 40 0N 7 0W
Portuguese-Guinea = Guinea-Bissau ■ 50 12 0N 15 0W
Portuguese Timor ■ = Timor 35 9 0S 125 0 E
Portumna 9 53 5N 8 12W
Porvenir 80 53 10S 70 16W
Porvoo 21 60 24N 25 40 E
Posadas 80 27 30S 55 50W
Poshan = Boshan 38 36 28N 117 49 E
Poso 35 1 20S 120 55 E
Posse 79 14 4S 46 18W
Possel 54 5 5N 19 10 E
Post 71 33 13N 101 21W
Post Falls 72 47 46N 116 59W
Poste Maurice Cortier 50 22 14N 1 2 E
Postmasburg 56 28 18S 23 5 E
Postojna 19 45 46N 14 12 E
Potchefstroom 56 26 41S 27 7 E
Poteau 71 35 5N 94 37W
Poteet 71 29 4N 98 35W
Potenza 18 40 40N 15 50 E
Poteriteri, L. 43 46 5S 167 10 E
Potgietersrus 57 24 10S 28 55 E
Poti 23 42 10N 41 38 E
Potiskum 53 11 39N 11 2 E
Potomac → 68 38 0N 76 23W
Potosí 78 19 38S 65 50W
Pototan 35 10 54N 122 38 E
Potrerillos 80 26 30S 69 30W
Potsdam, Germany 14 52 23N 13 4 E
Potsdam, U.S.A. 68 44 40N 74 59W
Potter 70 41 15N 103 20W
Pottstown 68 40 17N 75 40W
Pottsville 68 40 39N 76 12W
Pottuvil 32 6 55N 81 50 E
Pouce Coupé 64 55 40N 120 10W
Poughkeepsie 68 41 40N 73 57W
Poulaphouca Res. 9 53 8N 6 30W
Poulsbo 72 47 45N 122 39W
Pouso Alegre 79 11 46S 57 16W
Povenets 22 62 50N 34 50 E
Poverty Bay 43 38 43S 178 2 E
Póvoa de Varzim 13 41 25N 8 46W
Powassan 62 46 5N 79 25W
Powder → 70 46 47N 105 12W
Powder River 72 43 5N 107 0W
Powell 72 44 45N 108 45W
Powell, L. 73 37 25N 110 45W
Powell River 64 49 50N 124 35W
Powers, Mich., U.S.A. 68 45 40N 87 32W
Powers, Oreg., U.S.A. 72 42 53N 124 2W
Powers Lake 70 48 37N 102 38W
Powys □ 7 52 20N 3 20W
Poyang Hu 39 29 5N 116 20 E
Poyarkovo 25 49 36N 128 41 E
Poza Rica 74 20 33N 97 27W
Požarevac 19 44 35N 21 18 E
Poznań 14 52 25N 16 55 E
Pozo Almonte 78 20 10S 69 50W
Pozoblanco 13 38 23N 4 51W
Prachuap Khiri Khan 34 11 49N 99 48 E
Prado 79 17 20S 39 13W
Prague = Praha 14 50 5N 14 22 E
Praha 14 50 5N 14 22 E
Praid 15 46 32N 25 10 E
Prainha, Amazonas, Brazil 78 7 10S 60 30W
Prainha, Pará, Brazil 79 1 45S 53 30W
Prairie 44 20 50S 144 35 E
Prairie → 71 34 30N 99 23W
Prairie City 72 44 27N 118 44W
Prairie du Chien 70 43 1N 91 9W
Prapat 34 2 41N 98 58 E
Prata 79 19 25S 48 54W
Prato 18 43 53N 11 5 E
Pratt 71 37 40N 98 45W
Prattville 69 32 30N 86 28W
Pravia 13 43 30N 6 12W
Praya 34 8 39S 116 17 E
Preeceville 65 51 57N 102 40W
Prelate 65 50 51N 109 24W
Premier 64 56 4N 129 56W
Premont 71 27 19N 98 8W
Prentice 70 45 31N 90 19W
Prenzlau 14 53 19N 13 51 E
Prepansko Jezero 19 40 55N 21 0 E
Preparis North Channel 33 15 12N 93 40 E
Preparis South Channel 33 14 36N 93 40 E
Přerov 15 49 28N 17 27 E
Prescott, Canada 62 44 45N 75 30W
Prescott, Ariz., U.S.A. 73 34 35N 112 30W
Prescott, Ark., U.S.A. 71 33 49N 93 22W
Preservation Inlet 43 46 8S 166 35 E
Presho 70 43 56N 100 4W
Presidencia Roque Saenz Peña 80 26 45S 60 30W
Presidente Epitácio 79 21 56S 52 6W
Presidente Hermes 78 11 17S 61 55W
Presidente Prudente 79 22 5S 51 25W
Presidio 71 29 30N 104 20W
Prespa, L. = Prepansko Jezero 19 40 55N 21 0 E
Presque Isle 63 46 40N 68 0W
Prestbury 7 51 54N 2 2W
Presteigne 7 52 17N 3 0W
Preston, U.K. 6 53 46N 2 42W
Preston, Idaho, U.S.A. 72 42 10N 111 55W
Preston, Minn., U.S.A. 70 43 39N 92 3W
Preston, Nev., U.S.A. 72 38 59N 115 2W
Preston, C. 46 20 51S 116 12 E
Prestonpans 8 55 58N 3 0W
Prestwick 8 55 30N 4 38W
Pretoria 57 25 44S 28 12 E
Préveza 19 38 57N 20 47 E
Příbram 14 49 41N 14 2 E
Price 72 39 40N 110 48W
Price I. 64 52 23N 128 41W
Prichard 69 30 47N 88 5W
Prieska 56 29 40S 22 42 E
Priest L. 72 48 30N 116 55W
Priest River 72 48 11N 116 55W
Priestly 64 54 8N 125 20W
Prikaspiyskaya Nizmennost 23 47 0N 48 0 E
Prilep 19 41 21N 21 37 E
Priluki 23 50 30N 32 24 E
Prime Seal I. 44 40 3S 147 43 E
Primrose L. 65 54 55N 109 45W
Prince Albert, Canada 65 53 15N 105 50W
Prince Albert, S. Africa 56 33 12S 22 2 E
Prince Albert Nat. Park 65 54 0N 106 25W
Prince Albert Pen. 60 72 30N 116 0W
Prince Albert Sd. 60 70 25N 115 0W
Prince Charles I. 61 67 47N 76 12W
Prince Edward I. □ 63 46 20N 63 20W
Prince Edward Is. 3 46 35S 38 0 E
Prince George 64 53 55N 122 50W
Prince of Wales I., Canada 60 73 0N 99 0W
Prince of Wales I., U.S.A. 60 55 30N 133 0W
Prince of Wales Is. 44 10 40S 142 10 E
Prince Rupert 64 54 20N 130 20W
Princess Charlotte B. 44 14 25S 144 0 E
Princess May Ranges 46 15 30S 125 30 E
Princess Royal I. 64 53 0N 128 40W
Princeton, Canada 64 49 27N 120 30W
Princeton, Ill., U.S.A. 70 41 25N 89 25W
Princeton, Ind., U.S.A. 68 38 20N 87 35W
Princeton, Ky., U.S.A. 68 37 6N 87 55W
Princeton, Mo., U.S.A. 70 40 23N 93 35W
Princeton, N.J., U.S.A. 68 40 18N 74 40W
Princeton, W. Va., U.S.A. 68 37 21N 81 8W
Principe, I. de 48 1 37N 7 27 E
Principe Chan. 64 53 28N 130 0W
Principe da Beira 78 12 20S 64 30W
Prineville 72 44 17N 120 50W
Priozersk 22 61 2N 30 7 E
Pripet = Pripyat → 22 51 20N 30 9 E
Pripet Marshes = Polesye 22 52 0N 28 10 E
Pripyat → 22 51 20N 30 9 E
Pripyat Marshes = Polesye 22 52 0N 28 10 E
Priština 19 42 40N 21 13 E
Privas 12 44 45N 4 37 E
Privolzhskaya Vozvyshennost 23 51 0N 46 0 E
Prizren 19 42 13N 20 45 E
Probolinggo 35 7 46S 113 13 E
Proddatur 32 14 45N 78 30 E
Progreso 74 21 20N 89 40W
Prokopyevsk 24 54 0N 86 45 E
Prome = Pyè 33 18 49N 95 13 E
Prophet → 64 58 48N 122 40W
Propriá 79 10 13S 36 51W
Proserpine 44 20 21S 148 36 E
Prosser 72 46 11N 119 52W
Prostějov 14 49 30N 17 9 E
Proston 45 26 8S 151 32 E
Protection 71 37 16N 99 30W
Provence 12 43 40N 5 46 E
Providence, Ky., U.S.A. 68 37 25N 87 46W
Providence, R.I., U.S.A. 68 41 50N 71 28W
Providence Bay 62 45 41N 82 15W
Providence Mts. 73 35 0N 115 30W
Providencia, I. de 75 13 25N 81 26W
Provideniya 25 64 23N 173 18W
Provins 12 48 33N 3 15 E
Provo 72 40 16N 111 37W
Provost 65 52 25N 110 20W
Prud'homme 65 52 20N 105 54W
Pruszków 15 52 9N 20 49 E
Prut → 15 45 28N 28 10 E
Pryor 71 36 17N 95 20W
Przemysl 15 49 50N 22 45 E
Przeworsk 15 50 6N 22 32 E
Przhevalsk 24 42 30N 78 20 E
Pskov 22 57 50N 28 25 E
Puán 80 37 30S 62 45W
Pucallpa 78 8 25S 74 30W
Pucheng 39 27 59N 118 31 E
Pudozh 22 61 48N 36 32 E
Pudukkottai 32 10 28N 78 47 E
Puebla 74 19 0N 98 10W
Puebla □ 74 18 30N 98 0W
Pueblo 70 38 20N 104 40W
Pueblo Hundido 80 26 20S 70 5W
Puelches 80 38 5S 65 51W
Puente Alto 80 33 32S 70 35W
Puente-Genil 13 37 22N 4 47W
Puerco → 73 34 22N 107 50W
Puerto Aisén 80 45 27S 73 0W
Puerto Armuelles 75 8 20N 82 51W
Puerto Ayacucho 78 5 40N 67 35W
Puerto Barrios 75 15 40N 88 32W
Puerto Bermejo 80 26 55S 58 34W
Puerto Bermúdez 78 10 20S 75 0W
Puerto Bolívar 78 3 19S 79 55W
Puerto Cabello 78 10 28N 68 1W
Puerto Cabezas 75 14 0N 83 30W
Puerto Carreño 78 6 12N 67 22W
Puerto Castilla 75 16 0N 86 0W
Puerto Chicama 78 7 45S 79 20W
Puerto Coig 80 50 54S 69 15W
Puerto Cortes, C. Rica 75 8 55N 84 0W
Puerto Cortés, Hond. 75 15 51N 88 0W
Puerto Cumarebo 78 11 29N 69 30W
Puerto de Santa María 13 36 36N 6 13W
Puerto del Rosario 50 28 30N 13 52W
Puerto Deseado 80 47 55S 66 0W
Puerto Heath 78 12 34S 68 39W
Puerto Juárez 74 21 11N 86 49W
Puerto La Cruz 78 10 13N 64 38W
Puerto Leguízamo 78 0 12S 74 46W
Puerto Lobos 80 42 0S 65 3W
Puerto Madryn 80 42 48S 65 4W
Puerto Maldonado 78 12 30S 69 10W
Puerto Montt 80 41 28S 73 0W
Puerto Morelos 74 20 49N 86 52W
Puerto Natales 80 51 45S 72 15W
Puerto Padre 75 21 13N 76 35W
Puerto Páez 78 6 13N 67 28W
Puerto Peñasco 74 31 20N 113 33W
Puerto Pinasco 80 22 36S 57 50W
Puerto Pirámides 80 42 35S 64 20W
Puerto Plata 75 19 48N 70 45W
Puerto Princesa 35 9 46N 118 45 E
Puerto Quellón 80 43 7S 73 37W
Puerto Quepos 75 9 29N 84 6W
Puerto Rico ■ 75 18 15N 66 45W
Puerto Sastre 78 22 2S 57 55W
Puerto Suárez 78 18 58S 57 52W
Puerto Vallarta 74 20 36N 105 15W
Puerto Wilches 78 7 21N 73 54W
Puertollano 13 38 43N 4 7W
Pueyrredón, L. 80 47 20S 72 0W
Pugachev 22 52 0N 48 49 E
Puget Sd. 72 47 15N 122 30W
Púglia □ 18 41 0N 16 30 E
Puigcerdá 13 42 24N 1 50 E
Pukaki L. 43 44 4S 170 1 E
Pukapuka 41 10 53S 165 49W
Pukatawagan 65 55 45N 101 20W
Pukekohe 43 37 12S 174 55 E
Pukou 39 32 7N 118 38 E
Pulaski, N.Y., U.S.A. 68 43 32N 76 9W
Pulaski, Tenn., U.S.A. 69 35 10N 87 0W
Pulaski, Va., U.S.A. 68 37 4N 80 49W
Pulicat, L. 32 13 40N 80 15 E
Pullman 72 46 49N 117 10W
Pulog, Mt. 35 16 40N 120 50 E
Pumlumon Fawr 7 52 29N 3 47W
Puna 78 19 45S 65 28W
Puná, I. 78 2 55S 80 5W
Punakha 33 27 42N 89 52 E
Punata 78 17 32S 65 50W
Punch 32 33 48N 74 4 E
Pune 32 18 29N 73 57 E
Puning 39 23 20N 116 12 E
Punjab □, India 32 31 0N 76 0 E
Punjab □, Pakistan 32 30 0N 72 0 E
Puno 78 15 55S 70 3W
Punta Alta 80 38 53S 62 4W
Punta Arenas 80 53 10S 71 0W
Punta de Díaz 80 28 0S 70 45W
Punta Gorda, Belize 74 16 10N 88 45W
Punta Gorda, U.S.A. 69 26 55N 82 0W
Puntabie 45 32 12S 134 13 E
Puntarenas 75 10 0N 84 50W
Punto Fijo 78 11 50N 70 13W
Punxsutawney 68 40 56N 79 0W
Puqi 39 29 40N 113 50 E
Puquio 78 14 45S 74 10W
Pur → 24 67 31N 77 55 E
Purace, Vol. 78 2 21N 76 23W
Purbeck, Isle of 7 50 40N 2 5W
Purcell 71 35 0N 97 25W
Puri 33 19 50N 85 58 E
Purmerend 11 52 30N 4 58 E

Purnia **33** 25 45N 87 31 E
Purukcahu **34** 0 35S 114 35 E
Puruliya **33** 23 17N 86 24 E
Purus → **78** 3 42S 61 28W
Purwakarta **35** 6 35S 107 29 E
Purwodadi, Jawa, Indonesia **35** 7 7S 110 55 E
Purwodadi, Jawa, Indonesia **35** 7 51S 110 0 E
Purwokerto **35** 7 25S 109 14 E
Purworejo **35** 7 43S 110 2 E
Pusan **38** 35 5N 129 0 E
Push, La **72** 47 55N 124 38W
Pushchino **25** 54 10N 158 0 E
Pushkino **23** 51 16N 47 0 E
Putahow L. **65** 59 54N 100 40W
Putao **33** 27 28N 97 30 E
Putaruru **43** 38 2S 175 50 E
Puthein Myit → **33** 15 56N 94 18 E
Putian **39** 25 23N 119 0 E
Putignano **18** 40 50N 17 5 E
Puting, Tanjung **34** 3 31S 111 46 E
Putorana, Gory **25** 69 0N 95 0 E
Puttalam **32** 8 1N 79 55 E
Putten **11** 52 16N 5 36 E
Puttgarden **14** 54 28N 11 15 E
Putumayo → **78** 3 7S 67 58W
Putussibau **34** 0 50N 112 56 E
Puy, Le **12** 45 3N 3 52 E
Puy-de-Dôme **12** 45 46N 2 57 E
Puy-de-Dôme □ **12** 45 40N 3 5 E
Puyallup **72** 47 10N 122 22W
Puyang **38** 35 40N 115 1 E
Pweto **54** 8 25S 28 51 E
Pwllheli **6** 52 54N 4 26W
Pya-ozero **22** 66 5N 30 58 E
Pyapon **33** 16 20N 95 40 E
Pyasina → **25** 73 30N 87 0 E
Pyatigorsk **23** 44 2N 43 6 E
Pyè **33** 18 49N 95 13 E
Pyinmana **33** 19 45N 96 12 E
Pyŏngyang **38** 39 0N 125 30 E
Pyote **71** 31 34N 103 5W
Pyramid L. **72** 40 0N 119 30W
Pyrénées **12** 42 45N 0 18 E
Pyrénées-Atlantiques □ **12** 43 10N 0 50W
Pyrénées-Orientales □ **12** 42 35N 2 26 E
Pyu **33** 18 30N 96 28 E

Q

Qabalān **28** 32 8N 35 17 E
Qabātiyah **28** 32 25N 35 16 E
Qachasnek **57** 30 6S 28 42 E
Qādib **29** 12 37N 53 57 E
Qā'emshahr **31** 36 30N 52 55 E
Qahremānshahr = Bākhtarān **30** 34 23N 47 0 E
Qaidam Pendi **37** 37 0N 95 0 E
Qalāt **31** 32 15N 66 58 E
Qal'at al Akhḍar **30** 28 0N 37 10 E
Qal'eh Shaharak **32** 34 10N 64 20 E
Qal'eh-ye Now **31** 35 0N 63 5 E
Qalqīlya **28** 32 12N 34 58 E
Qam **28** 32 36N 35 43 E
Qamar, Ghubbat al **29** 16 20N 52 30 E
Qamruddin Karez **32** 31 45N 68 20 E
Qāna **28** 33 12N 35 17 E
Qandahār **31** 31 32N 65 30 E
Qandahār □ **32** 31 0N 65 0 E
Qâra **51** 29 38N 26 30 E
Qarachuk **30** 37 0N 42 2 E
Qārah **30** 29 55N 40 3 E
Qarqan **37** 38 5N 85 20 E
Qarqan He → **37** 39 30N 88 30 E
Qāsim **28** 32 59N 36 2 E
Qaṣr-e Qand **31** 26 15N 60 45 E
Qasr Farâfra **51** 27 0N 28 1 E
Qatar ■ **31** 25 30N 51 15 E
Qattâra, Munkhafed el **51** 29 30N 27 30 E
Qattâra Depression = Qattâra, Munkhafed el **51** 29 30N 27 30 E
Qāyen **31** 33 40N 59 10 E
Qazvin **30** 36 15N 50 0 E
Qena **51** 26 10N 32 43 E
Qeshm **31** 26 55N 56 10 E
Qezi'ot **28** 30 52N 34 26 E
Qian Xian **39** 34 31N 108 15 E
Qianshan **39** 30 37N 116 35 E
Qianxi **39** 27 3N 106 3 E
Qianyang **39** 27 18N 110 10 E
Qijiang **39** 28 57N 106 35 E
Qila Safed **31** 29 0N 61 30 E
Qila Saifullāh **32** 30 45N 68 17 E
Qilian Shan **37** 38 30N 96 0 E
Qin Ling = Qinling Shandi **39** 33 50N 108 10 E
Qin'an **39** 34 48N 105 40 E
Qingdao **38** 36 5N 120 20 E
Qinghai □ **37** 36 0N 98 0 E
Qinghai Hu **37** 36 40N 100 10 E
Qingjiang, Jiangsu, China **39** 33 30N 119 2 E
Qingjiang, Jiangxi, China **39** 28 4N 115 29 E
Qingliu **39** 26 11N 116 48 E
Qingshuihe **38** 39 55N 111 35 E
Qingyang **38** 36 2N 107 55 E
Qingyuan **39** 23 40N 112 59 E
Qinhuangdao **38** 39 56N 119 30 E
Qinling Shandi **39** 33 50N 108 10 E
Qinyang **39** 35 7N 112 57 E
Qinyuan **38** 36 29N 112 20 E
Qinzhou **39** 21 58N 108 38 E
Qiongshan **39** 19 51N 110 26 E
Qiongzhou Haixia **39** 20 10N 110 15 E
Qiqihar **38** 47 26N 124 0 E
Qiryat 'Anavim **28** 31 49N 35 7 E
Qiryat Ata **28** 32 47N 35 6 E
Qiryat Bialik **28** 32 50N 35 5 E
Qiryat Gat **28** 31 32N 34 46 E
Qiryat Ḥayyim **28** 32 49N 35 4 E
Qiryat Mal'akhi **28** 31 44N 34 44 E
Qiryat Shemona **28** 33 13N 35 35 E
Qiryat Yam **28** 32 51N 35 4 E
Qishan **39** 22 52N 120 25 E
Qishon → **28** 32 49N 35 2 E
Qitai **37** 44 2N 89 35 E
Qiyahe **38** 53 0N 120 35 E
Qiyang **39** 26 35N 111 50 E
Qom **31** 34 40N 51 0 E
Qomsheh **31** 32 0N 51 55 E
Qondūz **31** 36 50N 68 50 E
Qondūz □ **31** 36 50N 68 50 E
Qu Jiang → **39** 30 1N 106 24 E
Qu Xian, Sichuan, China **39** 30 48N 106 58 E
Qu Xian, Zhejiang, China **39** 28 57N 118 54 E
Quairading **47** 32 0S 117 21 E
Qualeup **47** 33 48S 116 48 E
Quambatook **45** 35 49S 143 34 E
Quambone **45** 30 57S 147 53 E
Quan Long **34** 9 7N 105 8 E
Quanan **71** 34 20N 99 45W
Quandialla **45** 34 1S 147 47 E
Quang Ngai **34** 15 13N 108 58 E
Quantock Hills **7** 51 8N 3 10W
Quanzhou, Fujian, China **39** 24 55N 118 34 E
Quanzhou, Guangxi Zhuangzu, China **39** 25 57N 111 5 E
Quaraí **80** 30 15S 56 20W
Quartzsite **73** 33 44N 114 16W
Quatsino **64** 50 30N 127 40W
Quatsino Sd. **64** 50 25N 127 58W
Qubab = Mishmar Ayyalon **28** 31 52N 34 57 E
Qūchān **31** 37 10N 58 27 E
Queanbeyan **45** 35 17S 149 14 E
Québec **63** 46 52N 71 13W
Québec □ **63** 50 0N 70 0W
Queen Charlotte **64** 53 15N 132 2W
Queen Charlotte Is. **64** 53 20N 132 10W
Queen Charlotte Sd. **43** 41 10S 174 15 E
Queen Charlotte Str. **64** 51 0N 128 0W
Queen Elizabeth Is. **2** 76 0N 95 0W
Queen Maud G. **60** 68 15N 102 30W
Queens Chan. **46** 15 0S 129 30 E
Queenscliff **45** 38 16S 144 39 E
Queensland □ **44** 22 0S 142 0 E
Queenstown, Australia **44** 42 4S 145 35 E
Queenstown, N.Z. **43** 45 1S 168 40 E
Queenstown, S. Africa **56** 31 52S 26 52 E
Queimadas **79** 11 0S 39 38W
Quela **54** 9 10S 16 56 E
Quelimane **55** 17 53S 36 58 E
Quelpart = Cheju Do **39** 33 29N 126 34 E
Quemado, N. Mex., U.S.A. **73** 34 17N 108 28W
Quemado, Tex., U.S.A. **71** 28 58N 100 35W
Quequén **80** 38 30S 58 30W
Querétaro **74** 20 40N 100 23W
Querétaro □ **74** 20 30N 100 0W
Queshan **39** 32 55N 114 2 E
Quesnel **64** 53 0N 122 30W
Quesnel → **64** 52 58N 122 29W
Quesnel L. **64** 52 30N 121 20W
Questa **73** 36 45N 105 35W
Quetico Prov. Park **62** 48 30N 91 45W
Quetta **31** 30 15N 66 55 E
Quezaltenango **75** 14 50N 91 30W
Quezon City **35** 14 38N 121 0 E
Qui Nhon **34** 13 40N 109 13 E
Quiaca, La **80** 22 5S 65 35W
Quibaxe **54** 8 24S 14 27 E
Quibdo **78** 5 42N 76 40W
Quiberon **12** 47 29N 3 9W
Quick **64** 54 36N 126 54W
Quiet L. **64** 61 5N 133 5W
Quilán, C. **80** 43 15S 74 30W
Quilengues **55** 14 12S 14 12 E
Quillabamba **78** 12 50S 72 50W
Quillagua **78** 21 40S 69 40W
Quillota **80** 32 54S 71 16W
Quilon **32** 8 50N 76 38 E
Quilpie **45** 26 35S 144 11 E
Quimilí **80** 27 40S 62 30W
Quimper **12** 48 0N 4 9W
Quimperlé **12** 47 53N 3 33W
Quincy, Calif., U.S.A. **72** 39 56N 120 56W
Quincy, Fla., U.S.A. **69** 30 34N 84 34W
Quincy, Ill., U.S.A. **70** 39 55N 91 20W
Quincy, Mass., U.S.A. **68** 42 14N 71 0W
Quincy, Wash., U.S.A. **72** 47 22N 119 56W
Quines **80** 32 13S 65 48W
Quinga **55** 15 49S 40 15 E
Quintana Roo □ **74** 19 0N 88 0W
Quintanar de la Orden **13** 39 36N 3 5W
Quintanar de la Sierra **13** 41 57N 2 55W
Quintero **80** 32 45S 71 30W
Quinyambie **45** 30 15S 141 0 E
Quipungo **55** 14 37S 14 40 E
Quirindi **45** 31 28S 150 40 E
Quissanga **55** 12 24S 40 28 E
Quitilipi **80** 26 50S 60 13W
Quitman, Ga., U.S.A. **69** 30 49N 83 35W
Quitman, Miss., U.S.A. **69** 32 2N 88 42W
Quitman, Tex., U.S.A. **71** 32 48N 95 25W
Quito **78** 0 15S 78 35W
Quixadá **79** 4 55S 39 0W
Qumbu **57** 31 10S 28 48 E
Qumrān **28** 31 43N 35 27 E
Quneitra **28** 33 7N 35 48 E
Quoin I. **46** 14 54S 129 32 E
Quoin Pt. **56** 34 46S 19 37 E
Quondong **45** 33 6S 140 18 E
Quorn **45** 32 25S 138 0 E
Qûs **51** 25 55N 32 50 E
Quseir **51** 26 7N 34 16 E
Qusrah **28** 32 5N 35 20 E
Quthing **57** 30 25S 27 36 E

R

Raahe **20** 64 40N 24 28 E
Ra'ananna **28** 32 12N 34 52 E
Raasay **8** 57 25N 6 4W
Raasay, Sd. of **8** 57 30N 6 8W
Raba **35** 8 36S 118 55 E
Rabat, Malta **18** 35 53N 14 25 E
Rabat, Morocco **50** 34 2N 6 48W
Rabaul **40** 4 24S 152 18 E
Rabbit → **64** 59 41N 127 12W
Rabbit Lake **65** 53 8N 107 46W
Rabbitskin → **64** 61 47N 120 42W
Rābigh **30** 22 50N 39 5 E
Race, C. **63** 46 40N 53 5W
Rach Gia **34** 10 5N 105 5 E
Racine **68** 42 41N 87 51W
Radama, Nosy **57** 14 0S 47 47 E
Radama, Saikanosy **57** 14 16S 47 53 E
Rădăuţi **15** 47 50N 25 59 E
Radford **68** 37 8N 80 32W
Radhwa, Jabal **30** 24 34N 38 18 E
Radisson **65** 52 30N 107 20W
Radium Hot Springs **64** 50 35N 116 2W
Radnor Forest **7** 52 17N 3 10W
Radom **15** 51 23N 21 12 E
Radomir **19** 42 37N 23 4 E
Radomsko **15** 51 5N 19 28 E
Radstock **7** 51 17N 2 25W
Radstock, C. **45** 33 12S 134 20 E
Radville **65** 49 30N 104 15W
Rae **64** 62 50N 116 3W
Rae Bareli **33** 26 18N 81 20 E
Rae Isthmus **61** 66 40N 87 30W
Raeren **11** 50 41N 6 7 E
Raeside, L. **47** 29 20S 122 0 E
Raetihi **43** 39 25S 175 17 E
Rafaela **80** 31 10S 61 30W
Rafai **54** 4 59N 23 58 E
Rafḥā **30** 29 35N 43 35 E
Rafsanjān **31** 30 30N 56 5 E
Raft Pt. **46** 16 4S 124 26 E
Ragama **32** 7 0N 79 50 E
Ragged Mt. **47** 33 27S 123 25 E
Raglan, Australia **44** 23 42S 150 49 E
Raglan, N.Z. **43** 37 55S 174 55 E
Ragusa **18** 36 56N 14 42 E
Raha **35** 4 55S 123 0 E
Rahad al Bardī **51** 11 20N 23 40 E
Rahaeng = Tak **34** 16 52N 99 8 E
Rahimyar Khan **32** 28 30N 70 25 E
Raichur **32** 16 10N 77 20 E
Raigarh **33** 21 56N 83 25 E
Raijua **35** 10 37S 121 36 E
Railton **44** 41 25S 146 28 E
Rainbow Lake **64** 58 30N 119 23W
Rainier **72** 46 4N 122 58W
Rainier, Mt. **72** 46 50N 121 50W
Rainy L. **65** 48 42N 93 10W
Rainy River **65** 48 43N 94 29W
Raipur **33** 21 17N 81 45 E
Ra'is **30** 23 33N 38 43 E
Raj Nandgaon **33** 21 0N 81 0 E
Raja, Ujung **34** 3 40N 96 25 E
Raja Ampat, Kepulauan **35** 0 30S 130 0 E
Rajahmundry **33** 17 1N 81 48 E
Rajang → **34** 2 30N 112 0 E
Rajapalaiyam **32** 9 25N 77 35 E
Rajasthan □ **32** 26 45N 73 30 E
Rajasthan Canal **32** 28 0N 72 0 E
Rajgarh **32** 24 2N 76 45 E
Rajkot **32** 22 15N 70 56 E
Rajojooseppi **20** 68 25N 28 30 E
Rajpipla **32** 21 50N 73 30 E
Rajshahi **33** 24 22N 88 39 E
Rajshahi □ **33** 25 0N 89 0 E
Rakaia **43** 43 45S 172 1 E
Rakaia → **43** 43 36S 172 15 E
Rakan, Ra's **31** 26 10N 51 20 E
Rakaposhi **32** 36 10N 74 25 E
Rakata, Pulau **34** 6 10S 105 20 E
Rakops **56** 21 1S 24 28 E
Raleigh **69** 35 47N 78 39W
Raleigh B. **69** 34 50N 76 15W
Ralls **71** 33 40N 101 20W
Ram → **64** 62 1N 123 41W
Rām Allāh **28** 31 55N 35 10 E
Ram Hd. **45** 37 47S 149 30 E
Rama **28** 32 56N 35 21 E
Ramanathapuram **32** 9 25N 78 55 E
Ramanetaka, B. de **57** 14 13S 47 52 E
Ramat Gan **28** 32 4N 34 48 E
Ramat HaSharon **28** 32 7N 34 50 E
Ramatlhabama **56** 25 37S 25 33 E
Rambipuji **35** 8 12S 113 37 E
Ramea **63** 47 31N 57 23W
Ramechhap **33** 27 25N 86 10 E
Ramelau **35** 8 55S 126 22 E
Ramgarh, Bihar, India **33** 23 40N 85 35 E
Ramgarh, Raj., India **32** 27 30N 70 36 E
Rāmhormoz **30** 31 15N 49 35 E
Ramla **28** 31 55N 34 52 E
Rammūn **28** 31 55N 35 17 E
Ramnad = Ramanathapuram **32** 9 25N 78 55 E
Ramon, Har **28** 30 30N 34 38 E
Ramona **73** 33 1N 116 56W
Ramore **62** 48 30N 80 25W
Ramotswa **56** 24 50S 25 52 E
Rampart **60** 65 0N 150 15W
Rampur **32** 28 50N 79 5 E
Rampur Hat **33** 24 10N 87 50 E
Ramree Kyun **33** 19 0N 94 0 E
Ramsey, Canada **62** 47 25N 82 20W
Ramsey, U.K. **6** 54 20N 4 21W
Ramsgate **7** 51 20N 1 25 E
Ramtek **32** 21 20N 79 15 E
Ranaghat **33** 23 15N 88 35 E
Ranau **34** 6 2N 116 40 E
Rancagua **80** 34 10S 70 50W
Rancheria → **64** 60 13N 129 7W
Ranchester **72** 44 57N 107 12W
Ranchi **33** 23 19N 85 27 E
Randers **21** 56 29N 10 1 E
Randfontein **57** 26 8S 27 45 E
Randolph **72** 41 43N 111 10W
Råne älv → **20** 65 50N 22 20 E
Rangaunu B. **43** 34 51S 173 15 E
Rangeley **68** 44 58N 70 33W
Rangely **72** 40 3N 108 53W
Ranger **71** 32 30N 98 42W
Rangia **33** 26 28N 91 38 E
Rangiora **43** 43 19S 172 36 E
Rangitaiki → **43** 37 54S 176 49 E
Rangitata → **43** 43 45S 171 15 E
Rangkasbitung **35** 6 21S 106 15 E
Rangon → **33** 16 28N 96 40 E
Rangoon **33** 16 45N 96 20 E
Rangpur **33** 25 42N 89 22 E
Rangwe **52** 0 38S 34 35 E
Ranibennur **32** 14 35N 75 30 E
Raniganj **33** 23 40N 87 5 E
Raniwara **32** 24 50N 72 10 E
Ranken → **44** 20 31S 137 36 E
Rankin **71** 31 16N 101 56W
Rankin Inlet **60** 62 30N 93 0W
Rankins Springs **45** 33 49S 146 14 E
Rannoch, L. **8** 56 41N 4 20W
Rannoch Moor **8** 56 38N 4 48W
Ranobe, Helodranon' i **57** 23 3S 43 33 E
Ranohira **57** 22 29S 45 24 E
Ranomafana, Toamasina, Madag. **57** 18 57S 48 50 E
Ranomafana, Toliara, Madag. **57** 24 34S 47 0 E
Ranong **34** 9 56N 98 40 E
Ransiki **35** 1 30S 134 10 E
Rantau **34** 2 56S 115 9 E
Rantauprapat **34** 2 15N 99 50 E
Rantekombola **35** 3 15S 119 57 E
Rantis **28** 32 4N 35 3 E
Rantoul **68** 40 18N 88 10W
Raohe **38** 46 47N 134 0 E
Rapa Iti **41** 27 35S 144 20W
Rāpch **31** 25 40N 59 15 E
Rapid → **64** 59 15N 129 5W
Rapid City **70** 44 0N 103 0W
Rapid River **68** 45 55N 87 0W
Rapides des Joachims **62** 46 13N 77 43W
Rarotonga **41** 21 30S 160 0W
Ra's al Khaymah **31** 25 50N 56 5 E
Ra's al-Unuf **51** 30 25N 18 15 E
Ras Bânâs **51** 23 57N 35 59 E
Ras Dashen **54** 13 8N 38 26 E
Râs Timirist **50** 19 21N 16 30W
Rasa, Punta **80** 40 50S 62 15W
Rashad **51** 11 55N 31 0 E
Rashîd **51** 31 21N 30 22 E
Rasht **30** 37 20N 49 40 E
Rason, L. **47** 28 45S 124 25 E
Rat Is. **60** 51 50N 178 15 E
Rat River **64** 61 7N 112 36W
Ratangarh **32** 28 5N 74 35 E
Rath Luirc **9** 52 21N 8 40W
Rathdrum **9** 52 57N 6 13W
Rathenow **14** 52 38N 12 23 E
Rathkeale **9** 52 32N 8 57W
Rathlin I. **9** 55 18N 6 14W
Rathlin O'Birne I. **9** 54 40N 8 50W
Ratlam **32** 23 20N 75 0 E
Ratnagiri **32** 16 57N 73 18 E
Raton **71** 37 0N 104 30W
Rattray Hd. **8** 57 38N 1 50W
Ratz, Mt. **64** 57 23N 132 12W
Raufarhöfn **20** 66 27N 15 57W
Raukumara Ra. **43** 38 5S 177 55 E
Rauma **21** 61 10N 21 30 E
Raurkela **33** 22 14N 84 50 E
Rāvar **31** 31 20N 56 51 E
Ravenna, Italy **18** 44 28N 12 15 E
Ravenna, U.S.A. **70** 41 3N 98 58W
Ravensburg **14** 47 48N 9 38 E
Ravenshoe **44** 17 37S 145 29 E
Ravensthorpe **47** 33 35S 120 2 E
Ravenswood, Australia **44** 20 6S 146 54 E
Ravenswood, U.S.A. **68** 38 58N 81 47W
Ravi → **32** 30 35N 71 49 E
Rawalpindi **32** 33 38N 73 8 E
Rawāndūz **30** 36 40N 44 30 E
Rawdon **62** 46 3N 73 40W
Rawene **43** 35 25S 173 32 E
Rawlinna **47** 30 58S 125 28 E
Rawlins **72** 41 50N 107 20W
Rawlinson Range **47** 24 40S 128 30 E
Rawson **80** 43 15S 65 0W
Ray **70** 48 21N 103 6W
Ray, C. **63** 47 33N 59 15W
Rayadurg **32** 14 40N 76 50 E
Rayagada **33** 19 15N 83 20 E
Raychikhinsk **25** 49 46N 129 25 E
Raymond, Canada **64** 49 30N 112 35W
Raymond, U.S.A. **72** 46 45N 123 48W
Raymondville **71** 26 30N 97 50W
Raymore **65** 51 25N 104 31W
Rayne **71** 30 16N 92 16W
Rayville **71** 32 30N 91 45W
Raz, Pte. du **12** 48 2N 4 47W
Razgrad **19** 43 33N 26 34 E
Ré, I. de **12** 46 12N 1 30W
Reading, U.K. **7** 51 27N 0 57W
Reading, U.S.A. **68** 40 20N 75 53W
Realicó **80** 35 0S 64 15W
Rebecca L. **47** 30 0S 122 15 E
Rebi **35** 6 23S 134 7 E
Rebiana **51** 24 12N 22 10 E
Rebun-Tō **36** 45 23N 141 2 E
Recherche, Arch. of the **47** 34 15S 122 50 E
Recife **79** 8 0S 35 0W
Recklinghausen **11** 51 36N 7 10 E
Reconquista **80** 29 10S 59 45W
Recreo **80** 29 25S 65 10W
Red → = Hong → **26** 20 17N 106 34 E

Red →, Canada **65** 50 24N 96 48W
Red →, Minn., U.S.A. **70** 48 10N 97 0W
Red →, Tex., U.S.A. **71** 31 0N 91 40W
Red Bay **63** 51 44N 56 25W
Red Bluff **72** 40 11N 122 11W
Red Bluff L. **71** 31 59N 103 58W
Red Cliffs **45** 34 19S 142 11 E
Red Cloud **70** 40 8N 98 33W
Red Deer **64** 52 20N 113 50W
Red Deer →, Alta., Canada **65** 50 58N 110 0W
Red Deer →, Man., Canada **65** 52 53N 101 1W
Red Deer L. **65** 52 55N 101 20W
Red Indian L. **63** 48 35N 57 0W
Red Lake **65** 51 3N 93 49W
Red Lake Falls **70** 47 54N 96 15W
Red Lodge **72** 45 10N 109 10W
Red Oak **70** 41 0N 95 10W
Red Rock **62** 48 55N 88 15W
Red Rock, L. **70** 41 30N 93 15W
Red Rock's Pt. **47** 32 13S 127 32 E
Red Sea **29** 25 0N 36 0 E
Red Sucker L. **65** 54 9N 93 40W
Red Tower Pass = Turnu Rosu Pasul **15** 45 33N 24 17 E
Red Wing **70** 44 32N 92 35W
Redbridge **7** 51 35N 0 7 E
Redcar **6** 54 37N 1 4W
Redcliff **65** 50 10N 110 50W
Redcliffe **45** 27 12S 153 0 E
Redcliffe, Mt. **47** 28 30S 121 30 E
Reddersburg **56** 29 41S 26 10 E
Redding **72** 40 30N 122 25W
Redditch **7** 52 18N 1 57W
Redfield **70** 45 0N 98 30W
Redknife → **64** 61 14N 119 22W
Redlands **73** 34 0N 117 11W
Redmond, Australia **47** 34 55S 117 40 E
Redmond, U.S.A. **72** 44 19N 121 11W
Redonda **75** 16 58N 62 19W
Redondela **13** 42 15N 8 38W
Redondo **13** 38 39N 7 37W
Redrock Pt. **64** 62 11N 115 2W
Redruth **7** 50 14N 5 14W
Redvers **65** 49 35N 101 40W
Redwater **64** 53 55N 113 6W
Redwood City **73** 37 30N 122 15W
Redwood Falls **70** 44 30N 95 2W
Ree, L. **9** 53 35N 8 0W
Reed, L. **65** 54 38N 100 30W
Reed City **68** 43 52N 85 30W
Reeder **70** 46 7N 102 52W
Reedley **73** 36 36N 119 27W
Reedsburg **70** 43 34N 90 5W
Reedsport **72** 43 45N 124 4W
Reefton **43** 42 6S 171 51 E
Refugio **71** 28 18N 97 17W
Regavim **28** 32 32N 35 2 E
Regensburg **14** 49 1N 12 7 E
Réggio di Calábria **18** 38 7N 15 38 E
Réggio nell' Emilia **18** 44 42N 10 38 E
Regina **65** 50 27N 104 35W
Rehoboth **56** 23 15S 17 4 E
Rehovot **28** 31 54N 34 48 E
Rei-Bouba **51** 8 40N 14 15 E
Reichenbach **14** 50 36N 12 19 E
Reid **47** 30 49S 128 26 E
Reid River **44** 19 40S 146 48 E
Reidsville **69** 36 21N 79 40W
Reigate **7** 51 14N 0 11W
Reims **12** 49 15N 4 1 E
Reina **28** 32 43N 35 18 E
Reina Adelaida, Arch. **80** 52 20S 74 0W
Reinbeck **70** 42 18N 92 40W
Reindeer → **65** 55 36N 103 11W
Reindeer I. **65** 52 30N 98 0W
Reindeer L. **65** 57 15N 102 15W
Reine, La **62** 48 50N 79 30W
Reinga, C. **43** 34 25S 172 43 E
Reitz **57** 27 48S 28 29 E
Reivilo **56** 27 36S 24 8 E
Rekinniki **25** 60 51N 163 40 E
Reliance **65** 63 0N 109 20W
Remarkable, Mt. **45** 32 48S 138 10 E
Rembang **35** 6 42S 111 21 E
Remeshk **31** 26 55N 58 50 E
Remich **11** 49 32N 6 22 E
Remscheid **14** 51 11N 7 12 E
Rendsburg **14** 54 18N 9 41 E
Rene **25** 66 2N 179 25W
Renfrew, Canada **62** 45 30N 76 40W
Renfrew, U.K. **8** 55 52N 4 24W
Rengat **34** 0 30S 102 45 E
Renhuai **39** 27 48N 106 24 E
Renk **51** 11 50N 32 50 E
Renkum **11** 51 58N 5 43 E
Renmark **45** 34 11S 140 43 E
Rennell Sd. **64** 53 23N 132 35W
Renner Springs T.O. **44** 18 20S 133 47 E
Rennes **12** 48 7N 1 41W
Reno **72** 39 30N 119 50W
Reno → **18** 44 37N 12 17 E
Renovo **68** 41 20N 77 47W
Rensselaer **68** 40 57N 87 10W
Renton **72** 47 30N 122 9W
Republic, Mich., U.S.A. **68** 46 25N 87 59W
Republic, Wash., U.S.A. **72** 48 38N 118 42W
Republican → **70** 39 3N 96 48W
Republican City **70** 40 9N 99 20W
Repulse Bay **61** 66 30N 86 30W
Requena, Peru **78** 5 5S 73 52W
Requena, Spain **13** 39 30N 1 4W
Reserve, Canada **65** 52 28N 102 39W
Reserve, U.S.A. **73** 33 50N 108 54W
Resht = Rasht **30** 37 20N 49 40 E
Resistencia **80** 27 30S 59 0W
Reşiţa **15** 45 18N 21 53 E
Resolution I., Canada **61** 61 30N 65 0W
Resolution I., N.Z. **43** 45 40S 166 40 E
Ressano Garcia **57** 25 25S 32 0 E
Reston **65** 49 33N 101 6W
Retalhuleu **75** 14 33N 91 46W
Réthímnon **19** 35 18N 24 30 E
Réunion **3** 21 0S 56 0 E
Reutlingen **14** 48 28N 9 13 E
Reval = Tallinn **22** 59 22N 24 48 E
Revda **22** 56 48N 59 57 E
Revelstoke **64** 51 0N 118 10W
Revilla Gigedo, Is. **41** 18 40N 112 0W
Revillagigedo I. **64** 55 50N 131 20W
Rewa **33** 24 33N 81 25 E
Rewari **32** 28 15N 76 40 E
Rexburg **72** 43 55N 111 50W
Rey Malabo **54** 3 45N 8 50 E
Reykjahlið **20** 65 40N 16 55W
Reykjanes **20** 63 48N 22 40W
Reykjavík **20** 64 10N 21 57 E
Reynolds **65** 49 40N 95 55W
Reynolds Ra. **46** 22 30S 133 0 E
Reynosa **74** 26 5N 98 18W
Rhayader **7** 52 19N 3 30W
Rheden **11** 52 0N 6 3 E
Rhein **65** 51 25N 102 15W
Rhein → **11** 51 52N 6 2 E
Rheine **14** 52 17N 7 25 E
Rheinland-Pfalz □ **14** 50 0N 7 0 E
Rhin = Rhein → **11** 51 52N 6 2 E
Rhine = Rhein → **11** 51 52N 6 2 E
Rhineland-Palatinate □ = Rheinland-Pfalz □ **14** 50 0N 7 0 E
Rhinelander **70** 45 38N 89 29W
Rhode Island □ **68** 41 38N 71 37W
Rhodes = Ródhos **19** 36 15N 28 10 E
Rhodesia = Zimbabwe ■ **55** 19 0S 30 0 E
Rhodope Mts. = Rhodopi Planina **19** 41 40N 24 20 E
Rhodopi Planina **19** 41 40N 24 20 E
Rhondda **7** 51 39N 3 30W
Rhône □ **12** 45 54N 4 35 E
Rhône → **14** 43 28N 4 42 E
Rhum **8** 57 0N 6 20W
Rhyl **6** 53 19N 3 29W
Rhymney **7** 51 32N 3 7W
Riachão **79** 7 20S 46 37W
Riasi **32** 33 10N 74 50 E
Riau □ **34** 0 0 102 35 E
Riau, Kepulauan **34** 0 30N 104 20 E
Ribadeo **13** 43 35N 7 5W
Ribatejo □ **13** 39 15N 8 30W
Ribble → **6** 54 13N 2 20W
Ribe **21** 55 19N 8 44 E
Ribeirão Prêto **79** 21 10S 47 50W
Riberalta **78** 11 0S 66 0W
Riccarton **43** 43 32S 172 37 E
Rice Lake **70** 45 30N 91 42W
Rich Hill **71** 38 5N 94 22W
Richards Bay **57** 28 48S 32 6 E
Richards L. **65** 59 10N 107 10W
Richardson → **65** 58 25N 111 14W
Richardton **70** 46 56N 102 22W
Riche, C. **47** 34 36S 118 47 E
Richey **70** 47 42N 105 5W
Richfield, Idaho, U.S.A. **72** 43 2N 114 5W
Richfield, Utah, U.S.A. **73** 38 50N 112 0W
Richibucto **63** 46 42N 64 54W
Richland, Ga., U.S.A. **69** 32 7N 84 40W
Richland, Oreg., U.S.A. **72** 44 49N 117 9W
Richland, Wash., U.S.A. **72** 46 15N 119 15W
Richland Center **70** 43 21N 90 22W
Richlands **68** 37 7N 81 49W
Richmond, N.S.W., Australia **45** 33 35S 150 42 E
Richmond, Queens., Australia **44** 20 43S 143 8 E
Richmond, N.Z. **43** 41 20S 173 12 E
Richmond, S. Africa **57** 29 51S 30 18 E
Richmond, N. Yorks., U.K. **6** 54 24N 1 43W
Richmond, Surrey, U.K. **7** 51 28N 0 18W
Richmond, Calif., U.S.A. **72** 37 58N 122 21W
Richmond, Ind., U.S.A. **68** 39 50N 84 50W
Richmond, Ky., U.S.A. **68** 37 40N 84 20W
Richmond, Mo., U.S.A. **70** 39 15N 93 58W
Richmond, Tex., U.S.A. **71** 29 32N 95 42W
Richmond, Utah, U.S.A. **72** 41 55N 111 48W
Richmond, Va., U.S.A. **68** 37 33N 77 27W
Richmond Ra., Australia **45** 29 0S 152 45 E
Richmond Ra., N.Z. **43** 41 32S 173 22 E
Richton **69** 31 23N 88 58W
Richwood **68** 38 17N 80 32W
Ridgedale **65** 53 0N 104 10W
Ridgeland **69** 32 30N 80 58W
Ridgelands **44** 23 16S 150 17 E
Ridgetown **62** 42 26N 81 52W
Ridgway **68** 41 25N 78 43W
Riding Mt. Nat. Park **65** 50 50N 100 0W
Ridley Mt. **47** 33 12S 122 7 E
Ried **14** 48 14N 13 30 E
Riet → **56** 29 0S 23 54 E
Rieti **18** 42 23N 12 50 E
Rifle **72** 39 40N 107 50W
Rifstangi **20** 66 32N 16 12W
Rig Rig **51** 14 13N 14 25 E
Riga **22** 56 53N 24 8 E
Riga, G. of = Rīgas Jūras Līcis **22** 57 40N 23 45 E
Rīgas Jūras Līcis **22** 57 40N 23 45 E
Rigby **72** 43 41N 111 58W
Rīgestān □ **31** 30 15N 65 0 E
Riggins **72** 45 29N 116 26W
Rigolet **63** 54 10N 58 23W
Riihimäki **21** 60 45N 24 48 E
Rijeka **18** 45 20N 14 21 E
Rijn → **11** 52 12N 4 21 E
Rijssen **11** 52 19N 6 30 E
Rijswijk **11** 52 4N 4 22 E
Riley **72** 43 35N 119 33W
Rima → **53** 13 4N 5 10 E
Rimah, Wadi ar → **30** 26 5N 41 30 E
Rimbey **64** 52 35N 114 15W
Rímini **18** 44 3N 12 33 E
Rîmnicu Sărat **15** 45 26N 27 3 E
Rîmnicu Vîlcea **15** 45 9N 24 21 E
Rimouski **63** 48 27N 68 30W
Rinca **35** 8 45S 119 35 E
Rinconada **80** 22 26S 66 10W
Rineanna **9** 52 42N 85 7W
Ringkøbing **21** 56 5N 8 15 E
Ringling **72** 46 16N 110 56W
Ringvassøy **20** 69 56N 19 15 E
Rinía **19** 37 23N 25 13 E
Rinjani **34** 8 24S 116 28 E
Rio Branco, Brazil **78** 9 58S 67 49W
Río Branco, Uruguay **80** 32 40S 53 40W
Río Claro **75** 10 20N 61 25W
Río Colorado **80** 39 0S 64 0W
Río Cuarto **80** 33 10S 64 25W
Rio das Pedras **57** 23 8S 35 28 E
Rio de Janeiro **79** 23 0S 43 12W
Rio de Janeiro □ **79** 22 50S 43 0W
Rio do Sul **80** 27 13S 49 37W
Río Gallegos **80** 51 35S 69 15W
Río Grande, Argentina **80** 53 50S 67 45W
Rio Grande, Brazil **80** 32 0S 52 20W
Rio Grande → **71** 25 57N 97 9W
Rio Grande City **71** 26 23N 98 49W
Rio Grande del Norte → **66** 26 0N 97 0W
Rio Grande do Norte □ **79** 5 40S 36 0W
Rio Grande do Sul □ **80** 30 0S 53 0W
Rio Largo **79** 9 28S 35 50W
Río Mulatos **78** 19 40S 66 50W
Río Muni = Mbini □ **54** 1 30N 10 0 E
Rio Negro **80** 26 0S 50 0W
Rio Verde, Brazil **79** 17 50S 51 0W
Río Verde, Mexico **74** 21 56N 99 59W
Rio Vista **72** 38 11N 121 44W
Ríobamba **78** 1 50S 78 45W
Ríohacha **78** 11 33N 72 55W
Rioja, La **80** 29 20S 67 0W
Rioja, La □ **13** 42 20N 2 20W
Riosucio, Caldas, Colombia **78** 5 30N 75 40W
Ríosucio, Choco, Colombia **78** 7 27N 77 7W
Riou L. **65** 59 7N 106 25W
Ripley **71** 35 43N 89 34W
Ripon, U.K. **6** 54 8N 1 31W
Ripon, U.S.A. **68** 43 51N 88 50W
Rishiri-Tō **36** 45 11N 141 15 E
Rishon le Ziyyon **28** 31 58N 34 48 E
Rishpon **28** 32 12N 34 49 E
Rison **71** 33 57N 92 11W
Risør **21** 58 43N 9 13 E
Ritzville **72** 47 10N 118 21W
Rivadavia **80** 29 57S 70 35W
Rivas **75** 11 30N 85 50W
Rivera **80** 31 0S 55 50W
Riverdsale **56** 34 7S 21 15 E
Riverhead **68** 40 53N 72 40W
Riverhurst **65** 50 55N 106 50W
Riverina **47** 29 45S 120 40 E
Rivers **65** 50 2N 100 14W
Rivers □ **53** 5 0N 6 30 E
Rivers, L. of the **65** 49 49N 105 44W
Rivers Inlet **64** 51 42N 127 15W
Riverside, Calif., U.S.A. **73** 34 0N 117 22W
Riverside, Wyo., U.S.A. **72** 41 12N 106 57W
Riversleigh **44** 19 5S 138 40 E
Riverton, Australia **45** 34 10S 138 46 E
Riverton, Canada **65** 51 1N 97 0W
Riverton, N.Z. **43** 46 21S 168 0 E
Riverton, U.S.A. **72** 43 1N 108 27W
Riviera **14** 44 0N 8 30 E
Rivière-à-Pierre **63** 46 59N 72 11W
Rivière-au-Renard **63** 48 59N 64 23W
Rivière-du-Loup **63** 47 50N 69 30W
Rivière-Pentecôte **63** 49 57N 67 1W
Rivoli B. **45** 37 32S 140 3 E
Riyadh = Ar Riyāḍ **29** 24 41N 46 42 E
Rize **30** 41 0N 40 30 E
Rizhao **39** 35 25N 119 30 E
Rizzuto, C. **18** 38 54N 17 5 E
Rjukan **21** 59 54N 8 33 E
Roag, L. **8** 58 10N 6 55W
Roanne **12** 46 3N 4 4 E
Roanoke, Ala., U.S.A. **69** 33 9N 85 23W
Roanoke, Va., U.S.A. **68** 37 19N 79 55W
Roanoke → **69** 35 56N 76 43W
Roanoke I. **69** 35 55N 75 40W
Roanoke Rapids **69** 36 28N 77 42W
Roatán **75** 16 18N 86 35W
Robbins I. **44** 40 42S 145 0 E
Robe →, Australia **46** 21 42S 116 15 E
Robe →, Ireland **9** 53 38N 9 10W
Robert Lee **71** 31 55N 100 26W
Roberts **72** 43 44N 112 8W
Robertson **56** 33 46S 19 50 E
Robertson Ra. **46** 23 15S 121 0 E
Robertsport **50** 6 45N 11 26W
Robertstown **45** 33 58S 139 5 E
Roberval **63** 48 32N 72 15W
Robinson → **44** 16 3S 137 16 E
Robinson Crusoe I. **41** 33 38S 78 52W
Robinson Ranges **47** 25 40S 119 0 E
Robinson River **44** 16 45S 136 58 E
Robinvale **45** 34 40S 142 45 E
Robla, La **13** 42 50N 5 41W
Roblin **65** 51 14N 101 21W
Roboré **78** 18 10S 59 45W
Robson, Mt. **64** 53 10N 119 10W
Robstown **71** 27 47N 97 40W
Roca, C. da **13** 38 40N 9 31W
Rocas, I. **79** 4 0S 34 1W
Rocha **80** 34 30S 54 25W
Rochdale **6** 53 36N 2 10W
Rochefort, Belgium **11** 50 9N 5 12 E
Rochefort, France **12** 45 56N 0 57W
Rochelle **70** 41 55N 89 5W
Rochelle, La **12** 46 10N 1 9W
Rocher River **64** 61 23N 112 44W
Rochester, Canada **64** 54 22N 113 27W
Rochester, U.K. **7** 51 22N 0 30 E
Rochester, Ind., U.S.A. **68** 41 5N 86 15W
Rochester, Minn., U.S.A. **70** 44 1N 92 28W
Rochester, N.H., U.S.A. **68** 43 19N 70 57W
Rochester, N.Y., U.S.A. **68** 43 10N 77 40W
Rock → **64** 60 7N 127 7W
Rock Hill **69** 34 55N 81 2W
Rock Island **70** 41 30N 90 35W
Rock Port **70** 40 26N 95 30W
Rock Rapids **70** 43 25N 96 10W
Rock River **72** 41 49N 106 0W
Rock Sound **75** 24 54N 76 12W
Rock Sprs., Mont., U.S.A. **72** 46 55N 106 11W
Rock Sprs., Wyo., U.S.A. **72** 41 40N 109 10W
Rock Valley **70** 43 10N 96 17W
Rockall **4** 57 37N 13 42W
Rockdale **71** 30 40N 97 0W
Rockford **70** 42 20N 89 0W
Rockglen **65** 49 11N 105 57W
Rockhampton **44** 23 22S 150 32 E
Rockhampton Downs **44** 18 57S 135 10 E
Rockingham **47** 32 15S 115 38 E
Rockingham B. **44** 18 5S 146 10 E
Rockingham Forest **7** 52 28N 0 42W
Rocklake **70** 48 50N 99 13W
Rockland, Idaho, U.S.A. **72** 42 37N 112 57W
Rockland, Maine, U.S.A. **63** 44 6N 69 6W
Rockland, Mich., U.S.A. **70** 46 40N 89 10W
Rockmart **69** 34 1N 85 2W
Rockport **71** 28 2N 97 3W
Rocksprings **71** 30 2N 100 11W
Rockville **68** 39 7N 77 10W
Rockwall **71** 32 55N 96 30W
Rockwell City **70** 42 20N 94 35W
Rockwood **69** 35 52N 84 40W
Rocky Ford **70** 38 7N 103 45W
Rocky Gully **47** 34 30S 116 57 E
Rocky Lane **64** 58 31N 116 22W
Rocky Mount **69** 35 55N 77 48W
Rocky Mountain House **64** 52 22N 114 55W
Rocky Mts. **60** 55 0N 121 0W
Rockyford **64** 51 14N 113 10W
Rod **31** 28 10N 63 5 E
Roda, La **13** 39 13N 2 15W
Rødbyhavn **21** 54 39N 11 22 E
Roddickton **63** 50 51N 56 8W
Roderick I. **64** 52 38N 128 22W
Rodez **12** 44 21N 2 33 E
Ródhos **19** 36 15N 28 10 E
Rodney, C. **43** 36 17S 174 50 E
Rodriguez **3** 19 45S 63 20 E
Roe → **9** 55 10N 6 59W
Roebourne **46** 20 44S 117 9 E
Roebuck B. **46** 18 5S 122 20 E
Roebuck Plains **46** 17 56S 122 28 E
Roermond **11** 51 12N 6 0 E
Roes Welcome Sd. **61** 65 0N 87 0W
Roeselare **11** 50 57N 3 7 E
Rogagua, L. **78** 13 43S 66 50W
Rogaland fylke □ **21** 59 12N 6 20 E
Rogers **71** 36 20N 94 5W
Rogers City **68** 45 25N 83 49W
Rogerson **72** 42 10N 114 40W
Rogersville **69** 36 27N 83 1W
Roggan River **62** 54 25N 79 32W
Roggeveldberge **56** 32 10S 20 10 E
Rogoaguado, L. **78** 13 0S 65 30W
Rogue → **72** 42 30N 124 0W
Rohri **32** 27 45N 68 51 E
Rohtak **32** 28 55N 76 43 E
Roi Et **34** 16 4N 103 40 E
Rojas **80** 34 10S 60 45W
Rojo, C. **74** 21 33N 97 20W
Rokan → **34** 2 0N 100 50 E
Rokeby **44** 13 39S 142 40 E
Rolândia **80** 23 18S 51 23W
Rolette **70** 48 42N 99 50W
Rolla, Kans., U.S.A. **71** 37 10N 101 40W
Rolla, Mo., U.S.A. **71** 37 56N 91 42W
Rolla, N. Dak., U.S.A. **70** 48 50N 99 36W
Rolleston **44** 24 28S 148 35 E
Rollingstone **44** 19 2S 146 24 E
Roma, Australia **45** 26 32S 148 49 E
Roma, Italy **18** 41 54N 12 30 E
Roma, Sweden **21** 57 32N 18 26 E
Roman, Romania **15** 46 57N 26 55 E
Roman, U.S.S.R. **25** 66 4N 112 14 E
Romana, La **75** 18 27N 68 57W
Romang **35** 7 30S 127 20 E
Romania ■ **15** 46 0N 25 0 E
Romano, Cayo **75** 22 0N 77 30W
Romblon **35** 12 33N 122 17 E
Rome = Roma **18** 41 54N 12 30 E
Rome, Ga., U.S.A. **69** 34 20N 85 0W
Rome, N.Y., U.S.A. **68** 43 14N 75 29W
Romney **68** 39 21N 78 45W
Romney Marsh **7** 51 0N 1 0 E
Romorantin-Lanthenay **12** 47 21N 1 45 E
Romsdalen **20** 62 25N 8 0 E
Rona **8** 57 33N 6 0W
Ronan **72** 47 30N 114 6W
Roncador, Cayos **75** 13 32N 80 4W
Roncador, Serra do **79** 12 30S 52 30W
Ronceverte **68** 37 45N 80 28W
Ronda **13** 36 46N 5 12W
Rondane **21** 61 57N 9 50 E
Rondônia □ **78** 11 0S 63 0W
Rondonópolis **79** 16 28S 54 38W
Rong Xian **39** 29 23N 104 22 E
Rong'an **39** 25 14N 109 22 E
Ronge, L. la **65** 55 6N 105 17W

Ronge, La 65 55 5N 105 20W
Rongshui 39 25 5N 109 12 E
Ronsard, C. 47 24 46S 113 10 E
Ronse 11 50 45N 3 35 E
Roodepoort 57 26 11S 27 54 E
Roof Butte 73 36 29N 109 5W
Roorkee 32 29 52N 77 59 E
Roosendaal 11 51 32N 4 29 E
Roosevelt, Minn., U.S.A. 70 48 51N 95 2W
Roosevelt, Utah, U.S.A. 72 40 19N 110 1W
Roosevelt, Mt. 64 58 26N 125 20W
Roosevelt Res. 73 33 46N 111 0W
Roper → 44 14 43S 135 27 E
Ropesville 71 33 25N 102 10W
Roraima □ 78 2 0N 61 30W
Roraima, Mt. 78 5 10N 60 40W
Rorketon 65 51 24N 99 35W
Røros 20 62 35N 11 23 E
Rosa 54 9 33S 31 15 E
Rosa, Monte 14 45 57N 7 53 E
Rosalia 72 47 14N 117 25W
Rosario, Argentina 80 33 0S 60 40W
Rosário, Brazil 79 3 0S 44 15W
Rosario, Baja Calif. N., Mexico 74 30 0N 115 50W
Rosario, Sinaloa, Mexico 74 23 0N 105 52W
Rosario, Paraguay 80 24 30S 57 35W
Rosario de la Frontera 80 25 50S 65 0W
Rosário do Sul 80 30 15S 54 55W
Rosas 13 42 19N 3 10 E
Rosas, G. de 13 42 10N 3 15 E
Roscoe 70 45 27N 99 20W
Roscommon, Ireland 9 53 38N 8 11W
Roscommon, U.S.A. 68 44 27N 84 35W
Roscommon □ 9 53 40N 8 15W
Roscrea 9 52 58N 7 50W
Rose → 44 14 16S 135 45 E
Rose Blanche 63 47 38N 58 45W
Rose Harbour 64 52 15N 131 10W
Rose Pt. 64 54 11N 131 39W
Rose Valley 65 52 19N 103 49W
Roseau, Domin. 75 15 20N 61 24W
Roseau, U.S.A. 70 48 51N 95 46W
Rosebery 44 41 46S 145 33 E
Rosebud 71 31 5N 97 0W
Roseburg 72 43 10N 123 20W
Rosedale, Australia 44 24 38S 151 53 E
Rosedale, U.S.A. 71 33 51N 91 0W
Rosemary 64 50 46N 112 5W
Rosenberg 71 29 30N 95 48W
Rosenheim 14 47 51N 12 9 E
Rosetown 65 51 35N 107 59W
Rosetta = Rashîd 51 31 21N 30 22 E
Roseville 72 38 46N 121 17W
Rosewood, N. Terr., Australia 46 16 28S 128 58 E
Rosewood, Queens., Australia 45 27 38S 152 36 E
Rosh Haniqra, Kefar 28 33 5N 35 5 E
Rosh Pinna 28 32 58N 35 32 E
Rosignol 78 6 15N 57 30W
Roskilde 21 55 38N 12 3 E
Roslavl 22 53 57N 32 55 E
Roslyn 45 34 29S 149 37 E
Rosmead 56 31 29S 25 8 E
Ross, Australia 44 42 2S 147 30 E
Ross, N.Z. 43 42 53S 170 49 E
Ross L. 72 48 50N 121 5W
Ross on Wye 7 51 55N 2 34W
Rossan Pt. 9 54 42N 8 47W
Rossburn 65 50 40N 100 49W
Rossignol, L. 62 52 43N 73 40W
Rossignol Res. 63 44 12N 65 10W
Rossland 64 49 6N 117 50W
Rosslare 9 52 17N 6 23W
Rosso 50 16 40N 15 45W
Rossosh 23 50 15N 39 28 E
Rossport 62 48 50N 87 30W
Røssvatnet 20 65 45N 14 5 E
Rossville 44 15 48S 145 15 E
Rosthern 65 52 40N 106 20W
Rostock 14 54 4N 12 9 E
Rostov, Don, U.S.S.R. 23 47 15N 39 45 E
Rostov, Moskva, U.S.S.R. 22 57 14N 39 25 E
Roswell 71 33 26N 104 32W
Rosyth 8 56 2N 3 26W
Rotan 71 32 52N 100 30W
Rothaargebirge 14 51 0N 8 20 E
Rother → 7 50 59N 0 40 E
Rotherham 6 53 26N 1 21W
Rothes 8 57 31N 3 12W
Rothesay, Canada 63 45 23N 66 0W
Rothesay, U.K. 8 55 50N 5 3W
Roti 35 10 50S 123 0 E
Roto 45 33 0S 145 30 E
Rotoroa, L. 43 41 55S 172 39 E
Rotorua 43 38 9S 176 16 E
Rotorua, L. 43 38 5S 176 18 E
Rotterdam 11 51 55N 4 30 E
Rottnest I. 47 32 0S 115 27 E
Rottumeroog 11 53 33N 6 34 E
Rottweil 14 48 9N 8 38 E
Rotuma 40 12 25S 177 5 E
Roubaix 12 50 40N 3 10 E
Rouen 12 49 27N 1 4 E
Rouleau 65 50 10N 104 56W
Round Mt. 45 30 26S 152 16 E
Round Mountain 72 38 46N 117 3W
Roundup 72 46 25N 108 35W
Rousay 8 59 10N 3 2W
Roussillon 12 42 30N 2 35 E
Rouxville 56 30 25S 26 50 E
Rouyn 62 48 20N 79 0W
Rovaniemi 20 66 29N 25 41 E
Rovereto 18 45 53N 11 3 E
Rovigo 18 45 4N 11 48 E
Rovinj 18 45 5N 13 40 E
Rovno 23 50 40N 26 10 E
Rovuma → 54 10 29S 40 28 E
Rowena 45 29 48S 148 55 E
Rowley Shoals 46 17 30S 119 0 E
Roxas 35 11 36N 122 49 E
Roxboro 69 36 24N 78 59W
Roxborough Downs 44 22 30S 138 45 E
Roxburgh 43 45 33S 169 19 E
Roy, Mont., U.S.A. 72 47 17N 109 0W
Roy, N. Mex., U.S.A. 71 35 57N 104 8W
Roy, Le 71 38 8N 95 35W
Roy Hill 46 22 37S 119 58 E
Royan 12 45 37N 1 2W
Rtishchevo 22 55 16N 43 50 E
Ruacaná 56 17 20S 14 12 E
Ruahine Ra. 43 39 55S 176 2 E
Ruapehu 43 39 17S 175 35 E
Ruapuke I. 43 46 46S 168 31 E
Rub' al Khali 29 18 0N 48 0 E
Rubh a' Mhail 8 55 55N 6 10W
Rubha Hunish 8 57 42N 6 20W
Rubicone → 18 44 8N 12 28 E
Rubio 78 7 43N 72 22W
Rubtsovsk 24 51 30N 81 10 E
Ruby 60 64 40N 155 35W
Ruby L. 72 40 10N 115 28W
Ruby Mts. 72 40 30N 115 30W
Rudall 45 33 43S 136 17 E
Rudnichnyy 22 59 38N 52 26 E
Rudnogorsk 25 57 15N 103 42 E
Rudnyy 24 52 57N 63 7 E
Rudolf, Ostrov 24 81 45N 58 30 E
Rudyard 68 46 14N 84 35W
Rufa'a 51 14 44N 33 22 E
Rufiji → 54 7 50S 39 15 E
Rufino 80 34 20S 62 50W
Rufisque 50 14 40N 17 15W
Rugao 39 32 23N 120 31 E
Rugby, U.K. 7 52 23N 1 16W
Rugby, U.S.A. 70 48 21N 100 0W
Rügen 14 54 22N 13 25 E
Ruhama 28 31 31N 34 43 E
Ruhr → 14 51 25N 6 44 E
Rui'an 39 27 47N 120 40 E
Ruidosa 71 29 59N 104 39W
Ruidoso 73 33 19N 105 39W
Rukwa L. 54 8 0S 32 20 E
Rulhieres, C. 46 13 56S 127 22 E
Rum Cay 75 23 40N 74 58W
Rum Jungle 46 13 0S 130 59 E
Rumāḥ 30 25 29N 47 10 E
Rumania = Romania ■ 15 46 0N 25 0 E
Rumbalara 44 25 20S 134 29 E
Rumbêk 51 6 54N 29 37 E
Rumford 68 44 30N 70 30W
Rumoi 36 43 56N 141 39W
Rumsey 64 51 51N 112 48W
Rumula 44 16 35S 145 20 E
Rumuruti 52 0 17N 36 32 E
Runan 39 33 0N 114 30 E
Runanga 43 42 25S 171 15 E
Runcorn 6 53 20N 2 44W
Rungwa 54 6 55S 33 32 E
Runka 53 12 28N 7 20 E
Ruoqiang 37 38 55N 88 10 E
Rupa 33 27 15N 92 21 E
Rupat 34 1 45N 101 40 E
Rupert → 62 51 29N 78 45W
Rupert House = Fort Rupert 62 51 30N 78 40W
Rurrenabaque 78 14 30S 67 32W
Rusape 55 18 35S 32 8 E
Ruschuk = Ruse 19 43 48N 25 59 E
Ruse 19 43 48N 25 59 E
Rushden 7 52 17N 0 37W
Rushford 70 43 48N 91 46W
Rushville, Ill., U.S.A. 70 40 6N 90 35W
Rushville, Ind., U.S.A. 68 39 38N 85 22W
Rushville, Nebr., U.S.A. 70 42 43N 102 28W
Russas 79 4 55S 37 50W
Russell, Canada 65 50 50N 101 20W
Russell, N.Z. 43 35 16S 174 10 E
Russell, U.S.A. 70 38 56N 98 55W
Russell L., Man., Canada 65 56 15N 101 30W
Russell L., N.W.T., Canada 64 63 5N 115 44W
Russellkonda 33 19 57N 84 42 E
Russellville, Ala., U.S.A. 69 34 30N 87 44W
Russellville, Ark., U.S.A. 71 35 15N 93 8W
Russellville, Ky., U.S.A. 69 36 50N 86 50W
Russian S.F.S.R. □ 25 62 0N 105 0 E
Russkaya Polyana 24 53 47N 73 53 E
Rustavi 23 41 30N 45 0 E
Rustenburg 56 25 41S 27 14 E
Ruston 71 32 30N 92 58W
Ruteng 35 8 35S 120 30 E
Ruth 72 39 15N 115 1W
Rutherglen 8 55 50N 4 11W
Rutland Plains 44 15 38S 141 43 E
Rutledge → 65 61 4N 112 0W
Rutledge L. 65 61 33N 110 47W
Rutshuru 54 1 13S 29 25 E
Ruurlo 11 52 5N 6 24 E
Ruwenzori 54 0 30N 29 55 E
Ružomberok 15 49 3N 19 17 E
Rwanda ■ 54 2 0S 30 0 E
Ryan, L. 8 55 0N 5 2W
Ryazan 22 54 40N 39 40 E
Ryazhsk 22 53 45N 40 3 E
Rybache 24 46 40N 81 20 E
Rybachiy Poluostrov 22 69 43N 32 0 E
Rybinsk = Andropov 22 58 5N 38 50 E
Rybinskoye Vdkhr. 22 58 30N 38 25 E
Ryde 7 50 44N 1 9W
Rye 7 50 57N 0 46 E
Rye → 6 54 12N 0 53W
Rye Patch Res. 72 40 38N 118 20W
Ryegate 72 46 21N 109 15W
Rylstone 45 32 46S 149 58 E
Rypin 15 53 3N 19 25 E
Ryūkyū Is. = Nansei-Shotō 37 26 0N 128 0 E
Rzeszów 15 50 5N 21 58 E
Rzhev 22 56 20N 34 20 E

S

Sa Dec 34 10 20N 105 46 E
Sa'ad 28 31 28N 34 33 E
Sa'ādatābād 31 30 10N 53 5 E
Saale → 14 51 57N 11 56 E
Saar → 14 49 41N 6 32 E
Saarbrücken 14 49 15N 6 58 E
Saaremaa 22 58 30N 22 30 E
Saariselkä 20 68 16N 28 15 E
Saba 75 17 42N 63 26W
Sabadell 13 41 28N 2 7 E
Sabah □ 34 6 0N 117 0 E
Şabāḩ, Wadi → 30 23 50N 48 30 E
Sábana de la Mar 75 19 7N 69 24W
Sábanalarga 78 10 38N 74 55W
Sabang 34 5 50N 95 15 E
Sabará 79 19 55S 43 46W
Sabarania 35 2 5S 138 18 E
Sabasţīyah 28 32 17N 35 12 E
Sabáudia 18 41 17N 13 2 E
Sabhah 51 27 9N 14 29 E
Sabie 57 25 10S 30 48 E
Sabinal, Mexico 74 30 58N 107 25W
Sabinal, U.S.A. 71 29 20N 99 27W
Sabinas 74 27 50N 101 10W
Sabinas Hidalgo 74 26 33N 100 10W
Sabine → 71 30 0N 93 35W
Sabine L. 71 29 50N 93 50W
Sabine Pass 71 29 42N 93 54W
Sablayan 35 12 50N 120 50 E
Sable, C., Canada 63 43 29N 65 38W
Sable, C., U.S.A. 75 25 13N 81 0W
Sable I. 63 44 0N 60 0W
Sables-d'Olonne, Les 12 46 30N 1 45W
Sabolev 25 54 20N 155 30 E
Sabulubek 34 1 36S 98 40 E
Sabzevār 31 36 15N 57 40 E
Sabzvārān 31 28 45N 57 50 E
Sac City 70 42 26N 95 0W
Sachigo → 62 55 6N 88 58W
Sachigo, L. 62 53 50N 92 12W
Saco, Maine, U.S.A. 69 43 30N 70 27W
Saco, Mont., U.S.A. 72 48 28N 107 19W
Sacramento 72 38 33N 121 30W
Sacramento → 72 38 3N 121 56W
Sacramento Mts. 73 32 30N 105 30W
Sádaba 13 42 19N 1 12W
Sadani 54 5 58S 38 35 E
Sadd el Aali 51 23 54N 32 54 E
Sado 36 38 0N 138 25 E
Sado, Shima 36 38 15N 138 30 E
Sadon 33 25 28N 98 0 E
Säffle 21 59 8N 12 55 E
Safford 73 32 50N 109 43W
Saffron Walden 7 52 2N 0 15 E
Safi 50 32 18N 9 20W
Safīd Kūh 31 34 45N 63 0 E
Saga, Indonesia 35 2 40S 132 55 E
Saga, Japan 36 33 15N 130 16 E
Saga □ 36 33 15N 130 20 E
Sagaing □ 33 23 55N 95 56 E
Sagala 50 14 9N 6 38W
Sagar 32 14 14N 75 6 E
Sagil 37 50 15N 91 15 E
Saginaw 68 43 26N 83 55W
Saginaw B. 68 43 50N 83 40W
Sagīr, Zab as → 30 35 10N 43 20 E
Saglouc 61 62 14N 75 38W
Sagra, La 13 37 57N 2 35W
Sagres 13 37 0N 8 58W
Sagua la Grande 75 22 50N 80 10W
Saguache 73 38 10N 106 10W
Saguenay → 63 48 22N 71 0W
Sagunto 13 39 42N 0 18W
Sahagún 13 42 18N 5 2W
Saham 28 32 42N 35 46 E
Saḩam al Jawlān 28 32 45N 35 55 E
Sahand, Kūh-e 30 37 44N 46 27 E
Sahara 50 23 0N 5 0 E
Saharan Atlas 48 34 9N 3 29 E
Saharanpur 32 29 58N 77 33 E
Saharien, Atlas 50 33 30N 1 0 E
Sahasinaka 57 21 49S 47 49 E
Sahiwal 32 30 45N 73 8 E
Sahtaneh → 64 59 2N 122 28W
Sahuaripa 74 29 0N 109 13W
Sahuarita 73 31 58N 110 59W
Sahuayo 74 20 4N 102 43W
Sa'id Bundas 51 8 24N 24 48 E
Saïda 50 34 50N 0 11 E
Saīdābād 31 29 30N 55 45 E
Sa'idiyeh 30 36 20N 48 55 E
Saidpur 33 25 48N 89 0 E
Saidu 32 34 43N 72 24 E
Saigon = Phanh Bho Ho Chi Minh 34 10 58N 106 40 E
Saih-al-Malih 31 23 37N 58 31 E
Saijō 36 33 55N 133 11 E
Saikhoa Ghat 33 27 50N 95 40 E
Saiki 36 32 58N 131 51 E
Sailolof 35 1 7S 130 46 E
St. Abb's Head 8 55 55N 2 10W
St. Alban's, Canada 63 47 51N 55 50W
St. Albans, U.K. 7 51 44N 0 19W
St. Albans, Vt., U.S.A. 68 44 49N 73 7W
St. Albans, W. Va., U.S.A. 68 38 21N 81 50W
St. Alban's Head 7 50 34N 2 3W
St. Albert 64 53 37N 113 32W
St. Andrew's, Canada 63 47 45N 59 15W
St. Andrews, U.K. 8 56 20N 2 48W
St. Ann B. 63 46 22N 60 25W
St. Anthony, Canada 63 51 22N 55 35W
St. Anthony, U.S.A. 72 44 0N 111 40W
St. Arnaud 45 36 40S 143 16 E
St. Arnaud Ra. 43 42 1S 172 53 E
St. Arthur 63 47 33N 67 46W
St. Asaph 6 53 15N 3 27W
St-Augustin-Saguenay 63 51 13N 58 38W
St. Augustine 69 29 52N 81 20W
St. Austell 7 50 20N 4 48W
St.-Barthélemy, I. 75 17 50N 62 50W
St. Bee's Hd. 6 54 30N 3 38 E
St. Boniface 65 49 53N 97 5W
St. Bride's 63 46 56N 54 10W
St. Brides B. 7 51 48N 5 15W
St.-Brieuc 12 48 30N 2 46W
St. Catharines 62 43 10N 79 15W
St. Catherines I. 69 31 35N 81 10W
St. Catherine's Pt. 7 50 34N 1 18W
St. Charles, Ill., U.S.A. 68 41 55N 88 21W
St. Charles, Mo., U.S.A. 70 38 46N 90 30W
St. Christopher 75 17 20N 62 40W
St. Christopher-Nevis ■ 75 17 20N 62 40W
St. Clair, L. 62 42 30N 82 45W
St. Claude 65 49 40N 98 20W
St. Cloud, Fla., U.S.A. 69 28 15N 81 15W
St. Cloud, Minn., U.S.A. 70 45 30N 94 11W
St-Coeur de Marie 63 48 39N 71 43W
St. Cricq, C. 47 25 17S 113 6 E
St. Croix 75 17 45N 64 45W
St. Croix → 70 44 45N 92 50W
St. Croix Falls 70 45 18N 92 22W
St. David's, Canada 63 48 12N 58 52W
St. David's, U.K. 7 51 54N 5 16W
St. David's Head 7 51 55N 5 16W
St.-Denis, France 12 48 56N 2 22 E
St.-Denis, Réunion 3 20 52S 55 27 E
St. Elias, Mt. 60 60 14N 140 50W
St. Elias Mts. 64 60 33N 139 28W
St.-Étienne 12 45 27N 4 22 E
St. Eustatius 75 17 20N 63 0W
St-Félicien 62 48 40N 72 25W
St.-Flour 12 45 2N 3 6 E
St. Francis 70 39 48N 101 47W
St. Francis → 71 34 38N 90 36W
St. Francis, C. 56 34 14S 24 49 E
St. Francisville 71 30 48N 91 22W
St-Gabriel-de-Brandon 62 46 17N 73 24W
St. George, Australia 45 28 1S 148 30 E
St. George, Canada 63 45 11N 66 50W
St. George, S.C., U.S.A. 69 33 13N 80 37W
St. George, Utah, U.S.A. 73 37 10N 113 35W
St. George, C., Canada 63 48 30N 59 16W
St. George, C., U.S.A. 69 29 36N 85 2W
St. George Ra. 46 18 40S 125 0 E
St-Georges 11 50 37N 5 20 E
St. George's 63 48 26N 58 31W
St-Georges 63 46 8N 70 40W
St.-Georges, Fr. Gui. 79 4 0N 52 0W
St. George's, Grenada 75 12 5N 61 43W
St. George's B. 63 48 24N 58 53W
St. George's Channel 9 52 0N 6 0W
St. Georges Head 45 35 12S 150 42 E
St. Gotthard P. = San Gottardo, Paso del 14 46 33N 8 33 E
St. Helena, Atl. Oc. 2 15 55S 5 44W
St. Helena, U.S.A. 72 38 29N 122 30W
St. Helena B. 56 32 40S 18 10 E
St. Helens, Australia 44 41 20S 148 15 E
St. Helens, U.K. 6 53 28N 2 44W
St. Helens, U.S.A. 72 45 55N 122 50W
St. Helier 7 49 11N 2 6W
St-Hubert 11 50 2N 5 23 E
St-Hyacinthe 62 45 40N 72 58W
St. Ignace 68 45 53N 84 43W
St. Ignace I. 62 48 45N 88 0W
St. Ignatius 72 47 19N 114 8W
St. Ives, Cambs., U.K. 7 52 20N 0 5W
St. Ives, Cornwall, U.K. 7 50 13N 5 29W
St. James 70 43 57N 94 40W
St-Jean 62 45 20N 73 20W
St-Jean → 63 50 17N 64 20W
St-Jean, L. 63 48 40N 72 0W
St. Jean Baptiste 65 49 15N 97 20W
St-Jean-Port-Joli 63 47 15N 70 13W
St-Jérôme, Qué., Canada 62 45 47N 74 0W
St-Jérôme, Qué., Canada 63 48 26N 71 53W
St. John, Canada 63 45 20N 66 8W
St. John, Kans., U.S.A. 71 37 59N 98 45W
St. John, N. Dak., U.S.A. 70 48 58N 99 40W
St. John → 63 45 15N 66 4W
St. John, C. 63 50 0N 55 32W
St. John's, Antigua 75 17 6N 61 51W
St. John's, Canada 63 47 35N 52 40W
St. Johns, Ariz., U.S.A. 73 34 31N 109 26W
St. Johns, Mich., U.S.A. 68 43 0N 84 31W
St. John's → 69 30 20N 81 30W
St. Johnsbury 68 44 25N 72 1W
St. Joseph, La., U.S.A. 71 31 55N 91 15W
St. Joseph, Mich., U.S.A. 68 42 5N 86 30W
St. Joseph, Mo., U.S.A. 70 39 46N 94 50W
St. Joseph → 68 42 7N 86 30W
St. Joseph, I. 62 46 12N 83 58W
St. Joseph, L. 62 51 10N 90 35W
St-Jovite 62 46 8N 74 38W
St. Kilda 43 45 53S 170 31 E
St. Kitts = St. Christopher 75 17 20N 62 40W
St. Laurent, Canada 65 50 25N 97 58W
St.-Laurent, Fr. Gui. 79 5 29N 54 3W
St. Lawrence, Australia 44 22 16S 149 31 E
St. Lawrence, Canada 63 46 54N 55 23W
St. Lawrence → 63 49 30N 66 0W

Sebastián Vizcaíno, B.

San Ygnacio **71** 27 6N 99 24W
Sana' **29** 15 27N 44 12 E
Sana → **18** 45 3N 16 23 E
Sanaga → **54** 3 35N 9 38 E
Sanak I. **60** 53 30N 162 30W
Sanana **35** 2 5S 125 59 E
Sanandaj **30** 35 18N 47 1 E
Sancha He → **39** 26 48N 106 7 E
Sanco Pt. **35** 8 15N 126 27 E
Sancti-Spíritus **75** 21 52N 79 33W
Sand → **57** 22 25S 30 5 E
Sand Springs **71** 36 12N 96 5W
Sandakan **34** 5 53N 118 4 E
Sanday **8** 59 15N 2 30W
Sanders **73** 35 12N 109 25W
Sanderson **71** 30 5N 102 30W
Sandfly L. **65** 55 43N 106 6W
Sandgate **45** 27 18S 153 3 E
Sandía **78** 14 10S 69 30W
Sandıklı **30** 38 30N 30 20 E
Sandnes **21** 58 50N 5 45 E
Sandness **8** 60 18N 1 38W
Sandoa **54** 9 41S 23 0 E
Sandomierz **15** 50 40N 21 43 E
Sandover → **44** 21 43S 136 32 E
Sandoway **33** 18 20N 94 30 E
Sandpoint **72** 48 20N 116 34W
Sandringham **6** 52 50N 0 30 E
Sandspit **64** 53 14N 131 49W
Sandstone **47** 27 59S 119 16 E
Sandusky, Mich., U.S.A. **62** 43 26N 82 50W
Sandusky, Ohio, U.S.A. **68** 41 25N 82 40W
Sandviken **21** 60 38N 16 46 E
Sandwich, C. **44** 18 14S 146 18 E
Sandwich B., Canada **63** 53 40N 57 15W
Sandwich B., Namibia **56** 23 25S 14 20 E
Sandwip Chan. **33** 22 35N 91 35 E
Sandy Bight **47** 33 50S 123 20 E
Sandy C., Queens., Australia **45** 24 42S 153 15 E
Sandy C., Tas., Australia **44** 41 25S 144 45 E
Sandy Cr. → **72** 41 15N 109 47W
Sandy L. **62** 53 2N 93 0W
Sandy Lake **62** 53 0N 93 15W
Sandy Narrows **65** 55 5N 103 4W
Sanford, Fla., U.S.A. **69** 28 45N 81 20W
Sanford, N.C., U.S.A. **69** 35 30N 79 10W
Sanford → **47** 27 22S 115 53 E
Sanford Mt. **60** 62 30N 143 0W
Sanga → **54** 1 5S 17 0 E
Sanga-Tolon **25** 61 50N 149 40 E
Sangamner **32** 19 37N 74 15 E
Sangar **25** 64 2N 127 31 E
Sangasangadalam **34** 0 36S 117 13 E
Sangeang **35** 8 12S 119 6 E
Sanger **73** 36 41N 119 35W
Sanggan He → **38** 38 12N 117 15 E
Sanggau **34** 0 5N 110 30 E
Sangihe, Kepulauan **35** 3 0N 126 0 E
Sangihe, P. **35** 3 45N 125 30 E
Sangkapura **34** 5 52S 112 40 E
Sangli **32** 16 55N 74 33 E
Sangmélina **54** 2 57N 12 1 E
Sangonera → **13** 37 59N 1 4W
Sangre de Cristo Mts. **71** 37 0N 105 0W
Sangudo **64** 53 50N 114 54W
Sangzhi **39** 29 25N 110 12 E
Sanjiang **39** 25 48N 109 37 E
Sankt Gallen **14** 47 26N 9 22 E
Sankt Moritz **14** 46 30N 9 50 E
Sankuru → **54** 4 17S 20 25 E
Sanlúcar de Barrameda **13** 36 46N 6 21W
Sanmenxia **39** 34 47N 111 12 E
Sannaspos **56** 29 6S 26 34 E
Sannicandro Gargánico **18** 41 50N 15 34 E
Sannieshof **56** 26 30S 25 47 E
Sanok **15** 49 35N 22 10 E
Sanquhar **8** 55 21N 3 56W
Sanshui **39** 23 10N 112 56 E
Santa Ana, Bolivia **78** 13 50S 65 40W
Santa Ana, Ecuador **78** 1 16S 80 20W
Santa Ana, El Salv. **75** 14 0N 89 31W
Santa Ana, Mexico **74** 30 31N 111 8W
Santa Ana, U.S.A. **73** 33 48N 117 55W
Santa Bárbara, Mexico **74** 26 48N 105 50W
Santa Barbara, U.S.A. **73** 34 25N 119 40W
Santa Catalina **74** 25 40N 110 50W
Santa Catalina, G. of **73** 33 0N 118 0W
Santa Catalina I. **73** 33 20N 118 30W
Santa Catarina □ **80** 27 25S 48 30W
Santa Clara, Cuba **75** 22 20N 80 0W
Santa Clara, Calif., U.S.A. **73** 37 21N 122 0W
Santa Clara, Utah, U.S.A. **73** 37 10N 113 38W
Santa Clotilde **78** 2 33S 73 45W
Santa Coloma de Gramanet **13** 41 27N 2 13 E
Santa Cruz, Argentina **80** 50 0S 68 32W
Santa Cruz, Bolivia **78** 17 43S 63 10W
Santa Cruz, C. Rica **75** 10 15N 85 35W
Santa Cruz, Phil. **35** 14 20N 121 24 E
Santa Cruz, U.S.A. **73** 36 55N 122 1W
Santa Cruz □ **78** 17 43S 63 10W
Santa Cruz → **80** 50 10S 68 20W
Santa Cruz, Is. **40** 10 30S 166 0 E
Santa Cruz de Tenerife **50** 28 28N 16 15W
Santa Cruz del Sur **75** 20 44N 78 0W
Santa Cruz do Sul **80** 29 42S 52 25W
Santa Cruz I. **73** 34 0N 119 45W
Santa Domingo, Cay **75** 21 25N 75 15W
Santa Elena **78** 2 16S 80 52W
Santa Elena, C. **75** 10 54N 85 56W
Santa Eugenia, Pta. **74** 27 50N 115 5W
Santa Fe, Argentina **80** 31 35S 60 41W
Santa Fe, U.S.A. **73** 35 40N 106 0W
Santa Filomena **79** 9 6S 45 50W
Santa Inés, I. **80** 54 0S 73 0W
Santa Isabel = Rey Malabo **54** 3 45N 8 50 E
Santa Isabel, Argentina **80** 36 10S 66 54W
Santa Isabel, Brazil **79** 11 45S 51 30W
Santa Lucia Range **73** 36 0N 121 20W
Santa Magdalena, I. **74** 24 40N 112 15W
Santa Margarita **74** 24 30N 111 50W
Santa Maria, Brazil **80** 29 40S 53 48W
Santa Maria, U.S.A. **73** 34 58N 120 29W
Santa María → **74** 31 0N 107 14W
Santa María, B. de **74** 25 10N 108 40W
Santa Maria da Vitória **79** 13 24S 44 12W
Santa Maria di Leuca, C. **19** 39 48N 18 20 E
Santa Marta **78** 11 15N 74 13W
Santa Marta, Sierra Nevada de **78** 10 55N 73 50W
Santa Maura = Levkás **19** 38 40N 20 43 E
Santa Monica **73** 34 0N 118 30W
Santa Rita **73** 32 50N 108 0W
Santa Rosa, La Pampa, Argentina **80** 36 40S 64 17W
Santa Rosa, San Luis, Argentina **80** 32 21S 65 10W
Santa Rosa, Bolivia **78** 10 36S 67 20W
Santa Rosa, Brazil **80** 27 52S 54 29W
Santa Rosa, Calif., U.S.A. **72** 38 26N 122 43W
Santa Rosa, N. Mex., U.S.A. **71** 34 58N 104 40W
Santa Rosa de Copán **75** 14 47N 88 46W
Santa Rosa I., Calif., U.S.A. **73** 34 0N 120 6W
Santa Rosa I., Fla., U.S.A. **69** 30 23N 87 0W
Santa Rosa Ra. **72** 41 45N 117 30W
Santa Rosalía **74** 27 20N 112 20W
Santa Tecla = Nueva San Salvador **75** 13 40N 89 18W
Santa Vitória do Palmar **80** 33 32S 53 25W
Santai **39** 31 5N 104 58 E
Santana, Coxilha de **80** 30 50S 55 35W
Santana do Livramento **80** 30 55S 55 30W
Santander **13** 43 27N 3 51W
Santander Jiménez **74** 24 11N 98 29W
Santaquin **72** 40 0N 111 51W
Santarém, Brazil **79** 2 25S 54 42W
Santarém, Portugal **13** 39 12N 8 42W
Santaren Channel **75** 24 0N 79 30W
Santiago, Brazil **80** 29 11S 54 52W
Santiago, Chile **80** 33 24S 70 40W
Santiago, Panama **75** 8 0N 81 0W
Santiago → **78** 4 27S 77 38W
Santiago de Compostela **13** 42 52N 8 37W
Santiago de Cuba **75** 20 0N 75 49W
Santiago de los Cabelleros **75** 19 30N 70 40W
Santiago del Estero **80** 27 50S 64 15W
Santiago Ixcuintla **74** 21 50N 105 11W
Santiago Papasquiaro **74** 25 0N 105 20W
Santiaguillo, L. de **74** 24 50N 104 50W
Santo Amaro **79** 12 30S 38 43W
Santo Ângelo **80** 28 15S 54 15W
Santo Antonio **79** 15 50S 56 0W
Santo Corazón **78** 18 0S 58 45W
Santo Domingo, Dom. Rep. **75** 18 30N 69 59W
Santo Domingo, Baja Calif. N., Mexico **74** 30 43N 116 2W
Santo Domingo, Baja Calif. S., Mexico **74** 25 32N 112 2W
Santo Domingo, Nic. **75** 12 14N 84 59W
Santo Tomás **78** 14 26S 72 8W
Santo Tomé **80** 28 40S 56 5W
Santo Tomé de Guayana = Ciudad Guayana **78** 8 0N 62 30W
Santoña **13** 43 29N 3 27W
Santos **80** 24 0S 46 20W
Santos Dumont **80** 22 55S 43 10W
Sānūr **28** 32 22N 35 15 E
Sanyuan **39** 34 35N 108 58 E
Sanza Pombo **54** 7 18S 15 56 E
São Anastácio **80** 22 0S 51 40W
São Bernado de Campo **79** 23 45S 46 34W
São Borja **80** 28 39S 56 0W
São Carlos **80** 22 0S 47 50W
São Cristóvão **79** 11 1S 37 15W
São Domingos **79** 13 25S 46 19W
São Francisco **79** 16 0S 44 50W
São Francisco → **79** 10 30S 36 24W
São Francisco do Sul **80** 26 15S 48 36W
São Gabriel **80** 30 20S 54 20W
São João del Rei **79** 21 8S 44 15W
São João do Araguaia **79** 5 23S 48 46W
São João do Piauí **79** 8 21S 42 15W
São José do Rio Prêto **80** 20 50S 49 20W
São Leopoldo **80** 29 50S 51 10W
São Lourenço **79** 22 7S 45 3W
São Lourenço → **79** 17 53S 57 27W
São Luís **79** 2 39S 44 15W
São Marcos → **79** 18 15S 47 37W
São Marcos, B. de **79** 2 0S 44 0W
São Mateus **79** 18 44S 39 50W
São Paulo **80** 23 32S 46 37W
São Paulo □ **80** 22 0S 49 0W
Sao Paulo, I. **2** 0 50N 31 40W
São Roque, C. de **79** 5 30S 35 16W
São Sebastião, I. de **80** 23 50S 45 18W
São Tomé & Principe ■ **3** 0 12N 6 39 E
São Vicente, C. de **13** 37 0N 9 0W
Saona, I. **75** 18 10N 68 40W
Saône → **12** 45 44N 4 50 E
Saône-et-Loire □ **12** 46 30N 4 50 E
Saonek **35** 0 22S 130 55 E
Saparua **35** 3 33S 128 40 E
Sapele **53** 5 50N 5 40 E
Sapelo I. **69** 31 28N 81 15W
Saposoa **78** 6 55S 76 45W
Sapporo **36** 43 0N 141 21 E
Sapudi **35** 7 6S 114 20 E
Sapulpa **71** 36 0N 96 0W
Saqqez **30** 36 15N 46 20 E
Sar-e Pol **31** 36 10N 66 0 E
Sar Planina **19** 42 10N 21 0 E
Sarāb **30** 38 0N 47 30 E
Sarada → **33** 27 21N 81 23 E
Saragossa = Zaragoza **13** 41 39N 0 53W
Saraguro **78** 3 35S 79 16W
Sarajevo **19** 43 52N 18 26 E
Saran, G. **34** 0 30S 111 25 E
Saranac Lake **68** 44 20N 74 10W
Sarandí del Yi **80** 33 18S 55 38W
Sarangani B. **35** 6 0N 125 13 E
Sarangani Is. **35** 5 25N 125 25 E
Sarangarh **33** 21 30N 83 5 E
Saransk **22** 54 10N 45 10 E
Sarapul **22** 56 28N 53 48 E
Sarasota **69** 27 20N 82 30W
Saratoga **72** 41 30N 106 48W
Saratoga Springs **68** 43 5N 73 47W
Saratov **22** 51 30N 46 2 E
Saravane **34** 15 43N 106 25 E
Sarawak □ **34** 2 0N 113 0 E
Sarbāz **31** 26 38N 61 19 E
Sarbīsheh **31** 32 30N 59 40 E
Sardalas **50** 25 60N 10 34 E
Sardarshahr **32** 28 30N 74 29 E
Sardegna **18** 39 57N 9 0 E
Sardinia = Sardegna **18** 39 57N 9 0 E
Sargent **70** 41 42N 99 24W
Sargodha **32** 32 10N 72 40 E
Sarh **51** 9 5N 18 23 E
Sārī **31** 36 30N 53 4 E
Sarida → **28** 32 4N 34 45 E
Sarikamiş **30** 40 22N 42 35 E
Sarikei **34** 2 8N 111 30 E
Sarina **44** 21 22S 149 13 E
Sarita **71** 27 14N 97 49W
Sark **7** 49 25N 2 20W
Sarlat-la-Canéda **12** 44 54N 1 13 E
Sarles **70** 48 58N 99 0W
Sarmi **35** 1 49S 138 44 E
Sarmiento **80** 45 35S 69 5W
Sarnia **62** 42 58N 82 23W
Sarny **22** 51 17N 26 40 E
Sarolangun **34** 2 19S 102 42 E
Saronikós Kólpos **19** 37 45N 23 45 E
Saros Körfezi **19** 40 30N 26 15 E
Sarpsborg **21** 59 16N 11 12 E
Sarre = Saar → **14** 49 41N 6 32 E
Sarre, La **62** 48 45N 79 15W
Sarro **50** 13 40N 5 15W
Sartène **18** 41 38N 8 58 E
Sarthe □ **12** 47 58N 0 10 E
Sarthe → **12** 47 33N 0 31W
Sartynya **24** 63 22N 63 11 E
Sarvestān **31** 29 20N 53 10 E
Sary-Tash **24** 39 44N 73 15 E
Saryshagan **24** 46 12N 73 38 E
Sasa **28** 33 2N 35 23 E
Sasabeneh **29** 7 59N 44 43 E
Sasaram **33** 24 57N 84 5 E
Sasebo **36** 33 10N 129 43 E
Saser Mt. **32** 34 50N 77 50 E
Saskatchewan □ **65** 54 40N 106 0W
Saskatchewan → **65** 53 37N 100 40W
Saskatoon **65** 52 10N 106 38W
Saskylakh **25** 71 55N 114 1 E
Sasolburg **57** 26 46S 27 49 E
Sasovo **22** 54 25N 41 55 E
Sassandra **50** 5 0N 6 8W
Sassandra → **50** 4 58N 6 5W
Sássari **18** 40 44N 8 33 E
Sassnitz **14** 54 29N 13 39 E
Sata-Misaki **36** 30 59N 130 40 E
Satadougou **50** 12 25N 11 25W
Satanta **71** 37 30N 101 0W
Satara **32** 17 44N 73 58 E
Satilla → **69** 30 59N 81 28W
Satka **22** 55 3N 59 1 E
Satmala Hills **32** 20 15N 74 40 E
Satna **33** 24 35N 80 50 E
Sátoraljaújhely **15** 48 25N 21 41 E
Satpura Ra. **32** 21 25N 76 10 E
Satu Mare **15** 47 46N 22 55 E
Satui **34** 3 50S 115 27 E
Saturnina → **78** 12 15S 58 10W
Saucillo **74** 28 1N 105 17W
Sauda **21** 59 40N 6 20 E
Sauðarkrókur **20** 65 45N 19 40W
Saudi Arabia ■ **29** 26 0N 44 0 E
Saugerties **68** 42 4N 73 58W
Sauk Centre **70** 45 42N 94 56W
Sauk Rapids **70** 45 35N 94 10W
Sault Ste. Marie, Canada **62** 46 30N 84 20W
Sault Ste. Marie, U.S.A. **68** 46 27N 84 22W
Saumlaki **35** 7 55S 131 20 E
Saumur **12** 47 15N 0 5W
Saunders C. **43** 45 53S 170 45 E
Saunders Point, Mt. **47** 27 52S 125 38 E
Saurbær, Borgarfjarðarsýsla, Iceland **20** 64 24N 21 35W
Saurbær, Eyjafjarðarsýsla, Iceland **20** 65 27N 18 13W
Sauri **53** 11 42N 6 44 E
Saurimo **54** 9 40S 20 12 E
Sava → **19** 44 50N 20 26 E
Savage **70** 47 27N 104 20W
Savage I. = Niue I. **2** 19 2S 169 54W
Savai'i **43** 13 28S 172 24W
Savalou **53** 7 57N 1 58 E
Savanna **70** 42 5N 90 10W
Savanna la Mar **75** 18 10N 78 10W
Savannah, Ga., U.S.A. **69** 32 4N 81 4W
Savannah, Mo., U.S.A. **70** 39 55N 94 46W
Savannah, Tenn., U.S.A. **69** 35 12N 88 18W
Savannah → **69** 32 2N 80 53W
Savannakhet **34** 16 30N 104 49 E
Savant L. **62** 50 16N 90 44W
Savant Lake **62** 50 14N 90 40W
Savanur **32** 14 59N 75 21 E
Savé **53** 8 2N 2 29 E
Save → **57** 21 16S 34 0 E
Sāveh **30** 35 2N 50 20 E
Savelugu **53** 9 38N 0 54W
Savoie □ **12** 45 26N 6 25 E
Savona **18** 44 19N 8 29 E
Savonlinna **22** 61 52N 28 53 E
Sawahlunto **34** 0 40S 100 52 E
Sawai **35** 3 0S 129 5 E
Sawai Madhopur **32** 26 0N 76 25 E
Sawara **36** 35 55N 140 30 E
Sawatch Mts. **73** 38 30N 106 30W
Sawel, Mt. **9** 54 48N 7 5W
Sawmills **55** 19 30S 28 2 E
Sawu **35** 10 35S 121 50 E
Sawu Sea **35** 9 30S 121 50 E
Saxby → **44** 18 25S 140 53 E
Say **53** 13 8N 2 22 E
Sayabec **63** 48 35N 67 41W
Sayán **78** 11 8S 77 12W
Sayan, Vostochnyy **25** 54 0N 96 0 E
Sayan, Zapadnyy **25** 52 30N 94 0 E
Saydā **30** 33 35N 35 25 E
Sayghān **31** 35 10N 67 55 E
Sayḥut **29** 15 12N 51 10 E
Saynshand **37** 44 55N 110 11 E
Sayre, Okla., U.S.A. **71** 35 20N 99 40W
Sayre, Pa., U.S.A. **68** 42 0N 76 30W
Sayula **74** 19 50N 103 40W
Sazan **19** 40 30N 19 20 E
Sázava → **14** 49 53N 14 24 E
Sazin **32** 35 35N 73 30 E
Scafell Pikes **6** 54 26N 3 14W
Scalpay **8** 57 51N 6 40W
Scandia **64** 50 20N 112 0W
Scandinavia **20** 64 0N 12 0 E
Scapa Flow **8** 58 52N 3 6W
Scarborough, Trin. & Tob. **75** 11 11N 60 42W
Scarborough, U.K. **6** 54 17N 0 24W
Scenic **70** 43 49N 102 32W
Schaffhausen **14** 47 42N 8 39 E
Schagen **11** 52 49N 4 48 E
Schefferville **63** 54 48N 66 50W
Schelde → **11** 51 15N 4 16 E
Schell Creek Ra. **72** 39 15N 114 30W
Schenectady **68** 42 50N 73 58W
Scheveningen **11** 52 6N 4 16 E
Schiedam **11** 51 55N 4 25 E
Schiermonnikoog **11** 53 30N 6 15 E
Schio **18** 45 42N 11 21 E
Schleswig **14** 54 32N 9 34 E
Schleswig-Holstein □ **14** 54 10N 9 40 E
Schofield **70** 44 54N 89 39W
Schouten I. **44** 42 20S 148 20 E
Schouwen **11** 51 43N 3 45 E
Schreiber **62** 48 45N 87 20W
Schuler **65** 50 20N 110 6W
Schumacher **62** 48 30N 81 16W
Schurz **72** 38 57N 118 48W
Schuyler **70** 41 30N 97 3W
Schwäbische Alb **14** 48 30N 9 30 E
Schwaner, Pegunungan **34** 1 0S 112 30 E
Schwarzwald **14** 48 0N 8 0 E
Schweinfurt **14** 50 3N 10 12 E
Schweizer-Reneke **56** 27 11S 25 18 E
Schwerin **14** 53 37N 11 22 E
Schwyz **14** 47 2N 8 39 E
Sciacca **18** 37 30N 13 3 E
Scie, La **63** 49 57N 55 36W
Scilla **18** 38 18N 15 44 E
Scilly, Isles of **7** 49 55N 6 15W
Scioto → **68** 38 44N 83 0W
Scobey **70** 48 47N 105 30W
Scone, Australia **45** 32 5S 150 52 E
Scone, U.K. **8** 56 25N 3 26W
Scotia **72** 40 36N 124 4W
Scotland **70** 43 10N 97 45W
Scotland □ **8** 57 0N 4 0W
Scotland Neck **69** 36 6N 77 32W
Scott, C. **46** 13 30S 129 49 E
Scott City **70** 38 30N 100 52W
Scott Inlet **61** 71 0N 71 0W
Scott Is. **64** 50 48N 128 40W
Scott L. **65** 59 55N 106 18W
Scott Reef **46** 14 0S 121 50 E
Scottburgh **57** 30 15S 30 47 E
Scottsbluff **70** 41 55N 103 35W
Scottsboro **69** 34 40N 86 0W
Scottsburg **68** 38 40N 85 46W
Scottsdale **44** 41 9S 147 31 E
Scottsville **69** 36 48N 86 10W
Scottville **68** 43 57N 86 18W
Scranton **68** 41 22N 75 41W
Scunthorpe **6** 53 35N 0 38W
Scusciuban **29** 10 18N 50 12 E
Scutari = Üsküdar **30** 41 0N 29 5 E
Seabrook, L. **47** 30 55S 119 40 E
Seaford **68** 38 37N 75 36W
Seaforth **62** 43 35N 81 25W
Seagraves **71** 32 56N 102 30W
Seal → **65** 59 4N 94 48W
Seal Cove **63** 49 57N 56 22W
Seal L. **63** 54 20N 61 30W
Sealy **71** 29 46N 96 9W
Searchlight **73** 35 31N 114 55W
Searcy **71** 35 15N 91 45W
Searles L. **73** 35 47N 117 17W
Seaside **72** 45 59N 123 55W
Seaspray **45** 38 25S 147 15 E
Seattle **72** 47 41N 122 15W
Seaview Ra. **44** 18 40S 145 45 E
Sebastián Vizcaíno, B. **74** 28 0N 114 30W

Sombrero

Sombrero 75 18 37N 63 30W
Somers 72 48 4N 114 18W
Somerset, Canada 65 49 25N 98 39W
Somerset, Colo., U.S.A. 73 38 55N 107 30W
Somerset, Ky., U.S.A. 68 37 5N 84 40W
Somerset □ 7 51 9N 3 0W
Somerset East 56 32 42S 25 35 E
Somerset I. 60 73 30N 93 0W
Somerset West 56 34 8S 18 50 E
Somerton 73 32 35N 114 47W
Someş → 15 47 49N 22 43 E
Sommariva 45 26 24S 146 36 E
Somme □ 12 50 0N 2 20 E
Somport, Puerto de 13 42 48N 0 31W
Sondag → 56 33 44S 25 51 E
Sønderborg 21 54 55N 9 49 E
Sonepur 33 20 55N 83 50 E
Song Cau 34 13 27N 109 18 E
Song Xian 39 34 12N 112 8 E
Songea 54 10 40S 35 40 E
Songhua Hu 38 43 35N 126 50 E
Songhua Jiang → 38 47 45N 132 30 E
Songjiang 39 31 1N 121 12 E
Songkhla 34 7 13N 100 37 E
Songling 38 48 2N 121 9 E
Songpan 37 32 40N 103 30 E
Songtao 39 28 11N 109 10 E
Songzi 39 30 12N 111 45 E
Sonipat 32 29 0N 77 5 E
Sonmiani 32 25 25N 66 40 E
Sono → 79 9 58S 48 11W
Sonora, Calif., U.S.A. 73 37 59N 120 27W
Sonora, Tex., U.S.A. 71 30 33N 100 37W
Sonora □ 74 29 0N 111 0W
Sonora → 74 28 50N 111 33W
Sonsomate 75 13 43N 89 44W
Soochow = Suzhou 39 31 19N 120 38 E
Sopi 35 2 34N 128 28 E
Sopot 15 54 27N 18 31 E
Sop's Arm 63 49 46N 56 56W
Sør-Trøndelag fylke □ 20 63 0N 10 0 E
Sorata 78 15 50S 68 40W
Sorel 62 46 0N 73 10W
Sorento 45 38 22S 144 47 E
Soreq, N. → 28 31 57N 34 43 E
Soria 13 41 43N 2 32W
Sorkh, Kuh-e 31 35 40N 58 30 E
Sorocaba 80 23 31S 47 27W
Sorochinsk 22 52 26N 53 10 E
Sorong 35 0 55S 131 15 E
Soroti 54 1 43N 33 35 E
Sørøya 20 70 40N 22 30 E
Sørøysundet 20 70 25N 23 0 E
Sorrento 18 40 38N 14 23 E
Sorsele 20 65 31N 17 30 E
Sorsogon 35 13 0N 124 0 E
Sortavala 22 61 42N 30 41 E
Soscumica, L. 62 50 15N 77 27W
Sosnogorsk 22 63 37N 53 51 E
Sosnovka 25 54 9N 109 35 E
Sosnowiec 15 50 20N 19 10 E
Sosva 22 59 10N 61 50 E
Soto la Marina → 74 23 40N 97 40W
Sotuta 74 20 29N 89 43W
Souanké 54 2 10N 14 3 E
Soúdhas, Kólpos 19 35 25N 24 10 E
Sŏul 38 37 31N 126 58 E
Sound, The 21 56 7N 12 30 E
Sources, Mt. aux 57 28 45S 28 50 E
Soure 79 0 35S 48 30W
Souris, Man., Canada 65 49 40N 100 20W
Souris, P.E.I., Canada 63 46 21N 62 15W
Souris → 70 49 40N 99 34W
Sousa 79 6 45S 38 10W
Sousel 79 2 38S 52 29W
Sousse 51 35 50N 10 38 E
South Africa, Rep. of ■ 56 32 0S 23 0 E
South America 76 10 0S 60 0W
South Aulatsivik I. 63 56 45N 61 30W
South Australia □ 45 32 0S 139 0 E
South Baldy, Mt. 73 34 6N 107 27W
South Bend, Ind., U.S.A. 68 41 38N 86 20W
South Bend, Wash., U.S.A. 72 46 44N 123 52W
South Boston 69 36 42N 78 58W
South Branch 63 47 55N 59 2W
South Brook 63 49 26N 56 5W
South Carolina □ 69 33 45N 81 0W
South Charleston 68 38 20N 81 40W
South China Sea 34 10 0N 113 0 E
South Dakota □ 70 45 0N 100 0W
South Downs 7 50 53N 0 10W
South East C. 44 43 40S 146 50 E
South-East Indian Rise 40 43 0S 80 0 E
South East Is. 47 34 17S 123 30 E
South Esk → 8 56 44N 3 3W
South Foreland 7 51 7N 1 23 E
South Fork → 72 47 54N 113 15W
South Gamboa 74 9 4N 79 40W
South Glamorgan □ 7 51 30N 3 20W
South Haven 68 42 22N 86 20W
South Henik, L. 65 61 30N 97 30W
South Honshu Ridge 40 23 0N 143 0 E
South Horr 54 2 12N 36 56 E
South I. 43 44 0S 170 0 E
South Invercargill 43 46 26S 168 23 E
South Knife → 65 58 55N 94 37W
South Korea ■ 38 36 0N 128 0 E
South Loup → 70 41 4N 98 40W
South Milwaukee 68 42 50N 87 52W
South Molton 7 51 1N 3 50W
South Nahanni → 64 61 3N 123 21W
South Negril Pt. 75 18 14N 78 30W
South Pass 72 42 20N 108 58W
South Pines 69 35 10N 79 25W
South Pittsburg 69 35 1N 85 42W
South Platte → 70 41 7N 100 42W
South Porcupine 62 48 30N 81 12W
South River 62 45 52N 79 23W
South Ronaldsay 8 58 46N 2 58W
South Sandwich Is. 2 57 0S 27 0W
South Saskatchewan → 65 53 15N 105 5W
South Seal → 65 58 48N 98 8W
South Shields 6 54 59N 1 26W
South Sioux City 70 42 30N 96 24W
South Taranaki Bight 43 39 40S 174 5 E
South Thompson → 64 50 40N 120 20W
South Twin I. 62 53 7N 79 52W
South Tyne → 6 54 46N 2 25W
South Uist 8 57 20N 7 15W
South West Africa = Namibia ■ 56 22 0S 18 9 E
South West C. 44 43 34S 146 3 E
South Yemen ■ 29 15 0N 48 0 E
South Yorkshire □ 6 53 30N 1 20W
Southampton, Canada 62 44 30N 81 25W
Southampton, U.K. 7 50 54N 1 23W
Southampton, U.S.A. 68 40 54N 72 22W
Southampton I. 61 64 30N 84 0W
Southbridge 43 43 48S 172 16 E
Southeast Pacific Basin 41 16 30S 92 0W
Southend 65 56 19N 103 22W
Southend-on-Sea 7 51 32N 0 42 E
Southern Alps 43 43 41S 170 11 E
Southern Cross 47 31 12S 119 15 E
Southern Hills 47 32 15S 122 40 E
Southern Indian L. 65 57 10N 98 30W
Southern Ocean 3 62 0S 60 0 E
Southern Uplands 8 55 30N 3 3W
Southport, Australia 45 27 58S 153 25 E
Southport, U.K. 6 53 38N 3 1W
Southport, U.S.A. 69 33 55N 78 0W
Southwestern Pacific Basin 40 42 0S 170 0W
Southwold 7 52 19N 1 41 E
Soutpansberg 57 23 0S 29 30 E
Sovetsk, Lithuania, U.S.S.R. 22 55 6N 21 50 E
Sovetsk, R.S.F.S.R., U.S.S.R. 22 57 38N 48 53 E
Sovetskaya Gavan 25 48 50N 140 0 E
Soviet Union = Union of Soviet Socialist Republics ■ 25 60 0N 100 0 E
Soweto 57 26 14S 27 54 E
Sōya-Kaikyō = Perouse Str., La 40 45 40N 142 0 E
Sōya-Misaki 36 45 30N 142 0 E
Soyo 54 6 13S 12 20 E
Sozh → 22 51 57N 30 48 E
Spa 11 50 29N 5 53 E
Spain ■ 13 40 0N 5 0W
Spalding, Australia 45 33 30S 138 37 E
Spalding, U.K. 6 52 47N 0 9W
Spalding, U.S.A. 70 41 45N 98 27W
Spaniard's Bay 63 47 38N 53 20W
Spanish 62 46 12N 82 20W
Spanish Fork 72 40 10N 111 37W
Spanish Town 75 18 0N 76 57W
Sparks 72 39 30N 119 45W
Sparta = Spárti 19 37 5N 22 25 E
Sparta, Ga., U.S.A. 69 33 18N 82 59W
Sparta, Wis., U.S.A. 70 43 55N 90 47W
Spartanburg 69 35 0N 82 0W
Spárti 19 37 5N 22 25 E
Spartivento, C., Calabria, Italy 18 37 56N 16 4 E
Spartivento, C., Sard., Italy 18 38 52N 8 50 E
Spassk-Dalniy 25 44 40N 132 48 E
Spátha, Akra 19 35 42N 23 43 E
Spatsizi → 64 57 42N 128 7W
Spearfish 70 44 32N 103 52W
Spearman 71 36 15N 101 10W
Speers 65 52 43N 107 34W
Speightstown 75 13 15N 59 39W
Spenard 60 61 11N 149 50W
Spence Bay 60 69 32N 93 32W
Spencer, Idaho, U.S.A. 72 44 18N 112 8W
Spencer, Iowa, U.S.A. 70 43 5N 95 19W
Spencer, Nebr., U.S.A. 70 42 52N 98 43W
Spencer, W. Va., U.S.A. 68 38 47N 81 24W
Spencer, C. 45 35 20S 136 53 E
Spencer B. 56 25 30S 14 47 E
Spencer G. 45 34 0S 137 20 E
Spences Bridge 64 50 25N 121 20W
Spenser Mts. 43 42 15S 172 45 E
Sperrin Mts. 9 54 50N 7 0W
Spessart 14 50 10N 9 20 E
Spey → 8 57 26N 3 25W
Speyer 14 49 19N 8 26 E
Spézia, La 18 44 8N 9 50 E
Spinazzola 18 40 58N 16 5 E
Spirit Lake 72 47 56N 116 56W
Spirit River 64 55 45N 118 50W
Spiritwood 65 53 24N 107 33W
Spithead 7 50 43N 1 5W
Spitzbergen = Svalbard 3 78 0N 17 0 E
Split 18 43 31N 16 26 E
Split L. 65 56 8N 96 15W
Splügenpass 14 46 30N 9 20 E
Spoffard 71 29 10N 100 27W
Spokane 72 47 45N 117 25W
Spoleto 18 42 46N 12 47 E
Spooner 70 45 49N 91 51W
Sporyy Navolok, Mys 24 75 50N 68 40 E
Spragge 62 46 15N 82 40W
Sprague 72 47 18N 117 59W
Sprague River 72 42 28N 121 31W
Spratly, I. 34 8 20N 112 0 E
Spray 72 44 50N 119 46W
Spree → 14 52 32N 13 13 E
Spremberg 14 51 33N 14 21 E
Spring City 72 39 31N 111 28W
Spring Mts. 73 36 20N 115 43W
Spring Valley 70 43 40N 92 23W
Springbok 56 29 42S 17 54 E
Springdale, Canada 63 49 30N 56 6W
Springdale, Ark., U.S.A. 71 36 10N 94 5W
Springdale, Wash., U.S.A. 72 48 1N 117 50W
Springer 71 36 22N 104 36W
Springerville 73 34 10N 109 16W
Springfield, N.Z. 43 43 19S 171 56 E
Springfield, Colo., U.S.A. 71 37 26N 102 40W
Springfield, Ill., U.S.A. 70 39 48N 89 40W
Springfield, Mass., U.S.A. 68 42 8N 72 37W
Springfield, Mo., U.S.A. 71 37 15N 93 20W
Springfield, Ohio, U.S.A. 68 39 58N 83 48W
Springfield, Oreg., U.S.A. 72 44 2N 123 0W
Springfield, Tenn., U.S.A. 69 36 35N 86 55W
Springfontein 56 30 15S 25 40 E
Springhill 63 45 40N 64 4W
Springhouse 64 51 56N 122 7W
Springhurst 45 36 10S 146 31 E
Springs 57 26 13S 28 25 E
Springsure 44 24 8S 148 6 E
Springvale, Queens., Australia 44 23 33S 140 42 E
Springvale, W. Austral., Australia 46 17 48S 127 41 E
Springville, N.Y., U.S.A. 68 42 31N 78 41W
Springville, Utah, U.S.A. 72 40 14N 111 35W
Springwater 65 51 58N 108 23W
Spur 71 33 28N 100 50W
Spurn Hd. 6 53 34N 0 8 E
Spuzzum 64 49 37N 121 23W
Squamish 64 49 45N 123 10W
Square Islands 63 52 47N 55 47W
Squires, Mt. 47 26 14S 127 28 E
Sragen 35 7 26S 111 2 E
Srbija □ 19 43 30N 21 0 E
Sre Umbell 34 11 8N 103 46 E
Sredinnyy Khrebet 25 57 0N 160 0 E
Sredinnyy Ra. = Sredinnyy Khrebet 25 57 0N 160 0 E
Sredne Tambovskoye 25 50 55N 137 45 E
Srednekolymsk 25 67 27N 153 40 E
Srednevilyuysk 25 63 50N 123 5 E
Sretensk 25 52 10N 117 40 E
Sri Lanka ■ 32 7 30N 80 50 E
Srikakulam 33 18 14N 83 58 E
Srinagar 32 34 5N 74 50 E
Staaten → 44 16 24S 141 17 E
Staðarhólskirkja 20 65 23N 21 58W
Stadlandet 20 62 10N 5 10 E
Stadskanaal 11 53 4N 6 55 E
Stafafell 20 64 25N 14 52W
Staffa 8 56 26N 6 21W
Stafford, U.K. 6 52 49N 2 9W
Stafford, U.S.A. 71 38 0N 98 35W
Stafford □ 6 52 53N 2 10W
Staines 7 51 26N 0 30W
Stakhanov 23 48 35N 38 40 E
Stalingrad = Volgograd 23 48 40N 44 25 E
Staliniri = Tskhinvali 23 42 14N 44 1 E
Stalino = Donetsk 23 48 0N 37 45 E
Stalinogorsk = Novomoskovsk 22 54 5N 38 15 E
Stalybridge 6 53 29N 2 4W
Stamford, Australia 44 21 15S 143 46 E
Stamford, U.K. 7 52 39N 0 29W
Stamford, Conn., U.S.A. 68 41 5N 73 30W
Stamford, Tex., U.S.A. 71 32 58N 99 50W
Stamps 71 33 22N 93 30W
Stanberry 70 40 12N 94 32W
Standerton 57 26 55S 29 7 E
Standish 68 43 58N 83 57W
Stanford 72 47 11N 110 10W
Stanger 57 29 27S 31 14 E
Stanislav = Ivano-Frankovsk 23 48 40N 24 40 E
Stanke Dimitrov 19 42 17N 23 9 E
Stanley, Australia 44 40 46S 145 19 E
Stanley, N.B., Canada 63 46 20N 66 44W
Stanley, Sask., Canada 65 55 24N 104 22W
Stanley, Falk. Is. 80 51 40S 59 51W
Stanley, Idaho, U.S.A. 72 44 10N 114 59W
Stanley, N. Dak., U.S.A. 70 48 20N 102 23W
Stanley, Wis., U.S.A. 70 44 57N 91 0W
Stanovoy Khrebet 25 55 0N 130 0 E
Stanovoy Ra. = Stanovoy Khrebet 25 55 0N 130 0 E
Stansmore Ra. 46 21 23S 128 33 E
Stanthorpe 45 28 36S 151 59 E
Stanton 71 32 8N 101 45W
Staples 70 46 21N 94 48W
Stapleton 70 41 30N 100 31W
Star City 65 52 50N 104 20W
Stara Planina 19 43 15N 23 0 E
Stara Zagora 19 42 26N 25 39 E
Staraya Russa 22 57 58N 31 23 E
Starbuck I. 41 5 37S 155 55W
Staritsa 22 56 33N 35 0 E
Starke 69 30 0N 82 10W
Starkville, Colo., U.S.A. 71 37 10N 104 31W
Starkville, Miss., U.S.A. 69 33 26N 88 48W
Starogard 15 53 59N 18 30 E
Start Pt. 7 50 13N 3 38W
Stary Sącz 13 49 33N 20 35 E
Staryy Kheydzhan 25 60 0N 144 50 E
Staryy Oskol 22 51 19N 37 55 E
State College 68 40 47N 77 1W
Staten, I. = Estados, I. de Los 80 54 40S 64 30W
Statesboro 69 32 26N 81 46W
Statesville 69 35 48N 80 51W
Staunton, Ill., U.S.A. 70 39 0N 89 49W
Staunton, Va., U.S.A. 68 38 7N 79 4W
Stavanger 21 58 57N 5 40 E
Staveley 43 43 40S 171 32 E
Stavelot 11 50 23N 5 55 E
Staveren 11 52 53N 5 22 E
Stavern 21 59 0N 10 1 E
Stavropol 23 45 5N 42 0 E
Stawell 45 37 5S 142 47 E
Stawell → 44 20 20S 142 55 E
Steamboat Springs 72 40 30N 106 50W
Steele 70 46 56N 99 52W
Steelton 68 40 17N 76 50W
Steelville 71 37 57N 91 21W
Steen River 64 59 40N 117 12W
Steenkool = Bintuni 35 2 7S 133 32 E
Steenwijk 11 52 47N 6 7 E
Steep Pt. 47 26 8S 113 8 E
Steep Rock 65 51 30N 98 48W
Stefanie L. = Chew Bahir 51 4 40N 36 50 E
Steiermark □ 14 47 26N 15 0 E
Steinbach 65 49 32N 96 40W
Steinfort 11 49 39N 5 55 E
Steinkjer 20 63 59N 11 31 E
Steinkopf 56 29 18S 17 43 E
Stellarton 63 45 32N 62 30W
Stellenbosch 56 33 58S 18 50 E
Stendal 14 52 36N 11 50 E
Stensele 20 65 3N 17 8 E
Stepanakert 23 39 40N 46 25 E
Stephan 70 48 30N 96 53W
Stephens Creek 45 31 50S 141 30 E
Stephens I. 64 54 10N 130 45W
Stephenville, Canada 63 48 31N 58 35W
Stephenville, U.S.A. 71 32 12N 98 12W
Stepnoi = Elista 23 46 16N 44 14 E
Stepnyak 24 52 50N 70 50 E
Steppe 26 50 0N 50 0 E
Sterkstroom 56 31 32S 26 32 E
Sterling, Colo., U.S.A. 70 40 40N 103 15W
Sterling, Ill., U.S.A. 70 41 45N 89 45W
Sterling, Kans., U.S.A. 70 38 17N 98 13W
Sterling City 71 31 50N 100 59W
Sterlitamak 22 53 40N 56 0 E
Stettin = Szczecin 14 53 27N 14 27 E
Stettler 64 52 19N 112 40W
Steubenville 68 40 21N 80 39W
Stevens Port 70 44 32N 89 34W
Stevenson L. 65 53 55N 96 0W
Stewart, B.C., Canada 64 55 56N 129 57W
Stewart, N.W.T., Canada 60 63 19N 139 26W
Stewart, C. 44 11 57S 134 56 E
Stewart, I. 80 54 50S 71 15W
Stewart I. 43 46 58S 167 54 E
Stewiacke 63 45 9N 63 22W
Steynsburg 56 31 15S 25 49 E
Steyr 14 48 3N 14 25 E
Steytlerville 56 33 17S 24 19 E
Stigler 71 35 19N 95 6W
Stikine → 60 56 40N 132 30W
Stilfontein 56 26 51S 26 50 E
Stillwater, N.Z. 43 42 27S 171 20 E
Stillwater, Minn., U.S.A. 70 45 3N 92 47W
Stillwater, Okla., U.S.A. 71 36 5N 97 3W
Stillwater Ra. 72 39 45N 118 6W
Stilwell 71 35 52N 94 36W
Štip 19 41 42N 22 10 E
Stirling, Australia 44 17 12S 141 35 E
Stirling, Canada 64 49 30N 112 30W
Stirling, U.K. 8 56 7N 3 57W
Stirling Ra. 47 34 23S 118 0 E
Stockerau 14 48 24N 16 12 E
Stockett 72 47 23N 111 7W
Stockholm 21 59 20N 18 3 E
Stockport 6 53 25N 2 11W
Stockton, Calif., U.S.A. 73 38 0N 121 20W
Stockton, Kans., U.S.A. 70 39 30N 99 20W
Stockton, Mo., U.S.A. 71 37 40N 93 48W
Stockton-on-Tees 6 54 34N 1 20W
Stoke-on-Trent 6 53 1N 2 11W
Stokes Bay 62 45 0N 81 28W
Stokes Pt. 44 40 10S 143 56 E
Stokes Ra. 46 15 50S 130 50 E
Stokkseyri 20 63 50N 21 2W
Stokksnes 20 64 14N 14 58W
Stolac 19 43 8N 17 59 E
Stolbovaya 25 64 50N 153 50 E
Stolbovoy, Ostrov 25 56 44N 163 14 E
Stonehaven 8 56 58N 2 11W
Stonehenge 44 24 22S 143 17 E
Stonewall 65 50 10N 97 19W
Stony L. 65 58 51N 98 40W
Stony Rapids 65 59 16N 105 50W
Stony Tunguska = Tunguska, Podkamennaya → 25 61 36N 90 18 E
Stora Lulevatten 20 67 10N 19 30 E
Stora Sjöfallet 20 67 29N 18 40 E
Storavan 20 65 45N 18 10 E
Store Bælt 21 55 20N 11 0 E
Store Creek 45 32 54S 149 6 E
Støren 20 63 3N 10 18 E
Storm B. 44 43 10S 147 30 E
Storm Lake 70 42 35N 95 11W
Stormberge 56 31 16S 26 17 E
Stormsrivier 56 33 59S 23 52 E
Stornoway 8 58 12N 6 23W
Storsjön 20 62 50N 13 8 E
Storuman 20 65 5N 17 10 E
Stoughton 65 49 40N 103 0W
Stour →, Dorset, U.K. 7 50 48N 2 7W

Taikang

Stour →, Hereford & Worcs., U.K. 7 52 25N 2 13W
Stour →, Kent, U.K. 7 51 15N 1 20 E
Stour →, Suffolk, U.K. 7 51 55N 1 5 E
Stourbridge 7 52 28N 2 8W
Stout, L. 65 52 0N 94 40W
Stowmarket 7 52 11N 1 0 E
Strabane 9 54 50N 7 28W
Strabane □ 9 54 45N 7 25W
Strahan 44 42 9S 145 20 E
Stralsund 14 54 17N 13 5 E
Strand 56 34 9S 18 48 E
Strangford, L. 9 54 30N 5 37W
Stranraer 8 54 54N 5 0W
Strasbourg, Canada 65 51 4N 104 55W
Strasbourg, France 12 48 35N 7 42 E
Strasburg 70 46 12N 100 9W
Stratford, Canada 62 43 23N 81 0W
Stratford, N.Z. 43 39 20S 174 19 E
Stratford, Calif., U.S.A. 73 36 10N 119 49W
Stratford, Tex., U.S.A. 71 36 20N 102 3W
Stratford-on-Avon 7 52 12N 1 42W
Strath Spey 8 57 15N 3 40W
Strathalbyn 45 35 13S 138 53 E
Strathclyde □ 8 56 0N 4 50W
Strathcona Prov. Park 64 49 38N 125 40W
Strathmore, Australia 44 17 50S 142 35 E
Strathmore, Canada 64 51 5N 113 18W
Strathmore, U.K. 8 56 40N 3 4W
Strathnaver 64 53 20N 122 33W
Strathpeffer 8 57 35N 4 32W
Strathroy 62 42 58N 81 38W
Strathy Pt. 8 58 35N 4 0W
Stratton, U.K. 6 51 41N 1 45W
Stratton, U.S.A. 70 39 20N 102 36W
Straumnes 20 66 26N 23 8W
Strawberry Res. 72 40 10N 111 7W
Strawn 71 32 36N 98 30W
Streaky B. 45 32 51S 134 18 E
Streaky Bay 45 32 48S 134 13 E
Streator 70 41 9N 88 52W
Streeter 70 46 39N 99 21W
Strelka 25 58 5N 93 3 E
Strezhevoy 24 60 42N 77 34 E
Strómboli 18 38 48N 15 12 E
Stromeferry 8 57 20N 5 33W
Stromness 8 58 58N 3 18W
Ströms vattudal 20 64 15N 14 55 E
Strömstad 21 58 55N 11 15 E
Strömsund 20 63 51N 15 33 E
Stronsay 8 59 8N 2 38W
Stronsburg 70 41 7N 97 36W
Stroud 7 51 44N 2 12W
Stroud Road 45 32 18S 151 57 E
Struer 21 56 30N 8 35 E
Strumica 19 41 28N 22 41 E
Struthers, Canada 62 48 41N 85 51W
Struthers, U.S.A. 68 41 6N 80 38W
Stryker 72 48 40N 114 44W
Strzelecki Cr. → 45 29 37S 139 59 E
Stuart, Fla., U.S.A. 69 27 11N 80 12W
Stuart, Nebr., U.S.A. 70 42 39N 99 8W
Stuart → 64 54 0N 123 35W
Stuart L. 64 54 30N 124 30W
Stuart Range 45 29 10S 134 56 E
Stull, L. 62 54 24N 92 34W
Stung Treng 34 13 31N 105 58 E
Stupart → 65 56 0N 93 25W
Sturgeon B. 65 52 0N 97 50W
Sturgeon Bay 68 44 52N 87 20W
Sturgeon Falls 62 46 25N 79 57W
Sturgeon L., Alta., Canada 64 55 6N 117 32W
Sturgeon L., Ont., Canada 62 50 0N 90 45W
Sturgis, Mich., U.S.A. 68 41 50N 85 25W
Sturgis, S. Dak., U.S.A. 70 44 25N 103 30W
Sturt Cr. → 46 19 8S 127 50 E
Sturt Creek 46 19 12S 128 8 E
Stutterheim 56 32 33S 27 28 E
Stuttgart, Germany 14 48 46N 9 10 E
Stuttgart, U.S.A. 71 34 30N 91 33W
Stykkishólmur 20 65 2N 22 40W
Styria = Steiermark □ 14 47 26N 15 0 E
Su Xian 39 33 41N 116 59 E
Suakin 51 19 8N 37 20 E
Suaqui 74 29 12N 109 41W
Subang 35 6 34S 107 45 E
Subansiri → 33 26 48N 93 50 E
Subi 34 2 58N 108 50 E
Subotica 19 46 6N 19 49 E
Success 65 50 28N 108 6W
Suceava 15 47 38N 26 16 E
Suchitoto 75 13 56N 89 0W
Suchou = Suzhou 39 31 19N 120 38 E
Süchow = Xuzhou 39 34 18N 117 10 E
Suck → 9 53 17N 8 18W
Sucre 78 19 0S 65 15W
Sud, Pte. 63 49 3N 62 14W
Sud-Ouest, Pte. du 63 49 23N 63 36W
Sudair 30 26 0N 45 0 E
Sudan 71 34 4N 102 32W
Sudan ■ 51 15 0N 30 0 E
Sudbury, Canada 62 46 30N 81 0W
Sudbury, U.K. 7 52 2N 0 44 E
Sûdd 51 8 20N 30 0 E
Sudetan Mts. = Sudety 14 50 20N 16 45 E
Sudety 14 50 20N 16 45 E
Sudirman, Pegunungan 35 4 30S 137 0 E
Sueca 13 39 12N 0 21W
Sueur, Le 70 44 25N 93 52W
Suez = El Suweis 51 29 58N 32 31 E
Suez, G. of = Suweis, Khalîg el 51 28 40N 33 0 E
Sūf 28 32 19N 35 49 E
Suffield 65 50 12N 111 10W
Suffolk 68 36 47N 76 33W
Suffolk □ 7 52 16N 1 0 E
Sufuk 31 23 50N 51 50 E
Sugar City 70 38 18N 103 38W
Sugluk = Saglouc 61 62 14N 75 38W
Suhār 31 24 20N 56 40 E
Suhbaatar 37 50 17N 106 10 E
Sui Xian, Henan, China 39 34 25N 115 2 E
Sui Xian, Henan, China 39 31 42N 113 24 E
Suichang 39 28 29N 119 15 E
Suichuan 39 26 20N 114 32 E
Suide 38 37 30N 110 12 E
Suifenhe 38 44 25N 131 10 E
Suihua 38 46 32N 126 55 E
Suining, Hunan, China 39 26 35N 110 10 E
Suining, Sichuan, China 39 30 26N 105 35 E
Suiping 39 33 10N 113 59 E
Suir → 9 52 15N 7 10W
Suixi 39 21 19N 110 18 E
Suizhong 38 40 21N 120 20 E
Sukabumi 35 6 56S 106 50 E
Sukadana, Kalimantan, Indonesia 34 1 10S 110 0 E
Sukadana, Sumatera, Indonesia 34 5 5S 105 33 E
Sukaraja 34 2 28S 110 25 E
Sukarnapura = Jayapura 35 2 28S 140 38 E
Sukhona → 22 60 30N 45 0 E
Sukhumi 23 43 0N 41 0 E
Sukkur 32 27 42N 68 54 E
Sukkur Barrage 32 27 50N 68 45 E
Sukunka → 64 55 45N 121 15W
Sula, Kepulauan 35 1 45S 125 0 E
Sulaiman Range 32 30 30N 69 50 E
Sulam Tsor 28 33 4N 35 6 E
Sulawesi □ 35 2 0S 120 0 E
Sulima 50 6 58N 11 32W
Sulina 15 45 10N 29 40 E
Sulitälma 20 67 17N 17 28 E
Sulitjelma 20 67 9N 16 3 E
Sullana 78 4 52S 80 39W
Sullivan, Ill., U.S.A. 70 39 40N 88 40W
Sullivan, Ind., U.S.A. 68 39 5N 87 26W
Sullivan, Mo., U.S.A. 70 38 10N 91 10W
Sullivan Bay 64 50 55N 126 50W
Sulphur, La., U.S.A. 71 30 13N 93 22W
Sulphur, Okla., U.S.A. 71 34 35N 97 0W
Sulphur Pt. 64 60 56N 114 48W
Sulphur Springs 71 33 5N 95 36W
Sulphur Springs Draw → 71 32 12N 101 36W
Sultan 62 47 36N 82 47W
Sultanpur 33 26 18N 82 4 E
Sultsa 22 63 27N 46 2 E
Sulu Arch. 35 6 0N 121 0 E
Sulu Sea 35 8 0N 120 0 E
Suluq 51 31 44N 20 14 E
Sumalata 35 1 0N 122 31 E
Sumatera □ 34 0 40N 100 20 E
Sumatra = Sumatera □ 34 0 40N 100 20 E
Sumatra 72 46 38N 107 31W
Sumba 35 9 45S 119 35 E
Sumba, Selat 35 9 0S 118 40 E
Sumbawa 34 8 26S 117 30 E
Sumbawa Besar 34 8 30S 117 26 E
Sumbe 54 11 10S 13 48 E
Sumburgh Hd. 8 59 52N 1 17W
Sumedang 35 6 52S 107 55 E
Šumen 19 43 18N 26 55 E
Sumenep 35 7 1S 113 52 E
Sumgait 23 40 34N 49 38 E
Summer L. 72 42 50N 120 50W
Summerland 64 49 32N 119 41W
Summerside 63 46 24N 63 47W
Summerville, Ga., U.S.A. 69 34 30N 85 20W
Summerville, S.C., U.S.A. 69 33 2N 80 11W
Summit Lake 64 54 20N 122 40W
Summit Pk. 73 37 20N 106 48W
Sumner 70 42 49N 92 7W
Sumperk 14 49 59N 17 0 E
Sumter 69 33 55N 80 22W
Sumy 23 50 57N 34 50 E
Sun City 73 33 41N 112 16W
Sunart, L. 8 56 42N 5 43W
Sunburst 72 48 56N 111 59W
Sunbury, Australia 45 37 35S 144 44 E
Sunbury, U.S.A. 68 40 50N 76 46W
Sunchon 39 34 52N 127 31 E
Sunda, Selat 34 6 20S 105 30 E
Sunda Is. 3 5 0S 105 0 E
Sundance 70 44 27N 104 27W
Sundarbans, The 33 22 0N 89 0 E
Sundargarh 33 22 4N 84 5 E
Sundays = Sondag → 56 33 44S 25 51 E
Sunderland 6 54 54N 1 22W
Sundre 64 51 49N 114 38W
Sundridge 62 45 45N 79 25W
Sundsvall 20 62 23N 17 17 E
Sungaigerong 34 2 59S 104 52 E
Sungailiat 34 1 51S 106 8 E
Sungaipakning 34 1 19N 102 0 E
Sungaipenuh 34 2 1S 101 20 E
Sungaitiram 34 0 45S 117 8 E
Sungari = Songhua Jiang → 38 47 45N 132 30 E
Sungguminasa 35 5 17S 119 30 E
Sunghua Chiang = Songhua Jiang → 38 47 45N 132 30 E
Sungtao Hu 39 19 20N 109 35 E
Sungurlu 30 40 12N 34 21 E
Sunnyside, Utah, U.S.A. 72 39 34N 110 24W
Sunnyside, Wash., U.S.A. 72 46 24N 120 2W
Sunnyvale 73 37 23N 122 2W
Sunray 71 36 1N 101 47W
Suntar 25 62 15N 117 30 E
Suoyarvi 22 62 12N 32 23 E
Supai 73 36 14N 112 44W
Supaul 33 26 10N 86 40 E
Superior, Ariz., U.S.A. 73 33 19N 111 9W
Superior, Mont., U.S.A. 72 47 15N 114 57W
Superior, Nebr., U.S.A. 70 40 3N 98 2W
Superior, Wis., U.S.A. 70 46 45N 92 5W
Superior, L. 67 47 40N 87 0W
Suphan Daği 30 38 54N 42 48 E
Supriori, Kepulauan 35 1 0S 136 0 E
Suqian 39 33 54N 118 8 E
Sūr, Lebanon 28 33 19N 35 16 E
Sūr, Oman 31 22 34N 59 32 E
Sur, Pt. 73 36 18N 121 54W
Sura → 22 56 6N 46 0 E
Surabaja = Surabaya 35 7 17S 112 45 E
Surabaya 35 7 17S 112 45 E
Surakarta 35 7 35S 110 48 E
Surat, Australia 45 27 10S 149 6 E
Surat, India 32 21 12N 72 55 E
Surat Thani 34 9 6N 99 20 E
Suratgarh 32 29 18N 73 55 E
Sûre → 11 49 44N 6 31 E
Surgut 24 61 14N 73 20 E
Suriapet 32 17 10N 79 40 E
Şūrīf 28 31 40N 35 4 E
Surigao 35 9 47N 125 29 E
Surinam ■ 79 4 0N 56 0W
Suriname → 79 5 50N 55 15W
Surprise L. 64 59 40N 133 15W
Surrey □ 7 51 16N 0 30W
Surt 51 31 11N 16 39 E
Surt, Khalīj 17 31 40N 18 30 E
Surtsey 20 63 20N 20 30W
Suruga-Wan 36 34 45N 138 30 E
Susa 18 45 8N 7 3 E
Süsangerd 30 31 35N 48 6 E
Susanino 25 52 50N 140 14 E
Susanville 72 40 28N 120 40W
Susquehanna → 68 39 33N 76 5W
Susques 80 23 35S 66 25W
Sussex 63 45 45N 65 37W
Sussex, E. □ 7 51 0N 0 20 E
Sussex, W. □ 7 51 0N 0 30W
Sustut → 64 56 20N 127 30W
Susuman 25 62 47N 148 10 E
Susunu 35 3 20S 133 25 E
Sutherland, S. Africa 56 32 24S 20 40 E
Sutherland, U.S.A. 70 41 12N 101 11W
Sutherland Falls 43 44 48S 167 46 E
Sutherlin 72 43 28N 123 16W
Sutlej → 32 29 23N 71 3 E
Sutton 70 40 40N 97 50W
Sutton → 62 55 15N 83 45W
Sutton-in-Ashfield 6 53 7N 1 20W
Suttor → 44 21 36S 147 2 E
Suva 43 18 6S 178 30 E
Suva Planina 19 43 10N 22 5 E
Suvorov Is. = Suwarrow Is. 41 15 0S 163 0W
Suwałki 15 54 8N 22 59 E
Suwannee → 69 29 18N 83 9W
Suwanose-Jima 36 29 38N 129 43 E
Suwarrow Is. 41 15 0S 163 0W
Suweis, Khalîg el 51 28 40N 33 0 E
Suwŏn 38 37 17N 127 1 E
Suzdal 22 56 29N 40 26 E
Suzhou 39 31 19N 120 38 E
Suzu-Misaki 36 37 31N 137 21 E
Suzuka 36 34 55N 136 36 E
Svalbard 3 78 0N 17 0 E
Svalbarð 20 66 12N 15 43W
Svanvik 20 69 25N 30 3 E
Svappavaara 20 67 40N 21 3 E
Svartisen 20 66 40N 13 50 E
Svealand □ 21 59 55N 15 0 E
Sveg 21 62 2N 14 21 E
Svendborg 21 55 4N 10 35 E
Sverdlovsk 22 56 50N 60 30 E
Sverdrup Is. 58 79 0N 97 0W
Svir → 22 60 30N 32 48 E
Svishtov 19 43 36N 25 23 E
Svobodnyy 25 51 20N 128 0 E
Svolvær 20 68 15N 14 34 E
Swabian Alps = Schwäbische Alb 14 48 30N 9 30 E
Swainsboro 69 32 38N 82 22W
Swakopmund 56 22 37S 14 30 E
Swale → 6 54 5N 1 20W
Swan Hill 45 35 20S 143 33 E
Swan Hills 64 54 42N 115 24W
Swan Is. 75 17 22N 83 57W
Swan L. 65 52 30N 100 40W
Swan River 65 52 10N 101 16W
Swanage 7 50 36N 1 59W
Swansea, Australia 45 33 3S 151 35 E
Swansea, U.K. 7 51 37N 3 57W
Swartberge 56 33 20S 22 0 E
Swartmodder 56 28 1S 20 32 E
Swartruggens 56 25 39S 26 42 E
Swastika 62 48 7N 80 6W
Swatow = Shantou 38 23 18N 116 40 E
Swaziland ■ 57 26 30S 31 30 E
Sweden ■ 20 57 0N 15 0 E
Sweet Home 72 44 26N 122 25W
Sweetwater 71 32 30N 100 28W
Sweetwater → 72 42 31N 107 2W
Swellendam 56 34 1S 20 26 E
Świdnica 14 50 50N 16 30 E
Świebodzin 14 52 15N 15 31 E
Swift Current 65 50 20N 107 45W
Swiftcurrent → 65 50 38N 107 44W
Swilly, L. 9 55 12N 7 35W
Swindle, I. 64 52 30N 128 35W
Swindon 7 51 33N 1 47W
Swinemünde = Świnoujście 14 53 54N 14 16 E
Świnoujście 14 53 54N 14 16 E
Switzerland ■ 14 46 30N 8 0 E
Swords 9 53 27N 6 15W
Sydney, Australia 45 33 53S 151 10 E
Sydney, Canada 63 46 7N 60 7W
Sydney Mines 63 46 18N 60 15W
Sydra G. of = Surt, Khalīj 17 31 40N 18 30 E
Syktyvkar 22 61 45N 50 40 E
Sylacauga 69 33 10N 86 15W
Sylarna 20 63 2N 12 13 E
Sylhet 33 24 54N 91 52 E
Sylvan Lake 64 52 20N 114 3W
Sylvania 69 32 45N 81 37W
Sylvester 69 31 31N 83 50W
Sym 24 60 20N 88 18 E
Synnott Ra. 46 16 30S 125 20 E
Syracuse, Kans., U.S.A. 71 38 0N 101 46W
Syracuse, N.Y., U.S.A. 68 43 4N 76 11W
Syrdarya → 24 46 3N 61 0 E
Syria ■ 30 35 0N 38 0 E
Syrian Desert 26 31 0N 40 0 E
Syul'dzhyukyor 25 63 14N 113 32 E
Syzran 22 53 12N 48 30 E
Szczecin 14 53 27N 14 27 E
Szczecinek 14 53 43N 16 41 E
Szechwan = Sichuan □ 39 31 0N 104 0 E
Szeged 15 46 16N 20 10 E
Székesfehérvár 15 47 15N 18 25 E
Szekszárd 15 46 22N 18 42 E
Szentes 15 46 39N 20 21 E
Szolnok 15 47 10N 20 15 E
Szombathely 14 47 14N 16 38 E

T

Tabacal 80 23 15S 64 15W
Tabaco 35 13 22N 123 44 E
Ţābah 30 26 55N 42 38 E
Tabarka 50 36 56N 8 46 E
Ţabas, Khorāsān, Iran 31 32 48N 60 12 E
Ţabas, Khorāsān, Iran 31 33 35N 56 55 E
Tabasará, Serranía de 75 8 35N 81 40W
Tabasco □ 74 17 45N 93 30W
Tabatinga, Serra da 79 10 30S 44 0W
Taber 64 49 47N 112 8W
Tablas 35 12 25N 122 2 E
Table B. = Tafelbaai 56 33 35S 18 25 E
Table B. 63 53 40N 56 25W
Table Mt. 56 34 0S 18 22 E
Table Top, Mt. 44 23 24S 147 11 E
Tableland 46 17 16S 126 51 E
Tábor, Czech. 14 49 25N 14 39 E
Tabor, Israel 28 32 42N 35 24 E
Tabora 54 5 2S 32 50 E
Tabou 50 4 30N 7 20W
Tabrīz 30 38 7N 46 20 E
Tabūk 30 28 23N 36 36 E
Tacheng 37 46 40N 82 58 E
Tach'ing Shan = Daqing Shan 38 40 40N 111 0 E
Tacloban 35 11 15N 124 58 E
Tacna 78 18 0S 70 20W
Tacoma 72 47 15N 122 30W
Tacuarembó 80 31 45S 56 0W
Tademaït, Plateau du 50 28 30N 2 30 E
Tadjoura 29 11 50N 42 55 E
Tadmor 43 41 27S 172 45 E
Tadoule, L. 65 58 36N 98 20W
Tadoussac 63 48 11N 69 42W
Tadzhik S.S.R. □ 24 35 30N 70 0 E
Taegu 38 35 50N 128 37 E
Taejŏn 38 36 20N 127 28 E
Tafalla 13 42 30N 1 41W
Ţafas 28 32 44N 36 5 E
Tafelbaai 56 33 35S 18 25 E
Tafermaar 35 6 47S 134 10 E
Taft, Phil. 35 11 57N 125 30 E
Taft, Calif., U.S.A. 73 35 9N 119 28W
Taft, Tex., U.S.A. 71 27 58N 97 23W
Taga Dzong 33 27 5N 89 55 E
Taganrog 23 47 12N 38 50 E
Tagbilaran 35 9 39N 123 51 E
Tagish 64 60 19N 134 16W
Tagish L. 60 60 10N 134 20W
Tagliamento → 18 45 38N 13 5 E
Taguatinga 79 12 16S 42 26W
Tagum 35 7 33N 125 53 E
Tagus = Tajo → 13 38 40N 9 24W
Tahakopa 43 46 30S 169 23 E
Tahan, Gunong 34 4 34N 102 17 E
Tahat 50 23 18N 5 33 E
Tāherī 31 27 43N 52 20 E
Tahiti 41 17 37S 149 27W
Tahoe, L. 72 39 0N 120 9W
Tahoe City 72 39 12N 120 9W
Tahoua 50 14 57N 5 16 E
Tahta 51 26 44N 31 32 E
Tahulandang 35 2 27N 125 23 E
Tahuna 35 3 38N 125 30 E
Taï 50 5 55N 7 30W
Tai Hu 39 31 5N 120 10 E
Tai Shan 38 36 25N 117 20 E
Tai'an 38 36 12N 117 8 E
Taibei 39 25 4N 121 29 E
Taibus Qi 38 41 54N 115 22 E
T'aichung = Taizhong 39 24 12N 120 35 E
Taidong 39 22 43N 121 9 E
Taieri → 43 46 3S 170 12 E
Taigu 38 37 28N 112 30 E
Taihang Shan 38 36 0N 113 30 E
Taihape 43 39 41S 175 48 E
Taihe 39 26 47N 114 52 E
Taihu 39 30 22N 116 20 E
Taijiang 39 26 39N 108 21 E
Taikang, Heilongjiang, China 38 46 50N 124 25 E
Taikang, Henan, China 39 34 5N 114 50 E

Tonantins

Tepalcatepec → 74 18 35N 101 59W
Tepic 74 21 30N 104 54W
Teplice 14 50 40N 13 48 E
Tepoca, C. 74 30 20N 112 25W
Tequila 74 20 54N 103 47W
Ter → 13 42 0N 3 12 E
Ter Apel 11 52 53N 7 5 E
Téra 53 14 0N 0 45 E
Teraina, I. 41 4 43N 160 25W
Téramo 18 42 40N 13 40 E
Terang 45 38 15S 142 55 E
Terek → 23 44 0N 47 30 E
Teresina 79 5 9S 42 45W
Terewah, L. 45 29 52S 147 35 E
Terhazza 50 23 38N 5 22W
Teridgerie Cr. → 45 30 25S 148 50 E
Termez 24 37 15N 67 15 E
Términos, L. de 74 18 35N 91 30W
Térmoli 18 42 0N 15 0 E
Ternate 35 0 45N 127 25 E
Terneuzen 11 51 20N 3 50 E
Terney 25 45 3N 136 37 E
Terni 18 42 34N 12 38 E
Ternopol 22 49 30N 25 40 E
Terowie 45 32 27S 147 52 E
Terrace 64 54 30N 128 35W
Terrace Bay 62 48 47N 87 5W
Terracina 18 41 17N 13 12 E
Terralba 18 39 42N 8 38 E
Terranova = Ólbia 18 40 55N 9 30 E
Terre Haute 68 39 28N 87 24W
Terrebonne B. 71 29 15N 90 28W
Terrell 71 32 44N 96 19W
Terrenceville 63 47 40N 54 44W
Terrick Terrick 44 24 44S 145 5 E
Territoire de Belfort □ 12 47 40N 6 55 E
Terry 70 46 47N 105 20W
Terschelling 11 53 25N 5 20 E
Teruel 13 40 22N 1 8W
Tervola 20 66 6N 24 49 E
Teryaweyna L. 45 32 18S 143 22 E
Tešanj 19 44 38N 17 59 E
Teshio 36 44 53N 141 44 E
Teshio-Gawa → 36 44 53N 141 45 E
Tesiyn Gol → 37 50 40N 93 20 E
Teslin 60 60 10N 132 43W
Teslin → 64 61 34N 134 35W
Teslin L. 64 60 15N 132 57W
Tessalit 50 20 12N 1 0 E
Tessaoua 53 13 47N 7 56 E
Test → 7 51 7N 1 30W
Tetachuck L. 64 53 18N 125 55W
Tetas, Pta. 80 23 31S 70 38W
Tete 55 16 13S 33 33 E
Teteven 19 42 58N 24 17 E
Tethul → 64 60 35N 112 12W
Teton → 72 47 58N 111 0W
Tétouan 50 35 35N 5 21W
Tetovo 19 42 1N 21 2 E
Tetuán = Tétouan 50 35 35N 5 21W
Teuco → 80 25 35S 60 11W
Teulon 65 50 23N 97 16W
Teun 35 6 59S 129 8 E
Teutoburger Wald 14 52 5N 8 20 E
Tevere → 18 41 44N 12 14 E
Teverya 28 32 47N 35 32 E
Teviot → 8 55 21N 2 51W
Tewantin 45 26 27S 153 3 E
Tewkesbury 7 51 59N 2 8W
Texada I. 64 49 40N 124 25W
Texarkana, Ark., U.S.A. 71 33 25N 94 0W
Texarkana, Tex., U.S.A. 71 33 25N 94 3W
Texas 45 28 49S 151 9 E
Texas □ 71 31 40N 98 30W
Texas City 71 29 20N 94 55W
Texel 11 53 5N 4 50 E
Texhoma 71 36 32N 101 47W
Texline 71 36 26N 103 0W
Texoma L. 71 34 0N 96 38W
Teyvareh 31 33 30N 64 24 E
Teziutlán 74 19 50N 97 22W
Tezpur 33 26 40N 92 45 E
Tezzeron L. 64 54 43N 124 30W
Tha-anne → 65 60 31N 94 37W
Thaba Nchu 56 29 17S 26 52 E
Thaba Putsoa 57 29 45S 28 0 E
Thabana Ntlenyana 57 29 30S 29 16 E
Thabazimbi 57 24 40S 27 21 E
Thailand ■ 34 16 0N 102 0 E
Thailand, G. of 34 11 30N 101 0 E
Thakhek 34 17 25N 104 45 E
Thal 32 33 28N 70 33 E
Thala La 33 28 25N 97 23 E
Thallon 45 28 39S 148 49 E
Thame → 7 51 35N 1 8W
Thames 43 37 7S 175 34 E
Thames →, Canada 62 42 20N 82 25W
Thames →, U.K. 7 51 30N 0 35 E
Thane 32 19 12N 72 59 E
Thanet, I. of 7 51 21N 1 20 E
Thangoo 46 18 10S 122 22 E
Thangool 44 24 38S 150 42 E
Thanh Pho Ho Chi Minh = Phanh Bho Ho Chi Minh 34 10 58N 106 40 E
Thanjavur 32 10 48N 79 12 E
Thanlwin Myit → 33 20 0N 98 0 E
Thar Desert 32 28 0N 72 0 E
Tharad 32 24 30N 71 44 E
Thargomindah 45 27 58S 143 46 E
Tharrawaddy 33 17 38N 95 48 E
Thásos 19 40 40N 24 40 E
Thatcher, Ariz., U.S.A. 73 32 54N 109 46W
Thatcher, Colo., U.S.A. 71 37 38N 104 6W
Thaton 33 16 55N 97 22 E
Thaungdut 33 24 30N 94 40 E
Thayer 71 36 34N 91 34W
Thayetmyo 33 19 20N 95 10 E
Thazi 33 21 0N 96 5 E
The Alberga → 45 27 6S 135 33 E
The Bight 75 24 19N 75 24W
The Dalles 72 45 40N 121 11W
The English Company's Is. 44 11 50S 136 32 E
The Frome → 45 29 8S 137 54 E
The Grenadines, Is. 75 12 40N 61 20W
The Hague = 's-Gravenhage 11 52 7N 4 17 E
The Hamilton → 45 26 40S 135 19 E
The Lynd 44 19 12S 144 20 E
The Macumba → 45 27 52S 137 12 E
The Neales → 45 28 8S 136 47 E
The Officer → 47 27 46S 132 30 E
The Pas 65 53 45N 101 15W
The Rock 45 35 15S 147 2 E
The Salt Lake 45 30 6S 142 8 E
The Stevenson → 45 27 6S 135 33 E
The Warburton → 45 28 4S 137 28 E
Thebes = Thívai 19 38 19N 23 19 E
Thedford 70 41 59N 100 31W
Theebine 45 25 57S 152 34 E
Thekulthili L. 65 61 3N 110 0W
Thelon → 65 62 35N 104 3W
Theodore 44 24 55S 150 3 E
Thermaïkos Kólpos 19 40 15N 22 45 E
Thermopolis 72 43 35N 108 10W
Thermopylae P. 19 38 48N 22 35 E
Thessalía □ 19 39 30N 22 0 E
Thessalon 62 46 20N 83 30W
Thessaloníki 19 40 38N 22 58 E
Thessaloniki, Gulf of = Thermaïkos Kólpos 19 40 15N 22 45 E
Thessaly = Thessalía □ 19 39 30N 22 0 E
Thetford 7 52 25N 0 44 E
Thetford Mines 63 46 8N 71 18W
Theunissen 56 28 26S 26 43 E
Thevenard 45 32 9S 133 38 E
Thibodaux 71 29 48N 90 49W
Thicket Portage 65 55 19N 97 42W
Thief River Falls 70 48 15N 96 48W
Thiérache 12 49 51N 3 45 E
Thies 50 14 50N 16 51W
Thika 54 1 1S 37 5 E
Thikombia 43 15 44S 179 55W
Thimphu 33 27 31N 89 45 E
þingvallavatn 20 64 11N 21 9W
Thionville 12 49 20N 6 10 E
Thíra 19 36 23N 25 27 E
Thirsk 6 54 15N 1 20W
Thisted 21 56 58N 8 40 E
Thistle I. 45 35 0S 136 8 E
Thívai 19 38 19N 23 19 E
þjórsá → 20 63 47N 20 48W
Thlewiaza →, Man., Canada 65 59 43N 100 5W
Thlewiaza →, N.W.T., Canada 65 60 29N 94 40W
Thoa → 65 60 31N 109 47W
Thomas, Okla., U.S.A. 71 35 48N 98 48W
Thomas, W. Va., U.S.A. 68 39 10N 79 30W
Thomas, L. 45 26 4S 137 58 E
Thomaston 69 32 54N 84 20W
Thomasville, Ala., U.S.A. 69 31 55N 87 42W
Thomasville, Ga., U.S.A. 69 30 50N 84 0W
Thomasville, N.C., U.S.A. 69 35 55N 80 4W
Thompson, Canada 65 55 45N 97 52W
Thompson, U.S.A. 73 39 0N 109 50W
Thompson →, Canada 64 50 15N 121 24W
Thompson →, U.S.A. 70 39 46N 93 37W
Thompson Falls 72 47 37N 115 20W
Thompson Landing 65 62 56N 110 40W
Thompson Pk. 72 41 0N 123 3W
Thomson → 44 25 11S 142 53 E
Thomson's Falls = Nyahururu 54 0 2N 36 27 E
þórisvatn 20 64 20N 18 55W
þorlákshöfn 20 63 51N 21 22W
Thornaby on Tees 6 54 36N 1 19W
þórshöfn 20 66 12N 15 20W
Thouin, C. 46 20 20S 118 10 E
Thrace = Thráki □ 19 41 9N 25 30 E
Thráki □ 19 41 9N 25 30 E
Three Forks 72 45 55N 111 32W
Three Hills 64 51 43N 113 15W
Three Hummock I. 44 40 25S 144 55 E
Three Lakes 70 45 48N 89 10W
Three Points, C. 50 4 42N 2 6W
Three Rivers, Australia 47 25 10S 119 5 E
Three Rivers, U.S.A. 71 28 30N 98 10W
Three Sisters, Mt. 72 44 10N 121 46W
Throssell, L. 47 27 33S 124 10 E
Throssell Ra. 46 22 3S 121 43 E
Thubun Lakes 65 61 30N 112 0W
Thuin 11 50 20N 4 17 E
Thun 14 46 45N 7 38 E
Thundelarra 47 28 53S 117 7 E
Thunder B. 68 45 0N 83 20W
Thunder Bay 62 48 20N 89 15W
Thung Song 34 8 10N 99 40 E
Thunkar 33 27 55N 91 0 E
Thüringer Wald 14 50 35N 11 0 E
Thurles 9 52 40N 7 53W
Thurloo Downs 45 29 15S 143 30 E
Thursday I. 44 10 30S 142 3 E
Thurso, Canada 62 45 36N 75 15W
Thurso, U.K. 8 58 34N 3 31W
Thutade L. 64 57 0N 126 55W
Thylungra 45 26 4S 143 28 E
Thysville = Mbanza Ngungu 54 5 12S 14 53 E
Tia 45 31 10S 150 34 E
Tian Shan 37 43 0N 84 0 E
Tiandu 39 18 18N 109 36 E
Tian'e 39 25 1N 107 9 E
Tianhe 39 24 48N 108 40 E
Tianjin 38 39 8N 117 10 E
Tianshui 39 34 32N 105 40 E
Tianyang 39 23 42N 106 53 E
Tianzhen 38 40 24N 114 5 E
Tiaret 50 35 20N 1 21 E
Tiassalé 50 5 58N 4 57W
Tibati 51 6 22N 12 30 E
Tiber = Tevere → 18 41 44N 12 14 E
Tiber Res. 72 48 20N 111 15W
Tiberias = Teverya 28 32 47N 35 32 E
Tiberias, L. = Yam Kinneret 28 32 45N 35 35 E
Tibesti 51 21 0N 17 30 E
Tibet = Xizang □ 37 32 0N 88 0 E
Tibnīn 28 33 12N 35 24 E
Tibooburra 45 29 26S 142 1 E
Tiburón 74 29 0N 112 30W
Tichît 50 18 21N 9 29W
Ticino → 14 45 9N 9 14 E
Ticonderoga 68 43 50N 73 28W
Ticul 74 20 20N 89 31W
Tiddim 33 23 28N 93 45 E
Tidjikja 50 18 29N 11 35W
Tidore 35 0 40N 127 25 E
Tiel, Neth. 11 51 53N 5 26 E
Tiel, Senegal 50 14 55N 15 5W
Tieling 38 42 20N 123 55 E
Tielt 11 51 0N 3 20 E
Tien Shan 31 42 0N 80 0 E
Tien-tsin = Tianjin 38 39 8N 117 10 E
T'ienching = Tianjin 38 39 8N 117 10 E
Tienen 11 50 48N 4 57 E
Tientsin = Tianjin 38 39 8N 117 10 E
Tierra Amarilla 73 36 42N 106 33W
Tierra de Campos 13 42 10N 4 50W
Tierra del Fuego, I. Gr. de 80 54 0S 69 0W
Tiétar → 13 39 50N 6 1W
Tieyon 45 26 12S 133 52 E
Tiffin 68 41 8N 83 10W
Tiflis = Tbilisi 23 41 43N 44 50 E
Tifrah 28 31 19N 34 42 E
Tifton 69 31 28N 83 32W
Tifu 35 3 39S 126 24 E
Tigil 25 57 49N 158 40 E
Tignish 63 46 58N 64 2W
Tigre → 78 4 30S 74 10W
Tigris = Dijlah, Nahr → 30 31 0N 47 25 E
Tigyaing 33 23 45N 96 10 E
Tîh, Gebel el 51 29 32N 33 26 E
Tijuana 74 32 30N 117 10W
Tikal 75 17 13N 89 24W
Tikamgarh 32 24 44N 78 50 E
Tikhoretsk 23 45 56N 40 5 E
Tiko 53 4 4N 9 20 E
Tikrīt 30 34 35N 43 37 E
Tiksi 25 71 40N 128 45 E
Tilamuta 35 0 32N 122 23 E
Tilburg 11 51 31N 5 6 E
Tilbury, Canada 62 42 17N 82 23W
Tilbury, U.K. 7 51 27N 0 24 E
Tilden, Nebr., U.S.A. 70 42 3N 97 45W
Tilden, Tex., U.S.A. 71 28 28N 98 33W
Tilichiki 25 60 27N 166 5 E
Till → 6 55 35N 2 3W
Tillabéri 53 14 28N 1 28 E
Tillamook 72 45 29N 123 55W
Tillsonburg 62 42 53N 80 44W
Tílos 19 36 27N 27 27 E
Tilpa 45 30 57S 144 24 E
Tilsit = Sovetsk 22 55 6N 21 50 E
Tilt → 8 56 50N 3 50W
Timagami L. 62 47 0N 80 10W
Timanskiy Kryazh 22 65 58N 50 5 E
Timaru 43 44 23S 171 14 E
Timau 52 0 4N 37 15 E
Timbedgha 50 16 17N 8 16W
Timber Lake 70 45 29N 101 6W
Timboon 45 38 30S 142 58 E
Timbuktu = Tombouctou 50 16 50N 3 0W
Timimoun 50 29 14N 0 16 E
Timişoara 15 45 43N 21 15 E
Timmins 62 48 28N 81 25W
Timok → 19 44 10N 22 40 E
Timon 79 5 8S 42 52W
Timor 35 9 0S 125 0 E
Timor □ 35 9 0S 125 0 E
Timor Sea 46 10 0S 127 0 E
Tinaca Pt. 35 5 30N 125 25 E
Tindouf 50 27 42N 8 10W
Tingo Maria 78 9 10S 75 54W
Tinjoub 50 29 45N 5 40W
Tinkurrin 47 32 59S 117 46 E
Tinnevelly = Tirunelveli 32 8 45N 77 45 E
Tinnoset 21 59 55N 9 3 E
Tinogasta 80 28 5S 67 32W
Tínos 19 37 33N 25 8 E
Tintinara 45 35 48S 140 2 E
Tioman, Pulau 34 2 50N 104 10 E
Tipongpani 33 27 20N 95 55 E
Tipperary 9 52 28N 8 10W
Tipperary □ 9 52 37N 7 55W
Tipton, U.K. 7 52 32N 2 4W
Tipton, Calif., U.S.A. 73 36 3N 119 19W
Tipton, Ind., U.S.A. 68 40 17N 86 0W
Tipton, Iowa, U.S.A. 70 41 45N 91 12W
Tiptonville 71 36 22N 89 30W
Tīrān 31 32 45N 51 8 E
Tirana 19 41 18N 19 49 E
Tiranë = Tirana 19 41 18N 19 49 E
Tiraspol 23 46 55N 29 35 E
Tirat Karmel 28 32 46N 34 58 E
Tirat Yehuda 28 32 1N 34 56 E
Tirat Zevi 28 32 26N 35 31 E
Tire 30 38 5N 27 50 E
Tirebolu 30 40 58N 38 45 E
Tiree 8 56 31N 6 55W
Tîrgovişte 15 44 55N 25 27 E
Tîrgu-Jiu 15 45 5N 23 19 E
Tîrgu Mureş 15 46 31N 24 38 E
Tirich Mir 31 36 15N 71 55 E
Tirodi 32 21 40N 79 44 E
Tirol □ 14 47 3N 10 43 E
Tirso → 18 39 52N 8 33 E
Tiruchchirappalli 32 10 45N 78 45 E
Tirunelveli 32 8 45N 77 45 E
Tirupati 32 13 39N 79 25 E
Tiruppur 32 11 5N 77 22 E
Tiruvannamalai 32 12 15N 79 5 E
Tisa → 15 45 15N 20 17 E
Tisdale 65 52 50N 104 0W
Tishomingo 71 34 14N 96 38W
Tisza → 15 46 8N 20 2 E
Tit-Ary 25 71 55N 127 2 E
Titicaca, L. 78 15 30S 69 30W
Titiwa 53 12 14N 12 53 E
Titograd 19 42 30N 19 19 E
Titov Veles 19 41 46N 21 47 E
Titovo Užice 19 43 55N 19 50 E
Titule 54 3 15N 25 31 E
Titusville, Fla., U.S.A. 69 28 37N 80 49W
Titusville, Pa., U.S.A. 68 41 35N 79 39W
Tivaouane 50 14 56N 16 45W
Tiverton 7 50 54N 3 30W
Tívoli 18 41 58N 12 45 E
Tiwī 31 22 45N 59 12 E
Tizi-Ouzou 50 36 42N 4 3 E
Tizimín 74 21 0N 88 1W
Tiznit 50 29 48N 9 45W
Tjeggelvas 20 66 37N 17 45 E
Tjirebon = Cirebon 35 6 45S 108 32 E
Tlahualilo 74 26 20N 103 30W
Tlaxcala 74 19 20N 98 14W
Tlaxcala □ 74 19 30N 98 20W
Tlaxiaco 74 17 18N 97 40W
Tlell 64 53 34N 131 56W
Tlemcen 50 34 52N 1 21W
Tmassah 51 26 19N 15 51 E
Toad → 64 59 25N 124 57W
Toamasina 57 18 10S 49 25 E
Toamasina □ 57 18 0S 49 0 E
Toay 80 36 43S 64 38W
Toba 36 34 30N 136 51 E
Toba Kakar 32 31 30N 69 0 E
Tobago 75 11 10N 60 30W
Tobelo 35 1 45N 127 56 E
Tobermorey 44 22 12S 138 0 E
Tobermory, Canada 62 45 12N 81 40W
Tobermory, U.K. 8 56 37N 6 4W
Tobin, L. 46 21 45S 125 49 E
Tobin L. 65 53 35N 103 30W
Toboali 34 3 0S 106 25 E
Tobol 24 52 40N 62 39 E
Tobol → 24 58 10N 68 12 E
Toboli 35 0 38S 120 5 E
Tobolsk 24 58 15N 68 10 E
Tobruk = Tubruq 51 32 7N 23 55 E
Tocantinópolis 79 6 20S 47 25W
Tocantins → 79 1 45S 49 10W
Toccoa 69 34 32N 83 17W
Tochigi 36 36 25N 139 45 E
Tochigi □ 36 36 45N 139 45 E
Tocopilla 80 22 5S 70 10W
Tocumwal 45 35 51S 145 31 E
Tocuyo → 78 11 3N 68 23W
Todd → 44 24 52S 135 48 E
Todeli 35 1 38S 124 34 E
Todenyang 54 4 35N 35 56 E
Todos los Santos, B. de 79 12 48S 38 38W
Todos Santos 74 23 27N 110 13W
Tofield 64 53 25N 112 40W
Tofino 64 49 11N 125 55W
Tofua 43 19 45S 175 5W
Togba 50 17 26N 10 12W
Togian, Kepulauan 35 0 20S 121 50 E
Togliatti 22 53 32N 49 24 E
Togo ■ 53 8 30N 1 35 E
Togtoh 38 40 15N 111 10 E
Toinya 51 6 17N 29 46 E
Tojo 35 1 20S 121 15 E
Tokachi-Gawa → 36 42 44N 143 42 E
Tokaj 15 48 8N 21 27 E
Tokala 35 1 30S 121 40 E
Tōkamachi 36 37 8N 138 43 E
Tokanui 43 46 34S 168 56 E
Tokar 51 18 27N 37 56 E
Tokara Kaikyō 36 30 0N 130 0 E
Tokarahi 43 44 56S 170 39 E
Tokat 30 40 22N 36 35 E
Tokelau Is. 2 9 0S 171 45W
Tokmak 24 42 49N 75 15 E
Toko Ra. 44 23 5S 138 20 E
Tokushima 36 34 4N 134 34 E
Tokushima □ 36 34 15N 134 0 E
Tokuyama 36 34 3N 131 50 E
Tōkyō 36 35 45N 139 45 E
Tōkyō □ 36 35 40N 139 30 E
Tolbukhin 19 43 37N 27 49 E
Toledo, Spain 13 39 50N 4 2W
Toledo, Ohio, U.S.A. 68 41 37N 83 33W
Toledo, Oreg., U.S.A. 72 44 40N 123 59W
Toledo, Wash., U.S.A. 72 46 29N 122 51W
Toledo, Montes de 13 39 33N 4 20W
Tolga 50 34 40N 5 22 E
Toliara 57 23 21S 43 40 E
Toliara □ 57 21 0S 45 0 E
Tolima, Vol. 78 4 40N 75 19W
Tolitoli 35 1 5N 120 50 E
Tolleson 73 33 29N 112 10W
Tolo 54 2 55S 18 34 E
Tolo, Teluk 35 2 20S 122 10 E
Tolosa 13 43 8N 2 5W
Toluca 74 19 20N 99 40W
Tom Burke 57 23 5S 28 0 E
Tom Price 46 22 40S 117 48 E
Tomah 70 43 59N 90 30W
Tomahawk 70 45 28N 89 40W
Tomakomai 36 42 38N 141 36 E
Tomar 13 39 36N 8 25W
Tomaszów Mazowiecki 15 51 30N 19 57 E
Tombé 51 5 53N 31 40 E
Tombigbee → 69 31 4N 87 58W
Tombouctou 50 16 50N 3 0W
Tombstone 73 31 40N 110 4W
Tombua 56 15 55S 11 55 E
Tomelloso 13 39 10N 3 2W
Tomingley 45 32 6S 148 16 E
Tomini 35 0 30N 120 30 E
Tomini, Teluk 35 0 10S 122 0 E
Tomkinson Ranges 47 26 11S 129 5 E
Tommot 25 59 4N 126 20 E
Tomnavoulin 8 57 19N 3 18W
Tomsk 24 56 30N 85 5 E
Tonalá 74 16 8N 93 41W
Tonalea 73 36 17N 110 58W
Tonantins 78 2 45S 67 45W

Tonasket

Tonasket 72 48 45N 119 30W
Tonawanda 68 43 0N 78 54W
Tonbridge 7 51 12N 0 18 E
Tondano 35 1 35N 124 54 E
Tonekābon 31 36 45N 51 12 E
Tong Xian 38 39 55N 116 35 E
Tonga ■ 43 19 50S 174 30W
Tonga Trench 40 18 0S 175 0W
Tongaat 57 29 33S 31 9 E
Tongareva 41 9 0S 158 0W
Tongatapu 43 21 10S 174 0W
Tongcheng 39 31 4N 116 56 E
Tongchuan 39 35 6N 109 3 E
Tongdao 39 26 10N 109 42 E
Tongeren 11 50 47N 5 28 E
Tongguan 39 34 40N 110 25 E
Tonghua 38 41 42N 125 58 E
Tongjiang, Heilongjiang, China 38 47 40N 132 27 E
Tongjiang, Sichuan, China 39 31 58N 107 11 E
Tongking, G. of = Tonkin, G. of 39 20 0N 108 0 E
Tongliao 38 43 38N 122 18 E
Tongling 39 30 55N 117 48 E
Tonglu 39 29 45N 119 37 E
Tongnan 39 30 9N 105 50 E
Tongobory 57 23 32S 44 20 E
Tongoy 80 30 16S 71 31W
Tongren 39 27 43N 109 11 E
Tongres = Tongeren 11 50 47N 5 28 E
Tongsa Dzong 33 27 31N 90 31 E
Tongue 8 58 29N 4 25W
Tongue → 70 46 24N 105 52W
Tongyu 38 44 45N 123 4 E
Tongzi 39 28 9N 106 49 E
Tonk 32 26 6N 75 54 E
Tonkawa 71 36 44N 97 22W
Tonkin, G. of 39 20 0N 108 0 E
Tonlé Sap 34 13 0N 104 0 E
Tonopah 73 38 4N 117 12W
Tønsberg 21 59 19N 10 25 E
Tooele 72 40 30N 112 20W
Toompine 45 27 15S 144 19 E
Toonpan 44 19 28S 146 48 E
Toora 45 38 39S 146 23 E
Toora-Khem 25 52 28N 96 17 E
Toowoomba 45 27 32S 151 56 E
Top-ozero 22 65 35N 32 0 E
Topeka 70 39 3N 95 40W
Topki 24 55 20N 85 35 E
Topley 64 54 49N 126 18W
Topock 73 34 46N 114 29W
Topolobampo 74 25 40N 109 4W
Toppenish 72 46 27N 120 16W
Toraka Vestale 57 16 20S 43 58 E
Torata 78 17 23S 70 1W
Torbat-e Heydārīyeh 31 35 15N 59 12 E
Torbat-e Jām 31 35 16N 60 35 E
Torbay, Canada 63 47 40N 52 42W
Torbay, U.K. 7 50 26N 3 31W
Tordesillas 13 41 30N 5 0W
Torey 25 50 33N 104 50 E
Torfajökull 20 63 54N 19 0W
Torgau 14 51 32N 13 0 E
Torhout 11 51 5N 3 7 E
Torin 74 27 33N 110 15W
Torino 18 45 4N 7 40 E
Torit 51 4 27N 32 31 E
Tormes → 13 41 18N 6 29W
Tornado Mt. 64 49 55N 114 40W
Torne älv → 20 65 50N 24 12 E
Torneå = Tornio 20 65 50N 24 12 E
Torneträsk 20 68 24N 19 15 E
Tornio 20 65 50N 24 12 E
Tornionjoki → 20 65 50N 24 12 E
Tornquist 80 38 8S 62 15W
Toro, Cerro del 80 29 10S 69 50W
Toro, Pta. 74 9 22N 79 57W
Toroníios Kólpos 19 40 5N 23 30 E
Toronto, Australia 45 33 0S 151 30 E
Toronto, Canada 62 43 39N 79 20W
Toronto, U.S.A. 68 40 27N 80 36W
Toropets 22 56 30N 31 40 E
Tororo 54 0 45N 34 12 E
Toros Dağlari 30 37 0N 35 0 E
Torowie 45 33 8S 138 55 E
Torquay, Canada 65 49 9N 103 30W
Torquay, U.K. 7 50 27N 3 31W
Tôrre de Moncorvo 13 41 12N 7 8W
Torre del Greco 18 40 47N 14 22 E
Torrelavega 13 43 20N 4 5W
Torremolinos 13 36 38N 4 30W
Torrens, L. 45 31 0S 137 50 E
Torrens Cr. → 44 22 23S 145 9 E
Torrens Creek 44 20 48S 145 3 E
Torreón 74 25 33N 103 25W
Torres 74 28 46N 110 47W
Torres Strait 40 9 50S 142 20 E
Torres Vedras 13 39 5N 9 15W
Torrevieja 13 37 59N 0 42W
Torrey 73 38 18N 111 25W
Torridge → 7 50 51N 4 10W
Torridon, L. 8 57 35N 5 50W
Torrington, Conn., U.S.A. 68 41 50N 73 9W
Torrington, Wyo., U.S.A. 70 42 5N 104 8W
Tortola 75 18 19N 65 0W
Tortosa 13 40 49N 0 31 E
Tortosa, C. 13 40 41N 0 52 E
Tortue, I. de la 75 20 5N 72 57W
Tortuga, La 75 11 0N 65 22W
Ţorūd 31 35 25N 55 5 E
Toruń 15 53 0N 18 39 E
Tory I. 9 55 17N 8 12W
Tosa-Wan 36 33 15N 133 30 E
Toscana 18 43 30N 11 5 E
Tostado 80 29 15S 61 50W
Tosya 30 41 1N 34 2 E
Toteng 56 20 22S 22 58 E
Totma 22 60 0N 42 40 E
Totnes 7 50 26N 3 41W
Totonicapán 75 14 58N 91 12W
Tottenham 45 32 14S 147 21 E
Tottori 36 35 30N 134 15 E
Tottori □ 36 35 30N 134 12 E
Touba 50 8 22N 7 40W
Toubkal, Djebel 50 31 0N 8 0W
Tougan 50 13 11N 2 58W
Touggourt 50 33 6N 6 4 E
Tougué 50 11 25N 11 50W
Toul 12 48 40N 5 53 E
Toulepleu 50 6 32N 8 24W
Toulon 12 43 10N 5 55 E
Toulouse 12 43 37N 1 27 E
Toummo 51 22 45N 14 8 E
Toungoo 33 19 0N 96 30 E
Touraine 12 47 20N 0 30 E
Tourane = Da Nang 34 16 4N 108 13 E
Tourcoing 12 50 42N 3 10 E
Tournai 11 50 35N 3 25 E
Tournon 12 45 4N 4 50 E
Tours 12 47 22N 0 40 E
Touwsrivier 56 33 20S 20 2 E
Towamba 45 37 6S 149 43 E
Towanda 68 41 46N 76 30W
Towang 33 27 37N 91 50 E
Tower 70 47 49N 92 17W
Towerhill Cr. → 44 22 28S 144 35 E
Towner 70 48 25N 100 26W
Townsend 72 46 25N 111 32W
Townshend I. 44 22 10S 150 31 E
Townsville 44 19 15S 146 45 E
Towson 68 39 26N 76 34W
Toyah 71 31 20N 103 48W
Toyahvale 71 30 58N 103 45W
Toyama 36 36 40N 137 15 E
Toyama □ 36 36 45N 137 30 E
Toyama-Wan 36 37 0N 137 30 E
Toyohashi 36 34 45N 137 25 E
Toyokawa 36 34 48N 137 27 E
Toyonaka 36 34 50N 135 28 E
Toyooka 36 35 35N 134 48 E
Toyota 36 35 3N 137 7 E
Tozeur 50 33 56N 8 8 E
Trabzon 30 41 0N 39 45 E
Tracadie 63 47 30N 64 55W
Tracy, Calif., U.S.A. 73 37 46N 121 27W
Tracy, Minn., U.S.A. 70 44 12N 95 38W
Trafalgar, C. 13 36 10N 6 2W
Trail 64 49 5N 117 40W
Trainor L. 64 60 24N 120 17W
Tralee 9 52 16N 9 42W
Tralee B. 9 52 17N 9 55W
Tramore 9 52 10N 7 10W
Tranås 21 58 3N 14 59 E
Trancas 80 26 11S 65 20W
Trang 34 7 33N 99 38 E
Trangahy 57 19 7S 44 31 E
Trangan 35 6 40S 134 20 E
Trangie 45 32 4S 148 0 E
Trani 18 41 17N 16 24 E
Tranoroa 57 24 42S 45 4 E
Transcaucasia = Zakavkazye 23 42 0N 44 0 E
Transcona 65 49 55N 97 0W
Transilvania 15 46 19N 25 0 E
Transkei □ 57 32 15S 28 15 E
Transvaal □ 56 25 0S 29 0 E
Transylvania = Transilvania 15 46 19N 25 0 E
Transylvanian Alps 4 45 30N 25 0 E
Trápani 18 38 1N 12 30 E
Trapper Peak 72 45 56N 114 29W
Traralgon 45 38 12S 146 34 E
Tras os Montes e Alto Douro □ 13 41 25N 7 20W
Trasimeno, L. 18 43 10N 12 5 E
Traveller's L. 45 33 20S 142 0 E
Travers, Mt. 43 42 1S 172 45 E
Traverse City 68 44 45N 85 39W
Travnik 19 44 17N 17 39 E
Trayning 47 31 7S 117 16 E
Trébbia → 18 45 4N 9 41 E
Trebinje 19 42 44N 18 22 E
Třeboň 14 48 59N 14 48 E
Tredegar 7 51 47N 3 16W
Tregaron 7 52 14N 3 56W
Tregrosse Is. 44 17 41S 150 43 E
Tréguier 12 48 47N 3 16W
Treherne 65 49 38N 98 42W
Treinta y Tres 80 33 16S 54 17W
Trekveld 56 30 35S 19 45 E
Trelew 80 43 10S 65 20W
Trelleborg 21 55 20N 13 10 E
Tremonton 72 41 45N 112 10W
Tremp 13 42 10N 0 52 E
Trenche → 62 47 46N 72 53W
Trenggalek 35 8 3S 111 43 E
Trenque Lauquen 80 36 5S 62 45W
Trent → 6 53 33N 0 44W
Trentino-Alto Adige □ 18 46 30N 11 0 E
Trento 18 46 5N 11 8 E
Trenton, Canada 62 44 10N 77 34W
Trenton, Mo., U.S.A. 70 40 5N 93 37W
Trenton, N.J., U.S.A. 68 40 15N 74 41W
Trenton, Nebr., U.S.A. 70 40 14N 101 4W
Trenton, Tenn., U.S.A. 71 35 58N 88 57W
Trepassey 63 46 43N 53 25W
Tréport, Le 12 50 3N 1 20 E
Tres Arroyos 80 38 26S 60 20W
Três Corações 79 21 44S 45 15W
Três Lagoas 79 20 50S 51 43W
Tres Marías 74 21 25N 106 28W
Tres Montes, C. 80 46 50S 75 30W
Tres Puentes 80 27 50S 70 15W
Tres Puntas, C. 80 47 0S 66 0W
Três Rios 79 22 6S 43 15W
Treungen 21 59 1N 8 31 E
Treviso 18 45 40N 12 15 E
Triabunna 44 42 30S 147 55 E
Tribulation, C. 44 16 5S 145 29 E
Tribune 70 38 30N 101 45W
Trichinopoly = Tiruchchirappalli 32 10 45N 78 45 E
Trichur 32 10 30N 76 18 E
Trida 45 33 1S 145 1 E
Trier 14 49 45N 6 37 E
Trieste 18 45 39N 13 45 E
Triglav 18 46 21N 13 50 E
Tríkkala 19 39 34N 21 47 E
Trikora, Puncak 35 4 15S 138 45 E
Trim 9 53 34N 6 48W
Trincomalee 32 8 38N 81 15 E
Trindade, I. 2 20 20S 29 50W
Trinidad, Bolivia 78 14 46S 64 50W
Trinidad, Colombia 78 5 25N 71 40W
Trinidad, Cuba 75 21 48N 80 0W
Trinidad, Uruguay 80 33 30S 56 50W
Trinidad, U.S.A. 71 37 15N 104 30W
Trinidad, W. Indies 75 10 30N 61 15W
Trinidad → 74 17 49N 95 9W
Trinidad, I. 80 39 10S 62 0W
Trinidad & Tobago ■ 75 10 30N 61 20W
Trinity, Canada 63 48 59N 53 55W
Trinity, U.S.A. 71 30 59N 95 25W
Trinity →, Calif., U.S.A. 72 41 11N 123 42W
Trinity →, Tex., U.S.A. 71 30 30N 95 0W
Trinity B. 63 48 20N 53 10W
Trinity Mts. 72 40 20N 118 50W
Trinkitat 51 18 45N 37 51 E
Trion 69 34 35N 85 18W
Tripoli = Tarābulus, Lebanon 30 34 31N 35 50 E
Tripoli = Tarābulus, Libya 51 32 49N 13 7 E
Trípolis 19 37 31N 22 25 E
Tripp 70 43 16N 97 58W
Tripura □ 33 24 0N 92 0 E
Tristan da Cunha 2 37 6S 12 20W
Trivandrum 32 8 41N 77 0 E
Trnava 15 48 23N 17 35 E
Trochu 64 51 50N 113 13W
Trodely I. 62 52 15N 79 26W
Troglav 18 43 56N 16 36 E
Troilus, L. 62 50 50N 74 35W
Trois-Pistoles 63 48 5N 69 10W
Trois-Rivières 62 46 25N 72 34W
Troitsk 24 54 10N 61 35 E
Troitsko Pechorsk 22 62 40N 56 10 E
Trölladyngja 20 64 54N 17 16W
Trollhättan 21 58 17N 12 20 E
Tromelin I. 3 15 52S 54 25 E
Troms fylke □ 20 68 56N 19 0 E
Tromsø 20 69 40N 18 56 E
Tronador 80 41 10S 71 50W
Trondheim 20 63 36N 10 25 E
Trondheimsfjorden 20 63 35N 10 30 E
Troon 8 55 33N 4 40W
Tropic 73 37 36N 112 4W
Trossachs, The 8 56 14N 4 24W
Trostan 9 55 4N 6 10W
Trotternish 8 57 32N 6 15W
Troup 71 32 10N 95 3W
Trout → 64 61 19N 119 51W
Trout L., N.W.T., Canada 64 60 40N 121 14W
Trout L., Ont., Canada 65 51 20N 93 15W
Trout Lake 62 46 10N 85 2W
Trout River 63 49 29N 58 8W
Trouville-sur-Mer 12 49 21N 0 5 E
Trowbridge 7 51 18N 2 12W
Troy, Turkey 30 39 57N 26 12 E
Troy, Ala., U.S.A. 69 31 50N 85 58W
Troy, Idaho, U.S.A. 72 46 44N 116 46W
Troy, Kans., U.S.A. 70 39 47N 95 2W
Troy, Mo., U.S.A. 70 38 56N 90 59W
Troy, Mont., U.S.A. 72 48 30N 115 58W
Troy, N.Y., U.S.A. 68 42 45N 73 39W
Troy, Ohio, U.S.A. 68 40 0N 84 10W
Troyes 12 48 19N 4 3 E
Trucial States = United Arab Emirates ■ 31 23 50N 54 0 E
Truckee 72 39 20N 120 11W
Trujillo, Hond. 75 16 0N 86 0W
Trujillo, Peru 78 8 6S 79 0W
Trujillo, Spain 13 39 28N 5 55W
Trujillo, U.S.A. 71 35 34N 104 44W
Trujillo, Venezuela 78 9 22N 70 38W
Trumann 71 35 42N 90 32W
Trumbull, Mt. 73 36 25N 113 8W
Trundle 45 32 53S 147 35 E
Trung-Phan 34 16 0N 108 0 E
Truro, Canada 63 45 21N 63 14W
Truro, U.K. 7 50 17N 5 2W
Truslove 47 33 20S 121 45 E
Truth or Consequences 73 33 9N 107 16W
Trutnov 14 50 37N 15 54 E
Tryon 69 35 15N 82 16W
Tsaratanana 57 16 47S 47 39 E
Tsaratanana, Mt. de 57 14 0S 49 0 E
Tsau 56 20 8S 22 22 E
Tselinograd 24 51 10N 71 30 E
Tsetserleg 37 47 36N 101 32 E
Tshabong 56 26 2S 22 29 E
Tshane 56 24 5S 21 54 E
Tshela 54 4 57S 13 4 E
Tshesebe 57 21 51S 27 32 E
Tshikapa 54 6 28S 20 48 E
Tshofa 54 5 13S 25 16 E
Tshwane 56 22 24S 22 1 E
Tsigara 56 20 22S 25 54 E
Tsihombe, Madag. 55 25 10S 45 41 E
Tsihombe, Madag. 57 25 18S 45 29 E
Tsimlyanskoye Vdkhr. 23 48 0N 43 0 E
Tsinan = Jinan 38 36 38N 117 1 E
Tsineng 56 27 5S 23 5 E
Tsinghai = Qinghai □ 37 36 0N 98 0 E
Tsingtao = Qingdao 38 36 5N 120 20 E
Tsinjomitondraka 57 15 40S 47 8 E
Tsiroanomandidy 57 18 46S 46 2 E
Tsivory 57 24 4S 46 5 E
Tskhinvali 23 42 14N 44 1 E
Tsna → 22 54 55N 41 58 E
Tsodilo Hill 56 18 49S 21 43 E
Tsolo 57 31 18S 28 37 E
Tsomo 57 32 0S 27 42 E
Tsu 36 34 45N 136 25 E
Tsu L. 64 60 40N 111 52W
Tsuchiura 36 36 5N 140 15 E
Tsugaru-Kaikyō 36 41 35N 141 0 E
Tsumeb 56 19 9S 17 44 E
Tsumis 56 23 39S 17 29 E
Tsuruga 36 35 45N 136 2 E
Tsuruoka 36 38 44N 139 50 E
Tsushima 36 34 20N 129 20 E
Tual 35 5 38S 132 44 E
Tuam 9 53 30N 8 50W
Tuamotu Arch. 41 17 0S 144 0W
Tuamotu Ridge 41 20 0S 138 0W
Tuao 35 17 55N 122 22 E
Tuapse 23 44 5N 39 10 E
Tuatapere 43 46 8S 167 41 E
Tuba City 73 36 8N 111 18W
Tuban 35 6 54S 112 3 E
Tubarão 80 28 30S 49 0W
Tūbās 28 32 20N 35 22 E
Tubau 34 3 10N 113 40 E
Tübingen 14 48 31N 9 4 E
Tubruq 51 32 7N 23 55 E
Tubuaeran I. 41 3 51N 159 22W
Tubuai Is. 41 25 0S 150 0W
Tucacas 78 10 48N 68 19W
Tuchodi → 64 58 17N 123 42W
Tucson 73 32 14N 110 59W
Tucumcari 71 35 12N 103 45W
Tucupita 78 9 2N 62 3W
Tucuruí 79 3 42S 49 44W
Tudela 13 42 4N 1 39W
Tudmur 30 34 36N 38 15 E
Tudor, L. 63 55 50N 65 25W
Tuen 45 28 33S 145 37 E
Tugela → 57 29 14S 31 30 E
Tuguegarao 35 17 35N 121 42 E
Tugur 25 53 44N 136 45 E
Tukangbesi, Kepulauan 35 6 0S 124 0 E
Tukarak I. 62 56 15N 78 45W
Tūkrah 51 32 30N 20 37 E
Tuktoyaktuk 60 69 27N 133 2W
Tukuyu 54 9 17S 33 35 E
Tula, Hidalgo, Mexico 74 20 0N 99 20W
Tula, Tamaulipas, Mexico 74 23 0N 99 40W
Tula, U.S.S.R. 22 54 13N 37 38 E
Tulak 31 33 55N 63 40 E
Tulancingo 74 20 5N 99 22W
Tulare 73 36 15N 119 26W
Tulare Lake Bed 73 36 0N 119 48W
Tularosa 73 33 4N 106 1W
Tulbagh 56 33 16S 19 6 E
Tulcán 78 0 48N 77 43W
Tulcea 15 45 13N 28 46 E
Tulemalu L. 65 62 58N 99 25W
Tuli, Indonesia 35 1 24S 122 26 E
Tuli, Zimbabwe 55 21 58S 29 13 E
Tulia 71 34 35N 101 44W
Ţulkarm 28 32 19N 35 2 E
Tullahoma 69 35 23N 86 12W
Tullamore, Australia 45 32 39S 147 36 E
Tullamore, Ireland 9 53 17N 7 30W
Tulle 12 45 16N 1 46 E
Tullibigeal 45 33 25S 146 44 E
Tullow 9 52 48N 6 45W
Tully 44 17 56S 145 55 E
Ţulmaythah 51 32 40N 20 55 E
Tulmur 44 22 40S 142 20 E
Tulsa 71 36 10N 96 0W
Tulsequah 64 58 39N 133 35W
Tulua 78 4 6N 76 11W
Tulun 25 54 32N 100 35 E
Tulungagung 34 8 5S 111 54 E
Tum 35 3 36S 130 21 E
Tuma → 75 13 6N 84 35W
Tumaco 78 1 50N 78 45W
Tumatumari 78 5 20N 58 55W
Tumba, L. 54 0 50S 18 0 E
Tumbarumba 45 35 44S 148 0 E
Túmbes 78 3 37S 80 27W
Tumby Bay 45 34 21S 136 8 E
Tumen 38 43 0N 129 50 E
Tumen Jiang → 38 42 20N 130 35 E
Tumeremo 78 7 18N 61 30W
Tumkur 32 13 18N 77 6 E
Tummel, L. 8 56 43N 3 55W
Tump 31 26 7N 62 16 E
Tumpat 34 6 11N 102 10 E
Tumu 50 10 56N 1 56W
Tumucumaque, Serra 79 2 0N 55 0W
Tumut 45 35 16S 148 13 E
Tumwater 72 47 0N 122 58W
Tunas de Zaza 75 21 39N 79 34W
Tunbridge Wells 7 51 7N 0 16 E
Tuncurry 45 32 17S 152 29 E
Tunduma 52 9 20S 32 48 E
Tunduru 54 11 8S 37 25 E
Tundzha → 19 41 40N 26 35 E
Tunga Pass 33 29 0N 94 14 E
Tungabhadra → 32 15 57N 78 15 E
Tungaru 51 10 9N 30 52 E
Tungla 75 13 24N 84 21W
Tungnafellsjökull 20 64 45N 17 55W
Tungsten 64 61 57N 128 16W
Tunguska, Nizhnyaya → 25 65 48N 88 4 E
Tunguska, Podkamennaya → 25 61 36N 90 18 E
Tunica 71 34 43N 90 23W
Tunis 50 36 50N 10 11 E
Tunisia ■ 50 33 30N 9 10 E
Tunja 78 5 33N 73 25W
Tunliu 38 36 13N 112 52 E
Tunnsjøen 20 64 45N 13 25 E
Tunungayualok I. 63 56 0N 61 0W
Tunuyán → 80 33 33S 67 30W
Tunxi 39 29 42N 118 25 E
Tuolumne 73 37 59N 120 16W
Tuoy-Khaya 25 62 32N 111 25 E
Tupelo 69 34 15N 88 42W
Tupik 25 54 26N 119 57 E
Tupinambaranas 78 3 0S 58 0W
Tupiza 80 21 30S 65 40W
Tupper 64 55 32N 120 1W
Tupper Lake 68 44 18N 74 30W
Tupungato, Cerro 80 33 15S 69 50W
Tuquan 38 45 18N 121 38 E
Tuque, La 62 47 30N 72 50W
Túquerres 78 1 5N 77 37W
Tura 25 64 20N 100 17 E

Valle Hermoso

Turabah 30 28 20N 43 15 E
Tūrān, Iran 31 35 39N 56 42 E
Turan, U.S.S.R. 25 51 55N 95 0 E
Turayf 30 31 41N 38 39 E
Turda 15 46 34N 23 47 E
Turek 15 52 3N 18 30 E
Turfan = Turpan 37 43 58N 89 10 E
Turfan Depression =
Turpan Hami 37 42 40N 89 25 E
Turgutlu 30 38 30N 27 48 E
Turhal 30 40 24N 36 5 E
Turia → 13 39 27N 0 19W
Turiaçu 79 1 40S 45 19W
Turiaçu → 79 1 36S 45 19W
Turin = Torino 18 45 4N 7 40 E
Turin 64 49 58N 112 31W
Turkana, L. 54 3 30N 36 5 E
Turkestan 24 43 17N 68 16 E
Turkey ■ 30 39 0N 36 0 E
Turkey Creek 46 17 2S 128 12 E
Turkmen S.S.R. □ 24 39 0N 59 0 E
Turks Is. 75 21 20N 71 20W
Turks Island
Passage 75 21 30N 71 30W
Turku 21 60 30N 22 19 E
Turlock 73 37 30N 120 55W
Turnagain → 64 59 12N 127 35W
Turnagain, C. 43 40 28S 176 38 E
Turneffe Is. 74 17 20N 87 50W
Turner, Australia 46 17 52S 128 16 E
Turner, U.S.A. 72 48 52N 108 25W
Turner Pt. 44 11 47S 133 32 E
Turner Valley 64 50 40N 114 17W
Turnhout 11 51 19N 4 57 E
Turnor L. 65 56 35N 108 35W
Tŭrnovo 19 43 5N 25 41 E
Turnu Măgurele 15 43 46N 24 56 E
Turnu Rosu Pasul 15 45 33N 24 17 E
Turnu-Severin 15 44 39N 22 41 E
Turon 71 37 48N 98 27W
Turpan 37 43 58N 89 10 E
Turpan Hami 37 42 40N 89 25 E
Turriff 8 57 32N 2 28W
Turtle Hd. I. 44 10 56S 142 37 E
Turtle L. 65 53 36N 108 38W
Turtle Lake, N. Dak.,
U.S.A. 70 47 30N 100 55W
Turtle Lake, Wis.,
U.S.A. 70 45 22N 92 10W
Turtleford 65 53 23N 108 57W
Turukhansk 25 65 21N 88 5 E
Turun ja Porin
lääni □ 21 60 27N 22 15 E
Tuscaloosa 69 33 13N 87 31W
Tuscany = Toscana 18 43 30N 11 5 E
Tuscola, Ill., U.S.A. 68 39 48N 88 15W
Tuscola, Tex., U.S.A. 71 32 15N 99 48W
Tuscumbia 69 34 42N 87 42W
Tuskar Rock 9 52 12N 6 10W
Tuskegee 69 32 24N 85 39W
Tuticorin 32 8 50N 78 12 E
Tutóia 79 2 45S 42 20W
Tutong 34 4 47N 114 40 E
Tutrakan 19 44 2N 26 40 E
Tutshi L. 64 59 56N 134 30W
Tuttle 70 47 9N 100 0W
Tuttlingen 14 47 59N 8 50 E
Tutuala 35 8 25S 127 15 E
Tutuila 43 14 19S 170 50W
Tuva A.S.S.R. □ 25 51 30N 95 0 E
Tuvalu ■ 3 8 0S 178 0 E
Tuxpan 74 20 58N 97 23W
Tuxtla Gutiérrez 74 16 50N 93 10W
Tuy 13 42 3N 8 39W
Tuya L. 64 59 7N 130 35W
Tuz Gölü 30 38 45N 33 30 E
Ţūz Khurmātū 30 34 56N 44 38 E
Tuzla 19 44 34N 18 41 E
Tweed → 8 55 42N 2 10W
Tweed Heads 45 28 10S 153 31 E
Tweedsmuir Prov.
Park 64 53 0N 126 20W
Twentynine Palms 73 34 10N 116 4W
Twillingate 63 49 42N 54 45W
Twin Bridges 72 45 33N 112 23W
Twin Falls 72 42 30N 114 30W
Twin Valley 70 47 18N 96 15W
Twisp 72 48 21N 120 5W
Two Harbors 70 47 1N 91 40W
Two Hills 64 53 43N 111 52W
Two Rivers 68 44 10N 87 31W
Twofold B. 45 37 8S 149 59 E
Tychy 15 50 9N 18 59 E
Tyler, Minn., U.S.A. 70 44 18N 96 8W
Tyler, Tex., U.S.A. 71 32 18N 95 18W
Tynda 25 55 10N 124 43 E
Tyne → 6 54 58N 1 28W
Tyne & Wear □ 6 54 55N 1 35W
Tynemouth 6 55 1N 1 27W
Tyre = Sūr 28 33 19N 35 16 E
Tyrifjorden 21 60 2N 10 8 E
Tyrol = Tirol □ 14 47 3N 10 43 E
Tyrrell → 45 35 26S 142 51 E
Tyrrell, L. 45 35 20S 142 50 E
Tyrrell Arm 65 62 27N 97 30W
Tyrrell L. 65 63 7N 105 27W
Tyrrhenian Sea 16 40 0N 12 30 E
Tysfjorden 20 68 7N 16 25 E
Tyulgan 22 52 22N 56 12 E
Tyumen 24 57 11N 65 29 E
Tywi → 7 51 48N 4 20W
Tywyn 7 52 36N 4 5W
Tzaneen 57 23 47S 30 9 E
Tzukong = Zigong 39 29 15N 104 48 E

U

Uanda 44 21 37S 144 55 E
Uarsciek 29 2 28N 45 55 E
Uato-Udo 35 9 7S 125 36 E
Uatumã → 78 2 26S 57 37W
Uaupés 78 0 8S 67 5W
Uaupés → 78 0 2N 67 16W
Ubá 80 21 8S 43 0W
Ubaitaba 79 14 18S 39 20W
Ubangi =
Oubangi → 54 0 30S 17 50 E
Ubauro 32 28 15N 69 45 E
Ube 36 33 56N 131 15 E
Ubeda 13 38 3N 3 23W
Uberaba 79 19 50S 47 55W
Uberlândia 79 19 0S 48 20W
Ubombo 57 27 31S 32 4 E
Ubon Ratchathani 34 15 15N 104 50 E
Ubundu 54 0 22S 25 30 E
Ucayali → 78 4 30S 73 30W
Uchi Lake 65 51 5N 92 35W
Uchiura-Wan 36 42 25N 140 40 E
Uchur → 25 58 48N 130 35 E
Ucluelet 64 48 57N 125 32W
Uda → 25 54 42N 135 14 E
Udaipur 32 24 36N 73 44 E
Udaipur Garhi 33 27 0N 86 35 E
Uddevalla 21 58 21N 11 55 E
Uddjaur 20 65 25N 21 15 E
Udgir 32 18 25N 77 5 E
Udhampur 32 33 0N 75 5 E
Udi 53 6 17N 7 21 E
Údine 18 46 5N 13 10 E
Udmurt A.S.S.R. □ 22 57 30N 52 30 E
Udon Thani 34 17 29N 102 46 E
Udupi 32 13 25N 74 42 E
Ueda 36 36 24N 138 16 E
Uele → 54 3 45N 24 45 E
Uelen 25 66 10N 170 0W
Uelzen 14 53 0N 10 33 E
Ufa 22 54 45N 55 55 E
Ufa → 22 54 40N 56 0 E
Ugab → 56 20 55S 13 30 E
Ugalla → 54 5 8S 30 42 E
Uganda ■ 54 2 0N 32 0 E
Ugie 57 31 10S 28 13 E
Uglegorsk 25 49 5N 142 2 E
Ugolyak 25 64 33N 120 30 E
Uhrichsville 68 40 23N 81 22W
Uíge 54 7 30S 14 40 E
Ŭiju 38 40 15N 124 35 E
Uinta Mts. 72 40 45N 110 30W
Uitenhage 56 33 40S 25 28 E
Uithuizen 11 53 24N 6 41 E
Ujjain 32 23 9N 75 43 E
Ujpest 15 47 32N 19 6 E
Ujung Pandang 35 5 10S 119 20 E
Uka 25 57 50N 162 0 E
Ukerewe I. 54 2 0S 33 0 E
Ukhrul 33 25 10N 94 25 E
Ukhta 22 63 55N 54 0 E
Ukiah 72 39 10N 123 9W
Ukrainian S.S.R. □ 23 49 0N 32 0 E
Ukwi 56 23 29S 20 30 E
Ulaanbaatar 37 47 55N 106 53 E
Ulaangom 37 50 0N 92 10 E
Ulan Bator =
Ulaanbaatar 37 47 55N 106 53 E
Ulan Ude 25 51 45N 107 40 E
Ulcinj 19 41 58N 19 10 E
Ulco 56 28 21S 24 15 E
Ulhasnagar 32 19 15N 73 10 E
Ulladulla 45 35 21S 150 29 E
Ullapool 8 57 54N 5 10W
Ullswater 6 54 35N 2 52W
Ullung-do 38 37 30N 130 30 E
Ulm 14 48 23N 10 0 E
Ulmarra 45 29 37S 153 4 E
Ulonguè 55 14 37S 34 19 E
Ulricehamn 21 57 46N 13 26 E
Ulster □ 9 54 35N 6 30W
Ulungur → 37 47 1N 87 24 E
Ulutau 24 48 39N 67 1 E
Ulverston 6 54 13N 3 7W
Ulverstone 44 41 11S 146 11 E
Ulya 25 59 10N 142 0 E
Ulyanovsk 22 54 20N 48 25 E
Ulyasutay 37 47 56N 97 28 E
Ulysses 71 37 39N 101 25W
Umala 78 17 25S 68 5W
Uman 23 48 40N 30 12 E
Umaria 33 23 35N 80 50 E
Umarkot 32 25 15N 69 40 E
Umatilla 72 45 58N 119 17W
Umba 22 66 50N 34 20 E
Umbrella Mts. 43 45 35S 169 5 E
Umbria □ 18 42 53N 12 30 E
Ume älv → 20 63 45N 20 20 E
Umeå 20 63 45N 20 20 E
Umera 35 0 12S 129 37 E
Umkomaas 57 30 13S 30 48 E
Umm al Qaywayn 31 25 30N 55 35 E
Umm Bel 51 13 35N 28 0 E
Umm el Fahm 28 32 31N 35 9 E
Umm Lajj 30 25 0N 37 23 E
Umm Qays 28 32 40N 35 41 E
Umm Ruwaba 51 12 50N 31 20 E
Umnak 60 53 20N 168 20W
Umniati → 55 16 49S 28 45 E
Umpqua → 72 43 42N 124 3W
Umtata 57 31 36S 28 49 E
Umuarama 79 23 45S 53 20W
Umzimvubu = Port
St. Johns 57 31 38S 29 33 E
Umzinto 57 30 15S 30 45 E
Unac → 18 44 30N 16 9 E
Unalaska 60 53 40N 166 40W
Uncía 78 18 25S 66 40W
Uncompahgre Pk. 73 38 5N 107 32W
Underberg 57 29 50S 29 22 E
Underbool 45 35 10S 141 51 E
Ungarie 45 33 38S 146 56 E
Ungarra 45 34 12S 136 2 E
Ungava B. 61 59 30N 67 30W
Ungava Pen. 61 60 0N 74 0W
Unggi 38 42 16N 130 28 E
União da Vitória 80 26 13S 51 5W
Unimak 60 55 0N 164 0W
Unimak Pass. 60 53 30N 165 15W
Union, Miss., U.S.A. 71 32 34N 89 14W
Union, Mo., U.S.A. 70 38 25N 91 0W
Union, S.C., U.S.A. 69 34 43N 81 39W
Unión, La, Chile 80 40 10S 73 0W
Unión, La, El Salv. 75 13 20N 87 50W
Union, Mt. 73 34 34N 112 21W
Union City, Pa.,
U.S.A. 68 41 53N 79 50W
Union City, Tenn.,
U.S.A. 71 36 25N 89 0W
Union Gap 72 46 38N 120 29W
Union of Soviet
Socialist
Republics ■ 25 60 0N 100 0 E
Union Springs 69 32 9N 85 44W
Uniondale 56 33 39S 23 7 E
Uniontown 68 39 54N 79 45W
Unionville 70 40 29N 93 1W
United Arab
Emirates ■ 31 23 50N 54 0 E
United Kingdom ■ 5 55 0N 3 0W
United States of
America ■ 67 37 0N 96 0W
United States Trust
Terr. of the Pacific
Is. □ 40 10 0N 160 0 E
Unity 65 52 30N 109 5W
Unnao 33 26 35N 80 30 E
Unst 8 60 50N 0 55W
Unuk → 64 56 5N 131 3W
Ünye 30 41 5N 37 15 E
Upata 78 8 1N 62 24W
Upemba, L. 54 8 30S 26 20 E
Upington 56 28 25S 21 15 E
Upolu 43 13 58S 172 0W
Upper Alkali Lake 72 41 47N 120 8W
Upper Arrow L. 64 50 30N 117 50W
Upper Foster L. 65 56 47N 105 20W
Upper Hutt 43 41 8S 175 5 E
Upper Klamath L. 72 42 16N 121 55W
Upper L. Erne 9 54 14N 7 22W
Upper Lake 72 39 10N 122 55W
Upper
Musquodoboit 63 45 10N 62 58W
Upper Red L. 70 48 0N 95 0W
Upper Sandusky 68 40 50N 83 17W
Upper Taimyr → 25 74 15N 99 48 E
Upper Volta =
Burkina Faso ■ 50 12 0N 1 0W
Uppsala 21 59 53N 17 38 E
Uppsala län □ 21 60 0N 17 30 E
Upstart, C. 44 19 41S 147 45 E
Upton 70 44 8N 104 35W
Ur 30 30 55N 46 25 E
Uracara 78 2 20S 57 50W
Urad Qianqi 38 40 40N 108 30 E
Urakawa 36 42 9N 142 47 E
Ural → 23 47 0N 51 48 E
Ural, Mt. 45 33 21S 146 12 E
Ural Mts. = Uralskie
Gory 22 60 0N 59 0 E
Ural Mts. 4 60 0N 59 0 E
Uralla 45 30 37S 151 29 E
Uralsk 22 51 20N 51 20 E
Uralskie Gory 22 60 0N 59 0 E
Urandangi 44 21 32S 138 14 E
Uranium City 65 59 34N 108 37W
Uranquinty 45 35 10S 147 12 E
Urawa 36 35 50N 139 40 E
Uray 24 60 5N 65 15 E
Urbana, Ill., U.S.A. 68 40 7N 88 12W
Urbana, Ohio, U.S.A. 68 40 9N 83 44W
Urbana, La 78 7 8N 66 56W
Urbino 18 43 43N 12 38 E
Urbión, Picos de 13 42 1N 2 52W
Urcos 78 13 40S 71 38W
Urda 23 48 52N 47 23 E
Urdzhar 24 47 5N 81 38 E
Ure → 6 54 20N 1 25W
Urengoy 24 65 58N 28 25 E
Ures 74 29 30N 110 30W
Urfa 30 37 12N 38 50 E
Urfahr 14 48 19N 14 17 E
Urgench 24 41 40N 60 41 E
Uribia 78 11 43N 72 16W
Urim 28 31 18N 34 32 E
Urique → 74 26 29N 107 58W
Urk 11 52 39N 5 36 E
Urla 30 38 20N 26 47 E
Urmia = Orūmīyeh 30 37 40N 45 0 E
Urmia, L. =
Orūmīyeh,
Daryācheh-ye 30 37 50N 45 30 E
Uruana 79 15 30S 49 41W
Uruapan 74 19 30N 102 0W
Urubamba 78 13 20S 72 10W
Urubamba → 78 10 43S 73 48W
Uruçuí 79 7 20S 44 28W
Uruguai → 80 26 0S 53 30W
Uruguaiana 80 29 50S 57 0W
Uruguay ■ 80 32 30S 56 30W
Uruguay → 80 34 12S 58 18W
Urumchi = Ürümqi 37 43 45N 87 45 E
Ürümqi 37 43 45N 87 45 E
Urup, Os. 25 46 0N 151 0 E
Uryung-Khaya 25 72 48N 113 23 E
Usa → 22 65 57N 56 55 E
Uşak 30 38 43N 29 28 E
Usakos 56 21 54S 15 31 E
Usedom 14 53 50N 13 55 E
Ush-Tobe 24 45 16N 78 0 E
Ushant = Ouessant,
I. d' 12 48 28N 5 6W
Ushuaia 80 54 50S 68 23W
Ushumun 25 52 47N 126 32 E
Usk → 7 51 37N 2 56W
Üsküdar 30 41 0N 29 5 E
Usman 22 52 5N 39 48 E
Usoke 54 5 8S 32 24 E
Usolye Sibirskoye 25 52 48N 103 40 E
Usoro 53 5 33N 6 11 E
Uspallata, P. de 80 32 37S 69 22W
Uspenskiy 24 48 41N 72 43 E
Ussuriysk 25 43 48N 131 59 E
Ust-Aldan =
Batamay 25 63 30N 129 15 E
Ust Amginskoye =
Khandyga 25 62 42N 135 35 E
Ust-Bolsheretsk 25 52 50N 156 15 E
Ust chaun 25 68 47N 170 30 E
Ust'-Ilga 25 55 5N 104 55 E
Ust Ilimpeya = Yukti 25 63 26N 105 42 E
Ust-Ilimsk 25 58 3N 102 39 E
Ust Ishim 24 57 45N 71 10 E
Ust-Kamchatsk 25 56 10N 162 28 E
Ust-Kamenogorsk 24 50 0N 82 36 E
Ust-Karenga 25 54 25N 116 30 E
Ust Khayryuzova 25 57 15N 156 45 E
Ust-Kut 25 56 50N 105 42 E
Ust Kuyga 25 70 1N 135 43 E
Ust Maya 25 60 30N 134 28 E
Ust-Mil 25 59 40N 133 11 E
Ust-Nera 25 64 35N 143 15 E
Ust-Nyukzha 25 56 34N 121 37 E
Ust Olenek 25 73 0N 119 48 E
Ust-Omchug 25 61 9N 149 38 E
Ust Port 24 69 40N 84 26 E
Ust Tsilma 22 65 25N 52 0 E
Ust-Tungir 25 55 25N 120 36 E
Ust Urt = Ustyurt,
Plato 24 44 0N 55 0 E
Ust Usa 22 66 0N 56 30 E
Ust Vorkuta 24 67 24N 64 0 E
Ústí nad Labem 14 50 41N 14 3 E
Ustica 18 38 42N 13 10 E
Ustinov 22 56 51N 53 14 E
Ustroń 15 49 43N 18 48 E
Ustye 25 57 46N 94 37 E
Ustyurt, Plato 24 44 0N 55 0 E
Usu 37 44 27N 84 40 E
Usuki 36 33 8N 131 49 E
Usulután 75 13 25N 88 28W
Usumacinta → 74 17 0N 91 0W
Usumbura =
Bujumbura 54 3 16S 29 18 E
Uta 35 4 33S 136 0 E
Utah □ 72 39 30N 111 30W
Utah, L. 72 40 10N 111 58W
Ute Cr. → 71 35 21N 103 45W
Utete 54 8 0S 38 45 E
Utiariti 78 13 0S 58 10W
Utica 68 43 5N 75 18W
Utik L. 65 55 15N 96 0W
Utikuma L. 64 55 50N 115 30W
Utrecht, Neth. 11 52 5N 5 8 E
Utrecht, S. Africa 57 27 38S 30 20 E
Utrecht □ 11 52 6N 5 7 E
Utrera 13 37 12N 5 48W
Utsjoki 20 69 51N 26 59 E
Utsunomiya 36 36 30N 139 50 E
Uttar Pradesh □ 32 27 0N 80 0 E
Uttaradit 34 17 36N 100 5 E
Uttoxeter 6 52 53N 1 50W
Uudenmaan lääni □ 21 60 25N 25 0 E
Uusikaarlepyy 20 63 32N 22 31 E
Uusikaupunki 21 60 47N 21 25 E
Uva 22 56 59N 52 13 E
Uvalde 71 29 15N 99 48W
Uvat 24 59 5N 68 50 E
Uvinza 54 5 5S 30 24 E
Uvira 54 3 22S 29 3 E
Uvs Nuur 37 50 20N 92 30 E
Uwajima 36 33 10N 132 35 E
Uxin Qi 38 38 50N 109 5 E
Uxmal 74 20 22N 89 46W
Uyandi 25 69 19N 141 0 E
Uyo 53 5 1N 7 53 E
Uyuni 78 20 28S 66 47W
Uzbek S.S.R. □ 24 41 30N 65 0 E
Uzen 23 43 27N 53 10 E
Uzerche 12 45 25N 1 34 E
Uzhgorod 22 48 36N 22 18 E

V

Vaal → 56 29 4S 23 38 E
Vaal Dam 57 27 0S 28 14 E
Vaalwater 57 24 15S 28 8 E
Vaasa 20 63 6N 21 38 E
Vaasan lääni □ 20 63 2N 22 50 E
Vác 15 47 49N 19 10 E
Vacaville 72 38 21N 122 0W
Vach → 24 60 45N 76 45 E
Vache, I.-à- 75 18 2N 73 35W
Vadodara 32 22 20N 73 10 E
Vadsø 20 70 3N 29 50 E
Værøy 20 67 40N 12 40 E
Váh → 15 47 55N 18 0 E
Vaigach 24 70 10N 59 0 E
Val-de-Marne □ 12 48 45N 2 28 E
Val-d'Oise □ 12 49 5N 2 10 E
Val d'Or 62 48 7N 77 47W
Val Marie 65 49 15N 107 45W
Valahia 15 44 35N 25 0 E
Valcheta 80 40 40S 66 8W
Valdayskaya
Vozvyshennost 22 57 0N 33 30 E
Valdepeñas 13 38 43N 3 25W
Valdés, Pen. 80 42 30S 63 45W
Valdez 60 61 14N 146 17W
Valdivia 80 39 50S 73 14W
Valdosta 69 30 50N 83 20W
Vale 72 44 0N 117 15W
Valença 79 13 20S 39 5W
Valença do Piauí 79 6 20S 41 45W
Valence 12 44 57N 4 54 E
Valencia, Spain 13 39 27N 0 23W
Valencia, Venezuela 78 10 11N 68 0W
Valencia □ 13 39 20N 0 40W
Valencia, Albufera
de 13 39 20N 0 27W
Valencia, G. de 13 39 30N 0 20 E
Valencia de
Alcántara 13 39 25N 7 14W
Valenciennes 12 50 20N 3 34 E
Valentia Harbour 9 51 56N 10 17W
Valentia I. 9 51 54N 10 22W
Valentim, Sa. do 79 6 0S 43 30W
Valentine, Nebr.,
U.S.A. 70 42 50N 100 35W
Valentine, Tex.,
U.S.A. 71 30 36N 104 28W
Valera 78 9 19N 70 37W
Valier 72 48 25N 112 9W
Valjevo 19 44 18N 19 53 E
Valkeakoski 21 61 16N 24 2 E
Valkenswaard 11 51 21N 5 29 E
Valladolid, Mexico 74 20 40N 88 11W
Valladolid, Spain 13 41 38N 4 43W
Valle d'Aosta □ 18 45 45N 7 22 E
Valle de la Pascua 78 9 13N 66 0W
Valle de Santiago 74 20 25N 101 15W
Valle Hermoso 74 25 35N 97 40W

Vallecas

Vallecas 13 40 23N 3 41W
Valledupar 78 10 29N 73 15W
Vallejo 72 38 12N 122 15W
Vallenar 80 28 30S 70 50W
Valletta 16 35 54N 14 30 E
Valley City 70 46 57N 98 0W
Valley Falls 72 42 33N 120 16W
Valleyview 64 55 5N 117 17W
Valls 13 41 18N 1 15 E
Valognes 12 49 30N 1 28W
Valparaíso, Chile 80 33 2S 71 40W
Valparaíso, Mexico 74 22 50N 103 32W
Valparaiso, U.S.A. 68 41 27N 87 2W
Vals → 56 27 23S 26 30 E
Vals, Tanjung 35 8 26S 137 25 E
Valsad 32 20 40N 72 58 E
Valverde del Camino 13 37 35N 6 47W
Van 30 38 30N 43 20 E
Van, L. = Van Gölü 30 38 30N 43 0 E
Van Alstyne 71 33 25N 96 36W
Van Bruyssel 63 47 56N 72 9W
Van Buren, Canada 63 47 10N 67 55W
Van Buren, Ark., U.S.A. 71 35 28N 94 18W
Van Buren, Maine, U.S.A. 69 47 10N 68 1W
Van Buren, Mo., U.S.A. 71 37 0N 91 0W
Van Diemen, C., N. Terr., Australia 46 11 9S 130 24 E
Van Diemen, C., Queens., Australia 44 16 30S 139 46 E
Van Diemen G. 46 11 45S 132 0 E
Van Gölü 30 38 30N 43 0 E
Van Horn 71 31 3N 104 55W
Van Reenen P. 57 28 22S 29 27 E
Van Rees, Pegunungan 35 2 35S 138 15 E
Van Tassell 70 42 40N 104 3W
Van Wert 68 40 52N 84 31W
Vanavara 25 60 22N 102 16 E
Vancouver, Canada 64 49 15N 123 10W
Vancouver, U.S.A. 72 45 44N 122 41W
Vancouver, C. 47 35 2S 118 11 E
Vancouver I. 64 49 50N 126 0W
Vandalia, Ill., U.S.A. 70 38 57N 89 4W
Vandalia, Mo., U.S.A. 70 39 18N 91 30W
Vanderbijlpark 57 26 42S 27 54 E
Vandergrift 68 40 36N 79 33W
Vanderhoof 64 54 0N 124 0W
Vanderlin I. 44 15 44S 137 2 E
Vandyke 44 24 10S 147 51 E
Vänern 21 58 47N 13 30 E
Vänersborg 21 58 26N 12 19 E
Vanga 54 4 35S 39 12 E
Vangaindrano 57 23 21S 47 36 E
Vanguard 65 49 55N 107 20W
Vanier 62 45 27N 75 40W
Vankarem 25 67 51N 175 50 E
Vankleek Hill 62 45 32N 74 40W
Vanna 20 70 6N 19 50 E
Vännäs 20 63 58N 19 48 E
Vannes 12 47 40N 2 47W
Vanrhynsdorp 56 31 36S 18 44 E
Vanrook 44 16 57S 141 57 E
Vansbro 21 60 32N 14 15 E
Vansittart B. 46 14 3S 126 17 E
Vanua Levu 43 16 33S 179 15 E
Vanua Mbalavu 43 17 40S 178 57W
Vanuatu ■ 3 15 0S 168 0 E
Vanwyksvlei 56 30 18S 21 49 E
Vanzylsrus 56 26 52S 22 4 E
Var □ 12 43 27N 6 18 E
Varanasi 33 25 22N 83 0 E
Varangerfjorden 20 70 3N 29 25 E
Varaždin 18 46 20N 16 20 E
Varberg 21 57 6N 12 20 E
Vardak □ 31 34 0N 68 0 E
Vardar → 19 40 35N 22 50 E
Varese 18 45 49N 8 50 E
Variadero 71 35 43N 104 17W
Värmlands län □ 21 60 0N 13 20 E
Varna 19 43 13N 27 56 E
Värnamo 21 57 10N 14 3 E
Varzaneh 31 32 25N 52 40 E
Vasa 20 63 6N 21 38 E
Vasa Barris → 79 11 10S 37 10W
Vascongadas □ 13 42 50N 2 45W
Vasht = Khāsh 31 28 15N 61 15 E
Vaslui 15 46 38N 27 42 E
Vassar, Canada 65 49 10N 95 55W
Vassar, U.S.A. 68 43 23N 83 33W
Västerås 21 59 37N 16 38 E
Västerbottens län □ 20 64 58N 18 0 E
Västernorrlands län □ 20 63 30N 17 30 E
Västervik 21 57 43N 16 43 E
Västmanlands län □ 21 59 45N 16 20 E
Vasto 18 42 8N 14 40 E
Vatnajökull 20 64 30N 16 48W
Vatneyri 20 65 35N 24 0W
Vatoa 43 19 50S 178 13W
Vatoloha, Mt. 57 17 52S 47 48 E
Vatomandry 57 19 20S 48 59 E
Vatra-Dornei 15 47 22N 25 22 E
Vättern 21 58 25N 14 30 E
Vaucluse □ 12 43 50N 5 20 E
Vaughn, Mont., U.S.A. 72 47 37N 111 36W
Vaughn, N. Mex., U.S.A. 73 34 37N 105 12W
Vaupés → = Uaupés → 78 0 2N 67 16W
Vauxhall 64 50 5N 112 9W
Vava'u 43 18 36S 174 0W
Växjö 21 56 52N 14 50 E
Vaygach, Ostrov 24 70 0N 60 0 E
Vechte → 11 52 34N 6 6 E
Vedea → 15 43 53N 25 59 E
Veendam 11 53 5N 6 52 E
Veenendaal 11 52 2N 5 34 E
Vefsna → 20 65 48N 13 10 E
Vega, Norway 20 65 40N 11 55 E
Vega, U.S.A. 71 35 18N 102 26W
Vega, La 75 19 20N 70 30W
Vegafjorden 20 65 37N 12 0 E
Veghel 11 51 37N 5 32 E
Vegreville 64 53 30N 112 5W
Vejer de la Frontera 13 36 15N 5 59W
Vejle 21 55 43N 9 30 E
Velay, Mts. du 12 45 0N 3 40 E
Velddrif 56 32 42S 18 11 E
Velebit Planina 18 44 50N 15 20 E
Vélez 78 6 1N 73 41W
Vélez Málaga 13 36 48N 4 5W
Vélez Rubio 13 37 41N 2 5W
Velhas → 79 17 13S 44 49W
Velikaya → 22 57 48N 28 20 E
Veliki Ustyug 22 60 47N 46 20 E
Velikiye Luki 22 56 25N 30 32 E
Velikonda Range 32 14 45N 79 10 E
Velletri 18 41 43N 12 43 E
Vellore 32 12 57N 79 10 E
Velsen-Noord 11 52 27N 4 40 E
Velsk 22 61 10N 42 5 E
Velva 70 48 6N 100 56W
Venado Tuerto 80 33 50S 62 0W
Venda □ 57 22 40S 30 35 E
Vendée □ 12 46 50N 1 35W
Vénéto □ 18 45 40N 12 0 E
Venézia 18 45 27N 12 20 E
Venézia, G. di 18 45 20N 13 0 E
Venezuela ■ 78 8 0N 66 0W
Venezuela, G. de 78 11 30N 71 0W
Vengurla 32 15 53N 73 45 E
Venice = Venézia 18 45 27N 12 20 E
Venkatapuram 33 18 20N 80 30 E
Venlo 11 51 22N 6 11 E
Venraij 11 51 31N 6 0 E
Ventana, Punta de la 74 24 4N 109 48W
Ventana, Sa. de la 80 38 0S 62 30W
Ventersburg 56 28 7S 27 9 E
Venterstad 56 30 47S 25 48 E
Ventnor 7 50 35N 1 12W
Ventspils 22 57 25N 21 32 E
Ventuarí → 78 3 58N 67 2W
Ventura 73 34 16N 119 18W
Venus B. 45 38 40S 145 42 E
Vera, Argentina 80 29 30S 60 20W
Vera, Spain 13 37 15N 1 51W
Veracruz 74 19 10N 96 10W
Veracruz □ 74 19 0N 96 15W
Veraval 32 20 53N 70 27 E
Vercelli 18 45 19N 8 25 E
Verdalsøra 20 63 48N 11 30 E
Verde →, Argentina 80 41 56S 65 5W
Verde →, Chihuahua, Mexico 74 26 29N 107 58W
Verde →, Oaxaca, Mexico 74 15 59N 97 50W
Verde →, Veracruz, Mexico 74 21 10N 102 50W
Verde, Cay 75 23 0N 75 5W
Verden 14 52 58N 9 18 E
Verdigre 70 42 38N 98 0W
Verdon-sur-Mer, Le 12 45 33N 1 4W
Verdun 12 49 9N 5 24 E
Vereeniging 57 26 38S 27 57 E
Vérendrye, Parc Prov. de la 62 47 20N 76 40W
Verga, C. 50 10 30N 14 10W
Vergemont 44 23 33S 143 1 E
Vergemont Cr. → 44 24 16S 143 16 E
Verkhnevilyuysk 25 63 27N 120 18 E
Verkhneye Kalinino 25 59 54N 108 8 E
Verkhniy Baskunchak 23 48 14N 46 44 E
Verkhoyansk 25 67 35N 133 25 E
Verkhoyansk Ra. = Verkhoyanskiy Khrebet 25 66 0N 129 0 E
Verkhoyanskiy Khrebet 25 66 0N 129 0 E
Verlo 65 50 19N 108 35W
Vermilion 65 53 20N 110 50W
Vermilion →, Alta., Canada 65 53 22N 110 51W
Vermilion →, Qué., Canada 62 47 38N 72 56W
Vermilion, B. 71 29 45N 91 55W
Vermilion Bay 65 49 51N 93 34W
Vermilion Chutes 64 58 22N 114 51W
Vermilion L. 70 47 53N 92 25W
Vermillion 70 42 50N 96 56W
Vermont □ 68 43 40N 72 50W
Vernal 72 40 28N 109 35W
Verner 62 46 25N 80 8W
Verneukpan 56 30 0S 21 0 E
Vernon, Canada 64 50 20N 119 15W
Vernon, U.S.A. 71 34 10N 99 20W
Vero Beach 69 27 39N 80 23W
Véroia 19 40 34N 22 12 E
Verona 18 45 27N 11 0 E
Veropol 25 65 15N 168 40 E
Versailles 12 48 48N 2 8 E
Vert, C. 50 14 45N 17 30W
Verulam 57 29 38S 31 2 E
Verviers 11 50 37N 5 52 E
Veselovskoye Vdkhr. 23 47 0N 41 0 E
Vesoul 12 47 40N 6 11 E
Vest-Agder fylke □ 21 58 30N 7 15 E
Vesterålen 20 68 45N 15 0 E
Vestfjorden 20 67 55N 14 0 E
Vestfold fylke □ 21 59 15N 10 0 E
Vestmannaeyjar 20 63 27N 20 15W
Vestvågøy 20 68 18N 13 50 E
Vesuvio 18 40 50N 14 22 E
Vesuvius, Mt. = Vesuvio 18 40 50N 14 22 E
Veszprém 15 47 8N 17 57 E
Vetlanda 21 57 24N 15 3 E
Veurne 11 51 5N 2 40 E
Veys 30 31 30N 49 0 E
Vezhen 19 42 50N 24 20 E
Viacha 78 16 39S 68 18W
Viamão 80 30 5S 51 0W
Viana, Brazil 79 3 13S 45 0W
Viana, Portugal 13 38 20N 8 0W
Viana do Castelo 13 41 42N 8 50W
Vianópolis 79 16 40S 48 35W
Vibank 65 50 20N 103 56W
Viborg 21 56 27N 9 23 E
Vicenza 18 45 32N 11 31 E
Vich 13 41 58N 2 19 E
Vichy 12 46 9N 3 26 E
Vicksburg, Mich., U.S.A. 68 42 10N 85 30W
Vicksburg, Miss., U.S.A. 71 32 22N 90 56W
Viçosa 79 9 28S 36 14W
Victor, India 32 21 0N 71 30 E
Victor, U.S.A. 70 38 43N 105 7W
Victor Harbor 45 35 30S 138 37 E
Victoria, Canada 64 48 30N 123 25W
Victoria, Chile 80 38 13S 72 20W
Victoria, Guinea 50 10 50N 14 32W
Victoria, Ind. Oc. 3 5 0S 55 40 E
Victoria, Malaysia 34 5 20N 115 14 E
Victoria, Kans., U.S.A. 70 38 52N 99 8W
Victoria, Tex., U.S.A. 71 28 50N 97 0W
Victoria → 46 15 10S 129 40 E
Victoria, Grand L. 62 47 31N 77 30W
Victoria, L., Australia 45 33 57S 141 15 E
Victoria, L., E. Afr. 54 1 0S 33 0 E
Victoria Beach 65 50 40N 96 35W
Victoria de Durango 74 24 3N 104 39W
Victoria de las Tunas 75 20 58N 76 59W
Victoria Falls 55 17 58S 25 52 E
Victoria Harbour 62 44 45N 79 45W
Victoria I. 60 71 0N 111 0W
Victoria Nile → 52 2 14N 31 26 E
Victoria Ra. 43 42 12S 172 7 E
Victoria Res. 63 48 20N 57 27W
Victoria River Downs 46 16 25S 131 0 E
Victoria Taungdeik 33 21 15N 93 55 E
Victoria West 56 31 25S 23 4 E
Victoriaville 63 46 4N 71 56W
Victorica 80 36 20S 65 30W
Victorville 73 34 32N 117 18W
Vicuña 80 30 0S 70 50W
Vidalia 69 32 13N 82 25W
Vidin 19 43 59N 22 50 E
Vidisha 32 23 28N 77 53 E
Viedma 80 40 50S 63 0W
Viedma, L. 80 49 30S 72 30W
Vienna = Wien 14 48 12N 16 22 E
Vienna 71 37 29N 88 54W
Vienne 12 45 31N 4 53 E
Vienne □ 12 46 30N 0 42 E
Vienne → 12 47 13N 0 5 E
Vientos, Paso de los 75 20 0N 74 0W
Vierzon 12 47 13N 2 5 E
Vietnam ■ 34 19 0N 106 0 E
Vigan 35 17 35N 120 28 E
Vigia 79 0 50S 48 5W
Vigo 13 42 12N 8 41W
Vijayawada 33 16 31N 80 39 E
Viking 64 53 7N 111 50W
Vikna 20 64 55N 10 58 E
Vikulovo 24 56 50N 70 40 E
Vila da Maganja 55 17 18S 37 30 E
Vila de João Belo = Xai-Xai 57 25 6S 33 31 E
Vila do Chibuto 57 24 40S 33 33 E
Vila Franca de Xira 13 38 57N 8 59W
Vila Gomes da Costa 57 24 20S 33 37 E
Vila Machado 55 19 15S 34 14 E
Vila Real 13 41 17N 7 48W
Vila Real de Santo António 13 37 10N 7 28W
Vila Velha 79 20 20S 40 17W
Vilaine → 12 47 30N 2 27W
Vilanandro, Tanjona 57 16 11S 44 27 E
Vilanculos 57 22 1S 35 17 E
Vilhelmina 20 64 35N 16 39 E
Vilhena 78 12 40S 60 5W
Viliga 25 61 36N 156 56 E
Villa Ahumada 74 30 38N 106 30W
Villa Ángela 80 27 34S 60 45W
Villa Bella 78 10 25S 65 22W
Villa Bens = Tarfaya 50 27 55N 12 55W
Villa Cisneros = Dakhla 50 23 50N 15 53W
Villa Colón 80 31 38S 68 20W
Villa de María 80 29 55S 63 43W
Villa Dolores 80 31 58S 65 15W
Villa Hayes 80 25 0S 57 20W
Villa María 80 32 20S 63 10W
Villa Mazán 80 28 40S 66 30W
Villa Montes 80 21 10S 63 30W
Villa Ocampo 80 28 30S 59 20W
Villach 14 46 37N 13 51 E
Villagarcía de Arosa 13 42 34N 8 46W
Villagrán 74 24 29N 99 29W
Villaguay 80 32 0S 59 0W
Villahermosa 74 18 0N 92 50W
Villalba 13 43 26N 7 40W
Villanueva 73 35 16N 105 23W
Villanueva de la Serena 13 38 59N 5 50W
Villarreal 13 39 55N 0 3W
Villarrica, Chile 80 39 15S 72 15W
Villarrica, Paraguay 80 25 40S 56 30W
Villarrobledo 13 39 18N 2 36W
Villavicencio 78 4 9N 73 37W
Villaviciosa 13 43 32N 5 27W
Villazón 80 22 0S 65 35W
Ville-Marie 62 47 20N 79 30W
Ville Platte 71 30 45N 92 17W
Villena 13 38 39N 0 52W
Villiers 57 27 2S 28 36 E
Villisca 70 40 55N 94 59W
Vilna 64 54 7N 111 55W
Vilnius 22 54 38N 25 19 E
Vilskutskogo, Proliv 25 78 0N 103 0 E
Vilvoorde 11 50 56N 4 26 E
Vilyuy → 25 64 24N 126 26 E
Vilyuysk 25 63 40N 121 35 E
Viña del Mar 80 33 0S 71 30W
Vinaroz 13 40 30N 0 27 E
Vincennes 68 38 42N 87 29W
Vindel älven → 20 63 55N 19 50 E
Vindeln 20 64 12N 19 43 E
Vindhya Ra. 32 22 50N 77 0 E
Vineland 68 39 30N 75 0W
Vinita 71 36 40N 95 12W
Vinkovci 19 45 19N 18 48 E
Vinnitsa 23 49 15N 28 30 E
Vinton, Iowa, U.S.A. 70 42 8N 92 1W
Vinton, La., U.S.A. 71 30 13N 93 35W
Viqueque 35 8 52S 126 23 E
Virac 35 13 30N 124 20 E
Virago Sd. 64 54 0N 132 30W
Viramgam 32 23 5N 72 0 E
Viranşehir 30 37 13N 39 45 E
Virden 65 49 50N 100 56W
Vire 12 48 50N 0 53W
Vírgenes, C. 80 52 19S 68 21W
Virgin →, Canada 65 57 2N 108 17W
Virgin →, U.S.A. 73 36 50N 114 10W
Virgin Gorda 75 18 30N 64 26W
Virgin Is. 75 18 40N 64 30W
Virginia, S. Africa 56 28 8S 26 55 E
Virginia, U.S.A. 70 47 30N 92 32W
Virginia □ 68 37 45N 78 0W
Virginia Beach 68 36 54N 75 58W
Virginia City, Mont., U.S.A. 72 45 18N 111 58W
Virginia City, Nev., U.S.A. 72 39 19N 119 39W
Virginia Falls 64 61 38N 125 42W
Virginiatown 62 48 9N 79 36W
Viroqua 70 43 33N 90 57W
Virton 11 49 35N 5 32 E
Virudunagar 32 9 30N 78 0 E
Vis 18 43 0N 16 10 E
Visalia 73 36 25N 119 18W
Visayan Sea 35 11 30N 123 30 E
Visby 21 57 37N 18 18 E
Viscount Melville Sd. 58 74 10N 108 0W
Visé 11 50 44N 5 41 E
Višegrad 19 43 47N 19 17 E
Viseu, Brazil 79 1 10S 46 5W
Viseu, Portugal 13 40 40N 7 55W
Vishakhapatnam 33 17 45N 83 20 E
Viso, Mte. 18 44 38N 7 5 E
Vistula = Wisła → 15 54 22N 18 55 E
Vitebsk 22 55 10N 30 15 E
Viterbo 18 42 25N 12 8 E
Viti Levu 43 17 30S 177 30 E
Vitim 25 59 28N 112 35 E
Vitim → 25 59 26N 112 34 E
Vitória, Brazil 79 20 20S 40 22W
Vitoria, Spain 13 42 50N 2 41W
Vitória da Conquista 79 14 51S 40 51W
Vittória 18 36 58N 14 30 E
Vittório Véneto 18 45 59N 12 18 E
Vivero 13 43 39N 7 38W
Vizcaíno, Desierto de 74 27 40N 113 50W
Vizcaíno, Sierra 74 27 30N 114 0W
Vizianagaram 33 18 6N 83 30 E
Vlaardingen 11 51 55N 4 21 E
Vladimir 22 56 15N 40 30 E
Vladivostok 25 43 10N 131 53 E
Vlieland 11 53 16N 4 55 E
Vlissingen 11 51 26N 3 34 E
Vltava → 14 50 21N 14 30 E
Vogelkop = Doberai, Jazirah 35 1 25S 133 0 E
Vogelsberg 14 50 37N 9 15 E
Vohibinany 57 18 49S 49 4 E
Vohimarina 57 13 25S 50 0 E
Vohimena, Tanjon' i 57 25 36S 45 8 E
Vohipeno 57 22 22S 47 51 E
Voi 54 3 25S 38 32 E
Voisey B. 63 56 15N 61 50W
Vojmsjön 20 64 55N 16 40 E
Volborg 70 45 50N 105 44W
Volcano Is. 40 25 0N 141 0 E
Volchayevka 25 48 40N 134 30 E
Volda 20 62 9N 6 5 E
Volga → 23 48 30N 46 0 E
Volga Hts. = Privolzhskaya Vozvyshennost 23 51 0N 46 0 E
Volgodonsk 23 47 33N 42 5 E
Volgograd 23 48 40N 44 25 E
Volgogradskoye Vdkhr. 23 50 0N 45 20 E
Volkhov → 22 60 8N 32 20 E
Volksrust 57 27 24S 29 53 E
Vollenhove 11 52 40N 5 58 E
Volochanka 25 71 0N 94 28 E
Vologda 22 59 10N 40 0 E
Vólos 19 39 24N 22 59 E
Volsk 22 52 5N 47 22 E
Volta → 53 5 46N 0 41 E
Volta, L. 53 7 30N 0 15 E
Volta Redonda 79 22 31S 44 5W
Voltaire, C. 46 14 16S 125 35 E
Volterra 18 43 24N 10 50 E
Volturno → 18 41 1N 13 55 E
Volvo 45 31 41S 143 57 E
Volzhskiy 23 48 56N 44 46 E
Vondrozo 57 22 49S 47 20 E
Voorburg 11 52 5N 4 24 E
Vopnafjörður 20 65 45N 14 40W
Vorarlberg □ 14 47 20N 10 0 E
Voríai Sporádhes 19 39 15N 23 30 E
Vorkuta 22 67 48N 64 20 E
Voronezh 22 51 40N 39 10 E
Voroshilovgrad 23 48 38N 39 15 E
Vorovskoye 25 54 30N 155 50 E
Vosges 12 48 20N 7 10 E
Vosges □ 12 48 12N 6 20 E
Voss 21 60 38N 6 26 E
Vostochnyy Sayan 25 54 0N 96 0 E
Vostok I. 41 10 5S 152 23W
Votkinsk 22 57 0N 53 55 E
Votkinskoye Vdkhr. 22 57 30N 55 0 E
Vouga → 13 40 41N 8 40W
Vozhe Oz. 22 60 45N 39 0 E
Voznesenka 25 56 40N 95 3 E
Voznesensk 23 47 35N 31 21 E
Voznesenye 22 61 0N 35 45 E
Vrangelya, Ostrov 25 71 0N 180 0 E
Vranje 19 42 34N 21 54 E
Vratsa 19 43 13N 23 30 E
Vrbas → 19 45 8N 17 29 E
Vrede 57 27 24S 29 6 E
Vredefort 56 27 0S 27 22 E
Vredenburg 56 32 56S 18 0 E
Vredendal 56 31 41S 18 35 E
Vršac 19 45 8N 21 18 E
Vryburg 56 26 55S 24 45 E
Vryheid 57 27 45S 30 47 E
Vught 11 51 38N 5 20 E
Vulcan, Canada 64 50 25N 113 15W

Wendell

Vulcan, U.S.A. 68 45 46N 87 51W
Vulcano 18 38 25N 14 58 E
Vung Tau 34 10 21N 107 4 E
Vyatka → 22 56 30N 51 0 E
Vyatskiye Polyany 22 56 5N 51 0 E
Vyazemskiy 25 47 32N 134 45 E
Vyazma 22 55 10N 34 15 E
Vyborg 22 60 43N 28 47 E
Vychegda → 22 61 18N 46 36 E
Vychodné Beskydy 15 49 30N 22 0 E
Vyg-ozero 22 63 30N 34 0 E
Vyrnwy, L. 6 52 48N 3 30W
Vyshniy Volochek 22 57 30N 34 30 E
Vyshzha = imeni 26 Bakinskikh Komissarov 23 39 22N 54 10 E
Vytegra 22 61 0N 36 27 E

W

W.A.C. Bennett Dam 64 56 2N 122 6W
Wa 50 10 7N 2 25W
Waal → 11 51 59N 4 30 E
Wabakimi L. 62 50 38N 89 45W
Wabana 63 47 40N 53 0W
Wabasca 64 55 57N 113 56W
Wabash 68 40 48N 85 46W
Wabash → 68 37 46N 88 2W
Wabeno 68 45 25N 88 40W
Wabigoon L. 65 49 44N 92 44W
Wabowden 65 54 55N 98 38W
Wąbrzeźno 15 53 16N 18 57 E
Wabuk Pt. 62 55 20N 85 5W
Wabush 63 52 55N 66 52W
Wabuska 72 39 9N 119 13W
Waco 71 31 33N 97 5W
Waconichi, L. 62 50 8N 74 0W
Wad Banda 51 13 10N 27 56 E
Wad Hamid 51 16 30N 32 45 E
Wâd Medanî 51 14 28N 33 30 E
Waddeneilanden 11 53 25N 5 10 E
Waddenzee 11 53 6N 5 10 E
Wadderin Hill 47 32 0S 118 25 E
Waddington, Mt. 64 51 23N 125 15W
Waddy Pt. 45 24 58S 153 21 E
Wadena, Canada 65 51 57N 103 47W
Wadena, U.S.A. 70 46 25N 95 8W
Wadesboro 69 35 2N 80 2W
Wadhams 64 51 30N 127 30W
Wadi Halfa 51 21 53N 31 19 E
Wadsworth 72 39 38N 119 22W
Wafrah 30 28 33N 47 56 E
Wageningen 11 51 58N 5 40 E
Wager B. 61 65 26N 88 40W
Wager Bay 61 65 56N 90 49W
Wagga Wagga 45 35 7S 147 24 E
Waghete 35 4 10S 135 50 E
Wagin 47 33 17S 117 25 E
Wagon Mound 71 36 1N 104 44W
Wagoner 71 36 0N 95 20W
Wah 32 33 45N 72 40 E
Wahai 35 2 48S 129 35 E
Wahiawa 66 21 30N 158 2W
Wahoo 70 41 15N 96 35W
Wahpeton 70 46 20N 96 35W
Waiau → 43 42 47S 173 22 E
Waibeem 35 0 30S 132 59 E
Waigeo 35 0 20S 130 40 E
Waihi 43 37 23S 175 52 E
Waihou → 43 37 15S 175 40 E
Waikabubak 35 9 45S 119 25 E
Waikaremoana 43 38 42S 177 12 E
Waikari 43 42 58S 172 41 E
Waikato → 43 37 23S 174 43 E
Waikerie 45 34 9S 140 0 E
Waikokopu 43 39 3S 177 52 E
Waikouaiti 43 45 36S 170 41 E
Waimate 43 44 45S 171 3 E
Wainganga → 32 18 50N 79 55 E
Waingapu 35 9 35S 120 11 E
Wainwright, Canada 65 52 50N 110 50W
Wainwright, U.S.A. 60 70 39N 160 1W
Waiouru 43 39 28S 175 41 E
Waipara 43 43 3S 172 46 E
Waipawa 43 39 56S 176 38 E
Waipiro 43 38 2S 178 22 E
Waipu 43 35 59S 174 29 E
Waipukurau 43 40 1S 176 33 E
Wairakei 43 38 37S 176 6 E
Wairarapa, L. 43 41 14S 175 15 E
Wairoa 43 39 3S 177 25 E
Waitaki → 43 44 56S 171 7 E
Waitara 43 38 59S 174 15 E
Waitsburg 72 46 15N 118 0W
Waiuku 43 37 15S 174 45 E
Wajima 36 37 30N 137 0 E
Wajir 54 1 42N 40 5 E
Wakasa-Wan 36 35 40N 135 30 E
Wakatipu, L. 43 45 5S 168 33 E
Wakaw 65 52 39N 105 44W
Wakayama 36 34 15N 135 15 E
Wakayama-ken □ 36 33 50N 135 30 E
Wake Forest 69 35 58N 78 30W
Wake I. 3 19 18N 166 36 E
Wakefield, N.Z. 43 41 24S 173 5 E
Wakefield, U.K. 6 53 41N 1 31W
Wakefield, U.S.A. 70 46 28N 89 53W
Wakema 33 16 30N 95 11 E
Wakkanai 36 45 28N 141 35 E
Wakkerstroom 57 27 24S 30 10 E
Wakool 45 35 28S 144 23 E
Wakool → 45 35 5S 143 33 E
Wakre 35 0 19S 131 5 E
Wakuach L. 63 55 34N 67 32W
Wałbrzych 14 50 45N 16 18 E
Walbury Hill 7 51 22N 1 28W
Walcha 45 30 55S 151 31 E
Walcheren 11 51 30N 3 35 E
Walcott 72 41 50N 106 55W
Waldburg Ra. 47 24 40S 117 35 E
Walden 72 40 47N 106 20W
Waldport 72 44 30N 124 2W
Waldron 71 34 52N 94 4W
Wales □ 7 52 30N 3 30W
Walgett 45 30 0S 148 5 E
Walhalla, Australia 45 37 56S 146 29 E
Walhalla, U.S.A. 65 48 55N 97 55W
Walkaway 47 28 59S 114 48 E
Walker 70 47 4N 94 35W
Walker L., Man., Canada 65 54 42N 95 57W
Walker L., Qué., Canada 63 50 20N 67 11W
Walker L., U.S.A. 72 38 56N 118 46W
Walkerston 44 21 11S 149 8 E
Wall 70 44 0N 102 14W
Walla Walla 72 46 3N 118 25W
Wallabadah 44 17 57S 142 15 E
Wallace, Idaho, U.S.A. 72 47 30N 116 0W
Wallace, N.C., U.S.A. 69 34 44N 77 59W
Wallace, Nebr., U.S.A. 70 40 51N 101 12W
Wallaceburg 62 42 34N 82 23W
Wallachia = Valahia 15 44 35N 25 0 E
Wallal 45 26 32S 146 7 E
Wallal Downs 46 19 47S 120 40 E
Wallambin, L. 47 30 57S 117 35 E
Wallaroo 45 33 56S 137 39 E
Wallasey 6 53 26N 3 2W
Wallerawang 45 33 25S 150 4 E
Wallhallow 44 17 50S 135 50 E
Wallingford 6 51 40N 1 15W
Wallis & Futuna 40 13 18S 176 10W
Wallowa 72 45 40N 117 35W
Wallowa, Mts. 72 45 20N 117 30W
Wallsend, Australia 45 32 55S 151 40 E
Wallsend, U.K. 6 54 59N 1 30W
Wallula 72 46 3N 118 59W
Wallumbilla 45 26 33S 149 9 E
Walmsley, L. 65 63 25N 108 36W
Walney, Isle of 6 54 5N 3 15W
Walnut Ridge 71 36 7N 90 58W
Walsall 7 52 36N 1 59W
Walsenburg 71 37 42N 104 45W
Walsh 71 37 28N 102 15W
Walsh → 44 16 31S 143 42 E
Walsh P.O. 44 16 40S 144 0 E
Walterboro 69 32 53N 80 40W
Walters 71 34 25N 98 20W
Waltham Sta. 62 45 57N 76 57W
Waltman 72 43 8N 107 15W
Walvisbaai 56 23 0S 14 28 E
Wamba 54 2 10N 27 57 E
Wamego 70 39 14N 96 22W
Wamena 35 4 4S 138 57 E
Wamsasi 35 3 27S 126 7 E
Wana 32 32 20N 69 32 E
Wanaaring 45 29 38S 144 9 E
Wanaka L. 43 44 33S 169 7 E
Wan'an 39 26 26N 114 49 E
Wanapiri 35 4 30S 135 59 E
Wanapitei L. 62 46 45N 80 40W
Wanbi 45 34 46S 140 17 E
Wanda Shan 38 46 0N 132 0 E
Wandoan 45 26 5S 149 55 E
Wangal 35 6 8S 134 9 E
Wanganella 45 35 6S 144 49 E
Wanganui 43 39 56S 175 3 E
Wangaratta 45 36 21S 146 19 E
Wangdu 38 38 40N 115 7 E
Wangerooge 14 53 47N 7 52 E
Wangiwangi 35 5 22S 123 37 E
Wangjiang 39 30 10N 116 42 E
Wangqing 38 43 12N 129 42 E
Wanless 65 54 11N 101 21W
Wanning 39 18 48N 110 22 E
Wanquan 38 40 50N 114 40 E
Wanxian 39 30 42N 108 20 E
Wanyuan 39 32 4N 108 3 E
Wanzai 39 28 7N 114 30 E
Wapakoneta 68 40 35N 84 10W
Wapato 72 46 30N 120 25W
Wapawekka L. 65 54 55N 104 40W
Wapikopa L. 62 52 56N 87 53W
Wapsipinicon → 70 41 44N 90 19W
Warangal 32 17 58N 79 35 E
Waratah 44 41 30S 145 30 E
Waratah B. 45 38 54S 146 5 E
Warburton, Vic., Australia 45 37 47S 145 42 E
Warburton, W. Austral., Australia 47 26 8S 126 35 E
Warburton Ra. 47 25 55S 126 28 E
Ward 43 41 49S 174 11 E
Ward → 45 26 28S 146 6 E
Ward Cove 64 55 25N 132 43W
Warden 57 27 50S 29 0 E
Wardha 32 20 45N 78 39 E
Wardha → 32 19 57N 79 11 E
Wardlow 64 50 56N 111 31W
Ware 64 57 26N 125 41W
Warialda 45 29 29S 150 33 E
Wariap 35 1 30S 134 5 E
Warkopi 35 1 12S 134 9 E
Warley 7 52 30N 2 0W
Warm Springs 73 38 16N 116 32W
Warman 65 52 19N 106 30W
Warmbad, Namibia 56 28 25S 18 42 E
Warmbad, S. Africa 57 24 51S 28 19 E
Warnambool Downs 44 22 48S 142 52 E
Warnemünde 14 54 9N 12 5 E
Warner 64 49 17N 112 12W
Warner Mts. 72 41 30N 120 20W
Warner Robins 69 32 41N 83 36W
Waroona 47 32 50S 115 58 E
Warragul 45 38 10S 145 58 E
Warrawagine 46 20 51S 120 42 E
Warrego → 45 30 24S 145 21 E
Warrego Ra. 44 24 58S 146 0 E
Warren, Australia 45 31 42S 147 51 E
Warren, Ark., U.S.A. 71 33 35N 92 3W
Warren, Mich., U.S.A. 68 42 31N 83 2W
Warren, Minn., U.S.A. 70 48 12N 96 46W
Warren, Ohio, U.S.A. 68 41 18N 80 52W
Warren, Pa., U.S.A. 68 41 52N 79 10W
Warrenpoint 9 54 7N 6 15W
Warrensburg 70 38 45N 93 45W
Warrenton, S. Africa 56 28 9S 24 47 E
Warrenton, U.S.A. 72 46 11N 123 59W
Warrenville 45 25 48S 147 22 E
Warri 53 5 30N 5 41 E
Warrina 45 28 12S 135 50 E
Warrington, U.K. 6 53 25N 2 38W
Warrington, U.S.A. 69 30 22N 87 16W
Warrnambool 45 38 25S 142 30 E
Warroad 70 48 54N 95 19W
Warsa 35 0 47S 135 55 E
Warsaw = Warszawa 15 52 13N 21 0 E
Warsaw 68 41 14N 85 50W
Warszawa 15 52 13N 21 0 E
Warta → 14 52 35N 14 39 E
Warthe = Warta → 14 52 35N 14 39 E
Waru 35 3 30S 130 36 E
Warwick, Australia 45 28 10S 152 1 E
Warwick, U.K. 7 52 17N 1 36W
Warwick, U.S.A. 68 41 43N 71 25W
Warwick □ 7 52 20N 1 30W
Wasatch Ra. 72 40 30N 111 15W
Wasbank 57 28 15S 30 9 E
Wasco, Calif., U.S.A. 73 35 37N 119 16W
Wasco, Oreg., U.S.A. 72 45 36N 120 46W
Waseca 70 44 3N 93 31W
Wasekamio L. 65 56 45N 108 45W
Wash, The 6 52 58N 0 20 E
Washburn, N. Dak., U.S.A. 70 47 17N 101 0W
Washburn, Wis., U.S.A. 70 46 38N 90 55W
Washim 32 20 3N 77 0 E
Washington, D.C., U.S.A. 68 38 52N 77 0W
Washington, Ga., U.S.A. 69 33 45N 82 45W
Washington, Ind., U.S.A. 68 38 40N 87 8W
Washington, Iowa, U.S.A. 70 41 20N 91 45W
Washington, Mo., U.S.A. 70 38 35N 91 1W
Washington, N.C., U.S.A. 69 35 35N 77 1W
Washington, Pa., U.S.A. 68 40 10N 80 20W
Washington, Utah, U.S.A. 73 37 10N 113 30W
Washington □ 72 47 45N 120 30W
Washington, Mt. 68 44 15N 71 18W
Washington I. 68 45 24N 86 54W
Wasian 35 1 47S 133 19 E
Wasior 35 2 43S 134 30 E
Waskaiowaka, L. 65 56 33N 96 23W
Waskesiu Lake 65 53 55N 106 5W
Wassenaar 11 52 8N 4 24 E
Waswanipi 62 49 40N 76 29W
Waswanipi, L. 62 49 35N 76 40W
Watangpone 35 4 29S 120 25 E
Water Park Pt. 44 22 56S 150 47 E
Water Valley 71 34 9N 89 38W
Waterberge 57 24 10S 28 0 E
Waterbury 68 41 32N 73 0W
Waterbury L. 65 58 10N 104 22W
Waterford 9 52 16N 7 8W
Waterford □ 9 52 10N 7 40W
Waterford Harb. 9 52 10N 6 58W
Waterhen L., Man., Canada 65 52 10N 99 40W
Waterhen L., Sask., Canada 65 54 28N 108 25W
Waterloo, Belgium 11 50 43N 4 25 E
Waterloo, Canada 62 43 30N 80 32W
Waterloo, S. Leone 50 8 26N 13 8W
Waterloo, Ill., U.S.A. 70 38 22N 90 6W
Waterloo, Iowa, U.S.A. 70 42 27N 92 20W
Watersmeet 70 46 15N 89 12W
Waterton Glacier Int. Peace Park 72 48 35N 113 40W
Watertown, N.Y., U.S.A. 68 43 58N 75 57W
Watertown, S. Dak., U.S.A. 70 44 57N 97 5W
Watertown, Wis., U.S.A. 70 43 15N 88 45W
Waterval-Boven 57 25 40S 30 18 E
Waterville, Maine, U.S.A. 63 44 35N 69 40W
Waterville, Wash., U.S.A. 72 47 38N 120 1W
Watervliet 68 42 46N 73 43W
Wates 35 7 51S 110 10 E
Watford 7 51 38N 0 23W
Watford City 70 47 50N 103 23W
Wathaman → 65 57 16N 102 59W
Watheroo 47 30 15S 116 0W
Watkins Glen 68 42 25N 76 55W
Watling I. = San Salvador 75 24 0N 74 40W
Watonga 71 35 51N 98 24W
Watrous, Canada 65 51 40N 105 25W
Watrous, U.S.A. 71 35 50N 104 55W
Watsa 54 3 4N 29 30 E
Watseka 68 40 45N 87 45W
Watson, Australia 47 30 29S 131 31 E
Watson, Canada 65 52 10N 104 30W
Watson Lake 60 60 6N 128 49W
Watsonville 73 36 55N 121 49W
Wattiwarriganna Cr. → 45 28 57S 136 10 E
Watuata = Batuata 35 6 12S 122 42 E
Watubela, Kepulauan 35 4 28S 131 35 E
Waubay 70 45 22N 97 17W
Waubra 45 37 21S 143 39 E
Wauchope 45 31 28S 152 45 E
Wauchula 69 27 35N 81 50W
Waugh 65 49 40N 95 11W
Waukegan 68 42 22N 87 54W
Waukesha 68 43 0N 88 15W
Waukon 70 43 14N 91 33W
Wauneta 70 40 27N 101 25W
Waupaca 70 44 22N 89 8W
Waupun 70 43 38N 88 44W
Waurika 71 34 12N 98 0W
Wausau 70 44 57N 89 40W
Wautoma 70 44 3N 89 20W
Wauwatosa 68 43 6N 87 59W
Wave Hill 46 17 32S 131 0 E
Waveney → 7 52 24N 1 20 E
Waverley 43 39 46S 174 37 E
Waverly, Iowa, U.S.A. 70 42 40N 92 30W
Waverly, N.Y., U.S.A. 68 42 0N 76 33W
Wavre 11 50 43N 4 38 E
Wâw 51 7 45N 28 1 E
Wâw al Kabir 51 25 20N 16 43 E
Wawa 62 47 59N 84 47W
Wawanesa 65 49 36N 99 40W
Waxahachie 71 32 22N 96 53W
Way, L. 47 26 45S 120 16 E
Wayabula Rau 35 2 29N 128 17 E
Wayatinah 44 42 19S 146 27 E
Waycross 69 31 12N 82 25W
Wayne, Nebr., U.S.A. 70 42 16N 97 0W
Wayne, W. Va., U.S.A. 68 38 15N 82 27W
Waynesboro, Ga., U.S.A. 69 33 6N 82 1W
Waynesboro, Miss., U.S.A. 69 31 40N 88 39W
Waynesboro, Pa., U.S.A. 68 39 46N 77 32W
Waynesboro, Va., U.S.A. 68 38 4N 78 57W
Waynesburg 68 39 54N 80 12W
Waynesville 69 35 31N 83 0W
Waynoka 71 36 38N 98 53W
Wazirabad 32 32 30N 74 8 E
We 34 5 51N 95 18 E
Weald, The 7 51 7N 0 9 E
Wear → 6 54 55N 1 22W
Weatherford, Okla., U.S.A. 71 35 30N 98 45W
Weatherford, Tex., U.S.A. 71 32 45N 97 48W
Weaverville 72 40 44N 122 56W
Webb City 71 37 9N 94 30W
Webster, S. Dak., U.S.A. 70 45 24N 97 33W
Webster, Wis., U.S.A. 70 45 53N 92 25W
Webster City 70 42 30N 93 50W
Webster Green 70 38 38N 90 20W
Webster Springs 68 38 30N 80 25W
Weda 35 0 21N 127 50 E
Weda, Teluk 35 0 30N 127 50 E
Weddell I. 80 51 50S 61 0W
Wedderburn 45 36 26S 143 33 E
Wedgeport 63 43 44N 65 59W
Wee Waa 45 30 11S 149 26 E
Weed 72 41 29N 122 22W
Weemelah 45 29 2S 149 15 E
Weenen 57 28 48S 30 7 E
Weert 11 51 15N 5 43 E
Wei He →, Hebei, China 38 36 10N 115 45 E
Wei He →, Shaanxi, China 39 34 38N 110 15 E
Weifang 38 36 44N 119 7 E
Weihai 38 37 30N 122 6 E
Weimar 14 51 0N 11 20 E
Weinan 39 34 31N 109 29 E
Weipa 44 12 40S 141 50 E
Weir →, Australia 45 28 20S 149 50 E
Weir →, Canada 65 56 54N 93 21W
Weir River 65 56 49N 94 6W
Weiser 72 44 10N 117 0W
Weishan 39 34 47N 117 5 E
Weiyuan 38 35 7N 104 10 E
Weizhou Dao 39 21 0N 109 5 E
Wejherowo 15 54 35N 18 12 E
Wekusko L. 65 54 40N 99 50W
Welbourn Hill 45 27 21S 134 6 E
Welch 68 37 29N 81 36W
Welkom 56 28 0S 26 46 E
Welland 62 43 0N 79 15W
Welland → 6 52 43N 0 10W
Wellesley Is. 44 16 42S 139 30 E
Wellin 11 50 5N 5 6 E
Wellingborough 7 52 18N 0 41W
Wellington, Australia 45 32 35S 148 59 E
Wellington, Canada 62 43 57N 77 20W
Wellington, N.Z. 43 41 19S 174 46 E
Wellington, S. Africa 56 33 38S 19 1 E
Wellington, Salop, U.K. 6 52 42N 2 31W
Wellington, Somerset, U.K. 7 50 58N 3 13W
Wellington, Colo., U.S.A. 70 40 43N 105 0W
Wellington, Kans., U.S.A. 71 37 15N 97 25W
Wellington, Nev., U.S.A. 72 38 47N 119 28W
Wellington, Tex., U.S.A. 71 34 55N 100 13W
Wellington □ 43 40 8S 175 36 E
Wellington, I. 80 49 30S 75 0W
Wellington, L. 45 38 6S 147 20 E
Wells, Norfolk, U.K. 6 52 57N 0 51 E
Wells, Somerset, U.K. 7 51 12N 2 39W
Wells, Minn., U.S.A. 70 43 44N 93 45W
Wells, Nev., U.S.A. 72 41 8N 115 0W
Wells Gray Prov. Park 64 52 30N 120 15W
Wells L. 47 26 44S 123 15 E
Wellsboro 68 41 45N 77 20W
Wellsville, Mo., U.S.A. 70 39 4N 91 30W
Wellsville, N.Y., U.S.A. 68 42 9N 77 53W
Wellsville, Ohio, U.S.A. 68 40 36N 80 40W
Wellsville, Utah, U.S.A. 72 41 35N 111 59W
Wellton 73 32 39N 114 6W
Wels 14 48 9N 14 1 E
Welshpool 7 52 40N 3 9W
Wem 6 52 52N 2 45W
Wen Xian 39 32 43N 104 36 E
Wenatchee 72 47 30N 120 17W
Wenchang 39 19 38N 110 42 E
Wenchi 50 7 46N 2 8W
Wenchow = Wenzhou 39 28 0N 120 38 E
Wendell 72 42 50N 114 42W

Yokote

Wood Is. **46** 16 24S 123 19 E
Wood L. **65** 55 17N 103 17W
Wood Lake **70** 42 38N 100 14W
Woodah I. **44** 13 27S 136 10 E
Woodanilling **47** 33 31S 117 24 E
Woodburn **45** 29 6S 153 23 E
Woodenbong **45** 28 24S 152 39 E
Woodend **45** 37 20S 144 33 E
Woodgreen **44** 22 26S 134 12 E
Woodland **72** 38 40N 121 50W
Woodlands **47** 24 46S 118 8 E
Woodpecker **64** 53 30N 122 40W
Woodridge **65** 49 20N 96 9W
Woodroffe, Mt. **47** 26 20S 131 45 E
Woodruff, Ariz., U.S.A. **73** 34 51N 110 1W
Woodruff, Utah, U.S.A. **72** 41 30N 111 4W
Woods, L., Australia **44** 17 50S 133 30 E
Woods, L., Canada **63** 54 30N 65 13W
Woods, L. of the **65** 49 15N 94 45W
Woodside **45** 38 31S 146 52 E
Woodstock, Queens., Australia **44** 19 35S 146 50 E
Woodstock, W. Austral., Australia **46** 21 41S 118 57 E
Woodstock, N.B., Canada **63** 46 11N 67 37W
Woodstock, Ont., Canada **62** 43 10N 80 45W
Woodstock, U.K. **7** 51 51N 1 20W
Woodstock, U.S.A. **70** 42 17N 88 30W
Woodsville **68** 44 10N 72 0W
Woodville, N.Z. **43** 40 20S 175 53 E
Woodville, U.S.A. **71** 30 45N 94 25W
Woodward **71** 36 24N 99 28W
Woolamai, C. **45** 38 30S 145 23 E
Woolgoolga **45** 30 6S 153 11 E
Woombye **45** 26 40S 152 55 E
Woomera **45** 31 30S 137 10 E
Woonsocket, R.I., U.S.A. **68** 42 0N 71 30W
Woonsocket, S. Dak., U.S.A. **70** 44 5N 98 15W
Wooramel **47** 25 45S 114 17 E
Wooramel → **47** 25 47S 114 10 E
Wooroloo **47** 31 48S 116 18 E
Wooster **68** 40 48N 81 55W
Worcester, S. Africa **56** 33 39S 19 27 E
Worcester, U.K. **7** 52 12N 2 12W
Worcester, U.S.A. **68** 42 14N 71 49W
Workington **6** 54 39N 3 34W
Worksop **6** 53 19N 1 9W
Workum **11** 52 59N 5 26 E
Worland **72** 44 0N 107 59W
Worms **14** 49 37N 8 21 E
Wortham **71** 31 48N 96 27W
Worthing **7** 50 49N 0 21W
Worthington **70** 43 35N 95 36W
Wosi **35** 0 15S 128 0 E
Wou-han = Wuhan **39** 30 31N 114 18 E
Wour **51** 21 14N 16 0 E
Wowoni **35** 4 5S 123 5 E
Woy Woy **45** 33 30S 151 19 E
Wrangel I. **26** 71 0N 180 0 E
Wrangell **60** 56 30N 132 25W
Wrangell, I. **64** 56 20N 132 10W
Wrangell Mts. **60** 61 40N 143 30W
Wrath, C. **8** 58 38N 5 0W
Wray **70** 40 8N 102 18W
Wrekin, The **6** 52 41N 2 35W
Wrens **69** 33 13N 82 23W
Wrexham **6** 53 5N 3 0W
Wright, Canada **64** 51 52N 121 40W
Wright, Phil. **35** 11 42N 125 2 E
Wrightson, Mt. **73** 31 43N 110 56W
Wrigley **60** 63 16N 123 37W
Wrocław **14** 51 5N 17 5 E
Września **15** 52 21N 17 36 E
Wu Jiang → **39** 29 40N 107 20 E
Wubin **47** 30 6S 116 37 E
Wuchang **38** 44 55N 127 5 E
Wuchuan **39** 28 25N 108 3 E
Wuding He → **38** 37 2N 110 23 E
Wugang **39** 26 44N 110 35 E
Wugong Shan **39** 27 30N 114 0 E
Wuhan **39** 30 31N 114 18 E
Wuhsi = Wuxi **39** 31 33N 120 18 E
Wuhu **39** 31 22N 118 21 E
Wukari **53** 7 51N 9 42 E
Wuliaru **35** 7 27S 131 0 E
Wulumuchi = Ürümqi **37** 43 45N 87 45 E
Wum **53** 6 24N 10 2 E
Wuning **39** 29 17N 115 5 E
Wunnummin L. **62** 52 55N 89 10W
Wuntho **33** 23 55N 95 45 E
Wuping **39** 25 5N 116 5 E
Wuppertal, Germany **14** 51 15N 7 8 E
Wuppertal, S. Africa **56** 32 13S 19 12 E
Wuqing **38** 39 23N 117 4 E
Wurung **44** 19 13S 140 38 E
Würzburg **14** 49 46N 9 55 E
Wushan **39** 31 7N 109 54 E
Wuting = Huimin **38** 37 27N 117 28 E
Wutongqiao **37** 29 22N 103 50 E
Wuwei, Anhui, China **39** 31 18N 117 54 E
Wuwei, Gansu, China **37** 37 57N 102 34 E
Wuxi, Jiangsu, China **39** 31 33N 120 18 E
Wuxi, Sichuan, China **39** 31 23N 109 35 E
Wuxing **39** 30 51N 120 8 E
Wuyi, Hebei, China **38** 37 46N 115 56 E
Wuyi, Zhejiang, China **39** 28 52N 119 50 E
Wuyi Shan **37** 27 0N 117 0 E
Wuying **38** 47 53N 129 56 E
Wuyuan **38** 41 2N 108 20 E
Wuzhai **38** 38 54N 111 48 E
Wuzhi Shan **39** 18 45N 109 45 E
Wuzhong **38** 38 2N 106 12 E
Wuzhou **39** 23 30N 111 18 E
Wyaaba Cr. → **44** 16 27S 141 35 E
Wyalkatchem **47** 31 8S 117 22 E
Wyandotte **68** 42 14N 83 13W
Wyandra **45** 27 12S 145 56 E
Wyangala Res. **45** 33 54S 149 0 E
Wyara, L. **45** 28 42S 144 14 E
Wycheproof **45** 36 0S 143 17 E
Wye → **7** 51 36N 2 40W
Wyemandoo, Mt. **47** 28 28S 118 29 E
Wymondham **7** 52 45N 0 42W
Wymore **70** 40 10N 96 40W
Wynbring **45** 30 33S 133 32 E
Wyndham, Australia **46** 15 33S 128 3 E
Wyndham, N.Z. **43** 46 20S 168 51 E
Wyndmere **70** 46 23N 97 7W
Wynne **71** 35 15N 90 50W
Wynnum **45** 27 27S 153 9 E
Wynyard, Australia **44** 41 5S 145 44 E
Wynyard, Canada **65** 51 45N 104 10W
Wyola, L. **47** 29 8S 130 17 E
Wyoming □ **66** 42 48N 109 0W
Wyong **45** 33 14S 151 24 E
Wytheville **68** 37 0N 81 3W

X

Xai-Xai **57** 25 6S 33 31 E
Xainza **37** 30 58N 88 35 E
Xangongo **56** 16 45S 15 5 E
Xánthi **19** 41 10N 24 58 E
Xapuri **78** 10 35S 68 35W
Xau, L. **56** 21 15S 24 44 E
Xenia **68** 39 42N 83 57W
Xhora **57** 31 55S 28 38 E
Xhumo **56** 21 7S 24 35 E
Xi Jiang → **39** 22 5N 113 20 E
Xi Xian **38** 36 41N 110 58 E
Xiachengzi **38** 44 40N 130 18 E
Xiachuan Dao **39** 21 40N 112 40 E
Xiaguan **37** 25 32N 100 16 E
Xiajiang **39** 27 30N 115 10 E
Xiamen **38** 24 25N 118 4 E
Xi'an **39** 34 15N 109 0 E
Xianfeng **39** 29 40N 109 8 E
Xiang Jiang → **39** 28 55N 112 50 E
Xiangfan **39** 32 2N 112 8 E
Xiangning **38** 35 58N 110 50 E
Xiangtan **39** 27 51N 112 54 E
Xiangxiang **39** 27 43N 112 28 E
Xiangyang **39** 32 1N 112 8 E
Xiangyin **39** 28 38N 112 54 E
Xiangzhou **39** 23 58N 109 40 E
Xianju **39** 28 51N 120 44 E
Xianyang **39** 34 20N 108 40 E
Xiao Hinggan Ling **38** 49 0N 127 0 E
Xiaogan **39** 30 52N 113 55 E
Xiapu **39** 26 54N 119 59 E
Xichang **37** 27 51N 102 19 E
Xichuan **39** 33 0N 111 30 E
Xifeng **39** 27 7N 106 42 E
Xigazê **37** 29 5N 88 45 E
Xihe **39** 34 2N 105 20 E
Xiliao He → **38** 43 32N 123 35 E
Xilin **39** 24 30N 105 6 E
Xin Xian **38** 38 22N 112 46 E
Xinavane **57** 25 2S 32 47 E
Xinbin **38** 41 40N 125 2 E
Xincheng **39** 24 5N 108 39 E
Xinfeng **39** 25 27N 114 58 E
Xing'an, Guangxi Zhuangzu, China **39** 25 38N 110 40 E
Xingan, Jiangxi, China **39** 27 46N 115 20 E
Xingcheng **38** 40 40N 120 45 E
Xingguo **39** 26 21N 115 21 E
Xinghua **39** 32 58N 119 48 E
Xinghua Wan **39** 25 15N 119 20 E
Xingning **39** 24 3N 115 42 E
Xingren **37** 25 24N 105 11 E
Xingshan **39** 31 15N 110 45 E
Xingtai **38** 37 3N 114 32 E
Xingu → **79** 1 30S 51 53W
Xingyang **39** 34 45N 112 52 E
Xinhua **39** 27 42N 111 13 E
Xining **37** 36 34N 101 40 E
Xinjiang **38** 35 34N 111 11 E
Xinjiang Uygur Zizhiqu □ **37** 42 0N 86 0 E
Xinjin **38** 39 25N 121 58 E
Xinle **38** 38 25N 114 40 E
Xinmin **38** 41 59N 122 50 E
Xinning **39** 26 28N 110 50 E
Xinxiang **39** 35 18N 113 50 E
Xinyang **39** 32 6N 114 3 E
Xinzheng **39** 34 20N 113 45 E
Xinzhou **39** 19 43N 109 17 E
Xinzhu **39** 24 49N 120 57 E
Xiongyuecheng **38** 40 12N 122 5 E
Xiping **39** 33 22N 114 0 E
Xique-Xique **79** 10 50S 42 40W
Xiuyan **38** 40 18N 123 11 E
Xixabangma Feng **33** 28 20N 85 40 E
Xixiang **39** 33 0N 107 44 E
Xizang □ **37** 32 0N 88 0 E
Xuancheng **39** 30 56N 118 43 E
Xuan'en **39** 30 0N 109 30 E
Xuanhan **39** 31 18N 107 38 E
Xuanhua **38** 40 40N 115 2 E
Xuchang **39** 34 2N 113 48 E
Xuguit Qi **38** 49 17N 120 44 E
Xunke **38** 49 35N 128 27 E
Xupu **39** 27 53N 110 32 E
Xuwen **39** 20 20N 110 10 E
Xuyong **39** 28 10N 105 22 E
Xuzhou **39** 34 18N 117 10 E

Y

Ya 'Bad **28** 32 27N 35 10 E
Yaamba **44** 23 8S 150 22 E
Ya'an **37** 29 58N 103 5 E
Yaapeet **45** 35 45S 142 3 E
Yabelo **51** 4 50N 38 8 E
Yablonovy Khrebet **25** 53 0N 114 0 E
Yablonovy Ra. = Yablonovy Khrebet **25** 53 0N 114 0 E
Yacheng **39** 18 22N 109 6 E
Yacuiba **80** 22 0S 63 43W
Yadgir **32** 16 45N 77 5 E
Yadkin → **69** 35 23N 80 3W
Yagodnoye **25** 62 33N 149 40 E
Yagoua **54** 10 20N 15 13 E
Yagur **28** 32 45N 35 4 E
Yahk **64** 49 6N 116 10W
Yahuma **54** 1 0N 23 10 E
Yakima **72** 46 42N 120 30W
Yakima → **72** 47 0N 120 30W
Yakut A.S.S.R. □ **25** 62 0N 130 0 E
Yakutat **60** 59 29N 139 44W
Yakutsk **25** 62 5N 129 50 E
Yala **34** 6 33N 101 18 E
Yalbalgo **47** 25 10S 114 45 E
Yalboroo **44** 20 50S 148 40 E
Yalgoo **47** 28 16S 116 39 E
Yalinga **51** 6 33N 23 10 E
Yalkubul, Punta **74** 21 32N 88 37W
Yalleroi **44** 24 3S 145 42 E
Yalobusha → **71** 33 30N 90 12W
Yalong Jiang → **37** 26 40N 101 55 E
Yalta **23** 44 30N 34 10 E
Yalu He → **38** 46 56N 123 30 E
Yalu Jiang → **38** 40 0N 124 22 E
Yalutorovsk **24** 56 41N 66 12 E
Yam Ha Melaḥ = Dead Sea **28** 31 30N 35 30 E
Yam Kinneret **28** 32 45N 35 35 E
Yamagata **36** 38 15N 140 15 E
Yamagata □ **36** 38 30N 140 0 E
Yamaguchi **36** 34 10N 131 32 E
Yamaguchi □ **36** 34 20N 131 40 E
Yamal, Poluostrov **24** 71 0N 70 0 E
Yamanashi □ **36** 35 40N 138 40 E
Yamantau **22** 54 20N 57 40 E
Yamantau, Gora **22** 54 15N 58 6 E
Yamba, N.S.W., Australia **45** 29 26S 153 23 E
Yamba, S. Austral., Australia **45** 34 10S 140 52 E
Yambah **44** 23 10S 133 50 E
Yambarran Ra. **46** 15 10S 130 25 E
Yâmbiô **51** 4 35N 28 16 E
Yambol **19** 42 30N 26 36 E
Yamdena **35** 7 45S 131 20 E
Yamethin **33** 20 29N 96 18 E
Yamma-Yamma, L. **45** 26 16S 141 20 E
Yamoussoukro **50** 6 49N 5 17W
Yampa → **72** 40 37N 108 59W
Yampi Sd. **46** 16 8S 123 38 E
Yamuna → **33** 25 30N 81 53 E
Yamzho Yumco **37** 28 48N 90 35 E
Yan **53** 10 5N 12 11 E
Yana → **25** 71 30N 136 0 E
Yanac **45** 36 8S 141 25 E
Yanai **36** 33 58N 132 7 E
Yan'an **38** 36 35N 109 26 E
Yanaul **22** 56 25N 55 0 E
Yanbu 'al Baḥr **30** 24 0N 38 5 E
Yancannia **45** 30 12S 142 35 E
Yanchang **38** 36 43N 110 1 E
Yancheng, Henan, China **39** 33 35N 114 0 E
Yancheng, Jiangsu, China **39** 33 23N 120 8 E
Yanchi **38** 37 48N 107 20 E
Yanchuan **38** 36 51N 110 10 E
Yanco Cr. → **45** 35 14S 145 35 E
Yandal **47** 27 35S 121 10 E
Yandanooka **47** 29 18S 115 29 E
Yandaran **44** 24 43S 152 6 E
Yandoon **33** 17 0N 95 40 E
Yangambi **54** 0 47N 24 20 E
Yangch'ü = Taiyuan **38** 37 52N 112 33 E
Yangchun **39** 22 11N 111 48 E
Yanggao **38** 40 21N 113 55 E
Yangi-Yer **24** 40 17N 68 48 E
Yangjiang **39** 21 50N 110 59 E
Yangquan **38** 37 58N 113 31 E
Yangshan **39** 24 30N 112 40 E
Yangshuo **39** 24 48N 110 29 E
Yangtze Kiang = Chang Jiang → **39** 31 48N 121 10 E
Yangxin **39** 29 50N 115 12 E
Yangzhou **39** 32 21N 119 26 E
Yanji **38** 42 59N 129 30 E
Yankton **70** 42 55N 97 25W
Yanna **45** 26 58S 146 0 E
Yanqi **37** 42 5N 86 35 E
Yanqing **38** 40 30N 115 58 E
Yanshan **39** 28 15N 117 41 E
Yantabulla **45** 29 21S 145 0 E
Yantai **38** 37 34N 121 22 E
Yanting **39** 31 11N 105 24 E
Yanzhou **38** 35 35N 116 49 E
Yao **51** 12 56N 17 33 E
Yaoundé **54** 3 50N 11 35 E
Yap Is. **40** 9 30N 138 10 E
Yapen **35** 1 50S 136 0 E
Yapen, Selat **35** 1 20S 136 10 E
Yappar → **44** 18 22S 141 16 E
Yaqui → **74** 27 37N 110 39W
Yar-Sale **24** 66 50N 70 50 E
Yaraka **44** 24 53S 144 3 E
Yarangüme **30** 37 35N 29 8 E
Yaransk **22** 57 22N 47 49 E
Yardea P.O. **45** 32 23S 135 32 E
Yare → **7** 52 36N 1 28 E
Yarensk **22** 61 10N 49 8 E
Yarí → **78** 0 20S 72 20W
Yarkand = Shache **37** 38 20N 77 10 E
Yarkhun → **32** 36 17N 72 30 E
Yarmouth **63** 43 50N 66 7W
Yarmūk → **28** 32 42N 35 40 E
Yaroslavl **22** 57 35N 39 55 E
Yarra Yarra Lakes **47** 29 40S 115 45 E
Yarraden **44** 14 17S 143 15 E
Yarraloola **46** 21 33S 115 52 E
Yarram **45** 38 29S 146 9 E
Yarraman **45** 26 50S 152 0 E
Yarranvale **45** 26 50S 145 20 E
Yarras **45** 31 25S 152 20 E
Yarrowmere **44** 21 27S 145 53 E
Yartsevo **25** 60 20N 90 0 E
Yasawa Group **43** 17 0S 177 23 E
Yasinski, L. **62** 53 16N 77 35W
Yass **45** 34 49S 148 54 E
Yas'ur **28** 32 54N 35 10 E
Yates Center **71** 37 53N 95 45W
Yathkyed L. **65** 62 40N 98 0W
Yatsushiro **36** 32 30N 130 40 E
Yaṭṭah **28** 31 27N 35 6 E
Yauyos **78** 12 19S 75 50W
Yavari → **78** 4 21S 70 2W
Yavatmal **32** 20 20N 78 15 E
Yavne **28** 31 52N 34 45 E
Yawatahama **36** 33 27N 132 24 E
Yazd **31** 31 55N 54 27 E
Yazd □ **31** 32 0N 55 0 E
Yazdān **31** 33 30N 60 50 E
Yazoo → **71** 32 35N 90 50W
Yazoo City **71** 32 48N 90 28W
Yding Skovhøj **21** 55 59N 9 46 E
Ye Xian **38** 37 8N 119 57 E
Yealering **47** 32 36S 117 36 E
Yebyu **33** 14 15N 98 13 E
Yecla **13** 38 35N 1 5W
Yeeda **46** 17 31S 123 38 E
Yeelanna **45** 34 9S 135 45 E
Yegros **80** 26 20S 56 25W
Yehuda, Midbar **28** 31 35N 35 15 E
Yei **51** 4 9N 30 40 E
Yelanskoye **25** 61 25N 128 0 E
Yelarbon **45** 28 33S 150 38 E
Yelets **22** 52 40N 38 30 E
Yell **8** 60 35N 1 5W
Yell Sd. **8** 60 33N 1 15W
Yellow Sea **38** 35 0N 123 0 E
Yellowhead P. **64** 52 53N 118 25W
Yellowknife **64** 62 27N 114 29W
Yellowknife → **60** 62 31N 114 19W
Yellowstone → **70** 47 58N 103 59W
Yellowstone L. **72** 44 30N 110 20W
Yellowstone National Park **72** 44 35N 110 0W
Yellowtail Res. **72** 45 6N 108 8W
Yelvertoft **44** 20 13S 138 45 E
Yemen ■ **29** 15 0N 44 0 E
Yenangyaung **33** 20 30N 95 0 E
Yenda **45** 34 13S 146 14 E
Yenisey → **24** 71 50N 82 40 E
Yeniseysk **25** 58 27N 92 13 E
Yeniseyskiy Zaliv **24** 72 20N 81 0 E
Yenyuka **25** 57 57N 121 15 E
Yeo, L. **47** 28 0S 124 30 E
Yeola **32** 20 0N 74 30 E
Yeovil **7** 50 57N 2 38W
Yeppoon **44** 23 5S 150 47 E
Yerbent **24** 39 30N 58 50 E
Yerbogachen **25** 61 16N 108 0 E
Yerevan **23** 40 10N 44 31 E
Yerilla **47** 29 24S 121 47 E
Yermak **24** 52 2N 76 55 E
Yermakovo **25** 52 25N 126 20 E
Yermo **73** 34 58N 116 50W
Yerofey Pavlovich **25** 54 0N 122 0 E
Yershov **23** 51 22N 48 16 E
Yerushalayim **28** 31 47N 35 10 E
Yes Tor **7** 50 41N 3 59W
Yeso **71** 34 29N 104 37W
Yessey **25** 68 29N 102 10 E
Yeu, I. d' **12** 46 42N 2 20W
Yevpatoriya **23** 45 15N 33 20 E
Yeysk **23** 46 40N 38 12 E
Yezd = Yazd **31** 31 55N 54 27 E
Yi Xian **38** 41 30N 121 22 E
Yiannitsa **19** 40 46N 22 24 E
Yibin **37** 28 45N 104 32 E
Yichang **39** 30 40N 111 20 E
Yicheng **38** 35 42N 111 40 E
Yichuan **38** 36 2N 110 10 E
Yichun, Heilongjiang, China **38** 47 44N 128 52 E
Yichun, Jiangxi, China **39** 27 48N 114 22 E
Yidu **38** 36 43N 118 28 E
Yihuang **39** 27 30N 116 12 E
Yijun **38** 35 28N 109 8 E
Yilan, China **38** 46 19N 129 34 E
Yilan, Taiwan **39** 24 51N 121 44 E
Yilehuli Shan **38** 51 20N 124 20 E
Yimianpo **38** 45 7N 128 2 E
Yinchuan **38** 38 30N 106 15 E
Yindarlgooda, L. **47** 30 40S 121 52 E
Ying He → **39** 32 30N 116 30 E
Ying Xian **38** 39 32N 113 10 E
Yingcheng **39** 30 56N 113 35 E
Yingde **39** 24 10N 113 25 E
Yingkou **38** 40 37N 122 18 E
Yingshan **39** 30 41N 115 32 E
Yingshang **39** 32 38N 116 12 E
Yingtan **37** 28 12N 117 0 E
Yining **37** 43 58N 81 10 E
Yinjiang **39** 28 1N 108 21 E
Yinmabin **33** 22 10N 94 55 E
Yinnietharra **47** 24 39S 116 12 E
Yipinglang **37** 25 10N 101 52 E
Yirshi **38** 47 18N 119 49 E
Yishan **39** 24 28N 108 38 E
Yíthion **19** 36 46N 22 34 E
Yitong **38** 43 13N 125 20 E
Yitulihe **38** 50 38N 121 34 E
Yixing **39** 31 21N 119 48 E
Yiyang, Henan, China **39** 34 27N 112 10 E
Yiyang, Hunan, China **39** 28 35N 112 18 E
Yizhang **39** 25 27N 112 57 E
Yizre'el **28** 32 34N 35 19 E
Ylitornio **20** 66 19N 23 39 E
Ylivieska **20** 64 4N 24 28 E
Ynykchanskiy **25** 60 15N 137 35 E
Yoakum **71** 29 20N 97 20W
Yog Pt. **35** 14 6N 124 12 E
Yogyakarta **35** 7 49S 110 22 E
Yoho Nat. Park **64** 51 25N 116 30W
Yojoa, L. de **75** 14 53N 88 0W
Yokadouma **54** 3 26N 14 55 E
Yokkaichi **36** 35 0N 136 38 E
Yoko **51** 5 32N 12 20 E
Yokohama **36** 35 27N 139 28 E
Yokosuka **36** 35 20N 139 40 E
Yokote **36** 39 20N 140 30 E